The Editors

JOHN P. RUMRICH is author of *Matter of Glory: A New Preface to Paradise Lost* and *Milton Unbound: Controversy and Reinterpretation* as well as editor of *Texas Studies in Literature and Language*. He is Arthur J. and Wilhelmina Doré Thaman Professor of English at the University of Texas at Austin, where he teaches courses in early modern British literature and cultural history.

GREGORY CHAPLIN is an assistant professor of British literature at Bridgewater State College in Massachusetts. He has published articles on Ben Jonson and John Milton in *ELH* and *Modern Philology*.

W. W. NORTON & COMPANY, INC.
Also Publishes

ENGLISH RENAISSANCE DRAMA: A NORTON ANTHOLOGY
edited by David Bevington et al.

THE NORTON ANTHOLOGY OF AFRICAN AMERICAN LITERATURE
edited by Henry Louis Gates Jr. and Nellie Y. McKay et al.

THE NORTON ANTHOLOGY OF AMERICAN LITERATURE
edited by Nina Baym et al.

THE NORTON ANTHOLOGY OF CHILDREN'S LITERATURE
edited by Jack Zipes et al.

THE NORTON ANTHOLOGY OF ENGLISH LITERATURE
edited by M. H. Abrams and Stephen Greenblatt et al.

THE NORTON ANTHOLOGY OF LITERATURE BY WOMEN
edited by Sandra M. Gilbert and Susan Gubar

THE NORTON ANTHOLOGY OF MODERN AND CONTEMPORARY POETRY
edited by Jahan Ramazani, Richard Ellmann, and Robert O'Clair

THE NORTON ANTHOLOGY OF POETRY
edited by Margaret Ferguson, Mary Jo Salter, and Jon Stallworthy

THE NORTON ANTHOLOGY OF SHORT FICTION
edited by R. V. Cassill and Richard Bausch

THE NORTON ANTHOLOGY OF THEORY AND CRITICISM
edited by Vincent B. Leitch et al.

THE NORTON ANTHOLOGY OF WORLD LITERATURE
edited by Sarah Lawall et al.

THE NORTON FACSIMILE OF THE FIRST FOLIO OF SHAKESPEARE
prepared by Charlton Hinman

THE NORTON INTRODUCTION TO LITERATURE
edited by Alison Booth, J. Paul Hunter, and Kelly J. Mays

THE NORTON INTRODUCTION TO THE SHORT NOVEL
edited by Jerome Beaty

THE NORTON READER
edited by Linda H. Peterson and John C. Brereton

THE NORTON SAMPLER
edited by Thomas Cooley

THE NORTON SHAKESPEARE, BASED ON THE OXFORD EDITION
edited by Stephen Greenblatt et al.

For a complete list of Norton Critical Editions, visit
wwnorton.com/college/English/nce_home.htm

A NORTON CRITICAL EDITION

SEVENTEENTH-CENTURY BRITISH POETRY: 1603–1660

AUTHORITATIVE TEXTS
CRITICISM

Edited by

JOHN P. RUMRICH
UNIVERSITY OF TEXAS AT AUSTIN

and

GREGORY CHAPLIN
BRIDGEWATER STATE COLLEGE

W. W. NORTON & COMPANY • *New York* • *London*

W. W. Norton & Company has been independent since its founding in 1923, when William Warder Norton and Mary D. Herter Norton first published lectures delivered at the People's Institute, the adult education division of New York City's Cooper Union. The Nortons soon expanded their program beyond the Institute, publishing books by celebrated academics from America and abroad. By mid-century, the two major pillars of Norton's publishing program—trade books and college texts—were firmly established. In the 1950s, the Norton family transferred control of the company to its employees, and today—with a staff of four hundred and a comparable number of trade, college, and professional titles published each year—W. W. Norton & Company stands as the largest and oldest publishing house owned wholly by its employees.

First Edition.

The text of this book is composed in Fairfield Medium
with the display set in Bernhard Modern.
Composition by Binghamton Valley Composition LLC.
Manufacturing by LSC Communications - Crawfordsville, IN
Production manager: Benjamin Reynolds.

Library of Congress Cataloging-in-Publication Data

Seventeenth-century British poetry, 1603–1660 : authoritative texts, criticism /
selected and edited by
John P. Rumrich and Gregory Chaplin.
p. cm. — (A Norton critical edition)
Includes bibliographical references.

ISBN 0-393-97998-9 (pbk.)

1. English poetry—Early modern, 1550–1700. 2. English poetry—Early modern, 1500–1700—History and criticism. 3. Great Britain—Civilization—17th century—Sources. I. Rumrich, John Peter, 1954– II. Chaplin, Gregory. III. Series.

PR1209.S515 2005
821'.408—dc22
2005053926

W. W. Norton & Company, Inc., 500 Fifth Avenue,
New York, N.Y. 10110-0017
www.wwnorton.com

W. W. Norton & Company Ltd.,
15 Carlisle Street, London W1D 3BS

6 7 8 9 0

Contents

Textual Notes

Criticism

Preface

Seventeenth-Century British Poetry: 1603–1660 succeeds two earlier Norton Critical Editions: *Ben Jonson and the Cavalier Poets* (ed. Hugh Maclean) and *George Herbert and the Seventeenth-Century Religious Poets* (ed. Mario A. Di Cesare). Ben Jonson and George Herbert charted new directions for English poetry during the early seventeenth century, and these volumes have long served as valuable guides to their poetry and their influence on the next generation of poets. But ideas about seventeenth-century literature have developed rapidly over the last twenty years: the poets in these volumes have remained central, but they now inhabit a literary landscape recognized to be richer and more crowded than it once was. Not only has the canon expanded, but the range of texts that constitute seventeenth-century literature has grown. Our response to these changes has been to fashion a single Norton Critical Edition that encompasses the poets and poems essential to the study of British poetry from 1603 to 1660. The rich diversity of the poetry in its topical concerns and forms reflects an extraordinarily eventful period of English history: the end of the long reign of Elizabeth I and of the Tudor dynasty, the increasingly absolutist reigns of the first two Stuart monarchs, the outbreak of civil war, the levelling of church hierarchy, the trial and execution of Charles I, the rule of Cromwell, and finally, the Restoration of the monarchy.

Readers familiar with *Ben Jonson and the Cavalier Poets* and *George Herbert and the Seventeenth-Century Religious Poets* will find that we have retained the majority of the poems from those volumes and that we have added newly edited selections from Aemilia Lanyer, John Donne, Lady Mary Wroth, John Milton, Anne Bradstreet, Margaret Cavendish, John Dryden, and Katherine Philips. In doing so, we have sought to provide ample selections by the poets most frequently taught in courses in seventeenth-century literature. The result is a volume with over six hundred poems by nearly thirty poets. Other poets might well have been included and quite properly so, but including them would have forced us to undermine one of the distinctive strengths of the earlier editions—their balance between depth and diversity. So while some readers may find their favorite poem or poet missing, they will also find, for many of the poets we have included, the most extensive selection of their poetry available in a single anthology: almost half of Donne's *Songs and Sonnets*, all of the poems from Jonson's *The Forest*, over a third of Herbert's *The Temple*, and eighty poems from Herrick's *Hesperides* and *Noble Numbers*. We have also included rarely anthologized pieces—for example, Donne's "Sappho to Philaenis," Cowley's "Ode. Upon Dr. Harvey," and Cavendish's atomic poems—that enrich our understanding of subjects as culturally salient and topically diverse as early modern eroticism and scientific speculation.

Our primary goal has been to provide modernized and well-annotated texts of the poems; details concerning our editorial practices, the copy texts of the poems, and substantive variants can be found in the Textual Notes. Choosing critical essays for this volume has been especially difficult. A representative selection of major essays on individual poems in this edition—Jonson's "To Penshurst," Herbert's "The Collar," or Milton's "Lycidas," for instance—would fill a volume of its own. In general, rather than studies of individual poems, we have provided essays that treat multiple poets, illustrate different critical approaches, and open avenues of discussion. As a primer in seventeenth-century assumptions about the mind and body, we have also included Lawrence Babb's concise "The Physiology and Psychology of the Renaissance." The Select Bibliography provides a starting point for research in the period.

We are indebted to Mario Di Cesare for providing us with updated texts for the poets included in his original edition—although we take final responsibility for how these poems appear in this volume. The Harry Ransom Humanities Research Center at the University of Texas at Austin, particularly the helpful staff of its reading room, has been an indispensable resource throughout the long preparation of this volume. Gregory Chaplin would like to thank the Center for the Advancement of Research and Teaching at Bridgewater State College for supporting this project, and he is deeply grateful to Kathleen Vejvoda for her advice and support. John Rumrich wishes to acknowledge the substantial assistance of Mary Maddox, Suzanne Penuel, Matthew Tucker, and Roger Rouland in preparing this edition. The College of Liberal Arts and Office of Graduate Studies at the University of Texas at Austin subsidized this assistance, for which we are much obliged. Finally, Rumrich wishes to thank Alicia, Gabriel, and Nathaniel; his part in this work is dedicated to them.

JOHN RUMRICH
GREGORY CHAPLIN

THE TEXTS OF THE POEMS

Aemilia Lanyer

1569 In January, Aemilia Basano is born to Margaret Johnson, common-law wife of Baptista Basano, a court musician who came to London from Venice (he died when Aemilia was seven).

1587 Her mother dies. By this time, Aemilia is mistress to Henry Carey, Lord Hunsdon, Queen Elizabeth's Lord Chamberlain. He is forty-five years her senior.

1592 Pregnant by Lord Hunsdon, she enters an arranged marriage with Alphonso Lanyer, a court musician. Her son, Henry, is born soon after.

1597 Consults the astrologer Simon Forman, whose diary is the source of most of what is known about Lanyer.

1598 Her only daughter is born; she does not survive infancy.

1611 Publishes her only known volume of poems, *Salve Deus Rex Judaeorum*.

1613 Alphonso Lanyer dies. Aemilia begins to suffer financial difficulties that will persist for the rest of her days.

1617 Founds a school in St. Giles. This endeavor ends in 1619.

1645 Dies on 3 April, aged seventy-six.

FROM *SALVE DEUS REX JUDAEORUM* (1611)

To the Queen's Most Excellent Majesty[1]

Renowned empress, and great Britain's Queen,
Most gracious mother of succeeding kings;
Vouchsafe[2] to view that which is seldom seen,
A woman's writing of divinest[3] things:
  Read it, fair Queen, though it defective be,
  Your Excellence can grace both it and me.

For you have rifled Nature of her store,
And all the goddesses have dispossest[4]
Of those rich gifts which they enjoyed before,
But now, great Queen, in you they all do rest.
  If now they strived for the golden ball,[5]
  Paris would give it you before them all.

From Juno you have state and dignities;
From warlike Pallas, wisdom, fortitude;
And from fair Venus, all her excellencies;
With their best parts your Highness is indu'd:[6]
  How much are we to honor those that springs
  From such rare beauty, in the blood of kings?

The Muses do attend upon your throne,
With all the artists at your beck and call;
The sylvan gods, and satyrs[7] every one,
Before your fair triumphant chariot fall:
  And shining Cynthia[8] with her nymphs attend
  To honor you, whose honor hath no end.

From your bright sphere of greatness where you sit,
Reflecting light to all those glorious stars
That wait upon your throne, to virtue yet
Vouchsafe that splendor which my meanness[9] bars:
  Be like fair Phoebe, who doth love to grace
  The darkest night with her most beauteous face.

Apollo's beams do comfort every creature,
And shines upon the meanest things that be;

1. Anne of Denmark (1574–1619), Queen to James I and patron of writers and musicians.
2. Be willing.
3. Most divine.
4. Disposed.
5. Paris was to award a golden apple (inscribed "for the fairest") to one of three goddesses. Each promised him a gift if he chose her: Minerva (Athena), wisdom; Juno (Hera), power; and Venus (Aphrodite), the most beautiful woman in the world, Helen of Troy.
6. Endowed.
7. Woodland gods supposed to be the companions of Bacchus, the god of wine.
8. Goddess of the moon, also called Diana or Phoebe.
9. Low birth or social status.

Since in estate[1] and virtue none is greater,
I humbly wish that yours may light on me:
That so these rude unpolished lines of mine,
Graced by you, may seem the more divine.

Look in this mirror[2] of a worthy mind,
Where some of your fair virtues will appear;
Though all it is impossible to find,
Unless my glass[3] were crystal, or more clear:
Which is dim steel, yet full of spotless truth,
And for one look from your fair eyes it su'th.

Here may your sacred Majesty behold
That mighty Monarch[4] both of heav'n and earth,
He that all nations of the world controlled,
Yet took our flesh in base and meanest birth:
Whose days were spent in poverty and sorrow,
And yet all kings their wealth of him do borrow.

For he is crown and crowner of all kings,
The hopeful haven of the meaner sort,
It's he that all our joyful tidings brings
Of happy reign within his royal court:
It's he that in extremity[5] can give
Comfort to them that have no time to live.

And since my wealth within his region stands,
And that his cross my chiefest comfort is,
Yea in his kingdom only rests my lands,
Of honor there I hope I shall not miss:
Though I on earth do live unfortunate,
Yet there I may attain a better state.

In the meantime, accept most gracious Queen
This holy work, virtue presents to you,
In poor apparel, shaming to be seen,
Or once t'appear in your judicial view:
But that fair virtue, though in mean attire,
All princes of the world do most desire.

And sith[6] all royal virtues are in you,
The natural, the moral, and divine,
I hope how plain soever,[7] being true,
You will accept even of the meanest line

1. Social class.
2. The "mirror" is the *Salve Deus* poem.
3. Mirror.
4. Christ.
5. On the verge of death.
6. Since.
7. However plain.

Fair virtue yields; by whose rare gifts you are
So highly graced, t'exceed the fairest fair.

Behold, great Queen, fair Eve's apology,[8]
Which I have writ in honor of your sex,
And do refer unto your Majesty,
To judge if it agree not with the text:[9]
And if it do, why are poor women blamed,
Or by more faulty men so much defamed?

And this great lady I have here attired,
In all her richest ornaments of honor,
That you fair Queen, of all the world admired,
May take the more delight to look upon her:
For she must entertain you to this feast,
To which your Highness is the welcomest guest.

For here I have prepared my Paschal Lamb,[1]
The figure of that living sacrifice;
Who dying, all th'infernal powers o'ercame,
That we with him t'eternity might rise:
This precious Passover[2] feed upon, O Queen,
Let your fair virtues in my glass be seen.

And she[3] that is the pattern of all beauty, *The Lady Elizabeth's Grace*
The very model of your Majesty
Whose rarest parts enforceth love and duty,
The perfect pattern of all piety:
O let my book by her fair eyes be blest,
In whose pure thoughts all innocency rests.

Then shall I think my glass a glorious sky,
When two such glitt'ring suns at once appear;
The one replete with sovereign majesty,
Both shining brighter than the clearest clear:
And both reflecting comfort to my spirits,
To find their grace so much above my merits;

Whose untuned voice the doleful notes doth sing
Of sad affliction in an humble strain;
Much like unto a bird that wants a wing,
And cannot fly, but warbles forth her pain:
Or he that barrèd from the sun's bright light,
Wanting day's comfort, doth commend the night.

8. Defense.
9. Scripture.
1. Lamb prepared for Passover, emblematic of Christ.
2. Jewish festival celebrating the escape of the Israelites from Egyptian bondage (Exodus 12:22–27), interpreted by Christians as foreshadowing Christ's liberation of humanity from sin.
3. Princess Elizabeth, the Queen's daughter.

So I that live closed up in sorrow's cell,
Since great Eliza's[4] favor blest my youth;
And in the confines of all cares do dwell,
Whose grievèd eyes no pleasure ever view'th:
But in Christ's suff'rings, such sweet taste they have,
As makes me praise pale sorrow and the grave.

And this great lady whom I love and honor,
And from my very tender years have known,
This holy habit still to take upon her,
Still to remain the same, and still her own:
And what our fortunes do enforce us to,
She of devotion and mere zeal doth do.

Which makes me think our heavy burden light,
When such a one as she will help to bear it:
Treading the paths that make our way go right,
What garment is so fair but she may wear it;
Especially for her that entertains
A glorious queen,[5] in whom all worth remains;

Whose power may raise my sad dejected Muse,
From this low mansion of a troubled mind;
Whose princely favor may such grace infuse,
That I may spread her virtues in like kind:
But in this trial of my slender skill,
I wanted[6] knowledge to perform my will.

For even as they that do behold the stars,
Not with the eye of learning, but of sight,
To find their motions, want of knowledge bars
Although they see them in their brightest light:
So, though I see the glory of her state,
It's she that must instruct and elevate.

My weak distempered brain and feeble spirits,
Which all unlearnèd have adventured, this
To write of Christ, and of his sacred merits,
Desiring that this book her hands may kiss:
And though I be unworthy of that grace,
Yet let her blessèd thoughts this book embrace.

And pardon me (fair Queen) though I presume,
To do that which so many better can;
Not that I learning to myself assume,
Or that I would compare with any man:

4. Queen Elizabeth I.
5. Queen Anne.
6. Lacked.

But as they are scholars, and by art do write,
So Nature yields my soul a sad[7] delight.

And since all arts at first from Nature came,
That goodly creature, mother of perfection,
Whom Jove's almighty hand[8] at first did frame,
Taking both her and hers[9] in his protection,
Why should not she now grace my barren Muse,
And in a woman all defects excuse.

So peerless princess humbly I desire,
That your great wisdom would vouchsafe t'omit
All faults; and pardon if my spirits retire,
Leaving to aim at what they cannot hit:
To write your worth, which no pen can express,
Were but t'eclipse your fame, and make it less.

To All Virtuous Ladies in General

Each blessed lady that in Virtue spends
Your precious time to beautify your souls,
Come wait on her[1] whom wingèd Fame attends
And in her hand the book where she enrolls
Those high deserts that majesty commends:
Let this fair queen not unattended be,
When in my glass[2] she deigns[3] herself to see.

Put on your wedding garments everyone,
The Bridegroom[4] stays to entertain you all;
Let Virtue be your guide, for she alone
Can lead you right that you can never fall;
And make no stay for fear he should be gone:
But fill your lamps with oil of burning zeal,[5]
That to your faith he may his truth reveal.

Let all your robes be purple scarlet white,
Those perfect colors purest Virtue wore;[6]
Come decked with lilies that did so delight
To be preferred in beauty, far before
Wise Solomon[7] in all his glory dight:[8]

The robes Christ wore before his death.

7. Solemn.
8. Jove refers to God, the creator of nature (and of the first woman, Eve).
9. Nature and those nature influences.
1. Virtue.
2. Mirror.
3. Condescends.
4. Christ.
5. An allusion to the parable of the wise and foolish virgins (Matthew 25:1–13). Cf. Milton, Sonnet 9, p. 397.
6. The ladies are asked to come dressed in colors associated with Christ's passion (Matthew 6:28–29; Luke 12:27).
7. King of Israel, celebrated for wisdom.
8. Dressed.

Whose royal robes did no such pleasure yield,
As did the beauteous lily of the field.[9]

Adorn your temples with fair Daphne's crown, *In token of constancy.*
The never changing laurel, always green;[1]
Let constant hope all worldly pleasures drown,
In wise Minerva's[2] paths be always seen;
Or with bright Cynthia, though fair Venus frown:[3]
With Aesop cross the posts of[4] every door,
Where Sin would riot, making Virtue poor.

And let the Muses your companions be,
Those sacred sisters that on Pallas[5] wait,
Whose virtues with the purest minds agree,
Whose godly labors do avoid the bait
Of worldly pleasures, living always free
From sword, from violence, and from ill report;
To these nine worthies all fair minds resort.

Anoint your hair with Aaron's precious oil,[6]
And bring your palms of vict'ry in your hands,
To overcome all thoughts that would defile
The earthly circuit of your souls' fair lands;
Let no dim shadows your clear eyes beguile:
Sweet odors, myrrh, gum, aloes, frankincense,[7]
Present that King who died for your offense.

Behold, bright Titan's[8] shining chariot stays,
All decked with flowers of the freshest hue,
Attended on by Age, Hours, Nights, and Days,
Which alters not your beauty, but gives you
Much more, and crowns you with eternal praise:
This golden chariot wherein you must ride,
Let simple[9] doves, and subtle[1] serpents guide.

Come swifter than the motion of the sun,
To be transfigured with our loving Lord,
Lest glory end what grace in you begun;
Of heav'nly riches make your greatest hoard,
In Christ all honor, wealth, and beauty's won:
By whose perfections you appear more fair
Than Phoebus,[2] if he sev'n times brighter were.

9. Cf. Matthew 6:28–29.
1. Rather than submit to the enamored Apollo, Daphne was transformed into a laurel tree.
2. Chaste Roman goddess of wisdom.
3. *Cynthia*: chaste goddess of the moon; *Venus*: goddess of love.
4. I.e., pass by without entering.
5. Pallas Athena, Greek goddess of wisdom.
6. Moses anointed Aaron with oil, making him the first priest of Israel (Leviticus 8:12).
7. Traditionally, gifts fit for a king.
8. The sun.
9. Harmless.
1. Shrewd.
2. Another name for Apollo, the sun god.

God's holy angels will direct your doves,
And bring your serpents to the fields of rest,
Where he[3] doth stay that purchased all your loves
In bloody torments, when he died oppressed;
There shall you find him in those pleasant groves
  Of sweet Elysium,[4] by the Well of Life,[5]
  Whose crystal springs do purge from worldly strife.

Thus may you fly from dull and sensual earth,
Whereof at first your bodies formèd were,
That new regen'rate in a second birth,
Your blessèd souls may live without all fear,
Being immortal, subject to no death:
  But in the eye of heaven so highly placed,
  That others by your virtues may be graced.

Where worthy ladies I will leave you all,
Desiring you to grace this little book;
Yet some of you methinks I hear to call
Me by my name, and bid me better look,
Lest unawares I in an error fall:
  In general terms, to place you with the rest,
  Whom Fame commends to be the very best.

'Tis true, I must confess (O noble Fame)
There are a number honorèd by thee,
Of which, some few thou didst recite by name,
And willed my Muse they should remembered be,
Wishing some would their glorious trophies frame:
  Which if I should presume to undertake,
  My tired hand for very fear would quake.

Only by name I will bid some of those,
That in true honor's seat have long been placed,
Yea even such as thou hast chiefly chose,
By whom my Muse may be the better graced;
Therefore, unwilling longer time to lose,
  I will invite some ladies that I know,
  But chiefly those as thou hast gracèd so.

From *Salve Deus Rex Judaeorum*

Now Pontius Pilate[6] is to judge the cause
Of faultless Jesus, who before him stands,
Who neither hath offended prince, nor laws,
Although he now be brought in woeful bands:

3. Christ.
4. Abode of the blessed dead.
5. Cf. Revelation 22:1.
6. Roman governor of Jerusalem from A.D. 26 to A.D. 36, he presided over the trial of Jesus.

O noble governor, make thou yet a pause,
Do not in innocent blood imbrue[7] thy hands;
But hear the words of thy most worthy wife,
Who sends to thee, to beg her Savior's life.[8]

Let barb'rous cruelty far depart from thee,
And in true justice take affliction's part;
Open thine eyes, that thou the truth may'st see;
Do not the thing that goes against thy heart,
Condemn not him that must thy Savior be;
But view his holy life, his good desert.
Let not us women glory in men's fall,
Who had power given to overrule us all.

Eve's Apology

Till now your indiscretion sets us free,
And makes our former fault much less appear;[9]
Our mother Eve, who tasted of the tree,
Giving to Adam what she held most dear,
Was simply good, and had no power to see;
The after-coming harm[1] did not appear:
The subtle serpent that our sex betrayed,
Before our fall so sure a plot had laid.

That undiscerning ignorance[2] perceived
No guile or craft that was by him intended;
For had she known of what we were bereaved,
To his request she had not condescended.[3]
But she (poor soul) by cunning was deceived;
No hurt therein her harmless heart intended:
For she alleged God's word,[4] which he denies,
That they should die, but even as gods, be wise.

But surely Adam cannot be excused,
Her fault though great, yet he was most to blame;
What weakness offered, strength might have refused;
Being lord of all, the greater was his shame:
Although the serpent's craft had her abused,
God's holy word ought all his actions frame,
For he was lord and king of all the earth,
Before poor Eve had either life or breath.[5]

Who being framed by God's eternal hand,
The perfect'st man that ever breathed on earth,

7. Stain.
8. "When [Pilate] was set down on the judgment seat, his wife sent unto him, saying, Have you nothing to do with that just man: for I have suffered many things this day in a dream because of him" (Matthew 27:19).
9. I.e., man's lack of judgment makes Eve's crime seem less grievous.
1. The consequences of the Fall.
2. Refers to Eve's ignorance.
3. I.e., would not have agreed.
4. I.e., (initially) resisted the serpent's argument by citing God's warning.
5. Cf. Genesis 2:7–22.

And from God's mouth received that straight[6] command,
The breach whereof he knew was present death:
Yea having power to rule both sea and land,
Yet with one apple won to lose that breath
  Which God had breathed in his beauteous face,
  Bringing us all in danger and disgrace.

And then to lay the fault on Patience[7] back,
That we (poor women) must endure it all;
We know right well he did discretion lack,
Being not persuaded thereunto at all;
If Eve did err, it was for knowledge sake;
The fruit being fair, persuaded him to fall:
  No subtle serpent's falsehood did betray him;
  If he would eat it, who had power to stay him?

Not Eve, whose fault was only too much love,
Which made her give this present to her dear,
That what she tasted, he likewise might prove,[8]
Whereby his knowledge might become more clear;
He never sought her weakness to reprove,[9]
With those sharp words, which he of God did hear:
  Yet men will boast of knowledge, which he took
  From Eve's fair hand, as from a learnèd book.

If any evil did in her remain,
Being made of him, he was the ground of all;[1]
If one of many worlds[2] could lay a stain
Upon our sex and work so great a fall
To wretched man by Satan's subtle train;[3]
What will so foul a fault amongst you all?
  Her weakness did the serpent's words obey;
  But you in malice God's dear Son betray.

Whom, if unjustly you condemn to die,
Her sin was small, to what you do commit;
All mortal sins that do for vengeance cry,
Are not to be comparèd unto it:
If many worlds would altogether try
By all their sins the wrath of God to get,
  This sin of yours surmounts them all as far
  As doth the sun another little star.

6. Direct.
7. Patience's.
8. Try.
9. Admonish.
1. Cf. Genesis 2:7, 21–23.
2. Ages, long periods of time.
3. Course of action (in tempting Eve); also, the body of the serpent.

Then let us have our liberty again,
And challenge[4] to yourselves no sovereignty;
You came not in the world without our pain;
Make that a bar against your cruelty.
Your fault being greater, why should you disdain
Our being your equals, free from tyranny?
If one weak woman simply did offend,
This sin of yours hath no excuse nor end.

To which (poor souls) we never gave consent,
Witness thy wife (O Pilate) speaks for all,
Who did but dream, and yet a message sent,
That thou should'st have nothing to do at all
With that just man, which, if thy heart relent,
Why wilt thou be a reprobate[5] with Saul?[6]
To seek the death of him that is so good,
For thy soul's health to shed his dearest blood.

The Description of Cookham[7]

Farewell (sweet Cookham) where I first obtained
Grace from that grace where perfect grace remained;[8]
And where the Muses gave their full consent,
I should have pow'r the virtuous to content;
Where princely palace willed me to indite,[9]
The sacred story of the soul's delight.
Farewell (sweet place) where virtue then did rest,
And all delights did harbor in her breast;
Never shall my sad eyes again behold
Those pleasures which my thoughts did then unfold:
Yet you (great Lady) mistress of that place,
From whose desires did spring this work of grace;
Vouchsafe[1] to think upon those pleasures past
As fleeting worldly joys that could not last:
Or, as dim shadows of celestial pleasures,
Which are desired above all earthly treasures.
Oh how (me thought) against you thither came,[2]
Each part did seem some new delight to frame!
The house received all ornaments to grace it,
And would endure no foulness to deface it.

4. Attribute.
5. One rejected by God.
6. King of Israel, rejected by God for disobedience (1 Samuel 15:23–26).
7. Country house visited by Lanyer when her patron, Margaret Clifford, Countess of Cumberland, was in residence (see line 11). The manor was leased for the Countess by her brother, William Russell, while she was estranged from her husband.
8. Evoking social and religious senses of grace, Lanyer credits her host with inspiring her spiritually and as a poet. "Remained" may retain its archaic sense of dwelled or resided.
9. "Palace" may refer simply to Cookham and the active influence of an ideal setting. It may also be read as a metonymy for the Countess, who asked Lanyer to write (indite) the sacred story (line 12).
1. Deign or agree.
2. In preparation for your arrival.

The walks put on their summer liveries,[3]
And all things else did hold like similes:[4]
The trees with leaves, with fruits, with flowers clad,
Embraced each other, seeming to be glad,
Turning themselves to beauteous canopies,
To shade the bright sun from your brighter eyes;
The crystal streams with silver spangles graced,
While by the glorious sun they were embraced;
The little birds in chirping notes did sing,
To entertain both you and that sweet spring.
And Philomela with her sundry lays,[5]
Both you and that delightful place did praise.
Oh how me thought each plant, each flower, each tree
Set forth their beauties then to welcome thee!
The very hills right humbly did descend,
When you to tread upon them did intend,
And as you set your feet, they still did rise,
Glad that they could receive so rich a prize.
The gentle winds did take delight to be
Among those woods that were so graced by thee.
And in sad murmur uttered pleasing sound,
That pleasure in that place might more abound:
The swelling banks delivered all their pride,
When such a phoenix once they had espied.[6]
Each arbor, bank, each seat, each stately tree,
Thought themselves honored in supporting thee.
The pretty birds would oft come to attend thee,
Yet fly away for fear they should offend thee:
The little creatures in the burrow by
Would come abroad to sport them in your eye,
Yet fearful of the bow in your fair hand
Would run away when you did make a stand.
Now let me come unto that stately tree,
Wherein such goodly prospects you did see;
That oak that did in height his fellows pass,
As much as lofty trees, low growing grass:
Much like a comely cedar straight and tall,
Whose beauteous stature far exceeded all:
How often did you visit this fair tree,
Which seeming joyful in receiving thee,
Would like a palm tree spread his arms abroad,
Desirous that you there should make abode:
Whose fair green leaves much like a comely veil,
Defended Phoebus when he would assail:[7]

3. Distinctive uniforms identifying servants of a noble house.
4. I.e., comported themselves in a similarly celebratory way.
5. Philomela was raped by her brother-in-law, Tereus, who tore out her tongue to ensure secrecy. Subsequently, she was transformed into a nightingale. *Lays*: songs.
6. The pride of the swelling banks could refer to fish in the streams (specifically the fresh water lamprey, or sand-pride, common in England) or to flowers blossoming in response to the Countess, who is likened to a phoenix, a mythical bird reborn from its own ashes, often invoked by Renaissance poets to praise subjects of unique excellence.
7. I.e., the leaves block the rays of Phoebus, the Greek sun god.

Whose pleasing boughs did yield a cool fresh air,
Joying[8] his happiness when you were there.
Where being seated, you might plainly see,
Hills, vales, and woods, as if on bended knee
They had appeared, your honor to salute,
Or to prefer some strange unlooked for suit:[9]
All interlaced with brooks and crystal springs,
A prospect fit to please the eyes of kings:
And thirteen shires appeared all in your sight,
Europe could not afford much more delight.
What was there then but gave you all content,
While you the time in meditation spent,
Of their Creator's power, which there you saw,
In all his creatures held a perfect law;
And in their beauties did you plain descry,[1]
His beauty, wisdom, grace, love, majesty.
In these sweet woods how often did you walk,
With Christ and his apostles there to talk;
Placing his holy writ in some fair tree,
To meditate what you therein did see:
With Moses you did mount his holy hill,
To know his pleasure, and perform his will.[2]
With lovely David[3] did you often sing,
His holy hymns to heav'n's eternal King.
And in sweet music did your soul delight,
To sound his praises, morning, noon, and night.
With blessed Joseph you did often feed
Your pinèd brethren, when they stood in need.[4]
And that sweet lady sprung from Clifford's race,
Of noble Bedford's blood, fair stem of grace,
To honorable Dorset now espoused,[5]
In whose fair breast true virtue then was housed:
Oh what delight did my weak spirits find,
In those pure parts of her well framèd mind.
And yet it grieves me that I cannot be
Near unto her, whose virtues did agree
With those fair ornaments of outward beauty,
Which did enforce from all both love and duty.
Unconstant Fortune, thou art most to blame,
Who casts us down into so low a frame:
Where our great friends we cannot daily see,

8. Enjoying. *His*: the oak's.
9. I.e., to make an odd, unanticipated request.
1. Discern or detect.
2. Like Moses, who climbed Mt. Sinai to receive God's law, the Countess seeks to discover and obey God's will (Exodus 24, 25).
3. King David, the psalmist.
4. Sold into slavery by his jealous brothers, Joseph nonetheless prospers in Egypt and ultimately rescues his brothers, and thus all of Israel, from starvation (Genesis 42:1–28).
5. The sweet lady (line 93) is the Countess's daughter, Anne Clifford, by George Clifford, third Earl of Cumberland. The Countess herself is a Russell (of "Bedford's blood"). Anne married the Earl of Dorset in 1609.

So great a diff'rence is there in degree.[6]
Many are placèd in those orbs of state,
Parters in honor, so ordained by fate
Nearer in show, yet farther off in love,
In which, the lowest always are above.[7]
But whither am I carried in conceit?
My wit too weak to conster of the great.[8]
Why not? Although we are but born of earth,
We may behold the heavens, despising death;
And loving heaven that is so far above,
May in the end vouchsafe us entire love.[9]
Therefore sweet memory do thou retain
Those pleasures past, which will not turn again:
Remember beauteous Dorset's former sports,[1]
So far from being touched by ill reports,
Wherein myself did always bear a part,
While reverend Love presented my true heart.
Those recreations let me bear in mind,
Which her sweet youth and noble thoughts did find;
Whereof deprived, I evermore must grieve,
Hating blind Fortune, careless to relieve.
And you sweet Cookham, whom these ladies leave,
I now must tell the grief you did conceive
At their departure; when they went away,
How everything retained a sad dismay.
Nay long before, when once an inkling came,
Methought each thing did unto sorrow frame:
The trees that were so glorious in our view,
Forsook both flowers and fruit, when once they knew
Of your depart, their very leaves did wither,
Changing their colors as they grew together.
But when they saw this had no power to stay you,
They often wept, though speechless, could not pray you,
Letting their tears in your fair bosoms fall,
As if they said, "Why will ye leave us all?"
This being vain, they cast their leaves away,
Hoping that pity would have made you stay:
Their frozen tops, like age's hoary hairs,
Shows their disaster, languishing in fears:

6. Lanyer laments her relatively low social status, which prevents her from enjoying a full friendship with Anne.
7. Lines 107–110 are difficult to paraphrase with confidence. Lanyer compares human society to the (geocentric) cosmos, similarly divided into distinct orbs or spheres, the "parters" or dividers that distinguish class from class, lowest to highest. But Lanyer complicates the comparison by insisting on the Christian paradox that when it comes to love, the lower are actually higher. The lines may also be taken to suggest that Lanyer (the lower) loves Anne (the higher) more than Anne loves her, as is naturally fitting.
8. "Conceit" signifies thought or conception. Conster is a variant of construe, here meaning interpret or understand.
9. Human beings, made of clay, can nonetheless aspire to eternal life and ultimately find it through divine love. The implication is that if God, who is infinitely higher than any human being, nonetheless can love his lowborn creature fully, loving relations between aristocrats and those of lower classes should be possible.
1. Anne is referred to by her husband's title, Dorset.

A swarthy riveled ryne[2] all overspread,
Their dying bodies half alive, half dead.
But your occasions[3] called you so away,
That nothing there had power to make you stay:
Yet did I see a noble grateful mind,
Requiting each according to their kind,
Forgetting not to turn and take your leave
Of these sad creatures, powerless to receive
Your favor, when with grief you did depart,
Placing their former pleasures in your heart,
Giving great charge to noble memory,
There to preserve their love continually:
But specially the love of that fair tree,
That first and last you did vouchsafe to see,
In which it pleased you oft to take the air,
With noble Dorset, then a virgin fair,
Where many a learnèd book was read and scanned
To this fair tree, taking me by the hand,
You did repeat the pleasures which had past,
Seeming to grieve they could no longer last.
And with a chaste, yet loving kiss took leave,
Of which sweet kiss I did it soon bereave:
Scorning a senseless creature should possess
So rare a favor, so great happiness.
No other kiss it could receive from me,
For fear to give back what it took of thee:
So I ingrateful creature did deceive it,
Of that which you vouchsafed in love to leave it.
And though it oft had giv'n me much content,
Yet this great wrong I never could repent:
But of the happiest made it most forlorn,
To show that nothing's free from Fortune's scorn,
While all the rest with this most beauteous tree,
Made their sad consort sorrow's harmony.
The flowers that on the banks and walks did grow,
Crept in the ground, the grass did weep for woe.
The winds and waters seemed to chide together,
Because you went away they know not whither:
And those sweet brooks that ran so fair and clear,
With grief and trouble wrinkled did appear.
Those pretty birds that wonted[4] were to sing,
Now neither sing, nor chirp, nor use their wing;
But with their tender feet on some bare spray,
Warble forth sorrow, and their own dismay.
Fair Philomela leaves her mournful ditty,
Drowned in dead sleep, yet can procure no pity:
Each arbor, bank, each seat, each stately tree,

2. A shriveled and wrinkled bark. Ryne was an alternative spelling for rind.
3. Circumstances. After her husband's death in 1605, Margaret Clifford resided in the north, where she had inherited property. Daughter Anne married Dorset in 1609.
4. Accustomed.

Looks bare and desolate now for want of thee;
Turning green tresses into frosty gray,
While in cold grief they wither all away.
The sun grew weak, his beams no comfort gave,
While all green things did make the earth their grave:
Each brier, each bramble, when you went away,
Caught fast your clothes, thinking to make you stay:
Delightful Echo wonted to reply
To our last words, did now for sorrow die:
The house cast off each garment that might grace it,
Putting on dust and cobwebs to deface it.
All desolation then there did appear,
When you were going whom they held so dear.
This last farewell to Cookham here I give,
When I am dead thy name in this may live
Wherein I have performed her noble hest,
Whose virtues lodge in my unworthy breast,
And ever shall, so long as life remains,
Tying my heart to her by those rich chains.

John Donne

1572 Born in Bread Street, London, to a devout Catholic family, related through Donne's mother to Sir Thomas More. Her brother (Jasper Heywood) was the leader of the Jesuit mission in England.

1576 Father dies suddenly. Six months later, Donne's mother marries John Syminges, a Catholic physician.

1583 Having been tutored by Jesuits, Donne enters Hart Hall (now Hertford College), University of Oxford. He may also have studied at Cambridge. As a Catholic, he was ineligible for a degree at either university.

1591 Admitted to study law as a member of Thavies Inn and, in 1592, Lincoln's Inn. Donne's satires, and some of his elegies and songs and sonnets, date from this period of residency in London.

1593 Having been imprisoned for giving refuge to a Catholic priest, Donne's brother Henry dies of a fever in prison. Donne's skepticism toward the Roman Catholic Church grows.

1596 Joins Robert Devereux, Second Earl of Essex, in the naval expedition against Cadiz, and, in the following year, sails with Raleigh in search of Spanish treasure ships. "The Storm" and "The Calm" date from this period.

1598 Returns to England and is appointed private secretary to Sir Thomas Egerton, Lord Keeper of the Great Seal.

1601 Secretly marries Lady Egerton's niece, seventeen-year-old Anne More, and is dismissed from Egerton's service, and briefly imprisoned. For the next fifteen years Donne struggles to find employment, often depending on the charity of relations and patrons, including Magdalen Herbert, George Herbert's mother.

1611 *An Anatomy of the World* published in honor of the deceased Elizabeth Drury, daughter of Donne's patron, Sir Robert Drury. Many of the Holy Sonnets were likely written around this time.

1614 At the insistence of King James, Cambridge confers the degree of Doctor of Divinity on Donne.

1615 Enters the ministry, is appointed Royal Chaplain. Through the influence of powerful friends, holds multiple livings in the Church.

1616 Appointed Reader in Divinity at Lincoln's Inn.

1617 Anne Donne dies 15 August (age thirty-three) after the birth of their twelfth child. Holy Sonnet 17 composed at this time.

1618 Travels to Germany as chaplain to the embassy of Viscount Doncaster. "Hymn to Christ at the Author's Last Going into Germany" composed.

1621 Donne wins the favor of the Duke of Buckingham and is appointed Dean of Saint Paul's.

1624 Appointed vicar of St. Dunstan's-in-the-West.

1631 After having his portrait made while wearing a shroud and standing on a funeral urn, Donne dies in London, 31 March.

FROM *POEMS* (1633)

FROM *SONGS AND SONNETS*

The Good-Morrow

I wonder, by my troth,[1] what thou and I
Did, till we loved? were we not weaned till then?
But sucked on country pleasures, childishly?
Or snorted we in the Seven Sleepers' den?[2]
'Twas so; but this,[3] all pleasures fancies be.
If ever any beauty I did see,
Which I desired, and got, 'twas but a dream of thee.

And now good-morrow to our waking souls,
Which watch not one another out of fear;
For love, all love of other sights controls,
And makes one little room an everywhere.
Let sea-discoverers to new worlds have gone,
Let maps to others, worlds on worlds have shown,[4]
Let us possess one world, each hath one, and is one.[5]

My face in thine eye, thine in mine appears,
And true plain hearts do in the faces rest;
Where can we find two fitter hemispheres,[6]
Without sharp north, without declining west?
Whatever dies[7] was not mixed equally;[8]
If our two loves be one, or, thou and I
Love so alike that none do slacken, none can die.

Song

Go and catch a falling star,
Get with child a mandrake root,[9]

1. In truth. "Troth" can also mean engagement or mutual pledge to marry.
2. Legend tells of seven second-century Christian youths who fled Roman persecution, took refuge in a cave or den, and miraculously slept there unharmed for two centuries.
3. Except for this.
4. Let maps reveal to other people many worlds.
5. According to conventional wisdom of Donne's time, every man is in himself a little cosmos, or microcosm, corresponding to the larger cosmos, or macrocosm.
6. Hemisphere here refers to the celestial sphere, particularly the half that stretches from horizon to horizon. The lovers united are like the two halves of the sky, which neither decline to the west nor disappear to the north (line 18), change color (line 19), or "slacken" (line 21). The two halves together thus overcome the defects of being only half of a whole.
7. Older manuscripts have "dyes" instead of "dies."
8. Scholastic doctrine held that death follows from the imbalance of constituent elements. Alchemic doctrine held that by changing the elements or a composition of a given thing the color of that thing would also change or be "dyed." Spiritually oriented alchemists sought self-transformation, a purified spirit that like an eternal love (line 21) cannot die.
9. The mandrake's fleshy, sometimes forked root was thought to resemble the human form and to possess various pharmacological and magical properties, especially relating to erotic love and reproduction. John Gerard's *Herball* (London, 1597) describes male and female mandrakes but debunks such lore (pp. 280–282).

Tell me where all past years are,
Or who cleft the Devil's foot,
Teach me to hear mermaids singing,
Or to keep off envy's stinging,
And find
What wind
Serves to advance an honest mind.

If thou be'st born to strange sights,
Things invisible to see,
Ride ten thousand days and nights,
Till age snow white hairs on thee,
Thou, when thou return'st, wilt tell me
All strange wonders that befell thee,
And swear
No where
Lives a woman true, and fair.

If thou findst one, let me know,
Such a pilgrimage were sweet.
Yet do not; I would not go,
Though at next door we might meet;
Though she were true, when you met her,
And last, till you write your letter,
Yet she
Will be
False, ere I come, to two, or three.

The Undertaking

I have done one braver thing
Than all the Worthies[1] did,
And yet a braver thence doth spring,
Which is, to keep that hid.

It were but madness now to impart
The skill of specular stone,[2]
When he which can have learned the art
To cut it can find none.

So, if I now should utter this,
Others (because no more
Such stuff to work upon there is)
Would love but as before.

But he who loveliness within
Hath found, all outward loathes,

1. Exemplary heroes of antiquity.
2. A transparent crystal capable of reflecting light like a mirror, used for glazing in ancient times but no longer available in Donne's era.

For he who color loves, and skin,
  Loves but their oldest clothes.

If, as I have, you also do
  Virtue attired in woman see,
And dare love that, and say so too,
  And forget the He and She,

And if this love, though placèd so,
  From profane men you hide,
Which will no faith on this bestow,
  Or, if they do, deride:

Then you have done a braver thing
  Than all the Worthies did;
And a braver thence will spring,
  Which is, to keep that hid.

The Sun Rising

    Busy old fool, unruly sun,
    Why dost thou thus,
Through windows, and through curtains, call on us?
Must to thy motions lovers' seasons run?
    Saucy pedantic wretch, go chide
    Late schoolboys, and sour prentices,
  Go tell court-huntsmen that the king will ride,
  Call country ants to harvest offices;
Love, all alike, no season knows, nor clime,
Nor hours, days, months, which are the rags of time.

    Thy beams, so reverend and strong
    Why shouldst thou think?
I could eclipse and cloud them with a wink,
But that I would not lose her sight so long:
    If her eyes have not blinded thine,
    Look, and tomorrow late, tell me
  Whether both the Indias of spice and mine[3]
  Be where thou leftst them, or lie here with me.
Ask for those kings whom thou saw'st yesterday,
And thou shalt hear, "All here in one bed lay."

    She's all states, and all princes I,
    Nothing else is.
Princes do but play us; compared to this,
All honor's mimic, all wealth alchemy.[4]
    Thou, sun, art half as happy as we,

3. The East Indies (spices) and the West Indies (precious metals).
4. Metallic composition that looks like gold, "alchemy gold" (e.g., the brass of a trumpet); glittering dross.

In that the world's contracted thus;
Thine age asks[5] ease, and since thy duties be
To warm the world, that's done in warming us.
Shine here to us, and thou art everywhere;
This bed thy center is, these walls thy sphere.

The Indifferent

I can love both fair and brown,
Her whom abundance melts, and her whom want betrays,
Her who loves loneness best, and her who masks and plays,
Her whom the country formed, and whom the town,
Her who believes, and her who tries,
Her who still weeps with spongy eyes,
And her who is dry cork, and never cries;
I can love her, and her, and you, and you;
I can love any, so she be not true.

Will no other vice content you?
Will it not serve your turn to do as did your mothers?
Or have you all old vices spent, and now would find out others?
Or doth a fear, that men are true, torment you?
Oh we are not; be not you so;
Let me, and do you, twenty know.
Rob me, but bind me not, and let me go.
Must I, who came to travail[6] thorough[7] you,
Grow your fixed subject, because you are true?

Venus heard me sigh this song,
And by love's sweetest part, variety, she swore
She heard not this till now; and that it should be so no more.
She went, examined, and returned ere long,
And said, "Alas, some two or three
Poor heretics in love there be,
Which think to 'stablish[8] dangerous constancy.
But I have told them, 'Since you will be true,
You shall be true to them who are false to you.'"

The Canonization

For God's sake, hold your tongue, and let me love,
Or chide my palsy,[9] or my gout,
My five gray hairs, or ruined fortune flout,
With wealth your state, your mind with arts improve,

5. Demands.
6. Severe toil or exertion (with a pun on "travel" as a verb).
7. Through.
8. Establish.
9. Short form of "paralysis." Palsy can also refer to involuntary tremors.

Take you a course, get you a place,[1]
Observe his honor, or his grace,[2]
Or the king's real, or his stampèd[3] face
Contemplate; what you will, approve,[4]
So you will let me love.

Alas, alas, who's injured by my love?
What merchant's ships have my sighs drowned?
Who says my tears have overflowed his ground?
When did my colds a forward[5] spring remove?
When did the heats which my veins fill
Add one more to the plaguy bill?[6]
Soldiers find wars, and lawyers find out still
Litigious men, which quarrels move,
Though she and I do love.

Call us what you will, we are made such by love;
Call her one, me another fly,
We're tapers too, and at our own cost die,[7]
And we in us find the eagle and the dove.[8]
The phoenix[9] riddle hath more wit[1]
By us; we two being one, are it.
So, to one neutral thing both sexes fit.[2]
We die and rise the same, and prove
Mysterious by this love.[3]

We can die by it, if not live by love,
And if unfit for tombs and hearse
Our legend be, it will be fit for verse;
And if no piece of chronicle we prove,
We'll build in sonnets pretty rooms;[4]
As well a well-wrought urn becomes
The greatest ashes, as half-acre tombs,
And by these hymns, all shall approve
Us canonized for Love.

1. Follow a plan of action, obtain a position for yourself.
2. "His honor" and "his grace" are forms of address applied to those in high office or of exalted social rank. "Observe" thus signifies careful attention to and a properly reverential attitude toward an influential person.
3. Impressed (on coins).
4. Sanction; put to test.
5. Early.
6. List of victims of the plague, a highly contagious, usually fatal disease marked by high fevers ("heats"). Lovers conventionally endure extremes of cold and hot.
7. Refers to moths, symbolic of lust and transience. They are fatally attracted to burning candles ("tapers"), whose flames consume their substance. In Donne's time, "to die" could mean "to experience sexual climax," which was thought to shorten one's life.
8. Symbols of opposing qualities: active strength and submissive peace.
9. A bird fabled to exist single, to be consumed by fire by its own act, and to rise again from its ashes. Hence, an emblem of immortality.
1. Aptitude or applicability.
2. Together, the lovers constitute a hermaphrodite: part male, part female.
3. Just as the phoenix rises reborn from its own ashes, so the lovers, made one by love, are consumed in their fire of passion but revive.
4. By "sonnets" Donne refers generally to "love poems"; "stanza" in Italian means "room."

And thus invoke us: "You, whom reverend love
Made one another's hermitage;
You, to whom love was peace, that now is rage;
Who did the whole world's soul contract, and drove[5]
Into the glasses of your eyes
(So made such mirrors, and such spies,
That they did all to you epitomize)
Countries, towns, courts: beg from above
A pattern of your love!"

Air and Angels

Twice or thrice had I loved thee,
Before I knew thy face or name,
So in a voice, so in a shapeless flame
Angels affect us oft, and worshipped be;
Still when, to where thou wert, I came,
Some lovely glorious nothing I did see.
But since my soul, whose child love is,
Takes limbs of flesh, and else could nothing do,
More subtle than the parent is
Love must not be, but take a body too,
And therefore what thou wert, and who,
I bid Love ask, and now
That it assume thy body, I allow,
And fix itself in thy lip, eye, and brow.

Whilst thus to ballast[6] love, I thought,
And so more steadily to have gone,
With wares which would sink admiration,
I saw I had love's pinnace[7] overfraught;[8]
Every thy hair[9] for love to work upon
Is much too much, some fitter[1] must be sought;
For, nor in nothing, nor in things
Extreme, and scatt'ring[2] bright, can love inhere;
Then as an angel, face, and wings
Of air, not pure as it, yet pure doth wear,[3]
So thy love may be my love's sphere;[4]
Just such disparity
As is 'twixt air and angels' purity,
'Twixt women's love and men's will ever be.

5. Compelled (transitive, with "countries, towns, courts" in line 44, as its objects).
6. Stabilize a vessel, typically by placing weighty goods ("wares") in its hold.
7. Ship's boat, used as a tender or scout for merchant and war vessels on which it was carried. In Donne's era, "pinnace" was figuratively applied to mean "woman" or, specifically, "procuress" or "prostitute."
8. Overloaded.
9. Each one of your hairs.
1. Fitter objects (than every hair) for love to inhabit.
2. Dazzlingly.
3. According to scholastic doctrine, angels, in order to appear to men, assumed bodies of air, which were pure but not as pure as the angelic essence.
4. Angels were thought to inhabit and govern the celestial spheres.

The Anniversary

All kings, and all their favorites,
All glory of honors, beauties, wits,
The sun itself, which makes times,[5] as they pass,
Is elder by a year, now, than it was
When thou and I first one another saw:
All other things to their destruction draw,
Only our love hath no decay;
This, no tomorrow hath, nor yesterday;
Running it never runs from us away,
But truly keeps his first, last, everlasting day.

Two graves must hide thine and my corse;[6]
If one might, death were no divorce:
Alas, as well as other princes, we
(Who prince enough in one another be)
Must leave at last in death, these eyes, and ears,
Oft fed with true oaths, and with sweet salt tears;
But souls where nothing dwells but love
(All other thoughts being inmates[7]) then shall prove
This, or a love increased there above,[8]
When bodies to their graves, souls from their graves remove.

And then we shall be throughly[9] blest,
But we no more than all the rest;
Here upon earth, we're kings, and none but we
Can be such kings, nor of such subjects be;
Who is so safe as we, where none can do
Treason to us, except one of us two?
True and false fears let us refrain,
Let us love nobly, and live, and add again
Years and years unto years, till we attain
To write threescore: this is the second of our reign.

Twickenham[1] Garden

Blasted with sighs, and surrounded with tears,
Hither I come to seek the spring,[2]
And at mine eyes, and at mine ears,
Receive such balms[3] as else cure everything;

5. Units of time defined by reference to the sun, e.g., days and years.
6. Corpse. Donne's spelling ("corse") could mean "course" as well as "corpse"; some early manuscripts spell it "coarse," which also meant the physical quality ("coarse").
7. Only temporary lodgers, not originally or properly belonging to the place where they dwell; "prove" here probably means "find out," "discover."
8. In heaven.
9. Thoroughly, completely, perfectly; throughout; through all time (henceforth).
1. Twickenham (or "Twicknam") was the home of Lucy, Countess of Bedford, Donne's patroness and friend. Cf. "To the Countess of Bedford," line 70, p. 63.
2. Season of first growth; beginning; source.
3. Aromatic resin exuded by various trees and shrubs; soothing, healing, or comforting agent.

But oh, self-traitor, I do bring
The spider[4] love, which transubstantiates[5] all,
And can convert manna[6] to gall,[7]
And that this place may thoroughly be thought
True Paradise, I have the serpent[8] brought.

'Twere wholesomer for me, that winter did
Benight the glory of this place,
And that a grave frost did forbid
These trees to laugh, and mock me to my face;
But that I may not this disgrace
Endure, nor leave this garden, Love, let me
Some senseless piece of this place be;
Make me a mandrake,[9] so I may groan here,
Or a stone fountain weeping out my year.

Hither with crystal vials, lovers, come,
And take my tears, which are love's wine,
And try your mistress' tears at home,
For all are false, that taste not just like mine;
Alas, hearts do not in eyes shine,
Nor can you more judge woman's thoughts by tears,
Than by her shadow, what she wears.
O perverse sex, where none is true but she,
Who's therefore true, because her truth kills me.

Confined Love

Some man unworthy to be possessor
Of old or new love, himself being false or weak,
Thought his pain and shame would be lesser,
If on womankind he might his anger wreak,
And thence a law did grow,
One might but one man know;
But are other creatures so?

Are sun, moon, or stars by law forbidden
To smile where they list,[1] or lend away their light?
Are birds divorced, or are they chidden[2]
If they leave their mate, or lie abroad a night?

4. Believed to produce poison.
5. Changes into another substance; in Roman Catholic theology, transubstantiation refers to the conversion of the sacramental bread and wine into the body and blood of Christ.
6. Divinely supplied food (Exodus 16:15); hence, spiritual nourishment.
7. Bile or any intensely bitter substance; poison.
8. The biblical serpent instigates the fall of humanity and is a general source of woe.
9. Plant whose fleshy, sometimes forked root was thought to resemble the human form. Though a vegetable, it supposedly shrieked when uprooted. Cf. "Song," line 2, p. 23.
1. Please, choose.
2. Rebuked, scolded.

Beasts do no jointures[3] lose
Though they new lovers choose,
But we are made worse than those.

Who e'er rigged fair ship to lie in harbors,
And not to seek new lands, or not to deal withal?[4]
Or built fair houses, set trees, and arbors,
Only to lock up, or else to let them fall?
Good is not good, unless
A thousand it possess,
But doth waste with greediness.

A Valediction: Of Weeping

Let me pour forth
My tears before thy face, whilst I stay here,
For thy face coins them, and thy stamp they bear,
And by this mintage they are something worth,
For thus they be
Pregnant of thee;
Fruits of much grief they are, emblems of more,
When a tear falls, that thou falls which it bore,[5]
So thou and I are nothing then, when on a diverse shore.

On a round ball
A workman that hath copies by, can lay
An Europe, Afric, and an Asia,
And quickly make that, which was nothing, All;[6]
So doth each tear
Which thee doth wear,[7]
A globe, yea world, by that impression grow,
Till thy tears mixed with mine do overflow
This world, by waters sent from thee, my heaven dissolved so.

O more than Moon,
Draw not up seas to drown me in thy sphere,[8]
Weep me not dead, in thine arms, but forbear
To teach the sea what it may do too soon;
Let not the wind
Example find

3. An estate settled on a wife, for use after her husband's death.
4. Seek trade with.
5. The impending separation of the lovers moves the speaker to tears, which reflect his beloved's face before him; when a tear drops, the woman's image (the "thou" borne by the "pregnant" tear) falls with it.
6. In gluing maps onto a blank globe ("round ball"), a mapmaker renders "that which was nothing," an empty globe, into "All"—a representation of the entire world.
7. Which bears your image; or, which your tears generate and you wear on your face.
8. The speaker compares his beloved weeping to the action of the moon in causing high tides. Being greater than the moon, she is capable of drawing water up to her sphere, i.e., to her eyes, in which his reflection appears.

To do me more harm than it purposeth;
Since thou and I sigh one another's breath,
Who'er sighs most is cruellest, and hastes the other's death.[9]

Love's Alchemy[1]

Some that have deeper digged love's mine than I,
Say where his centric[2] happiness doth lie:
    I have loved, and got, and told,[3]
But should I love, get, tell, till I were old,
I should not find that hidden mystery;[4]
    Oh,'tis imposture all:
And as no chemic[5] yet the elixir got[6]
    But glorifies his pregnant pot,[7]
    If by the way to him befall
Some odoriferous thing, or medicinal,
  So lovers dream a rich and long delight,
  But get a winter-seeming summer's night.

Our ease, our thrift, our honor, and our day,
Shall we for this vain bubble's shadow pay?
    Ends love in this, that my man[8]
Can be as happy as I can, if he can
Endure the short scorn of a bridegroom's play?
    That loving wretch that swears
'Tis not the bodies marry, but the minds,
    Which he in her angelic finds,
    Would swear as justly, that he hears,
In that day's rude hoarse minstrelsy, the spheres.[9]
  Hope not for mind in women; at their best
  Sweetness and wit, they're but *Mummy*, possessed.[1]

9. A sigh was thought to shorten life.
1. Alchemy was commonly understood to be the art or science of transforming base metals into gold; esoteric alchemy, however, was concerned with spiritual transformation, the salvation and immortal bliss of the alchemist himself. Alchemy was often deemed a fraudulent practice; hence in line 6 the notion of lasting happiness in love is deemed an "imposture" comparable to the alchemist's promise to produce the elixir of life.
2. At the center; central. In the Ptolemaic cosmos, Earth's center was the center of the universe. Digging a mine would bring one closer to it.
3. Possible senses of "got" include "obtained," "procured," and "begot." Possible senses of "told" include "disclosed," "related," and "counted." Donne compares love to alchemy as a three-part chronological process of desire, possession, and accounting.
4. The secret of producing an immortal love; love's alchemy.
5. Alchemist.
6. I.e., as no alchemist has yet found out the medicine capable of extending life indefinitely (the elixir). "Got" can also mean "begot" (see lines 3–4).
7. "Glorify" can mean "extol," "make something seem more splendid," or, in alchemical contexts, "refine," "sublimate." *Pregnant pot*: alchemic vessel ready to produce new forms.
8. Servant.
9. I.e., in the wedding day's raucous music, the heavenly music of the celestial spheres.
1. *Mummy* is the title of the poem in most manuscripts. In Donne's time, it meant, among other things, dead flesh; mummified corpse; medicinal substance prepared from mummified flesh; a universal medicine or balm. Lines 23–24 are often taken to mean that women at their best are merely dead flesh, inhabited by a spirit or demon.

The Flea

Mark but this flea, and mark in this
How little that which thou deny'st me is;
It sucked me first, and now sucks thee,
And in this flea our two bloods mingled be;
Thou know'st that this cannot be said
A sin, nor shame, nor loss of maidenhead,
  Yet this enjoys before it woo,
  And pampered swells with one blood made of two,[2]
  And this, alas, is more than we would do.

Oh stay, three lives in one flea spare,
Where we almost, yea more than married are.
This flea is you and I, and this
Our marriage bed, and marriage temple is;
Though parents grudge, and you, we're met
And cloistered in these living walls of jet.[3]
  Though use[4] make you apt to kill me,
  Let not to that, self-murder added be,
  And sacrilege, three sins in killing three.

Cruel and sudden, hast thou since
Purpled thy nail in blood of innocence?
Wherein could this flea guilty be,
Except in that drop which it sucked from thee?
Yet thou triumph'st, and say'st that thou
Find'st not thyself, nor me, the weaker now;
  'Tis true; then learn how false, fears be;
  Just so much honor, when thou yield'st to me,
  Will waste, as this flea's death took life from thee.

A Nocturnal upon St. Lucy's Day,[5] Being the Shortest Day

'Tis the year's midnight, and it is the day's,
Lucy's, who scarce seven hours herself unmasks;
  The sun is spent, and now his flasks[6]
  Send forth light squibs,[7] no constant rays;
    The world's[8] whole sap is sunk;

2. Early medical theory held that sexual intercourse caused mingling of blood.
3. Black marble; a deep glossy black.
4. Habit; also, employment or exploitation for sexual purposes.
5. St. Lucy's Day, 13 December on the old style (Julian) calendar, was deemed the shortest day of the year. Lucy is the patron saint of light and vision, and her feast was celebrated by burning calendars to hasten the arrival of longer days.
6. Flasks for gunpowder but also for liquor or medicinal balms.
7. Small, unimpressive fireworks.
8. "World" refers to the cosmos, not the earth. Sap may be a figure for light.

The general balm the hydroptic[9] earth hath drunk,[1]
Whither, as to the bed's-feet,[2] life is shrunk,
Dead and interred; yet all these seem to laugh,
Compared with me, who am their epitaph.[3]

Study me then, you who shall lovers be
At the next world, that is, at the next spring:
For I am every dead thing,
In whom love wrought new alchemy.[4]
For his art did express[5]
A quintessence[6] even from nothingness,
From dull privations,[7] and lean emptiness;
He ruined[8] me, and I am re-begot
Of absence, darkness, death; things which are not.[9]

All others, from all things, draw all that's good,
Life, soul, form, spirit, whence they being have;
I, by love's limbeck,[1] am the grave
Of all that's nothing. Oft a flood
Have we two wept, and so
Drowned the whole world,[2] us two; oft did we grow
To be two chaoses,[3] when we did show
Care to aught[4] else; and often absences
Withdrew our souls, and made us carcasses.

But I am by her death (which word wrongs her)
Of the first nothing the elixir grown;[5]
Were I a man, that I were one
I needs must know; I should prefer,
If I were any beast,
Some ends, some means; yea plants, yea stones detest,
And love; all, all some properties invest;
If I an ordinary nothing were,
As shadow, a light and body must be here.[6]

9. Dropsical, suffering an insatiable thirst.
1. The thirsty earth has entirely consumed the general balm (that which sustains and repairs all things).
2. It was thought that a dying person shrank toward the foot of the bed.
3. Inscription upon a tomb.
4. In whom love worked a transformation and renewal. "Alchemy" is the art or science of transmuting base substances into purer ones, especially gold.
5. Press out.
6. Literally, the "fifth essence." In ancient and medieval philosophy, quintessence was the highest element—above the four elements of earth, air, fire, and water—latent in all things and the constitutive substance of heavenly bodies. Expression of latent quintessence, usually by distillation, was a primary objective of alchemy.
7. Want of the usual comforts or even necessities of life; the absence of a quality.
8. Ruined is probably used in an alchemical sense of reducing something to its elements.
9. Christian doctrine taught that God creates out of nothing (*ex nihilo*).
1. Alembic, an alchemical apparatus used in distilling.
2. Noah's flood threatened to return the world to its condition prior to creation.
3. Chaos is the classical analogue for the watery deep of Genesis 1.
4. Anything.
5. The quintessence out of which God created the world.
6. If I were a common example of nothingness, such as a shadow, a light and body would have to exist to produce it.

But I am none; nor will my Sun renew.
You lovers, for whose sake the lesser sun
  At this time to the Goat[7] is run
  To fetch new lust, and give it you,
    Enjoy your summer all;
Since she enjoys her long night's festival,
Let me prepare towards her, and let me call
This hour her Vigil, and her Eve, since this
Both the year's, and the day's deep midnight is.

The Bait[8]

Come live with me, and be my love,
And we will some new pleasures prove[9]
Of golden sands, and crystal brooks,
With silken lines, and silver hooks.

There will the river whispering run
Warmed by thy eyes, more than the sun.
And there the enamored fish will stay,
Begging themselves they may betray.

When thou wilt swim in that live bath,
Each fish, which every channel hath,
Will amorously to thee swim,
Gladder to catch thee, than thou him.

If thou to be so seen be'st loath
By sun, or moon, thou dark'nest both,
And if myself have leave to see,
I need not their light, having thee.

Let others freeze with angling reeds,
And cut their legs, with shells and weeds,
Or treacherously poor fish beset,
With strangling snare, or windowy net:

Let coarse bold hands, from slimy nest
The bedded fish in banks out-wrest,[1]
Or curious traitors, sleave-silk[2] flies,
Bewitch poor fishes' wand'ring eyes.

For thee, thou need'st no such deceit,
For thou thyself art thine own bait;
That fish that is not catched thereby,
Alas, is wiser far than I.

7. The zodiacal sign Capricorn, ushered in by the winter solstice. Goats symbolized lust.
8. The poem is a parodic response to Marlowe's "The Passionate Shepherd to his Love."
9. Discover, find.
1. To draw out or extract as with a forcible twist, to extract by superior force.
2. Untwisted silk.

The Apparition

When by thy scorn, O murd'ress, I am dead,
    And that thou thinkst thee free
From all solicitation[3] from me,
Then shall my ghost come to thy bed,
And thee, feigned vestal,[4] in worse arms shall see;
Then thy sick taper[5] will begin to wink,[6]
And he, whose thou art then, being tired before,
Will, if thou stir, or pinch to wake him, think
    Thou call'st for more,
And in false sleep will from thee shrink,
And then, poor aspen[7] wretch, neglected thou
Bathed in a cold quicksilver sweat wilt lie,
    A verier[8] ghost than I;
What I will say, I will not tell thee now,
Lest that preserve thee; and since my love is spent,
I had rather thou shouldst painfully repent,
Than by my threat'nings rest still innocent.

A Valediction: Forbidding Mourning[9]

As virtuous men pass mildly away,
    And whisper to their souls to go,
Whilst some of their sad friends do say,
    "The breath goes now," and some say, "No,"

So let us melt, and make no noise,
    No tear-floods, nor sigh-tempests move;
'Twere profanation of our joys
    To tell the laity our love.

Moving of the earth[1] brings harms and fears,
    Men reckon what it did and meant,
But trepidation[2] of the spheres,
    Though greater far, is innocent.[3]

3. Courting or begging the favor (of a woman), particularly with immoral intention.
4. Pretended virgin. A vestal virgin was one of the priestesses who had charge of the sacred fire in the temple of Vesta at Rome; more generally, one having the qualities of such: chaste, pure, virginal.
5. Candle; wick of a candle.
6. Flicker.
7. Trembling like the leaves of one of these trees.
8. Truer.
9. According to Isaac Walton, Donne wrote this poem for his wife in 1611, before he left for France.
1. Earthquakes.
2. Oscillation. In Ptolemaic astronomy, the term "trepidation" referred to a slow oscillation of the ecliptic. It was introduced by Arabian astronomers to explain an apparent variation in the occurrences of equinoxes.
3. Oscillation of the celestial spheres, though more momentous than earthquakes, "is innocent," i.e., causes no "harms and fears."

Dull sublunary[4] lovers' love
  (Whose soul is sense) cannot admit
Absence, because it doth remove
  Those things which elemented[5] it.

But we, by a love so much refined
  That our selves know not what it is,
Inter-assurèd of the mind,
  Care less, eyes, lips, and hands to miss.

Our two souls therefore, which are one,
  Though I must go, endure not yet
A breach, but an expansion,
  Like gold to airy thinness beat.

If they be two, they are two so
  As stiff twin compasses are two:
Thy soul, the fixed foot, makes no show
  To move, but doth, if the other do;

And though it in the center sit,
  Yet when the other far doth roam,
It leans, and hearkens after it,
  And grows erect, as that comes home.

Such wilt thou be to me, who must,
  Like the other foot, obliquely run;
Thy firmness makes my circle just,
  And makes me end where I begun.

The Ecstasy

Where, like a pillow on a bed,
  A pregnant bank swelled up, to rest
The violet's reclining head,
  Sat we two, one another's best.

Our hands were firmly cemented
  With a fast balm,[6] which thence did spring;
Our eye-beams twisted, and did thread
  Our eyes, upon one double string;[7]

4. Beneath the moon and thus subject to the moon's influence; belonging to the temporal realm of growth and decay.
5. Composed it, through the four elements: fire, air, water, and earth.
6. Gripping, gluelike, resinous ointment; sweat.
7. According to one early theory of vision (*extromission*), the eyes emit invisible beams that fetch images for the beholder. The lovers are thus physically joined not simply by holding hands, but by gazing into one another's eyes and intertwining their visual rays.

So to intergraft our hands,[8] as yet
  Was all the means to make us one,
And pictures in our eyes to get[9]
  Was all our propagation.

As,'twixt two equal armies, Fate
  Suspends uncertain victory,
Our souls (which to advance their state
  Were gone out) hung 'twixt her and me.

And whilst our souls negotiate there,
  We like sepulchral statues lay;
All day, the same our postures were,
  And we said nothing, all the day.

If any, so by love refined
  That he souls' language understood,
And by good love were grown all mind,
  Within convenient distance stood,

He (though he knew not which soul spake,
  Because both meant, both spake the same)
Might thence a new concoction[1] take,
  And part far purer than he came.

This Ecstasy doth unperplex,[2]
  We said, and tell us what we love;
We see by this it was not sex;
  We see we saw not what did move:[3]

But as all several[4] souls contain
  Mixture of things, they know not what,
Love these mixed souls doth mix again,
  And makes both one, each this and that.

A single violet transplant,
  The strength, the color, and the size,
(All which before was poor, and scant)
  Redoubles still, and multiplies.[5]

When love, with one another so
  Interinanimates two souls,

8. To graft one hand to the other's hand. The botanical procedure of grafting was a common figure for sex, but is here limited to hand holding ("as yet").
9. Beget.
1. Level of refinement, state of perfection.
2. To uncomplicate, clarify. Donne is credited with the first usage.
3. We now perceive what we did not previously recognize as the motive of our love.
4. Separate.
5. The stanza claims that a single violet (see stanza one), transplanted, will continue to grow and even multiply. Donne's use of "transplant" as a noun predates by more than a century the first such example in the *OED*.

That abler soul, which thence doth flow,
   Defects of loneliness controls.[6]

We then, who are this new soul, know
   Of what we are composed, and made,
For the atomies[7] of which we grow
   Are souls, whom no change can invade.

But oh, alas, so long, so far
   Our bodies why do we forbear?
They're ours, though they're not we, we are
   The intelligences, they the sphere.[8]

We owe them thanks because they thus
   Did us to us at first convey,
Yielded their forces, sense, to us,
   Nor are dross[9] to us, but allay.[1]

On man heaven's influence works not so,
   But that it first imprints the air,[2]
So soul into the soul may flow,
   Though it to body first repair.

As our blood labors to beget
   Spirits,[3] as like souls as it can,
Because such fingers need[4] to knit
   That subtle knot which makes us man:

So must pure lovers' souls descend
   To affections, and to faculties,
Which sense may reach and apprehend,
   Else a great Prince in prison lies.

To our bodies turn we then, that so
   Weak men on love revealed may look;
Love's mysteries in souls do grow,
   But yet the body is his book.

And if some lover, such as we,
   Have heard this dialogue of one,
Let him still mark us, he shall see
   Small change, when we're to bodies gone.

6. When love joins two souls in mutual animation, the new soul that proceeds from the union prevents, by its very nature, the defect of loneliness.
7. Atoms.
8. The celestial spheres were thought to be governed by angels or intelligences. Donne portrays the human body as similarly governed by the soul or essential self.
9. Impurity that is discarded in the process of refining a metal.
1. Alloy, a baser metal mixed with a finer.
2. Astrology held that the influence of the stars on humanity was mediated by the air.
3. Animal spirits; vapors refined or concocted from the blood, linking body and soul.
4. Are needed.

The Funeral

Whoever comes to shroud me, do not harm
Nor question much
That subtle wreath of hair, which crowns my arm;
The mystery, the sign, you must not touch,
For 'tis my outward Soul,
Viceroy to that, which then to heaven being gone,
Will leave this to control,
And keep these limbs, her provinces, from dissolution.[5]

For if the sinewy thread[6] my brain lets fall
Through every part
Can tie those parts, and make me one of all,
These hairs, which upward grew, and strength and art
Have from a better brain,
Can better do it; except she meant that I
By this should know my pain,
As prisoners then are manacled, when they're condemned to die.

Whate'er she meant by it, bury it with me,
For since I am
Love's martyr, it might breed idolatry,
If into others' hands these relics came;
As 'twas humility
To afford to it all that a soul can do,
So,'tis some bravery,[7]
That since you would save none of me, I bury some of you.

The Blossom

Little think'st thou, poor flower,
Whom I have watched six or seven days,
And seen thy birth, and seen what every hour
Gave to thy growth, thee to this height to raise,
And now dost laugh and triumph on this bough,
Little think'st thou
That it will freeze anon,[8] and that I shall
Tomorrow find thee fal'n, or not at all.

Little think'st thou, poor heart,
That labor'st yet to nestle thee,
And think'st by hovering here to get a part
In a forbidden or forbidding tree,
And hop'st her stiffness by long siege to bow,

5. Decomposition; reduction of the body to constituent elements.
6. The spinal cord and nervous system.
7. Bravado.
8. Straightaway, at once.

Little think'st thou
That thou tomorrow, ere that Sun[9] doth wake,
Must with this sun and me a journey take.

But thou which lov'st to be
Subtle to plague thyself, wilt say,
"Alas, if you must go, what's that to me?
Here lies my business, and here I will stay;
You go to friends, whose love and means present
Various content
To your eyes, ears, and tongue, and every part.
If then your body go, what need you a heart?"

Well then, stay here; but know,
When thou hast stayed and done thy most,
A naked thinking heart, that makes no show,
Is to a woman but a kind of ghost;
How shall she know my heart; or, having none,
Know thee for one?
Practice may make her know some other part,
But take my word, she doth not know a heart.

Meet me at London, then,
Twenty days hence, and thou shalt see
Me fresher, and more fat, by being with men,
Than if I had stayed still with her and thee.
For God's sake, if you can, be you so too:
I would give you
There, to another friend, whom we shall find
As glad to have my body, as my mind.

The Relic

When my grave is broke up again
Some second guest to entertain[1]
(For graves have learned that woman-head,[2]
To be to more than one a bed)
And he that digs it spies
A bracelet of bright hair about the bone,[3]
Will he not let us alone,
And think that there a loving couple lies,
Who thought that this device might be some way
To make their souls, at the last busy day,[4]
Meet at this grave, and make a little stay?

9. The lady.
1. Refers to the reuse of burial ground.
2. Woman's manner or practice, with perhaps an ironic glance at "maidenhead."
3. Cf. "The Funeral," line 3, p. 40.
4. Doomsday, "busy" because on that day the bodies of all who ever lived were to be reanimated and summoned to judgment. Cf. Holy Sonnet 4 [VII], p. 71.

If this fall[5] in a time, or land,
Where mis-devotion doth command,
Then he that digs us up will bring
Us to the Bishop and the King
To make us relics; then
Thou shalt be a Mary Magdalen, and I
A something else[6] thereby;
All women shall adore us, and some men;
And, since at such time[7] miracles are sought,
I would have that age by this paper taught
What miracles we harmless lovers wrought.

First, we loved well and faithfully,
Yet knew not what we loved, nor why;
Difference of sex no more we knew,
Than our guardian angels do;
Coming and going, we
Perchance might kiss,[8] but not between those meals;[9]
Our hands ne'er touched the seals[1]
Which nature, injured by late law,[2] sets free.
These miracles we did; but now, alas,
All measure, and all language, I should pass,
Should I tell what a miracle she was.

The Damp

When I am dead, and doctors know not why,
And my friends' curiosity
Will have me cut up to survey each part,
When they shall find your picture in my heart,
You think a sudden damp[3] of love
Will through all their senses move,
And work on them as me, and so prefer[4]
Your murder to the name of massacre.

Poor victories! But if you dare be brave,
And pleasure in your conquest have,
First kill the enormous giant, your *Disdain*,
And let the enchantress *Honor* next be slain,
And like a Goth and Vandal[5] rise,

5. If this disinterment occur.
6. Donne leaves the hypothetical identification of his remains open to speculation. Jesus Christ (metrically equivalent to "something else") is one possibility. The blasphemous implications would account for Donne's lack of specificity.
7. The Catholic Church held that God worked miracles in honor of relics.
8. Kisses as conventional gestures of meeting and parting.
9. Refers to "coming and going."
1. Intact seals indicate that the contents have not been tampered with.
2. By human law, which comes after nature's law.
3. A poisonous exhalation or vapor; also, depression or dejection.
4. Promote, advance (applied to the category of her offense: from murder to massacre).
5. Goths and Vandals belonged to Germanic tribes that from A.D. 200 to A.D. 500 invaded and ultimately toppled the Roman Empire and its civilization.

Deface records, and histories
Of your own arts and triumphs over men,
And without such advantage kill me then.

For I could muster up as well as you
My giants, and my witches too,
Which are vast *Constancy,* and *Secretness,*
But these I neither look for, nor profess;
Kill me as woman; let me die[6]
As a mere[7] man; do you but try
Your passive valor, and you shall find then,
Naked you've odds enough of any man.

Farewell to Love

Whilst yet to prove,[8]
I thought there was some deity in love,
So did I reverence, and gave
Worship, as atheists at their dying hour
Call, what they cannot name, an unknown power,
As ignorantly did I crave:
Thus when
Things not yet known are coveted by men,
Our desires give them fashion,[9] and so
As they wax lesser, fall, as they size, grow.[1]

But, from late fair
His Highness sitting in a golden chair[2]
Is not less cared for after three days
By children, than the thing which lovers so
Blindly admire, and with such worship woo;
Being had, enjoying it decays:
And thence,
What before pleased them all, takes but one sense,[3]
And that so lamely, as it leaves behind
A kind of sorrowing dullness to the mind.

Ah, cannot we,
As well as cocks and lions, jocund[4] be
After such pleasures? Unless wise
Nature decreed (since each such act, they say,
Diminisheth the length of life a day)[5]

6. With a play on "undergo sexual climax."
7. Unaided.
8. Before I put my ideas to the test.
9. Appearance.
1. I.e., as the desires wane, the fashioned apparitions also decrease, and as the desires grow, they increase.
2. I.e., a toy bought at a recent fair.
3. What before pleased every sense, now appeals to only one (touch, presumably).
4. Mirthful, merry, cheerful.
5. Cf. "The Canonization," line 21n, p. 27.

This, as she would man should despise
The sport,
Because that other curse of being short,
And only for a minute made to be
Eager, desires to raise posterity.[6]

Since so, my mind
Shall not desire what no man else can find,
I'll no more dote and run
To pursue things which had endamaged me.
And when I come where moving beauties be,
As men do when summer's sun
Grows great,
Though I admire their greatness, shun their heat;
Each place can afford shadows. If all fail,
'Tis but applying wormseed[7] to the tail.

1635

A Lecture upon the Shadow

Stand still, and I will read to thee
A lecture, Love, in love's philosophy.
These three hours that we have spent
In walking here, two shadows went
Along with us, which we ourselves produced;
But, now the sun is just above our head,
We do those shadows tread;
And to brave[8] clearness all things are reduced.
So whilst our infant loves did grow,
Disguises did, and shadows, flow
From us, and our cares; but now 'tis not so.

That love hath not attained the high'st degree,
Which is still diligent lest others see.

Except our loves at this noon stay,
We shall new shadows make the other way.
As the first were made to blind
Others, these which come behind[9]
Will work upon ourselves, and blind our eyes.

6. "Unless . . . posterity": generally regarded as the most difficult lines in Donne's poetry. Does "the other curse" refer to the brevity of life or to the brevity of sexual pleasure? Is "desires to raise posterity" a euphemistic expression for "demands repetition," or does it mean, more literally, "wishes to beget children"? Grierson emends "Eager, desires" to "Eagers desire," meaning "provokes desire" (to repeat the act). But the line can mean as much without the emendation, if "desires" is accepted as a verb meaning "demands."
7. Primarily used medically for the expulsion of intestinal worms, wormseed was also thought to inhibit sexual desire. "Tail" could refer to the genitalia of either sex.
8. Splendid, intrepid.
9. Follow or come after, referring to the shadows they will cast after noon; perhaps also suggesting that those shadows will fall behind rather than go before them.

If our loves faint, and westwardly decline,
To me thou, falsely, thine,
And I to thee mine actions shall disguise.
The morning shadows wear away,
But these[1] grow longer all the day,
But oh, love's day is short, if love decay.

Love is a growing, or full constant light;
And his first minute, after noon, is night.

1635

FROM *ELEGIES*

Elegy 6. Nature's Lay Idiot

Nature's lay idiot,[2] I taught thee to love,
And in that sophistry,[3] oh, thou dost prove
Too subtle: Fool, thou didst not understand
The mystic language of the eye nor hand:
Nor couldst thou judge the difference of the air
Of sighs, and say, "This lies; this sounds[4] despair."
Nor by th'eye's water[5] call a malady
Desperately hot, or changing feverously.
I had not taught thee then, the alphabet
Of flowers, how they devisefully[6] being set
And bound up, might with speechless secrecy
Deliver errands mutely and mutually.[7]
Remember since[8] all thy words used to be
To every suitor, "Ay, if my friends[9] agree":
Since household charms thy husband's name to teach[1]
Were all the love-tricks that thy wit could reach,
And since an hour's discourse could scarce have made
One answer in thee, and that ill arrayed
In broken proverbs, and torn sentences.[2]
Thou art not by so many duties his
That from the world's common having severed thee,
Inlaid[3] thee, neither to be seen nor see,
As mine:[4] who have with amorous delicacies

1. Afternoon shadows.
2. Uneducated fool.
3. Cunning, craft.
4. Signifies, imports; renders audible.
5. Tears.
6. Ingeniously.
7. Convey messages back and forth without resorting to words.
8. When, the time when (as in lines 13, 15, 17).
9. Relatives, kinfolk.
1. Familiar incantations or rituals for divining the name of one's future husband.
2. Aphorisms or conventional sayings.
3. Placed or situated inside.
4. In opposition to "his" (line 20).

Refined thee into a blissful paradise.
Thy graces and good words my creatures be;
I planted knowledge and life's tree in thee,
Which oh, shall strangers taste? Must I alas
Frame and enamel plate,[5] and drink in glass?
Chafe wax for others' seals? Break a colt's force
And leave him then, being made a ready horse?

Elegy 8. To His Mistress Going to Bed[6]

Come, Madam, come, all rest my powers defy;
Until I labor, I in labor lie.
The foe oft-times having the foe in sight,
Is tired with standing though he never fight.
Off with that girdle, like heaven's zone[7] glistering,
But a far fairer world encompassing.
Unpin that spangled breastplate which you wear,
That the eyes of busy fools may be stopped there.
Unlace yourself, for that harmonious chime[8]
Tells me from you that now 'tis your bed time.
Off with that happy busk,[9] which I envy
That still can be, and still can stand so nigh.
Your gown going off, such beauteous state reveals
As when from flow'ry meads th'hill's shadow steals.
Off with that wiry coronet[1] and show
The hairy diadem[2] which on you doth grow;
Now off with those shoes, and then safely tread
In this love's hallowed temple, this soft bed.
In such white robes, heaven's angels used to be
Received by men; thou, angel, bring'st with thee
A heaven like Mahomet's Paradise;[3] and though
Ill spirits walk in white, we easily know
By this these angels from an evil sprite:
Those set our hairs, but these our flesh upright.
License my roving hands, and let them go
Behind, before, above, between, below.
O my America, my new found land,
My kingdom, safeliest when with one man manned.
My mine of precious stones, my empery,[4]

5. Utensils for table, typically of gold or silver.
6. Denied license for publication in 1633; printed in *The Harmony of the Muses* (1654) and in the 1669 edition of Donne's poems.
7. Donne writes in terms of the Ptolemaic cosmos, whose concentric spheres (hence "zone") structure and contain the heavens.
8. Chiming watches were an invention of the late sixteenth century.
9. Corset; more precisely, the stiff piece of wood (in later centuries, whalebone) that kept the front of the corset rigid.
1. Ornamental or honorary headdress, crownlike and indicative of high rank lower than sovereignty.
2. Crown, indicative of royal dignity.
3. A place of sensual fulfillment.
4. Empire.

How blest am I in this discovering[5] thee!
To enter in these bonds[6] is to be free;
Then where my hand is set, my seal shall be.[7]
Full nakedness, all joys are due to thee;
As souls unbodied, bodies unclothed must be,
To taste whole joys. Gems which you women use
Are like Atlanta's balls,[8] cast in men's views,
That when a fool's eye lighteth on a gem,
His earthly soul may covet theirs, not them.
Like pictures, or like books' gay coverings made
For lay[9] men, are all women thus arrayed;
Themselves are mystic books, which only we
Whom their imputed[1] grace will dignify
Must see revealed. Then since that I may know,
As liberally as to a midwife show
Thyself. Cast all, yea, this white linen hence;
There is no penance due to innocence.[2]
To teach thee, I am naked first; why then,
What needst thou have more covering than a man?

1669

Elegy 13. The Autumnal

No spring, nor summer beauty, hath such grace
As I have seen in one autumnal face.
Young beauties force your love, and that's a rape;
This doth but counsel, yet you cannot scape.[3]
If 'twere a shame to love, here 'twere no shame;
Affections here take reverence's name.
Were her first years the Golden Age?[4] That's true:
But now she's gold oft tried,[5] and ever new.
That was her torrid, and inflaming time;
This is her habitable[6] tropic clime.
Fair eyes, who asks more heat than comes from hence,
He in a fever wishes pestilence.
Call not these wrinkles, graves;[7] if graves they were

5. Uncovering; rendering visible or known.
6. Anything with which one's body or limbs are bound in restraint of personal liberty.
7. Invocation of "hand" (signature) and "seal" is common in legal documents.
8. In Greek myth, the golden apples dropped by Hippomenes to delay fleet Atlanta so that he might outrace her and win her hand.
9. Not of the clergy; unlettered.
1. Attributed by vicarious substitution (common Protestant theological term).
2. Some manuscripts read: "Here is no penance much less innocence."
3. Common substitution for "escape" (aphesis).
4. The first age, an era of concord, abundance, and ease.
5. The purity of gold could be tested in two ways: by touchstone and by fire.
6. The torrid zone, deemed intolerably hot by Aristotle and thus uninhabitable, is opposed to the habitable tropics. Some manuscripts read "tolerable." Cf. Dryden, "To . . . Dr. Charleton," line 10n, p. 651.
7. A French word for wrinkles.

They were Love's graves, for else he is no where.
Yet lies not Love dead here, but here doth sit
Vowed to this trench like an anachorite.[8]
And here, till hers, which must be his, death come,
He doth not dig a grave, but build a tomb.
Here dwells he, though he sojourn ev'rywhere,
In progress, yet his standing house[9] is here.
Here, where still evening is, not noon, nor night,
Where no voluptuousness, yet all delight.
In all her words, unto all hearers fit,
You may at revels, you at council sit.
This is love's timber, youth his underwood;[1]
There he, as wine in June, enrages blood,
Which then comes seasonabliest, when our taste
And appetite to other things is past.
Xerxes' strange Lydian love, the platane tree,[2]
Was loved for age, none being so large as she,
Or else because being young, nature did bless
Her youth with age's glory, barrenness.
If we love things long sought, age is a thing
Which we are fifty years in compassing;
If transitory things, which soon decay,
Age must be loveliest at the latest day.
But name not winter faces, whose skin's slack,
Lank, as an unthrift's purse, but a soul's sack,
Whose eyes seek light within, for all here's shade,
Whose mouths are holes, rather worn out, than made,
Whose every tooth to a several place is gone,
To vex their souls at Resurrection;[3]
Name not these living death's-heads unto me,
For these not ancient, but antiques be.
I hate extremes; yet I had rather stay
With tombs than cradles, to wear out a day.
Since such love's natural lation[4] is, may still
My love descend and journey down the hill,
Not panting after growing beauties, so,
I shall ebb on, with them who homeward go.

8. Recluse (usually religious). In Donne's time, a common alternative for "anchorite."
9. "Standing house" (fixed residence) is opposed to "progress" (an official tour).
1. Undergrowth. Ben Jonson, in *Underwoods* (1637), wrote, "I am bold to entitle these lesser poems, of later growth, by this [name] of Underwood, out of the analogie they hold to the Forest in my former booke."
2. The plane, favorite shade tree of the Greeks and Romans, commonly described as barren (e.g., Vergil, *Georgics* II.70, IV.146). Xerxes delayed his invasion of Greece to honor an especially lofty, spreading, and thus quite mature one, adorning it with gold.
3. When at the Resurrection a soul goes to reanimate its body, every part, however scattered, must be recovered.
4. Action of moving or transporting.

Elegy 14. Love's Progress[5]

Whoever loves, if he do not propose
The right true end of love, he's one that goes
To sea for nothing but to make him sick.
And love's a bear-whelp born; if we o'er lick[6]
Our love, and force it new strange shapes to take,
We err, and of a lump a monster make.
Were not a calf a monster that were grown
Faced like a man, though better than his own?[7]
Perfection is in unity: prefer
One woman first, and then one thing in her.
I, when I value gold, may think upon
The ductileness, the application,[8]
The wholesomeness, the ingenuity,[9]
From rust, from soil, from fire ever free.
But if I love it, 'tis because 'tis made
By our new nature, use, the soul of trade.
All these in women we might think upon
(If women had them) and yet love but one.
Can men more injure women than to say
They love them for that, by which they are not they?
Makes virtue woman? Must I cool my blood
Till I both be, and find one, wise and good?
May barren angels love so. But if we
Make love to woman, virtue is not she,
As beauty's not, nor wealth. He that strays thus
From her to hers,[1] is more adulterous
Than if he took her maid. Search every sphere
And firmament; our Cupid is not there:
He's an infernal god, and underground
With Pluto dwells, where gold and fire abound.
Men to such gods, their sacrificing coals
Did not in altars lay, but pits and holes.
Although we see celestial bodies move
Above the earth, the earth we till and love:
So we her airs contemplate, words and heart,
And virtues; but we love the centric[2] part.
Nor is the soul more worthy, or more fit
For love, than this,[3] as infinite as it.
But in attaining this desirèd place
How much they stray, that set out at the face!
The hair a forest is of ambushes

5. Denied license for publication in 1633; printed in *The Harmony of the Muses* (1654) and in the 1669 edition of Donne's poems.
6. It was believed that mother bears licked cubs, born unformed, into proper bear shape.
7. I.e., though a man's face is in itself better than a calf's.
8. The capacity of gold to be shaped, and its usefulness.
9. Gold was considered medicinal (wholesome) and noble in quality (ingenious).
1. The woman in herself, versus her attributes.
2. In or at the center, central.
3. I.e., "the centric part" (l. 36).

Of springs, snares, fetters, and manacles.
The brow becalms us when 'tis smooth and plain,
And when 'tis wrinkled, shipwrecks us again;
Smooth, 'tis a paradise, where we would have
Immortal stay, and wrinkled, 'tis our grave.
The nose, like to the first meridian,[4] runs
Not 'twixt an east and west,[5] but 'twixt two suns;
It leaves a cheek, a rosy hemisphere
On either side, and then directs us, where
Upon the Islands Fortunate[6] we fall,
(Not faint Canary,[7] but ambrosial)
Her swelling lips, to which when we are come
We anchor there, and think ourselves at home,
For they seem all: there sirens' songs, and there
Wise Delphic oracles do fill the ear.
There in a creek where chosen pearls do swell,
The remora,[8] her cleaving tongue, doth dwell.
These and the glorious promontory, her chin
O'erpast; and the Strait Hellespont[9] between
The Sestos and Abydos[1] of her breasts,
(Not of two lovers, but two loves the nests)
Succeeds a boundless sea, but that thine eye
Some island moles may scattered there descry:
And sailing towards her India, in that way
Shall at her fair Atlantic navel stay.
Though thence the current be thy pilot made,[2]
Yet ere thou be where thou wouldst be embayed,
Thou shalt upon another forest set,
Where some do shipwreck, and no further get.
When thou art there, consider what this chase
Misspent by thy beginning at the face.
Rather set out below; practice my art,
Some symmetry[3] the foot hath with that part
Which thou dost seek, and is thy map[4] for that:
Lovely enough to stop, but not stay at;
Least subject to disguise and change it is;
Men say the devil never can change his.
It is the emblem that hath figurèd
Firmness; 'tis the first part that comes to bed.
Civility, we see, refined the kiss,

4. The "first meridian" of longitude (the prime meridian). Some thought it crossed the Canaries, off the northwest coast of Africa.
5. East and west hemispheres, divided by the "first meridian."
6. Fabulous isles of the Western ocean, abode of the blessed dead; often identified with the Canary Islands.
7. Light sweet wine from the Canary Islands.
8. Sucking fish; according to ancient legend, they could stop a ship.
9. Ancient name for the Dardanelles Strait.
1. Island towns on opposite shores of the Hellespont (where legendary lovers Hero and Leander pined for each other).
2. In sailing from Europe to the Orient, ships could follow the South Atlantic current, which flows into the Indian Ocean.
3. Correspondence.
4. Representation in abridged form, summation.

Which, at the face begun, transplanted is
Since to the hand, since to the imperial knee,
Now at the papal foot delights to be.[5]
If kings think that the nearer way,[6] and do
Rise from the foot, lovers may do so too.
For as free spheres[7] move faster far than can
Birds, whom the air resists, so may that man
Which goes this empty, and ethereal way,
Than if at beauty's elements he stay.[8]
Rich Nature hath in women wisely made
Two purses, and their mouths aversely[9] laid;
They then which to the lower tribute owe,
That way, which that exchequer[1] looks, must go;
He which doth not, his error is as great
As who by clyster[2] gave the stomach meat.

1669

Sappho to Philaenis[3]

Where is that holy fire, which verse is said
To have? Is that enchanting force decayed?
Verse, that draws Nature's works from Nature's law,
Thee, her best work, to her work cannot draw.[4]
Have my tears quenched my old poetic fire?
Why quenched they not as well that of desire?
Thoughts, my mind's creatures, often are with thee,
But I, their maker, want[5] their liberty.
Only thine image in my heart doth sit,
But that is wax, and fires environ it.
My fires have driven, thine have drawn it hence;
And I am robbed of picture, heart, and sense;
Dwells with me still mine irksome memory,
Which both to keep and lose grieves equally.
That tells me how fair thou art: thou art so fair

5. I.e., the kiss as a sign of deference has moved steadily downward: from the face, to the hand, to the knee (of the emperor), to the foot (of the Pope).
6. Shortest route to what they want (even kings kissed the Pope's foot).
7. In Ptolemaic astronomy, concentric celestial globes that without wind resistance move the stars and planets at enormous speed.
8. The man who moves upward from the foot resembles the "free spheres" in his unimpeded and thus swift course. The path from the head downward, with all its diverting beauties, is comparable to travel through the denser regions of the four elements.
9. In opposite directions.
1. Office for collection of royal revenue. Here, the lower purse receiving its "tribute."
2. Enema.
3. In this epistolary poem, reminiscent of Ovid's *Heroides*, Donne assumes the voice of Sappho, celebrated classical poetess of Lesbos. Philaenis was renowned in the ancient world as the author of a systematic guide to the art of love.
4. The repetitions of "Nature," "draw," "work," and "her" make this couplet difficult to understand precisely, but the main point is clear enough: Sappho is frustrated by the failure of her verse to affect Philaenis, who remains unmoved despite poetry's fabled power to sway natural phenomena (see, e.g., the myth of Orpheus).
5. Lack.

As[6] gods, when gods to thee I do compare,
Are gracèd thereby; and to make men see
What things gods are, I say they are like to thee;
For if we justly call each silly[7] man
A little world, what shall we call thee then?
Thou art not soft, and clear, and straight, and fair
As down, as stars, cedars, and lilies are,
But thy right hand, and cheek, and eye only
Are like thy other hand, and cheek, and eye.
Such was my Phao[8] awhile, but shall be never
As thou wast, art, and oh, mayst be ever.
Here lovers swear in their idolatry
That I am such, but grief discolors me,
And yet I grieve the less, lest grief remove
My beauty and make me unworthy of thy love.
Plays some soft boy with thee, oh, there wants[9] yet
A mutual feeling, which should sweeten it.
His chin, a thorny-hairy unevenness
Doth threaten, and some daily change possess.
Thy body is a natural paradise,
In whose self, unmanured,[1] all pleasure lies,
Nor needs perfection;[2] why shouldst thou then
Admit the tillage of a harsh rough man?
Men leave behind them that which their sin shows
And are as thieves traced, which rob when it snows.
But of our dalliance, no more signs there are,
Than fishes leave in streams, or birds in air:
And between us all sweetness may be had;
All, all that nature yields, or art can add:
My two lips, eyes, thighs differ from thy two
But so as thine from one another do,
And, oh, no more: the likeness being such,
Why should they not alike in all parts touch?
Hand to strange hand, lip to lip none denies;
Why should they breast to breast, or thighs to thighs?
Likeness begets such strange self-flattery,
That touching myself all seems done to thee.
Myself I embrace, and my own hands I kiss,
And amorously thank my self for this.
Me in my glass, I call thee; but alas,
When I would kiss, tears dim my eyes and glass.
O cure this loving madness and restore
Me to me; thee my half, my all, my more.[3]
So may thy cheeks' red outwear scarlet dye,
And their white, whiteness of the galaxy,

6. That.
7. Insignificant.
8. Phaon, a male lover of Sappho.
9. Lacks.
1. Untilled.
2. Completion.
3. The maiden name of Donne's wife was Anne More.

So may thy mighty, amazing beauty move
  Envy in all women, and in all men, love,
And so be change, and sickness far from thee,
  As thou by coming near, keep'st them from me.

From *Satires*

Satire 3

Kind pity chokes my spleen,[4] brave scorn forbids
Those tears to issue which swell my eyelids;
I must not laugh, nor weep sins, and be wise,
Can railing[5] then cure these worn maladies?
Is not our mistress, fair Religion,
As worthy of all our soul's devotion,
As virtue was to the first blinded age?[6]
Are not heaven's joys as valiant to assuage
Lusts, as earth's honor[7] was to them? Alas,
As we do them in means, shall they surpass
Us in the end, and shall thy father's spirit
Meet blind philosophers[8] in heaven, whose merit
Of strict life may be imputed[9] faith, and hear
Thee, whom he taught so easy ways and near
To follow, damned? O if thou dar'st, fear this;
This fear great courage and high valor is.
Dar'st thou aid mutinous Dutch,[1] and dar'st thou lay
Thee in ships, wooden sepulchers, a prey
To leaders' rage, to storms, to shot, to dearth?
Dar'st thou dive seas and dungeons of the earth?
Hast thou courageous fire to thaw the ice
Of frozen north discoveries?[2] And thrice
Colder than salamanders,[3] like divine
Children in the oven,[4] fires of Spain, and the line,[5]
Whose countries limbecks[6] to our bodies be,
Canst thou for gain bear? And must every he
Which cries not "Goddess!" to thy mistress, draw,[7]
Or eat thy poisonous words? Courage of straw!
O desperate coward, wilt thou seem bold, and

4. The spleen was considered the organ of bile and thus the seat of scorn.
5. Uttering abuse, ranting.
6. The era of classical ethics, "blinded" because pre-Christian and therefore morally handicapped.
7. The honor of this world, as opposed to heavenly rewards.
8. Classical pre-Christian philosophers who discerned natural law rationally and strove to obey it.
9. Counted as. Protestants stressed faith as the basis of Christian justification.
1. English volunteers, Donne himself among them, sailed with the Dutch in their struggle against Spanish dominion.
2. Attempts to find a way through the northern ice to the Pacific.
3. Lizards thought to inhabit, or able to endure, fire; alchemical symbol.
4. The "children in the oven," Shadrach, Meshach, and Abednego, were thrown into a fiery furnace for refusing to worship a golden idol but remained unharmed (Daniel 3).
5. The fires of the Spanish Inquisition and the heat of the equator (objects of "bear," line 26).
6. Alembics, flasks used for boiling during alchemical distillation.
7. I.e., draw his sword.

To thy foes and his (who made thee to stand
Sentinel in his world's garrison) thus yield,
And for forbidden wars, leave the appointed field?
Know thy foes: the foul Devil, whom thou
Strivest to please, for hate, not love, would allow
Thee fain his whole realm to be quit;[8] and as
The world's all parts[9] wither away and pass,
So the world's self, thy other loved foe, is
In her decrepit wane,[1] and thou, loving this,
Dost love a withered and worn strumpet; last,
Flesh (itself's death)[2] and joys which flesh can taste,
Thou lovest; and thy fair goodly soul, which doth
Give this flesh power to taste joy, thou dost loathe.
Seek true religion. O where? Mirreus,[3]
Thinking her unhoused here, and fled from us,
Seeks her at Rome; there, because he doth know
That she was there a thousand years ago;
He loves her rags so, as we here obey
The statecloth[4] where the prince sat yesterday.
Crantz to such brave[5] loves will not be enthralled,
But loves her only, who at Geneva is called
Religion, plain, simple, sullen, young,
Contemptuous, yet unhandsome; as among
Lecherous humors,[6] there is one that judges
No wenches wholesome but coarse country drudges.
Graius stays still at home here, and because
Some preachers, vile ambitious bawds,[7] and laws,
Still[8] new like fashions, bid him think that she
Which dwells with us is only[9] perfect, he
Embraceth her whom his godfathers will
Tender to him, being tender,[1] as wards still
Take such wives as their guardians offer, or
Pay values.[2] Careless Phrygius doth abhor
All, because all cannot be good, as one,
Knowing some women whores, dares marry none.
Gracchus loves all as one, and thinks that so
As women do in diverse countries go
In divers[3] habits, yet are still one kind,

8. I.e., Satan for hate not love's sake would gladly reward your sinful efforts with his kingdom.
9. All parts of the world.
1. Old age.
2. The flesh destroys itself by yielding to the sins of the flesh.
3. Mirreus, Crantz (line 49), and Graius (line 55) represent followers of, in order, Roman Catholicism, Calvinism (centered in Geneva), Anglicanism. The sceptical Phrygius (line 62), seeing their divergence, would accept none. The Erastian Gracchus (line 65) discounts the divergence and would follow any.
4. Just as we signify our submission to the cloth over the throne when the ruler is absent.
5. Showy, ornate.
6. Lecherous dispositions; men of lecherous disposition.
7. Procurers, pimps.
8. Always (cf. line 60).
9. Alone.
1. Offer to him in his youth.
2. Sums paid for refusing an arranged marriage, here compared to fines on English recusants for not attending the national Church.
3. Different; differing from or opposed to what is right, good, or profitable.

So doth, so is Religion; and this blind-
ness too much light breeds;[4] but unmoved thou
Of force must one, and forced but one allow;
And the right; ask thy father which is she;
Let him ask his, though truth and falsehood be
Near twins, yet truth a little elder is;
Be busy to seek her, believe me this,
He's not of none, nor worst,[5] that seeks the best.
To adore, or scorn an image, or protest,
May all be bad; doubt wisely; in strange way[6]
To stand inquiring right is not to stray;
To sleep, or run wrong is. On a huge hill,
Cragged and steep, Truth stands, and he that will
Reach her, about must, and about must go;
And what the hill's suddenness resists, win so;
Yet strive so, that before age, death's twilight,
Thy soul rest, for none can work in that night.[7]
To will implies delay; therefore now do.
Hard deeds, the body's pains; hard knowledge too
The mind's endeavors reach,[8] and mysteries
Are like the sun, dazzling, yet plain to all eyes.
Keep the truth which thou hast found; men do not stand
In so ill case here that God hath with his hand
Signed kings' blank charters to kill whom they hate,
Nor are they vicars,[9] but hangmen to fate.
Fool and wretch, wilt thou let thy soul be tied
To man's laws, by which she shall not be tried
At the last day? Oh, will it then boot[1] thee
To say a Philip, or a Gregory,
A Harry, or a Martin[2] taught thee this?
Is not this excuse for mere[3] contraries
Equally strong? Cannot both sides say so?
That thou mayest rightly obey power, her bounds know;
Those passed, her nature, and name is changed;[4] to be
Then humble to her is idolatry.
As streams are, power is; those blest flowers that dwell
At the rough stream's calm head, thrive and do well,
But having left their roots, and themselves given
To the stream's tyrannous rage, alas, are driven
Through mills, and rocks, and woods, and at last, almost
Consumed in going, in the sea are lost:
So perish souls, which more choose men's unjust
Power from God claimed, than God himself to trust.

4. I.e., the blindness of Gracchus originates in his acceptance of too many sources of light.
5. I.e., he is not of no religion, nor the worst religion.
6. On an unfamiliar path.
7. "The night cometh, when no man can work" (John 9:4).
8. "Difficult deeds are accomplished by the body's efforts; difficult knowledge is similarly attained at the mind's expense."
9. Deputies, representatives.
1. Profit.
2. Philip II of Spain; Pope Gregory XIII or Gregory XIV; Henry VIII of England; Martin Luther.
3. Utter, absolute.
4. I.e., power that exceeds its proper jurisdiction is tyranny.

VERSE LETTERS

The Storm

To Mr. Christopher Brooke, from the Island voyage with the Earl of Essex[5]

Thou which art I ('tis nothing to be so),
Thou which art still thyself, by these shalt know
Part of our passage; and a hand, or eye
By Hilliard[6] drawn, is worth an history
By a worse painter made; and (without pride)
When by thy judgment they are dignified,
My lines are such: 'tis the pre-eminence
Of friendship only to impute excellence.
England to whom we owe what we be and have,
Sad that her sons did seek a foreign grave
(For fate's or fortune's drifts none can soothsay;
Honor and misery have one face and way),
From out her pregnant entrails sighed a wind
Which at the air's middle marble room did find
Such strong resistance that itself it threw
Downward again;[7] and so when it did view
How in the port our fleet dear time did leese,[8]
Withering like prisoners, which lie but for fees,[9]
Mildly it kissed our sails, and, fresh and sweet,
As to a stomach starved, whose insides meet,
Meat comes, it came, and swole[1] our sails, when we
So joyed as Sarah her swelling joyed to see.[2]
But 'twas but so kind as our countrymen
Which bring friends one day's way, and leave them then.
Then like two mighty kings which, dwelling far
Asunder, meet against a third to war,
The south and west winds joined, and, as they blew,
Waves like a rolling trench before them threw.
Sooner than you read this line, did the gale,
Like shot, not feared till felt, our sails assail;
And what at first was called a gust, the same

5. Like "The Calm," this poem relates an episode during the British Navy's famous "Islands Expedition" of 1597. Brooke, to whom "The Calm" seems also to have been addressed, was Donne's particular friend and, later, best man at his wedding. During the Renaissance, friends liked to think of themselves as sharing one soul; hence, in the first line Donne identifies Brooke as also himself.
6. Nicholas Hilliard (1537–1619), celebrated English painter.
7. It was thought that winds blew when Earth's warm exhalations were rebuffed by the cold middle region of the air. "Marble" (line 14) here suggests lucid, sparkling, and cold—qualities associated with the stone.
8. Lose.
9. I.e., fees owed the jailer to defray the cost of imprisonment.
1. Swelled.
2. Though over ninety, Sarah bore Abraham a son, Isaac (Genesis 17:17, 21:1–5).

Hath now a storm's, anon a tempest's name.
Jonas,[3] I pity thee, and curse those men
Who when the storm raged most, did wake thee then;
Sleep is pain's easiest salve, and doth fulfill
All offices of death, except to kill.
But when I waked, I saw that I saw not;
I, and the sun, which should teach me, had forgot
East, west, day, night, and I could only say,
If the world had lasted, now it had been day.
Thousands our noises were, yet we 'mongst all
Could none by his right name, but thunder, call.
Lightning was all our light, and it rained more
Than if the sun had drunk the sea before.
Some coffined in their cabins lie, equally
Grieved that they are not dead and yet must die;
And as sin-burdened souls from graves will creep
At the last day, some forth their cabins peep
And tremblingly ask what news, and do hear so,
Like jealous husbands, what they would not know.
Some, sitting on the hatches, would seem there
With hideous gazing to fear away fear.
Then note they the ship's sicknesses, the mast
Shaked with this ague, and the hold[4] and waist[5]
With a salt dropsy clogged, and all our tacklings
Snapping, like too-high-stretched treble strings.
And from our tattered sails, rags drop down so,
As from one hanged in chains a year ago.
Even our ordnance, placed for our defense,
Strive to break loose and 'scape away from thence.
Pumping hath tired our men, and what's the gain?
Seas into seas thrown, we suck in again;
Hearing hath deafed our sailors; and if they
Knew how to hear, there's none knows what to say.
Compared to these storms, death is but a qualm,[6]
Hell somewhat lightsome, and the Bermudas[7] calm.
Darkness, light's elder brother,[8] his birthright
Claims o'er this world, and to heaven hath chased light.
All things are one, and that one none can be,
Since all forms, uniform deformity
Doth cover, so that we, except God say
Another *fiat*, shall have no more day.
So violent, yet long these furies be,
That though thine absence starve me, I wish not thee.

3. The prophet Jonah, awakened during a storm and later cast into the sea (Jonah 1).
4. Cargo compartment.
5. The middle part of the ship; between the quarterdeck and the forecastle.
6. A feeling of faintness or sickness.
7. The seas around the Bermuda Islands were notorious for continual storms.
8. Darkness prevailed prior to the creation of light by divine fiat (see line 72 and Genesis 1).

The Calm

Our storm is past, and that storm's tyrannous rage,
A stupid calm, but nothing it, doth 'suage.[9]
The fable is inverted, and far more
A block afflicts, now, than a stork before.[1]
Storms chafe,[2] and soon wear out themselves, or us;
In calms, Heaven laughs to see us languish thus.
As steady as I can wish that my thoughts were,
Smooth as thy mistress' glass,[3] or what shines there,
The sea is now. And, as the Isles which we
Seek when we can move, our ships rooted be.
As water did in storms, now pitch runs out
As lead when a fired church becomes one spout.[4]
And all our beauty and our trim decays,
Like courts removing, or like ended plays.
The fighting place now seamen's rags supply;
And all the tackling is a frippery.[5]
No use of lanterns; and in one place lay
Feathers and dust, today and yesterday.
Earth's hollownesses, which the world's lungs are,
Have no more wind than the upper vault of air.
We can nor lost friends nor sought foes recover,
But meteor-like, save that we move not, hover.
Only the calenture[6] together draws
Dear friends, which meet dead in great fishes' jaws.
And on the hatches as on altars lies
Each one, his own priest and own sacrifice.
Who live, that miracle do multiply
Where walkers in hot ovens do not die.[7]
If in despite of these, we swim, that hath
No more refreshing than our brimstone bath,
But from the sea into the ship we turn
Like parboiled[8] wretches on the coals to burn.
Like Bajazet encaged, the shepherd's scoff,[9]
Or like slack-sinewed Samson, his hair off,
Languish our ships. Now, as a myriad
Of ants durst the emperor's lovèd snake invade,[1]
The crawling galleys, sea-jails, finny chips,

9. Assuage: to pacify, appease.
1. In a traditional version of Aesop's fable, frogs ask Jove for a king and are given a log, which they dance on in disdain. Jove replaces the log with a stork, which eats them.
2. Vex by friction or wear. Storms wear themselves out.
3. Mirror.
4. Pitch was used as caulk in ships. In hot, still weather, the pitch melted and ran from the seams. Church roofs were generally made of lead.
5. A shop that sells old clothes (sailors' rags hang from the rigging, as in a shop).
6. Tropical fever that causes sailors deliriously to mistake the sea for green fields and leap overboard.
7. In Daniel 3, three men cast into a fiery furnace miraculously walk about unharmed; cf. Satire 3, line 24n, p. 53.
8. Boiled, either thoroughly or partly.
9. In Marlowe's *Tamburlaine*, the Turkish emperor Bajazeth is caged by the former shepherd, Tamburlaine. A "scoff" is an object of mockery and derision.
1. In Suetonius's *Life of Tiberius* (section 72), a multitude of ants devours the emperor's pet serpent.

Might brave our pinnaces,[2] now bed-rid ships.
Whether a rotten state and hope of gain,
Or to disuse me from the queasy pain
Of being beloved, and loving, or the thirst
Of honor or fair death out-pushed me first,
I lose my end: for here as well as I
A desperate may live, and a coward die.
Stag, dog, and all which from, or towards flies,
Is paid with life, or prey, or doing dies.
Fate grudges us all, and doth subtly lay
A scourge, 'gainst which we all forget to pray.
He that at sea prays for more wind, as well
Under the poles may beg cold, heat in hell.
What are we then? How little more, alas,
Is man now than before he was! He was
Nothing; for us, we are for nothing fit;
Chance or ourselves still disproportion it.
We have no power, no will, no sense; I lie,
I should not then thus feel this misery.

To Sir Henry Wotton

Sir, more than kisses, letters mingle souls,
For thus, friends absent speak.[3] This ease controls
The tediousness of my life: but for these
I could ideate[4] nothing which could please,
But I should wither in one day, and pass
To a bottle[5] of hay, that am a lock of grass.
Life is a voyage, and in our life's ways
Countries, courts, towns are rocks, or remoras;[6]
They break or stop all ships, yet our state's such,
That though than pitch they stain worse, we must touch.
If in the furnace of the even line,[7]
Or under the adverse icy poles thou pine,[8]
Thou know'st two temperate regions, girded in,
Dwell there: but oh, what refuge canst thou win
Parched in the court, and in the country frozen?
Shall cities, built of both extremes, be chosen?
Can dung and garlic be a perfume? Or can
A scorpion and torpedo[9] cure a man?

2. Prisoners (in "sea-jail") sometimes rowed becalmed galleys, which thus looked like chips of wood with fins. Propelled by their oars, they could outrun their pinnaces, the light and ordinarily swift-sailing vessels that accompanied larger vessels as scouts.
3. Donne's friend, Wotton was a poet, diplomat, and translator with experience in the collection of foreign intelligence.
4. Form an idea of; in early use, often with reference to Platonic "ideas," eternally existing patterns or forms of phenomena, more authentic than the phenomena themselves.
5. Bundle.
6. Impediments. Remoras are sucking fish; according to ancient legend, they could stop a ship.
7. The equator, the center of the torrid zone, deemed intolerably hot by Aristotle. Cf. "The Autumnal," lines 9–10, p. 47.
8. Suffer.
9. The electric ray, whose shock numbs, and the scorpion, whose sting causes great pain.

Cities are worst of all three; of all three
(O knotty riddle) each is worst equally.
Cities are sepulchres; they who dwell there
Are carcasses, as if no such[1] there were.
And courts are theaters, where some men play
Princes, some slaves, all to one end, and of one clay.
The country is a desert, where no good,
Gained as habits, not borne, is understood.[2]
There men become beasts, and prone to more evils;
In cities blocks,[3] and in a lewd court, devils.
As in the first chaos confusedly
Each element's qualities were in the other three,[4]
So pride, lust, covetise,[5] being several[6]
To these three places, yet all are in all,
And mingled thus, their issue incestuous.
Falsehood is denizened. Virtue is barbarous.[7]
Let no man say there, "Virtue's flinty wall
Shall lock vice in me; I'll do none, but know all."
Men are sponges, which to pour out, receive;
Who[8] know false play, rather than lose, deceive.
For in best understandings, sin began;
Angels sinned first, then devils, and then man.
Only perchance beasts sin not; wretched we
Are beasts in all but white integrity.[9]
I think if men, which in these places live
Durst look for themselves, and themselves retrieve,
They would like strangers greet themselves, seeing then
Utopian youth grown old Italian.[1]
   Be thou thine own home, and in thyself dwell;
Inn[2] anywhere; continuance[3] maketh hell.
And seeing the snail, which everywhere doth roam,
Carrying his own house still,[4] still is at home,
Follow (for he is easy paced) this snail,
Be thine own palace, or the world's thy jail.
And in the world's sea, do not like cork sleep
Upon the water's face, nor in the deep
Sink like a lead without a line, but as
Fishes glide, leaving no print where they pass,

1. I.e., no living inhabitants.
2. In the country, goodness, which is acquired by habitual practice, not by being carried, is not understood (because country wits recognize only "goods" that are carried as commodities or carried as titles).
3. Dolts.
4. Before the order of creation was imposed, the qualities that distinguish the elements from each other were present in all of them.
5. Avarice.
6. Belonging respectively.
7. Falsehood is naturalized. Virtue is foreign.
8. Those who.
9. Sinlessness.
1. Unlike the ideal state of Utopia (Latin: "not a place"), Italy was associated with all corruption.
2. Find lodging.
3. Remaining in one place.
4. Always.

Nor making sound, so closely[5] thy course go;
Let men dispute whether thou breathe, or no.
Only in this one thing, be no Galenist:[6] to make
Courts' hot ambitions wholesome, do not take
A dram of country's dullness; do not add
Correctives, but as chemics,[7] purge the bad.
But, Sir, I advise not you, I rather do
Say o'er those lessons, which I learned of you:
Whom, free from German schisms, and lightness
Of France, and fair Italy's faithlessness,
Having from these sucked all they had of worth,
And brought home that faith, which you carried forth,
I thoroughly love. But if myself I've won
To know my rules, I have, and you have

Donne.

To the Countess of Bedford[8]

Madam,
You have refined me, and to worthiest things
(Virtue, art, beauty, fortune) now I see
Rareness, or use, not nature value brings;[9]
And such, as they are circumstanced, they be.
Two ills can ne'er perplex us, sin to excuse;[1]
But of two good things, we may leave and choose.

Therefore at court, which is not virtue's clime,
(Where a transcendent height, (as, lowness me)
Makes her not be, or not show)[2] all my rhyme
Your virtues challenge,[3] which there rarest be;
For, as dark[4] texts need notes, there some must be
To usher virtue, and say, "This is she."

So in the country is beauty;[5] to this place
You are the season (Madam), you the day,
'Tis but a grave of spices, till your face
Exhale them, and a thick close bud display.[6]

5. With closed lips; secretly.
6. Physicians in the Galenic tradition would attempt to balance an excess in one bodily humor by augmentation of its opposite.
7. Physicians in the Paracelsian, or chemical, tradition would attempt to purge a bodily illness by administration of an antagonistic substance.
8. See "Twickenham Garden," n. 1, p. 29.
9. The countess, like an alchemist refining a base metal, has improved the poet; he now perceives that rarity and utility (not inherent worth) determine value.
1. Two evils cannot compel a choice between them; if they could, that would justify a sin.
2. The virtues of the countess transcend the court and its recognition; Donne, by contrast, is beneath its notice.
3. Assert, proclaim.
4. Cryptic.
5. The court values her rare virtue; in the country, her beauty wins such admiration.
6. Her face acts like the sun, moving buds to blossom and breathe fragrance.

Widowed and reclused else, her sweets she enshrines
As China, when the sun at Brazil dines.

Out from your chariot, morning breaks at night,
And falsifies both computations so;[7]
Since a new world doth rise here from your light,
We your new creatures, by new reckonings go.
This shows that you from nature loathly[8] stray,
That suffer not an artificial day.

In this you have made the court the antipodes,[9]
And willed your delegate, the vulgar sun,[1]
To do profane autumnal offices,
Whilst here to you, we sacrificers run;
And whether priests, or organs, you we obey,
We sound your influence, and your dictates say.

Yet to that deity which dwells in you,
Your virtuous soul, I now not sacrifice;
These are petitions and not hymns; they sue
But that I may survey the edifice.[2]
In all religions as much care hath been
Of temples' frames, and beauty, as rites within.

As all which go to Rome, do not thereby
Esteem religions, and hold fast the best,
But serve discourse, and curiosity,
With that which doth religion but invest,
And shun the entangling labyrinths of schools,[3]
And make it wit, to think the wiser fools:

So in this pilgrimage I would behold
You as you're virtue's temple, not as she,
What walls of tender crystal her enfold,
What eyes, hands, bosom, her pure altars be;
And after this survey, oppose to all
Babblers of chapels, you the Escurial.[4]

Yet not as consecrate, but merely as fair,
On these I cast a lay and country eye.[5]
Of past and future stories, which are rare,

7. The countess's nocturnal arrival restores day to the countryside. This reversal renders "both computations"—daily and historical—inaccurate: the light she brings not only turns night into day; it restarts the world from its first moment.
8. Reluctantly, unwillingly.
9. Region on the opposite side of the globe.
1. I.e., the common sun, serving as the delegate of the more brilliant countess. Hence while the countess brings a fresh spring to the country, it is autumn at court.
2. Ask to visit the countess in person.
3. Schools of religious thought. Scholastic theology was notoriously complicated.
4. El Escorial, vast palace and mausoleum of the kings of Spain, constructed outside Madrid by Philip II. By comparison, other grand religious edifices seem like chapels.
5. The speaker takes a natural rather than a religious perspective on her beauties.

I find you all record, all prophecy.
Purge but the Book of Fate,[6] that it admit
No sad nor guilty legends, you are it.

If good and lovely were not one, of both
You were the transcript, and original,
The elements, the parent, and the growth,
And every piece of you, is both their all:
So entire are all your deeds, and you, that you
Must do the same thing still; you cannot two.

But these[7] (as nice thin school divinity
Serves heresy to further or repress)
Taste of poetic rage, or flattery,
And need not, where all hearts one truth profess;
Oft from new proofs, and new phrase, new doubts grow,
As strange attire aliens the men we know.

Leaving then busy praise, and all appeal
To higher courts, sense's decree is true,
The mine, the magazine,[8] the commonweal,
The story of beauty, in Twicknam is, and you.
Who hath seen one, would both; as, who had been
In Paradise, would seek the cherubin.

From An Anatomy of the World:[9] The First Anniversary

The entry into the work.

When that rich soul which to her heaven is gone,
Whom all they celebrate who know they have one
(For who is sure he hath a soul, unless
It see, and judge, and follow worthiness,
And by deeds praise it? He who doth not this,
May lodge an inmate[1] soul, but 'tis not his);
When that queen ended here her progress[2] time,
And, as to her standing house,[3] to heaven did climb,
Where, loath to make the saints attend[4] her long,
She's now a part both of the choir and song,
This world in that great earthquake languished;

6. Book in which all history is recorded.
7. The poet's praises.
8. The storehouse.
9. The 1611 edition includes a subtitle: "Wherein, by occasion of the untimely death of Mistress Elizabeth Drury, the frailty and decay of this whole world is represented." Elizabeth died in 1610, at age fifteen; her father was Sir Robert Drury, Donne's benefactor. Although she is the nominal subject of this poem, and of "The Progress of the Soul: The Second Anniversary" (published in 1612), Donne had never met her. To Jonson's complaint that the praise of the girl was blasphemously excessive, Donne replied "that he described the Idea of Woman and not as she was."
1. Dwelling in the same lodging with, or in the lodging of, another.
2. State journey by a royal personage.
3. Permanent dwelling.
4. Await.

For in a common bath of tears it bled,
Which drew the strongest vital spirits[5] out:
But succored then with a perplexèd doubt,
Whether the world did lose or gain in this
(Because since now no other way there is
But goodness to see her, whom all would see,
All must endeavor to be good as she),
This great consumption to a fever turned,
And so the world had fits; it joyed, it mourned.
And as men think that agues physic are,[6]
And the ague being spent, give over care,
So thou, sick world, mistak'st thyself to be
Well, when, alas, thou art in a lethargy.
Her death did wound and tame thee then, and than[7]
Thou might'st have better spared the sun, or man;
That wound was deep, but 'tis more misery,
That thou hast lost thy sense and memory.
'Twas heavy[8] then to hear thy voice of moan,
But this is worse, that thou art speechless grown.
Thou hast forgot thy name thou hadst; thou wast
Nothing but she, and her thou hast o'erpast.
For as a child kept from the font,[9] until
A prince, expected long, come to fulfill
The ceremonies, thou unnamed had'st laid,
Had not her coming, thee her palace made:
Her name defined thee, gave thee form and frame,
And thou forget'st to celebrate thy name.
Some months she hath been dead (but being dead,
Measures of times are all determinèd[1])
But long she hath been away, long, long, yet none
Offers to tell us who it is that's gone.
But as in states doubtful of future heirs,
When sickness without remedy impairs
The present prince, they're loath it should be said,
The prince doth languish, or the prince is dead:
So mankind feeling now a general thaw,
A strong example gone, equal to law,
The cement which did faithfully compact
And glue all virtues, now resolved, and slacked,
Thought it some blasphemy to say she was dead,
Or that our weakness was discovered
In that confession; therefore spoke no more
Than tongues, the soul being gone, the loss deplore.
But though it be too late to succor thee,
Sick world, yea dead, yea putrefied, since she

5. Refined, subtle agents of the heart and blood, thought to sustain life.
6. Acute fevers with fits of shaking were considered medicinal.
7. In Donne's time, "then" and "than," originally the same word, were not fully distinguished. Cf. also lines 199–200, where "then" rhymes with "man."
8. Grievous, distressing.
9. Baptismal font, where a child receives its Christian name.
1. Terminated, brought to an end.

Thy intrinsic balm and thy preservative,
Can never be renewed, thou never live,
I (since no man can make thee live) will try
What we may gain by thy anatomy.[2]
Her death hath taught us dearly that thou art
Corrupt and mortal in thy purest part.
Let no man say, the world itself being dead,
'Tis labor lost to have discoverèd
The world's infirmities, since there is none
Alive to study this dissection;
For there's a kind of world remaining still, *What life the world hath still.*
Though she which did inanimate[3] and fill
The world be gone, yet in this last long night,
Her ghost doth walk; that is, a glimmering light,
A faint weak love of virtue and of good
Reflects from her on them which understood
Her worth; and though she have shut in all day,
The twilight of her memory doth stay;[4]
Which, from the carcass of the old world, free,
Creates a new world; and new creatures be
Produced: the matter and the stuff of this,
Her virtue, and the form our practice is:
And though to be thus elemented,[5] arm
These creatures from home-born intrinsic harm,
(For all assumed[6] unto this dignity,
So many weedless Paradises be,
Which of themselves produce no venomous sin,
Except some foreign serpent bring it in)
Yet, because outward storms the strongest break,
And strength itself by confidence grows weak,
This new world may be safer, being told
The dangers and diseases of the old: *The sicknesses of the world.*
For with due temper[7] men do then forgo,
Or covet things, when they their true worth know.
There is no health; physicians say that we *The impossibility of health.*
At best enjoy but a neutrality.
And can there be worse sickness than to know
That we are never well, nor can be so?
We are born ruinous:[8] poor mothers cry
Except they headlong come and fall upon[9]
An ominous precipitation.
How witty's ruin! how importunate
Upon mankind! It labored to frustrate
Even God's purpose; and made woman, sent

2. By postmortem dissection of the world.
3. Infuse life into (Donne's coinage).
4. I.e., though she is gone, memory of her remains.
5. Compounded (with "her virtue" as matter and "our practice" as form).
6. Raised, taken up.
7. Proper or fit condition (such as creatures so "elemented" exemplify).
8. With a tendency to fall.
9. Pass suddenly into, begin upon (an action or a state).

For man's relief, cause of his languishment.
They were to good ends, and they are so still,
But accessory, and principal in ill.
For that first marriage[1] was our funeral:
One woman at one blow then killed us all,
And singly, one by one, they kill us now.
We do delightfully ourselves allow
To that consumption; and profusely blind,
We kill ourselves to propagate our kind.[2]
And yet we do not that; we are not men:
There is not now that mankind which was then,
Whenas[3] the sun and man did seem to strive
(Joint tenants of the world) who should survive; *Shortness of life.*
When stag, and raven,[4] and the long-lived tree,
Compared with man, died in minority;
When, if a slow-paced star[5] had stolen away
From the observer's marking, he might stay
Two or three hundred years to see it again,
And then make up his observation plain;[6]
When, as the age was long, the size was great
(Man's growth confessed, and recompensed the meat),[7]
So spacious and large that every soul
Did a fair kingdom and large realm control;
And when the very stature thus erect,
Did that soul a good way towards heaven direct.
Where is this mankind now? Who lives to age,
Fit to be made Methusalah his page?[8]
Alas, we scarce live long enough to try
Whether a new made clock run right, or lie.
Old grandsires talk of yesterday with sorrow,
And for our children we reserve tomorrow.
So short is life that every peasant strives,
In a torn house, or field, to have three lives.[9]
And as in lasting, so in length is man
Contracted to an inch, who was a span;[1] *Smallness of stature.*
For had a man at first in forests strayed,
Or shipwrecked in the sea, one would have laid
A wager that an elephant, or whale,
That met him, would not hastily assail
A thing so equal to him: now, alas,
The fairies and the pigmies well may pass
As credible; mankind decays so soon,

1. Adam and Eve's.
2. Sexual orgasm (the "little death") was thought to shorten life.
3. At the time when.
4. Considered long-lived animals.
5. Comet.
6. Complete his observation fully or directly.
7. I.e., man's growth attested to and made a suitable return for his food. (The nutritional value of food was thought to have declined over the centuries.)
8. Methusalah's serving boy. Methusalah lived 969 years (Genesis 5:27).
9. Houses and land could be leased for the joint lives of three persons (generally chosen to maximize the length of the lease).
1. Nine inches.

We're scarce our fathers' shadows cast at noon.
Only death adds to our length: nor are we grown
In stature to be men, till we are none.
But this were light,[2] did our less volume hold
All the old text; or had we changed to gold
Their silver,[3] or disposed into less glass
Spirits of virtue, which then scattered was.[4]
But 'tis not so: we're not retired, but damped;[5]
And as our bodies, so our minds are cramped:
'Tis shrinking, not close weaving, that hath thus
In mind and body both bedwarfèd us.
We seem ambitious God's whole work t'undo;
Of nothing he made us, and we strive too,
To bring ourselves to nothing back; and we
Do what we can to do't so soon as he.
With new diseases on ourselves we war,
And with new physic, a worse engine[6] far.
Thus man, this world's vice-emperor, in whom
All faculties, all graces are at home—
And if in other creatures they appear,
They're but man's ministers and legates there,
To work on their rebellions, and reduce
Them to civility, and to man's use.
This man, whom God did woo, and loath t'attend[7]
Till man came up, did down to man descend,
This man, so great that all that is, is his,
Oh what a trifle and poor thing he is!
If man were anything, he's nothing now:
Help, or at least some time to waste,[8] allow
T'his other wants, yet when he did depart
With her, whom we lament, he lost his heart.
She, of whom the ancients seemed to prophesy
When they called virtues by the name of *she*,
She in whom virtue was so much refined
That for alloy[9] unto so pure a mind
She took the weaker sex, she that could drive
The poisonous tincture,[1] and the stain of Eve,
Out of her thoughts and deeds; and purify
All, by a true religious alchemy;
She, she is dead; she's dead: when thou knowest this,
Thou knowest how poor a trifling thing man is,
And learn'st thus much by our anatomy,

2. Insignificant.
3. The alchemist sought to reduce baser metals into gold.
4. Concentrate potent spirits into a smaller bottle than before, when their virtue was diffused in a larger vessel.
5. Not concentrated, but stifled.
6. New medicine, a far more effective means of war (than disease).
7. Wait.
8. Diminish.
9. Inferior metal mixed with one of greater value.
1. In alchemy, a spiritual principle or immaterial substance whose character or quality may be infused into material things, which are then said to be tinctured.

The heart being perished, no part can be free.
And that except thou feed (not banquet) on
The supernatural food, religion,
Thy better growth grows witherèd and scant;
Be more than man, or thou'rt less than an ant.
Then, as mankind, so is the world's whole frame
Quite out of joint, almost created lame:
For, before God had made up all the rest,
Corruption entered, and depraved the best:
It seized the angels, and then first of all
The world did in her cradle take a fall,
And turned her brains, and took a general maim,
Wronging each joint of th'universal frame.
The noblest part, man, felt it first; and then
Both beasts and plants, curst in the curse of man. *Decay of nature in other parts.*
So did the world from the first hour decay,
That evening was beginning of the day,
And now the springs and summers which we see,
Like sons of women after fifty be.[2]
And new philosophy[3] calls all in doubt,
The element of fire is quite put out;[4]
The sun is lost, and th'earth, and no man's wit
Can well direct him where to look for it.
And freely men confess that this world's spent,
When in the planets and the firmament
They seek so many new; they see that this
Is crumbled out again to his atomies.[5]
'Tis all in pieces, all coherence gone,
All just supply,[6] and all relation:
Prince, subject, father, son are things forgot,
For every man alone thinks he hath got
To be a phoenix, and that there can be
None of that kind of which he is, but he.[7]
This is the world's condition now, and now
She that should all parts to reunion bow;
She that had all magnetic force alone,
To draw and fasten sundered parts in one;
She whom wise nature had invented then
When she observed that every sort of men
Did in their voyage in this world's sea stray,
And needed a new compass for their way;
She that was best, and first original
Of all fair copies; and the general
Steward to Fate; she whose rich eyes and breast

2. I.e., lacking in vigor.
3. Natural philosophy or science.
4. The concentric order of the elements, fire encircling the rest, had been rejected. As the next lines suggest, the new astronomy also held that the sun was at the center and that the earth moved around it.
5. Atoms.
6. Proper filling up of a place or position.
7. According to myth, the phoenix is unique.

Gilt the West Indies, and perfumed the East;[8]
Whose having breathed in this world did bestow
Spice on those Isles, and bade them still smell so,
And that rich Indy which doth gold inter,
Is but as single money,[9] coined from her:
She to whom this world must itself refer,
As suburbs, or the microcosm of her,
She, she is dead; she's dead: when thou know'st this,
Thou know'st how lame a cripple this world is,
And learn'st thus much by our anatomy,
That this world's general sickness doth not lie
In any humor,[1] or one certain part;
But, as thou saw'st it rotten at the heart,
Thou seest a hectic fever hath got hold
Of the whole substance, not to be controlled,
And that thou hast but one way not to admit
The world's infection, to be none of it.

1611

DIVINE POEMS

HOLY SONNETS[2]

I [II]

As due by many titles I resign
Myself to thee, O God, first I was made
By thee, and for thee, and when I was decayed
Thy blood bought that, the which before was thine;
I am thy son, made with thyself to shine,
Thy servant, whose pains thou hast still[3] repaid,
Thy sheep, thine image, and, till I betrayed
Myself, a temple of thy Spirit divine;
Why doth the Devil then usurp on[4] me?
Why doth he steal, nay ravish that's[5] thy right?

8. The West Indies were associated with precious metals; the East Indies, with fragrant spices.
9. Small change.
1. Medical theory of the time held that four bodily fluids, or "humors," accounted for the variety of human temperament.
2. The first sixteen "Holy Sonnets" date from about 1609–1611, prior to Donne's ordination. Although it is not clear that they were composed as units in a coherent sequence, we follow the order of the 1633 text, justified in Helen Gardner's edition of Donne's *Divine Poems*. For convenience, we also include in brackets the Roman numerals assigned in Grierson's widely cited edition. Only the first twelve of the sonnets appeared in 1633. Sonnets 13–16, not included here, were first published in the 1635 edition. Sonnets 17–19, evidently composed later in Donne's life (e.g., Sonnet 17 addresses the death of his wife in 1617), did not come to light until the discovery of the Westmoreland manuscript (1894). Note that Donne follows the Italian rhyme scheme, which formally divides the poem into two sections, of eight (*octave*) and six lines (*sestet*). A distinctive turn (*volta*) and change of tone typically occur at the start of the sestet.
3. Always, invariably.
4. Unjustly assume authority over.
5. That which is.

Except thou rise and for thine own work fight,
Oh I shall soon despair, when I do see
That thou lov'st mankind well, yet wilt not choose me,
And Satan hates me, yet is loath to lose me.

2 [IV]

Oh my black soul! Now thou art summoned
By sickness, death's herald, and champion;
Thou art like a pilgrim, which abroad hath done
Treason, and durst not turn to whence he is fled,
Or like a thief, which till death's doom be read,
Wisheth himself delivered from prison;
But damned and haled[6] to execution,
Wisheth that still he might be imprisoned.
Yet grace, if thou repent, thou canst not lack;
But who shall give thee that grace to begin.[7]
Oh make thyself with holy mourning black,
And red with blushing, as thou art with sin;
Or wash thee in Christ's blood, which hath this might
That being red, it dyes red souls to white.[8]

3 [VI]

This is my play's last scene, here heavens appoint
My pilgrimage's last mile; and my race,
Idly yet quickly run, hath this last pace,
My span's last inch, my minute's last point,[9]
And gluttonous death will instantly unjoint
My body and soul, and I shall sleep a space,
But my ever-waking part shall see that face
Whose fear[1] already shakes my every joint:
Then, as my soul to heaven, her first seat, takes flight,
And earth-born body in the earth shall dwell,
So, fall my sins, that all may have their right,
To where they're bred, and would press me, to hell.
Impute me righteous,[2] thus purged of evil,
For thus I leave the world, the flesh, the Devil.

6. Dragged or pulled with force or violence.
7. Theologically, "grace to begin," or *prevenient* grace, enables the sinner to repent in the first place.
8. Red is construed as the color of sin, but Christ's blood (line 13), despite its red color, can dye sinful souls white, the color of purity (line 14).
9. Instant.
1. The fear of whom.
2. Attribute righteousness to me.

4 [VII]

At the round earth's imagined corners,[3] blow
Your trumpets, angels, and arise, arise
From death, you numberless infinities
Of souls, and to your scattered bodies go,
All whom the flood did, and fire shall o'erthrow,
All whom war, dearth, age, agues,[4] tyrannies,
Despair, law, chance, hath slain, and you whose eyes
Shall behold God and never taste death's woe.[5]
But let them sleep, Lord, and me mourn a space,
For if above all these my sins abound,
'Tis late to ask abundance of thy grace
When we are there; here on this lowly ground,
Teach me how to repent; for that's as good
As if thou hadst sealed[6] my pardon with thy blood.

5 [IX]

If poisonous minerals, and if that tree
Whose fruit threw death on else immortal us,
If lecherous goats, if serpents envious
Cannot be damned, alas, why should I be?
Why should intent or reason, born in me,
Make sins, else equal, in me more heinous?
And mercy being easy, and glorious
To God, in his stern wrath why threatens he?
But who am I that dare dispute with thee
O God? Oh! of thine only worthy blood,[7]
And my tears, make a heavenly Lethean[8] flood,
And drown in it my sin's black memory.
That thou remember them, some claim as debt;[9]
I think it mercy, if thou wilt forget.

3. Cf. Revelation 7:1: "I saw four angels standing on the four corners of the earth."
4. Acute or violent fevers.
5. Cf. Luke 9:27: "there be some standing here, which shall not taste of death, till they see the kingdom of God."
6. Affixed a seal (to a document); irrevocably determined.
7. I.e., "Your uniquely sufficient blood."
8. In myth, drinking of the river Lethe erases memory.
9. In context, the likely sense of this line may be paraphrased as follows: "some claim you are obliged to remember sins (in order to forgive them)." The line can also be construed to say simply that "some claim you are obliged to remember them."

6 [X]

Death be not proud, though some have called thee
Mighty and dreadful, for thou art not so;
For those whom thou think'st thou dost overthrow
Die not, poor death, nor yet canst thou kill me.
From rest and sleep, which but thy pictures be,
Much pleasure;[1] then from thee much more must flow,
And soonest our best men with thee do go,
Rest of their bones, and soul's delivery.[2]
Thou art slave to fate, chance, kings, and desperate men,
And dost with poison, war, and sickness dwell;
And poppy[3] or charms can make us sleep as well,
And better than thy stroke; why swell'st[4] thou then?
One short sleep past, we wake eternally,
And death shall be no more; death, thou shalt die.

7 [XI]

Spit in my face you Jews, and pierce my side,
Buffet, and scoff, scourge, and crucify me,
For I have sinned, and sinned, and only he
Who could do no iniquity hath died:
But by my death cannot be satisfied
My sins,[5] which pass the Jews' impiety:
They killed once an inglorious man, but I
Crucify him daily, being now glorified.
Oh let me then his strange love still admire:
Kings pardon, but he bore our punishment.
And Jacob came clothed in vile harsh attire
But to supplant, and with gainful intent:[6]
God clothed himself in vile man's flesh that so
He might be weak enough to suffer woe.

1. I.e., "From rest and sleep, which are merely images of death, flow much pleasure."
2. Good men struggle least against death, which rests the weary body ("bones") and liberates or gives birth to the soul.
3. A plant with narcotic or sleep-inducing qualities.
4. Inflate with pride.
5. I.e., "My death does not suffice as payment for my sins."
6. Jacob disguised himself as his older brother, Esau, to win his father's blessing (Genesis 27).

8 [XII]

Why are we by all creatures waited on?
Why do the prodigal elements supply
Life and food to me, being more pure than I,
Simple, and further from corruption?
Why brook'st thou,[7] ignorant horse, subjection?
Why dost thou, bull and boar, so sillily
Dissemble weakness,[8] and by one man's stroke die,
Whose whole kind you might swallow and feed upon?
Weaker I am, woe is me, and worse than you,
You have not sinned, nor need be timorous.
But wonder at a greater wonder, for to us
Created nature doth these things subdue,
But their Creator, whom sin nor nature tied,
For us, his creatures, and his foes, hath died.

9 [XIII]

What if this present were the world's last night?
Mark in my heart, O soul, where thou dost dwell,
The picture of Christ crucified, and tell
Whether that countenance can thee affright,
Tears in his eyes quench the amazing light,
Blood fills his frowns, which from his pierced head fell.[9]
And can that tongue adjudge thee unto hell,
Which prayed forgiveness for his foes' fierce spite?
No, no; but as in my idolatry
I said to all my profane[1] mistresses,
Beauty, of pity, foulness only is
A sign of rigor:[2] so I say to thee,
To wicked spirits are horrid shapes assigned,
This beauteous form assures a piteous[3] mind.

10 [XIV]

Batter my heart, three-personed God; for you
As yet but knock, breathe, shine, and seek to mend;
That I may rise and stand, o'erthrow me, and bend

7. I.e., "Why do you tolerate . . . ?"
8. Senselessly pretend to be weak.
9. I.e., "The blood that dropped from his pierced head fills the wrinkles in his brow."
1. Not holy; worldly.
2. Beauty signifies compassion; ugliness, severity.
3. Compassionate.

Your force, to break, blow, burn, and make me new.
I, like an usurped town, to another due,
Labor to admit you, but oh, to no end!
Reason, your viceroy[4] in me, me should defend,
But is captived, and proves weak or untrue.
Yet dearly I love you, and would be loved fain,[5]
But am betrothed unto your enemy:
Divorce me, untie or break that knot again,
Take me to you, imprison me, for I,
Except you enthrall me, never shall be free,
Nor ever chaste, except you ravish me.

17 [XVII]

Since she whom I loved hath paid her last debt
To nature, and to hers and my good is dead,[6]
And her soul early into heaven ravished,
Wholly on heavenly things my mind is set.
Here the admiring her my mind did whet[7]
To seek thee, God; so streams do show the head;
But though I have found thee, and thou my thirst hast fed,
A holy thirsty dropsy melts[8] me yet.
But why should I beg more love, when as thou
Dost woo my soul, for hers off'ring all thine:
And dost not only fear lest I allow
My love to saints and angels, things divine,
But in thy tender jealousy dost doubt
Lest the world, flesh, yea Devil put thee out.[9]

Westmoreland MS.

18 [XVIII]

Show me, dear Christ, thy spouse, so bright and clear.
What! is it she which on the other shore
Goes richly painted?[1] or which robbed and tore
Laments and mourns in Germany and here?[2]

4. One who acts as the governor of a country, province, etc., in the name and by the authority of the supreme ruler.
5. Would be glad to be loved [by you].
6. Donne's wife, Anne More, died on 15 August 1617, at age thirty-three, a few days after delivering her twelfth child.
7. Sharpen, make more eager.
8. I.e., a holy, insatiable thirst or craving (dropsy) weakens (melts) me.
9. Donne suggests that God in his jealousy would prevent competition not only from saints and angels, but also from the world, the flesh, and even the devil. Hence Donne's wife is removed as a potential distraction from his devotion to God.
1. The Church of Rome, described as "painted" (wearing makeup) because of its lavish trappings.
2. The Protestant Church, relatively impoverished, tattered and suffering from persecution.

Sleeps she a thousand, then peeps up one year?
Is she self-truth and errs? Now new, now outwore?
Doth she, and did she, and shall she evermore
On one, on seven, or on no hill appear?[3]
Dwells she with us, or like adventuring knights
First travail[4] we to seek, and then make love?
Betray, kind husband, thy spouse to our sights,
And let mine amorous soul court thy mild dove,
Who is most true and pleasing to thee then
When she is embraced and open to most men.

Westmoreland MS.

19 [XIX]

Oh, to vex me, contraries meet in one;
Inconstancy unnaturally hath begot
A constant habit; that when I would not
I change in vows and in devotion.
As humorous[5] is my contrition[6]
As my profane[7] love, and as soon forgot:
As riddlingly distempered,[8] cold and hot;
As praying, as mute; as infinite, as none.
I durst[9] not view heaven yesterday; and today
In prayers and flattering speeches I court God;
Tomorrow I quake with true fear of his rod.
So my devout fits come and go away
Like a fantastic ague:[1] save that here
Those are my best days when I shake with fear.

Westmoreland MS.

Good Friday, 1613. Riding Westward[2]

Let man's soul be a sphere, and then, in this,
The intelligence that moves, devotion is,[3]
And as the other spheres, by being grown
Subject to foreign motions,[4] lose their own,

3. God's first institutional dwelling was Solomon's Temple on Mount Zion. The Catholic Church is identified with the seven hills of Rome. Protestantism is not associated with any hilltop(s).
4. Travel (its old spelling); toil.
5. I.e., based upon the inconstant physiological humors that govern human dispositions.
6. Penitence for sin.
7. Worldly (presumably referring to love affairs with women; cf. Holy Sonnet 9, line 10, p. 73).
8. Disordered, immoderate.
9. Dared.
1. A capricious fever, with hot and cold spells accompanied by shivering and trembling.
2. Composed during a journey westward, from Warwickshire into Wales.
3. Before Newton's theories rendered them superfluous, incorporeal intelligences (angels) were thought to move the celestial spheres. If man's soul were deemed a sphere per this paradigm, devotion to God would properly be its motivating principle.
4. I.e., motions of other spheres.

And being by others hurried every day,
Scarce in a year their natural form[5] obey:
Pleasure or business, so our souls admit
For their first mover, and are whirled by it.[6]
Hence is't that I am carried towards the west
This day, when my soul's form bends toward the east.
There I should see a Sun by rising, set,
And by that setting endless day beget;[7]
But that Christ on this cross did rise and fall,
Sin had eternally benighted all.
Yet dare I almost be glad I do not see
That spectacle of too much weight for me.
Who sees God's face, that is self life, must die;[8]
What a death were it then to see God die?
It made his own lieutenant, Nature, shrink;
It made his footstool crack, and the sun wink.[9]
Could I behold those hands which span the poles,[1]
And tune[2] all spheres at once, pierced with those holes?
Could I behold that endless height which is
Zenith[3] to us, and our antipodes,[4]
Humbled below us? or that blood which is
The seat of all our souls, if not of his,
Make dirt of dust, or that flesh which was worn
By God, for his apparel, ragg'd and torn?
If on these things I durst not look, durst I
Upon his miserable mother cast mine eye,
Who was God's partner here, and furnished thus
Half of that sacrifice which ransomed us?
Though these things, as I ride, be from mine eye,
They're present yet unto my memory,
For that looks towards them; and thou look'st towards me,
O Savior, as thou hang'st upon the tree;
I turn my back to thee but to receive
Corrections, till thy mercies bid thee leave.[5]
O think me worth thine anger, punish me,
Burn off my rusts and my deformity,
Restore thine image so much, by thy grace,
That thou may'st know me, and I'll turn my face.

5. Inherent principle of motion, as opposed to "foreign motions."
6. Instead of devotion to God (the prime mover), pleasure or business governs our souls.
7. The association of the sun as the light of the world with the Son of God was traditional. Riding with his back to the breaking day, Donne ponders the paradox that by rising (on the cross), the Son set (died), and in setting, undid the darkness of death.
8. God's face is life itself, yet anyone who sees it must die. Cf. Exodus 33:20.
9. On the earth as God's footstool, see Isaiah 66:1. When Christ was crucified, "the sun's light failed" and "the earth shook" (Luke 23:45, Matthew 27:51).
1. Referring to the poles at opposite ends of the entire Ptolemaic cosmos.
2. It was thought that the harmony of creation produced the music of the spheres, inaudible to fallen humanity. A variant and perhaps preferable reading is "turn."
3. The highest point of the celestial sphere as viewed from any particular place.
4. Here "antipodes" signifies the point of the celestial sphere precisely opposite the zenith.
5. Cease.

A Hymn to Christ, at the Author's Last Going into Germany[6]

In what torn ship soever I embark,
That ship shall be my emblem of thy ark;
What sea soever swallow me, that flood
Shall be to me an emblem of thy blood;
Though thou with clouds of anger do disguise
Thy face, yet through that mask I know those eyes,
  Which, though they turn away sometimes,
    They never will despise.

I sacrifice this island[7] unto thee,
And all whom I loved there, and who loved me;
When I have put our seas 'twixt them and me,
Put thou thy sea[8] betwixt my sins and thee.
As the tree's sap doth seek the root below
In winter, in my winter now I go
  Where none but thee, the eternal root
    Of true love, I may know.

Nor thou nor thy religion dost control[9]
The amorousness of an harmonious soul,
But thou would'st have that love thyself; as thou
Art jealous, Lord, so I am jealous now;
Thou lov'st not, till from loving more, thou free
My soul: whoever gives, takes liberty:
  O, if thou car'st not whom I love,
    Alas, thou lov'st not me.

Seal then this bill of my divorce to all
On whom those fainter beams of love did fall;
Marry those loves which in youth scattered be
On fame, wit, hopes (false mistresses) to thee.
Churches are best for prayer that have least light:
To see God only, I go out of sight;
  And to 'scape stormy days, I choose
    An everlasting night.

6. Donne was in Germany during 1619–1620, serving as chaplain on a diplomatic mission.
7. England.
8. The blood shed by Christ on the cross.
9. Forbid.

Hymn to God My God, in My Sickness[1]

Since I am coming to that holy room
 Where, with thy choir of saints for evermore,
I shall be made thy music, as I come
 I tune the instrument here at the door,
 And what I must do then, think now before.

Whilst my physicians by their love are grown
 Cosmographers, and I their map,[2] who lie
Flat on this bed, that by them may be shown
 That this is my south-west discovery
 Per fretum febris, by these straits to die,[3]

I joy, that in these straits, I see my west;
 For, though their current yield return to none,
What shall my west hurt me? As west and east[4]
 In all flat maps (and I am one) are one,
 So death doth touch the resurrection.

Is the Pacific Sea my home? Or are
 The eastern riches? Is Jerusalem?
Anyan,[5] and Magellan, and Gibraltar,
 All straits, and none but straits, are ways to them,
 Whether where Japhet dwelt, or Cham, or Shem.[6]

We think that Paradise and Calvary,
 Christ's cross and Adam's tree, stood in one place;[7]
Look, Lord, and find both Adams met in me;
 As the first Adam's sweat surrounds my face,
 May the last Adam's[8] blood my soul embrace.

So, in his purple[9] wrapped, receive me, Lord,
 By these his thorns give me his other crown;
And as to others' souls I preached thy word,
 Be this my text, my sermon to mine own,
 Therefore that he may raise, the Lord throws down.

1635

1. According to Isaac Walton, Donne wrote this poem eight days before his death on 31 March 1631. Other evidence suggests that he composed it during the same illness (in 1623) in which "A Hymn to God the Father" was composed.
2. Cosmographers mapped the features of celestial and terrestrial worlds (the universe or macrocosm). Human beings were thought to represent the greater world in miniature (microcosm).
3. Donne will make a southwest voyage of discovery "through the straits of fever" (*per fretum febris*). He alludes to Magellan, who, before dying in the Philippines, navigated a southwest passage to the Pacific between mainland South America and Tierra del Fuego, the land of fire.
4. West is the direction conventionally linked with death; east with birth, or in this case rebirth.
5. Bering Strait.
6. The descendents of Noah's sons were thought to dwell in Europe (Japheth), Africa (Cham or Ham), and Asia (Shem).
7. According to some traditions, the tree from which Adam and Eve ate the forbidden fruit grew from the same ground that would later hold Christ's cross on Golgotha.
8. Christ is the second, or "last," Adam. God's curse on Adam includes having to sweat for his food (Genesis 3:19).
9. Christ's blood. Roman soldiers mock Christ by dressing him in royal purple (Mark 15:17).

A Hymn to God the Father[1]

Wilt thou forgive that sin where I begun,
  Which is my sin, though it were done before?[2]
Wilt thou forgive that sin through which I run,[3]
  And do run still, though still[4] I do deplore?
    When thou hast done, thou hast not done,
      For I have more.

Wilt thou forgive that sin by which I have won
  Others to sin? and made my sin their door?
Wilt thou forgive that sin which I did shun
  A year or two, but wallowed in a score?
    When thou hast done, thou hast not done,
      For I have more.

I have a sin of fear, that when I have spun
  My last thread, I shall perish on the shore;
Swear by thyself that at my death thy sun[5]
  Shall shine as he shines now and heretofore;
    And, having done that, thou hast done,
      I have[6] no more.

1. According to Isaac Walton, the poem was written in 1623, during a serious illness.
2. Original sin, passed down from Adam and Eve.
3. Ran. A variant of lines 3–4 reads "those sins through which I run, / And do them still."
4. Always.
5. The original spelling, "sunn," could signify either "sun" or "son." We have chosen "sun" because it better fits the literal sense of the passage and because Donne does not generally belabor wordplay into explicitness.
6. An alternative reading is "fear."

Ben Jonson

1572	Born in London, a month or so after the death of his father, a minister. Attends Westminster School, perhaps through the good offices of William Camden (then second master), until 1589.
1589	Apprenticed to the bricklayer's trade, that of his stepfather.
1591–1592	Serves with the army in the Low Countries.
1594	Marriage to Anne Lewis.
1597	Playwright and actor in London. Imprisoned for more than six weeks in consequence of his connection with the (lost) play *The Isle of Dogs,* held by the Privy Council to be "lewd . . . seditious and slanderous."
1598	*The Case Is Altered* acted by the boys' company, the Children of the Chapel Royal; *Every Man in His Humor* acted by the Lord Chamberlain's Men (Shakespeare took one of the roles). Kills a fellow actor, Gabriel Spencer, in a duel, escaping the gallows only by pleading benefit of clergy, a legal loophole that enabled those who were literate in Latin to avoid capital punishment. Branded on thumb and released. Converted to Roman Catholicism while awaiting trial; remains a Catholic until about 1610. Included in Francis Meres's list, in *Palladis Tamia,* of those who are "our best for tragedy."
1599	*Every Man Out of His Humor* acted by the Lord Chamberlain's Men.
1600	*Cynthia's Revels* acted by the Children of the Chapel Royal, who perform *Poetaster* in 1601.
1602–1607	Living in the house of his patron, Esmé Stewart, Lord of Aubigny.
1603	Death of Queen Elizabeth, 24 March. Commissioned to write *An Entertainment at Althorpe* in connection with James I's journey from Edinburgh to London for his coronation; thereafter a regular contributor of masques (twenty-four in all) for entertainments at the royal court, often in uneasy collaboration with the designer Inigo Jones. *Sejanus* acted by the Lord Chamberlain's Men. Death of Jonson's first son.
1605	Imprisoned during late spring or summer with Chapman, for supposedly anti-Scottish elements in the play *Eastward Ho!* acted at this time by the boys' company, now termed the Children of the Queen's Revels.
1606	*Volpone* performed by the King's Men (formerly the Lord Chamberlain's Men).

1609–1610	*Epicoene* and *The Alchemist* acted by, respectively, the Children of the Queen's Revels and the King's Men.
1611	*Catiline* acted by the King's Men.
1612–1613	In France, serving as tutor and companion to Sir Walter Raleigh's son.
1614	*Bartholomew Fair* acted by Lady Elizabeth's Men.
1616	Publication of Jonson's *Works*. Awarded a royal pension.
1618–1619	Walking tour to Scotland; well received by persons of standing in Edinburgh and honored by the town council of that city. Resides for two or three weeks with William Drummond of Hawthornden. Awarded an honorary M.A. by Oxford University.
1620	Residing in Gresham College, London; perhaps lecturing in rhetoric at that institution. Until at least 1625, the central figure of a congenial group ("the Tribe of Ben") meeting in the "Apollo Room" of the Devil Tavern in London.
1623	Jonson's books and manuscripts destroyed by fire.
1625	Death of James I; Jonson's influence at court declines steadily from this time.
1626	*The Staple of News* acted by the King's Men.
1628	Suffers a paralytic stroke. Appointed historiographer of the City of London (a sinecure).
1629	*The New Inn* acted by the King's Men; a resounding failure.
1630	Jonson's pension increased to £100 annually, together with a tierce of Canary wine.
1631–1635	Years of declining health and influence. *A Tale of a Tub* acted by Queen Henrietta's Men in 1633; Jonson's last masque, *Love's Welcome at Bolsover*, presented in 1634. Death of Jonson's second son, 1635.
1637	Death, 6 August. Buried three days later in Westminster Abbey.
1640–1641	Publication of Jonson's *Works* in two volumes, under the direction of Sir Kenelm Digby.

FROM *THE WORKS OF BENJAMIN JONSON* (1616)

FROM *EPIGRAMS*[1]

I: To the Reader

Pray thee, take care, that tak'st my book in hand,
To read it well: that is, to understand.[2]

II: To My Book

It will be looked for, book, when some but see
  Thy title, *Epigrams*, and named of me,
Thou should'st be bold, licentious, full of gall,
  Wormwood and sulphur,[3] sharp, and toothed withal;
Become a petulant[4] thing, hurl ink and wit
  As madmen stones, not caring whom they hit.
Deceive their malice, who could wish it so.
  And by thy wiser temper, let men know
Thou are not covetous of least self-fame
  Made from the hazard of another's shame;
Much less, with lewd, profane, and beastly praise,
  To catch the world's loose laughter, or vain gaze.
He that departs with[5] his own honesty
  For vulgar praise, doth it too dearly buy.

IV: To King James[6]

How, best of kings, dost thou a scepter bear!
  How, best of poets, dost thou laurel wear!
But two things, rare, the Fates had in their store,
  And gave thee both, to show they could no more.
For such a poet, while thy days were green,

1. Johnson dedicated his *Epigrams* to William Herbert, third Earl of Pembroke (1580–1630), son of that Countess of Pembroke who was Sir Philip Sidney's sister; in the dedicatory epistle, Jonson calls these poems "the ripest of [his] studies." In form and spirit, they reflect primarily the work of the Roman epigrammatist Martial (c. 40–c. 104); for a useful account of Jonson's conception of the epigram, cf. *Ben Jonson*, ed. C. H. Herford, P. and E. M. Simpson, 11 vols. (Oxford, 1925–1952), II, pp. 342–360. This edition is cited hereafter as *H & S*.
2. Cf. *The Alchemist*. To the Reader: "If thou beest more, thou art an understander, and then I trust thee."
3. I.e., full of bitterness derived from several aspects of being; with that rancor supposed to have its seat in the gall bladder are conjoined the bitter-tasting plant *Artemisia absinthium* and the pungently odorous mineral sulphur, respectively associated in Jonson's day with whatever is bitter and grievous to the soul, and with Satan's abode in hell. The expression is ultimately scriptural: cf. Deuteronomy 29:18.
4. Peevishly aggressive.
5. I.e., gives up.
6. James I (James VI of Scotland) had published *His Majesties Poeticall Exercises* in 1591, and *Essayes of a Prentise in the Divine Art of Poesie* in 1584, at the age of eighteen.

Thou wert, as chief of them are said t'have been.
And such a prince thou art, we daily see,
As chief of those still promise they will be.
Whom should my Muse then fly to, but the best
Of kings for grace; of poets for my test?

IX: To All, To Whom I Write

May none, whose scattered names honor my book,
For strict degrees of rank or title look;
'Tis 'gainst the manners of an epigram;
And I a poet here, no herald am.

XI: On Something that Walks Somewhere

At court I met it, in clothes brave[7] enough
To be a courtier, and looks grave enough
To seem a statesman; as I near it came,
It made me a great face; I asked the name.
"A lord," it cried, "buried in flesh and blood,
And such from whom let no man hope least good,
For I will do none: and as little ill,
For I will dare none." Good lord, walk dead still.

XIV: To William Camden[8]

Camden, most reverend head, to whom I owe
All that I am in arts, all that I know
(How nothing's that?); to whom my country owes
The great renown and name wherewith she goes.[9]
Than thee the age sees not that thing more grave,
More high, more holy, that she more would crave.
What name, what skill, what faith hast thou in things![1]
What sight in searching the most antique springs!
What weight and what authority in thy speech!
Man scarce can make that doubt, but thou canst teach.
Pardon free truth, and let thy modesty,
Which conquers all, be once overcome by thee.
Many of thine this better could than I,
But for their powers, accept my piety.

7. Fine.
8. William Camden (1551–1623), antiquarian and historian, was Jonson's teacher at Westminster School. Jonson dedicated *Every Man in His Humor* to him.
9. Jonson here alludes to the international reputation of Camden's *Britannia* (1586), and probably also to the equally admired *Remaines of a Greater Worke concerning Britaine* (1605).
1. Facts, events.

XVIII: To My Mere[2] English Censurer

To thee, my way in epigrams seems new,
When both it is the old way, and the true.
Thou say'st, that cannot be; for thou hast seen
Davies, and Weever,[3] and the best have been,
And mine come nothing like. I hope so. Yet,
As theirs did with thee, mine might credit get,
If thou'dst but use thy faith, as thou didst then,
When thou wert wont t'admire, not censure men.
Prithee believe still, and not judge so fast;
Thy faith is all the knowledge that thou hast.

XXII: On My First Daughter

Here lies, to each her parents' ruth,[4]
Mary, the daughter of their youth;
Yet all heaven's gifts being heaven's due,
It makes the father less to rue.
At six months' end,[5] she parted hence
With safety of her innocence;
Whose soul heaven's queen, whose name she bears,
In comfort of her mother's tears,
Hath placed amongst her virgin-train:
Where, while that severed doth remain,[6]
This grave partakes the fleshly birth;
Which cover lightly, gentle earth!

XLV: On My First Son

Farewell, thou child of my right hand, and joy;[7]
My sin was too much hope of thee, loved boy.
Seven years thou wert lent to me, and I thee pay,
Exacted by thy fate, on the just day.
O, could I lose all father now![8] For why

2. Absolute; no more than.
3. The epigrams of Sir John Davies (1569–1626) had appeared c. 1590; John Weever (1576–1632) published *Epigrammes in the oldest cut, and newest fashion* in 1599.
4. Grief.
5. The dates of Mary's life are not known.
6. I.e., while the soul remains separate from the body (until souls and bodies are reunited at the Resurrection).
7. Jonson's son Benjamin (literally "child of the right hand" in Hebrew), born in 1596, died of the plague in 1603, while Jonson was absent from London. Drummond observes that the poet, "being in the country at Sir Robert Cotton's house with old Camden . . . saw in a vision his eldest son, then a child and at London, appear unto him with the mark of a bloody cross on his forehead as if it had been cutted with a sword; at which amazed, he prayed unto God, and in the morning he came to Mr. Camden's chamber to tell him, who persuaded him it was but an apprehension of his fantasy, at which he should not be dejected. In the meantime comes there letters from his wife of the death of that boy in the plague. He appeared to him, he said, of a manly shape, and of that growth that he thinks he shall be at the Resurrection" (*H & S*, I, pp. 139–140).
8. I.e., relinquish every thought of fatherhood.

Will man lament the state he should envy?
To have so soon 'scaped world's and flesh's rage,
And, if no other misery, yet age?
Rest in soft peace, and asked, say, "Here doth lie
Ben Jonson his best piece of poetry,
For whose sake, henceforth, all his vows be such
As what he loves may never like too much."[9]

LIX: On Spies[1]

Spies, you are lights in state, but of base stuff,
Who, when you've burnt yourselves down to the snuff,[2]
Stink, and are thrown away. End fair enough.

LXIX: To Pertinax Cob[3]

Cob, thou nor soldier, thief, nor fencer art,
Yet by thy weapon liv'st! Th'hast one good part.

LXXVI: On Lucy, Countess of Bedford[4]

This morning, timely rapt with holy fire,
I thought to form unto my zealous Muse
What kind of creature I could most desire
To honor, serve, and love; as poets use.
I meant to make her fair, and free, and wise,
Of greatest blood, and yet more good than great;
I meant the day-star should not brighter rise,
Nor lend like influence from his lucent seat.
I meant she should be courteous, facile,[5] sweet,
Hating that solemn vice of greatness, pride;
I meant each softest virtue there should meet,
Fit in that softer bosom to reside.
Only a learned and a manly soul
I purposed her; that should, with even powers,

9. These lines (with their echo of line 2) appear to reflect the classical belief that excessive good fortune is likely to excite the jealousy of the gods. Cf. Martial, *Epigrams*. VI.xxix.8: *Quidquid amas, cupias non placuisse nimis* ("Whatever you love, may you wish not to have been overly pleased by [it]").
1. Drummond reports that "in the time of [Jonson's] close imprisonment under Queen Elizabeth [i.e., in 1598], his judges could get nothing of him to all their demands but aye and no; they placed two damned villains to catch advantage of him, with him, but he was advertised [i.e., warned] by his keeper. Of the spies he hath an epigram" (*H & S*, I, p. 139). Cf. Epigram CI, line 36n, p. 90.
2. Candle end.
3. Latin *pertinax* means "stubborn, obstinate" (also "stiff"); "cob" has the double sense of "something big or stout" and "something forming a rounded lump." In northern English rustic dialect, "cob" came to mean "testicle."
4. Daughter (1581–1627) of Sir John Harington, the Countess of Bedford was friend and patron to Jonson, Donne, Daniel, and other literary figures; she took part in several of Jonson's masques. Cf. Epigram XCIV, p. 88, and Donne's "To the Countess of Bedford," p. 61.
5. Affable, unconstrained.

The rock, the spindle, and the shears[6] control
Of destiny, and spin her own free hours.
Such when I meant to feign, and wished to see,
My Muse bade, "Bedford write," and that was she.

LXXIX: To Elizabeth, Countess of Rutland[7]

That poets are far rarer births than kings
Your noblest father proved; like whom, before,
Or then, or since, about our Muses' springs,
Came not that soul exhausted so their store.
Hence was it that the destinies decreed
(Save that most masculine issue of his brain)[8]
No male unto him, who could so exceed
Nature, they thought, in all that he would feign.
At which she, happily[9] displeased, made you;
On whom if he were living now to look,
He should those rare and absolute numbers[1] view,
As he would burn, or better far his book.

LXXXIII: To a Friend

To put out the word, *whore*, thou dost me woo,
Throughout my book. 'Troth, put out *woman* too.

XCI: To Sir Horace Vere[2]

Which of thy names I take, not only bears
A Roman sound, but Roman virtue wears,
Illustrous Vere, or Horace; fit to be
Sung by a Horace, or a Muse as free,
Which thou art to thyself: whose fame was won
In th'eye of Europe, where thy deeds were done.
When on thy trumpet she did sound a blast,
Whose relish[3] to eternity shall last.

6. Distaff ("rock"), spindle, and shears are the emblems of the three Fates—Clotho spins the thread of life; Lachesis determines its length; Atropos cuts it with her shears. Cf. Hesiod, *Theogony*, 217–223, 904–906; and Plato, *Republic*, X.617–621.
7. The daughter (1584–1612) of Sir Philip Sidney; according to Drummond, Jonson thought her "nothing inferior to her father . . . in poesie" (*H & S*. I, p. 138).
8. I.e., Sidney's prose romance *Arcadia*.
9. By good fortune.
1. I.e., perfectly harmonious proportions.
2. A distinguished English soldier (1565–1635), Vere campaigned with considerable success against the forces of Spain in the Netherlands. Thomas Fuller notices his "excellent temper, it being true of him what is said of the Caspian Sea, that it doth never ebb nor flow; observing a constant tenor, neither elated nor depressed with success." Comparing him to his brother, Sir Francis Vere, Fuller observes, "Sir Francis was more feared, Sir Horace more loved, by the soldiery" (*The Worthies of England*. ed. J. Freeman [London, 1952], p. 180). The *Odes* and *Satires* of Horace (65–8 B.C.) were admired and imitated by Jonson, who translated the Roman poet's *Ars Poetica*. Latin *vere* means "truly."
3. Lingering and agreeable trace or echo.

I leave thy acts, which should I prosecute[4]
Throughout, might flatt'ry seem; and to be mute
To any one were envy, which would live
Against my grave, and time could not forgive.
I speak thy other graces, not less shown,
Nor less in practice, but less marked, less known:
Humanity and piety, which are
As noble in great chiefs as they are rare;
And best become the valiant man to wear,
Who more should seek men's reverence, than fear.

XCIV: To Lucy, Countess of Bedford, with Mr. Donne's *Satires*[5]

Lucy,[6] you brightness of our sphere, who are
Life of the Muses' day, their morning-star!
If works, not th'author's, their own grace should look,[7]
Whose poems would not wish to be your book?
But these, desired by you, the maker's ends
Crown with their own. Rare poems ask rare friends.
Yet satires, since the most of mankind be
Their unavoided subject, fewest see;
For none e'er took that pleasure in sin's sense,
But, when they heard it taxed, took more offence.
They, then, that living where the matter is bred,[8]
Dare for these poems, yet, both ask, and read,
And like them too, must needfully, though few,
Be of the best; and 'mongst those, best are you,
Lucy, you brightness of our sphere, who are
The Muses' evening, as their morning-star.

XCVI: To John Donne

Who shall doubt, Donne, where[9] I a poet be,
When I dare send my epigrams to thee?
That so alone canst judge, so alone dost make;
And, in thy censures, evenly, dost take
As free simplicity to disavow,
As thou hast best authority t'allow.
Read all I send; and if I find but one
Marked by thy hand, and with the better stone,[1]

4. Pursue in detail.
5. Donne's *Satires*, perhaps composed c. 1593–1595, were circulating in manuscript before their publication in 1633.
6. "Lucy" derives from Latin *lux*, "light, brightness."
7. Seek.
8. I.e., in the society being satirized.
9. Whether.
1. The ancient Romans marked joyful or successful days on their calendars with white stones (thought to be auspicious); cf. Pliny, *Natural History*, VII.40; and *Letters*, VI.11.

My title's sealed. Those that for claps do write,
Let puisnees',[2] porters', players' praise delight,
And, till they burst, their backs, like asses load,[3]
A man should seek great glory, and not broad.

CI: Inviting a Friend to Supper[4]

Tonight, grave sir, both my poor house and I
Do equally desire your company;
Not that we think us worthy such a guest,
But that your worth will dignify our feast
With those that come, whose grace may make that seem
Something, which else could hope for no esteem.
It is the fair acceptance, sir, creates
The entertainment perfect; not the cates.[5]
Yet shall you have, to rectify your palate,
An olive, capers, or some better salad
Ushering the mutton; with a short-legged hen,
If we can get her, full of eggs, and then
Lemons and wine for sauce; to these, a coney[6]
Is not to be despaired of, for our money;
And though fowl, now, be scarce, yet there are clerks,
The sky not falling, think we may have larks.
I'll tell you of more, and lie, so you will come:
Of partridge, pheasant, woodcock, of which some
May yet be there; and godwit, if we can,
Knat, rail, and ruff too.[7] Howsoe'er, my man
Shall read a piece of Vergil, Tacitus,
Livy, or of some better book[8] to us,
Of which we'll speak our minds, amidst our meat;
And I'll profess no verses to repeat;
To this, if ought appear which I not know of,
That will the pastry, not my paper, show of.
Digestive cheese, and fruit there sure will be;
But that which most doth take my Muse, and me
Is a pure cup of rich Canary wine,
Which is the Mermaid's[9] now, but shall be mine;

2. Inferiors, underlings.
3. I.e., (as foolish men overload beasts of burden), accept ever greater loads (of vulgar praise) until their back breaks.
4. The versified invitation to share a frugal or lavish repast is a popular variety of the classical and Renaissance verse epistle. Jonson took several hints from Martial's poems in this kind, e.g., *Epigrams*, V.xxviii; XI.lii. Cf. also Habington, "To a Friend, Inviting Him to a Meeting upon Promise," p. 354.
5. Dainties, delicacies.
6. Rabbit.
7. Edible birds of English marshlands and waterways; in modern usage, curlew, sandpiper, corncrake, pigeon.
8. With Vergil (70–19 B.C.), author of the *Aeneid*, Jonson conjoins the Roman historian Livy (59 B.C.–A.D. 17) and Tacitus (c. A.D. 60–c. 120), whom he especially admired; cf. *H & S*, I, p. 136. By "some better book" is meant, perhaps, the Bible.
9. The Mermaid Tavern in London was frequented by Jonson and his fellows. For Horace, cf. Epigram XCIn, p. 87. The lyric poet Anacreon of Teos (born c. 550 B.C.) wrote convivial verse in praise of wine and women.

Of which had Horace or Anacreon tasted,
  Their lives, as do their lines, till now had lasted.
Tobacco, nectar, or the Thespian spring[1]
  Are all but Luther's beer[2] to this I sing.
Of this we will sup free, but moderately,
  And we will have no Pooly, or Parrot by;[3]
Nor shall our cups make any guilty men,
  But at our parting we will be as when
We innocently met. No simple word
  That shall be uttered at our mirthful board
Shall makes us sad next morning, or affright
  The liberty that we'll enjoy tonight.

CXX: Epitaph on S. P., a Child of Q. El. Chapel[4]

Weep, with me, all you that read
  This little story;
And know, for whom a tear you shed
  Death's self is sorry.
'Twas a child that so did thrive
  In grace and feature,
As Heaven and Nature seemed to strive
  Which owned the creature.
Years he numbered scarce thirteen
  When Fates turned cruel,
Yet three filled zodiacs[5] had he been
  The stage's jewel;
And did act (what now we moan)
  Old men so duly,
As, sooth, the Parcae[6] thought him one,
  He played so truly.
So, by error, to his fate
  They all consented;
But viewing him since (alas, too late),
  They have repented,
And have sought, to give new birth,
  In baths to steep him;
But, being so much too good for earth,
  Heaven vows to keep him.

1. Thespiae lies at the foot of Mount Helicon, in Greece; the "Thespian spring" was associated with the Muses. Tobacco appears in this context, perhaps, because it was often said to be drunk; cf. *Every Man In His Humour*, III.v.137: "The most divine tobacco that ever I drunk."
2. I.e., German beer.
3. Robert Pooly and (probably) Henry Parrot were government spies; Pooly was present when Christopher Marlowe was killed in a tavern brawl. Jonson punningly suggests the loose chatter associated with ("polly") parrots.
4. Salomon Pavy, a boy actor with the Children of Queen Elizabeth's Chapel, took part in two of Jonson's plays: *Cynthia's Revels*, in 1600, and *Poetaster*, in 1601. He died in 1602. On his name and career, cf. G. E. Bentley, "A Good Name Lost," *Times Literary Supplement* (*TLS*) (30 May 1942).
5. I.e., he had acted for three years.
6. The Fates. Cf. Epigram LXXVI, line 15n, p. 87.

CXXVIII: To William Roe[7]

Roe (and my joy to name), th'art now to go
Countries, and climes, manners, and men to know,
T'extract, and choose the best of all these known,
And those to turn to blood, and make thine own:
May winds as soft as breath of kissing friends
Attend thee hence; and there, may all thy ends,
As the beginnings here, prove purely sweet,
And perfect in a circle always meet.
So, when we, blessed with thy return, shall see
Thy self, with thy first thoughts, brought home by thee,
We each to other may this voice inspire:
"This is that good Aeneas, passed through fire,
Through seas, storms, tempests; and, embarked for hell,
Came back untouched. This man hath travailed[8] well."

CXXXIII: On the Famous Voyage

No more let Greece her bolder fables tell
Of Hercules, or Theseus going to hell,
Orpheus, Ulysses; or the Latin Muse.
With tales of Troy's just knight,[9] our faiths abuse;
We have a Shelton[1] and a Heyden got,
Had power to act, what they to feign had not.
All that they boast of Styx, of Acheron,
Cocytus, Phlegethon,[2] ours have proved in one;[3]
The filth, stench, noise: save only what was there
Subtly distinguished, was confusèd here.
Their wherry[4] had no sail, too; ours had none;
And in it, two more horrid knaves than Charon.[5]
Arses were heard to croak instead of frogs;[6]
And for one Cerberus,[7] the whole coast was dogs.
Furies there wanted not; each scold[8] was ten.

7. William Roe (1585–1667) was the brother of Sir John Roe, Jonson's close friend; cf. *H & S*, I, pp. 136–137. Jonson appeared as a witness on William Roe's behalf in a lawsuit, in 1610. Cf. Donne's "To Sir Henry Wotton," p. 59.
8. I.e., worked (travailed) and traveled to good purpose.
9. Aeneas, the virtuous hero of the *Aeneid*, composed by Vergil ("the Latin Muse"). In the course of his mock epic, Jonson makes play with the apparatus of classical epic (invocation, heroic quest, descent to the underworld, etc.).
1. Sir Ralph Shelton was knighted in 1607; Heyden's identity is unknown.
2. I.e., the four rivers of Hades; cf. Homer, *Odyssey*, X.513–515.
3. I.e., ours have experienced in the Fleet Ditch, a thoroughly polluted stream running south into the Thames. "The Fleet . . . had become a shallow, silt-choked, rubbish-filled abomination 'very stinking and noisome' . . . little better, indeed, than a sewer. As early as 1390 the White Friars had complained that the stench arising from it, impossible to deaden with the strongest incense, had been responsible for the death of several of their brethren" (Christopher Hibbert, *London: The Biography of a City* [New York, 1969], p. 74).
4. I.e., the vessel(s) in which the figures named in lines 2–4 were embarked.
5. The boatman who ferried the souls of the dead across the river of Hades is a familiar figure in classical literature; cf. Vergil, *Aeneid*, VI.298–315.
6. The allusion refers to Aristophanes' comedy *The Frogs*.
7. The monstrous watchdog of Hades; cf. Hesiod, *Theogony*, 311.
8. A woman who disturbs the peace with loud abusive language.

And, for the cries of ghosts, women and men,
Laden with plague-sores, and their sins, were heard,
Lashed by their consciences, to die affeard.
Then let the former age with this content her,
She brought the poets forth, but ours th'adventer.[9]

The Voyage Itself

I sing the brave adventure of two wights,
And pity 'tis, I cannot call 'em knights:
One was; and he, for brawn and brain, right able
To have been stylèd of King Arthur's table.
The other was a squire of fair degree,
But in the action greater man than he
Who gave, to take at his return from hell,
His three for one.[1] Now, lordings, listen well.
It was the day, what time the powerful moon
Makes the poor Bankside creature wet its shoon
In its own hall,[2] when these (in worthy scorn
Of those that put out moneys on return
From Venice, Paris, or some inland passage
Of six times to and fro without embassage,[3]
Or him that backward went to Berwick,[4] or which
Did dance the famous morris unto Norwich)[5]
At Bread Street's Mermaid, having dined, and merry,
Proposed to go to Holborn[6] in a wherry:
A harder task than either his to Bristo',
Or his to Antwerp.[7] Therefore, once more, list ho.
A dock[8] there is that callèd is Avernus,
Of some Bridewell, and may, in time, concern us
All, that are readers; but methinks 'tis odd
That all this while I have forgot some god
Or goddess to invoke, to stuff my verse;
And with both bombard-style and phrase rehearse
The many perils of this port, and how,
Sans help of Sibyl, or a golden bough,[9]
Or magic sacrifice, they passed along!
Alcides,[1] be thou succoring to my song.

9. Adventure.
1. I.e., his large profit.
2. I.e., at high tide. The Bankside, or southern bank of the Thames, was a notoriously raffish district.
3. I.e., without acting as official ambassadors.
4. William Rowley, in *A Search for Money* (London, 1609), discussing the contemporary passion for eccentrically conceived travels, alludes to "the fellows going backward to Berwick, another hopping from York to London" (A 4).
5. Rowley also mentions Will Kemp's "wild morris to Norwich"; Kemp's exploit took place in 1599. In 1600 he published *Kemps nine daies wonder. Performed in a daunce from London to Norwich.*
6. In Jonson's day, Holborn was a residential area lying to the northwest of the city walls.
7. These feats of rowing are noticed by Samuel Rowlands in verses prefixed to John Taylor, *The Sculler, Rowing from Tiber to Thames* (London, 1612), A 4.
8. Bridewell Dock was situated at the junction of the Fleet Ditch and the Thames. The pun on "dock" (the place where prisoners stand in a court of law) would have reminded Jonson's readers that Bridewell Prison stood nearby.
9. Aeneas was so aided; cf. *Aeneid*, VI.1ff.
1. I.e., Hercules, who rescued Alcestis from Hades; cf. Euripides, *Alcestis*.

Thou hast seen hell, some say, and know'st all nooks there,
Canst tell me best how every Fury looks there,
And art a god, if fame thee not abuses,
Always at hand to aid the merry Muses.
Great club-fist,[2] though thy back and bones be sore
Still with thy former labors; yet once more
Act a brave work, call it thy last adventry;[3]
But hold my torch, while I describe the entry
To this dire passage. Say, thou, stop thy nose:
'Tis but light pains; indeed this dock's no rose.
In the first jaws appeared that ugly monster
Yclepèd[4] Mud, which, when their oars did once stir,
Belched forth an air as hot as at the muster
Of all your night-tubs, when the carts do cluster,
Who shall discharge first his merde-urinous[5] load;
Thorough her womb they make their famous road
Between two walls; where, on one side, to scare men,
Were seen your ugly Centaurs, ye call carmen,[6]
Gorgonian scolds, and Harpies; on the other
Hung stench, diseases, and old Filth, their mother,
With famine, wants, and sorrows many a dozen,
The least of which was to the plague a cousin.
But they unfrighted pass, though many a privy
Spake to 'em louder than the ox in Livy,[7]
And many a sink[8] poured out her rage anenst[9] 'em.
But still their valor and their virtue fenced[1] 'em
And on they went, like Castor brave and Pollux,[2]
Plowing the main. When, see, the worst of all lucks,
They met the second prodigy, would fear a
Man that had never heard of a Chimaera.[3]
One said it was bold Briareus,[4] or the beadle[5]
Who hath the hundred hands when he doth meddle;
The other thought it Hydra,[6] or the rock
Made of the trull that cut her father's lock;[7]

2. Hercules, usually represented as carrying a club cut from a wild olive tree, accidentally killed Eurynomus with a blow of his fist; cf. Diodorus Siculus, *Bibliotheca Historica*, IV.36.
3. Adventure.
4. Called.
5. I.e., composed of feces and urine.
6. I.e., men who drive carts carrying dung. Centaurs, Gorgons, and Harpies, monstrous beings from the realm of classical mythology, variously combine the characteristics of beasts and men.
7. Cf. Livy's history of Rome, XXXV.21.
8. Sewage drain.
9. Against.
1. Protected.
2. In classical mythology, Castor and Pollux, the Dioscuri, were the sons of Zeus; by a variant account, Pollux alone was Zeus's offspring and, therefore, immortal, while Castor, the son of Tyndareus, was mortal. Cf. *Odyssey*. XI.300 ff.; Pindar, *Nemean Odes*, X.80.
3. A fire-breathing monster combining the head of a lion, the body of a goat, and a dragon's tail.
4. A huge monster with a hundred hands and fifty heads, Briareus was the son of Uranus (Heaven) and Gaea (Earth); cf. Hesiod, *Theogony*, 149–150.
5. Parish official.
6. Hydra, a sea monster with nine heads, was slain by Hercules; cf. Ovid, *Metamorphoses*, IX.67–74.
7. Jonson confuses the sea monster Scylla, guardian of a dangerous rock in the Straits of Messina (Ovid, *Metamorphoses*, XIII.897–968; XIV.1–74), with Scylla, the daughter of King Nisus, who, to win the love of Minos, cut off a lock of her father's hair, on which his life depended (*Metamorphoses*, VIII.1–151).

But coming near, they found it but a lighter,
So huge, it seemed, they could by no means quite[8] her.
"Back," cried their brace of Charons; they cried, "No,
No going back; on still, you rogues, and row.
How hight[9] the place?" A voice was heard, "Cocytus."[1]
"Row close then, slaves." "Alas, they will beshite us."
"No matter, stinkards, row. What croaking sound
Is this we hear? of frogs?" "No, guts windbound,
Over your heads." "Well, row." At this loud
Crack did report itself, as if a cloud
Had burst with storm, and down fell, *ab excelsis*,[2]
Poor Mercury, crying out on Paracelsus[3]
And all his followers, that had so abused him;
And, in so shitten sort, so long had used him,
For (where he[4] was the god of eloquence,
And subtlety of metals) they dispense
His spirits, now, in pills, and eke in potions,
Suppositories, cataplasms,[5] and lotions.
"But many moons there shall not wane," quoth he,
"(In the meantime, let 'em imprison me)
But I will speak, and know I shall be heard,
Touching this cause, where they will be afeared
To answer me." And sure, it was the intent
Of the grave fart, late let in parliament,[6]
Had it been seconded, and not in fume
Vanished away; as you must all presume
Their Mercury did now. By this, the stem
Of the hulk touched, and, as by Polypheme
The sly Ulysses stole in a sheepskin,[7]
The well-greased wherry now had got between,
And bade her farewell sough unto the lurden; [8]
Never did bottom more betray her burden;
The meat-boat of bears' college, Paris Garden,[9]
Stunk not so ill; nor when she kissed, Kate Arden.[1]
Yet, one day in the year, for sweet 'tis voiced,

8. Avoid.
9. I.e., what is the name of.
1. The river of lamentation, in Hades.
2. I.e., from the heavens.
3. Mercurial compounds were employed as purgatives; the followers of Paracelsus (Theophrastus Bombastus von Hohenheim, 1493–1541), physician and alchemist, assigned special importance to the role of mercury in medical and alchemical processes. Jonson's view of the alchemist's art is dramatically set out in his comedy *The Alchemist*.
4. I.e., whereas Mercury. Mercury was also the divinity of commerce and gain.
5. Cataplasms, or poultices, are masses of organic material (flour, bran, etc.) applied to wounds or sores.
6. This alludes to "a discussion [in 1607] in the House of Commons on the peculiar manner in which Henry Ludlow said 'no' to a message brought . . . from the Lords" (*H & S*, X, p. 74).
7. Cf. *Odyssey*, IX.431–434.
8. I.e., gave a parting sigh to the clumsy slowness (of the lighter).
9. Offal from the meat markets in London was transported across the Thames to Paris Garden, in Southwark, where bears and bulls were "baited" by mastiffs.
1. A celebrated prostitute.

And that is when it is the Lord Mayor's foist.[2]
  By this time had they reached the Stygian pool
By which the Masters swear, when, on the stool
Of worship,[3] they their nodding chins do hit
Against their breasts. Here several ghosts did flit
About the shore, of farts but late departed,
White, black, blue, green, and in more forms outstarted
Than all those atomi ridiculous,
Whereof old Democrite and Hill Nicholas,[4]
One said, the other swore, the world consists.
These be the cause of those thick frequent mists
Arising in that place, through which who goes
Must try the unused valor of a nose,
And that ours did. For yet no nare[5] was tainted,
Nor thumb nor finger to the stop acquainted,
But open and unarmed encountered all,
Whether it languishing stuck upon the wall
Or were precipitated down the jakes,[6]
And, after, swum abroad in ample flakes,
Or that it lay, heaped like an usurer's mass,
All was to them the same, they were to pass;
And so they did, from Styx to Acheron,
The ever-boiling flood, whose banks upon
Your Fleet Lane Furies[7] and hot cooks do dwell
That, with still-scalding steams, make the place hell.
The sinks ran grease and hair of measled[8] hogs,
The heads, houghs,[9] entrails, and the hides of dogs;
For to say truth, what scullion is so nasty
To put the skins and offal in a pasty?
Cats there lay divers had been flayed and roasted,
And, after moldy grown, again were toasted;
Then, selling not, a dish was ta'en to mince 'em,
But still it seemed the rankness did convince[1] 'em.
For here they were thrown in with the melted pewter,
Yet drowned they not. They had five lives in future.
  But 'mongst these tiberts,[2] who do you think there was?
Old Banks the juggler,[3] our Pythagoras,
Grave tutor to the learnèd horse. Both which,

2. I.e., used as the Lord Mayor's barge. "Foist" means also "stink."
3. I.e., on the toilet.
4. Democritus (born c. 460 B.C.) is generally regarded as the founder of the atomic theory of matter; Nicholas Hill (c. 1570–1610) in 1601 published a philosophical text touching on Democritus and other ancient thinkers.
5. Nostril.
6. Privy.
7. I.e., the cooks of Fleet Lane.
8. Leprous.
9. Hocks.
1. Convict.
2. Cats.
3. Entertainer. Banks trained and exhibited the famous performing horse, Morocco, over a period of years toward the close of the sixteenth century. Notwithstanding the allusion to Pythagoras (540–510 B.C.), who believed in the transmigration of souls, Banks was still living in 1625.

Being beyond sea, burned for one witch,
Their spirits transmigrated to a cat;
And now above the pool a face right fat,
With great gray eyes, is lifted up, and mewed;
Thrice did it spit; thrice dived. At last it viewed
Our brave heroes with a milder glare,
And in a piteous tune began. "How dare
Your dainty nostrils (in so hot a season,
When every clerk eats artichokes and peason,[4]
Laxative lettuce, and such windy meat[5])
Tempt such a passage, when each privy's seat
Is filled with buttock, and the walls do sweat
Urine and plasters;[6] when the noise doth beat
Upon your ears of discords so unsweet,
And outcries of the damnèd in the Fleet?[7]
Cannot the plague-bill[8] keep you back; nor bells
Of loud Sepulchre's[9] with their hourly knells,
But you will visit grisly Pluto's hall?
Behold where Cerberus, reared on the wall
Of Holborn (three sergeants'[1] heads), looks o'er,
And stays but till you come unto the door!
Tempt not his fury, Pluto is away;
And Madame Caesar, great Proserpina,[2]
Is now from home. You lose your labors quite,
Were you Jove's sons, or had Alcides' might."
They cried out, "Puss!" He told them he was Banks,
That had so often showed 'em merry pranks.
They laughed at his laugh-worthy fate, and passed
The triple head without a sop.[3] At last,
Calling for Rhadamanthus,[4] that dwelt by,
A soap-boiler; and Aeacus him nigh
Who kept an alehouse; with my little Minos,
An ancient purblind fletcher,[5] with a high nose;
They took 'em all to witness of their action;
And so went bravely back, without protraction.[6]
  In memory of which most liquid deed,
The city since hath raised a pyramid.
And I could wish for their eternized sakes,
My Muse had plowed with his that sung A-jax.[7]

4. Peas.
5. Food.
6. I.e., excrement.
7. I.e., the Fleet Prison.
8. I.e., the weekly list of those dead of the plague.
9. Saint Sepulchre's Church stood just to the west of the city proper.
1. Lawyers'; but here alluding to the three judges named in lines 187–190.
2. I.e., the queen of Hades.
3. I.e., a bribe of food. Cerberus was propitiated in this way; cf. *Aeneid*, VI.415–425.
4. Rhadamanthus, Aeacus, and Minos were the three judges of Hades; cf. Plato, *Apology*, 41a.
5. I.e., blind or partly blind makers of arrows.
6. Delay.
7. I.e., with that of Sir John Harington (c. 1561–1612), who wrote the Rabelaisian *The Metamorphosis of Ajax* (with a pun on "a jakes," i.e., a privy).

The Forest[8]

I: Why I Write Not of Love

Some act of Love's bound to rehearse,[9]
I thought to bind him in my verse;
Which when he felt, "Away," quoth he,
"Can poets hope to fetter me?
It is enough they once did get
Mars and my mother in their net;[1]
I wear not these my wings in vain."
With which he fled me; and again
Into my rhymes could ne'er be got
By any art. Then wonder not
That since, my numbers[2] are so cold,
When Love is fled, and I grow old.

II: To Penshurst[3]

Thou are not, Penshurst, built to envious show
  Of touch,[4] or marble; nor canst boast a row
Of polished pillars, or a roof of gold;
  Thou hast no lantern,[5] whereof tales are told,
Or stair, or courts, but stand'st an ancient pile,
  And, these grudged at, art reverenced the while.[6]
Thou joy'st in better marks, of soil, of air,
  Of wood, of water: therein thou art fair.
Thou hast thy walks for health, as well as sport;

8. It seems likely that Jonson regarded the fifteen poems that comprise *The Forest* with special affection; he appears to have thought them superior to those "lesser poems, of later growth," that make up *Underwood* (as he remarks in his prefatory note to that collection), and also to have regarded them as in some ways more serious and exploratory even than the *Epigrams*, from which *The Forest* diverges in range, tone, and variety of verse form. The clipped brevity of the epigrammatic mode yields here, though the verse is as delicately chiseled as before, to the ampler design of the verse epistle and the ode, and to lyric poetry in various kinds; the dominantly critical stance of the *Epigrams* is less in evidence than are forthright expressions of allegiance to the highest standards of moral conduct, often exemplified by aristocratic figures whom Jonson especially admired. Then, too, while the couplet is not abandoned, other verse forms and structural patterns come into view; and these anticipate the haunting measures of such poems as "The Hourglass" or "The Dream" as well as the complexities of the "Epithalamion" for the Weston-Stuart nuptials. It may be, finally, that the arrangement of these fifteen poems is deliberate; certainly it is of interest that the first poem bids a sad farewell to Cupid while the last affirms the poet's love of God.
9. I.e., bound to relate some act performed by Cupid, the god of love.
1. Discovering his consort Venus in the embraces of her lover Mars, Vulcan threw a net over the guilty pair and invited the other gods to witness the scene; cf. Ovid, *Metamorphoses*, IV.171–189.
2. Verses.
3. Penshurst Place in Kent was, and remains, the home of the Sidney family. Although this poem has traditionally been regarded as the first "country house" poem in English, Lanyer's "The Description of Cookham," p. 14, was published, and perhaps written, earlier. "To Penshurst" was much admired and imitated by Jonson's contemporaries: cf. Carew's "To Saxham," p. 300, and "To My Friend G. N., from Wrest," p. 315; Waller's "At Penshurst," p. 363; and Marvell's "Upon Appleton House," p. 559.
4. Touchstone; here, fine black marble or basalt.
5. I.e., a glassed-in cupola or small room on the top of a house. To what other storied "lantern" the line may refer is unknown.
6. I.e., while other buildings are envied, you are admired.

Thy Mount,[7] to which the dryads[8] do resort,
Where Pan and Bacchus their high feasts have made
Beneath the broad beech and the chestnut shade;
That taller tree, which of a nut was set,
At his[9] great birth, where all the Muses met.
There in the writhèd bark are cut the names
Of many a sylvan, taken with his flames.[1]
And thence the ruddy satyrs oft provoke
The lighter fauns to reach thy Lady's oak.[2]
Thy copse, too, named of Gamage,[3] thou hast there,
That never fails to serve thee seasoned deer
When thou wouldst feast, or exercise thy friends.
The lower land, that to the river bends,
Thy sheep, thy bullocks, kine, and calves do feed;
The middle grounds thy mares and horses breed.
Each bank doth yield thee coneys;[4] and the tops
Fertile of wood, Ashore and Sidney's copse,[5]
To crown thy open table, doth provide
The purpled pheasant with the speckled side;
The painted partridge lies in every field,
And, for thy mess, is willing to be killed.
And if the high-swol'n Medway[6] fail thy dish,
Thou hast thy ponds, that pay thee tribute fish,
Fat, agèd carps, that run into thy net,
And pikes, now weary their own kind to eat,
As loath the second draught or cast to stay,[7]
Officiously[8] at first themselves betray;
Bright eels that emulate them, and leap on land
Before the fisher, or into his hand.
Then hath thy orchard fruit, thy garden flowers,
Fresh as the air, and new as are the hours.
The early cherry, with the later plum,
Fig, grape, and quince, each in his time doth come;
The blushing apricot and woolly peach
Hang on thy walls[9] that every child may reach.
And though thy walls be of the country stone,
They're reared with no man's ruin, no man's groan;
There's none that dwell about them wish them down;

7. Some high ground on the estate.
8. Wood nymphs.
9. I.e., Sir Philip Sidney's (on 30 November 1554, when an oak was planted to commemorate the occasion).
1. I.e., of many woodsmen, or country folk, stirred by Sidney's love poetry.
2. According to tradition, Lady Leicester's labor pains began under an oak on the estate, afterward called "My Lady's Oak."
3. Sir Robert Sidney (1563–1626), brother of the poet and owner of Penshurst when Jonson wrote this poem, had married Barbara Gamage in 1584. A grove near the entrance of the park bore her name.
4. Rabbits.
5. These two small groves still survive.
6. The river Medway borders the estate.
7. I.e., as if they were reluctant to wait for the second cast and drawing-in of the net.
8. Dutifully.
9. I.e., on the espaliered walls.

But all come in, the farmer, and the clown,[1]
And no one empty-handed to salute
Thy lord and lady, though they have no suit.[2]
Some bring a capon, some a rural cake,
Some nuts, some apples; some that think they make
The better cheeses bring 'em, or else send
By their ripe daughters whom they would commend
This way to husbands, and whose baskets bear
An emblem of themselves, in plum or pear.
But what can this (more than express their love)
Add to they free provisions, far above
The need of such whose liberal board doth flow
With all that hospitality doth know!
Where comes no guest but is allowed to eat
Without his fear, and of thy lord's own meat;
Where the same beer and bread and self-same wine
That is his lordship's shall be also mine.
And I not fain to sit, as some, this day,
At great men's tables, and yet dine away.[3]
Here no man tells[4] my cups; nor, standing by,
A waiter doth my gluttony envy,
But gives me what I call and lets me eat,
He knows, below, he shall find plenty of meat.
Thy tables hoard not up for the next day,
Nor when I take my lodging need I pray
For fire, or lights, or livery;[5] all is there
As if thou, then, wert mine, or I reigned here;
There's nothing I can wish, for which I stay.
That found King James, when hunting late this way
With his brave son, the Prince,[6] they saw thy fires
Shine bright on every hearth as the desires
Of thy Penates[7] had been set on flame
To entertain them; or the country came,
With all their zeal, to warm their welcome here.
What (great, I will not say, but) sudden cheer
Didst thou then make them! and what praise was heaped
On thy good lady then! who therein reaped
The just reward of her high huswifery;
To have her linen, plate, and all things nigh,
When she was far; and not a room but dressed,
As if it had expected such a guest!
These, Penshurst, are thy praise, and yet not all.
Thy lady's noble, fruitful, chaste withal.

1. I.e., the rustic.
2. Request or special petition.
3. I.e., to be given less satisfying or choice fare than that reserved for the host (and so be forced to go elsewhere for a full meal). Drummond reports that Jonson complained of such treatment by the Earl of Salisbury; cf. *H & S*, I, p. 141.
4. Counts.
5. Food, provisions.
6. I.e., Prince Henry, who died in November 1612.
7. The Roman household gods.

His children thy great lord may call his own,
  A fortune in this age but rarely known.
They are and have been taught religion; thence
  Their gentler spirits have sucked innocence.
Each morn and even they are taught to pray
  With the whole household, and may, every day,
Read, in their virtuous parents' noble parts,
  The mysteries[8] of manners, arms and arts.
Now, Penshurst, they that will proportion[9] thee
  With other edifices, when they see
Those proud, ambitious heaps, and nothing else,
  May say, their lords have built, but thy lord dwells.

III: To Sir Robert Wroth[1]

How blest are thou, canst love the country, Wroth,
  Whether by choice, or fate, or both;
And, though so near the city and the court,
  Art ta'en with neither's vice nor sport;
That, at great times, are no ambitious guest
  Of sheriff's dinner or mayor's feast,
Nor com'st to view the better cloth of state,
  The richer hangings, or crown-plate,
Nor throng'st, when masquing is, to have a sight
  Of the short bravery[2] of the night,
To view the jewels, stuffs, the pains, the wit
  There wasted, some not paid for yet;
But canst at home in thy securer[3] rest
  Live, with un-bought provision blessed,
Free from proud porches, or their gilded roofs,
  'Mongst lowing herds and solid hoofs,
Alongst the curlèd woods and painted meads
  Through which a serpent river leads
To some cool, courteous shade, which he calls his,
  And makes sleep softer than it is!
Or, if thou list the night in watch to break,
  Abed canst hear the loud stag speak
In spring, oft rousèd for thy master's[4] sport,

8. Crafts, arts; but there is also the sense of "high mysteries," implying a set of cultural attainments into which one must be initiated.
9. Compare.
1. Sir Robert Wroth (1576–1614) married Lady Mary Sidney, the daughter of Sir Robert Sidney, in 1604; cf. Lady Mary Wroth. Wroth's country estate at Durrants, northeast of London, is the setting for this tribute. While the poem has something in common with "To Penshurst," its informing idea is rather that of "the happy life," which is good "because it possesses, or may possess, enjoyments and a fullness of comfort," and which reflects the Stoic ideal of Cicero's *De Senectute*: "How blessed it is for the soul, after having, as it were, finished its campaigns of lust and ambition, of strife and enmity and of all the passions, to return within itself, and, as the saying is, 'to live apart!'" (XIV.49). The theme often recurs in the work of Jonson's followers: cf. Herrick's "The Country Life," p. 210; Fane's "To Retiredness," p. 334; Randolph's "An Ode to . . . Stafford," p. 342; and Philips's "A Country Life," p. 664.
2. I.e., ephemeral and showy appearance.
3. More free from care.
4. I.e., the king's.

Who, for it, makes thy house his court;
Or with thy friends, the heart of all the year,[5]
Divid'st upon the lesser deer;
In autumn at the partridge makes a flight,
And giv'st thy gladder guests the sight;
And in the winter hunt'st the flying hare
More for thy exercise than fare,
While all that follow their glad ears apply
To the full greatness of the cry;[6]
Or hawking at the river, or the bush,
Or shooting at the greedy thrush,
Thou dost with some delight the day out-wear,
Although the coldest of the year!
The whilst the several seasons thou hast seen
Of flow'ry fields, of copses green,
The mowèd meadows with the fleecèd sheep,
And feasts that either shearers keep,
The ripened ears, yet humble in their height,
And furrows laden with their weight,
The apple-harvest, that doth longer last,
The hogs returned home fat from mast,[7]
The trees cut out in log; and those boughs made
A fire now, that lent a shade!
Thus Pan and Sylvan having had their rites,
Comus[8] puts in for new delights,
And fills thy open hall with mirth and cheer
As if in Saturn's reign[9] it were;
Apollo's harp and Hermes' lyre resound,
Nor are the Muses strangers found;
The rout of rural folk come thronging in
(Their rudeness[1] then is thought no sin),
Thy noblest spouse affords them welcome grace,
And the great heroes of her race
Sit mixed with loss of state or reverence:
Freedom doth with degree dispense.
The jolly wassail walks the often round,[2]
And in their cups their cares are drowned;
They think not, then, which side the cause shall leese,[3]
Nor how to get the lawyer fees.
Such, and no other, was that age of old
Which boasts t'have had the head of gold;
And such, since thou canst make thine own content,
Strive, Wroth, to live long innocent.

5. I.e., in summer.
6. I.e., the baying of hounds.
7. Nuts, mashed to serve as food for hogs.
8. In later antiquity, Comus was the god of festive mirth and jollification.
9. I.e., in the Golden Age; cf. lines 63–64.
1. Rustic, unsophisticated manner.
2. I.e., the drinking cups are regularly refilled.
3. Lose; i.e., they forget everyday cares.

Let others watch in guilty arms, and stand
  The fury of a rash command,
Go enter breaches, meet the cannon's rage,
  That they may sleep with scars in age,
And show their feathers shot, and colors torn,
  And brag that they were therefore born.
Let this man sweat and wrangle at the bar
  For every price, in every jar,
And change possessions oftener with his breath
  Than either money, war, or death;
Let him than hardest sires more disinherit,[4]
  And each where boast it as his merit
To blow up orphans, widows, and their states,[5]
  And think his power doth equal Fate's.
Let that go heap a mass of wretched wealth,
  Purchased by rapine, worse than stealth,
And brooding o'er it sit with broadest[6] eyes,
  Not doing good, scarce when he dies.
Let thousands more go flatter vice, and win
  By being organs[7] to great sin;
Get place, and honor, and be glad to keep
  The secrets that shall break their sleep,
And, so they ride in purple, eat in plate,[8]
  Though poison, think it a great fate.
But thou, my Wroth, if I can truth apply,
  Shalt neither that nor this envy;
Thy peace is made; and when man's state is well,
  'Tis better if he there can dwell.
God wisheth none should wreck on a strange shelf;[9]
  To him, man's dearer than t'himself.
And howsoever we may think things sweet,
  He always gives what he knows meet,
Which who can use is happy: such be thou.
  Thy morning's and thy evening's vow
Be thanks to him, and earnest prayer to find
  A body sound, with sounder mind;
To do thy country service, thyself right,
  That neither want do thee affright
Nor death; but when thy latest sand is spent,
  Thou may'st think life a thing but lent.[1]

4. I.e., let him disinherit more children than the most severe fathers do.
5. I.e., deprive orphans and widows of their property and possessions.
6. Wide open, staring.
7. Instruments.
8. I.e., dine off gold or silver platters.
9. Shoal.
1. The view that man's life is lent to him by God, and that God takes account of the fashion in which man uses it, often recurs in Jonson's poetry; cf. Epigrams XXII and XLV, p. 85.

IV: To the World: A Farewell for a Gentlewoman,[2] Virtuous and Noble

False world, good-night; since thou hast brought
That hour upon my morn of age,
Henceforth I quit thee from my thought,
My part is ended on thy stage.
Do not once hope that thou canst tempt
A spirit so resolved to tread
Upon thy throat, and live exempt
From all the nets that thou canst spread.
I know thy forms are studied arts,
Thy subtle ways be narrow straits,
Thy courtesy but sudden starts,
And what thou call'st thy gifts are baits.
I know, too, though thou strut and paint,
Yet art thou both shrunk up and old,
That only fools make thee a saint,
And all thy good is to be sold.
I know thou whole[3] art but a shop
Of toys and trifles, traps and snares,
To take the weak, or make them stop;
Yet art thou falser than thy wares.
And, knowing this, should I yet stay,
Like such as blow away their lives,
And never will redeem a day,
Enamored of their golden gyves?[4]
Or, having 'scaped, shall I return
And thrust my neck into the noose
From whence, so lately, I did burn
With all my powers myself to loose?
What bird or beast is known so dull,
That fled his cage or broke his chain,
And, tasting air and freedom, wull
Render[5] his head in there again?
If these, who have but sense,[6] can shun
The engines that have them annoyed,[7]
Little for me had reason done
If I could not thy gins[8] avoid.
Yes, threaten, do. Alas, I fear
As little as I hope from thee;
I know thou canst nor show nor bear
More hatred than thou hast to me.

2. The unidentified gentlewoman is the speaker of the poem, which advocates an austerely Stoic self-sufficiency, derived primarily from Horace. Lines 25–32 may be compared with Horace, *Satires*, II.vii.68–71.
3. Wholly.
4. Fetters.
5. I.e., will put back. "Wull" is a Scottish variant of "will" (*OED*).
6. I.e., who lack reasoning power.
7. I.e., the devices that have troubled them.
8. Snares.

My tender, first, and simple years
  Thou didst abuse, and then betray;
Since, stirr'dst up jealousies and fears,
  When all the causes were away.
Then in a soil[9] hast planted me
  Where breathe the basest of thy fools,
Where envious arts professèd be,
  And pride and ignorance the schools
Where nothing is examined, weighed,
  But as 'tis rumored, so believed;
Where every freedom is betrayed,
  And every goodness taxed or grieved.
But what we're born for, we must bear;
  Our frail condition it is such
That, what to all may happen here,
  If't chance to me, I must not grutch.[1]
Else, I my state should much mistake,
  To harbor a divided thought
From all my kind, that for my sake
  There should a miracle be wrought.
No, I do know that I was born
  To age, misfortune, sickness, grief;
But I will bear these with that scorn
  As shall not need thy false relief.
Nor for my peace will I go far,
  As wand'rers do, that still do roam,
But make my strengths, such as they are,
  Here in my bosom, and at home.

V: Song: To Celia[2]

Come, my Celia, let us prove,[3]
While we may, the sports of love;
Time will not be ours forever;
He at length our good will sever.
Spend not then his gifts in vain.
Suns that set may rise again;
But if once we lose this light,
'Tis with us perpetual night.
Why should we defer our joys?
Fame[4] and rumor are but toys.
Cannot we delude the eyes
Of a few poor household spies?

9. I.e., at court.
1. Complain.
2. These lines appear in Jonson's *Volpone*, III.vii.166–183; Volpone employs the song as part of his campaign to seduce the virtuous Celia; wife to Corvino. The lines are based on Catullus, *Odes*, iv.3–6. The poem was set to music by Alphonso Ferrabosco (d. 1628) and published in that composer's *Ayres* (1609); Jonson addressed two epigrams to Ferrabosco (CXXX and CXXXI).
3. Experience.
4. Reputation.

Or his[5] easier ears beguile,
So removèd by our wile?
'Tis no sin love's fruit to steal;
But the sweet theft to reveal,
To be taken, to be seen,
These have crimes accounted been.

VI: To the Same[6]

Kiss me, sweet; the wary lover
Can your favors keep, and cover,
When the common courting jay
All your bounties will betray.
Kiss again; no creature comes.
Kiss, and score up wealthy sums
On my lips, thus hardly sundered
While you breathe. First give a hundred,
Then a thousand, then another
Hundred, then unto the t'other
Add a thousand, and so more;
Till you equal with the store
All the grass that Romney[7] yields,
Or the sands in Chelsea fields,
Or the drops in silver Thames,
Or the stars that gild his streams
In the silent summer nights
When youths ply their stol'n delights;
That the curious may not know
How to tell 'em[8] as they flow,
And the envious, when they find
What their number is, be pined.[9]

VII: Song: That Women Are but Men's Shadows[1]

Follow a shadow, it still flies you;
  Seem to fly it, it will pursue;
So court a mistress, she denies you;
  Let her alone, she will court you.

5. I.e., Corvino's.
6. The poem is based on Catullus, *Odes*, v.7–13, and vii. Lines 19–22 appear in *Volpone*, III.vii.236–239.
7. Romney Marsh is in Kent; Chelsea, in Jonson's time "but a group of isolated houses amidst six hundred acres of arable fields and pasture, orchards, gardens, and riverside meadows" (Hibbert, *London*, p. 93), derives its name from "chesil" (gravel).
8. I.e., count them.
9. I.e., be pained or dismayed.
1. The lines are based on a Latin poem by Barthelemi Aneau; cf. the note by O. Wallace, *Notes and Queries* (*N & Q*), III/8 (1865), 187. Drummond describes the occasion of the poem's composition: "Pembroke and his Lady discoursing, the Earl said [that] women were men's shadows, and she maintained them; both appealing to Jonson, he affirmed it true, for which my Lady gave a penance to prove it in verse; hence his epigram" (*H & S*, I, p. 142).

Say, are not women truly, then,
  Styled but the shadows of us men?
At morn, and even, shades are longest;
  At noon, they are or short or none;
So men at weakest, they are strongest,
  But grant us perfect, they're not known.
Say, are not women truly, then,
  Styled but the shadows of us men?

VIII: To Sickness

Why, Disease, dost thou molest
Ladies, and of them the best?
Do not men enough of rites
To thy altars, by their nights
Spent in surfeits, and their days,
And nights too, in worser ways?
  Take heed, Sickness, what you do;
  I shall fear you'll surfeit too.
Live not we, as all thy stalls,
Spitals,[2] pest-house, hospitals
Scarce will take our present store?
  And this age will build no more;
Pray thee, feed contented, then,
Sickness, only on us men;
  Or if needs thy lust will taste
  Womankind, devour the waste
  Livers[3] round about the town.
But forgive me; with thy crown[4]
They maintain the truest trade,
And have more diseases made.
  What should yet thy palate please?
  Daintiness, and softer ease,
  Sleekèd limbs, and finest blood?
  If thy leanness love such food,
  There are those that for thy sake
  Do enough, and who would take
  Any pains, yea, think it price,[5]
  To become thy sacrifice:
  That distill their husbands' land
  In decoctions,[6] and are manned

2. Hospitals for poor folk.
3. I.e., prostitutes.
4. I.e., with your authority, or following your leadership. Also a play on "crown" as a piece of money and as slang for syphilis, which could cause baldness: cf. "French Crown" in Shakespeare, *Measure for Measure*, I.ii.50.
5. Choice, highly desirable.
6. I.e., by their luxurious habits, ruin their husbands financially. Lines 29–33 employ alchemical expressions: *decoction* means "reduction by boiling down"; an *empiric* is an experimenter (here in a sexual sense); *spirit of amber* is an acid formed by dry distillation of amber; *oil of talk* (i.e., talc) a cosmetic (here, figuratively, courtly compliment and gossip).

With ten emp'ricks, in their chamber,
Lying for the spirit of amber;
That for th'oil of talk dare spend
More than citizens dare lend
Them, and all their officers;
That to make all pleasure theirs,
Will by coach and water go,
Every stew in town to know;
Dare entail[7] their loves on any,
Bald, or blind, or ne'er so many,
And for thee, at common game,
Play away health, wealth, and fame.
These, Disease, will thee deserve;
And will, long ere thou should'st starve[8]
On their beds, most prostitute,
Move it as their humblest suit
In they justice to molest
None but them, and leave the rest.

IX: Song: To Celia[9]

Drink to me only with thine eyes,
And I will pledge with mine;
Or leave a kiss but in the cup,
And I'll not look for wine.
The thirst that from the soul doth rise
Doth ask a drink divine:
But might I of Jove's nectar sup,
I would not change for thine.
I sent thee, late, a rosy wreath,
Not so much honoring thee,
As giving it a hope that there
It could not withered be.
But thou thereon did'st only breathe,
And sent'st it back to me;
Since when it grows, and smells, I swear,
Not of itself, but thee.

7. In law, to entail is to settle lands inalienably on a person and his descendents; the term is employed here in a sexual sense.
8. Die.
9. Jonson's poem is based on five separate passages in the *Epistles* of the Greek rhetorician Philostratus (c. A.D. 170–c. 245). For a variant manuscript version, cf. Textual Notes.

X[1]

And must I sing? What subject shall I choose?
Or whose great name in poets' heaven use
For the more countenance to[2] my active Muse?

Hercules? Alas, his bones are yet sore
With his old earthly labors.[3] T'exact more
Of his dull godhead were sin. I'll implore

Phoebus. No: tend thy cart[4] still. Envious day
Shall not give out[5] that I have made thee stay,
And foundered thy hot team, to tune my lay.

Nor will I beg of thee, lord of the vine,[6]
To raise my spirits with thy conjuring wine,
In the green circle of thy ivy twine.

Pallas, nor thee I call on, mankind[7] maid,
That at thy birth mad'st the poor smith afraid,
Who, with his axe, thy father's midwife played.[8]

Go, cramp dull Mars, light Venus, when he snorts,[9]
Or with thy tribade trine[1] invent new sports,
Thou nor thy looseness with my making sorts.[2]

Let the old boy, your son,[3] ply his old task,
Turn the stale prologue to some painted mask,
His absence in my verse is all I ask.

Hermes, the cheater,[4] shall not mix with us,
Though he would steal his sisters' Pegasus[5]
And riffle him; or pawn his petasus.[6]

1. This poem (together with "Epode" and two other poems by Jonson) first appeared in 1601, in an appendix to Robert Chester's poem "Love's Martyr"; the appendix also includes Shakespeare's "The Phoenix and the Turtle" and other verses on that theme by Marston and Chapman, all of which allegorically figure the phoenix and turtledove as idealized types of female and male virtue. An earlier version of this poem, preserved in manuscript, appears in *H & S*, VIII, p. 108.
2. I.e., for the higher repute of.
3. The twelve labors of Hercules were performed for Eurystheus, at the behest of Juno; cf. Apollodorus, *The Library*, 11.iv–v; also Ovid, *Metamorphoses*, IX.182–198.
4. Chariot (of the sun, pulled by Phoebus Apollo's team of horses; cf. Ovid, *Metamorphoses*, II.47–48).
5. I.e., report.
6. I.e., Bacchus, ordinarily represented as wearing an ivy garland.
7. Masculine.
8. Pallas Athene, goddess of wisdom, was born from the head of Zeus when Hephaestus (Vulcan) struck it with an axe; cf. Apollodorus, *The Library*, I.iii.
9. I.e., Go, wanton Venus, pinch dull Mars (to awaken him) when he snores. Cf. "Why I Write Not of Love," line 6n, p. 97.
1. I.e, the three Graces, who attended Venus after Vulcan had revealed her infidelity; cf. *Odyssey*, VIII.364–365. A *tribade* is "a woman who practices unnatural vice with other women" (*OED*). Jonson's is the first recorded use of the term in English.
2. I.e., is suitable for my poetry.
3. Cupid was the eldest of the gods according to Plato (*Symposium*, 178b–c).
4. Hermes (Mercury) was the god of merchants and thieves.
5. The winged horse Pegasus created the Hippocrene spring for the Muses by striking the ground with his hoof; cf. Ovid, *Metamorphoses*, V.257–258.
6. I.e., and gamble him away; or pawn his own winged hat.

Nor all the ladies of the Thespian lake[7]
Though they were crushed into one form could make
A beauty of that merit that should take

My Muse up by commission;[8] no, I bring
My own true fire. Now my thought takes wing,
And now an *Epode*[9] to deep[1] ears I sing.

XI: Epode

Not to know vice at all, and keep true state,
    Is virtue, and not fate;[2]
Next to that virtue is to know vice well,
    And her black spite expel.
Which to effect, since no breast is so sure
    Or safe but she'll procure[3]
Some way of entrance, we must plant a guard
    Of thoughts to watch and ward
At th'eye and ear, the ports[4] unto the mind,
    That no strange or unkind[5]
Object arrive there, but the heart, our spy,
    Give knowledge instantly
To wakeful reason, our affections' king;
    Who, in th'examining,
Will quickly taste[6] the treason, and commit
    Close, the close cause of it.[7]
'Tis the securest policy we have
    To make our sense our slave.
But this true course is not embraced by many;
    By many? scarce by any.
For either our affections do rebel,
    Or else the sentinel
That should ring 'larum to the heart doth sleep,
    Or some great[8] thought doth keep
Back the intelligence, and falsely swears
    They're base and idle fears
Whereof the loyal conscience so complains.
    Thus, by these subtle trains,[9]

7. I.e., the Muses; cf. Epigram CI, line 33n, p. 90.
8. I.e., by command.
9. The Greek poet Archilochus (c. 714–c. 676 B.C.) invented the epode, a lyric poem in lines alternately long and short, on a serious subject.
1. Wise, profound.
2. I.e., the virtue that is altogether untouched by vice achieves that condition by exercise of the will (not by the force of an external influence).
3. I.e., vice will obtain (as a pimp practices his trade).
4. Gates. Lines 9–30 are based on Renaissance "faculty psychology": reason ought properly to restrain and control the senses and the emotions, but in fact most men and women, for various reasons, are ruled by their emotions or passions.
5. Unnatural.
6. Apprehend, identify.
7. I.e., and bring its immediate cause under strict control.
8. Dominant.
9. Stratagems, deceitful tricks.

Do several passions invade the mind,
And strike our reason blind.
Of which usurping rank some have thought love
The first, as prone to move
Most frequent tumults, horrors, and unrests
In our enflamèd breasts;
But this doth from the cloud of error grow,
Which thus we overblow.[1]
The thing they here call love is blind desire,[2]
Armed with bow, shafts, and fire;
Inconstant, like the sea of whence 'tis born,
Rough, swelling, like a storm;
With whom who sails, rides on a surge of fear,
And boils, as if he were
In a continual tempest. Now, true love
No such effects doth prove;[3]
That is an essence far more gentle, fine,
Pure, perfect, nay divine;
It is a golden chain let down from heaven,[4]
Whose links are bright and even;
That falls like sleep on lovers, and combines
The soft and sweetest minds
In equal knots; this bears no brands, nor darts
To murder different hearts,
But, in a calm and godlike unity,
Preserves community.
O, who is he that, in this peace, enjoys
Th'elixir[5] of all joys?
A form more fresh than are the Eden bowers,
And lasting[6] as her flowers;
Richer than time, and as time's virtue[7] rare.
Sober as saddest[8] care,
A fixèd thought, an eye untaught to glance;
Who, blessed with such high chance,

1. Overcome.
2. Lines 37–48 are based on a passage from *In Praise of Demosthenes*, a work of the fourth century A.D. attributed to an imitator of the Greek satirist Lucian (died c. A.D. 185): "You could wax philosophical in your discourse about the two impulses of love that come upon men, the one that of a love like the sea, frenzied, savage, and raging like stormy waves in the soul, a veritable sea of earthy Aphrodite surging with the fevered passions of youth, the other the pull of a heavenly cord of gold that does not bring with fiery shafts affecting wounds hard to cure, but impels man to the pure and unsullied Form of absolute beauty . . ." (*Lucian*, ed. and trans. M. D. MacLeod, 8 vols. [Cambridge, Mass., 1921–1967], VIII, p. 253).
3. I.e., produce.
4. Homer's is the earliest reference to the "golden rope" of Zeus, suspended from heaven, to which gods, men, and the entire universe are attached; cf. *Iliad*, VIII.18–27. The figure was variously interpreted by later writers; in a note to line 320 of his masque *Hymenaei*, Jonson indicates his sympathy with the view of the Roman grammarian Macrobius (fl. c. A.D. 400), who emphasizes the divine origin of *mens* (mind), which "forms and suffuses all below with life . . . from the Supreme God even to the bottom-most dregs of the universe there is one tie, binding at every link and never broken. This is the golden chain of Homer" (*Commentary on the Dream of Scipio*, ed. and trans. W. H. Stahl [New York, 1952], p. 145).
5. Quintessence.
6. I.e., eternal.
7. I.e., Truth, the daughter of time. Cf. Aulus Gellius, *Noctes Atticae*, XII.xi.
8. Most firmly fixed.

Would, at suggestion of a steep[9] desire,
Cast himself from the spire
Of all his happiness?[1] But soft: I hear
Some vicious fool draw near,
That cries, we dream, and swears there's no such thing
As this chaste love we sing.
Peace, Luxury,[2] thou art like one of those
Who, being at sea, suppose,
Because they move, the continent doth so;
No, Vice, we let thee know,
Though thy wild thoughts with sparrow's[3] wings do fly,
Turtles can chastely die;[4]
And yet (in this t'express ourselves more clear)
We do not number here
Such spirits as are only continent
Because lust's means are spent,
Or those who doubt the common mouth of fame,[5]
And for their place and name
Cannot so safely sin. Their chastity
Is mere necessity.
Nor mean we those whom vows and conscience
Have filled with abstinence;
Though we acknowledge, who can so abstain
Makes a most blessèd gain.
He that for love of goodness hateth ill
Is more crown-worthy still
Then he which for sin's penalty forbears;
His heart sins, though he fears.
But we propose a person like our dove,[6]
Graced with a phoenix[7] love;
A beauty of that clear and sparkling light
Would make a day of night,
And turn the blackest sorrows to bright joys;
Whose odorous breath destroys
All taste of bitterness, and makes the air
As sweet as she is fair;
A body so harmoniously composed,
As if nature disclosed
All her best symmetry in that one feature!
O, so divine a creature
Who could be false to; chiefly, when he knows

9. Headlong.
1. Jonson alludes to Satan's temptation of Christ, in Luke 4:9: "And he brought him to Jerusalem, and set him on a pinnacle of the temple, and said unto him, If thou be the Son of God, cast thyself down from hence." Cf. also Matthew 4:5–6.
2. Lust.
3. The sparrow was a symbol of lechery.
4. I.e., turtledoves (symbolic of conjugal affection and constancy) can achieve sexual consummation and yet remain chaste.
5. I.e., who fear scandal.
6. I.e., the turtledove, symbol of man's faith.
7. The phoenix, traditionally an emblem of immortality, here represents primarily a Platonic ideal of womanly perfection.

How only she bestows
The wealthy treasure of her love on him,
Making his fortunes swim
In the full flood of her admired perfection?
What savage, brute affection
Would not be fearful to offend a dame
Of this excelling frame?
Much more a noble and right generous mind,
To virtuous moods inclined,
That knows the weight of guilt; he will refrain
From thoughts of such a strain,
And to his sense object this sentence ever:[8]
Man may securely[9] sin but safely never.

XII: Epistle to Elizabeth, Countess of Rutland[1]

Madame:
Whilst that for which all virtue now is sold,
And almost every vice, almighty gold,
That which, to boot[2] with hell, is thought worth heaven,
And for it, life, conscience, yea, souls are given,
Toils, by grave custom, up and down the court
To every squire or groom that will report
Well or ill only, all the following year,
Just to the weight their this day's presents bear;[3]
While it makes ushers[4] serviceable men,
And some one apteth[5] to be trusted, then,
Though never after; while it gains the voice
Of some grand peer, whose air[6] doth make rejoice
The fool that gave it, who will want and weep
When his proud patron's favors are asleep;
While thus it buys great grace and hunts poor frame,
Runs between man and man, 'tween dame and dame,
Solders cracked friendship, makes love last a day,
Or perhaps less; whilst gold bears all this sway,
I, that have none to send you, send you verse.
A present which (if elder writs rehearse
The truth of times) was once of more esteem
Than this our gilt nor golden[7] age can deem;
When gold was made no weapon to cut throats,

8. I.e., and always present to his senses this (controlling) maxim.
9. Carelessly, confidently.
1. Cf. Epigram LXXIX, p. 87. Elizabeth Sidney had married the fifth Earl of Rutland in 1599; this poem was a gift for New Year's Day, 1600. Jonson evidently considered the genre of the verse epistle well suited to his personality, his moral convictions, and what he conceived to be his social role. For a full discussion of the epistolary tradition, cf. W. Trimpli, *Ben Jonson's Poems: A Study of the Plain Style* (Stanford, Calif., 1962), pp. 60–75.
2. I.e., to be of avail.
3. I.e., precisely in proportion to the gifts bestowed today.
4. Servants, attendants.
5. Most fit.
6. Manner.
7. I.e., neither gilded nor golden. The text of 1616 has "our guilt, nor golden age."

Or put to flight Astraea;[8] when her ingots
Were yet unfound, and better placed in earth
Than, here, to give pride fame, and peasants birth.[9]
But let this dross carry what price it will
With noble ignorants, and let them still
Turn upon scorned verse their quarter-face;[1]
With you, I know, my off'ring will find grace.
For what a sin 'gainst your great father's[2] spirit
Were it to think that you should not inherit
His love unto the Muses, when his skill
Almost you have, or may have when you will;
Wherein wise nature you a dowry gave
Worth an estate treble to that you have.
Beauty, I know, is good, and blood is more;
Riches thought most. But, madame, think what store
The world hath seen, which all these had in trust,
And now lie lost in their forgotten dust.
It is the Muse alone can raise to heaven,
And, at her strong arms' end, hold up, and even,
The souls she loves. Those other glorious[3] notes
Inscribed in touch or marble, or the coats[4]
Painted or carved upon our great mens' tombs,
Or in their windows, do but prove the wombs
That bred them, graves; when they were born, they died,
That had no Muse to make their fame abide.
How many, equal with the Argive queen,[5]
Have beauty known, yet none so famous seen?
Achilles was not first that valiant was,
Or, in an army's head, that locked in brass[6]
Gave killing strokes. There were brave men before
Ajax or Idomen,[7] or all the store
That Homer brought to Troy; yet none so live,
Because they lacked the sacred pen could give
Like life unto them. Who heaved Hercules[8]
Unto the stars? or the Tyndarides?
Who placèd Jason's Argo in the sky,

8. Astraea, the goddess of justice, lived among men during the Golden Age; but when their wickedness increased, she returned to heaven and was stellified as the constellation Virgo; cf. Ovid, *Metamorphoses*, I.127–150.
9. I.e., to give high reputation and place to the proud and to those of low character.
1. I.e., all but turn away, contemptuously, from poetry.
2. I.e., Sir Philip Sidney's.
3. Pompous, boastful; cf. "To Penshurst," lines 1–2, p. 97.
4. Coats of arms.
5. I.e., Helen of Troy; "Argive" by metonymy for "Grecian."
6. I.e., in armor, leading an army.
7. Ajax, the son of Telamon, and Idomeneus of Crete commanded subdivisions of the Greek host; cf. *Iliad. passim.*
8. For Hercules, in this regard, cf. Ovid, *Metamorphoses*, IX.241–273. The Tyndarides are Castor and Pollux (sons of Leda, whose consort was Tyndareus), placed in the constellation Gemini; cf. Apollodorus, *Library*, III.xi.2. According to Hyginus, *Fables*, xiv, Minerva (Pallas Athene) placed the Argonauts' vessel in the heavens. Ariadne, deserted by Theseus on the isle of Naxos, became the consort of Dionysus, who placed her marriage crown among the stars; cf. Ovid, *Metamorphoses*. VIII.177–179. Berenice (c. 273–221 B.C.) married Ptolemy III of Egypt, who named a star "the lock of Berenice" in her honor; in *The Masque of Queens*. 546–560, Jonson gives Catullus (*Odes*, lxvi) as his source. For the story of Cassiopeia, culminating in her elevation to the heavens ("Cassiopeia's chair"), cf. Ovid, *Metamorphoses*, IV.663–803.

Or set bright Ariadne's crown so high?
Who made a lamp of Berenice's hair,
Or lifted Cassiopeia in her chair,
But only poets, rapt with rage divine?[9]
And such, or my hopes fail, shall make you shine.
You and that other star, that purest light
Of all Lucina's[1] train, Lucy the bright,[2]
Than which a nobler, heaven itself knows not,
Who, though she have a better verser[3] got
(Or poet, in the court account) than I,
And who doth me, though I not him, envy,
Yet, for the timely favors she hath done
To my less sanguine Muse, wherein she'hath won
My grateful soul, the subject of her powers,
I have already used some happy hours
To her remembrance; which, when time shall bring
To curious light, to notes[4] I then shall sing
Will prove old Orpheus' act[5] no tale to be,
For I shall move stocks, stones no less than he.
Then all that have but done my Muse least grace
Shall thronging come, and boast the happy place
They hold in my strange poems, which as yet
Had not their form touched by an English wit.[6]
There, like a rich and golden pyramid
Borne up by statues, shall I rear your head
Above your under-carvèd ornaments,
And show how, to the life, my soul presents
Your form impressed there; not with tickling rhymes
Or commonplaces filched, that take these times,
But high and noble matter, such as flies
From brains entranced and filled with ecstasies;
Moods which the godlike Sidney oft did prove,[7]
And your brave friend[8] and mine so well did love.
Who, wheresoe'er he be. . . .

The rest is lost.[9]

9. I.e., ravished by divine inspiration.
1. I.e., Queen Elizabeth's. "Lucina" derives from *lux*, "light, brightness."
2. I.e., Lucy Harington, Countess of Bedford.
3. Jonson may allude to Samuel Daniel, whom he thought "no poet," according to Drummond (*H & S*, I, p. 132); or to Michael Drayton, as R. W. Short suggests in "Ben Jonson in Drayton's Poems," *RES*, XV (1939), 149–158.
4. In *The Masque of Queens*, 666–669, Jonson refers to plans for a poem celebrating British ladies.
5. According to legend, stones and trees moved in response to the power of Orpheus' musical art; cf. Ovid, *Metamorphoses*, XI.1–2.
6. I.e., my poems, unfamiliar in mode, which exemplify an art not attained by other English poets.
7. Experience.
8. I.e., the Earl of Rutland.
9. Cf. Textual Notes for the concluding lines, dropped from the poem in the *Works* of 1616 since by that time it had become known that the Earl was impotent. Cf. *H & S*, I, pp. 139, 163.

XIII: Epistle to Katharine, Lady Aubigny[1]

'Tis grown almost a danger to speak true
Of any good mind, now: there are so few.
The bad by number are so fortified
As what they've lost t'expect, they dare deride.
So both the praised and praisers suffer. Yet
For others' ill, ought none their good forget.
I, therefore, who profess my self in love
With every virtue, wheresoe'er it move
And howsoever; as I am at feud
With sin and vice, though with a throne endued,
And, in this name, am given out[2] dangerous
By arts and practice of the vicious,
Such as suspect themselves, and think it fit
For their own capital crimes t'indict my wit;
I, that have suffered this, and, though forsook
Of fortune, have not altered yet my look
Or so my self abandoned, as because
Men are not just, or keep no holy laws
Of nature and society, I should faint,
Or leave to draw true lines 'cause others paint;
I, madame, am become your praiser. Where
If it may stand with your soft blush to hear
Your self but told unto yourself, and see
In my character[3] what your features be,
You will not from the paper slightly[4] pass;
No lady but at some time loves her glass,[5]
And this shall be no false one, but as much
Removed as you from need to have it such.
Look, then, and see your self. I will not say
"Your beauty," for you see that every day,
And so do many more; all which[6] can call
It perfect, proper, pure, and natural,
Not taken up o' th'doctors,[7] but as well
As I can say and see it doth excel.
That asks but to be censured by the eyes,
And in those outward forms all fools are wise.
Nor that your beauty wanted not a dower[8]

1. Jonson lived in the house of his patron, Esme Lord Aubigny (1574–1624), from 1602 to 1607; the poet acknowledged these favors in Epigram CXXVII, and dedicated his tragedy *Sejanus* to Lord Aubigny, who married Katharine Clifton in 1609. Three of Lady Aubigny's four sons, who fought on the royalist side in the civil wars, were killed in battle. Her daughter Frances was married to Jerome Weston, son of Richard Lord Weston, Lord High Treasurer (from 1628); Jonson celebrated the nuptials in his "Epithalamion," p. 144.
2. I.e., reputed to be.
3. I.e., in my detailed description of your qualities. The "character" was an ancient literary genre revived and polished in the seventeenth century by, for example, Sir Thomas Overbury and John Earle.
4. Indifferently, uncaringly.
5. Mirror.
6. Of whom.
7. I.e., not dependent on artificial or medical aids.
8. I.e., a natural gift.

Do I reflect. Some alderman has power,
Or coz'ning farmer of the customs[9] so,
T'advance his doubtful issue, and o'erflow
A prince's fortune; these are gifts of chance,
And raise not virtue; they may vice enhance.
My mirror is more subtle, clear, refined,
And takes and gives the beauties of the mind,
Though it reject not those of fortune: such
As blood, and match.[1] Wherein, how more than much
Are you engagèd to your happy fate
For such a lot![2] that mixed you with a state
Of so great title, birth, but virtue most,
Without which all the rest were sounds, or lost.
'Tis only that can time and chance defeat,
For he that once is good is ever great.
Wherewith then, madame, can you better pay
This blessing of your stars than by that way
Of virtue which you tread? What if alone,
Without companions? 'Tis safe to have none.
In single paths, dangers with ease are watched;
Contagion in the press[3] is soonest catched.
This makes that wisely you decline[4] your life
Far from the maze of custom, error, strife,
And keep an even and unaltered gait,
Not looking by,[5] or back (like those that wait
Times and occasions, to start forth, and seem);
Which though the turning world may disesteem,
Because that studies spectacles and shows,
And after varied as fresh objects goes,
Giddy with change, and therefore cannot see
Right, the right way; yet must your comfort be
Your conscience, and not wonder if none asks
For truth's complexion, where they all wear masks.
Let who will follow fashions and attires,
Maintain their ledgers forth, for foreign wires,[6]
Melt down their husbands' land to pour away
On the close-groom[7] and page, on New Year's Day,
And almost all days after, while they live
(They find it both so witty and safe to give).
Let 'em on powders, oils, and paintings[8] spend
Till that no usurer nor his bawds[9] dare lend

9. I.e., a deceitful exciseman who holds his post by virtue of having paid a fee for the right to collect customs duties.
1. Marriage.
2. Destiny, role in life.
3. Crowd.
4. Turn aside.
5. Aside.
6. I.e., keep agents in other places, to be informed of changing fashions. "Wires" refers to a metal framework supporting hair or a ruff.
7. Manservant (by implication, a lover).
8. Cosmetics.
9. Agents.

Them, or their officers;[1] and no man know
Whether it be a face they wear or no.
Let 'em waste body and state; and after all,
When their own parasites laugh at their fall,
May they have nothing left whereof they can
Boast but how oft they have gone wrong to man,[2]
And call it their brave[3] sin. For such there be
That do sin only for the infamy,
And never think how vice doth every hour
Eat on her clients, and some one devour.
You, madame, young have learned to shun these shelves[4]
Whereon the most of mankind wreck themselves,
And, keeping a just course, have early put
Into your harbor, and all passage shut
'Gainst storms, or pirates, that might charge[5] your peace;
For which you worthy are the glad increase
Of your blessed womb, made fruitful from above,
To pay your lord the pledges of chaste love,
And raise a noble stem to give the fame
To Clifton's blood, that is denied their name.[6]
Grow, grow, fair tree, and as thy branches shoot,
Hear what the Muses sing about thy root
By me, their priest (if they can ought divine):
Before the moons have filled their triple trine[7]
To crown the burden which you go withal,
It shall a ripe and timely issue fall
T'expect the honors of great Aubigny;
And greater rites, yet writ in mystery,
But which the Fates forbid me to reveal.
Only thus much, out of a ravished[8] zeal
Unto your name, and goodness of your life,
They speak; since you are truly that rare wife
Other great wives may blush at, when they see
What your tried manners are, what theirs should be;
How you love one, and him you should; how still
You are depending on his word and will;
Not fashioned for the court, or strangers' eyes,
But to please him, who is the dearer prize
Unto himself by being so dear to you.
This makes that your affections still be new,
And that your souls conspire,[9] as they were gone
Each into other, and had now made one.
Live that one, still; and as long years do pass,

1. I.e., those whom they send in their stead.
2. I.e., have indulged their carnal desires.
3. Fine.
4. Shoals.
5. Threaten.
6. Lady Aubigny's father, Sir Gervase Clifton, had no sons.
7. I.e., have completed nine months.
8. I.e., an enraptured.
9. Harmonize (literally, "breathe together").

Madame, be bold to use this truest glass,
Wherein your form you still the same shall find,
Because nor it can change, nor such a mind.

XIV: Ode to Sir William Sydney,[1] on His Birthday

Now that the hearth is crowned with smiling fire,
And some do drink, and some do dance,
Some ring,
Some sing,
And all do strive t'advance
The gladness higher;
Wherefore should I
Stand silent by,
Who not the least
Both love the cause, and authors of the feast?
Give me my cup, but from the Thespian well,[2]
That I may tell to Sydney, what
This day
Doth say,
And he may think on that
Which I do tell,
When all the noise
Of these forced joys
Are fled and gone,
And he with his best Genius[3] left alone.
This day says, then, the number of glad years
Are justly summed, that make you man;
Your vow
Must now
Strive all right ways it can
T'outstrip your peers;
Since he doth lack
Of going back
Little, whose will
Doth urge him to run wrong, or to stand still.
Nor can a little of the common store
Of nobles' virtue show in you;
Your blood,
So good
And great, must seek for new,

1. Sir William Sidney (1590–1612), the son of Sir Robert Sidney, was knighted in January 1611. As W. B. Hunter, Jr., observes, this "early attempt to introduce the complex form of the classical ode into English" anticipates Jonson's later and more ambitious efforts in the genre (*Complete Poetry of Ben Jonson* [New York, 1968], p. 75). For a discussion of Jonson's contributions in this kind, cf. Carol Maddison, *Apollo and the Nine: A History of the Ode* (Baltimore, Md., 1960), pp. 296–304.
2. Cf. Epigram CI, line 33n, p. 90.
3. I.e., protecting spirit. "According to the opinion of the Romans, every human being at his birth obtained a genius, whom he worshipped as [the holiest of gods], especially on his birthday, with libations of wine, incense, and garlands of flowers" (*A Smaller Classical Dictionary*, ed. E. H. Blakeney *et al.* [London, 1949], p. 225).

And study more;
Not weary, rest
On what's deceased.
For they that swell
With dust of ancestors in graves but dwell.
'Twill be exacted of your name, whose son,
Whose nephew, whose grand-child you are;[4]
And men
Will, then,
Say you have followed far,
When well begun;
Which must be now;
They teach you how.
And he that stays
To live until tomorrow hath lost two days.
So may you live in honor, as in name,
If with this truth you be inspired;
So may
This day
Be more and long desired;
And with the flame
Of love be bright,
As with the light
Of bonfires. Then
The birthday shines, when logs not burn, but men.

XV: To Heaven

Good and great God, can I not think of thee,
But it must, straight, my melancholy be?
Is it interpreted in me disease,
That, laden with my sins, I seek for ease?
O, be thou witness, that the reins[5] dost know,
And hearts of all, if I be sad for show,
And judge me after: if I dare pretend
To ought but grace, or aim at other end.
As Thou art all, so be thou all to me,
First, midst, and last, converted[6] one, and three;
My faith, my hope, my love; and in this state,
My judge, my witness, and my advocate.
Where have I been this while exiled from thee?
And whither raped,[7] now thou but stoop'st to me?
Dwell, dwell here still: O, being everywhere,
How can I doubt to find thee ever here?
I know my state, both full of shame and scorn,

4. Sir William was the nephew of Sir Philip Sidney and the grandchild of Sir Henry Sidney, who was named Queen Elizabeth's Lord Deputy in Ireland three times.
5. Physiologically, the reins (or kidneys) were considered to be the seat of the affections or feelings; but Johnson has an eye to Psalms 7:9: "for the righteous God trieth the hearts and reins."
6. Appearing as.
7. Ravished (in the sense of "enraptured").

Conceived in sin, and unto labor born,
Standing with fear, and must with horror fall,
And destined unto judgment after all.
I feel my griefs too, and there scarce is ground
Upon my flesh t'inflict another wound.
Yet dare I not complain, or wish for death
With holy Paul,[8] lest it be thought the breath
Of discontent; or that these prayers be
For weariness of life, not love of thee.

FROM *THE WORKS OF BENJAMIN JONSON* (1640–1641)

FROM *UNDERWOOD*[9]

A Hymn on the Nativity of My Savior

I sing the birth was born tonight,
The Author both of life and light,
The angels so did sound it;
And like[1] the ravished shepherds said,
Who saw the light, and were afraid,
Yet searched, and true they found it.[2]

The Son of God, th'eternal King,
That did us all salvation bring,
And freed the soul from danger;
He whom the whole world could not take,[3]
The Word which heaven and earth did make,[4]
Was now laid in a manger.

The Father's wisdom willed it so,
The Son's obedience knew no No,
Both wills were in one stature;[5]

8. Cf. Romans 7:24: "O wretched man that I am: who shall deliver me from the body of this death?"
9. Sir Kenelm Digby (1603–1665), scientist, diplomat, and friend to Jonson, took charge of the poet's manuscripts after Jonson's death in 1637, and included the eighty-nine poems and translations comprising *Underwood* in the *Works* of 1640–1641. The order in which the earlier poems appear seems to reflect Jonson's own concern with establishing their connection to *The Forest* (as the poet's prefatory note to *Underwood* suggests); thus, three doctrinal poems are followed by a group of metrically various love poems, and these in turn by an epitaph and three verse epistles. Thereafter, to speak generally, the collection follows the poems' order of composition, although the five translations from Horace, Petronius, and Martial with which *Underwood* concludes were probably composed between 1612 and 1622.
1. I.e., similar things.
2. Cf. Luke 2:8–16.
3. I.e., contain.
4. Cf. John 1:3.
5. I.e., the wills of the First and Second Persons of the Trinity were perfectly at one.

And as that wisdom had decreed,
The Word was now made flesh indeed,[6]
And took on him our nature.

What comfort by him do we win,
Who made himself the price of sin,[7]
To make us heirs of glory!
To see this babe, all innocence,
A martyr born in our defence,
Can man forget this story?

A Celebration of Charis in Ten Lyric Pieces[8]

1. *His Excuse for Loving*

Let it not your wonder move,
Less your laughter, that I love.
Though I now write fifty years,
I have had, and have, my peers;
Poets, though divine, are men,
Some have loved as old again.[9]
And it is not always face,
Clothes, or fortune gives the grace,
Or the feature,[1] or the youth;
But the language and the truth,
With the ardor and the passion,
Gives the lover weight and fashion.
If you then will read the story,
First, prepare you to be sorry
That you never knew till now
Either whom to love or how;
But be glad, as soon with me,
When you know that this is she
Of whose beauty it was sung,
She shall make the old man young,
Keep the middle age at stay,
And let nothing high decay;
Till she be the reason why
All the world for love may die.

6. Cf. John 1:14.
7. Cf. 1 Corinthians 6:20.
8. Although Jonson may have arranged these lyrics as they stand, they were not composed as a unit: lines 11–30 of "Her Triumph" appear in *The Devil Is an Ass* (1616), at II.vi.94–113; and "His Excuse for Loving" was presumably written in 1623. The identity of Charis (from Latin *caritas*, "love") is unknown.
9. I.e., at the age of one hundred.
1. Beauty.

2. *How He Saw Her*

I beheld her on a day,
When her look out-flourished May;
And her dressing did out-brave[2]
All the pride the fields then have;
Far I was from being stupid,
For I ran and called on Cupid,
"Love, if thou wilt ever see
Mark of glory, come with me;
Where's thy quiver? Bend thy bow;
Here's a shaft, thou art too slow!"
And, withal, I did untie
Every cloud about his eye;[3]
But he had not gained his sight
Sooner than he lost his might
Or his courage; for away
Straight he ran and durst not stay,
Letting bow and arrow fall,
Nor for any threat or call
Could be brought once back to look.
I, foolhardy, there up took
Both the arrow he had quit
And the bow; with thought to hit
This my object. But she threw
Such a lightning, as I drew,
At my face, that took my sight
And my motion from me quite;
So that there I stood a stone,
Mocked of all; and called of one
(Which with grief and wrath I heard)
Cupid's statue with a beard,
Or else one that played his ape,
In a Hercules-his shape.

3. *What He Suffered*

After many scorns like these,
Which the prouder beauties please,
She content was to restore
Eyes and limbs to hurt me more,
And would on conditions be
Reconciled to Love,[4] and me.
First, that I must kneeling yield
Both the bow and shaft I held
Unto her; which Love might take
At her hand, with oath to make

2. Surpass.
3. Cupid was traditionally represented as blind; cf. E. Panofsky, "Blind Cupid," in *Studies in Iconology* (New York, 1962), pp. 95–128.
4. I.e., Cupid.

Me the scope of his next draught.[5]
Armèd with that self-same shaft
He no sooner heard the law,
But the arrow home did draw,
And, to gain her by his art,
Left it sticking in my heart;
Which when she beheld to bleed,
She repented of the deed,
And would fain have changed the fate,
But the pity comes too late.
Loser-like, now, all my wreak[6]
Is that I have leave to speak,
And in either prose or song
To revenge me with my tongue,
Which how dexterously I do,
Hear and make examples too.

4. *Her Triumph*

See the chariot at hand here of Love
Wherein my lady rideth!
Each that draws is a swan or a dove,[7]
And well the car Love guideth.
As she goes, all hearts do duty
Unto her beauty;
And enamored, do wish so they might
But enjoy such a sight,
That they still[8] were to run by her side,
Through swords, through seas, whither she would ride.

Do but look on her eyes, they do light
All that Love's world compriseth!
Do but look on her hair, it is bright
As Love's star[9] when it riseth!
Do but mark, her forehead's smoother
Than words that soothe her!
And from her arched brows, such a grace
Sheds itself through the face,
As alone there triumphs to the life
All the gain, all the good, of the elements' strife.[1]

Have you seen but a bright lily grow
Before rude hands have touched it?
Ha' you marked but the fall o' the snow
Before the soil hath smutched it?

5. I.e., the object at which he next aimed.
6. Revenge.
7. Venus's chariot was drawn by swans or doves; cf. Ovid, *Metamorphoses*, X.718.
8. Continuously.
9. I.e., Venus.
1. It was thought that from the original clash and conflict of the four elements emerged the harmonious order of the universe. Cf. Ovid, *Metamorphoses*, I.1–31.

Ha' you felt the wool of beaver?
Or swan's down ever?
Or have smelt o' the bud o' the brier?
Or the nard[2] in the fire?
Or have tasted the bag of the bee?
O so white! O so soft! O so sweet is she![3]

5. *His Discourse with Cupid*

Noblest Charis, you that are
Both my fortune and my star!
And do govern more my blood
Than the various[4] moon the flood!
Hear what late discourse of you
Love and I have had; and true.
'Mongst my Muses finding me,
Where he chanced your name to see
Set, and to this softer strain;
"Sure," said he, "if I have brain,
This here sung can be no other
By description than my mother![5]
So hath Homer praised her hair;
So Anacreon drawn the air[6]
Of her face, and made to rise,
Just about[7] her sparkling eyes,
Both her brows, bent like my bow.
By her looks I do her know,
Which you call my shafts. And see!
Such my mother's blushes be,
As the bath your verse discloses
In her cheeks, of milk and roses;
Such as oft I wanton in.
And, above her even chin,
Have you placed the bank of kisses,
Where, you say, men gather blisses,
Ripened with a breath more sweet
Than when flowers and west winds meet;
Nay, her white and polished neck
With the lace that doth it deck
Is my mother's! Hearts of slain
Lovers, made into a chain!
And between each rising breast
Lies the valley, called my nest,
Where I sit and proyne[8] my wings
After flight; and put new stings

2. An aromatic herb.
3. With this stanza cf. Suckling's "A Song to a Lute," p. 427.
4. Changing.
5. I.e., Venus, whose hair Homer calls "lovely as the Graces'"; cf. *Iliad*, XVII.51. For Anacreon, cf. Epigram CI, line 30n, p. 89.
6. Expression.
7. I.e., above.
8. Preen.

To my shafts! Her very name
With my mother's is the same."[9]
"I confess all," I replied,
"And the glass hangs by her side,
And the girdle 'bout her waist,
All is Venus; save unchaste.
But alas, thou seest the least
Of her good, who is the best
Of her sex; but could'st thou, Love,
Call to mind the forms that strove
For the apple,[1] and those three
Make in one, the same were she.
For this beauty yet doth hide
Something more than thou hast spied.
Outward grace weak love beguiles;
She is Venus, when she smiles,
But she's Juno, when she walks,
And Minerva, when she talks."

6. *Claiming a Second Kiss by Desert*

Charis, guess, and do not miss,
Since I drew a morning kiss
From your lips, and sucked an air
Thence, as sweet as you are fair,
    What my Muse and I have done;
Whether we have lost or won,
If by us the odds were laid,
That the bride, allowed a maid,
Looked not half so fresh and fair,
With th'advantage of her hair
And her jewels, to the view
Of th'assembly, as did you!
    Or that did you sit or walk,
You were more the eye and talk
Of the court, today, than all
Else that glistered in Whitehall;[2]
So as those that had your sight[3]
Wished the bride were changed tonight,
And did think such rites were due
To no other Grace[4] but you!
    Or if you did move tonight,
In the dances, with what spite
Of your peers you were beheld,

9. In the *Odyssey* (VIII.364) the name of Vulcan's consort is Venus; in the *Iliad* (XVIII.382) she is named Charis.
1. Eris, angered at not having been invited to the marriage of Thetis and Peleus, threw among the invited goddesses a golden apple inscribed, "Let it be given to the fairest." The subsequent contest between Juno, Minerva, and Venus, decided by Paris in favor of Venus (who had promised him Helen), led to the Trojan War. Cf. Ovid, *Heroides*, xvi; Hyginus, *Fables*, xcii.
2. The king's palace at Westminster.
3. I.e., saw you.
4. The Graces (Euphrosyne, Aglaia, and Thalia) personified grace and beauty to the ancients; cf. Hesiod, *Theogony*, 907–911, for an initial reference.

That at every motion swelled
So to see a lady tread
As might all the Graces lead,
And was worthy, being so seen,
To be envied of the queen.
Or if you would yet have stayed,
Whether any would upbraid
To himself his loss of time;
Or have charged his sight of crime,
To have left all sight for you.
Guess of these, which is the true;
And if such a verse as this
May not claim another kiss.

7. *Begging Another, on Color[5] of Mending the Former*

For love's sake, kiss me once again;
I long, and should not beg in vain,
Here's none to spy or see;
Why do you doubt, or stay?
I'll taste as lightly as the bee,
That doth but touch his flower and flies away.
Once more, and, faith, I will be gone:
Can he that loves ask less than one?
Nay, you may err in this,
And all your bounty wrong;
This could be called but half a kiss.
What we're but once to do, we should do long;
I will but mend the last, and tell
Where, how it would have relished well;
Join lip to lip, and try;
Each suck other's breath.
And whilst our tongues perplexèd lie,
Let who will think us dead, or wish our death.

8. *Urging Her of a Promise*

Charis one day in discourse
Had of Love, and of his force,
Lightly promised she would tell
What[6] a man she could love well;
And that promise set on fire
All that heard her, with desire.
With the rest, I long expected[7]
When the work would be effected;
But we find that cold delay
And excuse spun every day,
As, until she tell her one,
We all fear she loveth none.

5. Pretence.
6. What kind of.
7. I.e., eagerly awaited.

Therefore, Charis, you must do't,
For I will so urge you to't
You shall neither eat nor sleep,
No, nor forth your window peep
With your emissary[8] eye,
To fetch in the forms go by;[9]
And pronounce which band or lace
Better fits him than his face;
Nay, I will not let you sit
'Fore your idol glass a whit,
To say over every purl[1]
There, or to reform a curl;
Or with secretary Sis[2]
To consult, if fucus[3] this
Be as good as was the last.
All your sweet of life is past,
Make account unless you can,
And that quickly, speak[4] your man.

9. *Her Man Described by Her Own Dictamen*[5]

Of your trouble, Ben, to ease me,
I will tell what man would please me.
I would have him, if I could,
Noble, or of greater blood;
Titles, I confess, do take me,
And a woman God did make me;
French to boot, at least in fashion,
And his manners of that nation.
    Young I'd have him too, and fair,
Yet a man; with crispèd[6] hair
Cast in thousand snares and rings
For Love's fingers, and his wings;
Chestnut color, or more slack[7]
Gold, upon a ground of black.
Venus' and Minerva's eyes,[8]
For he must look wanton-wise.
    Eyebrows bent like Cupid's bow;
Front,[9] an ample field of snow;
Even nose and cheek withal
Smooth as is the billiard ball;
Chin, as woolly as the peach;

8. Spying.
9. I.e., to consider the men who pass by.
1. Loop of lace.
2. I.e., with a confidential maid named Sis (or Cis, the name originally assigned to the chambermaid Prudence in Jonson's play *The New Inn*).
3. Cosmetic.
4. Describe.
5. Pronouncement.
6. Curled.
7. I.e., duller.
8. I.e., bright blue.
9. Forehead.

And his lip should kissing teach,
Till he cherished too much beard,
And make Love or me afeard.
He would have a hand as soft
As the down, and show it oft;
Skin as smooth as any rush,
And so thin to see a blush
Rising through it ere it came;
All his blood should be a flame
Quickly fired, as in beginners
In love's school, and yet no sinners.
'Twere too long to speak of all;
What we harmony do call
In a body should be there.
Well he should his clothes to wear;
Yet[1] no tailor help to make him;
Dressed, you still for man should take him;
And not think h'had eat a stake,
Or were set up in a brake.[2]
Valiant he should be as fire,
Showing danger[3] more than ire;
Bounteous as the clouds to earth
And as honest as his birth.
All his actions to be such,
As to do nothing too much.
Nor o'er-praise, not yet condemn;
Nor outvalue, nor condemn;
Nor do wrongs, nor wrongs receive;
Nor tie knots, nor knots unweave;
And from baseness to be free,
As he durst love truth and me.
Such a man, with every part,
I could give my very heart;
But of one, if short he came,
I can rest me where I am.

10. *Another Lady's Exception Present at the Hearing*

For his mind, I do not care,
That's a toy that I could spare;
Let his title be but great,
His clothes rich, and band[4] sit neat,
Himself young, and face be good,
All I wish is understood.
What you please, you parts may call,
'Tis one good part I'd lie withal.

1. I.e., yet even if.
2. I.e., in a stiff framework.
3. Courage.
4. Collar (or ruff).

The Musical Strife, in a Pastoral Dialogue[5]

She

Come, with our voices let us war,
And challenge all the spheres,[6]
Till each of us be made a star
And all the world turn ears.

He

At such a call, what beast or fowl
Of reason empty is?
What tree or stone doth want[7] a soul?
What man but must lose his?

She

Mix then your notes, that we may prove[8]
To stay the running floods,
To make the mountain quarries move,
And call the walking woods.[9]

He

What need of me? Do you but sing,
Sleep and the grave will wake;
No tunes are sweet, nor words have sting,
But what those lips do make.

She

They say the angels mark each deed
And exercise[1] below,
And out of inward pleasure feed
On what they viewing know.

He

O sing not you, then, lest the best
Of angels should be driven
To fall again; at such a feast,
Mistaking earth for heaven.

5. According to Drummond, Jonson was especially fond of quoting this poem (*H & S*, I, p. 134). Cf. John Hollander, *The Untuning of the Sky: Ideas of Music in English Poetry 1500–1700* (New York, 1970), pp. 338–342, 408–409.
6. I.e., match our voices with the music of the spheres.
7. Lack.
8. Attempt.
9. Cf. *The Forest*, XII, lines 77–78, p. 114.
1. Action.

She

Nay, rather both our souls be strained
  To meet their high desire;
So they in state of grace retained
  May wish us of their choir.

In the Person of Womankind: A Song Apologetic

Men, if you love us, play no more
  The fools or tyrants with your friends,
To make us still sing o'er and o'er
  Our own false praises, for your ends;
    We have both wits and fancies too,
    And if we must, let's sing of you.

Nor do we doubt but that we can,
  If we would search with care and pain,
Find some one good, in some one man;
  So going thorough all your strain,[2]
    We shall, at last, of parcels[3] make
    One good enough for a song's sake.

And as a cunning painter takes
  In any curious[4] piece you see
More pleasure while the thing he makes
  Than when 'tis made, why, so will we.
    And having pleased our art, we'll try
    To make a new, and hang that by.[5]

Another, in Defense of Their Inconstancy: A Song

Hang up those dull and envious fools
  That talk abroad of woman's change;
We were not bred to sit on stools,
  Our proper virtue is to range;[6]
    Take that away, you take our lives:
    We are no women then, but wives.

Such as in valor would excel
  Do change,[7] though man, and often fight;

2. I.e., race, stock (of men).
3. I.e., of separate parts of individual men.
4. Intricate.
5. I.e., put the first one aside.
6. I.e., the virtue peculiarly appropriate to women is to rove at will (by implication, to embody changefulness).
7. I.e., vary their styles of combat.

Which we, in love, must do as well
If ever we will love aright.
The frequent varying of the deed
Is that which doth perfection breed.

Nor is't inconstancy to change
For what is better, or to make
(By searching) what before was strange,
Familiar, for the use's sake;
The good from bad is not descried
But as 'tis often vexed[8] and tried.

And this profession of a store[9]
In love doth not alone help forth[1]
Our pleasure; but preserves us more
From being forsaken than doth worth;
For were the worthiest woman cursed
To love one man, he'd leave her first.

A Nymph's Passion[2]

I love, and he loves me again,
Yet dare I not tell who;
For if the nymphs[3] should know my swain,
I fear they'd love him too;
Yet, if it be not known,
The pleasure is as good as none,
For that's a narrow joy is but[4] our own.

I'll tell, that if they be not glad,
They yet may envy me;
But then if I grow jealous mad,
And of them pitied be,
It were a plague 'bove scorn,
And yet it cannot be forborne,[5]
Unless my heart would as my thought be torn.

He is, if they can find him, fair
And fresh and fragrant too,
As summer's sky, or purgèd[6] air;
And looks as lilies do

8. I.e., searchingly examined.
9. I.e., an abundance.
1. I.e., contribute to.
2. S. T. Coleridge thought enough of this poem to revise it and publish the revision (in *Sibylline Leaves*, 1817), describing it merely as "a song modernized, with some additions, from one of our elder poets."
3. I.e., the other nymphs, or young girls.
4. Merely.
5. Avoided.
6. Purified.

That are this morning blown;[7]
Yet, yet I doubt he is not known,
And fear much more that more of him be shown.

But he hath eyes so round and bright
As make away my doubt,
Where Love may all his torches light,
Though hate had put them out;
But then, t'increase my fears,
What nymph soe'er his voice but hears
Will be my rival, though she have but ears.

I'll tell no more; and yet I love,
And he loves me; yet no
One unbecoming thought doth move
From either heart, I know;
But so exempt from blame
As it would be to each a fame,
If love, or fear, would let me tell his name.

The Hourglass[8]

Do but consider this small[9] dust,
Here running in the glass,
By atoms moved;
Could you believe that this
The body was
Of one that loved?
And in his mistress' flame, playing like a fly,
Turned to cinders by her eye?
Yes; and in death, as life, unblessed,
To have't expressed,
Even ashes of lovers find no rest.

My Picture Left in Scotland[1]

I now think Love is rather deaf than blind,
For else it could not be
That she,
Whom I adore so much, should so slight me
And cast my love behind;
I'm sure my language to her was as sweet,
And every close[2] did meet

7. I.e., fully open.
8. Drummond gives a slightly different version of this "madrigal"; cf. *H & S*, I, p. 150. Cf. also Herrick's "The Hourglass," p. 187.
9. Fine.
1. Jonson sent a version of this poem to Drummond on 19 January 1619 (*H & S*, I, p. 151).
2. I.e., concluding phrase (as in music).

In sentence[3] of as subtle feet,
As hath the youngest he
That sits in shadow of Apollo's[4] tree.

Oh, but my conscious fears,
That fly my thoughts between,
Tell me that she hath seen
My hundreds of gray hairs,
Told seven and forty years;
Read so much waste,[5] as she cannot embrace
My mountain belly, and my rocky face;
And all these through her eyes have stopped her ears.

The Dream

Or[6] scorn or pity on me take,
I must the true relation make:
I am undone tonight.
Love, in a subtle dream disguised,
Hath both my heart and me surprised,
Whom never yet he durst attempt t'awake;
Nor will he tell me for whose sake
He did me the delight,
Or spite,
But leaves me to inquire,
In all my wild desire
Of sleep again, who was his aide;
And sleep so guilty and afraid,
As[7] since he dares not come within my sight.

An Epistle to Master John Selden[8]

I know to whom I write. Here, I am sure,
Though I am short,[9] I cannot be obscure;
Less shall I for the art or dressing care:
Truth and the Graces best when naked are.
Your book, my Selden, I have read, and much
Was trusted that you thought my judgment such
To ask it; though in most of works it be
A penance, where a man may not be free,

3. The term combines the sense of pithy meaning with that of a period in music.
4. Apollo was the god of poetry and song.
5. Jonson puns on "waist."
6. Either.
7. That.
8. A famous legal authority and antiquarian, Selden (1584–1654) is best known to students of literature for *Table Talk* (1689), his secretary's record of Selden's observations on men and manners. According to Drummond, Jonson called Selden "the law book of the judges of England, the bravest man in all languages" (*H & S*, I, p. 149). This poem is prefixed to Selden's *Titles of Honor* (1614), a study of the history of regal and honorific titles.
9. Brief.

Rather than office, when it doth or may
Chance that the friend's affection proves allay
Unto the censure.[1] Yours all need doth fly
Of this so vicious humanity,[2]
Than which there is not unto study a more
Pernicious enemy. We see before
A many[3] of books, even good judgments wound
Themselves through favoring what is there not found;
But I on yours far otherwise shall do,
Not fly the crime, but the suspicion too,
Though I confess (as every Muse hath erred,
And mine not least) I have too oft preferred
Men past their terms,[4] and praised some names too much;
But 'twas with purpose to have made them such.
Since, being deceived, I turn a sharper eye
Upon myself, and ask to whom, and why,
And what I write; and vex[5] it many days
Before men get a verse, much less a praise;
So that my reader is assured I now
Mean what I speak, and still will keep that vow.
Stand forth, my object, then: you that have been
Ever at home, yet have all countries seen,
And, like a compass keeping one foot still
Upon your center,[6] do your circle fill
Of general knowledge; watched men, manners too,
Heard what times past have said, seen what ours do.
Which grace shall I make love to first? Your skill,
Or faith in things?[7] Or is't your wealth and will
T'instruct and teach? Or your unwearied pain
Of gathering? Bounty in pouring out again?
What fables have you vexed! What truth redeemed!
Antiquities searched! Opinions dis-esteemed!
Impostures branded! And authorities urged!
What blots and errors have you watched and purged
Records and authors of! How rectified
Times, manners, customs! Innovations spied!
Sought out the fountains, sources, creeks, paths, ways,
And noted the beginnings and decays!
Where is that nominal mark, or real rite,
Form, act, or ensign[8] that hath 'scaped your sight?

1. I.e., he who is asked for an opinion of another's work often feels constrained not to speak with candor; but if a friend requests that "office," the bonds of friendship will permit perfect frankness.
2. I.e., the need, rooted in imperfect human nature, to silence, or somehow account for, the free expression of perfect truth.
3. I.e., a number.
4. Limits; i.e., extravagantly.
5. I.e., examine stringently.
6. Drummond observes that Jonson's "Impresa [device] was a compass with one foot in center, the other broken; the word [motto] *Deest quod duceret orbem* [There is lacking that which would lead the world]" (*H & S*, I, p. 148).
7. I.e., facts, events.
8. Jonson alludes in these lines to Selden's ability (as demonstrated in *Titles of Honor*) to distinguish among confusing aspects of ceremonial procedures.

How are traditions there examined; how
Conjectures retrieved![9] And a story now
And then of times (besides the bare conduct
Of what it tells us) weaved in to instruct.
I wondered at the richness, but am lost
To see the workmanship so'xceed the cost;
To mark the excellent seas'ning of your style,
And manly elocution, not one while
With horror rough, then rioting with wit,
But to the subject still the colors fit[1]
In sharpness of all search, wisdom of choice,
Newness of sense, antiquity of voice!
  I yield, I yield: the matter of your praise
Flows in upon me, and I cannot raise
A bank against it. Nothing but the round
Large clasp of nature[2] such a wit can bound.
Monarch in Letters! 'Mongst thy titles shown
Of other honors, thus enjoy thine own.
I first salute thee so; and gratulate[3]
With that thy style, thy keeping of thy state,
In offering this thy work to no great name,[4]
That would, perhaps, have praised, and thanked the same,
But nought beyond. He thou hast given it to,
Thy learned chamber-fellow, knows to do
It true respects. He will not only love,
Embrace, and cherish; but he can approve[5]
And estimate thy pains, as having wrought
In the same mines of knowledge; and thence brought
Humanity enough to be a friend,
And strength to be a champion, and defend
Thy gift 'gainst envy. O, how I do count
Among my comings-in,[6] and see it mount,
The gain of your two friendships! Hayward and
Selden! Two names that so much understand!
On whom I could take up[7] and ne'er abuse
The credit what would furnish a tenth Muse!
But here's no time, nor place, my wealth to tell;
You both are modest. So am I. Farewell.

9. I.e., recovered from historical obscurity.
1. I.e., continuously employ suitable rhetorical figures of speech.
2. I.e., the entire creation.
3. Hail.
4. *Titles of Honor* was dedicated to Edward Hayward (d. 1658), who, like Selden, had studied law at the Inner Temple; cf. line 72.
5. Confirm.
6. Income; i.e., the fruitful aspects of my life.
7. I.e., get.

An Ode to Himself[8]

Where dost thou careless lie
Buried in ease and sloth?
Knowledge that sleeps doth die;
And this security,
It is the common moth
That eats on wits and arts, and destroys[9] them both.

Are all the Aonian[1] springs
Dried up? Lies Thespia waste?
Doth Clarius' harp want strings,
That not a nymph now sings?
Or droop they as disgraced,
To see their seats and bowers by chatt'ring pies defaced?[2]

If hence they silence be,
As 'tis too just a cause,
Let this thought quicken thee:
Minds that are great and free
Should not on fortune pause;
'Tis crown enough to virtue still, her own applause.

What though the greedy fry
Be taken with false baits
Of worded balladry,[3]
And think it poesy?
They die with their conceits,
And only piteous scorn upon their folly waits.

Then take in hand thy lyre,
Strike in thy proper strain,
With Japhet's line,[4] aspire
Sol's chariot for new fire
To give the world again;
Who aided him will thee, the issue of Jove's brain.[5]

And since our dainty age
Cannot endure reproof,
Make not thyself a page
To that strumpet, the stage,
But sing high and aloof,
Safe from the wolf's black jaw, and the dull ass's hoof.

8. Cf. the later "Ode to Himself," p. 151, composed in 1629, on the failure of Jonson's play *The New Inn*.
9. Cf. Textual Notes. The figure of lines 5–6 recalls Matthew 6:19–21.
1. Mount Helicon and the Aganippean well, sacred to the Muses, were situated in Aonia; for Thespia, cf. Epigram CI, line 33n, p. 90. *Clarius* is a term for Apollo, from his temple at Claros, on the Ionian coast.
2. Magpies.
3. Jonson regularly distinguished between poets and poetasters; cf. his contemptuous remark to Drummond, "a poet should detest a ballad-maker" (*H & S*, 1, p. 145).
4. Prometheus, who stole fire from heaven, was the son of Iapetus (Japhet).
5. I.e., Minerva (Pallas Athena); cf. *The Forest*, X, line 15, p. 108.

A Sonnet to the Noble Lady, the Lady Mary Wroth[6]

I that have been a lover, and could show it,
Though not in these,[7] in rhythms not wholly dumb,
Since I exscribe[8] your sonnets, am become
A better lover, and much better poet.
Nor is my Muse or I ashamed to owe it
To those true numerous graces, whereof some
But charm the senses, others overcome
Both brains and hearts; and mine now best do know it:
For in your verse all Cupid's armory,
His flames, his shafts, his quiver, and his bow,
His very eyes are yours to overthrow.
But then his mother's sweets you so apply,
Her joys, her smiles, her loves, as readers take
For Venus' ceston[9] every line you make.

An Epistle Answering to One That Asked to Be Sealed of the Tribe of Ben[1]

Men that are safe and sure in all they do
Care not what trials they are put unto;
They meet the fire, the test, as martyrs would,
And, though opinion stamp them not, are gold.
I could say more of such, but that I fly[2]
To speak myself out too ambitiously,
And showing so weak an act to vulgar eyes,
Put conscience and my right to compromise.[3]
Let those that merely talk and never think,
That live in the wild anarchy of drink,
Subject to quarrel only; or else such
As make it their proficiency how much
They've glutted in and lechered out that week,
That never yet did friend or friendship seek
But for a sealing: let these men protest.
Or th'other on their borders,[4] that will jest
On all souls that are absent, even the dead,
Like flies or worms which man's corrupt parts fed;
That to speak well, think it above all sin,
Of any company but that they are in,
Call every night to supper in these fits,

6. Jonson dedicated *The Alchemist* to Wroth, and she danced at court in his *Masque of Blackness*; cf. the sonnets that compose Wroth's *Pamphilia to Amphilanthus*, pp. 167–176.
7. I.e., not in the rhyme scheme and metrical arrangement of the sonnet. "Rhythms" refers to rhyming verses.
8. Copy out.
9. Girdle (from Latin *cestus*).
1. "Sealed" here means "assured, accepted." Cf. Revelation 7:8: "Of the tribe of Benjamin were sealed twelve thousand."
2. I.e., prefer not.
3. I.e., compromise myself (by boasting).
4. I.e., or others like them.

And are receivèd for the covey[5] of wits;
That censure all the town, and all th'affairs,
And know whose ignorance is more than theirs:
Let these men have their ways, and take their times
To vent their libels, and to issue rhymes;
I have no portion in them, nor their deal
Of news they get to strew out the long meal;
I study other friendships, and more one[6]
Than these can ever be, or else with none.
What is't to me whether the French design
Be, or be not, to get the Valteline?[7]
Or the States'[8] ships sent forth belike to meet
Some hopes of Spain in their West Indian fleet?
Whether the dispensation[9] yet be sent,
Or that the match from Spain was ever meant?
I wish all well, and pray high heaven conspire
My prince's safety and my king's desire;
But if, for honor, we must draw the sword,
And force back that which will not be restored,[1]
I have a body yet that spirit draws
To live, or fall a carcass, in the cause.
So far without inquiry what the States,
Brunsfield and Mansfield[2] do this year, my fates
Shall carry me at call; and I'll be well,
Though I do neither hear these news, nor tell
Of Spain or France, or were not pricked down[3] one
Of the late mystery of reception,[4]
Although my fame, to his, not under-hears,[5]
That guides the motions and directs the bears.[6]
But that's a blow by which in time I may
Lose all my credit with my Christmas clay
And animated porcelain of the court;
Aye, and for this neglect, the coarser sort
Of earthen jars there may molest me too.[7]
Well, with mine own frail pitcher, what to do

5. I.e., and are considered to be the fashionable group.
6. I.e., friendships which more truly embody that ideal; or (perhaps) friendships which more completely exemplify a unity of character.
7. A valley near Lake Como, of some strategical importance, the Valteline was seized from Spanish control by the French in 1624.
8. I.e., Dutch.
9. Permission from Rome was necessary to make possible the projected marriage of Prince Charles to the Spanish Infanta.
1. I.e., any aggressively ambitious power, but in particular, the forces of Catholic Spain.
2. Ernest, Count of Mansfield, commanded the army of the Palatinate and Bohemia; the identity of "Brunsfield" is uncertain, although W. B. Hunter, Jr., suggests Christian of Brunswick (*Complete Poetry of Ben Jonson, ed. cit.*, p. 202).
3. I.e., singled out.
4. I.e., the committee (including the designer and architect Inigo Jones, whom Jonson bitterly resented) that, in 1623, arranged for the reception of the Spanish Infanta at Southampton.
5. I.e., is not inferior.
6. Jonson contemptuously likens Inigo Jones to a cheap showman, whose undertakings are no better than puppet shows ("motions") and bear baitings.
7. In lines 51–55, Jonson acknowledges the uncertainty of his own position at court, notably the likelihood (given Jones's influence) that he may no longer be commissioned to compose masques for the festivities of Christmas.

I have decreed: keep it from waves, and press,[8]
Lest it be jostled, cracked, made nought or less;
Live to that point I will for which I am man,
And dwell as in my center as I can,
Still looking to and ever loving heaven,
With reverence using all the gifts thence given;
'Mongst which, if I have any friendships sent,
Such as are square, well-tagged,[9] and permanent,
Not built with canvas, paper, and false lights[1]
As are the glorious scenes at the great sights,
And that there be no fev'ry heats nor colds,
Oily expansions,[2] or shrunk dirty folds,
But all so clear, and led by reason's flame,
As but to stumble in her sight were shame;
These I will honor, love, embrace, and serve,
And free it[3] from all question to preserve.
So short you read my character, and theirs
I would call mine, to which not many stairs
Are asked to climb. First give me faith, who know
Myself a little; I will take you so
As you have writ yourself. Now stand; and then,
Sir, you are sealèd of the Tribe of Ben.

An Epigram to the Household[4]

What can the cause be, when the king hath given
His poet sack,[5] the household will not pay?
Are they so scanted[6] in their store, or driven
For want of knowing the poet, to say him nay?
Well, they should know him, would the king but grant
His poet leave to sing his household true;
He'd frame such ditties of their store, and want,
Would make the very green cloth[7] to look blue,
And rather wish, in their expense of sack,
So the allowance from the king to use
As the old bard should no Canary lack.
'Twere better spare a butt than spill[8] his Muse,
For in the genius of a poet's verse
The king's fame lives. Go now, deny his tierce!

8. Crowds.
9. Well knit.
1. I.e., not depending on insubstantial devices (like those favored by Inigo Jones).
2. I.e., the stretching of painted canvas.
3. I.e., friendship.
4. I.e., the household of King Charles I.
5. By a royal patent of 26 March 1630, Jonson was to receive £100 and "one tierce [42 gallons] of Canary Spanish wine" (*H & S*, I, pp. 245–247).
6. Diminished.
7. The Board of Green Cloth controlled domestic expenses of the royal household.
8. I.e., spare a large cask than spoil (but Jonson's taste for punning adds point to the line).

To the Immortal Memory and Friendship of That Noble Pair, Sir Lucius Cary and Sir H. Morison[9]

The Turn[1]

Brave infant of Saguntum,[2] clear
Thy coming forth in that great year,
When the prodigious[3] Hannibal did crown
His rage, with razing your immortal town.
Thou, looking then about,
Ere thou wert half got out,
Wise child, didst hastily return,
And mad'st thy mother's womb thine urn.
How summed a circle didst thou leave mankind
Of deepest lore, could we the center find!

The Counter-Turn

Did wiser Nature draw thee back
From out the horror of that sack?
Where shame, faith, honor, and regard of right
Lay trampled on; the deeds of death and night
Urged, hurried forth, and hurled
Upon th'affrighted world;
Sword, fire, and famine with fell fury met,
And all on utmost ruin set;
As, could they but life's miseries foresee,
No doubt all infants would return like thee.

The Stand

For what is life, if measured by the space,[4]
Not by the act?
Or maskèd man, if valued by his face
Above his fact?[5]
Here's one outlived his peers,

9. Sir Lucius Cary, second Viscount Falkland (c. 1610–1643), in the view of Douglas Bush "the example *par excellence* of the noble and philosophical cavalier" (*English Literature in the Earlier Seventeenth Century 1600–1660*, 2nd ed., rev. [New York, 1962], p. 343), was the guiding spirit of an intellectual group that met in the 1630s at Cary's estate, Great Tew, in Oxfordshire. Cary contributed an elegy to *Jonsonus Virbius*, the collection of memorial poems published in 1638. Although he was not in sympathy with the views of Archbishop Laud and the Earl of Strafford, Cary allied himself with the royalist forces when the civil war began; he was killed at the battle of Newbury in September 1643. Sir Henry Morison (c. 1608–1629) was knighted in 1627; Cary married his sister in 1630.
1. The odes of Pindar (c. 522–442 B.C.), on which this poem is modeled, are typically arranged in groups of three stanzas: strophe, antistrophe, and a formally distinct epode. Jonson's "turn," "counterturn," and "stand" correspond to these terms and divisions. The complex metrical structure and the elevated tone of Pindar's odes evidently excited the particular admiration of Jonson, who refers more than once to the "fire" of Pindar's genius (cf. "Ode to Himself," line 44, p. 152).
2. According to Pliny (*Natural History*, VII.iii.), when Hannibal destroyed the Spanish city of Saguntum (modern Murviedro), in 217 B.C. (and so began the Second Punic War), a newly born child, after witnessing the sack of the city, returned to its mother's womb.
3. Like a prodigy; i.e., extraordinary, ominous.
4. I.e., by the length in time.
5. Deed.

And told forth fourscore years;
He vexèd time, and busied the whole state,
Troubled both foes and friends,
But ever to no ends;
What did this stirrer, but die late?
How well at twenty had he fall'n or stood!
For three of his fourscore he did no good.

The Turn

He entered well, by virtuous parts,
Got up, and thrived with honest arts;
He purchased friends, and fame, and honors then,
And had his noble name advanced with men;
But weary of that flight,
He stooped in all men's sight
To sordid flatteries, acts of strife,
And sunk in that dead sea of life
So deep, as he did then death's waters sup,
But that the cork of title buoyed him up.

The Counter-Turn

Alas, but Morison fell young!
He never fell; thou fall'st, my tongue.
He stood, a soldier to the last right end,
A perfect patriot, and a noble friend,
But most, a virtuous son.
All offices were done
By him, so ample, full, and round,
In weight, in measure, number, sound,
As, though his age imperfect might appear,
His life was of humanity the sphere.[6]

The Stand

Go now, and tell out days summed up with fears,
And make them years;
Produce thy mass of miseries on the stage,
To swell thine age;
Repeat of things a throng,
To show thou hast been long,
Not lived; for life doth her great actions spell[7]
By what was done and wrought
In season, and so brought
To light; her measures are, how well
Each syllabe answered, and was formed, how fair;
These make the lines of life, and that's her air.[8]

6. I.e., the perfect model.
7. Signify.
8. I.e., her element (or, perhaps, "manner").

The Turn

It is not growing like a tree
In bulk, doth make man better be;
Or standing long an oak, three hundred year,
To fall a log at last, dry, bald, and sere;
A lily of a day
Is fairer far in May,
Although it fall and die that night;
It was the plant and flower of light.
In small proportions, we just beauties see;
And in short measures, life may perfect be.

The Counter-Turn

Call, noble Lucius, then for wine,
And let thy looks with gladness shine;
Accept this garland, plant it on thy head,
And think, nay know, thy Morison's not dead.
He leaped the present age,
Possessed with holy rage
To see that bright eternal day
Of which we priests and poets say
Such truths, as we expect for happy men;
And there he lives with memory, and Ben

The Stand

Jonson, who sung this of him, ere he went
Himself to rest,
Or taste a part of that full joy he meant
To have expressed
In this bright asterism,[9]
Where it were friendship's schism,
Were not his Lucius long with us to tarry,
To separate these twi-
Lights, the Dioscuri,[1]
And keep the one half from his Harry.
But fate doth so alternate the design,
Whilst that in heav'n, this light on earth must shine.

9. Constellation.
1. Castor and Pollux; cf. *The Forest*, XII, line 58, p. 113.

The Turn

And shine as you exalted are;
Two names of friendship, but one star:
Of hearts the union. And those not by chance
Made, or indentured, or leased out t'advance
The profits for a time;
No pleasures vain did chime
Of rhymes, or riots at your feasts,
Orgies of drink, or feigned protests;
But simple love of greatness, and of good;
That knits brave minds, and manners, more than blood.

The Counter-Turn

This made you first to know the why
You liked, then after to apply
That liking; and approach so one the tother,
Till either grew a portion of the other;
Each stylèd by his end,[2]
The copy of his friend.
You lived to be the great surnames
And titles, by which all made claims
Unto the virtue; nothing perfect done
But as a Cary or a Morison.

The Stand

And such a force the fair example had,
As they that saw
The good, and durst not practise it, were glad
That such a law
Was left yet to mankind,
Where they might read, and find
Friendship in deed was written, not in words;
And with the heart, not pen,
Of two so early[3] men,
Whose lines her rolls were, and records,
Who, ere the first down bloomèd on the chin,
Had sowed these fruits, and got the harvest in.

2. Aim, intention.
3. Young.

Epithalamion, or a Song Celebrating the Nuptials of that Noble Gentleman, Mr. Jerome Weston, Son and Heir of the Lord Weston, Lord High Treasurer of England, with the Lady Frances Stuart, Daughter of Esme Duke of Lenox, Deceased, and Sister of the Surviving Duke of the Same Name[4]

Though thou hast passed thy summer standing,[5] stay
Awhile with us, bright sun, and help our light;
Thou canst not meet more glory, on the way
Between thy tropics,[6] to arrest thy sight
Than thou shalt see today.
We woo thee, stay,
And see what can be seen,
The bounty of a King, and beauty of his Queen!

See, the procession! What a holy day,
Bearing the promise of some better fate,
Hath fillèd, with caroches,[7] all the way
From Greenwich hither to Roehampton gate!
When looked the year, at best,
So like a feast;
Or were affairs in tune,
By all the spheres' consent, so in the heart of June?

What bevy of beauties and bright youths, at charge[8]
Of summer's liveries and gladding[9] green,
Do boast their loves and brav'ries[1] so at large
As they came all to see, and to be seen!
When looked the earth so fine,
Or so did shine
In all her bloom and flower,
To welcome home a pair, and deck the nuptial bower?

It is the kindly season of the time,
The month of youth, which calls all creatures forth
To do their offices in nature's chime,

4. An epithalamion is a nuptial song in honor of the bride and groom; the term, literally "on the bed chamber," derives from Latin and Greek. Edmund Spenser's is the first use of the term in English; the structure and stanzaic form of Jonson's poem generally recall the *Epithalamion* of his Elizabethan predecessor, although the particular emphases of Jonson's marriage ode differ from those of Spenser's poem. Richard Lord Weston (1577–1635) extended patronage to Jonson in the poet's later years; several poems in *Underwood* (not included here) compliment Lord Weston or request his aid. His son Jerome (1605–1663) conducted diplomatic negotiations in France and Italy during 1632–1633, just prior to his marriage, which took place at Roehampton on 25 June 1632. Frances Stuart was the daughter of that Lady Aubigny to whom Jonson addressed *The Forest*, XIII, p. 115. The marriage, according to Clarendon (*History of the Rebellion* . . . , 7 vols. [Oxford, 1849], I, p. 75), was arranged by King Charles I.
5. I.e., the solstice.
6. I.e., the Tropics of Cancer and Capricorn.
7. Carriages.
8. I.e., who have the expense.
9. Pleasing.
1. Finery (of clothing).

And celebrate (perfection at the worth)
Marriage, the end[2] of life,
That holy strife,
And the allowèd war,
Through which not only we but all our species are.

Hark, how the bells upon the waters play
Their sister-tunes, from Thames his either side,
As they had learned new changes[3] for the day,
And all did ring th'approaches of the bride,
The Lady Frances, dressed
Above the rest
Of all the maidens fair,
In graceful ornament of garland, gems, and hair.

See how she paceth forth in virgin white,
Like what she is, the daughter of a Duke,
And sister; darting forth a dazzling light
On all that come her simplesse[4] to rebuke.
Her tresses trim her back
As she did lack
Nought of a maiden queen,
With modesty so crowned and adoration seen.

Stay, thou wilt see what rites the virgins do,
The choicest virgin-troop of all the land,
Porting the ensigns of united two,[5]
Both crowns and kingdoms in their either hand,
Whose majesties appear,
To make more clear[6]
This feast than can the day,
Although that thou, O sun, at our entreaty stay.

See, how with roses and with lilies shine
(Lilies and roses, flowers of either sex)[7]
The bright bride's paths, embellished more than thine
With light of love, this pair doth intertexe![8]
Stay, see the virgins sow,
Where she shall go,
The emblems of their way.
O now thou smil'st, fair sun, and shin'st as thou wouldst stay!

With what full hands, and in how plenteous showers
Have they bedewed the earth where she doth tread,

2. Purpose, object.
3. Sequences (in the "change ringing" of church bells, an ancient English pursuit demanding concentration and stamina).
4. I.e., her simple and pure dress.
5. I.e., carrying the banners of England and France, symbolizing the union of Charles I and his French consort Henrietta Maria.
6. Bright.
7. The English rose is matched by the French fleur-de-lis.
8. Interweave.

As if her airy steps did spring the flowers,
And all the ground were garden, where she led!
See, at another door,
On the same floor,
The bridegroom meets the bride
With all the pomp of youth, and all our Court beside.

Our Court and all the grandees;[9] now, sun, look,
And looking with thy best inquiry tell,
In all thy age of journals[1] thou hast took,
Saw'st thou that pair became these rites so well
Save the preceding two?
Who, in all they do,
Search, sun, and thou wilt find
They are th'exampled pair[2] and mirror of their kind.

Force from the phoenix,[3] then, no rarity
Of sex, to rob the creature; but from man,
The king of creatures, take his parity
With angels, Muse, to speak these; nothing can
Illustrate these but they
Themselves today,
Who the whole act express;
All else we see beside are shadows, and go less.[4]

It is their grace and favor that makes seen
And wondered at the bounties of this day;
All is a story of the King and Queen,
And what of dignity and honor may
Be duly done to those
Whom they have chose,
And set the mark upon
To give a greater name and title to: their own.

Weston, their treasure, as their Treasurer,
That mine of wisdom and of counsels deep,
Great say-master[5] of state, who cannot err,
But doth his carract[6] and just standard keep
In all the proved assays
And legal ways
Of trials to work down[7]
Men's loves unto the laws, and laws to love the Crown.

9. Nobility, great ones.
1. Daily rounds (from Latin *diurnalis*).
2. I.e., the pair held up as an example.
3. According to legend, the phoenix, after an existence of 500 years, was consumed in its own flames, after which it miraculously emerged youthfully alive to renew its cycle of existence. Jonson, however, refers to the phoenix here primarily as an (ultimately Platonic) ideal of human perfection (cf. *The Forest*, XI, line 92n, p. 111), which is inappropriate, because insufficient, as a figure to describe this occasion.
4. I.e., are worth less.
5. Assay master (in his capacity as Lord High Treasurer of the realm).
6. Carat; i.e., worth. Jonson perhaps employs the term to allow also the sense "character."
7. I.e., bring into proper relationship.

And this well moved the judgment of the King
To pay with honors, to his noble son,
Today, the father's service; who could bring
Him up to do the same himself had done.
That far-all-seeing eye
Could soon espy
What kind of waking man
He had so highly set, and in what barbican.[8]

Stand there; for when a noble nature's raised,
It brings friends joy, foes grief, posterity fame;
In him the times, no less than Prince, are praised,
And by his rise, in active men his name
Doth emulation stir;
To the dull, a spur
It is; to th'envious meant,[9]
A mere upbraiding grief and torturing punishment.

See, now the chapel opens, where the King
And Bishop[1] stay to consummate the rites;
The holy prelate prays, then takes the ring,
Asks first, "Who gives her? "I, Charles."[2] Then he plights
One in the other's hand,
Whilst they both stand
Hearing their charge, and then
The solemn choir cries, "Joy!" and they return, "Amen."

O happy bands! And thou more happy place
Which to this use were built and consecrate!
To have thy God to bless, thy King to grace,
And this their chosen Bishop celebrate
And knit the nuptial knot,
Which time shall not,
Or cankered jealousy
With all corroding arts, be able to untie!

The chapel empties; and thou may'st begone
Now, sun, and post away the rest of day;
These two, now holy church hath made them one,
Do long to make themselves so, another way;
There is a feast behind[3]
To them of kind,
Which their glad parents taught
One to the other, long ere these to light were brought.

8. Watchtower.
9. I.e., interpreted by the envious as.
1. The presiding bishop on this occasion was William Laud, at this date Bishop of London, who became Archbishop of Canterbury.
2. Charles I gave the bride away since her father was deceased.
3. I.e., still to come.

Haste, haste, officious sun, and send them night
Some hours before it should, that these may know
All that their fathers and their mothers might
Of nuptial sweets, at such a season, owe,
To propagate their names,
And keep their fames
Alive, which else would die,
For fame keeps virtue up, and it posterity.

Th'ignoble never lived; they were a while,
Like swine or other cattle, here on earth;
Their names are not recorded on the file
Of life, that fall[4] so. Christians know their birth
Alone; and such a race
We pray may grace
Your fruitful spreading vine,
But dare not ask our wish in language fescennine.[5]

Yet as we may, we will,[6] with chaste desires
(The holy perfumes of the marriage-bed)
Be kept alive those sweet and sacred fires
Of love between you and your lovelihead,
That, when you both are old,
You find no cold
There, but, renewèd, say,
After the last child born, "This is our wedding day."

Till you behold a race to fill your hall,
A Richard[7] and a Jerome, by their names
Upon a Thomas or a Francis call;
A Kate, a Frank to honor their grand-dames,
And 'tween their grandsire's thighs,
Like pretty spies,
Peep forth a gem,[8] to see
How each one plays his part of the large pedigree.

And never may there want one of the stem[9]
To be a watchful servant for this state,
But, like an arm of eminence 'mongst them,
Extend a reaching virtue, early and late,
Whilst the main tree still found
Upright and sound,
By this sun's noon stead's[1] made
So great: his body now alone projects the shade.

4. Perish.
5. Obscene, licentious. Marriage ceremonies in ancient Rome included bawdy songs, which were thought to avert evil (cf. Catullus, *Odes*, lxi).
6. I.e., we desire that.
7. The names given here include those of the bride and groom, and several of their relatives. Jerome and Frances had one son, whom they named Charles.
8. I.e. (probably), each like a gem.
9. I.e., the family stock or line.
1. I.e., place is.

They both are slipped to bed. Shut fast the door
And let him freely gather love's first-fruits;
He's master of the office, yet no more
Exacts than she is pleased to pay; no suits,
Strifes, murmurs or delay
Will last till day;
Night, and the sheets, will show
The longing couple all that elder lovers know.[2]

FROM *MR. WILLIAM SHAKESPEARE'S COMEDIES, HISTORIES, AND TRAGEDIES* (1623)

To the Memory of My Beloved, The Author, Mr. William Shakespeare, and What He Hath Left Us[3]

To draw no envy (Shakespeare) on thy name,
Am I thus ample[4] to thy book, and fame;
While I confess thy writings to be such,
As neither man nor Muse can praise too much.
'Tis true, and all men's suffrage.[5] But these ways
Were not the paths I meant unto thy praise:
For seeliest[6] ignorance on these may light,
Which, when it sounds at best, but echoes right;
Or blind affection, which doth ne'er advance
The truth, but gropes, and urgeth all by chance;
Or crafty malice might pretend this praise,
And think to ruin where it seemed to raise.
These are as[7] some infamous bawd or whore
Should praise a matron. What could hurt her more?
But thou art proof against them, and indeed
Above th'ill fortune of them, or the need.
I, therefore, will begin. Soul of the age!
The applause, delight, the wonder of our stage!
My Shakespeare, rise; I will not lodge thee by
Chaucer, or Spenser, or bid Beaumont[8] lie
A little further, to make thee a room:
Thou art a monument without a tomb,

2. By art or hap the last phrase echoes Marlowe, "Hero and Leander," II.69.
3. While there is little reason to doubt that this famous tribute to Shakespeare's genius and art, published in the "First Folio" edition of Shakespeare's plays, represents (in language appropriate to the occasion) Jonson's honest opinion of his fellow dramatist's achievement, the lines should be read in conjunction with those comments on Shakespeare that appear elsewhere in Jonson's work: cf. *Timber*, 647–668, and also the brusque remark, recorded by Drummond, that "Shakespeare wanted art."
4. Copious (i.e., in this relatively lengthy poem).
5. I.e., all men acknowledge it.
6. Simplest.
7. I.e., as if.
8. These three poets are buried in Westminster Abbey; Shakespeare's remains lie in Holy Trinity Church, Stratford-on-Avon. The fancy rejected by Jonson (i.e., that the other three should make room for Shakespeare) is that with which William Basse (d. 1653) began his "Elegy on Shakespeare," printed in the 1633 edition of the poems of John Donne.

And art alive still, while thy book doth live,
  And we have wits to read, and praise to give.
That I not mix thee so, my brain excuses;
  I mean with great, but disproportioned[9] muses:
For if I thought my judgment were of years,[1]
  I should commit thee surely with thy peers,
And tell how far thou didst our Lyly outshine,
  Or sporting Kyd, or Marlowe's mighty line.[2]
And though thou hadst small Latin and less Greek,[3]
  From thence to honor thee, I would not seek
For names, but call forth thund'ring Aeschylus,
  Euripides, and Sophocles to us,
Pacuvius, Accius, him of Cordova dead,[4]
  To life again, to hear thy buskin[5] tread
And shake a stage; or, when thy socks were on,
  Leave thee alone for the comparison
Of all that insolent Greece or haughty Rome
  Sent forth, or since did from their ashes come.
Triumph, my Britain, thou hast one to show
  To whom all scenes of Europe homage owe.
He was not of an age, but for all time!
  And all the Muses still were in their prime
When like Apollo he came forth to warm
  Our ears, or like a Mercury to charm!
Nature herself was proud of his designs,
  And joyed to wear the dressing of his lines,
Which were so richly spun and woven so fit,
  As, since, she will vouchsafe no other wit;
The merry Greek, tart Aristophanes,
  Neat Terence, witty Plautus,[6] now not please,
But antiquated and deserted lie,
  As they were not of nature's family.
Yet must I not give nature all; thy art,
  My gentle Shakespeare, must enjoy a part;
For though the poet's matter nature be,
  His art doth give the fashion. And that he[7]
Who casts[8] to write a living line, must sweat

9. I.e., not comparable.
1. I.e., a judgment in the context of extended periods of time (whereas in fact Shakespeare "was not of an age, but for all time," line 43).
2. John Lyly (c. 1554–1606), author of the prose romance *Euphues*, was the prime exponent of Elizabethan "high comedy" (e.g., *Endymion*); Thomas Kyd (c. 1557–c. 1595) wrote *The Spanish Tragedy*. Christopher Marlowe (1564–1593) was universally admired for the quality of his dramatic blank verse, in *Tamburlaine* and later works.
3. This observation should be read in the context of Jonson's own considerable attainments in classical languages and literatures; Shakespeare's learning was by no means inconsiderable.
4. Aeschylus (525–456 B.C.), Sophocles (495–406 B.C.), and Euripides (480–406 B.C.), the masters of Greek tragedy, are grouped with three Roman tragic authors, Pacuvius (c. 220–130 B.C.), Accius (170–c. 90 B.C.), and Lucius Annaeus Seneca, born in Córdoba, Spain (c. 3 B.C.–A.D. 65).
5. The buskin was the high shoe traditionally worn by actors in Greek tragedy; "socks" (line 37) refers to its counterpart in comedy. The terms in this context represent Shakespeare's tragedies and comedies.
6. Aristophanes (c. 444–c. 380 B.C.), Publius Terentius Afer, called Terence (195–159 B.C.), and Titus Maccius Plautus (c. 254–184 B.C.) were the most renowned comic writers of classical times.
7. I.e., that man.
8. Undertakes.

(Such as thine are), and strike the second heat
Upon the Muses' anvil, turn the same
(And himself with it) that he thinks to frame;
Or for the laurel he may gain a scorn,
For a good poet's made, as well as born.
And such wert thou. Look how the father's face
Lives in his issue; even so, the race
Of Shakespeare's mind and manners brightly shines
In his well-turnèd and true-filèd lines,
In each of which he seems to shake a lance,[9]
As brandished at the eyes of ignorance.
Sweet swan of Avon! what a sight it were
To see thee in our waters yet appear,
And make those flights upon the banks of Thames,
That so did take Eliza and our James!
But stay, I see thee in the hemisphere
Advanced, and made a constellation[1] there!
Shine forth, thou star of poets, and with rage
Or influence, chide or cheer the drooping stage;
Which, since thy flight from hence, hath mourned like night,
And despairs day, but for thy volume's light.

FROM *BEN JONSON'S EXECRATION AGAINST VULCAN* (1640)

Ode to Himself[2]

Come leave the loathèd stage,
And the more loathsome age,
Where pride and impudence in faction knit
Usurp the chair of wit,
Indicting and arraigning, every day,
Something they call a play.
Let their fastidious, vain
Commission of the brain
Run on, and rage, sweat, censure, and condemn:
They were not made for thee, less thou for them.

Say that thou pour'st 'em wheat,
And they would acorns eat;
'Twere simple[3] fury, still thyself to waste
On such as have no taste;
To offer them a surfeit of pure bread,

9. The pun on Shakespeare's name looks back to another in line 37. Robert Greene, in *Greene's Groatsworth of Wit Bought with a Million of Repentance* (1592), had attacked Shakespeare for counting himself, "in his own conceit, the only Shake-scene in a county."
1. I.e., Cygnus, the swan.
2. Outraged by the failure of *The New Inn* in 1629, Jonson appended this poem as an epilogue to the published version of that play (1631).
3. Foolish.

Whose appetites are dead;
No, give them grains[4] their fill,
Husks, draff[5] to drink, and swill;
If they love lees, and leave the lusty wine,
Envy them not, their palate's with the swine.

No doubt a moldy tale,
Like *Pericles*,[6] and stale
As the shrive's crusts,[7] and nasty as his fish,
Scraps out of every dish
Thrown forth, and raked into the common tub,[8]
May keep up the Play Club.[9]
Broome's[1] sweepings do as well
There as his master's meal;
For who the relish of these guests will fit
Needs set them but the alms-basket of wit.

And much good do't ye then,
Brave plush and velvet men
Can feed on orts,[2] and safe in your scene clothes,[3]
Dare quit upon your oaths
The stagers, and the stage-wrights too (your peers)
Of stuffing your large ears
With rage of comic socks,[4]
Wrought upon twenty blocks;[5]
Which, if they're torn, and foul, and patched enough,
The gamesters share your guilt,[6] and you their stuff.

Leave things so prostitute,
And take th'Alcaic lute;[7]
Or thine own Horace, or Anacreon's lyre;
Warm thee by Pindar's fire;
And though thy nerves[8] be shrunk, and blood be cold,
Ere years have made thee old,
Strike that disdainful heat
Throughout, to their defeat;

4. I.e., refuse malt left after brewing (commonly thrown to hogs).
5. Dregs.
6. Acts III, IV, and V of the romance *Pericles* were substantially Shakespeare's work; but the play's verse and movement are notably uneven.
7. I.e., the stale bread served in prisons (under a sheriff's authority).
8. I.e., leavings collected for the poor.
9. Jonson apparently alludes to a group of critics and "wits" whom he scorned.
1. Richard Brome (died c. 1652), formerly Jonson's servant, attained some modest success as a playwright, notably with the comedy *The Joviall Crew* (1641).
2. Table scraps.
3. I.e., probably, clothes worn to attend plays.
4. Cf. "To Shakespeare," lines 36–37n, p. 150.
5. I.e., blockheads (with a pun on "molds").
6. I.e., (punningly), your "gilt" (gold) as well as guilt.
7. Alcaeus (fl. c. 611 B.C.) was a Greek lyric poet whose meter was imitated by Horace (65–8 B.C.); for Anacreon, cf. Epigram CI, line 30n, p. 89; for Pindar, cf. "To the Immortal Memory . . . of Cary and . . . Morison," n.1, p. 140.
8. Sinews (from Latin *nervus*).

As curious fools, and envious of thy strain,
May, blushing, swear no palsy's in thy brain.[9]

But when they hear thee sing
The glories of thy King,
His zeal to God, and his just awe of[1] men,
They may be blood-shaken, then
Feel such a flesh-quake to possess their powers,
That no tuned harp like ours,
In sound of peace or wars,
Shall truly hit the stars
When they shall read the acts of Charles his reign,
And see his chariot triumph 'bove his wain.[2]

SONGS FROM THE PLAYS AND MASQUES

From *The Works* (1616)

"Slow, slow, fresh fount"[3]

Slow, slow, fresh fount, keep time with my salt tears;
Yet slower, yet, O faintly, gentle springs!
List to the heavy part the music bears,
Woe weeps out her division,[4] when she sings.
Droop herbs and flowers;
Fall grief in showers;
Our beauties are not ours;
O, I could still,
Like melting snow upon some craggy hill,
Drop, drop, drop, drop,
Since nature's pride is, now, a withered daffodil.

"If I freely may discover"[5]

If I freely may discover[6]
What would please me in my lover:
I would have her fair, and witty,
Savoring more of court than city;
A little proud, but full of pity;

9. Jonson had suffered a paralytic stroke in 1628.
1. I.e., over.
2. Wagon; i.e., above the constellation Charles's Wain (with a pun on "wane"). Cf. Textual Notes.
3. This song appears in *Cynthia's Revels* (1600), I.ii, where it is sung by Echo.
4. I.e., divides a succession of long (slow) notes into several short (quick) ones.
5. The first stanza of this song (from *The Poetaster* [1601], II.ii), is assigned to Crispinus; the second to Hermogenes.
6. Reveal.

Light and humorous in her toying,
Oft building hopes, and soon destroying;
Long, but sweet, in the enjoying;
Neither too easy nor too hard,
All extremes I would have barred.

She should be allowed her passions,
So they were but used as fashions;
Sometimes froward, and then frowning,
Sometimes sickish, and then swowning,
Every fit with change still crowning,
Purely jealous I would have her;
Then only constant when I crave her,
'Tis a virtue should not save her.
Thus, nor her delicates[7] would cloy me,
Neither her peevishness annoy me.

"Swell me a bowl with lusty wine"[8]

Swell me a bowl with lusty wine,
Till I may see the plump Lyaeus[9] swim
Above the brim;
I drink as I would write,
In flowing measure, filled with flame and sprite.

"Still to be neat, still to be dressed"[1]

Still to be neat, still to be dressed,
As you were going to a feast;
Still to be powdered, still perfumed;
Lady, it is to be presumed,
Though art's hid causes are not found,
All is not sweet, all is not sound.

Give me a look, give me a face,
That makes simplicity a grace;
Robes loosely flowing, hair as free;
Such sweet neglect more taketh me
Than all th'adulteries of art.
They strike mine eyes, but not my heart.

7. I.e., her sensuously pleasing parts.
8. This lyric is sung by Horace, Jonson's spokesman in *Poetaster*, III.i.
9. I.e., Bacchus; the term means "deliverer from care."
1. Sung by Clerimont's page in *Epicoene, or The Silent Woman* (1609), I.i, the lyric derives from an anonymous Latin poem in the *Anthologia Latina* (sixteenth century A.D.). For a contrasting treatment of the central motif, cf. Herrick's "Delight in Disorder," p. 185.

From *The Works* (1640–1641)

"Though I am young, and cannot tell"[2]

Though I am young, and cannot tell
  Either what Death or Love is well,
Yet I have heard they both bear darts,
  And both do aim at human hearts;
And then again, I have been told
  Love wounds with heat, as Death with cold;
So that I fear they do but bring
  Extremes to touch, and mean one thing.

As in a ruin, we it call
  One thing to be blown up, or fall;
Or to our end, like way may have
  By a flash of lightning, or a wave;
So Love's inflamèd shaft, or hand;
  May kill as soon as Death's cold hand;
Except Love's fires the virtue have
  To fright the frost out of the grave.

2. This lyric is part of *The Sad Shepherd*, I.v.

Richard Corbett

1582	Born in Ewell, Surrey. Educated at Westminster School in London.
1598	Enters Broadgates Hall, in Oxford University.
1599	Transfers to Christ Church, Oxford.
1605	Receives M.A. At this time, according to Anthony à Wood, the historian of academic Oxford, "esteemed one of the most celebrated wits in the University."
1609	First English poems of substance.
1613	Preaching the Passion sermon at Christ Church, aligns himself with the Arminian (anti-Puritan) party at Oxford, led by William Laud, later Archbishop of Canterbury. From this year, associated with the circle of scholars, lawyers, and poets (including Ben Jonson) that gathered regularly at the Mermaid Tavern in London.
1616	Recommended, by virtue of his Arminian sympathies, for membership in King James I's projected college of theological controversy at Chelsea.
1619	Ben Jonson, following his return from Scotland, resides for a time with Corbett in Oxford, "writing and composing plays."
1619–1620	Undertakes a journey through the Midlands, in company with Leonard Hutten, Canon of Christ Church, and two other clerics; subsequently records the expedition in his poem *Iter Boreale*.
1620	Appointed Dean of Christ Church, through the influence of the royal favorite George Villiers, Earl of Buckingham.
1623–1624	Marries Alice Hutten, daughter of his companion on the Midlands journey. A daughter, Alice, is born in 1625; a son, Vincent in 1627.
1628	Installed as Bishop of Oxford.
1632	Appointed Bishop of Norwich.
1635	Death, 28 July. Buried in Norwich Cathedral.
1647	Publication of *Certain Elegant Poems*, edited by John Donne, son of the poet.
1648	Publication of *Poetica Stromata*.

FROM *CERTAIN ELEGANT POEMS* (1647)

A Proper New Ballad, Intituled the Fairies' Farewell, or God-a-Mercy Will: to be sung or whistled, to the tune of *The Meadow Brow* by the learned, by the unlearned to the tune of *Fortune*.[1]

Farewell, rewards and fairies,
  Good housewives now may say,
For now foul sluts in dairies
  Do fare as well as they;
And though they sweep their hearths no less
  Than maids were wont to do,
Yet who of late for cleanliness
  Finds sixpence in her shoe?

Lament, lament, old abbeys,[2]
  The fairies lost command;
They did but change priests' babies,
  But some have changed your land;
And all your children sprung from thence
  Are now grown Puritans,
Who live as changelings ever since,
  For love of your demesnes.[3]

At morning and at evening both
  You merry were and glad,
So little care of sleep or sloth
  These pretty ladies had;
When Tom came home from labor,
  Or Ciss to milking rose,
Then merrily went their tabor,[4]
  And nimbly went their toes.

Witness those rings and roundelays[5]
  Of theirs, which yet remain,

1. In his own time, Corbett's best-known poem was *Iter Boreale* ("A Northern Journey"), some 500 lines in pentameter couplets, describing a journey through the English Midlands that Corbett and three Oxford companions undertook in the long vacation of (probably) 1619. But it is "The Fairies' Farewell" for which Corbett is chiefly remembered today; not inappropriately, given Aubrey's portrait of this convivial churchman. For comments on "The Meadow Brow" and "Fortune," cf. *The Poems of Richard Corbett*, eds. J. A. W. Bennett and H. R. Trevor-Roper (Oxford, 1955), p. 129.
2. Thomas Hobbes, toward the end of *Leviathan*, remarks on the association of the fairy world and the Roman Catholic Church, but in a tone sharply contrasting with that of Corbett's poem: an extended list of parallels is capped by the observation that "as the fairies have no existence, but in the fancies of ignorant people, rising from the traditions of old wives, or old poets; so the spiritual power of the Pope, without the bounds of his own civil dominion, consisteth only in the fear that seduced people stand in, of their excommunications, upon hearing of false miracles, false traditions, and false interpretations of the Scripture" (*Leviathan*, ed. M. Oakeshott [New York, 1962], pp. 501–502).
3. Domains, estates.
4. Small drum.
5. I.e., fairy circles or rings, for dancing.

Were footed in Queen Mary's days[6]
  On many a grassy plain;
But since of late Elizabeth,
  And later James, came in,
They never danced on any heath
  As when the time hath been.

By which we note the fairies
  Were of the old profession;
Their songs were Ave Maries,
  Their dances were procession;
But now, alas, they all are dead,
  Or gone beyond the seas,
Or further from religion fled,
  Or else they take their ease.

A tell-tale in their company
  They never could endure,
And whoso kept not secretly
  Their mirth was punished sure;
It was a just and Christian deed
  To pinch such black and blue;
O, how the commonwealth doth need
  Such justices as you!

Now they have left our quarters,
  A register[7] they have,
Who can preserve their charters,
  A man both wise and grave;
A hundred of their merry pranks
  By one that I could name
Are kept in store; con[8] twenty thanks
  To William[9] for the same.

I marvel who his cloak would turn
  When Puck had led him round,
Or where those walking fires[1] would burn
  Where Cureton[2] would be found;
How Broker would appear to be,
  For whom this age doth mourn;
But that their spirits live in thee,
  In thee, old William Chourne.

6. I.e., in the reign of Mary Tudor (1553–1558), when the established religion was that of Rome.
7. Recorder.
8. Offer.
9. William Chourne was the servant of Dr. Leonard Hutten (Corbett's future father-in-law), one of the party that made the journey described in *Iter Boreale*. When the group lost its way in Charnwood Forest, "William found / A means for our deliverance: 'Turn your cloaks,' / Quoth he, 'for Puck is busy in these oaks'" (*Iter Boreale*, lines 306–308).
1. I.e., will-o'-the-wisps.
2. Cureton and Broker, presumably, were "Staffordshire worthies whose spirits Chourne could conjure up" (*Poems of Richard Corbett, ed. cit.*, p. 130).

To William Chourne of Staffordshire
Give laud and praises due,
Who every meal can mend your cheer
With tales both old and true;
To William all give audience,
And pray ye for his noddle,
For all the fairies' evidence
Were lost, if that were addle.[3]

An Elegy upon the Death of His Own Father[4]

Vincent Corbett, farther known
By Poynter's name than by his own,
Here lies engagèd till the day
Of raising bones and quickening clay.
Nor wonder, reader, that he hath
Two surnames in his epitaph,
For this one did comprehend[5]
All that two families could lend;
And if to know more arts than any
Could multiply one into many,
Here a colony lies, then,
Both of qualities and men.
Years he lived well-nigh fourscore,
But count his virtues, he lived more;
And number him by doing good,
He lived the age before the flood.
Should we undertake his story,
Truth would seem feigned, and plainness glory.
Beside, this tablet were too small:
Add too the pillars and the wall.
Yet of this volume much is found
Written in many a fertile ground,
Where the printer thee affords
Earth for paper, trees for words.
He was nature's factor[6] here,
And ledger lay[7] for every shire,
To supply the ingenious[8] wants
Of soon-sprung fruits and foreign plants.
Simple he was, and wise withal;
His purse nor base nor prodigal;
Poorer in substance than in friends,
Future and public were his ends;

3. I.e., if his head were addled or confused.
4. Cf. Jonson's "An Epitaph on Master Vincent Corbett." Why Vincent Corbett assumed the surname "Poynter" is not known.
5. I.e., for this one man encompassed.
6. Agent.
7. I.e., acted as an agent.
8. Sensible.

His conscience, like his diet, such
As neither took nor left too much,
So that made laws were useless grown
To him; he needed but his own.
Did he his neighbors bid, like those
That feast them only to enclose,[9]
Or with their roast meat rack[1] their rents,
And cozen[2] them with their consents?
No; the free meetings at his board
Did but one literal sense afford;
No close or acre understood,[3]
But only love and neighborhood.
His alms were such as Paul defines,[4]
Not causes to be saved, but signs;
Which alms, by faith, hope, love laid down,
Laid up, what now he wears, a crown.
Besides his fame, his goods, his life,
He left a grieved son and a wife;
Strange sorrow, not to be believed,
When the son and heir is grieved.
Read then, and mourn, whate'er thou art
That dost hope to have a part
In honest epitaphs, lest, being dead,
Thy life be written, and not read.

FROM *POETICA STROMATA* (1648)

Upon Fairford Windows[5]

Tell me, you anti-saints,[6] why glass
With you is longer lived than brass?
And why the saints have scaped their falls
Better from windows than from walls?
Is it because the brethren's fires
Maintain a glass-house at Blackfriars,[7]

9. I.e., to fence in or "enclose" their neighbors' arable land for the pasturage of sheep.
1. Raise unreasonably.
2. Cheat.
3. Cf. n. 9 above.
4. Cf. I Corinthians 13:3: "And though I bestow all my goods to feed the poor, and though I give my body to be burned, and have not charity, it profiteth me nothing."
5. The church of Saint Mary the Virgin in Fairford, Gloucestershire, contains twenty-eight stained-glass windows, which depict biblical scenes and were created between 1495 and 1505. Saint Mary's is the only English parish church to have retained its complete set of such medieval windows; other churches suffered in at least some degree from the excesses of Puritan zeal in the civil war. Since Corbett died in 1635, however, he is perhaps speaking of civil disorders in a sense not narrowly limited to sectarian intransigence.
6. The expression reflects Corbett's opinion of those Puritan zealots who described themselves as "saints," i.e., among the elect. Elaborately designed memorial tablets of brass, set in the floors or walls of churches, were regularly defaced by the Puritans.
7. Jonson also alludes to the glass factory near Blackfriars Church, a center of Puritan activity; cf. Jonson's "An Execration Upon Vulcan."

Next which the church stands north and south,
And east and west the preachers mouth?
Or is't because such painted ware
Resembles something what you are,
So pied,[8] so seeming, so unsound
In manners, and in doctrine, found,
That, out of emblematic wit,
You spare yourselves in sparing it?
If it be so, then, Fairford, boast
Thy church hath kept what all have lost,
And is preservèd from the bane
Of either war[9] or Puritan,
Whose life is colored in thy paint:
The inside dross, the outside saint.

The Distracted Puritan

Am I mad, oh noble Festus,[1]
When zeal and godly knowledge
Have put me in hope
To deal with the Pope,
As well as the best in the College?[2]
   Boldly I preach, hate a cross, hate a surplice,
      Miters, copes, and rochets;[3]
   Come, hear me pray nine times a day,
      And fill your heads with crotchets.

In the house of pure Emmanuel
I had my education,
Where my friends surmise
I dazzled mine eyes
With the light of revelation.
   Boldly I preach, &c.

They bound me like a bedlam,[4]
They lashed my four poor quarters;
Whilst this I endure,
Faith makes me sure
To be one of Foxe's martyrs.[5]
   Boldly I preach, &c.

8. I.e., diversely colored.
9. I.e., (perhaps), any violent civil unrest.
1. Cf. Acts 26:25–26: "Festus said . . . Paul, thou art beside thyself; much learning doth make thee mad. But he said, I am not mad, most noble Festus; but speak forth the words of truth and soberness."
2. I.e., Emmanuel College, known in Corbett's day as the most puritanically inclined of the colleges in Cambridge University.
3. Vestments (worn by Anglican bishops).
4. Lunatic (so called from the name of the London hospital for the insane, Saint Mary of Bethlehem).
5. John Foxe (1516–1587) was the author of *Actes and Monuments of these latter perilous times touching matters of the Church*, popularly known as "the Book of Martyrs"; first published (in

These injuries I suffer
Through Anti-Christ's invasions;
Take off this chain,
Neither Rome nor Spain
Can resist my strong persuasions.
  Boldly I preach, &c.

Of the beast's ten horns[6] (God bless us)
I have knocked off three already.
If they let me alone,
I'll leave him none;
But they say I am too heady.
  Boldly I preach, &c.

When I sacked the seven-hilled city,
I met the great red dragon;[7]
I kept him aloof
With the armor of proof,
Though here I have never a rag on.
  Boldly I preach, &c.

With a fiery sword and target,
There fought I with this monster;
But the sons of pride
My zeal deride,
And all my deeds misconster.
  Boldly I preach, &c.

I unhorsed the whore of Babel
With a lance of inspirations;
I made her stink,
And spill her drink
In the cup of abominations.[8]
  Boldly I preach, &c.

I have seen two in a vision,
With a flying book between them;[9]
I have been in despair
Five times a year,
And cured by reading Greenham.[1]
  Boldly I preach, &c.

Latin) at Strasbourg in 1559, the volume was printed in English in 1563. Foxe places special emphasis on the sufferings of Protestant martyrs during the reign of Mary Tudor.

6. Cf. Revelation 13:1: "And I . . . saw a beast rise up out of the sea, having seven heads and ten horns, and upon his horns ten crowns, and upon his heads the name of blasphemy." Puritan preachers commonly associated this beast with the Church of Rome, and with the Catholic nations of Europe.
7. Cf. Revelation 12:3: "And there appeared . . . a great red dragon, having seven heads and ten horns, and seven crowns upon his heads"; also Ephesians 6:11: "Put on the whole armor of God, that ye may be able to stand against the wiles of the devil."
8. Cf. Revelation 17:3–5.
9. Cf. Zechariah 5:1: "Then I turned, and lifted up mine eyes, and looked, and behold a flying roll."
1. The *Works* of Richard Greenham (c. 1535–c. 1574), Puritan divine and Fellow of Pembroke College, Cambridge, first published in 1599, had appeared in five editions by 1612.

I observed in Perkins' tables[2]
The black lines of damnation;
Those crooked veins
So stuck in my brains
That I feared my reprobation.
  Boldly I preach, &c.

In the holy tongue of Canaan[3]
I placed my chiefest pleasure;
Till I pricked my foot
With an Hebrew root,
That I bled beyond all measure.
  Boldly I preach, &c.

I appeared before the Archbishop
And all the High Commission;[4]
I gave him no grace,
But told him to's face
That he favored superstition.
  Boldly I preach, hate a cross, hate a surplice,
    Miters, copes, and rochets;
  Come, hear me pray nine times a day,
    And fill your heads with crotchets.

2. William Perkins (1558–1602), Fellow of Christ's College, Cambridge, was the most highly regarded teacher and theologian among the Puritan divines of his day. "The black lines of damnation" refer to Perkins's chart of the causes of damnation in *A Golden Chain* (1600).
3. I.e., in Hebrew.
4. The Court of High Commission was an ecclesiastical tribunal with broad powers, often exercised arbitrarily.

Lady Mary Wroth

1587 (?)	Born 18 October, eldest daughter of Sir Robert Sidney (Philip Sidney's younger brother) and Lady Barbara Gamage.
1604	Marriage to Sir Robert Wroth at Penshurst, 27 September.
1605	Takes part in Ben Jonson's *Masque of Blackness* with Queen Anne and other courtiers.
1608	Performs in the *Masque of Beauty*, Jonson's sequel to the *Masque of Blackness*.
1612	Jonson dedicates *The Alchemist* to Wroth, whom he terms "the grace, and glory of women."
1614	February brings the birth of James, her only child with Sir Robert, who dies a month later. Wroth later bore two illegitimate children to her first cousin, William Herbert, Earl of Pembroke.
1616	Wroth's son James dies, 5 July. Sir Robert Wroth died owing around £23,000, and with James's death much of the estate (though not the debt) reverted to Robert's uncle, John Wroth.
1618–1620	Probably engaged in writing *Urania*.
1621	Wroth's *The Countess of Montgomery's Urania* appears. A long prose romance that features various songs as well as the sonnet sequence *Pamphilia to Amphilanthus*, it is her only published work. Her unpublished works were a pastoral play—*Love's Victory*—and an unfinished sequel to *Urania*.
1621	Accused of slander by Edward Denny, Baron of Waltham, who complains that Wroth modeled characters in *Urania* on himself and his son-in-law, John Hay. On 15 December Wroth writes to the Duke of Buckingham, noting that "I have with all care caused the sale of them [i.e., copies of *Urania*] to be forbidden, and the books left to be shut up."
1623	Granted a warrant of protection against her creditors; she petitions for and receives additional warrants of protection in 1624, 1627, and 1628.
1651–1653	Death; no records of the exact time or place have survived.

FROM *PAMPHILIA TO AMPHILANTHUS*[1] (1621)

1

When night's black mantle could most darkness prove,[2]
And sleep, death's image, did my senses hire
From knowledge of myself, then thoughts did move
Swifter than those, most swiftness need require.
In sleep, a chariot drawn by winged desire
I saw, where sat bright Venus, Queen of Love,
And at her feet her son,[3] still adding fire
To burning hearts, which she did hold above.
But one heart flaming more than all the rest
The goddess held, and put it to my breast:
"Dear son, now shut," said she, "thus must we win."[4]
He her obeyed, and martyred my poor heart.
I, waking, hoped as dreams it would depart,
Yet since, O me, a lover I have been.

7

Song

"The spring now come at last
To trees, fields, to flowers,
And meadows makes to taste
His pride, while sad showers
Which from mine eyes do flow
Makes known with cruel pains
Cold winter yet remains;
No sign of spring we know."

"The sun which to the earth
Gives heat, light, and pleasure,
Joys in spring, hateth dearth,
Plenty makes his treasure.
His heat to me is cold,
His light all darkness is;
Since I am barred of bliss,
I heat nor light behold."

A shepherdess thus said,
Who was with grief oppressed,
For truest love betrayed,

1. The title of the sonnet sequence in *Urania*. The steadfast Pamphilia (All-loving) is the heroine of the romance. Her inconstant beloved, Amphilanthus (Lover of two), brings her heartache. He is also her first cousin. We follow the numbering in Josephine Roberts's edition.
2. Establish.
3. Cupid (Eros).
4. I.e., now enclose (her flaming heart) in her breast; that's the way we prevail.

Barred from her quiet rest.
And weeping thus said she,
"My end approaching near
Now willow[5] must I wear,
My fortune so will be."

"With branches of this tree
I'll dress my hapless head,
Which shall my witness be,
My hopes in love are dead:
My clothes embroidered all
Shall be with garlands round:
Some scattered, others bound;
Some tied, some like to fall."

"The bark my book shall be
Where daily I will write
This tale of hapless me,
True slave to Fortune's spite.
The root shall be my bed
Where nightly I will lie
Wailing inconstancy,
Since all true love is dead."

"And these lines I will leave,
If some such lover come
Who may them right conceive,
And place them on my tomb:
'She who still[6] constant loved,
Now dead with cruel care,
Killed with unkind despair
And change, her end here proved.'"[7]

16

Am I thus conquered? Have I lost the powers
That to withstand, which joys to ruin me?
Must I be still, while it my strength devours,
And captive leads me prisoner, bound, unfree?
Love first shall leave men's fancies to them free,[8]
Desire shall quench love's flames, spring hate sweet showers,
Love shall loose all his darts, have sight, and see
His shame and wishings hinder happy hours.
Why should we not Love's purblind[9] charms resist?

5. Willow signifies forsaken love.
6. Always.
7. Experienced.
8. I.e., before I am thus conquered, Love will stop affecting human imaginations (and other impossibilities will follow).
9. Entirely blind.

Must we be servile, doing what he list?[1]
No, seek some host to harbor thee: I fly
Thy babish tricks, and freedom do profess;
But O, my hurt makes my lost heart confess:
I love, and must; so farewell liberty.

24

When last I saw thee, I did not thee see:
It was thine image, which in my thoughts lay
So lively figured, as no time's delay
Could suffer me in heart to parted be,[2]
And sleep so favorable is to me,
As not to let thy loved remembrance stray,
Lest that I waking might have cause to say
There was one minute found to forget thee.
Then since my faith is such, so kind my sleep
That gladly thee presents unto my thought,
And still true lover-like thy face doth keep
So as some pleasure shadow-like is wrought.
Pity my loving, nay of conscience give
Reward to me in whom thy self doth live.

25

Like to the Indians scorched with the sun,
The sun which they do as their God adore:
So am I used by Love, for ever more
I worship him, less favors have I won.
Better are they who thus to blackness run,
And so can only whiteness' want[3] deplore
Than I who pale and white am with grief's store,
Nor can have hope, but to see hopes undone.
Besides their sacrifice received in sight
Of their chose saint,[4] mine hid as worthless rite;
Grant me to see where I my offerings give.
Then let me wear the mark of Cupid's might
In heart, as they in skin[5] of Phoebus'[6] light,
Not ceasing offerings to Love while I live.

1. Doing what he demands.
2. I.e., as if in my heart I could endure no period of separation from you.
3. I.e., lack of white color.
4. I.e., their sacrifice (of whiteness) occurs in sight of the sun.
5. Black skin signifies Apollo's favor in Jonson's *Masque of Blackness* (1606), a court entertainment in which Wroth participated: the river god Niger observes that in his daughters' "firm hues," Apollo "draws signs of his fervent'st love."
6. Apollo, god of the sun.

26

When everyone to pleasing pastime hies,[7]
Some hunt, some hawk, some play, while some delight
In sweet discourse, and music shows joy's might;
Yet I my thoughts do far above these prize.
The joy which I take is that free from eyes
I sit and wonder at this day-like night,
So to dispose themselves as void of right,[8]
And leave true pleasure for poor vanities.
When others hunt, my thoughts I have in chase;
If hawk, my mind at wishèd end doth fly;
Discourse, I with my spirit talk; and cry
While others music choose as greatest grace.
"O God," say I, "can these fond pleasures move,
Or music be but in sweet thoughts of love?"

39

Take heed mine eyes, how you your looks do cast,
Lest they betray my heart's most secret thought:
Be true unto yourselves; for nothing's bought
More dear than doubt, which brings a lover's fast.
Catch you all watching eyes ere they be past,
Or take yours fixed where your best love hath sought
The pride of your desires; let them be taught
Their faults for shame they could no truer last.
Then look, and look with joy, for conquest won,
Of those that searched your hurt in double kind;
So you kept safe, let them themselves look blind,
Watch, gaze, and mark till they to madness run,
While you, mine eyes, enjoy full sight of love,
Contented that such happinesses move.

40

False hope, which feeds but to destroy and spill[9]
What it first breeds; unnatural to the birth
Of thine own womb, conceiving but to kill,
And plenty gives to make the greater dearth.
So tyrants do who, falsely ruling earth,
Outwardly grace them,[1] and with profits fill,
Advance those who appointed are to death,
To make their greater fall to please their will.

7. Goes quickly.
8. I.e., to put those pleasures in their proper place, without a compelling claim.
9. Kill.
1. Those whom they intend to have killed.

Thus shadow they their wicked vile intent,
Coloring evil with a show of good
While in fair shows their malice so is spent;[2]
Hope kills the heart, and tyrants shed the blood.
For hope deluding brings us to the pride[3]
Of our desires, the farther down to slide.

68

My pain, still smothered in my grievèd breast,
Seeks for some ease, yet cannot passage find
To be discharged of this unwelcome guest;
When most I strive, more fast his burdens bind.
Like to a ship on Goodwins[4] cast by wind—
The more she strives, more deep in sand is pressed,
Till she be lost—so am I, in this kind,
Sunk, and devoured, and swallowed by unrest,
Lost, shipwrecked, spoiled, debarred of smallest hope;
Nothing of pleasure left, save[5] thoughts have scope,
Which wander may. Go then, my thoughts, and cry
Hope's perished, love tempest-beaten, joy lost.
Killing despair hath all these blessings crossed,
Yet faith still cries, love will not falsify.

74

Song

Love,[6] a child, is ever crying;
Please him, and he straight[7] is flying;
Give him, he the more is craving,
Never satisfied with having.

His desires have no measure;
Endless folly is his treasure;
What he promiseth he breaketh;
Trust not one word that he speaketh.

He vows nothing but false matter,
And to cozen[8] you he'll flatter;
Let him gain the hand,[9] he'll leave you,
And still glory to deceive you.

2. I.e., with shows of favor, they thus apply their malice.
3. Highest pitch.
4. The "Goodwins" are sandbars off the coast of Kent. After running aground on them, sailing ships would work deeper into the sand while striving to come off.
5. Except that.
6. Cupid, god of erotic love, is conventionally depicted as a winged child.
7. Immediately.
8. Cheat.
9. Take control.

He will triumph in your wailing,
  And yet be cause of your failing;
  These his virtues are, and slighter
  Are his gifts, his favors lighter;

Feathers are as firm in staying;
  Wolves no fiercer in their preying.
  As a child then leave him crying,
  Nor seek him so giv'n to flying.

77

In this strange labyrinth how shall I turn?[1]
  Ways are on all sides, while the way I miss:
  If to the right hand, there in love I burn;
  Let me go forward, therein danger is;
If to the left, suspicion hinders bliss;
  Let me turn back, shame cries I ought return,
  Nor faint, though crosses with my fortune kiss;[2]
  Stand still is harder, although sure to mourn.
Thus let me take the right, or left hand way,
  Go forward, or stand still, or back retire:
  I must these doubts endure without allay[3]
  Or help, but travail find for my best hire.[4]
Yet that which most my troubled sense doth move,
Is to leave all, and take the thread of love.[5]

90

Except[6] my heart, which you bestowed before,
  And for a sign of conquest gave away
  As worthless to be kept in your choice store,[7]
  Yet one more spotless with you doth not stay.
The tribute which my heart doth truly pay
  Is faith untouched; pure thoughts discharge the score
  Of[8] debts for me where Constancy bears sway,
  And rules as lord, unharmed by envy's sore.
Yet other mischiefs fail not to attend,
  As enemies to you, my foes must be:[9]

1. This is the first sonnet in a series of fourteen, *A Crown of Sonnets Dedicated to Love*. Italian in origin, the crown (*corona*) forms a discrete circular structure within the larger sonnet sequence. Each sonnet opens with the line that concludes the previous one.
2. I.e., nor falter, though adversities intersect my path.
3. Abatement.
4. I.e., receive toil as my best recompense. "Travail" meant "travel" as well as "toil."
5. An allusion to the legend of Theseus, who escaped from King Minos's labyrinth by following the thread given him by the devoted Ariadne.
6. In the seventeenth century, "except" sometimes meant "accept" or "receive."
7. I.e., unworthy to be kept in your most excellent collection.
8. *discharge the score / Of*: requite.
9. Though they (the forces of jealousy) "attend" (wait upon) her, they are enemies to her love and she regards them as foes.

Curst[1] jealousy doth all her forces bend
To my undoing; thus my harms I see.
So though in love I fervently do burn,
In this strange labyrinth how shall I turn?[2]

94

Song

Lovers learn to speak but[3] truth;
Swear not, and your oaths forgo;
Give your age a constant youth;
Vow no more than what you'll do.

Think it sacrilege to break
What you promise shall in love,
And in tears what you do speak,
Forget not when ends you prove.[4]

Do not think it glory is
To entice, and then deceive;
Your chief honors lie in this:
By worth what won is,[5] not to leave.

'Tis not for your fame to try
What we weak not oft refuse;
In our bounty[6] our faults lie
When you to do a fault will choose.

Fie, leave this, a greater gain
'Tis to keep when you have won
Than what purchased is with pain
Soon after all in scorn to shun.

For if worthless to be prized
Why at first will you it move,
And if worthy, why despised?
You cannot swear, and lie, and love.

Love alas you cannot like,
'Tis but for a fashion[7] moved,
None can choose and then dislike
Unless it be by falsehood proved.

1. Malignant.
2. The sonnet's final line repeats the first line of sonnet 77, thus completing the circular structure that contains the labyrinth.
3. Only.
4. I.e., when you are put to the test of action.
5. I.e., what you win by merit.
6. Generosity.
7. I.e., for the sake of appearance.

But your choice is, and your love,
How most number to deceive,
As if honor's claim did move
Like Popish law,[8] none safe to leave.

Fly this folly and return
Unto truth in love, and try;[9]
None but martyrs happy burn,
More shameful ends have they that lie.

99

Like to huge clouds of smoke which well may hide
The face of fairest day, though for a while,
So wrong may shadow me, till truth do smile,
And justice, sun-like, hath those vapors tied.
O doting Time, canst thou for shame let slide
So many minutes, while ills do beguile
Thy age and worth, and falsehoods thus defile
Thy ancient good, where now but crosses[1] bide?
Look but once up, and leave thy toiling pace,
And on my miseries thy dim eye place;
Go not so fast, but give my care some end;
Turn not thy glass, alas, unto my ill,
Since thou with sand it canst not so far fill,
But to each one my sorrows will extend.

103

My Muse, now happy, lay thyself to rest;
Sleep in the quiet of a faithful love;
Write you no more, but let the fancies move
Some other hearts; wake not to new unrest.
But if you study, be those thoughts addressed
To truth, which shall eternal goodness prove,[2]
Enjoying of true joy, the most and best,
The endless gain which never will remove.
Leave the discourse of Venus and her son
To young beginners, and their brains inspire
With stories of great love, and from that fire
Get heat to write the fortunes they have won.
And thus leave off; what's past shows you can love,
Now let your constancy your honor prove.

8. Law of the Roman Catholic Church.
9. Trial.
1. Afflictions. Time used to be benevolent; now it brings difficulties.
2. Establish, verify.

FROM *THE COUNTESS OF MONTGOMERY'S URANIA* (1621)

Song[3]

Love, what art thou? A vain thought
In our minds by fancy wrought.
Idle smiles did thee beget,
While fond wishes made the net
Which so many fools have caught.

Love what art thou? Light and fair,
Fresh as morning, clear as th' air.
But too soon thy evening change
Makes thy worth with coldness range;
Still[4] thy joy is mixed with care.

Love what art thou? A sweet flower
Once full blown,[5] dead in an hour.
Dust in wind as staid remains
As thy pleasure or our gains,
If thy humor changes to lour.[6]

Love what art thou? Childish, vain,
Firm as bubbles made by rain,
Wantonness thy greatest pride.
These foul faults thy virtue hide,
But babes can no staidness gain.

Love what art thou? Causeless cursed,[7]
Yet alas these not the worst.
Much more of thee may be said,
But thy law I once obeyed,
Therefore say no more at first.

3. This shepherd's song appears with others at the close of *Urania*'s first book.
4. Always.
5. In full bloom.
6. I.e., the pleasure of love and lovers' achievements are as stable (staid) as dust in the wind, if love's mood (humor) becomes threatening (lours).
7. Wantonly wicked.

Robert Herrick

1591	Born in London, the fourth son of Nicholas Herrick, a well-to-do London goldsmith.
1592	Nicholas Herrick dies, after a fall from the fourth floor of his house in Goldsmith's Row; although suicide is suspected, his estate goes to his wife Julian and her children, in accordance with the terms of the will. Details of Robert Herrick's early education are unknown.
1607	Apprenticed, for the customary term of ten years, to his uncle, the eminently successful goldsmith Sir William Herrick, who had been knighted in 1605.
1613	Enters Saint John's College, Cambridge, as a fellow commoner (i.e., a relatively affluent student).
1615–1616	Transfers to Trinity Hall; graduates B.A. in 1617.
1620	Receives M.A. Consorts in the early 1620s with Ben Jonson and the group meeting regularly at the Devil Tavern in London.
1623	Ordained deacon, 24 April; and with exceptional dispatch, ordained priest on the next day by the Bishop of Peterborough. Presumably residing in London, perhaps employed as a nobleman's chaplain, for some three or four years.
1625	Richard James, in a poem, "The Muses' Dirge," on the death of James I, links Herrick's name to those of (the established poets) Jonson and Drayton.
1627	As chaplain to the Duke of Buckingham, takes part in the unsuccessful military expedition led by that lord against the Île de Ré.
1629	Appointed Vicar of Dean Prior in Devonshire; installed on 29 October 1630.
1633–1634	First published poems: "Upon His Kinswoman Mistress Elizabeth Herrick," in John Stow's *Survey of London* (1633), and an early version of "Oberon's Feast," in *A Description of the King and Queene of Fayries* . . . (1634).
1640	Probably in London; an entry in the Stationers' Register alludes to a forthcoming volume of "Poems written by Master Robert Herrick" (not known to have been published).
1647	Expelled, as a royalist sympathizer, from his vicarage at Dean Prior; returns to London.
1648	Publication of *Hesperides*. Apparently resident in and about Westminster, until the Restoration.
1660	Returns to his Devonshire parish.
1674	Death; buried on 15 October, presumably in the churchyard at Dean Prior (no stone marks his grave).

Robert Herrick

[illegible]

FROM *HESPERIDES*[1] (1648)

The Argument[2] of His Book

I sing of brooks, of blossoms, birds, and bowers;
Of April, May, of June, and July flowers.
I sing of Maypoles, hock-carts,[3] wassails,[4] wakes,
Of bridegrooms, brides, and of their bridal cakes.
I write of youth, of love, and have access
By these to sing of cleanly wantonness.
I sing of dews, of rains, and piece by piece
Of balm, of oil, of spice, and ambergris.[5]
I sing of times trans-shifting,[6] and I write
How roses first came red, and lilies white.[7]
I write of groves, of twilights, and I sing
The court of Mab, and of the fairy king.[8]
I write of hell; I sing (and ever shall)
Of heaven, and hope to have it after all.

When He Would Have His Verses Read

In sober mornings, do not thou rehearse[9]
The holy incantation of a verse;
But when that men have both well drunk and fed,
Let my enchantments then be sung, or read.
When laurel spirts i'th'fire, and when the hearth
Smiles to itself, and gilds the roof with mirth;
When up the thyrse[1] is raised, and when the sound

1. The Hesperides, daughters of Night (or, by another tradition, of Atlas and Hesperis), guarded an orchard in the west, "across the fabulous stream of the Ocean," in which was planted a tree with golden apples, originally presented by Earth to Hera (Juno) at her marriage to Zeus: cf. Hesiod, *Theogony*, 215–216; Diodorus Siculus, IV.xxvii.2. Herrick's title indicates that his poems also are golden apples from a western garden, i.e., Devonshire, where many of these verses were made.
2. Theme, subject matter. Herrick's art was, for the most part, undervalued or dismissed until the early years of the nineteenth century; Edward Phillips, for instance, observed in 1675, "That which is chiefly pleasant in these poems is now and then a pretty flowery and pastoral gale of fancy, a vernal prospect of some hill, cave, rock, or fountain; which but for the interruption of other trivial passages might have made up none of the worst poetic landscapes" ("The Modern Poets," in *Theatrum Poetarum*, p. 162). In fact, as this first poem indicates, Herrick is concerned not merely with the charm and (often rude) vitality of nature, or with the sensuous thrust of human desire, but (and more deeply) with the causes and origins of things, the reality behind appearances. The forms and modes of classical verse are evidently congenial to Herrick, in some ways the closest to Jonson of all the "Sons of Ben"; as a churchman, he regularly draws into his verse the ceremonies of the Christian year; at the same time, he is fascinated by the timeless realm of myth and legend reflected in the folklore of the English countryside. The arrangement of the 1,100-odd poems in *Hesperides*, finally, appears in some degree to reflect Herrick's conscious design.
3. I.e., wagons bringing in the last load of the harvest. Cf. "The Hock-Cart," p. 197.
4. I.e., the drinking of healths on festive occasions.
5. A waxy substance used in perfumes.
6. I.e., (1) the transience of history; (2) the interrelated aspects and attributes of time.
7. Cf. "How Lilies Came White," p. 191, "How Roses Came Red," p. 198, and "How Violets Came Blue," p. 199.
8. Oberon and Mab are king and queen of the fairies.
9. Repeat, recite.
1. "A javelin twined with ivy" (Herrick's note); i.e., a symbol of Bacchus, god of revelry and wine.

Of sacred orgies[2] flies—a round, a round![3]
When the rose reigns,[4] and locks with ointments shine,
Let rigid Cato[5] read these lines of mine.

To Perilla

Ah my Perilla! dost thou grieve to see
Me, day by day, to steal away from thee?
Age calls me hence, and my gray hairs bid come,
And haste away to mine eternal home;
'Twill not be long, Perilla, after this,
That I must give thee the supremest kiss;
Dead when I am, first cast in salt, and bring
Part of the cream from that religious spring,[6]
With which, Perilla, wash my hands and feet;
That done, then wind me in that very sheet
Which wrapped thy smooth limbs, when thou didst implore
The gods' protection but the night before.
Follow me weeping to my turf, and there
Let fall a primrose, and with it a tear;
Then lastly, let some weekly strewings[7] be
Devoted to the memory of me;
Then shall my ghost not walk about, but keep
Still in the cool and silent shades of sleep.

No Loathsomeness in Love[8]

What I fancy, I approve,
No dislike there is in love:
Be my mistress short or tall,
And distorted therewithal;
Be she likewise one of those
That an acre hath of nose;
Be her forehead and her eyes
Full of incongruities;
Be her cheeks so shallow, too
As to show her tongue wag through;
Be her lips ill hung, or set,

2. "Songs to Bacchus" (Herrick's note).
3. Rounds are songs for three or more singers, in which the voices enter in succession with the same music and words, sing through the entire song, and return to the first phrase.
4. On Herrick's employment of flower imagery in the context of pagan ceremonies, cf. K. Wentersdorf, "Herrick's Floral Imagery," *Studia Neophilologica (SN)*, XXXVI (1964), 69–81.
5. Cato the Censor (234–149 B.C.) was an especially severe Roman administrator.
6. I.e., your eyes, from which salt tears flow. The sprinkling of salt is, ultimately, an echo of Roman ritual; in his poetry, Herrick regularly draws together elements from classical and Christian ceremony: cf. R. H. Deming, "Robert Herrick's Classical Ceremony," *ELH*, XXXIV (1967), 327–348.
7. I.e., strewings of flowers on my grave.
8. The poem in ironic praise of an ugly woman is something of a convention in the period; "The Deformed Mistress," by Sir John Suckling, and "Upon A Very Deformed Gentlewoman," by Thomas Randolph, illustrate the genre, which Donne's "The Autumnal," p. 47, may be said to transcend.

And her grinders[9] black as jet;
Has she thin hair, hath she none,
She's to me a paragon.

Upon the Loss of His Mistresses[1]

I have lost, and lately, these
Many dainty mistresses:
Stately Julia, prime of all;
Sappho next, a principal;
Smooth Anthea, for a skin
White, and heaven-like crystalline;
Sweet Electra, and the choice
Myrrha, for the lute, and voice;
Next, Corinna, for her wit,
And the graceful use of it;
With Perilla: all are gone;
Only Herrick's left alone,
For to number sorrow by
Their departures hence, and die.

The Vine

I dreamed this mortal part of mine
Was metamorphosed to a vine,
Which crawling one and every way
Enthralled my dainty Lucia.
Methought her long small legs and thighs
I with my tendrils did surprise;
Her belly, buttocks, and her waist
By my soft nervelets[2] were embraced;
About her head I writhing hung,
And with rich clusters, hid among
The leaves, her temples I behung,
So that my Lucia seemed to me
Young Bacchus ravished by his tree.[3]
My curls about her neck did crawl,
And arms and hands they did enthrall,
So that she could not freely stir,
All parts there made one prisoner.
But when I crept with leaves to hide
Those parts which maids keep unespied,
Such fleeting pleasures there I took
That with the fancy I awoke,

9. Teeth.
1. It is generally accepted that Herrick's Julia, Anthea, Electra, Dianeme, etc. are imaginative creations.
2. Tendrils.
3. I.e., by the grapevine.

And found (ah me!) this flesh of mine
More like a stock[4] than like a vine.

Discontents in Devon

More discontents I never had
  Since I was born, than here;
Where I have been, and still am sad,
  In this dull Devonshire;
Yet justly too I must confess,
  I ne'er invented such
Ennobled numbers[5] for the press
  Than where I loathed so much.

Cherry-Ripe

"Cherry-ripe, ripe, ripe," I cry,
"Full and fair ones; come and buy."[6]
If so be you ask me where
They do grow, I answer, "There,
Where my Julia's lips do smile;
There's the land, or cherry-isle,
Whose plantations fully show
All the year where cherries grow."

His Request to Julia

Julia, if I chance to die
Ere I print my poetry,
I most humbly thee desire
To commit it to the fire;
Better 'twere my book were dead
Than to live not perfected.

Dreams

Here we are all, by day; by night, we're hurled
By dreams, each one, into a sev'ral[7] world.

4. "Hardened stalk or stem of a plant" (*OED*).
5. Verses. *His Noble Numbers*. Herrick's collected religious verse, was published in 1648 (together with *Hesperides*), the year following the poet's expulsion from his vicarage in Dean Prior, Devonshire.
6. The street vendors of London cried their wares in such terms as these.
7. I.e., separate and distinctly individual. Plutarch reports the view of Heraclitus that "men while awake are in one common world; but asleep, each man has a world to himself" (*De Superstitione*, iii).

To the King, Upon His Coming with His Army into the West[8]

Welcome, most welcome to our vows and us,
Most great and universal Genius![9]
The drooping west, which hitherto has stood
As one in long-lamented widowhood,
Looks like a bride now, or a bed of flowers,
Newly refreshed both by the sun and showers.
War, which before was horrid,[1] now appears
Lovely in you, brave prince of cavaliers!
A deal[2] of courage in each bosom springs
By your access, O you the best of kings!
Ride on with all white[3] omens, so that where
Your standard's up, we fix a conquest there.

Delight in Disorder[4]

A sweet disorder in the dress
Kindles in clothes a wantonness:[5]
A lawn[6] about the shoulders thrown
Into a fine distraction;[7]
An erring lace, which here and there
Enthralls the crimson stomacher;[8]
A cuff neglectful, and thereby
Ribbons to flow confusedly;
A winning wave (deserving note)
In the tempestuous petticoat;
A careless shoestring, in whose tie
I see a wild civility:
Do more bewitch me than when art
Is too precise in every part.

Dean-bourn, a Rude River in Devon, By Which Sometimes He Lived

Dean-bourn, farewell; I never look to see
Dean, or thy warty incivility.

8. Charles I came to Exeter in the summer of 1644, before marching on into Cornwall.
9. Cf. Jonson, *The Forest*, XIV, line 20n, p. 118. Herrick identifies Charles I as the guardian spirit of all England.
1. I.e., hideous to behold.
2. I.e., a great amount.
3. I.e., auspicious. Cf. Jonson, Epigram XCVI, line 8n, p. 88.
4. Cf. Jonson's "Still to be neat," p. 154.
5. I.e., an unfettered gaiety (with the secondary sense of "unruliness").
6. I.e., a scarf of fine linen.
7. Confusion.
8. I.e., an ornamental item of dress worn under the lacings of the bodice.

Thy rocky bottom, that doth tear thy streams,
And makes them frantic, ev'n to all extremes,
To my content I never should behold,
Were thy streams silver, or thy rocks all gold.
Rocky thou art, and rocky we discover
Thy men, and rocky are thy walls all over.
O men, O manners;[9] now and ever known
To be a rocky generation![1]
A people currish, churlish as the seas,
And rude, almost, as rudest savages,
With whom I did, and may re-sojourn, when
Rocks turn to rivers, rivers turn to men.

The Definition of Beauty

Beauty no other thing is than a beam
Flashed out between the middle and extreme.

To Anthea Lying in Bed[2]

So looks Anthea, when in bed she lies
O'ercome or half betrayed by tiffanies,[3]
Like to a twilight, or that simp'ring dawn
That roses show when misted o'er with lawn.[4]
Twilight is yet, till that her lawns give way;
Which done, that dawn turns then to perfect day.

Upon Scobble. Epigram[5]

Scobble for whoredom whips his wife, and cries
He'll slit her nose. But, blubb'ring, she replies,
"Good sir, make no more cuts i'th'outward skin;
One slit's enough to let adult'ry in."

9. The expression echoes Cicero's phrase, *O tempora, O mores*, in the *First Oration Against Catiline*.
1. Cf. Jeremiah 5:31: "they have made their faces harder than a rock"; also Robert Burton's description of "those ordinary boors and peasants" as "a rude, brutish, uncivil, wild, a currish generation" (*Anatomy of Melancholy*, ed. H. Jackson, 3 vols. [London, 1964], II, p. 343). Echoes of Burton's work (published in 1621) often sound in *Hesperides*.
2. Cf. "Upon Electra," p. 206, for a contrasting view of clothed and unclothed beauty. "Delight in Disorder," p. 185, "Julia's Petticoat," p. 189, and "Upon Julia's Clothes," p. 214, also touch on this theme.
3. I.e., by fine silks or muslins.
4. I.e., with fine linen.
5. The harsh realism of these lines (not to mention their compressed precision) recalls Jonson's Epigram LXXXIII, p. 87. Herrick seems deliberately to have interspersed such coarse epigrammatic reflections on individual members of his country parish with the delicately charming fancies more often singled out as typical of his art.

The Hourglass[6]

That hourglass which there ye see
With water filled (sirs, credit me),
The humor[7] was, as I have read,
But lovers' tears encrystallèd,
Which, as they drop by drop do pass
From th'upper to the under-glass,
Do in a trickling manner tell,
By many a wat'ry syllable,
That lovers' tears in lifetime shed
Do restless run when they are dead.

His Farewell to Sack

Farewell thou thing, time-past so known, so dear
To me, as blood to life and spirit;[8] near,
Nay, though more near than kindred, friend, man, wife,
Male to the female, soul to body, life
To quick action, or the warm soft side
Of the resigning, yet resisting bride.
The kiss of virgins, first-fruits of the bed,
Soft speech, smooth touch, the lips, the maidenhead:
These, and a thousand sweets, could never be
So near, or dear, as thou wast once to me.
O thou the drink of gods, and angels! Wine
That scatter'st spirit and lust,[9] whose purest shine
More radiant than the summer's sunbeams shows;
Each way illustrious, brave;[1] and like to those
Comets we see by night, whose shagged[2] portents
Foretell the coming of some dire events;
Or some full flame, which with a pride aspires,[3]
Throwing about his wild and active fires.
'Tis thou, above nectar, O divinest soul!
Eternal in thyself, that canst control
That which subverts whole nature, grief and care,
Vexation of the mind, and damned despair.
'Tis thou alone who, with thy mystic fan,[4]
Work'st more than wisdom, art, or nature can
To rouse the sacred madness, and awake
The frost-bound blood spirits; and to make

6. Cf. Jonson, "The Hourglass," p. 132.
7. Moisture.
8. I.e., as blood is to "vital spirit" (a substance, thought to be formed in the heart, that brings natural heat to every part of the body) and to "animal spirit" (a more refined substance, formed in the brain, that flows through the nerves).
9. I.e., that distributes animal spirit and vital spirit throughout the body.
1. Magnificent.
2. Hairy(-tailed).
3. I.e., which rises in splendor.
4. I.e., the thyrsus of Bacchus (figured here as a winnowing fan for grain).

Them frantic with thy raptures, flashing through
The soul like lightning, and as active too.
'Tis not Apollo can, or those thrice three
Castalian sisters,[5] sing, if wanting thee.
Horace, Anacreon,[6] both had lost their fame,
Hadst thou not filled them with thy fire and flame.
Phoebean splendor! and thou Thespian spring![7]
Of which sweet swans[8] must drink before they sing
Their true-paced numbers and their holy lays,
Which makes them worthy cedar,[9] and the bays.
But why, why longer do I gaze upon
Thee with the eye of admiration?
Since I must leave thee, and enforced, must say
To all thy witching beauties, "Go, away."
But if thy whimp'ring looks do ask me why,
Then know that Nature bids thee go, not I.
'Tis her erroneous self has made a brain
Uncapable of such a sovereign
As is thy powerful self. Prithee not smile;
Or smile more inly, lest thy looks beguile
My vows denounced[1] in zeal, which thus much show thee,
That I have sworn but by thy looks to know thee.
Let others drink thee freely, and desire
Thee and their lips espoused; while I admire
And love thee, but not taste thee. Let my Muse
Fail of thy former helps, and only use
Her inadult'rate[2] strength: what's done by me
Hereafter shall smell of the lamp, not thee.

To Dianeme

Sweet, be not proud of those two eyes
Which, star-like, sparkle in their skies;
Nor be you proud that you can see
All hearts your captives, yours yet free;
Be you not proud of that rich hair
Which wantons with the love-sick air;
Whenas that ruby which you wear,
Sunk from the tip of your soft ear,
Will last to be a precious stone,
When all your world of beauty's gone.

5. I.e., the Muses, who frequented the Castalian spring, sacred to Phoebus Apollo, god of poetry and song.
6. Cf. Jonson, Epigrams XCI (note 2 on p. 87) and CI (line 30n, p. 89).
7. Cf. Jonson, Epigrams CI, line 33n, p. 90.
8. I.e., poets.
9. Oil of cedar was used to preserve ancient manuscripts.
1. Proclaimed.
2. Pure, not debased.

Julia's Petticoat

Thy azure robe I did behold,
As airy as the leaves of gold,[3]
Which erring here, and wand'ring there,
Pleased with transgression ev'rywhere.
Sometimes 'twould pant, and sigh, and heave,
As if to stir it scarce had leave;
But having got it, thereupon
'Twould make a brave expansion,
And pounced[4] with stars, it showed to me
Like a celestial canopy.
Sometimes 'twould blaze, and then abate,
Like to a flame grown moderate;
Sometimes away 'twould wildly fling,
Then to thy thighs so closely cling
That some conceit[5] did melt me down,
As lovers fall into a swoon,
And all confused I there did lie
Drowned in delights, but could not die.
That leading cloud[6] I followed still,
Hoping t'have seen of it my fill,
But ah! I could not; should it move
To life eternal, I could love.

Corinna's Going A-Maying

Get up, get up for shame; the blooming morn
Upon her wings presents the god unshorn.[7]
  See how Aurora[8] throws her fair
  Fresh-quilted colors through the air:
  Get up, sweet slug-a-bed, and see
  The dew bespangling herb and tree.
Each flower has wept, and bowed toward the east,
Above an hour since; yet you not dressed,
  Nay! not so much as out of bed?
  When all the birds have matins said,
  And sung their thankful hymns, 'tis sin,
  Nay, profanation to keep in,
Whenas a thousand virgins on this day
Spring, sooner than the lark, to fetch in May.[9]

3. I.e. (probably), the decorative golden leaves on Julia's blue gown.
4. Powdered.
5. Fancy.
6. Cf. Exodus 13:21: "And the Lord went before them by day in a pillar of a cloud to lead them the way."
7. I.e., Phoebus Apollo, god of the sun (whose long hair conventionally figures the sun's rays, as well as youthful vitality).
8. Goddess of the dawn.
9. I.e., to gather the white hawthorn flowers (and so to celebrate the coming of full spring).

Rise, and put on your foliage, and be seen
To come forth, like the springtime, fresh and green,
And sweet as Flora.[1] Take no care
For jewels for your gown or hair:
Fear not; the leaves will strew
Gems in abundance upon you;
Besides, the childhood of the day has kept,
Against[2] you come, some orient[3] pearls unwept;
Come, and receive them while the light
Hangs on the dew-locks of the night,
And Titan[4] on the eastern hill
Retires himself, or else stands still
Till you come forth. Wash, dress, be brief in praying:
Few beads[5] are best when once we go a-Maying.

Come, my Corinna, come; and coming, mark
How each field turns a street, each street a park
Made green, and trimmed with trees; see how
Devotion gives each house a bough
Or branch; each porch, each door, ere this,
An ark, a tabernacle is,[6]
Made up of white-thorn neatly interwove,
As if here were those cooler shades of love.
Can such delights be in the street
And open fields, and we not see't?
Come, we'll abroad; and let's obey
The proclamation made for May,[7]
And sin no more, as we have done, by staying;
But my Corinna, come, let's go a-Maying.

There's not a budding boy or girl this day
But is got up, and gone to bring in May.
A deal[8] of youth, ere this, is come
Back, and with white-thorn laden home.
Some have dispatched their cakes and cream,
Before that we have left to dream;
And some have wept, and wooed, and plighted troth,
And chose their priest, ere we can cast off sloth.
Many a green-gown[9] has been given;
Many a kiss, both odd and even;
Many a glance too has been sent
From out the eye, love's firmament;

1. Roman goddess of flowers and spring.
2. Until.
3. Lustrous (also, "eastern").
4. I.e., the sun.
5. I.e., prayers (with an allusion to the beads of a rosary).
6. I.e., each porch and door is thus transformed and made holy. For the Hebraic "Ark of the Covenant" and "Tabernacle," cf. Exodus 37, 40. Herrick combines the religious ceremonies of Holy Scripture with those of a religion of nature.
7. I.e., a proclamation authorizing Mayday festivities.
8. I.e., a great number.
9. I.e., a dress stained with green, from rolling in the grass.

Many a jest told of the keys betraying
This night, and locks picked, yet we're not a-Maying.

Come, let us go, while we are in our prime,
And take the harmless folly of the time.
We shall grow old apace, and die
Before we know our liberty.
Our life is short; and our days run
As fast away as does the sun;
And as a vapor, or a drop of rain
Once lost, can ne'er be found again,
So when or you or I are made
A fable, song, or fleeting shade,
All love, all liking, all delight
Lies drowned with us in endless night.
Then while time serves, and we are but decaying,
Come, my Corinna, come, let's go a-Maying.[1]

How Lilies Came White

White though ye be, yet, lilies, know
From the first ye were not so;
But I'll tell ye
What befell ye:
Cupid and his mother lay
In a cloud, while both did play;
He with his pretty finger pressed
The ruby niplet of her breast,
Out of the which, the cream of light,
Like to a dew,
Fell down on you,
And made ye white.

Upon Some Women

Thou who wilt not love, do this:
Learn of me what woman is.
Something made of thread and thrum,[2]
A mere botch of all and some.
Pieces, patches, ropes of hair;
Inlaid garbage ev'rywhere.
Outside silk and outside lawn;
Scenes[3] to cheat us, neatly drawn.
False in legs, and false in thighs,

1. Classical expressions of the theme informing Herrick's poem include Catullus, *Odes*, v, and Ovid, *Fasti*, VI.771. In Holy Scripture, it is the ungodly who cling to the thought of carpe diem: cf. Proverbs 7:18, and (in the Apocrypha) the Wisdom of Solomon, 2:1–8.
2. I.e., bits and pieces of yarn.
3. Veils.

False in breast, teeth, hair, and eyes,
False in head, and false enough;
Only true in shreds and stuff.

The Welcome to Sack

So soft streams meet, so springs with gladder smiles
Meet after long divorcement by the isles,
When love, the child of likeness, urgeth on
Their crystal natures to an union;
So meet stol'n kisses, when the moony nights
Call forth fierce lovers to their wished delights;
So kings and queens meet, when desire convinces[4]
All thoughts but such as aim at getting princes:
As I meet thee. Soul of my life and fame!
Eternal lamp of love! whose radiant flame
Outglares the heav'n's Osiris,[5] and thy gleams
Outshine the splendor of his mid-day beams.
Welcome, O welcome, my illustrious spouse;
Welcome as are the ends unto my vows;
Aye! far more welcome than the happy soil
The sea-scourged merchant,[6] after all his toil,
Salutes with tears of joy, when fires betray
The smoky chimneys of his Ithaca.
Where hast thou been so long from my embraces,
Poor pitied exile? Tell me, did thy graces
Fly discontented hence, and for a time
Did rather choose to bless another clime?
Or went'st thou to this end, the more to move me,
By thy short absence, to desire and love thee?
Why frowns my sweet? Why won't my saint confer
Favors on me, her fierce idolater?
Why are those looks, those looks the which have been
Time-past so fragrant, sickly now drawn in
Like a dull twilight? Tell me, and the fault
I'll expiate with[7] sulphur, hair, and salt;
And with the crystal humor of the spring[8]
Purge hence the guilt, and kill this quarreling.
Wo't thou not smile, or tell me what's amiss?
Have I been cold to hug thee, too remiss,
Too temp'rate in embracing? Tell me, has desire
To thee-ward died i'th'embers, and no fire
Left in this raked-up ash-heap, as a mark
To testify the glowing of a spark?
Have I divorced thee only to combine

4. Conquers.
5. "The Sun" (Herrick's note). Cf. Spenser, *The Faerie Queene*. V.vii.4: "Like as Osyris signifies the Sun."
6. I.e., Odysseus.
7. I.e., with offerings of (echoing classical ceremonies).
8. I.e., with water.

In hot adult'ry with another wine?
True, I confess I left thee,[9] and appeal
'Twas done by me more to confirm my zeal
And double my affection on thee, as do those
Whose love grows more inflamed by being foes.
But to forsake thee ever, could there be
A thought of such like possibility?
When thou thyself dar'st say, thy isles shall lack
Grapes, before Herrick leaves Canary sack.
Thou mak'st me airy, active to be borne,
Like Iphiclus,[1] upon the tops of corn.
Thou mak'st me nimble, as the wingèd hours,[2]
To dance and caper on the heads of flowers,
And ride the sunbeams. Can there be a thing
Under the heavenly Isis[3] that can bring
More love unto my life, or can present
My genius with a fuller blandishment?
Illustrious idol! could th'Egyptians seek
Help from the garlic, onion, and the leek,[4]
And pay no vows to thee, who wast their best
God, and far more transcendent than the rest?
Had Cassius,[5] that weak water-drinker, known
Thee in thy vine, or had but tasted one
Small chalice of thy frantic liquor, he
As the wise Cato[6] had approved of thee.
Had not Jove's son,[7] that brave Tyrinthian swain,
Invited to the Thespian banquet, ta'en
Full goblets of thy gen'rous blood, his sprite
Ne'er had kept heat for fifty maids that night.
Come, come and kiss me; love and lust commends
Thee and thy beauties; kiss, we will be friends
Too strong for fate to break us; look upon
Me with that full pride of complexion
As queens meet queens; or come thou unto me
As Cleopatra came to Antony,
When her high carriage did at once present
To the triumvir, love and wonderment.
Swell up my nerves with spirit; let my blood
Run through my veins like to a hasty flood.
Fill each part full of fire, active to do
What thy commanding soul shall put it to.

9. Cf. "His Farewell to Sack," p. 187.
1. A celebrated runner, Iphiclus won the longer of two footraces at the funeral games of Pelias; cf. Hyginus, *Fables*, cclxxviii.
2. I.e., the goddesses of the seasons; cf. Ovid, *Metamorphoses*, II.26–30.
3. "The Moon" [Herrick's note].
4. Cf. Numbers 11:5: "We remember the fish, which we did eat in Egypt freely; the cucumbers, and the melons, and the leeks, and the onions, and the garlic."
5. Cassius, who conspired with Brutus to assassinate Caesar, drank only water.
6. Cato the Censor (cf. "When He Would Have His Verses Read") found time to write *De Agri Cultura*, which includes information on vineyards and winemaking.
7. "Hercules" (Herrick's note) was brought up in Tiryns (in Argolis); he enjoyed the favors of King Thespius' fifty daughters in return for ridding that monarch's land of a ravaging lion. Cf. Apollodorus, *Library*, II.iv.10.

And till I turn apostate to thy love,
Which here I vow to serve, do not remove
Thy fires from me, but Apollo's curse
Blast these-like actions; or a thing that's worse,
When these circumstants[8] shall but live to see
The time that I prevaricate from thee,
Call me the son of beer, and then confine
Me to the tap, the toast, the turf;[9] let wine
Ne'er shine upon me; may my numbers all
Run to a sudden death and funeral.
And last, when thee, dear spouse, I disavow,
Ne'er may prophetic Daphne[1] crown my brow.

To Live Merrily, and to Trust to Good Verses[2]

Now is the time for mirth,
  Nor cheek or tongue be dumb;
For with the flow'ry earth
  The golden pomp is come.

The golden pomp is come;
  For now each tree does wear,
Made of her pap[3] and gum,
  Rich beads of amber here.

Now reigns the rose,[4] and now
  Th'Arabian dew besmears
My uncontrollèd brow
  And my retorted[5] hairs.

Homer, this health to thee,
  In sack of such a kind
That it would make thee see
  Though thou wert ne'er so blind.

Next, Vergil I'll call forth,
  To pledge this second health
In wine, whose each cup's worth
  An Indian commonwealth.

A goblet next I'll drink
  To Ovid, and suppose,

8. Bystanders.
9. I.e., to beer, to beer-soaked bread, and to earth (as distinct from the "airy" element with which wine is associated in line 49).
1. Daphne, pursued by Apollo, was changed into a laurel tree, which Apollo adopted as his sacred tree. Cf. Ovid, *Metamorphoses*, I.548–567. Poets' achievements were rewarded with laurel garlands.
2. Herrick's poem at several points (notably lines 5, 10, 41–44) echoes the language of Ovid's *Amores* and *Heroides*; cf. *The Poetical Works of Robert Herrick*, ed. L. C. Martin (Oxford, 1956), p. 517.
3. Pulp.
4. Cf. "When He Would Have His Verses Read," line 9n, p. 182.
5. I.e., bent backward.

Made he the pledge, he'd think
The world had all one nose.[6]

Then this immensive cup
Of aromatic wine,
Catullus, I quaff up
To that terse Muse of thine.

Wild I am now with heat;
O Bacchus! cool thy rays!
Or frantic I shall eat
Thy thyrse,[7] and bite the bays.

Round, round the roof does run;
And being ravished thus,
Come, I will drink a tun[8]
To my Propertius.[9]

Now, to Tibullus, next,
This flood I drink to thee;
But stay, I see a text[1]
That this presents to me.

Behold, Tibullus lies
Here burnt, whose small return
Of ashes scarce suffice
To fill a little urn.

Trust to good verses, then;
They only will aspire,
When pyramids, as men,
Are lost i'th'funeral fire.

And when all bodies meet
In Lethe to be drowned,
Then only numbers sweet
With endless life are crowned.

To the Virgins, to Make Much of Time[2]

Gather ye rosebuds while ye may,
Old time is still a-flying;

6. Herrick puns on Ovid's full name, Publius Ovidius Naso ("nose").
7. Cf. "When He Would Have His Verses Read," line 7n, p. 181.
8. Large cask.
9. Propertius (born c. 51 B.C.) and Tibullus (c. 54–18 B.C.) were, with Catullus (87–c. 47 B.C.), the most celebrated of the Roman elegiac poets.
1. I.e., Ovid, *Amores*, III.ix.39–40, translated in the next stanza.
2. Cf. "Corinna's Going A-Maying," lines 57–70n, p. 191: also, for further examples of the carpe diem motif in classical poetry, *The Complete Poetry of Robert Herrick*, ed. J. Max Patrick (New York, 1968), p. 118.

And this same flower that smiles today,
  Tomorrow will be dying.

The glorious lamp of heaven, the sun,
  The higher he's a-getting,
The sooner will his race be run,
  And nearer he's to setting.

That age is best which is the first,
  When youth and blood are warmer,
But being spent, the worse, and worst
  Times still succeed the former.

Then be not coy, but use your time,
  And while ye may, go marry;
For having lost but once your prime,
  You may for ever tarry.

His Poetry His Pillar

Only a little more
  I have to write,
  Then I'll give o'er,
And bid the world good-night.

'Tis but a flying minute
  That I must stay,
  Or linger in it;
And then I must away.

O Time that cut'st down all!
  And scarce leav'st here
  Memorial
Of any men that were.

How many lie forgot
  In vaults beneath,
  And piecemeal rot
Without a fame in death?

Behold this living stone
  I rear for me,
  Ne'er to be thrown
Down, envious Time, by thee.

Pillars let some set up,
  If so they please;
  Here is my hope
And my pyramides.

To the Rose. Song[3]

Go, happy rose, and interwove
With other flowers, bind my love.
Tell her, too, she must not be
Longer flowing, longer free,
That so oft has fettered me.

Say (if she's fretful) I have bands
Of pearl and gold to bind her hands;
Tell her, if she struggle still,
I have myrtle rods at will,
For to tame, though not to kill.

Take thou my blessing, thus, and go,
And tell her this; but do not so,
Lest a handsome anger fly
Like a lightning from her eye,
And burn thee up, as well as I.

The Hock-Cart, or Harvest Home: To the Right Honorable Mildmay, Earl of Westmorland[4]

Come, sons of summer, by whose toil
We are the lords of wine and oil;
By whose tough labors and rough hands
We rip up first, then reap our lands;
Crowned with the ears of corn, now come,
And, to the pipe, sing harvest home.
Come forth, my lord, and see the cart
Dressed up with all the country art.
See here a maukin,[5] there a sheet,
As spotless pure as it is sweet;
The horses, mares, and frisking fillies,
Clad all in linen, white as lilies;
The harvest swains and wenches bound
For joy to see the hock-cart crowned.
About the cart, hear how the rout
Of rural younglings raise the shout;
Pressing before, some coming after,
Those with a shout, and these with laughter.
Some bless the cart; some kiss the sheaves;
Some prank them up with oaken leaves;

3. The opening lines of this poem echo Martial, *Epigrams*, VII.lxxxix. Cf. Waller's "Go, lovely rose!," p. 369.
4. The celebration of "harvest home" began with the return from the fields of the hock-cart, bringing the last load of the harvest. Herrick's poem, based generally on Tibullus, *Odes*, II.i, bears some slight resemblance to Jonson's "To Penshurst," p. 97, and "To Sir Robert Wroth," p. 100.
5. I.e., a pole bound with cloth, used as a scarecrow.

Some cross the fill-horse;[6] some with great
Devotion stroke the home-borne wheat;
While other rustics, less attent[7]
To prayers than to merriment,
Run after with their breeches rent.
Well, on, brave boys, to your lord's hearth,
Glitt'ring with fire; where, for your mirth,
Ye shall see first the large and chief
Foundation of your feast, fat beef,
With upper stories, mutton, veal,
And bacon, which makes full the meal;
With sev'ral dishes standing by,
As here a custard, there a pie,
And here all-tempting frumenty.[8]
And for to make the merry cheer,
If smirking wine be wanting here,
There's that which drowns all care, stout beer,
Which freely drink to your lord's health;
Then to the plow, the commonwealth,
Next to your flails, your fans, your fats;[9]
Then to the maids with wheaten hats;
To the rough sickle, and crook'd scythe,
Drink, frolic boys, till all be blithe.
Feed, and grow fat; and as ye eat,
Be mindful that the laboring neat,[1]
As you, may have their fill of meat.
And know, besides, ye must revoke[2]
The patient ox unto the yoke,
And all go back unto the plow
And harrow, though they're hanged up now.
And, you must know, your lord's word's true,
Feed him ye must, whose food fills you,
And that this pleasure is like rain,
Not sent ye for to drown your pain,
But for to make it spring again.

How Roses Came Red

Roses at first were white,
  Till they could not agree
Whether my Sappho's breast
  Or they more white should be.

But being vanquished quite,
  A blush their cheeks bespred;

6. I.e., some bless the horse that draws the cart.
7. Attentive.
8. I.e., pudding made of wheat, milk, and spices.
9. I.e., your winnowing fans, your vats (for storing grain).
1. Cattle.
2. Call back (next year).

Since which, believe the rest,
  The roses first came red.

How Violets Came Blue

Love on a day, wise poets tell,
  Some time in wrangling spent,
Whether the violets should excel,
  Or she, in sweetest scent.

But Venus having lost the day,
  Poor girls, she fell on you,
And beat ye so, as some dare say,
  Her blows did make ye blue.

A Nuptial Song, or Epithalamie, on Sir Clipsby Crew and His Lady[3]

What's that we see from far? the spring of day
Bloomed from the east, or fair enjewelled May
    Blown out of April, or some new
    Star filled with glory to our view,
                Reaching at heaven,
To add a nobler planet to the seven?
    Say, or do we not descry
Some goddess in a cloud of tiffany[4]
            To move, or rather the
    Emergent Venus from the sea?[5]

'Tis she! 'Tis she! or else some more divine
Enlightened substance; mark how from the shrine
    Of holy saints she paces on,
    Treading upon vermilion
                And amber; spice-
ing the chafed[6] air with fumes of Paradise.
    Then come on, come on, and yield
A savor like unto a blessèd field,[7]
            When the bedabbled morn
    Washes the golden ears of corn.

See where she comes, and smell how all the street
Breathes vineyards and pomegranates: O how sweet!
    As a fired altar is each stone,

3. Sir Clipsby Crewe (1599–1649) married Jane Pulteney on 7 July 1625.
4. I.e., of fine silk or muslin.
5. Venus was said to have sprung from the sea foam; cf. Ovid, *Metamorphoses* IV.537.
6. Warmed.
7. Cf. Genesis 27:27: "the smell of a field which the Lord hath blessed."

Perspiring pounded cinnamon.
The phoenix' nest,
Built up of odors, burneth in her breast.
Who therein would not consume
His soul to ash-heaps in that rich perfume,
Bestroking fate the while
He burns to embers on the pile?

Hymen, O Hymen! Tread the sacred ground;[8]
Show thy white feet, and head with marjoram crowned;
Mount up thy flames, and let thy torch[9]
Display the bridegroom in the porch,
In his desires
More tow'ring, more disparkling[1] than thy fires;
Show her how his eyes do turn
And roll about, and in their motions burn
Their balls to cinders; haste,
Or else to ashes he will waste.

Glide by the banks of virgins, then, and pass
The showers of roses, lucky four-leaved grass,[2]
The while the cloud of younglings sing,
And drown ye with a flow'ry spring;
While some repeat
Your praise, and bless you, sprinkling you with wheat;
While that others do divine,[3]
"Blest is the bride on whom the sun doth shine";
And thousands gladly wish
You multiply, as doth a fish.[4]

And beauteous bride, we do confess y'are wise
In dealing forth these bashful jealousies;
In love's name do so, and a price
Set on yourself, by being nice;[5]
But yet take heed,
What now you seem, be not the same indeed,
And turn apostate; love will
Part of the way be met, or sit stone-still.
On then, and though you slow-
ly go, yet, howsoever, go.

And now y'are entered; see, the coddled[6] cook
Runs from his torrid zone to pry and look,
And bless his dainty mistress; see,

8. The practice of going barefoot on sacred ground, common in classical ceremonies, is also enjoined by Holy Scripture; cf. Exodus 3:5 and Acts 7:33.
9. Hymen, god of marriage, is typically represented as a youth bearing a torch.
1. I.e., higher and more widespread.
2. I.e., four-leaf clovers.
3. Prophesy.
4. Cf. Luke 9:13–17.
5. I.e., modestly reserved.
6. Parboiled.

The aged point out, "This is she
Who now must sway
The house (love shield her) with her yea and nay":
And the smirk[7] butler thinks it
Sin, in's napery, not to express his wit;
Each striving to devise
Some gin[8] wherewith to catch your eyes.

To bed, to bed, kind turtles[9] now, and write
This the short'st day, and this the longest night,
But yet too short for you; 'tis we
Who count this night as long as three,
Lying alone,
Telling the clock strike ten, eleven, twelve, one.
Quickly, quickly then, prepare,
And let the young men and the bride-maids share
Your garters, and their joints
Encircle with the bridegroom's points.[1]

By the bride's eyes, and by the teeming life
Of her green hopes, we charge ye that no strife,
Farther than gentleness tends, gets place
Among ye, striving for her lace;
O do not fall
Foul in these noble pastimes, lest ye call
Discord in, and so divide
The youthful bridegroom and the fragrant bride,
Which love forfend; but spoken,
Be't to your praise, no peace was broken.

Strip her of springtime, tender-whimp'ring maids;
Now autumn's come, when all those flow'ry aids
Of her delays must end; dispose
That lady-smock, that pansy, and that rose
Neatly apart;
But for prick-madam, and for gentle-heart,
And soft maiden's-blush,[2] the bride
Makes holy these, all others lay aside;
Then strip her, or unto her
Let him come who dares undo her.

And to enchant ye more, see everywhere
About the roof a Siren[3] in a sphere,

7. Spruce.
8. Snare.
9. I.e., turtledoves.
1. Tagged laces called "points" were used to fasten items of clothing.
2. "Maiden's-blush" is a country name for a rose of a delicate pink shade; "lady-smock," "prick-madam," and "gentle-heart" are rustic names for various flowers and herbs of the English countryside.
3. I.e., an angelic being who sings sweetly. Cf. Plato, *Republic*. X.617; and Milton's "At a Solemn Music," lines 1–8.

As we think, singing to the din[4]
Of many a warbling Cherubim;
O mark ye how
The soul of nature melts in numbers![5] Now
See, a thousand Cupids fly
To light their tapers at the bride's bright eye.
To bed, or her they'll tire,
Were she an element of fire.

And to your more bewitching, see, the proud
Plump bed bear up, and, swelling like a cloud,
Tempting the two too modest; can
Ye see it brusle[6] like a swan,
And you be cold
To meet it, when it woos and seems to fold
The arms to hug it? Throw, throw
Yourselves into the mighty overflow
Of that white pride, and drown
The night with you in floods of down.

The bed is ready, and the maze of love
Looks for the treaders; everywhere is wove
Wit and new mystery;[7] read,[8] and
Put in practice, to understand
And know each wile,
Each hieroglyphic[9] of a kiss or smile,
And do it to the full; reach
High in your own conceit,[1] and some way teach
Nature and art one more
Play than they ever knew before.

If needs we must for ceremony's sake
Bless a sack-posset,[2] luck go with it; take
The night-charm quickly; you have spells
And magics for to end, and hells
To pass, but such
And of such torture as no one would grutch[3]
To live therein forever; fry
And consume, and grow again to die
And live, and in that case
Love the confusion of the place.

4. I.e., the loud, resonant sound.
5. I.e., in harmonious measures.
6. Ruffle up (as feathers).
7. I.e. (primarily), craft or skill.
8. I.e., look with discernment.
9. Sign (of meaning conveyed by kisses and smiles).
1. Fancy.
2. I.e., a mixture of spiced hot milk curdled by sack, traditionally offered to the bridegroom on his wedding night.
3. Resent.

But since it must be done, despatch, and sew
Up in a sheet your bride; and what if so
    It be with rock, or walls of brass
    Ye tower her up,[4] as Danae was,
                                Think you that this
Or hell itself a powerful bulwark is?
    I tell ye no; but like a
Bold bolt of thunder he will make his way,
                        And rend the cloud, and throw
    The sheet about like flakes of snow.

All now is hushed in silence; midwife-moon,
With all her owl-eyed issue, begs a boon
    Which you must grant, that's entrance; with
    Which extract all we can call pith
                                And quintessence
Of planetary bodies. So commence,
    All fair constellations
Looking upon ye, that two nations[5]
                        Springing from two such fires
    May blaze the virtue of their sires.

Oberon's Feast[6]

Shapcot,[7] to thee the fairy state
I with discretion dedicate,
Because thou prizest things that are
Curious and unfamiliar.
Take first the feast; these dishes gone,
We'll see the fairy court anon.

A little mushroom table spread,
After short prayers, they set on bread;
A moon-parched grain of purest wheat,
With some small glitt'ring grit,[8] to eat
His choice bits with; then in a trice
They make a feast less great than nice.
But all this while his eye is served,
We must not think his ear was starved,

4. I.e., confine in a fortified building. Danae's father thought to keep his daughter safe from the attentions of Zeus by so confining her; but the god visited Danae in a shower of gold. Cf. Apollodorus, *Library,* II.iv.1.
5. Cf. Genesis 25:23: "The Lord said unto Rebekah, Two nations are in thy womb." The implicit promise of this scriptural allusion caps and confirms the poet's desire that the stars shed propitious influence on the wedded pair.
6. A briefer version was published in 1635; cf. *Poetical Works of Robert Herrick.* ed. Martin, p. 454.
7. Herrick elsewhere describes Thomas Shapcot (c. 1586–c. 1669) as a "peculiar" [i.e., particular] friend; "Oberon's Palace," to which Herrick alludes in line 6, is also addressed to Shapcot.
8. Unground oats.

But that there was in place to stir
His spleen,[9] the chirring grasshopper,
The merry cricket, puling[1] fly
The piping gnat, for minstrelsy.
And now we must imagine first,
The elves present to quench his thirst
A pure seed-pearl of infant dew,
Brought and besweetened in a blue
And pregnant[2] violet; which done,
His kitling[3] eyes begin to run
Quite through the table, where he spies
The horns of papery butterflies,
Of which he eats, and tastes a little
Of that we call the cuckoo's spittle.[4]
A little fuzz-ball[5] pudding stands
By, yet not blessèd by his hands;
That was too coarse; but then forthwith
He ventures boldly on the pith
Of sugared rush, and eats the sag
And well-bestrutted[6] bee's sweet bag,
Gladding his palate with some store
Of emmets'[7] eggs; what would he more?
But beards of mice, a newt's stewed thigh,
A bloated earwig, and a fly,
With the red-capped worm that's shut
Within the concave of a nut,
Brown as his tooth. A little moth,
Late fattened in a piece of cloth;
With withered cherries, mandrakes' ears,
Moles' eyes; to these, the slain stag's tears,
The unctuous dewlaps of a snail;
The broke-heart of a nightingale
O'ercome in music; with a wine
Ne'er ravished from the flattering vine,
But gently pressed from the soft side
Of the most sweet and dainty bride,[8]
Brought in a dainty daisy, which
He fully quaffs up to bewitch
His blood to height; this done, commended
Grace by his priest; the feast is ended.

9. I.e., to keep him amused (since cheerful as well as gloomy emotions were thought to originate in the spleen).
1. Buzzing.
2. Full-blown.
3. Diminutive.
4. I.e., insects' cocoons.
5. Puffball (a species of edible fungus).
6. Swollen.
7. Ants'.
8. I.e., meadowsweet or meadowwort, used for flavoring wine.

Upon a Child That Died

Here she lies, a pretty bud,
Lately made of flesh and blood;
Who as soon fell fast asleep
As her little eyes did peep.
Give her strewings; but not stir
The earth that lightly covers her.

To Daffodils

Fair daffodils, we weep to see
You haste away so soon;
As yet the early-rising sun
Has not attained his noon.
Stay, stay,
Until the hasting day
Has run
But to the even-song;
And, having prayed together, we
Will go with you along.

We have short time to stay, as you;
We have as short a spring;
As quick a growth to meet decay,
As you, or any thing.
We die,
As your hours do, and dry
Away,
Like to the summer's rain;
Or as the pearls of morning's dew,
Ne'er to be found again.

Upon Master Ben Jonson: Epigram

After the rare arch-poet Jonson died,
The sock[9] grew loathsome, and the buskin's pride,
Together with the stage's glory, stood
Each like a poor and pitied widowhood.
The cirque[1] profaned was, and all postures racked,
For men did strut, and stride, and stare, not act.
Then temper flew from words, and men did squeak,
Look red, and blow and bluster, but not speak;

9. Sock (the high shoe worn by actors of comedy in ancient times) and buskin (the high boot worn by actors of tragedy) in this context symbolize English comic and tragic drama.
1. Circus (i.e., theater).

No holy rage or frantic fires did stir
Or flash about the spacious theater.
No clap of hands, or shout, or praise's proof
Did crack the playhouse sides, or cleave her roof.
Artless the scene was, and that monstrous sin
Of deep and arrant ignorance came in;
Such ignorance as theirs was, who once hissed
At thy unequalled play, *The Alchemist.*
Oh, fie upon 'em! Lastly too, all wit
In utter darkness did, and still will sit
Sleeping the luckless age out, till that she
Her resurrection has again with thee.

Upon Electra

When out of bed my love doth spring,
'Tis but as day a-kindling;
But when she's up and fully dressed,
'Tis then broad day throughout the east.

Upon Parson Beanes

Old Parson Beanes hunts six days of the week,
And on the seventh, he has his notes to seek.
Six days he hollows[2] so much breath away
That on the seventh he can nor preach or pray.

To Daisies, Not to Shut So Soon

Shut not so soon; the dull-eyed night
   Has not as yet begun
To make a seizure on the light,
   Or to seal up the sun.

No marigolds yet closèd are,
   No shadows great appear;
Nor doth the early shepherd's star
   Shine like a spangle here.

Stay but till my Julia close
   Her life-begetting eye,
And let the whole world then dispose
   Itself to live or die.

2. I.e., shouts, "Halloo!" (as the huntsmen pursue the fox).

To the Right Honorable Mildmay, Earl of Westmorland[3]

You are a lord, an earl, nay more, a man,
Who writes sweet numbers well as any can;
If so, why then are not these verses hurled,
Like sibyls' leaves, throughout the ample world?[4]
What is a jewel if it be not set
Forth by a ring, or some rich carcanet?[5]
But being so, then the beholders cry,
"See, see a gem as rare as Belus' eye!"[6]
Then public praise does run upon the stone
For a most rich, a rare, a precious one.
Expose your jewels then unto the view,
That we may praise them, or themselves prize you.
Virtue concealed (with Horace you'll confess)
Differs not much from drowsy slothfulness.[7]

To Blossoms

Fair pledges of a fruitful tree,
 Why do ye fall so fast?
 Your date is not so past
But you may stay yet here a while,
 To blush and gently smile,
  And go at last.

What, were ye born to be
 An hour or half's delight,
 And so to bid good-night?
'Twas pity nature brought ye forth
 Merely to show your worth,
  And lose you quite.

But you are lovely leaves, where we
 May read how soon things have
 Their end, though ne'er so brave;[8]
And after they have shown their pride,
 Like you a while, they glide
  Into the grave.

3. It is arguable that this poem contributed to Mildmay Fane's decision to publish *Otia Sacra* in 1648.
4. Of the various prophetesses or sibyls to whom ancient authors allude, the most celebrated was the Sibyl of Cumae, in Campania; her prophecies were written on palm leaves and placed at the entrance to her cave, whence the wind often carried them away. Cf. Vergil, *Aeneid*, VI.73–76.
5. Necklace, ornamental chain.
6. The Assyrians, who worshiped Baal (Bel, Belus), dedicated to their god a certain white stone with a glittering black center; cf. Pliny, *Natural History*, XXXVII.55.
7. Lines 13–14 translate Horace, *Carmina*, IV.ix.29–30.
8. Beautiful.

Kissing and Bussing

Kissing and bussing differ both in this:
We buss[9] our wantons, but our wives we kiss.

Art above Nature: To Julia

When I behold a forest spread
With silken trees upon thy head,
And when I see that other dress
Of flowers set in comeliness;
When I behold another grace
In the ascent of curious lace,
Which like a pinnacle doth shew
The top, and the top-gallant[1] too;
Then, when I see thy tresses bound
Into an oval, square, or round,
And knit in knots far more than I
Can tell by tongue, or true-love tie;
Next, when those lawny films I see
Play with a wild civility,
And all those airy silks to flow,
Alluring me, and tempting so:
I must confess, mine eye and heart
Dotes less on nature, than on art.

His Prayer to Ben Jonson

When I a verse shall make,
Know I have prayed thee,
For old religion's[2] sake,
Saint Ben, to aid me.

Make the way smooth for me,
When, I, thy Herrick,
Honoring thee, on my knee
Offer my lyric.

Candles I'll give to thee,
And a new altar;
And thou, Saint Ben, shalt be
Writ in my psalter.

9. Although "buss" and "kiss" are synonyms, Herrick suggests a distinction.
1. I.e., the platforms at the heads of the mainmast and mizzenmast.
2. I.e. (primarily), for the sake of our old friendship, implicitly a sacred bond; but the expression glances also, very aptly, at a classical ideal of duty as well as at the faith and ceremonies of Roman times.

The Bad Season Makes the Poet Sad

Dull to myself, and almost dead to these
My many fresh and fragrant mistresses,
Lost to all music now, since every thing
Puts on the semblance here of sorrowing;
Sick is the land to th'heart, and doth endure
More dangerous faintings by her desp'rate cure.
But if that golden age would come again,
And Charles here rule, as he before did reign;
If smooth and unperplexed the seasons were
As when the sweet Maria[3] livèd here;
I should delight to have my curls half drowned
In Tyrian dews, and head with roses crowned,
And once more yet, ere I am laid out dead,
Knock at a star with my exalted head.[4]

The Night-Piece, To Julia

Her eyes the glow-worm lend thee;
The shooting stars attend thee;
  And the elves also,
  Whose little eyes glow
Like the sparks of fire, befriend thee.

No will-o'-the-wisp mis-light thee;
Nor snake or slow-worm[5] bite thee:
  But on, on thy way,
  Not making a stay,
Since ghost there's none to affright thee.

Let not the dark thee cumber;
What though the moon does slumber?
  The stars of the night
  Will lend thee their light,
Like tapers clear without number.

Then, Julia, let me woo thee,
Thus, thus to come unto me;
  And when I shall meet
  Thy silv'ry feet,
My soul I'll pour into thee.

3. I.e., Henrietta Maria, wife of Charles I.
4. Cf. Horace, *Carmina*, I.i.36.
5. Adder (or possibly the blindworm, a small lizard).

The Hag

The hag[6] is astride,
This night for to ride,
The devil and she together;
Through thick and through thin,
Now out and then in,
Though ne'er so foul be the weather.

A thorn or a burr
She takes for a spur;
With a lash of a bramble she rides now,
Through brakes and through briers,
O'er ditches and mires,
She follows the spirit that guides now.

No beast for his food
Dares now range the wood,
But hushed in his lair he lies lurking;
While mischiefs by these,
On land and on seas,
At noon of night[7] are a-working.

The storm will arise
And trouble the skies
This night, and more for the wonder,
The ghost from the tomb
Affrighted shall come,
Called out by the clap of the thunder.

The Country Life, To the Honored Mr. Endymion Porter,[8] Groom of the Bedchamber to His Majesty

Sweet country life, to such unknown,
Whose lives are others', not their own!
But, serving courts and cities, be
Less happy, less enjoying thee.
Thou never plow'st the ocean's foam
To seek and bring rough pepper home;
Nor to the Eastern Ind dost rove
To bring from thence the scorchèd clove;
Nor, with the loss of thy loved rest,
Bring'st home the ingot from the West.
No, thy ambition's masterpiece
Flies no thought higher than a fleece;

6. Witch.
7. I.e., at midnight.
8. Endymion Porter (1587–1649), an influential courtier during the reigns of James I and, especially, Charles I, extended support to Sir William Davenant and Thomas Randolph; to Herrick he appears to have been friend as well as patron.

Or how to pay thy hinds,[9] and clear
All scores, and so to end the year;
But walk'st about thine own dear bounds,
Not envying others' larger grounds,
For well thou know'st, 'tis not th'extent
Of land makes life, but sweet content.
When now the cock, the plowman's horn,
Calls forth the lily-wristed morn,
Then to thy corn-fields thou dost go,
Which, though well soiled,[1] yet thou dost know
That the best compost for the lands
Is the wise master's feet and hands.
There at the plow thou find'st thy team,
With a hind whistling there to them,
And cheer'st them up by singing how
The kingdom's portion is the plow.
This done, then to th'enameled meads
Thou go'st, and as thy foot there treads,
Thou seest a present godlike power
Imprinted in each herb and flower,
And smell'st the breath of great-eyed kine,
Sweet as the blossoms of the vine.
Here thou behold'st thy large sleek neat
Unto the dewlaps up in meat;
And as thou look'st, the wanton steer,
The heifer, cow, and ox draw near
To make a pleasing pastime there.
These seen, thou go'st to view thy flocks
Of sheep, safe from the wolf and fox,
And find'st their bellies there as full
Of short, sweet grass as backs with wool,
And leav'st them, as they feed and fill,
A shepherd piping on a hill.
For sports, for pageantry, and plays,
Thou hast thy eves, and holy-days,
On which the young men and maids meet
To exercise their dancing feet,
Tripping the comely country round,
With daffodils and daisies crowned.
Thy wakes, thy quintals,[2] here thou hast,
Thy May-poles, too, with garlands graced;
Thy morris-dance, thy Whitsun-ale,
Thy shearing-feast, which never fail;
Thy harvest home, thy wassail bowl,
That's tossed up after fox-i'-th'hole,[3]
Thy mummeries,[4] thy Twelfth-tide kings
And queens, thy Christmas revelings,

9. Farm laborers.
1. Manured.
2. Posts used as targets in rustic tilting-matches.
3. I.e., an ancient game similar to hopscotch.
4. I.e., ceremonies performed by masked actors.

Thy nut-brown mirth, thy russet[5] wit,
And no man pays too dear for it.
To these, thou hast thy times to go
And trace the hare i'th'treacherous snow;
Thy witty wiles to draw, and get
The lark into the trammel net;[6]
Thou hast thy cockrood[7] and thy glade,
To take the precious pheasant made;
Thy lime-twigs,[8] snares, and pitfalls then,
To catch the pilf'ring birds, not men.
O happy life! if that their good
The husbandmen but understood,
Who all the day themselves do please,
And younglings, with such sports as these;
And, lying down, have naught t'affright
Sweet sleep, that makes more short the night.
Caetera desunt[9]—

The Maypole

The Maypole is up,
Now give me the cup,
I'll drink to the garlands around it;
But first unto those
Whose hands did compose
The glory of flowers that crowned it.

A health to my girls,
Whose husbands may earls
Or lords be (granting my wishes);
And when that ye wed
To the bridal bed,
Then multiply all, like to fishes.[1]

His Return to London[2]

From the dull confines of the drooping west,
To see the day spring from the pregnant east,
Ravished in spirit, I come, nay more, I fly
To thee, blest place of my nativity!
Thus, thus with hallowed foot I touch the ground,

5. Homespun.
6. I.e., a net combining coarse and fine mesh.
7. Nets were stretched across a "cockrood," or open space in a wood, to catch woodcocks.
8. Branches were smeared with sticky substances made from holly bark to catch birds (cf. Wyatt's lyric, "Tangled I was in love's snare").
9. I.e., the rest is wanting.
1. Cf. "A Nuptial Song," line 50, p. 200.
2. Herrick presumably returned from Devonshire to London in 1647, the year in which he was expelled from his living at Dean Prior.

With thousand blessings by thy fortune crowned.
O fruitful Genius! that bestowest here
An everlasting plenty, year by year.
O Place! O People! Manners![3] framed to please
All nations, customs, kindreds, languages!
I am a free-born Roman; suffer then
That I amongst you live a citizen.
London my home is, though by hard fate sent
Into a long and irksome banishment;
Yet since called back; henceforward let me be,
O native country, repossessed by thee!
For, rather than I'll to the west return,
I'll beg of thee first here to have mine urn.
Weak I am grown, and must in short time fall;
Give thou my sacred relics burial.

His Grange,[4] or Private Wealth

Though clock
To tell how night draws hence, I've none,
A cock
I have, to sing how day draws on.
I have
A maid, my Prue, by good luck sent
To save
That little, Fates me gave or lent.
A hen
I keep, which creaking[5] day by day,
Tells when
She goes her long white egg to lay.
A goose
I have, which with a jealous ear
Let's loose
Her tongue, to tell what danger's near.
A lamb
I keep, tame, with my morsels fed,
Whose dam
An orphan left him, lately dead.
A cat
I keep, that plays about my house,
Grown fat
With eating many a miching[6] mouse.
To these
A Tracy[7] I do keep, whereby
I please

3. Cf. "Dean-bourn," line 9, p. 186.
4. I.e., his country dwelling (the vicarage of Dean Prior).
5. Clucking.
6. Thieving.
7. "His Spaniel" (Herrick's note). Cf. "Upon His Spaniel Tracy," p. 219.

The more my rural privacy;
Which are
But toys to give my heart some ease:
Where care
None is, slight things do lightly please.

Upon Julia's Clothes

Whenas in silks my Julia goes,
Then, then, methinks, how sweetly flows
That liquefaction of her clothes.

Next, when I cast mine eyes and see
That brave vibration each way free;
O, how that glittering taketh me!

Upon Prue, His Maid[8]

In this little urn is laid
Prudence Baldwin, once my maid,
From whose happy spark here let
Spring the purple violet.

Ceremonies for Christmas

Come, bring with a noise,[9]
My merry, merry boys,
The Christmas log to the firing;
While my good dame, she
Bids ye all be free,
And drink to your hearts' desiring.

With the last year's brand
Light the new block, and
For good success in his spending,[1]
On your psalt'ries[2] play,
That sweet luck may
Come while the log is a-tinding.[3]

Drink now the strong beer,
Cut the white loaf here,
The while the meat is a-shredding;

8. The Parish Register at Dean Prior indicates that Prudence Baldwin was in fact buried on 6 January 1678; Herrick had died almost four years earlier.
9. I.e., a joyful noise.
1. I.e., consuming (by the fire).
2. The psaltery was a string instrument akin to the zither.
3. Kindling.

For the rare mince-pie
And the plums stand by
To fill the paste that's a-kneading.

Poetry Perpetuates the Poet

Here I myself might likewise die,
And utterly forgotten lie,
But that eternal poetry
Repullulation[4] gives me here
Unto the thirtieth thousand year,[5]
When all now dead shall reappear.

Kisses

Give me the food that satisfies a guest;
Kisses are but dry banquets to a feast.

The Amber Bead

I saw a fly within a bead
Of amber cleanly burièd;
The urn was little, but the room
More rich than Cleopatra's tomb.

Upon Love

Love brought me to a silent grove,
And showed me there a tree
Where some had hanged themselves for love,
And gave a twist to me.

The halter was of silk and gold
That he reached forth to me,
No otherwise than if he would
By dainty things undo me.

He bade me then that necklace use,
And told me, too, he maketh
A glorious end by such a noose,
His death for love that taketh.

4. Regeneration.
5. I.e., the period of time required, according to some ancient authorities, for the heavenly bodies to return to their original positions; sometimes referred to as a "great Year." Cf. Plato, *Republic*, VIII.546.

'Twas but a dream; but had I been
There, really alone,
My desperate fears in love had seen
Mine execution.

Charms[6]

Bring the holy crust of bread,
Lay it underneath the head;
'Tis a certain charm to keep
Hags away while children sleep.

Another

Let the superstitious wife
Near the child's heart lay a knife,
Point be up, and haft be down,
While she gossips in the town;
This, 'mongst other mystic charms,
Keeps the sleeping child from harms.

Another to Bring in the Witch

To house[7] the hag, you must do this:
Commix with meal a little piss
Of him bewitched; then forthwith make
A little wafer or a cake;
And this, rawly baked, will bring
The old hag in. No surer thing.

Another Charm for Stables

Hang up hooks and shears to scare
Hence the hag that rides the mare,
Till they be all over wet
With the mire and the sweat;
This observed, the manes shall be
Of your horses all knot-free.

6. This poem and the three that follow reflect the continuing strength in Herrick's time, especially in country parishes such as Dean Prior, of pre-Christian folklore and ritual designed to ward off evil spirits. Cf. "The Hag," p. 210.
7. I.e., to attract into the house (where the witch might be destroyed).

Ceremonies for Candlemas Eve[8]

Down with the rosemary and bays,
Down with the mistletoe;
Instead of holly, now upraise
The greener box, for show.

The holly hitherto did sway;
Let box now domineer
Until the dancing Easter Day,[9]
Or Easter's Eve appear.

Then youthful box which now hath grace
Your houses to renew,
Grown old, surrender must his place
Unto the crispèd[1] yew.

When yew is out, then birch comes in,
And many flowers beside,
Both of a fresh and fragrant kin
To honor Whitsuntide.

Green rushes then, and sweetest bents,[2]
With cooler oaken boughs,
Come in for comely ornaments,
To re-adorn the house.
Thus times do shift; each thing his turn does hold;
New things succeed, as former things grow old.

Upon Ben Jonson

Here lies Jonson with the rest
Of the poets; but the best.
Reader, would'st thou more have known?
Ask his story, not this stone.
That will speak what this can't tell
Of his glory. So farewell.

8. Candlemas, which falls on 2 February, commemorates the Purification of the Virgin Mary; candles, especially for the altar, are blessed on this day. It seems probable, however, that Herrick also has in view the pre-Christian symbolic associations of the various flowers and trees mentioned in the course of the poem.
9. It was popularly believed that the sun dances on Easter Day: cf. Sir Thomas Browne, *Pseudodoxia Epidemica*, V.xxii.16.
1. Curled.
2. Bent grass.

An Ode for Him

Ah, Ben!
Say how or when
Shall we, thy guests,
Meet at those lyric feasts
Made at the Sun,
The Dog, the Triple Tun,[3]
Where we such clusters[4] had
As made us nobly wild, not mad;
And yet each verse of thine
Outdid the meat, outdid the frolic wine.

My Ben!
Or come again,
Or send to us
Thy wit's great overplus;
But teach us yet
Wisely to husband it,
Lest we that talent spend;
And having once brought to an end
That precious stock, the store
Of such a wit the world should have no more.

To the King, Upon His Welcome to Hampton Court[5]

Welcome, great Caesar, welcome now you are
As dearest peace after destructive war;
Welcome as slumbers, or as beds of ease
After our long and peevish sicknesses.
O pomp of glory! Welcome now, and come
To repossess once more your longed-for home.
A thousand altars smoke; a thousand thighs
Of beeves here ready stand for sacrifice.
Enter and prosper, while our eyes do wait
For an ascendant throughly auspicate,[6]
Under which sign we may the former stone
Lay of our safety's new foundation.[7]
That done, O Caesar, live, and be to us
Our Fate, our Fortune, and our Genius,
To whose free knees we may our temples tie
As to a still protecting deity.
That should you stir, we and our altars too

3. The Sun, The Dog, and The Triple Tun were taverns in London.
4. Bunches (of grapes)—i.e., wine.
5. On 24 August 1647 by Parliamentary order, Charles I was sent with a military escort to Hampton Court.
6. I.e., for an altogether auspicious aspect of the heavens.
7. Herrick alludes to the ancients' practice of noting the aspect of the stars under which a city was founded, in order to ascertain the most propitious occasions for later actions affecting the city's well-being.

May, great Augustus,[8] go along with you.
Long live the King! and to accomplish this,
We'll from our own add far more years to his.

On Himself

Lost to the world; lost to myself; alone
Here now I rest under this marble stone:
In depth of silence, heard and seen of none.

Upon His Spaniel Tracy

Now thou art dead, no eye shall ever see,
For shape and service, spaniel like to thee.
This shall my love do, give thy sad death one
Tear, that deserves of me a million.

The Pillar of Fame[9]

Fame's pillar here at last we set,
Out-during[1] marble, brass or jet;
Charmed and enchanted so
As to withstand the blow
Of overthrow;
Nor shall the seas,
Or outrages
Of storms, o'erbear
What we uprear;
Tho' kingdoms fall,
This pillar never shall
Decline or waste at all;
But stand for ever by his own
Firm and well-fixed foundation.

To his book's end this last line he'd have placed:
Jocund his Muse was; but his life was chaste.

8. Caesar Augustus (63 B.C.–A.D. 14) was considered to have been the most successful of his line.
9. The poem is "shaped" to resemble a column.
1. Outlasting.

FROM *HIS NOBLE NUMBERS*[2] (1647; WITH *HESPERIDES*, 1648)

His Prayer for Absolution

For those my unbaptizèd rhymes,
Writ in my wild unhallowed times;
For every sentence, clause, and word,
That's not inlaid with Thee, my Lord,
Forgive me, God, and blot each line
Out of my book that is not Thine.
But if, 'mongst all, Thou find'st here one
Worthy Thy benediction,
That one of all the rest shall be
The glory of my work and me.

To Find God[3]

Weigh me the fire; or canst thou find
A way to measure out the wind?
Distinguish all those floods that are
Mixed in that wat'ry theater,[4]
And taste thou them as saltless there,
As in their channel first they were.
Tell[5] me the people that do keep
Within the kingdoms of the deep;
Or fetch me back that cloud again,
Beshivered into seeds of rain.
Tell me the motes, dust, sands, and spears
Of corn, when summer shakes his ears;
Show me that world of stars, and whence
They noiseless spill their influence.
This if thou canst;[6] then show me Him
That rides the glorious cherubim.[7]

2. The title page of *His Noble Numbers*, which comprises 272 "pious pieces" in which Herrick "sings the birth of his Christ, and sighs for his Savior's sufferings on the cross," bears an epigraph in Greek, drawn from the *Theogony* of Hesiod: "We know how to say many false things that seem like true sayings, but we know also how to speak the truth when we wish to" (*Hesiod*, trans. R. Lattimore [Ann Arbor, 1970], p. 124). In these poems we have retained Herrick's capitalization of references to God and to religious doctrines.
3. Cf. Donne's "Song," p. 23, which also (in quite another context) confronts the reader initially with a series of impossible demands, the better to enforce the poet's concluding emphasis. Herrick's poem, however, looks in the first instance specifically to II Esdras, in the Apocrypha: "Weigh me the weight of fire, or measure me a measure of wind, or call back for me the day that is past. . . . How many dwellings are there in the heart of the sea, or how many streams at the source of the deep, or how many ways above the firmament . . ." (4:5–7).
4. I.e., the oceans.
5. Count.
6. Lines 10–15 probably echo Ecclesiasticus 1:2–3: "The sand of the seas, and the drops of rain, and the days of eternity—who can count them? The height of the heavens, and the breadth of the earth, and the deep, and wisdom—who can track them out?"
7. Cf. Psalms 18:10: "[The Lord] rode upon a cherub."

What God Is

God is above the sphere of our esteem,
And is the best known, not defining Him.

Calling, and Correcting

God is not only merciful, to call
Men to repent, but when He strikes withal.[8]

Upon Time

Time was upon
The wing, to fly away,
And I called on
Him but a while to stay;
But he'd be gone,
For ought that I could say.

He held out then
A writing, as he went,
And asked me when
False man would be content
To pay again[9]
What God and Nature lent.

An hourglass,
In which were sands but few,
As he did pass,
He showed; and told me too
Mine end near was,
And so away he flew.

To His Savior, a Child; A Present by a Child

Go, pretty child, and bear this flower
Unto thy little Savior,
And tell Him, by that bud now blown
He is the *Rose of Sharon*[1] known;
When thou hast said so, stick it there
Upon His bib, or stomacher,[2]

8. Cf. Hebrews 12:11: "Now no chastening for the present seemeth to be joyous, but grievous; nevertheless afterward it yieldeth the peaceable fruit of righteousness unto them which are exercised thereby."
9. I.e., to repay.
1. Cf. Song of Solomon 2:1: "I am the rose of Sharon, and the lily of the valleys."
2. Pinafore (in this context).

And tell Him, for good handsel[3] too,
That thou hast brought a whistle[4] new,
Made of a clean, straight, oaten reed,
To charm His cries, at time of need;
Tell Him, for coral, thou hast none,
But if thou hadst, He should have one;
But poor thou art, and known to be
Even as moneyless as He.
Lastly, if thou canst win a kiss
From those mellifluous lips[5] of His,
Then never take a second on,
To spoil the first impression.

To His Conscience

Can I not sin, but thou wilt be
My private protonotary?[6]
Can I not woo thee to pass by
A short and sweet iniquity?
I'll cast a mist and cloud upon
My delicate transgression,
So utter dark as that no eye
Shall see the hugged impiety;
Gifts blind the wise,[7] and bribes do please
And wind[8] all other witnesses,
And wilt not thou with gold be tied
To lay thy pen and ink aside,
That in the murk and tongueless night,
Wanton I may, and thou not write?
It will not be; and therefore now,
For times to come I'll make this vow:
From aberrations to live free,
So I'll not fear the Judge, or thee.

His Creed

I do believe that die I must,
And be returned from out my dust;
I do believe that when I rise
Christ I shall see with these same eyes;
I do believe that I must come

3. Pledge, gift.
4. "Small silver whistles seem to have been one of the two *sine qua non* of seventeenth-century babyhood. Trinculo adds the other when [Dryden, *The Tempest*, III.iii] he cries, 'It shall be a Whistle for our first Babe, and when the next Shipwrack puts us again to swimming, I'll dive to get a coral to it'" (*Plays and Poems of William Cartwright*, ed. G. Blakemore Evans [Madison, Wis., 1951], p. 694).
5. Cf. Song of Solomon 4:3: "Thy lips are like a thread of scarlet, and thy speech is comely."
6. The protonotary was chief recording clerk in a court of law.
7. Cf. Deuteronomy 16:19: "A gift doth blind the eye of the wise."
8. Corrupt.

With others to the dreadful Doom;
I do believe the bad must go
From thence to everlasting woe;
I do believe the good, and I,
Shall live with Him eternally;
I do believe I shall inherit
Heaven, by Christ's mercies, not my merit;
I do believe the One in Three,
And Three in perfect Unity;
Lastly, that Jesus is a deed
Of gift from God. And here's my creed.

Another Grace for a Child

Here a little child I stand,
Heaving up my either hand;
Cold as paddocks[9] though they be,
Here I lift them up to Thee,
For a benison[1] to fall
On our meat, and on us all. Amen.

The Bellman

Along the dark and silent night,
With my lantern, and my light,
And the tinkling of my bell,
Thus I walk, and this I tell:
Death and dreadfulness call on
To the gen'ral Session,[2]
To whose dismal bar, we there
All accounts must come to clear.
Scores of sins we've made here many;
Wiped out few, God knows, if any.
Rise, ye debtors, then, and fall
To make payment, while I call.
Ponder this when I am gone;
By the clock 'tis almost one.

The White Island, or Place of the Blest

In this world, the isle of dreams,
While we sit by sorrow's streams,
Tears and terrors are our themes,
Reciting;

9. Toads.
1. Blessing.
2. I.e., the Last Judgment.

But when once from hence we fly,
More and more approaching nigh
Unto young eternity,
Uniting

In that whiter island, where
Things are evermore sincere,
Candor here and lustre there
Delighting:

There no monstrous fancies shall
Out of hell an horror call
To create, or cause at all,
Affrighting.

There in calm and cooling sleep
We our eyes shall never steep,
But eternal watch shall keep,
Attending

Pleasures, such as shall pursue
Me immortalized, and you;
And fresh joys, as never, too,
Have ending.

George Herbert

1593 Born 3 April, fifth son of Richard (d. 1596) and Magdalen Herbert, in Montgomery, Wales.
1605 Attends Westminster School.
1608 Magdalen Herbert weds Sir John Danvers.
1609 Enrolls at Trinity College, Cambridge (B.A., 1613; M.A., 1616).
1612 Heir apparent, Prince Henry, dies. Herbert composes two Latin memorial poems, his first published verses.
1616 Elected major fellow of Trinity College, Cambridge.
1618 Appointed Reader in Rhetoric at Cambridge.
1620 Elected Public Orator at Cambridge (keeps the post until 1628).
1625 Sir Francis Bacon dedicates *Translation of Certain Psalms* to Herbert.
1627 Magdalen Herbert dies; John Donne gives the funeral sermon.
1629 Marries Jane Danvers (cousin to his stepfather).
1630 Forsaking worldly ambition, becomes Rector of Bemerton, in Wiltshire. Helps rebuild the church there out of his own funds and attends his pastoral duties with extraordinary conscientiousness.
1633 Dies (1 March) of consumption. *The Temple* published posthumously and is remarkably well received.

FROM *THE TEMPLE* (1633)

The Altar

A broken ALTAR, Lord, thy servant rears,
Made of a heart, and cemented with tears:[1]
Whose parts are as thy hand did frame;
No workman's tool hath touched the same.
A HEART alone
Is such a stone,
As nothing but
Thy power doth cut.
Wherefore each part
Of my hard heart
Meets in this frame,
To praise thy Name.
That, if I chance to hold my peace,
These stones to praise thee may not cease.[2]
Oh let thy blessed SACRIFICE be mine,
And sanctify this ALTAR to be thine.

The Sacrifice[3]

Oh all ye, who pass by,[4] whose eyes and mind
To worldly things are sharp, but to me blind,
To me, who took eyes[5] that I might you find.
Was ever grief[6] like mine?
The Princes of my people make a head[7]
Against their Maker: they do wish me dead,
Who cannot wish, except I give them bread.
Was ever grief like mine?
Without me each one, who doth now me brave,[8]
Had to this day been an Egyptian slave.
They use that power against me, which I gave.
Was ever grief like mine?
Mine own Apostle, who the bag did bear,[9]

1. "And if thou wilt make me an altar of stone, thou shalt not build it of hewn stone: for if thou lift up thy tool upon it, thou hast polluted it" (Exodus 20:25); "a broken and a contrite heart, O God, thou wilt not despise" (Psalms 51:7).
2. "I tell you, that if these should hold their peace, the stones would immediately cry out" (Luke 19: 40).
3. "The Sacrifice" is a dramatic monologue spoken by Christ. The form and details evoke the liturgy for Holy Week, specifically the ironic *Improperia,* or Reproaches of the Good Friday liturgy, which Christ addresses to the ungrateful people as he undergoes the Passion and Crucifixion. Interwoven in the text are many details from the Gospel narratives of the Passion—Matthew 26–27, Mark 14–15, Luke 22–23, and John 18–19. See also Textual Notes.
4. Cf. Jeremiah, Lamentations 1:12, "All ye that pass by, behold, and see if there be any sorrow like unto my sorrow."
5. I.e., became man.
6. Besides the usual meanings, "grief" includes physical distress.
7. *Make a head*: rebel, as militarily.
8. Defy.
9. Judas carried the apostles' money (John 12:6).

Though he had all I had, did not forbear
To sell me also, and to put me there:
Was ever grief like mine?
For thirty pence he did my death devise,
Who at three hundred did the ointment prize,[1]
Not half so sweet as my sweet sacrifice.
Was ever grief, &c.
Therefore my soul melts, and my heart's dear treasure
Drops blood (the only beads) my words to measure.
O let this cup pass, if it be thy pleasure.[2]
Was ever grief, &c.
These drops being tempered with a sinner's tears
A balsam are for both the hemispheres;
Curing all wounds, but mine, all, but my fears.
Was ever grief, &c.
Yet my Disciples sleep: I cannot gain
One hour of watching, but their drowsy brain
Comforts not me, and doth my doctrine stain.
Was ever grief, &c.
Arise, arise, they come. Look how they run.
Alas! what haste they make to be undone!
How with their lanterns do they seek the sun!
Was ever grief, &c.
With clubs and staves they seek me, as a thief,
Who am the way and Truth,[3] the true relief,
Most true to those, who are my greatest grief.
Was ever grief, &c.
Judas, dost thou betray me with a kiss?
Canst thou find hell about my lips? and miss
Of life, just at the gates of life and bliss?
Was ever grief, &c.
See, they lay hold on me, not with the hands
Of faith, but fury: yet at their commands
I suffer binding, who have loosed their bands.
Was ever grief, &c.
All my Disciples fly: fear puts a bar
Betwixt my friends and me; they leave the star,
That brought the wise men of the East from far.
Was ever grief, &c.
Then from one ruler to another bound
They lead me, urging, that it was not sound
What I taught: comments would the text confound.[4]
Was ever grief, &c.
The Priests and rulers all false witness seek[5]

1. Judas, who betrays Christ for thirty pieces of silver (Matthew 26:15), had previously complained that ointment used on Christ's feet might have been sold for "three hundred pence" (John 12:5).
2. Drops of blood are here compared to the "beads" of a rosary. In the Garden of Gethsemane, Christ sweats blood (Luke 22:44) while praying to his father to "let this cup pass" (Matthew 26:39).
3. "I am the way, the truth, and the life" (John 14:6).
4. Christ was accused of teachings that subverted Mosaic law.
5. *Priests*: most editors follow the Bodleian manuscript and use the singular, identifying the Priest as Caiaphas (Matthew 26:57). The context indicates that Herbert has in mind Matthew 26:59,

Gainst him, who seeks not life, but is the meek
And ready Paschal Lamb of this great week.[6]
Was ever grief like mine?
Then they accuse me of great blasphemy,
That I did thrust into the Deity,
Who never thought that any robbery.[7]
Was ever grief, &c.
Some said, that I the Temple to the floor
In three days razed, and raisèd as before.
Why, he that built the world can do much more.
Was ever grief, &c.
Then they condemn me all with that same breath,
Which I do give them daily, unto death:
Thus Adam my first breathing rendereth.[8]
Was ever grief, &c.
They bind, and lead me unto Herod: he
Sends me to Pilate. This makes them agree;
But yet their friendship is my enmity.
Was ever grief, &c.
Herod and all his bands do set me light,
Who teach all hands to war, fingers to fight,
And only am the Lord of Hosts and might.
Was ever grief, &c.
Herod in judgment sits, while I do stand,
Examines me with a censorious hand:
I him obey, who all things else[9] command.
Was ever grief, &c.
The Jews accuse me with despitefulness,
And vying malice with my gentleness,
Pick quarrels with their only happiness.
Was ever grief, &c.
I answer nothing, but with patience prove[1]
If stony hearts will melt with gentle love.
But who does hawk at eagles with a dove?
Was ever grief, &c.
My silence rather doth augment their cry:
My dove doth back into my bosom fly:
Because the raging waters still are high.[2]
Was ever grief, &c.
Hark how they cry aloud still, "Crucify.
It is not fit he live a day," they cry,
Who cannot live less than eternally.

however: "now the chief priests, and elders, and all the council, sought false witness against Jesus, to put him to death."
6. The week of Passover and the first Christian passion week.
7. This stanza combines Jesus' answer to the priests and false witnesses, which asserted his place as Son of God (Matthew 26:59 ff.), with the observation in Philippians 2:6: "Who, being in the form of God, thought it not robbery to be equal with God." In the original Greek, the last clause literally means "did not consider equality with God something to be seized."
8. Returns or gives back the breath of life. Cf. "Prayer [I]," line 2, p. 243.
9. Otherwise.
1. Try to discover.
2. The dove, unable to alight, returns to Noah's ark (Genesis 8:9).

Was ever grief like mine?
Pilate a stranger holdeth off; but they,
Mine own dear people, cry, "Away, away,"
With noises confusèd frighting the day.
Was ever grief, &c.
Yet still they shout, and cry, and stop their ears,
Putting my life among their sins and fears,
And therefore wish my blood on them and theirs.[3]
Was ever grief, &c.
See how spite cankers things. These words, aright
Used, and wishèd, are the whole world's light.[4]
But honey is their gall, brightness their night.
Was ever grief, &c.
They choose a murderer,[5] and all agree
In him to do themselves a courtesy:
For it was their own cause who killèd me.
Was ever grief, &c.
And a seditious murderer he was.
But I the Prince of peace, peace that doth pass
All understanding, more than heav'n doth glass.[6]
Was ever grief, &c.
Why, Caesar is their only King, not I:
He clave the stony rock, when they were dry.[7]
But surely not their hearts, as I well try.
Was ever grief, &c.
Ah! How they scourge me! Yet my tenderness[8]
Doubles each lash: and yet their bitterness
Winds up my grief to a mysteriousness.
Was ever grief, &c.
They buffet him, and box him as they list,
Who grasps the earth and heaven with his fist,
And never yet, whom he[9] would punish, missed.
Was ever grief, &c.
Behold, they spit on me in scornful wise,
Who by my spittle[1] gave the blind man eyes,
Leaving his blindness to my enemies.
Was ever grief, &c.
My face they cover, though it be divine.
As Moses' face was veilèd so is mine,
Lest on their double-dark souls either[2] shine.

3. Cf. Matthew 27:25 (the basis of the blood libel historically used to justify Jewish persecution).
4. In Christian theology, Christ's blood is the basis of salvation.
5. In keeping with a custom of amnesty at festival time, Pilate offers a choice between Jesus and the murderer Barabbas (Matthew 27:15 ff.; Mark 15:7).
6. See Isaiah 9:6 (the "Messianic" prophecy) and Philippians 4:7 for the peace that passes all understanding. *Glass*: reflect, as in a mirror; cf. 1 Corinthians 13:12.
7. "We have no king but Caesar" (John 19:15). God "smote the rock that the waters gushed out" (Psalms 78:20).
8. Compassion, love (not physical weakness).
9. *Him . . . he*: in the 1633 and most subsequent editions, the pronouns are first person, which clouds the irony of the passage. We follow the manuscripts in using the third person.
1. John 9 relates the curing of the man born blind. Note the pun on "spittle" as hospital; cf. "The Thanksgiving," line 33, p. 234.
2. I.e., either Moses' face or Christ's. Moses veils his face when he talks to the people, who were fearful because after his meetings with God "the skin of his face shone" (Exodus 34:29).

Was ever grief like mine?
Servants and abjects flout me; they are witty:
"Now prophesy who strikes thee," is their ditty.
So they in me deny themselves all pity.
Was ever grief, &c.
And now I am delivered unto death,
Which each one calls for so with utmost[3] breath,
That he before me well nigh suffereth.
Was ever grief, &c.
Weep not, dear friends, since I for both have wept
When all my tears were blood, the while you slept:
Your tears for your own fortunes should be kept.
Was ever grief, &c.
The soldiers lead me to the common hall,
There they deride me, they abuse me all;
Yet for twelve heav'nly legions I could call.
Was ever grief, &c.
Then with a scarlet robe they me array:
Which shows my blood to be the only way
And cordial left to repair man's decay.
Was ever grief, &c.
Then on my head a crown of thorns I wear:
For these are all the grapes Sion doth bear,
Though I my vine planted and watered there.[4]
Was ever grief, &c.
So sits the earth's great curse in Adam's fall[5]
Upon my head; so I remove it all
From th'earth unto my brows, and bear the thrall.
Was ever grief, &c.
Then with the reed they gave to me before,
They strike my head, the rock from whence all store
Of heav'nly blessings issue evermore.
Was ever grief, &c.
They bow their knees to me, and cry, "Hail king."
Whatever scoffs and scornfulness can bring,
I am the floor, the sink, where they it fling.
Was ever grief, &c.
Yet since man's scepters are as frail as reeds,
And thorny all their crowns, bloody their weeds,[6]
I, who am Truth turn into truth their deeds.
Was ever grief, &c.
The soldiers also spit upon that face,
Which Angels did desire to have the grace,
And Prophets once to see, but found no place.
Was ever grief, &c.
Thus trimmèd forth they bring me to the rout,

3. *Utmost*: suggests both the vehemence of the outcry and the last (or dying) breath (cf. line 229).
4. God planted and watered the Vine of Sion (House of Israel), but Christ's crown of thorns is its only fruit (cf. Isaiah 5:1–7).
5. "Thorns . . . shall [the earth] bring forth" (Genesis 3:18).
6. Clothing.

Who "Crucify him," cry with one strong shout.
God holds his peace at man, and man cries out.
Was ever grief like mine?
They lead me in once more, and putting then
Mine own clothes on, they lead me out again.
Whom devils fly, thus is he tossed of men.
Was ever grief, &c.
And now weary of sport, glad to engross[7]
All spite in one, counting my life their loss,
They carry me to my most bitter cross.
Was ever grief, &c.
My cross I bear my self, until I faint:
Then Simon bears it for me, by constraint,[8]
The decreed burden of each mortal saint.
Was ever grief, &c.
Oh all ye who pass by, behold and see;
Man stole the fruit, but I must climb the tree,
The tree of life to all, but only me.[9]
Was ever grief, &c.
Lo, here I hang, charged with a world of sin,
The greater world o'th'two: for that came in
By words, but this by sorrow I must win.[1]
Was ever grief, &c.
Such sorrow, as if sinful man could feel,
Or feel his part, he would not cease to kneel,
Till all were melted, though he were all steel.
Was ever grief, &c.
But, O my God, my God! why leav'st thou me,
The Son, in whom thou dost delight to be?
My God, my God—[2]
Never was grief like mine.
Shame tears my soul, my body many a wound,
Sharp nails pierce this, but sharper that confound,
Reproaches, which are free, while I am bound.
Was ever grief, &c.
"Now heal thy self, Physician; now come down."[3]
Alas! I did so, when I left my crown,
And father's smile to feel for you his frown.
Was ever grief, &c.
In healing not my self, there doth consist
All that salvation, which ye now resist.

7. Concentrate, collect.
8. A bystander, Simon of Cyrene, is "compelled to bear his cross" (Matthew 27:32) and assist Christ.
9. The cross and the forbidden tree (where "Man stole the fruit") are often linked in Christian literature and art. *But only*: except for.
1. I.e., the world was first created by God's spoken commands; once fallen, it is redeemed by Christ's suffering.
2. Cf. Matthew 27:46.
3. Jesus quotes the proverb "Physician, heal thyself" during his ministry (Luke 4:23); on Calvary, he is taunted, "if thou be the Son of God, come down from the cross" (Matthew 27:40).

Your safety in my sickness doth subsist.
Was ever grief like mine?
Betwixt two thieves I spend my utmost breath,
As he that for some robbery suffereth.
Alas! what have I stolen from you? Death.
Was ever grief, &c.
A King my title is, prefixed on high,[4]
Yet by my subjects am condemned to die,
A servile death in servile company.
Was ever grief, &c.
They give me vinegar, mingled with gall,
But more with malice: yet, when they did call,
With Manna, Angels' food,[5] I fed them all.
Was ever grief, &c.
They part my garments, and by lot dispose
My coat, the type of love, which once cured[6] those
Who sought for help, never malicious foes.
Was ever grief, &c.
Nay, after death their spite shall further go:
For they will pierce my side, I full well know.
That as sin came, so Sacraments[7] might flow.
Was ever grief, &c.
But now I die: now all is finishèd.
My woe, man's weal. And now I bow my head.
Only let others say, when I am dead,
Never was grief like mine.

The Thanksgiving[8]

Oh King of grief (a title strange, yet true
To thee, of all kings, only due)
Oh King of wounds, how shall I grieve for thee,
Who in all grief preventest[9] me?
Shall I weep blood? Why thou hast wept such store[1]
That all thy body was one door.[2]
Shall I be scourgèd, flouted, boxèd, sold?
Tis but to tell the tale is told.
"My God, my God, why dost thou part from me,"
Was such a grief as cannot be.

4. Cf. Matthew 27:37 for the accusation fixed over Christ's head on the cross. "Prefixed on high" may also suggest that his kingship and sacrifice were predestined by God.
5. *Manna*: dewlike food divinely supplied to the Hebrews in the desert (Exodus 16:35). Prefigured by manna, the Eucharist in the liturgy of Holy Thursday is called the "bread of angels."
6. On the healing power of Christ's coat, see Matthew 14:36.
7. Eve, who begins human sinning, came from Adam's side. At the piercing of the second Adam's side, blood and water flowed (John 19:34), signifying the Church and the Sacraments.
8. Herbert uses the word nowhere else in his poetry.
9. Anticipate, go before; also, surpass.
1. Abundance.
2. "I am the door" (John 10:9). Cf. "The Bag," line 38, p. 276.

Shall I then sing, skipping thy doleful story,
    And side with thy triumphant glory?[3]
Shall thy strokes be my stroking? Thorns, my flower?
    Thy rod, my posy?[4] Cross, my bower?
But how then shall I imitate thee, and
    Copy thy fair though bloody hand?
Surely I will revenge me on thy love,
    And try, who shall victorious prove.
If thou dost give me wealth, I will restore
    All back unto thee by[5] the poor.
If thou dost give me honor, men shall see,
    That honor doth belong to thee.
I will not marry: or if she be mine,
    She and her children shall be thine.
My bosom friend, if he blaspheme thy name,
    I will tear thence his love and fame.
One half of me being gone, the rest I'll give
    Unto some chapel, die or live.
As for thy Passion—but of that anon
    When with the other I have done.
For thy predestination[6] I'll contrive,
    That three years hence if I survive,
I'll build a spittle,[7] or mend common ways,
    But mend mine own without delays.
Then will I use the works of thy creation
    As if I used them but for fashion.
The world and I will quarrel: and the year
    Shall not perceive that I am here.
My music shall find thee, and ev'ry string
    Shall have his attribute[8] to sing
That all together may accord in thee,
    And prove one God, one harmony.
If thou shalt give me wit, it shall appear
    If thou hast giv'n it me,'tis here.[9]
Nay, I will read thy book, and never move
    Till I have found therein thy love,
Thy art of love, which I'll turn back on thee,
    O my dear Savior, Victory!
Then for thy Passion—I will do for that—
    Alas, my God, I know not what.

3. The two lines allude to the parallel traditions: *Christus patiens*, or Christ suffering, emphasizing the Passion; *Christus gloriosus* (sometimes *Christus triumphans*), Christ in glory or triumphant, emphasizing the Resurrection.
4. Bunch of flowers; a short motto; poetical collection.
5. By means of.
6. Election to salvation through grace.
7. Hospital.
8. Particular characteristic.
9. In this book of poems.

The Reprisal[1]

I have considered it and find
There is no meddling with thy mighty Passion.
For though I die for thee, I am behind,
My sins deserve the condemnation.

O make me innocent, that I
May give a disentangled state and free:
And yet thy wounds still my attempts defy,
For by thy death I die for thee.

Ah was it not enough, that thou
By thy eternal glory didst outgo me?
Couldst thou not grief's sad conquests me allow,
But in all victories overthrow me?

Yet by confession will I come
Into thy conquest. Though I can do naught
Against thee, in thee I will overcome
The man, who once against thee fought.

The Agony[2]

Philosophers[3] have measured mountains,
Fathomed the depths of seas, of states, and kings,
Walked with a staff[4] to heav'n and traced fountains,
But there are two vast, spacious things
The which to measure it doth more behove,
Yet few there are that sound them, Sin and Love.

Who would know Sin, let him repair
Unto Mount Olivet,[5] there shall he see
A man so wrung with pains that all his hair,
His skin, his garments bloody be.
Sin is that press and vice[6] which forceth pain
To hunt his cruel food through ev'ry vein.

1. Herbert uses the word nowhere else in his works.
2. Herbert uses the word nowhere else in his works. The main metaphor of this poem is that of the winepress, a traditional symbol of Christ's Passion (cf. Isaiah 63:3).
3. Men learned in the sciences.
4. A "Jacob's staff" (Genesis 32:10), i.e., an instrument for taking altitude as well as a pilgrim's staff.
5. Place of the agony and betrayal of Jesus.
6. *Press and vice*: instruments of torture.

Who knows not Love, let him assay
And taste that juice which on the cross a pike
Did set again abroach;[7] then let him say
If ever he did taste the like.
Love is that liquor sweet and most divine
Which my God feels as blood, but I, as wine.

The Sinner

Lord how I am all ague, when I seek
What I have treasured in my memory;
Since if my soul make even with the week,
Each seventh note by right is due to thee.
I find there quarries of piled vanities
But shreds of holiness, that dare not venture
To show their face, since cross to thy decrees.
There the circumference earth is: heav'n the center.
In so much dregs, the quintessence is small,
The spirit and good extract of my heart
Comes to about the many hundredth part,
Yet Lord restore thine image, hear my call
And though my hard heart scarce to thee can groan,
Remember that thou once didst write in stone.

Good Friday

Oh my chief good
How shall I measure out thy blood?
How shall I count what thee befell
And each grief tell?

Shall I thy woes
Number according to thy foes?
Or since one star showed thy first breath,
Shall all, thy death?

Or shall each leaf
Which falls in Autumn score[8] a grief?
Or cannot leaves, but fruit be sign
Of the True Vine?

Then let each hour
Of my whole life one grief devour
That thy distress through all may run
And be my sun.

7. *Set . . . abroach*: to let out, as liquor (cf. John 19:34).
8. Record; perhaps also, cut.

Or rather let
My several sins their sorrows get,
That as each beast his cure doth know
Each sin may so.

The Passion

Since blood is fittest, Lord, to write
Thy sorrows in, and bloody fight;
My heart hath store, write there, where in
One box doth lie both ink and sin.

That when sin spies so many foes,
Thy whips, thy nails, thy wounds, thy woes,
All come to lodge there, sin may say,
"No room for me," and fly away.

Sin being gone oh fill the place,
And keep possession with thy grace
Lest sin take courage and return,
And all the writings blot or burn.

Redemption

Having been tenant[9] long to a rich Lord,
Not thriving, I resolved to be bold
And make a suit unto him, to afford
A new small-rented lease, and cancel th' old.
In heaven at his manor I him sought:
They told me there, that he was lately gone
About some land which he had dearly bought
Long since on earth to take possession.
I strait[1] returned, and knowing his great birth
Sought him accordingly in great resorts,
In cities, theatres, gardens, parks, and courts.
At length I heard a ragged noise and mirth
Of thieves and murderers. There I him espied,
Who strait, "Your suit is granted," said and died.

9. This narrative sonnet weaves two metaphors: tenancy and redemption, i.e., payment or ransom.
1. Immediately; in straitened circumstances. Cf. line 14.

Sepulcher[2]

Oh blessed body! Whither art thou thrown?
No lodging for thee, but a cold hard stone?
So many hearts on earth, and yet not one
Receive thee?
Sure there is room within our hearts good store:[3]
For they can lodge transgressions by the score.
Thousands of toys[4] dwell there; yet out of door
They leave thee.
But that, which shows them large, shows them unfit.
What ever sin did this pure rock commit,
Which holds thee now? Who hath indicted it
Of murder?
Where our hard hearts have took up stones to brain thee,[5]
And missing this, most falsely did arraign thee,
Only these stones in quiet entertain thee,
And order.
And as of old, the Law by heav'nly art
Was writ in stone: so thou, which also art
The letter of the word,[6] find'st no fit heart
To hold thee.
Yet do we still persist as we began,
And so should perish, but that nothing can,
Though it be cold, hard, foul, from loving man
Withhold thee.

Easter [I]

Rise heart, thy Lord is risen. Sing his praise
Without delays,
Who takes thee by the hand, that thou likewise
With him mayst rise:
That, as his death calcinèd thee to dust,
His life may make thee gold, and much more just.

Awake, my lute, and struggle for thy part
With all thy art.
The cross taught all wood[7] to resound his name,
Who bore the same.
His stretched sinews taught all strings what key
Is best to celebrate this most high day.

2. Herbert uses this word nowhere else in his works.
3. Sufficient or abundant supply (*OED*).
4. Trifles of little value.
5. Cf. John 10:31.
6. In 2 Corinthians 3:3 Paul describes his readers as "the epistle of Christ . . . written not with ink, but with the Spirit of the living God: not in tables of stone, but in fleshy tables of the heart." Cf. Exodus 31:18 for the tablets of stone on which God writes the law.
7. I.e., not just the wood of the lute.

Consort[8] both heart and lute and twist a song[9]
Pleasant and long
Or since all music is but three parts vied[1]
And multiplied
Oh let thy blessèd Spirit bear a part
And make up our defects with his sweet art.

Easter [II][2]

I got me flowers to straw[3] thy way,
I got me boughs off many a tree:
But thou wast up by break of day
And brought'st thy sweets along with thee.

The sun arising in the East
Though he give light and th' East perfume,
If they should offer to contest
With thy arising, they presume.

Can there be any day but this,
Though many suns to shine endeavor?
We count three hundred, but we miss:
There is but one, and that one ever.

Easter-wings [I][4]

Lord who createdst man in wealth and store
Though foolishly he lost the same,
Decaying more and more
Till he became
Most poor.
With thee
O let me rise,
As larks, harmoniously
And sing this day thy victories.
Then shall the fall further the flight in me.[5]

8. Combine in musical harmony.
9. *Twist*: weave both heart and lute together to make a song.
1. *Vie*: "increase in number by addition or repetition" (*OED*, citing this text).
2. The bracketed numerals distinguish poems with similar titles.
3. Strew, scatter.
4. The 1633 edition printed the two "Easter-wings" poems vertically, in an X shape, but the scribes of both manuscripts wrote the texts horizontally, aligned right. The 1633 editor apparently wanted to mimic the shape of wings and upward flight and thus the spiritual act of rising and the X shape of the cross that made possible the rising. The scribes by contrast wrote the poems on facing pages, suggesting the flight of birds *across* the sky. Both "further the flight" and "advance the flight," in the respective last lines of the two poems, support the sense of horizontal flight.
5. In the liturgy of Holy Saturday, humanity's fall is described as a *felix culpa* (happy fault) because it brought so great a Redeemer.

Easter-wings [II]

My tender[6] age in sorrow did begin,
And still with sicknesses and shame
Thou didst so punish sin,
That I became
Most thin.
With thee,
Let me combine
And feel this day thy victory:
For if I imp[7] my wing on thine,
Affliction shall advance the flight in me.

H. Baptism [I][8]

As he that sees a dark and shady grove
Stays not but looks beyond it on the sky:
So when I view my sins, mine eyes remove
More backward still and to that water fly
Which is above the heav'ns, whose spring and vent
Is in my dear Redeemer's piercèd side.
O blessèd streams, either ye do prevent
And stop our sins from growing thick and wide
Or else give tears to drown them as they grow.
In you Redemption measures all my time
Spreading the plaster equal to the crime.
You taught the book of life[9] my name, that so
What ever future sins should me miscall
Your first acquaintance might discredit all.

H. Baptism [II]

Since, Lord, to thee
A narrow way and little gate[1]
Is all the passage, on my infancy
Thou didst lay hold, and antedate
My faith in me.

O let me still
Write thee great God, and me a child:
Let me be soft and supple to thy will,
Small to my self, to others mild,
Behither[2] ill.

6. Youthful; also, of delicate constitution.
7. Engraft.
8. H. = Holy.
9. The list of the saved (Philippians 4:3, Revelation 21:27).
1. "Strait is the gate, and narrow is the way" (Matthew 7:14).
2. Short of, barring.

Although by stealth
My flesh get on, yet let her sister
My soul bid nothing, but[3] preserve her wealth;
The growth of flesh is but a blister
Childhood is health.

Sin [I][4]

Lord, with what care hast thou begirt us round?
Parents first season us: then schoolmasters
Deliver us to laws: they send us bound
To rules of reason. Holy messengers.
Pulpits and Sundays. Sorrow dogging Sin.
Afflictions sorted, anguish of all sizes:
Fine nets and stratagems to catch us in.
Bibles laid open; millions of surprises.
Blessings beforehand: ties of gratefulness:
The sound of glory ringing in our ears:
Without, our shame: within, our consciences:
Angels and grace: eternal hopes and fears.
Yet all these fences and their whole array
One cunning bosom-sin blows quite away.

Affliction [I]

When first thou didst entice to thee my heart
I thought the service brave.[5]
So many joys I writ down for my part
Besides what I might have
Out of my stock of natural delights,
Augmented with thy gracious benefits.

I looked on thy furniture so fine,
And made it fine to me:
Thy glorious household-stuff did me entwine,
And 'tice me unto thee.
Such stars I counted mine; both heaven and earth
Paid me my wages in a world of mirth.

What pleasures could I want,[6] whose King I served?
Where joys my fellows were?
Thus argued into hopes, my thoughts reserved
No place for grief or fear.

3. *Bid . . . but*: pray for nothing, except to.
4. Coleridge (*Biographia Literaria*, XIX) admired this sonnet "for the purity of the language and the fullness of the sense."
5. Splendid.
6. Lack.

Therefore my sudden soul caught at the place
And made her youth and fierceness seek thy face.

At first thou gav'st me milk and sweetnesses,
I had my wish and way.
My days were strawed[7] with flow'rs and happiness,
There was no month but May.
But with my years sorrows did twist and grow,
And made a party unawares[8] for woe.

My flesh began unto[9] my soul in pain,
"Sicknesses cleave my bones:
Consuming agues dwell in ev'ry vein
And tune my breath to groans."
Sorrow was all my soul, I scarce believed,
Till grief did tell me roundly, that I lived.

When I got health, thou took'st away my life
And more, for my friends die.
My mirth and edge was lost, a blunted knife
Was of more use[1] than I.
Thus thin and lean, without a fence or friend
I was blown through with every storm and wind.

Whereas my birth and spirit rather took
The way that takes the Town
Thou didst betray me to a ling'ring book
And wrap me in a gown.[2]
I was entangled in the world of strife,
Before I had the power to change my life.

Yet for I threatened oft the siege to raise,
Not simp'ring all mine age,
Thou often didst with academic praise
Melt and dissolve my rage.
I took thy sweetened pill, till I came where
I could not go away, nor persevere.

Yet lest perchance, I should too happy be
In my unhappiness
Turning my purge to food: thou throwest me
Into more sicknesses,
Thus doth thy power cross-bias me: not making
Thine own gift good, yet me from my ways taking.[3]

7. As in "Easter [II]," line 1, p. 239, strewn.
8. Created a faction inadvertently.
9. *Began unto*: complained to.
1. See below, lines 57 ff.; cf. the "Employment" poems on the poet's concern that he be of some use.
2. I.e., an academic gown.
3. In the game of bowls, either a lead weight or the shape of the bowl biases it to go a particular way. Herbert complains that God is thwarting him from going the way of his God-given bias.

Now I am here; what thou wilt do with me
None of my books will show:
I read and sigh and wish I were a tree,
For sure, then I should grow
To fruit or shade: at least some bird would trust
Her household to me, and I should be just.

Yet though thou troublest me, I must be meek:
In weakness must be stout.
Well, I will change the service and go seek
Some other Master out.
Ah my dear God, though I am clean forgot,
Let me not love thee, if I love thee not.

Prayer [I]

Prayer, the Church's banquet, angels' age,
God's breath in man returning to his birth,
The soul in paraphrase,[4] heart in pilgrimage,
The Christian plummet sounding heav'n and earth,
Engine against th'Almighty, sinners' tower,
Reversèd thunder, Christ-side-piercing spear,
The six-days' world[5] transposing[6] in an hour,
A kind of tune which all things hear and fear
Softness and peace and joy and love and bliss,
Exalted manna, gladness of the best,
Heaven in ordinary,[7] man well dressed,
The milky way, the bird of Paradise,
Church-bells beyond the stars heard: the soul's blood,
The Land of Spices, something understood.

The H. Communion[8]

Not in rich furniture, or fine array,
Nor in a wedge of gold,
Thou, who for me wast sold,
To me dost now thy self convey;
For so thou should'st without me still have been,
Leaving within me sin.

But by the way of nourishment and strength
Thou creep'st into my breast,
Making thy way my rest,

4. Clarifying by expansion.
5. The world was created in the six days of the ordinary week.
6. Musically, changing keys.
7. In everyday practice.
8. See Textual Notes.

And thy small quantities my length,
Which spread their forces into every part,
Meeting sin's force and art.

Yet can these not get over to my soul
Leaping the wall that parts
Our souls and fleshy hearts,
But as th'outworks,[9] they may control
My rebel flesh, and carrying thy Name
Affright both sin and shame.

Only thy grace, which with these elements comes,
Knoweth the ready way,
And hath the privy key,
Opening the soul's most subtle rooms,
While those to spirits refined,[1] at door attend
Dispatches from their friend.

Prayer [II][2]

Give me my captive soul or take
My body also thither;
Another lift like this, will make
Them both to be together.

Before that sin turned flesh to stone
And all our lump to leaven,
A fervent sigh might well have blown
Our innocent earth to heaven.

For sure when Adam did not know
To sin or sin to smother,
He might to heav'n from Paradise go
As from one room t'another.

Thou hast restored us to this ease
By this thy heav'nly blood
Which I can go to when I please
And leave th'earth to their food.

9. Outer fortifications.
1. The elements of bread and wine (line 19) are refined into physiological spirits through the process of digestion.
2. Usually printed as part of the preceding poem, these stanzas in the Williams manuscript form a separate poem, entitled "Prayer." See Textual Notes.

Love I

Immortal Love, author of this great frame,
  Sprung from that beauty which can never fade,
  How hath man parceled out thy glorious name,
And thrown it on that dust, which thou hast made,
While mortal love doth all the title gain,
  Which siding with invention,[3] they together
  Bear all the sway, possessing heart and brain,
(Thy workmanship) and give thee share in neither.
Wit fancies[4] beauty, beauty raiseth wit.
  The world is theirs: they two play out the game,
  Thou standing by. And though thy glorious name
Wrought our deliverance from th'infernal pit,
  Who sings thy praise? Only a scarf or glove[5]
  Doth warm our hands and make them write of love.

[Love II][6]

Immortal Heat, O let thy greater flame
  Attract the lesser to it: let those fires
  Which shall consume the world, first make it tame
And kindle in our hearts such true desires
As may consume our lusts, and make thee way:[7]
  Then shall our hearts pant[8] thee: then shall our brain
  All her invention on thine Altar lay,
And there in hymns send back thy fire again.
Our eyes shall see thee, which before saw dust,
  Dust blown by wit, till that they both were blind.
  Thou shalt recover all thy goods in kind,
Who wert disseizèd[9] by usurping lust.
  All knees shall bow to thee, all wits shall rise,
  And praise him who did make and mend our eyes.

The Temper [I]

How should I praise thee Lord? How should my rimes
    Gladly engrave thy love in steel?
    If what my soul doth feel sometimes
        My soul might ever feel!

3. The power of mental creation. Cf. "wit" in line 9 and in "[Love II]," lines 10 and 13.
4. Takes a liking to; represents mentally.
5. Romantic tokens in conventional love poetry.
6. Entitled "2" in the manuscripts.
7. Make *way* for *thee*, or make *thee* the *way*.
8. Pant for.
9. Dispossessed, usually wrongfully or by force (legal term).

Although there were some forty heav'ns or more
Sometimes I peer above them all
Sometimes I hardly reach a score
Sometimes to Hell I fall.

O rack me not to such a vast extent;
Those distances belong to thee.
The world's too little for thy tent,
A grave too big for me.

Wilt thou meet arms with man? that thou dost stretch
A crumb of dust from heav'n to hell?
Will great God measure with[1] a wretch?
Shall he thy stature spell?[2]

O let me, when thy roof my soul hath hid,
O let me roost and nestle there:
Then of a sinner thou art rid,
And I of hope and fear.

Yet take thy way, for sure thy way is best,
Stretch or contract me, thy poor debtor.
This is but tuning of my breast
To make the music better.

Whether I fly with angels, fall with dust,
Thy hands made both, and I am there:
Thy power and love, my love and trust
Make one place ev'ry where.

The Temper [II]

It cannot be. Where is that mighty joy
Which just now took up all my heart?
Lord, if thou must needs use thy dart
Save that,[3] and me, or sin for both destroy.

The grosser world stands to[4] thy word and art:
But thy diviner world of grace
Thou suddenly dost raise and race,[5]
And ev'ry day a new creator art.

1. Be comparable to.
2. Tell; comprehend.
3. The mighty joy.
4. *Stands to*: is bound by; persists through.
5. Raze.

O fix thy chair of grace, that all my powers
May also fix their reverence:
For when thou dost depart from hence,
They grow unruly and sit in thy bowers.

Scatter, or bind them all to bend to thee:
Though elements change, and heaven move,
Let not thy higher court remove,[6]
But keep a standing Majesty in me.

Jordan [I][7]

Who says that fictions only and false hair
Become a verse; is there in Truth no beauty?
Is all good structure in a winding-stair?
May no lines pass except they do their duty
Not to a true but painted chair?[8]

Is it no verse, except enchanted groves
And sudden arbors shadow coarse-spun lines?[9]
Must purling streams refresh a lover's loves?
Must all be veiled, while he that reads, divines,
Catching the sense at two removes?

Shepherds are honest people, let them sing.
Riddle who list for me, and pull for Prime.[1]
I envy no man's nightingale or spring:
Nor let them punish me with loss of rime
Who plainly say, "My God, My King."

Employment [I]

If as a flower doth spread and die
Thou wouldst extend me to some good
Before I were by frost's extremity
Nipped in the bud,

6. Depart.
7. The river Jordan, at the border of the Promised Land, suggests conversion, healing, salvation, and religious rather than secular poetry (symbolized by the springs of Helicon). Jesus was baptized by John in the Jordan; cf. 2 Kings 5:10.
8. I.e., is no verse acceptable unless it defers, not to truth, but to an image? *Chair*: may refer to a seat of authority, e.g., a throne.
9. *Sudden*: appearing unexpectedly; *shadow*: overshadow (also, hide poor workmanship); *coarse-spun lines*: like poorly spun thread. The "groves" and "arbors" to which Herbert refers, like the "purling streams" of line 8, are clichés, especially in allegorical romance where readers grasp "the sense at two removes" (line 10).
1. I.e., As far as I'm concerned, let anyone riddle who wants to, or draw for the winning hand in the card game "primero" (*OED*).

The sweetness and the praise were[2] thine,
But the extension and the room
Which in thy garland I should fill, were mine
At thy great doom.[3]

For as thou dost impart thy grace
The greater shall our glory be.
The measure of our joys is in this place;
The stuff with thee.

Let me not languish then, and spend
A life as barren to thy praise
As is the dust, to which that life doth tend
But with delays.

All things are busy, only I
Neither bring honey with the bees
Nor flowers to make that, nor the husbandry
To water these.

I am no link of thy great chain,[4]
But all my company is a weed.
Lord place me in thy consort: give one strain
To my poor reed.[5]

The H. Scriptures I

Oh Book! infinite sweetness! Let my heart
Suck ev'ry letter and a honey gain
Precious for any grief in any part.
To clear the breast, to mollify all pain—
Thou art all health, health thriving till it make
A full eternity: thou art a mass
Of strange delights, where we may wish and take.
Ladies look here; this is the thankful glass,
That mends the looker's eyes: this is the well
That washes what it shows: who can endear[6]
Thy praise too much? Thou art Heav'n's Ledger[7] here
Working against the states of Death and Hell.
Thou art joy's handsel:[8] heav'n lies flat in thee,
Subject to ev'ry mounter's bended knee.

2. *Were* (and in line 7): would be.
3. Judgment Day.
4. The "great chain" links all creation to God in a hierarchical structure, from inanimate matter ("dust," line 15), through the various levels of creation (vegetable, animal, human, spiritual). "Chain" can also suggest the succession of notes in music.
5. *Consort*: concert. *Strain*: a sustained note or movement of music. *Reed*: pastoral pipe made of a hollow end of a plant.
6. Render precious.
7. Resident ambassador.
8. First installment.

[The H. Scriptures II]

O, that I knew how all thy lights combine,
And the configurations of their glory;
Seeing not only how each verse doth shine,
But all the constellations of the story.
This verse marks that: and both do make a motion
Unto a third, that ten leaves[9] off doth lie:
Then as dispersed herbs do watch a potion,
These three make up some Christian's destiny.[1]
Such are thy secrets, which my life makes good
And comments on thee: for in ev'ry thing
Thy words do find me out and parallels bring
And in another make me understood.
Stars are poor books, and oftentimes do miss:
This book of stars lights to eternal bliss.

Whitsunday[2]

Listen sweet Dove unto my song
And spread thy golden wings in me,
Hatching my tender heart so long
Till it get wing and fly away with thee.

Where is that fire, which once descended
On thy Apostles? Thou didst then
Keep open house, richly attended,
Feasting all comers by twelve chosen men.

Such glorious gifts thou didst bestow
That th'earth did like a heav'n appear,
The stars were coming down to know
If they might mend their wages and serve here.

The sun which once did shine alone
Hung down his head and wished for night,
When he beheld twelve suns for one
Going about the world and giving light.

But since those pipes of gold[3] which brought
That cordial water to our ground
Were cut and martyred by the fault
Of those who did themselves through their side wound,

9. Pages.
1. I.e., just as separate herbs wait ("watch") to join in a potion, so discrete scriptural verses wait to transform a Christian's life.
2. Whitsunday (Pentecost) commemorates the fiery descent of the Holy Spirit (the Dove, line 1) upon the apostles (Acts 2).
3. The apostles as conduits of God's grace.

Thou shut'st the door and keep'st within,
Scarce a good joy creeps through the chink,
And if the braves[4] of conqu'ring sin
Did not excite thee, we should wholly sink.

Lord though we change, thou art the same;
The same sweet God of love and light
Restore this day for thy great name
Unto his ancient and miraculous right.

Grace

My stock[5] lies dead, and no increase
Doth my dull husbandry improve:
O let thy graces without cease
Drop from above.

If still the sun should hide his face,
Thy house would but a dungeon prove,
Thy works, Night's captives: O let grace
Drop from above.

The Dew[6] doth ev'ry morning fall
And shall the Dew outstrip thy Dove?
The Dew, for which grass[7] cannot call,
Drop from above.

Death is still working like a mole
And digs my grave at each remove:
Let grace work too and on my soul
Drop from above.

Sin is still hammering my heart
Unto a hardness void of love:
Let suppling grace to cross his art
Drop from above.

O come for thou dost know the way:
Or if to me thou wilt not move,
Remove me where I need not say,
"Drop from above."

4. Challenges, threats.
5. Tree trunk (also, lineage); cf. Job 14:7–9.
6. "Drop down dew, ye heavens, from above" (Isaiah 45:8).
7. A near homophone with "grace."

Church-monuments[8]

While that my Soul repairs to her devotion,
Here I entomb my Flesh: that it betimes
May take acquaintance of this heap of Dust
To which the blast of Death's incessant motion,
Fed with the exhalation of our crimes,
Drives all at last. Therefore I gladly trust
My body to this school, that it may learn
To spell his elements, and find his birth
Written in dusty heraldry and lines,[9]
Which Dissolution sure doth best discern,
Comparing dust with dust, and earth with earth:
These laugh at jet and marble, put for signs,
To sever the good fellowship of Dust
And spoil the meeting: what shall point out them
When they shall bow and kneel and fall down flat
To kiss those heaps, which now they have in trust?
Dear Flesh, while I do pray, learn here thy stem
And true descent, that when thou shalt grow fat
And wanton in thy cravings, thou mayst know
That flesh is but the glass[1] which holds the dust
That measures all our time, which also shall
Be crumbled into dust. Mark here below
How tame these ashes are, how free from lust,[2]
That thou mayst fit thy self against[3] thy fall.

Church-music

Sweetest of sweets I thank you. When displeasure
    Did through my body wound my mind:
You took me thence, and in your house of pleasure
    A dainty lodging me assigned.

Now I in you without a body move,
    Rising and falling with your wings:
We both together sweetly live and love,
    Yet say sometimes, "God help poor Kings."[4]

Comfort,[5] I'll die: for if you post from me
    Sure I shall do so and much more.
But if I travel in your company,
    You know the way to heaven's door.

8. Unlike the manuscripts, 1633 and subsequent editions break the poem into six-line stanzas, but the poem's enjambment, syntax, and internal rhyming argue against that imposition.
9. Engraving; genealogy.
1. Hourglass. Note the echo of Isaiah 40:6: "all flesh is grass."
2. Cf. Marvell, "To His Coy Mistress," lines 25–32, p. 544.
3. In preparation for; opposed to.
4. Presumably because unlike them, we are happy (line 7).
5. He addresses a personification of the music as comfort.

Church-lock and Key

I know it is my sin, which locks thine ears,
And binds thy hands,
Out-crying my requests, drowning my tears;
Or else the chillness of my faint demands.

But as cold hands are angry[6] with the fire
And mend it still:
So I do lay the want of my desire
Not on my sins or coldness, but thy will.

Yet hear, O God, only for his blood's sake
Which pleads for me:
For though sins plead too, yet like stones[7] they make
His blood's sweet current much more loud to be.

The Windows

Lord how can man preach thy eternal word?
He is a brittle crazy[8] glass
Yet in thy Temple thou dost him afford
This glorious and transcendent place,
To be a window through thy grace.

But when thou dost anneal[9] in glass thy story,
Making thy life to shine within
The holy Preacher's; then the light and glory
More rev'rend grows and more doth win,
Which else shows wat'rish bleak and thin.

Doctrine and life, colors and light, in one
When they combine and mingle bring
A strong regard and awe: but speech alone
Doth vanish like a flaring thing
And in the ear not conscience ring.

The Quiddity[1]

My God a verse is not a crown,
No point of honor or gay suit:
Nor hawk, nor banquet, nor renown,
Nor a good sword, not yet a lute.

6. I.e., red, hot.
7. As in a brook.
8. Cracked.
9. Fix colors by heat.
1. In the Williams manuscript, the title is "Poetry." In scholastic philosophy, "quiddity" means the essence of a thing, literally, its "whatness": later, it came to mean a subtle distinction or quibble.

It cannot vault or dance, or play;
It never was in France or Spain;
Nor can it entertain the day
With my great stable or domain.

It is no office, art, or news,
Nor the Exchange or busy hall;
But it is that, which, while I use,
I am with thee: and "most take all."[2]

Sunday

O day most calm, most bright:
The fruit of this, the next world's bud,
Th' endorsement of supreme delight,
Writ by a friend and with his blood,
The couch of time, care's balm and bay:
The week were dark, but for thy light.
Thy torch doth show the way.

The other days and thou
Make up one man, whose face thou art
Knocking at heaven with thy brow:
The worky-days are the back-part,
The burden of the week lies there
Making the whole to stoop and bow
Till thy release appear.

Man had strait[3] forward gone
To endless death, but thou dost pull
And turn us round to look on one
Whom if we were not very dull
We could not choose but look on still
Since there is no place so alone
The which he doth not fill.

Sundays the pillars are
On which heav'n's palace archèd lies:
The other days fill up the spare
And hollow room with vanities.
They are the fruitful beds and borders
In God's rich garden: that is bare,
Which parts their ranks and orders.

The Sundays of man's life
Threaded together on Time's string,
Make bracelets to adorn the wife

2. I.e., winner take all.
3. Cf. "Redemption," line 9n, p. 237.

Of the eternal glorious King.
On Sunday heaven's gate stands ope,[4]
Blessings are plentiful and rife,
More plentiful than hope.

This day my Savior rose,
And did enclose this light for his:
That as each beast his manger knows
Man might not of his fodder miss.
Christ hath took in[5] this piece of ground
And made a garden there for those
Who want herbs for their wound.

The rest[6] of our creation
Our great Redeemer did remove
With the same shake[7] which at his Passion
Did th'earth and all things with it move:
As Samson bore the doors away
Christ's hands (though nailed) wrought our salvation
And did un-hinge that day.[8]

The brightness of that day
We sullied by our foul offence:
Wherefore that robe we cast away,
Having a new at his expense,
Whose drops of blood paid the full price[9]
That was required to make us gay
And fit for Paradise.

Thou art a day of mirth:
And where the weekdays trail on ground,
Thy flight is higher, as thy birth:
O let me take thee at the bound
Leaping with thee from sev'n to sev'n,
Till that we both being tossed from earth
Fly hand in hand to heav'n.

Employment [II]

He that is weary, let him sit.
My soul would stir;
And trade in courtesies and wit,

4. I.e., open.
5. Taken into cultivation.
6. Remainder, but also, Sunday as the day of rest.
7. The earth shook at Christ's death (Matthew 27:51).
8. Trapped in Gaza, Samson "took the doors of the gate of the city . . . and went away with them . . . upon his shoulders" (Judges 16:3). *That day*: refers to the Crucifixion and to the old Sabbath.
9. Cf. Revelation 7:14.

Quitting the fur[1]
To cold complexions[2] needing it.

Man is no star, but a quick coal[3]
Of mortal fire:
Who blows it not, nor doth control
A faint desire,
Lets his own ashes choke his soul.

When th'elements[4] did for place contest
With him, whose will
Ordained the highest to be best,
The Earth sat still,
And by the others is oppressed.

Life is a business, not good cheer,
Ever in wars.
The sun still shineth there or here:
Whereas the stars
Watch an advantage to appear.

Oh that I were an orange tree,
That busy[5] plant;
Then should I ever laden be
And never want
Some fruit for him that dressèd me.

But we are still too young or old:
The man is gone,
Before we do our wares unfold:[6]
So we freeze on,
Until the grave increase our cold.

Denial[7]

When my devotions could not pierce
Thy silent ears,
Then was my heart broken as was my verse
My breast was full of fears
And disorder.

My bent thoughts like a brittle bow
Did fly asunder:

1. Academic dress; warm clothing.
2. Constitutions (from the theory of humors).
3. A piece of carbon glowing but without flame.
4. Earth, air, fire, water.
5. Usefully active; the orange tree bears fruit and blossoms at the same time.
6. I.e., we always make excuses that we are too young or too old, until suddenly life has slipped by.
7. As is the case with so many of Herbert's titles, this word is used nowhere else in Herbert's works. Note the "denial" of poetic rhythm in the last line of each stanza except the last.

Each took his way: some would to pleasures go,
Some to the wars and thunder
Of alarmès.[8]

As good go anywhere, they say:
As to benumb
Both knees and heart, in crying night and day,
"Come, come my God, O come,"
But no hearing.

Oh that thou shouldst give dust a tongue
To cry to thee,
And then not hear it crying; all day long
My heart was in my knee,
But no hearing.

Therefore my soul lay out of sight,
Untuned, unstrung:
My feeble spirit, unable to look right,
Like a nipped blossom, hung
Discontented.

O cheer and tune my heartless breast,
Defer no time:
That so thy favors granting my request,
They and my mind may chime
And mend my rime.

Christmas[9]

All after pleasures as I rid[1] one day,
My horse and I both tired, body and mind,
With full cry of affections, quite astray,
I took up[2] in the next inn I could find.
There when I came, whom found I, but my dear
My dearest Lord, expecting[3] till the grief
Of pleasures brought me to him, ready there
To be all passengers' most sweet relief.
Oh thou, whose glorious yet contracted light
Wrapped in night's mantle stole into a manger,
Since my dark soul and brutish is thy right,
To man of all beasts be not thou a stranger:

8. I.e., *alarums*, calls to arms. We retain the spelling of both manuscripts to indicate the scansion (trochaic dimeter; cf. lines 5, 15, 20, 25).
9. The word is used nowhere else in Herbert's poetry.
1. Rode.
2. Settled.
3. Waiting.

Furnish and deck my soul that thou mayst have
A better lodging than a rack[4] or grave.

The shepherds sing; and shall I silent be?
My God, no hymn for thee?
My soul's a shepherd too; a flock it feeds
Of thoughts and words and deeds.
The pasture is thy word: the streams, thy grace
Enriching all the place.
Shepherd and flock shall sing and all my powers
Outsing the day-light hours.
Then we will chide the sun for letting night
Take up his place and right,
We sing one common Lord: wherefore he should
Himself the candle hold.
I will go searching till I find a sun
Shall stay, till we have done:
A willing shiner, that shall shine as gladly
As frost-nipped suns look sadly.
Then we will sing and shine all our own day
And one another pay:
His beams shall cheer my breast, and both so twine,
Till ev'n his beams sing and my music shine.

The World

Love built a stately house; where Fortune came,
And spinning fancies, she was heard to say
That her fine cobwebs did support the frame:
Whereas they were supported by the same.
But Wisdom quickly swept them all away.

Then Pleasure came, who liking not the fashion,
Began to make balconies, terraces,
Till she had weakened all by alteration,
But reverend Laws and many a Proclamation
Reformèd all at length with menaces.

Then entered Sin and with that sycamore[5]
Whose leaves first sheltered man from drought and dew.
Working and winding slyly evermore,
The inward walls and sommers[6] cleft and tore:
But Grace shored these, and cut that as it grew.

Then Sin combined with Death in a firm band
To raze the building to the very floor:

4. Place for hay or straw, like Christ's manger.
5. Adam and Eve use sycamore (fig) leaves to cover their nakedness (Genesis 3:7).
6. Supporting beams.

Which they effected; none could them withstand
But Love and Grace took Glory by the hand,
And built a braver palace than before.

Vanity [I][7]

The fleet astronomer can bore
And thread the spheres with his quick-piercing mind:
He views their stations, walks from door to door,
Surveys, as if he had designed
To make a purchase there: he sees their dances
And knoweth long before
Both their full-eyed aspects and secret glances.

The nimble diver with his side
Cuts through the working waves, that he may fetch
His dearly-earnèd pearl, which God did hide
On purpose from the vent'rous wretch
That he might save his life, and also hers
Who with excessive pride
Her own destruction and his danger wears.

The subtle chemic[8] can divest
And strip the creature naked till he find
The callow[9] principles within their nest:
There he imparts to them his mind,
Admitted to their bed-chamber before
They appear trim and dressed
To ordinary suitors at the door.

What hath not Man sought out and found
But his dear God? Who yet his glorious law
Embosoms in us, mellowing the ground
With showers and frosts, with love and awe
So that we need not say, "Where's this command?"
Poor Man, thou searchest round
To find out death, but missest life at hand.

Virtue

Sweet day so cool, so calm, so bright,
The bridal of the earth and sky:
The dew shall weep thy fall[1] to night
For thou must die.

7. Alan Rudrum sees the poem as "illustrating both the witty use of *double entendre*" and Herbert's alertness "to the range of contemporary meanings of the words he uses." See "The Problem of Sexual Reference in George Herbert's Verse," *George Herbert Journal* 21 (1998): 19–32.
8. Alchemist.
9. Without feathers; in its native condition.
1. Musically, each stanza's final line is a "dying fall."

Sweet rose, whose hue angry and brave[2]
Bids the rash gazer wipe his eye:
Thy root is ever in its grave
And thou must die.

Sweet spring full of sweet days and roses,
A box, where sweets compacted lie;
My music shows ye have your closes[3]
And all must die.

Only a sweet and virtuous soul,
Like seasoned timber, never gives;
But though the whole world turn to coal,[4]
Then chiefly lives.

The Pearl. Matthew 13:45[5]

I know the ways of learning, both the head
And pipes that feed the press and make it run;[6]
What reason hath from nature borrowèd
Or of it self like a good housewife spun
In laws and policy; what the stars conspire;
What willing Nature speaks; what forced by fire:[7]
Both th'old discoveries, and the new-found seas,
The stock and surplus, cause and history.
All these stand open, or I have the keys.
Yet I love thee.

I know the ways of honor: what maintains
The quick returns of courtesy and wit;
In vies of favors whether party gains,[8]
When glory[9] swells the heart and moldeth it
To all expressions both of hand and eye,
Which on the world a true-love-knot may tie
And bear the bundle wheresoe'er it goes.
How many drams of spirit there must be
To sell my life unto my friends or foes.
Yet I love thee.

I know the ways of pleasure: the sweet strains,
The lullings and the relishes of it.

2. *Angry*: red, with hue of anger; *brave*: splendid.
3. In music, concluding cadences.
4. I.e., in the general conflagration at the Last Judgment.
5. "The kingdom is like unto a merchant man seeking goodly pearls: who when he had found one pearl of great price, went and sold all that he had and bought it" (Matthew 13:45–46).
6. *Head and pipes*: source and conduits. The "press" is presumably the printing press.
7. I.e., in an alchemical procedure.
8. I.e., in rivalries for privileges, I know which side is winning.
9. Ambition.

The propositions of hot blood and brains:[1]
What mirth and music mean, what love and wit
Have done these twenty hundred years, and more:
I know the projects of unbridled store.
My stuff is flesh not brass; my senses live
And grumble oft that they have more in me
Than he that curbs them, being but one to five.
Yet I love thee.

I know all these and have them in my hand.
Therefore not seelèd[2] but with open eyes
I fly to thee, and fully understand
Both the main sale and the commodities,[3]
And at what rate and price I have thy love
With all the circumstances that may move.
Yet through these labyrinths, not my groveling wit,
But thy silk-twist,[4] let down from heaven to me
Did both conduct, and teach me how by it
To climb to thee.

Affliction [IV]

Broken in pieces, all asunder,
Lord hunt me not
A thing forgot
Once a poor creature, now a wonder,
A wonder tortured in the space
Betwixt this world and that of grace.

My thoughts are all a case of knives
Wounding my heart
With scattered smart
As wat'ring pots give flowers their lives.
Nothing their fury can control
While they do wound and pink[5] my soul.

All my attendants are at strife
Quitting their place
Unto my face.
Nothing performs the task of life.
The elements are let loose to fight
And while I live, try out their right.

1. *Strains, lullings, relishes, propositions*: terms of both pleasure and music. *Lulling*: a soothing song.
2. Eyes sewn shut, as a falcon's are in training.
3. Advantages.
4. *Silk-twist*: cord made of plaited silk thread.
5. Pierce or stab.

Oh help my God! Let not their plot
Kill them and me
And also thee
Who art my life. Dissolve the knot
As the sun scatters by his light
All the rebellions of the night.

Then shall those powers, which work for grief,
Enter thy pay
And day by day
Labor[6] thy praise and my relief
With care and courage building me
Till I reach heav'n: and much more, thee.

Man

My God I heard this day
That no man builds a stately habitation
But he that means to dwell therein.
What house more stately hath there been
Or can be, than is Man? to[7] whose creation
All things are in decay.

For Man is ev'ry thing
And more: he is a tree, yet bears more fruit;
A beast, yet is, or should be more;
Reason and speech we only[8] bring.
Parrots may thank us. If they are not mute,
They go upon the score.[9]

Man is all symmetry,
Full of proportions, one limb to another
And all to all the world besides.
Each part may call the farthest, brother:
For Head with Foot hath private amity
And both with moons and tides.[1]

Nothing hath got so far
But Man hath caught and kept it as his prey:
His eyes dismount[2] the highest star.
He is in little all the Sphere:
Herbs gladly cure our flesh, because that they
Find their acquaintance there.[3]

6. Labor for.
7. Compared to.
8. As often in Herbert's poems, "only" (alone) can modify *we* or *bring* or both.
9. They are in our debt.
1. The parts of a human being, who is a microcosm of all creation, correlate with the greater world. Cf. line 22.
2. Bring down to Earth.
3. The "acquaintance" owes to the analogy between microcosm and macrocosm ("all the Sphere").

For us the winds do blow
The earth doth rest, heav'n move, and fountains flow:[4]
Nothing we see but means our good
As our delight, or as our treasure:
The whole is either our cupboard of food
Or cabinet of pleasure.

The stars have us to bed
Night draws the curtain, which the sun withdraws:
Music and light attend our head.
All things unto our flesh are kind[5]
In their descent and being: to our mind
In their ascent and cause.

Each thing is full of duty:
Waters united are our navigation,
Distinguished, our habitation;
Below our drink, above[6] our meat,
Both are our cleanliness; if one have beauty,
Then how are all things neat![7]

More servants wait on man
Than he'll take notice of: in ev'ry path
He treads down that, which doth befriend him
When sickness makes him pale and wan.
Oh mighty love! Man is one world and hath
Another to attend him.

Since then, my God thou hast
So brave a palace[8] built, o dwell in it,
That it may dwell with thee at last:
Till then afford us so much wit,
That as the world serves us, we may serve thee,
And both thy servants be.

Life

I made a posy,[9] while the day ran by:
Here will I smell my remnant out and tie
My life within this band.
But time did beckon to the flowers and they
By noon most cunningly did steal away
And withered in my hand.

4. The four elements: air, earth, fire (heaven), water.
5. Gentle; but also naturally related, kin.
6. Because rain contributes to producing food.
7. If just one element (water) has such beauty, what proportion must there be in all.
8. Cf. 1 Corinthians 3:16, "Know ye not that ye are the temple of God, and that the Spirit of God dwelleth in you?"
9. Either a bouquet or a poem.

My hand was next to them, and then my heart:
I took without more thinking in good part
Time's gentle admonition
Who did so sweetly death's sad taste convey,
Making my mind to smell my fatal day,
Yet sug'ring the suspicion.

Farewell dear flowers, sweetly your time ye spent
Fit, while ye lived, for smell or ornament
And after death for cures:
I follow straight without complaints or grief,
Since if my scent be good, I care not if
It be as short as yours.

Mortification[1]

How soon does Man decay!
When clothes are taken from a chest of sweets[2]
To swaddle infants, whose young breath
Scarce knows the way;
Those clouts[3] are little winding sheets
Which do consign and send them unto death.

When boys go first to bed
They step into their voluntary graves:
Sleep binds them fast: only their breath
Makes them not dead.
Successive nights like rolling waves
Convey them quickly who are bound for death.

When youth is frank and free
And calls for music, while his veins do swell,
All day exchanging mirth and breath
In company,
That music summons to the knell[4]
Which shall befriend him at the house[5] of death.

When man grows staid and wise,
Getting a house and home, where he may move
Within the circle of his breath,
Schooling his eyes:
That dumb enclosure maketh love
Unto the coffin, that attends his death.

1. In Christianity, this often refers to ascetic practices, but here the emphasis recalls the Latin root, *mortificare* (to put to death).
2. Sweet-smelling herbs.
3. Swaddling clothes.
4. The "passing-bell" tolled to mark a death.
5. Some editions read *hour*, from the Williams manuscript, but *house* (in *B* and *1633*) fits the house imagery, both overt and subtle, that pervades the poem.

When age grows low and weak
Marking his grave, and thawing ev'ry year,
Till all do melt and drown his breath
When he would speak:
A chair or litter shows the bier
Which shall convey him to the house of death.

Man, ere he is aware,
Hath put together a solemnity
And dressed his hearse, while he has breath
As yet to spare.
Yet Lord, instruct us so to die
That all these dyings may be life in death.[6]

Jordan [II]

When first my lines of heav'nly joys made mention
Such was their luster, they did so excel,
That I sought out quaint words and trim invention,
My thoughts began to burnish,[7] sprout and swell,
Curling with metaphors a plain intention
Decking the sense, as if it were to sell.

Thousands of notions in my brain did run,
Off'ring their service, if I were not sped:[8]
I often blotted what I had begun,
This was not quick[9] enough, and that was dead.
Nothing could seem too rich to clothe the sun,
Much less those joys which trample on his head.[1]

As flames do work and wind when they ascend,
So did I weave my self into the sense:
But while I bustled, I might hear a friend
Whisper, "How wide[2] is all this long pretence!
There is in love a sweetness ready penned:
Copy out only that and save expense."

Obedience

My God, if writings may
Convey[3] a Lordship any way
Whither the buyer and the seller please;

6. So that the intimations of death at each age may render life a preparation for death.
7. Spread out, grow in vigor.
8. If I did not meet with success.
9. Alive, lively.
1. Presumably the joys are heavenly; *his head*: the sun's.
2. Wide of the mark.
3. Transfer by deed or other legal process.

Let it not thee displease
If this poor paper do as much as they.

On it my heart doth bleed
As many lines as there doth need
To pass[4] it self and all it hath to thee:
To which I do agree,
And here present it as my special Deed.

If that[5] hereafter Pleasure
Cavil and claim her part and measure
As if this passed with a reservation[6]
Or some such words in fashion:
I here shut out the wrangler from thy treasure.

Oh let thy sacred will
All thy delight in me fulfill:
Let me not think an action mine own way,
But as thy love shall sway,
Resigning up the rudder to thy skill.

Lord what is man to thee[7]
That thou shouldst mind[8] a rotten tree?
Yet since thou canst not choose but see my actions,
So great are thy perfections:
Thou mayst as well my actions guide as see.

Besides thy death and blood
Showed a strange love to all our good:
Thy sorrows were in earnest, no faint proffer
Or superficial offer
Of what we might not take, or be withstood.

Wherefore I all forego:
To one word only I say no:
Where in the Deed there was an intimation
Of a gift or donation
Lord let it now by way of purchase go.

He that will pass his land
As I have mine, may set his hand
And heart unto this Deed, when he hath read
And make the purchase spread
To both our goods, if he to it will stand.

4. Convey, as in previous note; cf. lines 13 and 36.
5. If.
6. Codicil, or rider.
7. "Lord what is man, that thou takest knowledge of him!" (Psalms 144:3).
8. Be mindful of.

How happy were my part
If some kind man would thrust his heart
Into these lines: till in Heav'n's Court of Rolls[9]
They were by wingèd souls
Entered for both: far above their desert.

The British Church

I joy, dear Mother, when I view
Thy perfect lineaments and hue
Both sweet and bright.
Beauty in thee takes up the place
And dates[1] her letters from thy face
When she doth write.

A fine aspect in fit array,
Neither too mean nor yet too gay,
Shows who is best.
Outlandish[2] looks may not compare:
For all they either painted are
Or else undressed.

She on the Hills,[3] which wantonly
Allureth all in hope to be
By her preferred,
Hath kissed so long her painted shrines
That ev'n her face by kissing shines
For her reward.

She in the valley[4] is so shy
Of dressing that her hair doth lie
About her ears:
While she avoids her neighbor's pride,
She wholly goes on th' other side
And nothing wears.

But dearest Mother what those miss,
The mean, thy praise and glory is
And long may be.
Blessèd be God, whose love it was
To double-moat thee with his grace
And none but thee.

9. Where deeds are recorded.
1. 25 March (Feast of the Annunciation, Lady Day) marked the new year in the Anglican calendar.
2. Foreign; bizarre.
3. The seven hills of Rome; i.e., the Roman church.
4. Geneva; i.e., Calvinist religion.

The Quip

The merry World did on a day
With his train-bands[5] and mates agree
To meet together where I lay
And all in sport to jeer at me.

First Beauty crept into a rose
Which when I plucked not, "Sir," said she,
"Tell me, I pray, whose hands are those?"
But thou shalt answer, Lord, for me.[6]

Then Money came and chinking still,
"What tune is this, poor man," said he:
"I heard in music you had skill."
But thou shalt answer, Lord, for me.

Then came brave Glory puffing by
In silks that whistled, who but he:
He scarce allowed me half an eye.
But thou shalt answer, Lord, for me.

Then came quick Wit-and-Conversation
And he would needs a comfort be
And to be short make an oration.
But thou shalt answer, Lord, for me.

Yet when the hour of thy design
To answer these fine things shall come
Speak not at large; say, "I am thine":[7]
And then they have their answer home.

Dullness

Why do I languish thus drooping and dull
As if I were all earth?
O give me quickness that I may with mirth
Praise thee brim-full.

The wanton lover in a curious strain[8]
Can praise his fairest fair
And with quaint metaphors her curled hair
Curl o'er again.

5. Trained bands of citizen soldiers.
6. "Thou shalt answer for me, O Lord my God" (Psalms 38:15).
7. *"I am thine"*: the main "quip" of the poem, since it means both that the speaker is God's and that God is the speaker's.
8. Elaborate or intricate melody.

Thou art my loveliness, my life, my light,
Beauty alone to me.
Thy bloody death and undeserved, makes thee
Pure red and white.[9]

When all perfections as but one appear
That those thy form doth show,
The very dust where thou dost tread and go
Makes beauties here.

Where are my lines then, my approaches, views,
Where are my window-songs?
Lovers are still pretending[1] and ev'n wrongs
Sharpen their Muse.

But I am lost in flesh, whose sugared lies
Still mock me and grow bold.
Sure thou didst put a mind there if I could
Find where it lies.

Lord, clear thy gift, that with a constant wit
I may but look towards thee.
Look only: for to love thee who can be,
What angel fit?

Sin's Round[2]

Sorry I am, my God, sorry I am
That my offenses course it in a ring.
My thoughts are working like a busy flame
Until their cockatrice[3] they hatch and bring:
And when they once have perfected their draughts
My words take fire from my inflamèd thoughts.

My words take fire from my inflamèd thoughts
Which spit it forth like the Sicilian Hill.[4]
They vent[5] the wares and pass them with their faults
And by their breathing ventilate[6] the ill.
But words suffice not where are lewd intentions:
My hands do join to finish the inventions.

My hands do join to finish the inventions
And so my sins ascend three stories high

9. Commonplace colors in secular love poetry, also traditional for Christ as lover; cf. Song of Solomon 5:10.
1. Always wooing.
2. The repetition of lines, as in a "round," reflects the self-perpetuating character of sin.
3. Fabulous creature hatched by a serpent from a cock's egg.
4. The volcanic Mount Etna.
5. Discharge, with secondary meaning of "sell" (the wares).
6. Make the fire burn better.

As Babel grew, before there were dissensions.
Yet ill deeds loiter not: for they supply
New thoughts of sinning. Wherefore to my shame
Sorry I am, my God, sorry I am.

Peace

Sweet Peace, where dost thou dwell, I humbly crave
Let me once know.
I sought thee in a secret cave
And asked, if Peace were there.
A hollow wind did seem to answer, "No
Go seek elsewhere."

I did; and going did a rainbow note:
Surely, thought I,
This is the lace of Peace's coat:
I will search out the matter.
But while I looked the clouds immediately
Did break and scatter.

Then went I to a garden and did spy
A gallant flower,
The Crown Imperial: "Sure," said I,
"Peace at the root must dwell."
But when I digged, I saw a worm devour
What showed so well.

At length I met a reverend good old man,
Whom when for Peace
I did demand, he thus began,
"There was a Prince of old[7]
At Salem dwelt, who lived with good increase
Of flock and fold.

He sweetly lived; yet sweetness did not save
His life from foes.
But after death out of his grave
There sprang twelve stalks of wheat,[8]
Which many wond'ring at, got some of those
To plant and set.

It prospered strangely and did soon disperse
Through all the earth:
For they that taste it do rehearse
That virtue[9] lies therein,

7. Melchisedec, "King of Salem, which is, King of peace" (Hebrews 7:2), "brought forth bread and wine" (Genesis 14:18), prefiguring Christ.
8. The twelve Apostles.
9. Power, potency.

A secret virtue bringing Peace and mirth
By flight of sin.

Take of this grain which in my garden grows
And grows for you;
Make bread of it: and that repose
And Peace which ev'ry where
With so much earnestness you do pursue
Is only there."

The Bunch of Grapes[1]

Joy, I did lock thee up. But some bad man
Hath let thee out again.
And now, methinks, I am where I began
Sev'n years ago; one vogue[2] and vein,
One air of thoughts usurps my brain.
I did towards Canaan draw but now I am
Brought back to the Red Sea, the sea of shame.[3]

For as the Jews of old by God's command
Travailed and saw no town:
So now each Christian hath his journeys spanned:
Their story pens and sets us down.
A single deed is small renown.[4]
God's works are wide and let in future times,
His ancient justice overflows our crimes.

Then have we too our guardian fires and clouds;
Our Scripture-dew drops fast.[5]
We have our sands and serpents, tents and shrouds;[6]
Alas our murmurings come not last.
But where's the cluster? Where's the taste
Of mine inheritance? Lord, if I must borrow,
Let me, as well take up their joy as sorrow.

But can he want the grape who hath the wine?[7]
I have their fruit and more.
Blessèd be God, who prospered Noah's vine
And made it bring forth grapes good store.
But much more him I must adore,

1. Cf. Numbers 13:23.
2. General tendency.
3. After they rebelled, God sent the ancient Hebrews, nearing the Promised Land, wandering back toward the Red Sea.
4. *Spanned*: measured or bounded. *Pens*: encloses; writes. Cf. 1 Corinthians 10:11.
5. *Guardian fires and clouds*: cf. Exodus 13:21. *Scripture-dew*: cf. Exodus 16:14–15.
6. *Shrouds*: temporary shelters.
7. Cf. Numbers 18:20.

Who of the Law's sour juice sweet wine did make
Ev'n God himself being pressèd[8] for my sake.

The Storm

If as the winds and waters here below
Do fly and flow,
My sighs and tears as busy were above;
Sure they would move
And much affect thee, as tempestuous times
Amuse poor mortals and object[9] their crimes.

Stars have their storms[1] ev'n in a high degree
As well as we.
A throbbing conscience spurrèd by remorse
Hath a strange force:
It quits the earth and mounting more and more
Dares to assault thee and besiege thy door.

There it stands knocking to thy music's wrong
And drowns the song.
Glory and honor are set by, till it
An answer get.
Poets have wronged poor storms: such days are best;
They purge the air without, within the breast.

Paradise

I bless thee Lord because I Grow
Among thy trees which in a Row
To thee both fruit and order Ow.[2]

What open force or hidden Charm
Can blast my fruit or bring me Harm
While the enclosure is thine Arm?

Enclose me still for fear I Start.
Be to me rather sharp and Tart
Than let me want thy hand and Art.

When thou dost greater judgments Spare
And with thy knife but prune and Pare
Even fruitful trees more fruitful Are.

8. I.e., made into the wine of communion.
9. *Amuse*: bewilder; *object*: place before, make conscious of.
1. Such as meteor showers.
2. Herbert uses an alternate spelling of *owe*. Cf. line 13, "Frend" for "friend."

Such sharpness shows the sweetest Frend.
Such cuttings rather heal than Rend.
And such beginnings touch their End.

The Size[3]

Content thee, greedy heart.
Modest and moderate joys to those that have
Title to more hereafter when they part
Are passing brave.
Let th'upper springs into the low
Descend and fall, and thou dost flow.

What though some have a fraught[4]
Of cloves and nutmegs and in cinnamon sail;
If thou hast wherewithal to spice a draught
When griefs prevail
And for the future time art heir
To th'Isle of spices. Is't not fair?

To be in both worlds full
Is more than God was, who was hungry here.
Wouldst thou his laws of fasting disannul?
Exact good cheer?
Lay out thy joy yet hope to save it?
Wouldst thou both eat thy cake and have it?

Great joys are all at once
But little do reserve themselves for more:
Those have their hopes; these, what they have, renounce
And live on score:[5]
Those are at home; these journey still
And meet the rest on Sion's hill.

Thy Savior sentenced joy
And in the flesh condemned it as unfit
At least in lump: and such doth oft destroy;
Whereas a bit
Doth tice[6] us on to hopes of more
And for the present health restore.

A Christian's state and case
Is not a corpulent, but a thin and spare
Yet active strength, whose long and bony face
Content and care

3. Status or condition; "portion of bread, ale, etc." (*OED*).
4. Freight.
5. On credit.
6. Entice.

Do seem to equally divide
Like a pretender[7] not a bride.

Wherefore sit down good heart;
Grasp not at much for fear thou losest all
If comforts fell according to desert,[8]
They would great frosts and snows destroy:
For we should count, since the last joy.

Then close again the seam
Which thou hast opened: do not spread thy robe
In hope of great things. Call to mind thy dream,
An earthly globe,
On whose meridian[9] was engraven
"These seas are tears, and heav'n the haven."[1]

Artillery

As I one ev'ning sat before my cell,
Methoughts a star did shoot into my lap.
I rose, and shook my clothes, as knowing well
That from small fires comes oft no small mishap.
When suddenly I heard one say,
"Do as thou usest, disobey,
Expel good motions from thy breast
Which have the face of fire but end in rest."

I, who had heard of music in the spheres
But not of speech in stars, began to muse:
But turning to my God, whose ministers
The stars and all things are; "If I refuse
Dread Lord," said I, "so oft my good,
Then I refuse not ev'n with blood
To wash away my stubborn thought:
For I will do or suffer what I ought.

But I have also stars and shooters[2] too
Born, where thy servants both artilleries use.
My tears and prayers night and day do woo
And work up to thee, yet thou dost refuse.
Not, but I am, I must say still
Much more obliged to do thy will
Than thou to grant mine, but because
Thy promise now hath ev'n set thee thy laws.

7. Wooer.
8. A four-syllable line is missing after this.
9. "A graduated ring . . . in which an artificial globe is suspended" (*OED*).
1. Gerard Manley Hopkins (1844–1888), who greatly admired Herbert, titled one of his poems from this concluding phrase; compare also his "Pied Beauty" and Herbert's "Bitter-sweet," p. 282.
2. Shooting stars, but also those who use artillery.

Then we are shooters both, and thou dost deign
To enter combat with us and contest
With thine own clay. But I would parley fain.
Shun not my arrows, and behold my breast.
Yet if thou shunnest, I am thine.
I must be so if I am mine:
There is no articling[3] with thee:
I am but finite yet thine infinitely."

The Pilgrimage

I travailed on seeing the hill, where lay
My expectation.
A long it was and weary way.
The gloomy cave of Desperation
I left on th'one and on the other side
The rock of Pride.

And so I came to Fancy's[4] meadow strowed
With many a flower.
Fain would I here have made abode
But I was quickened by my hour.
So to Care's copse I came and there got through
With much ado.

That led me to the wild of Passion,[5] which
Some call the wold[6]
A wasted place, but sometimes rich.
Here I was robbed of all my gold
Save one good angel,[7] which a friend had tied
Close to my side.

At length I got unto the gladsome hill
Where lay my hope,
Where lay my heart, and climbing still,
When I had gained the brow and top,
A lake of brackish waters on the ground
Was all I found.

With that abashed and struck with many a sting
Of swarming fears
I fell, and cried, Alas my King,
Can both the way and end be tears?
Yet taking heart I rose, and then perceived,
I was deceived.

3. Negotiating, arranging by treaty.
4. *Fancy*: fantasy, imagination.
5. *Wild of Passion*: the wilderness of intense desire or of suffering (with a suggestion of Christ's Passion).
6. Treeless plain, moorland.
7. A gold coin; also, guardian angel.

My Hill was further: So I flung away
Yet heard a cry
Just as I went, "None goes that way
And lives." "If that be all," said I,
"After so foul a journey, death is fair
And but a chair."[8]

The Bag[9]

Away Despair! my gracious Lord doth hear.
Though winds and waves assault my keel,
He doth preserve it: he doth steer
Ev'n when the boat seems most to reel.
Storms are the triumph of his art,
Well may he close his eyes but not his heart.[1]

Hast thou not heard that my Lord Jesus died?
Then let me tell thee a strange story.
The God of power as he did ride
In his majestic robes of glory,
Resolved to light; and so one day
He did descend, undressing all the way.

The stars his tire[2] of light and rings obtained.
The cloud his bow, the fire[3] his spear,
The sky his azure mantle gained.
And when they asked what he would wear,
He smiled and said as he did go,
He had new clothes a making here below.

When he was come, as travelers are wont,
He did repair unto an inn.
Both then and after, many a brunt
He did endure to cancel sin.
And having giv'n the rest before
Here he gave up his life to pay our score.

But as he was returning there came one
That ran upon him with a spear.
He, who came hither all alone,
Bringing nor man nor arms nor fear,
Received the blow upon his side
And straight he turned and to his brethren cried,

8. Place of rest; sedan chair.
9. The title may allude to Job 14:17.
1. See Matthew 8:24, where Christ sleeps in the boat during the storm on Galilee; *not his heart*: awakened, Christ calms the storm.
2. Attire.
3. Lightning.

"If ye have any thing to send or write,
I have no bag, but here is room:
Unto my Father's hands and sight,
Believe me, it shall safely come.
That I shall mind, what you impart,
Look you may put it very near my heart.

Or if hereafter any of my friends
Will use me in this kind, the door
Shall still be open; what he sends
I will present, and somewhat more
Not to his hurt. Sighs will convey
Anything to me. Hark, Despair away."

The Collar[4]

I struck the board,[5] and cried, "No more."
I will abroad.
What[6] shall I ever sigh and pine?
My lines and life are free: free as the road
Loose as the wind, as large as store.
Shall I be still in suit?[7]
Have I no harvest but a thorn
To let me blood and not restore,
What I have lost with cordial[8] fruit?
Sure there was wine
Before my sighs did dry it. There was corn
Before my tears did drown it.
Is the year only lost to me?
Have I no bays to crown it?
No flowers, no garlands gay? All blasted?
All wasted?[9]
Not so my heart: but there is fruit,
And thou hast hands.
Recover all thy sigh-blown age
On double pleasures. Leave thy cold dispute
Of what is fit, and not. Forsake thy cage,
Thy rope of sands,
Which petty thoughts have made, and made to thee
Good cable to enforce and draw
And be thy law
While thou didst wink and wouldst not see.

4. As often with Herbert's titles, the word is used nowhere else in his works. "Collar" suggests choler or anger; a badge of office; a restraint, such as a yoke (cf. Matthew 11:29–30); or, aurally, caller.
5. Table; presumably, the communion table.
6. Most editors punctuate "What" as if it were an exclamation, but there is no punctuation in *B*. "What" may mean "why."
7. *Still*: continuously, or silently; *suit*: a petitioner, waiting on another (cf. line 31).
8. Invigorating.
9. Exceptionally, this line consists of three syllables only and in *B* is placed much farther to the right than the parallel short lines.

Away, "Take Heed,"[1]
I will abroad,
Call in thy death's head there: tie up thy fears.
He, that forbears
To suit and serve his need,
Deserves his load.
But as I raved and grew more fierce and wild
At every word,
Methoughts I heard one calling, "Child!"
And I replied, "My Lord."

Joseph's Coat[2]

Wounded I sing, tormented I indite,[3]
Thrown down I fall into a bed and rest:
Sorrow hath changed its note: such is his will
Who changeth all things as him pleaseth best.
For well he knows if but one grief and smart
Among my many had his full career,
Sure it would carry with it ev'n my heart
And both would run until they found a bier,
To fetch the body, both being due to grief.
But he hath spoiled the race; and giv'n to anguish
One of joy's coats, ticing[4] it with relief
To linger in me and together languish.
I live to show his power, who once did bring
My joys to weep, and now my griefs to sing.

The Pulley

When God at first made man,
Having a glass[5] of blessings standing by,
"Let us" (said he) "pour on him all we can:
Let the world's riches, which dispersèd lie,
Contract into a span."[6]

So strength first made a way;
Then beauty flowed, then wisdom, honor, pleasure:
When almost all was out God made a stay
Perceiving that alone of all his treasure
Rest[7] in the bottom lay.

1. *"Take Heed"*: an exhortation or motto that might serve as legend to a skull, per line 29. Buck and most other editors print the line as if it were a command (to someone) to *go away! look out!*
2. Joseph's "coat of many colors," given him by Jacob "because he was the son of his old age" (Genesis 37:3). Joseph was considered a type of Christ; his coat, a type of Christ's humanity.
3. Write; compose a poem.
4. Enticing.
5. Jar.
6. A small space; literally, a hand span or about eight inches.
7. In this poem, three different meanings apply to "rest."

"For if I should" (said he)
"Bestow this jewel also on my creature,
He would adore my gifts instead of me
And rest in Nature not the God of Nature.
So both should losers be.

Yet let him keep the rest
But keep them with repining restlessness:
Let him be rich and weary: that at least
If goodness lead him not, yet weariness
May toss him to my breast."[8]

The Search

Whither, o whither art thou fled,
My Lord, my Love?
My searches are my daily bread
Yet never prove.

My knees pierce th'earth: mine eyes the sky
And yet the sphere
And center[9] both to me deny,
That thou art there.

Yet can I mark how herbs below
Grow green and gay,
As if to meet thee they did know
While I decay.

Yet can I mark how stars above
Simper[1] and shine,
As having keys unto thy love
While poor I pine.

I sent a sigh to seek thee out
Deep drawn, in pain,
Winged like an arrow: but my scout
Returns in vain.

I tuned another (having store)
Into a groan:
Because the search was dumb before:
But all was one.[2]

8. "Thou hast made us for thyself and restless is our heart until it comes to rest in thee" (Augustine, *Confessions*, trans. Albert C. Outler [1995], I, 1).
9. *Sphere . . . center*: the cosmos and the earth at its center. According to one traditional definition, God is a circle whose center is everywhere and circumference nowhere.
1. Glimmer, twinkle.
2. The result was the same.

Lord dost thou some new fabric mold
Which favor wins
And keeps thee present, leaving th'old
Unto their sins?

Where is my God? what hidden place
Conceals thee still?
What covert dare eclipse thy face?
Is it thy will?

O let not that of any thing;[3]
Let rather brass
Or steel or mountains be thy ring
And I will pass.

Thy will such an entrenching is
As passeth thought:
To it,[4] all strength, all subtleties
Are things of naught.

Thy will such a strange distance is,
As that to it
East and West touch, the poles do kiss,
And parallels meet.

Since then my grief must be as large
As is thy space,
Thy distance from me; see my charge,[5]
Lord, see my case.

O take these bars, these lengths away,
Turn and restore me:
Be not almighty, let me say
Against, but for me.

When thou dost turn and wilt be near,
What edge so keen,
What point so piercing can appear
To come between?

For as thy absence doth excel
All distance known:
So doth thy nearness bear the bell[6]
Making two one.

3. *Of any thing*: above all.
4. Compared to it; also in line 42.
5. Burden.
6. *Bear the bell*: is preeminent.

The Flower

How fresh, O Lord, how sweet and clean
Are thy returns! Ev'n as the flowers in spring
To which, besides their own demean,[7]
The late-past frosts tributes of pleasure bring.
Grief melts away
Like snow in May
As if there were no such cold thing.

Who would have thought my shriveled heart
Could have recovered greenness! It was gone
Quite under ground: as flowers depart
To see their mother-root, when they have blown;[8]
Where they together
All the hard weather,
Dead to the world, keep house unknown.

These are thy wonders, Lord of Power,[9]
Killing and quick'ning,[1] bringing down to hell
And up to heaven in an hour:
Making a chiming of a passing bell.[2]
We say amiss
This or that is,
Thy word is all, if we could spell.[3]

O that I once past changing were
Fast in thy Paradise, where no flower can wither,
Many a spring I shoot up fair
Offering at[4] heaven, growing and groaning thither.
Nor doth my flower
Want a spring-shower,
My sins and I joining together.

But while I grow in a strait line
Still upwards bent, as if heav'n were mine own,
Thy anger comes and I decline:
What frost to that? What pole is not the zone,[5]
Where all things burn,
When thou dost turn
And the least frown of thine is shown.

7. Demeanor; domain.
8. Bloomed; "under ground" in the preceding line suggests the myth of Persephone, as do lines 12–14.
9. Cf. line 43.
1. Giving life to.
2. Unlike bells that chime, the passing bell tolls a single tone.
3. "Engage in the study or contemplation of" (*OED* II.6.b).
4. Aiming at.
5. *Pole*: polar extremes of cold; *zone*: equatorial regions.

And now in age I bud again,
After so many deaths I live and write,
I once more smell the dew and rain
And relish[6] versing: O my only light,
It cannot be
That I am he
On whom thy tempests fell all night.

These are thy wonders, Lord of Love,
To make us see, we are but flowers that glide.
Which when we once can find and prove,[7]
Thou hast a garden for us where to bide.
Who would be more
Swelling through store
Forfeit their Paradise by their pride.

The Son

Let foreign nations of their language boast
What fine variety each tongue affords;
I like our language, as our men and coast,
Who cannot dress it well, want wit not words.
How neatly do we give one only name
To parents' issue and the son's bright star!
A son is light and fruit: a fruitful flame
Chasing[8] the father's dimness, carried far
From the first man in th'East, to fresh and new
Western discoveries of posterity.
So in one word our Lord's humility
We turn upon him in a sense most true:
For what Christ once in humbleness began,
We him in glory call, "The Son of Man."

A True Hymn

My joy, my life, my crown!
My heart was meaning all the day,
Somewhat it fain would say:
And still it runneth muttering up and down
With only this, "My joy, my life, my crown."

Yet slight not these few words:
If truly said, they may take part
Among the best in art.

6. *Relish*: enjoy; also, in music, "a grace, ornament, or embellishment" (*OED*).
7. Experience.
8. Chasing away, dispelling.

The fineness[9] which a hymn or psalm affords
Is, when the soul unto the lines accords.[1]

He who craves all the mind
And all the soul and strength and time,
If the words only rhyme,
Justly complains, that somewhat is behind[2]
To make his verse, or write a hymn in kind.

Whereas if th'heart be moved,
Although the verse be somewhat scant,
God doth supply the want.
As when th'heart says (sighing to be approved)
"O could I love!" and stops: God writeth, "Loved."

Bitter-sweet

Ah my dear angry Lord,
Since thou dost love yet strike,
Cast down yet help afford,
Sure I will do the like.

I will complain yet praise:
I will bewail, approve:
And all my sour-sweet days
I will lament and love.

Mary Magdalene

When Blessèd Mary wiped her Savior's feet,
(Whose precepts she had trampled on before)
And wore them for a jewel on her head,
Showing his steps should be the street,
Wherein she thenceforth evermore
With pensive humbleness would live and tread,

She being stained her self, why did she strive
To make him clean, who could not be defiled?
Why kept she not her tears for her own faults,
And not his feet? Though we could dive
In tears, like seas, our sins are piled
Deeper than they, in words, and works, and thoughts.

9. Delicacy or subtlety, splendor.
1. *Accord*: includes a sense of singing or playing in harmony.
2. *Somewhat is behind*: something is lacking or needed.

Dear soul, she knew who did vouchsafe and deign
To bear her filth: and her sins did dash[3]
Ev'n God himself. Wherefore she was not loath,
As she had brought wherewith to stain,
So to bring in wherewith to wash
And yet in washing one, she washèd both.

Aaron[4]

Holiness on the head,
Light and perfections on the breast,
Harmonious bells below raising the dead,
To lead them unto life and rest,
Thus are true Aarons dressed.

Profaneness in my head,
Defects and darkness in my breast,
A noise[5] of passions ringing me for dead
Unto a place where is no rest,
Poor priest thus am I dressed.

Only another head
I have, another heart and breast,
Another music, making live not dead,
Without whom I could have no rest,
In him I am well dressed.

Christ is my only head,
My alone only heart and breast,
My only music, striking[6] me ev'n dead,
That to the old man I may rest,
And be in him new dressed.[7]

So holy in my head,
Perfect and light in my dear breast,
My doctrine tuned by Christ (who is not dead
But lives in me while I do rest)
Come people; Aaron's dressed.

3. Splash or splatter, here implying violence.
4. Brother of Moses and first high priest. The stanzas suggest the swelling and dying sound of a bell, visually take the shape of a bell, and use the same words to rhyme. Aaron's priestly garb is divinely prescribed in Exodus 28.
5. Band of musicians (group noun); cf. "Another music" (line 13).
6. Like the clapper of a bell.
7. "Ye have put off the old man with his deeds; and have put on the new man" (Colossians 3:9–10).

The Forerunners

The harbingers[8] are come. See, see their mark,
White is their color. And behold my head.
But must they have my brain? Must they dispark[9]
Those sparkling notions which therein were bred?
Must dullness turn me to a clod?
Yet have they left me, thou art still my God.

Good men ye be, to leave me my best room,
Ev'n all my heart and what is lodged there:
I pass[1] not, I, what of the rest become,
So (thou art still my God) be out of fear.
He will be pleased with that ditty,
And if I please him I write fine and witty.

Farewell sweet phrases, lovely metaphors.
But will ye leave me thus? When ye before
Of stews and brothels only knew the doors,
Then did I wash you with my tears: and more
Brought you to Church well dressed and clad;
My God must have my best, ev'n all I had.

Lovely enchanting language, sugar-cane,
Honey of roses, whither wilt thou fly?
Hath some fond lover ticed[2] thee to thy bane?
And wilt thou leave the Church and love a sty?
Fie, thou wilt soil thy broidered coat
And hurt thy self and him, that sings thy note.

Let foolish lovers if they will love dung
With canvas, not with arras,[3] clothe their shame:
Let folly speak in her own native tongue.
True beauty dwells on high. Ours is a flame
But borrowed thence to light us thither;
Beauty and beauteous words should go together.

Yet, if you go, I pass not. Take your way.
For (Thou art still my God) is all, that ye
Perhaps with more embellishment can say.
Go birds of spring: let winter have his fee:
Let a bleak paleness chalk the door
So all within be livelier than before.

8. Messengers in advance of a royal progress. They secured lodging by chalking doors. It was also customary to chalk doors on January 6, the feast of the Epiphany (lines 34–35).
9. Disimpark; to turn deer out of a park.
1. Care, with a play on die (cf. 31).
2. Enticed.
3. Expensive cloth, used for wall hangings or draperies.

Discipline

Throw away thy rod,
Throw away thy wrath:
O my God,
Take the gentle path.

For my heart's desire
Unto thine is bent:
I aspire
To a full consent.

Not a word or look
I affect to own,
But by book
And thy book alone.

Though I fail, I weep:
Though I halt in pace,
Yet I creep
To the throne of grace.

Then let wrath remove;
Love will do the deed
For with love
Stony hearts will bleed.

Love is swift of foot,
Love's a man of war[4]
And can shoot
And can hit from far.

Who can scape his bow?
That, which wrought on thee,
Brought thee low,
Needs, must work on me.

Throw away thy rod;
Though man frailties hath
Thou art God:
Throw away thy wrath.

4. "The Lord is a man of war" (Exodus 15:3).

The Banquet

Welcome sweet and sacred cheer,[5]
Welcome dear,
With me, in me live and dwell:
For thy neatness passeth sight,
Thy delight
Passeth tongue to taste, or tell.

O what sweetness from the bowl
Fills my soul,
Such as is and makes divine:
Is some star (fled from the sphere)
Melted there
As we sugar melt in wine?

Or hath sweetness in the bread
Made a head[6]
To subdue the smell of sin,
Flowers and gums and powders giving
All their living
Lest the enemy should win?

Doubtless, neither star nor flower
Hath the power
Such a sweetness to impart:
Only God, who gives perfumes,
Flesh assumes,
And with it perfumes my heart.

But as pomanders and wood
Still are good,
Yet being bruised are better scented:
God to show how far his love
Could improve,
Here, as broken, is presented.

When I had forgot my birth,
And on earth
In delights of earth was drowned,
God took blood and needs would be
Spilt with me,
And so found me on the ground.

Having raised me to look up
In a cup
Sweetly he doth meet my taste.
But I still being low and short,

5. Food and drink; here the bread and wine of the Eucharist.
6. *Made a head*: raised troops; thus, opposed.

Far from court
Wine becomes a wing at last.

For with it alone I fly
To the sky:
Where I wipe mine eyes and see
What I seek, for what I sue,
Him I view
Who hath done so much for me.

Let the wonder of his pity
Be my ditty
And take up my lines and life:
Hearken under pain of death,
Hands and breath.
Strive in this and love the strife.

The Elixir[7]

Teach me my God and King
In all things thee to see
And what I do in any thing
To do it as for thee.

Not rudely as a beast
To run into an action:
But still to make thee prepossesed[8]
And give it his[9] perfection.

A man that looks on glass
On it may stay his eye:
Or if he pleaseth, through it pass
And then the heaven espy.

All may of thee partake:
Nothing can be so mean
Which with his tincture[1] (for thy sake)
Will not grow bright and clean.

A servant with this clause,
Makes drudgery divine.
Who sweeps a room as for thy laws,
Makes that, and th'action fine.

7. The philosopher's stone, with which alchemists hoped to transmute baser metals into gold; also, "essence with property of indefinitely prolonging life" (*OED*). See Textual Notes for another version of this poem.
8. Always to grant you a prior claim.
9. The antecedent is "action" (line 6).
1. In alchemy, a spiritual principle whose quality may be infused into material things (then said to be "tinctured"); the elixir could be referred to as a universal tincture.

This is the famous stone
That turneth all to gold
For that which God doth touch[2] and own
Cannot for less be told.

A Wreath[3]

A wreathèd garland of deservèd praise
Of praise deservèd unto thee I give
I give to thee who knowest all my ways
My crooked winding ways wherein I live
Wherein I die not live: for life is straight
Straight as a line, and ever tends to thee
To thee who art more far above deceit
Than deceit seems above simplicity.
Give me simplicity, that I may live
So live and like, that I may know thy ways
Know them and practice them, then shall I give
For this poor wreath, give thee a crown of praise.

Death

Death thou wast once an uncouth[4] hideous thing,
Nothing but bones,
The sad effect of sadder groans:
Thy mouth was open but thou couldst not sing.

For we considered thee as at some six
Or ten years hence
After the loss of life and sense,
Flesh being turned to dust and bones to sticks.

We looked on this side of thee shooting short
Where we did find
The shells of fledge[5] souls left behind,
Dry dust which sheds no tears, but may extort.

But since our Savior's death did put some blood
Into thy face,
Thou art grown fair and full of grace
Much in request, much sought for as a good.

For we do now behold thee gay and glad
As at Doomsday

2. Try or prove gold, as with a touchstone.
3. The poem weaves diction, phrasing, and rhyme.
4. Unknown, strange.
5. Feathered; fit to fly.

When souls shall wear their new array,
And all thy bones with beauty shall be clad.

Therefore we can go die as sleep: and trust
Half that we have
Unto an honest faithful grave:
Making our pillows either down or dust.

Doomsday

Come away,
Make no delay.
Summon all the dust to rise,
Till it stir, and rub the eyes:
While this member jogs the other,
Each one whisp'ring: "Live you brother?"

Come away
Make this the day.
Dust, alas, no music feels
But thy trumpet, then it kneels.
As peculiar notes and strains
Cure tarantula's[6] raging pains.

Come away
O make no stay.
Let the graves make their confession
Lest at length they plead possession:[7]
Flesh's stubbornness may have
Read that lesson to the grave.

Come away
Thy flock doth stray.
Some to winds their bodies lend,
And in them may drown a friend.
Some in noisome vapors grow
To a plague and public woe.

Come away
Help our decay.
Man is out of order hurled
Parceled out to all the world.
Lord thy broken consort[8] raise
And the music shall be praise.

6. It was believed that the tarantula bite caused madness that could be cured by wild music and dancing (Hutchinson).
7. On the grounds that the bodies will have been there so long.
8. Concert, harmonious music.

Judgment

Almighty Judge, how shall poor wretches brook
Thy dreadful look
Able a heart of iron to appall
When thou shalt call
For every man's peculiar book.

What others mean to do, I know not well,
Yet I hear tell,
That some will turn thee to some leaves therein
So void of sin
That they in merit shall excel.

But I resolve, when thou shalt call for mine,
That to decline,
And thrust a Testament into thy hand:
Let that be scanned,
There thou shalt find, my faults are thine.

Heaven

O who will show me those delights on high?
Echo. I.
Thou Echo, thou art mortal, all men know.
Echo. No.
Wert thou not born among the trees and leaves?
Echo. Leaves.
And are there any leaves, that still abide?
Echo. Bide.
What leaves are they? Impart the matter wholly?
Echo. Holy.
Are holy leaves the Echo then of bliss?
Echo. Yes.
Then tell me, what is that supreme delight?
Echo. Light.
Light to the mind: what shall the will enjoy?
Echo. Joy.
But are there cares and business with the pleasure?
Echo. Leisure.
Light, joy, and leisure, but shall they persever?
Echo. Ever.

Love [III][9]

Love bade me welcome: yet my soul drew back,
Guilty of dust and sin.
But quick-eyed Love, observing me grow slack
From my first entrance in,
Drew nearer to me, sweetly questioning
If I lacked any thing.

"A guest," I answered, "worthy to be here":
Love said, "You shall be he."
"I the unkind, ungrateful? Ah, my Dear,
I cannot look on thee."
Love took my hand, and smiling did reply,
"Who made the eyes but I?"

"Truth Lord, but I have marred them: let my shame
Go, where it doth deserve."
"And know you not," says Love, "who bore the blame?"
"My Dear, then I will serve."
"You must sit down," says Love, "and taste my meat":
So I did sit and eat.

9. "Blessed are those servants, whom the lord when he cometh shall find watching: verily I say unto you, that he shall gird himself, and make them to sit down to meat, and will come forth and serve them" (Luke 13:37).

Thomas Carew

1594–1595	Born, possibly at West Wickham, Kent. His father, Matthew Carew, a lawyer of some distinction, had been a Master in Chancery (i.e., an officer in the Lord Chancellor's Court) since 1576, and was knighted by James I in 1603. The family took up residence in London about 1598, but nothing is known of Thomas Carew's early education.
1608	Matriculates at Merton College, Oxford; graduates B.A. in January 1610/1611.
1612	Incorporated B.A. of Cambridge (i.e., Cambridge recognizes his Oxford B.A. and grants him the same status). Admitted to the Middle Temple, presumably intending to enter the legal profession.
1613	Probably in consequence of his father's financial difficulties, accepts the offer of Sir Dudley Carleton, English ambassador in Venice, to join Carleton's entourage as a secretary.
1615	On completion of the embassy's official business, returns to England with Carleton, in December.
1616	Accompanies Carleton's embassy to the Netherlands. By consequence of some written indiscretions bearing on Carleton's character, returns to England in August, having been discreetly but effectively dismissed from his post.
1616–1618	Unsuccessfully seeks employment from various noblemen; recurrently in attendance at court. Father dies, August 1618.
1619	Makes one of an embassy to Paris headed by Sir Edward Herbert (later Lord Herbert of Cherbury). Perhaps meets the Italian poet Giambattista Marino, resident in Paris from 1615 to 1623.
1622	First published poem: commendatory verses prefixed to *The Heir*, a comedy by Thomas May. "A Rapture" probably composed between 1622 and 1624. Associates in the early 1620s with Jonson and his circle; frequents the court and cultivates influential persons there.
1630	Appointed a Gentleman of the Privy Chamber Extraordinary (i.e., a private servant of the King) and Sewer in Ordinary to the King (i.e., a household official in charge of the royal dining arrangements).
1634	Carew's masque, *Coelum Britannicum*, performed at court; published later in the year.

1639	Accompanies Charles I's military expedition against Scotland, brought to a bloodless conclusion at Berwick with the Articles of Pacification, 18 June.
1640	Death. Buried in Saint Dunstan's-in-the-West, Westminster, 23 March. Publication of *Poems*.
1642	Publication of *Poems*, "the second edition revised and enlarged."

FROM *POEMS* (1640)

The Spring[1]

Now that the winter's gone, the earth hath lost
Her snow-white robes, and now no more the frost
Candies[2] the grass, or casts an icy cream
Upon the silver lake or crystal stream;
But the warm sun thaws the benumbèd earth,
And makes it tender; gives a sacred[3] birth
To the dead swallow; wakes in hollow tree
The drowsy cuckoo and the humble-bee.
Now do a choir of chirping minstrels bring
In triumph to the world the youthful spring.
The valleys, hills, and woods in rich array
Welcome the coming of the longed-for May.
Now all things smile; only my love doth lour;
Nor hath the scalding noonday sun the power
To melt that marble ice, which still doth hold
Her heart congealed, and makes her pity cold.
The ox, which lately did for shelter fly
Into the stall, doth now securely lie
In open fields; and love no more is made
By the fireside, but in the cooler shade
Amyntas now doth with his Chloris sleep
Under a sycamore, and all things keep
Time with the season; only she doth carry
June in her eyes, in her heart January.

A Divine Mistress[4]

In Nature's pieces still I see
Some error, that might mended be;
Something my wish could still remove,
Alter or add; but my fair love
Was framed by hands far more divine,
For she hath every beauteous line;
Yet I had been far happier,
Had Nature, that made me, made her.

1. While Carew's poetry reflects the influence of Jonson and Donne, many of his lyrics echo themes and mannerisms favored by French and Italian poets, notably Giambattista Marino (1569–1625). "The Spring" reflects the influence of Pierre de Ronsard (1524–1585); cf. "Amourette" and Amour XXXIII.
2. I.e., coats with ice.
3. Cf. Textual Notes. "Sacred," the reading of both early editions, gains support by the fact that in ancient times the swallow was "held sacred to the gods of the household and to Aphrodite, for she also is one of them" (Aelian, *On the Characteristics of Animals*, ed. A. F. Scholfield, 3 vols. [London, 1959], II, p. 331). A twelfth-century bestiary observes that the swallow "is exalted by an uncommonly devout state of mind" (*The Bestiary: A Book of Beasts*, trans. and ed. T. H. White [New York, 1960], p. 147).
4. Henry Lawes (1596–1662), who composed the music for Milton's masque *Comus*, set this lyric to music (together with others by Carew) in *Ayres and Dialogues*, published 1653.

Then likeness might, that love creates,
Have made her love what now she hates;
Yet, I confess, I cannot spare
From her just shape the smallest hair;
Nor need I beg from all the store
Of heaven for her one beauty more.
She hath too much divinity for me;
You gods, teach her some more humanity.

Song: Mediocrity[5] in Love Rejected

Give me more love, or more disdain;
  The torrid or the frozen zone
Bring equal ease unto my pain,
  The temperate affords me none;
Either extreme, of love or hate,
Is sweeter than a calm estate.

Give me a storm; if it be love,
  Like Danaë in that golden shower,[6]
I swim in pleasure; if it prove
  Disdain, that torrent will devour
My vulture-hopes; and he's possessed
Of heaven, that's but from hell released.
  Then crown my joys, or cure my pain;
  Give me more love, or more disdain.

To My Mistress Sitting by a River's Side: An Eddy[7]

Mark how yon eddy steals away
From the rude stream into the bay;
There locked up safe, she doth divorce
Her waters from the channel's course,
And scorns the torrent that did bring
Her headlong from her native spring.
Now doth she with her new love play,
Whilst he runs murmuring away.
Mark how she courts the banks, whilst they
As amorously their arms display,
T'embrace and clip her silver waves;
See how she strokes their sides, and craves
An entrance there, which they deny;
Whereat she frowns, threat'ning to fly
Home to her stream, and 'gins to swim
Backward, but from the channel's brim,

5. Moderation.
6. Cf. Herrick, "A Nuptial Song," line 144n, p. 203.
7. The informing conceit of this poem is taken from Donne's Elegy VI ("Oh, let me not serve so"), lines 21–34.

Smiling, returns into the creek,
With thousand dimples on her cheek.
Be thou this eddy, and I'll make
My breast thy shore, where thou shalt take
Secure repose, and never dream
Of the quite forsaken stream;
Let him to the wide ocean haste,
There lose his color, name, and taste;
Thou shalt save all, and, safe from him,
Within these arms forever swim.

Song: To My Inconstant Mistress[8]

When thou, poor excommunicate
From all the joys of love, shalt see
The full reward, and glorious fate,
Which my strong faith shall purchase me,
Then curse thine own inconstancy.

A fairer hand than thine shalt cure
That heart which thy false oaths did wound;
And to my soul, a soul more pure
Than thine shall by Love's hand be bound,
And both with equal glory crowned.

Then shalt thou weep, entreat, complain
To Love, as I did once to thee;
When all thy tears shall be as vain
As mine were then, for thou shalt be
Damned for thy false apostasy.

Song: Persuasions to Enjoy

If the quick[9] spirits in your eye
Now languish, and anon[1] must die;
If every sweet, and every grace
Must fly from that forsaken face;
Then, Celia, let us reap our joys
Ere Time such goodly fruit destroys.

Or if that golden fleece must grow
Forever, free from aged snow;
If those bright suns must know no shade,
Nor your fresh beauties ever fade;
Then fear not, Celia, to bestow

8. This poem bears comparison with Donne's "The Apparition," p. 36.
9. Lively, vital.
1. Straightway.

What, still[2] being gathered, still must grow.
Thus, either Time his sickle brings
In vain, or else in vain his wings.

Ingrateful Beauty Threatened

Know, Celia, since thou art so proud,
'Twas I that gave thee thy renown;
Thou hadst, in the forgotten crowd
Of common beauties, lived unknown,
Had not my verse exhaled thy name,
And with it imped[3] the wings of fame.

That killing power is none of thine,
I gave it to thy voice, and eyes;
Thy sweets, thy graces, all are mine;
Thou art my star, shin'st in my skies;
Then dart not from thy borrowed sphere[4]
Lightning on him that fixed thee there.

Tempt me with such affrights no more,
Lest what I made, I uncreate;
Let fools thy mystic forms adore,
I'll know thee in thy mortal state;
Wise poets that wrapped truth in tales
Knew her themselves, through all her veils.[5]

Disdain Returned

He that loves a rosy cheek,
Or a coral lip admires,
Or from star-like eyes doth seek
Fuel to maintain his fires;
As old Time makes these decay,
So his flames must waste away.

But a smooth and steadfast mind,
Gentle thoughts, and calm desires,
Hearts with equal love combined,
Kindle never-dying fires.

2. Continuously.
3. I.e., grafted feathers onto (as falconers repair a bird's injured wing).
4. Cf. Herrick, "A Nuptial Song," line 102n, p. 201. Herrick's "Siren," however, sings sweetly in her sphere; Carew's Celia combines the attributes of a star that sheds malign influence with (by implication) those of the enticing and dangerous Sirens of Homer's *Odyssey*, XII.39–46, 184–200.
5. Renaissance mythographers regularly insist that poetry "veils truth in a fair and fitting garment of fiction" (Boccaccio, *Genealogia Deorum Gentilium, XIV–XV*, ed. C. G. Osgood [Indianapolis, 1956], p. 39).

Where these are not, I despise
Lovely cheeks, or lips, or eyes.

No tears, Celia, now shall win
  My resolved heart to return;
I have searched thy soul within,
  And find nought but pride and scorn;
I have learned thy arts, and now
  Can disdain as much as thou.
Some power,[6] in my revenge, convey
That love to her, I cast away.

To My Mistress in Absence[7]

Though I must live here, and by force
Of your command suffer divorce;
Though I am parted, yet my mind,
That's more myself, still stays behind.
I breathe in you, you keep my heart;
'Twas but a carcass that did part.
Then though our bodies are disjoined,
As things that are to place confined,
Yet let our boundless spirits meet,
And in love's sphere each other greet;
There let us work a mystic wreath,
Unknown unto the world beneath;
There let our clasped loves sweetly twin,
There let our secret thoughts unseen
Like nets be weaved and intertwined,
Wherewith we'll catch each other's mind.
There whilst our souls do sit and kiss,
Tasting a sweet and subtle bliss
Such as gross lovers cannot know,
Whose hands and lips meet here below,
Let us look down, and mark what pain
Our absent bodies here sustain,
And smile to see how far away
The one doth from the other stray;
Yet burn and languish with desire
To join, and quench their mutual fire.
There let us joy to see from far
Our emulous flames at loving war,
Whilst both with equal lustre shine,
Mine bright as yours, yours bright as mine.
There seated in those heavenly bowers,
We'll cheat the lag and lingering hours,

6. I.e., may some god.
7. Carew's poem recalls, but interestingly diverges from, Donne's "The Ecstasy," p. 37. Lines 23–24 may owe something to Donne's "A Valediction: Forbidding Mourning," p. 36.

Making our bitter absence sweet,
Till souls and bodies both may meet.

Song: Eternity of Love Protested

How ill doth he deserve a lover's name,
Whose pale weak flame
Cannot retain
His heat, in spite of absence or disdain;
But doth at once, like paper set on fire,
Burn and expire;
True love can never change his seat,
Nor did he ever love, that could retreat.

That noble flame which my breast keeps alive
Shall still survive
When my soul's fled;
Nor shall my love die when my body's dead,
That shall wait on me to the lower shade,
And never fade;
My very ashes in their urn
Shall, like a hallowed lamp, forever burn.[8]

To Saxham[9]

Though frost and snow locked from mine eyes
That beauty which without door lies,
Thy gardens, orchards, walks, that so
I might not all thy pleasures know,
Yet, Saxham, thou within thy gate
Art of thyself, so delicate,
So full of native sweets, that bless
Thy roof with inward happiness,
As neither from nor to thy store
Winter takes aught, or spring adds more.
The cold and frozen air had starved[1]
Much poor, if not by thee preserved,
Whose prayers have made thy table blest
With plenty, far above the rest.

8. Sir Thomas Browne inquires, in *Pseudodoxia Epidemica*, "Why some lamps included in close bodies have burned many hundred years, as that discovered in the sepulchre of Tullia the sister of Cicero . . ." (*The Prose of Sir Thomas Browne*, ed. N. J. Endicott [New York, 1967], p. 202). Donne also alludes to the lamp "in Tullia's tomb": cf. "Epithalamion," lines 215–218.
9. Little Saxham, near Bury Saint Edmunds in Suffolk, was the country residence of Sir John Crofts (1563–1628), with whose family Carew maintained friendly relations. The poem is modeled on Jonson's "To Penshurst," p. 97.
1. I.e., had caused to die.

The season hardly did afford
Coarse cates[2] unto thy neighbors' board,
Yet thou hadst dainties, as the sky
Had only been thy volary;[3]
Or else the birds, fearing the snow
Might to another Deluge grow,
The pheasant, partridge, and the lark
Flew to thy house, as to the Ark.[4]
The willing ox of himself came
Home to the slaughter, with the lamb,
And every beast did thither bring
Himself, to be an offering.
The scaly herd more pleasure took,
Bathed in thy dish, than in the brook;
Water, earth, air, did all conspire
To pay their tributes to thy fire,
Whose cherishing flames themselves divide
Through every room, where they deride
The night, and cold abroad; whilst they,
Like suns within, keep endless day.
Those cheerful beams send forth their light
To all that wander in the night,[5]
And seem to beckon from aloof[6]
The weary pilgrim to thy roof,
Where if, refreshed, he will away,
He's fairly welcome; or if stay,
Far more; which he shall hearty find
Both from the master and the hind.[7]
The stranger's welcome each man there
Stamped on his cheerful brow doth wear,
Nor doth this welcome or his cheer
Grow less 'cause he stays longer here;
There's none observes, much less repines,
How often this man sups or dines.
Thou hast no porter at the door
T'examine or keep back the poor;
Nor locks nor bolts: thy gates have been
Made only to let strangers in;
Untaught to shut, they do not fear
To stand wide open all the year,
Careless who enters, for they know
Thou never didst deserve a foe;
And as for thieves, thy bounty's such,
They cannot steal, thou giv'st so much.

2. Victuals, food.
3. Aviary.
4. Cf. Genesis 7:7.
5. Cf. Matthew 5:16: "Let your light so shine before men, that they may see your good works. . . ."
6. I.e., from a distance.
7. Servant (or farm laborer on the estate).

Upon a Ribbon

This silken wreath, which circles in mine arm,[8]
Is but an emblem of that mystic charm,
Wherewith the magic of your beauties binds
My captive soul, and round about it winds
Fetters of lasting love. This hath entwined
My flesh alone, that hath empaled[9] my mind.
Time may wear out these soft weak bands, but those
Strong chains of brass, Fate shall not discompose.
This holy relic may preserve my wrist,
But my whole frame doth by that power subsist;
To that my prayers and sacrifice, to this
I only pay a superstitious kiss.
This but the idol, that's the deity;
Religion there is due; here, ceremony;
That I receive by faith, this but in trust;
Here I may tender duty, there I must;
This order as a layman I may bear,
But I become Love's priest when that I wear.
This moves like air; that as the center[1] stands;
That knot your virtue tied, this but your hands;
That, nature framed; but this was made by art;
This makes my arm your prisoner; that, my heart.

A Rapture[2]

I will enjoy thee now, my Celia, come,
And fly with me to Love's Elysium.[3]
The giant, Honor, that keeps cowards out,
Is but a masquer,[4] and the servile rout
Of baser subjects only bend in vain
To the vast idol, whilst the nobler train
Of valiant lovers daily sail between
The huge colossus' legs,[5] and pass unseen
Unto the blissful shore. Be bold, and wise,[6]
And we shall enter; the grim Swiss[7] denies

8. Cf. Donne's "The Funeral" (notably line 3: "That subtle wreath of hair, which crowns my arm"), p. 40, and "The Relic," p. 41.
9. Enclosed.
1. I.e., the earth (by Ptolemaic reckoning situated at the center of the created universe).
2. Carew's poem has some affinity with Donne's Elegy XIX ("Going to Bed"), p. 46. Not very surprisingly, "The Rapture" excited the admiration of many among Carew's contemporaries; Randolph, Cartwright, John Cleveland, and others composed verses that clearly reflect the influence of its language and tone.
3. I.e., love's paradise. In the Latin poets, Elysium is that part of the underworld reserved for those whose earthly lives had been heroic or markedly righteous (cf. Vergil, *Aeneid*, VI.637–678).
4. I.e., one who plays a part in a courtly entertainment.
5. The Colossus of Rhodes, one of the seven wonders of the ancient world, was a statue of Apollo, some 120 feet high, made by Chares in the third century B.C.
6. It is not unlikely that Carew ironically recalls that inscription in the House of Busirane, which challenged the wit of chaste Britomart: *"Be bold, be bold,* and every where *Be bold . . . Be not too bold"* (*The Faerie Queene*, III.xi.54).
7. The Swiss guards at the Vatican, in Rome, were renowned for their stature.

Only to tame fools a passage, that not know
He is but form, and only frights in show
The duller eyes that look from far; draw near,
And thou shalt scorn what we were wont to fear.
We shall see how the stalking pageant[8] goes
With borrowed legs, a heavy load to those
That made and bear him; not, as we once thought,
The seed of gods, but a weak model wrought
By greedy men, that seek to enclose the common,[9]
And within private arms impale[1] free woman.
   Come, then, and mounted on the wings of Love
We'll cut the flitting air, and soar above
The monster's head, and in the noblest seats
Of those blest shades quench and renew our heats.
There shall the Queen of Love, and Innocence,
Beauty, and Nature, banish all offence
From our close ivy-twines; there I'll behold
Thy barèd snow and thy unbraided gold;
There my enfranchised hand on every side
Shall o'er thy naked polished ivory slide.
No curtain there, though of transparent lawn,[2]
Shall be before thy virgin-treasure drawn;
But the rich mine, to the inquiring eye
Exposed, shall ready still for mintage lie,
And we will coin young Cupids. There a bed
Of roses and fresh myrtles shall be spread
Under the cooler shade of cypress groves;
Our pillows, of the down of Venus' doves,[3]
Whereon our panting limbs we'll gently lay,
In the faint respites of our active play;
That so our slumbers may in dreams have leisure
To tell the nimble fancy our past pleasure,
And so our souls that cannot be embraced
Shall the embraces of our bodies taste.
Meanwhile the bubbling stream shall court the shore,
Th'enamored chirping wood-choir shall adore
In varied tunes the deity of love;
The gentle blasts of western winds shall move
The trembling leaves, and through their close boughs breathe
Still music, whilst we rest ourselves beneath
Their dancing shade; till a soft murmur, sent
From souls entranced in amorous languishment,
Rouse us, and shoot into our veins fresh fire,
Till we in their sweet ecstasy expire.
   Then, as the empty bee, that lately bore
Into the common treasure all her store,

8. I.e., honor, mere show without substance.
9. I.e., to seize for personal gain that which is properly common to all (as rich men "enclosed" common land for pasturage).
1. I.e., (1) enclose; (2) penetrate.
2. Fine linen.
3. Cf. Jonson's "A Celebration of Charis," no. 4, line 3n, p. 123.

Flies 'bout the painted field with nimble wing,
Deflow'ring the fresh virgins of the spring,
So will I rifle all the sweets that dwell
In my delicious paradise, and swell
My bag with honey, drawn forth by the power
Of fervent kisses, from each spicy flower.
I'll seize the rose-buds in their perfumed bed,
The violet knots, like curious mazes spread
O'er all the garden, taste the ripened cherry,
The warm, firm apple, tipped with coral berry;
Then will I visit with a wand'ring kiss
The vale of lilies and the bower of bliss;
And where the beauteous region doth divide
Into two milky ways, my lips shall slide
Down those smooth alleys, wearing as I go
A tract[4] for lovers on the printed snow;
Thence climbing o'er the swelling Apennine,
Retire into thy grove of eglantine,[5]
Where I will all those ravished sweets distill
Through Love's alembic,[6] and with chemic skill
From the mixed mass one sovereign balm derive,
Then bring that great elixir to thy hive.
   Now in more subtle wreaths I will entwine
My sinewy thighs, my legs and arms with thine;
Thou like a sea of milk shalt lie displayed,
Whilst I the smooth, calm ocean invade
With such tempest, as when Jove of old
Fell down on Danaë in a storm of gold;[7]
Yet my tall pine shall in the Cyprian[8] strait
Ride safe at anchor, and unlade her freight;
My rudder, with thy bold hand, like a tried
And skillful pilot, thou shalt steer, and guide
My bark into love's channel, where it shall
Dance, as the bounding waves do rise or fall.
Then shall thy circling arms embrace and clip
My willing body, and thy balmy lip
Bathe me in juice of kisses, whose perfume
Like a religious incense shall consume,
And send up holy vapors to those powers
That bless our loves, and crown our sportful hours,
That with such halcyon[9] calmness fix our souls
In steadfast peace, as no affright controls.
There no rude sounds shake us with sudden starts;

4. Path.
5. Sweetbriar.
6. An alembic was a vessel used in alchemical ("chemic") distillation.
7. Cf. Herrick's "A Nuptial Song," line 144n, p. 203.
8. The island of Cyprus was a center of the worship of Venus.
9. According to legend, during that period when the halcyon (a seabird) makes and maintains her nest, the ocean's waves are calm; cf. Ovid, *Metamorphoses*, XI.415–748.

No jealous ears, when we unrip our hearts,
Suck our discourse in; no observing spies
This blush, that glance traduce; no envious eyes
Watch our close meetings; nor are we betrayed
To rivals by the bribèd chambermaid.
No wedlock bonds unwreathe our twisted loves;
We seek no midnight arbor, no dark groves
To hide our kisses: there the hated name
Of husband, wife, lust, modest, chaste, or shame,
Are vain and empty words, whose very sound
Was never heard in the Elysian ground.
All things are lawful there that may delight
Nature or unrestrainèd appetite;
Like and enjoy, to will and act is one:
We only sin when Love's rites are not done.
  The Roman Lucrece[1] there reads the divine
Lectures of love's great master, Aretine,[2]
And knows as well as Lais[3] how to move
Her pliant body in the act of love.
To quench the burning ravisher, she hurls
Her limbs into a thousand winding curls,
And studies artful postures, such as be
Carved on the bark of every neighboring tree
By learned hands, that so adorned the rind
Of those fair plants, which, as they lay entwined,
Have fanned their glowing fires. The Grecian dame,[4]
That in her endless web toiled for a name
As fruitless as her work, doth there display
Herself before the youth of Ithaca,
And th'amorous sport of gamesome nights prefer
Before dull dreams of the lost traveller.
Daphne[5] hath broke her bark, and that swift foot,
Which th'angry gods had fastened with a root
To the fixed earth, doth now unfettered run
To meet th'embraces of the youthful sun.
She hangs upon him like his Delphic lyre;
Her kisses blow the old, and breathe new fire;
Full of her god, she sings inspirèd lays,
Sweet odes of love, such as deserve the bays,
Which she herself was. Next her, Laura[6] lies

1. The name of Lucretia, who took her own life after she was raped by Tarquin, became a byword for chastity in later times.
2. Pietro Aretino (1492–1556) composed mock-moralistic sonnets to accompany a set of lascivious engravings by Marcantonio Raimondi. Robert Burton notes that "Aretine's Lucretia [in another of Aretino's works] sold her maidenhead a thousand times before she was twenty-four years old" (*Anatomy of Melancholy*, *ed. cit.*, III, p. 54).
3. Lais was a beautiful and talented courtesan of Corinth in the fifth century B.C. Cf. Athenaeus, *The Learned Banquet*, XIII, for an account of her career (and of other celebrated courtesans of ancient times).
4. A number of classical writers deny that Penelope, the wife of Odysseus, remained faithful to her husband during his long absence from Ithaca.
5. Cf. Herrick, "The Welcome to Sack," line 92n, p. 194.
6. Petrarch (1304–1374) addressed his celebrated sonnets to Laura.

In Petrarch's learnèd arms, drying those eyes
That did in such sweet smooth-paced numbers flow,
As made the world enamored of his woe.
These, and ten thousand beauties more, that died
Slave to the tyrant, now enlarged, deride
His cancelled laws, and for their time misspent
Pay into Love's exchequer double rent.
  Come then, my Celia, we'll no more forbear
To taste our joys, struck with a panic fear,
But will depose from his imperious sway
This proud usurper,[7] and walk free as they,
With necks unyoked; nor is it just that he
Should fetter your soft sex with chastity,
Which Nature made unapt for abstinence;
When yet this false imposter can dispense
With human justice and with sacred right,
And, maugre[8] both their laws, command me fight
With rivals, or with emulous loves, that dare
Equal with thine their mistress' eyes or hair.
If thou complain of wrong, and call my sword
To carve out thy revenge, upon that word
He bids me fight and kill, or else he brands
With marks of infamy my coward hands,
And yet religion bids from bloodshed fly,
And damns me for that act. Then tell me why
This goblin Honor, which the world adores,
Should make men atheists, and not women whores.

Epitaph on the Lady Mary Villiers[9]

The Lady Mary Villiers lies
Under this stone, with weeping eyes
The parents that first gave her birth,
And their sad friends, laid her in earth.
If any of them, reader, were
Known unto thee, shed a tear;
Or if thyself possess a gem
As dear to thee as this to them,
Though a stranger to this place,
Bewail in theirs, thine own hard case;
For thou perhaps at thy return
Mayest find thy darling in an urn.

7. I.e., honor.
8. In spite of.
9. Mary Villiers, the daughter of the Earl and Countess of Anglesey (who were Carew's patrons), died on 4 August 1630, about five months after her second birthday.

Another[1]

The purest soul that e'er was sent
Into a clayey tenement
Informed this dust; but the weak mold
Could the great guest no longer hold;
The substance was too pure, the flame
Too glorious that thither came;
Ten thousand Cupids brought along
A grace on each wing, that did throng
For place there, till they all oppressed
The seat in which they sought to rest;
So the fair model[2] broke, for want
Of room to lodge th'inhabitant.

Another

This little vault, this narrow room,
Of love and beauty is the tomb;
The dawning beam that 'gan to clear
Our clouded sky, lies darkened here,
Forever set to us, by death
Sent to inflame the world beneath.
'Twas but a bud, yet did contain
More sweetness than shall spring again;
A budding star that might have grown
Into a sun, when it had blown.[3]
This hopeful beauty did create
New life in Love's declining state;
But now his empire ends, and we
From fire and wounding darts are free;
His brand, his bow, let no man fear:
The flames, the arrows, all lie here.

To Ben Jonson: Upon Occasion of His Ode of Defiance Annexed to His Play of *The New Inn*[4]

'Tis true, dear Ben, thy just chastising hand
Hath fixed upon the sotted age a brand,
To their swoll'n pride and empty scribbling due;
It can nor judge nor write, and yet 'tis true
Thy comic Muse, from the exalted line
Touched by thy *Alchemist*, doth since decline

1. Cf. Textual Notes.
2. Mold.
3. Fully opened.
4. Cf. Jonson's "Ode to Himself," p. 151.

From that her zenith, and foretells a red
And blushing evening, when she goes to bed;
Yet such as shall outshine the glimmering light
With which all stars shall gild the following night.
Nor think it much, since all thy eaglets may
Endure the sunny trial,[5] if we say
This hath the stronger wing, or that doth shine
Tricked up in fairer plumes, since all are thine.
Who hath his flock of cackling geese compared
With thy tuned choir of swans?[6] or else who dared
To call thy births deformed? But if thou bind
By city-custom, or by gavelkind,[7]
In equal shares thy love on all thy race,
We may distinguish of their sex and place;
Though one hand form them, and though one brain strike
Souls into all, they are not all alike.
Why should the follies, then, of this dull age
Draw from thy pen such an immodest rage,
As seems to blast thy (else-immortal) bays,[8]
When thine own tongue proclaims thy itch of praise?
Such thirst will argue drouth. No, let be hurled
Upon thy works, by the detracting world,
What malice can suggest; let the rout[9] say,
The running sands, that, ere thou make a play,
Count the slow minutes, might a Goodwin[1] frame,
To swallow, when th'hast done, thy shipwrecked name.
Let them the dear expense of oil upbraid,
Sucked by thy watchful lamp, that hath betrayed
To theft the blood of martyred authors, spilt
Into thy ink, whilst thou growest pale with guilt.
Repine not at the taper's thrifty waste,
That sleeks thy terser poems; nor is haste
Praise, but excuse;[2] and if thou overcome
A knotty writer, bring the booty home;
Nor think it theft, if the rich spoils so torn
From conquered authors be as trophies worn.
Let others glut on the extorted praise
Of vulgar breath; trust thou to after-days:
Thy labored works shall live, when Time devours
Th'abortive offspring of their hasty hours.
Thou art not of their rank, the quarrel lies

5. It was believed that eagles confirmed the nature of their young by forcing them to gaze directly at the sun. Cf. *The Bestiary, ed. cit.*, p. 107.
6. "In the Northern parts of the world, once the lute players have tuned up, a great many swans are invited in, and they play a concert together in strict measure" (*The Bestiary, ed. cit.*, p. 119).
7. I.e., according to the London regulation by which a citizen's estate was divided equally among his wife, children, and executors; or the Kentish practice, by which each heir received an equal share of the estate.
8. I.e., the laurel wreath, symbolic of excellence in poetry.
9. Rabble.
1. The notorious Goodwin Sands, near Ramsgate, posed a continuous threat to coastal shipping.
2. Cf. Jonson's distinction, in *Timber*, between "common rhymers" who "pour forth verses, such as they are, *ex tempore*," and the true poet, who understands the importance of careful revision.

Within thine own verge;[3] then let this suffice,
The wiser world doth greater thee confess
Than all men else, than thyself only less.

An Elegy upon the Death of Dr. Donne, Dean of Paul's[4]

Can we not force from widowed poetry,
Now thou art dead, great Donne, one elegy
To crown thy hearse? Why yet dare we not trust,
Though with unkneaded dough-baked[5] prose, thy dust,
Such as the unscissored[6] churchman, from the flower
Of fading rhetoric, short-lived as his hour,
Dry as the sand that measures it, should lay
Upon thy ashes on the funeral day?
Have we no voice, no tune? Didst thou dispense
Through all our language both the words and sense?
'Tis a sad truth. The pulpit may her plain
And sober Christian precepts still retain;
Doctrines it may, and wholesome uses, frame,
Grave homilies and lectures, but the flame
Of thy brave[7] soul, that shot such heat and light
As burnt our earth, and made our darkness bright,
Committed holy rapes upon our will,
Did through the eye the melting heart distill,
And the deep knowledge of dark truths so teach,
As sense might judge what fancy could not reach,
Must be desired forever. So the fire
That fills with spirit and heat the Delphic choir,[8]
Which, kindled first by thy Promethean[9] breath,
Glowed here awhile, lies quenched now in thy death.
The Muses' garden, with pedantic weeds
O'erspread, was purged by thee; the lazy seeds
Of servile imitation thrown away,
And fresh invention planted. Thou didst pay
The debts of our penurious bankrupt age;
Licentious thefts, that make poetic rage
A mimic fury, when our souls must be
Possessed, or with Anacreon's[1] ecstasy,
Or Pindar's, not their own; the subtle cheat

3. Domain.
4. Donne died on 31 March 1631. The text given here is that which appears in *Poems, by J[ohn]. D[onne]. with Elegies on the Authors Death* (1633), 385–388. Cf. Textual Notes for significant variants in the text printed in the 1640 edition of Carew's *Poems*.
5. I.e., tedious and flat. Cf. Donne, "A Letter to the Lady Carey, and Mrs. Essex Riche, from Amiens," lines 19–21.
6. Unshorn; i.e., with uncut hair.
7. Superior.
8. I.e., the echoing pronouncements of Apollo's oracle at Delphi.
9. Prometheus stole fire from heaven, in spite of Zeus' attempt to conceal it; cf. Hesiod, *Works and Days*, 47–53.
1. For Anacreon, cf. Jonson, Epigram CI, lines 30–31n, p. 89; for Pindar, cf. Jonson, "To the Immortal Memory [of] Sir Lucius Cary and Sir H. Morison," note 1, p. 140.

Of sly exchanges, and the juggling feat
Of two-edged words,[2] or whatsoever wrong
By ours was done the Greek, or Latin tongue,
Thou hast redeemed, and opened us a mine
Of rich and pregnant fancy; drawn a line
Of masculine expression,[3] which had good
Old Orpheus[4] seen, or all the ancient brood
Our superstitious fools admire, and hold
Their lead more precious than thy burnished gold,
Thou hadst been their exchequer, and no more
They each in other's dust had raked for ore.
Thou shalt yield no precedence, but of time,
And the blind fate of language, whose tuned chime
More charms the outward sense; yet thou mayst claim
From so great disadvantage greater fame,
Since to the awe of thy imperious wit
Our stubborn language bends, made only fit
With her tough thick-ribbed hoops to gird about
Thy giant fancy, which had proved too stout
For their soft melting phrases. As in time
They had the start, so did they cull the prime
Buds of invention many a hundred year,
And left the rifled fields, besides the fear
To touch their harvest; yet from those bare lands
Of what is purely thine, thy only hands,
(And that thy smallest work) have gleanèd more
Than all those times and tongues could reap before.
   But thou art gone, and thy strict laws will be
Too hard for libertines in poetry.
They will repeal[5] the goodly exiled train
Of gods and goddesses, which in thy just reign
Were banished nobler poems; now, with these,
The silenced tales o'th'*Metamorphoses*[6]
Shall stuff their lines, and swell the windy page,
Till verse, refined by thee, in this last age
Turn ballad-rhyme,[7] or those old idols be
Adored again with new apostasy.[8]
   O pardon me, that break with untuned verse
The reverend silence that attends thy hearse,
Whose awful[9] solemn murmurs were to thee,
More than these faint lines, a loud elegy,
That did proclaim in a dumb eloquence

2. I.e., perhaps, puns and ambiguous terms (although these are often encountered in Donne's poetry).
3. Cf. Jonson's reference to "strong lines" in "An Execration Upon Vulcan," line 78.
4. Cf. Jonson, *The Forest*, XII, line 77n, p. 114.
5. Call back.
6. Ovid's storehouse of myth and legend, first translated into English by Arthur Golding in 1567, had been translated c. 1621–1626 by George Sandys.
7. I.e., altogether decline into a condition of crude rhyming and versing.
8. I.e., apostasy from Donne's exemplary rule.
9. I.e., awestruck.

The death of all the arts, whose influence,
Grown feeble, in these panting numbers lies
Gasping short-winded accents, and so dies.
So doth the swiftly turning wheel not stand
In th'instant we withdraw the moving hand,
But some small time maintain a faint weak course,
By virtue of the first impulsive force;
And so, whilst I cast on thy funeral pile
Thy crown of bays, oh, let it crack awhile,
And spit disdain, till the devouring flashes
Suck all the moisture up, then turn to ashes.
  I will not draw the envy to engross[1]
All thy perfections, or weep all our loss;
Those are too numerous[2] for an elegy,
And this too great to be expressed by me.
Though every pen should share a distinct part,
Yet art thou theme enough to 'tire[3] all art;
Let others carve the rest; it shall suffice
I on thy tomb this epitaph incise:
    Here lies a king, that ruled as he thought fit
    The universal monarchy of wit;
    Here lie two flamens,[4] *and both those the best:*
    Apollo's first, at last the true God's priest.

In Answer of an Elegiacal Letter, upon the Death of the King of Sweden, from Aurelian Townshend, Inviting Me to Write on That Subject[5]

Why dost thou sound, my dear Aurelian,
In so shrill accents, from thy Barbican,[6]
A loud alarum to my drowsy eyes,
Bidding them wake in tears and elegies
For mighty Sweden's fall? Alas! how may
My lyric feet, that of the smooth soft way
Of love, and beauty, only know the tread,
In dancing paces celebrate the dead
Victorious king, or his majestic hearse
Profane with th'humble touch of their low verse?

1. I.e., to write large.
2. I.e., too many (also, punningly, "too largely poetical").
3. I.e., to attire, adorn (with a pun on "tire": to wear out).
4. Priests.
5. Gustavus II (Gustavus Adolphus), King of Sweden, led the Protestant armies to their first military successes against the forces of the Holy Roman Empire during the Thirty Years' War (1618–1648). He was killed at the battle of Lützen, near Leipzig, on 16 November 1632, although his troops defeated the Catholic army under Wallenstein on that occasion. Aurelian Townshend (c. 1583–c. 1651) was a minor poet who wrote two masques for the court in 1632, *Albion's Triumph* and *Tempe Restored*. The poem to which Carew here responds is printed in Rhodes Dunlap's edition of Carew's poetry, pp. 207–208.
6. Townshend resided for some years in the London parish of Saint Giles, Cripplegate; the Barbican (originally an armed watchtower) is an area within that parish.

Vergil, nor Lucan,[7] no, nor Tasso more
Than both, nor Donne, worth all that went before,
With the united labor of their wit,
Could a just poem to this subject fit.
His actions were too mighty to be raised
Higher by verse; let him in prose be praised,
In modest, faithful story, which his deeds
Shall turn to poems. When the next age reads
Of Frankfort, Leipzig, Würzburg, of the Rhine,
The Lech, the Danube, Tilly, Wallenstein,
Bavaria, Pappenheim, Lützen-field,[8] where he
Gained after death a posthume victory,
They'll think his acts things rather feigned than done,
Like our romances of the Knight o'th' Sun.[9]
Leave we him, then, to the grave chronicler,
Who, though to annals[1] he cannot refer
His too brief story, yet his journals may
Stand by the Caesars' years, and every day
Cut into minutes, each shall more contain
Of great designment than an emperor's reign.
And, since 'twas but his churchyard, let him have
For his own ashes now no narrower grave
Than the whole German continent's vast womb,
Whilst all her cities do but make his tomb.
Let us to supreme providence commit
The fate of monarchs, which first thought it fit
To rend the empire from the Austrian grasp;
And next from Sweden's, even when he did clasp
Within his dying arms the sovereignty
Of all those provinces, that men might see
The divine wisdom would not leave that land
Subject to any one king's sole command.
Then let the Germans fear if Caesar shall,
Or the united princes, rise and fall;
But let us, that in myrtle bowers sit
Under secure shades, use the benefit
Of peace and plenty, which the blessed hand
Of our good king gives this obdurate land;
Let us of revels sing, and let thy breath,
Which filled Fame's trumpet with Gustavus' death,
Blowing his name to heaven, gently inspire
Thy past'ral pipe, till all our swains admire

7. Marcus Annaeus Lucanus (A.D. 39–65), called Lucan, wrote the heroic poem *Pharsalia*, an account in ten books of the conflict between Pompey and Caesar; Torquato Tasso (1544–1595) was renowned primarily for his epic poem about the Crusades, *Gerusalemme Liberata* (1581).
8. The Catholic generals Tilly, Wallenstein, and Pappenheim, regularly victorious in the early stages of the Thirty Years' War, met their match in Gustavus Adolphus. Tilly died of wounds received at the crossing of the river Lech; Pappenheim was fatally wounded at Lützen, where the imperial army under Wallenstein was defeated. Wallenstein was assassinated in 1634.
9. The Knight of the Sun was the hero of a popular sixteenth-century Spanish romance, translated into English (c. 1580–1601) as *The Mirror of Princely Deeds and Knighthood*.
1. Carew probably alludes to the *Annales of Tacitus* (c. A.D. 59–c. 118).

Thy song and subject, whilst they both comprise
The beauties of the *Shepherd's Paradise*.[2]
For who like thee (whose loose discourse is far
More neat and polished than our poems are,
Whose very gait's more graceful than our dance)
In sweetly-flowing numbers may advance
The glorious night when, not to act foul rapes
Like birds or beasts, but in their angel-shapes,
A troop of deities came down to guide
Our steerless barks in passion's swelling tide
By virtue's card,[3] and brought us from above
A pattern of their own celestial love?
Nor lay it in dark, sullen precepts drowned,
But with rich fancy and clear action crowned,
Through a mysterious fable, that was drawn
Like a transparent veil of purest lawn
Before their dazzling beauties, the divine
Venus did with her heavenly Cupid shine.
The story's curious web, the masculine style,
The subtle sense, did time and sleep beguile;
Pinioned and charmed they stood to gaze upon
Th'angelic forms, gestures, and motion,
To hear those ravishing sounds that did dispense
Knowledge and pleasure to the soul and sense.
It filled us with amazement to behold
Love made all spirit, his corporeal mold,
Dissected into atoms, melt away
To empty air, and from the gross allay[4]
Of mixtures and compounding accidents,[5]
Refined to immaterial elements.
But when the Queen of Beauty[6] did inspire
The air with perfumes, and our hearts with fire,
Breathing from her celestial organ[7] sweet
Harmonious notes, our souls fell at her feet,
And did with humble reverent duty more
Her rare perfections than high state adore.
   These harmless pastimes let my Townshend sing
To rural tunes; not that thy Muse wants wing
To soar a loftier pitch, for she hath made
A noble flight, and placed th'heroic shade
Above the reach of our faint flagging rhyme;
But these are subjects proper to our clime:
Tourneys, masques, theaters, better become
Our halcyon[8] days. What though the German drum

2. I.e., Townshend's masque, *Tempe Restored*, presented at court in January 1633.
3. Compass.
4. Alloy.
5. Nonessential qualities.
6. Queen Henrietta Maria took this role in *Tempe Restored*.
7. I.e., throat.
8. Cf. "A Rapture," line 97n, p. 304.

Bellow for freedom and revenge? The noise
Concerns not us, nor should divert our joys;
Nor ought the thunder of their carabins[9]
Drown the sweet airs of our tuned violins.
Believe me, friend, if their prevailing powers
Gain them a calm security like ours,
They'll hang their arms up on the olive bough,
And dance, and revel then, as we do now.

To a Lady That Desired I Would Love Her

Now you have freely given me leave to love,
    What will you do?
Shall I your mirth or pastime move
    When I begin to woo?
Will you torment, or scorn, or love me too?

Each petty beauty can disdain, and I,
    Spite of your hate,
Without your leave can see, and die;
    Dispense a nobler fate:
'Tis easy to destroy, you may create.

Then give me leave to love, and love me too,
    Not with design
To raise, as love's curst rebels do
    When puling poets whine,
Fame to their beauty from their blubbered eyne.

Grief is a puddle, and reflects not clear
    Your beauty's rays;
Joys are pure streams, your eyes appear
    Sullen in sadder lays;
In cheerful numbers they shine bright with praise,

Which shall not mention, to express you fair,
    Wounds, flames, and darts,
Storms in your brow, nets in your hair,
    Suborning all your parts,
Or to betray or torture captive hearts.

I'll make your eyes like morning suns appear,
    As mild and fair,
Your brow as crystal smooth and clear,
    And your disheveled hair
Shall flow like a calm region of the air.

9. Carbines (short firearms).

Rich nature's store, which is the poet's treasure,
I'll spend to dress
Your beauties; if your mine of pleasure
In equal thankfulness
You but unlock, so we each other bless.

To My Friend G. N., from Wrest[1]

I breathe, sweet Ghib, the temperate air of Wrest,
Where I no more, with raging storms oppressed,
Wear the cold nights out by the banks of Tweed,[2]
On the bleak mountains where fierce tempests breed,
And everlasting winter dwells; where mild
Favonius[3] and the vernal winds exiled
Did never spread their wings, but the wild north
Brings sterile fern, thistles, and brambles forth.
Here, steeped in balmy dew, the pregnant earth
Sends from her teeming womb a flow'ry birth,
And cherished with the warm sun's quick'ning heat,
Her porous bosom doth rich odors sweat,
Whose perfumes through the ambient[4] air diffuse
Such native aromatics as we use;
No foreign gums, nor essence fetched from far,
No volatile spirits, nor compounds that are
Adulterate, but at nature's cheap expense
With far more genuine sweets refresh the sense.
Such pure and uncompounded beauties bless
This mansion with an useful comeliness,
Devoid of art, for here the architect
Did not with curious skill a pile erect
Of carvèd marble, touch,[5] or porphyry,
But built a house for hospitality.
No sumptuous chimney-piece of shining stone
Invites the stranger's eye to gaze upon,
And coldly entertains his sight, but clear
And cheerful flames cherish and warm him here;
No Doric nor Corinthian pillars grace
With imag'ry this structure's naked face;
The lord and lady of this place delight
Rather to be in act, than seem in sight.
Instead of statues to adorn their wall,
They throng with living men their merry hall,
Where at large tables filled with wholesome meats

1. The identity of "G. N." remains uncertain, although Rhodes Dunlap (*ed. cit.*, p. 256) makes a plausible case for Gilbert North, "who like Carew served Charles I as a gentleman of the privy chamber." The manor of Wrest Park, in Bedfordshire, belonged to Anthony de Grey, Earl of Kent. Carew's poem owes something to Jonson's "To Penshurst," p. 97.
2. Carew had taken part in Charles I's expedition against the Scots (the "first bishops' war"), an ill-advised venture terminated by the inconclusive Treaty of Berwick, in June 1639.
3. I.e., Zephyrus, the west wind.
4. Encompassing.
5. Cf. Jonson, "To Penshurst," line 2n, p. 97.

The servant, tenant, and kind neighbor eats.
Some of that rank, spun of a finer thread,
Are with the women, steward, and chaplain fed
With daintier cates;[6] others of better note,
Whom wealth, parts,[7] office, or the herald's coat[8]
Have severed from the common, freely sit
At the lord's table, whose spread sides admit
A large access of friends to fill those seats
Of his capacious circle, filled with meats
Of choicest relish, till his oaken back
Under the load of piled-up dishes crack.
Nor think, because our pyramids and high
Exalted turrets threaten not the sky,
That therefore Wrest of narrowness complains,
Or straitened walls, for she more numerous trains
Of noble guests daily receives, and those
Can with far more conveniency dispose,[9]
Than prouder piles, where the vain builder spent
More cost in outward gay embellishment
Than real use; which was the sole design
Of our contriver, who made things not fine,
But fit for service. Amalthea's horn
Of plenty[1] is not in effigy worn
Without the gate, but she within the door
Empties her free and unexhausted store.
Nor, crowned with wheaten wreaths, doth Ceres[2] stand
In stone, with a crook'd sickle in her hand;
Nor on a marble tun,[3] his face besmeared
With grapes, is curled unscissored[4] Bacchus reared;
We offer not in emblems to the eyes,
But to the taste those useful deities:
We press the juicy god, and quaff his blood,
And grind the yellow goddess into food.
Yet we decline not all the work of art,
But where more bounteous Nature bears a part
And guides her handmaid, if she but dispense
Fit matter, she with care and diligence
Employs her skill; for where the neighbor source
Pours forth her waters, she directs their course,
And entertains the flowing streams in deep
And spacious channels, where they slowly creep
In snaky windings, as the shelving ground

6. Viands.
7. Talents, abilities.
8. I.e., noble or gentle lineage.
9. Accommodate.
1. According to one version of this myth, Amalthea was a nymph who fed Zeus with goat's milk; in return, Zeus endowed one of the goat's horns with the power of being filled with whatever the nymph might wish. This horn was called the cornucopia, or horn of plenty. Cf., for a basic reference, Apollodorus, *Library*, I.i.6; but the myth has several variant forms.
2. Ceres is goddess of agriculture and of the fruits of the earth, as Bacchus is god of wine.
3. Large cask.
4. I.e., with uncut hair.

Leads them in circles, till they twice surround
This island mansion, which i'th'center placed
Is with a double crystal heaven embraced,
In which our watery constellations float,
Our fishes, swans, our waterman and boat,
Envied by those above, which wish to slake
Their starburnt limbs in our refreshing lake.
But they stick fast nailed to the barren sphere,[5]
Whilst our increase in fertile waters here
Disport, and wander freely where they please
Within the circuit of our narrow seas.
    With various trees we fringe the water's brink,
Whose thirsty roots the soaking moisture drink,
And whose extended boughs in equal ranks
Yield fruit, and shade, and beauty to the banks.
On this side young Vertumnus[6] sits, and courts
His ruddy-cheeked Pomona; Zephyr sports
On th'other, with loved Flora, yielding there
Sweets for the smell, sweets for the palate here.
But did you taste the high and mighty drink
Which from that fountain flows, you'd clearly think
The god of wine did his plump clusters bring
And crush the Falerne grape[7] into our spring;
Or else disguised in watery robes did swim
To Ceres' bed, and make her big of him,
Begetting so himself on her; for know
Our vintage here in March doth nothing owe
To theirs in autumn, but our fire boils here
As lusty liquor as the sun makes there.
    Thus I enjoy myself, and taste the fruit
Of this blest peace, whilst toiled in the pursuit
Of bucks and stags, th'emblem of war,[8] you strive
To keep the memory of our arms alive.

A Song[9]

Ask me no more where Jove bestows,
When June is past, the fading rose;
For in your beauty's orient[1] deep
These flowers, as in their causes,[2] sleep.

5. I.e., (by Ptolemaic astronomy), the eighth sphere, containing the fixed stars.
6. Vertumnus, god of the seasons, courted and eventually won the wood nymph Pomona; cf. Ovid, *Metamorphoses*, XIV.625–771.
7. The "Falernian fields" in Campania were famous for the wine made from grapes grown there.
8. I.e., the hunt.
9. Like Donne's "Go and catch a falling star," and Herrick's "To Find God," this poem is built about a series of impossible demands. Cf. Textual Notes for variants of language and stanza arrangement, probably representing earlier drafts of the text given here.
1. Lustrous.
2. Carew probably alludes to Aristotle's "formal cause": "the form or the archetype" of a thing (or, possibly, to the "material cause": "that out of which a thing comes to be and which persists"). Cf. *Physics*, II.ii.3, in *Basic Works of Aristotle*, ed. R. McKeon (New York, 1941), p. 240.

Ask me no more whither doth stray
The golden atoms of the day;
For in pure love heaven did prepare
Those powders to enrich your hair.

Ask me no more whither doth haste
The nightingale, when May is past;
For in your sweet dividing[3] throat
She winters, and keeps warm her note.

Ask me no more where those stars light,
That downwards fall in dead of night;
For in your eyes they sit, and there
Fixèd become, as in their sphere.[4]

Ask me no more if east or west
The phoenix[5] builds her spicy nest;
For unto you at last she flies,
And in your fragrant bosom dies.

3. Harmonious (as in singing).
4. I.e., as in their appropriate place in the heavens.
5. According to Egyptian fable, the phoenix builds her nest of aromatic twigs; every 500 years she dies by fiery self-immolation, only to be at once reborn from the ashes of her funeral pyre.

James Shirley

1596	Born 18 September in London.
1608–1612	Attends the Merchant Taylors' School in London.
1612	Enters Saint John's College, Oxford; subsequently transfers to Catharine Hall (now Saint Catharine's), Cambridge.
c. 1618	Graduates B.A., Catharine Hall. First poem published: perhaps an early version (no copy survives) of "Narcissus," published in 1646.
c. 1620	Receives M.A. About this time, according to Anthony à Wood, "a minister . . . in or near St. Albans in Hertfordshire."
1623–1625	Headmaster of a grammar school in Saint Albans. Converted to Roman Catholicism. Married, probably in 1623.
1625	Moves to London and becomes a playwright. First play, *Love Tricks, with Complements*, licensed in February 1626 (first published play, *The Wedding*, 1629).
1626–1636	Years of greatest success: composes fifteen comedies, four tragedies, two masques (notably "The Triumph of Peace," presented at Whitehall in February 1634), and a pastoral play, all acted in London. Associating with William Habington, Thomas Randolph, and other poets and playwrights. In high favor with Queen Henrietta Maria.
1636–1640	Living in Dublin and writing plays (two comedies, two tragedies) for production in that city. Returns to London probably before March 1640.
1641	Shirley's best-known tragedy, *The Cardinal*, licensed in November.
1642	Stage plays suppressed by Parliament. Shirley apparently campaigns with royalist forces led by the Earl of Newcastle until July 1644, when he returns to London. Befriended and aided by the poet and scholar Thomas Stanley.
1646	Publication of *Poems*. Maintains himself from about this time as a schoolteacher, residing at Whitefriars, in London. Continues to write plays as well as pedagogical texts dealing with grammar.
1666	Shirley's house destroyed in the Great Fire of London. A few weeks later, he and his wife, homeless and in straitened circumstances, die on the same day; they are buried in the churchyard of Saint Giles on 29 October.

FROM *POEMS* (1646)

Cupid's Call[1]

Ho! Cupid calls; come, lovers, come,
Bring his wanton harvest home;
The west wind blows, the birds do sing,
The earth's enameled, 'tis high spring;
    Let hinds[2] whose soul is corn and hay
    Expect their crop another day.

Into Love's spring-garden[3] walk,
Virgins dangle on their stalk,
Full-blown, and playing at fifteen;
Come, bring your amorous sickles then!
    See, they are pointing to their beds,
    And call to reap their maidenheads.

Hark, how in yonder shady grove
Sweet Philomel[4] is warbling love,
And with her voice is courting kings;
For since she was a bird, she sings,
    "There is no pleasure but in men;
    Oh, come and ravish me again."

Virgins that are young and fair
May kiss, and grow into a pair;
Then warm and active use your blood,
No sad thought congeal the flood;
    Nature no med'cine can impart
    When age once snows upon our heart.

To Odelia[5]

Health to my fair Odelia! Some that know
    How many months are past
  Since I beheld thy lovely brow,
    Would count an age at least;
      But unto me,
    Whose thoughts are still on thee,
        I vow
By thy black eyes, 'tis but an hour ago.

1. To make this poem, Shirley revised and combined two separate sets of verses, "The Courtesan" and "Another"; cf. Textual Notes.
2. Farm laborers, peasants.
3. Lovers' trysts often took place at the "Spring Garden" in London.
4. Philomela, raped and maimed by Tereus, was subsequently turned into a nightingale; cf. Ovid, *Metamorphoses*, VI.438–670.
5. This poem was probably composed in 1642–1644, while Shirley was in northern England with a royalist force commanded by the Earl of Newcastle. The identity of Odelia has not been established.

That mistress I pronounce but poor in bliss,
That when her servant parts,
Gives not as much with her last kiss,
As will maintain two hearts
Till both do meet
To taste what else is sweet.
Is't fit
Time measure love, or our affection it?

Cherish that heart, Odelia, that is mine;
And if the north thou fear,
Dispatch but from thy southern clime
A sigh, to warm thine here;
But be so kind
To send by the next wind:
'Tis far,
And many accidents do wait on war.

Love for Enjoying

Fair lady, what's your face to me?
I was not only made to see;
Every silent stander-by
May thus enjoy as much as I.
That blooming nature on your cheek
Is still inviting me to seek
For unknown wealth; within the ground
Are all the royal metals found.
Leave me to search; I have a thread
Through all the labyrinth shall lead,
And through every winding vein
Conduct me to the golden mine;
Which, once enjoyed, will give me power
To make new Indies every hour.
Look on those jewels that abound
Upon your dress: that diamond
No flame, no lustre could impart,
Should not the lapidary's[6] art
Contribute here and there a star;
And just such things ye women are,
Who do not in rude quarries shine,
But meeting us y'are made divine.
Come, let us mix ourselves, and prove
That action is the soul of love;
Why do we coward-gazing stand
Like armies in the Netherland,
Contracting fear at either's sight,
Till we both grow too weak to fight?

6. A lapidary cuts, polishes, and engraves precious stones.

Let's charge, for shame; and choose you whether
One shall fall, or both together:
This is love's war! Whoever dies,
If the survivor be but wise,
He may reduce the spirit fled,
For t'other kiss will cure the dead.

To the Excellent Pattern of Beauty and Virtue, Lady Elizabeth, Countess of Ormonde[7]

Madam,
Were you but only great, there are some men,
Whose heat is not the Muses', nor their pen
Steered by chaste truth, could flatter you in prose
Or glorious verse; but I am none of those.
I never learned that trick of court to wear
Silk at the cost of flattery; or make dear
My pride, by painting a great lady's face
When she had done't before, and swear the grace
Was nature's; anagram upon her name,
And add to her no virtue, my own shame.
I could not make this lord a god, then try
How to commit new court idolatry,
And, when he dies, hang on his silent hearse
Wet elegies, and haunt his ghost in verse.
These, some hold witty, thriving garbs; but I
Choose (to my loss) a modest poesy,
And place my genius upon subjects fit
For imitation,[8] rather than bold wit;
And such are you, who both in name and blood
Born great, have learned this lesson, to be good.
   Armed with this knowledge, madam, I not fear
To hold fair correspondence with the year,
And bring my gift, hearty as you are fair;
A servant's wish, for all my wealth is prayer,
Which with the year thus enters.[9] May you be
Still the same flowing goodness that we see;
In your most noble lord be happy still,
And heaven chain your hearts into one will;
Be rich in your two darlings of the spring,
Which, as it waits, perfumes their blossoming,
The growing pledges of your love and blood;[1]

7. James Butler (1610–1688), twelfth Earl (later, first Duke) of Ormonde, led the royalist armies in Ireland with vigor and skill. He married Elizabeth, only child of the Earl of Desmond, in 1630. Shirley appears to have moved in their social circle during his years in Dublin. With this poem may be compared Jonson's verse epistle to Lady Aubigny (*The Forest*, XIII, p. 115), which probably served Shirley as a model.
8. I.e., subjects that, by virtue of their intrinsic merit, are appropriate models for poetical imitation (in the Aristotelian sense, as well as in a social context).
9. I.e., which is presented on New Year's Day (1640).
1. Thomas Butler was born in July 1634; Richard Butler in June 1639. A third son ("that unborn blessing" of line 32) was named John.

And may that unborn blessing timely bud,
The chaste and noble treasure of your womb,
Your own, and th'age's expectation come;
And when your days and virtues have made even,[2]
Die late, beloved of earth, and change for heaven.

To a Lady upon a Looking-Glass Sent

When this crystal shall present
Your beauty to your eye,
Think that lovely face was meant
To dress another by.
For not to make them proud,
These glasses are allowed
To those are fair,
But to compare
The inward beauty with the outward grace,
And make them fair in soul as well as face.[3]

Two Gentlemen That Broke Their Promise of a Meeting, Made When They Drank Claret[4]

There is no faith in claret, and it shall
Henceforth with me be held apocryphal.
I'll trust a small-beer[5] promise, nay, a troth
Washed in the Thames, before a French wine oath.
That grape, they say, is binding; yes, 'tis so,
And it has made your souls thus costive[6] too.
Circe transformed the Greeks;[7] no hard design,
For some can do as much with claret wine
Upon themselves; witness you two, allowed
Once honest, now turned air, and *à la mode*.[8]
Begin no health in this, or if by chance
The King's, 'twill question your allegiance;
And men will, after all your ruffling,[9] say
You drink as some do fight, in the French way:
Engage and trouble many, when 'tis known
You spread their interest to wave your own.
Away with this false Christian:[1] it shall be

2. I.e., have harmoniously come to the evening of life.
3. In medieval and Renaissance poetry and pictorial art forms, mirrors regularly symbolize both worldly vanity and discerning self-knowledge: cf. Shakespeare's *Richard II*, IV.i.276–290. Cf. also, for another kind of example, the painting by Diego de Velázquez (1599–1660), "The Toilet of Venus."
4. Cf. William Habington's reply to this poem, "To a Friend, Inviting Him to a Meeting upon Promise," p. 354. For an earlier version of Shirley's poem, cf. Textual Notes.
5. I.e., beer of inferior quality.
6. I.e., reticent, uncommunicative (with a glance at the primary meaning, "constipated").
7. Cf. Homer, *Odyssey*, X.
8. I.e., in the fashion.
9. Swaggering.
1. I.e., French claret wine (with an allusion to the "Most Christian" King of France).

An excommunicate from mirth, and me;
Give me the Catholic[2] diviner flame,
To light me to the fair Odelia's name;
'Tis sack that justifies both man and verse,
Whilst you in Lethe-claret still converse.
Forget your own names next; and when you look
With hope to find, be lost in the church-book.[3]

The Garden[4]

This garden does not take[5] my eyes,
Though here you show how art of men
Can purchase nature at a price
Would stock old Paradise again.

These glories while you dote upon,
I envy not your spring nor pride,
Nay, boast the summer all your own;
My thoughts with less are satisfied.

Give me a little plot of ground
Where might I with the sun agree,
Though every day he walk the round,
My garden he should seldom see.

Those tulips that such wealth display
To court my eye, shall lose their name,
Though now they listen as if they
Expected I should praise their flame.

But I would see myself appear
Within the violet's drooping head,
On which a melancholy tear
The discontented morn hath shed.

Within their buds let roses sleep,
And virgin lilies on their stem,
Till sighs from lovers glide and creep
Into their leaves to open them.

I'th' center of my ground compose
Of bays[6] and yew my summer room,
Which may, so oft as I repose,
Present my arbor and my tomb.

2. I.e., Spanish wine, notably sack (with an allusion to the "Most Catholic" King of Spain).
3. Parish register.
4. Cf. Andrew Marvell's "The Garden," p. 553, in connection particularly with the first and eighth stanzas of Shirley's poem.
5. Delight.
6. Laurels.

No woman here shall find me out,
Or if a chance do bring one hither,
I'll be secure, for round about
I'll moat it with my eyes' foul weather.

No bird shall live within my pale[7]
To charm me with their shames of art,
Unless some wand'ring nightingale
Come here to sing, and break her heart.

Upon whose death I'll try to write
An epitaph, in some funeral stone,
So sad and true it may invite
Myself to die, and prove mine own.

FROM *THE CONTENTION OF AJAX AND ULYSSES FOR THE ARMOR OF ACHILLES*[8] (1659)

Dirge

The glories of our blood and state
Are shadows, not substantial things;
There is no armor against fate;
Death lays his icy hand on kings;
Scepter and crown
Must tumble down,
And in the dust be equals made
With the poor crooked scythe and spade.

Some men with swords may reap the field,
And plant fresh laurels where they kill;
But their strong nerves at last must yield,
They tame but one another still;
Early or late,
They stoop to fate,
And must give up their murmuring breath,
When they, pale captives, creep to death.

The garlands wither on your brow,
Then boast no more your mighty deeds;
Upon death's purple altar now,
See where the victor-victim bleeds;
Your heads must come
To the cold tomb;
Only the actions of the just
Smell sweet, and blossom in their dust.

7. Enclosure.
8. Cf. Ovid, *Metamorphoses*, XIII.1–398. This poem, Shirley's most celebrated lyric, concludes the drama.

Mildmay Fane, Earl of Westmorland

c. 1600	Born, probably in Kent. His father, Francis Fane, first Earl of Westmorland, descended from a powerful Kentish family, had augmented his fortune and influence by his marriage, in 1599, to Mary, the granddaughter of Sir Walter Mildmay, Queen Elizabeth's Treasurer and the founder of Emmanuel College, Cambridge. The Mildmays held large estates in Northamptonshire.
c. 1615–1617	Attends Emmanuel College, Cambridge.
1620–1621	Member of Parliament for Peterborough (and again in 1626–1628).
1625	Member of Parliament for Kent.
1626	Created a Knight of the Bath at the time of Charles I's coronation.
1628	Marries Grace Thornhurst, of Herne, Kent, who subsequently bore a son, Charles, and five daughters; she dies in 1637.
1638	Marries Mary Townshend (daughter of Sir Horace Vere), who bore a son, Vere, and four daughters.
1642	Having sided with Charles I at the outbreak of the civil war, imprisoned in the Tower of London by Parliamentary order until April 1643; for some months thereafter restricted to an area within five miles around London. Fined £2,000.
1644	Set at liberty, having subscribed to the (Presbyterian) covenant, probably to save his property from appropriation by the Parliamentary government.
1648	Publication of *Otia Sacra*.
1660	At the Restoration, appointed Lord Lieutenant of Northamptonshire.
1666	Death, 12 February.

FROM *OTIA SACRA*[1] (1648)

My Country Audit[2]

Blest privacy! Happy retreat, wherein
I may cast up my reck'nings,[3] audit sin,
Count o'er my debts, and how arrears increase
In nature's book, towards the God of peace;
What through perverseness hath been waived,[4] or done
To my first covenant's contradiction;
How many promised resolutions broke
Of keeping touch,[5] almost as soon as spoke.
    Thus, like that tenant who, behind-hand cast,[6]
    Entreats so oft forbearance till at last
    The sum surmounts his hopes, and then no more
    Expects, but mercy to strike off the score,[7]
So here, methinks, I see the Landlord's grace
Full of compassion to my drooping case,
Bidding me be of comfort, and not grieved:
My rent his Son should pay if I believed.

My Observation at Sea

Though every thing we see or hear may raise
        The Maker's praise,
    For without lightning or thunder,
        His works are all of wonder;
        Yet amongst those there's none
        Like to the ocean,

    Where, not a catalogue to keep
Of several shapes inhabiting the deep,
        Let but our thoughts confer[8]
With what once graveled[9] the philosopher;

1. The title subtly combines two meanings: "sacred poems" (cf. Ovid, *Tristia*, II.224) and "the poetical fruits of leisure" (cf. *Tristia*, IV.x.19). The poems in Book I of *Otia Sacra* are, in fact, predominantly devotional in character; the greater number of those in Book II are concerned with secular matters and the simple pleasures of life in the country. The collection includes a number of "emblematic" poems, which have some affinity with Francis Quarles's *Emblems* (1635); of the "metaphysical" poets it is Marvell, however, with whose outlook Fane is most clearly in sympathy. Robert Herrick may perhaps have persuaded Fane to publish his verses; cf. "To the Right Honorable Mildmay, Earl of Westmorland," p. 207.
2. This poem and "To Retiredness" were probably composed at Fane's country estate of Apthorpe, Northamptonshire, which had belonged to his mother's family. The Fanes were originally a Kentish family, having settled in and around Tonbridge, c. 1425.
3. I.e., calculate my accounts.
4. I.e., either (1) put aside, neglected; or (2) flaunted.
5. I.e., keeping agreements sealed by clasping of hands.
6. I.e., fallen into debt.
7. Account.
8. Compare.
9. Baffled. Ancient philosophers were unable to account satisfactorily for the regular ebb and flow of the tides, although by the first century A.D. the connection between tidal motion and the action of sun and moon was generally recognized.

And we must straight confess
Amazement more, but apprehension less.

The fire for heat and light
Most exquisite;
And the all-temp'ring air
Beyond compare;
Earth, composition and solidity,
Bountiful mixèd with humidity;
But here, for profit and content,
Each must give place to th'liquid element,

Whose admirable course, that steers
Within twelve hours[1] mariners
Outwards and homewards bound,
May be sufficient ground
To raise conclusion from thence
At once of mighty power and providence.

For as the Cynthian queen[2]
Her bounty less or more vouchsafes be seen,
So by her wane she brings
The tides to neaps, and by her full to springs;[3]
Yet not but as he please
Who set her there, chief governess of seas;

Which understood
Truly by such would seek for traffic good,
They must their anchors weigh
Out of the oozy dirt and clay,
Earth's contemplations yield,
And hoisting sails, they'll straightway have them filled
With a fresh-mackerel gale,[4] whose blast
May port them in true happiness at last.

There th'in a bay of bliss,
Where a sweet calm our welcome is,
Let us at length the cables veer[5]
Fore and abaft, that may our moorage clear
From warp[6] or winding, so ride, fixed upon
Our hope's sheet-anchor of salvation.

1. The tide ebbs and flows twice in each lunar day.
2. I.e., the moon.
3. Neap tides, the lowest high tide in a lunar month, occur when the moon is at first or third quarter; spring tides, highest tide in a lunar month, occur when the moon is full or new.
4. I.e., "a strong breeze, such as mackerel are best caught in" (*OED*).
5. Pay out.
6. Twist, tangle.

A Dedication of My First Son[7]

Is it not fit the mold and frame
Of man should dedicate the same
To God, who first created it; and t'give
To him the first fruit of that span we live?

In the world's infancy, could Hannah tell
She ought to offer her son Samuel
To him that made him, and refine
That sacrifice with flour and wine?[8]

Was Abrams long-expected seed
From Sarah's womb condemned to bleed?[9]
And shall the times, now they grow old, conclude
In faithlessness, and in ingratitude?

Let shame awake us, and where blessings fall,
Let everyone become a prodigal
In paying vows of thanks, and bring
The first and best for offering.[1]

Where am I, then, whom God hath deigned to bless
With hopes of a succeeding happiness
Unto my house? Why is't I stand
At th'altar with an empty hand?

Have I no herds, no flocks, no oil,
No incense-bearing Sheba-soil?[2]
Is not my granary stored with flour that's fine?
Are not my strutted[3] vessels full of wine?

What temporal blessing's wanting to suffice
And furnish out a lively sacrifice,
Save only this, to make a free-
Will-offering of an infancy?

Which if I should not do, that piled-
Up wood, whereon lay Sarah's child,
The Temple would accuse me, where the son
Of Elk'na first had dedication.

7. Fane married twice; his first wife, Grace Thornhurst, who died in 1637, bore him a son, Charles (the subject of this poem), and five daughters.
8. Hannah, the barren wife of Elkanah, prayed that she might bear a son, vowing that the child should be dedicated to God's service; when Samuel was born, she brought him (together with "three bullocks, and one ephah of flour, and a bottle of wine") to the priest Eli, in fulfillment of her vow. Cf. 1 Samuel 1:11, 24–28.
9. Cf. Genesis 20:1–14.
1. Cf. Luke 15:11–32.
2. Shebam (Hebrew "balsam") was located in the center of the Moabite vineyards; cf. Numbers 32:3.
3. Distended.

Wherefore accept, I pray thee, this
Thou'st given, and my first son is;
Let him be thine, and from his cradling,
Begin his service's first reckoning.

Grant, with his days, thy grace increase, and fill
His heart, or leave there room to harbor ill,
That in the progress of his years,
He may express whose badge he wears.

Upon the Times

Awake, thou best of sense,
Intelligence,
And let no fancy-vapor steer
Thy contemplation t'think that peace is near,
Whilst war in words we do bemoan,
There's nothing less left in invention.

England that was, not is,
Unless in metamorphosis,
Changed from the bower of bliss and rest,
To become now Bellona's interest,[4]
In danger of a funeral pile,
Unless some happy swift means reconcile.

Which how to bring to pass,
Beyond man's hopes, alas!
Therefore be pleased, Thou who didst make
Atonement for his sake,
To silence this unnatural spell,
As Thou didst once the Delphian Oracle.[5]

My Close-Committee[6]

How busied's man
To seek and find
An accusation
Against all those
He deems his body's good, or goods oppose;
And winks at such as hazard soul and mind.

4. Bellona was the Roman goddess of war.
5. In *De Defectu Oraculorum* ("On the Cessation of the Oracles"), Plutarch (c. 50–c. 120) alludes to a mysterious voice that, about the time of Christ's crucifixion, cried that the great Pan was dead. The tradition was elaborated by many Christian poets. Cf. John Milton, "On the Morning of Christ's Nativity," line 173n, p. 384.
6. I.e., a committee meeting in private session.

Nothing, of late,
Is done or spoke
But either king or state
Concernèd are,
The while each 'gainst his neighbor wages war;
So're all the bonds of love and friendship broke.

And how comes this,
But that we do
Or utter what's amiss
In every thing,
Making each fancy lord, each will a king,
And all that checks not reason, treason too?

Were't not more wise
To lay about
Which way for to surprise
That trait'rous band
Of sins, that in our bosoms bear command,
And, entertaining grace, t'cause those march out?

Our lust, our pride,
Ambition,
Or whatsoe'er beside,
Seems to give way
To that unjust militia and array,
Bring we t'our close committee's inquisition:
Thus, when our hearts these for malignants brand,
Commit them not, but banish them thy land.

In Praise of Fidelia

Get thee a ship well-rigged and tight,
With ordnance[7] stored, and manned for fight,
Snug in her timbers' mold for th'seas,
Yet large in hold for merchandise;
Spread forth her cloth, and anchors weigh,
And let her on the curled waves play
Till, fortune-towed, she chance to meet
Th' Hesperian[8] home-bound western fleet;
Then let her board 'em, and for price
Take gold ore, sugar-canes, and spice:
Yet when all these sh'hath brought ashore,
In my Fidelia I'll find more.

7. Guns, ammunition.
8. I.e. (in this context), West Indian; whence Spanish fleets brought home spices and precious metals.

To Retiredness[9]

Next unto God, to whom I owe
What e'er I here enjoy below,
I must indebted stand to thee,
Great patron of my liberty;
For in the cluster of affairs,
Whence there are dealing[1] several shares,
As in a trick thou hast conveyed
Into my hand what can be said;
Whilst he who doth himself possess,
Makes all things pass[2] him seem far less.

Riches and honors that appear,
Rewards to the adventurer,
On either tide of court or seas,
Are not attained nor held with ease,
But, as unconstancy bears sway,
Quickly will fleet and ebb away;
And oft when fortune those confers,
She gives them but for torturers;
When, with a mind ambition-free,
These, and much more, come home to me.

Here I can sit; and sitting under
Some portions of His works of wonder,
Whose all are such, observe by reason
Why every plant obeys its season;
How the sap rises, and the fall
Wherein they shake off leaves and all;
Then how again they bud and spring,
Are laden for an offering;
Which whilst my contemplation sees,
I am taught thankfulness from trees.

Then, turning over nature's leaf,
I mark the glory of the sheaf,
For every field's a several[3] page
Deciphering the Golden Age;
So that without a miner's pains,
Or Indies' reach, here plenty reigns;
Which, watered from above, implies
That our acknowledgments should rise
To Him that thus creates a birth
Of mercies for us out of earth.

9. Cf. Andrew Marvell, "The Garden," p. 553.
1. Contending (with a punning allusion to cardplay).
2. I.e., (1) that surpass; (2) that pass by.
3. Separate, distinct.

Here is no other case in law
But what the sunburnt hat of straw
With crooked sickle reaps and binds
Up into sheaves to help the hinds,[4]
Whose arguing alone's in this,
Which cop[5] lies well, and which amiss,
How the hock-cart[6] with all its gear
Should be tricked up, and what good cheer
Bacon with cook's reports express,
And how to make the tenth go less.[7]

There are no other wars or strifes,
Encouragers, shrill trumpets, fifes,
Or horrid drums, but what excels
All music, nature's minstrels
Piping and chirping, as they sit
Embower'd in branches, dance to it;
And if at all those do contest,
It is in this, but which sings best;
And when they have contended long,
I, though unseen, must judge the song.

Thus out of fears or noise of war,
Crowds, and the clamorings at bar,
The merchant's dread, th'unconstant tides,
With all vexations besides,
I hug my quiet, and alone
Take thee for my companion,
And deem, in doing so, I've all
I can true conversation[8] call;
For so my thoughts by this retreat
Grow stronger, like contracted heat.

Whether on nature's book I muse,
Or else some other writes on 't use
To spend the time in,[9] every line
Is not eccentric but divine;
And though all others[1] downward tend,
These look to heaven, and ascend
From when they came; where, pointed high,
They ravish into mystery,
To see the footsteps here are trod
Of mercy by a gracious God.

4. Farm laborers.
5. Conical heap of unbound grain or straw.
6. I.e., the wagon bringing in the last load of the harvest.
7. I.e., how to reduce the tithe (the tenth part of one's produce, paid over to ecclesiastical authorities).
8. I.e., social intercourse.
9. I.e., or else employ my time in reading another man's writings about nature.
1. I.e., all artificial constructs.

Thomas Randolph

1605	Born, Newnham-cum-Badby, Northamptonshire; baptized on 15 June. His father, William Randolph, was steward (i.e., estate manager) to Lord Zouch.
c. 1614	Writes a verse "History of our Savior's Incarnation" (not extant).
c. 1618–1623	Educated at Westminster School, London, as a "King's Scholar."
1623	Attains the highest rating among those Westminster schoolboys competing for places at Cambridge and Oxford.
1624	Matriculates at Trinity College, Cambridge.
1628	Graduates B.A.; created a "minor fellow" in 1629.
1630	First published work in English: *Aristippus, or the Joviall Philosopher*, a dramatic satire in prose and verse on university education, the pleasures of drinking, and other matters. Probably makes the acquaintance of Ben Jonson at about this time.
1631	Takes M.A. at Cambridge. Incorporated M.A. at Oxford.
1632	His blank-verse drama, *The Jealous Lovers*, presented at Cambridge, in March, on the occasion of the visit to the University by Charles I and Henrietta Maria: a great success. The play is published later in the year by Cambridge University.
1633	*Amyntas*, Randolph's pastoral play, presented at Whitehall. Health and fortunes in decline from this time by consequence of his "irregular" life.
1635	Dies, while visiting his friend William Stafford in Blatherwick, Northamptonshire; buried in the Stafford vault in Blatherwick Church on 17 March.
1638	Publication of *Poems, with The Muses' Looking-Glass and Amyntas*.

FROM *POEMS, WITH THE MUSES' LOOKING-GLASS AND AMYNTAS* (1638)

A Gratulatory[1] to Mr. Ben Jonson for His Adopting of Him To Be His Son

I was not born to Helicon,[2] nor dare
Presume to think myself a Muse's heir.
I have no title to Parnassus hill,
Nor any acre of it by the will
Of a dead ancestor, nor could I be
Aught but a tenant unto poetry.
But thy adoption quits me of all fear,
And makes me challenge a child's portion there.
I am akin to heroes, being thine,
And part of my alliance is divine.
Orpheus, Musaeus,[3] Homer too, beside
Thy brothers by the Roman mother's side,
As Ovid, Vergil, and the Latin lyre
That is so like thee, Horace: the whole choir
Of poets are by thy adoption all
My uncles; thou hast given me pow'r to call
Phoebus[4] himself my grandsire; by this grant
Each sister of the Nine is made my aunt.
Go, you that reckon from a large descent
Your lineal honors, and are well content
To glory in the age of your great name,
Though on a herald's faith you build the same;
I do not envy you, nor think you blest,
Though you may bear a gorgon on your crest
By direct line from Pegasus;[5] I will boast
No farther than my father; that's the most
I can or should be proud of, and I were
Unworthy his adoption if that here
I should be dully modest; boast I must,
Being son of his adoption, not his lust.
And to say truth, that which is best in me
May call you father; 'twas begot by thee.
Have I a spark of that celestial flame

1. I.e., an expression of gratitude. For an account (possibly apocryphal) of the circumstances leading to Randolph's "adoption," which took place in c. 1630, cf. W. Winstanley, *Lives of the Most Famous English Poets* [1687], ed. W. R. Parker (Gainesville, Fla., 1963), pp. 143–144. Being "somewhat addicted to libertine indulgences," Randolph never fulfilled the promise of his early years, when he had given "proof of an amazing quickness of parts" (D. E. Baker, *Biographia Dramatica*, 2 vols. [London, 1792], I, p. 366).
2. Mount Helicon, in Boeotia, and Mount Parnassus, near Delphi, were sacred to the nine Muses and to Apollo, god of poetry and song.
3. For Orpheus, cf. Jonson, *The Forest*, XII, line 77n, p. 114. The Musaeus referred to is probably not the fifth-century author of "Hero and Leander," but the mythical singer to whom Aristophanes alludes in his comedy *The Frogs* (lines 1032–1033).
4. Phoebus Apollo.
5. The winged horse Pegasus sprang from the blood of the gorgon Medusa, when Perseus struck off her head; cf. Ovid, *Metamorphoses*, IV.785–786.

Within me, I confess I stole the same,
Prometheus-like,[6] from thee; and may I feed
His vulture when I dare deny the deed.
Many more moons thou hast, that shine by night,
All bankrupts, were't not for a borrowed light,
Yet can forswear it; I the debt confess
And think my reputation ne'er the less.
For, father, let me be resolved by you:
Is't a disparagement from rich Peru
To ravish gold; or theft, for wealthy ore
To ransack Tagus', or Pactolus' shore?[7]
Or does he wrong Alcinous,[8] that for want
Doth take from him a sprig or two, to plant
A lesser orchard? Sure it cannot be;
Nor is it theft to steal some flames from thee.
Grant this, and I'll cry guilty, as I am,
And pay a filial reverence to thy name.
For when my Muse upon obedient knees
Asks not a father's blessing, let her leese
The fame of this adoption; 'tis a curse
I wish her 'cause I cannot think a worse.
And here, as piety bids me, I entreat
Phoebus to lend thee some of his own heat,
To cure thy palsy,[9] else I will complain
He has no skill in herbs; poets in vain
Make him the god of physic. 'Twere his praise
To make thee as immortal as thy bays,[1]
As his own Daphne; 'twere a shame to see
The god not love his priest more than his tree.
  But if heaven take thee, envying us thy lyre,
  'Tis to pen anthems for an angels' choir.

Upon the Loss of His Little Finger[2]

Arithmetic nine digits, and no more,
Admits of; then I still have all my store.
For what mischance hath ta'en from my left hand,
It seems did only for a cipher stand.
But this I'll say for thee, departed joint,
Thou wert not given to steal, nor pick, nor point
At any in disgrace; but thou didst go
Untimely to thy death only to show
The other members what they once must do:

6. Cf. Jonson, "Ode to Himself," line 27n, p. 136.
7. The Spanish and Portuguese river Tagus and the Lydian river Pactolus (in what is now western Turkey) were celebrated for the gold ore in their sands.
8. The garden of Alcinous, king of the Phaeacians, is described in Homer, *Odyssey*, VII.112–134.
9. Cf. Jonson, "Ode to Himself," line 50n, p. 153.
1. Laurels. Cf. Herrick, "The Welcome to Sack," line 92n, p. 194.
2. According to Winstanley (p. 142), the finger was cut off during a violent quarrel that took place while Randolph was drinking in "gentlemen's company." In line 16, the expression "made a hand of" means "done away with."

Hand, arm, leg, thigh, and all must follow too.
Oft didst thou scan my verse, where, if I miss
Henceforth, I will impute the cause to this.
A finger's loss (I speak it not in sport)
Will make a verse a foot too short.
Farewell, dear finger: much I grieve to see
How soon mischance hath made a hand of thee.

An Elegy[3]

Love, give me leave to serve thee, and be wise,
To keep thy torch in but restore blind eyes.
I will a flame into my bosom take
That martyrs court when they embrace the stake:
Not dull and smoky fires, but heat divine,
That burns not to consume but to refine.
I have a mistress for perfections rare
In every eye, but in my thoughts most fair,
Like tapers on the altar shine her eyes;
Her breath is the perfume of sacrifice.
And wheresoe'er my fancy would begin,
Still her perfection lets religion in.
I touch her like my beads with devout care,
And come unto my courtship as my prayer.
We sit, and talk, and kiss away the hours,
As chastely as the morning dews kiss flowers.
Go, wanton lover, spare thy sighs and tears,
Put on the livery which thy dotage wears,
And call it love; where heresy gets in,
Zeal's but a coal to kindle greater sin.
We wear no flesh, but one another greet,
As blessed souls in separation meet.
Were't possible that my ambitious sin
Durst commit rapes upon a cherubin,
I might have lustful thoughts to her, of all
Earth's heav'nly choir the most angelical.
Looking into my breast, her form I find
That like my guardian angel keeps my mind
From rude attempts; and when affections stir,
I calm all passions with one thought of her.
Thus they whose reasons love, and not their sense,
The spirits love; thus one intelligence
Reflects upon his like, and by chaste loves
In the same sphere this and that angel moves.

3. This poem, entitled "A Platonic Elegy" in later editions, reflects that fashionable concern with "Platonic love" which was encouraged by Queen Henrietta Maria and her circle. James Howell, writing in the last year of Randolph's life, remarks, "The court affords little news at present, but that there is a love called Platonic love, which much sways there of late. It is a love abstracted from all corporal gross impressions and sensual appetite, but consists in contemplations and ideals of the mind, not in any carnal fruition" (*Epistolae Ho-Elianae, or Familiar Letters*, ed. J. Jacobs [London, 1890], p. 317).

Nor is this barren love; one noble thought
Begets another, and that still is brought
To bed of more; virtues and grace increase,
And such a numerous issue ne'er can cease,
Where children, though great blessings, only be
Pleasures reprieved to some posterity.
Beasts love like men, if men in lust delight,
And call that love which is but appetite.
When essence meets with essence, and souls join
In mutual knots, that's the true nuptial twine:
Such, lady, is my love, and such is true;
All other love is to your sex, not you.

An Ode to Mr. Anthony Stafford[4] to Hasten Him into the Country

Come, spur away,
I have no patience for a longer stay,
But must go down,
And leave the chargeable[5] noise of this great town.
I will the country see,
Where old simplicity,
Though hid in gray,
Doth look more gay
Than foppery in plush and scarlet clad.
Farewell, you city-wits that are
Almost at civil war;
'Tis time that I grow wise, when all the world grows mad.

Most of my days
I will not spend to gain an idiot's praise,
Or to make sport
For some slight puny[6] of the Inns of Court.
Then, worthy Stafford, say,
How shall we spend the day;
With what delights
Shorten the nights?
When from this tumult we are got secure
Where mirth with all her freedom goes,
Yet shall no finger lose,[7]
Where every word is thought, and every thought is pure.

There from the tree
We'll cherries pluck, and pick the strawberry,

4. Anthony Stafford (1587–1645), author of various moral and historical works, is described by Anthony à Wood as "a good scholar . . . well read in ancient history, poets and other authors" (*Athenae Oxoniensis* [1691–1692; ed. P. Bliss, 4 vols., Oxford, 1813], 4 vols. [New York, 1967], III, pp. 33–34).
5. Burdensome.
6. Puisne—i.e., a first-year law student.
7. Cf. Randolph's poem, "Upon the Loss of His Little Finger," p. 340.

And every day
Go see the wholesome country girls make hay,
Whose brown hath lovelier grace
Than any painted face
That I do know
Hyde Park can show;
Where I had rather gain a kiss than meet,
Though some of them in greater state
Might court my love with plate,
The beauties of the Cheap, and wives of Lombard Street.[8]

But think upon
Some other pleasures, these to me are none;
Why do I prate
Of women, that are things against my fate?
I never mean to wed
That torture to my bed.
My Muse is she
My love shall be.
Let clowns[9] get wealth, and heirs; when I am gone,
And this great bugbear, grisly death,
Shall take this idle breath,
If I a poem leave, that poem is my son.

Of this, no more;
We'll rather taste the bright Pomona's[1] store;
No fruit shall 'scape.
Our palates, from the damson[2] to the grape.
Then, full, we'll seek a shade
And hear what music's made;
How Philomel[3]
Her tale doth tell,
And how the other birds do fill the choir;
The thrush and blackbird lend their throats,
Warbling melodious notes;
We will all sports enjoy, which others but desire.

Ours is the sky,
Where at what fowl we please our hawk shall fly;
Nor will we spare
To hunt the crafty fox or timorous hare,
But let our hounds run loose
In any ground they'll choose;
The buck shall fall,

8. Hyde Park, given to the people of London by Charles I in 1637, was a fashionable promenade; Lombard Street was predominantly given over to merchants' offices; Cheapside and Eastcheap were known for their markets and shops.
9. I.e. (in this context), crass fellows.
1. The wood nymph Pomona was the Roman divinity of fruit trees; cf. Carew, "To My Friend G. N., from Wrest," line 93n, p. 317.
2. Small plum.
3. Cf. Shirley, "Cupid's Call," line 14n, p. 321.

The stag and all;
Our pleasures must from their own warrants be,
For to my Muse, if not to me,
I'm sure all game is free;
Heaven, earth, are all but parts of her great royalty.

And when we mean
To taste of Bacchus' blessings now and then,
And drink by stealth
A cup or two to noble Berkeley's[4] health,
I'll take my pipe and try
The Phrygian[5] melody,
Which he that hears
Lets through his ears
A madness to distemper all the brain,
Then I another pipe will take
And Doric music make,
To civilize with graver notes our wits again.

On the Death of a Nightingale[6]

Go, solitary wood, and henceforth be
Acquainted with no other harmony
Than the pies'[7] chattering, or the shrieking note
Of boding owls, and fatal raven's throat.
Thy sweetest chanter's dead, that warbled forth
Lays that might tempests calm, and still the north,
And call down angels from their glorious sphere[8]
To hear her songs, and learn new anthems there.
That soul is fled, and to Elysium[9] gone;
Thou a poor desert left; go then and run,
Beg there to stand a grove, and if she please
To sing again beneath thy shadowy trees;
The souls of happy lovers crowned with blisses
Shall flock about thee, and keep time with kisses.

A Mask for Lydia

Sweet Lydia, take this mask, and shroud
Thy face within the silken cloud,
And veil those powerful skies;

4. Stafford dedicated *The Guide of Honor* (1634) to George, eighth Baron Berkeley (1601–1658).
5. In ancient Greek music, the Phrygian mode was that suited "to express peaceful action under no stress of hard necessity"; the Dorian mode was appropriate rather for the "brave man in warlike action or in any hard and dangerous task" (Plato, *Republic*, III. 378–399 [ed. F. M. Cornford, Oxford, 1941]).
6. Cf. Henry Vaughan, "To My Ingenuous Friend, R. W.," lines 33–36, pp. 585–86.
7. Magpies'.
8. Cf. Herrick, "A Nuptial Song," line 102n, p. 201.
9. Cf. Carew, "A Rapture," line 2n, p. 302.

For he whose gazing dares so high aspire
  Makes burning-glasses of his eyes,
And sets his heart on fire.

Veil, Lydia, veil, for unto me
There is no basilisk[1] but thee:
  Thy very looks do kill.
Yet in those looks so fixed is my delight,
  Poor soul, alas, I languish still
In absence of thy sight.

Close up those eyes, or we shall find
Too great a lustre strike us blind;
  Or if a ray so good
Ought to be seen, let it but then appear
  When eagles do produce their brood
To try their young ones there.[2]

Or if thou would'st have me to know
How great a brightness thou canst show
  When they have lost the sun,
Then do thou rise, and give the world this theme:
  Sol from th'Hesperides[3] is run,
And back hath whipped his team.

Yet through the Goat when he shall stray,
Thou through the Crab must take thy way;[4]
  For should you both shine bright
In the same tropic, we poor moles should get
  Not so much comfort by the light,
As torment by the heat.

Where's Lydia now? Where shall I seek
Her charming lip, her tempting cheek
  That my affections bowed?
So dark a sable hath eclipsed my fair,
  That I can gaze upon the cloud
That durst not see the star.

But yet methinks my thoughts begin
To say there lies a white within,
  Though black her pride control;
And what care I how black a face I see,
  So there be whiteness in the soul,
Still such an Ethiope be.

1. According to legend, the glance or breath of the basilisk (a monstrous serpent or dragon) was fatal.
2. Cf. Carew, "To Ben Jonson," line 12n, p. 308.
3. I.e., from the legendary garden of golden apples, in the west.
4. Capricorn, the goat, is the sign of the zodiac for the wintry period from 23 December to 20 January; Cancer, the Crab, is the zodiacal sign for the midsummer period from 22 June to 23 July.

Upon Love Fondly[5] Refused for Conscience's Sake

Nature, creation's law, is judged by sense,
Not by the tyrant conscience.
Then our commission[6] gives us leave to do
What youth and pleasure prompts us to,
For we must question, else, heaven's great decree,
And tax it with a treachery,
If things made sweet to tempt our appetite
Should with a guilt stain the delight.
Higher powers rule us, ourselves can nothing do;
Who made us love made't lawful too.
It was not love, but love transformed to vice,
Ravished by envious avarice,
Made women first impropriate;[7] all were free;
Enclosures man's inventions be.
I'th'Golden Age no action[8] could be found
For trespass on my neighbor's ground;
'Twas just with any fair to mix our blood;
The best is most diffusive good.
She that confines her beams to one man's sight
Is a dark-lantern[9] to a glorious light.
Say, does the virgin-spring less chaste appear
'Cause many thirsts are quenchèd there?
Or have you not with the same odors met
When more have smelt your violet?
The phoenix[1] is not angry at her nest
'Cause her perfumes make others blest:
Though incense to th'eternal gods be meant,
Yet mortals revel in the scent.
Man is the lord of creatures, yet we see
That all his vassals' loves are free;
The severe wedlock's fetters do not bind
The pard's[2] inflamed and amorous mind,
But that he may be like a bridegroom led
Even to the royal lion's bed.
The birds may for a year their loves confine,
But make new choice each Valentine.
If our affections then more servile be
Than are our slaves', where's man's sovereignty?
Why, then, by pleasing more should you less please,

5. Foolishly. The argument and "witty" rhetoric of Randolph's poem may be compared with those of Leander's persuasive address to Hero, in Marlowe's *Hero and Leander*; also with the extended appeal made by Comus to the Lady, in Milton's *Comus*.
6. Warrant (by implication, "assigned task").
7. I.e., assigned to be the property of particular men.
8. I.e., no basis for legal proceedings.
9. I.e., a lantern with an opening that may be closed to conceal the light.
1. Cf. Carew, "A Song," line 18n, p. 318.
2. Leopard's.

And spare the sweets, being more sweet than these?
If the fresh trunk have sap enough to give
That each insertive[3] branch may live,
The gard'ner grafts not only apples there,
But adds the warden[4] and the pear;
The peach and apricot together grow,
The cherry and the damson too,
Till he hath made by skilful husbandry
An entire orchard of one tree.
So, lest our paradise perfection want,
We may as well inoculate as plant.
What's conscience but a beldame's[5] midnight theme,
Or nodding nurse's idle dream?
So feigned, as are the goblins, elves, and fairies,
To watch their orchards and their dairies,
For who can tell when first her reign begun?
I'th'state of innocence was none;
And since large conscience, as the proverb shows,
In the same sense with bad one goes,[6]
The less the better, then, whence this will fall:
'Tis to be perfect to have none at all.
Suppose it be a virtue, rich and pure,
'Tis not for spring or summer, sure,
Nor yet for autumn: love must have his prime,
His warmer heats, and harvest time.
Till we have flourished, grown, and reaped our wishes,
What conscience dares oppose our kisses?
But when time's colder hand leads us near home,
Then let that winter-virtue come;
Frost is till then prodigious;[7] we may do
What youth and pleasure prompts us to.

3. Grafted.
4. A variety of baking pear.
5. I.e., an elderly matron's.
6. I.e., a pliable conscience. Cf. for example, in Shakespeare's *Henry VIII*, the Old Lady's suggestion that Anne Boleyn should "stretch" her "soft cheveril conscience" by giving in to the king's desire for her (II.iii.29–33).
7. I.e., unnatural.

William Habington

1605	Born, 4 or 5 November at Hindlip, Worcestershire. The Habingtons were Roman Catholics: William's uncle had been executed in 1586 for his connection with the Babington Plot against Queen Elizabeth's life; his father had been imprisoned for six years at that time. Educated at Saint Omer and at Paris, Habington subsequently resides at Hindlip, where his father indulges a passion for antiquarian research.
1630–1633	At some time during this period marries Lucy Herbert ("Castara"), youngest daughter of William Herbert, first Baron Powis.
1634	Publication of *Castara*.
1635	Second (enlarged) edition of *Castara*.
1640	Third (further enlarged) edition of *Castara*. Also publishes a tragicomedy, *The Queen of Aragon*, which appears to have been acted at court.
1641	Publication of *Observations Upon History*.
c. 1644–1650	According to Anthony à Wood, "not unknown to Oliver the usurper."
1654	Death, 30 November; buried at Hindlip.

FROM *CASTARA*[1] (1640)

To Roses in the Bosom of Castara

Ye blushing virgins happy are
In the chaste nunn'ry of her breasts,
For he'd profane so chaste a fair,
Whoe'er should call them Cupid's nests.

Transplanted thus, how bright ye grow,
How rich a perfume do ye yield!
In some close[2] garden cowslips so
Are sweeter than i'th'open field.

In these white cloisters live secure
From the rude blasts of wanton breath,
Each hour more innocent and pure,
Till you shall wither into death.

Then that which living gave you room,
Your glorious sepulcher shall be;
There wants no marble for a tomb,
Whose breast hath marble been to me.

To Castara

Do not their profane orgies hear,
Who but[3] to wealth no altars rear;
The soul's oft poisoned through the ear.

Castara, rather seek to dwell
I'th' silence of a private cell;
Rich discontent's a glorious hell.

Yet Hindlip[4] doth not want extent
Of room, though not magnificent,
To give free welcome to content.

1. "Chaste altar." The third (augmented) edition of *Castara*, published in 1640, is divided into three parts: three prose "characters" ("A Mistress," "A Wife," "A Holy Man") successively introduce and in some sense epitomize the central emphasis of each part. The first grouping includes fifty-seven poems; the second, fifty (together with the prose "character," "A Friend," and eight elegies to the memory of Habington's friend George Talbot); the third, twenty-two, of which a majority are based on passages in the Psalms and the Book of Job. In his preface to the collection, Habington observes that when poetry "is wholly employed in the soft strains of love, his soul who entertains it loseth much of that strength which should confirm him man"; he offers rather "the innocency of a chaste Muse." "In all those flames in which I burnt, I never felt a wanton heat, nor was my invention ever sinister [i.e., corrupted away] from the strait way of chastity. And when love builds upon that rock, it may safely contemn the battery of the waves and threatenings of the wind."
2. Secluded.
3. Except.
4. Hindlip Hall, near Worcester, was the country estate of the Habington family.

There shalt thou see the early spring
That wealthy stock of nature bring,
Of which the Sybil's books did sing.[5]

From fruitless palms shall honey flow,
And barren winter harvest show,
While lilies in his bosom grow;

No north wind shall the corn infest,[6]
But the soft spirit of the east
Our scent with perfumed banquets feast.

A satyr here and there shall trip,
In hope to purchase leave to sip
Sweet nectar from a fairy's lip.

The nymphs with quivers shall adorn
Their active sides, and rouse the morn
With the shrill music of their horn.

Wakened with which, and viewing thee,
Fair Daphne[7] her fair self shall free
From the chaste prison of a tree,

And with Narcissus[8] to thy face
Who humbly will ascribe all grace
Shall once again pursue the chase.

So they whose wisdom did discuss
Of these as fictions, shall in us
Find they were more than fabulous.

To a Wanton

In vain, fair sorceress, thy eyes speak charms,
In vain thou mak'st loose circles with thy arms,
I'm 'bove thy spells. No magic him can move
In whom Castara hath inspired her love.
As she, keep thou strict sent'nel o'er thy ear,
Lest it the whispers of soft courtiers hear;
Read not his raptures,[9] whose invention must
Write journeywork, both for his patron's lust
And his own plush; let no admirer feast
His eye o'th'naked banquet of thy breast.

5. Cf. Herrick, "To the Right Honorable Mildmay, Earl of Westmorland," line 4n, p. 207.
6. Disturb.
7. Cf. Ovid, *Metamorphoses*, I.452–567.
8. The story of Narcissus, who fell in love with his own image reflected in the water and who was eventually changed into the flower that bears his name, appears in Ovid, *Metamorphoses*, III.339–510.
9. Habington perhaps alludes to Carew's poem "A Rapture," p. 302.

If[1] this fair precedent, nor yet my want
Of love to answer thine, make thee recant
Thy sorc'ries, pity shall to justice turn,
And judge thee, witch, in thy own flames to burn.

To the World. The Perfection of Love[2]

You who are earth, and cannot rise
  Above your sense,
Boasting the envied wealth which lies
Bright in your mistress' lips or eyes,
Betray a pitied eloquence.

That which doth join our souls, so light
  And quick doth move,
That like the eagle in his flight
It doth transcend all human sight,
Lost in the element of love.

You poets reach not this, who sing
  The praise of dust
But kneaded, when by theft you bring
The rose and lily from the spring
T'adorn the wrinkled face of lust.

When we speak love, nor art nor wit
  We gloss upon:
Our souls engender, and beget
Ideas, which you counterfeit
In your dull propagation.

While time seven ages[3] shall disperse,
  We'll talk of love,
And when our tongues hold no commerce,[4]
Our thoughts shall mutually converse,
And yet the blood no rebel prove.

And though we be of several kind
  Fit for offence,
Yet are we so by love refined,
From impure dross we are all mind;
Death could not more have conquered sense.

How suddenly those flames expire
  Which scorch our clay;

1. I.e., if neither.
2. This poem first appears in the 1635 edition of *Castara*. Cf. Donne, "The Ecstasy," especially lines 19–21 and 22–30, pp. 37–39.
3. It was believed that the world would pass through six "ages" (i.e., eras), and that the Last Judgment would usher in the seventh, and final, age.
4. I.e., are silent.

Prometheus-like, when we steal fire
From heaven, 'tis endless and entire:
It may know age, but not decay.

To a Friend, Inviting Him to a Meeting upon Promise[5]

May you drink beer, or that adult'rate wine
Which makes the zeal of Amsterdam divine,[6]
If you make breach of promise. I have now
So rich a sack that even yourself will bow
T'adore my Genius.[7] Of this wine should Prynne[8]
Drink but a plenteous glass, he would begin
A health to Shakespeare's ghost. But you may bring
Some excuse forth, and answer me, the King
Today will give you audience, or that on
Affairs of state you and some serious Don[9]
Are to resolve, or else, perhaps, you'll sin
So far as to leave word you're not within.
The least of these will make me only think
Him subtle who can in his closet[1] drink,
Drunk even alone; and, thus made wise, create
As dangerous plots as the Low Country state,
Projecting for such baits[2] as shall draw o'er
To Holland all the herrings from our shore.
But you're too full of candor, and I know
Will sooner stones at Sal'sbury casements throw,[3]
Or buy up for the silenced Levites[4] all
The rich impropriations, than let pall
So pure Canary, and break such an oath,
Since charity is sinned against in both.
Come, therefore, blest even in the Lollards'[5] zeal,
Who canst with conscience safe, 'fore hen and veal,
Say grace in Latin, while I faintly sing
A penitential verse in oil and ling.[6]

5. This piece and the four that follow are drawn from the second grouping of poems that comprise *Castara*. Habington here responds to Shirley's poem, "Two Gentlemen That Broke Their Promise of a Meeting, Made When They Drank Claret," p. 324.
6. Habington alludes sardonically to those English Puritans who had fled to the Netherlands to escape persecution by the Anglican authorities.
7. I.e., my protecting spirit.
8. William Prynne (1600–1669) was a Puritan pamphleteer whose fierce attacks on contemporary mores (notably stage plays and the theaters in London, in *Histriomastix*, published in 1623) led at length to savage reprisals by the government, which imposed fines amounting to £10,000, and sentenced him to have his ears cut off and to be branded.
9. I.e., some solemn Spanish grandee.
1. Private chamber.
2. I.e., devising such alluring temptations.
3. Church windows in Salisbury, Wiltshire, had been broken (in 1630) by a local official of Puritanical inclinations.
4. I.e., Puritan ministers who had been officially removed from their parishes.
5. The Lollards (from Dutch, "mumblers") were followers of the English reformer John Wycliffe (c. 1320–1384).
6. A North Sea fish, ling is a member of the cod family. Habington is making game of Puritan asceticism.

Come, then, and bring with you, prepared for fight,
Unmixed Canary; Heaven send both prove right!
This I am sure: my sack will disengage
All human thoughts, inspire so high a rage
That Hippocrene[7] shall henceforth poets lack,
Since more enthusiasms are in my sack.
  Heightened with which, my raptures shall commend
  How good Castara is, how dear my friend.

To Castara, upon Beauty

Castara, see that dust the sportive wind
So wantons with; 'tis haply all you'll find
Left of some beauty; and how still[8] it flies,
To trouble, as it did in life, our eyes.
Oh, empty boast of flesh! Though our heirs gild
The far-fetched Phrygian[9] marble, which shall build
A burden to our ashes, yet will death
Betray them to the sport of every breath.
Dost thou, poor relic of our frailty, still
Swell up with glory? Or is it thy skill
To mock weak man, whom every wind of praise
Into the air doth 'bove his center raise?
  If so, mock on, and tell him that his lust
  To beauty's[1] madness; for it courts but dust.

Against Them Who Lay Unchastity to the Sex of Women[2]

They meet but with unwholesome springs,
And summers which infectious are,[3]
They hear but when the mermaid sings,
And only see the falling star,
  Whoever dare
Affirm no woman chaste and fair.

Go, cure your fevers, and you'll say
The dog-days[4] scorch not all the year;
In copper mines no longer stay,
But travel to the west,[5] and there
  The right ones see;
And grant all gold's not alchemy.

7. The Hippocrene spring, created when the winged horse Pegasus struck the ground with his hoof, was situated on the slopes of Mount Helicon, in Boeotia.
8. Continuously.
9. Phrygia was located in Asia Minor.
1. I.e., beauty is.
2. The poem responds to the challenges posed by Donne in his lyric "Go and catch a falling star," p. 23.
3. Bubonic plague was a particular threat during the hot summer months.
4. I.e., the most sultry weeks of the summer.
5. I.e., to Worcestershire, Habington's county of residence.

What madman, 'cause the glowworm's flame
Is cold, swears there's no warmth in fire?
'Cause some make forfeit of their name,
And slave themselves to man's desire,
  Shall the sex, free
From guilt, damned to the bondage be?

Nor grieve, Castara, though 'twere frail,
Thy virtue then would brighter shine,
When thy example should prevail,
And every woman's faith be thine;
  And were there none,
'Tis majesty to rule alone.

To Castara, upon an Embrace

  'Bout th'husband oak the vine
Thus wreathes to kiss his leafy face;
  Their streams thus rivers join,
And lose themselves in the embrace.
  But trees want sense when they enfold,
  And waters, when they meet, are cold.

  Thus turtles[6] bill, and groan
Their loves into each other's ear;
  Two flames thus burn in one,
When their curled heads to heaven they rear;
  But birds want soul, though not desire,
  And flames material soon expire.

  If not profane, we'll say
When angels close, their joys are such;
  For we not love obey
That's bastard to[7] a fleshly touch.
  Let's close, Castara, then, since thus
  We pattern[8] angels, and they us.

Nox Nocti Indicat Scientiam.[9] David

  When I survey the bright
    Celestial sphere,
So rich with jewels hung that night
Doth like an Ethiop bride appear,

6. Turtledoves.
7. I.e., that is the illegitimate consequence of.
8. Imitate.
9. "Night unto night sheweth knowledge" (Psalms 19:2). This poem is part of the third and final section of *Castara*.

My soul her wings doth spread
And heavenward flies,
Th'Almighty's mysteries to read
In the large volumes of the skies.

For the bright firmament
Shoots forth no flame
So silent, but is eloquent
In speaking the Creator's name.

No unregarded star
Contracts its light
Into so small a character,[1]
Removed far from our human sight,

But if we steadfast look,
We shall discern
In it, as in some holy book,
How man may heavenly knowledge learn.

It tells the conqueror
That far-stretched power
Which his proud dangers traffic for,[2]
Is but the triumph of an hour.

That from the farthest north
Some nation may,
Yet undiscovered, issue forth,
And o'er his new-got conquest sway.

Some nation yet shut in
With hills of ice
May be let out to scourge his sin,
Till they shall equal him in vice.

And then they likewise shall
Their ruin have,
For as yourselves, your empires fall,
And every kingdom hath a grave.

Thus those celestial fires,
Though seeming mute,
The fallacy of our desires
And all the pride of life confute.

For they have watched since first
The world had birth;
And found sin in itself accurst,
And nothing permanent on earth.

1. Sign, symbol.
2. I.e., undertake to maintain (in the sense of sordid commercial enterprise).

Edmund Waller

1606	Born 3 March, at Coleshill, Hertfordshire; baptized 9 March at Amersham. Eldest son of a wealthy landowner.
1616	Father dies.
1616–1620	Attends Eton, and (from March 1620) King's College, Cambridge, as a fellow commoner. Leaves without taking a degree.
1621	Represents Amersham in Parliament.
1622	Admitted to Lincoln's Inn.
1624–1628	Member of Parliament for Ilchester in the last Parliament of James I; for Chipping Wycombe and Amersham in the first and third Parliaments of Charles I.
1631	Enabled by the intervention of Charles I to marry the wealthy heiress Anne Banks, without her guardians' consent, in July.
1634	Death of his wife.
1635	From about this time, associated with Lucius Cary, Lord Falkland, and the group of philosophers and poets meeting at Great Tew. Becomes acquainted with Lady Dorothy Sidney ("Sacharissa"), whom he intermittently courts in verse until 1638.
1640	Member of Parliament for Amersham in the "Short Parliament," and for Saint Ives in the "Long Parliament," convened in November.
1643	Centrally active in a conspiracy designed to secure London for the King, while serving as one of the Parliamentary commission designated to reach an agreement with the sovereign; subsequently (the plot discovered) betrays his associates, two of whom are hanged. Imprisoned in the Tower of London from September 1643, until November 1644; fined £10,000 and banished from the realm. For some years thereafter lives comfortably with his second wife in France and Italy.
1645	Publication of first, second (augmented), and third editions of *Poems*. Later editions appear in 1664, 1668, 1682, 1686.
1651	Chiefly by consequence of his mother's influence with Cromwell, receives a pardon; returns to England in the year following.
1653	Death of his mother.

1661	Member of Parliament for Hastings; regularly in Parliament until his death. Welcomed and respected in courtly and literary circles.
1687	Death, 21 October; buried at his estate in Beaconsfield, Hertfordshire.
1690	*The Second Part of Mr. Waller's Poems* published.

FROM *POEMS*[1] (1686)

To the King, on His Navy[2]

Where'er thy navy spreads her canvas wings,
Homage to thee, and peace to all she brings;
The French and Spaniard, when thy flags appear,
Forget their hatred, and consent to fear.
So Jove from Ida did both hosts survey,
And when he pleased to thunder, part the fray.[3]
Ships heretofore in seas like fishes sped,
The mighty still upon the smaller fed;
Thou on the deep imposest nobler laws,
And by that justice hast removed the cause
Of those rude tempests, which for rapine sent,
Too oft, alas, involved the innocent.
Now shall the ocean, as thy Thames, be free
From both those fates, of storms and piracy;
But we most happy, who can hear no force
But wingèd troops, or Pegasean horse.[4]
'Tis not so hard for greedy foes to spoil
Another nation, as to touch our soil.
Should nature's self invade the world again,
And o'er the center spead the liquid main,
Thy power were safe, and her destructive hand
Would but enlarge the bounds of thy command;
Thy dreadful fleet would style thee lord of all,
And ride in triumph o'er the drownèd ball;[5]
Those towers of oak o'er fertile plains might go,
And visit mountains where they once did grow.
  The world's Restorer never could endure
That finished Babel[6] should those men secure,
Whose pride designed that fabric to have stood
Above the reach of any second flood;[7]
To thee, His chosen, more indulgent, He
Dares trust such power with so much piety.

1. Waller's poetry was extravagantly admired in his own lifetime and in the eighteenth century: Dryden wrote, in 1664, that "the excellence and dignity of rhyme were never fully known till Mr. Waller taught it; he first made writing easily an art" (*Essays of John Dryden*, ed. W. P. Ker, 2 vols. [Oxford, 1926], I, p. 7). His employment of the pentameter couplet served (with Denham's "Cooper's Hill") as a model for Dryden, Pope, and the poets of the Augustan Age.
2. Noting the allusion in line 4 to a period of truce, in 1627, between France and Spain, G. Thorn-Drury assigns the poem to that year, when the Earl of Buckingham was making the English fleet ready for sea (*Poems of Edmund Waller*, 2 vols. [London, 1893], II, pp. 160–161).
3. In Homer's *Iliad*, the gods look on from Mount Ida as Greeks and Trojans engage in battle on the plain below.
4. Cf. Randolph, "A Gratulatory," line 25n, p. 339.
5. Globe.
6. I.e., the Tower of Babel.
7. Cf. Genesis 11:1–9.

The Story of Phoebus and Daphne Applied[8]

Thyrsis, a youth of the inspirèd train,[9]
Fair Sacharissa[1] loved, but loved in vain:
Like Phoebus sung the no less amorous boy;
Like Daphne she, as lovely and as coy:
With numbers[2] he the flying nymph pursues,
With numbers such as Phoebus' self might use.
Such is the chase, when love and fancy leads,
O'er craggy mountains, and through flowery meads,[3]
Invoked to testify the lover's care,
Or form some image of his cruel fair:
Urged with his fury like a wounded deer,
O'er these he fled, and now approaching near,
Had reached the nymph with his harmonious lay,
Whom all his charms[4] could not incline to stay.
Yet what he sung in his immortal strain,
Though unsuccessful, was not sung in vain:
All but the nymph, that should redress his wrong,
Attend his passion, and approve his song.
Like Phoebus thus, acquiring unsought praise,
He catched at love, and filled his arm with bays.

Upon Ben Jonson[5]

Mirror of poets! Mirror of our age!
Which her whole face beholding on thy stage,
Pleased, and displeased, with her own faults, endures
A remedy like those whom music cures.
Thou hast alone those various inclinations
Which nature gives to ages, sexes, nations,
So tracèd with thy all-resembling pen,[6]
That whate'er custom has imposed on men,
Or ill-got habit (which deforms them so
That scarce a brother can his brother know),
Is represented to the wondering eyes
Of all that see, or read, thy comedies.
Whoever in those glasses[7] looks may find

8. The nymph Daphne finally escaped Phoebus Apollo's pursuit when her father, a river god, transformed her into a laurel (or bay) tree. Sacred to Apollo, god of poetry, the tree became emblematic of poetic fame, and its leaves were used to crown successful poets.
9. I.e., a poet. Thyrsis is a conventional pastoral name.
1. Derived from the Latin for sugar, Sacharissa is Waller's name for Lady Dorothy Sidney, eldest daughter of the Earl of Leicester, whom he courted in verse from 1635 until her marriage to Lord Spencer in 1639. Cf. "At Penshurst," p. 363.
2. Verses.
3. Meadows.
4. Songs, incantations.
5. This poem was first published in *Jonsonus Virbius* (1638), a collection of tributes in Greek, Latin, and English, dedicated to Jonson's memory. Of the authors represented in the present edition, Habington and Cartwright also contributed English verses to the memorial volume.
6. I.e., thy pen, which can represent every aspect of nature.
7. Mirrors.

The spots returned, or graces, of his mind;
And by the help of so divine an art,
At leisure view, and dress, his nobler part.
Narcissus,[8] cozened by that flattering well,
Which nothing could but of his beauty tell,
Had here, discovering the deformed estate
Of his fond mind, preserved himself with hate.
But virtue too, as well as vice, is clad
In flesh and blood so well, that Plato had
Beheld what his high fancy once embraced,
Virtue with colors, speech, and motion graced.[9]
The sundry postures of thy copious Muse
Who would express, a thousand tongues must use;
Whose fate's no less peculiar[1] than thy art;
For as thou couldst all characters impart,
So none could render thine, which still escapes,
Like Proteus,[2] in variety of shapes;
Who was not this, nor that, but all we find,
And all we can imagine, in mankind.

At Penshurst[3]

Had Sacharissa[4] lived when mortals made
Choice of their deities, this sacred shade
Had held an altar to her power, that gave
The peace and glory which these alleys have;
Embroidered so with flowers where she stood,
That it became a garden of a wood.
Her presence has such more than human grace,
That it can civilize the rudest place;
And beauty too, and order, can impart,
Where nature ne'er intended it, nor art.
The plants acknowledge this, and her admire,
No less than those of old did Orpheus' lyre;[5]
If she sit down, with tops all towards her bowed,
They round about her into arbors crowd;
Or if she walk, in even ranks they stand,
Like some well-marshaled and obsequious band.
Amphion so made stones and timber leap
Into fair figures from a confused heap;[6]

8. Cf. Habington, "To Castara," line 28n, p. 352.
9. Waller perhaps has in view Plato's account of "the poet and taleteller who would imitate the action of the good man and would tell his tale in the [virtuous] patterns" that appropriately match the austere principles of Plato's ideal state. Cf. *Republic,* III.398b; II.378c–e; in *Collected Dialogues of Plato,* ed. Edith Hamilton and H. Cairns (New York, 1961), pp. 643, 625.
1. Distinctive.
2. Proteus, old man of the sea, could change into every kind of shape: cf. Homer, *Odyssey,* IV.456–458.
3. Cf. Jonson, "To Penshurst," p. 97.
4. I.e., Dorothy Sidney.
5. Cf. Jonson, *The Forest,* XII, line 77n, p. 114.
6. Amphion's skill in music was such that, moved by his lyre, stones of their own accord formed the walls of Thebes; cf. Homer, *Odyssey,* XI.260.

And in the symmetry of her parts is found
A power like that of harmony in sound.
   Ye lofty beeches, tell this matchless dame,
That if together ye fed all one flame,
It could not equalize the hundredth part
Of what her eyes have kindled in my heart.
Go, boy, and carve this passion on the bark
Of yonder tree, which stands the sacred mark
Of noble Sidney's birth;[7] when such benign,
Such more than mortal-making stars did shine,
That there they cannot but forever prove
The monument and pledge of humble love;
His humble love whose hope shall ne'er rise higher
Than for a pardon that he dares admire.

The Battle of the Summer Islands[8]

CANTO I

What fruits they have, and how heaven smiles
Upon those late-discovered isles.

Aid me, Bellona![9] while the dreadful fight
Betwixt a nation and two whales I write.
Seas stained with gore I sing, adventurous toil,
And how these monsters did disarm an isle.
   Bermudas, walled with rocks, who does not know?
That happy island where huge lemons grow,
And orange trees, which golden fruit do bear,
The Hesperian garden[1] boasts of none so fair;
Where shining pearl, coral, and many a pound,
On the rich shore, of ambergris[2] is found.
The lofty cedar, which to heaven aspires,
The prince of trees, is fuel for their fires;
The smoke by which their loaded spits do turn,
For incense might on sacred altars burn;
Their private roofs on odorous timber borne,
Such as might palaces for kings adorn.
The sweet palmettos a new Bacchus yield,
With leaves as ample as the broadest shield,
Under the shadow of whose friendly boughs
They sit, carousing where their liquor grows.
Figs there unplanted through the fields do grow,
Such as fierce Cato[3] did the Romans show,

7. Cf. Jonson, "To Penshurst," line 14n, p. 98.
8. I.e., the Bermudas, named for the Spanish navigator Juan de Bermúdez, who discovered them in 1515. They became known in England as the Somers (or "Summer") Islands, after the ships of Sir George Somers, en route for Virginia, were wrecked there in 1609.
9. The Roman goddess of war.
1. Cf. Herrick, *Hesperides*, first note, p. 181.
2. A waxy substance derived from the sperm whale, ambergris is used in making perfume.
3. Marcus Porcius Cato (234–149 B.C.), known for his austerity, regularly called for the destruction of Carthage, Rome's rival in the Mediterranean world. He was the author of *De Agri Cultura*.

With the rare fruit inviting them to spoil
Carthage, the mistress of so rich a soil.
The naked rocks are not unfruitful there,
But, at some constant seasons, every year
Their barren tops with luscious food abound,
And with the eggs of various fowl are crowned.
Tobacco is the worst of things[4] which they
To English landlords, as their tribute, pay.
Such is the mold, that the blest tenant feeds
On precious fruits, and pays his rent in weeds.
With candied plantains, and the juicy pine,[5]
On choicest melons, and sweet grapes, they dine,
And with potatoes fat their wanton swine.
Nature these cates[6] with such a lavish hand
Pours out among them, that our coarser land
Tastes of that bounty, and does cloth return,
Which not for warmth but ornament is worn;
For the kind spring, which but salutes us here,
Inhabits there, and courts them all the year.
Ripe fruits and blossoms on the same trees live;
At once they promise what at once they give.
So sweet the air, so moderate the clime,
None sickly lives, or dies before his time.
Heaven sure has kept this spot of earth uncursed
To show how all things were created first.
The tardy plants in our cold orchards placed
Reserve their fruit for the next age's taste.
There a small grain in some few months will be
A firm, a lofty, and a spacious tree.
The palma-christi, and the fair papaw,[7]
Now but a seed, preventing[8] nature's law,
In half the circle of the hasty year
Project a shade, and lovely fruit do wear.
And as their trees, in our dull region set,
But faintly grow, and no perfection get,
So in this northern tract our hoarser throats
Utter unripe and ill-constrainèd notes,
Where the supporter of the poets' style,
Phoebus, on them eternally does smile.
Oh! how I long my careless limbs to lay
Under the plantain's shade, and all the day
With amorous airs my fancy entertain,
Invoke the Muses, and improve my vein!
No passion there in my free breast should move,
None but the sweet and best of passions, love.
There while I sing, if gentle love be by,
That tunes my lute, and winds the strings so high;

4. I.e., tobacco (by implication delightful and desirable) is the most common commodity.
5. Pineapple.
6. Delicacies.
7. I.e., the castor-oil plant and the papaya.
8. Anticipating.

With the sweet sound of Sacharissa's name
I'll make the listening savages grow tame.
But while I do these pleasing dreams indite,
I am diverted from the promised fight.

CANTO II

Of their alarm, and how their foes
Discovered were, this Canto shows.

Though rocks so high about this island rise
That well they may the numerous Turk despise,
Yet is no human fate exempt from fear,
Which shakes their hearts, while through the isle they hear
A lasting noise, as horrid and as loud
As thunder makes before it breaks the cloud.
Three days they dread this murmur, ere they know
From what blind cause th'unwonted sound may grow.
At length two monsters of unequal size,
Hard by the shore, a fisherman espies:
Two mighty whales! which swelling seas had tossed,
And left them prisoners on the rocky coast.
One as a mountain vast; and with her came
A cub, not much inferior to his dam.
Here in a pool, among the rocks engaged,
They roared, like lions caught in toils, and raged.
The man knew what they were, who heretofore
Had seen the like lie murdered on the shore,
By the wild fury of some tempest cast,
The fate of ships and shipwrecked men to taste.
As careless dames, whom wine and sleep betray
To frantic dreams, their infants overlay,[9]
So there, sometimes, the raging ocean fails,
And her own brood exposes; when the whales
Against sharp rocks, like reeling vessels quashed,[1]
Though huge as mountains, are in pieces dashed;
Along the shore their dreadful limbs lie scattered,
Like hills with earthquakes shaken, torn, and shattered.
Hearts sure of brass they had, who tempted first
Rude seas that spare not what themselves have nursed.
The welcome news through all the nation spread,
To sudden joy and hope converts their dread;
What lately was their public terror, they
Behold with glad eyes as a certain prey,
Dispose already of th'untaken spoil,
And, as the purchase of their future toil,
These share the bones, and they divide the oil.
So was the huntsman by the bear oppressed,
Whose hide he sold—before he caught the beast!
They man their boats, and all their young men arm

9. I.e., lie upon (and smother) their young ones.
1. Crushed.

With whatsoever may the monsters harm:
Pikes, halberds, spits, and darts that wound so far,
The tools of peace, and instruments of war.
Now was the time for vigorous lads to show
What love or honor could invite them to;
A goodly theater, where rocks are round
With reverend age, and lovely lasses, crowned.
Such was the lake which held this dreadful pair
Within the bounds of noble Warwick's[2] share,
Warwick's bold earl! than which no title bears
A greater sound among our British peers;
And worthy he the memory to renew
The fate and honor, to that title due,
Whose brave adventures have transferred his name,
And through the new world spread his growing fame.
  But how they fought, and what their valor gained,
Shall in another Canto be contained.

CANTO III

The bloody fight, successful toil,
And how the fishes sacked the isle.

The boat which on the first assault did go
Struck with a harping-iron[3] the younger foe,
Who, when he felt his side so rudely gored,
Loud as the sea that nourished him he roared.
As a broad bream,[4] to please some curious taste,
While yet alive in boiling water cast,
Vexed with unwonted heat, bounds, flings about
The scorching brass, and hurls the liquor out,
So with the barbed javelin stung, he raves,
And scourges with his tail the suffering waves.
Like Spenser's Talus with his iron flail,[5]
He threatens ruin with his ponderous tail,
Dissolving at one stroke the battered boat,
And down the men fall, drenchèd in the moat;
With every fierce encounter they are forced
To quit their boats, and fare like men unhorsed.
  The bigger whale like some huge carrack[6] lay,
Which wanteth sea-room with her foes to play;
Slowly she swims, and when, provoked, she would
Advance her tail, her head salutes the mud;
The shallow water doth her force infringe,
And renders vain her tail's impetuous swinge;[7]
The shining steel her tender sides receive,

2. Robert Rich, second Earl of Warwick (1587–1658), was one of the principal proprietors of the English colony in the Bermudas.
3. Harpoon.
4. The sea bream, a saltwater fish.
5. Talus, "made of iron mold," is Artegall's squire in *The Faerie Queene*.
6. Galleon.
7. Sweep.

And there, like bees, they all their weapons leave.
This sees the cub, and does himself oppose
Betwixt his cumbered mother and her foes;
With desperate courage he receives her wounds,
And men and boats his active tail confounds.
Their forces joined, the seas with billows fill
And make a tempest, though the winds be still.
Now would the men with half their hopèd prey
Be well content, and wish this cub away;
Their wish they have: he, to direct his dam
Unto the gap through which they thither came,
Before her swims, and quits the hostile lake,
A prisoner there, but for his mother's sake.
She, by the rocks compelled to stay behind,
Is by the vastness of her bulk confined.
They shout for joy! and now on her alone
Their fury falls, and all their darts are thrown.
Their lances spent, one bolder than the rest
With his broadsword provoked the sluggish beast;
Her oily side devours both blade and haft,
And there his steel the bold Bermudian left.
Courage the rest from his example take,
And now they change the color of the lake;
Blood flows in rivers from her wounded side,
As if they would prevent the tardy tide,
And raise the flood to that propitious height
As might convey her from this fatal strait.
She swims in blood, and blood does spouting throw
To heaven, that heaven men's cruelties might know.
Their fixèd javelins in her side she wears,
And on her back a grove of pikes appears:
You would have thought, had you the monster seen
Thus dressed, she had another island been.
Roaring, she tears the air with such a noise,
As well resembled the conspiring voice
Of routed armies, when the field is won,
To reach the ears of her escapèd son.
He, though a league removèd from the foe,
Hastes to her aid; the pious Trojan[8] so,
Neglecting for Creusa's life his own,
Repeats the danger of the burning town.
The men, amazèd, blush to see the seed
Of monsters human piety exceed.
Well proves this kindness what the Grecians sung,
That Love's bright mother from the ocean sprung.[9]
Their courage droops, and, hopeless now, they wish
For composition with th'unconquered fish,
So she their weapons would restore again;
Through rocks they'd hew her passage to the main.

8. Aeneas returned to burning Troy to seek his wife, Creusa (*Aeneid*, II.749–794).
9. Venus was reputed to have sprung from the sea foam: cf. Ovid, *Metamorphoses*, IV.537.

But how instructed in each other's mind,
Or what commerce can men with monsters find?
Not daring to approach their wounded foe,
Whom her courageous son protected so,
They charge their muskets, and with hot desire
Of fell revenge, renew the fight with fire;
Standing aloof, with lead they bruise the scales
And tear the flesh of the incensèd whales.
But no success their fierce endeavors found,
Nor this way could they give one fatal wound.
Now to their fort they are about to send
For the loud engines which their isle defend;
But what those pieces, framed to batter walls,
Would have effected on those mighty whales,
Great Neptune will not have us know, who sends
A tide so high that it relieves his friends.
And thus they parted with exchange of harms:
Much blood the monsters lost, and they their arms.

On a Girdle

That which her slender waist confined
Shall now my joyful temples bind;
No monarch but would give his crown,
His arms might do what this has done.

It was my heaven's extremest sphere,
The pale[1] which held that lovely deer;
My joy, my grief, my hope, my love,
Did all within this circle move!

A narrow compass! and yet there
Dwelt all that's good, and all that's fair;
Give me but what this ribbon bound,
Take all the rest the sun goes round.

Song

Go, lovely rose!
Tell her that wastes her time and me
That now she knows,
When I resemble her to thee,
How sweet and fair she seems to be.

Tell her that's young,
And shuns to have her graces spied,
That hadst thou sprung

1. Enclosure.

In deserts where no men abide,
Thou must have uncommended died.

Small is the worth
Of beauty from the light retired;
Bid her come forth,
Suffer herself to be desired,
And not blush so to be admired.

Then die, that she
The common fate of all things rare
May read in thee;
How small a part of time they share,
That are so wondrous sweet and fair!

On St. James's Park, As Lately Improved by His Majesty[2]

Of the first Paradise there's nothing found;
Plants set by Heaven are vanished, and the ground;
Yet the description lasts; who knows the fate
Of lines that shall this paradise relate?
Instead of rivers rolling by the side
Of Eden's garden, here flows in the tide;[3]
The sea, which always served his empire, now
Pays tribute to our Prince's pleasure too.
Of famous cities we the founders know;
But rivers, old as seas, to which they go,
Are nature's bounty; 'tis of more renown
To make a river than to build a town.
For future shade, young trees upon the banks
Of the new stream appear in even ranks;
The voice of Orpheus, or Amphion's hand,[4]
In better order could not make them stand;
May they increase as fast, and spread their boughs,
As the high fame of their great owner grows!
May he live long enough to see them all
Dark shadows cast, and as his palace tall!
Methinks I see the love that shall be made,
The lovers walking in that amorous shade,
The gallants dancing by the river's side;

2. Immediately following his accession to the throne in 1660, Charles II set about making improvements in Saint James's Park in London. "Advised . . . by André Le Nôtre, Louis XIV's garden designer, he planted it with fruit trees, stocked it with deer, made a lake on which he could feed his ducks and round which he could walk his spaniels, and built an avenue, lined with trees and covered with powdered cockleshells, where he could play pall mall, a game something like croquet that had originated in Italy as *palla a maglio* (ball to mallet) and had become a fashionable craze in France" (C. Hibbert, *London, The Biography of a City* [New York, 1969], p. 81).
3. Among his other improvements, Charles had arranged to divert into the park a stream of water from the Thames.
4. Cf. "At Penshurst," lines 12n and 18n, p. 363.

They bathe in summer, and in winter slide.
Methinks I hear the music in the boats,
And the loud echo which returns the notes;
Whilst overhead a flock of new-sprung fowl
Hangs in the air, and does the sun control,
Darkening the sky; they hover o'er, and shroud
The wanton sailors with a feathered cloud.
Beneath, a shoal of silver fishes glides,
And plays about the gilded barges' sides;
The ladies, angling in the crystal lake,
Feast on the waters with the prey they take;
At once victorious with their lines and eyes,
They make the fishes, and the men, their prize.
A thousand Cupids on the billows ride,
And sea-nymphs enter with the swelling tide,
From Thetis[5] sent as spies, to make report,
And tell the wonders of her sovereign's court.
All that can, living, feed the greedy eye,
Or dead, the palate, here you may descry;
The choicest things that furnished Noah's ark,
Or Peter's sheet,[6] inhabiting this park;
All with a border of rich fruit-trees crowned,
Whose loaded branches hide the lofty mound.
Such various ways the spacious alleys lead,
My doubtful Muse knows not what path to tread.
Yonder, the harvest of cold months laid up,
Gives a fresh coolness to the royal cup;
There ice, like crystal firm, and never lost,
Tempers hot July with December's frost;
Winter's dark prison, whence he cannot fly
Though the warm spring, his enemy, draws nigh.
Strange! that extremes should thus preserve the snow,
High on the Alps, or in deep caves below.
  Here, a well-polished Mall gives us the joy
To see our Prince his matchless force employ;
His manly posture, and his graceful mien,
Vigor and youth, in all his motions seen;
His shape so lovely, and his limbs so strong,
Confirm our hopes we shall obey him long.
No sooner has he touched the flying ball,
But 'tis already more than half the Mall;
And such a fury from his arm has got,
As from a smoking culverin[7] 'twere shot.
  Near this my Muse, what most delights her, sees
A living gallery of aged trees;
Bold sons of earth that thrust their arms so high,

5. Thetis, a sea nymph, was the mother of Achilles.
6. Simon Peter "saw heaven opened, and a certain vessel descending unto him, as it had been a great sheet knit at the four corners, and let down to the earth: Wherein were all manner of fourfooted beasts of the earth, and wild beasts, and creeping things, and fowls of the air" (Acts 10:11–12).
7. Cannon.

As if once more they would invade the sky.[8]
In such green palaces the first kings reigned,
Slept in their shades, and angels entertained;
With such old counsellors they did advise,
And, by frequenting sacred groves, grew wise.
Free from th'impediments of light and noise,
Man, thus retired, his nobler thoughts employs.
Here Charles contrives the ordering of his states,
Here he resolves his neighboring princes' fates;
What nation shall have peace, where war be made,
Determined is in this oraculous shade;[9]
The world, from India to the frozen north,
Concerned in what this solitude brings forth.
His fancy, objects from his view receives;
The prospect, thought and contemplation gives.
That seat of empire here salutes his eye,
To which three kingdoms[1] do themselves apply;
The structure by a prelate[2] raised, Whitehall,
Built with the fortune of Rome's capitol;
Both, disproportioned to the present state
Of their proud founders, were approved by Fate.
From hence he does that antique pile[3] behold
Where royal heads receive the sacred gold;
It gives them crowns, and does their ashes keep;
There made like gods, like mortals there they sleep,
Making the circle of their reign complete,
Those suns of empire; where they rise, they set.
When others fell, this, standing, did presage
The crown should triumph over popular rage;
Hard by that house[4] where all our ills were shaped,
Th'auspicious temple stood, and yet escaped.
So snow on Etna does unmelted lie,
Whence rolling flames and scattered cinders fly;
The distant country in the ruin shares
What falls from heaven the burning mountain spares.
Next, that capacious hall[5] he sees, the room
Where the whole nation does for justice come;
Under whose large roof flourishes the gown,
And judges grave, on high tribunals, frown.
Here, like the people's pastor he does go,
His flock subjected to his view below;[6]

8. Waller perhaps has in mind the revolt against the gods by the giants, earth's children, who "darted rocks and burning oaks at the sky" (Apollodorus, *Library*, I.vi.1).
9. I.e., grove where royal decisions, like the oracles' utterances in ancient times, are made.
1. I.e., England, Scotland, and Ireland.
2. I.e., Cardinal Wolsey (1472–1530), Lord Chancellor to Henry VIII.
3. I.e., Westminster Abbey.
4. I.e., the Houses of Parliament, within the precincts of the Palace of Westminster. The Commons met in Saint Stephen's Chapel; the Lords, in the Parliament Chamber. These buildings, save for Westminster Hall, were destroyed by fire in 1834.
5. I.e., Westminster Hall.
6. At the coronation of Charles II, a medal was struck representing the king as a shepherd tending his flock.

On which reflecting in his mighty mind,
No private passion does indulgence find;
The pleasures of his youth suspended are,
And made a sacrifice to public care.
Here, free from court compliances, he walks,
And with himself, his best adviser, talks;
How peaceful olive may his temples shade,
For mending laws, and for restoring trade;
Or how his brows may be with laurel charged,[7]
For nations conquered, and our bounds enlarged.
Of ancient prudence here he ruminates,
Of rising kingdoms, and of falling states;
What ruling arts gave great Augustus fame,
And how Alcides[8] purchased such a name.
His eyes, upon his native palace bent,
Close by, suggest a greater argument.
His thoughts rise higher, when he does reflect
On what the world may from that star[9] expect
Which at his birth appeared to let us see
Day, for his sake, could with the night agree;
A prince, on whom such different lights did smile,
Born the divided world to reconcile!
Whatever Heaven or high extracted blood
Could promise or foretell, he will make good;
Reform these nations, and improve them more
Than this fair park, from what it was before.

Of English Verse

Poets may boast, as safely vain,
Their work shall with the world remain;
Both, bound together, live or die,
The verses and the prophecy.

But who can hope his lines should long
Last in a daily changing tongue?
While they are new, envy prevails;
And as that dies, our language fails.

When architects have done their part,
The matter may betray their art;
Time, if we use ill-chosen stone,
Soon brings a well-built palace down.

7. I.e., crowned with the laurel garland, emblematic (in this context) of power and victory. In heraldry, to "charge" is to assume as an armorial bearing.
8. Hercules.
9. In 1630, as Charles I was returning, at midday, from Saint Paul's, after having given thanks for the birth of his son, the future Charles II, a star was widely reported to have been observed in the sky.

Poets that lasting marble seek
Must carve in Latin or in Greek;[1]
We write in sand, our language grows,
And, like the tide, our work o'erflows.

Chaucer his sense can only boast,
The glory of his numbers lost;[2]
Years have defaced his matchless strain,
And yet he did not sing in vain.

The beauties which adorned that age,
The shining subjects of his rage,
Hoping they should immortal prove,
Rewarded with success his love.

This was the generous poet's scope,
And all an English pen can hope,
To make the fair approve his flame,
That can so far extend their fame.

Verse, thus designed, has no ill fate
If it arrive but at the date
Of fading beauty; if it prove
But as long-lived as present love.

Of the Last Verses in the Book[3]

When we for age could neither read nor write,
The subject made us able to indite;
The soul, with nobler resolutions decked,
The body stooping, does herself erect.
No mortal parts are requisite to raise
Her that, unbodied, can her Maker praise.

The seas are quiet when the winds give o'er;
So, calm are we when passions are no more,
For then we know how vain it was to boast
Of fleeting things, so certain to be lost.
Clouds of affection from our younger eyes
Conceal that emptiness which age descries.

1. The traditional view that poetry written in Greek or (especially) Latin would survive that written in the vernacular tongues of Europe had been very generally abandoned by the end of the seventeenth century.
2. Chaucer's technical mastery of his medium was generally obscured throughout the sixteenth and seventeenth centuries, in part because of a failure to recognize the principles of Chaucerian pronunciation.
3. I.e., of the "Divine Poems," first published in 1685.

The soul's dark cottage, battered and decayed,
Lets in new light through chinks that time has made;
Stronger by weakness, wiser, men become,
As they draw near to their eternal home.
Leaving the old, both worlds at once they view,
That stand upon the threshold of the new.

—*Miratur Limen Olympi.*
Vergil.[4]

4. Cf. Vergil, *Eclogues*, v. 56: *Candidus insuetum miratur limen Olympi* ("Arrayed in dazzling white, he stands enraptured at Heaven's unfamiliar threshold").

John Milton

1608	Born in London (9 December), to John and Sara Milton.
1620 (?)	Begins studies at St. Paul's School.
1625	Admitted to Christ's College, Cambridge. Charles I succeeds to the throne.
1629	Receives the B.A. (March). Begins the "Nativity Ode" (25 December).
1632	Completes studies at Cambridge; receives the M.A., cum laude (July). "L'Allegro" and "Il Penseroso" composed around this time. "On Shakespeare" printed in the second folio of Shakespeare's plays.
1634	Milton's *Mask* performed at Ludlow Castle, Wales (29 September).
1637	Sara Milton dies (April); Edward King drowns (August). Milton composes "Lycidas" (November). Publishes his *Mask* with the help of Henry Lawes, who composed the music.
1638	"Lycidas" first published; Milton begins year-long European tour, spending most of the time in Italy.
1639	Returns to London and begins teaching his nephews at home.
1641–1642	Writes the antiprelatical tracts. Weds Mary Powell (summer 1642), who leaves after about a month. The civil war begins.
1643–1645	Publishes a series of divorce tracts. *Areopagitica* first published (November 1644). Cromwell decisively defeats royalist forces at Naseby (June 1645). Mary Powell returns (summer 1645). *Poems* registered for publication (actually published, January 1646).
1646	First child, Anne, born (July).
1647	John Milton, Sr., dies (March).
1648	Second child, Mary, born (October).
1649	Charles I executed (30 January); Milton publishes *Tenure of Kings and Magistrates* (February). Appointed Secretary for Foreign Tongues (March). Publishes *Eikonoklastes* (October).
1651	Publishes *Defense of the English People* in Latin, defending the regicide of Charles I (March). Third child, John, born (March).
1652	Becomes totally blind (February). Fourth child, Deborah, born (2 May); wife, Mary, dies (5 May). Son, John, dies (June).
1653	Recommends that the government make Andrew Marvell his assistant.

1656	Marries Katherine Woodcock (November).
1657	Fifth child, Katherine, born (October).
1658	Wife, Katherine, dies (February); daughter Katherine dies (March).
1659	*Eikonoklastes* and *Defense of the English People* burned by the London hangman (27 June). Arrested and imprisoned (October); released (December).
1660	Restoration of Charles II (May).
1663	Marries Elizabeth Minshull (February).
1667	Publishes *Paradise Lost* (in ten books).
1671	Publishes *Paradise Regained* and *Samson Agonistes* together.
1674	Publishes second edition of *Paradise Lost* (in twelve books). Dies (November).

FROM *POEMS* (1645)

On the Morning of Christ's Nativity[1]

I

This is the month, and this the happy morn[2]
Wherein the Son of Heav'n's eternal King,
Of wedded maid, and virgin mother born,
Our great redemption from above did bring;
For so the holy sages[3] once did sing,
 That he our deadly forfeit[4] should release,
And with his Father work us a perpetual peace.

II

That glorious form, that light unsufferable,
And that far-beaming blaze of Majesty,
Wherewith he wont at Heav'n's high council table,
To sit the midst of trinal unity,[5]
He laid aside; and here with us to be,
 Forsook the courts of everlasting day,
And chose with us a darksome house of mortal clay.[6]

III

Say Heav'nly Muse, shall not thy sacred vein[7]
Afford a present to the infant God?
Hast thou no verse, no hymn, or solemn strain,
To welcome him to this his new abode,
Now while the heav'n by the sun's team untrod,[8]
 Hath took no print of the approaching light,
And all the spangled host keep watch in squadrons bright?

IV

See how from far upon the eastern road
The star-led wizards haste with odors sweet:[9]
O run, prevent[1] them with thy humble ode,

1. Although not the earliest of Milton's English poems, this ode appears first in the 1645 edition of his collected poetry. More than other early works, it anticipates Milton's late masterpieces in its explicitly Christian topic and high classical form. Cf. Jonson's "Hymn on the Nativity of My Savior," p. 120; Herbert's "Christmas," p. 256; and Crashaw's "In the Holy Nativity of Our Lord God: A Hymn Sung as by the Shepherds," p. 459.
2. Milton informed his friend Charles Diodati that the poem was begun on Christmas morning, 1629.
3. Biblical prophets.
4. Death, the penalty of sin.
5. A reference to Christ's middle position in the Trinity, an orthodox doctrine Milton would later reject.
6. I.e., a body of flesh and blood.
7. Milton refers to his source of inspiration as heavenly, and her characteristic theme as sacred, to distinguish her from the Muses of classical mythology.
8. In classical myth, a team of horses pulls the chariot of the sun across the sky.
9. The Magi, astrologers from the east whose gifts for the infant Jesus include aromatic frankincense and myrrh (Matthew 2:11).
1. Arrive before.

And lay it lowly at his blessèd feet;
Have thou the honor first, thy Lord to greet,
And join thy voice unto the angel choir,
From out his secret altar touched with hallowed fire.[2]

THE HYMN

I

It was the winter wild,
While the Heav'n-born-child,
All meanly wrapped in the rude manger lies;
Nature in awe to him
Had doffed her gaudy trim
With her great master so to sympathize:
It was no season then for her
To wanton with the sun, her lusty paramour.

II

Only with speeches fair
She woos the gentle air
To hide her guilty front[3] with innocent snow,
And on her naked shame,
Pollute with sinful blame,
The saintly veil of maiden white to throw,
Confounded, that her maker's eyes
Should look so near upon her foul deformities.

III

But he her fears to cease,
Sent down the meek-eyed Peace;
She crowned with olive green, came softly sliding
Down through the turning sphere[4]
His ready harbinger,
With turtle[5] wing the amorous clouds dividing,
And waving wide her myrtle[6] wand,
She strikes a universal peace through sea and land.

IV

No war, or battle's sound
Was heard the world around:
The idle spear and shield were high up hung,
The hookèd chariot[7] stood
Unstained with hostile blood,

2. I.e., the speaker of the ode is purified by fire from God's holy altar; cf. Isaiah 6:6–7.
3. Face.
4. The outermost sphere of the Ptolemaic cosmos imparted motion to the rest. Earth stood at the stationary center.
5. Turtle dove, emblematic of constant love and, with an olive branch (as in line 47), of peace.
6. The myrtle was sacred to Venus, goddess of love.
7. War chariot armed with hooks (sickles).

The trumpet spake not to the armèd throng,
And kings sat still with awful[8] eye,
As if they surely knew their sov'reign Lord was by.

V

But peaceful was the night
Wherein the Prince of Light
His reign of peace upon the earth began:
The winds with wonder whist,[9]
Smoothly the waters kissed,
Whispering new joys to the mild ocean,
Who now hath quite forgot to rave,
While birds of calm sit brooding on the charmèd wave.[1]

VI

The Stars with deep amaze
Stand fixed in steadfast gaze,
Bending one way their precious influence,[2]
And will not take their flight,
For all the morning light,
Or Lucifer[3] that often warned them thence;
But in their glimmering orbs did glow,
Until their Lord himself bespake, and bid them go.

VII

And though the shady gloom
Had given day her room,
The Sun himself withheld his wonted speed,
And hid his head for shame,
As his inferior flame,
The new-enlightened world no more should need;
He saw a greater sun appear
Than his bright throne, or burning axletree could bear.

VIII

The shepherds on the lawn,
Or ere the point of dawn,
Sat simply chatting in a rustic row;
Full little thought they then,
That the mighty Pan[4]
Was kindly[5] come to live with them below;

8. Awestruck.
9. Hushed, silent.
1. Halcyons ("bird of calm") were anciently supposed to charm midwinter seas to a calm so that they might brood quietly upon the eggs in their floating nests.
2. An invisible fluid thought by astrologers to flow down from the stars and influence the world.
3. The morning star.
4. Classical god of shepherds, often associated with Christ by Renaissance poets.
5. As one of their kind; sympathetically.

Perhaps their loves, or else their sheep,
Was all that did their silly[6] thoughts so busy keep.

IX

When such music sweet
Their hearts and ears did greet,
As never was by mortal finger struck,
Divinely-warbled voice
Answering the stringèd noise,
As all their souls in blissful rapture took:
The air such pleasure loth to lose,
With thousand echoes still prolongs each heav'nly close.[7]

X

Nature that heard such sound
Beneath the hollow round
Of Cynthia's seat, the airy region thrilling,[8]
Now was almost won
To think her part was done,
And that her reign had here its last fulfilling;
She knew such harmony alone
Could hold all heav'n and earth in happier union.

XI

At last surrounds their sight
A globe[9] of circular light,
That with long beams the shame-faced Night arrayed;
The helmèd Cherubim
And sworded Seraphim,
Are seen in glittering ranks with wings displayed,
Harping in loud and solemn choir,
With unexpressive[1] notes to Heav'n's new-born heir.

XII

Such music (as 'tis said)
Before was never made,
But when of old the sons of morning sung,[2]
While the Creator great
His constellations set,
And the well-balanced world on hinges[3] hung,

6. Simple and rustic, unlearned.
7. Conclusion of a strain of music, cadence.
8. I.e., the entire atmosphere, believed to extend to the sphere of the moon ("the hollow round / Of Cynthia's seat"), was vibrant with the music.
9. As in Latin usage (*globus*), "globe" here means "troops in compact formation" (the Cherubim and Seraphim) as well as "sphere."
1. Beyond description.
2. Cf. Job 38:4–8.
3. The two poles about which the world revolves, and, by extension, the four cardinal points: east, west, north, and south.

And cast the dark foundations deep,
And bid the welt'ring waves their oozy channel keep.

XIII

Ring out, ye crystal spheres,[4]
Once bless our human ears,
(If ye have power to touch our senses so)
And let your silver chime
Move in melodious time,
And let the base[5] of Heav'n's deep organ blow,
And with your ninefold harmony
Make up full consort to th'angelic symphony.

XIV

For if such holy song
Enwrap our fancy long,
Time will run back, and fetch the age of gold,[6]
And speckled Vanity
Will sicken soon and die,
And lep'rous Sin will melt from earthly mold,
And Hell itself will pass away,
And leave her dolorous mansions to the peering day.

XV

Yea Truth and Justice then
Will down return to men,[7]
Orbed in a rainbow; and, like glories wearing,
Mercy will sit between,[8]
Throned in celestial sheen,
With radiant feet the tissued clouds down steering,
And Heav'n as at some festival,
Will open wide the gates of her high palace hall.

XVI

But wisest Fate says no,
This must not yet be so,
The babe lies yet in smiling infancy,
That on the bitter cross

4. The nine spheres of the Ptolemaic cosmos were thought to correspond to the nine angelic hierarchies. Each sphere rang with its own clear and gentle ("silver") sound, and together they produced a perfect harmony, inaudible to fallen humanity. Milton imagines the angels and the spheres making music together in full concert ("consort").
5. The earth itself, at the bottom of the geocentric cosmos, was cut off from the celestial harmony after the Fall.
6. The first age of classical myth, a time of blissful innocence and plenty.
7. According to classical myth, Astraea, goddess of justice, lived among men during the golden age but departed when human society became increasingly wicked.
8. For lines 143–144 the 1645 text instead has "Th'enamelled arras of the rainbow wearing / And Mercy set between." The lines were revised for the 1673 edition. Peace, Truth, Justice, and Mercy had long been allegorized as the four daughters of God, with Justice and Mercy often represented as being at odds over the fate of fallen humanity.

Must redeem our loss;
So both himself and us to glorify:
Yet first to those ychained[9] in sleep,
The wakeful[1] trump of doom must thunder through the deep.

XVII

With such a horrid clang
As on Mount Sinai rang
While the red fire, and smold'ring[2] clouds out brake:
The agèd earth aghast
With terror of that blast,
Shall from the surface to the center shake;
When at the world's last session,
The dreadful judge in middle air shall spread his throne.

XVIII

And then at last our bliss
Full and perfect is,
But now begins; for from this happy day
Th' old Dragon underground
In straiter limits bound,
Not half so far casts his usurpèd sway,
And wroth to see his kingdom fail,
Swinges[3] the scaly horror of his folded tail.

XIX

The Oracles are dumb,[4]
No voice or hideous hum
Runs through the archèd roof in words deceiving.
Apollo from his shrine
Can no more divine,
With hollow shriek the steep of Delphos leaving.[5]
No nightly trance, or breathèd spell,
Inspires the pale-eyed priest from the prophetic cell.

XX

The lonely mountains o'er,
And the resounding shore,
A voice of weeping heard, and loud lament;

9. Archaic form of the past participle of *chain*.
1. Rousing.
2. Suffocating (the only usage current in Milton's century). The scriptural episode to which Milton compares the apocalypse occurs when Moses receives the law on Mount Sinai (Exodus 19:16; cf. Hebrews 12).
3. Moves as a lash. The "Dragon" is Satan, per Revelation 20:2. Christ's advent was supposed to mitigate the worldly authority he "usurped" at the Fall.
4. Citing Plutarch's *Obsolescence of the Oracles*, Christians held that pagan oracles fell silent when the authentic Word of God had become flesh.
5. The classical god of prophecy, Apollo had his most celebrated shrine near the city of Delphi ("Delphos"), on the steep southern slope of Mount Parnassus.

From haunted spring, and dale
Edged with poplar pale,
The parting Genius[6] is with sighing sent;
With flow'r-inwoven tresses torn
The Nymphs in twilight shade of tangled thickets mourn.[7]

XXI

In consecrated earth,
And on the holy hearth,
The Lars and Lemures[8] moan with midnight plaint;
In urns, and altars round,
A drear and dying sound
Affrights the flamens at their service quaint;[9]
And the chill marble seems to sweat,
While each peculiar power forgoes his wonted seat.

XXII

Peor and Baälim[1]
Forsake their temples dim,
With that twice-battered god of Palestine,[2]
And moonèd Ashtaroth,[3]
Heav'n's queen and mother both,
Now sits not girt with tapers' holy shine,
The Libyc Hammon[4] shrinks his horn,
In vain the Tyrian maids their wounded Thammuz mourn.[5]

XXIII

And sullen Moloch[6] fled,
Hath left in shadows dread,
His burning idol all of blackest hue;
In vain with cymbals' ring,
They call the grisly king,
In dismal dance about the furnace blue;
The brutish gods of Nile as fast,
Isis and Orus, and the dog Anubis haste.[7]

6. Spirit or guardian deity of a particular place. Cf. "Lycidas," line 183, p. 403.
7. Classically, mourning is a characteristic action of nymphs, and a convention of such mourning is to tear hair. Here, however, the nymphs mourn their own passing.
8. Lars (or Lares) were ghosts of ancestors revered at the hearth as household gods; Lemures wandered by night and troubled the living.
9. As priests devoted to specific deities, flamens performed elaborate ("quaint") rituals.
1. Peor was a local (Moabite) manifestation of Baäl (pl. "Baälim"), a Phoenician sun god whose worship became widespread and diverse in the ancient Middle East. In *Paradise Lost*, lines 457–466, Milton will expand on this catalogue of pagan gods (XXII–XXIV).
2. Dagon, god of the Philistines whose image is twice cast down before the ark of God.
3. Plural of Ashtareth, Phoenician moon goddess (Syrian Astarté). Cf. Jeremiah 7:18.
4. Libyan version of the ram-headed (hence horned) Egyptian god, Ammon.
5. Phoenician god (hence "Tyrian"), original of Greek Adonis. Cf. Ezekiel 8:14.
6. Ammonite brass idol, hollow and filled with fire. The Hebrews sacrificed children on this furnace-idol as priests drowned out the victims' screams with "cymbals' ring." Cf. 1 Kings 11:7.
7. Egyptian gods, "brutish" because worshipped in the shapes of animals. Isis, wife and sister to Osiris, was represented with a cow's horns. Horus (Orus), son of Isis and Osiris, had a hawk's head. Anubis, another son of Osiris, bore the head of a jackal (mistaken for a dog by the Greeks).

XXIV

Nor is Osiris[8] seen
In Memphian grove, or green,
  Trampling the unshow'red grass with lowings loud:
Nor can he be at rest
Within his sacred chest,[9]
  Naught but profoundest Hell can be his shroud;
In vain with timbrelled[1] anthems dark
The sable-stolèd sorcerers bear his worshipped ark.

XXV

He feels from Judah's land
The dreaded infant's hand,
  The rays of Bethlehem blind his dusky eyne;
Nor all the gods beside,
Longer dare abide,
  Not Typhon huge ending in snaky twine:[2]
Our babe to show his Godhead true,
Can in his swaddling bands control the damnèd crew.

XXVI

So when the Sun in bed,
Curtained with cloudy red,
  Pillows his chin upon an orient wave,
The flocking shadows pale,
Troop to th'infernal jail,
  Each fettered ghost slips to his several grave,
And the yellow-skirted fays
Fly after the Night-steeds, leaving their moon-loved maze.[3]

XXVII

But see the virgin blest,
Hath laid her babe to rest.
  Time is our tedious song should here have ending:
Heav'n's youngest teemèd star,
Hath fixed her polished car,[4]
  Her sleeping Lord with handmaid lamp attending:
And all about the courtly stable,
Bright-harnessed angels sit in order serviceable.[5]

8. Osiris, worshiped in the form of a bull (hence his "lowings loud"). "Memphian" refers to the ancient Egyptian capital of Memphis.
9. Osiris is lured into a chest and drowned by his brother Set (later identified with Typhon; see line 226).
1. Accompanied by timbrels, an ancient kind of drum or tambourine.
2. Typhon, with whom the Greeks identified Set, was monstrously serpentine.
3. I.e., the fairies ("yellow-skirted fays") follow the horses of the night in fleeing the dawn, leaving only the mazy imprint of their nocturnal dancing.
4. I.e., heaven's newest star has assumed a stationary position over the stable; cf. Matthew 2:9. "Polished car" is conventional poetic diction meaning "shining chariot."
5. I.e., clad in bright armor, the angels sit in an order expressing their readiness to serve.

On Time[6]

Fly envious Time, till thou run out thy race,
Call on the lazy leaden-stepping hours,
Whose speed is but the heavy plummet's pace;[7]
And glut thy self with what thy womb[8] devours,
Which is no more than what is false and vain,
And merely mortal dross;
So little is our loss,
So little is thy gain.
For when as each thing bad thou hast entombed,
And last of all, thy greedy self consumed,
Then long eternity shall greet our bliss
With an individual[9] kiss;
And joy shall overtake us as a flood,
When everything that is sincerely good
And perfectly divine,
With Truth, and Peace, and Love shall ever shine
About the supreme throne
Of him, t'whose happy-making sight[1] alone,
When once our Heav'nly-guided soul shall climb,
Then all this earthy grossness quit,
Attired with stars, we shall forever sit,
  Triumphing over Death, and Chance, and thee, O Time.

On Shakespeare[2]

What needs my Shakespeare for his honored bones,
The labor of an age in pilèd stones,
Or that his hallowed relics should be hid
Under a star-ypointing[3] pyramid?
Dear son of Memory,[4] great heir of Fame,
What need'st thou such weak witness of thy name?
Thou in our wonder and astonishment
Hast built thyself a livelong[5] monument.

6. In Milton's manuscript, the heading "To be set on a clock case" is deleted, and "On Time" written above it.
7. Early clocks were driven by the regulated descent of a lead-weighted line.
8. Stomach.
9. Indivisible and so everlasting.
1. I.e., the beatific vision (of God's face in heaven).
2. The first of Milton's poems to be printed, "On Shakespeare" appears anonymously in the Second Folio of Shakespeare's plays (1632) as "An Epitaph on the Admirable Dramatic Poet W. Shakespeare." Milton's connection with those responsible for the Second Folio remains unknown, but in retrospect it seems proper that England's greatest nondramatic poet should begin his public career with a tribute to her greatest dramatic poet.
3. I.e., pointing to the stars. An archaism popularized by Spenser, the y prefix is a metrically handy vestige of Middle English. Usually joined to past participles (cf. "Nativity Ode," line 155, "L'Allegro," line 12), here it is used with the present.
4. In classical myth, the goddess of Memory (Mnemosyne) is mother of the Muses. Milton thus makes Shakespeare the Muses' brother.
5. Milton's nonce use of "livelong" to mean "durable" underscores Shakespeare's *living* presence. The 1632 Folio has "lasting."

For whilst to th'shame of slow-endeavoring art,
Thy easy numbers[6] flow, and that[7] each heart[8]
Hath from the leaves of thy unvalued[9] book
Those Delphic[1] lines with deep impression took,
Then thou our fancy of itself bereaving,
Dost make us marble[2] with too much conceiving;
And so sepulchered in such pomp dost lie,
That kings for such a tomb would wish to die.

L'Allegro[3]

Hence loathèd Melancholy
  Of Cerberus, and blackest Midnight born,[4]
In Stygian[5] cave forlorn
  'Mongst horrid shapes, and shrieks, and sights unholy,
Find out some uncouth[6] cell,
  Where brooding Darkness spreads his jealous wings,
And the night-raven[7] sings;
  There under ebon shades, and low-browed rocks,
As ragged as thy locks,
  In dark Cimmerian[8] desert ever dwell.
But come thou goddess fair and free,
In Heav'n yclept Euphrosyne,[9]
And by men, heart-easing Mirth,
Whom lovely Venus at a birth
With two sister Graces more
To ivy-crownèd Bacchus bore;[1]
Or whether (as some sager sing)
The frolic wind that breathes the spring,
Zephyr with Aurora playing,[2]

6. Rhythmic verses.
7. "That" is used in substitution for "whilst."
8. The 1632 version has "part."
9. Invaluable. "Not valued" was also a current sense (so used by Shakespeare).
1. Oracular, like the oracle at Delphi.
2. Stone used for tombs and tombstones. Cf. "Il Penseroso," line 42, p. 393.
3. "L'Allegro" (Italian for "the cheerful man") and "Il Penseroso" ("the pensive man") are companion poems: the first chronicles typical daily pursuits inspired by Mirth; the second, those inspired by Melancholy. Highly original poems, their deceptive simplicity has been often rather than successfully imitated. One of Milton's less recognized triumphs as a crafter of verses is his mastery of iambic tetrameter couplets—the predominant lyric meter of the age, fully and variously exploited in these poems.
4. Melancholy here descends from the guard dog of hell (Cerberus) and Midnight (the darkest hour). The infernal genealogy distinguishes her from the pensive disposition celebrated in "Il Penseroso," lines 22–30, pp. 392–393.
5. In the region of the infernal river Styx, where, according to Vergil, the cave of Cerberus resounds with shrieks of dead children's souls (*Aeneid* VI.418).
6. Unknown, desolate.
7. A bird (not a raven) supposed to croak or cry at night, of evil omen.
8. Homer places the Cimmerians on the far shore of the western ocean, where the sun does not shine (*Odyssey* XI.13–22).
9. A common archaism, "yclept" means "called." Euphrosyne (Greek for mirth) is one of the three Graces, divine attendants on Aphrodite (Latin Venus).
1. Different writers assigned the Graces different parents, among them Bacchus, god of wine, and Venus, goddess of love. One of the Graces' good effects on society was to moderate the exciting effects of wine.
2. Milton's own alternative genealogy identifies Mirth's parents as the god of the west wind (Zephyr) and the goddess of the dawn (Aurora).

As he met her once a-Maying.
There on beds of violets blue,
And fresh-blown roses washed in dew,
Filled her with thee a daughter fair,
So buxom, blithe, and debonair.[3]
Haste thee nymph, and bring with thee
Jest and youthful Jollity,
Quips and Cranks,[4] and wanton Wiles,
Nods, and Becks, and wreathèd Smiles,
Such as hang on Hebe's[5] cheek,
And love to live in dimple sleek;
Sport that wrinkled Care derides,
And Laughter holding both his sides.
Come, and trip it as ye go[6]
On the light fantastic[7] toe,
And in thy right hand lead with thee,
The mountain nymph, sweet Liberty,
And if I give thee honor due,
Mirth, admit me of thy crew
To live with her, and live with thee,
In unreprovèd[8] pleasures free;
To hear the lark begin his flight,
And singing startle the dull night,
From his watch-tower in the skies,
Till the dappled dawn doth rise;
Then to come in spite of[9] sorrow,
And at my window bid good morrow,
Through the sweet-briar, or the vine,
Or the twisted eglantine.
While the cock with lively din,
Scatters the rear of darkness thin,
And to the stack, or the barn door,
Stoutly struts his dames before,
Oft list'ning how the hounds and horn,
Cheerly rouse the slumb'ring morn,
From the side of some hoar hill,
Through the high wood echoing shrill.
Some time walking not unseen
By hedge-row elms, on hillocks green,
Right against the eastern gate,
Where the great sun begins his state,[1]
Robed in flames, and amber light,

3. *Buxom*: jolly and compliant; *debonair*: affable (with a play on "of good air").
4. Witty verbal twists of form and meaning.
5. Greek goddess of youth, she serves beverages on Olympus.
6. I.e., dance your way.
7. Moving whimsically, fancifully.
8. Irreprovable, blameless. This couplet alludes distinctly to Marlowe's "The Passionate Shepherd to His Love."
9. In defiance of. Opinion is divided on whether L'Allegro or the lark comes to the window. The series of infinitives preceding "to come" suggests that L'Allegro is still petitioning Mirth. Also, skylarks do not as a rule announce themselves at windows.
1. Procession, official tour.

The clouds in thousand liveries dight.[2]
While the plowman near at hand,
Whistles o'er the furrowed land,
And the milkmaid singeth blithe,
And the mower whets his scythe,
And every shepherd tells his tale[3]
Under the hawthorn in the dale.
Straight mine eye hath caught new pleasures
Whilst the landscape round it measures,
Russet lawns, and fallows gray,
Where the nibbling flocks do stray,
Mountains on whose barren breast
The laboring clouds do often rest:
Meadows trim with daisies pied,
Shallow brooks, and rivers wide.
Towers and battlements it sees
Bosomed high in tufted trees,
Where perhaps some beauty lies,
The cynosure[4] of neighboring eyes.
Hard by, a cottage chimney smokes,
From betwixt two agèd oaks,
Where Corydon and Thyrsis[5] met,
Are at their savory dinner set
Of herbs, and other country messes,
Which the neat-handed Phyllis dresses;
And then in haste her bower she leaves,
With Thestylis to bind the sheaves;
Or if the earlier season lead
To the tanned haycock in the mead,
Sometimes with secure[6] delight
The upland hamlets will invite,
When the merry bells ring round,
And the jocund rebecks[7] sound
To many a youth, and many a maid,
Dancing in the checkered shade;
And young and old come forth to play
On a sunshine holiday,
Till the livelong daylight fail,
Then to the spicy nut-brown ale,
With stories told of many a feat,
How fairy Mab the junkets[8] atc,

2. I.e., arrayed in a thousand colors, as attendants on a prince would wear standard uniforms of distinctive color.
3. Tallies his sheep or recounts his story.
4. The Little Bear, the constellation of the polestar (by which mariners navigated); thus, something that attracts attention.
5. Traditional pastoral names, like Phyllis and Thestylis (lines 86–88).
6. Carefree.
7. Three-stringed fiddles.
8. "Mab" is Queen of the Fairies; "junkets" are cream cheeses or other cream-based dishes. In Ben Jonson's masque "The Satyr" (1603), Mab is introduced as "the Mistress Fairy / That doth nightly rob the dairy / . . . / She that pinches country wenches / If they rub not clean their benches."

She[9] was pinched, and pulled she said,
And he by friar's lantern led,
Tells how the drudging goblin sweat,
To earn his cream-bowl duly set,
When in one night, ere glimpse of morn,
His shadowy flail hath threshed the corn
That ten day-laborers could not end,
Then lies him down the lubber fiend,[1]
And stretched out all the chimney's length,
Basks at the fire his hairy strength;
And crop-full[2] out of doors he flings,
Ere the first cock his matin rings.
Thus done the tales, to bed they creep,
By whispering winds soon lulled asleep.
Towered cities please us then,
And the busy hum of men,
Where throngs of knights and barons bold,
In weeds of peace high triumphs hold,[3]
With store of ladies, whose bright eyes
Rain influence,[4] and judge the prize
Of wit, or arms, while both contend
To win her grace, whom all commend.
There let Hymen oft appear
In saffron robe, with taper clear,[5]
And pomp, and feast, and revelry,
With mask, and antique pageantry,
Such sights as youthful poets dream
On summer eves by haunted stream.
Then to the well-trod stage anon,
If Jonson's learnèd sock be on,[6]
Or sweetest Shakespeare, Fancy's child,
Warble his native wood-notes wild.
And ever against eating cares,[7]
Lap me in soft Lydian airs,[8]
Married to immortal verse
Such as the meeting soul may pierce
In notes, with many a winding bout[9]

9. A woman telling her supernatural tale to the group, just as, in the next line, "he" is a man telling his. *Friar's lantern*: an *ignis fatuus*, or will-o'-the-wisp; today it might be called a UFO.
1. A "lubber" is an inferior household servant, a drudge. Here the "lubber" is a supernatural agent ("goblin" or "fiend") who for a bowl of cream (line 106) performs prodigious farmwork by night and then lies by the fire. Milton in this passage may have in mind Shakespeare's Puck as described in *A Midsummer Night's Dream* II.i.32–41.
2. Entirely full (with cream), to the top.
3. I.e., in peacetime clothing (no armor) put on stately shows or pageants.
4. Love poets often compared ladies' eyes to stars. Astrologically, stars pour down "influence," an invisible but potent fluid that affects everything in the world. Cf. "Nativity Ode," line 71, p. 381.
5. "Hymen" is the marriage god, routinely depicted in a "saffron robe" and bearing a torch or candle ("taper"). When her taper burns "clear," without smoke, it bodes well.
6. The low-heeled shoe worn by Greek comic actors symbolizes the comedies of Jonson, deeply informed with classical learning. In contrast, Shakespeare is represented as a natural genius of the imagination (cf. "On Shakespeare," lines 9–14, p. 388).
7. "Eating cares" translates Horace's *curas edacis* (*Odes* 2.11.18).
8. Lydian music was considered soft and relaxed (and so unfit for warriors—Plato, *Republic* 3.398–399).
9. A turn or round.

Of linkèd sweetness long drawn out,
With wanton heed, and giddy cunning,
The melting voice through mazes running;
Untwisting all the chains that tie
The hidden soul of harmony;
That Orpheus' self may heave his head
From golden slumber on a bed
Of heaped Elysian flowers, and hear
Such strains as would have won the ear
Of Pluto, to have quite set free
His half-regained Eurydice.[1]
These delights, if thou canst give,
Mirth with thee, I mean to live.[2]

Il Penseroso

Hence vain deluding joys,
The brood of Folly without father bred,[3]
How little you bestead,[4]
Or fill the fixèd mind with all your toys;
Dwell in some idle brain,
And fancies fond[5] with gaudy shapes possess,
As thick and numberless
As the gay motes that people the sunbeams,
Or likest hovering dreams
The fickle pensioners of Morpheus' train.[6]
But hail thou goddess, sage and holy,
Hail divinest Melancholy,
Whose saintly visage is too bright
To hit the sense of human sight;
And therefore to our weaker view,
O'erlaid with black, staid Wisdom's hue.
Black, but such as in esteem,
Prince Memnon's sister[7] might beseem,
Or that starred Ethiop queen that strove
To set her beauty's praise above
The sea nymphs, and their powers offended.[8]
Yet thou art higher far descended,

1. Moved by Orpheus's music, Pluto frees Eurydice (four syllables) from his realm on the condition that Orpheus not look back at her as they depart. At the brink of the world of the living, he glances back and loses her. Cf. "Il Penseroso," lines 105–108, p. 395. After his death, Orpheus goes to Elysium; hence the flowers in line 147.
2. Another allusion to Marlowe's "Passionate Shepherd" (see above, lines 39–40).
3. The poem begins, like "L'Allegro," by exorcizing a scandalous misrepresentation of its subject's opposite. Mirth is not even named (cf. "L'Allegro," line 1, p. 388).
4. Profit, satisfy.
5. Imaginations that are weak and foolish.
6. Dependents of Morpheus, god of dreams.
7. Himera (Greek daylight) is the beautiful sister of the handsome Ethiopian king, Memnon (a son of Aurora, and thus, by one lineage, half brother to Mirth).
8. Cassiopeia boasted herself more beautiful than the Nereids (sea nymphs), who then arranged for a sea monster to afflict her realm. At her death, she was transformed into a constellation near the polestar or "cynosure" ("L'Allegro," line 80, p. 390).

Thee bright-haired Vesta long of yore,
To solitary Saturn bore;
His daughter she (in Saturn's reign,
Such mixture was not held a stain);[9]
Oft in glimmering bow'rs, and glades
He met her, and in secret shades
Of woody Ida's inmost grove,
While yet there was no fear of Jove.
Come pensive nun, devout and pure,
Sober, steadfast, and demure,
All in a robe of darkest grain,[1]
Flowing with majestic train,
And sable stole of cypress lawn,[2]
Over thy decent shoulders drawn.
Come, but keep thy wonted state,
With even step, and musing gait,
And looks commercing with the skies,
Thy rapt soul sitting in thine eyes:
There held in holy passion still,
Forget thyself to marble,[3] till
With a sad leaden downward cast,[4]
Thou fix them on the earth as fast.
And join with thee calm Peace, and Quiet,
Spare Fast, that oft with gods doth diet,
And hears the Muses in a ring,
Ay round about Jove's altar sing.
And add to these retired Leisure,
That in trim gardens takes his pleasure;
But first, and chiefest, with thee bring,
Him that yon soars on golden wing,
Guiding the fiery-wheelèd throne,
The Cherub Contemplatïon,[5]
And the mute Silence hist[6] along,
'Less Philomel[7] will deign a song,
In her sweetest, saddest plight,
Smoothing the rugged brow of Night,
While Cynthia checks her dragon yoke,[8]
Gently o'er th'accustomed oak;
Sweet bird that shunn'st the noise of folly,
Most musical, most melancholy!

9. The virgin Vesta is Roman goddess of the hearth (its sacred fire, rather). Saturn ruled from Crete's Mount Ida until, in fulfillment of prophecy, Jove overthrew him (cf. lines 29–30). Her incestuous conception of Melancholy is Milton's invention.
1. Dye, color.
2. Black ("sable") linen so fine as to be transparent, like crape; used for mourning.
3. I.e., to such an extent that you are motionless as a statue (cf. "On Shakespeare," line 14, p. 388).
4. Lead is associated with Saturn, melancholy, and motion downward (cf. "On Time," lines 2–3, p. 387), which is where this daughter of Saturn now casts her solemn ("sad") eyes.
5. The cherubim (cherub is singular) constitute the order of angels traditionally thought to be devoted to contemplation of God. Cf. the account of God's chariot in Ezekiel 1.
6. The interjection "hist" ("hush") is here used as a verb meaning "bring without sound."
7. Philomela was raped and had her tongue torn out by her brother-in-law. She was metamorphosed into the nightingale, noted for its melodious nocturnal song.
8. Goddess of the moon, Cynthia was associated with Hecate, whose chariot was drawn by dragons.

Thee chantress oft the woods among,
I woo to hear thy evensong;
And missing thee, I walk unseen
On the dry smooth-shaven green,
To behold the wand'ring moon,
Riding near her highest noon,
Like one that had been led astray
Through the heav'n's wide pathless way;
And oft, as if her head she bowed,
Stooping through a fleecy cloud.
Oft on a plat of rising ground,
I hear the far-off curfew sound,
Over some wide-watered shore,
Swinging slow with sullen roar;[9]
Or if the air will not permit,
Some still removèd place will fit,
Where glowing embers through the room
Teach light to counterfeit a gloom,
Far from all resort of mirth,
Save the cricket on the hearth,
Or the bellman's drowsy charm,
To bless the doors from nightly harm:[1]
Or let my lamp at midnight hour,
Be seen in some high lonely tow'r,
Where I may oft outwatch the Bear,[2]
With thrice-great Hermes,[3] or unsphere
The spirit of Plato[4] to unfold
What worlds, or what vast regions hold
The immortal mind that hath forsook
Her mansion in this fleshly nook:
And of those daemons that are found
In fire, air, flood, or under ground,
Whose power hath a true consent
With planet, or with element.[5]
Sometime let gorgeous Tragedy
In sceptered pall[6] come sweeping by,
Presenting Thebes, or Pelops' line,
Or the tale of Troy divine.[7]
Or what (though rare) of later age,
Ennobled hath the buskined[8] stage.
But, O sad virgin, that thy power

9. The lonely, solemn sound of the curfew bell.
1. Cf. Herrick, "The Bellman," p. 223.
2. I.e., stay awake all night. The constellation of the Great Bear never sets.
3. Hermes Trismegistus, supposed author of the *Hermetica*, esoteric works of Neoplatonism, including the magical arts.
4. I.e., summon Plato's ghost from the heavenly sphere in which it resides.
5. Daemons (also spelled demons) are intermediary spirits that in Neoplatonic philosophy inhabit and have sympathetic connection ("consent") with the elements and planets.
6. Regal robe. Classical tragedies concern kings and other noble heroes.
7. The great Greek tragedians all set works in the city of Thebes. Descendents of Pelops (e.g., Agamemnon, Orestes, and Electra) are among the most famous tragic characters. Troy was the site of tragedies by Sophocles and Euripides.
8. The buskin is a high boot worn by Greek tragic actors. Cf. "L'Allegro," line 132, p. 391.

Might raise Musaeus[9] from his bower,
Or bid the soul of Orpheus sing
Such notes as warbled to the string,
Drew iron tears down Pluto's cheek,
And made Hell grant what love did seek.[1]
Or call up him that left half-told[2]
The story of Cambuscan bold,
Of Camball, and of Algarsife,
And who had Canace to wife,
That owned the virtuous ring and glass,
And of the wondrous horse of brass,
On which the Tartar king did ride;
And if aught else, great bards beside,
In sage and solemn tunes have sung,
Of tourneys and of trophies hung;
Of forests, and enchantments drear,
Where more is meant than meets the ear.[3]
Thus, Night, oft see me in thy pale career,
Till civil-suited Morn appear,
Not tricked and frounced[4] as she was wont,
With the Attic boy[5] to hunt,
But kerchiefed in a comely cloud,
While rocking winds are piping loud,
Or ushered with a shower still,
When the gust hath blown his fill,
Ending on the rustling leaves,
With minute[6] drops from off the eaves.
And when the Sun begins to fling
His flaring beams, me goddess bring
To archèd walks of twilight groves,
And shadows brown that Sylvan[7] loves
Of pine, or monumental oak,
Where the rude axe with heavèd stroke,
Was never heard the nymphs to daunt,
Or fright them from their hallowed haunt.
There in close covert by some brook,
Where no profaner eye may look,
Hide me from Day's garish eye,
While the bee with honeyed thigh,
That at her flow'ry work doth sing,
And the waters murmuring
With such consort as they keep,[8]

9. Legendary Greek poet, pupil of Orpheus.
1. I.e., a song like that which persuaded Pluto to return Eurydice to Orpheus. Cf. "L'Allegro," lines 148–150, p. 392, where the song desired would improve upon that potent music.
2. Chaucer's unfinished "Squire's Tale" features the characters mentioned in lines 110–115.
3. As in allegorical romance such as Spenser wrote.
4. In fancy clothes and done-up hair.
5. Cephalus, Greek prince beloved of the goddess of the dawn.
6. Editors are split between "minute" as "small drops" and as "drops that fall at minute intervals"; for metrical and thematic reasons, we think the interval of time is correct.
7. Sylvanus, Roman god of forests.
8. I.e., with such natural sounds as accompany the sound of the bee and the waters.

Entice the dewy-feathered Sleep;
And let some strange mysterious dream
Wave at his wings[9] in airy stream,
Of lively portraiture displayed,
Softly on my eyelids laid.
And as I wake, sweet music breathe
Above, about, or underneath,
Sent by some spirit to mortals good,
Or th'unseen Genius[1] of the wood.
But let my due feet never fail,
To walk the studious cloister's pale,[2]
And love the high embowèd[3] roof,
With antic pillars massy proof,[4]
And storied windows richly dight,[5]
Casting a dim religious light.
There let the pealing organ blow,
To the full-voiced choir below,
In service high, and anthems clear,
As may with sweetness, through mine ear,
Dissolve me into ecstasies,
And bring all Heav'n before mine eyes.
And may at last my weary age
Find out the peaceful hermitage,
The hairy gown and mossy cell,
Where I may sit and rightly spell,[6]
Of every star that heav'n doth show,
And every herb that sips the dew;
Till old experience do attain
To something like prophetic strain.
These pleasures Melancholy give,
And I with thee will choose to live.

Sonnet 7[7]

How soon hath Time, the subtle thief of youth,
Stol'n on his wing my three and twentieth year!
My hasting days fly on with full career,
But my late spring no bud or blossom shew'th.
Perhaps my semblance might deceive the truth,
That I to manhood am arrived so near,
And inward ripeness doth much less appear,

9. The wings of sleep, on which the dream arrives. The description is of a dream that begins as a series of images on the brink of sleep.
1. Presiding local spirit.
2. Enclosure.
3. Vaulted.
4. The pillars are old and oddly decorated (antique and antic were both spelled "antick"), huge and strong enough ("massy proof") to support the roof.
5. The windows are stained glass, ornamented ("dight") with stories told in images.
6. *Spell*: study in detail.
7. Written in observance of the poet's twenty-fourth birthday (9 December 1632).

That some more timely-happy spirits endu'th.[8]
Yet be it less or more, or soon or slow,
It shall be still in strictest measure even[9]
To that same lot, however mean or high,
Toward which Time leads me, and the will of Heaven;
All is, if I have grace to use it so,
As ever in my great Taskmaster's eye.[1]

Sonnet 8[2]

Captain or colonel,[3] or knight in arms,
Whose chance on these defenseless doors[4] may seize,
If deed of honor did thee ever please,
Guard them, and him within protect from harms;
He can requite thee, for he knows the charms
That call fame on such gentle[5] acts as these,
And he can spread thy name o'er lands and seas,
Whatever clime the sun's bright circle warms.
Lift not thy spear against the Muses' bower:
The great Emathian conqueror bid spare
The house of Pindarus,[6] when temple and tower
Went to the ground: and the repeated air
Of sad Electra's poet had the power
To save th'Athenian walls from ruin bare.[7]

Sonnet 9

Lady that in the prime of earliest youth,
Wisely hast shunned the broad way and the green,[8]
And with those few art eminently seen,
That labor up the hill of heav'nly truth,
The better part with Mary, and with Ruth,[9]

8. I.e., the "inner ripeness" with which some are endowed, those whose accomplishments better suit their years. "Inner ripeness" is the antecedent of "it" in subsequent lines.
9. It shall always be exactly equal.
1. The concluding lines have been variously construed. They suggest that despite anxiety over his slow development, Milton hopes for grace to recognize that from the divine perspective everything is as it should be. On "Taskmaster," see Matthew 20:1–16.
2. In October of 1642, Londoners frantically prepared defenses against Charles's advancing royalist army. Milton composed the poem during this time of anxious expectation.
3. Trisyllabic, accented on the last syllable.
4. Milton's lodgings lay outside the city walls.
5. Noble.
6. When Alexander the Great sacked Thebes, he spared a house once occupied by the Greek poet Pindar. "Emathia" is Homer's name for Macedon, Alexander's native land.
7. A besieged resident's continuous singing of the first chorus ("air") from Euripides' *Electra* prevented an army of Spartans, Thebans, and Corinthians from razing Athens. The city was spared because it had produced such poets.
8. "Broad is the way that leadeth to destruction" (Matthew 7:13). For the green paths of those who neglect God, see Job 8:12–13. The identity of the lady to whom Milton addresses this sonnet is unknown.
9. On Martha's sister Mary (not Christ's mother) and her devotion to Jesus, see Luke 10:39–42. The widowed Ruth's decision to devote herself to her Hebrew mother-in-law, Naomi, leads to her becoming an ancestor of King David and thus of Jesus.

Chosen thou hast, and they that overween,[1]
And at thy growing virtues fret their spleen,[2]
No anger find in thee, but pity and ruth.
Thy care is fixed, and zealously attends
To fill thy odorous lamp with deeds of light,[3]
And hope that reaps not shame.[4] Therefore be sure
Thou, when the bridegroom with his feastful friends
Passes to bliss at the mid-hour of night,
Hast gained thy entrance, virgin wise and pure.

Lycidas[5]

In this monody the author bewails a learned friend, unfortunately drowned in his passage from Chester on the Irish Seas, 1637. And by occasion foretells the ruin of our corrupted clergy, then in their height.[6]

Yet once more,[7] O ye laurels, and once more
Ye myrtles brown, with ivy never sere,[8]
I come to pluck your berries harsh and crude,[9]
And with forced fingers rude,
Shatter your leaves before the mellowing year.
Bitter constraint, and sad occasion dear,[1]
Compels me to disturb your season due:
For Lycidas is dead, dead ere his prime,
Young Lycidas, and hath not left his peer:
Who would not sing for Lycidas? He knew
Himself to sing, and build the lofty rhyme.
He must not float upon his wat'ry bier

1. Arrogantly presume (to criticize the lady).
2. Aggravate their ill humor.
3. For the parable of the wise virgins (those with fuel for their lamps) and the foolish (those without), see Matthew 25:1–13. When the bridegroom is delayed until midnight, the wise ones are ready to greet him and attend the marriage feast, as in lines 12–14.
4. "Hope maketh none ashamed" (Romans 5:5).
5. This pastoral elegy (strictly defined, a poem lamenting the death of a fellow shepherd) is one of the most diversely conventional and yet singularly innovative poems in English. It first appeared without title or headnote, over the initials IM, in *Obsequies to the Memory of Mr. Edward King* (1638), the English-language side of a dual-volume collection mourning the drowning at sea of twenty-five-year-old Edward King (Lycidas). Milton knew of King because both had attended Christ's College, Cambridge University. "Lycidas" was a fairly common pastoral name, applied to King as representative of the ideal poet-priest, shockingly cut down in youth. The title and italicized note were added for the 1645 edition of Milton's poems, which we follow.
6. The claim of prophetic foresight refers to the Long Parliament's abolishment of the Episcopal hierarchy in 1642, five years after Milton composed the poem. A "monody" is a funeral song for one voice. As was characteristic of Protestant meditations, its indictment of religious corruption is "occasional"—driven by events, not preset. Cf. the subtitle to Donne's *Anatomy of the World*.
7. The opening phrase, repeated at key moments in Milton's later works (e.g., Sonnet 23, line 7), alludes to an apocalyptic scriptural verse: "he hath promised, saying, 'Yet once more I shake not the earth only, but also heaven.' And this word, 'Yet once more,' signifieth the removing of those things that are shaken, as of things that are made, that those things which cannot be shaken may remain" (Hebrews 12:26–27; cf. Haggai 2:6–7).
8. Laurel is sacred to Apollo, myrtle to Venus, ivy to Bacchus. All are evergreens ("never sere") and signify realms of poetic inspiration appropriate to their patron gods.
9. Unripe. The speaker goes on to claim that he is compelled to scatter ("shatter") the leaves that shelter the unripe fruit.
1. Costly, heartfelt, dire.

Unwept, and welter[2] to the parching wind,
Without the meed of some melodious tear.[3]
Begin then, sisters of the sacred well,
That from beneath the seat of Jove doth spring;[4]
Begin, and somewhat loudly sweep the string.
Hence with denial vain, and coy[5] excuse;
So may some gentle muse[6]
With lucky words favor my destined urn,
And as he passes turn,
And bid fair peace be to my sable shroud.
For we were nursed upon the self-same hill,
Fed the same flock, by fountain, shade, and rill.
Together both, ere the high lawns[7] appeared
Under the opening eyelids of the morn,
We drove afield, and both together heard
What time the grayfly winds her sultry horn,[8]
Batt'ning[9] our flocks with the fresh dews of night,
Oft till the star[1] that rose, at evening, bright
Toward heav'n's descent had sloped his westering wheel.
Meanwhile the rural ditties were not mute,
Tempered to th'oaten flute,[2]
Rough satyrs danced, and fauns with cloven heel
From the glad sound would not be absent long,
And old Damoetas[3] loved to hear our song.
But O the heavy change, now thou art gone,
Now thou art gone, and never must return!
Thee shepherd, thee the woods, and desert caves,
With wild thyme and the gadding[4] vine o'ergrown,
And all their echoes mourn.
The willows, and the hazel copses green,
Shall now no more be seen,
Fanning their joyous leaves to thy soft lays.
As killing as the canker to the rose,
Or taint-worm to the weanling herds that graze,
Or frost to flowers, that their gay wardrobe wear,
When first the whitethorn blows;[5]
Such, Lycidas, thy loss to shepherd's ear.
Where were ye nymphs when the remorseless deep

2. Roll on the waves.
3. I.e., without the fitting tribute of a funeral song.
4. The Muses were associated with various springs, among them the Pierian on Mount Olympus (site of Zeus's throne) and Aganippe on Mount Helicon (site of an altar to Zeus). Either could be deemed a "sacred well . . . beneath the seat of Jove."
5. Shy, modest.
6. Courteous poet.
7. Glades in the wooded hills, where sheep were pastured.
8. The grayfly, also known as the trumpet fly, makes its distinctive sound, or blows ("winds") its horn, in the humid summer heat.
9. Fattening.
1. Hesperus (Venus), the evening star, sets in the west.
2. Shepherd's pipe made from oat straw.
3. Conventional pastoral name, possibly referring to a tutor at Christ's College.
4. Wandering, uncontrolled.
5. Hawthorn blossoms.

Closed o'er the head of your loved Lycidas?
For neither were ye playing on the steep
Where your old bards, the famous Druids lie,[6]
Nor on the shaggy top of Mona high,[7]
Nor yet where Deva spreads her wizard stream:[8]
Ay me, I fondly dream!
Had ye been there—for what could that have done?
What could the Muse herself that Orpheus bore,[9]
The Muse herself, for her enchanting son
Whom Universal nature did lament,
When by the rout that made the hideous roar,
His gory visage down the stream was sent,
Down the swift Hebrus to the Lesbian shore.[1]
   Alas! What boots[2] it with uncessant care
To tend the homely slighted shepherd's trade,
And strictly meditate the thankless Muse?
Were it not better done as others use,
To sport with Amaryllis in the shade,
Or with the tangles of Neaera's hair?[3]
Fame is the spur that the clear spirit doth raise
(That last infirmity of noble mind)
To scorn delights, and live laborious days;
But the fair guerdon[4] when we hope to find,
And think to burst out into sudden blaze,
Comes the blind Fury with th'abhorrèd shears,
And slits the thin-spun life.[5] "But not the praise,"
Phoebus replied, and touched my trembling ears.[6]
"Fame is no plant that grows on mortal soil,
Nor in the glistering foil[7]
Set off to th'world, nor in broad rumor lies,
But lives and spreads aloft by those pure eyes,
And perfect witness of all-judging Jove;
As he pronounces lastly on each deed,
Of so much fame in Heav'n expect thy meed."
   O Fountain Arethuse, and thou honored flood,

6. Sharp slope or high elevation ("steep") used as a burial ground for the Druids, presumably in coastal Wales, near the site of King's drowning.
7. The Isle of Anglesey (called "Mona" by the Romans), ancient stronghold of the Druids in the Irish Sea. It was known for its thick forests ("shaggy").
8. The river Dee, associated with wizards, empties into the Irish Sea. Changes in its course were thought to predict the flow of future events.
9. Calliope, Muse of epic poetry.
1. Orpheus was dismembered by a throng ("rout") of Maenads, frenzied female devotees of Bacchus. The bloody head of Orpheus, thrown into the river Hebrus, sang its way to Lesbos in the Aegean sea.
2. Profits, avails.
3. *Amaryllis* and *Neaera*: generic names for girls wooed by shepherds.
4. Reward (fame).
5. In Greek myth, the shears that cut the thread of life are held by Atropos, one of the three Fates. Furies, by contrast, are fierce agents of vengeance. A blind one with Atropos's shears would be terrifyingly prone to unfortunate mistakes.
6. Phoebus Apollo, classical god of poetry. In ancient Rome, touching the ears urged remembrance of something forgotten.
7. Shiny, thin-leaf metal used by jewelers to add brilliancy to inferior stones.

Smooth-sliding Mincius, crowned with vocal reeds,[8]
That strain I heard was of a higher mood:
But now my oat[9] proceeds,
And listens to the herald of the sea[1]
That came in Neptune's plea.
He asked the waves, and asked the felon[2] winds,
"What hard mishap hath doomed this gentle swain?"
And questioned every gust of rugged wings
That blows from off each beakèd promontory:
They knew not of his story,
And sage Hippotades[3] their answer brings,
That not a blast was from his dungeon strayed;
The air was calm, and on the level brine,
Sleek Panope[4] with all her sisters played.
It was that fatal and perfidious bark
Built in th'eclipse,[5] and rigged with curses dark,
That sunk so low that sacred head of thine.
   Next Camus,[6] reverend sire, went footing slow,
His mantle hairy, and his bonnet sedge,
Inwrought with figures dim, and on the edge
Like to that sanguine flower inscribed with woe.[7]
"Ah! Who hath reft," quoth he, "my dearest pledge?"[8]
Last came, and last did go,
The pilot of the Galilean lake;[9]
Two massy keys he bore of metals twain
(The golden opes, the iron shuts amain).
He shook his mitered locks, and stern bespake,
"How well could I have spared for thee, young swain,
Enow[1] of such as for their bellies' sake,
Creep and intrude, and climb into the fold?
Of other care they little reck'ning make,
Than how to scramble at the shearer's feast,
And shove away the worthy bidden guest.
Blind mouths![2] that scarce themselves know how to hold
A sheep-hook, or have learned aught else the least

8. According to legend, the nymph Arethusa bathed in the river Alpheus in Arcadia, Greece. Pursued by the smitten river god, she fled undersea to Syracuse (birthplace of Theocritus) on the southeastern coast of Sicily. There she surfaced as a freshwater fountain on the island of Ortygia. "Mincius" is a river in north-central Italy (birthplace of Vergil). Its tall reeds are "vocal" perhaps because they whisper in the wind.
9. The shepherd's oaten flute (cf. line 33).
1. Triton, Neptune's son, usually represented as blowing a conch shell. He calls witnesses ("waves" and "winds") in making a defense ("plea") for Neptune.
2. Capable of heinous crime.
3. Son of Hippotes, Aeolus (god of the winds).
4. Sea nymph associated with calm seas.
5. Eclipses were considered unlucky.
6. The river Cam (of Cambridge University), "slow" and weedy.
7. The academic gown ("mantle") and hood ("bonnet") are conventionally symbolic in color and design. The hyacinth, bloody in color ("sanguine"), represents a mythical boy accidentally slain by Apollo. Its streaks suggest the letters AI, the Greek sound of woe.
8. I.e., who has snatched away my precious child?
9. St. Peter fished the Sea of Galilee and became the Church's first bishop (cf. the "mitred locks" of line 112). Christ hands him "the keys of the kingdom of heaven" (Matthew 16:19).
1. Archaic plural of "enough," referring to the ample number of bad shepherds.
2. John Ruskin (*Sesame and Lilies*, first lecture) observed that etymologically bishop means "one who sees" and pastor "one who feeds." "Blind mouths" reverses what clergy ought to be.

That to the faithful herdman's art belongs!
What recks it them? What need they? They are sped;[3]
And when they list,[4] their lean and flashy songs
Grate on their scrannel[5] pipes of wretched straw;
The hungry sheep look up, and are not fed,
But swoll'n with wind, and the rank mist they draw,
Rot inwardly, and foul contagion spread:
Besides what the grim wolf with privy[6] paw
Daily devours apace, and nothing said.
But that two-handed engine[7] at the door,
Stands ready to smite once, and smite no more."
   Return Alpheus,[8] the dread voice is past
That shrunk thy streams; return Sicilian muse,
And call the vales, and bid them hither cast
Their bells, and flow'rets of a thousand hues.
Ye valleys low, where the mild whispers use[9]
Of shades and wanton winds, and gushing brooks,
On whose fresh lap the swart star sparely looks,[1]
Throw hither all your quaint enameled eyes,[2]
That on the green turf suck the honeyed showers,
And purple all the ground with vernal flowers.
Bring the rath[3] primrose that forsaken dies,
The tufted crow-toe, and pale jessamine,[4]
The white pink, and the pansy freaked with jet,[5]
The glowing violet,
The musk-rose, and the well-attired woodbine,
With cowslips wan that hang the pensive head,
And every flower that sad embroidery wears:
Bid amaranthus[6] all his beauty shed,
And daffadillies fill their cups with tears,
To strew the laureate hearse where Lycid lies.
For so to interpose a little ease,
Let our frail thoughts dally with false surmise.
Ay me! Whilst thee the shores, and sounding seas
Wash far away, where'er thy bones are hurled,
Whether beyond the stormy Hebrides,[7]

3. I.e., What do they care? Do they lack anything? They've got all they want.
4. Please.
5. Thin, harsh (first recorded written use of this grating word).
6. Clandestine, acting in secret; usually taken as a reference to agents of the outlawed Catholic Church.
7. The single most disputed phrase in Milton, "two-handed engine" signifies some offensive weapon, literal or figurative, "ready to smite" corrupt clergy.
8. See lines 85–86n. After St. Peter's denunciation of the clergy, the elegy returns to the pastoral mode and its Sicilian origins.
9. Speak (a language).
1. "Whose" refers back to valleys (line 136). Sirius, the dog star, is called "swart" (dark) because when it rises (the "dog days" of August), summer heat scorches the fields—though less so ("sparely") in shady valleys.
2. I.e., your elegant, brightly colored flowers. Counterpointing the "blind mouths" of line 119, these eyes "suck."
3. Early.
4. The wild hyacinth ("crow-toe") grows in clusters ("tufted"). "Jessamine" is jasmine.
5. I.e., the pansy with black ("jet") streaks.
6. An imaginary flower supposed never to fade.
7. Islands off the west coast of Scotland, north of where King drowned.

Where thou perhaps under the whelming tide
Visit'st the bottom of the monstrous world;
Or whether thou to our moist vows denied,
Sleep'st by the fable of Bellerus old,[8]
Where the great vision of the guarded mount
Looks toward Namancos and Bayona's hold:[9]
Look homeward Angel now, and melt with ruth;
And, O ye dolphins, waft the hapless youth.[1]
Weep no more, woeful shepherds, weep no more,
For Lycidas your sorrow is not dead,
Sunk though he be beneath the wat'ry floor,
So sinks the day-star in the ocean bed,
And yet anon repairs his drooping head,
And tricks his beams, and with new-spangled ore,
Flames in the forehead of the morning sky:
So Lycidas sunk low, but mounted high,
Through the dear might of him that walked the waves,[2]
Where other groves, and other streams along,
With nectar pure his oozy locks he laves,
And hears the unexpressive[3] nuptial song,
In the blest kingdoms meek of joy and love.
There entertain him all the saints above,
In solemn troops, and sweet societies
That sing, and singing in their glory move,
And wipe the tears for ever from his eyes.[4]
Now Lycidas the shepherds weep no more;
Henceforth thou art the genius[5] of the shore,
In thy large recompense, and shalt be good
To all that wander in that perilous flood.
Thus sang the uncouth swain[6] to th'oaks and rills,
While the still Morn went out with sandals gray;
He touched the tender stops of various quills,
With eager thought warbling his Doric lay:[7]
And now the sun had stretched out all the hills,
And now was dropped into the western bay;
At last he rose, and twitched his mantle blue:
Tomorrow to fresh woods, and pastures new.

8. Land's End promontory at the southern tip of Cornwall was in Roman times called Bellerium. "Bellerus" appears to be Milton's coinage from that place-name. In the manuscript of the poem, Bellerus is inserted for the crossed-out "Corineus," a fabled warrior who slew one of the giants inhabiting Cornwall and threw him into the sea.
9. St. Michael's Mount lies off the south coast of Cornwall, where the angel Michael was supposed to have appeared in a vision. Here he peers across the Atlantic toward the northern coast of Spain ("Namancos" and "Bayona"), England's old enemy.
1. The kindness of dolphins to strangers is legendary (e.g., the rescue of the poet Arion or the retrieval of Melicertes, subsequently transformed into a marine god). Here dolphins are asked to buoy ("waft") the sunken Lycidas. Dolphins were common in early Christian symbolism of salvation.
2. "Jesus went unto them, walking on the sea" (Matthew 14:25).
3. Inexpressible. For the "nuptial" or marriage song, see Revelation 19:5.
4. "God shall wipe away all tears from their eyes" (Revelation 21:4).
5. Guardian spirit.
6. The unknown shepherd.
7. His rustic song. Doric was the plain dialect used by Theocritus.

FROM *POEMS* (1673)

Sonnet 12[8]

I did but prompt the age to quit their clogs[9]
By the known rules of ancient liberty,[1]
When straight a barbarous noise[2] environs me
Of owls and cuckoos, asses, apes and dogs.
As when those hinds that were transformed to frogs
Railed at Latona's twin-born progeny
Which after held the sun and moon in fee.[3]
But this is got by casting pearl to hogs,[4]
That bawl for freedom in their senseless mood,
And still revolt when truth would set them free.[5]
License they mean when they cry liberty;
For who loves that, must first be wise and good;
But from that mark how far they rove we see
For all this waste of wealth, and loss of blood.[6]

Sonnet 13

To Mr. H. Lawes, on his Airs[7]

Harry, whose tuneful and well-measured song
First taught our English music how to span
Words with just note and accent, not to scan
With Midas' ears,[8] committing short and long,[9]

8. Probably written in 1646, this is the second of Milton's sonnets on his divorce tracts. Response to his arguments on marriage and divorce was overwhelmingly negative and derisive rather than reasoned.
9. Leave behind their impediments (such as were used to keep animals from straying).
1. I.e., Mosaic divorce law.
2. Cf. "Lycidas," line 61, p. 400.
3. After the birth of Apollo and Diana (Artemis), who became the deities of the sun and the moon, their mother, Latona, sought to drink water from a pool. Peasants ("hinds") refused and reviled her. The peasants were transformed into frogs, who then croaked their insults (see Ovid, *Metamorphoses* VI.317–381). To hold "in fee" means to possess as one's own.
4. "Neither cast ye your pearls before swine, lest they trample them under their feet, and turn again and rend you" (Matthew 7:6).
5. "The truth shall make you free" (John 8:32). *Still*: always, ever.
6. I.e., in spite of all this destruction of wealth and life. Milton complains that the sacrifices of the civil war have been wasted because those now in power (his critics, the Presbyterians) have returned to customary habits of spiritual bondage rather than instituting liberty.
7. This sonnet was written in 1646 and first printed as a prefatory poem for a 1648 volume of Lawes's arrangements for the Psalms (dedicated to King Charles). In the 1630s, aside from composing music for court entertainments, Henry Lawes was music tutor to the Earl of Bridgewater's children. In that capacity, he chose Milton, then a young unknown, to write the book for *Arcades* and *A Mask*. Their long-standing friendship was evidently not disturbed by their political differences. Lawes also set to music works of Herrick, Waller, and Carew, among others.
8. Lawes was notable for composing musical arrangements that preserved poets' rhythm and stress (spanning their "words with just note and accent"). "To scan" verse is to recognize its metrical pattern, an ability that, according to Apollo, Midas lacked. The god therefore gave him the ears of an ass.
9. I.e., combining short syllables with long notes (and vice versa).

Thy worth and skill exempts thee[1] from the throng,
With praise enough for Envy to look wan;
To after-age thou shalt be writ the man
That with smooth air couldst humor best our tongue.
Thou honor'st verse, and verse must lend her wing
To honor thee, the priest of Phoebus' choir[2]
That tun'st their happiest lines in hymn or story.
Dante shall give Fame leave to set thee higher
Than his Casella, whom he wooed to sing
Met in the milder shades of Purgatory.[3]

Sonnet 16[4]

To the Lord General Cromwell, May 1652,
On the proposals of certain ministers at the Committee for Propagation of the Gospel

Cromwell, our chief of men, who through a cloud[5]
Not of war only, but detractions rude,
Guided by faith and matchless fortitude,
To peace and truth thy glorious way hast ploughed,
And on the neck of crownèd Fortune proud[6]
Hast reared God's trophies[7] and his work pursued,
While Darwen stream with blood of Scots imbrued,[8]
And Dunbar[9] field resounds thy praises loud,
And Worcester's[1] laureate wreath; yet much remains
To conquer still: peace hath her victories
No less renowned than war; new foes arise
Threat'ning to bind our souls with secular chains.
Help us to save free conscience from the paw
Of hireling wolves[2] whose Gospel is their maw.

1. Distinguishes you.
2. I.e., the choir of Apollo, god of poetry and music.
3. At the entrance to Purgatory, Dante meets the spirit of his friend Casella, a Florentine musician, and requests a song; Casella proceeds to sing a work of Dante's that he had set to music (*Purgatorio* II.76–117).
4. Like Tasso in the *Heroic Sonnets*, Milton addresses several sonnets to great men. He typically begins, as Jonson often began his poems, with the name of the person addressed. Here the Puritans' unstoppable military leader is appealed to as a member of the parliamentary committee for the propagation of the Gospel. Against the proposal that Parliament establish a national church and pay its clergy, Milton urges Cromwell to embrace separation of church and state for the sake of "free conscience" and to repudiate the "hireling wolves" of a state-funded clergy. The sonnet was not printed until 1694.
5. Cf. Marvell's "Horatian Ode," lines 13–16, p. 556.
6. Perhaps an allusion to the beheading of Charles I in January 1649.
7. A "trophy" was a memorial of victory raised on the battlefield or public place.
8. At the battle of Preston, along the river Darwen, Cromwell routed the invading Scottish army in August 1648.
9. In September 1650, Cromwell defeated the Scottish army at Dunbar.
1. On the anniversary of his victory at Dunbar in 1651, Cromwell decisively defeated Charles II at Worcester.
2. Cf. "Lycidas," lines 128–129, p. 402.

Sonnet 18

On the Late Massacre in Piedmont[3]

Avenge, O Lord, thy slaughtered saints, whose bones
Lie scattered on the Alpine mountains cold,
Even them who kept thy truth so pure of old
When all our fathers worshipped stocks[4] and stones,
Forget not: in thy book[5] record their groans
Who were thy sheep and in their ancient fold
Slain by the bloody Piemontese that rolled
Mother with infant down the rocks. Their moans
The vales redoubled to the hills, and they
To Heaven. Their martyred blood and ashes sow
O'er all th'Italian fields where still doth sway
The triple tyrant:[6] that from these may grow
A hundredfold,[7] who having learnt thy way
Early may fly the Babylonian woe.[8]

Sonnet 19[9]

When I consider how my light is spent,[1]
Ere half my days, in this dark world and wide,
And that one talent which is death to hide,
Lodged with me useless,[2] though my soul more bent
To serve therewith[3] my Maker, and present
My true account, lest he returning chide,
"Doth God exact day labor, light denied,"[4]
I fondly[5] ask; but patience to prevent
That murmur[6] soon replies, "God doth not need
Either man's work or his own gifts; who best

3. The Vaudois, or Waldensians, are adherents of a religious sect that originated in the late twelfth century in the south of France. The sect had long had the right to settle in parts of the Italian Alps. But when its membership spread into the Piedmont valley, beyond agreed-upon borders, the Duke of Savoy sent an army, which massacred more than 1,700 Vaudois. Milton's sonnet registers the outrage of English Protestants, also expressed in letters of protest he wrote for Cromwell's government.
4. Blocks of wood, posts. See Jeremiah 2:27. It was believed that the Vaudois had maintained purity of worship from the time of the apostles.
5. A record of human actions to be consulted on doomsday; see Revelation 5:1.
6. The Pope wears a three-tiered mitre.
7. In lines 10–13 Milton allusively combines Tertullian's claim that "the blood of the martyrs is the seed of the Church" with the parable of the sower, in which the seed that falls on good ground sometimes yields "a hundredfold" (Matthew 13:8).
8. Many Protestants identified the Church of Rome with the Babylon whose doom is prophesied in Revelation 16:19.
9. The sonnet is generally thought to have been written shortly after the forty-four-year-old Milton went totally blind in 1652, which makes "ere half my days" (line 2) notably optimistic.
1. Milton assumes that the power of vision is active, effected via beams emitted by ("spent") the eyes of the beholder.
2. In the parable of the talents (Matthew 25:14–30), a servant buries the one talent with which his lord entrusts him. He is cast into "outer darkness" for his profitless ("useless") action.
3. I.e., to serve his Maker with the talent.
4. "I must work the works of him that sent me, while it is day: the night cometh when no man can work" (John 9:4). See also the parable of the vineyard (Matthew 20:1–16).
5. Foolishly.
6. Complaint.

Bear his mild yoke,[7] they serve him best. His state
Is kingly; thousands at his bidding speed
And post o'er land and ocean without rest:
They also serve who only stand and wait."

Sonnet 20

Lawrence of virtuous father virtuous son,[8]
Now that the fields are dank, and ways are mire,
Where shall we sometimes meet, and by the fire
Help waste[9] a sullen day, what may be won
From the hard season[1] gaining? Time will run
On smoother, till Favonius[2] reinspire
The frozen earth, and clothe in fresh attire
The lily and rose, that neither sowed nor spun.[3]
What neat repast shall feast us, light and choice,
Of Attic[4] taste, with wine, whence we may rise
To hear the lute well touched, or artful voice
Warble immortal notes and Tuscan air?[5]
He who of those delights can judge, and spare
To interpose them oft, is not unwise.

Sonnet 23

Methought I saw my late espousèd saint[6]
Brought to me like Alcestis[7] from the grave,
Whom Jove's great son to her glad husband gave,
Rescued from death by force though pale and faint.
Mine as whom washed from spot of child-bed taint
Purification in the Old Law did save,[8]
And such, as yet once more[9] I trust to have
Full sight of her in Heaven without restraint,

7. "My yoke is easy" (Matthew 11:30).
8. The "virtuous father" is Henry Lawrence (1600–1664), who became Lord President of the Council of State in 1653. His "virtuous son" is Milton's young friend and frequent visitor, Edward Lawrence (1633–1657), who became a Member of Parliament in 1656.
9. Spend.
1. Staying indoors during winter to enjoy food, wine, music, poetry, and conversation is a common Cavalier literary theme. Cf. Lovelace, "The Grasshopper," p. 494, and Herrick, "To Live Merrily, and to Trust to Good Verses," p. 194. Jonson, and ultimately Horace, was the inspiration for such verse. Milton's sonnet suggests that some Puritans also valued such fellowship.
2. The west wind, Zephyrus. Cf. "L'Allegro," lines 18–19, p. 388.
3. See Matthew 6:28–29.
4. Refined, such as would have been enjoyed in classical Athens.
5. A song from the Tuscan region of Italy.
6. "Them that are sanctified in Christ Jesus, called to be saints" (1 Corinthians 1:2). Milton probably refers to Katherine Woodcock, his second wife. They were married in 1656, when Milton was totally blind, and she died in 1658, several months after giving birth to a daughter, who also died.
7. In Euripides' *Alcestis*, the heroine dies, but Hercules ("Jove's great son") rescues her from Hades and restores her, veiled, to Admetus ("her glad husband").
8. The scriptural reference is to the ceremonial purification of women after childbirth (Leviticus 12). Women were not to be seen by their husbands during this time. (The name "Katherine" means pure.)
9. A phrase suggestive of the apocalypse (etymologically, the removal of the veil); cf. the first line of "Lycidas," p. 398.

Came vested all in white, pure as her mind:
Her face was veiled, yet to my fancied sight,
Love, sweetness, goodness in her person[1] shined
So clear, as in no face with more delight.
But O, as to embrace me she inclined,
I waked, she fled, and day brought back my night.[2]

1. Body.
2. Failed embraces of a deceased beloved are common in classical literature, the original instance being Achilles' attempt to embrace the dream image of Patroclus (*Iliad* XXIII. 99–107). Milton differs from his predecessors in that he represents the vision as attempting to embrace him, not the other way round, and failing because the dreamer waked.

Sir John Suckling

1609	Born in Twickenham, Middlesex; baptized February 10. His father, descended from a prominent Norfolk family, was appointed Comptroller of James I's Household in 1622; his mother (deceased, 1613) was the sister of Lionel Cranfield, who became the Lord Treasurer.
1623	Matriculates at Trinity College, Cambridge; leaves in 1626 without taking a degree.
1627	On his father's death, inherits extensive estates in Suffolk, Lincoln, and Middlesex. Probably accompanies Buckingham's expedition to the Île de Ré.
1629–1630	With Lord Wimbledon's regiment in the Low Countries until May 1630; subsequently studying astrology at the University of Leyden. Knighted, September 1630.
1631–1632	In Germany, with Sir Henry Vane's embassy to Gustavus Adolphus.
1633–1634	Devotes himself to gambling on a grand scale, and to the (unsuccessful) courtship of Anne Willoughby, a wealthy heiress.
1637	Writes the prose *Account of Religion by Reason*.
1638	Publication of his play, *Aglaura*, presented before Charles I and Henrietta Maria in February and again in April. First separately published poems: commendatory verses to Lord Lepington's translation of Malvezzi's *Romulus and Tarquin*, and to Davenant's *Madagascar, with Other Poems*.
1639	Recruits and equips a troop of cavalrymen for the King's expedition against the Scots.
1640	Member of Parliament for Bramber. Takes part in the unsuccessful action against the Scots at Newburn Ford, near Newcastle, 28 August.
1641	Involved with royalist plans to make use of the army on behalf of Charles I. Pressed by Parliament to account for his movements, flees to Dieppe on 6 May; arrives in Paris on 14 May. Apparently takes his own life, by poison, in late July or shortly thereafter.
1646	Publication of *Fragmenta Aurea*.
1659	Publication of *The Last Remains of Sir John Suckling*.

FROM *FRAGMENTA AUREA*[1] (1646)

Loving and Beloved

There never yet was honest man
That ever drove the trade of love;
It is impossible, nor can
Integrity our ends promove;[2]
For kings and lovers are alike in this,
That their chief art in reign dissembling is.

Here we are loved, and there we love;
Good nature now and passion strive
Which of the two should be above,
And laws unto the other give.
So we false fire with art sometimes discover,
And the true fire with the same art do cover.

What rack[3] can fancy find so high?
Here we must court, and here engage,
Though in the other place we die.
Oh, 'tis torture all, and cozenage,[4]
And which the harder is I cannot tell,
To hide true love, or make false love look well.

Since it is thus, God of Desire,
Give me my honesty again,
And take thy brands back, and thy fire;
I'm weary of the state I'm in:
Since (if the very best should now befall)
Love's triumph must be Honor's funeral.

1. "Golden remains." John Aubrey's account of Suckling's character and career (not to mention the poet's description of himself in "A Sessions of the Poets," lines 83–88, p. 414) tends to reinforce the popular conception of Suckling as gallant, gamester, and libertine, and as a poet whose best work is charming but trivial. Congreve's Millamant, however, meant more than this when she spoke of "natural, easy Suckling" (*The Way of the World*, IV.i), and it is of interest that Pope explicitly placed Suckling in "another school" from that including Waller and Carew, while Joseph Spence drew attention to the formal "purity" of Suckling's verse (J. Spence, *Observations, Anecdotes, and Characters of Books and Men*, ed. J. M. Osborn, 2 vols. [Oxford, 1966], I, pp. 196, 274).
2. Promote. The line, however, punningly reinforces the brutal realism informing line 2.
3. The rack was an instrument of torture devised to stretch (and, if need be, pull apart) the bodies of those bound upon it.
4. Trickery.

A Sessions[5] of the Poets

A sessions was held the other day,
And Apollo[6] himself was at it, they say;
The laurel that had been so long reserved,
Was now to be given to him best deserved.
And

Therefore the wits of the town came thither;
'Twas strange to see how they flocked together.
Each strongly confident of his own way,
Thought to gain the laurel away that day.

There was Selden,[7] and he sat hard by the chair;
Wenman not far off, which was very fair;
Sandys with Townshend, for they kept no order;
Digby and Chillingworth a little further.
And

There was Lucan's translator[8] too, and he
That makes God speak so big in's poetry;
Selwin and Waller, and Berkeleys both the brothers;
Jack Vaughan and Porter, and divers others.

The first that broke silence was good old Ben,
Prepared before with Canary wine,
And he told them plainly he deserved the bays,
For his were called *Works*, where others' were but plays.[9]
And

Bid them remember how he had purged the stage
Of errors that had lasted many an age;
And he hoped they did not think *The Silent Woman*,
The Fox, and *The Alchemist* outdone by no man.

5. The poem, composed in 1637, seems originally to have been entitled "The Wits"; the title given here, by which the piece is generally known, was probably of editorial origin, in 1648. Thomas Clayton, citing Dr. Johnson in support, observes that the poem "introduced a much-imitated minor genre—'the trial for the bays'—into English poetry" (*Works of Sir John Suckling: The Non-Dramatic Works*,) ed. T. Clayton [Oxford, 1971], pp. 266, 268). The complicated textual problems are discussed by L. A. Beaurline in *SB*, XVI (1963), 43–60; cf. Textual Notes.
6. Excellence in the art of poetry was traditionally rewarded with the garland of laurel ("bays"), which was sacred to Apollo, god of poetry and song. Ben Jonson and his admirers habitually foregathered in the "Apollo Room" of the Devil Tavern, near Temple Bar, in London; in this room, it appears, a bust of Apollo was set over Jonson's place.
7. I.e., John Selden (1584–1654); cf. Jonson, "Epistle to Master John Selden," p. 133. The other persons named in this stanza are Sir Francis Wenman (fl. 1615–1640); George Sandys (1577–1644), whose translation of the Psalms was praised in verse by Carew; Aurelian Townshend (c. 1583–c. 1651), whose "Elegiacal Letter" (p. 311) had elicited Carew's diffident but characteristic response; Sir Kenelm Digby (1603–1665), general editor of the 1640–1641 edition of Jonson's *Works*; and William Chillingworth (1602–1644), Protestant theologian and, with Wenman, one of Lord Falkland's circle at Great Tew.
8. I.e., Thomas May (1595–1650), who had translated Lucan's epic poem *Pharsalia* in 1626–1627. "He that makes God speak so big in's poetry" is unidentified, as is "Selwin." Other persons named in this stanza are Samuel Waller; Sir William Berkeley (d. 1677), and his brother John, first Baron Berkeley of Stratton (d. 1678); Selden's friend Sir John Vaughan (1605–1674); and Endymion Porter (1587–1649), for whom cf. Herrick, "The Country Life," p. 210.
9. Jonson, the first English poet to publish his *Works* (1616), was widely criticized on that account. A contemporary gibe, "Pray tell me, Ben, where does the mystery lurk, / What others call a play you call a work?" drew this anonymous response: "The author's friend thus for the author says: / Ben's plays are works, when others' works are plays."

Apollo stopped him there, and bade him not go on,
'Twas merit, he said, and not presumption
Must carry't; at which Ben turned about,
And in great choler offered to go out;
But
Those that were there thought it not fit
To discontent so ancient a wit;
And therefore Apollo called him back again,
And made him mine host of his own New Inn.[1]

Tom Carew was next, but he had a fault
That would not well stand with a laureate;
His Muse was hard bound,[2] and th'issue of 's brain
Was seldom brought forth but with trouble and pain.
And
All that were present there did agree,
A laureate's Muse should be easy and free;
Yet sure 'twas not that, but 'twas thought that his grace
Considered, he was well he had a cup-bearer's place.[3]

Will Davenant,[4] ashamed of a foolish mischance
That he had got lately travelling in France,
Modestly hoped the handsomeness of 's Muse
Might any deformity about him excuse.
And
Surely the company would have been content,
If they could have found any precedent;
But in all their records, either in verse or prose,
There was not one laureate without a nose.

To Will Berkeley sure all the wits meant well,
But first they would see how his snow would sell;[5]
Will smiled and swore in their judgments they went less
That concluded of merit upon success.
So
Suddenly taking his place again,
He gave way to Selwin, who straight stepped in,
But alas! he had been so lately a wit
That Apollo hardly knew him yet.

Tobie Matthew[6] (pox on him, how came he there?)
Was whispering nothing in somebody's ear,

1. Jonson's play, *The New Inn*, had been poorly received in 1629. Cf. Jonson's "Ode to Himself," p. 151.
2. I.e., Carew composed his verses slowly and with some painstaking revision.
3. Carew had been appointed "Sewer in Ordinary" (i.e., an honorary steward at the royal dining table) in c. 1630.
4. The poet and playwright Sir William Davenant (1606–1688), who in fact became poet laureate in 1637, had "got a terrible clap of a black handsome wench that lay in Axe Yard, Westminster . . . which cost him his nose, with which mischance many wits were too cruelly bold" (John Aubrey, *Brief Lives*, ed. Oliver Dick [London, 1950], p. 76).
5. This allusion has not been definitively explained.
6. Sir Tobie Mathew (1577–1655), son of the Archbishop of Canterbury, had become a Roman

When he had the honor to be named i'th court;
But, sir, you may thank my Lady Carlisle for't;
For
Had not her care furnished you out
With something of handsome, without all doubt
You and your sorry Lady Muse had been
In the number of those that were not let in.

In haste from the court two or three came in,
And they brought letters, forsooth, from the Queen;
'Twas discreetly done, too, for if th'had come
Without them, th'had scarce been let into the room.
This
Made a dispute, for 'twas plain to be seen
Each man had a mind to gratify the Queen;
But Apollo himself could not think it fit;
There was difference, he said, betwixt fooling and wit.

Suckling next was called, but did not appear,
But straight one whispered Apollo i'th'ear,
That of all men living he cared not for't,
He loved not the Muses so well as his sport;
And
Prized black eyes, or a lucky hit
At bowls, above all the trophies of wit;
But Apollo was angry, and publicly said,
'Twere fit that a fine were set upon 's head.

Wat Montague[7] now stood forth to his trial,
And did not so much as suspect a denial;
But witty Apollo asked him first of all,
If he understood his own pastoral.
For
If he could do it, 'twould plainly appear
He understood more than any man there,
And did merit the bays above all the rest;
But the Monsieur[8] was modest, and silence confessed.

During these troubles, in the crowd was hid
One that Apollo soon missed, little Sid;[9]
And having spied him, called him out of the throng,
And advised him in his ear not to write so strong.
Then

Catholic priest in 1614. He assiduously courted the favor of Lucy Hay, Countess of Carlisle (1599–1660), a reigning beauty and wit at the court of Charles I.
7. Walter Montagu (c. 1603–1677) was the author of a pastoral comedy, *The Shepherd's Paradise*, performed at court in 1633.
8. I.e., the Frenchified fellow.
9. The poet Sidney Godolphin (1610–1643) was of small stature. A member of Parliament and royalist, he died in a skirmish with parliamentary forces.

Murray[1] was summoned, but 'twas urged that he
Was chief already of another company.

Hales[2] set by himself, most gravely did smile
To see them about nothing keep such a coil;[3]
Apollo had spied him, but knowing his mind
Passed by, and called Falkland[4] that sat just behind.
But
He was of late so gone with divinity,[5]
That he had almost forgot his poetry;
Though to say the truth (and Apollo did know it)
He might have been both his priest and his poet.

At length who but an alderman[6] did appear,
At which Will Davenant began to swear;
But wiser Apollo bade him draw nigher,
And when he was mounted a little higher,
He
Openly declared that 'twas the best sign
Of good store of wit to have good store of coin;[7]
And without a syllable more or less said,
He put the laurel on the alderman's head.

At this all the wits were in such a maze
That for a good while they did nothing but gaze
One upon another; not a man in the place
But had discontent writ in great[8] in his face.
Only
The small poets cleared up again,
Out of hope, as 'twas thought, of borrowing;
But sure they were out, for he forfeits his crown,
When he lends any poets about the town.

Sonnets[9]

I

Dost see how unregarded now
That piece of beauty passes?
There was a time when I did vow

1. William Murray (c. 1600–1651), subsequently first Earl of Dysart, made one of the circle of courtly advisers to Charles I.
2. John Hales (1584–1656) was one of Lord Falkland's circle at Great Tew.
3. I.e., became so excited.
4. I.e., Lucius Cary (c. 1610–1643), second Viscount Falkland. Cf. Jonson's poem "To the Immortal Memory . . . of . . . Sir Lucius Cary and Sir H. Morison," p. 140.
5. I.e., so concerned with theological disputation (explicitly with the role of reason in theology).
6. I.e., the chief officer of a city ward, concerned primarily with the material well-being of the citizenry.
7. Proverbs on this theme abound in every literature; cf., for example, Pope, *Imitations of Horace*, Epistle I.i.81.
8. I.e., in large letters.
9. I.e., short lyrics. Musical settings of Sonnets I and II appear in *Select Ayres and Dialogues* (London, 1659), and in other midcentury song collections.

To that alone;
But mark the fate of faces:
The red and white[1] works now no more on me,
Than if it could not charm, or I not see.

And yet the face continues good,
And I have still desires,
Am still the selfsame flesh and blood,
As apt to melt
And suffer from those fires;
Oh! some kind power unriddle where it lies,
Whether my heart be faulty, or her eyes?

She every day her man does kill,
And I as often die;
Neither her power, then, nor my will
Can questioned be;
What is the mystery?
Sure beauties' empires, like to greater states,
Have certain periods set, and hidden fates.

II

Of thee, kind boy,[2] I ask no red and white,
To make up my delight;
No odd becoming graces,
Black eyes, or little know-not-whats,[3] in faces;
Make me but mad[4] enough, give me good store
Of love for her I court;
I ask no more,
'Tis love in love that makes the sport.

There's no such thing as that we beauty call,
It is mere cozenage[5] all;
For though some, long ago,
Liked certain colors mingled so and so,
That doth not tie me now from choosing new;
If I a fancy take
To black and blue,
That fancy doth it beauty make.

'Tis not the meat, but 'tis the appetite
Makes eating a delight,

1. I.e., the lady's complexion. The Petrarchan convention of praising "red and white" female beauty, regularly a feature of Elizabethan poetry, was largely repudiated, for various reasons, by seventeenth-century English poets. Cf. Marvell's "The Garden," lines 17–18: "No white nor red was ever seen / So amorous as this lovely green" (p. 554).
2. I.e., Cupid.
3. I.e. (perhaps), beauty patches.
4. Frantic.
5. Trickery.

And if I like one dish
More than another, that a pheasant is;
What in our watches, that in us is found:[6]
So to the height and nick
We up be wound,
No matter by what hand or trick.

III

Oh! for some honest lover's ghost,
Some kind unbodied post[7]
Sent from the shades below:
I strangely long to know
Whether the nobler chaplets[8] wear,
Those that their mistress' scorn did bear,
Or those that were used kindly.

For whatsoe'er they tell us here
To make those sufferings dear,
'Twill there, I fear, be found,
That to the being crowned
T'have loved alone will not suffice,
Unless we also have been wise,
And have our loves enjoyed.

What posture can we think him in,
That here unloved again
Departs, and's thither gone
Where each sits by his own?
Or how can that Elysium[9] be,
Where I my mistress still must see
Circled in others' arms?

For there the judges all are just,
And Sophonisba[1] must
Be his whom she held dear,
Not his who loved her here;
The sweet Philoclea,[2] since she died,
Lies by her Pyrocles his side,
Not by Amphialus.

6. The conceit of man's likeness to a timepiece occurs in Suckling's verse with some frequency. Thomas Hobbes, in the Introduction to *Leviathan* (1651), inquired, "What is the heart, but a spring; and the nerves, but so many strings; and the joints, but so many wheels, giving motion to the whole body, such as was intended by the artificer?"
7. Messenger.
8. Garlands.
9. Cf. Carew, "A Rapture," line 2n, p. 302.
1. Sophonisba, daughter of the Carthaginian general Hasdrubal, loved the Numidian prince Masinissa; when, in 204 B.C., Scipio Africanus demanded that she should be surrendered to Rome, she took her life by poison.
2. Philoclea, Pyrocles, and Amphialus are characters in Sir Philip Sidney's romance, *Arcadia*.

Some bays, perchance, or myrtle bough,
For difference crowns the brow
Of those kind souls that were
The noble martyrs here;
And if that be the only odds
(As who can tell?), ye kinder gods,
Give me the woman here.

Against Fruition [1]

Stay here, fond[3] youth, and ask no more; be wise:
Knowing too much long since lost paradise.
The virtuous joys thou hast, thou would'st should still
Last in their pride; and would'st not take it ill,
If rudely from sweet dreams (and for a toy)
Thou wert waked? he wakes himself, that does enjoy.

Fruition adds no new wealth, but destroys,
And while it pleaseth much the palate, cloys;
Who thinks he shall be happier for that,
As reasonably might hope he might grow fat
By eating to a surfeit; this once past,
What relishes? even kisses lose their taste.

Urge not 'tis necessary: alas! we know
The homeliest thing which mankind does is so;
The world is of a vast extent, we see,
And must be peopled; children there must be;
So must bread too; but since there are enough
Born to the drudgery, what need we plough?

Women enjoyed, whate'er before they've been,
Are like romances read, or sights once seen;
Fruition's dull, and spoils the play much more
Than if one read or knew the plot before.
'Tis expectation makes a blessing dear;
Heaven were not heaven, if we knew what it were.

And as in prospects we are there pleased most
Where something keeps the eye from being lost,
And leaves us room to guess, so here restraint
Holds up delight, that with excess would faint.
They who know all the wealth they have, are poor;
He's only rich that cannot tell his store.[4]

3. Foolish.
4. Suckling glances at Ovid, *Metamorphoses*, III.466: *inopem me copia fecit* ("plenty makes me poor").

Upon My Lady Carlisle's[5] Walking in Hampton Court Garden

Dialogue
T.C. J.S.[6]

THOM.

Didst thou not find the place inspired,
And flowers, as if they had desired
No other sun, start from their beds,
And for a sight steal out their heads?
Heard'st thou not music when she talked?
And didst not find that, as she walked,
She threw rare perfumes all about,
Such as bean-blossoms newly out
Or chafèd[7] spices give—?

J.S.

I must confess those perfumes, Tom,
I did not smell; nor found that from
Her passing by, aught sprung up new;
The flowers had all their birth from you,
For I passed o'er the selfsame walk,
And did not find one single stalk
Of anything that was to bring
This unknown after after-spring.

THOM.

Dull and insensible, could'st see
A thing so near a deity
Move up and down, and feel no change?

J.S.

None and so great were alike strange.
I had my thoughts, but not your way;
All are not born, sir, to the bay.[8]
Alas! Tom, I am flesh and blood,
And was consulting how I could
In spite of masks and hoods descry
The parts denied unto the eye;
I was undoing all she wore;
And, had she walked but one turn more,

5. Cf. "A Sessions of the Poets," line 64n, p. 413. Suckling's cynical view of Lady Carlisle is at odds with the admiring note struck in poems addressed to her by Herrick, Waller, and Carew (who wrote two New Year's poems to the lady).
6. I.e., Thomas Carew and Sir John Suckling.
7. Warmed.
8. I.e., to poetical excellence, symbolized by the laurel (or "bays"); by implication, with highly developed imaginative powers.

Eve in her first state had not been
More naked, or more plainly seen.

THOM.

'Twas well for thee she left the place,
There is great danger in that face;
But hadst thou viewed her leg and thigh
And, upon that discovery,
Searched after parts that are more dear
(As fancy seldom stops so near),
No time or age had ever seen
So lost a thing as thou hadst been.[9]

J.S.[1]

'Troth, in her face I could descry
No danger, no divinity.
But since the pillars were so good
On which the lovely fountain stood,
Being once come so near, I think
I should have ventured hard to drink.
What ever fool like me had been
If I'd not done as well as seen?
There to be lost why should I doubt
When fools with ease go in and out?

"That none beguilèd be by time's quick flowing"

That none beguilèd be by time's quick flowing,
Lovers have in their hearts a clock still going;
For, though time be nimble, his motions
Are quicker
And thicker
Where love hath his notions.

Hope is the mainspring on which moves desire,
And these do the less wheels, fear, joy, inspire;
The balance is thought, evermore
Clicking
And striking,
And ne'er giving o'er.

Occasion's the hand which still's moving round,
Till by it the critical hour may be found;
And, when that falls out, it will strike

9. The stanza recalls the story of Actaeon, who chanced to see the goddess Diana naked; he was consequently transformed into a stag and torn to pieces by his own hounds: cf. Ovid, *Metamorphoses*, III.155–252.
1. This final stanza appears only in manuscript.

Kisses,
Strange blisses,
And what you best like.

Against Fruition [2]

Fie upon hearts that burn with mutual fire!
I hate two minds that breathe but one desire.
Were I to curse th'unhallowed sort of men,
I'd wish them to love, and be loved again.
Love's a chameleon, that lives on mere air,[2]
And surfeits when it comes to grosser fare;
'Tis petty jealousies, and little fears,
Hopes joined with doubts, and joys with April tears,
That crowns our love with pleasures: these are gone
When once we come to full fruition,
Like waking in a morning, when all night
Our fancy hath been fed with true delight.
Oh, what a stroke 'twould be! Sure I should die,
Should I but hear my mistress once say, "Aye."
That monster expectation feeds too high
For any woman e'er to satisfy;
And no brave spirit ever cared for that
Which in down beds with ease he could come at.
She's but an honest whore that yields, although
She be as cold as ice, as pure as snow;
He that enjoys her hath no more to say
But keep us fasting, if you'll have us pray.[3]
Then, fairest mistress, hold the power you have,
By still denying what we still do crave;
In keeping us in hopes strange things to see,
That never were, nor are, nor e'er shall be.

A Ballad upon a Wedding[4]

I tell thee, Dick, where I have been,
Where I the rarest things have seen,
Oh, things without compare!
Such sights again cannot be found
In any place on English ground,
Be it at wake[5] or fair.

2. This popular belief is often encountered in literature of the period; cf., for example, *Hamlet*, III.ii.91–92.
3. I.e., beg for more.
4. The poem probably celebrates the wedding of John Lord Lovelace to Lady Anne Wentworth, on 11 July 1638; cf. *Works of Suckling, ed. cit.*, pp. 280–281. "Dick" may be the poet Richard Lovelace, brother to the groom; but that identification need not be insisted upon since the speaker and his companion are evidently rustics (presumably from the West Country, Devonshire or Somerset). Clayton observes that Suckling's poem initiates "a minor genre, that of the 'rusticated epithalamion,' a gently burlesqued version of the traditional pastoral epithalamion" (*ed. cit.*, p. 279).
5. Parish festival.

At Charing Cross,[6] hard by the way
Where we, thou know'st, do sell our hay,
There is a house with stairs;
And there did I see coming down
Such folk as are not in our town,
Forty, at least, in pairs.

Amongst the rest, one pest'lent fine[7]
(His beard no bigger, though, than thine)
Walked on before the rest:
Our landlord looks like nothing to him;
The King (God bless him!), 'twould undo him,
Should he go still[8] so dressed.

At course-a-park,[9] without all doubt,
He should have first been taken out
By all the maids i'th'town,
Though lusty Roger there had been,
Or little George upon the Green,
Or Vincent of the Crown.[1]

But wot[2] you what? the youth was going
To make an end of all his wooing;
The parson for him stayed;
Yet by his leave, for all his haste,
He did not so much wish all past,
Perchance, as did the maid.

The maid (and thereby hangs a tale,
For such a maid no Whitsun-ale[3]
Could ever yet produce):
No grape that's kindly[4] ripe could be
So round, so plump, so soft as she,
Nor half so full of juice.

Her finger was so small, the ring
Would not stay on which they did bring,
It was too wide a peck;[5]

6. Originally the site of a stone cross erected by Edward I in memory of his consort, Queen Eleanor, Charing Cross had at an early date become a busy center in the city of Westminster. The Haymarket is situated nearby.
7. I.e., exceptionally fine.
8. Constantly.
9. "A country game, in which a girl called out one of the other sex to choose her" (*OED*).
1. "As good as George of Green" was an English proverb or folk saying; it seems that the other names refer also to generalized types of male prowess.
2. Know.
3. I.e., no Whitsuntide festival. Held on the seventh Sunday after Easter, to commemorate Pentecost (cf. Acts 2:1–4), these celebrations were characterized by merrymaking, and drinking on a heroic scale.
4. Naturally.
5. I.e., it was much too large.

And to say truth (for out it must),
It looked like the great collar (just)
About our young colt's neck.

Her feet beneath her petticoat
Like little mice stole in and out,
As if they feared the light;
But oh! she dances such a way,
No sun upon an Easter day
Is half so fine a sight.[6]

He would have kissed her once or twice,
But she would not, she was so nice,[7]
She would not do't in sight;
And then she looked as who should say,
I will do what I list today,
And you shall do't at night.

Her cheeks so rare a white was on,
No daisy makes comparison
(Who sees them is undone[8]),
For streaks of red were mingled there,
Such as are on a Katherine pear[9]
(The side that's next the sun).

Her lips were red, and one was thin,
Compared to that was next her chin
(Some bee had stung it newly);
But, Dick, her eyes so guard her face,
I durst no more upon them gaze
Than on the sun in July.

Her mouth so small, when she does speak,
Thou'dst swear her teeth her words did break,
That they might passage get;
But she so handled still the matter,
They came as good as ours, or better,
And are not spent a whit.

If wishing should be any sin,
The parson himself had guilty been
(She looked that day so purely);
And did the youth so oft the feat
At night, as some did in conceit,[1]
It would have spoiled him, surely.

6. Cf. Herrick, "Ceremonies for Candlemas Eve," line 7n, p. 217.
7. Demure.
8. I.e., is overcome.
9. I.e., a small and early variety of pear.
1. Fancy.

Passion, oh me! how I run on!
There's that that would be thought upon,
I trow,[2] besides the bride:
The business of the kitchen's great,
For it is fit that men should eat,
Nor was it there denied.

Just in the nick the cook knocked thrice,
And all the waiters in a trice
His summons did obey;
Each servingman, with dish in hand,
Marched boldly up, like our trained band,[3]
Presented, and away.

When all the meat was on the table,
What man of knife or teeth was able
To stay to be entreated?
And this the very reason was,
Before the parson could say grace,
The company was seated.

Now hats fly off, and youths carouse;
Healths first go round, and then the house,
The bride's came thick and thick;
And when 'twas named another's health,
Perhaps he made it hers by stealth;
And who could help it, Dick?

O'th' sudden up they rise and dance;
Then sit again, and sigh, and glance;
Then dance again and kiss;
Thus several ways the time did pass,
Whilst every woman wished her place,
And every man wished his.

By this time all were stol'n aside
To counsel and undress the bride,
But that he must not know;
But yet 'twas thought he guessed her mind,
And did not mean to stay behind
Above an hour or so.

When in he came, Dick, there she lay
Like new-fall'n snow melting away
('Twas time, I trow, to part);

2. Reckon.
3. I.e., our village militia (trained in the rudiments of close-order drill and the use of firearms).

Kisses were now the only stay,
Which soon she gave, as who would say,
"Good Boy!" with all my heart.[4]

But just as heav'ns would have, to cross it,
In came the bridesmaids with the posset;[5]
The bridegroom eat[6] in spite,
For had he left the women to't,
It would have cost two hours to do't,
Which were too much that night.

At length the candle's out, and now
All that they had not done, they do:
What that is, who can tell?
But I believe it was no more
Than thou and I have done before
With Bridget and with Nell.

"My dearest rival, lest our love"

My dearest rival, lest our love
Should with eccentric motion move,[7]
Before it learn to go astray
We'll teach and set it in a way,
And such directions give unto't
That it shall never wander foot.[8]
Know first, then, we will serve as true
For one poor smile, as we would do
If we had what our higher flame
Or our vainer wish could frame.
Impossible shall be our hope,
And love shall only have his scope
To join with fancy now and then,
And think what reason would condemn;
And on these grounds we'll love as true,
As if they were most sure t'ensue;
And chastely for these things we'll stay,
As if tomorrow were the day.
Meantime we two will teach our hearts
In love's burdens bear their parts:[9]
Thou first shall sigh, and say, "She's fair";
And I'll still answer, "Past compare."

4. Cf. Textual Notes.
5. Cf. Herrick, "A Nuptial Song," line 132n, p. 202.
6. Ate.
7. I.e., deviate.
8. I.e., go astray.
9. I.e., in love's choral refrains sing their individual melodies.

Thou shalt set out each part o'th' face
While I extol each little grace;
Thou shalt be ravished at her wit,
And I, that she so governs it;
Thou shalt like well that hand, that eye,
That lip, that look, that majesty,
And in good language them adore;
While I want words, and do it more.
Yea, we will sit and sigh a while,
And with soft thoughts some time beguile,
But straight again break out and praise
All we had done before, new ways.
Thus will we do till paler death
Come with a warrant for our breath;
And then whose fate shall be to die
First of us two, by legacy
Shall all his store bequeath, and give
His love to him that shall survive;
For no one stock[1] can ever serve
To love so much as she'll deserve.

Song[2]

Why so pale and wan, fond lover?
    Prithee, why so pale?
Will, when looking well can't move her,
    Looking ill prevail?
    Prithee, why so pale?

Why so dull and mute, young sinner?
    Prithee, why so mute?
Will, when speaking well can't win her,
    Saying nothing do't?
    Prithee, why so mute?

Quit, quit, for shame; this will not move,
    This cannot take her;
If of herself she will not love,
    Nothing can make her:
    The devil take her!

1. Lineage.
2. First printed in Suckling's play *Aglaura* (1638), this most famous of the poet's lyrics was set to music by William Lawes.

FROM *THE LAST REMAINS OF SIR JOHN SUCKLING* (1659)

"Out upon it! I have loved"[3]

Out upon it! I have loved
  Three whole days together;[4]
And am like to love three more,
  If it prove fair weather.

Time shall molt away his wings
  Ere he shall discover
In the whole wide world again
  Such a constant lover.

But the spite on't is, no praise
  Is due at all to me:
Love with me had made no stay,
  Had it any been but she.

Had it any been but she,
  And that very very face,
There had been at least ere this
  A dozen dozen in her place.

A Song to a Lute[5]

Hast thou seen the down i'th'air
  When wanton blasts have tossed it,
Or the ship on the sea
  When ruder winds have crossed it?
Hast thou marked the crocodile's weeping,
  Or the fox's sleeping?
Or hast viewed the peacock in his pride,
  Or the dove by his bride,
  When he courts for his lechery?
Oh, so fickle, oh, so vain, oh, so false, so false, is she!

3. Cf. Textual Notes.
4. The poem may have been based on a proverb, "After three days men grow weary of a wench, a quest, and weather rainy" (*Works of Suckling*, *ed. cit.*, p. 254).
5. This lyric is part of Suckling's play *The Sad One* (IV.iii.47–56). Cf. Jonson, "A Celebration of Charis," 4.21–30, pp. 123–124.

William Cartwright

1611	Born in Northway, Gloucestershire, on or about 23 December. Financial reverses may account for family's subsequent move to Cirencester, where father becomes an innkeeper and Cartwright receives his early education.
1623–1624	Enters Westminster School, London, on scholarship. Probably comes to the attention of Ben Jonson at this period.
1628	Elected to a studentship (i.e., recognized as a potentially outstanding scholar) at Christ Church, Oxford.
1629	Leader of a student protest against certain disciplinary arrangements at Christ Church.
1632	Receives the B.A. degree.
1635	Receives M.A. First published English poem: commendatory verses to Francis Kynaston's *Amorum Troili et Cresseidae*. Two plays, *The Lady-Errant* and *The Ordinary*, probably composed about this time.
1636	*The Royal Slave* presented on the occasion of a royal visit to Oxford in August, and again in November at Hampton Court.
1638	Takes holy orders. Contributes a poem to the Jonson memorial volume, *Jonsonus Virbius*.
1639	Publication of *The Royal Slave*.
1642	Appointed succentor (a choral leader) in Salisbury Cathedral. Preaches the "victory sermon" on the king's return to Oxford after the Battle of Edgehill. Appointed Reader in Metaphysic at Oxford University; serves as a member of the academic "Council of War," which cooperates with the royal military authorities in the city of Oxford.
1643	Appointed Junior Proctor in Oxford University. Dies of a fever, 29 November; buried in Christ Church.
1651	Publication of *Comedies, Tragi-Comedies, with Other Poems*.

FROM *COMEDIES, TRAGI-COMEDIES, WITH OTHER POEMS*[1] (1651)

To Mr. W. B.,[2] at the Birth of His First Child

You're now transcribed, and public view
Persuing finds the copy true,
Without erratas new crept in,
Fully complete and genuine,
And nothing wanting can espy
But only bulk and quantity;
The text in letters small we see,
And the arts in one epitome.
Oh, what pleasure do you take
To hear the nurse discovery make,
How the nose, the lip, the eye,
The forehead full of majesty,
Shows the father; how to this
The mother's beauty added is;
And after all, with gentle numbers,[3]
To woo the infant into slumbers.
  And these delights he yields you now,
The swathe[4] and cradle this doth show;
But hereafter, when his force
Shall wield the rattle and the horse,
When his vent'ring tongue shall speak
All synalaephaes,[5] and shall break
This word short off, and make that two,
Prattling as obligations[6] do,
'Twill ravish the delighted sense
To view these sports of innocence,
And make the wisest dote upon
Such pretty imperfection.
  Those hopeful cradles promise such
Future goodness, and so much,
That they prevent[7] my prayers, and I
Must wish but for[8] formality.
  I wish religion timely be

1. According to Humphrey Moseley, who published the 1651 edition of Cartwright's plays and poems, Ben Jonson once said, "My Son Cartwright writes all like a man." The poetical reputation of this Son of Ben declined rapidly after his untimely death in 1643, but the poems selected here indicate something of the grace and ingenuity that Cartwright, looking to Donne as well as to Jonson, could bring to bear on a variety of themes. Academic and courtly connections no doubt contributed to his success as preacher and lecturer at Oxford; yet, as his modern editor observes, he was evidently "a person of engaging charm and force," for whom (according to John Aubrey) "the king [Charles I] dropped a tear at the news of his death" (*Plays and Poems of William Cartwright*, ed. G. Blakemore Evans [Madison, Wis., 1951], p. 21).
2. The identity of this person has not been established.
3. I.e., lullabies.
4. Swaddling band.
5. I.e., confused sounds: "the coalescence or contraction of two syllables into one" (*OED*).
6. I.e., as legal documents (which include conventionally abbreviated fragments of Latin terms).
7. Anticipate.
8. I.e., merely to satisfy.

Taught him with his A B C.
I wish him good and constant health,
His father's learning, but more wealth,
And that to use, nor hoard; a purse
Open to bless, not shut to curse.
May he have many and fast friends,
Meaning good will, not private ends,
Such as scorn to understand,
When they name love, a piece of land.
May the swathe and whistle[9] be
The hardest of his bonds. May he
Have no sad cares to break his sleep,
Nor other cause, than now, to weep.
May he ne'er live to be again
What he is now, a child; may pain,
If it do visit, as a guest
Only call in, not dare to rest.

To Chloe, Who Wished Herself Young Enough for Me[1]

Chloe, why wish you that your years
  Would backwards run till they meet mine,
That perfect likeness, which endears
  Things unto things, might us combine?
Our ages so in date agree
That twins do differ more than we.

There are two births: the one when light
  First strikes the new-awakened sense;
The other when two souls unite,
  And we must count our life from thence;
When you loved me and I loved you,
Then both of us were born anew.

Love then to us did new souls give,
  And in those souls did plant new pow'rs;
Since when another life we live,
  The breath we breathe is his, not ours;
Love makes those young men whom age doth chill,

And whom he finds young, keeps young still.
Love, like that angel that shall call
  Our bodies from the silent grave,
Unto one age doth raise us all,
  None too much, none too little have;

9. Cf. Herrick, "To His Savior, a Child," line 8n, p. 222.
1. The thought and expression of this poem may be compared with those of Donne's lyric "The Good-Morrow," p. 23.

Nay, that the difference may be none,
He makes two not alike, but one.[2]

And now, since you and I are such,
Tell me what's yours and what is mine?
Our eyes, our ears, our taste, smell, touch,
Do, like our souls, in one combine;
So by this, I as well may be
Too old for you, as you for me.

A Valediction

Bid me not go where neither suns nor showers
Do make or cherish flowers,
Where discontented things in sadness lie,
And nature grieves as I;
When I am parted from those eyes,
From which my better day doth rise,
Though some propitious power
Should plant me in a bower,
Where amongst happy lovers I might see
How showers and sunbeams bring
One everlasting spring,
Nor would those fall, nor these shine forth to me;
Nature herself to him is lost
Who loseth her he honors most.
Then fairest to my parting view display
Your graces all in one full day,
Whose blessed shapes I'll snatch and keep, till when
I do return and view again;
So by this art fancy shall fortune cross,[3]
And lovers live by thinking on their loss.

No Platonic Love[4]

Tell me no more of minds embracing minds,
And hearts exchanged for hearts;
That spirits spirits meet, as winds do winds,
And mix their subtlest parts;
That two unbodied essences may kiss,
And then, like angels, twist and feel one bliss.

I was that silly[5] thing that once was wrought
To practice this thin love;

2. Cf. Donne, "The Good-Morrow," lines 20–21: "If our two loves be one, or, thou and I / Love just alike in all, none of these loves can die" (p. 23).
3. Thwart.
4. Cf. Randolph, "An Elegy," p. 341.
5. Witless (also, "innocent").

I climbed from sex to soul, from soul to thought;
    But thinking there to move,
Headlong I rolled from thought to soul, and then
From soul I lighted at the sex again.

As some strict down-looked men pretend to fast
    Who yet in closets[6] eat,
So lovers who profess they spirits taste
    Feed yet on grosser meat;
I know they boast they souls to souls convey,
Howe'er they meet, the body is the way.

Come, I will undeceive thee: they that tread
    Those vain aerial ways
Are, like young heirs and alchemists, misled
    To waste their wealth and days;
For searching thus to be forever rich,
They only find a med'cine for the itch.

6. I.e., in private rooms.

James Graham, Marquis of Montrose

1612	Born, probably in October, at Montrose, on the east coast of Scotland; the only son of the fourth Earl of Montrose and of Lady Margaret Ruthven (deceased, 1618).
1624–1626	Attends school in Glasgow. Father dies, 1626.
1627–1628	Attends Saint Andrew's University.
1629	Marries Magdalene Carnegie, November.
1633–1636	Traveling on the continent.
1638–1639	Actively supports the Scottish Covenanters in opposition to efforts by Charles I and Archbishop Laud to impose uniformity of worship on Scotland. Campaigns successfully in the vicinity of Aberdeen.
1640–1643	Increasingly disenchanted with the Presbyterian principles of the Covenanters, and with their leader, the Duke of Argyll, offers his services to Charles I. "My dear and only love" probably composed in this period.
1644	Appointed Lieutenant General in Scotland by Charles I; created Marquis of Montrose.
1644–1646	Defeats Covenanter armies in six battles between September 1644 (Tippermuir) and August 1645 (Kilsyth). Subsequently defeated at Philiphaugh in September 1645, by superior forces under Leslie; obliged to leave Scotland in September 1646.
1646–1649	After various unsuccessful efforts to raise money and troops, commissioned Lieutenant Governor of Scotland in March 1649, by the future Charles II at the Hague.
1650	Sails in March from Bergen, Norway, to Kirkwall, in the Orkney Islands. Crosses into northern Scotland with a small force, which is crushed by Leslie's troops at Carbisdale, northwest of Inverness, on 27 April. Betrayed to the government by Neil Macleod of Assynt, he is hanged, drawn, and quartered in Edinburgh, on 21 May. His head, impaled on a spike on the Tollbooth, is not taken down until 1661.

FROM *A CHOICE COLLECTION OF COMIC AND SERIOUS SCOTS POEMS* (1711)

"My dear and only love, I pray"[1]

My dear and only love, I pray
  This noble world of thee
Be governed by no other sway
  But purest monarchy;
For if confusion have a part,
  Which virtuous souls abhor,
And hold a synod[2] in thy heart,
  I'll never love thee more.

Like Alexander I will reign,
  And I will reign alone:
My thoughts shall evermore disdain
  A rival on my throne.
He either fears his fate too much,
  Or his deserts are small,
That puts it not unto the touch[3]
  To win or lose it all.

But I must rule and govern still,
  And always give the law,
And have each subject at my will,
  And all to stand in awe.
But 'gainst my battery, if I find
  Thou shunn'st the prize so sore
As that thou sett'st me up a blind,[4]
  I'll never love thee more.

Or in the empire of thy heart,
  Where I should solely be,
Another do pretend a part
  And dares to vie with me;
Or if committees thou erect,
  And go on such a score,[5]

1. "As a soldier Montrose ranks by common consent with the greatest of his age" (John Buchan, *Montrose* [London, 1928], p. 389); as a poet, although he wrote a few other pieces, he is remembered almost exclusively for this lyric. Whether the loyalties it affirms are given to an unnamed mistress or to a political ideal, "the stanzas are typical of the Cavaliers of the mid-seventeenth century, in their passionate, at times incoherent loyalty" (*Poems of James Graham, Marquis of Montrose [1612–1650]*. ed. J. L. Weir [London, 1938], p. 51). Critical opinion generally concurs with Buchan's view that the poem, written c. 1642, "is a political and not a love poem" (*op. cit.*, p. 152n); it is of interest that Montrose wrote to the future Charles II, on 28 January 1649 (two days before the execution of Charles I), "I never had passion upon earth so strong as to do the King, your father, service" (Buchan, *op. cit.*, p. 328).
2. I.e., an assembly of ecclesiastics.
3. Touchstone; i.e., that shrinks from a challenge.
4. I.e., that you are deceitful.
5. I.e., and proceed in that fashion.

I'll sing and laugh at thy neglect,
  And never love thee more.

But if thou wilt be constant then,
  And faithful of thy word,
I'll make thee glorious by my pen
  And famous by my sword:
I'll serve thee in such noble ways
  Was never heard before;
I'll crown and deck thee all with bays,[6]
  And love thee evermore.

6. I.e., with laurel garlands (in this context, the emblem of victory).

Anne Bradstreet

1612/13	Born to Thomas Dudley and Dorothy Yorke in Northamptonshire, England. Dudley became steward to the Puritan Earl of Lincoln, and Anne, tutored in aristocratic households, was unusually well educated for a woman of her time.
1628	Marries Simon Bradstreet (age twenty-five), son of a minister, graduate of Emmanuel College, Cambridge University, and assistant to her father.
1630	Emigrates to Massachusetts with her husband and father in John Winthrop's fleet, which carries the first settlers of the Massachusetts Bay Colony. Winthrop, Dudley, and Simon Bradstreet would all serve as colonial governors of Massachusetts.
1633	Her first son, Samuel, is born. She would bear seven more children.
1650	Without Anne's knowledge, John Woodbridge, her brother-in-law, publishes a volume of her poetry in London, *The Tenth Muse Lately Sprung up in America*.
1672	Dies of consumption, 16 September, in Andover.
1678	A substantially augmented and revised version of *The Tenth Muse* is published in Boston under the title *Several Poems Compiled with Great Variety of Wit and Learning*.

FROM *THE TENTH MUSE LATELY SPRUNG UP IN AMERICA* (1650)

The Prologue

To sing of wars, of captains, and of kings,
Of cities founded, commonwealths begun,[1]
For my mean pen are too superior things;
Or how they all or each their dates have run,
Let poets and historians set these forth.
My obscure lines shall not so dim their worth.

But when my wond'ring eyes and envious heart
Great Bartas'[2] sugared lines do but read o'er,
Fool[3] I do grudge the Muses did not part
'Twixt him and me that over-fluent store;
A Bartas can do what a Bartas will,
But simple I, according to my skill.

From schoolboys' tongues no rhet'ric we expect,
Nor yet a sweet consort[4] from broken strings,
Nor perfect beauty where's a main defect:
My foolish, broken, blemished Muse so sings
And this to mend, alas, no art is able,
'Cause nature made it so irreparable.

Nor can I, like that fluent sweet-tongued Greek[5]
Who lisped at first, speak afterwards more plain;
By art he gladly found what he did seek,
A full requital of his striving pain.
Art can do much, but this maxim's most sure:
A weak or wounded brain admits no cure.

I am obnoxious[6] to each carping tongue
Who says my hand a needle better fits.
A poet's pen, all scorn, I should thus wrong,
For such despite they cast on female wits:
If what I do prove well, it won't advance;
They'll say it's stolen, or else it was by chance.

But sure the antique Greeks were far more mild,
Else of our sex, why feignèd they those nine,

1. Bradstreet inventories the traditional subjects of heroic poetry.
2. Guillaume de Salluste du Bartas (1544–1590). A French poet, his most famous work was a creation epic, *La Semaine* (1578). Joshua Sylvester published an English translation in 1605. A Huguenot, Du Bartas was more influential in England than in France.
3. Foolish, silly.
4. Harmony.
5. Demosthenes (384–322 B.C.), the greatest Athenian orator. Legend has it that he began life with a speech impediment that he trained himself to overcome.
6. Exposed.

And poesy made Calliope's[7] own child?
So 'mongst the rest they placed the arts divine,
But this weak knot they will full soon untie.
The Greeks did naught but play the fools and lie.

Let Greeks be Greeks, and women what they are:
Men have precedency and still excel;
It is but vain unjustly to wage war.
Men can do best, and women know it well.
Preeminence in all and each is yours,
Yet grant some small acknowledgment of ours.

And oh ye high-flown quills[8] that soar the skies,
And ever with your prey still catch your praise,
If e'er you deign these lowly lines your eyes,
Give thyme or parsley wreath, I ask no bays.
This mean and unrefinèd ore[9] of mine
Will make your glistering gold but more to shine.

A Dialogue between Old England and New, Concerning their Present Troubles. Anno. 1642

New England.

Alas, dear mother, fairest queen and best,
With honor, wealth, and peace happy and blessed,
What ails thee hang thy head and cross thine arms,
And sit i'the dust to sigh these sad alarms?
What deluge of new woes thus overwhelm
The glories of thy ever-famous realm?
What means this wailing tone, this mournful guise?
Ah, tell thy daughter, she may sympathize.

Old England.

Art ignorant indeed of these my woes?
Or must my forcèd tongue these griefs disclose?
And must myself dissect my tattered state,
Which 'mazed Christendom stands wondering at?
And thou a child, a limb, and dost not feel
My weakened, fainting body now to reel?
This physic purging potion I have taken
Will bring consumption, or an ague quaking,
Unless some cordial thou fetch from high
Which present help may ease my malady.
If I decease, dost think thou shalt survive?

7. The nine Muses are female; Calliope is conventionally deemed the Muse of epic poetry.
8. Pens were made by sharpening the points of birds' large feathers (quills).
9. The 1650 edition has "stuff."

Or by my wasting state dost think to thrive?
Then weigh our case, if't be not justly sad,
Let me lament alone, while thou art glad.

New England.

And thus, alas, your state you much deplore
In general terms, but will not say wherefore.
What medicine shall I seek to cure this woe,
If th'wound's so dangerous, I may not know?
But you, perhaps, would have me guess it out.
What, hath some Hengist[1] like that Saxon stout
By fraud and force usurped thy flow'ring crown,
Or by tempestuous wars thy fields trod down?
Or hath Canutus,[2] that brave valiant Dane,
The regal peaceful scepter from thee ta'en?
Or is't a Norman[3] whose victorious hand
With English blood bedews thy conquered land?
Or is't intestine wars that thus offend?
Do Maud and Stephen for the crown contend?[4]
Do barons rise and side against their king,[5]
And call in foreign aid to help the thing?
Must Edward be depos'd?[6] Or is't the hour
That second Richard must be clapped i'th' Tower?[7]
Or is it the fatal jar, again begun,
That from the red, white pricking roses sprung?[8]
Must Richmond's aid the nobles now implore
To come and break the tushes of the boar?[9]
If none of these, dear mother, what's your woe?
Pray, do not fear Spain's bragging Armado.[1]
Doth your ally, fair France, conspire your wrack,
Or doth the Scots play false behind your back?
Doth Holland quit you ill for all your love?
Whence is this storm, from earth or heaven above?
Is't drought, is't famine, or is't pestilence?
Dost feel the smart, or fear the consequence?
Your humble child entreats you show your grief.
Though arms nor purse she hath for your relief—

1. Hengist was leader of a Saxon tribe (the Jutes) that imposed itself in Kent during the fifth century through double-dealing and conquest.
2. Canute, Danish King of England (1016–1035).
3. A reference to the Norman Conquest (1066), led by William the Conqueror.
4. Matilda (Maud), daughter to Henry I and mother of the future Henry II, contested the right to the throne of her father's nephew, Stephen (1135–1143). Civil war ensued. The dispute was settled when Stephen named Maud's son heir to the throne.
5. During the reign of King John (1199–1216), outraged nobles compelled the king to sign the Magna Carta (1215).
6. Edward II (1307–1327) was deposed, imprisoned, and murdered after his queen, Isabella, and her lover, Mortimer, warred against him.
7. Richard II (1377–1399), deposed by Henry IV (1399–1413), was murdered in prison.
8. "Fatal jar," or fateful conflict, refers to the War of the Roses (1455–1485), a series of dynastic conflicts between the ducal houses of York (the white rose) and Lancaster (red rose).
9. In 1485, Henry Tudor, Earl of Richmond, took the throne from Richard III, "the Boar," and so ended the War of the Roses; *tushes*: tusks.
1. The Spanish Armada, defeated in 1588

Such is her poverty—yet shall be found
A suppliant for your help, as she is bound.

Old England.

I must confess, some of those sores you name
My beauteous body at this present maim,
But foreign foe nor feignèd friend I fear,
For they have work enough, thou knowest, elsewhere.
Nor is it Alcie's son and Henry's daughter[2]
Whose proud contention cause this slaughter;
Nor nobles siding to make John no king,
French Louis[3] unjustly to the crown to bring;
No Edward, Richard, to lose rule and life,
Nor no Lancastrians to renew old strife;
No crook-backed[4] tyrant now usurps the seat,
Whose tearing tusks did wound, and kill, and threat.
No Duke of York nor Earl of March to soil
Their hands in kindred's blood whom they did foil;
No need of Tudor, roses to unite:
None knows which is the red or which the white.
Spain's braving fleet a second time is sunk.
France knows how of my fury she hath drunk
By Edward Third and Henry Fifth of fame;
Her lilies in mine arms[5] avouch the same.
My sister Scotland hurts me now no more,
Though she hath been injurious heretofore.
What Holland is, I am in some suspense,
But trust not much unto his excellence.
For wants, sure some I feel, but more I fear;
And for the pestilence, who knows how near?
Famine and plague, two sisters of the sword,
Destruction to a land doth soon afford.
They're for my punishments ordained on high,
Unless thy tears prevent it speedily.
But yet I answer not what you demand
To show the grievance of my troubled land.
Before I tell the effect, I'll show the cause,
Which are my sins—the breach of sacred Laws:
Idolatry, supplanter of a nation,
With foolish superstitious adoration,
Are liked and countenanced by men of might,
The Gospel is trod down and hath no right.
Church offices are sold and bought for gain
That Pope had hope to find Rome here again.
For oaths and blasphemies did ever ear

2. Stephen and Maud (36). Lines 61–86 reply to New England's list of historical woes (lines 36–52).
3. Louis VII of France (1187–1226) invaded England in 1216.
4. Richard III was hunchbacked.
5. French lilies in the royal coat of arms signified English claims on France.

From Beelzebub[6] himself such language hear?
What scorning of the saints of the most high!
What injuries did daily on them lie!
What false reports, what nick-names did they take,
Not for their own, but for their master's sake!
And thou, poor soul, wast jeered among the rest;
Thy flying for the truth I made a jest.
For Sabbath-breaking and for drunkenness
Did ever land profaneness more express?
From crying bloods[7] yet cleansèd am not I,
Martyrs and others dying causelessly.
How many princely heads on blocks laid down
For naught but title to a fading crown!
'Mongst all the cruelties which I have done,
Oh, Edward's babes, and Clarence' hapless son,[8]
O Jane,[9] why didst thou die in flow'ring prime?—
Because of royal stem, that was thy crime.
For bribery, adultery, for thefts, and lies,
Where is the nation I can't parallize?[1]
With usury, extortion, and oppression,
These be the Hydras[2] of my stout transgression;
These be the bitter fountains, heads, and roots
Whence flowed the source, the sprigs, the boughs, and fruits
Of more than thou canst hear, or I relate,
That with high hand I still[3] did perpetrate;
For these were threatenèd the woeful day
I mocked the preachers, put it far away;[4]
The sermons yet upon record do stand
That cried destruction to my wicked land.
These prophets' mouths (alas the while) was stopped,
Unworthily, some backs whipped, and ears cropped;
Their reverent cheeks bear the glorious marks
Of stinking, stigmatizing Romish clerks;
Some lost their livings, some in prison pent,
Some grossly fined, from friends to exile went:
Their silent tongues to heaven did vengeance cry,
Who heard their cause, and wrongs judged righteously,
And will repay it sevenfold in my lap.
This is forerunner of my afterclap.[5]
Nor took I warning by my neighbors' falls.
I saw sad Germany's dismantled walls,

6. Name for the devil, "lord of the flies" (Matthew 12:24, 27).
7. Scripturally, the blood of those unjustly killed cries out for vengeance (Genesis 4:10).
8. "Edward's babes" are the murdered sons of Edward IV. Clarence's son, Edward, Earl of Warwick, was executed for treason in 1499.
9. Lady Jane Grey (1538–1554), Henry VII's great-granddaughter, was proclaimed successor to Edward VI in 1553 and executed the next year.
1. Match, equal.
2. In Greek myth, the Hydra is a many-headed, poisonous serpent.
3. Constantly.
4. "If iniquity be in thine hand, put it far away" (Job 11:14).
5. An unexpected subsequent event; something disagreeable happening after an affair is supposed to be at an end.

I saw her people famished, nobles slain,
Her fruitful land a barren heath remain.
I saw (unmoved) her armies foiled and fled,
Wives forced, babes tossed, her houses calcinèd.
I saw strong Rochelle yielded to her foe,[6]
Thousands of starvèd Christians there also.
I saw poor Ireland bleeding out her last,
Such cruelty as all reports have past.[7]
Mine heart obdurate stood not yet aghast.
Now sip I of that cup, and just 't may be
The bottom dregs reservèd are for me.

New England.

To all you've said, sad mother, I assent.
Your fearful sins great cause there's to lament.
My guilty hands (in part) hold up with you,
A sharer in your punishments my due.
But all you say amounts to this effect,
Not what you feel, but what you do expect.
Pray, in plain terms, what is your present grief?
Then let's join heads and hands for your relief.

Old England.

Well, to the matter, then. There's grown of late
'Twixt king and peers a question of state:
Which is the chief, the law, or else the king?
One saith, it's he; the other, no such thing.
My better part in court of Parliament
To ease my groaning land show their intent
To crush the proud, and right to each man deal,
To help the Church, and stay the Commonweal.
So many obstacles comes in their way
As puts me to a stand what I should say.
Old customs, new prerogatives stood on.
Had they not held law fast, all had been gone,
Which by their prudence stood them in such stead
They took high Strafford[8] lower by the head,
And to their Laud be't spoke they held'n th'Tower
All England's metropolitan that hour.[9]
This done, an Act they would have passèd fain
No prelate should his Bishopric retain.
Here tugged they hard indeed, for all men saw
This must be done by Gospel, not by law.

6. In 1627–1628, French Protestants (Huguenots) were besieged at La Rochelle.
7. The murder of English settlers during the Irish rebellion in 1641 was exaggerated in report as a deliberate, widespread massacre.
8. Thomas Wentworth (1593–1641), first Earl of Strafford and chief minister of Charles I, was convicted of treason by Parliament and executed.
9. As Archbishop of Canterbury, William Laud (1573–1645) was England's chief prelate. Imprisoned in 1641, he was executed for treason in 1645. In lines 175–186 Bradstreet relates the growing conflict between Parliament and King Charles (1641–1642) that led to civil war.

Next the militia they urgèd sore.
This was denied, I need not say wherefore.
The king, displeased, at York himself absents.
They humbly beg return, show their intents.
The writing, printing, posting to and fro,
Shows all was done; I'll therefore let it go.
But now I come to speak of my disaster.
Contention's grown 'twixt subjects and their master:
They worded it so long, they fell to blows,
That thousands lay on heaps. Here bleeds my woes.
I that no wars so many years have known
Am now destroyed and slaughtered by mine own.
But could the field alone this strife decide,
One battle, two, or three I might abide,
But these may be beginnings of more woe;
Who knows, the worst, the best may overthrow!
Religion, Gospel, here lies at the stake,
Pray now, dear child, for sacred Zion's sake,
Oh, pity me in this sad perturbation,
My plundered towns, my houses' devastation,
My ravished virgins, and my young men slain,
My wealthy trading fallen, my dearth of grain.
The seed time's come, but ploughman hath no hope
Because he knows not who shall in[1] his crop.
The poor they want their pay, their children bread,
Their woeful mothers' tears unpitièd.
If any pity in thy heart remain,
Or any childlike love thou dost retain,
For my relief now use thy utmost skill,
And recompense me good for all my ill.

New England.

Dear mother, cease complaints, and wipe your eyes,
Shake off your dust, cheer up, and now arise.
You are my mother, nurse; I once your flesh,
Your sunken bowels gladly would refresh.
Your griefs I pity much but should do wrong,
To weep for that we both have prayed for long,
To see these latter days of hoped-for good,
That Right may have its right, though't be with blood.
After dark Popery the day did clear;
But now the sun in's brightness shall appear.
Blest be the nobles of thy noble land
With (ventured lives) for truth's defense that stand.
Blest be thy Commons, who for common good
And thy infringèd laws have boldly stood.
Blest be thy counties, who do aid thee still
With hearts and states to testify their will.
Blest be thy preachers, who do cheer thee on,

1. Harvest.

O cry, "the sword of God and Gideon!"[2]
And shall I not on them wish Mero's curse[3]
That help thee not with prayers, arms, and purse?
And for myself, let miseries abound
If mindless of thy state I e'er be found.
These are the days the Church's foes to crush,
To root out prelates, head, tail, branch, and rush.
Let's bring Baal's vestments[4] out, to make a fire,
Their mitres, surplices, and all their tire,
Copes, rochets, croziers, and such trash,
And let their names consume, but let the flash
Light Christendom, and all the world to see
We hate Rome's Whore,[5] with all her trumpery.
Go on, brave Essex,[6] show whose son thou art,
Not false to king nor country in thy heart,
But those that hurt his people and his crown,
By force expel, destroy, and tread them down.
Let jails be filled with th'remnant of that pack,
And sturdy Tyburn[7] loaded till it crack.
And ye brave nobles, chase away all fear,
And to this blessed cause closely adhere.
O mother, can you weep and have such peers?
When they are gone, then drown yourself in tears;
If now you weep so much, that then no more
The briny ocean will o'erflow your shore.
These, these are they (I trust) with Charles our King,
Out of all mists such glorious days will bring
That dazzled eyes, beholding, much shall wonder
At that thy settled peace, thy wealth, and splendor,
Thy Church and weal established in such manner
That all shall joy that thou displayedst thy banner,
And discipline erected so, I trust,
That nursing kings shall come and lick thy dust.
Then justice shall in all thy courts take place
Without respect of persons or of case.
Then bribes shall cease, and suits shall not stick long,
Patience and purse of clients for to wrong.
Then High Commissions shall fall to decay,
And pursuivants and catchpoles[8] want their pay.
So shall thy happy nation ever flourish,
When truth and righteousness they thus shall nourish.

2. Gideon led Israel against the Midianites; his name means "one who cuts down" (cf. Judges 7:18).
3. "Curse ye Meroz, said the angel of the Lord, curse ye bitterly the inhabitants thereof; because they came not to the help of the Lord, to the help of the Lord against the mighty" (Judges 5:23).
4. I.e., apparel worn by idolatrous priest. Scripturally, Baal is a god of the Canaanites. As the following lines detail, Bradstreet means ceremonial finery worn by bishops.
5. The Scarlet Whore of Babylon (Revelation 17:3–6), identified by Protestants as the Catholic Church.
6. Robert Devereux, Earl of Essex (1591–1646), led parliamentary forces (1642–1645).
7. London's gallows.
8. The High Commission was the supreme ecclesiastical court in England from 1570 until 1641, when it was abolished. "Pursuivants and catchpoles" are warrant officers.

When thus in Peace, thine armies brave send out
To sack proud Rome, and all her vassals rout.
There let thy name, thy fame, and valor shine,
As did thine ancestors' in Palestine,
And let her spoils full pay, with interest be,
Of what unjustly once she polled[9] from thee.
Of all the woes thou canst, let her be sped,
Execute to th'full the vengeance threat'ned.
Bring forth the beast[1] that ruled the world with's beck,
And tear his flesh, and set your feet on's neck,
And make his filthy den so desolate
To th'stonishment of all that knew his state.
This done, with brandished swords to Turkey go,—
(For then what is it but English blades dare do?)
And lay her waste, for so's the sacred doom,
And do to Gog[2] as thou hast done to Rome.
Oh Abraham's seed, lift up your heads on high,
For sure the day of your redemption's nigh.[3]
The scales shall fall from your long blinded eyes,
And him you shall adore who now despise.
Then fullness of the nations in shall flow,
And Jew and Gentile to one worship go.
Then follows days of happiness and rest.
Whose lot doth fall to live therein is blest.
No Canaanite shall then be found 'n th'land,
And holiness on horses' bells shall stand.[4]
If this[5] make way thereto, then sigh no more,
But, if at all, thou didst not see't before.[6]
Farewell, dear mother; Parliament, prevail,
And in a while you'll tell another tale.

9. Taxed.
1. The Whore of Babylon is carried by the beast (Revelation 17:7–8).
2. Satan incites "the nations which are in the four quarters of the earth, Gog and Magog" against the New Jerusalem (Revelation 20:8). English Protestants associated Gog with Turkey.
3. "And if ye be Christ's, then are ye Abraham's seed, and heirs according to the promise" (Galatians 3:29). Bradstreet in lines 282–287 alludes to the conversion of the Jews as a precondition of the apocalyptic establishment of the ideal state. Saul, who persecuted Christians until his blinding conversion on the road to Damascus, regained his sight after baptism (Acts 9:18).
4. For the ideal state where Canaanites do not reside and "holiness unto the Lord" is on horses' bells, see Zechariah 14:20–21.
5. The civil war.
6. I.e., if you are going to sigh about anything, sigh that you did not see true religion stir sooner.

Richard Crashaw

1612 (or 1613)	Born in London, the only child of a prominent Puritan preacher and virulent anti-Catholic; both parents die by the time he is fourteen.
1629–1631	Educated at the Charterhouse, an English boarding school founded in 1611.
1631	Enters Pembroke College, Cambridge, a High Church college.
1634	Takes his B.A. and publishes *Epigrammatum sacrorum liber*, a book of Latin epigrams on scriptural subjects.
1634	Elected to a fellowship at Peterhouse, Cambridge, also a High Church college. During the next several years, he teaches poetry, music, and painting, and serves in some official capacity at Little Saint Mary's, Cambridge. He becomes a friend of Nicholas Ferrar and a frequent visitor to the Little Gidding religious community.
1643	Leaves Cambridge, just before he would have been ejected by the Puritans intent on stripping Peterhouse and other colleges of Laudian trappings.
1646	Lives in Paris along with Cowley and other exiles from England, including the Countess of Denbigh and Queen Henrietta Maria. By this time he had already entered the Roman Catholic Church. Publishes poems in a combined volume, *Steps to the Temple* and *The Delights of the Muses*.
1648	Publishes a much revised and enlarged edition of *Steps to the Temple* and *The Delights of the Muses*.
1649	Dies on 21 August, at Loreto, Italy, where he held a minor post at the cathedral.
1652	The final volume of his poems, *Carmen Deo Nostro*, published in Paris.

FROM *STEPS TO THE TEMPLE* (1646)

Upon the Infant Martyrs

To see both blended in one flood
The mothers' milk, the children's blood,
Makes me doubt if Heaven will gather,
Roses hence, or lilies rather.

Upon the Ass that Bore Our Savior[1]

Hath only anger an omnipotence
In eloquence?
Within the lips of love and joy doth dwell
No miracle?
Why else had Baalam's ass[2] a tongue to chide
His master's pride?
And thou (heaven-burdened beast) hast ne'er a word
To praise thy Lord?
That he should find a tongue and vocal thunder,
Was a great wonder.
But oh methinks 'tis a far greater one
That thou find'st none.

Upon Lazarus His Tears

Rich Lazarus![3] richer in those gems, thy tears,
Than Dives in the robes he wears:
He scorns them now, but oh they'll suit full well
With the purple he must wear in hell.

On the Wounds of Our Crucified Lord

O these wakeful wounds of thine!
Are they mouths? or are they eyes?
Be they mouths, or be they eyen,[4]
Each bleeding part some one supplies.

1. Christ's entry into Jerusalem (Matthew 21:1–11).
2. See Numbers 22:23–30.
3. Lazarus, epitome of suffering poverty, goes to Abraham's bosom after death; but Dives, who "was clothed in purple and fine linen," arrives in hell, where he futilely begs Abraham that "Lazarus dip the tip of his finger in water, and cool my tongue" (Luke 16:19–31).
4. Eyes.

Lo! a mouth, whose full-bloomed lips
At too dear a rate are roses.
Lo! a blood-shot eye! that weeps
And many a cruel tear discloses.

O thou[5] that on this foot hast laid
Many a kiss, and many a tear,
Now thou shalt have all repaid,
Whatsoe'er thy charges[6] were.

This foot hath got a mouth and lips,
To pay the sweet sum of this kisses:
To pay thy tears, an eye that weeps
Instead of tears such gems as this is.

The difference only this appears,
(Nor can the change offend)
The debt is paid in ruby-tears,
Which thou in pearls didst lend.

On Mr. G. Herbert's Book[7]

Know you, fair, on what you look?
Divinest love lies in this book:
Expecting fire from your eyes,
To kindle this his sacrifice.
When your hands untie these strings,[8]
Think you have an angel by th'wings.
One that gladly will be nigh,
To wait upon each morning sigh.
To flutter in the balmy air,
Of your well perfumèd prayer.
These white plumes of his he'll lend you,
Which every day to heaven will send you:
To take acquaintance of the sphere,
And all the smooth faced kindred there.
And though Herbert's name do owe[9]
These devotions, fairest; know
That while I lay them on the shrine
Of your white hand, they are mine.

5. Mary Magdalene.
6. I.e., sins. Mary Magdalene was traditionally thought to have been a prostitute.
7. Cf. Textual Notes.
8. The ribbons tying the book together.
9. Own.

FROM *DELIGHTS OF THE MUSES* (1646)

Music's Duel[1]

Now westward Sol[2] had spent the richest beams
Of noon's high glory, when hard by the streams
Of Tiber, on the scene of a green plat,
Under protection of an oak, there sat
A sweet lute's-master: in whose gentle airs[3]
He lost the day's heat, and his own hot cares.
Close in the covert of the leaves there stood
A nightingale, come from the neighboring wood:
(The sweet inhabitant of each glad tree,
Their Muse, their Siren, harmless Siren she)
There stood she listening, and did entertain
The music's soft report: and mold the same
In her own murmurs, that whatever mood
His curious[4] fingers lent, her voice made good:
The man perceived his rival, and her art,
Disposed to give the light-foot lady sport
Awakes his lute, and 'gainst the fight to come
Informs it, in a sweet *praeludium*[5]
Of closer strains, and ere the war begin,
He lightly skirmishes on every string
Charged with a flying touch: and straightway she
Carves out her dainty voice as readily,
Into a thousand sweet distinguished tones,
And reckons up in soft divisions,[6]
Quick volumes of wild notes; to let him know
By that shrill taste, she could do something too.
His nimble hands instinct then taught each string
A cap'ring cheerfulness; and made them sing
To their own dance; now negligently rash
He throws his arm, and with a long drawn dash
Blends all together; then distinctly trips
From this to that; then quick returning skips
And snatches this again, and pauses there.
She measures every measure, everywhere
Meets art with art; sometimes as if in doubt
Not perfect yet, and fearing to be out
Trails her plain ditty[7] in one long-spun note
Through the sleek passage of her open throat:

1. Based loosely on a popular Latin poem, this is a contest between a nightingale and a lutenist in the traditions of nature versus art; the subject was a frequent one in the seventeenth century. For the Latin text, cf. the edition of Crashaw by George Walton Williams (New York, 1970). The poem is replete with musical terms, only some of which are noted here.
2. The Roman god of the Sun.
3. *Whose*: the lute's; *airs*: tunes or breezes.
4. Careful, artful.
5. Prelude or introduction.
6. Improvised elaborations of the melody.
7. Simple melody, without divisions.

A clear unwrinkled song, then doth she point it
With tender accents, and severely joint it
By short diminutives, that being reared
In controverting warbles evenly shared,
With her sweet self she wrangles; he amazed
That from so small a channel should be raised
The torrent of a voice, whose melody
Could melt into such sweet variety,
Strains higher yet; that tickled with rare art
The tattling[8] strings (each breathing in his part)
Most kindly do fall out; the grumbling bass
In surly groans disdains the treble's grace.
The high-perched treble chirps at this, and chides,
Until his finger (moderator) hides
And closes the sweet quarrel, rousing all
Hoarse, shrill, at once; as when the trumpets call
Hot Mars to th'harvest of death's field, and woo
Men's hearts into their hands; this lesson too
She gives him back; her supple breast thrills out
Sharp airs, and staggers in a warbling doubt
Of dallying sweetness, hovers o'er her skill,
And folds in waved notes with a trembling bill,
The pliant series of her slippery song.
Then starts she suddenly into a throng
Of short thick sobs, whose thundering volleys float,
And roll themselves over her lubric[9] throat
In panting murmurs, stilled[1] out of her breast,
That ever-bubbling spring; the sugared nest
Of her delicious soul, that there does lie
Bathing in streams of liquid melody;
Music's best seed-plot, whence in ripened airs
A golden-headed harvest fairly rears
His honey-dropping tops, plowed by her breath
Which there reciprocally laboreth
In that sweet soil. It seems a holy choir
Founded to th'name of great Apollo's[2] lyre.
Whose silver-roof rings with the sprightly notes
Of sweet-lipped angel-imps, that swill their throats
In cream of morning Helicon,[3] and then
Prefer soft anthems to the ears of men,
To woo them from their beds, still murmuring
That men can sleep while they their Matins sing:
(Most divine service) whose so early lay
Prevents[4] the eyelids of the blushing day.

8. Prattling.
9. Smooth.
1. Distilled.
2. God of music, poetry, and prophecy, as well as of manly beauty and of the sun.
3. Mountain home of the Muses in Greece; sometimes, the fountains there; also, a stringed instrument.
4. Comes before.

There might you hear her kindle her soft voice,
In the close murmur of a sparkling noise,
And lay the groundwork of her hopeful song,
Still keeping in the forward stream, so long
Till a sweet whirlwind (striving to get out)
Heaves her soft bosom, wanders round about,
And makes a pretty earthquake in her breast,
Till the fledged notes at length forsake their nest;
Fluttering in wanton shoals, and to the sky
Winged with their own wild echoes prattling fly.
She opes the floodgate, and lets loose a tide
Of streaming sweetness, which in state doth ride
On the waved back of every swelling strain,
Rising and falling in a pompous train.
And while she thus discharges a shrill peal
Of flashing airs, she qualifies their zeal
With the cool epode of a graver note,
Thus high, thus low, as if her silver throat
Would reach the brazen voice of war's hoarse bird;[5]
Her little soul is ravished: and so poured
Into loose ecstasies, that she is placed
Above herself, music's enthusiast.
Shame now and anger mixed a double stain
In the musician's face; yet once again
(Mistress) I come; now reach a strain, my lute,
Above her mock, or be forever mute.
Or tune a song of victory to me,
Or to thyself sing thine own obsequy;[6]
So said, his hands sprightly as fire he flings,
And with a quavering coyness tastes the strings.
The sweet-lipped sisters[7] musically frighted,
Singing their fears are fearfully delighted.
Trembling as when Apollo's golden hairs[8]
Are fanned and frizzled, in the wanton airs
Of his own breath: which married to his lyre
Doth tune the spheres, and make heaven's self look higher.
From this to that, from that to this he flies,
Feels music's pulse in all her arteries,
Caught in a net which there Apollo spreads,
His fingers struggle with the vocal threads,
Following those little rills, he sinks into
A sea of Helicon; his hand does go
Those parts of sweetness, which with nectar drop,
Softer than that which pants in Hebe's[9] cup.

5. The raven.
6. I.e., if the lutenist loses.
7. The Muses.
8. I.e., the sun's rays.
9. Greek goddess of youth and cupbearer to the gods.

The humorous strings expound his learned touch
By various glosses; now they seem to grutch[1]
And murmur in a buzzing din, then jingle
In shrill-tongued accents: striving to be single.
Every smooth turn, every delicious stroke
Gives life to some new grace; thus doth h'invoke
Sweetness by all her names; thus, bravely thus
(Fraught with a fury so harmonious)
The lute's light genius[2] now does proudly rise,
Heaved on the surges of swollen rhapsodies.
Whose flourish (meteor-like) doth curl the air
With flash of high-borne fancies: here and there
Dancing in lofty measures, and anon
Creeps on the soft touch of a tender tone:
Whose trembling murmurs melting in wild airs
Runs to and fro, complaining his sweet cares
Because those precious mysteries that dwell,
In music's ravished soul he dare not tell,
But whisper to the world: thus do they vary
Each string his note, as if they meant to carry
Their master's blest soul (snatched out at his ears
By a strong ecstasy) through all the spheres
Of music's heaven; and seat it there on high
In th'*empyraeum*[3] of pure harmony.
At length (after so long, so loud a strife
Of all the strings, still breathing the best life
Of blest variety attending on
His finger's fairest revolution
In many a sweet rise, many as sweet a fall)
A full-mouth diapason[4] swallows all.
This done, he lists what she would say to this,
And she, although her breath's late exercise
Had dealt too roughly with her tender throat,
Yet summons all her sweet powers for a note
Alas! in vain! for while (sweet soul) she tries
To measure all those wild diversities
Of chatt'ring strings, by the small size of one
Poor simple voice, raised in a natural tone,
She fails, and failing grieves, and grieving dies.
She dies; and leaves her life the victor's prize,
Falling upon his lute; o fit to have
(That lived so sweetly) dead, so sweet a grave!

1. Grumble.
2. Spirit.
3. The highest heaven.
4. Grand burst of harmony.

FROM *CARMEN DEO NOSTRO* (1652)

In the Holy Nativity of Our Lord God: A Hymn Sung as by the Shepherds

Chorus.

Come we shepherds whose blest sight
Hath met love's noon in nature's night;
Come lift we up our loftier song
And wake the sun that lies too long.

To all our world of well-stol'n joy
He slept, and dreamt of no such thing,
While we found out Heav'n's fairer eye,
And kissed the cradle of our King.
Tell him he rises now, too late
To show us aught worth looking at.

Tell him we now can show him more
Than he e'er showed to mortal sight;
Than he himself e'er saw before;
Which to be seen needs not his light.
Tell him, Tityrus, where th'hast been;
Tell him, Thyrsis, what th'hast seen.

Tityrus. Gloomy night embraced the place
Where the noble infant lay.
The babe looked up and showed his face;
In spite of darkness, it was day.
It was thy day, sweet! and did rise
Not from the East, but from thine eyes.

Chorus. It was thy day, sweet, *etc.*

Thyrsis. Winter chid aloud; and sent
The angry North to wage his wars.
The North forgot his fierce intent,
And left perfumes instead of scars.
By those sweet eyes' persuasive pow'rs
Where he meant frost, he scattered flow'rs.

Chorus. By those sweet eyes', *etc.*

Both. We saw thee in thy balmy nest,
Young dawn for our eternal day!
We saw thine eyes break from their East
And chase the trembling shades away.
We saw thee: and we blest the sight;
We saw thee by thine own sweet light.

Tityrus. Poor world (said I) what wilt thou do
To entertain this starry stranger?
Is this the best thou canst bestow,
A cold, and not too cleanly, manger?
Contend, ye powers of Heav'n and earth,
To fit a bed for this huge birth.

Chorus. Contend, ye powers, *etc.*

Thyrsis. Proud world, said I; cease your contest
And let the mighty babe alone.
The Phoenix builds the Phoenix' nest.[5]
Love's architecture is his own.
The babe whose birth embraces this morn,
Made his own bed e'er he was born.

Chorus. The babe whose, *etc.*

Tityrus. I saw the curled drops, soft and slow,
Come hovering o'er the place's head;
Off'ring their whitest sheets of snow
To furnish the fair infant's bed:
Forbear, said I, be not too bold;
Your fleece is white but 'tis too cold.

Chorus. Forbear, said I, *etc.*

Thyrsis. I saw the obsequious Seraphims
Their rosy fleece of fire bestow.
For well they now can spare their wings
Since Heav'n itself lies here below.
Well done, said I: but are you sure
Your down so warm, will pass for pure?

Chorus. Well done, said I, *etc.*

Tityrus. No, no, your King's not yet to seek
Where to repose his royal head;
See, see, how soon his new-bloomed cheek
'Twixt mother's breasts is gone to bed.
Sweet choice, said we! no way but so
Not to lie cold, yet sleep in snow.

Chorus. Sweet choice, said we, *etc.*

Both. We saw thee in thy balmy nest,
Bright dawn of our eternal day!
We saw thine eyes break from their East,

5. The Phoenix is a mythological bird, reputedly only one of a kind, that lived for 500 (or 1,000) years, consumed itself in fire, and rose renewed from its own ashes to begin again another long life.

And chase the trembling shades away.
We saw thee: and we blest the sight.
We saw thee, by thine own sweet light.

Chorus. We saw thee, *etc.*

Full Chorus.

Welcome, all wonders in one sight!
Eternity shut in a span.
Summer in winter. Day in night.
Heaven in earth, and God in man.
Great little one! whose all-embracing birth
Lifts earth to Heaven, stoops Heav'n to earth.

Welcome. Though nor to gold nor silk,
To more than Caesar's birthright is;
Two sister-seas of virgin-milk,
With many a rarely-tempered kiss,
That breathes at once both maid and mother,
Warms in the one, cools in the other.

Welcome, though not to those gay flies[6]
Gilded i'th'beams[7] of earthly kings;
Slippery souls in smiling eyes;
But to poor shepherds, home-spun things:
Whose wealth's their flock; whose wit, to be
Well read in their simplicity.

Yet when young April's husband show'rs
Shall bless the fruitful Maia's bed,[8]
We'll bring the first-born of her flowers
To kiss thy feet and crown thy head.
To thee, dread Lamb! whose love must keep
The shepherds; more than they the sheep.

To thee, meek majesty! soft King
Of simple graces and sweet loves.
Each of us his lamb will bring,
Each his pair of silver doves;
Till burnt at last in fire of thy fair eyes,
Ourselves become our own best sacrifice.

6. Parasites.
7. I.e., in the beams.
8. Maia was one of the earliest ancient deities, usually described as an earth goddess; the month of May was named for her.

Saint Mary Magdalene or The Weeper[9]

Lo where a wounded heart with bleeding eyes conspire,
Is she a flaming fountain, or a weeping fire?

1

Hail, sister springs!
Parents of silver-forded rills!
Ever bubbling things!
Thawing crystal! snowy hills,
Still spending, never spent! I mean
Thy fair eyes, sweet Magdalene!

2

Heavens thy fair eyes be;
Heav'n's bosom drinks the gentle stream.
'Tis seed-time still with thee,
And stars thou sow'st, whose harvest dares
Promise to earth to countershine
Whatever makes heav'n's forehead fine.

3

But we're deceivèd all.
Stars indeed they are too true;
For they but seem to fall.
As heav'n's other spangles do.
It is not for our earth and us
To shine in things so precious.

4

Upwards thou dost weep.
Heav'n's bosom drinks the gentle stream.
Where the milky rivers creep,
Thine floats above and is the cream.
Waters above the heav'ns, what they be
We're taught best by thy tears and thee.

5

Every morn from hence
A brisk Cherub something sips
Whose sacred influence
Adds sweetness to his sweetest lips,

9. The weeper is Mary Magdalene, notorious sinner, who anointed Christ's feet with her tears and dried them with her hair (Luke 7:36 ff.) and later, according to legend, did penance in the desert for thirty years. Apparently an amalgam of several scriptural Marys, she became the pattern of the Christian penitent, very popular in religious poetry of the sixteenth and seventeenth centuries, especially Crashaw's. The poem abounds in images of moisture, especially lachrymose images.

Then to his music. And his song
Tastes of this breakfast all day long.

6

Not in the evening's eyes
When they red with weeping are
For the sun that dies,
Sits sorrow with a face so fair,
Nowhere but here did ever meet
Sweetness so sad, sadness so sweet.

7

When sorrow would be seen
In her brightest majesty
(For she is a queen)
Then is she drest by none but thee.
Then, and only then, she wears
Her proudest pearls; I mean, thy tears.

8

The dew no more will weep
The primrose's pale cheek to deck,
The dew no more will sleep
Nuzzled in the lily's neck;
Much rather would it be thy tear,
And leave them both to tremble here.

9

There is no need at all
That the balsam-sweating bough
So coyly should let fall
His medicinable tears; for now
Nature hath learnt t'extract a dew
More sovereign and sweet from you.

10

Yet let the poor drops weep
(Weeping is the ease of woe),
Softly let them creep,
Sad that they are vanquished so.
They, though to others no relief,
Balsam may be, for their own grief.

11

Such the maiden gem[1]
By the purpling vine put on,

1. A flower.

Peeps from her parent stem
And blushes at the bridegroom sun.
This wat'ry blossom of thy eyn,[2]
Ripe, will make the richer wine.

12

When some new bright guest
Takes up among the stars a room,
And Heav'n will make a feast,
Angels with crystal vials come
And draw from these full eyes of thine
Their master's water: their own wine.

13

Golden though he be,
Golden Tagus[3] murmurs though;
Were his way by thee,
Content and quiet he would go.
So much more rich would he esteem
Thy silver, than his golden stream.

14

Well does the May[4] that lies
Smiling in thy cheeks, confess
The April in thine eyes.
Mutual sweetness they express.
No April e'er lent kinder showers,
Nor May returned more faithful flowers.

15

O cheeks! beds of chaste loves
By your own showers seasonably dashed;
Eyes! nests of milky doves
In your own wells decently washed,
O wit of love! that thus could place
Fountain and garden in one face.

16

Oh sweet contest: of woes
With loves, of tears with smiles disputing!
O fair, and friendly foes,
Each other kissing and confuting!
While rain and sunshine, cheeks and eyes
Close in kind contrarieties.

2. Eyes.
3. A river in Spain and Portugal famous for its golden sand.
4. I.e., flowers.

17

But can these fair floods be
Friends with the bosom fires that fill thee!
Can so great flames agree
Eternal tears should thus distill thee?
O floods, o fires! O suns, o showers!
Mixed and made friends by love's sweet powers.

18

'Twas his well-pointed dart
That digged these wells and drest this vine,
And taught the wounded Heart
The way into these weeping eyn.
Vain loves avaunt! bold hands forbear!
The lamb hath dipped his white foot here.

19

And now where'er he strays,
Among the Galilean mountains,
Or more unwelcome ways,
He's followed by two faithful fountains;
Two walking baths; two weeping motions;
Portable and compendious oceans.

20

O thou, thy lord's fair store!
In thy so rich and rare expenses,
Even when he showed most poor,
He might provoke the wealth of princes.
What prince's wanton'st pride e'er could
Wash with silver, wipe with gold?

21

Who is that King, but he
Who call'st his crown to be called thine,
That thus can boast to be
Waited on by a wandering mine,
A voluntary mint, that strows
Warm silver showers where'er he goes!

22

O precious prodigal!
Fair spendthrift by thyself! Thy measure
(Merciless love!) is all.
Even to the last pearl in thy treasure.
All places, times, and objects be
Thy tear's sweet opportunity.

23

Does the daystar rise?
Still thy stars do fall and fall.
Does day close his eyes?
Still the fountain weeps for all.
Let night or day do what they will,
Thou hast thy task; thou weepest still.

24

Does thy song lull the air?
Thy falling tears keep faithful time.
Does thy sweet-breathèd prayer
Up in clouds of incense climb?
Still at each sigh, that is, each stop,
A bead, that is, a tear, does drop.

25

At these thy weeping gates,
(Watching their wat'ry motion)
Each wingèd moment waits,
Takes his tear, and gets him gone.
By thine eye's tinct ennobled thus
Time lays him up; he's precious.

26

Not, so long she lived,
Shall thy tomb report of thee;
But, so long she grieved,
Thus must we date thy memory.
Others by moments, months, and years
Measure their ages; thou, by tears.

27

So do perfumes expire,
So sigh tormented sweets, oppressed
With proud unpitying fire.
Such tears the suff'ring rose that's vexed
With ungentle flames does shed,
Sweating in a too warm bed.

28

Say, ye bright brothers,
The fugitive sons of those fair eyes
Your fruitful mothers!
What make you here? what hopes can 'tice[5]
You to be born? what cause can borrow
You from those nests of noble sorrow?

5. Entice.

29

Whither away so fast?
For sure the sordid earth
Your sweetness cannot taste
Nor does the dust deserve your birth.
Sweet, whither haste you then? O say
Why you trip so fast away?

30

We go not to seek
The darlings of Aurora's bed,[6]
The rose's modest cheek
Nor the violet's humble head,
Though the field's eyes too weepers be
Because they want[7] such tears as we.

31

Much less mean we to trace
The fortune of inferior gems,
Preferred[8] to some proud face
Or perched upon feared diadems.
Crowned heads are toys.[9] We go to meet
A worthy object, our Lord's feet.[1]

A Hymn to the Name and Honor of the Admirable Saint Teresa[2]

Love, thou art absolute sole lord
Of life and death. To prove the word,
We'll now appeal to none of all
Those thy old soldiers, great and tall,
Ripe men of martyrdom, that could reach down
With strong arms, their triumphant crown;
Such as could with lusty breath
Speak loud into the face of death
Their great Lord's glorious name; to none
Of those whose spacious bosoms spread a throne
For love at large to fill; spare blood and sweat;

6. Aurora, bride of Tithonus, was the goddess of the dawn.
7. Lack.
8. Here meaning literally placed before or in front of.
9. Trifles.
1. I.e., Christ's crucified feet; cf. also the tear-washed feet of Luke 7:38.
2. The title continues, "Foundress of the Reformation of the Discalced Carmelites, both men and women; a woman for angelical height of speculation, for masculine courage of performance, more than a woman. Who yet a child, outran maturity, and durst plot a martyrdom." The poem is based on the *Autobiography* of Saint Teresa of Avila (1515–1582), translated into English in 1642 as *The Flaming Heart*. A mystic as well as a leader of the Counter-Reformation, Teresa was both reformer and head of the Carmelites, an ascetic, contemplative order. In the Office for her feast, 15 October, the hymn for both matins and lauds thematically contrasts her early desire for martyrdom and her later role as "love's victim."

And see him take a private seat,
Making his mansion in the mild
And milky soul of a soft child.
Scarce has she learnt to lisp the name
Of martyr; yet she thinks it shame
Life should so long play with that breath
Which spent can buy so brave a death.
She never undertook to know
What death with love should have to do;
Nor has she e'er yet understood
Why to show love, she should shed blood.
Yet though she cannot tell you why,
She can love, and she can die.
Scarce has she blood enough to make
A guilty sword blush for her sake;
Yet has she a heart dares hope to prove
How much less strong is death than love.
Be love but there; let poor six years
Be posed with maturest fears
Man trembles at, you straight shall find
Love knows no nonage,[3] nor the mind.
'Tis love, not years or limbs that can
Make the martyr, or the man.
Love touched her heart, and lo it beats
High, and burns with such brave heats;
Such thirsts to die, as dares drink up
A thousand cold deaths in one cup.
Good reason. For she breathes all fire.
Her weak breast heaves with strong desire
Of what she may with fruitless wishes
Seek for amongst her mother's kisses.
Since 'tis not to be had at home
She'll travail[4] to a martyrdom.
No home for her confesses she
But where she may a martyr be.
She'll to the Moors and try with them,
For this unvalued[5] diadem.
She'll offer them her dearest breath,
With Christ's name in't, in change for death.
She'll bargain with them; and will give
Them God; and teach them how to live
In him: or, if they this deny,
For him she'll teach them how to die.
So shall she leave amongst them sown
Her Lord's blood; or at least her own.
Farewell then, all the world! Adieu.
Teresa is no more for you.

3. The time when one is still legally under parents' or guardian's control.
4. "Travail" combines travel and the labor of childbirth. Teresa's older brother accompanied her on this adventure.
5. Invaluable, priceless.

Farewell, all pleasures, sports, and joys,
(Never till now esteemèd toys)
Farewell whatever dear may be,
Mother's arms or father's knee;
Farewell house, and farewell home!
She's for the Moors, and martyrdom.
Sweet, not so fast! lo thy fair spouse
Whom thou seek'st with so swift vows,
Calls thee back, and bids thee come
T'embrace a milder martyrdom.
Blest powers forbid, thy tender life
Should bleed upon a barbarous knife;
Or some base hand have power to rase[6]
Thy breast's chaste cabinet, and uncase
A soul kept there so sweet, o no;
Wise heav'n will never have it so.
Thou art Love's victim; and must die
A death more mystical and high.
Into Love's arms thou shalt let fall
A still-surviving funeral
He is the dart must make the death
Whose stroke shall taste thy hallowed breath;[7]
A dart thrice dipped in that rich flame
Which writes thy spouse's radiant name
Upon the roof of heav'n; where aye[8]
It shines, and with a sovereign ray
Beats bright upon the burning faces
Of souls which in that name's sweet graces
Find everlasting smiles. So rare,
So spiritual, pure, and fair
Must be th'immortal instrument
Upon whose choice point shall be sent
A life so loved; and that there be
Fit executioners for thee,
The fair'st and first-born sons of fire,
Blest Seraphim, shall leave their choir
And turn Love's soldiers, upon thee
To exercise their archery.
O how oft shalt thou complain
Of a sweet and subtle pain.
Of intolerable joys;
Of a death, in which who dies
Loves his death, and dies again,
And would forever so be slain.
And lives, and dies; and knows not why

6. Cut, slash.
7. In one of her visions, Teresa saw an angel "of very much beautie" with a "long Dart of gold in his hand" which he "thrust . . . some severall times, through my verie Hart, after such a manner, as that it passed the verie inwards, of my Bowells" and left her "wholy inflamed with a great love of Almightye God" (*The Flaming Heart*, 1642, chapter XXIX). Bernini's Baroque sculpture of Teresa in ecstasy is based on this passage, as is Crashaw's "The Flaming Heart," p. 471.
8. Forever.

To live, but that he thus may never leave to die.
   How kindly will thy gentle heart
Kiss the sweetly killing dart!
And close in his embraces keep
Those delicious wounds, that weep
Balsam to heal themselves with. Thus
When these thy deaths, so numerous,
Shall all at last die into one,
And melt thy soul's sweet mansion;
Like a soft lump of incense, hasted
By too hot a fire, and wasted
Into perfuming clouds, so fast
Shalt thou exhale to Heav'n at last
In a resolving sigh, and then
O what? Ask not the tongues of men,
Angels cannot tell: suffice,
Thyself shall feel thine own full joys
And hold them fast forever. There
So soon as thou shalt first appear,
The moon of maiden stars, thy white
Mistress,[9] attended by such bright
Souls as thy shining self, shall come
And in her first ranks make thee room;
Where 'mongst her snowy family
Immortal welcomes wait for thee.
   O what delight, when revealed life shall stand
And teach thy lips heav'n with his hand;
On which thou now may'st to thy wishes
Heap up thy consecrated kisses.
What joys shall seize thy soul, when she,
Bending her blessed eyes on thee
(Those second smiles of Heaven) shall dart
Her mild rays through thy melting heart!
   Angels, thy old friends, there shall greet thee
Glad at their own home now to meet thee.
   All thy good works which went before
And waited for thee at the door,
Shall own thee there; and all in one
Weave a constellation
Of crowns, with which the King thy spouse
Shall build up thy triumphant brows.
   All thy old woes shall now smile on thee
And thy pains sit bright upon thee.
All thy sorrows here shall shine,
All thy sufferings be divine.
Tears shall take comfort and turn gems,
And wrongs repent to diadems.
Even thy deaths shall live; and new
Dress the soul that erst they slew.

9. The Virgin Mary.

Thy wounds shall blush to such bright scars
As keep account of the Lamb's wars.[1]
Those rare works where thou shalt leave writ
Love's noble history, with wit
Taught thee by none but him, while here
They feed our souls, shall clothe thine there.
Each heav'nly word by whose hid flame
Our hard hearts shall strike fire, the same
Shall flourish on thy brows, and be
Both fire to us and flame to thee;
Whose light shall live bright in thy face
By glory, in our hearts by grace.
Thou shalt look around about, and see
Thousands of crowned souls throng to be
Themselves thy crown. Sons of thy vows,
The virgin births with which thy sovereign spouse
Made fruitful thy fair soul, go now
And with them all about thee bow
To him, put on (he'll say), put on
(My rosy love) that thy rich zone[2]
Sparkling with sacred flames
Of thousand souls, whose happy names
Heav'n keeps upon thy score. (Thy bright
Life brought them first to kiss the light
That kindled them to stars) and so
Thou with the Lamb,[3] thy Lord, shalt go;
And wheresoe'er he sets his white
Steps, walk with him those ways of light
Which who in death would live to see,
Must learn in life to die like thee.

The Flaming Heart[4]

Well meaning readers! you that come as friends
And catch the precious name that piece pretends;
Make not too much haste t'admire
That fair-cheek'd fallacy of fire.[5]
That is a Seraphim, they say
And this the great Teresia.
Readers, be ruled by me; and make
Here a well-placed and wise mistake,
You must transpose the picture quite,
And spell it wrong to read it right;
Read him for her, and her for him;

1. Cf. Revelation 12:10–11.
2. An encircling band (like a girdle), distinct in color or texture from its surroundings.
3. Cf. Revelation 19:7–10.
4. The full title reads, "The Flaming Heart upon the Book and Picture of the Seraphical Saint Teresa (as She Is Usually Expressed with a Seraphim beside Her)."
5. I.e., the "picture" referred to in the subtitle is mistaken; the poem will now undertake to put things right, largely by paradox.

And call the Saint the Seraphim.
Painter, what didst thou understand
To put her dart into his hand!
See, even the years and size of him
Shows this the Mother Seraphim.
This is the mistress flame; and duteous he
Her happier fire-works, here, comes down to see.
O most poor-spirited of men!
Had thy cold pencil kissed her pen
Thou couldst not so unkindly err
To show us this faint shade for her.
Why man, this speaks pure mortal frame;
And mocks with female frost love's manly flame.
One would suspect thou meant'st to paint
Some weak, inferior, woman saint.
But had thy pale-faced purple took
Fire from the burning cheeks of that bright book
Thou wouldst on her have heaped up all
That could be found seraphical;
Whate'er this youth of fire wears fair,
Rosy fingers, radiant hair,
Glowing cheeks, and glistering wings,
All those fair and flagrant things,
But before all, that fiery dart
Had filled the hand of this great heart.
Do then as equal right requires,
Since his the blushes be, and hers the fires,
Resume and rectify thy rude design;
Undress thy Seraphim into mine.
Redeem this injury of thy art;
Give him the veil,[6] give her the dart.
Give him the veil; that he may cover
The red cheeks of a rivaled lover.
Ashamed that our world, now, can show
Nests of new Seraphims here below.
Give her the dart, for it is she
(Fair youth) shoots both thy shaft and thee.
Say, all ye wise and well-pierced hearts
That live and die amidst her darts,
What is't your tasteful spirits do prove
In that rare life of her, and love?
Say and bear witness. Sends she not
A Seraphim at every shot?
What magazines of immortal arms there shine!
Heav'n's great artillery in each love-spun line.
Give him the veil, who kindly takes the shame.
But if it be the frequent fate
Of worst faults to be fortunate;

6. I.e., veil of the nun.

If all's prescription; and proud wrong
Hearkens not to an humble song;
For all the gallantry of him,
Give me the suff'ring Seraphim.
His be the bravery of all those bright things;
The glowing cheeks, the glittering wings;
The rosy hand, the radiant dart;
Leave her alone the Flaming Heart.
    Leave her that; and thou shalt leave her
Not one loose shaft but Love's whole quiver.
For in Love's field was never found
A nobler weapon than a wound.
Love's passives are his activ'st part.
The wounded is the wounding heart.
O heart! the equal poise[7] of love's both parts,[8]
Big alike with wounds and darts.
Live in these conquering leaves;[9] live all the same;
And walk through all tongues one triumphant flame.
Live here, great heart; and love and die and kill;
And bleed and wound, and yield and conquer still.
Let this immortal life, where'er it comes.
Walk in a crowd of loves and martyrdoms.
Let mystic deaths wait on't; and wise souls be
The love-slain witnesses of this life of thee.
O sweet incendiary! show here thy art,
Upon this carcass of a hard, cold heart;
Let all thy scattered shafts of light, that play
Among the leaves of thy large books of day,[1]
Combined against this breast at once break in
And take away from me myself and sin.
This gracious robbery shall thy bounty be;
And my best fortunes such fair spoils of me.
O thou undaunted daughter of desires!
By all thy dow'r of lights and fires;
By all the eagle in thee, all the dove;[2]
By all thy lives and deaths of love;
By thy large draughts of intellectual day,
And by thy thirsts of love more large than they;
By all thy brim-filled bowls of fierce desire,
By thy last morning's draught of liquid fire;
By the full kingdom of that final kiss
That seized thy parting soul, and sealed thee his;
By all the heav'ns thou hast in him,
(Fair sister of the Seraphim!)
By all of him we have in thee,

7. Weight, value.
8. Refers to active and passive aspects of love, as illustrated by the "wounds and darts."
9. Pages of the *Autobiography*.
1. Light, both spiritual and intellectual (cf. lines 96–97).
2. *Eagle . . . dove*: complex reference to symbols of fire and light, active and passive, vision and peace, John the Evangelist (the eagle could look at the sun) and the inspiring Holy Spirit.

Leave nothing of myself in me!
Let me so read thy life, that I
Unto all life of mine may die!

To the Noblest and Best of Ladies, The Countess of Denbigh[3]

What heaven-entreated heart[4] is this?
Stands trembling at the gate of bliss;
Holds fast the door, yet dares not venture
Fairly to open it, and enter.
Whose definition is a doubt
'Twixt life and death, 'twixt in and out.
Say, lingering fair! why comes the birth
Of your brave soul so slowly forth?
Plead your pretenses (oh you strong
In weakness) why you choose so long
In labor of yourself to lie,
Nor daring quite to live nor die?
Ah linger not, loved soul! a slow
And late consent was a long no.
Who grants at last, long time tried
And did his best to have denied.
What magic bolts, what mystic bars
Maintain the will in these strange wars!
What fatal, yet fantastic, bands
Keep the free heart from its own hands!
So when the year takes cold, we see
Poor waters their own prisoners be.
Fettered, and locked up fast they lie
In a sad self-captivity.
Th'astonished nymphs their flood's strange fate deplore,
To see themselves their own severer shore.
Thou that alone canst thaw this cold
And fetch the heart from its stronghold,
Almighty Love! End this long war,
And of a meteor make a star.
Oh fix this fair indefinite.
And 'mongst thy shafts of sovereign light
Choose out that sure decisive dart
Which has the key of this close heart,
Knows all the corners of't, and can control
The self-shut cabinet of an unsearched soul.
O let it be at last, love's hour.

3. The subtitle of the 1652 version reads, "Persuading her to Resolution in Religion, and to render herself without further delay into the Communion of the Catholic Church." There are two versions of the poem (cf. Textual Notes); this is the earlier. Both poems are parodies of the seduction poem. The countess's husband, the Earl of Denbigh, died in 1643 fighting for King Charles I; later the countess went with Queen Henrietta Maria to Paris, where she did become a Roman Catholic.
4. The poem is preceded by the emblem of a locked heart; cf. line 34.

Raise this tall trophy of thy power;
Come once the conquering way; not to confute
But kill this rebel-word, "irresolute,"
That so, in spite of all this peevish strength
Of weakness, she may write "resolved at length,"
Unfold at length, unfold fair flower
And use the season of love's shower,
Meet his well-meaning wounds, wise heart!
And haste to drink the wholesome dart,
That healing shaft, which heav'n till now
Hath in love's quiver hid for you.
Oh, dart of love! arrow of light!
Oh happy you, if it hit right;
It must not fall in vain, it must
Not mark the dry regardless dust.
Fair one, it is your fate; and brings
Eternal worlds upon its wings.
Meet it with wide-spread arms; and see
Its seat your soul's just center be.
Disband dull fears; give faith the day.
To save your life, kill your delay.
It is love's siege; and sure to be
Your triumph, though his victory.
'Tis cowardice that keeps this field
And want of courage not to yield.
Yield then, O yield, that love may win
The fort at last, and let life in.
Yield quickly. Lest perhaps you prove
Death's prey, before the prize of love.
This fort of your fair self, if't be not won,
He is repulsed indeed; but you're undone.

Sir John Denham

1615	Born in Dublin; brought to England, 1617, and educated initially in London. His father was Lord Chief Justice of the King's Bench in Ireland, 1612–1616; his mother, daughter of an Irish peer, died in 1619.
1631–1634	Attends Trinity College, Oxford; apparently leaves without taking a degree. Marries Anne Cotton, June 1634.
1634–1636	Studies law at Lincoln's Inn. Given to obsessive gambling, but writes a prose essay against that vice, *The Anatomy of Play* (published 1651), to calm his father's concern. Translates Book II of Vergil's *Aeneid*, in heroic couplets (published 1656).
1639	On the death of his father, inherits a large fortune and extensive lands; takes up residence at Egham, Surrey. Called to the bar (i.e., admitted as a barrister).
1641	First draft of "Cooper's Hill" perhaps written in this year. His blank-verse tragedy, *The Sophy*, acted at Blackfriars.
1642	Publication of *The Sophy* and of the first edition of "Cooper's Hill." As Sheriff of Surrey, attempts to defend Farnham Castle against parliamentary forces, but resists only briefly before surrendering to Sir William Waller. His estates confiscated by Parliament.
1643–1647	Employed in various capacities for the royalist cause. First wife dies in this period.
1648–1652	Living abroad, in attendance on the future Charles II.
1655–1656	Works for the royalist cause in England and Wales. Fourth (revised) edition of "Cooper's Hill" published.
1658	Given permission by Cromwell to reside in Bury Saint Edmunds, Suffolk.
1660	At the Restoration, appointed Surveyor of the Works (the post once held by Inigo Jones); knighted, and given various offices and lands by Charles II.
1661	Member of Parliament for Old Sarum, Wiltshire; in Parliament until his death.
1663	Elected to the Royal Society.
1665	Marries Margaret Brooke, a beauty of twenty-three, who shortly becomes the publicly acknowledged mistress of the Duke of York.
1666	Apparently insane (by consequence of paresis) for some months.
1667	Death of Lady Denham, 6 January; various highly placed

	personages, including Denham himself, suspected of having poisoned her.
1668	Publication of *Poems and Translations, with The Sophy*.
1669	Death, 10 March. Buried in Westminster Abbey.

FROM *POEMS AND TRANSLATIONS* (1668)

Cooper's Hill[1]

Sure there are poets which did never dream
Upon Parnassus, nor did taste the stream
Of Helicon;[2] we therefore may suppose
Those made not poets, but the poets those.
And as courts make not kings, but kings the court,
So where the Muses and their train resort,
Parnassus stands: if I can be to thee
A poet, thou Parnassus art to me.
Nor wonder, if (advantaged in my flight,
By taking wing from thy auspicious[3] height)
Through untraced ways and airy paths I fly,
More boundless in my fancy than my eye:
My eye, which swift as thought contracts the space
That lies between, and first salutes the place
Crowned with that sacred pile, so vast, so high,
That whether 'tis a part of earth or sky
Uncertain seems, and may be thought a proud
Aspiring mountain, or descending cloud,
Paul's, the late theme of such a Muse whose flight
Has bravely reached and soared above thy height;[4]
Now shalt thou stand though sword, or time, or fire,
Or zeal[5] more fierce than they, thy fall conspire,
Secure, whilst thee the best of poets sings,
Preserved from ruin by the best of kings.
Under his proud survey the city lies,
And like a mist beneath a hill doth rise,
Whose state and wealth, the business and the crowd,
Seems at this distance but a darker cloud;
And is to him who rightly things esteems
No other in effect than what it seems;
Where, with like haste, through several ways they run,
Some to undo and some to be undone;
While luxury and wealth, like war and peace,

1. Cooper's Hill is a rise of ground near Egham, Surrey. Denham's poetical reputation rests almost entirely upon this "topographical-reflective" poem, which Dr. Johnson called "the work that confers upon him the rank and dignity of an original author" (cf. Johnson's remarks on Denham, pp. 738–739). Dryden, in the dedicatory epistle to his play *The Rival Ladies* (1664), observed that the poem, "for the majesty of the style is, and ever will be, the exact standard of good writing"; in the dedication of his translation of the *Aeneid* (1697), he remarked particularly the "sweetness" of the most famous couplet in the poem (lines 191–192), adding that few "can find the reason of that sweetness." For variant readings in the (pirated) edition of 1642 and in the first authorized edition of 1655, cf. Textual Notes. A full account of the complicated textual problems is given in Brendan O Hehir, *Expans'd Hieroglyphicks: A Study of Sir John Denham's "Coopers Hill," with a Critical Edition of the Poem* (Berkeley, 1969).
2. In ancient Greece, Mount Parnassus and Mount Helicon were sacred to the Muses and to Apollo, god of poetry and song.
3. I.e., favorable for augury.
4. These lines refer to Edmund Waller's poem "Upon His Majesty's Repairing of Paul's" (c. 1640).
5. I.e., the zeal of those Puritans who considered the decorative and ceremonial aspects of Anglican worship to be idolatrous.

Are each the other's ruin and increase,
As rivers lost in seas, some secret vein
Thence reconveys, there to be lost again.[6]
Oh, happiness of sweet retired content!
To be at once secure and innocent.
Windsor[7] the next (where Mars with Venus dwells,
Beauty with strength) above the valley swells
Into my eye, and doth itself present
With such an easy and unforced ascent
That no stupendous precipice denies
Access, no horror turns away our eyes;
But such a rise as doth at once invite
A pleasure and a reverence from the sight.
Thy mighty master's emblem, in whose face
Sat meekness, heightened with majestic grace;
Such seems thy gentle height, made only proud
To be the basis of that pompous load,
Than which a nobler weight no mountain bears,
But Atlas only that supports the spheres.[8]
When nature's hand this ground did thus advance,
'Twas guided by a wiser power than chance,
Marked out for such a use as if 'twere meant
T'invite the builder, and his choice prevent.[9]
Nor can we call it choice when what we choose,
Folly or blindness only could refuse.
A crown of such majestic towers doth grace
The gods' great mother[1] when her heavenly race
Do homage to her; yet she cannot boast
Amongst that numerous and celestial host
More heroes than can Windsor, nor doth fame's
Immortal book record more noble names.
Not to look back so far, to whom this isle
Owes the first glory of so brave a pile,
Whether to Caesar, Albanact, or Brute,
The British Arthur, or the Danish Canute[2]
(Though this of old no less contest did move
Than when for Homer's birth seven cities strove;[3]
Like him in birth, thou should'st be like in fame,
As thine his fate, if mine had been his flame),
But whosoe'er it was, nature designed
First a brave place, and then as brave a mind.
Not to recount those several kings, to whom

6. Cf. Donne's lyric, "The Triple Fool," lines 6–7.
7. Charles I and his consort Henrietta Maria dwelt intermittently at the royal residence of Windsor Castle, westward from Cooper's Hill.
8. The Titan Atlas, brother to Prometheus, was condemned by Zeus to bear the heavens on his back (cf. Hesiod, *Theogony*, 517–520).
9. Anticipate.
1. I.e., the Asian goddess Cybele, known to the Greeks as Rhea.
2. According to Geoffrey of Monmouth (c. 1100–1154), Brute, the (legendary) descendant of Aeneas, founded London; his son Albanact ruled Scotland after the death of Brute (*Historia Regum Britanniae*, I.xviii, II.1). The Danish King Canute ruled England from 1018 to 1035.
3. Homer was probably born in Chios or Smyrna; Rhodes, Colophon, Salamis, Argos, and Athens also claimed the honor.

It gave a cradle, or to whom a tomb,
But thee, great Edward, and thy greater son[4]
(The lilies which his father wore, he won),
And thy Bellona,[5] who the consort came
Not only to thy bed, but to thy fame;
She to thy triumph led one captive king
And brought that son, which did the second bring.[6]
Then didst thou found that Order;[7] whether love
Or victory thy royal thoughts did move,
Each was a noble cause, and nothing less
Than the design has been the great success,
Which foreign kings and emperors esteem
The second honor to their diadem.
Had thy great destiny but given thee skill
To know, as well as power to act her will,
That from those kings, who then thy captives were,
In after-times should spring a royal pair[8]
Who should possess all that thy mighty power,
Or thy desires more mighty, did devour,
To whom their better fate reserves whate'er
The victor hopes for, or the vanquished fear;
That blood which thou and thy great grandsire[9] shed,
And all that since these sister nations bled,
Had been unspilt, had happy Edward known
That all the blood he spilt had been his own.
When he that patron[1] chose in whom are joined
Soldier and martyr, and his arms confined
Within the azure circle, he did seem
But to foretell and prophesy of him[2]
Who to his realms that azure round hath joined,
Which nature for their bound at first designed;
That bound, which to the world's extremest ends,
Endless itself, its liquid arms extends:
Nor doth he need those emblems which we paint,
But is himself the soldier and the saint.[3]
Here should my wonder dwell, and here my praise;
But my fixed thoughts my wandering eye betrays,
Viewing a neighboring hill,[4] whose top of late
A chapel crowned, till in the common fate

4. Edward III, who claimed France through his mother's lineage, was the father of the Black Prince, victor at Poitiers in 1356.
5. Bellona was the Roman goddess of war; the term here refers to Philippa of Hainault, consort of Edward III.
6. King David II of Scotland was taken prisoner at Neville's Cross in 1346; King John II of France was captured (by the Black Prince) at Poitiers.
7. I.e., the Order of the Garter, founded by Edward III in 1349; its badge is the red-cross shield of Saint George and England, surrounded by a blue garter inscribed *honi soit qui mal ye pense* ("evil be to him that evil thinks").
8. I.e., Charles I and Henrietta Maria.
9. I.e., Edward I.
1. I.e., Saint George of Cappadocia.
2. I.e., Charles I.
3. Peter Paul Rubens (1577–1640) had painted Charles I in the figure of Saint George.
4. I.e., Saint Anne's Hill, southeast from Cooper's Hill, the site of Chertsey Abbey, seized for the Crown when the monasteries were dissolved in the reign of Henry VIII.

The adjoining Abbey fell (may no such storm
Fall on our times, where ruin must reform).
Tell me, my Muse, what monstrous dire offense,
What crime could any Christian king incense
To such a rage? Was't luxury, or lust?
Was he so temperate, so chaste, so just?
Were these their crimes? They were his own much more;
But wealth is crime enough to him that's poor,
Who having spent the treasures of his crown,
Condemns their luxury to feed his own.
And yet this act, to vanish o'er the shame
Of sacrilege, must bear devotion's name.
No crime so bold but would be understood
A real, or at least a seeming good.
Who fears not to do ill, yet fears the name,
And free from conscience, is a slave to fame.
Thus he the church at once protects and spoils;
But princes' swords are sharper than their styles.[5]
And thus to th'ages past he makes amends,
Their charity destroys, their faith defends.
Then did religion in a lazy cell,
In empty, airy contemplations dwell,
And like the block, unmovèd, lay; but ours,
As much too active, like the stork devours.[6]
Is there no temperate region can be known
Betwixt their frigid and our torrid zone?
Could we not wake from that lethargic dream
But to be restless in a worse extreme?
And for that lethargy was there no cure
But to be cast into a calenture?
Can knowledge have no bound, but must advance
So far, to make us wish for ignorance?
And rather in the dark to grope our way
Than led by a false guide to err by day?
Who sees these dismal heaps, but would demand
What barbarous invader sacked the land?
But when he hears no Goth, no Turk did bring
This desolation, but a Christian king,
When nothing but the name of zeal[7] appears
'Twixt our best actions and the worst of theirs,
What does he think our sacrilege would spare,
When such th'effects of our devotions are?
Parting from thence 'twixt anger, shame, and fear,
Those for what's past, and this for what's too near,[8]
My eye, descending from the hill, surveys

5. I.e., (1) sharper than their pens; (2) sharper than their titles. Some years before Henry VIII broke with Rome, the Pope had conferred upon him the title "Defender of the Faith."
6. The fable, from Aesop, appears also in Donne's "The Calm," lines 3–4. Donne also alludes to "the calenture" (cf. line 144), a delirious fever "incident to sailors within the tropics" (*OED*); cf. "The Calm," line 23n, p. 58.
7. Cf. line 22.
8. I.e., anger and shame for what is past, and fear for what is too immediately threatening.

Where Thames amongst the wanton[9] valleys strays.
Thames, the most loved of all the ocean's sons
By his old sire, to his embraces runs,
Hasting to pay his tribute to the sea,
Like mortal life to meet eternity.
Though with those streams he no resemblance hold,
Whose foam is amber and their gravel gold;[1]
His genuine, and less guilty wealth to explore,
Search not his bottom, but survey his shore,
O'er which he kindly spreads his spacious wing,
And hatches plenty for th'ensuing spring.
Nor then destroys it with too fond a stay,
Like mothers which their infants overlay;[2]
Nor with a sudden and impetuous wave,
Like profuse kings, resumes the wealth he gave.
No unexpected inundations spoil
The mower's hopes, nor mock the plowman's toil;
But God-like his unwearied bounty flows;
First loves to do, then loves the good he does.
Nor are his blessings to his banks confined,
But free and common as the sea or wind;
When he to boast, or to disperse his stores,
Full of the tributes of his grateful shores,
Visits the world, and in his flying towers[3]
Brings home to us, and makes the Indies ours;
Finds wealth where 'tis, bestows it where it wants,
Cities in deserts, woods in cities plants,
So that to us no thing, no place is strange,
While his fair bosom is the world's exchange.
O could I flow like thee, and make thy stream
My great example, as it is my theme!
Though deep, yet clear, though gentle, yet not dull,
Strong without rage, without o'er-flowing full.
Heaven her Eridanus[4] no more shall boast,
Whose fame in thine, like lesser currents lost,
Thy nobler streams shall visit Jove's abodes,
To shine amongst the stars and bathe the gods.
Here nature, whether more intent to please
Us or herself with strange varieties
(For things of wonder give no less delight
To the wise Maker's, than beholder's sight,
Though these delights from several causes move;
For so our children, thus our friends we love),
Wisely she knew the harmony of things,
As well as that of sounds, from discords springs.
Such was the discord which did first disperse

9. Fertile.
1. I.e., the Spanish and Portuguese river Tagus and the Lydian river Pactolus, famous for their ore-bearing sands. Cf. Randolph, "A Gratulatory," line 44, p. 340.
2. Cf. Waller, "The Battle of the Summer Islands," Canto 2, lines 21–22, p. 366.
3. I.e., tall-masted sailing ships.
4. I.e., the Milky Way (also a classical name for the Italian river Po).

Form, order, beauty through the universe.
While dryness moisture, coldness heat resists,[5]
All that we have, and that we are, subsists;
While the steep horrid roughness of the wood
Strives with the gentle calmness of the flood,
Such huge extremes when nature doth unite,
Wonder from thence results, from thence delight.
The stream is so transparent, pure, and clear,
That had the self-enamored youth[6] gazed here,
So fatally deceived he had not been,
While he the bottom, not his face had seen.
But his proud head the airy mountain hides
Among the clouds; his shoulders and his sides
A shady mantle clothes; his curlèd brows
Frown on the gentle stream, which calmly flows,
While winds and storms his lofty forehead beat,
The common fate of all that's high or great.
Low at his foot a spacious plain[7] is placed,
Between the mountain and the stream embraced,
Which shade and shelter from the hill derives,
While the kind river wealth and beauty gives;
And in the mixture of all these appears
Variety, which all the rest endears.
This scene had some bold Greek, or British bard
Beheld of old, what stories had we heard
Of fairies, satyrs, and the nymphs, their dames,
Their feasts, their revels, and their amorous flames.
'Tis still the same, although their airy shape
All but a quick poetic sight escape.
There Faunus and Sylvanus keep their courts,
And thither all the hornèd host resorts
To graze the ranker mead; that noble herd
On whose sublime and shady fronts is reared
Nature's great masterpiece, to show how soon
Great things are made, but sooner are undone.
Here have I seen the King,[8] when great affairs
Give leave to slacken and unbend his cares,
Attended to the chase by all the flower
Of youth, whose hopes a nobler prey devour.
Pleasure with praise and danger they would buy,
And wish a foe that would not only fly.
The stag now conscious of his fatal growth,
At once indulgent to his fear and sloth,
To some dark covert his retreat had made,
Where nor man's eye, nor heaven's, should invade
His soft repose; when th'unexpected sound
Of dogs and men his wakeful ear doth wound.

5. Cf. Ovid, *Metamorphoses*, I.17–20.
6. I.e., Narcissus.
7. I.e., Egham Mead, or Runnymede, where the Magna Carta was signed in 1215.
8. For the allegorical significance of the stag hunt (lines 241–328), cf. Brendan O Hehir, *ed. cit.*, pp. 244–250.

Roused with the noise, he scarce believes his ear,
Willing to think th'illusions of his fear
Had given this false alarm; but straight his view
Confirms that more than all he fears is true.
Betrayed in all his strengths, the wood beset,
All instruments, all arts of ruin met,
He calls to mind his strength and then his speed,
His wingèd heels, and then his armèd head;
With these t'avoid, with that his fate to meet;
But fear prevails and bids him trust his feet.
So fast he flies that his reviewing[9] eye
Has lost the chasers, and his ear the cry;
Exulting, till he finds their nobler sense
Their disproportioned speed does recompense;
Then curses his conspiring feet, whose scent
Betrays that safety which their swiftness lent.
Then tries his friends: among the baser herd,
Where he so lately was obeyed and feared,
His safety seeks; the herd, unkindly[1] wise,
Or chases him from thence, or from him flies.
Like a declining statesman, left forlorn
To his friends' pity and pursuers' scorn,
With shame remembers, while himself was one
Of the same herd, himself the same had done.
Thence to the coverts and the conscious[2] groves,
The scenes of his past triumphs and his loves,
Sadly surveying where he ranged alone,
Prince of the soil, and all the herd his own,
And like a bold knight errant did proclaim
Combat to all, and bore away the dame,
And taught the woods to echo to the stream
His dreadful challenge and his clashing beam;[3]
Yet faintly now declines the fatal strife,
So much his love was dearer than his life.
Now every leaf and every moving breath
Presents a foe, and every foe a death.
Wearied, forsaken, and pursued, at last
All safety in despair of safety placed,
Courage he thence resumes, resolved to bear
All their assaults, since 'tis in vain to fear.
And now too late he wishes for the fight;
That strength he wasted in ignoble flight.
But when he sees the eager chase renewed,
Himself by dogs, the dogs by men pursued,
He straight revokes his bold resolve, and more
Repents his courage than his fear before;
Finds that uncertain ways unsafest are,

9. I.e., backward-looking.
1. Unnaturally.
2. Sympathetic.
3. Antlers.

And doubt a greater mischief than despair.
Then to the stream, when neither friends, nor force,
Nor speed, nor art avail, he shapes his course;
Thinks not their rage so desperate t'assay
An element more merciless than they.
But fearless they pursue, nor can the flood
Quench their dire thirst; alas, they thirst for blood.
So towards a ship the oar-finned galleys ply,
Which wanting sea to ride, or wind to fly,
Stands but to fall revenged on those that dare
Tempt the last fury of extreme despair.
So fares the stag among th'enragèd hounds,
Repels their force, and wounds returns for wounds.
And as a hero, whom his baser foes
In troops surround, now these assails, now those,
Though prodigal of life, disdains to die
By common hands; but if he can descry
Some nobler foe's approach, to him he calls
And begs his fate, and then contented falls;
So when the king a mortal shaft lets fly
From his unerring hand, then glad to die,
Proud of the wound, to it resigns his blood
And stains the crystal with a purple flood.
This a more innocent and happy chase
Than when of old, but in the self-same place,[4]
Fair liberty pursued, and meant a prey
To lawless power, here turned and stood at bay,
When in that remedy all hope was placed
Which was, or should have been at least, the last.
Here was that Charter sealed wherein the crown
All marks of arbitrary power lays down.
Tyrant and slave, those names of hate and fear,
The happier style of king and subject bear:
Happy when both to the same center move,
When kings give liberty, and subjects love.
Therefore not long in force this Charter stood;
Wanting that seal, it must be sealed in blood.
The subjects armed, the more their princes gave,
Th'advantage only took the more to crave,
Till kings by giving, give themselves away,
And even that power that should deny, betray.
"Who gives constrained, but his own fear reviles,
Not thanked, but scorned; nor are they gifts, but spoils."[5]
Thus kings, by grasping more than they could hold,
First made their subjects by oppression bold;
And popular sway, by forcing kings to give
More than was fit for subjects to receive,
Ran to the same extremes; and one excess
Made both, by striving to be greater, less.

4. I.e., Runnymede.
5. The author of the quoted lines is unidentified.

When a calm river, raised with sudden rains,
Or snows dissolved, o'erflows the adjoining plains,
The husbandmen with high-raised banks secure
Their greedy hopes, and this he can endure.
But if with bays[6] and dams they strive to force
His channel to a new or narrow course,
No longer then within his banks he dwells;
First to a torrent, then a deluge swells;
Stronger and fiercer by restraint he roars,
And knows no bound, but makes his power his shores.

6. Embankments.

Richard Lovelace

1618	Born in Woolwich, in the outskirts of London (or possibly born in Holland); the eldest son of Sir William Lovelace, who had served in the Low Countries under Sir Horace Vere and who was killed in action near Assen, Holland, in 1627. By royal warrant, receives his early education at Charterhouse School by virtue of his father's death on active service.
1634	Matriculates at Gloucester Hall (now Worcester College), Oxford, as a gentleman commoner.
1636	His comedy, *The Scholar*, acted at Oxford. Awarded the M.A. degree, apparently at the request of one of Queen Henrietta Maria's ladies in waiting, on the occasion of a royal visit to Oxford.
1637	Incorporated M.A. at Cambridge. At court, gains the support of Lord Goring, subsequently Earl of Norwich and, from 1647, general in the royalist army.
1638	First published poems: "An Elegy," printed in *Musarum Oxoniensis Charisteria Pro Serenissima Regina Maria*; and commendatory verses prefixed to Anthony Hodges's translation of *Clitophon and Leucippe* (a Greek romance of the third century A.D.).
1639–1640	As ensign in Goring's regiment, takes part in the King's military expeditions against Scotland. Writes a tragedy, *The Soldier*. Presumably makes Sir John Suckling's acquaintance at this time.
1640–1641	Residing at his estate in Kent.
1642	In April, presents the Kentish Petition (a royalist manifesto) to Parliament; consequently imprisoned in the Gatehouse Prison in Westminster for some two months. Writes "To Althea. From Prison" during this time. Following his release, resides briefly in London; then follows Goring to the Low Countries. Remains in Holland and France until 1646.
1646–1647	Returns to England; living in London.
1648	In October, committed by Parliament to Peterhouse Prison, Aldersgate (probably for his connection with disturbances in Kent).
1649	Released from prison, April. Publication of *Lucasta*. Financially ruined by his outlay on behalf of the royalist

	cause, exists thereafter in miserable circumstances, maintained by charity.
1657 or 1658	Death, in London. Buried in Saint Bride's Church.
1659	Publication of *Lucasta: Posthume Poems*.

FROM *LUCASTA*[1] (1649)

To Lucasta. Going Beyond the Seas. Song. Set by Mr. Henry Lawes[2]

If to be absent were to be
        Away from thee;
    Or that when I am gone,
    You or I were alone;
Then, my Lucasta, might I crave
Pity from blust'ring wind or swallowing wave.

But I'll not sigh one blast or gale
        To swell my sail,
    Or pay a tear to 'suage[3]
    The foaming blue-god's[4] rage;
For whether he will let me pass
Or no, I'm still as happy as I was.

Though seas and land betwixt us both,
        Our faith and troth,
    Like separated souls,
    All time and space controls;
Above the highest sphere we meet
Unseen, unknown, and greet as angels greet.

So then we do anticipate
        Our after-fate,
    And are alive i'the skies,
    If thus our lips and eyes
Can speak like spirits unconfined
In heaven, their earthy bodies left behind.

To Lucasta. Going to the Wars. Song. Set by Mr. John Lanière[5]

Tell me not, sweet, I am unkind,
    That from the nunnery

1. Lovelace and Suckling have traditionally been paired as in some sense archetypally representative of the "Cavalier" spirit. There is a measure of truth in this view, but the two poets are not, after all, much alike. If Suckling's verse is often lighthearted, his friend's poems are regularly serious and thoughtful, struck through with somber undertones. Suckling as a rule employs relatively simple diction, while that of Lovelace's poetry is often hard to disentangle. Much of Lovelace's verse, in fact, reflects its author's determination to present a cool and unruffled countenance to the world, betraying little of the terror induced by the spectacle of a disintegrating society.
2. The identity of Lucasta ("chaste light") has not been established. Henry Lawes (1596–1662) composed the music for Milton's *Comus* in 1634, and for Carew's masque, *Coelum Britannicum*, presented at Whitehall in the same year.
3. Assuage.
4. I.e., Neptune's.
5. The Lanière (Lanyer) family had been musicians to the royal household for several generations; John Lanière died in 1650. Cf. Aemilia Lanyer, p. 3.

Of thy chaste breast, and quiet mind,
  To war and arms I fly.

True, a new mistress now I chase,
  The first foe in the field;
And with a stronger faith embrace
  A sword, a horse, a shield.

Yet this inconstancy is such,
  As you too shall adore;
I could not love thee, dear, so much,
  Loved I not honor more.

To Amarantha, That She Would Dishevel Her Hair. Song. Set by Mr. Henry Lawes[6]

  Amarantha sweet and fair,
Ah, braid no more that shining hair!
  As my curious hand or eye,
Hovering round thee, let it fly.

  Let it fly as unconfined
As its calm ravisher, the wind,
  Who hath left his darling, th'East,
To wanton o'er that spicy nest.

  Ev'ry tress must be confessed
But neatly tangled at the best,
  Like a clue[7] of golden thread,
Most excellently ravelèd.

  Do not then wind up that light
In ribbons, and o'ercloud in night;
  Like the sun in's early ray,
But shake your head and scatter day.

  See, 'tis broke! Within this grove,
The bower and the walks of love,
  Weary lie we down and rest,
And fan each other's panting breast.

  Here we'll strip and cool our fire
In cream below, in milk-baths higher;
  And when all wells are drawn dry,
I'll drink a tear out of thine eye.

6. Lawes's musical setting was printed in his collection *Ayres and Dialogues* (1653).
7. Ball.

Which our very joys[8] shall leave,
That sorrows thus we can deceive;
Or our very sorrows weep,
That joys so ripe, so little keep.

Gratiana Dancing and Singing

See! with what constant motion,
Even and glorious as the sun,
Gratiana steers that noble frame,
Soft as her breast, sweet as her voice,
That gave each winding law and poise,
And swifter than the wings of fame.

She beat the happy pavement
By such a star made firmament,
Which now no more the roof envies,
But swells up high with Atlas even,
Bearing the brighter, nobler heaven,
And in her all the deities.

Each step trod out a lover's thought
And the ambitious hopes he brought;
Chained to her brave feet with such arts,
Such sweet command and gentle awe,
As when she ceased, we sighing saw
The floor lay paved with broken hearts.

So did she move; so did she sing
Like the harmonious spheres that bring
Unto their rounds their music's aid;
Which she performèd such a way
As all th'enamored world will say
The Graces danced, and Apollo played.

The Scrutiny. Song. Set by Mr. Thomas Charles[9]

Why should you swear I am forsworn,
Since thine I vowed to be?
Lady, it is already morn,
And 'twas last night I swore to thee
That fond[1] impossibility.

8. I.e., our deepest and truest joys.
9. First printed by John Playford in *Select Musical Ayres and Dialogues* (London, 1652), this song also appears in Playford's *Select Ayres and Dialogues* (1659), where the setting is attributed to Henry Lawes.
1. Foolish.

Have I not loved thee much and long,
A tedious twelve hours' space?
I must all other beauties wrong,
And rob thee of a new embrace,
Could I still dote upon thy face.

Not but all joy in thy brown hair
By others may be found;
But I must search the black and fair,
Like skillful mineralists that sound[2]
For treasure in unplowed-up ground.

Then, if when I have loved my round,
Thou prov'st the pleasant she,
With spoils of meaner beauties crowned
I laden will return to thee,
Ev'n sated with variety.

The Grasshopper.
Ode. To My Noble Friend, Mr. Charles Cotton[3]

O thou that swing'st upon the waving hair
Of some well-fillèd oaten beard,
Drunk every night with a delicious tear
Dropped thee from heav'n, where now th'art reared;

The joys of earth and air are thine entire,
That with thy feet and wings dost hop and fly;
And, when thy poppy works, thou dost retire
To thy carved acorn bed to lie.

Up with the day, the sun thou welcom'st then,
Sport'st in the gilt plats[4] of his beams,
And all these merry days mak'st merry men,
Thyself, and melancholy streams.[5]

But ah, the sickle! golden ears are cropped;
Ceres and Bacchus bid good-night;
Sharp frosty fingers all your flow'rs have topped,
And what scythes spared, winds shave off quite.

Poor verdant fool! and now green ice! thy joys,
Large and as lasting as thy perch of grass,

2. Probe, explore.
3. Lovelace apparently addresses, not Charles Cotton the poet (1630–1687), but his father (d. 1658). Clarendon says of the elder Cotton that he had "such a pleasantness and gaiety of humor, such a sweetness and gentleness of nature, and such a civility and delightfulness in conversation that no man in the court or out of it appeared a more accomplished person" (*Life, ed. cit.*, I, p. 25). The poem is based on verses by the Greek lyric poet Anacreon, whom Abraham Cowley also follows in his *Anacreontics* on this subject; cf. Cowley's "The Grasshopper," p. 520.
4. I.e., golden braids.
5. I.e., makes men, thyself, and melancholy streams merry.

Bid us lay in 'gainst winter, rain, and poise[6]
Their floods with an o'erflowing glass.

Thou best of men and friends! we will create
A genuine summer in each other's breast,
And spite of this cold time and frozen fate,
Thaw us a warm seat to our rest.

Our sacred hearths shall burn eternally
As vestal flames,[7] the north wind, he
Shall strike[8] his frost-stretched wings, dissolve, and fly
This Etna in epitome.

Dropping December shall come weeping in,
Bewail th'usurping of his reign;
But when in show'rs of old Greek we begin,
Shall cry, he hath his crown again![9]

Night as clear Hesper[1] shall our tapers whip
From the light casements where we play,
And the dark hag from her black mantle strip,
And stick there everlasting day.

Thus richer than untempted kings are we,
That asking nothing, nothing need:
Though lord of all what seas embrace, yet he
That wants[2] himself is poor indeed.

The Vintage to the Dungeon. A Song. Set by Mr. William Lawes[3]

Sing out, pent souls, sing cheerfully!
Care shackles you in liberty,
Mirth frees you in captivity;
Would you double fetters add?
Else why so sad?
Besides your pinioned arms you'll find
Grief, too, can manacle the mind.

Live then pris'ners uncontrolled,
Drink o'th'strong, the rich, the old,

6. Counterbalance.
7. The temple of Vesta, Roman goddess of the hearth, was attended by "Vestal Virgins" (appointed for a period of years), who swore to retain their virginity while they guarded the sacred flame.
8. I.e., shall abruptly spread.
9. In the 1640s, Parliament banned Christmas celebrations. Lovelace is thus alluding to both the usurpation of Charles I's reign and the abolition of the traditional festive calendar that the Stuarts supported. *Old Greek*: Greek wine.
1. The evening star.
2. Lacks.
3. If this song is to be connected with Lovelace's own career, it may relate to his imprisonment in the Gatehouse of Westminster in 1642.

Till wine too hath your wits in hold;
Then if still your jollity
And throats are free,
Triumph in your bonds and pains,
And dance to th'music of your chains.

To Lucasta. From Prison. An Epode[4]

Long in thy shackles, liberty
I ask, not from these walls but thee[5]
(Left for awhile another's bride),
To fancy all the world beside.

Yet ere I do begin to love,
See! how I all my objects prove;[6]
Then my free soul to that confine
'Twere possible I might call mine.

First I would be in love with Peace,
And her rich swelling breasts' increase;
But how, alas! how may that be,
Despising earth, will she love me?

Fain would I be in love with War,
As my dear just avenging star;
But War is loved so ev'rywhere,
Ev'n he disdains a lodging here.

Thee and thy wounds I would bemoan,
Fair thorough-shot[7] Religion;
But he lives only that kills thee,
And whoso binds thy hands is free.

I would love a Parliament
As a main prop from Heaven sent;
But ah! who's he that would be wedded
To th'fairest body that's beheaded?[8]

Next would I court my Liberty,
And then my birthright, Property;
But can that be, when it is known
There's nothing you can call your own?

4. This poem was presumably composed while Lovelace was confined in Peterhouse Prison, from June 1648 until April 1649.
5. I.e., Lucasta.
6. Test; i.e., consider carefully.
7. Shot through.
8. On 6 December 1648, by Cromwell's order, 141 members of Parliament were arrested or prevented from taking their seats ("Pride's Purge," so called because a Colonel Pride directed the operation); the remaining 78 members constituted the "Rump" Parliament. Charles I was executed on 30 January 1649.

A Reformation I would have,
As for our griefs a sov'reign salve;
That is, a cleansing of each wheel
Of state that yet some rust doth feel;

But not a Reformation so
As to reform were to o'erthrow;
Like watches by unskillful men
Disjointed, and set ill again.

The Public Faith[9] I would adore,
But she is bankrupt of her store;
Nor how to trust her can I see,
For she that cozens[1] all, must me.

Since then none of these can be
Fit objects for my love and me,
What then remains but th'only spring
Of all our loves and joys, the King?

He who, being the whole ball
Of day on earth, lends it to all;
When seeking to eclipse his right,
Blinded, we stand in our own light.

And now an universal mist
Of error is spread o'er each breast,
With such a fury edged as is
Not found in th'inwards of th'abyss.

Oh, from thy glorious starry wain,[2]
Dispense on me one sacred beam,
To light me where I soon may see
How to serve you, and you trust me.

To Althea. From Prison. Song. Set by Dr. John Wilson[3]

When Love with unconfinèd wings
Hovers within my gates,
And my divine Althea brings
To whisper at the grates;
When I lie tangled in her hair
And fettered to her eye,

9. The government habitually borrowed money on the "public faith," a practice widely derided by royalist sympathizers.
1. Cheats.
2. Wagon. The seven brightest stars in the constellation Ursa Major (i.e., the stars of the Big Dipper) were known as "Charles's Wain."
3. This most famous of Lovelace's poems was probably written while he was confined in the Gatehouse in 1642; Wilson's setting appears in Playford's *Select Ayres and Dialogues* (1659).

The gods that wanton in the air
Know no such liberty.

When flowing cups run swiftly round,
With no allaying Thames,[4]
Our careless heads with roses bound,[5]
Our hearts with loyal flames;
When thirsty grief in wine we steep,
When healths and draughts go free,
Fishes that tipple in the deep
Know no such liberty.

When, like committed[6] linnets, I
With shriller throat shall sing
The sweetness, mercy, majesty,
And glories of my King;
When I shall voice aloud how good
He is, how great should be,
Enlargèd winds that curl the flood
Know no such liberty.

Stone walls do not a prison make,
Nor iron bars a cage:
Minds innocent and quiet take
That for an hermitage.
If I have freedom in my love,
And in my soul am free,
Angels alone, that soar above,
Enjoy such liberty.

La Bella Bona Roba[7]

I cannot tell who loves the skeleton
Of a poor marmoset,[8] naught but bone, bone.
Give me a nakedness with her clothes on.[9]

Such whose white satin upper coat of skin,
Cut upon velvet rich incarnadine,
Has yet a body (and of flesh) within.

Sure it is meant good husbandry in men
Who do incorporate with airy lean,
T'repair their sides, and get their rib again.[1]

4. I.e., no water.
5. Cf. Herrick, "When He Would Have His Verses Read," line 9n, p. 182.
6. I.e., caged.
7. "Bona roba" was a common term for a prostitute; cf. Shakespeare's Justice Shallow, "We knew where the bona robas were and had the best of them at commandment" (*Henry IV, Part II*, III.ii.22–23).
8. Ordinarily implying playful endearment, the term in this context means "wanton."
9. I.e., give me a well-rounded (i.e., plump) nakedness.
1. Cf. Genesis 2:21–22.

Hard hap unto that huntsman that decrees
Fat joys for all his sweat, whenas he sees,
After his 'say, nought but his keeper's fees.[2]

Then Love, I beg, when next thou tak'st thy bow,
Thy angry shafts, and dost heart-chasing go,
Pass rascal[3] deer, strike me the largest doe.

The Fair Beggar

Commanding asker, if it be
  Pity that you fain would have,
Then I turn beggar unto thee,
  And ask the thing that thou dost crave;
I will suffice thy hungry need
So thou wilt but my fancy feed.

In all ill years, wast ever known
  On so much beauty such a dearth,
Which in that thrice-bequeathèd gown
  Looks like the sun eclipsed with earth,
Like gold in canvas, or with dirt
Unsoilèd ermines close begirt?

Yet happy he that can but taste
  This whiter skin, who thirsty is;
Fools dote on satin motions laced,
  The gods go naked in their bliss;
At th'barrel's head there shines the vine,
There only relishes the wine.

There quench my heat, and thou shalt sup,
  Worthy the lips that it must touch,
Nectar from out the starry cup;
  I beg thy breath not half so much;
So both our wants supplied shall be,
You'll give for love, I, charity.

Cheap, then, are pearl-embroideries
  That not adorn but cloud thy waist;
Thou shalt be clothed above all price
  If thou wilt promise me embraced;
We'll ransack neither chest nor shelf,
I'll cover thee with mine own self.

But, cruel, if thou dost deny
  This necessary alms to me,

2. I.e., after his assay (of the fatness of a slain deer's flesh), nothing but the meager portion allotted to a gamekeeper. Cf. Beaumont and Fletcher, *Philaster*, IV.ii.10–20.
3. Lean.

What soft-souled man but with his eye
And hand will hence be shut to thee?
Since all must judge you more unkind,
I starve your body, you my mind.

FROM *LUCASTA. POSTHUME POEMS* (1659)

The Snail

Wise emblem of our politic world,
Sage snail, within thine own self curled;
Instruct me softly to make haste,
Whilst these my feet go slowly fast.
Compendious snail! thou seem'st to me
Large Euclid's[4] strict epitome;
And in each diagram, dost fling
Thee from the point unto the ring.
A figure now triangular,
An oval now, and now a square,
And then a serpentine dost crawl,
Now a straight line, now crook'd, now all.
Preventing[5] rival of the day,
Th'art up and openest thy ray,
And ere the morn cradles the moon,
Th'art broke into a beauteous noon.
Then when the sun sups in the deep,
Thy silver horns ere Cynthia's peep;
And thou from thine own liquid bed,
New Phoebus, heav'st thy pleasant head.
Who shall a name for thee create,
Deep riddle of mysterious state?
Bold nature, that gives common birth
To all products of seas and earth,
Of thee, as earthquakes, is afraid,
Nor will thy dire deliv'ry aid.
Thou thine own daughter then, and sire,
That son and mother art entire,
That big still with thyself dost go,
And liv'st an agèd embryo;
That like the cubs of India,[6]
Thou from thyself a while dost play;
But frightened with a dog or gun,
In thine own belly thou dost run,

4. Euclid (fl. c. 300 B.C.) systematized and effectively founded the mathematical science of geometry.
5. Anticipating.
6. Lovelace may here recall Edward Topsell's account (based on that of Conrad Gesner) of the "Semivulpa or Apish-Fox," a denizen of "the country of Payran," which carries its young in "a skin like a bag or scrip . . . neither do they come forth of that receptacle, except it be to suck milk, or sport themselves" (Edward Topsell, *History of Four-Footed Beasts and Serpents and Insects*, ed. W. Ley, 3 vols. [New York, 1967], I, p. 16).

And as thy house was thine own womb,
So thine own womb concludes thy tomb.
But now I must, analyzed king,
Thy economic virtues sing;
Thou great staid husband[7] still within,
Thou thee, that's thine, dost discipline;
And when thou art to progress bent,
Thou mov'st thyself and tenement;
As warlike Scythians traveled,[8] you
Remove your men and city too;
Then after a sad dearth and rain,
Thou scatterest thy silver train;
And when the trees grow nak'd and old,
Thou clothest them with cloth of gold,
Which from thy bowels thou dost spin,
And draw from the rich mines within.
Now hast thou changed thee saint; and made
Thyself a fane[9] that's cupola'd,
And in thy wreathèd cloister thou
Walkest thine own gray friar too;
Strict, and locked up, th'art hood all o'er
And ne'er eliminat'st thy door.
On salads thou dost feed severe,
And 'stead of beads thou drop'st a tear,
And when to rest, each calls the bell,
Thou sleep'st within thy marble cell,
Where in dark contemplation placed,
The sweets of nature thou dost taste;
Who now with time thy days resolve,
And in a jelly thee dissolve
Like a shot star,[1] which doth repair
Upward, and rarefy the air.

A Loose Saraband[2]

Nay prithee, dear, draw nigher,
Yet closer, nigher yet,
Here is a double fire,
A dry one and a wet;
True lasting heavenly fuel
Puts out the vestal jewel,
When once we twining marry
Mad love with wild Canary.

7. Steward.
8. Cf. Herodotus, *Histories*, IV.1–142.
9. Temple.
1. It was thought that falling (shooting) stars became jellies on reaching the earth. Cf. Donne, "Epithalamion," lines 204–205.
2. Originally a stately Spanish dance, the saraband in seventeenth-century England was regarded somewhat differently. In Ben Jonson's play *The Staple of News*, for instance, Old Pennyboy observes, "How they are tickled / With a light air, the bawdy saraband" (IV.ii).

Off with that crownèd Venice[3]
  Till all the house doth flame,
We'll quench it straight in Rhenish,
  Or what we must not name;
Milk lightning still assuageth,
So when our fury rageth,
As th'only means to cross it,
We'll drown it in love's posset.[4]

Love never was well-willer
  Unto my nag or me,
Ne'er watered us i'th' cellar,[5]
  But the cheap buttery;
At th'head of his own barrels,
Where broached are all his quarrels,
Should a true noble master
Still make his guest his taster.

See! all the world how't staggers,
  More ugly drunk than we,
As if far gone in daggers
  And blood it seemed to be;
We drink our glass of roses
Which nought but sweets discloses,
Then in our loyal chamber
Refresh us with love's amber.

Now tell me, thou fair cripple,
  That dumb canst scarcely see
Th'almightiness of tipple,
  And th'odds 'twixt thee and thee,
What of Elysium's[6] missing?
Still drinking and still kissing,
Adoring plump October;
Lord! what is man and sober?

Now, is there such a trifle
  As honor, the fool's giant?[7]
What is there left to rifle
  When wine makes all parts pliant?
Let others glory follow,
In their false riches wallow,
And with their grief be merry;
Leave me but love and sherry.

3. I.e., that goblet of Venetian glass.
4. I.e., in milky sperm.
5. I.e., in the wine cellar (as distinct from the buttery, where beer and ale were stored).
6. Cf. Carew, "A Rapture," line 2n, p. 302.
7. Cf. Carew, "A Rapture," line 3, p. 302.

Love Made in the First Age. To Chloris

In the nativity of time,
Chloris, it was not thought a crime
In direct Hebrew for to woo.[8]
Now we make love as all on fire,
Ring retrograde our loud desire,
And court in English backward too.

Thrice happy was that golden age,
When compliment was construed rage,
And fine words in the center hid;
When cursèd *No* stained no maid's bliss,
And all discourse was summed in *Yes*,
And nought forbade, but to forbid.

Love then unstinted, love did sip,
And cherries plucked fresh from the lip,
On cheeks and roses free he fed;
Lasses like autumn plums did drop,
And lads indifferently[9] did crop
A flower and a maidenhead.

Then unconfinèd each did tipple
Wine from the bunch, milk from the nipple,
Paps tractable as udders were;
Then equally the wholesome jellies
Were squeezed from olive trees and bellies,
Nor suits of trespass did they fear.

A fragrant bank of strawberries,
Diapered[1] with violet's eyes
Was table, tablecloth, and fare;
No palace to the clouds did swell,
Each humble princess then did dwell
In the piazza[2] of her hair.

Both broken faith and th'cause of it,
All-damning gold, was damned to th'pit;
Their troth, sealed with a clasp and kiss,
Lasted until that extreme day
In which they smiled their souls away,
And, in each other, breathed new bliss.

Because no fault, there was no tear;
No groan did grate the granting ear;

8. It was believed (partly on the evidence of Genesis 11:1) that Hebrew, which reads from right to left, was the original language of humankind.
9. Impartially.
1. Patterned, strewn.
2. Arcade (hence "delicately artful structure").

No false foul breath their del'cate smell:
No serpent kiss poisoned the taste,
Each touch was naturally chaste,
And their mere sense a miracle.

Naked as their own innocence,
And unembroidered from offense
They went, above poor riches, gay;
On softer than the cygnet's down,
In beds they tumbled of their own;
For each within the other lay.

Thus did they live; thus did they love,
Repeating only joys above;
And angels were, but with clothes on,
Which they would put off cheerfully,
To bathe them in the galaxy,
Then gird them with the heavenly zone.

Now, Chloris, miserably crave
The offered bliss you would not have,
Which evermore I must deny,
Whilst ravished with these noble dreams,
And crownèd with mine own soft beams,
Enjoying of myself I lie.

A Mock-Song

Now Whitehall's in the grave,
And our head is our slave,[3]
The bright pearl in his close shell of oyster;
Now the miter is lost,
The proud prelates, too, crossed,
And all Rome's confined to a cloister;
He that Tarquin was styled,[4]
Our white land's exiled,
Yea undefiled,
Not a court ape's left to confute us;
Then let your voices rise high,
As your colors did fly,
And flourishing cry,
"Long live the brave Oliver-Brutus."

Now the sun is unarmed,
And the moon by us charmed,

3. With the execution of Charles I, in 1649, outside his own palace of Whitehall, Cromwell (considered by royalists to be a low fellow without breeding or culture) became master of England.
4. I.e., Charles II, regularly so described in the official newspaper of the Commonwealth, *Mercurius Politicus*.

All the stars dissolved to a jelly;[5]
Now the thighs of the crown
And the arms are lopped down,
And the body is all but a belly;
Let the Commons go on,
The town is our own,
We'll rule alone;
For the knights have yielded their spent gorge;[6]
And an order is ta'en
With *honi soit* profane,[7]
Shout forth amain,
For our dragon hath vanquished the St. George.

A Fly Caught in a Cobweb

Small type of great ones, that do hum
Within this whole world's narrow room,
That with a busy hollow noise
Catch at the people's vainer voice,
And with spread sails play with their breath,
Whose very hails new christen death,
Poor fly, caught in an airy net,
Thy wings have fettered now thy feet;
Where like a lion in a toil,[8]
Howe'er thou keep'st a noble coil[9]
And beat'st thy gen'rous breast, that o'er
The plains thy fatal buzzes roar,
Till thy all-bellied foe, round elf,
Hath quartered thee within himself.
Was it not better once to play
I'th'light of a majestic ray?
Where though too near and bold, the fire
Might singe thy upper down attire,
And thou i'th'storm to lose an eye,
A wing, or a self-trapping thigh,
Yet hadst thou fall'n like him, whose coil
Made fishes in the sea to broil;
When now th'hast 'scaped the noble flame,
Trapped basely in a slimy frame;
And free of air, thou art become
Slave to the spawn of mud and loam.
Nor is't enough thyself dost dress
To thy swol'n lord a num'rous mess,[1]
And by degrees thy thin veins bleed,

5. Cf. "The Snail," line 65n, p. 501.
6. I.e. (perhaps), for the privileged aristocracy has been destroyed.
7. Cf. Denham, "Cooper's Hill," line 83n, p. 481.
8. Net.
9. Tumult.
1. I.e., a large meal.

And piecemeal dost his poison feed;
But now devoured, art like to be
A net spun for thy family,
And straight expanded in the air
Hang'st for thy issue too a snare.
Strange witty death, and cruel ill,
That killing thee, thou thine dost kill!
Like pies[2] in whose entombèd ark
All fowl crowd downward to a lark,
Thou art thine en'mies' sepulcher,
And in thee buriest too thine heir.
  Yet Fates a glory have reserved
For one so highly hath deserved;
As the rhinoceros doth die
Under his castle[3] enemy,
As through the crane's trunk[4] throat doth speed
The asp doth[5] on his feeder feed;
Fall yet triumphant in thy woe,
Bound with the entrails of thy foe.

Advice to My Best Brother, Colonel Francis Lovelace[6]

  Frank, wilt live handsomely? Trust not too far
Thyself to waving[7] seas, for what thy star
Calculated by sure event must be,
Look in the glassy epithet[8] and see.

  Yet settle here your rest, and take your state,
And in calm halcyon's nest[9] ev'n build your fate;
Prithee lie down securely, Frank, and keep
With as much no noise the inconstant deep
As its inhabitants; nay, steadfast stand,
As if discovered were a Newfoundland
Fit for plantation here; dream, dream still,
Lulled in Dione's cradle,[1] dream, until
Horror awake your sense, and you now find
Yourself a bubbled pastime for the wind,

2. Magpies.
3. Elephant (known as the "carry-castle" from the howdah or pavilion on his back). Topsell observes that there is between rhinoceros and elephant "a natural . . . enmity" (*ed. cit.*, I, p. 463).
4. I.e., tubular.
5. I.e., that doth.
6. Colonel Francis Lovelace (c. 1618–c. 1675) commanded the royalist garrison at Carmarthen, in Wales, from June 1644 until October 1645. After the Restoration, he shipped over with his regiment to America, where it appears that he became (in 1668) the Governor of New York, serving in that capacity for some time. Cf. *Poems of Richard Lovelace*, ed. C. H. Wilkinson, 2 vols. (Oxford, 1925), I, pp. 4–6. This poem is based on Horace, *Odes*, II.x.
7. Rolling.
8. I.e., crystal ball. But cf. *Poems, ed. cit.*, I, p. 102.
9. Cf. Carew, "A Rapture," line 97n, p. 304.
1. I.e., in Aphrodite's cradle, the sea. Dione was the mother of Aphrodite (Venus), who is hence called Dionaea, and occasionally Dione.

And in loose Thetis'[2] blankets torn and tossed;
Frank, to undo thyself why art at cost?

Nor be too confident, fixed on the shore,
For even that too borrows from the store
Of her rich neighbor, since now wisest know,
And this to Galileo's judgment owe,[3]
The palsy earth itself is every jot
As frail, inconstant, waving as that blot
We lay upon the deep; that sometimes lies
Changed, you would think, with's bottom's properties,
But this eternal strange Ixion's wheel[4]
Of giddy earth, ne'er whirling leaves to reel
Till all things are inverted, till they are
Turned to that antic confused state they were.

Who loves the golden mean, doth safely want
A cobwebbed cot, and wrongs entailed upon't;
He richly needs a palace for to breed
Vipers and moths, that on their feeder feed;
The toy that we (too true) a mistress call,
Whose looking-glass and feather weighs up all;
And clothes which larks would play with in the sun,[5]
That mock him in the night when's course is run.

To rear an edifice by art so high
That envy should not reach it with her eye,
Nay, with a thought come near it, would'st thou know
How such a structure should be raised? Build low.
The blust'ring wind's invisible rough stroke
More often shakes the stubborn'st, proper'st oak,
And in proud turrets we behold withal,
'Tis the imperial top declines to fall;
Nor does heav'n's lightning strike the humble vales,
But high aspiring mounts batters and scales.

A breast of proof defies all shocks of fate,
Fears in the best, hopes in the worser state;
Heaven forbid that, as of old, time ever
Flourished in spring, so contrary, now never;
That mighty breath which blew foul winter hither
Can eas'ly puff it to a fairer weather.
Why dost despair then, Frank? Aeolus has
A Zephyrus as well as Boreas.[6]

2. The sea nymph Thetis was the mother of Achilles.
3. The telescopic observations of the heavens made by Galileo Galilei (1564–1642) were instrumental for change in humanity's conception of the universe.
4. For attempting to ravish Juno (Hera), Ixion was bound to a flaming wheel, which rolled eternally through the heavens. Cf. Ovid, *Metamorphoses*, IV.461, for an allusion to the story.
5. Falconers used pieces of scarlet cloth (or mirrors) to attract and entrap birds. Cf. Shakespeare's *Henry VIII*, III.ii.276–279.
6. I.e., the god of the winds has at command a (mild) west wind as well as a (harsh) north wind.

'Tis a false sequel, solecism, 'gainst those
Precepts by fortune giv'n us, to suppose
That, 'cause it is now ill, 'twill e'er be so;
Apollo doth not always bend his bow;
But oft uncrownèd of his beams divine,
With his soft harp awakes the sleeping Nine.[7]

In strictest things magnanimous appear,
Greater in hope, howe'er thy fate, than fear;
Draw all your sails in quickly, though no storm
Threaten your ruin with a sad alarm;
For tell me how they differ, tell me, pray,
A cloudy tempest, and a too fair day.

7. Phoebus Apollo combined with other attributes those of the god who punishes, the sun god, and (in conjunction with the nine Muses) the god of poetry and song.

Abraham Cowley

1618	Born in London, the posthumous son of a stationer.
1629	Admitted to Westminster School, in London, as a King's Scholar (i.e., a poor student on scholarship).
1633	Publication of *Poetical Blossoms* (five poems).
1636	Second (augmented) edition of *Poetical Blossoms*; third edition published in 1637.
1637	Matriculates at Trinity College, Cambridge.
1638	Publication of *Love's Riddle*, a pastoral drama, and of *Naufragium Joculare*, a Latin comedy (acted at Cambridge in this year).
1639	Takes the B.A. degree.
1641	A comedy, *The Guardian* (rewritten in 1658 as *The Cutter of Coleman Street*), presented at Cambridge before Prince Charles.
1642	Takes M.A.
1643	Publication of *The Puritan and the Papist*, a satire. In April, having been removed from Cambridge by official fiat, takes up residence at Saint John's College, Oxford, where he associates with Lord Falkland and other moderate royalists.
1646–1656	In France, actively employed by Queen Henrietta Maria and exiled members of the court.
1647	Publication of *The Mistress*.
1656	On return to England, arrested and (briefly) imprisoned; released on bail, but remains under bail until 1660. Publication of *Poems*.
1657	Receives M.D. (Master of Divinity) from Oxford.
1659–1660	Resides in France.
1661	Publication of *A Proposition for the Advancement of Experimental Philosophy*, and of *A Discourse by Way of Vision, Concerning the Government of Oliver Cromwell. The Cutter of Coleman Street* acted at Lincoln's Inn Fields.
1662	Publication of *A Couleii Plantarum Libri Duo*.
1663	Publication of *Verses lately Written upon Several Occasions*. Retirement to Barn Elms, Kent.
1665	Moves to Chertsey.
1667	Death, 28 July. Buried in Westminster Abbey.
1668	Publication of *The Works of Mr. Abraham Cowley*, edited by Thomas Sprat.

FROM *THE WORKS OF MR. ABRAHAM COWLEY* (1668)

FROM *MISCELLANIES*

The Motto

Tentanda via est, etc.[1]

What shall I do to be forever known,
And make the age to come my own?
I shall like beasts or common people die,
Unless you write my elegy,
Whilst others great by being born are grown,
Their mothers' labor, not their own.
In this scale gold, in th'other fame does lie,
The weight of that mounts this so high.
These men are fortune's jewels, molded bright,
Brought forth with their own fire and light;
If I her vulgar stone, for either look,
Out of myself it must be strook.
Yet I must on: what sound is't strikes mine ear?
Sure I Fame's trumpet hear;
It sounds like the last trumpet, for it can
Raise up the buried man.
Unpassed Alps stop me, but I'll cut through all
And march, the Muses' Hannibal.[2]
Hence, all the flattering vanities that lay
Nets of roses in the way;
Hence, the desire of honors or estate
And all that is not above fate;
Hence, Love himself, the tyrant of my days,
Which intercepts my coming praise.
Come, my best friends, my books, and lead me on:
'Tis time that I were gone.
Welcome, great Stagirite,[3] and teach me now
All I was born to know;
Thy scholar's vict'ries thou dost far outdo,
He conquered th'earth, the whole world you.
Welcome, learn'd Cicero,[4] whose blest tongue and wit
Preserve Rome's greatness yet:
Thou art the first of orators; only he
Who best can praise thee, next must be.

1. Cf. Vergil, *Georgics*, III.8–9: "A path must be found out whereby I too may rise from earth and fly in triumph on the lips of men."
2. The Carthaginian general Hannibal (247–c. 183 B.C.) led his troops across the Alps in the spring of 218 B.C., subsequently annihilating the Roman forces led by Flaminius at Lake Trasimene.
3. I.e., Aristotle (384–322 B.C.), born in the Macedonian town of Stagira. Alexander the Great (356–323 B.C.) was his pupil from 342–335 B.C.
4. Marcus Tullius Cicero (106–43 B.C.), orator and philosopher, was widely admired for the range, clarity, and style of his writings.

Welcome the Mantuan swan,[5] Vergil the wise,
Whose verse walks highest, but not flies;
Who brought green poesy to her perfect age,
And made that art which was a rage.[6]
Tell me, ye mighty three, what shall I do
To be like one of you?
But you have climbed the mountain's top, there sit
On the calm flour'shing head of it,
And whilst with wearied steps we upward go,
See us and clouds below.

Ode. Of Wit[7]

Tell me, O tell, what kind of thing is wit,
Thou[8] who master art of it,
For the first matter[9] loves variety less;
Less women love't, either in love or dress.
A thousand different shapes it bears,
Comely in thousand shapes appears.
Yonder we saw it plain; and here 'tis now,
Like spirits in a place, we know not how.

London, that vents[1] of false ware so much store,
In no ware deceives us more,
For men led by the color and the shape,
Like Zeuxis' birds fly to the painted grape;[2]
Some things do through our judgment pass
As through a multiplying[3] glass,
And sometimes, if the object be too far,
We take a falling meteor for a star.

Hence 'tis a wit, that greatest word of fame,
Grows such a common name;
And wits by our creation they become,
Just so, as tit'lar bishops[4] made at Rome.
'Tis not a tale, 'tis not a jest
Admired with laughter at a feast,
Nor florid talk, which can that title gain;
The proofs of wit forever must remain.

5. Vergil (70–19 B.C.) was born near Mantua.
6. I.e., the frenzied and uncontrolled expression of poetic inspiration.
7. "As true wit consists in the resemblance of ideas, and false wit in the resemblance of words, there is another kind of wit, which consists partly in the resemblance of ideas, and partly in the resemblance of words; which, for distinction's sake, I shall call mixed wit. This kind of wit is that which abounds in Cowley more than in any author that ever wrote" (Dr. Johnson, *The Spectator* 62).
8. It seems probable that Cowley's poem is not addressed to an actual person.
9. I.e., the original matter from which all things were created.
1. Vends, sells.
2. The Greek painter Zeuxis (fl. c. 400 B.C.) was accounted a master of realistic effect (trompe l'oeil).
3. Magnifying.
4. I.e., bishops who bear the title but have no see.

'Tis not to force some lifeless verses meet
   With their five gouty feet;
All ev'rywhere, like man's, must be the soul,
And reason the inferior powers control.
   Such were the numbers which could call
   The stones into the Theban wall;[5]
Such miracles are ceased; and now we see
No towns or houses raised by poetry.

Yet 'tis not to adorn and gild each part;
   That shows more cost than art.
Jewels at nose and lips but ill appear;
Rather than all things wit, let none be there.
   Several[6] lights will not be seen
   If there be nothing else between;
Men doubt, because they stand so thick i'th'sky,
If those be stars which paint the galaxy.

'Tis not when two like words make up one noise,
   Jests for Dutch men and English boys,
In which who finds out wit, the same may see
In an'grams and acrostics, poetry.
   Much less can that have any place
   At which a virgin hides her face:
Such dross the fire must purge away; 'tis just
The author blush, there where the reader must.

'Tis not such lines as almost crack the stage
   When Bajazet[7] begins to rage,
Nor a tall metaphor in the bombast way,
Nor the dry chips of short-lunged Seneca,[8]
   Nor upon all things to obtrude,
   And force some odd similitude.
What is it, then, which like the Power Divine
We only can by negatives define?

In a true piece of wit all things must be,
   Yet all things there agree;
As in the ark, joined without force or strife,
All creatures dwelt, all creatures that had life;
   Or as the primitive forms of all,
   If we compare great things with small,
Which without discord or confusion lie
In that strange mirror of the Deity.

5. Cf. Waller, "At Penshurst," line 17–18n, p. 363.
6. Separate, distinct.
7. Cowley alludes not to the actual Turkish Sultan Bajazet (1347–1403), but to the dramatic character in Marlowe's play *Tamburlaine*, whose speeches are marked by bombast and rant.
8. The literary style of Lucius Annaeus Seneca (d. A.D. 65) was terse and curt, in contrast to the urbane and balanced style associated with Cicero.

But love, that molds one man up out of two,
Makes me forget and injure you;
I took you for myself, sure, when I thought
That you in anything were to be taught.
Correct my error with thy pen;
And if any ask me then,
What thing right wit and height of genius is,
I'll only show your lines, and say, *'Tis this.*

On the Death of Mr. William Hervey

Immodicis brevis est aetas, et rara senectus[9]

It was a dismal and a fearful night;
Scarce could the morn drive on th'unwilling light,
When sleep, death's image, left my troubled breast
By something liker death possessed.
My eyes with tears did uncommanded flow,
And on my soul hung the dull weight
Of some intolerable fate.
What bell was that? Ah me! Too much I know.

My sweet companion, and my gentle peer,
Why hast thou left me thus unkindly here,
Thy end forever, and my life to moan?
Oh, thou hast left me all alone!
Thy soul and body, when death's agony
Besieged around thy noble heart,
Did not with more reluctance part
Than I, my dearest friend, do part from thee.

My dearest friend, would I had died for thee!
Life and this world henceforth will tedious be:
Nor shall I know hereafter what to do
If once my griefs prove tedious too.
Silent and sad I walk about all day,
As sullen ghosts stalk speechless by
Where their hid treasures lie.
Alas, my treasure's gone, why do I stay?

He was my friend, the truest friend on earth;
A strong and mighty influence joined our birth.
Nor did we envy the most sounding name
By friendship giv'n of old to fame.
None but his brethren he, and sisters, knew,
Whom the kind youth preferred to me;

9. "To the extraordinarily gifted, life is brief and old age rare" (Martial, *Epigrams*, VI.xxix.7). William Hervey (1616–1642), Cowley's close friend, attended Pembroke College, Cambridge.

And ev'n in that we did agree,
For much above myself I loved them too.

Say, for you saw us, ye immortal lights,
How oft unwearied have we spent the nights?
Till the Ledaean stars,[1] so famed for love,
Wondered at us from above.
We spent them not in toys, in lusts, or wine,
But search of deep philosophy,
Wit, eloquence, and poetry,
Arts which I loved, for they, my friend, were thine.

Ye fields of Cambridge, our dear Cambridge, say,
Have ye not seen us walking every day?
Was there a tree about which did not know
The love betwixt us two?
Henceforth, ye gentle trees, forever fade;
Or your sad branches thicker join,
And into darksome shades combine,
Dark as the grave wherein my friend is laid.

Henceforth no learned youths beneath you sing,
Till all the tuneful birds to your boughs they bring;
No tuneful birds play with their wonted cheer,
And call the learnèd youths to hear;
No whistling winds through the glad branches fly,
But all with sad solemnity,
Mute and unmovèd be,
Mute as the grave wherein my friend does lie.

To him my Muse made haste with every strain
Whilst it was new, and warm yet from the brain.
He loved my worthless rhymes, and like a friend
Would find out something to commend.
Hence now, my Muse, thou canst not me delight;
Be this my latest verse
With which I now adorn his hearse,
And this my grief without thy help shall write.

Had I a wreath of bays about my brow,
I should contemn[2] that flourishing honor now,
Condemn it to the fire, and joy to hear
It rage and crackle there.
Instead of bays, crown with sad cypress me,
Cypress which tombs does beautify;

1. I.e., Castor and Pollux (known also as the Dioscuri), Leda's twin sons, who were stellified as the constellation Gemini. Cf. Jonson, "To the Immortal Memory . . . of . . . Sir Lucius Cary and Sir H. Morison," lines 89–99, pp. 142–143.
2. Scorn.

Not Phoebus grieved so much as I
For him, who first was made that mournful tree.[3]

Large was his soul; as large a soul as e'er
Submitted to inform a body here.
High as the place 'twas shortly in heav'n to have,
But low and humble as his grave;
So high that all the virtues there did come
As to their chiefest seat,
Conspicuous and great;
So low that for me, too, it made a room.

He scorned this busy world below, and all
That we, mistaken mortals, pleasure call;
Was filled with innocent gallantry and truth,
Triumphant o'er the sins of youth.
He, like the stars to which he now is gone,
That shine with beams like flame,
Yet burn not with the same,
Had all the light of youth, of the fire none.

Knowledge he only sought, and so soon caught,
As if for him knowledge had rather sought;
Nor did more learning ever crowded lie
In such a short mortality.
Whene'er the skillful youth discoursed or writ,
Still did the notions throng
About his eloquent tongue,
Nor could his ink flow faster than his wit.

So strong a wit did nature to him frame
As all things but his judgment overcame;
His judgment like the heav'nly moon did show,
Temp'ring that mighty sea below.
Oh, had he lived in learning's world, what bound
Would have been able to control
His overpowering soul?
We have lost in him arts that not yet are found.

His mirth was the pure spirits of various wit,
Yet never did his God or friends forget,
And, when deep talk and wisdom came in view,
Retired and gave to them their due.
For the rich help of books he always took,
Though his own searching mind before
Was so with notions written o'er
As if wise nature had made that her book.

3. The remorse of Cyparissus at having accidentally killed his favorite stag was such that he prayed for death. Phoebus Apollo transformed him into a cypress tree (Ovid, *Metamorphoses*, X.106–142).

So many virtues joined in him, as we
Can scarce pick here and there in history;
More than old writers' practice e'er could reach,
As much as they could ever teach.
These did religion, queen of virtues, sway,
And all their sacred motions steer,
Just like the first and highest sphere,[4]
Which wheels about, and turns all heav'n one way.

With as much zeal, devotion, piety,
He always lived, as other saints do die.
Still with his soul severe account he kept,
Weeping all debts out ere he slept.
Then down in peace and innocence he lay,
Like the sun's laborious light,
Which still in water sets at night,
Unsullied with his journey of the day.

Wondrous young man, why wert thou made so good,
To be snatched hence ere better understood?
Snatched before half of thee enough was seen!
Thou ripe, and yet thy life but green!
Nor could thy friends take their last sad farewell,
But danger and infectious death
Maliciously seized on that breath
Where life, spirit, pleasure always used to dwell.

But happy thou, ta'en from this frantic age,
Where ignorance and hypocrisy does rage!
A fitter time for heav'n no soul e'er chose,
The place now only free from those.
There 'mong the blest thou dost forever shine,
And wheresoe'er thou casts thy view
Upon that white and radiant crew,
See'st not a soul clothed with more light than thine.

And if the glorious saints cease not to know
Their wretched friends who fight with life below,
Thy flame to me does still the same abide,
Only more pure and rarefied.
There whilst immortal hymns thou dost rehearse,
Thou dost with holy pity see
Our dull and earthly poesy,
Where grief and misery can be joined with verse.

4. I.e., the primum mobile, the outermost sphere by which all others in the Ptolemaic system were thought to be moved.

On the Death of Mr. Crashaw[5]

Poet and saint! to thee alone are given
The two most sacred names of earth and heaven,
The hard and rarest union which can be,
Next that of Godhead with humanity.
Long did the Muse's banished slaves abide,
And built vain pyramids to mortal pride;
Like Moses thou, though spells and charms withstand,
Hast brought them nobly home back to their Holy Land.
   Ah wretched we, poets of earth! but thou
Wert, living, the same poet which thou'rt now
Whilst angels sing to thee airs divine,
And joy in an applause so great as thine.
Equal society with them to hold,
Thou need'st not make new songs, but say the old;
And they (kind spirits!) shall all rejoice to see
How little less than they exalted man may be.
   Still the old heathen gods in numbers dwell,
The heav'nliest thing on earth still keeps up hell.
Nor have we yet quite purged the Christian land;
Still idols here like calves at Bethel stand.[6]
And though Pan's death long since all oracles broke,
Yet still in rhyme the fiend Apollo spoke;[7]
Nay, with the worst of heathen dotage we
(Vain men!) the monster woman deify;
Find stars, and tie our fates there in a face,[8]
And Paradise in them by whom we lost it, place.
What different faults corrupt our Muses thus?
Wanton as girls, as old wives fabulous![9]
   Thy spotless Muse, like Mary, did contain
The boundless Godhead; she[1] did well disdain
That her eternal verse employed should be
On a less subject than eternity;
And for a sacred mistress scorned to take
But her whom God himself scorned not his spouse to make.
It, in a kind, her miracle did do;
A fruitful mother was, and virgin too.
   How well, blest swan, did fate contrive thy death,
And made thee render up thy tuneful breath
In thy great mistress' arms, thou most divine
And richest off'ring of Loreto's shrine!

5. Crashaw became Cowley's friend at Cambridge, where he was a Fellow of Peterhouse from 1635 to 1643.
6. Jeroboam, King of Israel, set up two golden calves in Bethel and in Dan, which the Israelites were induced to worship with sacrifice and feasting (1 Kings 12:25–33).
7. In the essay "On the Cessation of the Oracles," Plutarch tells of the voice that cried that the great Pan was dead. Christians associated this account with Christ's mission on Earth. Cowley suggests that, while the Oracle of Apollo at Delphi has been silenced, the pagan deity continues to speak through the medium of love poetry (the "numbers" of line 17).
8. Cf., for example, Sidney's sonnet sequence, *Astrophil and Stella*.
9. I.e., given to recounting fables and legends.
1. I.e., Crashaw's muse.

Where, like some holy sacrifice t'expire,
A fever burns thee, and love lights the fire.
Angels, they say, brought the famed chapel there,
And bore the sacred load in triumph through the air.
'Tis surer much they brought thee there, and they,
And thou, their charge, went singing all the way.
Pardon, my mother church,[2] if I consent
That angels led him when from thee he went,
For even in error sure no danger is
When joined with so much piety as his.
Ah, mighty God, with shame I speak't, and grief,
Ah, that our greatest faults were in belief!
And our weak reason were ev'n weaker yet,
Rather than thus our wills too strong for it.
His faith perhaps in some nice[3] tenets might
Be wrong; his life, I'm sure, was in the right.
And I myself a Catholic will be,
So far at least, great saint, to pray to thee.
Hail, bard triumphant! and some care bestow
On us, the poets militant below!
Opposed by our old enemy, adverse chance,
Attacked by envy and by ignorance,
Enchained by beauty, tortured by desires,
Exposed by tyrant love to savage beasts and fires,
Thou from low earth in nobler flames didst rise,
And, like Elijah, mount alive the skies.[4]
Elisha-like (but with a wish much less,
More fit thy greatness and my littleness)
Lo, here I beg (I whom thou once didst prove
So humble to esteem, so good to love)
Not that thy spirit might on me doubled be,
I ask but half thy mighty spirit for me;
And when my Muse soars with so strong a wing,
'Twill learn of things divine, and first of thee to sing.

From *Anacreontics; Or, Some Copies of Verses Translated Periphrastically out of Anacreon*[5]

I. Love

I'll sing of heroes and of kings;
In mighty numbers,[6] mighty things;

2. I.e., the Church of England. Crashaw, a Roman Catholic, died at Loreto, site of a Marian shrine featuring the holy family's house, transported to the Italian city from Nazareth by angels, according to Catholic belief.
3. Oversubtle.
4. Cf. 2 Kings 2:11: "Elijah went up by a whirlwind into heaven." His successor Elisha prayed that "a double portion" of Elijah's spirit should be allotted to him (*ibid.*, 2:9).
5. Cowley translated and grouped together eleven poems attributed to the Greek lyric poet Anacreon of Teos (born c. 550 B.C.).
6. Verses.

Begin, my Muse; but lo, the strings
To my great song rebellious prove;
The strings will sound of nought but love.
I broke them all, and put on new;
'Tis this or nothing sure will do.
"These sure," said I, "will me obey,
These sure heroic notes will play."
Straight I began with thund'ring Jove
And all th'immortal pow'rs but Love.
Love smiled, and from my enfeebled lyre
Came gentle airs, such as inspire
Melting love, soft desire.
Farewell, then, heroes, farewell kings,
And mighty numbers, mighty things;
Love tunes my heart just[7] to my strings.

VIII. The Epicure

Fill the bowl with rosy wine,
Around our temples roses twine,
And let us cheerfully awhile
Like the wine and roses smile.
Crowned with roses, we contemn
Gyges'[8] wealthy diadem.
Today is ours; what do we fear?
Today is ours; we have it here.
Let's treat it kindly, that it may
Wish, at least, with us to stay.
Let's banish business, banish sorrow;
To the gods belongs tomorrow.

X. The Grasshopper[9]

Happy insect, what can be
In happiness compared to thee?
Fed with nourishment divine,
The dewy morning's gentle wine!
Nature waits upon thee still,
And thy verdant cup does fill;
'Tis filled wherever thou dost tread,
Nature self's thy Ganymede.[1]
Thou dost drink and dance and sing,
Happier than the happiest king!
All the fields which thou dost see,

7. Precisely; only.
8. The wealth of the Lydian King Gyges, who reigned in the seventh century B.C., inspired the proverbial expression "the riches of Gyges."
9. Cf. Lovelace, "The Grasshopper," p. 494.
1. I.e., Nature herself is thy Ganymede (Jove's cupbearer).

All the plants belong to thee,
All that summer hours produce,
Fertile made with early juice.
Man for thee does sow and plow,
Farmer he, and landlord thou!
Thou dost innocently joy,
Nor does thy luxury destroy;
The shepherd gladly heareth thee,
More harmonious than he.
Thee country hinds with gladness hear,
Prophet of the ripened year!
Thee Phoebus loves, and does inspire;
Phoebus is himself thy sire.
To thee of all things upon earth,
Life is no longer than thy mirth.
Happy insect, happy thou,
Dost neither age nor winter know.
But when thou'st drunk, and danced, and sung
Thy fill, the flow'ry leaves among
(Voluptuous, and wise withal,
Epicurean[2] animal!),
Sated with thy summer feast,
Thou retir'st to endless rest.

FROM *THE MISTRESS*

The Spring[3]

Though you be absent here, I needs must say
The trees as beauteous are, and flowers as gay
As ever they were wont to be;
Nay, the birds' rural music too
Is as melodious and free
As if they sung to pleasure you:
I saw a rosebud ope this morn; I'll swear
The blushing morning opened not more fair.

How could it be so fair, and you away?
How could the trees be beauteous, flowers so gay?
Could they remember but last year,
How you did them, they you delight,
The sprouting leaves which saw you here
And called their fellows to the sight,
Would, looking round for the same sight in vain,
Creep back into their silent barks again.

2. The Greek philosopher Epicurus (342–270 B.C.) in fact taught his followers to seek not merely sensual gratification but (and chiefly) that peace of mind that is the consequence of a virtuous life.
3. Cf. Carew, "The Spring," p. 295.

Where'er you walked, trees were as reverent made
As when of old gods dwelt in every shade;
Is't possible they should not know
What loss of honor they sustain,
That thus they smile and flourish now,
And still their former pride retain?
Dull creatures! 'Tis not without cause that she
Who fled the god of wit was made a tree.[4]

In ancient times sure they much wiser were,
When they rejoiced the Thracian verse to hear;
In vain did nature bid them stay,
When Orpheus[5] had his song begun;
They called their wond'ring roots away
And bade them silent to him run.
How would those learnèd trees have followed you?
You would have drawn them, and their poet too.

But who can blame them now? For, since you're
gone,
They're here the only fair, and shine alone.
You did their natural rights invade;
Wherever you did walk or sit,
The thickest boughs could make no shade,
Although the sun had granted it;
The fairest flowers could please no more, near you,
Than painted flowers set next to them could do.

Whene'er then you come hither, that shall be
The time, which this to others is, to me.
The little joys which here are now,
The name of punishments do bear,
When by their sight they let us know
How we deprived of greater are.
'Tis you the best of seasons with you bring;
This is for beasts, and that for men, the spring.

Platonic Love[6]

Indeed I must confess,
When souls mix 'tis an happiness;
But not complete till bodies too combine,
And closely as our minds together join.
But half of heaven the souls in glory taste,
Till by love in heaven at last
Their bodies too are placed.

4. The nymph Daphne fled Apollo and was transformed into a laurel.
5. Cf. Jonson, *The Forest*, XII, line 77n, p. 114.
6. Cf. Randolph, "An Elegy," p. 341.

In thy immortal part
Man, as well as I, thou art.
But something 'tis that differs thee and me,
And we must one even in that difference be.
I thee, both as a man and woman prize;
For a perfect love implies
Love in all capacities.

Can that for true love pass
When a fair woman courts her glass?
Something unlike must in love's likeness be,
His wonder is one and variety.
For he, whose soul nought but a soul can move,
Does a new Narcissus[7] prove,
And his own image love.

That souls do beauty know,
'Tis to the body's help they owe;
If when they know't they straight abuse that trust,
And shut the body from't, 'tis as unjust
As if I brought my dearest friend to see
My mistress, and at th'instant he
Should steal her quite from me.

Against Fruition[8]

No; thou'rt a fool, I'll swear, if e'er thou grant;
Much of my veneration thou must want,[9]
When once thy kindness puts my ignorance out,
For a learn'd age is always least devout.
Keep still thy distance; for at once to me
Goddess and woman too thou canst not be;
Thou'rt queen of all that sees thee, and as such
Must neither tyrannize nor yield too much;
Such freedom give as may admit command,
But keep the forts and magazines in thine hand.
Thou'rt yet a whole world to me, and dost fill
My large ambition; but 'tis dang'rous still,
Lest I like the Pellaean prince[1] should be,
And weep for other worlds, having conquered thee.
When Love has taken all thou hast away,
His strength by too much riches will decay.
Thou in my fancy dost much higher stand

7. Cf. Ovid, *Metamorphoses*, III.341–510.
8. Cf. the two poems by Sir John Suckling on this theme, pp. 418 and 421.
9. Lack.
1. I.e., Alexander the Great, born at Pella, in Macedonia.

Than women can be placed by Nature's hand;
And I must needs, I'm sure, a loser be,
To change thee, as thou'rt there, for very thee.
Thy sweetness is so much within me placed,
That shouldst thou nectar give, 'twould spoil the taste.
Beauty at first moves wonder and delight;
'Tis Nature's juggling trick to cheat the sight;
We admire it, whilst unknown, but after more
Admire ourselves for liking it before.
Love, like a greedy hawk, if we give way,
Does overgorge himself with his own prey;
Of very[2] hopes a surfeit he'll sustain
Unless by fears he cast them up again:
His spirit and sweetness dangers keep alone;
If once he lose his sting, he grows a drone.

From *Pindaric Odes*[3]

To Mr. Hobbes[4]

Vast bodies of philosophy
I oft have seen, and read,
But all are bodies dead;
Or bodies by art fashionèd;
I never yet the living soul could see,
But in thy books and thee.
'Tis only God can know
Whether the fair idea thou dost show
Agree entirely with his own or no.
This I dare boldly tell,
'Tis so like truth 'twill serve our turn as well.
Just,[5] as in nature, thy proportions be,
As full of concord their variety,
As firm the parts upon their center rest,
And all so solid are that they at least
As much as nature emptiness detest.

Long did the mighty Stagirite[6] retain
The universal intellectual reign,

2. Absolute.
3. Cowley gives some account of his purposes in undertaking to render the Pindaric mode in English verse in his Preface to *Pindaric Odes*, first published in 1656.
4. The philosopher Thomas Hobbes (1588–1679), known primarily for his treatise of political philosophy, *Leviathan* (1651), published a number of other important works in the fields of history, law, and science, not to mention his translations of Thucydides (1629), and Homer (1673–1676). For an intriguing account of Hobbes's character and career, see John Aubrey, *Brief Lives*, ed. Oliver Dick (London, 1950), pp. 237–262.
5. Precise, exact.
6. I.e., Aristotle.

Saw his own country's short-lived leopard slain;[7]
The stronger Roman eagle did outfly,[8]
Oft'ner renewed his age, and saw that die.
Mecca itself, in spite of Mahomet possessed,[9]
And chased by a wild deluge from the East,
His monarchy new planted in the West.
But as in time each great imperial race
Degenerates, and gives some new one place,
So did this noble empire waste,
Sunk by degrees from glories past,
And in the schoolmen's hands[1] it perished quite at last.
Then nought but words it grew,
And those all barb'rous too.
It perished, and it vanished there,
The life and soul breathed out, became but empty air.

The fields which answered well the ancients' plow,
Spent and outworn return no harvest now,
In barren age wild and unglorious lie,
And boast of past fertility,
The poor relief of present poverty.
Food and fruit we now must want
Unless new lands we plant.
We break up tombs with sacrilegious hands;
Old rubbish we remove;
To walk in ruins, like vain ghosts, we love,
And with fond[2] divining wands
We search among the dead
For treasures burièd,
Whilst still the liberal earth does hold
So many virgin mines of undiscovered gold.

The Baltic, Euxin,[3] and the Caspian,
And slender-limbed Mediterranean,
Seem narrow creeks to thee, and only fit
For the poor wretched fisher-boats of wit.
Thy nobler vessel the vast ocean tries,
And nothing sees but seas and skies,
Till unknown regions it descries,

7. "Outlasted the Grecian Empire, which in the Visions of Daniel is represented by a Leopard, with four wings upon the back, and four heads, vii.6" (Cowley's note).
8. "Was received even beyond the bounds of the Roman Empire, and outlived it" (Cowley's note).
9. "For Aristotle's philosophy was in great esteem among the Arabians or Saracens, witness those many excellent books upon him, or according to his principles, written by Averroes, Avicenna, Avempace, and divers others. *In spite of Mahomet*, because his law, being adapted to the barbarous humour of those people he had first to deal with, and aiming only at greatness of empire by the sword, forbids all the studies of learning; which (nevertheless) flourished admirably under the Saracen monarchy, and continued so, till it was extinguished with that empire, by the inundation of the Turks, and other nations" (Cowley's note).
1. I.e., in the hands of medieval scholasticism.
2. Foolish, futile.
3. The Black Sea.

Thou great Columbus of the golden lands of new philosophies.
Thy task was harder much than his,
For thy learned America is
Not only found out first by thee,
And rudely left to future industry,
But thy eloquence and thy wit
Has planted, peopled, built, and civilized it.

I little thought before
(Nor being my own self so poor,
Could comprehend so vast a store),
That all wardrobe of rich eloquence
Could have afforded half enough
Of bright, of new, and lasting stuff
To clothe the mighty limbs of thy gigantic sense;
Thy solid reason, like the shield from heaven
To the Trojan hero given,[4]
Too strong to take a mark from any mortal dart,
Yet shines with gold and gems in every part,
And wonders on it graved by the learn'd hand of art;
A shield that gives delight
Even to the enemies' sight,
Then when they're sure to lose the combat by't.

Nor can the snow which now cold age does shed
Upon thy reverend head
Quench or allay the noble fires within,
But all which thou hast been,
And all that youth can be, thou'rt yet,
So fully still dost thou
Enjoy the manhood, and the bloom of wit,
And all the natural heat, but not the fever too.
So contraries on Etna's top conspire,
Here hoary frosts, and by them[5] breaks out fire.
A secure peace the faithful neighbors keep,
Th'emboldened snow next to the flame does sleep.
And if we weigh, like thee,
Nature and causes, we shall see
That thus it needs must be,
To things immortal time can do no wrong,
And that which never is to die, forever must be young.

4. At the request of Venus, Vulcan forged a magnificently engraved shield for her son Aeneas; cf. *Aeneid*, VIII.600–731.
5. I.e., near them. Cowley gives Claudian, *De Raptu Proserpine*, as his source for this "description of fire and snow upon Etna (but not the application of it)."

From *Verses Written on Several Occasions*

Ode. Upon Dr. Harvey[6]

1.

Coy Nature, (which remained, though agèd grown,
A beauteous virgin still, enjoyed by none,
Nor seen unveiled by anyone)
When Harvey's violent passion she did see,
Began to tremble, and to flee,
Took sanctuary, like Daphne,[7] in a tree:
There Daphne's lover stopped, and thought it much
The very leaves of her to touch;
But Harvey, our Apollo, stopped not so,
Into the bark, and root, he after her did go:
No smallest fibers of a plant,
For which the eyebeam's point[8] doth sharpness want,
His passage after her withstood.
What should she do? Through all the moving wood,
Of lives endowed with sense, she took her flight;
Harvey pursues, and keeps her still in sight.
But as the deer long-hunted takes a flood,
She leapt at last into the winding streams of blood;
Of man's Meander[9] all the purple reaches[1] made,
Till at the heart she stayed,
Where turning head, and at a bay,[2]
Thus by well-purged ears[3] was she o'erheard to say.

2.

"Here sure shall I be safe," said she,
"None will be able sure to see
This my retreat, but only he
Who made both it and me.
The heart of man, what art can e'er reveal?
A wall impervious between
Divides the very parts within,[4]
And doth the heart of man ev'n from itself conceal."
She spoke, but ere she was aware,

6. William Harvey (1578–1657), physician to James I and Charles I, discovered the circulation of the blood, including the role of the heart, and published his results in *Exercitatio Anatomica de Motu Cordis et Sanguinis in Animalibus* (1628). In *Exercitationes de Generatione Animalium* (1651), he established the basis for modern embryology.
7. Cf. Waller, "The Story of Phoebus and Daphne Applied" and first note, p. 362.
8. The prevailing theory of vision held that the eyes emitted beams that brought back images to the imagination.
9. The Maeander is a river in southern Asia Minor: the verb "meander" ("to follow a winding course") derives from its name.
1. A continuous stretch of river.
2. "The position of a hunted animal" (*OED*). Also, Cowley may be punning on Daphne's transformation into a bay tree.
3. I.e., purified and receptive ears.
4. The septum dividing the chambers of the heart.

Harvey was with her there,
And held this slippery Proteus[5] in a chain,
Till all her mighty mysteries she descried,
Which from his wit th'attempt before to hide
Was the first thing that Nature did in vain.

3.

He the young practice of new life did see,[6]
Whil'st to conceal its toilsome poverty,
It for a living wrought,[7] both hard and privately.
Before the liver understood
The noble scarlet dye of blood,
Before one drop was by it made,
Or brought into it, to set up the trade;[8]
Before the untaught heart began to beat
The tuneful march to vital heat,[9]
From all the souls that living buildings rear,[1]
Whether implied[2] for earth, or sea, or air,
Whether it in the womb or egg be wrought,[3]
A strict account to him is hourly brought,
How the great fabric[4] does proceed;
What time and what materials it does need.
He so exactly does the work survey,
As if he hired the workers by the day.

4.

Thus Harvey sought for truth in truth's own book,
The creatures, which by God himself was writ;
And wisely thought 'twas fit,
Not to read comments only upon it,
But on th'original itself to look.
Methinks in art's great circle others stand
Locked up together, hand in hand;
Everyone leads as he is led;
The same bare path they tread,
And dance like fairies a fantastic round[5]
But neither change their motion, nor their ground:
Had Harvey to this road confined his wit,
His noble circle of the blood had been untrodden yet.
Great Doctor! Th'art of curing's cured by thee;

5. A shape-shifting sea god skilled in prophecy. In the *Odyssey* (IV.349–570), Menelaus captures Proteus and forces him to tell him how to return to Sparta.
6. This stanza foregrounds Harvey's work on the generation of animals.
7. Worked.
8. The liver was thought to convert digested nutrients from the stomach into blood.
9. The refined spirit in semen that Aristotle believed enabled generation.
1. I.e., souls (the power of vital animation) rear living buildings (bodies) intended for earth, sea, or air.
2. Intended.
3. Made.
4. I.e., the developing embryo.
5. A dance in which the dancers form one large circle. "Fantastic" can refer to the imagination as well.

We now thy patient Physic[6] see,
From all inveterate diseases free;
Purged of old errors by thy care,
New-dieted, put forth to clearer air,
It now will strong, and healthful prove;
Itself before lethargic lay and could not move.

5.

These useful secrets to his pen we owe,
And thousands more 'twas ready to bestow;
Of which, a barbarous war's unlearnèd rage[7]
Has robbed the ruined age;
O cruel loss! As if the Golden Fleece,[8]
With so much cost, and labor bought,
And from afar by a great hero brought,
Had sunk even in the ports of Greece.
O cursèd war! Who can forgive thee this?
Houses and towns may rise again,
And ten times easier it is
To rebuild Paul's[9] than any work of his.
That mighty task none but himself can do,
Nay, scarce himself too now,[1]
For though his wit the force of age withstand,
His body, alas, and time it must command,
And Nature now, so long by him surpassed,
Will sure have her revenge on him at last.

6. The theory and practice of medicine.
7. The English Civil War.
8. The Greek hero Jason's quest was to bring the Golden Fleece back from Colchis, a land beyond the Black Sea.
9. St. Paul's Cathedral.
1. Harvey published little after 1651.

Andrew Marvell

1621	Born on 31 March at Winestead-in-Holderness, Yorkshire. Son of the "Calvinstical" Reverend Andrew Marvell and his wife, Anne Pease.
1624	Father appointed Master of the Hull Charterhouse and lecturer in Holy Trinity Church; family moves to Hull.
1629–1633	Probably attends Hull Grammar School.
1633	Matriculates at Trinity College, Cambridge; graduates B.A. in 1639.
1639	Runs off to London and converts to Roman Catholicism. His father intervenes and sends him back to Cambridge.
1641	Father's accidental death by drowning; Marvell moves to London.
1642–1647	Travels in Holland, France, Italy, and Spain.
1648	Writes "To His Noble Friend Mr. Richard Lovelace" and "An Elegy upon the Death of My Lord Francis Villiers."
1651–1652	Serves as tutor to Mary Fairfax at Nun Appleton, Yorkshire.
1653	Milton recommends him for the post of Assistant Latin Secretary. He serves as tutor to William Dutton, who becomes Cromwell's ward. Living at Eton.
1656	Traveling in France with Dutton.
1657	Joins Milton as Latin Secretary to the Council of State.
1659	Elected member of Parliament for Hull; represents Hull in Parliament until 1678, vigorously fighting for constitutional liberties.
1662–1663	In Holland on state business.
1663–1665	As Secretary to the Earl of Carlisle, visits Russia, Sweden, and Denmark.
1672–1673	Publishes *The Rehearsal Transposed* anonymously, as part of a controversy with Samuel Parker, Archdeacon of Canterbury.
1674	Writes commendatory poem for *Paradise Lost*.
1677	Publishes *An Account of the Growth of Popery* anonymously.
1678	Dies on 16 August in his home in Great Russell Street, London.
1681	*Miscellaneous Poems* published by his former housekeeper as support for her (unsuccessful) claim to be his widow and heir.

Andrew Marvell

FROM *MISCELLANEOUS POEMS* (1681)

A Dialogue between the Resolved[1] Soul and Created Pleasure

Courage, my Soul, now learn to wield
The weight of thine immortal shield.
Close on thy head thy helmet bright.
Balance thy sword[2] against the fight.
See where an army, strong as fair,
With silken banners spreads the air.
Now, if thou be'st that thing divine,
In this day's combat let it shine:
And show that Nature wants[3] an art
To conquer one resolvèd heart.

Pleasure Welcome the creation's guest,
Lord of earth, and heaven's heir.
Lay aside that warlike crest,
And of Nature's banquet share:
Where the souls[4] of fruits and flowers
Stand prepared to heighten yours.[5]

Soul I sup above, and cannot stay
To bait[6] so long upon the way.

Pleasure On these downy pillows lie,
Whose soft plumes will thither fly:
On these roses, strowed so plain
Lest one leaf thy side should strain.[7]

Soul My gentler rest is on a thought,
Conscious of doing what I ought.

Pleasure If thou be'st with perfumes pleased,
Such as oft the gods appeased,
Thou in fragrant clouds shalt show
Like another god below.

Soul A soul that knows not to presume
Is heaven's and its own perfume.

1. Not only resolute but carrying a musical suggestion.
2. In Ephesians 6:11–17, Saint Paul describes the "whole armor of God," the "shield of faith . . . , helmet of salvation, and the sword of the Spirit."
3. Lacks.
4. Essences.
5. I.e., your lower soul. Pleasure appeals to the senses in turn, then to beauty, wealth, glory, knowledge.
6. To stop at an inn and take refreshment (*OED*).
7. *Strowed*: strewn; *plain*: flat; *leaf*: petal; *strain*: hurt.

Pleasure Everything does seem to vie
Which should first attract thine eye:
But since none deserves that grace,
In this crystal[8] view thy face.

Soul When the Creator's skill is prized,
The rest is all but earth disguised.

Pleasure Hark how music then prepares
For thy stay these charming airs;
Which the posting[9] winds recall,
And suspend the river's fall.

Soul Had I but any time to lose,
On this I would it all dispose.
Cease tempter. None can chain a mind
Whom this sweet chordage[1] cannot bind.

Chorus Earth cannot show so brave a sight
As when a single soul does fence
The batteries of alluring sense
And heaven views it with delight.
  Then persevere: for still new charges sound:
  And if thou overcomest thou shalt be crowned.

Pleasure All this fair, and soft, and sweet,
  Which scattering doth shine,
Shall within one beauty meet,
  And she be only thine.

Soul If things of sight such heavens be,
What heavens are those we cannot see?

Pleasure Wheresoe'er thy foot shall go
  The minted gold shall lie;
Till thou purchase all below,
  And want new words to buy.

Soul Were't not for price[2] who'd value gold?
And that's worth nought that can be sold.

Pleasure Wilt thou all the glory have
  That war or peace commend?
Half the world shall be thy slave
  The other half thy friend.

8. Mirror.
9. Hurrying, rushing.
1. Pun on chord and cord.
2. I.e., if it were not worth money.

Soul What friends, if to myself untrue?
What slaves, unless I captive you?

Pleasure Thou shalt know each hidden cause;
And see the future time;
Try what depth the center[3] draws;
And then to heaven climb.

Soul None thither mounts by the degree
Of knowledge, but humility.[4]

Chorus Triumph, triumph, victorious Soul;
The world has not one pleasure more:
The rest does lie beyond the pole,
And is thine everlasting store.

On a Drop of Dew

See how the orient[5] dew,
Shed from the bosom of the morn
Into the blowing[6] roses,
Yet careless of its mansion new,
For the clear region[7] where 'twas born
Round in itself incloses:
And in its little globe's extent,
Frames as it can its native element.[8]
How it the purple flower does slight,
Scarce touching where it lies,
But gazing back upon the skies,
Shines with a mournful light;
Like its own tear,
Because so long divided from the sphere.
Restless it rolls and unsecure,
Trembling lest it grow impure,
Till the warm sun pity its pain,
And to the skies exhale it back again.
So the soul, that drop, that ray
Of the clear fountain of eternal day,
Could it within the human flower be seen,
Remembering still[9] its former height,
Shuns the sweet leaves, and blossoms green;[1]
And recollecting[2] its own light,
Does, in its pure and circling thoughts, express

3. Of the earth.
4. But rather by humility.
5. "Orient" suggests sunrise and pearl-like.
6. Blossoming.
7. *For*: in preference to (*OED*); *clear region*: heaven.
8. Heaven.
9. Yet; always; quietly.
1. *Green*: a favorite word in Marvell's poetry.
2. Collecting again; perhaps, remembering.

The greater heaven in an heaven less,
In how coy[3] a figure wound,
Every way it turns away:
So the world excluding round,
Yet receiving in the day,
Dark beneath, but bright above:
Here disdaining, there in love.
How loose and easy hence to go:
How girt and ready to ascend,
Moving but on a point below,
It all about does upwards bend.[4]
Such did the manna's sacred dew distill,
White and entire, though congealed and chill,
Congealed on earth: but does, dissolving, run
Into the glories of the almighty sun.[5]

The Coronet

When for[6] the thorns with which I long, too long,
With many a piercing wound,
My Savior's head have crowned,
I seek with garlands to redress that wrong:
Through every garden, every mead,
I gather flowers (my fruits are only flowers),
Dismantling all the fragrant towers[7]
That once adorned my shepherdess's head.
And now when I have summed up all my store,
Thinking (so I myself deceive)
So rich a chaplet[8] thence to weave
As never yet the king of glory wore:
Alas I find the serpent old
That, twining in[9] his speckled breast,
About the flowers disguised does fold,
With wreaths of fame and interest.[1]
Ah, foolish man, that wouldst debase with them,
And mortal glory, heaven's diadem!
But thou who only couldst the serpent tame,
Either his slippery knots at once untie,
And disentangle all his winding snare:
Or shatter too with him my curious frame:[2]
And let these wither, so that he may die,

3. Quiet, still.
4. Cf. Herbert, "The Flower," line 30, p. 280.
5. For the manna, miraculous food provided to the Israelites in the wilderness, see Exodus 16. It covered the ground like dew in the morning; that which was not eaten melted as the sun grew hot.
6. In the place of, because of.
7. *Towers*: very tall headdresses worn by women (*OED*).
8. Coronet.
9. I.e., entwining.
1. Self-interest.
2. *Curious*: elaborately wrought (*OED*); "curious frame" suggests that *coronet* is also a metaphor for poetry.

Though set with skill and chosen out with care:
That they, while thou on both their spoils dost tread,
May crown thy feet, that could not crown thy head.

Eyes and Tears

How wisely Nature did decree,
With the same eyes to weep and see!
That, having viewed the object vain,
They might be ready to complain.

And, since the self-deluding sight,
In a false angle takes each height,
These tears which better measure all,
Like watery lines and plummets fall.

Two tears, which Sorrow long did weigh
Within the scales of either eye,
And then paid out in equal poise,
Are the true price of all my joys.

What in the world most fair appears,
Yea even laughter turns to tears:
And all the jewels which we prize,
Melt in these pendants of the eyes.

I have through every garden been,
Amongst the red, the white, the green;
And yet from all the flowers I saw,
No honey, but these tears could draw.

So the all-seeing sun each day
Distills the world with chymic[3] ray;
But finds the essence only showers,
Which straight in pity back he pours.

Yet happy they whom grief doth bless,
That weep the more, and see the less;
And, to preserve their sight more true,
Bathe still their eyes in their own dew.

So Magdalen, in tears more wise
Dissolved those captivating eyes,
Whose liquid chains could flowing meet
To fetter her Redeemer's feet.

Not full sails hasting loaden home,
Nor the chaste lady's pregnant womb,

3. Alchemical.

Nor Cynthia teeming[4] shows so fair,
As two eyes swollen with weeping are.

The sparkling glance that shoots desire,
Drenched in these waves, does lose its fire.
Yea oft the Thunderer pity takes
And here the hissing lightning slakes.

The incense was to heaven dear,
Not as a perfume, but a tear.
And stars show lovely in the night,
But as they seem the tears of light.

Ope[5] then mine eyes your double sluice,
And practice so your noblest use.
For others too can see, or sleep;
But only human eyes can weep.

Now like two clouds dissolving, drop,
And at each tear in distance stop:
Now like two fountains trickle down:
Now like two floods o'erturn and drown.

Thus let your streams o'erflow your springs,
Till eyes and tears be the same things:
And each the other's difference bears,
These weeping eyes, those seeing tears.

Bermudas[6]

Where the remote Bermudas ride
In the ocean's bosom unespied,
From a small boat, that rowed along,
The listening winds received this song.
"What should we do but sing his praise
That led us through the watery maze,
Unto an isle so long unknown,
And yet far kinder than our own?
Where he the huge sea-monsters wracks,
That lift the deep upon their backs.
He lands us on a grassy stage,
Safe from the storms, and prelate's rage.
He gave us this eternal spring,
Which here enamels everything;
And sends the fowls to us in care,
On daily visits through the air.

4. The full moon.
5. Open.
6. In Marvell's time, the Bermudas were a refuge for persecuted Puritans and an image of remoteness, associated with a type of Paradise.

He hangs in shades the orange bright,
Like golden lamps in a green night.
And does in the pomegranates close,
Jewels more rich than Ormus[7] shows.
He makes the figs our mouths to meet,
And throws the melons at our feet.
But apples[8] plants of such a price,
No tree could ever bear them twice.
With cedars, chosen by his hand,
From Lebanon, he stores the land;
And makes the hollow seas, that roar,
Proclaim the ambergris[9] on shore.
He cast (of which we rather boast)
The gospel's pearl[1] upon our coast.
And in these rocks for us did frame
A temple, where to sound his name.
Oh let our voice his praise exalt,
Till it arrive at heaven's vault:
Which thence (perhaps) rebounding, may
Echo beyond the Mexique Bay."[2]
Thus sung they, in the English boat,
An holy and a cheerful note,
And all the way, to guide their chime,
With falling oars they kept the time.

A Dialogue between the Soul and Body[3]

Soul O who shall from this dungeon raise
A soul enslaved so many ways?
With bolts of bones, that fettered stands
In feet; and manacled in hands.
Here blinded with an eye; and there
Deaf with the drumming of an ear.
A soul hung up, as 'twere, in chains
Of nerves, and arteries, and veins.
Tortured, besides each other part,
In a vain head, and double[4] heart.

Body O, who shall me deliver whole,
From bonds of this tyrannic soul?

7. Hormuz, on the Persian Gulf, a center for the pearl and jewel trade.
8. Pineapples.
9. Odorous substance that derives from the sperm whale.
1. Alludes to either, or both, the pearl of great price (Matthew 13:14–46) and the pearl cast before swine (Matthew 7:6).
2. The Gulf of Mexico. Presumably, their voice is to be heard by the heathen and the Roman Catholics in the Americas.
3. While the poem turns on Galatians 5:17 ("the flesh lusteth against the spirit, and the spirit against the flesh"), it explores the problem in paradoxical terms, playing off mutually restrictive elements of soul and body against each other. In the first two stanzas, both Soul and Body lay claim, by allusion, to Paul's outcry in Romans 7:24 (on the relation of the Law and sin), "O wretched man that I am! who shall deliver me from the body of this death?"
4. False, deceitful.

Which, stretched upright, impales me so,
That mine own precipice I go;[5]
And warms and moves this needless frame:
(A fever could but do the same),
And, wanting where its spite to try,
Has made me live to let me die,
A body that could never rest,
Since this ill spirit it possessed.

Soul What magic could me thus confine
Within another's grief to pine?
Where whatsoever it[6] complain,
I feel, that cannot feel, the pain.
And all my care itself employs,
That to preserve, which me destroys:
Constrained not only to endure
Diseases, but, what's worse, the cure:
And ready oft the port to gain,
Am shipwrecked into health again.

Body But physic yet could never reach
The maladies thou me dost teach;
Whom first the cramp of hope does tear:
And then the palsy shakes of fear.
The pestilence of love does heat:
Or hatred's hidden ulcer eat.
Joy's cheerful madness does perplex:
Or sorrow's other madness vex.
Which knowledge forces me to know;
And memory will not forego.
What but a soul could have the wit
To build me up for sin so fit?
So architects do square and hew,
Green trees that in the forest grew.

The Nymph Complaining for the Death of Her Fawn[7]

The wanton troopers[8] riding by
Have shot my fawn, and it will die.
Ungentle men! They cannot thrive
To kill thee. Thou never didst alive[9]
Them any harm; alas nor could
Thy death yet do them any good.
I'm sure I never wished them ill;

5. Lines 13–14 express both erectness and spiritual pride, both a reaching toward heaven and the danger of damnation.
6. The body.
7. Among points of reference, cf. the story of Silvia's deer killed wantonly by the Trojans (*Aeneid* VII.475 ff.), the immediate cause of a war.
8. Cromwell's soldiers were called troopers.
9. The syntax suggests that "alive" means "merely by being alive" as well as "while alive."

Nor do I for all this; nor will:
But if my simple prayers may yet
Prevail with heaven to forget
Thy murder, I will join my tears
Rather than fail. But, O my fears!
It cannot die so.[1] Heaven's King
Keeps register of everything:
And nothing may we use in vain.
Even beasts must be with justice slain,
Else men are made their deodands.[2]
Though they should wash their guilty hands
In this warm life blood which doth part
From thine, and wound me to the heart,
Yet could they not be clean: their stain
Is dyed in such a purple grain.
There is not such another in
The world, to offer for their sin.
Unconstant Sylvio, when yet
I had not found him counterfeit,
One morning (I remember well)
Tied in this silver chain and bell,
Gave it to me; nay and I know
What he said then; I'm sure I do:
Said he, "Look how your huntsman here
Hath taught a fawn to hunt his dear."
But Sylvio soon had me beguiled.
This waxèd tame, while he grew wild,
And quite regardless of my smart,
Left me his fawn, but took his heart.[3]
Thenceforth I set myself to play
My solitary time away,
With this: and very well content,
Could so mine idle life have spent.
For it was full of sport; and light
Of foot, and heart; and did invite
Me to its game: it seemed to bless
Itself in me. How could I less
Than love it? O I cannot be
Unkind, to a beast that loveth me.
Had it lived long, I do not know
Whether it too might have done so
As Sylvio did: his gifts might be
Perhaps as false or more than he.
But I am sure, for ought that I
Could in so short a time espy,
Thy love was far more better then[4]
The love of false and cruel men.

1. Unavenged.
2. Personal chattels that are forfeited (literally, *deodandus* means "due to be given to God") for causing the death of a human being (*OED*).
3. "Dear" (line 32) is a pun on *deer*; "heart," a pun on *hart*.
4. Than.

With sweetest milk, and sugar, first
I it at mine own fingers nursed.
And as it grew, so every day
It waxed more white and sweet than they.
It had so sweet a breath! And oft
I blushed to see its foot more soft
And white (shall I say than my hand?)
Nay, any lady's of the land.
It is a wondrous thing how fleet
'Twas on those little silver feet.
With what a pretty skipping grace,
It oft would challenge me the race:
And, when it had left me far away,
'Twould stay, and run again, and stay.
For it was nimbler much than hinds;
And trod, as if on the four winds.
I have a garden of my own,
But so with roses overgrown,
And lilies, that you would it guess
To be a little wilderness.
And all the springtime of the year
It only lovèd to be there.
Among the beds of lilies, I
Have sought it oft, where it should lie;
Yet could not, till itself would rise,
Find it, although before mine eyes.
For, in the flaxen lilies' shade,
It like a bank of lilies laid.
Upon the roses it would feed,
Until its lips even seemed to bleed:
And then to me 'twould boldly trip,
And print those roses on my lip.
But all its chief delight was still
On roses thus itself to fill:
And its pure virgin limbs to fold
In whitest sheets of lilies cold.
Had it lived long, it would have been
Lilies without, roses within.
O help! O help! I see it faint:
And die as calmly as a saint.
See how it weeps. The tears do come
Sad, slowly dropping like a gum.
So weeps the wounded balsam: so
The holy frankincense doth flow.
The brotherless Heliades[5]
Melt in such amber tears as these.
I in a golden vial will
Keep these two crystal tears; and fill
It till it do overflow with mine;

5. Disconsolate at the death of their brother Phaeton, the three daughters of Helios were metamorphosed into amber-dropping trees (poplars, perhaps, or weeping willows).

Then place it in Diana's shrine.
Now my sweet fawn is vanished to
Whither the swans and turtles[6] go:
In fair Elysium to endure,
With milk-white lambs, and ermines pure.
O do not run too fast: for I
Will but bespeak thy grave, and die.
First, my unhappy statue shall
Be cut in marble; and withal,
Let it be weeping too; but there
The engraver sure his art may spare;
For I so truly thee bemoan,
That I shall weep though I be stone:[7]
Until my tears, still dropping, wear
My breast, themselves engraving there.
There at my feet shalt thou be laid,
Of purest alabaster made:
For I would have thine image be
White as I can, though not as thee.

To His Coy Mistress[8]

Had we but world enough, and time,
This coyness, Lady, were no crime.
We would sit down, and think which way
To walk, and pass our long love's day.
Thou by the Indian Ganges' side
Shouldst rubies find: I by the tide
Of Humber[9] would complain. I would
Love you ten years before the Flood:
And you should if you please refuse
Till the conversion of the Jews.[1]
My vegetable[2] love should grow
Vaster than empires, and more slow.
An hundred years should go to praise
Thine eyes, and on thy forehead gaze.
Two hundred to adore each breast;
But thirty thousand to the rest.
An age at least to every part,
And the last age should show your heart.
For, lady, you deserve this state;[3]
Nor would I love at lower rate.
But at my back I always hear

6. Turtle doves.
7. Niobe, lamenting the death of her many children, was turned to stone.
8. Using arguments out of the carpe diem (literally, "seize the day") tradition, the poem has an apparently logical structure (if / but / therefore), its main images turning on the time and space motifs introduced in line 1.
9. A river in northern England, suggesting the other end of the world from the Ganges.
1. Lines 7–10: from nearly the beginning of time to nearly the end of time.
2. Like plant life; of the lowest soul, which has only the capacity to grow (and decay).
3. Dignity.

Time's wingèd chariot hurrying near:
And yonder all before us lie
Deserts of vast eternity.
Thy beauty shall no more be found;
Nor, in thy marble vault, shall sound
My echoing song: then worms shall try
That long-preserved virginity:
And your quaint honor[4] turn to dust,
And into ashes all my lust.
The grave's a fine and private place,
But none, I think, do there embrace.
  Now therefore, while the youthful hue
Sits on thy skin like morning dew,[5]
And while thy willing soul transpires
At every pore with instant[6] fires,
Now let us sport us while we may;
And now, like amorous birds of prey,
Rather at once our time devour,
Than languish in his slow-chapt[7] power.
Let us roll all our strength, and all
Our sweetness, up into one ball:
And tear our pleasures with rough strife,
Thorough[8] the iron gates of life.
Thus, though we cannot make our sun
Stand still, yet we will make him run.[9]

The Definition of Love

1

My love is of a birth as rare
As 'tis for object strange and high:
It was begotten by Despair
Upon Impossibility.

2

Magnanimous Despair alone
Could show me so divine a thing,
Where feeble Hope could ne'er have flown
But vainly flapped its tinsel wing.

4. Both "quaint" (cf. Middle English "queynte") and "honor" could mean the female genitals.
5. See Textual Notes.
6. Urgent, as well as sudden.
7. Slowly devouring; the slow jaws of, e.g., a bird of prey (cf. line 38) or of the god Kronos (mistakenly identified in the Renaissance with time), who, fearing his children, swallowed them.
8. Through.
9. The three actions in lines 38–46 include imaginative conquest of time and space ("ball" as "sphere" or "world"), while recognizing that the "rough strife" now envisaged (including defloration) must defy both time and world. The sun stood still for Joshua (10:12) and for Zeus and Alcmene when Hercules was conceived.

3

And yet I quickly might arrive
Where my extended soul is fixed,[1]
But Fate does iron wedges drive,
And always crowds itself betwixt.

4

For Fate with jealous eye does see
Two perfect loves; nor lets them close:
Their union would her ruin be,
And her tyrannic power depose.

5

And therefore her decrees of steel
Us as the distant poles have placed,
(Though Love's whole world on us doth wheel)
Not by themselves to be embraced.

6

Unless the giddy heaven fall,
And earth some new convulsion tear;
And, us to join, the world should all
Be cramped into a planisphere.[2]

7

As lines so loves oblique may well
Themselves in every angle greet:
But ours so truly parallel,
Though infinite, can never meet.

8

Therefore the love which us doth bind,
But Fate so enviously debars,
Is the conjunction of the mind,
And opposition[3] of the stars.

1. Paradoxically (extension is a property of matter) gone out of him and attached to his lady.
2. A flat sphere: a two-dimensional projection in which the poles are united.
3. "Conjunction" and "opposition" are terms from astronomy, indicating spiritual union but opposition between the stars and the lovers.

The Picture of Little T.C. in a Prospect of Flowers[4]

1

See with what simplicity
This nymph begins her golden days!
In the green grass she loves to lie,
And there with her fair aspect tames
The wilder flowers, and gives them names:[5]
But only with the roses plays;
    And them does tell
What color best becomes them, and what smell.

2

Who can foretell for what high cause
This darling of the gods was born!
Yet this is she whose chaster laws
The wanton Love shall one day fear,
And, under her command severe,
See his bow broke and ensigns torn.
    Happy, who can
Appease this virtuous enemy of man!

3

O then let me in time compound,
And parley with those conquering eyes;
Ere they have tried their force to wound,
Ere, with their glancing wheels, they drive
In triumph over hearts that strive,
And them that yield but[6] more despise.
    Let me be laid,
Where I may see thy glories from some shade.

4

Meantime, whilst every verdant thing
Itself does at thy beauty charm,
Reform the errors of the spring;
Make that the tulips may have share
Of sweetness, seeing they are fair;
And roses of their thorns disarm:
    But most procure
That violets may a longer age endure.

4. T.C. may be Theophila Cornewall, born 1644; "darling of the gods" (line 10) then would be a pun on her name. *Prospect*: landscape.
5. In Genesis 2:19–20, "Adam gave names to all cattle, and to the fowl of the air, and to every beast of the field; but for Adam there was not found an help meet for him." The last clause may be behind the tradition that Eve named the flowers.
6. Only.

5

But, O young beauty of the woods,
Whom Nature courts with fruits and flowers,
Gather the flowers, but spare the buds;
Lest Flora,[7] angry at thy crime,
To kill her infants in their prime,
Do quickly make the example yours;
And, ere we see,
Nip in the blossom all our hopes and thee.

The Mower against Gardens[8]

Luxurious man, to bring his vice in use,[9]
Did after him the world seduce;
And from the fields the flowers and plants allure,
Where Nature was most plain and pure.
He first enclosed within the garden's square
A dead and standing pool of air:
And a more luscious earth for them did knead,
Which stupefied them while it fed.
The pink grew then as double as his mind;
The nutriment did change the kind.
With strange perfumes he did the roses taint,
And flowers themselves were taught to paint.
The tulip, white, did for complexion seek,
And learned to interline its cheek;
Its onion root they then so high did hold,
That one was for a meadow sold.
Another world was searched, through oceans new,
To find the Marvel of Peru.[1]
And yet these rarities might be allowed,
To man, that sovereign thing and proud,
Had he not dealt[2] between the bark and tree,
Forbidden mixtures there to see.
No plant now knew the stock from which it came;
He grafts upon the wild the tame:
That the uncertain and adulterate fruit
Might put the palate in dispute.
His green seraglio[3] has its eunuchs too,
Lest any tyrant him outdo;
And in the cherry he does Nature vex,
To procreate without a sex.[4]

7. Goddess of flowers, wife of Zephyr, the west wind of springtime.
8. Since this poem appears to be the first of a sequence of four, the Mower is presumably Damon.
9. *Luxurious*: lustful; *in use*: into common practice, or (as in usury) to profit.
1. Exotic multicolored flower.
2. Intervened, perhaps in the sense of pandered.
3. Enclosure; "seraglio" was also used specifically for the enclosure where wives and concubines lived in a sultan's palace.
4. Propagate, e.g., by grafting.

'Tis all enforced, the fountain and the grot,
While the sweet fields do lie forgot:
Where willing Nature does to all dispense
A wild and fragrant innocence;
And fauns and fairies do the meadows till,
More by their presence than their skill.
Their statues polished by some ancient hand,
May to adorn the gardens stand;
But, howsoe'er the figures do excel,
The gods themselves with us do dwell.

Damon the Mower

1

Hark how the Mower Damon sung,
With love of Juliana stung!
While everything did seem to paint
The scene more fit for his complaint.
Like her fair eyes the day was fair,
But scorching like his amorous care.
Sharp like his scythe his sorrow was,
And withered like his hopes the grass.

2

"Oh what unusual heats are here,
Which thus our sunburned meadows sear!
The grasshopper its pipe gives o'er;
And hamstringed[5] frogs can dance no more:
But in the brook the green frog wades,
And grasshoppers seek out the shades.
Only the snake, that kept within,
Now glitters in its second skin.

3

"This heat the sun could never raise,
Nor Dog Star so inflames the days.
It from an higher beauty groweth,
Which burns the fields and mower both:
Which mads the Dog, and makes the sun
Hotter than his own Phaeton.[6]
Not July causeth these extremes,
But Juliana's scorching beams.

5. Crippled by the heat.
6. Charioteer of the sun.

4

"Tell me where I may pass the fires
Of the hot day, or hot desires.
To what cool cave shall I descend,
Or to what gelid fountain bend?
Alas! I look for ease in vain,
When remedies themselves complain.
No moisture but my tears do rest,
Nor cold but in her icy breast.

5

"How long wilt thou, fair shepherdess,
Esteem me, and my presents less?
To thee the harmless snake I bring,
Disarmèd of its teeth and sting.
To thee chameleons changing hue,
And oak leaves tipped with honey dew.
Yet thou, ungrateful, hast not sought
Nor what they are, nor who them brought.

6

"I am the Mower Damon, known
Through all the meadows I have mown.
On me the morn her dew distills
Before her darling daffodils:
And, if at noon my toil me heat,
The sun himself licks off my sweat.
While, going home, the evening sweet
In cowslip-water[7] bathes my feet.

7

"What though the piping shepherd stock
The plains with an unnumbered flock,
This scythe of mine discovers[8] wide
More ground than all his sheep do hide.
With this the golden fleece I shear
Of all these closes[9] every year.
And though in wool more poor than they,
Yet am I richer far in hay.

8

"Nor am I so deformed to sight,
If in my scythe I lookèd right;
In which I see my picture done,
As in a crescent moon the sun.

7. Cowslip plants grow wild in meadows; lotion made from their juice was used as a cleansing agent.
8. Uncovers.
9. Enclosures; here, enclosed fields.

The deathless fairies take me oft
To lead them in their dances soft;
And, when I tune myself to sing,
About me they contract their ring.

9

"How happy might I still have mowed,
Had not Love here his thistles sowed!
But now I all the day complain,
Joining my labor to my pain;
And with my scythe cut down the grass,
Yet still my grief is where it was;
But, when the iron blunter grows,
Sighing I whet my scythe and woes."

10

While thus he threw his elbow round,
Depopulating all the ground,
And, with his whistling scythe, does cut
Each stroke between the earth and root,
The edgèd steel by careless chance
Did into his own ankle glance;
And there among the grass fell down,
By his own scythe, the Mower mown.

11

"Alas!" said he, "these hurts are slight
To those that die by love's despite.
With shepherd's-purse, and clown's-all-heal,[1]
The blood I staunch, and wound I seal.
Only for him no cure is found,
Whom Juliana's eyes do wound.
'Tis death alone that this must do:
For Death, thou art a Mower too."

The Mower to the Glowworms

1

Ye living lamps, by whose dear light
The nightingale does sit so late,
And studying all the summer night,
Her matchless songs does meditate;

1. Herbs used to check bleeding and to heal wounds.

2

Ye country comets, that portend
No war, nor prince's funeral,
Shining unto no higher end
Than to presage the grass's fall;

3

Ye glowworms, whose officious[2] flame
To wandering mowers shows the way,
That in the night have lost their aim,
And after foolish fires[3] do stray;

4

Your courteous lights in vain you waste,
Since Juliana here is come,
For she my mind hath so displaced
That I shall never find my home.

The Mower's Song[4]

1

My mind was once the true survey
Of all these meadows fresh and gay;
And in the greenness of the grass
Did see its hopes as in a glass;[5]
When Juliana came, and she,
What I do to the grass, does to my thoughts and me.

2

But these, while I with sorrow pine,
Grew more luxuriant still and fine;
That not one blade of grass you spied,
But had a flower on either side;
When Juliana came, and she,
What I do to the grass, does to my thoughts and me.

3

Unthankful meadows, could you so
A fellowship so true forego,
And in your gaudy May-games meet,
While I lay trodden under feet?

2. Zealous, attentive.
3. Will-o'-the-wisps.
4. This poem has the only refrain in Marvell's poetry; "the rhythm [of the final, alexandrine line] suggests the long regular sweep of the scythe" (Margoliouth, 1971 Oxford edition).
5. Green is the color of hope. *Glass*: mirror.

When Juliana came, and she,
What I do to the grass, does to my thoughts and me.

4

But what you in compassion ought,
Shall now by my revenge be wrought:
And flowers, and grass, and I and all,
Will in one common ruin fall.
For Juliana comes, and she,
What I do to the grass, does to my thoughts and me.

5

And thus, ye meadows, which have been
Companions of my thoughts more green,
Shall now the heraldry become
With which I shall adorn my tomb;
For Juliana came, and she,
What I do to the grass, does to my thoughts and me.

Music's Empire

1

First was the world as one great cymbal made,
Where jarring winds to infant Nature played.
All Music was a solitary sound,
To hollow rocks and murmuring fountains bound.

2

Jubal[6] first made the wilder notes agree;
And Jubal tuned Music's jubilee:[7]
He called the echoes from their sullen cell,[8]
And built the organ's city where they dwell.

3

Each sought a consort[9] in that lovely place,
And virgin trebles wed the manly bass.
From whence the progeny of numbers new
Into harmonious colonies withdrew.

6. "The father of all such as handle the harp and organ" (Genesis 4:21). His name may be connected with the Hebrew word for "ram's horn."
7. *Jubilee*: "And ye shall hallow the fiftieth year, and proclaim liberty throughout all the land unto all the inhabitants thereof: it shall be a jubile unto you; and ye shall return every man unto his possession, and ye shall return every man unto his family" (Leviticus 25:10).
8. *Sullen*: implies gloomy, moody, obstinate, but may also suggest a "deep, dull, or mournful tone" (*OED*).
9. Mate, fellow, or partner; also, musical concert or harmony (*OED*).

4

Some to the lute, some to the viol went,
And others chose the cornet eloquent.
These practicing the wind, and those the wire,
To sing men's triumphs, or in heaven's choir.

5

Then music, the mosaic of the air,
Did of all these a solemn noise prepare:
With which she gained the empire of the ear,
Including all between the earth and sphere.

6

Victorious sounds! Yet here your homage do
Unto a gentler conqueror[1] than you;
Who though he flies the music of his praise,
Would with you heaven's hallelujahs raise.

The Garden[2]

1

How vainly men themselves amaze[3]
To win the palm, the oak, or bays,[4]
And their uncessant labors see
Crowned from some single herb or tree,
Whose short and narrow vergèd[5] shade
Does prudently their toils upbraid;
While all flowers and all trees do close[6]
To weave the garlands of repose.

2

Fair Quiet, have I found thee here,
And Innocence, thy sister dear!
Mistaken long, I sought you then
In busy companies of men.
Your sacred plants, if here below,[7]
Only among the plants will grow.
Society is all but rude
To[8] this delicious solitude.

1. Probably Fairfax, of Appleton House (cf. "Upon Appleton House," p. 559); perhaps Cromwell.
2. Interpretations range from a simple poem about the life of solitude to explorations of the profound meanings of, e.g., action and contemplation, art and nature.
3. "Bewilder, puzzle, or drive oneself stupid" (*OED*); lead into a maze or labyrinth.
4. *Palm . . . oak . . . or bays*: for military, political, or poetic achievement.
5. Edged.
6. Join, unite.
7. On Earth.
8. Compared to.

3

No white nor red[9] was ever seen
So amorous as this lovely green.[1]
Fond[2] lovers, cruel as their flame,
Cut in these trees their mistress' name.
Little, alas, they know, or heed,
How far these beauties hers exceed!
Fair trees! wheres'e'er your barks I wound,
No names shall but your own be found.

4

When we have run our passion's heat,[3]
Love hither makes his best retreat.[4]
The gods, that mortal beauty chase,
Still[5] in a tree did end their race.
Apollo hunted Daphne so,
Only that she might laurel grow.
And Pan did after Syrinx speed,
Not as a nymph, but for a reed.[6]

5

What wondrous life is this I lead!
Ripe apples drop about my head;
The luscious clusters of the vine
Upon my mouth do crush their wine;
The nectarine, and curious[7] peach,
Into my hands themselves do reach;
Stumbling on melons, as I pass,
Ensnared with flowers, I fall on grass.

6

Meanwhile the mind, from pleasure less,[8]
Withdraws into its happiness:
The mind, that ocean[9] where each kind
Does straight[1] its own resemblance find;

9. Emblematic of feminine beauty.
1. Of quiet rural solitude.
2. Doting; perhaps also foolish.
3. *Heat*: single intense effort; course in a race; fervor, vehemence; fit of passion (all *OED*).
4. A place of refuge or resort (*OED*); e.g., a cloister.
5. Always; but also suggesting "in stillness."
6. Apollo pursued Daphne, but she was turned into a laurel tree (sacred to him as god of poetry); Pan pursued Syrinx, who was turned into a reed, which he used for musical pipes.
7. Choice, excellent, fine (*OED*).
8. Lesser pleasure.
9. It was commonly thought that the oceans contained counterparts to all earthly creatures.
1. Immediately; compactly ("strait").

Yet it creates, transcending these,
Far other worlds, and other seas;[2]
Annihilating[3] all that's made
To a green thought in a green shade.[4]

7

Here at the fountain's sliding foot,
Or at some fruit-tree's mossy root,
Casting the body's vest[5] aside,
My soul into the boughs does glide:
There like a bird it sits, and sings,
Then whets,[6] and combs its silver wings;
And, till prepared for longer flight,[7]
Waves in its plumes the various light.[8]

8

Such was that happy garden-state,
While man there walked without a mate:
After a place so pure, and sweet,
What other help could yet be meet![9]
But 'twas beyond a mortal's share
To wander solitary there:
Two paradises 'twere in one
To live in Paradise alone.

9

How well the skillful gardener drew
Of flowers and herbs this dial[1] new;
Where from above the milder[2] sun
Does through a fragrant zodiac run;
And, as it works, the industrious bee
Computes its time[3] as well as we.
How could such sweet and wholesome hours
Be reckoned but with herbs and flowers!

2. Because the mind can imagine forms beyond all ordinary reality.
3. I.e., reducing, making the created world seem nothing in comparison to what the mind imagines; or reducing the material world to immaterial thought; or, perhaps, returning to the nothingness (*nihil*) before the Creation.
4. "Green" can mean naive, fresh, youthful; primarily, it describes the shade cast by foliage and is contrasted to the red of passion and the white of innocence (cf. line 17).
5. *Body's vest*: the body as the soul's garment or covering.
6. Preens.
7. Perhaps of the soul after death, perhaps of Platonic ascent.
8. *Various*: varied in color (*OED*), contrasted with the white light of eternity.
9. *Help . . . meet*: Genesis 2:18, "It is not good that the man should be alone; I will make him an help meet for him."
1. Sundial (the garden itself).
2. Because its rays are tempered by the trees and vegetation.
3. With a pun on the herb thyme.

An Horatian Ode upon Cromwell's Return from Ireland[4]

The forward[5] youth that would appear
Must now forsake his Muses dear,
    Nor in the shadows sing
    His numbers languishing.
'Tis time to leave the books in dust,
And oil the unused armor's rust:
    Removing from the wall
    The corslet[6] of the hall.
So restless Cromwell could not cease[7]
In the inglorious arts of peace,
    But through adventurous war
    Urged his active star:
And, like the three-forked lightning,[8] first
Breaking the clouds where it was nursed,
    Did through his own side
    His fiery way divide.[9]
For 'tis all one to courage high
The emulous or enemy;
    And with such to enclose
    Is more than to oppose.[1]
Then burning through the air he went,
And palaces and temples rent:
    And Caesar's head at last
    Did through his laurels blast.[2]
'Tis madness to resist or blame
The face of angry heaven's flame;
    And if we would speak true,
    Much to the man is due.
Who, from his private gardens, where
He lived reservèd and austere,
    As if his highest plot
    To plant the bergamot,[3]
Could by industrious valor climb

4. Oliver Cromwell returned from his Irish conquest in May 1650, not quite eighteen months after the execution of King Charles I; on 22 July 1650, as the new commander of the parliamentary forces, he invaded Scotland—a task his former superior, General Fairfax, had refused on principle. "Horatian" promises a balanced, even detached poem, and the work does manifest ambivalent attitudes, many puns, and a cool tone. There are allusions to Lucan's unfinished epic on the Roman Civil War, the *Pharsalia,* which celebrates as "hero" neither Caesar nor Pompey, but rather Liberty and her defender, the Stoic Cato of Utica. The remarkable meter of the poem is probably "Marvell's own invention, but he used it for no other extant poem" (Margoliouth).
5. Precocious; ambitious; presumptuous.
6. A piece of armor for the trunk.
7. Rest; Lucan's Caesar was notably "restless."
8. Of Zeus.
9. Cromwell early became a leader of the more radical revolutionaries; "side" includes the meaning of party or faction.
1. Frank Kermode suggests, "To pen him in will produce an even more violent reaction than to fight against him."
2. *Caesar*: Charles I, executed despite his "laurels," which are supposed to be immune to lightning. Both Caesar and the lightning wielder are figures of tyranny.
3. A fine species of pear, known as the "pear of kings."

To ruin the great work of Time,
And cast the kingdoms old
Into another mold.
Though Justice against Fate complain,
And plead the ancient rights in vain:
But those do hold or break
As men are strong or weak.
Nature that hateth emptiness,
Allows of penetration[4] less;
And therefore must make room
Where greater spirits come.
What field of all the Civil Wars,
Where his were not the deepest scars?
And Hampton shows what part
He had of wiser art:
Where, twining subtle fears with hope,
He wove a net of such a scope,
That Charles himself might chase
To Carisbrook's narrow case;[5]
That thence the royal actor borne
The tragic scaffold might adorn,
While round the armèd bands
Did clap[6] their bloody hands.
He nothing common did or mean
Upon that memorable Scene:
But with his keener eye
The axe's edge did try;[7]
Nor called the gods with vulgar spite
To vindicate his helpless right,
But bowed his comely head,
Down as upon a bed.
This was that memorable hour
Which first assured the forcèd power.[8]
So when they did design
The Capitol's first line,
A bleeding head where they begun
Did fright the architects to run;
And yet in that the State
Foresaw its happy fate.[9]
And now the Irish are ashamed
To see themselves in one year tamed:[1]

4. Occupation of the same space by two bodies at the same time (*OED*).
5. King Charles fled to Carisbrooke, which turned out to be a cage ("narrow case") for him. It was rumored that Cromwell had connived at this escape from Hampton Court to prod Parliament into the decision to execute him.
6. Besides continuing the theater metaphor, this may be an allusion to the story that the soldiers were ordered to clap so as to drown out the king's words.
7. *Keener*: than the axe's edge; *try*: test. The Latin *acies* can mean the front line of battle, the sharp edge of a blade, the pupil of the eye, and keen vision. *He*: Charles I.
8. I.e., the power won by force.
9. The story is told by Livy and Pliny about the digging of the foundations for the Temple of Jupiter in Rome; the omen was taken to mean that Rome would be the head (*caput*) of an empire, so the hill on which the Temple stood was called the Capitoline.
1. Cromwell's Irish campaign (August 1649 to May 1650) was ruthlessly efficient.

So much one man can do,
That does both act and know.
They[2] can affirm his praises best,
And have, though overcome, confessed
How good he is, how just,
And fit for highest trust:
Nor yet grown stiffer with command,
But still in the Republic's hand:
How fit he is to sway
That can so well obey.
He to the Commons' feet presents
A kingdom for his first year's rents;
And, what he may,[3] forbears
His fame, to make it theirs:
And has his sword and spoils ungirt,
To lay them at the public's skirt.
So when the falcon high
Falls heavy from the sky,
She, having killed, no more does search
But on the next green bough to perch,
Where, when he first does lure,
The falconer has her sure.
What may not then our isle presume
While victory his crest does plume!
What may not others fear
If thus he crowns each year!
A Caesar he ere long to Gaul,
To Italy an Hannibal,
And to all states not free
Shall climacteric[4] be.
The Pict no shelter now shall find
Within his party-colored mind;
But from this valor sad
Shrink underneath the plaid:[5]
Happy if in the tufted brake
The English hunter him mistake;[6]
Nor lay his hounds in near
The Caledonian[7] deer.
But thou the wars' and Fortune's son
March indefatigably on;
And for the last effect
Still keep the sword erect:[8]
Besides the force it has to fright
The spirits of the shady night,

2. The Irish.
3. So far as he can.
4. Crucial or critical period.
5. *Pict*: Scot; the Picts painted themselves (Latin *pictus* = "painted") various colors; contemporary Scots were divided by many factions; *sad*: severe.
6. Because of his colorful camouflage.
7. Scottish.
8. With blade (of power) upraised, not the cross hilt. In ancient myth, the drawn sword has special powers against the spirits of the dead. The Puritans were hostile to all representations of the cross.

The same arts that did gain
A power must it maintain.

Upon Appleton House[9]

TO MY LORD FAIRFAX

1

Within this sober[1] frame expect
Work of no foreign architect,
That unto caves the quarries drew,
And forests did to pastures hew;
Who of his great design in pain
Did for a model vault his brain,[2]
Whose columns should so high be raised
To arch the brows that on them gazed.

2

Why should of all things man unruled
Such unproportioned dwellings build?
The beasts are by their dens expressed,
And birds contrive an equal[3] nest;
The low-roofed tortoises do dwell
In cases fit of tortoise shell:
No creature loves an empty space;
Their bodies measure out their place.

3

But he, superfluously spread,
Demands more room alive than dead;
And in his hollow palace goes
Where winds as he themselves may lose.
What need of all this marble crust
T'impark the wanton mote of dust,

9. From 1651 to 1653, Marvell served as tutor to Mary Fairfax, daughter of Thomas, Lord Fairfax and Ann Vere. Lord Fairfax had been commander-in-chief of the parliamentary army, but he opposed the execution of the king (1649), and in June 1650, resigned in protest against the proposed invasion of Scotland (cf. "Horatian Ode"). Fairfax then retired to his Yorkshire properties, particularly Appleton House; the house may have been a small one built on the site of a Cistercian priory until the dissolution in 1542, or a large brick mansion built between 1637 and 1650.

The poem is loosely organized and highly eclectic. Within the broad genre of the country-house or topographical poem, the poet ranges from Christian Platonism and the Church Fathers to contemporary poets, ruminating about the active and the contemplative life, while immersed in (and transcending) the nature all around him. The framework is a guided tour: a description of the house itself (lines 1–80), modulating into moralized history—the story of the nunnery and the attempted seduction of the Fairfax ancestor, the "blooming Virgin Thwaites"—and into false and corrupted religion (81–280). The grounds are described: the gardens (281–368), laid out in military style; the meadows (369–480), where the order of the seasons prevails; the woods (481–624), image of the retired life; the river (625–648). Finally, at evening, returning to the mode of elaborate compliment, the poet describes Mary Fairfax, the epitome of the natural scene, the microcosm of the place, and the hope of a new and better order (649–776).

1. Modest, humble; cf. line 28.
2. Used his skull as model for the vault.
3. Appropriate.

That thinks by breadth the world t'unite
Though the first builders[4] failed in height?

4

But all things are composèd here
Like Nature, orderly and near:
In which we the dimensions find
Of that more sober age and mind,
When larger-sizèd men did stoop
To enter at a narrow loop;[5]
As practicing, in doors so strait,
To strain themselves through Heaven's Gate.[6]

5

And surely when the after age
Shall hither come in pilgrimage,
These sacred places to adore,
By Vere[7] and Fairfax trod before,
Men will dispute how their extent
Within such dwarfish confines went;
And some will smile at this as well
As Romulus his bee-like cell.[8]

6

Humility alone designs
Those short but admirable lines,
By which, ungirt and unconstrained,
Things greater are in less contained.
Let others vainly strive t'immure
The circle in the quadrature![9]
These holy mathematics can
In ev'ry figure equal man.

7

Yet thus the laden house does sweat,
And scarce endures the master great:
But where he comes the swelling hall
Stirs, and the square grows spherical;[1]
More by his magnitude distressed,
Than he is by its straitness pressed;
And too officiously it slights
That[2] in itself which him delights.

4. Of the Tower of Babel (Genesis 11).
5. Cf. *Aeneid* VIII.359ff., where Aeneas is exhorted to imitate Hercules and not disdain to stoop to enter King Evander's humble house.
6. Cf. Matthew 7:14: "Strait is the gate, and narrow is the way. . . ."
7. Ann Vere, Lady Fairfax.
8. The thatched hut of the founder of Rome resembled a beehive.
9. To square the circle.
1. This refers to the cupola.
2. Its humility.

8

So honor better lowness bears,
Than that unwonted greatness wears.
Height with a certain grace does bend,
But low things clownishly ascend.
And yet what needs there here excuse,
Where everything does answer use?
Where neatness nothing can condemn,
Nor pride invent what to contemn?

9

A stately frontispiece of poor
Adorns without the open door;[3]
Nor less the rooms within commends
Daily new furniture of friends.
The house was built upon the place
Only as for a mark of grace;
And for an inn to entertain
Its lord a while, but not remain.

10

Him Bishops-Hill, or Denton may,
Or Bilbrough,[4] better hold than they;
But Nature here hath been so free
As if she said, "Leave this to me."
Art would more neatly have defaced
What she had laid so sweetly waste;
In fragrant gardens, shady woods,
Deep meadows, and transparent floods.

11

While with slow eyes we these survey,
And on each pleasant footstep stay,
We opportunely may relate
The progress of this house's fate.
A nunnery first gave it birth
For virgin buildings oft brought forth.
And all that neighbor-ruin shows
The quarries whence this dwelling rose.

12

Near to this gloomy cloister's gates
There dwelt the blooming virgin Thwaites[5]
Fair beyond measure and an heir

3. The poor who await Fairfax's alms (with confidence: the door is open) make a frontispiece, decorating the entrance.
4. Fairfax estates.
5. Isabella Thwaites, Fairfax's ancestor.

Which might deformity make fair.
And oft she spent the summer suns
Discoursing with the subtle nuns.
Whence in these words one to her weaved,
(As 'twere by chance) thoughts long conceived.

13

"Within this holy leisure we
Live innocently as you see.
These walls restrain the world without,
But hedge our liberty about.
These bars inclose the wider den
Of those wild creatures, callèd men;
The cloister outward shuts its gates,
And, from us, locks on them the grates.

14

"Here we, in shining armor white,
Like virgin Amazons do fight:
And our chaste lamps we hourly trim,
Lest the great Bridegroom find them dim.[6]
Our orient breaths perfumèd are
With incense of incessant prayer.
And holy water of our tears
Most strangely our complexion clears:

15

"Not tears of grief; but such as those
With which calm pleasure overflows;
Or pity, when we look on you
That live without this happy vow.
How should we grieve that must be seen
Each one a spouse, and each a queen;
And can in Heaven hence behold
Our brighter robes and crowns of gold?

16

"When we have prayèd all our beads,
Some one the holy Legend[7] reads;
While all the rest with needles paint
The face and graces of the saint.
But what the linen can't receive
They in their lives do interweave.
This work the saints best represents;
That serves for altar's ornaments.

6. Cf. Milton, Sonnet 9, line 10n, p. 398.
7. The allusion is to the *Legenda aurea* of Jacobus de Voragine; see *The Golden Legend: Readings on the Saints*, trans. William Granger Ryan, 2 vols. (Princeton, 1993).

17

"But much it to our work would add
If here your hand, your face we had.
By it we would Our Lady touch;
Yet thus she you resembles much.
Some of your features, as we sewed,
Through every shrine should be bestowed:
And in one beauty we would take
Enough a thousand saints to make.

18

"And (for I dare not quench the fire
That me does for your good inspire)
'Twere sacrilege a man t'admit
To holy things, for Heaven fit.
I see the angels in a crown
On you the lilies showering down;
And round about you glory breaks,
That something more than human speaks.

19

"All beauty, when at such a height,
Is so already consecrate.
Fairfax I know; and long ere this
Have marked the youth, and what he is.
But can he such a rival seem
For whom you Heav'n should disesteem?
Ah, no! and 'twould more honor prove
He your *devoto*[8] were, than love.

20

"Here live belovèd, and obeyed,
Each one your sister, each your maid.
And, if our rule seem strictly penned,
The rule itself to you shall bend.
Our abbess too, now far in age,
Doth your succession near presage.
How soft the yoke on us would lie,
Might such fair hands as yours it tie!

21

"Your voice, the sweetest of the choir,
Shall draw Heaven nearer, raise us higher:
And your example, if our head,
Will soon us to perfection lead.
Those virtues to us all so dear,
Will straight grow sanctity when here:

8. Devotee.

And that, once sprung, increase so fast
Till miracles it work at last.

22

"Nor is our order yet so nice,
Delight to banish as a vice.
Here pleasure piety doth meet,
One perfecting the other sweet.
So through the mortal fruit we boil
The sugar's uncorrupting oil;
And that which perished while we pull,
Is thus preservèd clear and full.

23

"For such indeed are all our arts;
Still handling Nature's finest parts.
Flow'rs dress the altars; for the clothes,
The sea-born amber[9] we compose;
Balms for the grieved we draw; and pastes
We mold, as baits for curious tastes.
What need is here of man? unless
These as sweet sins we should confess.

24

"Each night among us to your side
Appoint a fresh and virgin bride;
Whom if our Lord at midnight find,
Yet neither should be left behind.
Where you may lie as chaste in bed,
As pearls together billeted.
All night embracing arm in arm,
Like crystal pure with cotton warm.

25

"But what is this to all the store
Of joys you see, and may make more!
Try but a while, if you be wise:
The trial neither costs, nor ties."
Now Fairfax seek her promised faith:
Religion that dispensèd hath,
Which she henceforward does begin:[1]
The nun's smooth tongue has sucked her in.

26

Oft, though he knew it was in vain,
Yet would he valiantly complain:

9. Ambergris (cf. "Bermudas," line 28n, p. 539), an odorous substance that derives from the sperm whale.
1. Unclear. Probably, since religion has dispensed her from her betrothal, she now enters the convent.

"Is this that sanctity so great,
An art by which you finelier cheat?
Hypocrite witches, hence avant,
Who though in prison yet enchant!
Death only can such thieves make fast,
As rob though in the dungeon cast.

27

"Were there but, when this house was made,
One stone that a just hand had laid,
It must have fallen upon her head
Who first thee from thy faith misled.
And yet, how well soever meant,
With them 'twould soon grow fraudulent:
For like themselves they alter all,
And vice infects the very wall.

28

"But sure those buildings last not long,
Founded by folly, kept by wrong.
I know what fruit their gardens yield,
When they it think by night concealed.
Fly from their vices. 'Tis thy estate,
Not thee, that they would consecrate.
Fly from their ruin. How I fear
Though guiltless lest thou perish there!"

29

What should he do? He would respect
Religion, but not right neglect;
For first religion taught him right,
And dazzled not but cleared his sight.
Sometimes resolved his sword he draws,
But reverenceth then the laws:
For justice still that courage led;
First from a judge, then soldier bred.[2]

30

Small honor would be in the storm.
The court him grants the lawful form,
Which licensed either peace or force,
To hinder the unjust divorce.
Yet still the nuns his right debarred,
Standing upon their holy guard.
Ill-counseled women, do you know
Whom you resist, or what you do?

2. Sir William Fairfax's father was a judge; his maternal grandfather, a heroic soldier.

31

Is not this he whose offspring fierce
Shall fight through all the universe,
And with successive valor try
France, Poland, either Germany;
Till one, as long since prophesied,
His horse through conquered Britain ride?
Yet, against Fate, his spouse they kept,
And the great race would intercept.

32

Some to the breach against their foes
Their wooden saints in vain oppose.
Another bolder stands at push
With their old holy-water brush.
While the disjointed[3] abbess threads
The jingling chain-shot of her beads.
But their loudest cannon were their lungs;
And sharpest weapons were their tongues.

33

But waving these aside like flies,
Young Fairfax through the wall does rise.
Then th'unfrequented vault appeared,
And superstitions vainly feared.
The relics false were set to view;
Only the jewels there were true—
But truly bright and holy Thwaites
That weeping at the altar waits.

34

But the glad youth away her bears
And to the nuns bequeaths her tears:
Who guiltily their prize bemoan,
Like gypsies that a child had stol'n.
Thenceforth (as when th'enchantment ends
The castle vanishes or rends)
The wasting cloister with the rest
Was in one instant dispossessed.

35

At the demolishing, this seat
To Fairfax fell as by escheat.[4]
And what both nuns and founders willed
'Tis likely better thus fulfilled:
For if the virgin proved not theirs,

3. Distracted.
4. Legally, in the absence of an heir, the property reverted to him as lord of the manor.

The cloister yet remainèd hers;
Though many a nun there made her vow,
'Twas no religious house till now.

36

From that blest bed the hero came,
Whom France and Poland yet does fame;
Who, when retirèd here to peace,
His warlike studies could not cease;
But laid these gardens out in sport
In the just figure of a fort;
And with five bastions it did fence,
As aiming one for every sense.[5]

37

When in the East the morning ray
Hangs out the colors of the day,
The bee through these known alleys hums,
Beating the *dian*[6] with its drums.
Then flowers their drowsy eyelids raise,
Their silken ensigns each displays,
And dries its pan[7] yet dank with dew,
And fills its flask[8] with odors new.

38

These, as their governor goes by,
In fragrant volleys they let fly;
And to salute their governess
Again as great a charge they press:
None for the virgin nymph;[9] for she
Seems with the flow'rs a flow'r to be.
And think so still! though not compare[1]
With breath so sweet, or cheek so fair.

39

Well shot ye firemen![2] Oh how sweet,
And round your equal fires do meet;
Whose shrill report no ear can tell,
But echoes to the eye and smell.
See how the flow'rs, as at parade,
Under their colors stand displayed:
Each regiment in order grows,
That of the tulip, pink, and rose.

5. The gardens are laid out in military style.
6. Reveille.
7. The part of the musket lock containing firing powder.
8. Powder flask.
9. Mary Fairfax, Marvell's pupil at Appleton House; at this time, twelve to fourteen years old.
1. *Think . . . compare*: addressed to the flowers.
2. Men who use firearms.

40

But when the vigilant patrol
Of stars walks round about the Pole,
Their leaves, that to the stalks are curled,
Seem to their staves the ensigns furled.
Then in some flow'r's beloved hut
Each bee as sentinel is shut;
And sleeps so too: but, if once stirred,
She runs you through, nor asks the word.[3]

41

Oh thou,[4] that dear and happy isle
The garden of the world ere while,
Thou paradise of four[5] seas,
Which Heaven planted us to please,
But, to exclude the world, did guard
With wat'ry if not flaming sword;
What luckless apple did we taste,
To make us mortal, and thee waste?

42

Unhappy! shall we never more
That sweet militia restore,
When gardens only had their tow'rs,
And all the garrisons were flow'rs,
When roses only arms might bear,
And men did rosy garlands wear?
Tulips, in several colors barred,
Were then the Switzers[6] of our guard.

43

The gardener had the soldier's place,
And his more gentle forts did trace.
The nursery of all things green
Was then the only magazine.
The winter quarters were the stoves
Where he the tender plants removes.
But war all this doth overgrow;
We ordnance plant, and powder sow.

44

And yet there walks one on the sod
Who, had it pleasèd him and God,
Might once have made our gardens spring

3. Password.
4. England.
5. Pronounced as two syllables.
6. The Papal Swiss Guards and their multicolored uniforms.

Fresh as his own and flourishing.
But he preferred to the Cinque Ports[7]
These five imaginary forts:
And, in those half-dry trenches, spanned[8]
Pow'r which the ocean might command.

45

For he did, with his utmost skill,
Ambition weed, but conscience till.
Conscience, that Heaven-nursèd plant,
Which most our earthly gardens want.[9]
A prickling leaf it bears, and such
As that which shrinks at every touch;
But flow'rs eternal, and divine,
That in the crowns of saints do shine.

46

The sight does from these bastions ply
The invisible artillery;
And at proud Cawood Castle[1] seems
To point the battery of its beams,
As if it quarreled in[2] the seat
Th'ambition of its prelate great;
But o'er the meads below it plays,
Or innocently seems to graze.

47

And now to the abyss I pass
Of that unfathomable grass,
Where men like grasshoppers appear,
But grasshoppers are giants[3] there:
They, in their squeaking laugh, contemn
Us as we walk more low than them:
And, from the precipices tall
Of the green spires, to us do call.

48

To see men through this meadow dive,
We wonder how they rise alive;
As, under water, none does know
Whether he fall through it or go;
But as the mariners that sound

7. The "Five Ports" on the southeast coast of England, of which Fairfax was Warden for a time; often used metaphorically (cf. the "five bastions" of line 287).
8. Restrained.
9. Need; lack.
1. Two miles from Appleton House, seat of the Archbishop of York.
2. Quarreled with.
3. Numbers 13:33: "And there we saw the giants . . . and we were in our own sights as grasshoppers, and so we were in their sight."

And show upon their lead the ground,
They bring up flowers so to be seen,
And prove they've at the bottom been.

49

No scene that turns with engines[4] strange
Does oftener than these meadows change:
For when the sun the grass hath vexed,
The tawny mowers enter next;
Who seem like Israelites to be
Walking on foot through a green sea.
To them the grassy deeps divide,
And crowd a lane to either side.[5]

50

With whistling scythe, and elbow strong,
These massacre the grass along:
While one, unknowing, carves the rail,[6]
Whose yet unfeathered quills her fail.
The edge all bloody from its breast
He draws, and does his stroke detest;
Fearing the flesh untimely mowed
To him a fate as black forebode.

51

But bloody Thestylis, that waits
To bring the mowing camp their cates,[7]
Greedy as kites has trussed it up,
And forthwith means on it to sup;
When on another quick[8] she lights,
And cries, "He[9] called us Israelites;
But now, to make his saying true,
Rails rain for quails, for manna, dew."[1]

52

Unhappy birds! what does it boot
To build below the grass's root,
When lowness is unsafe as height,
And chance o'ertakes what 'scapeth spite?
And now your orphan parents' call
Sounds your untimely funeral.

4. *Engines*: suggests ingenuity, artifice, and special equipment for theatrical effects.
5. Form a lane by "crowding" to either side.
6. The corncrake (land rail), a field bird.
7. Food. Thestylis is a camp follower.
8. Alive.
9. The poet (cf. line 389).
1. See Exodus 16:13–14 for the quails and the dew that miraculously fed the Israelites after they had crossed the Red Sea.

Death-trumpets creak in such a note,
And 'tis the sourdine[2] in their throat.

53

Or[3] sooner hatch or higher build:
The mower now commands the field;
In whose new traverse[4] seemeth wrought
A camp of battle newly fought:
Where, as the meads with hay, the plain
Lies quilted o'er with bodies slain;
The women that with forks it fling,
Do represent the pillaging.

54

And now the careless victors play,
Dancing the triumphs of the Hay;[5]
Where every mower's wholesome heat
Smells like an Alexander's sweat,[6]
Their females fragrant as the mead
Which they in Fairy Circles tread:
When at their dance's end they kiss,
Their new-made hay not sweeter is.

55

When after this 'tis piled in cocks,
Like a calm sea it shows the rocks:
We wondering in the river near
How boats among them safely steer.
Or, like the desert Memphis[7] sand,
Short pyramids of hay do stand.
And such the Roman camps do rise[8]
In hills for soldiers' obsequies.

56

This scene again withdrawing brings
A new and empty face of things;
A leveled space, as smooth and plain
As cloths for Lely[9] stretched to stain.
The world when first created sure
Was such a table rase[1] and pure;

2. A muted trumpet (*OED*).
3. Either.
4. Track.
5. A country dance (with a pun), involving figure S's.
6. Plutarch writes that Alexander's sweat was sweet.
7. A city near the pyramids.
8. Raise.
9. Canvases for the Dutch portrait painter Sir Peter Lely, who came to England in 1643.
1. *Tabula rasa*: clean or blank slate.

Or rather such is the *toril*
Ere the bulls enter at Madril.[2]

57

For to this naked equal flat,
Which Levellers[3] take pattern at,
The villagers in common[4] chase
Their cattle, which it closer rase;[5]
And what below the scythe increased
Is pinched yet nearer by the beast.
Such, in the painted world, appeared
Davenant with the universal herd.[6]

58

They seem within the polished grass
A landscape drawn in looking glass;
And shrunk in the huge pasture show
As spots, so shaped, on faces do.
Such fleas, ere they approach the eye,
In multiplying glasses[7] lie.
They feed so wide, so slowly move,
As constellations do above.

59

Then, to conclude these pleasant acts,
Denton[8] sets ope its cataracts;
And makes the meadow truly be
(What it but seemed before) a sea.
For, jealous of its lord's long stay,
It tries t'invite him thus away.
The river in itself is drowned
And isles the astonished cattle round.

60

Let others tell the paradox,
How eels now bellow in the ox;[9]
How horses at their tails do kick,
Turned as they hang to leeches quick;[1]
How boats can over bridges sail,
And fishes do the stables scale;

2. *Toril*: bull ring; *Madril*: Madrid.
3. The Levellers sought social and economic egalitarianism.
4. On the common pasture (also a "level" place).
5. Keep the grass closely cropped.
6. In *Gondibert*, a contemporary work, Davenant's creation scene includes a "universal herd."
7. Magnifying glasses or microscopes.
8. The river.
9. I.e., because the ox swallowed them while drinking.
1. Their tails hanging in the water became live (quick) leeches or eels (a popular superstition).

How salmons trespassing are found,
And pikes are taken in the pound.[2]

61

But I, retiring from the flood,
Take sanctuary in the wood;
And, while it lasts, myself embark
In this yet green, yet growing ark;
Where the first carpenter might best
Fit timber for his keel[3] have pressed;
And where all creatures might have shares,
Although in armies, not in pairs.

62

The double wood of ancient stocks
Linked in so thick an union[4] locks,
It like two pedigrees appears,
On one hand Fairfax, the other Veres:
Of whom though many fell in war,
Yet more to Heaven shooting are:
And, as they Nature's cradle decked,
Will in green age her hearse expect.

63

When first the eye this forest sees
It seems indeed as wood not trees;
As if their neighborhood[5] so old
To one great trunk them all did mould.
There the huge bulk takes place, as meant
To thrust up a fifth element;
And stretches still so closely wedged
As if the night within were hedged.

64

Dark all without it knits; within
It opens passable and thin;
And in as loose an order grows
As the Corinthian porticoes.
The arching boughs unite between
The columns of the temple green;
And underneath the wingèd choirs
Echo about their tunèd fires.[6]

2. Enclosure for cattle (*OED*).
3. *First carpenter*: Noah; *keel*: the ark. Cf. Genesis 6.
4. "An union" is the subject of lines 489–490.
5. Nearness to each other.
6. *Tunèd fires*: love songs.

65

The nightingale does here make choice
To sing the trials of her voice.
Low shrubs she sits in, and adorns
With music high the squatted thorns.
But highest oaks stoop down to hear,
And list'ning elders prick the ear.
The thorn, lest it should hurt her, draws
Within the skin its shrunken claws.

66

But I have for my music found
A sadder, yet more pleasing sound:
The stock doves, whose fair necks are graced
With nuptial rings their ensigns chaste;
Yet always, for some cause unknown,
Sad pair, unto the elms they moan.
O why should such a couple mourn,
That in so equal flames do burn!

67

Then as I careless on the bed
Of gelid strawberries do tread,
And through the hazels thick espy
The hatching throstle's[7] shining eye,
The heron from the ash's top
The eldest of its young lets drop,
As if it stork-like did pretend
That tribute to its lord to send.

68

But most the hewel's[8] wonders are,
Who here has the holt-felster's[9] care.
He walks still upright from the root,
Measuring the timber with his foot;
And all the way, to keep it clean,
Doth from the bark the wood-moths glean.
He, with his beak, examines well
Which fit to stand and which to fell.

69

The good he numbers up, and hacks;
As if he marked them with the ax.
But where he, tinkling with his beak,
Does find the hollow oak to speak,

7. *Throstle*: the song thrush (*OED*).
8. The hickwall or green woodpecker.
9. Woodcutter's.

That for his building he designs,
And through the tainted side he mines.
Who could have thought the tallest oak
Should fall by such a feeble stroke!

70

Nor would it, had the tree not fed
A traitor-worm, within it bred
(As first our flesh corrupt within
Tempts impotent and bashful sin).
And yet that worm triumphs not long,
But serves to feed the hewel's young;
While the oak seems to fall content,
Viewing the treason's punishment.

71

Thus I, easy philosopher,
Among the birds and trees confer;
And little now to make me, wants
Or of the fowls, or of the plants.
Give me but wings as they, and I
Straight floating on the air shall fly:
Or turn me but, and you shall see
I was but an inverted tree.[1]

72

Already I begin to call
In their most learned original:
And where I language want, my signs
The bird upon the bough divines;
And more attentive there doth sit
Than if she were with lime twigs knit.
No leaf does tremble in the wind
Which I returning cannot find.

73

Out of these scattered Sibyl's leaves[2]
Strange prophecies my fancy weaves:
And in one history consumes,
Like Mexique paintings, all the plumes.[3]
What Rome, Greece, Palestine ere said
I in this light mosaic[4] read.

1. A widely used metaphor in the Renaissance: cf. A. B. Chambers, *Studies in the Renaissance* 8 (1961), 291–299.
2. The Sibyl committed her prophecies to leaves. Vergil's Aeneas asks that the Cumaean Sibyl "speak" her prophecy to him (*Aeneid* VI. 77–102), lest the leaves be scattered.
3. Feathers.
4. *Mosaic*: the pattern formed by the leaves and by the light and shade; perhaps also the books of Moses, or the Scriptures, or the allegorical exegesis of them, and thus the poet's new Sibylline leaves.

Thrice happy he who, not mistook,
Hath read in Nature's mystic Book.[5]

74

And see how chance's better wit
Could with a mask[6] my studies hit!
The oak leaves me embroider all,
Between which caterpillars crawl;
And ivy, with familiar trails,
Me licks, and clasps, and curls, and hales.
Under this antic cope[7] I move
Like some great Prelate of the Grove.

75

Then, languishing with ease, I toss
On pallets swollen of velvet moss;
While the wind, cooling through the boughs,
Flatters with air my panting brows.
Thanks for my rest, ye mossy banks,
And unto you, cool zephyrs, thanks,
Who, as my hair, my thoughts too shed,[8]
And winnow from the chaff my head.

76

How safe, methinks, and strong, behind
These trees have I encamped my mind;
Where beauty, aiming at the heart,
Bends in some tree its useless dart;
And where the world no certain shot
Can make, or me it toucheth not.
But I on it securely play,
And gall its horsemen all the day.

77

Bind me ye woodbines in your twines,
Curl me about ye gadding vines,
And O so close your circles lace,
That I may never leave this place:
But lest your fetters prove too weak,
Ere I your silken bondage break,
Do you, O brambles, chain me too,
And courteous briars, nail me through.

5. "Nature's mystic Book" is the book of the creatures, or the book of God's works, as distinguished from the book of God's words, or Scripture.
6. Disguise, or costume for a masque.
7. *Antic cope*: ludicrously odd ecclesiastical vestment.
8. Part, separate.

78

Here in the morning tie my chain,
Where the two woods have made a lane;
While, like a guard on either side,
The trees before their lord divide;
This, like a long and equal thread,
Betwixt two labyrinths does lead.
But where the floods did lately drown,
There at the evening stake me down.

79

For now the waves are fall'n and dried,
And now the meadows fresher dyed;
Whose grass, with moister color dashed,
Seems as green silks but newly washed.
No serpent new nor crocodile
Remains behind our little Nile;[9]
Unless itself[1] you will mistake,
Among these meads the only snake.

80

See in what wanton harmless folds
It everywhere the meadow holds;
And its yet muddy back doth lick,
Till as a crystal mirror slick;
Where all things gaze themselves, and doubt
If they be in it or without.
And for his shade which therein shines,
Narcissus-like, the sun too pines.

81

Oh what a pleasure 'tis to hedge
My temples here with heavy sedge;
Abandoning my lazy side,
Stretched as a bank unto the tide;
Or to suspend my sliding foot
On the osier's underminèd root,
And in its branches tough to hang,
While at my lines the fishes twang!

82

But now away my hooks, my quills,
And angles,[2] idle utensils.

9. According to legend, the mud of the Nile bred serpents and crocodiles by spontaneous generation.
1. The river, "our little Nile."
2. *Quill*: the float of a fishing line (*OED*); *angle*: hook used in fishing, extended to fishing tackle.

The young Maria[3] walks tonight:
Hide trifling youth thy pleasures slight.
'Twere shame that such judicious eyes
Should with such toys a man surprise;
She that already is the law
Of all her sex, her age's awe.

83

See how loose Nature, in respect
To her, itself doth recollect;
And everything so whisht[4] and fine,
Starts forthwith to its *bonne mine*.[5]
The sun himself, of her aware,
Seems to descend with greater care;
And lest she see him go to bed,
In blushing clouds conceals his head.

84

So when the shadows laid asleep
From underneath these banks do creep,
And on the river as it flows
With ebon shuts[6] begin to close;
The modest halcyon[7] comes in sight,
Flying betwixt the day and night;
And such an horror calm and dumb,
Admiring Nature does benumb.

85

The viscous air, wheresoe'er she fly,
Follows and sucks her azure dye;
The jellying stream compacts below,
If it might fix her shadow so;
The stupid[8] fishes hang, as plain
As flies in crystal overta'en;
And men the silent scene assist,[9]
Charmed with the sapphire-wingèd mist.[1]

86

Maria such, and so doth hush
The world, and through the evening rush.
No new-born comet such a train

3. Mary Fairfax, to whom Marvell was tutor.
4. Hushed.
5. Good appearance. "*Bonne*" has two syllables.
6. *Ebon shuts*: black (ebony) shutters.
7. A bird that was thought to produce absolute calm on the sea.
8. Stupefied, amazed.
9. Observe, attend.
1. "Sapphire-wingèd mist" describes the halcyon (line 669) in its flight.

Draws through the sky, nor star new-slain.[2]
For straight those giddy rockets fail,
Which from the putrid earth exhale,
But by her flames, in Heaven tried,
Nature is wholly vitrified.[3]

87

'Tis she that to these gardens gave
That wondrous beauty which they have;
She straightness on the woods bestows;
To her the meadow sweetness owes;
Nothing could make the river be
So crystal-pure but only she;
She yet more pure, sweet, straight, and fair,
Than gardens, woods, meads, rivers are.

88

Therefore what first she on them spent,
They gratefully again present:
The meadow, carpets where to tread;
The garden, flow'rs to crown her head;
And for a glass, the limpid brook,
Where she may all her beauties look;
But, since she would not have them seen,
The wood about her draws a screen.

89

For she, to higher beauties raised,
Disdains to be for lesser praised.
She counts her beauty to converse
In all the languages as hers;
Not yet in those herself employs
But for the wisdom, not the noise;
Nor yet that wisdom would affect,
But as 'tis Heaven's dialect.

90

Blest nymph! that couldst so soon prevent
Those trains[4] by youth against thee meant:
Tears (watery shot that pierce the mind)
And sighs (love's cannon charged with wind)
True praise (that breaks through all defense)
And feigned complying innocence;
But knowing where this ambush lay,
She scaped the safe, but roughest way.

2. Meteor or shooting star.
3. Turned to glass.
4. *Prevent*: anticipate, avoid; *trains*: traps, baits, enticements (*OED*).

91

This 'tis to have been from the first
In a domestic heaven nursed,
Under the discipline severe
Of Fairfax, and the starry Vere;
Where not one object can come nigh
But pure, and spotless as the eye;
And goodness doth itself entail
On females, if there want a male.

92

Go now fond sex that on your face
Do all your useless study place,
Nor once at vice your brows dare knit
Lest the smooth forehead wrinkled sit;
Yet your own face shall at you grin,
Thorough the black-bag[5] of your skin;
When knowledge only could have filled
And virtue all those furrows tilled.

93

Hence she with graces more divine
Supplies beyond her sex the line;
And, like a sprig of mistletoe,
On the Fairfacian oak doth grow;
Whence, for some universal good,
The priest shall cut the sacred bud;
While her glad parents most rejoice,
And make their destiny their choice.

94

Meantime, ye fields, springs, bushes, flow'rs,
Where yet she leads her studious hours
(Till Fate her worthily translates,
And find a Fairfax for our Thwaites),
Employ the means you have by her,
And in your kind yourselves prefer;[6]
That, as all virgins she precedes,
So you all woods, streams, gardens, meads.

5. *Thorough*: through; *black-bag*: mask.
6. Make yourselves the best.

95

For you Thessalian Tempe's[7] seat
Shall now be scorned as obsolete;
Aranjuez, as less, disdained;
The Bel-Retiro[8] as constrained;
But name not the Idalian Grove,[9]
For 'twas the seat of wanton love;
Much less the dead's Elysian Fields,[1]
Yet nor to them your beauty yields.

96

'Tis not, what once it was, the world,
But a rude heap together hurled;
All negligently overthrown,
Gulfs, deserts, precipices, stone.
Your lesser world[2] contains the same,
But in more decent order tame;
You Heaven's center, Nature's lap,
And Paradise's only map.

97

But now the salmon-fishers moist
Their leathern boats begin to hoist;
And, like Antipodes[3] in shoes,
Have shod their heads in their canoes.
How tortoise-like, but not so slow,
These rational amphibii[4] go!
Let's in; for the dark hemisphere
Does now like one of them appear.

7. The Vale of Tempe, in Greece: a kind of ancient paradise.
8. *Aranjuez . . . Bel-Retiro*: Spanish palaces noted for their gardens.
9. A favorite place of Aphrodite (or Venus), goddess of love, in Cyprus.
1. Habitation of the blessed in the lower world after death (*Aeneid* VI).
2. Appleton House.
3. *Antipodes*: the upside-down side of the world.
4. Creatures that live on both land and water.

Henry Vaughan

1621 or 1622	Born (the twin of Thomas Vaughan) in Newton, in the parish of Llansantfraed, Breconshire, Wales. Initially educated by a local clergyman.
1638–1640	Probably at Jesus College, Oxford, where Thomas Vaughan matriculates in December 1638. Does not take a degree.
1640–1642	Studying law in London.
1642–1646	Law clerk to Sir Marmaduke Lloyd, Chief Justice of the Brecon circuit court. Probably serving with royalist forces, 1645–1646.
1646	Marries Catherine Wise; settles at Newton. Publication of *Poems, With the Tenth Satire of Juvenal Englished.*
1647	Writes dedicatory epistle later published with *Olor Iscanus.*
1650	First edition of *Silex Scintillans* published.
1651	Publication of *Olor Iscanus.* Practicing medicine from about this time.
1652	Publication of *The Mount of Olives: Or, Solitary Devotions.*
1654	Publication of *Flores Solitudinis* (including three prose translations, *Of Temperance and Patience*, *Of Life and Death*, and *The World Contemned*, and a life of Saint Paulinus of Nola). Wife dies about this time.
1655	Marries his wife's sister, Elizabeth Wise. Second (augmented) edition of *Silex Scintillans* published. Translates Henry Nollius's *Hermetical Physick*, a treatise dealing with the medical aspects of Hermetic doctrine.
1657	Translates Nollius's *The Chymists Key*, published by "Eugenius Philalethes" (Thomas Vaughan).
1666	Death of Thomas Vaughan.
1678	*Thalia Rediviva* published.
1695	Death, 23 April. Buried in Llansantfraed churchyard.

FROM *POEMS* (1646)[1]

To My Ingenuous Friend, R. W.[2]

When we are dead, and now no more
Our harmless mirth, our wit, and score[3]
Distracts the town; when all is spent
That the base niggard world hath lent
Thy purse or mine; when the loathed noise
Of drawers, 'prentices, and boys
Hath left us, and the clam'rous bar
Items no pints i'th'Moon or Star;[4]
When no calm whisp'rers wait the doors
To fright us with forgotten scores,
And such agèd, long bills[5] carry
As might start an antiquary;
When the sad tumults of the Maze,[6]
Arrests, suits, and the dreadful face
Of sergeants[7] are not seen, and we
No lawyers' ruffs or gowns must see;
When all these mulcts[8] are paid, and I
From thee, dear wit, must part, and die:
We'll beg the world would be so kind
To give's one grave, as we'd one mind;
There (as the wiser few suspect
That spirits after death affect)[9]
Our souls shall meet, and thence will they,
Freed from the tyranny of clay,
With equal wings and ancient love
Into the Elysian fields[1] remove,
Where in those blessèd walks they'll find
More of thy genius, and my mind.
First, in the shade of his own bays,[2]
Great Ben they'll see, whose sacred lays
The learnèd ghosts admire, and throng
To catch the subject of his song.
Then Randolph, in those holy meads,
His *Lovers*, and *Amyntas* reads,[3]

1. *Poems, With The Tenth Satire of Juvenal Englished* (1646) testifies to Vaughan's early affinities with some aspects of the Cavalier temperament: the claims and rewards of friendship, the social function of the gracefully figured compliment, the decorous and tender response to the death of a child.
2. The identity of "R. W." has not been established. *Ingenuous*: honorable and open.
3. Tally of debts.
4. Presumably, two taverns.
5. I.e., lists of debts extending over a long period of time.
6. The Maze was a building on the south bank of the Thames, in a raffish quarter of London.
7. Servants of the court charged with arresting offenders; attorneys.
8. Fines.
9. Are inclined.
1. Abode of the blessed dead. Cf. Carew, "A Rapture," line 2n, p. 302.
2. Laurels.
3. Randolph's comedy *The Jealous Lovers* was presented at Oxford in 1631; his pastoral *Amyntas* (published 1638) was acted at Whitehall in 1632–1633. Line 35 alludes to his poem "On the Death of a Nightingale," p. 344.

Whilst his nightingale close by
Sings his and her own elegy.
From thence dismissed by subtle roads,
Through airy paths and sad abodes,
They'll come into the drowsy fields
Of Lethe,[4] which such virtue yields
That (if what poets sing be true)
The streams all sorrow can subdue.
Here on a silent, shady green,
The souls of lovers oft are seen,
Who in their lives' unhappy space
Were murdered by some perjured face.
All these th'enchanted streams frequent,
To drown their cares and discontent,
That th'inconstant, cruel sex
Might not in death spirits vex.
  And here our souls, big with delight
Of their new state, will cease their flight;
And now the last thoughts will appear
They'll have of us, or any here;
But on those flowery banks will stay,
And drink all sense and cares away.
  So they that did of these discuss
  Shall find their fables true in us.

To Amoret, of the Difference 'twixt Him and Other Lovers, and What True Love Is

Mark, when the evening's cooler wings
  Fan the afflicted[5] air, how the faint sun,
    Leaving undone
    What he begun,
Those spurious flames sucked up from slime and earth[6]
    To their first, low birth,
    Resigns and brings.

They shoot their tinsel beams and vanities,
  Threading with those false fires their way;
    But as you stay
    And see them stray,
You lose the flaming track, and subtly they
    Languish away
    And cheat your eyes.

4. The river of forgetfulness in the classical underworld.
5. I.e., afflicted with either heat or darkness.
6. I.e., the glimmerings of the will-o'-the-wisp. Cf. Milton's "L'Allegro," line 103n, p. 391.

Just so,[7] base sublunary lovers' hearts,
Fed on loose, profane desires,
May for an eye
Or face comply;
But those removed, they will as soon depart,
And show their art
And painted fires.

Whilst I by powerful love so much refined
That my absent soul the same is,
Careless to miss
A glance or kiss,
Can with those elements of lust and sense
Freely dispense,
And court the mind.

Thus to the north the lodestones[8] move,
And thus to them th'enamored steel aspires;
Thus, Amoret,
I do affect;[9]
And thus, by wingèd beams and mutual fire,
Spirits and stars conspire;
And this is love.

FROM *SILEX SCINTILLANS*, PART I (1650)[1]

Regeneration

1

A ward and still in bonds,[2] one day
I stole abroad.
It was high spring, and all the way
Primrosed and hung with shade;
Yet was it frost within,
And surly winds
Blasted my infant buds, and sin
Like clouds eclipsed my mind.

7. I.e., in the manner of those spurious flames. This stanza and the next recall Donne's "A Valediction: Forbidding Mourning," p. 36.
8. Minerals that can be used as magnets.
9. I.e., I (also) am moved.
1. *Silex Scintillans: or Sacred Poems and Private Ejaculations* ("Part I" first appeared in 1650, "Part II" in 1655). By his subtitle, Vaughan calls attention to the profound influence of Herbert on himself and his work. *Silex scintillans* means flashing or sparkling flint. In the Latin "emblem" explicating his title page, Vaughan describes divine violence and alludes to both the Ezekiel 11: 19—"I will take the stony heart out of their flesh and will give them an heart of flesh"—and to Moses' striking the rock and producing water for the Israelites (Exodus 17:1–6).
2. The "spirit in bondage"—imprisoned by sin—is compared to the "spirit of adoption, whereby we cry, Abba, Father" (Romans 8:14-15). *Ward*: one in official custody.

2

Stormed[3] thus, I straight perceived my spring
Mere stage and show,
My walk a monstrous, mountained thing
Roughcast with rocks and snow;
And as a pilgrim's eye
Far from relief,
Measures the melancholy sky,
Then drops, and rains for grief,

3

So sighed I upwards still; at last
'Twixt steps and falls,
I reached the pinnacle, where placed
I found a pair of scales.
I took them up and laid
In th'one late pains;
The other smoke and pleasures weighed,
But proved the heavier grains.[4]

4

With that, some cried, "Away!" Straight I
Obeyed, and led
Full east, a fair, fresh field could spy;
Some called it Jacob's bed,[5]
A virgin soil which no
Rude feet ere trod,
Where, since he stepped there, only go
Prophets and friends of God.

5

Here I reposed; but scarce well set,
A grove descried
Of stately height, whose branches met
And mixed on every side;
I entered, and once in
(Amazed to see't),
Found all was changed, and a new spring
Did all my senses greet.

6

The unthrift sun shot vital gold[6]
A thousand pieces,
And heaven its azure did unfold

3. I.e., beset by storms.
4. Units of weight.
5. Cf. Jacob's dream of a ladder stretching from earth to heaven (Genesis 28:11–19).
6. *Unthrift*: prodigal, generous, spendthrift; *vital*: vitalizing, invigorating.

Checkered with snowy fleeces;
The air was all in spice
And every bush
A garland wore; thus fed my eyes,
But all the earth[7] lay hush.

7

Only a little fountain lent
Some use for ears,
And on the dumb shades language spent
The music of her tears;
I drew her near, and found
The cistern full
Of divers stones, some bright and round,
Others ill-shaped and dull.[8]

8

The first (pray mark) as quick as light
Danced through the flood,
But th'last, more heavy than the night,
Nailed to the center stood;
I wondered much, but tired
At last with thought,
My restless eye that still desired,[9]
As strange an object brought:

9

It was a bank of flowers, where I descried
(Though 'twas midday)
Some fast asleep, others broad-eyed
And taking in the ray;[1]
Here musing long, I heard
A rushing wind[2]
Which still increased, but whence it stirred,[3]
Nor[4] where I could not find;

10

I turned me round, and to each shade
Dispatched an eye,
To see if any leaf had made
Least motion or reply,

7. Cf. Textual Notes.
8. Editors generally deem this stanza and the next an allegory on the baptism of fit souls.
9. I.e., still sought something to see. Vaughan's diction presumes an extromission theory of vision, in which the eyes emit beams that bring back images.
1. Of sunlight.
2. "There came a sound from heaven like the rush of a mighty wind" (Acts 2:2).
3. "The wind bloweth where it listeth, and thou hearest the sound thereof, but canst not tell whence it cometh, and whither it goeth: so is every one that is born of the Spirit" (John 3:8).
4. Cf. Textual Notes.

But while I listening sought
My mind to ease
By knowing where 'twas or where not,
It whispered, "Where I please."

Lord, then said I, "on me one breath,
And let me die before my death!"

Song of Solomon 4:16.[5]
Arise O North, and come thou South-wind, and blow upon my garden, that the spices thereof may flow out.

The Search

'Tis now clear day: I see a rose
Bud in the bright east and disclose
The pilgrim sun; all night have I
Spent in a roving ecstasy[6]
To find my Savior; I have been
As far as Bethle'm, and have seen
His inn and cradle. Being there,
I met the wise men, asked them where
He might be found, or what star can
Now point him out, grown up a man?
To Egypt hence I fled, ran o'er
All her parched bosom to Nile's shore,
Her yearly nurse,[7] came back, inquired
Amongst the Doctors,[8] and desired
To see the Temple but was shown
A little dust, and for the Town
A heap of ashes, where some said
A small bright sparkle was abed,
Which would one day (beneath the pole,)
Awake, and then refine the whole.[9]
Tired here, I come to Sychar; thence
To Jacob's well, bequeathèd since
Unto his sons, (where often they
In those calm, golden evenings lay
Wat'ring their flocks, and having spent
Those white days, drove home to the tent
Their well-fleeced train). And here (O fate!)
I sit where once my Savior sat;
The angry spring in bubbles swelled

5. Vaughan's own citation uses a different title for the Song of Solomon and a different citation (Canticles 5:17).
6. "Withdrawal of the soul from the body" (*OED*).
7. I.e., the annual flooding of the Nile, which "nourishes" Egypt.
8. The learned men with whom the boy Jesus, age twelve, discoursed in the Temple (Luke 2:41–50).
9. Lines 15–20 allude to the destruction of the Temple by the Romans in A.D. 70, an act taken by "some" as foreshadowing the final destruction of the world by fire, which would "refine the whole." Cf. the "new heaven and new earth" of Revelation 21. *Beneath the pole*: under the heavens.

Which broke in sighs still, as they filled,
And whispered, "Jesus had been there
But Jacob's children would not hear."[1]
Loath hence to part, at last I rise
But with the fountain in my eyes,
And here a fresh search is decreed.
He must be found, where he did bleed;
I walk the garden,[2] and there see
Ideas of his agony,
And moving anguishments that set
His blest face in a bloody sweat;
I climbed the hill, perused the Cross
Hung with my gain, and his great loss:
Never did tree bear fruit like this;
Balsam[3] of souls, the body's bliss.
But, O his grave! where I saw lent
(For he had none) a monument,
An undefiled and new hewed one,
But there was not the cornerstone.[4]
"Sure" (then said I) "my quest is vain;
He'll not be found where he was slain;
So mild a Lamb can never be
'Midst so much blood and cruelty;
I'll to the wilderness[5] and can
Find beasts more merciful than man:
He lived there safe; 'twas his retreat
From the fierce Jew, and Hero's heat,
And forty days withstood the fell
And high temptations of hell;
With Seraphins[6] there talkèd he
His father's flaming ministry;
He heav'ned their walks and with his eyes
Made those wild shades a Paradise;
Thus was the desert sanctified
To be the refuge of his bride.[7]
I'll thither then; see, it is day,
The sun's broke through to guide my way."
    But as I urged thus, and writ down
What pleasures should my journey crown—
What silent paths, what shades, and cells,
Fair, virgin flowers, and hallowed wells
I should rove in, and rest my head

1. "Jacob's well" at Sychar is the site of Jesus' revelation to the Samaritan (foreign) woman: "the water I will give . . . shall become . . . a fountain . . . springing up into life everlasting" (John 4:5–15). The well symbolizes the disinheritance of the nonbelieving Jews.
2. The Garden of Gethesemane, where Jesus sweat blood and sought release from the coming Passion.
3. In alchemy, a "healthful preservative essence" (*OED*).
4. Joseph of Arimathea provided the tomb of hewn stone (Luke 23:53), but Christ, the cornerstone, arose from the dead (Acts 4:10–11, 1 Peter 2:4 ff.).
5. See Luke 4:1–13 or Matthew 4:1–11 for accounts of Jesus' forty days in the wilderness.
6. Class of angels. Usually, seraph is singular; seraphim, plural.
7. The woman of Revelation 12:1 f., "who fled into the wilderness," is commonly interpreted as the Church, the Bride of Christ.

Where my dear Lord did often tread,
Sug'ring all dangers with success—
Methought I heard one singing thus:

1

Leave, leave, thy gadding thoughts;
Who pores
and spies
Still[8] out of doors
descries
Within them naught.

2

The skin and shell of things,
Though fair,
are not
Thy wish nor prayer,
but got
By mere despair
of wings.

3

To rack old elements,
or dust
and say
Sure here he must
needs stay
Is not the way,
nor just.
Search well another world; who studies this,
Travels in clouds, seeks manna where none is.

Acts 17:27–28.
That they should seek the Lord, if haply they might feel after him, and find him, though he be not far from every one of us: for in him we live, and move, and have our being.

The Shower

'Twas so; I saw thy birth. That drowsy lake
From her faint bosom breathed thee, the disease
Of her sick waters and infectious ease;
But now at even,
Too gross for heaven,
Thou fall'st in tears and weep'st for thy mistake.

8. Always.

2

Ah! It is so with me. Oft have I pressed
Heaven with a lazy breath, but fruitless this
Pierced not; love only can with quick access
Unlock the way,
When all else stray,
The smoke and exhalations of the breast.

3

Yet if, as thou dost melt and with thy train
Of drops make soft the earth, my eyes could weep
O'er my hard heart that's bound up and asleep,
Perhaps at last
(Some such showers past)
My God would give a sunshine after rain.

Distraction

O knit me that am crumbled dust! The heap
Is all dispersed and cheap;
Give for a handful but a thought,
And it is bought.
Hadst thou
Made me a star, a pearl, or a rainbow,
The beams I then had shot[9]
My light had lessened not,
But now
I find my self the less, the more I grow;
The world
Is full of voices; man is called, and hurled[1]
By each; he answers all,
Knows every note and call;
Hence, still
Fresh dotage tempts, or old usurps, his will.
Yet, hadst thou clipped my wings, when coffined in
This quickened[2] mass of sin,
And saved that light, which freely thou
Didst then bestow,
I fear
I should have spurned and said thou didst forbear,
Or that thy store was less,
But now since thou didst bless
So much,
I grieve, my God! that thou hast made me such.
I grieve?

9. Emitted.
1. Upset, disturbed.
2. Given life.

O, yes! thou knowest I do; come and relieve
And tame and keep down with thy light
Dust that would rise and dim my sight,
Lest left alone too long
Amidst the noise and throng,
Oppressed I
Striving to save the whole, by parcels[3] die.

The Pursuit

Lord! What a busy, restless thing
Hast thou made man!
Each day and hour he is on wing,
Rests not a span;
Then having lost the sun, and light,
By clouds surprised,
He keeps a commerce in the night
With air disguised.
Hadst thou given to this active dust
A state untired,
The lost son had not left the husk
Nor home desired.[4]
That was thy secret, and it is
Thy mercy too,
For when all fails to bring to bliss,
Then this must do.
Ah, Lord! And what a purchase will that be
To take us sick, that sound would not take thee?

Vanity of Spirit[5]

Quite spent with thoughts, I left my cell and lay
Where a shrill spring tuned to the early day.
I begged here long and groaned to know
Who gave the clouds so brave[6] a bow,
Who bent the spheres and circled in
Corruption with this glorious ring,
What is his name and how I might
Descry some part of his great light.
I summoned nature; pierced through all her store;
Broke up some seals, which none had touched before.
Her womb, her bosom, and her head,
Where all her secrets lay abed,
I rifled quite, and, having passed
Through all the creatures, came at last

3. Piece by piece; see "crumbled" and "dispersed" (lines 1–2).
4. Cf. the parable of the prodigal son (Luke 15:11 ff.).
5. "[A]ll is vanity and vexation of spirit" (Ecclesiastes 1:14).
6. Splendid, handsome.

To search myself, where I did find
Traces and sounds of a strange kind.
Here of this mighty spring, I found some drills,[7]
With echoes beaten from th'eternal hills.
Weak beams and fires flashed to my sight,
Like a young east or moonshine night,
Which showed me in a nook cast by,
A piece of much antiquity,
With hieroglyphics quite dismembered
And broken letters scarce remembered.
I took them up and (much joyed) went about
T'unite those pieces, hoping to find out
The mystery; but this ne'er done,
That little light I had was gone.
It grieved me much. At last, said I,
"Since in these veils my eclipsed eye
May not approach thee (for at night
Who can have commerce with the light?),
I'll disapparel and, to buy
But one half glance, most gladly die."

The Retreat

Happy those early days! when I
Shined in my angel infancy.
Before I understood this place
Appointed for my second race,[8]
Or taught my soul to fancy ought
But a white, celestial thought;
When yet I had not walked above
A mile or two from my first love,
And looking back, at that short space,
Could see a glimpse of his bright-face;
When on some gilded cloud or flower
My gazing soul would dwell an hour,
And in those weaker glories spy
Some shadows of eternity;
Before I taught my tongue to wound
My conscience with a sinful sound,
Or had the black art to dispense
A several[9] sin to every sense,
But felt through all this fleshy dress
Bright shoots of everlastingness.
O, how I long to travel back,
And tread again that ancient track!
That I might once more reach that plain,
Where first I left my glorious train,

7. Rills, small streams.
8. The phrase "second race" implies Vaughan's belief in the soul's preexistence.
9. Different.

From whence th'enlightened spirit sees
That shady city of palm trees;[1]
But (ah!) my soul with too much stay[2]
Is drunk, and staggers in the way.
Some men a forward motion love,
But I by backward steps would move,
And when this dust falls to the urn
In that state I came, return.

The Morning Watch[3]

O joys! Infinite sweetness! With what flowers,
And shoots of glory my soul breaks and buds!
All the long hours
Of night, and rest,
Through the still shrouds
Of sleep, and clouds,
This dew fell on my breast;
O how it bloods,
And spirits all my earth! Hark! In what rings,
And hymning circulations[4] the quick world
Awakes, and sings;
The rising winds
And falling springs,
Birds, beasts, all things
Adore him in their kinds.
Thus all is hurled
In sacred hymns and order, the great chime
And symphony of nature. Prayer is
The world in tune,
A spirit voice
And vocal joys
Whose echo is heaven's bliss.
O let me climb[5]
When I lie down! The pious soul by night
Is like a clouded star, whose beams, though said
To shed their light
Under some cloud,
Yet are above,
And shine and move
Beyond that misty shroud.
So in my bed,

1. Jericho, "city of palm-trees," was shown to Moses in the vision of the Promised Land from the top of Mount Pisgah (Deuteronomy 34); here the phrase suggests the Heavenly City.
2. Delay.
3. Morning prayer.
4. *Bloods, spirits, circulations*: combines the old notion of blood creating "spirits" (highly rarefied substances linking soul and body) and Harvey's new theory of circulation of the blood.
5. I.e., pray.

That curtained grave, though sleep, like ashes, hide
My lamp and life, both shall in thee abide.

Peace

My soul, there is a country
Far beyond the stars,
Where stands a wingèd sentry[6]
All skillful in the wars.
There, above noise and danger,
Sweet Peace sits crowned with smiles,
And one born in a manger
Commands the beauteous files,[7]
He is thy gracious friend,
And (O my soul, awake!)
Did in pure love descend
To die here for thy sake.
If thou canst get but thither,
There grows the flower of peace,
The rose that cannot wither,
Thy fortress and thy ease.
Leave then thy foolish ranges;
For none can thee secure,
But one who never changes,
Thy God, thy life, thy cure.

["And do they so? Have they a sense"]

Roman 8:19.
Etenim res creatae exerto capite observantes expectant revelationem Filiorum Dei.[8]

And do they so? Have they a sense
Of aught but influence?[9]
Can they their heads lift and expect,[1]
And groan too?[2] Why, th'elect
Can do no more: my volumes said
They[3] were all dull and dead;
They[4] judged them senseless, and their state

6. Sentry. Presumably the Archangel Michael (Revelation 12:7).
7. *Files*: ranks.
8. "For created things, watching with head uplifted, look for the revelation of the Sons of God." The heading is Beza's Latin translation, inaccurately cited, as published by T. Vautrollier (London, 1576 and 1582). Other editions have different renderings of the Greek. In the King James Version, Romans 8:19 reads: "For the earnest expectation of the creature waiteth for the manifestation of the Sons of God."
9. The effects of stellar emanations.
1. Await, look for.
2. "We know that the whole creation groaneth" (Romans 8:22).
3. *They*: created things.
4. *They*: the books.

Wholly inanimate.
Go, go; seal up thy looks,
And burn thy books.

I would I were a stone or tree
Or flower, by pedigree,
Or some poor highway herb, or spring
To flow, or bird to sing!
Then should I (tied to one sure state)
All day expect my date;[5]
But I am sadly loose and stray
A giddy blast each way;
O let me not thus range!
Thou canst not change.

Sometimes I sit with thee and tarry
An hour or so, then vary.
Thy other creatures in this scene
Thee only aim and mean;
Some rise to seek thee, and with heads
Erect, peep from their beds;
Others, whose birth is in the tomb
And cannot quit the womb,
Sigh there and groan for thee,
Their liberty.

O let not me do less! Shall they
Watch while I sleep or play?
Shall I thy mercies still abuse
With fancies, friends, or news?
O brook it not! Thy blood is mine,
And my soul should be thine;
O brook it not! Why wilt thou stop
After whole showers one drop?
Sure, thou wilt joy to see
Thy sheep with thee.

Corruption

Sure it was so. Man in those early days
Was not all stone and earth;
He shined a little, and by those weak rays
Had some glimpse of his birth.
He saw heaven o'er his head and knew from whence
He came, condemnèd, hither,
And, as first love draws strongest, so from hence
His mind sure progressed thither.

5. Of death.

Things here were strange unto him: sweat and till;[6]
All was a thorn or weed,
Nor did those last, but (like himself) died still
As soon as they did seed.
They seemed to quarrel with him, for that act[7]
That felled him foiled them all:
He drew the curse upon the world and cracked
The whole frame with his fall.
This made him long for home, as loath to stay
With murmurers and foes;
He sighed for Eden and would often say,
"Ah! what bright days were those!"
Nor was Heaven cold unto him; for each day
The valley or the mountain
Afforded visits, and still Paradise lay
In some green shade, or fountain.
Angels lay leiger[8] here: each bush and cell,
Each oak and highway, knew them;
Walk but the fields or sit down at some well,
And he was sure to view them.
Almighty Love! where art thou now? Mad man
Sits down and freezeth on:
He raves and swears to stir nor fire nor fan,
But bids the thread be spun.[9]
I see thy curtains are close-drawn; thy bow
Looks dim, too, in the cloud;
Sin triumphs still, and man is sunk below
The center and his shroud;[1]
All's in deep sleep and night; thick darkness lies
And hatcheth o'er thy people.
But hark! What trumpet's that? What angel cries
"Arise! Thrust in thy sickle"?[2]

The World

I saw eternity the other night,
Like a great ring of pure and endless light,
All calm as it was bright,
And round beneath it, time in hours, days, years,
Driv'n by the spheres,[3]
Like a vast shadow moved, in which the world
And all her train were hurled.

6. Plow the ground; see Genesis 3:18–19.
7. Adam and Eve's disobedience.
8. As resident ambassadors.
9. In Greek myth, the three Fates spin the thread of life, measure out its length, and cut it.
1. In a geocentric cosmos, Earth is the center and lowest point, as well as the source of human flesh and its final shelter ("shroud").
2. "Another angel came out of the temple, crying with a loud voice . . . , Thrust in thy sickle, and reap . . . the harvest of the earth is ripe" (Revelation 14:15).
3. Time is the measure of motion, and motion derives from the spheres of the geocentric cosmos.

The doting lover in his quaintest[4] strain
Did there complain;
Near him, his lute, his fancy, and his flights,
Wit's sour delights,
With gloves and knots,[5] the silly snares of pleasure,
Yet his dear treasure,
All scattered lay, while he his eyes did pour
Upon a flower.

The darksome[6] statesman hung with weights and woe,
Like a thick midnight fog, moved there so slow
He did not stay nor go;
Condemning[7] thoughts (like sad eclipses) scowl
Upon his soul,
And clouds of crying witnesses without
Pursued him with one shout.
Yet digged the mole, and lest his ways be found,
Worked under ground,
Where he did clutch his prey. But one did see
That policy;[8]
Churches and altars fed him; perjuries
Were gnats and flies;
It rained about him blood and tears, but he
Drank them as free.[9]

The fearful miser on a heap of rust
Sat pining all his life there, did scarce trust
His own hands with the dust,
Yet would not place one piece above but lives
In fear of thieves.[1]
Thousands there were as frantic as himself
And hugged each one his pelf:[2]
The down-right epicure placed heaven in sense[3]
And scorned pretence,
While others, slipped into a wide excess,
Said little less;
The weaker sort, slight, trivial wares enslave,
Who think them brave;
And poor, despisèd truth sat counting by[4]
Their victory.

4. Most ingenious or clever.
5. Love knots.
6. Gloomy.
7. Used as an adjective, modifying "thoughts."
8. Strategy or plan.
9. I.e., as freely as they rained.
1. Cf. Matthew 6:20 (the Sermon on the Mount): "lay up for yourselves treasures in heaven, where thieves do not break through and steal."
2. Riches.
3. The senses.
4. Observing.

Yet some, who all this while did weep and sing,
And sing and weep, soared up into the ring,[5]
But most would use no wing.
"O fools," said I, "thus to prefer dark night
Before true light,
To live in grots and caves and hate the day
Because it shows the way,
The way which from this dead and dark abode
Leads up to God,
A way where you might tread the sun and be
More bright than he."
But as I did their madness so discuss,
One whispered thus,
"This ring the Bridegroom did for none provide
But for his bride."[6]

1 John 2:16–17.
All that is in the world, the lust of the flesh, the lust of the eyes, and the pride of life, is not of the Father, but is of the world. And the world passeth away, and the lust thereof, but he that doeth the will of God abideth for ever.

Man

Weighing the steadfastness and state[7]
Of some mean things which here below reside,
Where birds, like watchful clocks, the noiseless date
And intercourse of times divide,
Where bees at night get home and hive, and flowers
Early as well as late,
Rise with the sun and set in the same bowers;

"I would," said I, "my God would give
The staidness[8] of these things to man! For these
To his divine appointments ever cleave,
And no new business[9] breaks their peace;
The birds nor sow nor reap, yet sup and dine;
The flowers without clothes live,
Yet Solomon was never dressed so fine."[1]

5. In hermetic thought, those who escape the world, by ascending through the seven spheres, sing hymns to the Father in the eighth sphere ("the ring") before entering the substance of God himself.
6. I.e., the Church. Cf. Revelation 19:7–8 and 19:21 on the Marriage of the Lamb.
7. *State*: dignity.
8. Steadfastness.
9. Busyness, restlessness.
1. Cf. Matthew 6:26–29, part of the Sermon on the Mount; see "The World," line 35n, p. 600.

Man hath still either toys[2] or care,
He hath no root, nor to one place is tied,
But ever restless and irregular
About this earth doth run and ride.
He knows he hath a home but scarce knows where;
He says it is so far
That he hath quite forgot how to go there.

He knocks at all doors, strays and roams,
Nay hath not so much wit as some stones[3] have,
Which in the darkest night point to their homes,
By some hid sense their Maker gave;
Man is the shuttle, to whose winding quest
And passage through these looms
God ordered motion, but ordained no rest.

["I walked the other day . . ."]

I walked the other day, to spend my hour,[4]
Into a field
Where I sometimes had seen the soil to yield
A gallant flower;
But winter now had ruffled all the bower
And curious store
I knew there heretofore.

Yet I whose search loved not to peep and peer
I'th' face of things,
Thought with my self, "there might be other springs
Besides this here,
Which, like cold friends, sees us but once a year;
And so the flower
Might have some other bower."

Then taking up what I could nearest spy
I digged about
That place where I had seen him to grow out,
And by and by
I saw the warm recluse alone to lie
Where fresh and green
He lived of us unseen.

Many a question intricate and rare
Did I there strow,

2. Diversions.
3. Lodestones, with magnetic properties.
4. Hour of meditation.

But all I could extort[5] was that he now
Did there repair
Such losses as befell him in this air
And would ere long
Come forth most fair and young.

This past, I threw the clothes quite o'er his head,
And stung with fear
Of my own frailty dropt down many a tear
Upon his bed,
Then sighing whispered, "happy are the dead!
What peace doth now
Rock him asleep below?"

And yet, how few believe such doctrine springs
From a poor root,
Which all the winter sleeps here under foot,
And hath no wings
To raise it to the truth and light of things,
But is still trod
By every wand'ring clod.

O thou! whose spirit did at first inflame
And warm the dead,
And by a sacred incubation fed
With life this frame
Which once had neither being, form, nor name,[6]
Grant I may so
Thy steps track here below,

That in these masques and shadows I may see
Thy sacred way,
And by those hid ascents climb to that day
Which breaks from thee,
Who art in all things, though invisibly;
Show me thy peace,
Thy mercy, love, and ease,

And from this care, where dreams and sorrows reign
Lead me above
Where light, joy, leisure, and true comforts move
Without all pain,
There, hid in thee,[7] show me his life again,
At whose dumb urn
Thus all the year I mourn.

5. I.e., conclude.
6. Cf. Genesis 1:2.
7. "Your life is hid with Christ in God" (Colossians 3:3).

FROM *SILEX SCINTILLANS*, PART II (1655)

["They are all gone into the world of light!"][8]

They are all gone into the world of light!
And I alone sit ling'ring here;
Their very memory is fair and bright,
And my sad thoughts doth clear.

It[9] glows and glitters in my cloudy breast
Like stars upon some gloomy grove,
Or those faint beams in which this hill is dressed,
After the sun's remove.

I see them walking in an air of glory,
Whose light doth trample on my days:
My days, which are at best but dull and hoary,
Mere glimmering and decays.

O holy hope! and high humility,
High as the heavens above!
These are your walks, and you have showed them me
To kindle my cold love.

Dear, beauteous death! The jewel of the just,
Shining nowhere but in the dark;
What mysteries do lie beyond thy dust,
Could man outlook that mark!

He that hath found some fledged bird's nest, may know
At first sight, if the bird be flown;
But what fair well or grove he sings in now,
That is to him unknown.

And yet as angels in some brighter dreams
Call to the soul, when man doth sleep:
So some strange thoughts transcend our wonted themes,
And into glory peep.

If a star were confined into a tomb
Her captive flames must needs burn there;
But when the hand that locked her up, gives room,
She'll shine through all the sphere.

O Father of eternal life, and all
Created glories under thee!

8. The poem seems to be partly autobiographical, a meditation on the loss of individuals close to him.
9. Their memory.

Resume[1] thy spirit from this world of thrall[2]
Into true liberty.

Either disperse these mists, which blot and fill
My perspective[3] still as they pass,
Or else remove me hence unto that hill,[4]
Where I shall need no glass.[5]

Cock-crowing

Father of lights![6] what sunny seed,
What glance[7] of day hast thou confined
Into this bird? To all the breed
This busy ray thou hast assigned;
Their magnetism works all night
And dreams of Paradise and light.

Their eyes watch for the morning hue;
Their little grain expelling night
So shines and sings as if it knew
The path unto the house of light.
It seems their candle, however done,
Was tinned[8] and lighted at the sun.

If such a tincture,[9] such a touch,
So firm a longing can empower
Shall thy own image think it much
To watch for thy appearing hour?
If a mere blast so fill the sail,
Shall not the breath of God prevail?

O thou immortal light and heat!
Whose hand so shines through all this frame,[1]
That by the beauty of the seat,
We plainly see who made the same.
Seeing thy seed abides in me,
Dwell thou in it, and I in thee.

1. Take back.
2. Slavery.
3. Distant vision, as through a telescope.
4. Sion (heaven).
5. 1 Corinthians 13:12: "For now we see through a glass, darkly; but then, face to face; now I know in part; but then shall I know even as also I am known."
6. "Every good gift and every perfect gift . . . cometh down from the Father of lights" (James 1:17).
7. *Seed, glance* (and *grain* in line 8): these are hermetic terms for spiritual elements derived from the Father of lights and providing for the sympathetic attraction (or "magnetism," line 5) between earthly and spiritual things.
8. Given its brilliance.
9. Infused quality, spirit or soul of a thing.
1. Universe.

To sleep without thee is to die;
Yea, 'tis a death partakes of hell:
For where thou dost not close the eye,
It never opens, I can tell.
In such a dark Egyptian border,[2]
The shades of death dwell, and disorder.

If joys, and hopes, and earnest throes,
And hearts, whose pulse beats still for light
Are given to birds; who, but thee, knows
A lovesick soul's exalted flight?
Can souls be tracked by any eye
But his who gave them wings to fly?

Only this veil which thou hast broke,[3]
And must be broken yet in me,
This veil, I say, is all the cloak
And cloud which shadows thee from me.
This veil thy full-eyed love denies,
And only gleams and fractions spies.

O take it off! Make no delay,
But brush me with thy light, that I
May shine unto a perfect day,
And warm me at thy glorious eye!
O take it off! Or till it flee,
Though with no lily,[4] stay with me!

The Bird

Hither thou comest: the busy wind all night
Blew through thy lodging, where thy own warm wing
Thy pillow was. Many a sullen storm
(For which course man seems much the fitter born)
Rained on thy bed
And harmless head.

And now as fresh and cheerful as the light
Thy little heart in early hymns doth sing
Unto that Providence, whose unseen arm
Curbed them and clothed thee well and warm.
All things that be praise him and had
Their lesson taught them when first made.

So hills and valleys into singing break,
And though poor stones have neither speech nor tongue,

2. The plague of darkness over Egypt (Exodus 10:21 ff.).
3. The veil of physical being, which obscures the other world.
4. "My beloved is mine and I am his; he feedeth among the lilies" (Song of Solomon 2:16). The lily is the flower of light.

While active winds and streams both run and speak,
Yet stones are deep in admiration.
Thus praise and prayer here beneath the sun
Make lesser mornings when the great are done.

For each enclosèd spirit is a star
Enlightening his own little sphere,
Whose light, though fetched and borrowèd from far,
Both mornings makes and evenings there.

But as these birds of light make a land glad,
Chirping their solemn matins[5] on each tree:
So in the shades of night some dark fowls be,
Whose heavy notes make all that hear them sad.

The turtle[6] then in palm trees mourns,
While owls and satyrs[7] howl;
The pleasant land to brimstone turns,
And all her streams grow foul.

Brightness and mirth, and love and faith, all fly
Till the dayspring breaks forth again from high.

The Timber

Sure thou didst flourish once! And many springs,
Many bright mornings, much dew, many showers
Passed o'er thy head; many light hearts and wings,
Which now are dead, lodged in thy living bowers.

And still a new succession sings and flies;
Fresh groves grow up, and their green branches shoot
Towards the old and still enduring skies,
While the low violet thrives at their root.

But thou beneath the sad and heavy line
Of death, dost waste all senseless, cold, and dark;
Where not so much as dreams of light may shine,
Nor any thought of greenness, leaf, or bark.

And yet (as if some deep hate and dissent,
Bred in thy growth betwixt high winds and thee,
Were still alive) thou dost great storms resent[8]
Before they come, and knowest how near they be.

5. Morning prayer.
6. Turtledove.
7. Lecherous creatures, half goat and half man, who dwell in deserted or waste places. Cf. Isaiah 13:21 and 34:12, 14.
8. Perceive.

Else all at rest thou liest, and the fierce breath
Of tempests can no more disturb thy ease,
But this thy strange resentment after death
Means only those who broke (in life) thy peace.

So murdered man, when lovely life is done,
And his blood freezed, keeps in the center still
Some secret sense, which makes the dead blood run
At his approach that did the body kill.

And is there any murd'rer worse than sin?
Or any storms more foul than a lewd life?
Or what resentient[9] can work more within
Than true remorse, when with past sins at strife?

He that hath left life's vain joys and vain care
And truly hates to be detained on earth,
Hath got an house where many mansions are[1]
And keeps his soul unto eternal mirth.

But though thus dead unto the world and ceased
From sin, he walks a narrow, private way;
Yet grief and old wounds make him sore displeased,
And all his life a rainy, weeping day.

For though he should forsake the world and live
As mere[2] a stranger as men long since dead;
Yet by itself will make a right soul grieve
To think he should be so long vainly led.

But as shades set off light, so tears and grief
(Though of themselves but a sad blubbered story)
By showing the sin great, show the relief
Far greater, and so speak my Savior's glory.

If my way lies through deserts and wild woods
Where all the land with scorching heat is cursed,
Better the pools should flow with rain and floods
To fill my bottle, than I die with thirst.[3]

Blest showers they are, and streams sent from above
Begetting virgins where they use[4] to flow;
And trees of life no other waters love:
These upper springs and none else make them grow.

9. That which causes a change of feeling (*OED*).
1. "In my Father's house are many mansions" (John 14:2).
2. Complete.
3. Hagar and her son Ishmael had been turned out by Sarah and were dying of thirst in the wilderness. She is led by God to a well, "and she went, and filled the bottle with water, and gave the lad drink" (Genesis 21:19).
4. Are accustomed.

But these chaste fountains flow not till we die:
Some drops may fall before, but a clear spring,
And ever running till we leave to fling
Dirt in her way, will keep above the sky.[5]

Romans 6:7
He that is dead, is freed from sin.

The Dwelling Place

John 1:38–39.[6]

What happy secret fountain,
Fair shade, or mountain,
Whose undiscovered virgin glory
Boasts it this day, though not in story,
Was then thy dwelling? Did some cloud
Fixed to a tent[7] descend and shroud
My distressed Lord? Or did a star
Beckoned by thee, though high and far,
In sparkling smiles haste gladly down
To lodge light and increase her own?
My dear, dear God! I do not know
What lodged thee then, nor where, nor how;
But I am sure, thou dost now come
Oft to a narrow, homely room,
Where thou too hast but the least part,
My God, I mean my sinful heart.

The Night

John 3:2.[8]

Through that pure virgin shrine,
That sacred veil[9] drawn o'er thy glorious noon
That men might look and live as glowworms shine
And face the moon,[1]

5. The last two stanzas have some reference to these, among other, biblical texts: Revelation 14:3–4, the "hundred and forty and four thousand . . . not defiled with women; for they are virgins," and Revelation 22:1–2, the "pure river of water of life" with the tree of life growing on either side of it.
6. "They said unto him, 'Rabbi, . . . where dwellest thou?' He saith unto them, 'Come and see.' They came and saw where he dwelt, and abode with him that day" (John 1:38–39).
7. During the journey through the wilderness of Sinai, a cloud covers the "tent of the testimony" (Numbers 9:15 ff.).
8. John 3:2 tells of Nicodemus, who "came to Jesus by night, and said unto him, Rabbi, we know that thou art a teacher come from God."
9. Christ's flesh (per Hebrews 10:20).
1. "Thou canst not see my face: for there shall no man see me, and live" (Exodus 33:20). Glowworms shine at night.

Wise Nicodemus saw such light
As made him know his God by night.

Most blest believer he!
Who in that land of darkness and blind eyes
Thy long expected healing wings could see,
When thou didst rise,[2]
And what can never more be done,
Did at midnight speak with the sun!

O who will tell me where
He found thee at that dead and silent hour!
What hallowed solitary ground did bear
So rare a flower,
Within whose sacred leafs did lie
The fullness of the Deity?

No mercy seat[3] of gold,
No dead and dusty Cherub, nor carved stone,
But his own living works did my Lord hold
And lodge alone;[4]
Where trees and herbs did watch and peep
And wonder,[5] while the Jews did sleep.

Dear night! This world's defeat;[6]
The stop to busy fools; care's check and curb;
The day of spirits; my soul's calm retreat
Which none disturb!
Christ's progress, and his prayer time;[7]
The hours to which high Heaven doth chime.

God's silent, searching flight:
When my Lord's head is filled with dew, and all
His locks are wet with the clear drops of night;
His still, soft call;
His knocking time;[8] the soul's dumb watch,
When spirits their fair kindred catch.

Were all my loud, evil days
Calm and unhaunted as is thy dark tent,

2. Malachi 4:2: "Unto you that fear my name, shall the Sun of righteousness arise with healing in his wings."
3. The golden cover of the ark of the covenant, throne of the invisible presence of God, beneath the wings of cherubim. In the ark were the two stone tablets of the Mosaic law (1 Kings 8:6–9).
4. I.e., his own living work (a human being), and that alone, held and lodged the Lord (not the ark revered by the Jews).
5. Cf. "And do they so?" (p. 597), for inanimate creatures' awareness of the creator.
6. This stanza and the next are a series of appositions characterizing night.
7. In the 1655 edition, Vaughan cites Mark 1:35: "in the morning, rising up a great while before day, he went out, and departed into a solitary place, and there he prayed." *Progress*: region or distance traversed during a state journey.
8. "I sleep, but my heart waketh: it is the voice of my beloved that knocketh, saying, Open to me my sister, my love, my dove, my undefiled: for my head is filled with dew and my locks with the drops of the night" (Song of Solomon 5:2; see also 1 Kings 19:12).

Whose peace but by some angel's wing or voice
Is seldom rent,
Then I in Heaven all the long year
Would keep and never wander here.

But living where the sun
Doth all things wake, and where all mix and tire
Themselves and others, I consent and run
To every mire,
And by this world's ill-guiding light,
Err more than I can do by night.

There is in God (some say)[9]
A deep but dazzling darkness, as men here
Say it is late and dusky because they
See not all clear;
O for that night! where I in him
Might live invisible and dim.

Quickness

False life! a foil and no more, when
Wilt thou be gone?
Thou foul deception of all men
That would not have the true come on.

Thou art a moonlike toil; a blind
Self-posing[1] state;
A dark contest of waves and wind;
A mere tempestuous debate.

Life is a fixed, discerning light,
A knowing joy;
No chance or fit,[2] but ever bright
And calm and full, yet doth not cloy.

'Tis such a blissful thing, that still
Doth vivify
And shine and smile, and hath the skill
To please without eternity.

Thou art a toilsome mole or less,
A moving mist.
But life is, what none can express,
A quickness, which my God hath kissed.

9. E.g., Dionysius the Areopagite (also called Pseudo-Dionysius), highly influential among Renaissance Neoplatonists. In *Mystical Theology*, he develops the idea of a divine darkness so intense that it outshines all brilliance.
1. Baffling.
2. I.e., life is not subject to luck or irregularity.

The Book

Eternal God! Maker of all
That have lived here since the man's fall;
The Rock of ages! in whose shade
They live unseen, when here they fade.
Thou knew'st this paper, when it was
Mere seed and after that but grass;
Before 'twas dressed or spun, and when
Made linen, who did wear it then:[3]
What were their lives, their thoughts, and deeds,
Whether good corn or fruitless weeds.

Thou knew'st this tree when a green shade
Covered it, since a cover made,
And where it flourished, grew, and spread,
As if it never should be dead.

Thou knew'st this harmless beast when he
Did live and feed by thy decree
On each green thing; then slept (well fed)
Clothed with this skin, which now lies spread
A covering o'er this aged book;
Which makes me wisely weep and look
On my own dust; mere dust it is,
But not so dry and clean as this.
Thou knew'st and saw'st them all and though
Now scattered thus, dost know them so.

O knowing, glorious Spirit! When
Thou shalt restore trees, beasts and men,
When thou shalt make all new again,
Destroying only death and pain,
Give him amongst thy works a place,
Who in them loved and sought thy face!

3. Rather than belabor the conventional opposition of nature and book learning, Vaughan finds nature in the physical book: its pages were made of linen, which was originally a plant; its cover, boards made from trees, wrapped in leather made from the skin of cattle.

Margaret Cavendish, Duchess of Newcastle

1623 Born in Colchester, Essex, daughter of Sir Thomas Lucas and Elizabeth Leighton.

1643 Accepted as maid of honor to Queen Henrietta Maria; she follows the Queen into exile in Paris.

1645 Marries William Cavendish, a widower thirty years her senior; having served as a royalist general, he becomes Duke of Newcastle after the Restoration. They live in exile on the Continent until 1660.

1651 Returns to England in an unsuccessful attempt to save her husband's estates from being seized.

1653 Publishes *Poems and Fancies* and *Philosophical Fancies*. She writes extensively in numerous genres for the rest of her life.

1655 Publishes her autobiography, *A True Relation of My Birth, Breeding, and Life*.

1660 Returns to England.

1664 An "altered and corrected" edition of *Poems and Fancies* appears.

1666 Publishes her utopian romance, *The Blazing World*, along with *Observations on Experimental Philosophy*.

1667 Publishes *The Life of William Cavendish*.

1670 Her play, *The Forced Marriage*, produced.

1673 Dies on 15 December.

FROM *POEMS AND FANCIES* (1664)

The Poetress's Hasty Resolution

Reading my verses, I liked them so well,
Self-love did make my judgment to rebel;
And thinking them so good, thought more to make,
Considering not how others would them take.
I writ so fast, thought, lived I many a year,
A pyramid of fame thereon to rear;[1]
Reason observing which way I was bent,
Did stay my hand, and asked me what I meant;
"Will you," said he, "thus waste your time in vain,
On that which in the world small praise shall gain?
For shame leave off, and do the printer spare,
He'll lose by your ill poetry, I fear:
Besides, the world already hath great store
Of useless books, wherefore do write no more,
But pity take, do the world a good turn,
And all you write cast into th'fire, and burn."
Angry I was, and reason struck away,
When I did hear, what he to me did say;
Then all in haste I to the press it sent,
Fearing persuasion might my book prevent:
But now 'tis done, repent with grief do I,
Hang down my head with shame, blush, sigh, and cry.
Take pity, and my drooping spirits raise,
Wipe off my tears with handkerchiefs of praise.

The Poetress's Petition

Like to a fever's pulse my heart doth beat,
For fear my book some great repulse should meet:
If it be naught, let it in silence lie;
Disturb it not; let it in quiet die;
Let not the bells of your dispraise ring loud,
But wrap it up in silence as a shroud;
Cause black oblivion on its hearse to lie,
Instead of tapers, let dark night stand by;
Instead of flowers, on its grave to strew,
Before its hearse, sleepy, dull poppy throw;
Instead of scutcheons,[2] let my tears be hung,
Which grief and sorrow from my eyes out wrung:
Let those that bear its corpse, no jesters be,
But sober, sad, and grave mortality:

1. I.e., I wrote so fast that I thought that I would be able to build a poetic monument to myself if I lived long enough.
2. An escutcheon is an ornamental shield covered with a coat of arms.

No satyr[3] poets by its grave appear,
No altars raised, to write inscriptions there:
Let dust of all forgetfulness be cast
Upon its corpse, there let it lie and waste:
Nor let it rise again, unless some know,
At judgments some good merits it can show;
Then shall it live in heavens of high praise,
And for its glory, garlands have of bays.[4]

An Apology for Writing So Much upon This Book

Condemn me not, I make so much ado
About this book, it is my child, you know;
Just like a bird, when her young are in nest,
Goes in, and out, and hops, and takes no rest;
But when their young are fledged,[5] their heads out peep,
Lord! what a chirping does the old one keep:
So I, for fear my strengthless child should fall
Against a door, or stool, aloud I call,
Bid have a care of such a dangerous place:
Thus write I much, to hinder all disgrace.

A World Made by Atoms[6]

Small atoms of themselves a world may make,
For being subtle, every shape they take;
And as they dance about, they places find,
Of forms, that best agree, make every kind.
For when we build an house of brick or stone,
We lay them even, every one by one,
And when we find a gap that's big, or small,
We seek out stones to fit that place withal;
For when as they too big, or little be,
They fall away, and cannot stay, we see;
So atoms, as they dance, find places fit,
And there remaining close and fast will knit.
Those which not fit, the rest that rove about,
Do never leave, until they thrust them out;
Thus by their forms and motions they will be,
Like workmen, which amongst themselves agree;
And so by chance may a new world create,
Or else predestinate,[7] may work by fate.

3. Satirical.
4. Emblematic of poetic success.
5. Fully feathered and ready for flight.
6. Cavendish's atomic poems are informed by Epicurean philosophy, especially Lucretius's *De rerum natura*. Epicurean physics posits a materialist universe composed of an infinite quantity of atoms in an endless void. In this universe, creation and destruction are the products of motion and chance, not fate or divine design—although Cavendish equivocates on this point in this first poem.
7. Predestined.

What Atoms Make a Palsy, or Apoplexy[8]

When dull flat atoms do together join,
And with each other in a heap combine,
This body thick doth stop all passage so,
Keeps motion out, and makes the body grow
Numbed; for sharp atoms in which heat doth live,
Being close and smothered up, no heat can give;
But if these atoms flat meet in the brain,
The spirits[9] are choked, and can no heat obtain.

In All Other Diseases Atoms Are Mixed, Taking Parts and Factions

In all other diseases they are mixed,
And not in one united body fixed,
But do in factions part,[1] and when they rise,
Striving to beat each other out, man dies.

All Things Are Governed by Atoms

Thus life and death, and young and old,
Are, as the several[2] atoms hold;
Wit, understanding in the brain,
Are, as the several atoms reign;
And disposition good or ill,
Are as the several atoms still;
And every passion which doth rise,
Is as each sort of atoms lies:
Thus sickness, health, and peace and war,
Are as the several atoms are.[3]

A War betwixt Atoms

Some factious atoms 'mongst themselves combine,
And strive some formèd body to disjoin;
Round atoms do beat out the sharp; the long
With flat atoms do fight; thus all go wrong.
Those which make motion general[4] in their war,
By his directions much stronger are.

8. Both diseases attack the brain or nervous system, impairing muscular control and power.
9. Rarified, vaporous substances refined from the blood. Animal spirits, in particular, were based in the brain and thought to diffuse vital heat throughout the body. Cf. "Of the Motion of the Blood," line 6n, p. 619.
1. I.e., divide into factions. The image is one of partisan conflict or civil war.
2. Different.
3. I.e., depend on how the various types of atoms dispose themselves.
4. I.e., make motion their general.

Atoms and Motion Fall Out

When motion and all atoms disagree,
Thunder i'th' air, and sickness in men be;
Earthquakes and winds, which make disorder great,
Are,[5] when as motion doth all atoms beat;
And they great noise in this confusion make,
For motion lets them not their places take:
Like frighted flocks that do together keep,
Which motion worries, as a wolf doth sheep.

An Agreement of Some Kind of Motion with Some Kind of Atoms

Some motion with some atoms doth agree,
Fitting them to their place, just as may be,
Where they by motion's help so strong do grow,
As it shall hardly them again undo:
Motion's inconstancy oft gives such power
To atoms, as they may itself devour.[6]

Motion Directs while Atoms Dance

Atoms will in just[7] measures dance, and join
All one by one in a round circle line,
Run in and out, as we do dance the hay,[8]
Crossing about, yet keep just time and way,
Whilst motion doth direct; and thus they dance,
And meet all by consent, not by mere chance:
This consort's health,[9] which life depends upon,
But when 'tis out, 'tis death; so dancing's done.

If Infinite Worlds, There Must Be Infinite Centers[1]

If infinites of worlds, they must be placed
At such a distance, as between lies waste;[2]
If they were joinèd close, moving about,
By jostling they would push each other out;

5. Occur.
6. I.e., the empowered atoms may consume or suppress motion itself.
7. Appropriate, correct.
8. A country dance with winding, serpentine movements.
9. I.e., this harmonious combination (consort) is health.
1. The Italian philosopher Giordano Bruno (1548–1600) argued for the existence of an infinite universe and a plurality of worlds in *De l'infinito universo et mondi* (1585). In 1600, he was burned at the stake in Rome for his heretical views.
2. Uninhabited country, empty space.

And if they swim in air, as fishes do
In water, they would meet as they did go.
But if the air doth every world enclose
And compass[3] all about, as water flows,
It keeps them equal[4] in their proper seat,
That as they move shall not each other beat:
Or if like wheels which turn by water round,
So air about these worlds is running found,
Then by that motion they do turn about,
No further, than that motion's strength runs out;
Like to a bowl,[5] which will not further go,
But runs according as that strength did throw.
And thus like bowls the worlds do turn and run,
But still the jack[6] and center is the sun.

Of Infinite Matter

If matter be no more than we do see
This world, I pray, what must beyond it be?
For sure this world is limited and bound,
And like a ball is made in compass[7] round;
But matter, out of which the world is made,
If infinite, then more worlds may be said;[8]
Nay, infinites of worlds[9] there may be found,
If infinite of matter has no bound.

Of the Motion of the Blood

Some[1] by their industry and learning found,
That all the blood like to the sea runs round;
From two great arteries it doth begin,
Runs through all veins, and so comes back again.
The muscles like the tides do ebb and flow,
According as the several spirits go;[2]
The sinews as small pipes come from the head,
And they are all about the body spread,
Through which the animal spirits are conveyed

3. Encompass.
4. Undisturbed.
5. The hard wooden ball used in bowling.
6. "In the game of Bowls, a smaller bowl placed as a mark for the players to aim at" (*OED*).
7. Enclosed space, circuit.
8. Declared or made known.
9. I.e., no end of worlds.
1. William Harvey; cf. Cowley's "Ode. Upon Dr. Harvey," p. 527. Cavendish's omission of the heart in her description suggests that she may be more influenced by Harvey's *De circulatione sanguinis* (1649), which downplays the role of the heart, than by his *De motu cordis* (1628).
2. Traditional physiology held that vital spirits, which were refined from the blood in the heart, were further refined into animal spirits in the brain and then carried throughout the body via the nerves (Cavendish's "sinews").

To every member, as the pipes are laid;
And from those sinews' pipes each sense doth take
Of those pure spirits, as they us do make.[3]

Of Many Worlds in This World[4]

Just like as in a nest of boxes round,
Degrees of sizes in each box are found;
So in this world may many others be,
Thinner and less, and less still by degree;
Although they are not subject to our sense,
A world may be no bigger than two-pence.
Nature is curious,[5] and such works may shape,
Which our dull senses easily escape:
For creatures small as atoms may be there,
If every one a creature's figure bear.
If four atoms a world can make, then see,
What several worlds might in an earring be:
For millions of those atoms may be in
The head of one small, little, single pin.
And if thus small, then ladies may well wear
A world of worlds as pendants in each ear.

The Hunting of the Hare

Betwixt two ridges of plowed land sat Wat,[6]
Whose body pressed to th'earth, lay close, and squat,
His nose upon his two forefeet did lie,
With his gray eyes he glared obliquèly;
His head he always set against the wind,
His tail when turned, his hair blew up behind,
And made him to get cold; but he being wise,
Doth keep his coat still down, so warm he lies:
Thus rests he all the day, till th'sun doth set,
Then up he riseth his relief to get,
And walks about, until the sun doth rise,
Then coming back in's[7] former posture lies.
At last poor Wat was found, as he there lay,
By huntsmen, which came with their dogs that way,
Whom seeing, he got up and fast did run,
Hoping some ways the cruel dogs to shun;
But they by nature had so quick a scent,

3. I.e. (perhaps), we as conscious beings are constituted by the animal spirits that feed each of our five senses.
4. Epicurean atomic theory postulated the existence of other worlds beneath the appearance of things.
5. Intricately wrought.
6. Traditional name for a hare.
7. In his.

That by their nose they traced what way he went,
And with their deep wide mouths set forth a cry,
Which answered was by echo in the sky;
Then Wat was struck with terror and with fear,
Seeing each shadow, thought the dogs were there,
And running out some distance from their cry,
To hide himself his thoughts he did employ;
Under a clod of earth in sandpit wide
Poor Wat sat close, hoping himself to hide,
There long he had not been, but straight in's ears
The winding[8] horns and crying dogs he hears;
Then starting up with fear, he leaped, and such
Swift speed he made, the ground he scarce did touch;
Into a great thick wood straightways he got,
And underneath a broken bough he sat,
Where every leaf that with the wind did shake
Brought him such terror that his heart did ache;
That place he left, to champaign[9] plains he went,
Winding about, for to deceive their scent,
And while they snuffling were to find his track,
Poor Wat being weary, his swift pace did slack;
On his two hinder legs for ease he sat,
His forefeet rubbed his face from dust and sweat,
Licking his feet, he wiped his ears so clean,
That none could tell that Wat had hunted been;
But casting round about his fair gray eyes,
The hounds in full career he near him spies,
To Wat it was so terrible a sight,
Fear gave him wings and made his body light;
Though he was tired before by running long,
Yet now his breath he never felt more strong;
Like those that dying are, think health returns,
When 'tis but a faint blast which life out burns;
For spirits seek to guard the heart about,
Striving with death, but death doth quench them out.
The hounds so fast came on, and with such cry,
That he no hopes had left, nor help could spy;
With that the winds did pity poor Wat's case,
And with their breath the scent blew from that place;
Then every nose was busily employed,
And every nostril was set open wide,
And every head did seek a several way,
To find the grass or track where the scent lay;
For witty industry[1] is never slack,
'Tis like to witchcraft, and brings lost things back:
But though the wind had tied the scent up close,

8. Blowing.
9. Open.
1. Resourceful diligence.

A busy dog thrust in his snuffling nose
And drew it out, with that did foremost run,
Then horns blew loud, the rest to follow on:
The great slow hounds their throats did set a bass,
The fleet, swift hounds, as tenors next in place,
The little beagles did a treble sing,
And through the air their voices round did ring,
Which made such comfort as they ran along,
That, had they spoken words, 't had been a song;
The horns kept time, the men did shout for joy,
And seemed most valiant, poor Wat to destroy;
Spurring their horses to a full career,[2]
Swum rivers deep, leapt ditches without fear,
Endangered life and limbs, so fast they'd ride;
Only to see how patiently Wat died;
At last the dogs so near his heels did get,
That their sharp teeth they in his breech did set;
Then tumbling down he fell, with weeping eyes
Gave up his ghost; and thus poor Wat, he dies.
Men whooping loud, such acclamations made,
As if the devil they imprisoned had,
When they but did a shiftless[3] creature kill;
To hunt, there needs no valiant soldier's skill:
But men do think that exercise and toil,
To keep their health, is best, which makes most spoil,
Thinking that food and nourishment so good,
Which doth proceed from others' flesh and blood.
When they do lions, wolves, bears, tigers see
Kill silly sheep, they say, they cruel be;
But for themselves all creatures think too few,
For luxury, wish God would make more new;[4]
As if God did make creatures for man's meat,
And gave them life and sense for man to eat,[5]
Or else for sport or recreation's sake
For to destroy those lives that God did make,
Making their stomachs graves, which full they fill
With murdered bodies, which in sport they kill;
Yet man doth think himself so gentle and mild,
When of all creatures he's most cruel, wild,
Nay, so proud, that he only thinks to live,
That God a godlike nature him did give,
And that all creatures for his sake alone
Were made, for him to tyrannize upon.

2. Rush.
3. Lazy, lacking in ambition.
4. I.e., that God would create more animals or species for their sport; cf. Genesis 1:19–28. The dominion over animals that God grants "man" in Genesis 1:26–28 played a significant role in seventeenth-century debates over monarchical and individual sovereignty. "Luxury" (lasciviousness, lust) was pejorative in the period.
5. Prelapsarian existence was supposed to be vegetarian.

A Description of an Island[6]

There was an island rich by Nature's grace;
In all the world it was the sweetest place,
Surrounded with the seas, whose waves not missed
To do her homage, and her feet they kissed;
Each wave did seem by turn to bow down low,
And proud to touch her, when as they did flow;
Armies of waves in troops high tides brought on,
Whose wat'ry arms did glister as the sun,
And on their backs burdens of ships did bear,
Placing them in her havens with great care,
Not mercenary, for no pay they'd have,
But as her guard did watch, to keep her safe,
And in a ring they circled her about,
Strong as a wall, to keep her foes without;
The winds did serve her, and on clouds did ride,
Blowing their trumpets loud on every side,
Serving as scouts, they searched in every lane,
And galloped in the forests, fields and plain;
While she did please the gods, she did live safe,
And they all kind of pleasures to her gave;
For all this place was fertile, rich and fair,
Both woods, and hills, and dales in prospects[7] were;
Birds pleasure took, and with delight did sing,
In praises of this isle the woods did ring;
Trees thrived with joy, for she their roots well fed,
And tall with pride, their tops did overspread;
Danced with the winds, when they did sing and blow,
Played like a wanton kid, or a swift roe;
Their several branches several birds did bear,
Which hopped and skipped, and always merry were;
Their leaves did wave, and rushing make a noise,
And many ways strived to express their joys;
All flowers there looked fresh and gay with mirth,
Whilst they were danced upon the lap of earth;
Th'isle was their mother; they her children sweet,
Born from her loins, got by Apollo great,[8]
Who dressed and pruned them often with great care,
And washed their leaves with dew to make them fair;
Which being done, he wiped those drops away
With webs of heat which he weaves every day;
Paint them with several colors intermixed,
Veiled them with shadows every leaf betwixt;
Their heads he dressed, their hairy leaves spread out,
Wreathed round their crowns his golden beams about:
For he this isle esteemed above the rest;

6. This poem and the next are thinly veiled descriptions of England before and during the civil war.
7. Views.
8. I.e., the sun.

Of all his wives he had he loved her best;
Daily he did present her with some gift,
Twelve ells[9] of light to make her smocks for shift;
Which every time he came, he put on fair,
That lovely she and handsome might appear,
And when he from her went, the world to see,
He left his sister her for company,
Whose name is Cynthia,[1] though pale yet clear,
Which makes her always in dark clouds appear;
Besides, he left his stars to wait on her,
Lest she should grieve too much, when he's not there,
And from his bounty clothed them all with light,
Which makes them twinkle in a frosty night;
He never brought hot beams to do her harm,
Nor let her take a cold, but lapped her warm;
He mantles rich of equal heat o'erspread,
And covered her with color crimson red;
He gave another o'er her head to lie,
The color is a pure bright azure sky;
And with soft air did line them all within,
Like furs in winter, in summer satin thin;
With silver clouds he fringèd them about,
And spangled meteors glist'ring hung without:
Thus gave he change, lest she should weary grow,
Or think them old, and so away them throw.
Nature adorned this island all throughout
With landscapes, rivulets, prospects round about;
Hills overtopped the dales, which level were,
And covered all with cattle, feeding there;
Grass grew up even to the belly high,
Where beasts that chew their cud lay pleasantly,
Whisking their tails about, the flies to beat,
Or else to cool them from the sultry heat;
Nature, her love to th'gods willing to show,
Sent plenty in, like Nile's great overflow,[2]
And temperate seasons gave, and equal lights,
Warm sunshine days, and dewy moonshine nights;
And in this pleasant island peace did dwell,
No noise of war, or sad tale could it tell.

The Ruin of This Island

This island lived in peace full many a day,
So long as she unto the gods did pray;
But she grew proud with plenty and with ease,
Adored herself, and did the gods displease,

9. *Ell*: a unit for measuring the length of textiles (forty-five inches in England).
1. I.e., the moon. Cynthia is another name for Diana (Artemis).
2. The Nile flooded annually between June and September, leaving silt necessary to the fertility of the region.

She flung their altars down, and in their stead
Set up her own, and would be worshippèd:
The gods grew angry, and commanded Fate
To alter and to ruin quite the state,
For they had changed their mind of late, they said,
And did repent, unthankful man th'[3] had made;
Fates[4] wondered much to hear what said the gods,
That they and mortal men were at great odds,
And found them apt to change, thought it did show,
As if the gods did not poor men foreknow;
For why, said they, if men do evil grow,
The gods, foreseeing all, men's hearts did know
Long, long before they did man first create?
If so, what need they change or alter fate?
'Twas in their power to make them good or ill,
Wherefore men cannot do just what they will;
Then why do gods complain against them so,
Since men are made by them such ways to go?
If evil power hath gods to oppose,
Two equal deities it plainly shows;
The one pow'r cannot keep obedience long,
If disobedient power be as strong;
And being ignorant how men will prove,
Know not how strong or long will last their love:
But may't not be the course of God's decree,
To love obedience, wheresoe'er it be?
They from the first a changing power create,
And for that work make destiny and fate;
It is the mind of man that's apt to range,
The minds of gods are not subject to change.
Then did the Fates unto the planets go,
And told them they malignity must throw
Into this island, for the gods would take
Revenge on them, who did their laws forsake;
With that the planets drew like with a screw
Bad vapors from the earth, and then did view
What place to squeeze that poison on, which all
The venom had, got from the world's great ball;
Then through men's veins like molten lead it came,
And did like oil their spirits all inflame,
Where malice boiled with rancor, spleen and spite,
In war and fraud, injustice took delight,
Thinking which way their lusts they might fulfill,
Committed thefts, rapes, murders at their will;
Parents and children did unnat'ral grow,
And every friend was turned a cruel foe;
Nay, innocency[5] no protection had,
Religious men were thought to be stark mad;

3. They.
4. Presumably the three Fates: Clotho, Lachesis, and Atropos.
5. Innocence.

In witches, wizards, they did put their trust;
Extortions, bribes were thought to be most just;
Like Titan's race[6] all did in tumults rise,
And 'gainst the heavens utter blasphemies;
The gods in rage unbound the winds, to blow
In a strange nation, formerly their foe,
Where they themselves did plant, the natives all
Were by them killed, for th'gods had sworn their fall;
Compassion wept, and virtue wrung her hands,
To see that right was banished from their lands:
Thus winds, and seas, the planets, fates and all
Conspired to work her ruin and her fall;
But those that keep the laws of God on high,
Shall live in peace, i'th' grave rest quietly;
And ever after like the gods shall be,
Enjoy all pleasure, know no misery.

Upon the Funeral of My Dear Brother, Killed in These Unhappy Wars[7]

Alas! Who shall my funeral mourner be,
Since none is near that is allied to me?
Or who shall drop a sacrificing tear,
If none but enemies my hearse shall bear?

For here's no mourner to lament my fall,
But in my fate, though sad, rejoicèd all,
And think my heavy ruin far too light,
So cruel is their malice, spleen, and spite!

For men no pity nor compassion know,
But like fierce beasts in savage wildness go,
To wash and bathe themselves in my poor blood,
As if they health received from that red flood.

Yet will the winds my doleful knell ring out,
And showering rain fall on my hearse about;
The birds, as mourners on my tomb shall sit,
And grass, like as a covering grow on it.

Then let no spade nor pickaxe come near me,
But let my bones in peace rest quietly;
He, who the dead dislodges from their grave,
Shall neither blessedness nor honor have.

6. The elder generation of Greek gods, supplanted by Zeus and the Olympians.
7. Sir Charles Lucas (1613–1648), one of Cavendish's older brothers, was a successful royalist commander. Captured at Stow-on-the-Wold in 1646, he pledged to not bear arms against Parliament. He broke this pledge and, captured at Colchester in 1648, was executed.

Thomas Stanley

1625	Born at Cumberlow, Hertfordshire; baptized 8 September. The only son of Sir Thomas Stanley and his wife Mary, a cousin to Richard Lovelace. Initially educated by the classical scholar William Fairfax, son of Edward Fairfax, the translator of Tasso's *Gerusalemme Liberata*.
1639	Admitted to Pembroke Hall, Cambridge, as a gentleman commoner.
1642	Takes M.A. degree. At the outbreak of the civil war, leaves England; resides in France until 1646.
1646	Returns to England; takes up residence in the Middle Temple, London. Befriends and assists James Shirley; also, probably, Lovelace and Herrick.
1647	*Poems and Translations* published. Marries Dorothy Enyon, heiress of a titled and wealthy Northamptonshire family.
1648–1649	Working on translations of poetry by classical and contemporary authors. Following the execution of Charles I in January 1649, retires to Cumberlow.
1651	Publication of *Poems*. Turns his attention primarily to classical scholarship.
1655	Publication of *A History of Philosophy*, volume I; subsequent volumes appear in 1656, 1660, and 1662.
1661	Elected a charter member of the Royal Society.
1663	Publishes a scholarly edition of Aeschylus. Named a Fellow of the Royal Society.
1678	Death, 12 April. Buried in Saint Martin-in-the-Fields, London.

FROM *POEMS* (1651)

The Glowworm

Stay, fairest Charissa, stay and mark
This animated gem, whose fainter spark
Of fading light its birth had from the dark.

A star thought by the erring passenger,[1]
Which falling from its native orb dropped here,
And makes the earth, its center, now its sphere.

Should many of these sparks together be,
He that the unknown light far off should see
Would think it a terrestrial galaxy.

Take't up, fair saint; see how it mocks thy fright;
The paler flame doth not yield heat, though light,
Which thus deceives thy reason through thy sight.

But see how quickly it, ta'en up, doth fade,
To shine in darkness only being made,
By th'brightness of thy light turned to a shade;

And burnt to ashes by thy flaming eyes,
On the chaste altar of thy hand it dies,
As to thy greater light a sacrifice.

Changed, Yet Constant[2]

Wrong me no more
In thy complaint,
Blamed for inconstancy;
I vowed t'adore
The fairest saint,
Nor changed whilst thou wert she;
But if another thee outshine,
Th'inconstancy is only thine.

To be by such
Blind fools admired
Gives thee but small esteem,
By whom as much
Thou'dst be desired
Didst thou less beauteous seem;
Sure why they love they know not well,
Who why they should not cannot tell.

1. I.e., the wandering wayfarer.
2. Cf. Lovelace, "The Scrutiny," p. 493.

Women are by
Themselves betrayed,
And to their short joys cruel,
Who foolishly
Themselves persuade
Flames can outlast their fuel;
None, though Platonic their pretense,[3]
With reason love unless by sense.

And he, by whose
Command to thee
I did my heart resign,
Now bids me choose
A deity
Diviner far than thine;
No power can love from beauty sever;
I'm still love's subject, thine was never.

The fairest she
Whom none surpass
To love hath only right,
And such to me
Thy beauty was
Till one I found more bright;
But 'twere as impious to adore
Thee now, as not t'have done't before.

Nor is it just
By rules of love
Thou should'st deny to quit
A heart that must
Another's prove,
Ev'n in thy right to it;
Must not thy subjects captives be
To her who triumphs over thee?

Cease then in vain
To blot my name
With forged apostasy;
Thine is that stain
Who dar'st to claim
What others ask of thee.
Of lovers they are only true
Who pay their hearts where they are due.

3. Cf. Randolph, "An Elegy" and note, p. 341.

Celia Singing

Roses in breathing forth their scent,
Or stars their borrowed ornament;
Nymphs in the watery sphere that move,
Or angels in their orbs above;
The wingèd chariot of the light,
Or the slow, silent wheels of night;
The shade which from the swifter sun
Doth in a circular motion run;
Or souls that their eternal rest do keep,
Make far more noise than Celia's breath in sleep.

But if the angel which inspires
This subtle frame with active fires
Should mold this breath to words, and those
Into a harmony dispose,
The music of this heavenly sphere
Would steal each soul out at the ear,
And into plants and stones infuse
A life that cherubins[4] would choose;
And with new powers invert the laws of fate,
Kill those that live, and dead things animate.

Love's Innocence

See how this ivy strives to twine
Her wanton arms about the vine,
And her coy lover thus restrains,
Entangled in her amorous chains;
See how these neighb'ring palms do bend
Their heads, and mutual murmurs send,
As whisp'ring with a jealous fear
Their loves into each other's ear.
Then blush not such a flame to own[5]
As like thyself no crime hath known:
Led by these harmless guides, we may
Embrace and kiss as well as they.
And like those blessèd souls above,
Whose life is harmony and love,
Let us our mutual thoughts betray
And in our wills our minds display;
This silent speech is swifter far
Than the ears' lazy species are,
And the expression it affords
(As our desires) 'bove reach of words.
Thus we, my dear, of these may learn

4. I.e., the highest among the orders of angels.
5. Acknowledge.

A passion others not discern;
Nor can it shame or blushes move,
Like plants to live, like angels love;
Since all excuse with equal innocence
What above reason is, or beneath sense.

La Belle Confidente[6]

You earthly souls that court a wanton flame,
Whose pale weak influence
Can rise no higher than the humble name
And narrow laws of sense,
Learn by our friendship to create
An immaterial fire,
Whose brightness angels may admire,
But cannot emulate.

Sickness may fright the roses from her cheek,
Or make the lilies fade,
But all the subtle ways that death doth seek
Cannot my love invade;
Flames that are kindled by the eye
Through time and age expire;
But ours, that boast a reach far higher
Cannot decay or die.

For when we must resign our vital breath,
Our loves by fate benighted,
We by this friendship shall survive in death,
Even in divorce united.
Weak love, through fortune or distrust,
In time forgets to burn,
But this pursues us to the urn
And marries either's dust.

The Bracelet[7]

Rebellious fools that scorn to bow
Beneath love's easy sway,
Whose stubborn wills no laws allow,
Disdaining to obey,
Mark but this wreath of hair, and you shall see,
None that might wear such fetters would be free.

6. I.e., intimate female friend.
7. Cf. Donne, "The Funeral," p. 40.

I once could boast a soul like you,
As unconfined as air;
But mine, which force could not subdue,
Was caught within this snare;
And, by myself betrayed, I, for this gold,
A heart that many storms withstood have sold.

No longer now wise art inquire,
With this vain search delighted,
How souls that human breasts inspire
Are to their frames united;
Material chains such spirits well may bind,
When this soft braid can tie both arm and mind.

Now, beauties, I defy your charm,
Ruled by more powerful art;
This mystic wreath which crowns my arm
Defends my vanquished heart;
And I, subdued by one more fair, shall be
Secured from conquest by captivity.

FROM *POEMS AND TRANSLATIONS* (1647)

Expectation

Chide, chide no more away
The fleeting daughters of the day,
Nor with impatient thoughts outrun
The lazy sun,
Or think the hours do move too slow;
Delay is kind,
And we too soon shall find
That which we seek, yet fear to know.

The mystic dark decrees
Unfold not of the destinies,
Nor boldly seek to antedate
The laws of fate;
Thy anxious search awhile forbear;
Suppress thy haste,
And know that time at last
Will crown thy hope, or fix thy fear.

John Dryden

1631 Born on 9 August in Aldwincle, Northamptonshire. His parents, gentry of moderate fortune, sided with Parliament during the civil war.

1644 Enters Westminster School.

1650 Matriculates at Trinity College, Cambridge; takes his B.A. in 1654.

1657 Employed as a secretary for the Protectorate. Attends Cromwell's funeral, along with Milton and Marvell, in 1658.

1659 Publishes "Heroic Stanzas," on the death of Cromwell, in a volume that also includes elegies by Edmund Waller and Thomas Sprat.

1660 The Restoration of Charles II; Dryden publishes *Astraea Redux*.

1662 Nominated to the Royal Society by Walter Charleton; writes "To My Honored Friend, Dr. Charleton," a commendatory poem for Charleton's *Chorea Gigantum* (1663).

1663 Marries Lady Elizabeth Howard. His first play, *The Wild Gallant*, performed; he works primarily as a playwright through 1681.

1668 Appointed poet laureate; appointed historiographer royal in 1669. He publishes *An Essay of Dramatic Poesy*.

1673 Writes *The State of Innocence*, an opera based on Milton's *Paradise Lost*.

1681 Publishes *Absalom and Achitophel*.

1682 Publishes *Religio Laici*.

1685 James II takes the throne; Dryden converts to Roman Catholicism, perhaps out of loyalty to James. Dryden publishes *The Hind and the Panther* in 1687.

1688 James II deposed; Dryden loses his public offices in 1689.

1697 Publishes *The Works of Virgil*, a major translation and commercial success.

1700 Dies on 1 May.

FROM *THREE POEMS UPON THE DEATH OF HIS HIGHNESS OLIVER LORD PROTECTOR* (1659)

Heroic Stanzas[1]

1.

And now 'tis time;[2] for their officious haste,
Who would before have borne him to the sky,
Like eager Romans ere all rites were past
Did let too soon the sacred eagle fly.[3]

2.

Though our best notes are treason to his fame
Joined with the loud applause of public voice,
Since heaven, what praise we offer to his name,
Hath rendered too authentic[4] by its choice:

3.

Though in his praise no arts can liberal be,
Since they whose muses have the highest flown
Add not to his immortal memory,
But do an act of friendship to their own:

4.

Yet 'tis our duty and our interest too
Such monuments as we can build to raise,
Lest all the world prevent what we should do
And claim a title in him by their praise.

5.

How shall I then begin, or where conclude
To draw a fame so truly circular?[5]
For in a round what order can be showed,
Where all the parts so equal perfect are?

6.

His grandeur he derived from heaven alone,
For he was great ere fortune made him so;

1. Dryden published *Heroic Stanzas, Consecrated to the Glorious Memory of his Most Serene and Renowned Highness Oliver, Late Lord Protector of this Commonwealth, etc. Written after the Celebration of his Funeral* in early 1659 as part of a volume that also included elegies by Edmund Waller and Thomas Sprat.
2. Oliver Cromwell (1599–1658) died on 3 September, but his official funeral took place on 23 November. "Officious haste" refers to the poets who published their elegies before the funeral.
3. The Romans released an eagle from the funeral pyre of an emperor to carry his soul to the gods.
4. I.e., proper to heaven. Praising Cromwell infringes on a function that heaven has made its own.
5. The circle was emblematic of perfection; cf. Jonson, "To the Immortal Memory . . . of . . . Cary and . . . Morison," lines 9–10, p. 140.

And wars like mists that rise against the sun
Made him but greater seem, not greater grow.

7.

No borrowed bays his temples did adorn,
But to our crown he did fresh jewels bring,
Nor was his virtue poisoned soon as born
With the too early thoughts of being king.

8.

Fortune (that easy mistress of the young,
But to her ancient servants coy and hard)[6]
Him at that age her favorites ranked among
When she her best-loved Pompey did discard.[7]

9.

He, private, marked the faults of others' sway,
And set as sea-marks[8] for himself to shun;
Not like rash monarchs who their youth betray
By acts their age too late would wish undone.

10.

And yet dominion was not his design:
We owe that blessing not to him but heaven,
Which to fair acts unsought rewards did join,
Rewards that less to him than us were given.

11.

Our former chiefs[9] like sticklers[1] of the war
First sought t'inflame the parties, then to poise;
The quarrel loved, but did the cause abhor,
And did not strike to hurt but make a noise.

12.

War, our consumption, was their gainful trade,
We inward bled whilst they prolonged our pain:
He fought to end our fighting, and essayed
To stanch the blood by breathing the vein.[2]

6. Cf. Machiavelli, *The Prince*, Ch. XXV.
7. Cromwell emerged as a successful leader at age forty-five, the same age at which the Roman general Pompey's fortunes declined.
8. Discernible objects by which sailors can navigate.
9. Earlier parliamentary generals were unable to bring the first civil war to an end.
1. Umpires.
2. I.e., to cure a hemorrhage by bloodletting.

13.

Swift and resistless[3] through the land he past,
Like that bold Greek[4] who did the East subdue,
And made to battles such heroic haste
As if on wings of victory he flew.

14.

He fought secure of fortune as of fame,
Till by new maps the island might be shown,
Of conquests which he strewed where'er he came
Thick as the galaxy with stars is sown.[5]

15.

His palms, though under weights they did not stand,
Still thrived;[6] no winter could his laurels fade;
Heaven in his portrait showed a workman's hand
And drew it perfect yet without a shade.

16.

Peace was the prize of all his toils and care,
Which war had banished and did now restore;
Bologna's walls thus mounted in the air
To seat themselves more surely than before.[7]

17.

Her safety rescued Ireland to him owes;[8]
And treacherous Scotland to no interest true,
Yet blest that fate which did his arms dispose
Her land to civilize as to subdue.[9]

18.

Nor was he like those stars which only shine
When to pale mariners they storms portend;
He had his calmer influence, and his mien
Did love and majesty together blend.

3. Irresistible.
4. Alexander the Great.
5. I.e., until new maps would show the island as thickly marked by his victories as the galaxy is by stars.
6. Palms were the reward for victory, and because palm trees were thought to thrive when weighed down, they were also emblematic of constancy in the face of hardship. *Still*: always; undisturbed.
7. During the siege of 1512, the Spanish undermined part of the city walls that contained a chapel dedicated to the Blessed Virgin. The explosion carried this part of wall into the air, but miraculously it landed intact and in place.
8. Cromwell led the reconquest of Ireland in 1649–1650.
9. Cromwell conquered Scotland, uniting it with England in 1654.

19.

'Tis true, his countenance did imprint an awe,
And naturally all souls to his did bow,
As wands of divination downward draw
And point to beds where sovereign gold doth grow.

20.

When past all offerings to Feretrian Jove[1]
He Mars deposed, and arms to gowns made yield,
Successful councils did him soon approve
As fit for close intrigues as open field.

21.

To suppliant Holland he vouchsafed a peace,[2]
Our once bold rival in the British main
Now tamely glad her unjust claim to cease,
And buy our friendship with her idol, Gain.

22.

Fame of the asserted sea through Europe blown
Made France and Spain ambitious of his love;
Each knew that side must conquer he would own
And for him fiercely as for empire strove.

23.

No sooner was the Frenchman's cause embraced,
Than the light Monsieur the grave Don outweighed,
His fortune turned the scale where it was cast,
Though Indian mines were in the other laid.[3]

24.

When absent,[4] yet we conquered in his right:
For though some meaner artist's skill where shown
In mingling colors, or in placing light,
Yet still the fair designment was his own.

25.

For from all tempers[5] he could service draw;
The worth of each with its alloy[6] he knew;

1. The god to whom the Romans consecrated the spoils of war, especially the arms that a general won from an enemy commander in battle.
2. Cromwell ended the war with the United Provinces in 1654.
3. Cromwell made a military alliance with France in 1656; this led to the capture of Dunkirk from Spain and the English possession of it in 1658.
4. When Cromwell was absent.
5. Dryden is using the metallurgical sense of "temper": the strength or elasticity of a metal.
6. A baser metal mixed with a finer.

And as the confident of nature saw
How she complexions[7] did divide and brew.

26.

Or he their single virtues did survey
By intuition in his own large breast,
Where all the rich ideas of them lay,
That were the rule and measure to the rest.

27.

When such heroic virtue heaven sets out,
The stars, like Commons,[8] sullenly obey,
Because it drains them when it comes about,
And therefore is a tax they seldom pay.

28.

From this high spring our foreign-conquests flow
Which yet more glorious triumphs do portend,
Since their commencement to his arms they owe,
If springs as high as fountains may ascend.

29.

He made us freemen of the continent
Whom nature did like captives treat before,
To nobler preys the English Lion sent,
And taught him first in Belgian walks to roar.

30.

That old unquestioned pirate of the land,
Proud Rome, with dread, the fate of Dunkirk heard,
And trembling wished behind more Alps to stand,
Although an Alexander[9] were her guard.

31.

By his command we boldly crossed the line
And bravely fought where southern stars arise;[1]
We traced the far-fetched gold unto the mine
And that which bribed our fathers made our prize.

7. The temperaments produced by various combinations of bodily humors.
8. The House of Commons was traditionally averse to levying taxes.
9. Pope Alexander VII.
1. Cromwell sent a fleet to capture San Domingo from Spain. It failed, but it succeeded in capturing Jamaica in 1655.

32.

Such was our prince; yet owned[2] a soul above
The highest acts it could produce to show:
Thus poor mechanic arts[3] in public move,
Whilst the deep secrets beyond practice go.

33.

Nor died he when his ebbing fame went less,
But when fresh laurels courted him to live;
He seemed but to prevent[4] some new success,
As if above what triumphs earth could give.

34.

His latest victories still thickest came,
As near the center, motion does increase;
Till he, pressed down by his own weighty name,
Did, like the vestal,[5] under spoils decease.

35.

But first the ocean as tribute sent
That giant prince[6] of all her watery herd,
And the isle when her protecting genius went
Upon his obsequies[7] loud sighs conferred.

36.

No civil broils have since his death arose,
But faction now by habit does obey;
And wars have that respect for his repose,
As winds for halcyons[8] when they breed at sea.

37.

His ashes in a peaceful urn shall rest,
His name a great example stands to show
How strangely high endeavors may be blest,
Where piety and valor jointly go.

2. Possessed.
3. I.e., the work of manual laborers or artisans.
4. To go before.
5. The virgin Tarpeia betrayed Rome to the Sabines. Instead of throwing the gold bracelets that she demanded as a reward, the Sabines threw their shields, killing her.
6. A whale was captured in the Thames on 3 June 1658.
7. Funeral rites. The "loud sighs" refer to the windstorms that marked Cromwell's death.
8. A seabird symbolizing peace and calm; cf. Carew, "A Rapture," line 97n, p. 304.

ASTRAEA REDUX (1660)[9]

Now with a general peace the world was blest,
While ours, a world divided from the rest,
A dreadful quiet felt, and worser far
Than arms, a sullen interval of war:
Thus when black clouds draw down the lab'ring skies,
Ere yet abroad the wingèd thunder flies,
An horrid stillness first invades the ear,
And in that silence we the tempest fear.
The ambitious Swede[1] like restless billows tossed,
On this hand gaining what on that he lost,
Though in his life he blood and ruin breathed,
To his now guideless kingdom peace bequeathed.
And heaven that seemed regardless of our fate,
For France and Spain did miracles create,
Such mortal quarrels to compose in peace
As nature bred and int'rest did increase.
We sighed to hear the fair Iberian bride
Must grow a lily to the lily's side,[2]
While our cross stars denied us Charles his[3] bed
Whom our first flames and virgin love did wed.
For his long absence church and state did groan;
Madness the pulpit, faction seized the throne:
Experienced age in deep despair was lost
To see the rebel thrive, the loyal crossed:
Youth that with joys had unacquainted been
Envied gray hairs that once good days had seen:
We thought our sires, not with their own content,
Had ere we came to age our portion spent.
Nor could our nobles hope their bold attempt
Who ruined crowns would coronets exempt:
For when by their designing leaders taught
To strike at pow'r which for themselves they sought,
The vulgar gulled into rebellion, armed,
Their blood to action by the prize was warmed.
The sacred purple then and scarlet gown[4]
Like sanguine dye to elephants was shown.
Thus when the bold Typhoeus[5] scaled the sky
And forced great Jove from his own heaven to fly,

9. *Astraea Redux* ("The Return of Justice"): *A Poem on the Happy Restoration and Return of His Sacred Majesty Charles the Second* was published in June 1660. Charles II landed at Dover on 25 May 1660 and entered London on 29 May, his thirtieth birthday. Dryden took Virgil's *Eclogues* IV.6 as his epigram: "*Iam redite et virgo, redeunt Saturnia regna*" (Now the virgin [Astraea] returns, and Saturn reigns again). The return of Astraea was supposed to herald the return of the Golden Age.
1. After waging war on Denmark and Poland, Charles X of Sweden died in February 1660, leaving the throne to his young son.
2. In 1659, the Infanta Maria Theresa was betrothed to the French King Louis XIV as part of the Treaty of the Pyrenees, which ended a long war between Spain and France.
3. Charles's; cf. lines 111, 231, and 240.
4. Bishops' gowns were purple; peers' gowns, scarlet.
5. Typhon, a huge monster with numerous serpent heads, attacked Olympus, forcing the gods to hide in Egypt; cf. Hesiod, *Theogony*, 819–885, and Ovid, *Metamorphoses*, V.346–358.

(What king, what crown from treason's reach is free,
If Jove and heaven can violated be?)
The lesser gods that shared his prosperous state
All suffered in the exiled thund'rer's fate.
The rabble now such freedom did enjoy,
As winds at sea that use it to destroy:
Blind as the Cyclops,[6] and as wild as he,
They owned a lawless savage liberty,
Like that our painted ancestors so prized
Ere empire's arts their breasts had civilized.
How great were then our Charles his woes, who thus
Was forced to suffer for himself and us!
He tossed by fate and hurried up and down,
Heir to his father's sorrows, with his crown,
Could taste no sweets of youth's desirèd age,
But found his life too true a pilgrimage.
Unconquered yet in that forlorn estate,
His manly courage overcame his fate.
His wounds he took like Romans on his breast,
Which by his virtue were with laurels dressed.
As souls reach heaven while yet in bodies pent,
So did he live above his banishment.
That sun, which we beheld with cozened eyes,
Within the water, moved along the skies.
How easy 'tis when destiny proves kind,
With full-spread sails to run before the wind,
But those that 'gainst stiff gales laveering[7] go
Must be at once resolved and skillful too.
He would not like soft Otho hope prevent,
But stayed and suffered fortune to repent.
These virtues Galba in a stranger sought,
And Piso to adopted empire brought.[8]
How shall I then my doubtful thoughts express
That must suff'rings both regret and bless!
For when his early valor heav'n had crossed,
And all at Worc'ster[9] but the honor lost,
Forced into exile from his rightful throne,
He made all countries where he came his own.
And viewing monarchs' secret arts of sway,
A royal factor for their kingdoms lay.
Thus banished David[1] spent abroad his time,
When to be God's anointed was his crime,
And when restored made his proud neighbors rue
Those choice remarks he from his travels drew.

6. The blind Cyclops Polyphemus was frequently associated with the Puritans and the Commonwealth.
7. Tacking back and forth to make headway into the wind.
8. Marcus Salvius Otho (A.D. 32–69) helped Galba to become emperor of Rome, hoping to be adopted by him and named his successor. When he adopted Piso instead, Otho had Galba murdered.
9. After being defeated by parliamentary forces at Worcester on 3 September 1651, the future Charles II escaped to France.
1. Cf. II Samuel 15–21.

Nor is he only by afflictions shown
To conquer others' realms, but rule his own:
Recovering hardly what he lost before,
His right endears it much, his purchase more.
Inured to suffer ere he came to reign,
No rash procedure will his actions stain.
To bus'ness ripened by digestive thought,
His future rule is into method brought:
As they who first proportion understand,
With easy practice reach a master's hand.
Well might the ancient poets then confer
On night the honored name of counselor,
Since struck with rays of prosperous fortune blind,
We light alone in dark afflictions find.
In such adversities to scepters trained,
The name of Great his famous grandsire[2] gained,
Who yet a king alone in name and right,
With hunger, cold, and angry Jove did fight;
Shocked by a Convenanting League's vast pow'rs,
As holy and as catholic as ours,
Till fortune's fruitless spite had made it known,
Her blows not shook but riveted his throne.
Some lazy ages lost in sleep and ease
No action leave to busy chronicles;
Such whose supine felicity but makes
In story chasms, in epochs mistakes;
O'er whom time gently shakes his wings of down
Till with his silent sickle they are mown:
Such is not Charles his too too active age,
Which, governèd by wild distempered rage
Of some black star infecting all the skies,
Made him at his own cost like Adam wise.
Tremble, ye nations, who secure before,
Laughed at those arms that 'gainst ourselves we bore;
Roused by the lash of his own stubborn tail
Our lion now will foreign foes assail.
With alga[3] who the sacred altar strows?
To all the sea-gods Charles an off'ring owes:
A bull to thee, Portunus,[4] shall be slain,
A lamb to you, the tempests of the main:
For those loud storms that did against him roar
Have cast his shipwrecked vessel on the shore.
Yet as wise artists mix their colors so
That by degrees they from each other go,
Black steals unheeded from the neighb'ring white
Without offending the well-cozened sight:
So on us stole our blessèd change; while we

2. Henry IV of France (1553–1610), the maternal grandfather of Charles II, fought against the Catholic League, which Dryden compares with the Presbyterian Solemn League and Covenant that opposed Charles I in 1643.
3. Seaweed.
4. Roman god of harbors.

Th' effect did feel, but scarce the manner see.
Frosts that constrain the ground and birth deny
To flow'rs that in its womb expecting lie,
Do seldom their usurping pow'r withdraw,
But raging floods pursue their hasty thaw:
Our thaw was mild, the cold not chased away,
But lost in kindly heat of lengthened day.
Heav'n would no bargain for its blessings drive,
But what we could not pray for, freely give.
That prince of peace would like himself confer
A gift unhoped without the price of war.
Yet as he knew his blessings' worth, took care
That we should know it by repeated pray'r;
Which stormed the skies and ravished Charles from thence,
As heav'n itself is took by violence.
Booth's forward valor[5] only served to show
He durst that duty pay we all did owe:
Th'attempt was fair; but heav'n's prefixed hour
Not come; so like the watchful traveler
That by the moon's mistaken light did rise,
Lay down again, and closed his weary eyes.
'Twas Monck[6] whom providence designed to loose
Those real bonds false freedom did impose.
The blessèd saints that watched this turning scene
Did from their stars with joyful wonder lean
To see small clews[7] draw vastest weights along,
Not in their bulk but in their order strong.
Thus pencils can by one slight touch restore
Smiles to that changèd face that wept before.
With ease such fond chimeras[8] we pursue
As fancy frames for fancy to subdue,
But when ourselves to action we betake,
It shuns the mint like gold that chemists make:[9]
How hard was then his[1] task, at once to be
What in the body natural we see
Man's architect distinctly did ordain
The charge of muscles, nerves, and of the brain,
Through viewless conduits spirits[2] to dispense,
The springs of motion from the seat of sense.
'Twas not the hasty product of a day,
But the well-ripened fruit of wise delay.
He, like a patient angler, ere he struck,
Would let them play a while upon the hook.

5. Sir George Booth led a royalist uprising that was quickly suppressed in August 1659.
6. General George Monck (1608–1670) occupied London in 1660 and arranged for new parliamentary elections, which led to the return of Charles II.
7. A "clew" is the lower or corner part of the sail to which a line is attached.
8. Illusions.
9. I.e., like the false gold of alchemists.
1. Monck's.
2. "Spirit" was held to be a substance, refined from the blood, that allowed the brain to enact bodily motion via imperceptible conduits.

Our healthful food the stomach labors thus,
At first embracing what it strait doth crush.
Wise leeches[3] will not vain receipts obtrude,
While growing pains pronounce the humors[4] crude;
Deaf to complaints they wait upon the ill,
Till some safe crisis authorize their skill.
Nor could his acts too close a vizard[5] wear
To 'scape their eyes whom guilt had taught to fear,
And guard with caution that polluted nest
Whence Legion twice before was dispossessed,[6]
Once sacred house,[7] which when they entered in,
They thought the place could sanctify a sin;
Like those that vainly hoped kind heaven would wink,
While to excess on martyrs' tombs they drink.
And as devouter Turks first warn their souls
To part before they taste forbidden bowls,
So these when their black crimes they went about
First timely charmed their useless conscience out.
Religion's name against itself was made;
The shadow served the substance to invade:
Like zealous missions they did care pretend
Of souls in show, but made the gold their end.
Th'incensed pow'rs beheld with scorn from high
An heaven so far distant from the sky,
Which durst with horses' hoofs that beat the ground
And martial brass belie the thunder's sound.
'Twas hence at length just vengeance thought it fit
To speed their ruin by their impious wit.
Thus Sforza,[8] cursed with a too fertile brain,
Lost by his wiles the pow'r his wit did gain.
Henceforth their fogue[9] must spend at lesser rate
Than in its flames to wrap a nation's fate.
Suffered to live, they are like helots[1] set,
A virtuous shame within us to beget.
For by example most we sinned before,
And, glass-like, clearness mixed with frailty bore.
But since reformed by what we did amiss,
We by our suff'rings learn to prize our bliss,
Like early lovers whose unpracticed hearts
Were long the May-game of malicious arts,
When once they find their jealousies were vain,
With double heat renew their fires again.

3. Physicians. *Receipts*: recipes or prescriptions.
4. The four fluids thought to determine an individual's mental and physical characteristics.
5. A mask.
6. The Rump Parliament was dissolved first by Cromwell in 1653 and then by Major-General Lambert in 1659. For Legion, cf. Mark 5:9.
7. I.e., the House of Parliament.
8. Lodovico Sforza (1451–1508), Duke of Milan, was famous for his treachery.
9. Passion, ardor.
1. Slaves. The Spartans would intoxicate them and set them before Spartan children to illustrate the shameful effects of intemperance.

'Twas this produced the joy that hurried o'er
Such swarms of English[2] to the neighb'ring shore,
To fetch that prize, by which Batavia[3] made
So rich amends for our impoverish'd trade.
Oh had you seen from Scheveline's barren shore[4]
(Crowded with troops, and barren now no more,)
Afflicted Holland to his farewell bring
True sorrow, Holland to regret a King,
While waiting him his royal fleet did ride,
And willing winds to their low'red sails denied.
The wavering streamers, flags, and standard out,
The merry seaman's rude but cheerful shout,
And last the cannons' voice that shook the skies
And, as it fares in sudden ecstasies
At once bereft us both of ears and eyes.
The *Naseby*,[5] now no longer England's shame,
But better to be lost in Charles his name
(Like some unequal bride in nobler sheets)
Receives her Lord; the joyful *London* meets
The princely York,[6] himself alone a freight;
The *Swiftsure* groans beneath great Glouc'ster's weight.[7]
Secure as when the halcyon[8] breeds, with these
He that was born to drown might cross the seas.
Heav'n could not own a providence and take
The wealth three nations ventured at a stake.
The same indulgence Charles his voyage blessed,
Which in his right had miracles confessed.
The winds that never moderation knew,
Afraid to blow too much, too faintly blew;
Or out of breath with joy could not enlarge
Their straightened lungs, or conscious of their charge.
The British Amphitrite,[9] smooth and clear,
In richer azure never did appear;
Proud her returning prince to entertain
With the submitted fasces[1] of the main.

And welcome now, great monarch, to your own;
Behold th'approaching cliffs of Albion;[2]
It is no longer motion that cheats your view,
As you meet it, the land approacheth you.

2. Many loyal subjects preempted Charles's return by traveling to Holland.
3. Holland. There was a noticeable decline in English trade in the years leading up to 1660.
4. Charles embarked for England at Scheveningen, a port near The Hague, on May 23.
5. The *Naseby*, the warship sent to return Charles to England, was quickly renamed the *Royal Charles*. It was originally named after the battle of Naseby, where the New Model Army decimated the royalist army on 14 June 1645.
6. James Stuart (1633–1701), Duke of York, the second surviving son of Charles I. Later James II (1685–1688).
7. Henry Stuart (1640–1660), Duke of Gloucester, the third surviving son of Charles I.
8. Cf. "Heroic Stanzas," line 144, p. 642; cf. Carew, "A Rapture," line 97n, p. 304.
9. A sea nymph and the wife of Neptune.
1. Roman officials carried fasces, rods bundled with an axe, as a symbol of authority. They could be lowered ("submitted") to recognize superior authority.
2. Albion, the Latin name for Britain, stems from the white cliffs of Dover (from Latin *albus*, or white).

The land returns, and in the white it wears
The marks of penitence and sorrow bears.
But you, whose goodness your descent doth show,
Your heav'nly parentage and earthly too,
By that same mildness which your father's crown
Before did ravish, shall secure your own.[3]
Not tied to rules of policy, you find
Revenge less sweet than a forgiving mind.
Thus when th'almighty would to Moses give
A sight of all he could behold and live,
A voice before his entry did proclaim
"Long-suffering, goodness, mercy" in his name.[4]
Your pow'r to justice doth submit your cause,
Your goodness only is above the laws;
Whose rigid letter while pronounced by you
Is softer made. So winds that tempests brew,
When through Arabian groves they take their flight,
Made wanton with rich odors, lost their spite.
And as those lees that trouble it refine
The agitated soul of generous[5] wine
So tears of joy, for your returning spilt,
Work out and expiate our former guilt.
Methinks I see those crowds on Dover's strand
Who in their haste to welcome you to land
Choked up the beach with their still growing store,
And made a wilder torrent on the shore;
While spurred with eager thoughts of past delight,
Those who had seen you court a second sight;
Preventing still your steps and making hast
To meet you often wheresoe'er you passed.
How shall I speak of that triumphant day
When you renewed the expiring pomp of May!
(A month that owns an interest in your name:
You and the flow'rs are its peculiar claim.)
That star[6] that at your birth shone out so bright,
It stained the duller sun's meridian light,
Did once again its potent fires renew,
Guiding our eyes to find and worship you.
And now time's whiter[7] series is begun,
Which in soft centuries shall smoothly run;
Those clouds that overcast your morn shall fly,
Dispelled to farthest corners of the sky.
Our nation, with united int'rest blest,
Not now content to poise, shall sway the rest.
Abroad your empire shall no limits know,

3. Alluding to the Act of Indemnity and Oblivion, which Charles II issued to grant amnesty to most of Cromwell's supporters.
4. Cf. Exodus 33:20–23 and 34:6–7.
5. Powerful.
6. On the day of Charles's birth, 29 May 1630, a star was seen at noon. Some claimed that it was a new star; others, that it was the planet Venus.
7. More fortunate.

But like the sea in boundless circles flow.
Your much loved fleet shall with a wide command
Besiege the petty monarchs of the land;
And as old Time[8] his offspring swallowed down,
Our ocean in its depths all seas shall drown.
Their wealthy trade from pirates' rapine free,
Our merchants shall no more advent'rers be;
Nor in the farthest east those dangers fear,
Which humble Holland must dissemble here.
Spain to your gift alone her Indies owes,
For what the pow'rful takes not he bestows.
And France that did an exile's presence fear
May justly apprehend you still too near.[9]
At home the hateful names of parties cease
And factious souls are wearied into peace.
The discontented now are only they
Whose crimes before did your just cause betray;
Of those your edicts some reclaim from sins,
But most your life and blest example wins.
Oh happy prince whom Heav'n hath taught the way,
By paying vows, to have more vows to pay!
Oh happy age! Oh times like those alone
By fate reserved for great Augustus' throne![1]
When the joint growth of arms and arts foreshow
The world a monarch, and that monarch you.

FROM *CHOREA GIGANTUM* (1663)

To My Honored Friend, Dr. Charleton[2]

The longest tyranny that ever swayed
Was that wherein our ancestors betrayed
Their free-born reason to the Stagirite,[3]
And made his torch their universal light.
So truth, while only one supplied the state,
Grew scarce, and dear, and yet sophisticate,[4]
Until 'twas bought, like emp'ric wares or charms,[5]
Hard words sealed up with Aristotle's arms.
Columbus was the first that shook his throne

8. Kronos, the father of Zeus, swallowed his children to avoid being deposed.
9. The emerging alliance between Cromwell and France led to Charles's departure from the nation in 1654; cf. "Heroic Stanzas," lines 89–92, p. 640.
1. Alluding to Virgil's prophecy that Augustus's reign would prompt the return of the Golden Age; cf. *Aeneid* VI.791 ff.
2. First published as a commendatory poem for Charleton's *Chorea Gigantum* (1663), which argues that the Danes originally built Stonehenge as a coronation site for their kings. Walter Charleton (1620–1707), a physician, scientist, and antiquarian, joined the Royal Society in 1661, and he nominated Dryden for membership in November 1662.
3. Aristotle; cf. Cowley, "To Mr. Hobbes," line 17n, p. 524.
4. Sophisticated; corrupted by sophistry.
5. The wares of a charlatan or quack doctor.

And found a temp'rate in a torrid zone:[6]
The fev'rish air fanned by a cooling breeze;
The fruitful vales set round with shady trees;
And guiltless men, who danced away their time,
Fresh as their groves, and happy as their clime.
Had we still paid that homage to a name,
Which only God and nature justly claim,
The western seas had been our utmost bound,
Where poets still might dream the sun was drowned:
And all the stars that shine in southern skies
Had been admired by none but savage eyes.
   Among th'asserters of free reason's claim,
Th' English are not the least in worth or fame.
The world to Bacon[7] does not only owe
Its present knowledge, but its future too.
Gilbert[8] shall live, till loadstones cease to draw,
Or British fleets the boundless ocean awe;
And noble Boyle,[9] not less in nature seen,
Than his great brother read in states and men.
The circling streams, once thought but pools, of blood
(Whether life's fuel or the body's food),
From dark oblivion Harvey's name[1] shall save;
While Ent[2] keeps all the honor that he gave.
Nor are you, learnèd friend, the least renowned;
Whose fame, not circumscribed with English ground,
Flies like the nimble journeys of the light
And is, like that, unspent too in its flight.
Whatever truths have been, by art or chance,
Redeemed from error, or from ignorance,
Thin in their authors (like rich veins of ore),
Your works unite, and still discover more.
Such is the healing virtue of your pen,
To perfect cures on books, as well as men.
Nor is this work the least: you well may give
To men new vigor, who make stones to live.
Through you, the Danes (their short dominion lost)
A longer conquest than the Saxons boast.
Stonehenge, once thought a temple, you have found
A throne, where kings, our earthly gods, were crowned,

6. Aristotle maintained that an uninhabitable torrid zone existed between the Tropic of Cancer and the Tropic of Capricorn. During his third voyage, Columbus disproved this notion by discovering temperate weather within this equatorial zone, to which he ascribed the characteristics of the earthly paradise.
7. The Royal Society openly acknowledged its debt to Francis Bacon (1561–1626), whose works were pivotal to the development of experimental philosophy.
8. William Gilbert (1540–1603) published *De Magnete* (1600), which advanced the study of magnetism.
9. Robert Boyle (1627–1691), the famous chemist, was central to the founding of the Royal Society; his brother was Roger Boyle (1621–1679), Earl of Orrery, a dramatist and politician.
1. William Harvey (1578–1657) discovered the circulation of the blood; cf. Cowley, "Ode. Upon Dr. Harvey," p. 527.
2. George Ent (1604–1689) wrote *Apologia pro Circuitione Sanguinis* (1641), a defense of Harvey's theory.

Where by their wondering subjects they were seen,
Joyed with their stature, and their princely mien.
Our sovereign here above the rest might stand,
And here be chose again to rule the land.
  These ruins sheltered once his sacred head,
Then when from Worc'ster's fatal field he fled,[3]
Watched by the genius of this royal place,
And mighty visions of the Danish Race.
His refuge then was for a temple shown:
But, he restored, 'tis now become a throne.

3. The future Charles II visited Stonehenge following his defeat at Worcester in 1651.

Katherine Philips

1631 Born to a London merchant, John Fowler, and his wife, Katherine Oxenbridge. Raised as a Presbyterian and educated at Mrs. Salmon's Presbyterian School at Hackney, London.

1639 Father dies; her mother marries a Welsh baronet, Hector Philips, and moves to Wales.

1648 Marries James Philips, thirty-eight years her senior, a Presbyterian, magistrate, and member of Parliament. They reside in Cardigan, Wales.

1651 Receives praise from Henry Vaughan in *Olor Iscanus*. Despite her husband's support for Parliament—he signed the King's death warrant in 1649—she is a royalist, and throughout the Interregnum, she established relations with other royalist sympathizers.

1660 Celebrates the Restoration of Charles II in her poetry, while her husband narrowly escapes being executed as a regicide. His estates are seized, and he loses his seat in Parliament. Nonetheless, Katherine becomes popular at court.

1663 While in Ireland, she translates Corneille's *Pompey*, which is published in Dublin.

1664 She dies of smallpox. A pirated edition of her *Poems* appears in print.

1667 Publication of her *Poems*, an authorized edition directed by her friend, Sir Charles Cotterell.

FROM *POEMS* (1667)

Upon the Double Murder of K. Charles I in Answer to a Libelous Copy of Rhymes by Vavasor Powell[1]

I think not on the state, nor am concerned
Which way soever the great helm is turned,
But as that son whose father's danger nigh
Did force his native dumbness and untie
The fettered organs, so this is a cause
That will excuse the breach of nature's laws.[2]
Silence were now a sin: nay passion now
Wise men themselves for merit would allow.[3]
What noble eye could see (and careless pass)
The dying lion kicked by every ass?
Has Charles so broke God's laws, he must not have
A quiet crown, nor yet a quiet grave?
Tombs have been sanctuaries; thieves lie there
Secure from all their penalty and fear.
Great Charles his double misery was this:
Unfaithful friends, ignoble enemies.
Had any heathen been this prince's foe,
He would have wept to see him injured so.
His title was his crime, they'd reason good
To quarrel at the right they had withstood.
He broke God's laws, and therefore he must die;[4]
And what shall become of thee and I?
Slander must follow treason; but yet stay,
Take not our reason with our king away.
Though you have seized upon all our defense,
Yet do not sequester our common sense.
But I admire not at this new supply:
No bounds will hold those who at scepters fly.
Christ will be King, but I ne'er understood
His subjects build his kingdom up with blood,
Except their own; or that he would dispense
With his commands, though for his own defense.
Oh! to what height of horror are they come
Who dare pull down a crown, tear up a tomb![5]

1. Vavasor Powell (1617–1670), a Welsh Puritan preacher and Fifth Monarchist, defended the execution of Charles I (30 January 1649) on the grounds that Christ's second coming, and thus the end of all earthly monarchs, was imminent.
2. Natural law was thought to prohibit women from speaking about public affairs.
3. Classical philosophers, especially the Stoics, advocated the strict control of the passions.
4. This line seems to be a quote from Powell's poem, as does "Christ will be King" at line 29.
5. I.e., their slanders tear up Charles's tomb.

Arion on a Dolphin, To His Majesty at His Passage into England[6]

Whom does this stately navy bring?
O! 'tis Great Britain's glorious king.
Convey him then, ye winds and seas,
Swift as desire and calm as peace.
In your respect let him survey
What all his other subjects pay;
And prophesy to them again
The splendid smoothness of his reign.
Charles and his mighty hopes you bear:
A greater now than Caesar's here,[7]
Whose veins a richer purple boast
Than ever heroes yet engrossed;[8]
Sprung from a father so august,
He triumphs in his very dust.
In him two miracles we view,
His virtue and his safety too:
For when compelled by traitors' crimes
To breathe and bow in foreign climes,
Exposed to all the rigid fate
That does on withered greatness wait,
Plots against life and conscience laid,
By foes pursued, by friends betrayed;
Then heaven, his secret potent friend,
Did him from drugs and stabs defend;
And what's more yet, kept him upright
'Midst flattering hope and bloody fight.
Cromwell his whole right never gained,
Defender of the Faith remained,[9]
For which his predecessors fought
And writ, but none so dearly bought.
Never was prince so much besieged,
At home provoked, abroad obliged;
Nor ever man resisted thus,
No, not great Athanasius.[1]
No help of friends could, or foes' spite,
To fierce invasion him invite.
Revenge to him no pleasure is,
He spared their blood who gaped for his;
Blushed any hands the English crown

6. Arion, a Greek lyric poet, was rescued by a dolphin after having been thrown overboard by Corinthian sailors; cf. Herodotus, *Histories*, II.24. On the return of Charles II, cf. Dryden, "Astraea Redux," p. 643.
7. I.e., a greater sovereign than Julius Caesar is now in England. Sailing from Gaul (France), Caesar invaded Britain in 55 and 54 B.C.
8. Had possession of.
9. Pope Leo X granted this title to Henry VIII in 1621 as a reward for writing against Luther, and subsequent English monarchs retained it. Cromwell rejected the crown and thus the title.
1. St. Athanasius (c. 296–373), Bishop of Alexandria, remained steadfast in the face of political persecution and was exiled from his see five times.

Should fasten on him, but their own.
As peace and freedom with him went,
With him they came from banishment.
That he might his dominions win,
He with himself did first begin:
And that best victory obtained,
His kingdom quickly he regained.
Th'illustrious suff'rings of this prince
Did all reduce and all convince.
He only lived with such success,
That the whole world would fight with less.
Assistant kings could but subdue
Those foes which he can pardon too.[2]
He thinks no slaughter-trophies good,
Nor laurels dipped in subjects blood;
But with a sweet resistless art
Disarms the hand, and wins the heart;
And like a god doth rescue those
Who did themselves and him oppose.[3]

Go, wondrous prince, adorn that throne
Which birth and merit make your own,
And in your mercy brighter shine
Than in the glories of your line:
Find love at home, and abroad fear,
And veneration everywhere.
Th'united world will you allow
Their chief, to whom the English bow:
And monarchs shall to yours resort,
As Sheba's queen to Judah's court;[4]
Returning thence constrainèd more
To wonder, envy, and adore.
Discovered Rome will hate your crown,
But she shall tremble at your frown.
For England shall (ruled and restored by you)
The suppliant world protect, or else subdue.

On the Third of September, 1651[5]

As when the glorious magazine of light[6]
Approaches to his canopy of night,
He with new splendor clothes his dying rays,

2. I.e., Charles's mercy to his foes is a testament to his power. Such enemies would be threats to lesser kings and need to be subdued.
3. On 4 April 1660, Charles offered a general pardon as part of the Declaration of Breda. Parliament followed suit by passing the Act of Indemnity and Oblivion; cf. Dryden, "Astraea Redux," lines 258–259n, p. 649.
4. 1 Kings 10:1–13.
5. On 3 September 1651, the future Charles II and his army were soundly defeated at the Battle of Worcester. Charles became a fugitive and eventually fled to France; cf. Dryden "Astraea Redux," lines 73–74n, p. 644, and "To My Honored Friend, Dr. Charleton," lines 53–54n, p. 652.
6. I.e., the sun.

And double brightness to his beams conveys;
And (as to brave and check his ending fate)
Puts on his highest looks in's lowest state,
Dressed in such terror as to make us all
Be anti-Persians,[7] and adore his fall;
Then quits the world, depriving it of day,
While every herb and plant does droop away:
So when our gasping English royalty
Perceived her period[8] was now drawing nigh,
She summons her whole strength to give one blow,
To raise herself, or pull down others too.
Big with revenge and hope, she now spake more
Of terror than in many months before;[9]
And musters her attendants, or to save
Her from, or else attend her to the grave:
Yet but enjoyed the miserable fate
Of setting majesty, to die in state.
Unhappy kings, who cannot keep a throne,
Nor be so fortunate to fall alone!
Their weight sinks others: Pompey[1] could not fly,
But half the world must bear him company;
And captive Sampson[2] could not life conclude,
Unless attended with a multitude.
Who'd trust greatness now, whose food is air,
Whose ruin sudden, and whose end despair?
Who would presume upon his glorious birth,
Or quarrel for a spacious share of earth,
That sees such diadems become so cheap,
And heroes tumble in a common heap?
Oh give me virtue then, which sums up all,
And firmly stands when crowns and scepters fall.[3]

Friendship's Mystery, To My Dearest Lucasia[4]

SET BY MR. HENRY LAWES[5]

1.

Come, my Lucasia, since we see
That miracles men's faith do move,
By wonders and by prodigy
To the dull angry world let's prove
There's a religion in our love.

7. Persians were thought to worship the sun.
8. End.
9. Local uprisings preceded Charles II's invasion of England.
1. After his defeat at Pharsalus in 48 B.C., Pompey fled to Egypt.
2. Judges 16:25–30.
3. Cf. Shirley, "Dirge," p. 326.
4. Lucasia is Philips's name for Anne Owen, later Lady Dungannon. *Mystery*: "A religious truth known or understood only by divine revelation" (*OED*).
5. See the note on Carew's "A Divine Mistress," p. 295; Lawes set several of Philips's poems to music.

2.

For though we were designed t'agree,
  That fate no liberty destroys,
But our election is as free
  As angels, who with greedy choice
  Are yet determined to their joys.[6]

3.

Our hearts are doubled by their loss,
  Here mixture is addition grown;
We both diffuse, and both engross:
  And we whose minds are so much one,[7]
  Never, yet ever are alone.

4.

We court our own captivity
  Than greatest Thrones[8] more innocent:
'Twere banishment to be set free,
  Since we wear fetters whose intent
  Not bondage is, but ornament.

5.

Divided joys are tedious found,
  And griefs united easier grow:
We are ourselves but by rebound,
  And all our titles shuffled so,
  Both princes, and both subjects too.[9]

6.

Our hearts are mutual victims laid,
  While they (such power in friendship lies)
Are altars, priests, and off'rings made:
  And each heart which thus kindly[1] dies,
  Grows deathless by the sacrifice.

6. I.e., Orinda and Lucasia were created to love one another, and yet this fate does not change the fact that they freely choose to love. Thus they are like the angels who were created to love and serve God and actively elect to do so.
7. According to the classical friendship tradition, a perfect friendship would result in "one soul in two bodies."
8. One of the nine orders of angels; perhaps the thrones of earthly monarchs as well.
9. Cf. Donne, "The Sun Rising," lines 21–22, p. 25.
1. Naturally, benevolently.

A Retired Friendship, To Ardelia[2]

1.

Come, my Ardelia, to this bower,
Where kindly mingling souls a while,
Let's innocently spend an hour,
And at all serious follies smile.

2.

Here is no quarrelling for crowns,
Nor fear of changes in our fate;
No trembling at the great ones' frowns,
Nor any slavery of state.

3.

Here's no disguise, nor treachery,
Nor any deep concealed design;
From blood and plots this place is free,
And calm as are those looks of thine.

4.

Here let us sit and bless our stars,
Who did such happy quiet give,
As that removed from noise of wars
In one another's hearts we live.

5.

Why should we entertain a fear?
Love cares not how the world is turned:
If crowds of dangers should appear,
Yet friendship can be unconcerned.

6.

We wear about us such a charm,
No horror can be our offence;
For mischief's self can do no harm
To friendship or to innocence.

7.

Let's mark how soon Apollo's beams[3]
Command the flocks to quit their meat,[4]

2. Ardelia has not been identified. Manuscript versions of this poem are dated 23 August 1651.
3. I.e., sunbeams.
4. Food.

And not entreat the neighboring streams
To quench their thirst, but cool their heat.

8.

In such a scorching age as this,
Who would not ever seek a shade,
Deserve their happiness to miss,
As having their own peace betrayed.

9.

But we (of one another's mind
Assured), the boisterous world disdain;
With quiet souls, and unconfined,
Enjoy what princes wish in vain.

To the Excellent Mrs. Anne Owen, upon Her Receiving the Name of Lucasia, and Adoption into Our Society, December 28, 1651

We are complete, and fate hath now
No greater blessing to bestow:
No, the dull world must now confess
We have all worth, all happiness.
Annals of state are trifles to our fame,
Now 'tis made sacred by Lucasia's name.

But as though through a burning glass[5]
The sun more vigorous doth pass,
Yet still with general freedom shines;
For that contracts, but not confines:
So though by this her beams are fixed here,
Yet she diffuses glory everywhere.

Her mind is so entirely bright,
The splendor would but wound our sight,
And must to some disguise submit,
Or we could never worship it.
And we by this relation are allowed
Luster enough to be Lucasia's cloud.

Nations will own us now to be
A temple of divinity;
And pilgrims shall ten ages hence
Approach our tombs with reverence.

5. A lens that concentrates the rays of the sun on an object.

May then that time which did such bliss convey
Be kept by us perpetual holy day.[6]

To My Excellent Lucasia, on Our Friendship[7]

I did not live until this time
Crowned my felicity,
When I could say without a crime,
I am not thine, but thee.

This carcass[8] breathed, and walked, and slept,
So that the world believed
There was a soul the motions kept,
But they were all deceived.

For as a watch by art is wound
To motion, such was mine:[9]
But never had Orinda found
A soul till she found thine;

Which now inspires, cures, and supplies,
And guides my darkened breast:
For thou art all that I can prize,
My joy, my life, my rest.

No bridegroom's nor crown-conqueror's mirth
To mine compared can be:
They have but pieces of this earth;
I've all the world in thee.

Then let our flames still light and shine,
And no false fear control,
As innocent as our design,
Immortal as our soul.

To Mrs. M. A. at Parting[1]

1.

I have examined and do find,
Of all that favor me,
There's none I grieve to leave behind
But only, only thee.

6. Cf. Donne, "The Canonization," p. 26.
7. Manuscript versions of this poem are dated 17 July 1651.
8. Body.
9. Cf. Suckling, Sonnet II, lines 21–24n, p. 417.
1. M. A. stands for Mary Aubrey, a close friend and probably the first member of Philips's "Society of Friendship." Cf. Donne, "A Valediction: Forbidding Mourning," p. 36.

To part with thee I needs must die,
Could parting sep'rate thee and I.

2.

But neither chance nor complement[2]
Did element[3] our love;
'Twas sacred sympathy was lent
Us from the choir above.[4]
That friendship fortune did create,
Still fears a wound from time or fate.

3.

Our changed and mingled souls are grown
To such acquaintance now,
That if each would resume their own,
Alas! we know not how.
We have each other so engrossed,[5]
That each is in the union lost.

4.

And thus we can no absence know,
Nor shall we be confined;
Our active souls will daily go
To learn each other's mind.
Nay, should we never meet to sense,
Our souls would hold intelligence.[6]

5.

Inspired with a flame divine
I scorn to court a stay;
For from that noble soul of thine
I ne'er can be away.
But I shall weep when thou dost grieve;
Nor can I die whil'st thou dost live.

6.

By my own temper I shall guess
At thy felicity,
And only like my happiness
Because it pleaseth thee.
Our hearts at any time will tell
If thou, or I, be sick, or well.

2. Something that enhances or perfects something else.
3. Seal.
4. The music of the spheres was associated with celestial harmony and the angelic choir.
5. Absorbed.
6. I.e., even if our bodies never meet, our souls will still converse. Cf. Donne, "The Ecstasy," lines 13–14, p. 38.

7.

All honor sure I must pretend,[7]
All that is good or great;
She that would be Rosania's[8] friend,
Must be at least complete.
If I have any bravery,[9]
'Tis cause[1] I have so much of thee.

8.

Thy leiger[2] soul in me shall lie,
And all thy thoughts reveal;
Then back again with mine shall fly,
And thence to me shall steal.
Thus still to one another tend;
Such is the sacred name of friend.

9.

Thus our twin-souls in one shall grow,
And teach the world new love,
Redeem the age and sex, and show
A flame fate dares not move:
And courting death to be our friend,
Our lives together too shall end.

10.

A dew shall dwell upon our tomb
Of such a quality,
That fighting armies, thither come,
Shall reconcilèd be.
We'll ask no epitaph, but say
ORINDA and ROSANIA.

A Country Life[3]

How sacred and how innocent
A country life appears,
How free from tumult, discontent,
From flattery or fears!

7. Lay claim to.
8. The poetic name Philips gave to Aubrey.
9. I.e., if I have anything to boast of.
1. I.e., because.
2. Ambassadorial.
3. Cf. Jonson's "To Sir Robert Wroth," p. 100; Herrick's "The Country Life," p. 210; Fane's "To Retiredness," p. 334; and Randolph's "An Ode to . . . Stafford. . . . ," p. 342.

This was the first and happiest life,[4]
  When man enjoyed himself;
Till pride exchangèd peace for strife,
  And happiness for pelf.[5]
'Twas here the poets were inspired,
  Here taught the multitude;
The brave they here with honor fired,
  And civilized the rude.[6]
That golden age did entertain
  No passion but of love;
The thoughts of ruling and of gain
  Did ne'er their fancies move.
None then did envy neighbor's wealth,
  Nor plot to wrong his bed:
Happy in friendship and in health,
  On roots, not beasts, they fed.
They knew no law nor physic then;
  Nature was all their wit,
And if there yet remain to men
  Content, sure this is it.
What blessings doth this world afford
  To tempt or bribe desire?
Her[7] courtship is all fire and sword,
  Who would not then retire?
Then welcome dearest solitude,
  My great felicity;
Though some are pleased to call thee rude,
  Thou are not so, but we.
Them that do covet only rest,
  A cottage will suffice:
It is not brave to be possessed
  Of earth, but to despise.
Opinion is the rate of things,[8]
  From which our peace doth flow;
I have a better fate than kings,
  Because I think it so.
When all the stormy world doth roar,
  How unconcerned am I?
I cannot fear to tumble lower
  Who never could be high.
Secure in these unenvied walls
  I think not on the state,
And pity no man's case[9] that falls

4. I.e., the golden age described by classical poets, a primordial state of perfection from which humankind has declined.
5. A disparaging term for money.
6. For the didactic and civilizing power of poetry, cf. Horace, *The Arts of Poetry*, lines 301–401.
7. I.e., the world's.
8. I.e., opinion determines the value of things.
9. State, situation.

From his ambition's height.
Silence and innocence are safe;
A heart that's nobly true
At all these little arts[1] can laugh
That do the world subdue.
While others revel it in state,
Here I'll contented sit,
And think I have as good a fate
As wealth and pomp admit.
Let some in courtship take delight,
And to th'Exchange[2] resort,
Then revel out a winter's night,
Not making love, but sport.
These never know a noble flame,
'Tis lust, scorn, or design:
While vanity plays all their game,
Let peace and honor mine.
When the inviting spring appears,
To Hyde Park[3] let them go,
And hasting thence be full of fears
To lose Spring Garden[4] show.
Let others (nobler) seek to gain
In knowledge happy fate,
And others busy them in vain
To study ways of state.
But I, resolvèd from within,
Confirmèd from without,
In privacy intend to spin
My future minutes out.
And from this hermitage of mine
I banish all wild toys,
And nothing that is not divine
Shall dare to tempt my joys.
There are below but two things good,
Friendship and honesty,
And only those of all I would
Ask for felicity.[5]
In this retired and humble seat
Free from both war and strife,
I am not forced to make retreat
But choose to spend my life.

1. Strategies.
2. The New Exchange, built between 1566 and 1568, was a fashionable bazaar that was destroyed by the Great Fire of London (1666).
3. Hyde Park was a fashionable promenade; cf. Randolph, "An Ode to . . . Stafford . . . ," lines 32–36 and note, p. 343.
4. Part of St. James's Park; cf. Waller's "On St. James's Park, As Lately Improved by His Majesty," p. 370.
5. I.e., the only two things that I need for happiness are friendship and honesty.

Epitaph. On Her Son H. P. at St. Sith's Church[6]

What on earth deserves our trust?
Youth and beauty both are dust.
Long we gathering are with pain,
What one moment calls again.
Seven years childless marriage past,
A son, a son is born at last;
So exactly limned[7] and fair,
Full of good spirits, mien,[8] and air,
As a long life promisèd;
Yet, in less than six weeks, dead.
Too promising, too great a mind
In so small room to be confined:
Therefore, as fit in Heav'n to dwell,
He quickly broke the prison shell.
So the subtle alchemist,
Can't with Hermes' seal[9] resist
The powerful spirit's subtler flight,
But 'twill bid him long good night.
And so the sun, if it arise
Half so glorious as his eyes,
Like this infant, takes a shroud,
Buried in a morning cloud.

Against Love

Hence Cupid with your cheating toys,
Your real griefs, and painted joys,
Your pleasure which itself destroys.
  Lovers like men in fevers burn and rave,
  And only what will injure them do crave.
Men's weakness makes Love so severe;
They give him power by their fear,
And make the shackles, which they wear.
  Who to another does his heart submit,
  Makes his own idol and then worships it.
Him whose heart is all his own,
Peace and liberty does crown;
He apprehends no killing frown.
  He feels no raptures,[1] which are joys diseased,
  And is not much transported, but still pleased.

6. Philips's only son, Hector, was born on 23 April 1655 and died on 2 May 1655. St. Sith's Church burned down in the Great Fire (1666).
7. Drawn.
8. Expression.
9. Hermetic seal: a complete, airtight seal named after Hermes Trismegistus, the legendary founder of alchemy.
1. Cf. Carew, "A Rapture," p. 302.

An Answer to Another Persuading a Lady to Marriage

1.

Forbear bold youth, all's heaven here,
And what you do aver,[2]
To others courtship may appear,
'Tis sacrilege to her.

2.

She is a public deity,
And were't not very odd
She should depose herself to be
A petty household god?

3.

First make the sun in private shine,
And bid the world adieu,
That so he may his beams confine
In compliment to you.[3]

4.

But if of that you do despair,
Think how you did amiss,
To strive to fix her beams which are
More bright and large than his.

2. Assert.
3. Cf. Donne, "The Sun Rising," p. 25.

Thomas Traherne

1637 Born in Hereford, the son of a shoemaker of Welsh descent.
1656 Takes his B.A. from Brasenose College, Oxford.
1660 Ordained an Anglican priest.
1661 Becomes rector at Credenhill in Herefordshire; he holds this position until his death.
1667 In London as chaplain to Sir Orlando Bridgeman, Keeper of the Great Seal.
1669 Takes M.A. and B.D. at Oxford.
1673 Publishes *Roman Forgeries*, an anti-Catholic polemic.
1674 Dies in Sir Orlando's house at Teddington in Middlesex, where he served as vicar. Buried in the church there on 10 October.
1675 Publication of *Christian Ethics*.
1699 Publication of the *Thanksgivings*.
1897 The manuscripts of *Centuries of Meditations* and his poems are discovered in London bookstalls.

FROM THE *DOBELL FOLIO*

The Salutation[1]

1

These little limbs,
These eyes and hands which here I find,
These rosy cheeks wherewith my life begins,
Where have ye been? Behind
What curtain were ye from me hid so long!
Where was, in what abyss, my speaking tongue?

2

When silent I,
So many thousand thousand years,
Beneath the dust did in a chaos lie,
How could I smiles or tears,
Or lips or hands or eyes or ears perceive?
Welcome ye treasures which I now receive.

3

I that so long
Was nothing from eternity,
Did little think such joys as ear or tongue,
To celebrate or see:
Such sounds to hear, such hands to feel, such feet,
Beneath the skies, on such a ground to meet.

4

New burnished joys!
Which yellow gold and pearl excel!
Such sacred treasures are the limbs in boys,
In which a soul doth dwell;
Their organizèd joints and azure veins
More wealth include, than all the world contains.

5

From dust I rise,
And out of nothing now awake;
These brighter regions which salute mine eyes,
A gift from God I take;
The earth, the seas, the light, the day, the skies,
The sun and stars are mine; if those I prize.

1. The first six poems are from Thomas Traherne's manuscript. See Textual Notes.

6

Long time before
I in my mother's womb was born,
A God preparing did this glorious store,
The world for me adorn.
Into this Eden so divine and fair,
So wide and bright, I come his son and heir.

7

A stranger here
Strange things doth meet, strange glories see;
Strange treasures lodged in this fair world appear,
Strange all, and new to me.
But that they mine should be, who nothing was,
That strangest is of all, yet brought to pass.

Wonder

1

How like an angel came I down!
How bright are all things here!
When first among his works I did appear
O how their glory me did crown!
The world resembled his eternity,
In which my soul did walk;
And everything that I did see,
Did with me talk.

2

The skies in their magnificence,
The lively, lovely air;
Oh how divine, how soft, how sweet, how fair!
The stars did entertain my sense.[2]
And all the works of God so bright and pure,
So rich and great did seem,
As if they ever must endure,
In my esteem.

3

A native health and innocence
Within my bones did grow,
And while my God did all his glories show,
I felt a vigor in my sense
That was all spirit. I within did flow
With seas of life, like wine;

2. Sensory apprehension, especially sight.

I nothing in the world did know,
But 'twas divine.

4

Harsh ragged objects were concealed,
Oppressions, tears and cries,
Sins, griefs, complaints, dissensions, weeping eyes,
Were hid: and only things revealed,
Which heavenly spirits and the angels prize.
The state of innocence
And bliss, not trades and poverties,
Did fill my sense.

5

The streets were paved with golden stones,
The boys and girls were mine,
Oh how did all their lovely faces shine!
The sons of men were holy ones.
Joy, beauty, welfare did appear to me,
And everything which here I found,
While like an angel I did see,
Adorned the ground.

6

Rich diamond and pearl and gold
In everyplace was seen;
Rare splendors, yellow, blue, red, white, and green,
Mine eyes did everywhere behold;
Great wonders clothed with glory did appear;
Amazement was my bliss,
That and my wealth was everywhere:
No joy to this![3]

7

Cursed and devisèd proprieties,[4]
With envy, avarice
And fraud, those fiends that spoil even Paradise,
Fled from the splendor of mine eyes.
And so did hedges, ditches, limits, bounds:
I dreamed not aught of those,
But wandered over all men's grounds,
And found repose.

8

Proprieties themselves were mine,
And hedges ornaments;

3. I.e., in comparison to this.
4. *Devisèd*: legally willed, or (perhaps) contrived; *proprieties*: properties, possessions.

Walls, boxes, coffers, and their rich contents
Did not divide my joys, but shine.[5]
Clothes, ribbons, jewels, laces, I esteemed
My joys by others worn;
For me they all to wear them seemed
When I was born.

Eden

1

A learned and a happy ignorance[6]
Divided me,
From all vanity,
From all the sloth, care, pain and sorrow that advance,
The madness and the misery
Of men. No error, no distraction I
Saw soil the earth, or overcloud the sky.

2

I knew not that there was a serpent's sting,
Whose poison shed
On men, did overspread
The world: nor did I dream of such a thing
As sin; in which mankind lay dead.
They all were brisk and living wights[7] to me,
Yea pure, and full of immortality.

3

Joy, pleasure, beauty, kindness, glory, love,
Sleep, day, life, light,
Peace, melody, my sight,
My ears and heart did fill, and freely move.
All that I saw did me delight.
The universe was then a world of treasure,
To me an universal world of pleasure.

4

Unwelcome penitence was then unknown,
Vain costly toys,
Swearing and roaring boys,
Shops, markets, taverns, coaches were unshown;

5. In *The Third Century*, Traherne wrote: "I knew no Churlish Proprieties, nor Bounds nor Divisions: but all Proprieties and Divisions were mine: all Treasures and the Possessors of them" (H. M. Margoliouth, Oxford edition of Traherne [1958], vol. I, p. 111).
6. Nicholas of Cusa (c. 1401–1464) wrote *De docta ignorantia* (*Of Learned Ignorance*), a Neoplatonist work of rational speculation and intuition, on God's infinity, the tension of opposites, God's creative activity, and the necessity of thinking of God in analogies and negatives.
7. Persons.

So all things were that drowned my joys.
No briars choked up my path, nor hid the face
Of bliss and beauty, nor eclipsed the place.

5

Only what Adam in his first estate,
Did I behold;
Hard silver and dry gold
As yet lay underground; my blessed fate
Was more acquainted with the old
And innocent delights, which he did see
In his original simplicity.

6

Those things which first his Eden did adorn,
My infancy
Did crown. Simplicity
Was my protection when I first was born.
Mine eyes those treasures first did see
Which God first made. The first effects of love
My first enjoyments upon earth did prove;

7

And were so great, and so divine, so pure,
So fair and sweet,
So true; when I did meet
Them here at first, they did my soul allure,
And drew away my infant feet
Quite from the works of men; that I might see
The glorious wonders of the Deity.

The Rapture

1

Sweet infancy!
O fire of Heav'n! O sacred light!
How fair and bright!
How great am I,
Whom all the world doth magnify!

2

O heav'nly joy!
O great and sacred blessedness,
Which I possess!
So great a joy
Who did into my arms convey!

3

From God above
Being sent,[8] the heavens me enflame,
To praise his Name.
The stars do move![9]
The burning sun doth show his love.

4

O how divine
Am I! To all this sacred wealth,
This life and health,
Who raised? Who mine
Did make the same? What hand divine!

My Spirit[1]

1

My naked simple life was I.
That act so strongly shined
Upon the earth, the sea, the sky,
That was the substance of my mind.
The sense itself was I.
I felt no dross nor matter in my soul,
No brims nor borders, such as in a bowl
We see; my essence was capacity
That felt all things,
The thought that springs
Therefrom's itself. It hath no other wings
To spread abroad, nor eyes to see,
Nor hands distinct to feel,
Nor knees to kneel:
But being simple like the Deity
In its own center is a sphere
Not shut up here, but everywhere.[2]

2

It acts not from a center to
Its object as remote,
But present is, when it doth view
Being with the being it doth note.
Whatever it doth do,

8. The joy (of line 9).
9. I.e., move me to praise.
1. "This is Traherne's most comprehensive poem. It contains the experience of the Infant Eye reflected on in maturity, the mature experience of the Infant Eye regained, the mature man's mystical inner experience, and all three united in an act of the understanding which is itself a further experience" (Margoliouth, vol. II, p. 349).
2. God conventionally is described as a sphere whose center is everywhere.

It doth not by another engine work,
But by itself; which in the act doth lurk.
Its essence is transformed into a true
And perfect act.
And so exact
Hath God appeared in this mysterious fact,
That 'tis all eye, all act, all sight,
And what it please can be,
Not only see,
Or do; for 'tis more voluble[3] than light:
Which can put on ten thousand forms,
Being clothed with what itself adorns.

3

This made me present evermore
With whatsoe'er I saw,
An object, if it were before
My eye, was by Dame Nature's law,
Within my soul. Her store
Was all at once within me; all her treasures
Were my immediate and internal pleasures,
Substantial joys, which did inform my mind.
With all she wrought,
My soul was fraught,
And every object in my soul a thought
Begot, or was; I could not tell,
Whether the things did there
Themselves appear,
Which in my spirit truly seemed to dwell;
Or whether my conforming mind
Were not alone ev'n all that shined.

4

But yet of this I was most sure,
That at the utmost length,
(So worthy was it to endure)
My soul could best express its strength.
It was so quick and pure,
That all my mind was wholly everywhere
Whate'er it saw, 'twas ever wholly there;
The sun ten thousand legions[4] off, was nigh:
The utmost star,
Though seen from far,
Was present in the apple of my eye.
There was my sight, my life, my sense,
My substance and my mind,

3. Protean.
4. Multitudes, "presumably of miles, though leagues may have had something to do with suggesting the odd but effective use of the word here" (Margoliouth, vol. II, p. 350).

My spirit shined
Ev'n there, not by a transient[5] influence.
The act was immanent, yet there.
The thing remote, yet felt ev'n here.

5

O joy! O wonder and delight!
O sacred mystery!
My soul a spirit infinite!
An image of the Deity!
A pure substantial light!
That being greatest which doth nothing seem!
Why 'twas my all, I nothing did esteem
But that alone. A strange mysterious sphere!
A deep abyss
That sees and is
The only proper place or bower of bliss.
To its Creator 'tis so near
In love and excellence,
In life and sense,
In greatness, worth and nature; and so dear;
In it, without hyperbole,
The son and friend of God we see.

6

A strange extended orb of joy,
Proceeding from within,
Which did on every side convey
Itself, and being nigh of kin
To God did every way
Dilate itself ev'n in an instant, and
Like an indivisible center stand
At once surrounding all eternity.
'Twas not a sphere
Yet did appear
One infinite. 'Twas somewhat everywhere.
And though it had a power to see
Far more, yet still it shined
And was a mind
Exerted for it saw infinity
'Twas not a sphere, but 'twas a power
Invisible, and yet a bower.

7

O wondrous self! O sphere of light,
O sphere of joy most fair;
O act, O power infinite;

5. The text reads "Transeunt," a spelling used only when the word is opposed to "immanent" (line 67) rather than to "permanent."

O subtle, and unbounded air!
O living orb of sight!
Thou which within me art, yet me! Thou eye,
And temple of his whole infinity!
O what a world art thou! a world within!
All things appear,
All objects are
Alive in thee! Supersubstantial, rare,
Above themselves, and nigh of kin
To those pure things we find
In his great mind
Who made the world! though now eclipsed by sin.
There they are useful and divine,
Exalted there they ought to shine.

Love

1

O nectar! O delicious stream!
O ravishing and only pleasure! Where
Shall such another theme
Inspire my tongue with joys, or please mine ear!
Abridgement of delights!
And queen of sights!
O mine of rarities! O kingdom wide!
O more! O cause of all! O glorious bride!
O God! O Bride of God! O King!
O soul and crown of everything!

2

Did not I covet to behold
Some endless monarch, that did always live
In palaces of gold,
Willing all kingdoms, realms and crowns to give
Unto my soul! Whose love
A spring might prove
Of endless glories, honors, friendships, pleasures,
Joys, praises, beauties and celestial treasures!
Lo, now I see there's such a King,
The fountainhead of everything!

3

Did my ambition ever dream
Of such a Lord, of such a love! Did I
Expect so sweet a stream
As this at any time! Could any eye
Believe it? Why all power
Is used here

Joys down from heaven on my head to shower,
And Jove beyond the fiction doth appear
Once more in golden rain to come
To Danae's pleasing fruitful womb.[6]

4

His Ganymede![7] His life! His joy!
Or he comes down to me, or takes me up
That I might be his boy,
And fill, and taste, and give, and drink the cup.
But these (though great) are all
Too short and small,
Too weak and feeble pictures to express
The true mysterious depths of blessedness.
I am his image and his friend.
His son, bride, glory, temple, end.

FROM *THE THIRD CENTURY*

On News

1

News from a foreign country came,
As if my treasure and my wealth lay there:
So much it did my heart enflame!
'Twas wont to call my soul into mine ear.
Which thither went to meet
The approaching sweet:
And on the threshold stood,
To entertain[8] the unknown good.
It hovered there,
As if 'twould leave mine ear.
And was so eager to embrace
The joyful tidings as they came,
'Twould almost leave its dwelling place
To entertain the same.

2

As if the tidings were the things,
My very joys themselves, my foreign treasure,
Or else did bear them on their wings;

6. Jove, in the form of a shower of golden rain, visited Danaë in her bronze tower and lay with her; their offspring was Perseus.
7. The shepherd Ganymede was so beautiful that Jupiter fell in love with him and, in the form of an eagle, swooped down, carried him off to Olympus, and made him his cupbearer.
8. Receive.

With so much joy they came, with so much pleasure.
My soul stood at the gate
To recreate[9]
Itself with bliss: and to
Be pleased with speed. A fuller view
It fain would take
Yet journeys back would make
Unto my heart: as if 'twould fain
Go out to meet, yet stay within
To fit a place, to entertain,
And bring the tidings in.

3

What sacred instinct did inspire
My soul in childhood with a hope so strong?
What secret force moved my desire,
To expect my joys beyond the seas, so young?
Felicity I knew
Was out of view:
And being here alone,
I saw that happiness was gone,
From me! for this,
I thirsted[1] absent bliss,
And thought that sure beyond the seas,
Or else in something near at hand
I knew not yet (since naught did please
I knew) my bliss did stand.

4

But little did the infant dream
That all the treasures of the world were by:
And that himself was so the cream
And crown of all, which round about did lie.
Yet thus it was. The gem,
The diadem,
The ring enclosing all
That stood upon this earthy ball;
The heavenly eye,
Much wider than the sky,
Wherein they all included were;
The glorious soul that was the king
Made to possess them, did appear
A small and little thing!

9. Refresh.
1. Thirsted for.

FROM THE *BURNEY MANUSCRIPT*

The Return[2]

To infancy, O Lord, again I come,
That I my manhood may improve:
My early tutor is the womb;[3]
I still my cradle love.
'Tis strange that I should wisest be,
When least I could an error see.

Till I gain strength against temptation, I
Perceive it safest to abide
An infant still; and therefore fly
(A lowly state may hide
A man from danger) to the womb,
That I may yet new-born become.

My God, thy bounty then did ravish me!
Before I learnèd to be poor,
I always did thy riches see,
And thankfully adore:
Thy glory and thy goodness were
My sweet companions all the year.

Shadows in the Water[4]

In unexperienced infancy
Many a sweet mistake doth lie:
Mistake though false, intending[5] true;
A seeming somewhat more than view;
That doth instruct the mind
In things that lie behind,
And many secrets to us show
Which afterwards we come to know.

Thus did I by the water's brink
Another world beneath me think;
And while the lofty spacious skies
Reversèd there abused mine eyes,
I fancied other feet

2. On this and the following poems, see Textual Notes.
3. Margoliouth cites "not Freud, but John 3:3–4," where Christ says, "Except a man be born again, he cannot see the kingdom of God," and Nicodemus responds, "How can a man be born when he is old? Can he enter the second time into his mother's womb?"
4. "The reminiscence of childish, and probably also later, intense interest in reflections in water is linked with adult thought of worlds other than the world of our particular sense impressions. But even the child is at least half-consciously exercising his fancy in play (cf. lines 33–40) and so is the adult" (Margoliouth, vol. II, p. 377).
5. Meaning.

Came mine to touch and meet;
As by some puddle I did play
Another world within it lay.

Beneath the water people drowned,
Yet with another heaven crowned,
In spacious regions seemed to go
Freely moving to and fro:[6]
In bright and open space
I saw their very face;
Eyes, hands, and feet they had like mine;
Another sun did with them shine.

'Twas strange that people there should walk,
And yet I could not hear them talk:
That through a little wat'ry chink,
Which one dry ox or horse might drink,
We other worlds should see,
Yet not admitted be;
And other confines there behold
Of light and darkness, heat and cold.

I called them oft, but called in vain;
No speeches we could entertain:
Yet did I there expect to find
Some other world to please my mind.
I plainly saw by these
A new Antipodes,[7]
Whom, though they were so plainly seen,
A film kept off that stood between.

By walking men's reversèd feet
I chanced another world to meet;
Though it did not to view exceed
A phantasm, 'tis a world indeed,
Where skies beneath us shine,
And earth by art divine
Another face presents below,
Where people's feet against ours go.

Within the regions of the air,
Compassed about with heavens fair,
Great tracts of land there may be found
Enriched with fields and fertile ground;
Where many numerous hosts,
In those far distant coasts,
For other great and glorious ends,
Inhabit, my yet unknown friends.

6. The idea of a kingdom beneath the waves is a motif common in Celtic folklore.
7. Those "far distant coasts" (line 54) presumed to be on the other side of the world.

Oh ye that stand upon the brink,
Whom I so near me, through the chink,
With wonder see: what faces there,
Whose feet, whose bodies, do ye wear?
I my companions see
In you, another me.
They seemèd others, but are we;
Our second selves those shadows be.

Look how far off those lower skies
Extend themselves! Scarce with mine eyes
I can them reach. O ye my friends,
What secret borders on those ends?
Are lofty heavens hurled
'Bout your inferior[8] world?
Are ye the representatives
Of other peoples' distant lives?

Of all the playmates which I knew
That here I do the image view
In other selves; what can it mean?
But that below the purling stream
Some unknown joys there be
Laid up in store for me;
To which I shall, when that thin skin
Is broken, be admitted in.

On Leaping over the Moon[9]

I saw new worlds beneath the water lie;
New people; and another sky,
And sun, which seen by day
Might things more clear display.
Just such another[1]
Of late my brother
Did in his travel see, and saw by night
A much more strange and wondrous sight:
Nor could the world exhibit such another,
So great a sight, but in a brother.

Adventure strange! No such in store we
New or old, true or feignèd, see.
On earth he seemed to move
Yet heaven went above;[2]

8. Lower.
9. "The first four stanzas (lines 5–40) relate [Traherne's brother] Philip's youthful adventure and delight. It is pure fancy. The last three (lines 41–70) give it an imaginative application" (Margoliouth, vol. II, p. 378).
1. Another world.
2. I.e., he went above heaven.

Up in the skies
His body flies
In open, visible, yet magic sort:
As he along the way did sport
Like Icarus over the flood he soars
Without the help of wings or oars.

As he went tripping o'er the King's highway,
A little pearly river lay
O'er which, without a wing
Or oar, he dared to swim,
Swim through the air
On body fair;
He would not use nor trust Icarian wings[3]
Lest they should prove deceitful things;
For had he fall'n, it had been wondrous high,
Not from, but from above, the sky:

He might have dropped through that thin element
Into a fathomless descent;
Unto the nether sky
That did beneath him lie,
And there might tell
What wonders dwell
On earth above. Yet bold he briskly runs
And soon the danger overcomes;
Who, as he leapt, with joy related soon
How happy he o'er-leapt the moon.

What wondrous things upon the earth are done
Beneath, and yet above, the sun?
Deeds all appear again
In higher spheres; remain
In clouds as yet:
But there they get
Another light, and in another way
Themselves to us above display,
The skies themselves this earthly globe surround;[4]
We're even here within them found.

On heav'nly ground within the skies we walk,
And in this middle center talk:
Did we but wisely move,
On earth in heaven above,
We then should be
Exalted high

3. With wings fashioned by his father, Daedalus, Icarus flew too near the sun, and the wax fastening his wings melted.
4. "On the playful level because above us and also reflected below us, on the scientific level because all round the globe, on the spiritual level because heaven is all about us" (Margoliouth, vol. II, p. 379).

Above the sky: from whence whoever falls,
Through a long dismal precipice,
Sinks to the deep abyss where Satan crawls
Where horrid Death and Despair lies.

As much as others thought themselves to lie
Beneath the moon, so much more high
Himself he thought to fly
Above the starry sky,
As that he spied
Below the tide.
Thus did he yield me in the shady night
A wondrous and instructive light,
Which taught me that under our feet there is,
As o'er our heads, a place of bliss.

TEXTUAL NOTES

The texts of the poems in this edition are derived from the most authoritative early editions. In most cases, this means that our copy text is the first edition; but in instances where later editions are preferable, we have based our texts upon them. For example, we have taken the authorized 1667 edition of Philips's *Poems* as our copy text rather than the 1664 edition, and the 1668 edition of Waller's *Poems* has been preferred to the 1645 and 1664 editions. However, there are two major exceptions to this rule. As Mario Di Cesare explains in the textual note to George Herbert, the Bodleian and Williams manuscripts of Herbert's poems have more authority than the posthumous 1633 edition of *The Temple*, and thus we have given preference to the manuscripts. Since there were no published editions of Thomas Traherne's poetry until the twentieth century, the texts of his poems are also based on manuscripts. There are some minor exceptions as well. For instance, three of Donne's Holy Sonnets are based on the Westmoreland manuscript, while Milton's Sonnet 16 is based on the Cambridge manuscript. Textual notes on each author record the individual editions (or manuscripts) that we have taken as our copy texts.

The spelling and punctuation of the poems in this edition have been modernized. As consistently as possible, we have adhered to the principles that Hugh Maclean set out in his original edition. Spelling has been modernized throughout, except when such changes would obscure rhyme, meter, or meaning. Certain other emendations have been fairly straightforward: (1) italicized proper names are given in roman type; (2) the use of *i*, *u*, and *v* is regularized to conform with modern practice; (3) the ampersand is replaced by *and*; (4) diphthongs are replaced by separate characters; (5) quotations are punctuated in accord with modern practice; (6) the silent *e* is substituted for the apostrophe in such words as *annoy'd* and *abandon'd*; and (7) accents are inserted over the *e* of final *-ed* to indicate voicing of the extra syllable.

But imposing consistent punctuation upon the entire volume is problematic. As Maclean stressed, to modernize the work of a single seventeenth-century poet without altering its original meaning is itself a challenge; to do so with the work of numerous poets, while imposing a uniform standard of punctuation, is simply not practicable. The heterogeneous origin of this edition compounds the problem. Maclean and Di Cesare took different tacks in modernizing the texts in their original editions, while we have established our own procedures for modernizing the texts that we have added. Faced with reconciling three different editorial practices, we have occasionally sacrificed consistency for the sake of retaining the virtues of our precursors. This is particularly true for the Herbert poems and textual notes, which are informed by Mario Di Cesare's work on the Bodleian and Williams manuscripts. Nonetheless, we have worked to produce a coherent volume, and readers familiar with the Maclean and Di Cesare editions will recognize places where we have worked to resolve differences between those volumes. In emending punctuation, the goal of all the editors has been to produce accessible texts for modern readers without effacing the distinct style of individual poets. Whenever possible, we have let the seventeenth-century punctuation stand; but in numerous instances, we have removed or adjusted punctuation. Only rarely have we added punctuation. Capitalization in the seventeenth century is inconsistent, more so for some poets and early editors than others. We have generally followed modern practice, except when personifications (Nature, Fate, Love) are overt.

The breadth of this edition has made including a complete critical apparatus for each poet untenable. But we have provided textual variants that we believe are particularly salient, such as those for Donne, Herbert, and Denham. "MS." signifies one manuscript; "MSS." two or more manuscripts; "om.," omitted in; and "corr.," corrected.

AEMILIA LANYER

The text is based on a copy of *Salve Deus Rex Judaeorum* in the British Library, as photographed for Early English Books Online. There are no substantive variants from this edition.

JOHN DONNE

Establishing the texts for Donne's poems is notoriously challenging and a problem too vast and complicated to recount in detail here. Suffice it to say that three major and to some degree independent seventeenth-century editions of Donne's poems (1633, 1635, 1669) were published after Donne's death. Copies of all these editions, held in the Harry Ransom Humanities Research Center at the University of Texas at Austin, were consulted. With few exceptions (e.g., "The Anatomy of the World"), Donne's poems circulated in manuscript during his life, and as Donne's reputation grew, collections of his poetry in manuscript multiplied, some of them proving more authoritative than others.

For this edition, the 1633 edition is used as the copy text, except for those poems that were first printed in a later edition, or for which a text published during Donne's lifetime exists. These exceptions are listed below, with the copy text in parentheses.

Farewell to Love (*1635*)
A Lecture upon the Shadow (*1635*)
Elegy 8: To His Mistress Going to Bed (*1669*)
Elegy 14: Love's Progress (*1669*)
An Anatomy of the World (*1611*)
Holy Sonnet 17 (*Westmoreland MS.*)
Holy Sonnet 18 (*Westmoreland MS.*)
Holy Sonnet 19 (*Westmoreland MS.*)
Hymn to God My God, in My Sickness (*1635*)

The textual authority for each of these poems also appears in the right-hand margin beneath the last line of the poem as printed in this edition. The primary source of information regarding the manuscripts of Donne's poetry is Sir Herbert Grierson's edition, *The Poems of John Donne*. Theodore Redpath's edition of *The Songs and Sonnets of John Donne* was also consulted. Finally, for the text and numbering of the elegies, the copy here generally adheres to the Donne variorum. The variants listed below are substantive and indicate deviations from the copy text only. Where appropriate, other significant variants are discussed in the annotations of the poems.

Songs and Sonnets

The Good-Morrow

Division into stanzas *1635*; no division into stanzas *1633*.

17/ fitter hemispheres *1635–1669*; better hemispheres *1633*.

The Indifferent

4/ whom *1669*; who *1633–1635*.

The Anniversary

22/ But we no more *MSS.*; But now no more *1633–1669*.

Twickenham Garden

15/ Endure, nor leave this garden, *1635–1669 and MSS.*; Endure, nor yet leave loving, *1633*.
24/ woman's *MSS.*; women's *1633–1669 and MSS.*

The Bait

title/ The Bait *1635–1669*; no title *1633*.

The Ecstasy

Division into quatrains *MSS.*; no stanza breaks *1633*.

25/ knew *1635 and MSS.*; knows *1633*.
42/ Interinanimates *MSS.*; Interanimates *1633–1669 and MSS.*
51/ though they're not *MSS.*; though not *1633–1669*.
55/ forces, sense *MSS.*; senses force *1633–1669*.
59/ So *MSS.*; For *1633–1669*.

The Funeral

6/ then to *MSS.*; unto *1633–1669*.
12 / These *MSS.*; Those *1633–1669*.
17/ with me *1635–1669 and MSS.*; by me 1633.
24/ save *MSS.*; have *1633–1669 and MSS.*

The Blossom

10/ labor'st *MSS.*; labors *1633*.
23/ tongue *MSS.*; taste *1633–1669*.
24/ need you a *MSS.*; need your *1633–1669*.
38/ would *MSS.*; will *1633–1669*.

The Damp

24/ Naked *1635–1669 and MSS.*; In that *1633 and MSS.*

A Lecture upon the Shadow

4/ In walking *MSS.*; Walking *1635–1669 and MSS.*

Elegies

Elegy 8. To His Mistress Going to Bed

5/ glistering *MSS.*; glittering *1669*.
10/ 'tis your *MSS.*; it is *1669*.
14/ from *MSS.*; through *1669*.
17/ safely *MSS.*; softly *1669 and MSS.*
20/ Received by *MSS.*; Reveal'd to *1669*.
26/ Behind, before, above, between, below *MSS.*; Before, behind, between, above, below *1669*.
28/ safliest *MSS.*; safest *1669*.
30/ How blest am I in this *MSS.*; How am I blest thus *1669 and MSS.*
36/ balls *MSS.*; ball *1669*.
38/ covet *MSS.*; court *1669 and MSS.*
38/ theirs *MSS.*; that *1669 and MSS.*
41/ Themselves are mystic books, which only we *MSS.*; Themselves are only mystic books, which we *1669*.
44/ a *MSS.*; thy *1669*.

Elegy 13. The Autumnal

3/ your love *1635–1654 and MSS.*; our love *1633 and MSS.*
8/ she's *1635–1669 and MSS.*; they're *1633*.
10/ habitable *1635–1669 and MSS.*; tolerable *1633 and MSS.*
44/ ancient . . . antiquesy *MSS.*; ancient . . . antique *1633, 1669, and MSS.*
47/ natural lation *MSS.*; motion natural *1633*.
50/ on *1635–1669 and MSS.*; out *1633*.

Elegy 14. Love's Progress

47/ first meridian *MSS.*; sweet meridian *1669*.
60/ O'erpast . . . between *MSS.*; Being past the Straits of Hellespont between *1669*.
63/ that *MSS.*; yet *1669*.
70/ some do *MSS.*; many *1669*.
96/ clyster gave *MSS.*; glister gives *1669*.

Sappho to Philaenis

58/ thee *1635–1669 and MSS.*; she *1633*.

Satires

Satire 3

7/ to *1635–1669 and MSS.*; in *1633 and MSS.*
33/ Know thy foes: the foul Devil, whom thou *MSS.*; Know thy foe, the foul devil h'is, whom thou *1633*.
47/ her *MSS.*; the *1633–1669*.
57/ bid *MSS.*; bids *1633–1669*.
90/ here *MSS.*; om. *1633–1669*.
95/ Oh *MSS.*; om. *1633*.

Verse Letters

The Storm

47/ graves *1669 and MSS.*; grave *1633.*
66/ Bermudas *1635 and MSS.*; Bermuda *1633 and MSS.*
67/ elder *MSS.*; eldest *1633–1669 and MSS.*
68/ Claims *1635–1669 and MSS.*; Claim'd *1633.*

The Calm

38/ pinnaces *1635 and MSS.*; venices *1633 and MSS.*

To Sir Henry Wotton

11/ even *1669 and MSS.*; raging *1633.*
12/ poles *MSS.*; pole *1633–1669 and MSS.*
18/ and *MSS.*; or *1633–1669 and MSS.*
22/ there were *MSS.*; they were *1633.*
44/ for *MSS.*; in *1633–1669.*

To the Countess of Bedford ("Madame, You have refined me")

60/ thing *MSS.*; things *1633–1669 and MS.*

Divine Poems

Holy Sonnet 4 [VII]

6/ dearth *Westmoreland MS.*; death *1633–1669 and MSS.*

Holy Sonnet 6 [X]

10/ dost *1669*; doth *1633–1635.*

Holy Sonnet 9 [XIII]

4/ that *MSS.*; his *1633–1669 and MSS.*
14/ assures *MSS.*; assumes *1633–1669.*

Good Friday, 1613. Riding Westward

4/ motions *MSS.*; motion *1633–1669.*

A Hymn to Christ, at the Author's Last Going into Germany

12/ sea *MSS.*; seas *1633.*

Hymn to God My God, in My Sickness

12/ their current *MS.*; those currents *1635–1669.*

A Hymn to God the Father

2/ is *MSS.*; was *1633–1669.*
18/ have *MSS.*; fear *1633–1669.*

BEN JONSON

The text of the *Epigrams* and *The Forest* in this edition is based on a copy of the 1616 edition of the *Works* in the Cambridge University Library; the texts of poems in *Underwood* and (with one exception) those of the songs from Jonson's plays and masques are based on a copy of the 1640–1641 edition of the *Works* in the same library. The text of "To the Memory of . . . Mr. William Shakespeare" is based on a copy of the text in *Mr. William Shakespeare's Comedies, Histories, and Tragedies* (1623) in the Harry Ransom Humanities Research Center at the University of Texas at Austin; that of "Ode to Himself" ("Come leave the loathèd stage") on a microfilm copy of the text in *Ben Jonson's Execration against Vulcan* (1640, noted as Q in the list of variants) in the British Museum. Manuscript information (together with variants in the 1640 duodecimo edition of *Ben Jonson's Execration against Vulcan* [noted as D in the list of variants]) was obtained from *Ben Jonson*, ed. C. H. Herford and P. and E. M. Simpson, 11 vols. (Oxford, 1925–1952), VIII. A few of the emendations made by editors of Jonson's *Works* (notably Peter Whalley, 1756; William Gifford, 1816; Francis Cunningham, 1871; and Herford and Simpson) are included among the variants.

Epigrams

XCI: *To Sir Horace Vere*

9/ leave thy acts, *1616*; leave, then, acts; *B.M. MS. Add. 23229.*

CI: *Inviting a Friend to Supper*

16/ think *1616*; say *B.M. MS. Harleian 6917.*
17/ lie *1616*; buy *MS.*
19–20/ and godwit, if we can, / Knat, rail, and ruff too *1616*; and perhaps if we can / A duck and mallard *MS.*
36/ Pooly, or Parrot *1616*; fool, or parrot *MS.*

CXX: *Epitaph on S.P. . . .*

7/ seemed to *1616*; both did *Bodleian MS. Ashmole* 38.
11/ three filled *1616*; thrice past *MS.*
20–22/ They have repented, / And have sought, to give new birth, / In baths to steep him *1616*; since have repented / and would have given new breath / Nay they desire (not able) to give birth / In charms to sleep him *MS.*

CXXXIII: *On the Famous Voyage*

30/ the *1640*; thee *1616.*
161/ is *Gifford 1816*; are *1616.*
177/ Holborn *1616*, Holborn height *Gifford 1816*; Holborn bridge *Cunningham 1871*; Holborn (the three *H & S 1947.*

The Forest

III: *To Sir Robert Wroth*

6/ sheriff's . . . mayor's *1616*; sergeants . . . sheriff *MSS.*
9/ when *1616*; where *Bodleian MS. Rawl. poet. 31.*
24/ house *1616*; lodge *MSS.*
28/ gladder *1616*; welcome *MSS.* sight *1616*; right *B.M. MS. Harleian 4064.*
41/ ears, yet humble in their height *1616*; ears cut down in their most height *MSS.*
43/ that doth longer last *1616*; and ploughed lands up cast *MSS.*
46/ lent *MSS.*; lend *1616, 1640.*
55/ grace *1616*; place *MSS.*
60/ *After this line, some MSS. read:* The milk nor oil, did ever flow so free / Nor yellow honey from the tree
66/ live *1616*; be *MSS.*
77/ Let him than hardest sires more disinherit *1616*; Than hardest let him more disherit *MSS.*
87/ glad *1616*; proud *MSS.*
98/ knows *1616*; thinks *B.M.* MS.
99/ be thou *1616*; art thou *MSS.*
100/ Thy . . . thy *1616*; Whose . . . whose *MSS.*
101/ Be *1616*; Is *MSS.* and *1616, 1640*; an B.M. *MS.*

V: *Song: To Celia*

1/ my *1616*; sweet *MSS.*
2/ may *1616*; can *Volpone.*
4/ good *1616*; bliss *B.M. MS. Add. 10309.*
14/ So removèd by our wile *1616*; So removed by many a mile *MSS.*
15/ fruit *1616*; fruits *Volpone, MSS.*
16/ theft *1616*; thefts *Volpone.*

VI: *To the Same*

15/ Thames *1616*; streams *B.M. MS. Add. 10309.*
16/ his streams *1616*; the Thames *MS.*
19/ may *1616*; shall *Volpone, MS.*

VIII: *To Sickness*

11/ store *1616*; score *Bodleian MS. Rawl. poet. 31.*
27/ yea, *1616*; and *MSS.*
38/ stew *1616*; crank *MSS.*
41/ thee *1616*; that *Bodleian MS.*

IX: *Song: To Celia*

Another version, in B.M. MS. Sloane 1446, reads:

Drink to me Celia with thine eyes
  And I'll pledge thee with mine
  Leave but a kiss within the cup
  And I'll expect no wine
The thirst that from the soul proceeds
  Doth ask a drink divine
But might I of love's nectar sup
I would not change for thine
I sent to thee a rosy wreath
Not so to honor thee
But being well assured that there
It would not withered be
And thou thereon didst only breathe
  And sent'st it back to me
Since when it lives and smells I swear
  Not of itself but thee

XI: *Epode*

29/ passions *1616, 1640*; passions still *MSS.*
39/ 'tis *1616*; he's *MSS.*
45/ far more gentle *1616*; most gentle and *MSS.*
67/ we *1616*; I *MSS.*
68/ we *1616*; I *MSS.*
72/ we *1616*; I *MSS.*
75/ ourselves *1616*; myself *MSS.*
76/ We *1616*; I *MSS.*
83/ we *1616*; I *MSS.*
84/ filled *1616*; graced *MSS.*
85/ we *1616*; I *MSS.*
91/ we propose *1616*; I conceive *MSS.* our *1616*; my *MSS.*

XII: *Epistle to Elizabeth, Countess of Rutland*

15/ buys great *1616*; gets *MSS.*
22/ nor *1616*; not *MSS.*
25/ in *1616*; on *Bodleian MS. Rawl. poet. 31.*

63/ only *1616*; holy *MSS*. rage *1616*; sense *MSS*.
76/ to notes *1616*; the notes *Bodleian MS*.
77/ act *1616*; arts *Bodleian MS*.
79/ Muse *1616*; verse *MSS*. least *1616*; less *Bodleian MS*.
84/ Borne up by *1616*; beset with *MSS*.
87/ tickling *1616*; tinkling *MSS*.
The concluding lines in MSS. read:

Who, wheresoe'er he be, on what dear coast,
Now thinking on you, though to England lost,
For that firm grace he holds in your regard,
I, that am grateful for him, have prepared
This hasty sacrifice, wherein I rear
A vow as new and ominous as the year;
Before his swift and circled race be run,
My best of wishes: may you bear a son.

XIII: Epistle to Katharine, Lady Aubigny

100/ about *1616*; above *1640*.

Underwood

A Celebration of Charis

2. How He Saw Her
22/ with *Gifford 1816*; which *1640*.
3. What He Suffered
11/ draught. *Hunter 1963*; draught *1640*; draught, *H & S 1947*.
12/ Armèd *Hunter 1963*; Aimed, *1640*; aimed *H & S 1947*. shaft *1640*; shaft. *H & S 1947*.
4. Her Triumph
4/ car *1640*; coach *B. M. MS. Add. 15227*.
11/ light *1640*; delight *B. M. MS. Harleian 6057*
21/ bright *1640*; white *B.M. MS. Add. 15227*.
7. Begging Another, on Color of Mending the Former
2/ long *1640*; beg *Bodleian MS. Ashmole 38*. beg *1640*; ask *MSS*.
6/ touch *1640*; suck *MSS*.
17/ whilst our tongues *1640*; while we thus *MSS*.
9. Her Man Described by Her Own Dictamen
4/ greater *1640*; greatest *B.M. MS. Harleian 4955*.
18/ Front, an ample field of *1640*; forehead large, and white as *MS*.
32/ school *1640*; art *MS*.
37/ him; *MS*.; him *1640*.

The Musical Strife . . .

3/ each *1640*; one *Trinity College, Dublin MS. G.2.21*.
8/ but must lose *1640*; doth not want *Trin. Coll. MS*.
9/ then your *1640*; we our *MSS*.
15/ No tunes are sweet *1640*; no voice is sweet *MSS*; no ear hath sound *MSS*.
16/ those *1640*; your *MSS*.
19/ pleasure *1640*; passion *MSS*.
20/ On what they viewing know *1640*; On what they see or know *MSS*; Themselves with what they know *Trin. Coll. MS*.
21/ O sing not you, then *1640*; Sing we no more then *MSS*.
25/ souls *1640*; seat *Trin. Coll. MS*.
27/ state *1640*; seat *Trin. Coll. MS*.
28/ May *1640*; Shall *MSS*.

My Picture Left in Scotland

1/ now think *1640*; doubt that *Drummond, Conversations, 1619*.
5/ love *1640*; suit *Drummond, B.M. MS. Harleian 4955*.
6/ was *1640*; is *Drummond*.
7/ every close did *1640*; all my closes *Drummond, MS*.
8/ sentence *1640*; numbers *Drummond, MS*.
9/ hath *1640*; makes *Drummond, MS*. youngest *1640*; wisest *D, Q*.
13/ Tell *1640*; prompt *Drummond*.
14/ hundreds *1640, MS., D, Q*; hundred *Drummond*.
15/ seven *1640*; six *Drummond, MS., D, Q*.
16/ cannot *1640, Drummond*; could not *D, Q*.

An Epistle to Master John Selden

4/ Truth . . . naked *1640*; Since, naked, best Truth, and the Graces *Selden, "Titles of Honor," 1614*.
17/ far otherwise *1640*; far from this fault *1614*.
37/ T'instruct *1640*; To inform *1614*.
56/ manly elocution, *1640*; masculine elocution; *1614*.
66/ thine *1614*; their *1640*.
76/ same *1640*; rich *1614*.
81/ gain *1614*; grain *1640*.

An Ode to Himself ["Where dost thou careless lie"]

4/ security *1640*; obscurity *B.M. MS. Egerton 923*.
6/ and destroys *1640*; and oft destroys *MSS. H & S*.
12/ defaced *1640*; displaced *Egerton MS*.
13/ thy silence *1640*; they silent *B.M. MS. Rawl. poet. 31*.
16/ great *1640*; quick *Egerton MS*.
29/ give *1640*; guide *Egerton MS*.
30/ him *1640*; them *MSS*.

An Epistle . . . Tribe of Ben

62/ thence *Gifford 1816*; then *1640*.

To the Immortal Memory . . . of . . . Cary and . . . Morison

Title/ To . . . Morison *1640*; ODE PINDARICK To the Noble Sir Lucius Cary *D, Edinburgh Univ. MS. Dc. 7.94*; ODE PINDARICK On the Death of Sir Henry Morison *Q*; To Sir Lucius Cary, on the death of his Brother Morison *B.M. MS. Harleian 4955*.
The Turn *1640*; The turn of ten *D*.

10/ deepest *1640*; secret *Bodleian MS. Ashmole 36–7*.

The Counter-turn *1640*; The Counter-turn of ten *D*.

11/ wiser *1640*; wisest *MSS*.
15/ hurried *1640*; harried *Bodleian MS*.
The Stand *1640*; The Stand, of twelve *D*.

41/ So *1640*; Too *D, Q*.
44/ fall'st *1640*; tripst *MSS., D, Q*.
50/ measure *1640*; fashion *Bodleian MS*.
123/ in deed *Bodleian MS*.; indeed *1640, D, Q*.
126/ lines *1640*; lives *MSS*.

Epithalamion . . .

28/ (perfection at *1640*; perfection, (at *B.M. MS. Harleian* 4955.
46/ she *1640*; they *MS*.
166/ find *1640*; feel *MS*.
171/ Francis *1640*; sister *MS*.
184/ So . . . shade *1640*; So large: his body then, not boughs, project his shade *MS*.
187–188/ yet . . . pay *1640*; and the more / gently he asketh, she will pay *MS*.

Ben Jonson's Execration Against Vulcan

Ode to Himself ["Come leave the loathèd stage"]

27/ Broome's *Q, Bodleian MS. Ashmole* 38; There, *New Inn 1621*.
28/ There as his master's meal *D, Q, MSS*.; As the best ordered meal *New Inn*.
33/ scene clothes *D, Q*; stage-clothes *New Inn*.
36/ stuffing *D, Q, MSS*.; larding *New Inn*.
37/ With rage of *D, Q*; with rags of *MSS*.; With their foul *New Inn*.
39/ foul *D, Q, Ashmole MS*.; turned *New Inn:*
53/ of *D, Q, Ashmole MS*.; o'er *New Inn*.
54/ may . . . then *D, Q*; may, blood-shaken, then *New Inn*.
56/ That no tuned harp *D, Q, MSS*.; As they shall cry, *New Inn*.
58/ Shall truly *D, Q, MSS*.; No harp e'er *New Inn*.
59–60/ When . . . triumph *D, Q, MSS*.; In tuning forth the acts of his sweet reign, / And raising Charles his chariot *New Inn*.

RICHARD CORBETT

Texts in this edition are based either on a copy of *Certain Elegant Poems, Written by Dr. Corbet, Bishop of Norwich* (1647) in the Cambridge University Library, or on a microfilm copy of *Poetica Stromata or a Collection of Sundry Pieces in Poetry* (1648) in the Newberry Library. Manuscript and related information was obtained from *The Poems of Richard Corbett*, ed. J. A. W. Bennett and H. R. Trevor-Roper (Oxford, 1955).

Certain Elegant Poems

A Proper New Ballad . . .

13/ sprung *1648*; stol'n *1647*.
23/ merrily *1647*; merrily merrily *1648*.
47/ need *1647*; want *1648*.
51/ can preserve *1647*; looketh to *1648*.
57–64/ *omitted in 1647*.

An Elegy upon the Death of His Own Father

6/ his *1648*; one *1647*.
16/ the age before *1647*; their age beyond *1648*.
18/ plainness *1648*; feignedness *1647*.
20/ Add too *1648*; Adding *1647*.
28/ soon-sprung *B & T-R from MSS*.; some spring *1647*; some sprung *1648*.
40/ their *1648*; fed *1647*.
42/ literal *1648*; liberal *1647*.
45–48/ *omitted in 1648*.
46/ saved *B & T-R from MSS*.; said *1647*.
53–56/ *omitted in 1647*.

Poetica Stromata

Upon Fairford Windows [not in 1647]

1–2/ glass . . . brass *B & T-R from "Parnassus Biceps, or several choice pieces" 1656*; brass / With you is shorter lived than glass *1648*.
10/ what *B & T-R from 1656*; that *1648*.

LADY MARY WROTH

The selections from Mary Wroth's poetry follow, without substantive variant, *The Countesse of Mountgomeries Urania* (London, 1621), consulted at the Harry Ransom Humanities Research Center at the University of Texas at Austin.

ROBERT HERRICK

The text is based on copies of *Hesperides* and *His Noble Numbers* (*1648*) in the Library of Trinity College, Cambridge, and in the Harry Ransom Humanities Research Center at the University of Texas at Austin. A microfilm of another copy in the Huntington Library was also consulted. Manuscript and related information was obtained from *The Poetical Works of Robert Herrick*, ed. L. C. Martin (Oxford, 1956), and, for certain poems, from *The Complete Poetry of Robert Herrick*, ed. J. Max Patrick (New York, 1963).

Hesperides

The Vine

3/ Which . . . and *1648*; Spreading his branches *The Garden of Delight 1658*.
5/ long small *1648*; cedary *1658*.
9–12/ About . . . So that my *1648*; Her curious parts I so did twine / With the rich clusters of my vine, / That my sweet *1658*.
16–17/ could . . . one *1648*; lay and could not stir, / But yield her self my *1648*.

His Farewell to Sack

1/ known, so *1648*; true and *Recreation for Ingenious Headpieces 1650*.
3/ man *1648*; or *MSS*.
6/ resigning, yet resisting *1648*; yet chaste, and undefiled *1650*.
15/ shagged *1648*; sad *some MSS*.; sage *some MSS*.
19/ above *1648*; loved *MSS*. divinest *1648*; diviner *MSS*.
27/ flashing *1648*; striking *MSS*.; stretching *1650*.
38/ eye of admiration *1648*; eyes of adoration *MSS*.
43/ made *1648*; forged *MSS*.
45/ not smile *1648*; draw in *MSS*.
46/ *MSS*. and *1650 insert* (*with minor variants*):

Thy glaring fires, lest in their sight the sin
Of idolatry steal upon me, and
I turn apostate to the strict command
Of Nature; bid me now farewell, or smile
More inly, lest thy tempting looks beguile

12/ Outshine *1648*; Dash forth *MSS*.
17/ betray *1648*; display *MSS*.
25/ Why frowns . . . confer *1648*; O then no longer let my sweet defer *MSS*.
26/ Favors . . . idolater? *1648*; Her buxom smiles from me her worshipper *MSS*.
27/ are those looks, those looks *1648*; are those happy looks *some MSS*.; are those amber looks *some MSS*.
29/ Tell . . . fault *1648*; tell me hath my soul / Profaned in speech or done an act that's foul / Against thy purer essence, for that fault *MSS*. (*with minor variants*).
40/ In . . . wine *1648*; Or quench my thirst upon some other wine *some MSS*. (*with minor variants*); or quench my lust upon some other wine *some MSS*.
46/ possibility *1648*; probability *MSS*.
47/ When . . . lack *1648*; When all the world may know the vines shall lack *MSS*.
After l. 48 most MSS. read:

Sack is my life, my leaven, salt to all
My dearest dainties, 'tis the principal
Fire to all my functions, gives me blood
An active spirit full marrow and what is good

50/ Iphiclus . . . corn *1648*; Ixions upon the top of corn *Rosenbach MS*.
53/ And ride *1648*; Amid *Rosenbach MS*.
63/ Small . . . he *1648*; Full chalice of thy purer nectar, he *MSS*.
65/ Jove's *1648*; Juno's *Rosenbach MS*. brave *1648*; vast *MSS*.
67/ gen'rous blood, his *1648*; blood, his lustful *MSS*.
71/ fate to break us *1648*; hate to sunder *MSS*.
75/ carriage *1648*; visage *MSS*.
77/ nerves with spirit *1648*; feeble sinews *MSS*.
83/ fires *1648*; blessings *MSS*.
89/ may my numbers *1648*; let my verses *MSS*.

The Welcome to Sack

3/ likeness *1648*; liking *Rosenbach MS. 1083/16*.
4/ natures *1648*; waters *MSS*.
6/ fierce *1648*; hot *Rosenbach MS*. wished *1648*; stol'n *Rosenbach MS*.

To the Virgins, to Make Much of Time

11–12/ But . . . former *1648*; Expect not then the last and worst / Time still succeeds the former *MSS*. (*with minor variants*).

How Violets Came Blue

1–2/ Love . . . spent *1648*; The violets, as poets tell, / With Venus wrangling went *Recreation for Ingenious Headpieces 1650*.

A Nuptial Song . . .

Cf. Poetical Works, ed. Martin, pp. 476–480, for complete list of variants.

Oberon's Feast

8/ short prayers *1648*; the dance *MSS*.
9/ A moon-parched grain *1648*; A yellow corn *MSS*. purest *1648*; perky *MSS*.
10/ glitt'ring *1648*; sandy *MSS*.
16/ spleen, the chirring, *1648*; fire the pittering *MSS*.
After l. 18 MSS. read:

The humming dorr, the dying swan
And each a choice musician.

27/ . and tastes *1648*; but with *MSS*.
28/ Of that we call *1648*; Neat-cool allay *MSS*.
31–33/ then . . . sag *1648*; he not spares / To feed upon the candid hairs / Of a dried canker with a sag *MSS*.
35/ Gladding *1648*; Stroking *MSS*.
38/ A bloated . . . fly *1648*; A pickled maggot and a dry *MSS*.
41/ *After "tooth" MSS. read (with minor variants)*:

and with the fat
A well-boiled inkpin of a bat.
A bloated earwig with the pith
Of sugared rush he glads him with.
But most of all the glowworm's fire
As much betickling his desire
To know his queen mixed with the far-
Fetched binding jelly of a star
The silk-worm's seed, a little moth

51/ dainty daisy *1648*; daisy chalice *MSS*.

GEORGE HERBERT

George Herbert's English poems have come down to us in numerous seventeenth-century editions as well as in a manuscript containing more than half the poetry and a complete manuscript. The first edition was published in Cambridge in late 1633, six or (probably) more months after his death: *The Temple. Sacred Poems and Private Ejaculations . . . Printed by Thom. Buck and Roger Daniel, printers to the Universitie*; this edition has been reprinted in a Scolar Press facsimile. The edition may have been seen through the press by Herbert's friend, Nicholas Ferrar of Little Gidding. Whether or not it was, the rigid punctuation conventions and other features of the edition were certainly Thomas Buck's, as cursory examination of other texts printed by Buck at Cambridge amply shows.

The two important manuscripts are the Williams (*W*) or MS. Jones B 62 in Dr. Williams's Library, Gordon Square, London, and the Bodleian (*B*) or Tanner 307. The Williams manuscript is a volume of 120 leaves and includes 69 poems in *The Church*, the main section of *The Temple*. Herbert supervised the copying in the 1620s and made corrections and revisions. The poems sometimes contain substantial variants. The manuscript has been published by Scholars Facsimiles & Reprints (1977) with an introduction by Amy M. Charles.

The Bodleian manuscript is a folio of 155 leaves, bequeathed to the Bodleian Library, Oxford, by Thomas Tanner (MS. Tanner 307). It bears the inscription (in a later hand) "The Original of Mr George Herbert's Temple; as it was first Licenced for the presse." It was copied at Little Gidding from Herbert's papers in the months immediately following his death. While *1633* was certainly printed from *B*, the manuscript is clearly closer to Herbert's final intentions. *B* harmonizes very well in most features with *W* manuscript, while Thomas Buck, the printer of *B*, imposed a rigid kind of editorial, even grammatical, consistency on the poems, particularly in matters of punctuation. Preference is given in the texts here to the early manuscripts, particularly *W*, which Herbert supervised and revised. Punctuation is generally lighter than in either *B* or *1633*, or in the judicious Oxford edition of F. E. Hutchinson (*H*), which was also consulted. Spelling has generally been normalized. The copy texts follow the early texts closely in regard to physical format. The notes below record revisions, editorial choices, and significant variants.

All the poems edited here are from the central section, which Herbert called *The Church.* Where there are several poems with the same name, numerical distinctions are used, in square brackets. Contractions in *W* and *B* are expanded.

W Williams manuscript
B Bodleian manuscript
1633 1633 edition by Thomas Buck
H Hutchinson edition (Oxford, 1941, rev. 1945)

Title. *The Temple* is the general title assigned to Herbert's three-part collection ("The Church-porch," "The Church," and "The Church Militant"). However, it is most unlikely that Herbert assigned this title. See M. Di Cesare, *George Herbert, The Temple: A Diplomatic Edition of the Bodleian Manuscript* (1995), *5 (hereafter, *The Bodleian Manuscript*).

The Altar

W presents the text in the shape of an altar, as *B* generally does.

12/ name *W* / name. *1633* / Name. *B*

The Sacrifice

The *1633* edition and most subsequent editions print this poem as sixty-three quatrains separated by spaces, but in both manuscripts the text is continuous. That the decision to present it thus was Herbert's own is emphatic. In *W*, space between stanzas is otherwise clearly defined in all his other poems; in *B*, the scribes wrote the last line of each page (the abbreviated refrain) in what usually is a blank space elsewhere in the manuscript. Such continuity of text and the abbreviated refrain are two characteristics of liturgical texts.

38/ way & *W B H* / way of *1633*
57/ Priests *W* / Priest *B 1633 H* (Hutchinson identifies the priest as Caiaphas)
115/ cause *B 1633* / case *W H*
129$_{B}$131/ him . . . him . . . his . . . he *W B H* / me . . . me . . . my . . . I *1633*
130/ grasps *W B H* / grasp *1633*
171/ evermore *B 1633 H* / to the poore *W*
177$_{B}$178/ *W*:
Yet since in frailty, cruelty, shrowd turns,
All Scepters, Reeds: Cloths, Scarlet: Crowns are Thorns:
179/ deeds *B 1633 H* / scorns *W*
187/ *W*: With stronger blows strike mee as I come out
209/ sorrow, as if *W B 1633* / sorrow as, if *H*
217/ *W* reads: My soule is full of shame, my flesh of wound:
237/ give *W B H* / gave *1633*

The Thanksgiving

11/ sing, skipping *B H* / sing skipping, *1633* / sing, neglecting thy sad story *W*

The Reprisal

Title in *W* "The Second Thanks-giving"

14/ thy *W B H* / the *1633*

The Passion

Despite the strikingly different prosody and placement of the text, this poem is printed as lines 21$_{B}$32 of "Good Friday" in *1633* and subsequent editions. But *W* has it as a separate poem (24v) facing a second poem entitled "The Passion" (which appears below as "Redemption"). In *B*, the last two lines of "Good Friday" are squeezed into what is ordinarily blank space at the page bottom (56) and this poem begins, without title but with the usual enlarged first letter, on a new page (57). See *The Bodleian Manuscript*, LIII$_{B}$LV.

21$_{B}$22/ *W*:
Since nothing Lord can bee so good
To write thy sorrows in, as blood

7/ sin *B 1633 H* / he *W*
29$_{B}$32/ *W*:

> Sinn being gone o doe thou fill
> The Place, & keep possession still.
> ffor by the writings all may see
> Thou hast an ancient claime to mee.

Redemption

Title in *W* "The Passion." See above.

9, 14/ strait *W B* / straight *1633 H*
10$_{B}$11/ *W* originally read

Sought him in Citties, Theaters, resorts
In grottos, gardens, Palaces & Courts
but Herbert corrected these lines to the current text.

Sepulcher

B has no line spaces; *1633, H*, and most editors print as eight-line stanzas.

Easter [II]

Printed as part of "Easter" in *1633, H*, and most editions, this was a separate poem in *W* and was separated in *B* from the previous text by a large space. As in the two "Passion" poems, the prosody of these twelve lines differs considerably from that of the preceding poem. See *The Bodleian Manuscript*, LV$_{B}$LVII.

W:

I had prepared many a flowre
To strow thy way and Victorie,
But thou wa'st vp before myne houre
Bringinge (*corr. from* And brought) thy sweets along with thee. (1_B4)

Though hee bring light & th'other sents:
Can not make vp so braue a feast
As thy discouerie presents. (6_B8)

Yet though my flours be lost, they say
A hart can never come too late.
Teach it to sing thy praise, this day,
And then this day, my life shall date. (9_B12)

Easter-wings [I]

Though both *W* and *B* present the texts of this and the next poem horizontally, *1633*, all early editions, and some modern editions print the texts vertically. See *The Bodleian Manuscript*, LVII_BLIX.

8/ harmoniously *W corrected from* doe by degree
9/ victories *W corrected from* sacrifice
10/ the fall *B 1633 H* / my fall *W*

Easter-wings [II]

2/ And still *W corrected from* Yet thou
3/ Thou didst so *W corrected from* Dayly didst
4/ That *W corrected from* Till
8/ this day *B 1633 H* / *omitted W* (Hutchinson points out that the phrase makes the line parallel to line 9 of the preceding poem but makes this line a foot longer than the corresponding line in the preceding.)

H. Baptism [I]

Text much revised from the *W* version:

When backward on my sins I turne mine eyes
And then beyond them all my Baptisme view
As he that Heaven beyond much thicket spyes
I pass the shades, & fixe vpon the true
Waters aboue the Heavens. O sweet streams
You doe prevent most sins & for the rest
You give vs teares to wash them: lett those beams
Which then ioin'd with you still meet in my brest
And mend as rising starres & rivers doe. (*W* 1_B9)

5/ vent *B H* / rent *1633*
11/ Spredding the plaister *W* / And spreads the plaister *B 1633 H*

H. Baptism [II]

11/ Although *B 1633 H* / Though that *W*
13/ preserve her *B 1633 H* / keep hir first *W*

Sin [I]

7/ stratagems *B 1633 H* / casualties *W*
13_B14/ *W*:

Yet all these fences with one bosome sinne
Are blowne away, as if they nere had bin.'

Affliction [I]

6/ gracious benefits *B 1633 H* / graces perquisites *W*
7, 8/ fine *B 1633 H* / rich *W*
9_B10/ entwine, And 'tice me unto thee. *B 1633 H* / bewitch Into thy familie. *W*
23/ sorrows *W* / sorrow *B 1633 H*
65/ God *B 1633 H* / King *W*

Prayer [I]

5/ tower *B 1633* / fort *W*
7/ world transposing *B H* / world-transposing *1633; W*: Transposer of the world, wonders resort
8_B9/ Unlike *W, B 1633* and *H* all have commas within these two lines

The H. Communion

3/ for *B H* / from *1633*
16/ fleshy *B H* / fleshly *1633*

Prayer [II]

This poem appears in *1633* and *H* and most other editions as a continuation of "The H. Communion." As in previous combined poems, however, the large space before these lines, the enlarged initial letter, and the very different prosody argue that, as in *W*, this should be considered a separate poem. See *The Bodleian Manuscript*, LIX_BLXX.

13_B16/ *W*:

But wee are strangers grown, o Lord,
Lett Prayer help our losses,
Since thou hast taught us by thy word,
That wee may gaine by crosses.

Love I

2/ that *B 1633 H* / the *W*
4/ on *B 1633 H* / in *W*

The Temper [I]

Titles for both "Temper" poems in *W* "The Christian Temper"

5/ some forty *B 1633* / a hundred *W*
25/ Whether I Angell it, or fall to dust *W*

The Temper [II]

4/ Save that: and me, *W B* / Save that, and me; *1633 H*

Employment [I]

23_B24/ Lord that I may the Sunns perfection gaine
Give mee his speed. *W*

The H. Scriptures I

4/ mollify all pain *B 1633 H* / suple outward paine *W*
5/ health, health *W H* / health health, *B 1633*
11/ too much *B 1633 H* / enough *W*

[*The H. Scriptures II*]

10/ And comments on thee *B 1633 H* / And more then fancy *W*
14/ lights to *B 1633 H* / can spell *W*

Whitsunday

1/ Come blessed Dove charm'd with my song *W*
2/ Display . . . mee: *W* / And spred . . . mee, *B 1633 H*
4/ Till I gett wing to *W* / Till it get wing and *B 1633 H*
8/ With livery-graces furnishing thy men. *W*
13ff.:

But wee are falne from Heaven to Earth,
And if wee can stay there, it's well.
He that first fell from his great birth
Without thy help, leads vs his way to Hell.
Lord once more shake the Heaven & earth
Least want of Graces seeme thy thrift:
ffor sinn would faine remoue the dearth
And lay it on thy husbandry, for shift.
Show that thy brests can not be dry,
But that from them ioyes purle for ever
Melt into blessings all the sky,
So wee may cease to suck: to praise thee, never. *W*

Grace

5/ still the sun *B 1633 H* / the Sunne still *W*
6/ house would but *B 1633 H* / great house would
13_B16/ Not in W
Between stanzas 5 and 6, *W* had the following stanza, deleted by slanted lines drawn through it:

What if I say thou seek'st delayes;
Wilt thou not then my fault reproue?
Prevent my Sinn to thine owne praise,
Drop from aboue.

Church-monuments

W and *B* present this poem without stanza divisions and indent line 17, after the second of only two full-stopped lines. *1633 H* and most editions print as four six-line stanzas, based apparently on the rhyme scheme.

12/ Jet *W B* / Jeat *1633 H*
22/ crumbled *B 1633 H* / broken *W*

Church-music

The following stanza in *W* (after the second of our text) was dropped:

O what a state is this, which never knew
Sicknes, or shame, or sinn, or sorrow:
Where all my debts are payd, none can accrue
Which knoweth not, what means, too Morrow.

9/ post *B 1633 H* / part *W*
11/ travail *B* / travel *W 1633 H*

Church-lock and Key

Title in *W* "Prayer"
A substantial argument has been made, notably by Frank Huntley ("A Crux . . . , *ELH* 8 [1970], 13_B17), to return to the title and placement of this poem in *W*. But Herbert's final version, in *B*, included several revisions, omitted the second and fourth stanzas, and provided a new final stanza.

1/ locks *B 1633 H* / stops *W*
The original second stanza in *W*:

If either Innocence or ffervencie
did play their part.
Armies of blessings would contend & vye
Which of them soonest should attaine my hart.

5/ But *B 1633 H* / Yet *W*
6/ And mend *B 1633 H* / Mending *W*
The fourth stanza in *W*:

O make mee wholy guiltles, or at least
Guiltles so farr;
That zele and purenes circling my request
May guard it safe beyond the highest starr.

The Quiddity

Title in *W* "Poetry"

3/ Nor . . . , nor . . . , nor *W* / No . . . , no . . . , no *B 1633 H*
4/ not yet *W* / nor yet *B 1633 H*
8/ my *W B H* / a *1633*

Sunday

1/ most calm, most bright, *B 1633 H* / so calme, so bright: *W*
2_B7/ in *W*:

The Couch of Tyme, the balme of tears (*corr. from* teares),
Th'Indorsment of supreme Delight,
The parter [*corr. from* partner] of my wrangling feares
Setting in order what they tumble:
The week were dark, but that thy light
Teaches it not to stumble.

23/ palace . . . lies *B 1633 H* / Kingdome . . . doth stand *W*
25/ with vanities *B 1633 H* / on either hand *W*
26_B28/ *W*:

They are the rowes of fruitfull trees
Parted with alleys or with grass
In Gods rich Paradice.

31_B32/ *W*:

Make bracelets for the spouse & wife
Of the Immortall onely King.

Employment [II]

21_B25/ *W*:

O that I had the wing and thigh
Of laden Bees;
Then would I mount vp instantly
And by degrees
On men dropp blessings as I fly.

26/ still too *B 1633 H* / ever *W*
29/ So we freeze on *B 1633 H* Thus wee creep on *W*

Denial

10/ Alarmes *W B* / alarms *1633 H*
13/ knees and heart *B 1633 H* / hart & knees *W*
20/ But *B 1633 H* / Yet *W*
29/ mind *B 1633 H* / hart, *corr. to* soule *W*
30/ mend *B 1633 H* / meet *W*

Christmas

Title in *W* "Christmas-Day"

1/ as I rid one day *B 1633 H* / riding on a Day *W*
13_B14/ *W*:

ffurnish my soule to thee, that being drest
Of better lodging thou maist be possest.

15_B34/ These lines do not appear in *W*; they were added in *B* and, since some space was left at the top of the page, Herbert probably intended a separate poem.

The World

10/ Reformed all at length *B 1633 H* / Quickly reformed all *W*
19/ Love and Grace took Glory *B 1633 H* / Love took Grace & Glory *W*

Vanity [I]

22/ sought *1633 H* / wrought *B*

Virtue

7/ its *1633 H* / his *B*

The Pearl. Matthew 13:45

Title: 13. 45 *W H* / 13 *B 1633*

3/ borrowed *B 1633 H* / purchased *W*
26/ unbridled *1633 H* / vnbundled *B*
26_B29/ (the first three lines crossed out in *W*):

Where both their baskets are with all their store.
The smacks of dainties and their exaltation:
What both the stops and pegs of pleasure bee:
The ioyes of Company or Contemplation

32/ seeled *W* / sealed *B 1633 H*

Affliction [IV]

Title in *W* "Tentation"

12/ pink *W B H* / prick *1633*

Man

2/ no man builds *W* / none doth build *B 1633 H*
8/ more fruit *W H* / no fruit *B 1633* (Hutchinson, choosing *W*, summarizes at length arguments on both sides.)
26/ *W*: Earth resteth, Heaven moveth, fountains flow:
41/ if one have beauty, *W* / Hath one such beauty? *B 1633 H*
42/ neat! *W B* / neat? *1633 H*
53_B54/ *W*:

That as the world to vs is kind and free
So we may bee to Thee.

Mortification

W capitalizes Death at the end of each stanza; the practice is not followed in *B 1633* or *H*.

18/ house *B 1633* / houre *W H*, but cf. note in the text.
30/ house *B 1633* / place *W*

Jordan [II]

Title in *W* "Invention"

1/ lines *B 1633 H* / verse *W*
4/ sprout *B 1633 H* / spredd *W*
6/ Decking *B 1633 H* / Praising *W*
14/ So I bespoke me much insinuation: *W*
16/ long pretence *B 1633 H* / preparation *W*
18/ Coppy out that: there needs no alteration. *W*

Obedience

7/ as there doth *B 1633 H* / as it does *W*
15/ shutt out *W* / exclude *B 1633 H*
38/ hath read; *B 1633* / doth read *W*

The British Church

1633 organizes the poem in three-line stanzas; *B H* present it, as here, in six-line stanzas.

4/ the *B* / her *1633 H*

The Quip

The refrain, from Psalms 38:15 (*Book of Common Prayer*), is italicized in *1633,2d* and *H* but not in *B* or *1633*.

The Bunch of Grapes

9/ Travailed *B* / Travelled *1633 H*
18/ last *1633 H* / at last *B*

The Storm

6/ Amuse *B* / Amaze *1633 H*

Paradise

1633 and *H* set the last word of each line in small caps and place it symmetrically; in *B*, the last words are capitalized and enlarged; paring down each word provides the visual symmetry.

The Size

12/ spices. *B* / spices, *1633 H*
16/ Exact *B* / Enact *1633 H*
21/ have, renounce *B* / have renounce, *1633 H*
39/ A line of four syllables is obviously missing after this, but there is no space in *B* or *1633*.

The Pilgrimage

1/ travaild *B* / travelled *1633 H*
13/ Passion *B H* / passion *1633*

The Bag

1/ despair! *B H* / despair; *1633*
19/ travellers *1633 H* / travailers *B*

The Collar

3/ What *B* / What? *1633 H*
21/ not. Forsake *B* / not forsake *1633* (though clearly an error, the punctuation was not corrected until the fifth edition)
27/ Away, *Take Heed, B* / Away; take heed: *1633 H.*

The Flower

18/ bell *B* / bell. *1633 H*

The Son

6/ son's *B* / sun's *1633 H*

Aaron

3, 8, 18, 23/ Dead *B* / dead *1633 H*
4, 9, 14/ rest, *B* / rest. *1633* / rest: *H*

The Banquet

2/ dear, *B* / dear; *1633*
15/ sin, *B* / sin; *1633 H*
49/ his *B H* / this *1633*

The Elixir

In *W*, the title was first given as "Perfection"; Herbert added "The Elixir" without crossing out the copyist's title. The poem is heavily revised in *W*, the revisions in Herbert's own hand.

$1_{B}4$/ *W*:

> Lord teach mee to referr
> All things I doe to thee
> That I not onely may not erre
> But allso pleasing bee.

W lacks $5_{B}8$. Between $12_{B}13$, *W*:

> He that does ought for thee,
> Marketh that deed for thine:
> And when the Divel shakes the tree,
> Thou saist, this fruit is mine.

14/ mean *corrected from* low *W*
16/ grow bright and clean *corrected from* in Heaven grow *W*
19/ room as *corrected from* chamber *W*
$21_{B}24$/ *W*:

> But these are high perfections:
> Happy are they that dare
> Lett in the Light to all their actions
> And show them as they are.

These lines were struck out; Herbert wrote the final stanza in the space following.

A Wreath

This poem is squeezed in after "Employment [II]" in *W*. The text has little punctuation, perhaps to emphasize the *wreath* motif. In *B* and *1633*, lines $1_{B}7$, 9, 10 end in commas.

Death

Punctuation from *W* with some additions; heavier in *B 1633 H*

16/ sought for *B H* / sought for, *1633* / long'd for *W*

Heaven

The responses of *Echo* are italicized in *1633* and *H*

5/ trees *B 1633 H* / woods *W*
7/ that *B 1633 H* / which *W*

THOMAS CAREW

Texts are based, with one exception, on copies of *Poems* (1640) and *Poems. With a Maske* (1651) in the Cambridge University Library. The text of Carew's "Elegy" on Donne is based on that in *Poems, By J. D.* (1633). A microfilm of another copy of the 1640 edition in the Huntington Library was consulted. Manuscript and other textual information was obtained principally from *The Poems of Thomas Carew*, ed. Rhodes Dunlap (Oxford, 1949). The facsimile of portions of the Wyburd MS. (Bodleian MS. Don. b. 9), reproduced in the Scolar Press facsimile of the 1940 edition of Carew's *Poems* (Menston, 1969), was consulted as well.

Poems (1640)

The Spring

6/ sacred *1649*; second *MSS.*

A Rapture

25/ Queen *1642, MSS.*; Queens *1640.*
65/ cherry *1640*; cherries *MSS.*
66/ apple, tipped with coral berry *1640*; apples, tipped with crimson berries *MSS.*
92/ willing *1640*; naked *MSS.*
101/ spies *1640*; eyes *MSS.*
102/ envious eyes *1640*; politic spies *MSS.*

Another ["The purest soul that e'er was sent"]

5–10/ *C. L. Powell, in MLR, XI (1916), 286–287, proposes the following alternative version, based on B. M. MS. Harleian 6917:*

The substance was too pure, the frame
So glorious that thither came
Ten thousand Cupids, bringing along
A grace on each wing, that did throng
For place there, till they all oppressed
The seat in which they thought to rest.

To Ben Jonson . . .

19/ on *1640*; to *MSS.*
21/ form *1640*; shape *MSS.*

An Elegy upon the Death of Dr. Donne . . .

3/ dare *Poems, By, J. D. 1633*; did *1640.*
5/ churchman *1633*; lect'rer *1640.*
7/ should *1633*; might *1640.*
17/ our will *1633*; the will *1640.*
44/ dust had raked *1633*; dung had searched *1640.*
50/ stubborn *1633*; troublesome *1640.*
58/ is purely *1633*; was only *1640.*
59/ thy *1633*; their *1640.*
63/ repeal *1633*; recall *1640.*
65/ Were *1633*; Was *1640.*
74/ faint *1633*; rude *1640.*
81/ small *1633*; short *1640.* maintain *1633*; retain *1640.*
88/ our *1633*; the *1640.*
89/ an *1633*; one *1640.*
91–92/ *omitted in 1640.*
94/ tomb *1633*; grave *1640.*
95–98/ *not italicized in 1640.*
97/ lie *1633*; lies *1640.*

A Song ["Ask me no more where Jove bestows"]

Some MS. versions arrange the stanzas 2, 3, 1, 4, 5. B.M. MS. Add 23229, in Dunlap's view "an early draft," reads:

Ask me no more where Jove bestows
When June is past, the damask rose
For on your cheeks and lips they be
Fresher than on any tree.

Ask me no more where those stars light
That downwards fall in dark of night,
For in your eyes they sit and there
Fixed become, as in their sphere.

Ask me no more where nightingale
When June is past puts forth her tale,
For in your sweet dividing throat
She winters and keeps warm her note.

Nor ask me whether east or west,
The phoenix builds her spiced nest
For unto you she always flies,
And in your fragrant bosom dies.

Two MS. versions that arrange the stanzas 2, 3, 1, 4, 5 conclude with a (nearly identical) sixth stanza:

Ask me no more whether north or south
These vapors come from out thy mouth
For unto heaven they are sent from hence
And there are made Jove's frankincense.

JAMES SHIRLEY

The text is based on a copy of *Poems, &c.* (1946) in the Cambridge University Library. The Scolar Press facsimile of a copy of this edition in the Bodleian Library, together with poems by Shirley in Bodleian MS. Rawl. poet. 88 (Menston, 1970), was also consulted. Further textual information was obtained from *The Poems of James Shirley*, ed. R. L. Armstrong (New York, 1941), and from *The Dramatic Works and Poems of James Shirley*, ed. W. Gifford and A. Dyce, 6 vols. (London, 1833).

Poems

Cupid's Call

The Poem derives from two separate lyrics, given in Bodleian MS. Rawl. poet. 88 as follows:

THE COURTESAN

Cupid calls o young men come,
Bring his wanton, wanton harvest home.
When the birds most sweetly sing,
And flowers are in their prime,
No season, but the spring,
Is Cupid's harvest time.

Into Love's field, or garden walk,
Virgins dangle, dangle on their stalk,
Blown, and playing at fifteen,
And pointing to their beds,
Come bring your sickles then,
And reap their maidenheads.

ANOTHER

Hark, hark how in every grove,
Nightingales do sing of love,
They have lost their sullen note,
Warbling with a merry throat,
There is no bliss to men
O let them ravish me again.

Virgins, that are young and fair,
Kiss yourselves into a pair.
Warm, and active keep your blood,
Let no thought congeal the flood,
In youth refuse no art,
For age will snow upon your heart.

Love for Enjoying

Another version, in Bodleian MS. Rawl. poet. 88, reads:

Lady: what's your face to me?
I was not only made to see;
Every silent stander by
Thus enjoys, as much, as I.
Your rose and lilies are not mine,
By praising them into divine;
Nature's wealth upon your brow,
On your cheek, or lip, doth show
That within are to be found,
Rocks of pearl, and diamond,
To which, a lapidary's art
Must richness and the price impart.
Here a vein with golden threads,
To the mine of pleasure leads,
Which who once enjoys, has power
To make more Indies every hour.
Come let us mix our selves, and prove
'Tis action, that perfects love.
Your smiles, and kisses; fruitless toying,
Stay me not, but tempt enjoying.
Shall we on either gazing stand,
Like armies in the Netherland,
Taking fear, at either's sight,
Till we grow too weak to fight?
Give the signal, let us try
Who shall fall, yourself or I;
'Tis loves war, if either yield
We both lose, and win the field.

Two Gentlemen That Broke Their Promise . . .

An early version, in Bodleian MS Rawl. poet. 88, reads:

TO E. H. AND W. H.

There is no faith in claret, now I see
That blushing wine doth merely frenchify,
Can promises in wine, and wine, that should
Having no color, best agree with blood,
Make men so cold, that after, they appear
As dull as they which compliment in beer?
But 'tis no wonder, for we do not seek
A Christian, where there is no Catholic.
'Tis sack that justifies; and had you both
Promised in sack, each word had been an oath.

The Garden

Another version, in B.M. MS. Add. 33998, reads:

CHLORINDA'S GARDEN

Fain would I have a plot of ground
Which the sun did never see,
Nor by wanton lover found,
That alone my garden be.

No curious flowers do I crave,
To tempt my smelling, or my eye,
A little heart's ease let me have
But to look on, ere I die.

In the violet's drooping head
Will my counterfeit appear,
A little thyme, but withered;
But no woodbine shall grow there.

Weave a pretty robe of willow,
On each side let blackthorn grow,
Raise a bank, where for my pillow,
Wormwood, rue, and poppy strow.

No bird sing here but Philomel,
Or the orphan turtle groan,
Either of these two can tell
My sad story, by their own.

Here let no man find me out,
Or, if chance shall bring one hither,
I'll be secure, when round about
'Tis moated with my eyes' foul weather.

Thus let me sigh my heart away,
At last to one as sad as I,
I'll give my garden, that he may,
By my example, love and die.

MILDMAY FANE

The text is based on a microfilm of a copy of *Otia Sacra* (1648) in the University of Illinois Library. *The Poems of Mildmay, Second Earl of Westmoreland* (1648), ed. A. B. Grosart (Manchester, 1879), and the versions of Fane's poems included in *Rare Poems of the Seventeenth Century*, ed. L. B. Marshall (Cambridge, 1936), were also consulted.

Otia Sacra

My Country Audit

1/ privacy!; privacy, *1648*.
5/ waived; wav'd *1648*.

My Observation at Sea

6/ ocean; ocean. *1648*.

A Dedication of My First Son

8/ flour; flowre *1648*.

In Praise of Fidelia

2/ stored; store *1648*.

To Retiredness

72/ on't use; on't, use *1648*.

THOMAS RANDOLPH

The text is based on a copy of *Poems, with the Muses' Looking-Glass and Amyntas* (1638), in the Cambridge University Library. A microfilm of another copy of this edition, in the British Museum, was also consulted. Manuscript and further textual information was obtained from *The Poems and Amyntas of Thomas Randolph*, ed. J. J. Parry (New Haven, Conn., 1917), and *The Poems of Thomas Randolph*, ed. G. Thorn-Drury (London, 1929).

Poems, with The Muses' Looking-Glass and Amyntas

A Gratulatory to Mr. Ben Jonson . . .

6/ tenant unto *1638*; poor tenant to *B.M. MS. Add. 22602*.
14/ thee, Horace *Parry 1917*; thy Horace *1638*. whole *1638*; full *MS*.
27/ can or should *1638*; should or dare *MS*.
28/ adoption *1638*; election *MS*.

Upon the Loss of His Little Finger

3/ what mischance hath ta'en *1638*; that which chance did cut *Bodleian MS. Firth i.4*.
8/ death *1638*; grave *MSS*.
11/ verse *1638*; rhymes *MSS*.

An Elegy

2/ blind *1638*; thine *Bodleian MS. Firth i.4*.
3/ my *1638*; thy *MS*.
8/ most *1638*; more *MS*.
12/ her perfection *1638*; my affection *MS*.
15–16/ *MS. substitutes*: And when I send her verse, those that might be / Termed sonnets in the loose, are hymns in me.
After line 20 MS. inserts: My mistress' face is fair, but soul divine, / And I adore the saint above the shrine.
23/ my *1638*; mans *MS*.
26/ Earth's *1638*; The *MS*.

WILLIAM HABINGTON

The text is based on a microfilm of a copy of *Castara* (1640) in the Yale University Library. Microfilms of copies of the 1634 and 1635 editions in the Huntington Library were also consulted. Full textual apparatus is provided in K. Allott's edition of *Castara* (Liverpool, 1948).

Castara

To a Friend, Inviting Him to a Meeting upon Promise

23/ pure *1640*; sure *1635*.

EDMUND WALLER

The text is based on a copy of the 1686 edition of *Poems, &c.* in the Cambridge University Library. Other editions consulted include the first ("Works," pub. for T. Walkley) and second issues of the 1645 edition (in a microfilm of the Huntington Library copy, and in the Scolar Press facsimile of a copy in the British Museum [Menston, 1971], respectively), and a copy of the "first authorized" edition of 1664 in the Cambridge University Library. The Scolar Press facsimile of Bodleian MS. Don d 55 was also consulted. Further information was obtained from *The Poems of Edmund Waller*, ed. G. Thorn-Drury, 2 vols. (London, 1905).

Poems

To the King, on His Navy

8/mighty . . . smaller *1686*; mightiest . . . smallest *Bodleian MS. Don d 55, 1645, 1664*.
9/ nobler *1664, 1686*; stricter *MS., 1645*.
29/ designed that fabric to have stood *MS., 1664, 1686*; designed, that fabrics should have stood *1645*.

Upon Ben Jonson

5/ Thou hast alone *MS., 1645, 1664, 1686*; Thou not alone *Jonsonus Virbius 1638*.
7/ So tracèd *1664, 1686*; Hast tracked *MS., 1645*; Hast traced *1638*.
8/ That whate'er *1664, 1686*; What ever *MS., 1645*; But all that *1638*.
9/ habit *1645, 1664, 1686*; habits *MS., 1638*. deforms *1664, 1686*; distorts *MS.*; distort *1638*; deserts *1645*.
10/ a brother can his brother *1664, 1686*; one brother can the brother *MS., 1645*; the brother can the brother *1638*.
11/ represented *1638, 1664, 1686*; representing *MS., 1645*.
29/ which *1686*; who *MS., 1638, 1645, 1664*.

At Penshurst ["Had Sacharissa lived when mortals made"]

1/ Sacharissa *1664, 1668*; Dorothea *MS., 1645*.
22/ fed all one *1686*; feed all on *MS.*; feed all on one *1645*; fed all on one *1664*.

The Battle of the Summer Islands

II, Proem, 1/ alarm *1664, 1686*; affright *MS., 1645*.
36/ as the *MS., 1664, 1686*; as if *1645*.
III, 7/ bounds *MS.*; boils *1645, 1664, 1686*.
11/ Spenser's *1664, 1686*; fairy *MS., 1645*.
29/ forces *1664, 1686*; furies *MS.*; surges *1645*.

On a Girdle

5/ was *1664, 1686*; is *1645*.
8/ Did *1664, 1686*; Do *1645*.
10/ Dwelt *1664, 1686*; Dwells *1645*.
11/ bound *1664, 1686*; tied *1645*.
12/ Take . . . round *1664, 1686*; Take all the sun goes round beside *1645*.

On St. James's Park . . .

54/ draws *1664, 1686*; grows *A Poem on St. James Park 1661*.

61/ lovely *1664, 1686*; comely *1661*.
89–90/ state . . . Fate *1664, 1686*; state . . . Fates *1661*.
95–96/ *omitted in 1661*.
109/ Here . . . go *1664, 1686*; Here he does like the people's pastor go *1661*.
121/ ruminates *1664, 1686*; meditates *1661*.

JOHN MILTON

The copy text for most of the selections from Milton's works is the 1645 edition of his poems. For Sonnets 12–23, the 1673 edition was followed, with the lone exception of sonnet 16, which was not published during Milton's lifetime. For it, the authority is the MS. of Milton's poems held at Cambridge University (usually referred to as the Cambridge MS.) Copies of the 1645 and 1673 editions held in the Harry Ransom Humanities Research Center at the University of Texas at Austin, were consulted as has the Scolar Press facsimile of the Cambridge MS. (1970). Any substantive variants are noted in the annotations to the poems.

SIR JOHN SUCKLING

The text is based on copies of *Fragmenta Aurea* (1646) and *The Last Remains of Sir John Suckling* (1659) in the Cambridge University Library and the Harry Ransom Humanities Research Center at the University of Texas at Austin. A microfilm of a copy of the 1646 edition of *Fragmenta Aurea* in the Yale University Library was also consulted. Manuscript and other textual information was obtained from *The Works of Sir John Suckling: The Non-Dramatic Works*, ed. T. Clayton (Oxford, 1971).

Fragmenta Aurea

A Sessions of the Poets

The arrangement of "suspensions" (single words suspended between quatrains), imperfect in the 1646 edition of Fragmenta Aurea, follows that of Clayton's edition.

Title/ A Sessions of the Poets *1646*; The Wits *MSS.*
9/ Thought . . . day *1646*; That day thought to carry the laurel away *MSS., Fragmenta Aurea 1648*.
17/ Berkeleys *two MSS.*; Bartlets *most MSS., 1646, 1648*.
26/ did not *1646*; did *MSS., 1648*.
39/ hard *1646*; hide *1648*.
55/ Berkeley *two MSS.*; Bartlet *most MSS., 1646, 1648*.
60/ Suddenly *two MSS., 1646*; Sullenly *some MSS.*
63/ Apollo *1646*; Apollo himself *MSS., 1648*.
64/ on him *1646*; on't *MSS., 1648*. how came *1646*; what made *1648*.
65/ whispering nothing *1646, 1648*; busily whispering *most MSS.*
69/ care *1646*; character *MSS., 1648*.
72/ let in *1646*; to come in *MSS., 1648*.
77–81/ *omitted in 1646*.
83/ But *1646*; And *MSS., 1648*.
93/ But witty *1646*; But wise *1648*; Wise *MSS.* asked *1646*; then asked *MSS., 1648*.
99/ silence *some MSS., 1646, 1648*; silent *some MSS.*
100/ crowd *MSS., 1648*; court *1646*.
121/ that 'twas *MSS., 1648*; that *1646*.
122/ wit *MSS., 1648*; wit's *1646*.
128/ in great *MSS., 1646*; at large *1648*.
130/ poets *MSS., 1646*; ones *1648*. cleared *some MSS., 1646*; cheered *some MSS., 1648*.
133/ poets *1646*; poet *MSS., 1648*.

Sonnet I

14/ my heart be faulty, or her eyes *1646*; her face be guilty, or my eyes *MSS.*

Against Fruition [I]

10/ might grow *1646, some MSS.*; should grow *some MSS.*
16/ there *1646, some MSS.*; then *some MSS.*
24/ Heaven were *1646, most MSS.*; It were *some MSS.*

Upon My Lady Carlisle's Walking . . .

7–8/ all . . . out *1646*; everywhere / Such as Arabian gumtrees bear *Bodleian MS. Rawl. poet. 199*.

13/ had all their birth from *1646*; were wholly made by *MS*.
16–17/ was . . . after-spring *1646*; came to bring / News of this unknown after-spring *MS*.
26/ masks and hoods *1646*; silks and lawn *MS*.
36/ Searched after *1646*; Pressed on to *MS*.
37/ seldom stops *1646*; hardly steps *MS*.
40–49/ *omitted in 1646*.

A Ballad upon a Wedding

3/ without *1646*; beyond *MSS.*, *Fragmenta Aurea 1648*.
5/ In any place on *1646*; In any part of *MSS.*, *1648*.
12/ Forty *MSS.*, *1648*; Vorty *1646*.
46/ But oh! *MSS.*, *1646*; But Dick *1648*.
61–72/ *The order of these two stanzas is reversed in some MSS.*
65/ them *1646*; her *MSS.*, *1648*.
72/ spent a *1646*; spoiled one *MSS*.
79–84/ In *1646*, *this stanza, with first three and last three lines transposed, follows l. 96*.

107/ Whilst *MSS.*, *1648*; Till *1646*.
120/ Good Boy *1646*; God b'w'y' *MSS.*, *1648*; Good b'w'y *Bodleian MS. Rawl. poet.* 37.

The Last Remains of Sir John Suckling

"Out upon It! . . ."

4/ prove *1659*; hold *MSS*.
5/ molt *1659*; melt *MSS*.
6/ shall *some MSS.*, *1659*; can *some MSS*.
9/ the spite on't *1659*; a pox upon't *MSS*.
10/ Is due *1659*; There is due *MSS*.
14/ very very *MSS*; very *1659*.

A Song to a Lute

4/ winds *1659* (*Poems*); waves *1659* (*The Sad One*).

WILLIAM CARTWRIGHT

The text is based on a copy of *Comedies, Tragi-Comedies, with Other Poems* (1651), in the Cambridge University Library. Manuscript and other textual information was obtained from *The Plays and Poems of William Cartwright*, ed. G. Blakemore Evans (Madison, Wis., 1951).

Comedies, Tragi-Comedies, With Other Poems

No Platonic Love

15/ profess *1651*; protest *The Marrow of Compliments 1655*.
19/ Come . . . tread *1651*; Let all believe this truth that those that tread *1655*.

JAMES GRAHAM

The text is based on a copy of James Watson, *A Choice Collection of Comic and Serious Scots Poems* (Edinburgh, 1711), in the Cambridge University Library. Additional textual information is available in *The Poems of James Graham, Marquis of Montrose (1612–1650)*, ed. J. L. Weir (London, 1938). The poem first appeared, c. 1660, in broadside form, with the title, "An Excellent New Ballad to the Tune of 'I'll never love thee more.'"

ANNE BRADSTREET

The text for Bradstreet's poems is based on a microfilm copy of *The Tenth Muse Lately Sprung up in America . . . By a Gentlewoman in Those Parts* (London, 1650) held in the Library of Congress. No substantive variants from later editions are included because they are of doubtful authority and seem to reflect retrospective political considerations.

RICHARD CRASHAW

Crashaw's first English volume was *Steps to the Temple, Sacred Poems, With other Delights of the Muses*, published in 1646 and again, in a much revised and augmented edition, in 1648. These volumes were published in London while Crashaw was in Paris and then later in Italy (where he died in 1649). *Carmen Deo Nostro* was published in Paris, posthumously, in 1652; this contains many poems from the 1648 edition and several significant additions, especially the first version of "To . . . the Countess of Denbigh." The changes in individual poems from edition to edition are often extensive and sometimes bewildering, and in many cases the versions must simply be described as different versions. There is, for instance, a 1653 version of the poem to the Countess of Denbigh that is in many ways a different poem from the 1652 version. The textual notes indicate the main source for each text. These notes have relied, both for interpretation of the principal editions and for notes on the manuscripts, on the magisterial work of Martin and Williams. Williams helpfully provides parallel texts of poems extant in two versions.

Because of the variant versions and Crashaw's inconsistent practices in matters of orthography and other conventions, his texts present particular problems. While Crashaw meant to use capitals and italics for emphasis, the practice varies from text to text, so that sometimes it becomes next to impossible to divine his intent. Given the many inconsistencies, no attempt is made here to preserve his patterns of capitalization and italics. Instead, conservative modern practice is followed. The notes mainly provide a record of editorial choices and emendations.

1646 *Steps to the Temple. . . .* (1646)
1648 *Steps to the Temple. . . .* (the second edition, 1648)
1652 *Carmen Deo Nostro* (1652)
1653 The 1653 revision of "To . . . The Countess of Denbigh"
M *The Poems English Latin and Greek of Richard Crashaw*, 2nd edition, Oxford, 1957
W *The Complete Poetry of Richard Crashaw*, New York, 1970

On the Wounds

Text: *1646*

6/ too *M* / two *1646*

On . . . Herbert's book

Full title: *On Mr. G. Herberts booke intituled the Temple of Sacred Poems, sent to a Gentlewoman. M*

Music's Duel

Text: *1646*. The secular poems have a separate title page: *The Delights of the Muses. Or, Other Poems written on severall occasions. . . .*

69/ whence *M* (following manuscripts) / when *1646 1648*
99/ graver *1648 M* / grave *1646*
156/ full-mouth *1646 1648* / full-mouth'd *M*

In the Holy Nativity

Text: *1652*; substantially revised in *1648* from *1646*.

28/ eyes' *M W* / eye's *1652*
32/ Young *1652* / Bright *1648*
47/ his own *1652* / all one *1648*
54/ bed: *1648* / bed *1652*
60/ wings *1648* / wing *1652*
69/ we *1652* / I *1648*
85/ nor to *1652* / not to *1648*

Saint Mary Magdalene

Text: *1652*; substantially revised in *1648* from *1646*.

2/ silver-forded *1646* / sylver-footed *1652 M W* (The reading links *rills* and *fords*. *W* argues that the *1652* "footed" is preferable because of the emphasis on feet in this poem.)
22/ above *1646* / above; *1652*
27/ sacred *1652* / soft *1646*
65/ blossom *1652* / Balsome *1648*
70/ crystal vials *1652* / their Bottles *1646*
91/ contest: of woes / contest of woes. *1648* / contest; of woes *1652*
95/ While *1652* / white *1648*
101/ suns, / suns *1652*
118/ wealth *1652* / wrath *1648*
159/ fire. / fire *1648* / fires *1652*
172/ your *1648* / their *1652*

A Hymn to . . . Saint Teresa

Text: *1652*. The Pierpont Morgan Library in New York owns a manuscript of this poem with the following title: "A HYMN *to the name and honour of the renowned* S. TERESIA Foundres of the Reformation of the Order of barefoote Carmelites; *A Woman for* Angelicall *height of* Contemplation *for* Masculine *courage of* Performance *more then a woman. Who* yet a *Child outranne Maturity & durst plott a* Martyrdome; *but was reserved by God to dy the* living death *of the* life *of his* love. *of whose great impressions as her noble heart had most high experiment, so hath she in her life most heroically exprest them, in her Spirituall posterity most fruitfully propagated them, and in these her heavnly Writings most sublimely, most sweetly taught them to ye world.*"
The text of the poem does not undergo major changes from version to version, but Crashaw added "The Flaming Heart" to this and another Teresa poem in *1648*.

4/ great *1652* / stout *1646*
10/ spacious bosoms spread *1652* / large breasts built *1646*
31/ you *1652* / we *1646*
44/ travail *1652* / travel *1646 1648*
47/ try *1648* / trade *1646 1652*
61/ *Line omitted in 1652*
104/ he . . . Die *1652* / he still may die *1646*
107/ his *1652* / thine *1648*
117/ resolving *1652* / dissolving *1646*
122/ thou shalt first *1648* / you first *1652*
130/ his *1652* / her *1646 1648*
147/ *Line omitted 1652*
148/ All *1652* / Anhs *1648*
151/ Deaths *1648* / Death *1652*
175/ keeps *1648* / keep *1652*

The Flaming Heart

Text: *1652*. The first version, *1648*, was eighty-four lines long; *1652* adds 85_B108. Full title: "THE FLAMING HEART UPON THE BOOK AND Picture of the seraphicall saint TERESA, (AS SHE IS USUALLY EX-pressed with a SERAPHiM biside her.)"

3/ too *1652* / so *1648*
11/ Read *1652* / And *1648*
16/ Shows *1652* / Shew *1648*
18/ happier *1648* / happy *1652*
31/ What *1652* / But *1648* wears *1652* / wore *1648*
33/ cheeks *1648 W* / cheek *1652*
36/ Had *1652* / She *1648*
58/ kindlly takes *1648* / gives *1652*
66/ glittering *1648* / glistering *1652 M*
76/ wounds *1648* / wound *1652* darts. *1652* / darts, *1648*
90/ sin. / sin, *1648 1652*

To . . . The Countess of Denbigh

Text: *1652*. A greatly revised and expanded version (one-third longer) was published at London in 1653.

10/ weakness) / weaknes! *1652*
58/ delay. *W* / delay *1652 M*

SIR JOHN DENHAM

The text is based on copies of *Poems and Translations* (1668) in the Cambridge University Library and the Harry Ransom Humanities Research Center at the University of Texas at Austin. Microfilms of a copy of *Cooper's Hill* (1642) in the British Museum and of a copy of *Poems and Translations* (1668) in the Huntington Library were also consulted. Other textual information was obtained from *The Poetical Works of Sir John Denham*, ed. T. H. Banks, 2nd ed. (New Haven, 1969), and B. O Hehir, *Expans'd Hieroglyphicks: A Critical Edition of Sir John Denham's Coopers Hill* (Berkeley, 1969).

Poems and Translations

Cooper's Hill

1/ Sure . . . which *1668*; Sure we have poets, that *1642*; If there be poets, which *1655*.
3/ we . . . may *1668*; and therefore I *1642*; we justly may *1655*.
6/ train *1655, 1668*; troops *1642*.
13–18/ In *1655 and 1668 these lines replace the following couplet in 1642*:

Exalted to this height, I first look down
On Paul's, as men from thence upon the town.

18/ descending *1668*; a falling *1655*.
25–30/ Under . . . seems *1655, 1668; 1642 reads:*

As those who raised in body, or in thought
Above the earth, or the air's middle vault,
Behold how winds, and storms, and meteors grow,
How clouds condense to rain, congeal to snow,
And see the thunder formed, before it tear
The air, secure from danger and from fear,
So raised above the tumult and the crowd
I see the city in a thicker cloud
Of business, than of smoke, where men like ants

Toil to prevent imaginary wants;
Yet all in vain, increasing with their store,
Their vast desires, but make their wants the more.
As food to unsound bodies, though it please
The appetite, feeds only the disease,

36/ *After this line, 1642 reads:*

Some study plots, and some those plots t'undo,
Others to make 'em, and undo 'em too,
False to their hopes, afraid to be secure
Those mischiefs only which they make, endure,
Blinded with light, and sick of being well,
In tumults seek their peace, their heaven in hell.

41–60/ Into . . . race *1655, 1668; 1642 reads:*

Into my eye, as the late married dame,
(Who proud, yet seems to make that pride her shame)
When nature quickens in her pregnant womb
Her wishes past, and now her hopes to come:
With such an easy, and unforced ascent,
Windsor her gentle bosom doth present;
Where no stupendous cliff, no threat'ning heights
Access deny, no horrid steep affrights,
But such a rise, as doth at once invite
A pleasure, and a reverence from the sight.
Thy master's emblem, in whose face I saw
A friend-like sweetness, and a king-like awe,
Where majesty and love so mixed appear,
Both gently kind, both royally severe.
So Windsor, humble in itself, seems proud,
To be the base of that majestic load,
Than which no hill a nobler burden bears,
But Atlas only, that supports the spheres.
Nature this mount so fitly did advance,
We might conclude, that nothing is by chance
So placed, as if she did on purpose raise
The hill, to rob the builder of his praise.
For none commends his judgement, that doth choose
That which a blind man only could refuse;
Such are the towers which th'hoary temples graced
Of Cybele, when all her heavenly race

79–82/ And thy . . . bring *1655, 1668; 1642 reads:*

He that the lilies wore, and he that won,
And thy Bellona who deserves her share
In all thy glories, of that royal pair
Which waited on thy triumph, she brought one,
Thy son the other brought, and she that son
Nor of less hopes could her great offspring prove,
A royal eagle cannot breed a dove.

85–86/ Each was . . . success *1655, 1668; 1642 reads:*

Each was a noble cause, nor was it less
I'th'institution, than the great success,
Whilst every part conspires to give it grace,
The King, the cause, the patron, and the place,

101–113/ When he . . . of late *1655, 1668; 1642 reads:*

Thou hadst extended through the conquered East
Thine and the Christian name, and made them blest
To serve thee, while that loss this gain would bring,
Christ for their God, and Edward for their King;
When thou that saint thy patron didst design,
In whom the martyr, and the soldier join;
And when thou didst within the azure round,
(Who evil thinks may evil him confound)
The English arms encircle, thou didst seem
But to foretell, and prophesy of him
Who has within that azure round confined
These realms, which nature for their bound designed.
That bound which to the worlds extremest ends,
Endless herself, her liquid arms extends;
In whose heroic face I see the saint
Better expressed than in the liveliest paint,
That fortitude which made him famous here,
That heavenly piety, which saints him there,
Who when this Order he forsakes, may he
Companion of that sacred order be.
Here could I fix my wonder, but our eyes,
Nice as our tastes, affect varieties;
And though one please him most, the hungry guest
Tastes every dish, and runs through all the feast;
So having tasted Windsor, casting round
My wand'ring eye, an emulous hill doth bound,
My more contracted sight, whose top of late

122/ But . . . poor, *1655, 1668*; But they, alas, were rich, and he was poor, *1642*.

127–33/ No crime . . . amends *1655, 1668; 1642 reads:*

And he might think it just, the cause and time
Considered well, for none commits a crime
Appearing such, but as 'tis understood
A real or at least a seeming good.
While for the church his learned pen disputes,
His much more learned sword his pen confutes;
Thus to the ages past he makes amends

149–156/ Who sees . . . are? *1655, 1668; omitted in 1642*

165–166/ Though with . . . gold: *1655, 1668*; And though his clearer sand no golden veins,/ Like Tagus and Pactolus streams contains *1642*.

171–172/ Nor then . . . overlay *1655, 1668; omitted in 1642*.

173/ sudden and impetuous *1655, 1668*; furious and unruly *1642*.

177–186/ But God-like . . . plants *1655, 1668; 1642 reads:*

Then like a lover he forsakes his shores,
Whose stay with jealous eye his spouse implores,
Till with a parting kiss he saves her tears,
And promising return, secures her fears;
As a wise king first settles fruitful peace
In his own realms, and with their rich increase
Seeks wars abroad, and then in triumph brings
The spoils of kingdoms, and the crowns of kings;

So Thames to London doth at first present
Those tributes which the neighboring countries sent;
But at his second visit from the east,
Spices he brings, and treasures from the west;
Finds wealth where 'tis, and gives it where it wants,
Cities in deserts, woods in cities plants;
Rounds the whole globe, and with his flying towers
Brings home to us and makes both Indies ours.

189–196/ O could . . . gods *1668; 1655 omits 193–196; 1642 reads:*

O could my verse freely and smoothly flow,
As thy pure flood, heaven should no longer know
Her old Eridanus, thy purer stream
Should bathe the gods, and be the poet's theme.

217–233/ But his . . . shape *1655, 1668; 1642 reads:*

And such the roughness of the hill, on which
Diana her toils, and Mars his tents might pitch.
And as our surly, supercilious lords,
Big in their frowns, and haughty in their words,
Look down on those, whose humble fruitful pain
Their proud, and barren greatness must sustain:
So looks the hill upon the stream, between
There lies a spacious, and a fertile green;
Where from the woods, the Dryades oft meet
The Naiades, and with their nimble feet
Soft dances lead, although their airy shape

236/ hornèd *1655, 1668*; horrid *1642. After l. 236, 1642 reads:*

(When like the elixir, with his evening beams,
The sun has turned to gold the silver streams)

240/ are undone *1655, 1668*; much undone *1642.*
241/ the King *1655, 1668*; our Charles *1642.*
243–271/ Attended to . . . unkindly wise *1655, 1668; 1642 reads:*

Chasing the royal stag, the gallant beast,
Roused with the noise 'twixt hope and fear distressed,
Resolves 'tis better to avoid, than meet
His danger, trusting to his winged feet:
But when he sees the dogs, now by the view
Now by the scent his speed with speed pursue,
He tries his friends, amongst the lesser herd,
Where he but lately was obeyed, and feared,
Safety he seeks, the herd unkindly wise,

275–288/ With shame . . . death *1655, 1668; omitted in 1642.*
293–294/ And now . . . flight *1655, 1668; omitted in 1642.*
297–303/ He straight . . . t'assay *1655, 1668; 1642 reads:*

When neither speed, nor art, nor friends, nor force
Could help him towards the stream he bends his course;
Hoping those lesser beasts would not assay

307–312/ So towards . . . wounds *1655, 1668; omitted in 1642.*
316/ common *1655, 1668*; vulgar *1642.*
319–322/ So when . . . flood *1655, 1668; 1642 reads:*

So the tall stag, amids the lesser hounds
Repels their force, and wounds returns for wounds,
Till Charles from his unerring hand lets fly
A mortal shaft, then glad, and proud to die
By such a wound he falls, the crystal flood
Dying he dies, and purples with his blood:

326/ lawless power *1655, 1668*; tyranny *1642.*
328/ *After this line 1642 reads:*

For armed subjects can have no pretence
Against their princes, but their just defence,
And whether then, or no, I leave to them
To justify, who else themselves condemn:
Yet might the fact be just, if we may guess
The justness of an action from success

343–348/ Thus kings . . . less *1655, 1668; 1642 reads:*

And they, whom no denial can withstand,
Seem but to ask, while they indeed command.
Thus all to limit royalty conspire,
While each forgets to limit his desire.
Till kings like old Antaeus by their fall,
Being forced, their courage from despair recall.

After 358, 1642 reads:

Thus kings by grasping more than they can hold,
First made their subjects by oppressions bold,
And popular sway by forcing kings to give
More, than was fit for subjects to receive,
Ran to the same extreme, and one excess
Made both, by stirring to be greater, less;
Nor any way, but seeking to have more,
Makes either lose, what each possessed before.
Therefore their boundless power tell princes draw
Within the channel, and the shores of law,
And may that law, which teaches kings to sway
Their scepters, teach their subjects to obey.

RICHARD LOVELACE

The text is based on a copy of *Lucasta* (1649) in the Library of Emmanuel College, Cambridge, and a copy of *Lucasta. Posthume Poems* (1659) in the Library of Trinity College, Cambridge. Copies of the 1649 and 1659 editions held in the Harry Ransom Humanities Research Center at the University of Texas at Austin were also consulted. A microfilm of a copy of the 1659 volume in the Huntington Library was also consulted. Manuscript and other textual information was obtained from *The Poems of Richard Lovelace*, ed. C. H. Wilkinson, 2 vols. (Oxford, 1925).

Lucasta

The Scrutiny . . .

7/ hours' *1649, 1659*; months *Wits Interpreter 1655*.
8/ must *1649, 1659*; should *Select Musicall Ayres and Dialogues 1653, Wits Interpreter 1655*.
11/ Not but all joy *1649, 1659*; Not that all joys *Select Musicall Ayres and Dialogues 1652, Wits Interpreter 1655*.
12/ By *1649, 1659*; In *1655*.
13/ I must *1649, 1659*; I will *1652, 1655*.
18/ With spoils *1649, 1659*; In spoil *1652, 1655*.

To Lucasta. From Prison . . .

12/ will she *1659*; she will *1649*.

To Althea. From Prison . . .

Cf. Wilkinson's edition, 1, pp. 47–60, for full account of variants.

7/ gods *1649, 1659*; birds *MSS*.
18/ throat *1649, 1659*; notes *B.M. MS. Add. 22603*; note *MSS*.
27/ Minds innocent and quiet take *1649, 1659*; The spotless soul and innocent *MSS*.; A spotless mind and innocent *MSS*.
32/ Enjoy *MSS., 1649, 1659*; Know no *Bodleian MS. 1267 Rawl. D.*

ABRAHAM COWLEY

The text is based on copies of *The Works of Mr. Abraham Cowley* (1668) in the Cambridge University Library and in the Harry Ransom Humanities Research Center at the University of Texas at Austin. A microfilm of another copy of that edition in the British Museum was also consulted. Further textual information was obtained from A. R. Waller's edition of Cowley's *Poems* (Cambridge, 1905).

The Works of Mr. Abraham Cowley

Ode. Of Wit

51/ the bombast *1668*; th'Oxford *Poems 1656*.
On the Death of Mr. Crashaw

21/ broke *1668*; breaks *1656*.
22/ spoke *1668*; speaks *1656*.

Anacreontics I: Love

14/ soft *1668*; and soft *1656*.

Platonic Love

3–4/ too combine . . . join *1668*; to do join, / And both our wholes into one whole combine *The Mistress 1647, Poems 1656*.

ANDREW MARVELL

Only a few of Marvell's poems were published in his lifetime. The first edition was the posthumous *Miscellaneous Poems* of 1681, published by "Mary Marvell" to lay claim to his estate, and it provides the only text for most of the poems written before 1660. A Bodleian Library manuscript—MS. Engl. poet. d. 49—contains the 1681 text (with omissions), a hundred manuscript emendations in a hand imitating print, manuscript additions (including three Cromwell poems canceled from most copies of 1681), and some satires. This manuscript is apparently the text compiled by Marvell's nephew and friend

William Popple for a projected *Complete Poetry*. The Scolar Press has published the 1681 folio using the British Museum copy, the best copy available, together with the Bodleian manuscript material.

While the order of the poems in 1681 is not totally satisfactory, no reordering has been very satisfactory either. Except for placement of the "Horatian Ode" before "Appleton House," this text follows the 1681 order and uses that as copy text. The 1681 is erratic in spelling, punctuation, and other conventions; there are printer's devils such as unclosed parentheses. The Bodleian corrects many small errors, but the basic problem remains. Hence, this text is conservative in the matter of capitals and punctuation, dropping most of the (very numerous) capitals and italics of the 1681 but modifying punctuation only where necessary.

1681	*Miscellaneous Poems.* By Andrew Marvell, Esq; Late Member of the Honourable House of Commons. London, 1681.
Cooke	*The Works* . . . , ed. Thomas Cooke. London, 1726. Bodleian MS. Engl. poet. d. 49.
BMS	Bodleian MS. Don. b. 8.
M1927	*The Poems and Letters* . . . , ed. H. M. Margoliouth. Two volumes. Vol. I, *The Poems*, Oxford, 1927.
M	1952, 1963, revised edition of the Oxford edition.
ML	1973, third edition (revised by Pierre Legouis).

A Dialogue between the Resolved. . . .

51/ soft *BMS M* / cost *1681. Cooke* conjectures: "All that's costly, fair, and sweet"

On a Drop of Dew

23/ sweet *BMS* / sweat *1681* / swart *ML*

Eyes and Tears

4/ They *1681* / We *BMS*
5/ And *1681* / Thus *BMS*
35/ teeming *1681* / seeming *BMS*

Bermudas

15/ fowls / Fowl's *1681* / Fowle *BMS*
37/ Indent from *BMS*

A Dialogue. . . .

BMS: The amanuensis crossed out the last four lines and wrote *Desunt multa* (*Many things are missing*). This may have been a guess (if so, a wrong one), or it may have been based on a manuscript. No solid evidence has come to light.

The Nymph Complaining . . .

119/ Legouis (*ML*) suggests that *There* may be a misprint and that *Then* (corresponding to *Until*, 117) would make a better reading.

To His Coy Mistress

33/ hue *1681* / lew *M* / glew *BMS*
34/ dew *BMS Cooke M* / lew *M1927* / glew *1681*

hue . . . dew are a well-known crux. *1681* reads *hue . . . glew*; many editors have accepted the latter, since *glew* could be a dialectal variant of *glow* (on the analogy *shew: show*), and *glow* makes better sense in the context than *dew*. In the 1927 edition, Margoliouth, though he thought that *glew* may have been Marvell's for line 34, found it nonetheless improbable: "The word had its modern sense [of glue] . . . and would therefore be inadmissible in this context"; he emended first to *lew*, "warmth," conjecturing that the *g* was a mistaken repeat of the last letter of the previous word, and then, in the 1952 edition, to *dew*, the emendation suggested by Cooke. *BMS* emends the *1681* readings, changing *hew* (33) to *glew* and *glew* (34) to *dew*. In 1970, W. H. Kelleher described another Bodleian manuscript (Don. b. 8), a miscellany in the hand of Sir William Haward, which contains a transcription (1672) of an early version of this poem with the following:

> Now then whil'st ye youthfull Glue
> Stickes on your Cheeke, like Morning Dew,
> (*Notes and Queries*, 215 [1970], 254_C56).

In the 3rd Oxford edition, Legouis remarks that "this fact invites us to make Marvell responsible for 'glew,' at least in an earlier version," but Legouis keeps Margoliouth's considered reading, speculating that Marvell "may well not have felt happy about" the word. Margoliouth's original reluctance to accept *glew* as Marvell's final reading seems still right.

44/ gates *1681* / grates *BMS*

Damon the Mower

21/ mads *BMS* / made *1681*
38/ dew *BMS* / due *1681*

Music's Empire

5/ first *BMS* / *omitted 1681*

The Garden

33/ in *1681* / is (conjectured by several editors, beginning with Edward Thompson, 1776; an attractive but unnecessary emendation)
41/ pleasure *1681* / pleasures *BMS*

An Horatian Ode

This poem was excised from all extant copies of *1681* except two, the British Museum copy and the copy at the Henry Huntington Library.

15/ through *1681* / thorough *BMS*
25/ kingdoms *BMS* / Kingdom *1681*
26/ force *1681* / face *BMS*
44_B45/ Wars . . . scars *1681* / warre . . . scarre *BMS*
85/ *Commons BMS* / Common *1681*
100/ crown *1681* / crowns *BMS*

Upon Appleton House

22/ Mote *BMS M* / Mose *1681* / Mole *Cooke* (perhaps with allusion to *molis*, in *Aeneid* I, 33, with its sense not only of great bulk but also of great effort)
268/ had *BMS* / hath *1681 M*
320/ nor *Cooke* / or *1681 M*
328/ thee *BMS* / The *1681 M*
356/ Earthly *1681 M* / Earthy *BMS*
368/ graze *BMS* / gaze *1681 M*
454/ Beast *BMS M* / Breast *1681*
472/ astonish'd *BMS M* / astonish *1681*

HENRY VAUGHAN

The text for "To My Ingenuous Friend, R. W." and "To Amoret" is from the microfilm copy of *Poems, With the Tenth Satire of Juvenal Englished* (London, 1646) in the University of Illinois Library. *Silex Scintillans* was first published in 1650, then reissued with a second part in 1655. (The 1655 edition also includes four reset pages—Sig. B2 and B3—of the 1650 with substantial variants.) Vaughan's major works were printed during his lifetime, under his supervision, and his texts therefore present few problems. Texts of poems from *Silex Scintillans* are based on the British Museum copy of the 1650 (reproduced in 1968 by Scolar Press) and of the 1655 editions. The modern editions of L. C. Martin and French Fogle were also consulted. The notes below record substantive editorial decisions only.

1650 *Silex Scintillans: or Sacred Poems and Private Ejaculations.* By Henry Vaughan Silurist. London, 1650.
M *The Works of Henry Vaughan*, ed. by L. C. Martin. 2nd edition, Oxford. 1957.
F *The Complete Poetry of Henry Vaughan*, ed. by French Fogle. New York, 1964.

Regeneration

48/ Earth (emendation suggested by Grosart) / Eare *1650 M F*
72/ Nor (emendation suggested by Edgar Daniels) / No *1650 M F*

MARGARET CAVENDISH, DUCHESS OF NEWCASTLE

The copy text is *Poems and Fancies* (London, 1664), which was "much altered and corrected" by Cavendish herself. The differences between the 1653 and 1664 editions are numerous, but no variants from the 1653 edition have been preferred.

THOMAS STANLEY

The text is based on a copy of *Poems* (1651) in the Cambridge University Library; the text of "Expectation" is based on a microfilm of a copy of *Poems and Translations* (1647) in the University of Illinois Library. Manuscript and further textual information was obtained from *Poems and Translations of Thomas Stanley*, ed. G. M. Crump (Oxford, 1962). *Minor Poems of the Caroline Period*, ed. G. Saintsbury, 3 vols. (Oxford, 1921), was also consulted.

Poems

The Glowworm

2/ animated gem *1651*; living star of earth *MSS., 1647*.
4/ erring *1651*; deceived *MSS., 1647*.
11/ paler *1647, 1651*; purer *Bodleian MS. Mus. b.* 1.
15/ thy *1651*; the *1647*.

Changed, Yet Constant

12–13/ By whom . . . desired *1651*; Who would as much / With love be fired *Cambs. Univ. Lib. MS. Add.* 7514.
17–24/ *In MS. this stanza reads:* She thats most fair / Exacts above / The rest obedience / For none there are / With reason love / But they that love by sense / Nor think allegiance I decline / Who was loves subject never thine
31–32/ Now power . . . never *1651*; 'Twere the same sin should I adore / Thee now or not have done't before *MS*.
33–48/ *Omitted in MS.*
For another distinctive MS. version of the poem, cf. Crump's edition, pp. 7–9.

Celia Singing

Title/ Celia Singing *1651*; Celia sleeping or singing *1647*.
10/ more *1647*; less *1651*.
12/ frame *Cambs MS., 1647*; flame *1651*.
19/ powers *1651*; power *1647*.

Love's Innocence

1/ strive to *1651*; (Dear) doth *Cambs MS., 1647*.
7/ As . . . fear 1651; To one another, whisp'ring there *MS., 1647*.
9–11/ such a . . . guides *1651*; (Fair) that flame to show / Which like thyself no crime can know: / Thus led by those chaste guides *MS., 1647*.
12/ well *1651*; free *MS., 1647*.
20/ (As our desires) *1651*; (As are our flames) *MS., 1647*.
21/ we, my dear *1651*; Doris, we *MS., 1647*.

La Belle Confidente

15/ But ours, that boast a reach *1647, 1651*; Ours that a being boast *Cambs MS*.
17/ For *1651*; And *MS., 1647*.
18/ Our . . . benighted *1651*; (Even in divorce delighted) *MS., 1647*.
20/ Even in divorce *1651*; Still in the grave *MS., 1647*.

The Bracelet

7/ soul *1651*; heart *MSS., 1647*.
12/ A heart . . . sold *1651*; Have to mine enemy my freedom sold *MSS., 1647*.
15/ human breasts *1651*; do our life *MSS., 1647*.
22/ Defends my vanquished 1651; Guards and defends my *MSS., 1647*.

JOHN DRYDEN

The texts are based on copies of *Three Poems upon the Death of his late Highnesse Oliver Lord Protector of England, Scotland, and Ireland* (1659), *Astraea Redux* (1660; bound with *Annus Mirabilis* [1688]), and Charleton's *Chorea Gigantum* (1662) in the Harry Ransom Humanities Research Center at the University of Texas at Austin. *The Works of John Dryden*, ed. Edward Niles Hooker and H. T. Swedenberg, Jr., et al., 20 vols. (California, 1956–2000), were also consulted. There are no substantive variants.

KATHERINE PHILIPS

The copy text is *Poems* (London, 1667), which was the first authorized edition. The 1664 edition in the Harry Ransom Humanities Research Center at the University of Texas at Austin was also consulted. Manuscript information is available in Patrick Thomas, ed., *The Collected Works of Katherine Philips, Vol. 1: The Poems* (Essex: Stump Cross, 1990).

Poems

Upon the Double Murder of King Charles I . . .

27–28/ *1664*; om. in *1667*.

On the Third of September, 1651

25/ captivated *1667*; captive *MS*.

To the Excellent Mrs. Anne Owen . . .

3/ No *1664*; Nay *1667*.

THOMAS TRAHERNE

Apart from some verses in his prose works, Traherne's poetry was virtually unknown in the seventeenth century. A manuscript of his poems was discovered and identified by Bertram Dobell at the end of the nineteenth century and first published by him in 1903; the Dobell Folio is now in the Bodleian Library (Bodl. MS. Engl. Poet. c. 42). A separate collection of poems, including many of the Dobell Folio poems, had been available in Burney MS. 392, acquired by the British Museum in 1818, but it was not noticed until after Dobell's publication. This manuscript, entitled *Poems of Felicity*, was prepared for publication by Philip Traherne, Thomas's brother. In preparing the text, Philip made extensive and usually unfortunate changes; as Margoliouth said, "His editing and changing of the text is a disaster" (p. xv). Philip's redaction was published with a misguided introduction by H. I. Bell (Oxford, 1910).

This text follows the Dobell Folio for all but one poem, using photocopies kindly loaned to Mario Di Cesare by the late Professor Arthur Clements. Readings have been checked against the excellent editions of Margoliouth and Ridler. Margoliouth includes Philip's versions of the Dobell Folio poems on facing pages. The editions differ in choices made when Dobell contains corrections by Thomas of original words: Margoliouth sometimes prefers the original; Ridler rarely does.

Traherne's conventions, while idiosyncratic, are fairly regular in their idiosyncrasy—for example, he capitalizes virtually all nouns and many verbs. The text as presented here follows modern practice. Traherne's idiosyncratic orthography is also regular, usually omitting final silent *e* (even in words like *celebrate, live, love*), apparently in a deliberate attempt to simplify spelling, a project that seems to have been mainly Philip's. He regularly omits internal silent or elided *e* without signaling the omission (in words like *every, eyes, adorned, seemed)* and usually uses *ie* for *y*, as in *sky* or *vanity*. Philip corrects many slips—inserting apostrophes in possessives or emending *ie* to *y* or correcting odd spellings, for example, *feinds* to *fiends* ("Wonder," 51).

The first six poems in this text are from the Dobell Folio; "On News" is from *The Third Century*; the last three are from Philip's manuscript. All the poems except "Love" are in Philip's text. The texts of the last four poems must be considered suspect.

D Dobell Folio, published as *The Poetical Works of Thomas Traherne* (London, 1903)
DT Thomas's original word(s) in *D*
F Philip's manuscript, published as *Poems of Felicity*, ed. H. I. Bell (Oxford, 1910)
M *Centuries, Poems, and Thanksgivings*, ed. by H. M. Margoliouth, two volumes (Oxford, 1958)
R *Poems, Centuries, and Three Thanksgivings*, ed. by Anne Ridler (Oxford, 1966).

Eden

13/ wights *R* / Weights *D F M*

My Spirit

51/ Were not alone even all that shined. *M* / Were not even all that therein shind. *D* (Thomas's correction)
79/ or Bower of Bliss. *DT M* / of Heavenly Bliss *D* (Thomas's correction)

On News

Text from *The Third Century* (*M*, I, 125_C27)

On Leaping Over the Moon (from F)

3/ And / Another (canceled). *M* suggests that Thomas actually wrote:

Another Sun by Day
Did things more clear display.

If so, Philip's version loses the fourfold emphasis (2, 3, 5, 9).

55–56/ As first written in *F*; Philip's version:

Then soon should we
Exalted be.

CRITICISM

Seventeenth- and Eighteenth-Century Criticism

BEN JONSON

From *Timber, or Discoveries*†

[*Poets and "Wits"*]

Nothing in our age, I have observed, is more preposterous, than the running judgments upon poetry and poets; when we shall hear those things commended and cried up for the best writings, which a man would scarce vouchsafe to wrap any wholesome drug in; he would never light his tobacco with them. And those men almost named for miracles, who yet are so vile, that if a man should go about to examine and correct them, he must make all they have done, but one blot. Their good is so entangled with their bad, as forcibly one must draw on the other's death with it. A sponge dipped in ink will do all: *Comitetur punica librium spongia*. Et paulo post, *Non possunt . . . multae, una litura potest.*[1]

Yet their vices have not hurt them: nay, a great many they have profited; for they have been loved for nothing else. And this false opinion grows strong against the best men: if once it take root with the ignorant. Cestius,[2] in his time, was preferred to Cicero; so far, as the ignorant durst; they learned him without book and had him often in their mouths. But a man cannot imagine that thing so foolish, or rude, but will find and enjoy an admirer; at least, a reader, or spectator. The puppets are seen now in despite of the players; Heath's *Epigrams*[3] and the Sculler's poems have their applause. [They] are never wanting that dare prefer the worst preachers, the worst pleaders, the worst poets; not that the better have left to write, or speak better, but that they that hear them judge worse: *Non illi peius dicunt, sed hi corruptius judicant*. Nay, if it were put to the question of the Water-rhymer's works, against Spenser, I doubt not, but that they would find more suffrages; because the most favor common vices, out of

† *Timber, or Discoveries* (included in the third volume of Jonson's *Works*, published in 1640–1641) is a "commonplace book," i.e., a collection of pithy observations on manners, men, and art. While Jonson draws on Greek and Latin authors and on sixteenth-century humanists for much of his material, he has extensively reworked his sources, combining them with anecdotes and opinions that reflect his own experience. The text is based on *Ben Jonson*, ed. C. H. Herford, P. and E. M. Simpson, 11 vols. (Oxford, 1925–1952), VIII (hereafter cited as *H&S*).

1. "Let a Punic sponge go with the book"; (and, a little farther on) "No amount [of erasures] will serve; a general blotting out is needed" (Martial, *Epigrams*, IV.x) [*Editor*].
2. Cestius of Smyrna was a Greek rhetorician who responded to several of Cicero's orations [*Editor*].
3. John Heath's *Epigrams* were published in 1610; the Thames waterman John Taylor (1580–1653), known as "the water-poet," published his verses in 1630 [*Editor*].

a prerogative the vulgar have, to lose their judgments and like that which is naught.

Poetry, in this latter age, hath proved but a mean mistress, to such as have wholly addicted themselves to her, or given their names up to her family. They who have but saluted her on the by, and now and then tendered their visits, she hath done much for, and advanced in the way of their own professions (both the Law, and the Gospel) beyond all they could have hoped, or done for themselves, without her favor. Wherein she doth emulate the judicious, but preposterous bounty of the time's grandees: who accumulate all they can upon the parasite, or freshman in their friendship; but think an old client, or honest servant, bound by his place to write and starve.

Indeed, the multitude commend writers, as they do fencers, or wrestlers; who if they come in robustiously and put for it, with a deal of violence, are received for the braver fellows: when many times their own rudeness is a cause of their disgrace; and a slight touch of their adversary, gives all that boisterous force the foil. But in these things, the unskillful are naturally deceived, and judging wholly by the bulk, think rude things greater than polished; and scattered more numerous, than composed: nor think this only to be true in the sordid multitude, but the neater sort of our gallants: for all are the multitude; only they differ in clothes, not in judgment or understanding.

I remember, the players have often mentioned it as an honor to Shakespeare, that in his writing (whatsoever he penned), he never blotted out a line. My answer hath been, would he had blotted a thousand. Which they thought a malevolent speech. I had not told posterity this, but for their ignorance, who choose that circumstance to commend their friend by, wherein he most faulted. And to justify mine own candor (for I loved the man, and do honor his memory, on this side idolatry, as much as any.) He was (indeed) honest, and of an open, and free nature: had an excellent fancy; brave notions and gentle expressions: wherein he flowed with that facility, that sometimes it was necessary he should be stopped: *Sufflaminandus erat*, as Augustus said of Haterius.[4] His wit was in his own power; would the rule of it had been so too. Many times he fell into those things, could not escape laughter: as when he said in the person of Caesar, one speaking to him, "Caesar, thou dost me wrong." He replied, "Caesar did never wrong, but with just cause,"[5] and such like; which were ridiculous. But he redeemed his vices with his virtues. There was ever more in him to be praised, than to be pardoned.

In the difference of wits,[6] I have observed; there are many notes: and it is a little mastery to know them: to discern, what every nature, every disposition will bear: for before we sow our land, we should plough it. There are no fewer forms of minds, than of bodies amongst us. The variety is incredible; and therefore we must search. Some are fit to make divines, some poets, some lawyers, some physicians; some to be sent to the plough and trades.

4. The remark ("What he needed was a brake") occurs in Marcus Annaeus Seneca, *Controversiae*, IV. The Roman rhetorician Quintus Haterius died in A.D. 26 [*Editor*].
5. Cf. *Julius Caesar*, III.i.47–48 [*Editor*].
6. The remainder of this section is largely based on Books I and II of Quintillian's *Institutio Oratoria* and Seneca's *Controversiae*, III [*Editor*].

There is no doctrine will do good, where nature is wanting. Some wits are swelling and high; others low and still: some hot and fiery; others cold and dull: one must have a bridle, the other a spur.

There be some that are forward and bold; and these will do every little thing easily: I mean, that is hard by, and next them: which they will utter, unretarded, without any shamefastness. These never perform much, but quickly. They are, what they are on the sudden; they show presently, like grain, that, scattered on the top of the ground, shoots up, but takes no root; has a yellow blade, but the ear empty. They are wits of good promise at first, but there is an *Ingenistitium*.[7] They stand still at sixteen, they get no higher.

You have others, that labor only to ostentation; and are ever more busy about the colors and surface of a work, than in the matter and foundation: for that is hid, the other is seen.

Others that in composition are nothing, but what is rough and broken: *Quae per salebras, altaque, saxa cadunt*.[8] And if it would come gently, they trouble it of purpose. They would not have it run without rubs,[9] as if that style were more strong and manly, that struck the ear with a kind of unevenness. These men err not by chance, but knowingly and willingly; they are like men that affect a fashion by themselves, have some singularity in a ruff, cloak, or hat-band; or their beards, specially cut to provoke beholders and set a mark upon themselves. They would be reprehended, while they are looked on. And this vice, one that is in authority with the rest, loving, delivers over to them to be imitated: so that oft-times the faults which he fell into, the others seek for: this is the danger, when vice becomes a precedent.

Others there are, that have no composition at all; but a kind of tuning and rhyming fall in what they write. It runs and slides and only makes a sound. Women's poets they are called: as you have women's tailors.

> They write a verse, as smooth, as soft, as cream;
> In which there is no torrent, nor scarce stream.

You may sound these wits and find the depth of them with your middle finger. They are cream-bowl, or but puddle deep.

Some that turn over all books, and are equally searching in all papers, that write out of what they presently find or meet, without choice: by which means it happens, that what they have discredited, and impugned in one work, they have before, or after, extolled the same in another. Such are all the essayists, even their master Montaigne. These, in all they write, confess still what books they have read last; and therein their own folly, so much, that they bring it to the stake raw and undigested: not that the place did need it neither; but that they thought themselves furnished and would vent it.

Some again, who (after they have got authority, or, which is less, opinion, by their writings, to have read much) dare presently to feign whole books and authors and lie safely. For what never was, will not easily be found; not by the most curious.

And some, by a cunning protestation against all reading, and false ven-

7. "A wit-stand" [Jonson's note].
8. "Which fall over rough places and high rocks" (Martial, *Epigrams*, XI.xc.2) [*Editor*].
9. I.e., uneven places in the surface of a bowling green [*Editor*].

ditation of their own naturals,[1] think to divert the sagacity of their readers from themselves, and cool the scent of their own fox-like thefts; when yet they are so rank, as a man may find whole pages together usurped from one author, their necessities compelling them to read for present use, which could not be in many books; and so come forth more ridiculously, and palpably guilty, than those, who because they cannot trace, they yet would slander their industry.

But the wretcheder are the obstinate contemners of all helps and arts: such as presuming on their own naturals (which perhaps are excellent) dare deride all diligence, and seem to mock at the terms, when they understand not the things; thinking that way to get off wittily, with their ignorance. These are imitated often by such, as are their peers in negligence, though they cannot be in nature: and they utter all they can think with a kind of violence and indisposition; unexamined, without relation, either to person, place, or any fitness else; and the more willful, and stubborn, they are in it, the more learned they are esteemed of the multitude, through their excellent vice of judgment: who think those things the stronger, that have no art: as if to break, were better than to open; or to rent asunder, gentler than to loose.

It cannot but come to pass, that these men, who commonly seek to do more than enough, may sometimes happen on something that is good and great; but very seldom: and when it comes, it doth not recompense the rest of their ill. For their jests and their sentences (which they only and ambitiously seek for) stick out and are more eminent; because all is sordid and vile about them; as lights are more discerned in a thick darkness, than a faint shadow. Now because they speak all they can (however unfitly) they are thought to have the greater copy;[2] where the learned use ever election, and a mean;[3] they look back to what they intended at first and make all an even and proportioned body. The true artificer will not run away from nature, as he were afraid of her; or depart from life and the likeness of truth; but speak to the capacity of his hearers. And though his language differ from the vulgar somewhat; it shall not fly from all humanity, with the Tamerlanes, and Tamer-Chams[4] of the late age, which had nothing in them but the scenical strutting, and furious vociferation, to warrant them to the ignorant gapers. He knows it is his only art, so to carry it, as none but artificers perceive it. In the meantime perhaps he is called barren, dull, lean, a poor writer (or by what contumelious word can come in their cheeks) by these men, who without labor, judgment, knowledge, or almost sense, are received, or preferred before him. He gratulates them and their fortune. Another age, or juster men, will acknowledge the virtues of his studies: his wisdom, in dividing:[5] his subtlety, in arguing: with what strength he doth inspire his readers; with what sweetness he strokes them: in inveighing, what sharpness; in jest, what urbanity he uses. How he doth reign in men's affections; how invade, and break in upon them; and makes their minds like the thing he writes. Then in his elocution to behold, what word is proper: which hath ornament: which height: what is beautifully translated: where figures are fit: which gentle, which strong to show the

1. I.e., display of their natural gifts [*Editor*].
2. Abundance [*Editor*].
3. I.e., selection and moderation [*Editor*].
4. *Tamer-Cham*, a lost play, appears to have been an imitation of Marlowe's *Tamburlaine* [*Editor*].
5. I.e., in rhetorical *divisio* [*Editor*].

composition manly. And how he hath avoided faint, obscure, obscene, sordid, humble, improper, or effeminate phrase; which is not only praised of the most, but commended (which is worse), especially for that it is naught.

[*Knowledge and Ignorance*]

I know no disease of the soul, but ignorance; not of the arts and sciences, but itself; yet relating to those, it is a pernicious evil: the darkener of man's life, the disturber of his reason, and common confounder of truth; with which a man goes groping in the dark, no otherwise than if he were blind. Great understandings are most racked and troubled with it; nay, sometimes they will rather choose to die, than not to know the things they study for. Think then what an evil it is; and what good the contrary.

Knowledge is the action of the soul; and is perfect without the senses, as having the seeds of all science and virtue in itself; but not without the service of the senses: by those organs, the soul works. She is a perpetual agent, prompt and subtle; but often flexible and erring; entangling herself like a silkworm; but her reason is a weapon with two edges and cuts through. In her indagations[6] oft-times new scents put her by; and she takes in errors into her, by the same conduits she doth truths. * * *

[*Language and Learning*][7]

Language most shows a man: speak that I may see thee. It springs out of the most retired, and inmost parts of us, and is the image of the parent of it, the mind. No glass renders a man's form, or likeness, so true as his speech. Nay, it is likened to a man; and as we consider feature, and composition in a man; so words in language: in the greatness, aptness, sound, structure, and harmony of it. Some men are tall and big, so some language is high and great. Then the words are chosen, their sound ample, the composition full, the absolution plenteous,[8] and poured out, all grave, sinewy and strong. Some are little and dwarfs: so of speech it is humble and low, the words poor and flat; the members and periods, thin and weak, without knitting, or number. The middle are of a just stature. There the language is plain and pleasing: even without stopping, round without swelling; all well-turned, composed, elegant, and accurate. The vicious language is vast, and gaping, swelling, and irregular; when it contends to be high, full of rock, mountain, and pointedness: as it affects to be low, it is abject, and creeps, full of bogs, and holes. And according to their subject, these styles vary and lose their names: for that which is high and lofty, declaring excellent matter, becomes vast and tumorous,[9] speaking of petty and inferior things: so that which was even, and apt in a mean and plain subject, will appear most poor and humble in a high argument. Would you not laugh, to meet a great counsellor of state in a flat cap, with his trunk hose, and a hobbyhorse cloak,[1] his gloves under his girdle, and yond haberdasher in a velvet gown, furred with sables? There is a certain latitude in these

6. Investigations [*Editor*].
7. The first part of this section is based on a passage from Vives's *De Ratione Dicendi*; the second part on Bacon's *Advancement of Learning*, I.iv [*Editor*]
8. I.e., the delivery free [*Editor*].
9. Swollen [*Editor*].
1. I.e., a long cloak like that worn by the "hobby horse" performers in morris dances [*Editor*].

things, by which we find the degrees. The next thing to the stature, is the figure and feature in language: that is, whether it be round and straight, which consists of short and succinct periods, numerous, and polished; or square and firm, which is to have equal and strong parts, every where answerable and weighed. The third is the skin and coat, which rests in the well-joining, cementing, and coagmentation[2] of words; when as it is smooth, gentle, and sweet: like a table, upon which you may run your finger without rubs, and your nail cannot find a joint; not horrid, rough, wrinkled, gaping, or chapped. After these the flesh, blood, and bones come in question. We say it is a fleshy style, when there is much periphrasis, and circuit of words; and when with more than enough, it grows fat and corpulent; *arvina orationis*,[3] full of suet and tallow. It hath blood and juice, when the words are proper and apt, their sound sweet, and the phrase neat and picked. *Oratio uncta, et bene pasta*.[4] But where there is redundancy, both the blood and juice are faulty and vicious. *Redundant sanguine, quae multo plus dicit, quam necesse est*.[5] Juice in language is somewhat less than blood; for if the words be but becoming and signifying, and the sense gentle, there is juice: but where that wanteth, the language is thin, flagging, poor, starved, scarce covering the bone; and shows like stones in a sack. Some men, to avoid redundancy, run into that; and while they strive to have no ill blood, or juice, they lose their good. There be some styles, again, that have not less blood, but less flesh, and corpulence. These are bony and sinewy: *Ossa habent, et nervos*.

It was well noted by the late L. St. Alban,[6] that the study of words is the first distemper of learning: vain matter the second: and a third distemper is deceit, or the likeness of truth; imposture held up by credulity. All these are the cobwebs of learning, and to let them grow in us is either sluttish or foolish. Nothing is more ridiculous, than to make an author a dictator, as the schools have done Aristotle. The damage is infinite knowledge receives by it. For to many things a man should owe but a temporary belief, and a suspension of his own judgment, not an absolute resignation of himself, or a perpetual captivity. Let Aristotle and others have their dues; but if we can make farther discoveries of truth and fitness than they, why are we envied? Let us beware while we strive to add, we do not diminish, or deface; we may improve, but not augment. By discrediting falsehood, truth grows in request. We must not go about like men anguished and perplexed, for vicious affectation of praise: but calmly study the separation of opinions, find the errors have intervened, awake antiquity, call former times into question; but make no parties with the present, nor follow any fierce undertakers, mingle no matter of doubtful credit, with the simplicity of truth, but gently stir the mold about the root of the question, and avoid all digladiations,[7] facility of credit, or superstitious simplicity; seek the consonancy, and concatenation of truth; stoop only to point of necessity, and what leads to convenience. Then make exact animadversion where style hath degenerated, where flourished, and thrived in choiceness of phrase, round and clean composition of sentence, sweet falling of the clause, vary-

2. Combination [*Editor*].
3. "The fat of speech" [*Editor*].
4. "Speech sleek and well-fed" [*Editor*].
5. "That style which says more than is strictly required has too much blood in it" [*Editor*].
6. I.e., Sir Frances Bacon [*Editor*].
7. Disputations [*Editor*].

ing an illustration by tropes and figures, weight of matter, worth of subject, soundness of argument, life of invention, and depth of judgment. This is *monte potiri*, to get the hill. For no perfect discovery can be made upon a flat or a level. * * *

[*Poets and Poetry*]

WHAT IS A POET?

A poet is that, which by the Greeks is called κατ' ἐξοχὴν, ὁ ποιητὴς, a maker, or a feigner: his art, an art of imitation, or feigning; expressing the life of man in fit measure, numbers, and harmony, according to Aristotle: from the word ποιεῖν, which signifies to make or feign. Hence, he is called a poet, not he which writeth in measure only; but that feigneth and formeth a fable, and writes things like the truth. For the fable and fiction is (as it were) the form and soul of any poetical work, or poem.

WHAT MEAN YOU BY A POEM?

A poem is not alone any work, or composition of the poet's in many, or few verses; but even one alone verse sometimes makes a perfect poem. As, when Aeneas hangs up, and consecrates the arms of Abas, with this inscription: *Aeneas haec de Danais victoribus arma.*[8] And calls it a poem, or *carmen*. Such as those in Martial. *Omnia, Castor, emis: sic fiet, ut omnia vendas.*[9] And, *Pauper videri cinna vult, et est pauper.*[1]

So were Horace his *Odes* called, *Carmina*, his lyric songs. And Lucretius designs a whole book, in his sixth. *Quod in primo quoque carmine claret.*[2] And anciently, all the oracles were called, *Carmina*; or, whatever sentence was expressed, were it much, or little, it was called, an epic, dramatic, lyric, elegiac, or epigrammatic poem.

BUT, HOW DIFFERS A POEM FROM WHAT WE CALL POESY?

A poem, as I have told you, is the work of the poet; the end and fruit of his labor and study. Poesy is his skill, or craft of making: the very fiction itself, the reason, or form of the work. And these three voices differ, as the thing done, the doing, and the doer; the thing feigned, the feigning, and the feigner: so the poem, the poesy, and the poet. Now, the poesy is the habit, or the art: nay, rather the queen of arts, which had her original from heaven, received thence from the Hebrews, and had in prime estimation with the Greeks, transmitted to the Latins, and all nations, that professed civility. The study of it (if we will trust Aristotle) offers to mankind a certain rule, and pattern of living well, and happily; disposing us to all civil offices of society. If we will believe Tully,[3] it nourisheth and instructeth our youth; delights our age; adorns our prosperity; comforts our adversity; entertains us at home; keeps us company abroad, travels with us; watches; divides the times of our earnest and sports; shares in our country recesses and recreations; insomuch as the wisest and best learned have thought her

8. "Aeneas [won] these arms from the conquering Greeks" (*Aeneid*, III.288) [*Editor*].
9. "Castor, you buy everything; by the same token, you will sell everything" (Martial, *Epigrams*, VII.xcviii) [*Editor*].
1. "Cinna wishes to appear a pauper, and is a pauper" (*ibid.*, VIII.xix) [*Editor*].
2. "Which is set forth in the first part of my poem" [*Editor*].
3. I.e., Cicero [*Editor*].

the absolute mistress of manners and nearest of kin to virtue. And, whereas they entitle philosophy to be a rigid and austere poesy: they have (on the contrary) styled poesy, a dulcet and gentle philosophy, which leads on, and guides us by the hand to action, with a ravishing delight and incredible sweetness. But, before we handle the kinds of poems, with their special differences; or make court to the art itself, as a mistress, I would lead you to the knowledge of our poet, by a perfect information, what he is, or should be by nature, by exercise, by imitation, by study; and so bring him down through the disciplines of grammar, logic, rhetoric, and the ethics, adding somewhat, out of all, peculiar to himself, and worthy of your admittance, or reception.

1. *Ingenium.*[4] First, we require in our poet, or maker (for that title our language affords him, elegantly, with the Greek), a goodness of natural wit. For, whereas all other arts consist of doctrine and precepts: the poet must be able by nature and instinct, to pour out the treasure of his mind; and, as Seneca saith, *Aliquando secundum Anacreontem insanire, jucundum esse,*[5] by which he understands, the poetical rapture. And according to that of Plato; *Frustra Poeticas fores sui compos pulsavit.*[6] And of Aristotle: *Nullum magnum ingenium sine mixtura dementiae fuit. Nec potest grande aliquid, et supra caeteros loqui, nisi mota mens.*[7] Then it riseth higher, as by a divine instinct, when it contemns common and known conceptions. It utters somewhat above a mortal mouth. Then it gets aloft, and flies away with his rider, whether, before, it was doubtful to ascend. This the poets understood by their Helicon, Pegasus, or Parnassus; and this made Ovid to boast:

> *Est, Deus in nobis; agitante calescimus illo:*
> *Sedibus aethereis spiritus ille venit.*[8]

And Lipsius, to affirm; *Scio, Poetam neminem praestantem fuisse, sine parte quadam uberiore divinae aurae.*[9] And, hence it is, that the coming up of good poets (for I mind not *mediocres*, or *imos*)[1] is so thin and rare among us; every beggarly corporation affords the state a mayor, or two bailiffs, yearly: but, *Solus Rex, aut Poeta, non quotannis nascitur.*[2]

2. *Exercitatio.* To this perfection of nature in our poet, we require exercise of those parts and frequent. If his wit will not arrive suddenly at the dignity of the ancients, let him not yet fall out with it, quarrel, or be overhastily angry: offer, to turn it away from study, in a humor; but come to it again upon better cogitation; try another time, with labor. If then it succeed not, cast not away the quills, yet: nor scratch the wainscot, beat not the poor desk; but bring all to the forge, and file, again; turn it anew. There is no statue law of the kingdom bids you be a poet, against your will; or

4. I.e., "genius," or natural character [*Editor*].
5. "According to Anacreon, occasionally it is pleasing to be seized with madness" (Seneca, *De Tranquilitate Animi*, xvii) [*Editor*].
6. "A man in his senses knocks vainly at the gates of poetry" (*Phaedrus*, 245a) [*Editor*].
7. "There was never a great genius without a touch of madness. Nor may the mind achieve or express anything great unless emotion plays a part" [*Editor*].
8. "There is a god in us, by whose movement we are kept warm; that spirit comes from the heavenly realms" (cf. *Fasti*, vi.5–6, and *Ars Amatoria*, iii.549–550) [*Editor*].
9. "I know there has never been a great poet without a richer share than most possess of divine inspiration." Justus Lipsius (1547–1606) was a Flemish scholar and translator [*Editor*].
1. I.e., the ordinary or inferior [*Editor*].
2. "It is only a king or a poet that is not born every year" [*Editor*].

the first quarter.[3] If it come, in a year, or two, it is well. The common rhymers pour forth verses, such as they are (*ex tempore*), but there never comes from them one sense, worth the life of a day. A rhymer and a poet are two things. It is said of the incomparable Vergil, that he brought forth his verses like a bear, and after formed them with licking. Scaliger, the father,[4] writes it of him, that he made a quantity of verses in the morning, which afore night he reduced to a less number. But, that which Valerius Maximus[5] hath left recorded of Euripides, the tragic poet, his answer to Alcestis, another poet, is as memorable, as modest: who, when it was told to Alcestis, that Euripides had in three days brought forth but three verses, and those with some difficulty and throes; Alcestis, glorying he could with ease have sent forth a hundred in the space; Euripides roundly replied, "Like enough. But, here is the difference; thy verses will not last those three days; mine will to all time." Which was, as to tell him, he could not write a verse. I have met many of these rattles, that made a noise and buzzed. They had their hum; and, no more. Indeed, things, wrote with labor, deserve to be so read, and will last their age.

3. *Imitatio*. The third requisite in our poet, or maker, is imitation, to be able to convert the substance, or riches of another poet, to his own use. To make choice of one excellent man above the rest, and so to follow him, till he grow very he: or, so like him, as the copy may be mistaken for the principal. Not as a creature that swallows what it takes in crude, raw, or undigested; but, that feeds with an appetite, and hath a stomach to concoct,[6] divide, and turn all into nourishment. Not to imitate servilely, as Horace saith, and catch at vices, for virtue: but, to draw forth out of the best and choicest flowers with the bee and turn all into honey, work it into one relish and savor: make our imitation sweet: observe, how the best writers have imitated and follow them. How Vergil and Statius[7] have imitated Homer; how Horace, Archilochus; how Alcéus, and the other lyrics: and so of the rest.

4. *Lectio*. But, that, which we especially require in him is an exactness of study, and multiplicity of reading, which maketh a full man, not alone enabling him to know the history, or argument of a poem, and to report it: but so to master the matter and style, as to show, he knows, how to handle, place, or dispose of either, with elegancy, when need shall be. And not think he can leap forth suddenly a poet by dreaming he hath been in Parnassus, or having washed his lips (as they say) in Helicon. There goes more to his making, than so.

Ars corona.[8] For to nature, exercise, imitation, and study, art must be added, to make all these perfect. And, though these challenge to themselves much, in the making up of our maker, it is art only can lead him to perfection, and leave him there in possession, as planted by her hand. It is the assertion of Tully, if to an excellent nature, there happen an acces-

3. I.e., three months (relatively soon) [*Editor*].
4. I.e., J. C. Scaliger (1484–1558), Italian humanist [*Editor*].
5. Valerius Maximus (fl. c. A.D. 35) compiled an anthology of historical anecdotes [*Editor*].
6. Digest [*Editor*].
7. The epic poet Statius (c. A.D. 61–c. 96) composed the *Thebaid*; Archilocus was a Greek lyric poet of the seventh century B.C.; the Greek poet Alcaeus flourished late in the same century [*Editor*].
8. "Art [is] the crown" [*Editor*].

sion, or conformation of learning and discipline, there will then remain somewhat noble and singular. For, as Simylus saith in Stobaeus:[9]

> *Οὔτε φύσις ἱκανὴ γίνεται τέχνης ἄτερ,*
> *οὔτε πᾶν τέχνη μὴ φύσιν κεκτημένη·*

without art, nature can never be perfect; and, without nature, art can claim no being. But, our poet must beware, that his study be not only to learn of himself; for, he that shall affect to do that, confesseth his ever having a fool to his master. He must read many; but ever the best and choicest: those, that can teach him anything, he must ever account his masters and reverence: among whom Horace, and (he that taught him) Aristotle, deserve to be the first in estimation. Aristotle was the first accurate critic and truest judge; nay, the greatest philosopher, the world ever had: for, he noted the vices of all knowledges, in all creatures, and out of many men's perfections in a science, he formed still one art. So he taught us two offices[1] together, how we ought to judge rightly of others, and what we ought to imitate specially in ourselves. But all this in vain, without a natural wit, and a poetical nature in chief.

BEN JONSON

From *Conversations with William Drummond of Hawthornden*†

That he had an intention to perfect an epic poem entitled *Heroologia*, of the worthies of his country roused by fame and was to dedicate it to his country; it is all in couplets, for he detesteth all other rhymes. Said he had written a discourse of poesy both against Campion and Daniel, especially this last, where he proves couplets to be the bravest sort of verses, especially when they are broken, like hexameters; and that cross rhymes and stanzas (because the purpose would lead him beyond 8 lines to conclude) were all forced.

He recommended to my reading Quintilian (who, he said, would tell me the faults of my verses as if he had lived with me) and Horace, Plinius Secundus' *Epistles*, Tacitus, Juvenal, Martial, whose epigram . . . he hath translated.[1]

His censure of the English poets was this: that Sidney did not keep a decorum in making everyone speak as well as himself. Spenser's stanzas pleased him not, nor his matter, the meaning of which allegory he had delivered in papers to Sir Walter Raleigh. Samuel Daniel was a good honest man, had no children, but no poet.

That Michael Drayton's *Polyolbion* (if he had performed what he prom-

9. Stobaeus, about A.D. 500, compiled an anthology of Greek writings, including passages from the work of Simylus, who flourished in the fourth century B.C. [*Editor*].
1. Duties [*Editor*].
† During Jonson's visit to Scotland in 1618–1619, he stayed in Edinburgh (for some three weeks) with the Scottish poet and man of letters William Drummond (1585–1649), who recorded in note form his guest's opinions on literary and other matters. The text is based on that in *H & S*, I, pp. 132–151.
1. Cf. Martial, *Epigrams*, X.xlvii [*Editor*].

ised to write, the deeds of all the worthies) had been excellent; his long verses pleased him not.

That Silvester's translation of Du Bartas was not well done, and that he wrote his verses before it ere he understood to confer.

Nor that of Fairfax's.[2]

That the translations of Homer and Vergil in long Alexandrines were but prose.

That John Harington's Ariosto, under all translations, was the worst.

* * *

That Donne's *Anniversary* was profane and full of blasphemies.

That he told Mr. Donne, if it had been written of the Virgin Mary, it had been something. To which he answered that he described the idea of a woman and not as she was. That Donne for not keeping of accent deserved hanging.

That Shakespeare wanted art.

That Sharpham, Day, Dekker were all rogues, and that Minshew was one.[3]

That Abram Francis[4] in his English hexameters was a fool.

That next himself, only Fletcher and Chapman could make a masque.

* * *

His censure of my verses was that they were all good, especially my epitaph of the prince, save that they smelled too much of the schools and were not after the fancy of the time. For a child, says he, may write after the fashion of the Greeks and Latin verses in running;[5] yet that he wished, to please the king, that piece of *Forth Feasting* had been his own.

He esteemeth John Donne the first poet in the world in some things. His verses of the lost chain,[6] he hath by heart; and that passage of *The Calm*: that dust and feathers do not stir, all was so quiet. Affirmeth Donne to have written all his best pieces ere he was 25 years old. Sir Edward Wotton's verses of a happy life[7] he hath by heart, and a piece of Chapman's translation of the 13 of the *Iliad*, which he thinketh well done.

That Donne said to him he wrote that *Epitaph on Prince Henry* ("Look to me, faith") to match Sir Edward Herbert[8] in obscureness.

He hath by heart some verses of Spenser's *Calender*, about wine, between Colin and Pierce.[9]

2. I.e., the translation of Tasso's epic poem *Gerusalemme Liberata* by Edward Fairfax (c. 1575–1635) [*Editor*].
3. Edward Sharpham (1576–1608) and John Day (fl. 1606) were contemporary playwrights of no particular mark; Thomas Dekker (1570–1632), the author of *The Shoemakers' Holiday*, also wrote a number of prose pamphlets on social conditions in London; the lexicographer John Minsheu published a polyglot dictionary in 1617 [*Editor*].
4. Abraham Fraunce (c. 1587–1633), author of *The Arcadian Rhetorike*, was known in his day primarily for his translation of Thomas Watson's Latin play *Amynias* [*Editor*].
5. Samuel Daniel, in *A Defence of Ryme* (1603), objects to "those continual cadences of couplets used in long and continued poems," adding that "to beguile the ear with a running out, and passing over the rhyme . . . is rather graceful than otherwise" (*Poems and a Defence of Ryme*, ed. A. C. Sprague [Chicago, 1965], pp. 155–156) [*Editor*].
6. I.e., Elegy XI ("The Bracelet") [*Editor*].
7. I.e., the lyric beginning, "How happy is he born or taught," by Sir Henry Wotton (1568–1639) [*Editor*].
8. Douglas Bush describes Lord Herbert of Cherbury (1582–1648) as "the first disciple of Donne on the secular side" (*English Literature in the Earlier Seventeenth Century*, 2nd ed., rev. [New York, 1962], p. 160) [*Editor*].
9. The allusion is to *The Shepheardes Calender*, "October," lines 109–114 [*Editor*].

* * *

That Petronius, Plinius Secundus, Tacitus speak best Latin; that Quintilian's 6. 7. 8. books were not only to be read but altogether digested. Juvenal, Persius, Horace, Martial for delight, and so was Pindar. For health, Hippocrates. Of their nation, Hooker's *Ecclesiastical History* (whose children are now beggars) for church matters.

* * *

For a heroic poem, he said there was no such ground as King Arthur's fiction, and that Sir Philip Sidney had an intention to have transformed all his *Arcadia* to the stories of King Arthur.

His acquaintance and behavior with poets living with him.

Daniel was at jealousies with him.

That Francis Beaumont loved too much himself and his own verses.

That Sir John Roe[1] loved him, and when they two were ushered by my Lord Suffolk from a masque, Roe wrote a moral epistle to him, which began that next to plays the court and the state were the best: God threateneth kings, kings lords, and lords do us.

He beat Marston and took his pistol from him.

* * *

Ned Field[2] was his scholar and he had read to him the satires of Horace and some epigrams of Martial.

That Markham[3] (who added his *English Arcadia*) was not of the number of the faithful (i.e., poets) and but a base fellow.

That such were Day and Middleton.

That Chapman and Fletcher were loved of him.

Overbury[4] was first his friend, then turned his mortal enemy.

* * *

That in that paper Sir Walter Raleigh had of the allegories of his [Spenser's] *Fairie Queene*, by the Blatant Beast the Puritans were understood; by the false Duessa, the Queen of Scots.

That Southwell was hanged; yet, so he had written that piece of his *The Burning Babe*, he would have been content to destroy many of his.

* * *

That Donne himself, for not being understood, would perish.

That Sir Walter Raleigh esteemed more of fame than conscience: the best wits of England were employed for making of his history; Ben himself had written a piece to him of the Punic War, which he altered and set in his book.

1. The "moral epistle" by Sir John Roe, the brother of William Roe to whom Jonson's Epigram CXXVIII is addressed, appears in *The Poems of John Donne*, ed. Sir H. I. C. Grierson (London, 1933), pp. 383–384 [*Editor*].
2. Nathaniel Field (1587–1633) was a playwright and actor who took roles in plays by Jonson and Shakespeare [*Editor*].
3. Gervase Markham (1568–1637), who wrote voluminously on several subjects, is distinguished chiefly for having been the first to import an Arabian stallion into England [*Editor*].
4. Sir Thomas Overbury (1581–1613), known to literary history for his Theophrastian *Characters*, met his death by poison, administered over a lengthy period of time by agents of Lady Essex [*Editor*].

* * *

Marston wrote his father-in-law's preachings, and his father-in-law his comedies.

Shakespeare in a play brought in a number of men saying they had suffered shipwreck in Bohemia, where there is no sea near by some 100 miles.

Daniel wrote *Civil Wars*, and yet hath not one battle in his book.

* * *

His opinion of verses.

That he wrote all his first in prose, for so his master Camden had learned him.

That verses stood by sense without either colors or accent, which yet other times he denied.

A great many epigrams were ill, because they expressed in the end what should have been understood by what was said.

* * *

He was better versed and knew more in Greek and Latin than all the poets in England and quintessenced their brains.

* * *

He is a great lover and praiser of himself, a contemner and scorner of others, given rather to lose a friend than a jest; jealous of every word and action of those about him (especially after drink, which is one of the elements in which he liveth); a dissembler of ill parts which reign in him, a bragger of some good that he wanteth; thinketh nothing well but what either he himself, or some of his friends and countrymen, hath said or done. He is passionately kind and angry; careless either to gain or keep; vindicative,[5] but, if he be well answered, at himself.

EDWARD HYDE, EARL OF CLARENDON†

From *The Life of Edward, Earl of Clarendon*

Whilst he[1] was only a student of the law, and stood at gaze, and irresolute what course of life to take, his chief acquaintance were Ben Jonson, John Selden, Charles Cotton, John Vaughan, Sir Kenelm Digby, Thomas May, and Thomas Carew, and some others of eminent faculties in their several ways. Ben Jonson's name can never be forgotten, having by his very good learning, and the severity of his nature and manners, very much reformed the stage; and indeed the English poetry itself. His natural advantages were, judgment to order and govern fancy, rather than excess of fancy, his productions being slow and upon deliberation, yet then abounding with

5. Vindictive [*Editor*].

† The text is that of the edition published at Oxford in 1760.

1. I.e., Edward Hyde (subsequently Earl of Clarendon). For Selden, cf. Jonson, "An Epistle to Master John Selden," p. 133; for Vaughan, Digby, and May, cf. Suckling, "A Sessions of the Poets," p. 412 [*Editor*].

great wit and fancy and will live accordingly; and surely as he did exceedingly exalt the English language in eloquence, propriety, and masculine expressions; so he was the best judge of, and fittest to prescribe rules to poetry and poets, of any man who had lived with, or before him, or since: if Mr. Cowley had not made a flight beyond all men, with that modesty yet, to ascribe much of this, to the example and learning of Ben Jonson. His conversation was very good, and with the men of most note; and he had for many years an extraordinary kindness for Mr. Hyde, till he found he betook himself to business, which he believed ought never to be preferred before his company. He lived to be very old, and till the palsy made a deep impression upon his body, and his mind.

JOHN DRYDEN

[Observations on Jonson's Art]†

I must desire you to take notice, that the greatest man of the last age, Ben Jonson, was willing to give place to them in all things: he was not only a professed imitator of Horace, but a learned plagiary of all the others; you track him everywhere in their snow: if Horace, Lucan, Petronius Arbiter, Seneca, and Juvenal, had their own from him, there are few serious thoughts which are new in him: you will pardon me, therefore, if I presume he loved their fashion, when he wore their clothes.

* * *

As for Jonson, to whose character I am now arrived, if we look upon him while he was himself (for his last plays were but his dotages), I think him the most learned and judicious writer which any theatre ever had. He was a most severe judge of himself, as others. One cannot say he wanted wit, but rather that he was frugal of it. In his works you find little to retrench or alter. Wit and language, and humor also in some measure, we had before him; but something of art was wanting to the drama, till he came. He managed his strength to more advantage than any who preceded him. You seldom find him making love in any of his scenes, or endeavoring to move the passions; his genius was too sullen and saturnine to do it gracefully, especially when he came after those who had performed both to such an height. Humor was his proper sphere; and in that he delighted most to represent mechanic people. He was deeply conversant in the ancients, both Greek and Latin, and he borrowed boldly from them: there is scarce a poet or historian among the Roman authors of those times, whom he has not translated in *Sejanus* and *Catiline*. But he has done his robberies so openly, that one may see he fears not to be taxed by any law. He invades authors like a monarch; and what would be theft in other poets, is only victory in him. With the spoils of these writers he so represents old Rome to us, in its rites, ceremonies, and customs, that if one of their poets had

† The first three passages are excerpted from *An Essay of Dramatick Poesie*; the text follows that in vol. XVII of *The Works of John Dryden*, ed. S. H. Monk (Berkeley, 1971). The fourth passage is excerpted from the Preface to *An Evening's Love*, and follows the text in vol. X of *The Works of John Dryden*, ed. M. E. Novak (Berkeley, 1970).

written either of his tragedies, we had seen less of it than in him. If there was any fault in his language, it was, that he weaved it too closely and laboriously, in his comedies especially: perhaps, too, he did a little too much Romanize our tongue, leaving the words which he translated almost as much Latin as he found them: wherein, though he learnedly followed their language, he did not enough comply with the idiom of ours. If I would compare him with Shakespeare, I must acknowledge him the more correct poet, but Shakespeare the greater wit. Shakespeare was the Homer, or father of our dramatic poets; Jonson was the Vergil, the pattern of elaborate writing; I admire him, but I love Shakespeare. To conclude of him; as he has given us the most correct plays, so in the precepts which he has laid down in his *Discoveries*, we have as many and profitable rules for perfecting the stage, as any wherewith the French can furnish us.

* * *

And as for your instance of Ben Jonson, who, you say, writ exactly without the help of rhyme; you are to remember, it is only an aid to a luxuriant fancy, which his was not: as he did not want imagination, so none ever said he had much to spare.

* * *

But Ben Jonson is to be admired for many excellencies; and can be taxed with fewer failings than any English poet. I know I have been accused as an enemy of his writings; but without any other reason, than that I do not admire him blindly, and without looking into his imperfections. For why should there be *ipse dixit*[1] in our poetry, any more than there is in our philosophy? I admire and applaud him where I ought: those who do more, do but value themselves in their admiration of him; and, by telling you they extol Ben Jonson's way, would insinuate to you that they can practise it. For my part, I declare that I want judgment to imitate him; and should think it a great impudence in myself to attempt it. To make men appear pleasantly ridiculous on the stage, was, as I have said, his talent; and in this he needed not the acumen of wit but that of judgment. For the characters and representations of folly are only the effects of observation; and observation is an effect of judgment. * * * I think there is no folly so great in any poet of our age, as the superfluity and waste of wit was in some of our predecessors: particularly we may say of Fletcher and of Shakespeare, what was said of Ovid, *In omni ejus ingenio, facilius quod rejici, quam quod adjici potest, invenies*:[2] The contrary of which was true in Vergil, and our incomparable Jonson. . . .

[Donne "Affects the Metaphysics"]†

You [the Earl of Dorset] equal Donne in the variety, multiplicity, and choice of thoughts; you excel him in the manner and the words. I read you both with the same admiration, but not with the same delight. He affects

1. "He himself has said it" [*Editor*].
2. "In any case, as in regard to all the manifestations of his genius [his detractors will] find it easier to detect superfluities than deficiencies" (Quintilian, *Institutio Oratorio*, VI.iii.5) [*Editor*].
† From *A Discourse Concerning the Original and Progress of Satire* (1693).

the metaphysics, not only in his satires, but in his amorous verses, where nature only should reign; and perplexes the minds of the fair sex with nice speculations of philosophy, when he should engage their hearts, and entertain them with the softnesses of love.

* * *

Would not Donne's *Satires*, which abound with so much wit, appear more charming, if he had taken care of his words, and of his numbers? But he followed Horace so very close, that of necessity he must fall with him; and I may safely say it of this present age, that if we are not so great wits as Donne, yet certainly we are better poets.

DR. SAMUEL JOHNSON

From *Lives of The English Poets*†

[*Waller*]

Waller was not one of those idolaters of praise who cultivate their minds at the expence of their fortunes. Rich as he was by inheritance, he took care early to grow richer by marrying Mrs. Banks, a great heiress in the city, whom the interest of the court was employed to obtain for Mr. Crofts. Having brought him a son, who died young, and a daughter, who was afterwards married to Mr. Dormer of Oxfordshire, she died in childbed, and left him a widower of about five and twenty, gay and wealthy, to please himself with another marriage.

Being too young to resist beauty, and probably too vain to think himself resistible, he fixed his heart, perhaps half fondly and half ambitiously, upon the Lady Dorothea Sidney, eldest daughter of the Earl of Leicester, whom he courted by all the poetry in which Sacharissa is celebrated: the name is derived from the Latin appellation of *sugar*, and implies, if it means any thing, a spiritless mildness and dull good-nature, such as excites rather tenderness than esteem, and such as, though always treated with kindness, is never honoured or admired.

Yet he describes Sacharissa as a sublime predominating beauty, of lofty charms and imperious influence, on whom he looks with amazement rather than fondness, whose chains he wishes, though in vain, to break, and whose presence is 'wine that inflames to madness.'

His acquaintance with this high-born dame gave wit no opportunity of boasting its influence; she was not to be subdued by the powers of verse, but rejected his addresses, it is said, with disdain, and drove him away to solace his disappointment with Amoret or Phillis. She married in 1639 the Earl of Sunderland, who died at Newberry in the king's cause; and, in her old age, meeting somewhere with Waller, asked him when he would again write such verses upon her; 'When you are as young, Madam,' said he, 'and as handsome, as you were then.'

In this part of his life it was that he was known to Clarendon, among the rest of the men who were eminent in that age for genius and literature;

† The text is that of G. Birkbeck Hill's editions, 3 vols. (Oxford, 1905).

but known so little to his advantage, that they who read his character[1] will not much condemn Sacharissa that she did not descend from her rank to his embraces, nor think every excellence comprised in wit.

* * *

The poem on the death of the Protector[2] seems to have been dictated by real veneration for his memory. Dryden and Sprat[3] wrote on the same occasion; but they were young men, struggling into notice, and hoping for some favour from the ruling party. Waller had little to expect; he had received nothing but his pardon from Cromwell, and was not likely to ask any thing from those who should succeed him.

Soon afterwards the Restauration supplied him with another subject; and he exerted his imagination, his elegance, and his melody with equal alacrity for Charles the Second.[4] It is not possible to read, without some contempt and indignation, poems of the same author, ascribing the highest degree of 'power and piety' to Charles the First, then transferring the same 'power and piety' to Oliver Cromwell; now inviting Oliver to take the Crown, and then congratulating Charles the Second on his recovered right. Neither Cromwell nor Charles could value his testimony as the effect of conviction, or receive his praises as effusions of reverence; they could consider them but as the labour of invention and the tribute of dependence.

Poets, indeed, profess fiction, but the legitimate end of fiction is the conveyance of truth; and he that has flattery ready for all whom the vicissitudes of the world happen to exalt must be scorned as a prostituted mind that may retain the glitter of wit, but has lost the dignity of virtue.

The *Congratulation* was considered as inferior in poetical merit to the *Panegyrick*,[5] and it is reported that when the king told Waller of the disparity he answered, 'Poets, Sir, succeed better in fiction than in truth.'

* * *

The characters, by which Waller intended to distinguish his writings, are spriteliness and dignity: in his smaller pieces he endeavours to be gay; in the larger, to be great. Of his airy and light productions the chief source is gallantry; that attentive reverence of female excellence which has descended to us from the Gothick ages.[6] As his poems are commonly occasional and his addresses personal, he was not so liberally supplied with grand as with soft images; for beauty is more easily found than magnanimity.

The delicacy which he cultivated restrains him to a certain nicety and caution, even when he writes upon the slightest matter. He has therefore in his whole volume nothing burlesque, and seldom any thing ludicrous or familiar. He seems always to do his best, though his subjects are often unworthy of his care.

1. Clarendon acknowledges "the excellence and power of [Waller's] wit," but emphasizes "a narrowness in his nature to the lowest degree, an abjectness and want of courage to support him in any virtuous undertaking" (*Life of Edward Earl of Clarendon*, 2 vols. [Oxford, 1760], I, p. 38).
2. I.e., "Upon the Late Storm, and Of the Death of His Highness [Oliver Cromwell] Ensuing the Same" (not included in this edition) [*Editor*].
3. I.e., Bishop Thomas Sprat, the historian of the Royal Society [*Editor*].
4. Johnson alludes to the poem, "To the King, Upon His Majesty's Happy Return" (not included in this edition) [*Editor*].
5. I.e., Waller's "Panegyric to my Lord Protector" [*Editor*].
6. I.e., the Middle Ages [*Editor*].

* * *

As much of Waller's reputation was owing to the softness and smoothness of his numbers, it is proper to consider those minute particulars to which a versifier must attend.

He certainly very much excelled in smoothness most of the writers who were living when his poetry commenced. The poets of Elizabeth had attained an art of modulation, which was afterwards neglected or forgotten. Fairfax[7] was acknowledged by him as his model; and he might have studied with advantage the poem of Davis,[8] which, though merely philosophical, yet seldom leaves the ear ungratified.

But he was rather smooth than strong; of 'the full resounding line,' which Pope attributes to Dryden, he has given very few examples. The critical decision has given the praise of strength to Denham, and of sweetness to Waller.

* * *

The general character of his poetry is elegance and gaiety. He is never pathetick, and very rarely sublime. He seems neither to have had a mind much elevated by nature, nor amplified by learning. His thoughts are such as a liberal conversation and large acquaintance with life would easily supply. They had however then, perhaps, that grace of novelty, which they are now often supposed to want by those who, having already found them in later books, do not know or enquire who produced them first. This treatment is unjust. Let not the original author lose by his imitators.

* * *

He borrows too many of his sentiments and illustrations from the old mythology, for which it is vain to plead the example of ancient poets: the deities which they introduced so frequently were considered as realities, so far as to be received by the imagination, whatever sober reason might even then determine. But of these images time has tarnished the splendor. A fiction, not only detected but despised, can never afford a solid basis to any position, though sometimes it may furnish a transient allusion, or slight illustration. No modern monarch can be much exalted by hearing that, as Hercules had had his *club*, he has his *navy*.[9]

But of the praise of Waller, though much may be taken away, much will remain, for it cannot be denied that he added something to our elegance of diction, and something to our propriety of thought; and to him may be applied what Tasso said, with equal spirit and justice, of himself and Guarini,[1] when, having perused the *Pastor Fido*, he cried out, 'If he had not read *Aminta*, he had not excelled it.'

[*Denham*]

Denham is deservedly considered as one of the fathers of English poetry. 'Denham and Waller,' says Prior, 'improved our versification, and Dryden

7. Edward Fairfax (c. 1575–1635) translated Tasso's epic *Gerusalemme Liberata* [*Editor*].
8. I.e., "Nosce Teipsum," by Sir John Davies (1569–1626) [*Editor*].
9. The allusion is to Waller's "To the King" (not included in this edition) [*Editor*].
1. *Il Pastor Fido*, a pastoral drama by Giovanni Battista Guarini (1537–1612), was widely admired in the seventeenth century [*Editor*].

perfected it.'[2] He has given specimens of various composition, descriptive, ludicrous, didactick, and sublime.

* * *

His poem on the death of Cowley was his last, and among his shorter works his best performance: the numbers are musical, and the thoughts are just.

Cooper's Hill is the work that confers upon him the rank and dignity of an original author. He seems to have been, at least among us, the author of a species of composition that may be denominated *local poetry*, of which the fundamental subject is some particular landscape to be poetically described, with the addition of such embellishments as may be supplied by historical restrospection or incidental meditation.

To trace a new scheme of poetry has in itself a very high claim to praise, and its praise is yet more when it is apparently copied by Garth and Pope;[3] after whose names little will be gained by an enumeration of smaller poets, that have left scarce a corner of the island not dignified either by rhyme or blank verse.

Cooper's Hill if it be maliciously inspected will not be found without its faults. The digressions are too long, the morality too frequent, and the sentiments sometimes such as will not bear a rigorous enquiry.

The four verses, which, since Dryden has commended them, almost every writer for a century past has imitated, are generally known:

> 'O could I flow like thee, and make thy stream
> My great example, as it is my theme!
> Though deep, yet clear; though gentle, yet not dull;
> Strong without rage, without o'erflowing full.'

The lines are in themselves not perfect, for most of the words thus artfully opposed are to be understood simply on one side of the comparison, and metaphorically on the other; and if there be any language which does not express intellectual operations by material images, into that language they cannot be translated. But so much meaning is comprised in so few words; the particulars of resemblance are so perspicaciously collected, and every mode of excellence separated from its adjacent fault by so nice a line of limitation; the different parts of the sentence are so accurately adjusted; and the flow of the last couplet is so smooth and sweet—that the passage however celebrated has not been praised above its merit. It has beauty peculiar to itself, and must be numbered among those felicities which cannot be produced at will by wit and labour, but must arise unexpectedly in some hour propitious to poetry.

[*Cowley*]

Cowley, like other poets who have written with narrow views and, instead of tracing intellectual pleasure to its natural sources in the mind of man, paid their court to temporary prejudices, has been at one time too much praised and too much neglected at another.

2. Matthew Prior (1664–1721), in the Preface to his poem "Solomon," refers in fact not to Denham but to Sir William Davenant [*Editor*].
3. The allusion is to "Claremont" by Samuel Garth (1661–1719) and to Pope's "Windsor Forest" [*Editor*].

Wit, like all other things subject by their nature to the choice of man, has its changes and fashions, and at different times takes different forms. About the beginning of the seventeenth century appeared a race of writers that may be termed the metaphysical poets, of whom in a criticism on the works of Cowley it is not improper to give some account.

The metaphysical poets were men of learning, and to shew their learning was their whole endeavor; but, unluckily resolving to shew it in rhyme, instead of writing poetry they only wrote verses, and very often such verses as stood the trial of the finger better than of the ear; for the modulation was so imperfect that they were only found to be verses by counting the syllables.

If the father of criticism[4] has rightly denominated poetry *τέχνη μιμητική, an imitative art*, these writers will without great wrong lose their right to the name of poets, for they cannot be said to have imitated any thing: they neither copied nature nor life; neither painted the forms of matter nor represented the operations of intellect.

Those however who deny them to be poets allow them to be wits. Dryden confesses of himself and his contemporaries that they fall below Donne in wit, but maintains that they surpass him in poetry.

If wit be well described by Pope as being 'that which has been often thought, but was never before so well expressed,'[5] they certainly never attained nor ever sought it, for they endeavoured to be singular in their thoughts, and were careless of their diction. But Pope's account of wit is undoubtedly erroneous; he depresses it below its natural dignity, and reduces it from strength of thought to happiness of language.

If by a more noble and more adequate conception that be considered as wit which is at once natural and new, that which though not obvious is, upon its first production, acknowledged to be just; if it be that, which he that never found it, wonders how he missed; to wit of this kind the metaphysical poets have seldom risen. Their thoughts are often new, but seldom natural; they are not obvious, but neither are they just; and the reader, far from wondering that he missed them, wonders more frequently by what perverseness of industry they were ever found.

But wit, abstracted from its effects upon the hearer, may be more rigorously and philosophically considered as a kind of *discordia concors*; a combination of dissimilar images, or discovery of occult resemblances in things apparently unlike. Of wit, thus defined, they have more than enough. The most heterogeneous ideas are yoked by violence together; nature and art are ransacked for illustrations, comparisons, and allusions; their learning instructs, and their subtlety surprises; but the reader commonly thinks his improvement dearly bought, and though he sometimes admires, is seldom pleased.

From this account of their compositions it will be readily inferred that they were not successful in representing or moving the affections. As they were wholly employed on something unexpected and surprising they had no regard to that uniformity of sentiment, which enables us to conceive and to excite the pains and the pleasure of other minds: they never enquired what on any occasion they should have said or done, but wrote rather as beholders than partakers of human nature; as beings looking

4. I.e., Aristotle [*Editor*].
5. Cf. "An Essay on Criticism," line 297 [*Editor*].

upon good and evil, impassive and at leisure; as Epicurean deities making remarks on the actions of men and the vicissitudes of life, without interest and without emotion. Their courtship was void of fondness and their lamentation of sorrow. Their wish was only to say what they hoped had been never said before.

Nor was the sublime more within their reach than the pathetick; for they never attempted that comprehension and expanse of thought which at once fills the whole mind, and of which the first effect is sudden astonishment, and the second rational admiration. Sublimity is produced by aggregation, and littleness by dispersion. Great thoughts are always general, and consist in positions not limited by exceptions, and in descriptions not descending to minuteness. It is with great propriety that subtlety, which in its original import means exility[6] of particles, is taken in its metaphorical meaning for nicety of distinction. Those writers who lay on the watch for novelty could have little hope of greatness; for great things cannot have escaped former observation. Their attempts were always analytick: they broke every image into fragments, and could no more represent by their slender conceits and laboured particularities the prospects of nature or the scenes of life, than he who dissects a sun-beam with a prism can exhibit the wide effulgence of a summer noon.

What they wanted however of the sublime they endeavored to supply by hyperbole; their amplification had no limits: they left not only reason but fancy behind them, and produced combinations of confused magnificence that not only could not be credited, but could not be imagined.

Yet great labour directed by great abilities is never wholly lost: if they frequently threw away their wit upon false conceits, they likewise sometimes struck out unexpected truth: if their conceits were far-fetched, they were often worth the carriage. To write on their plan it was at least necessary to read and think. No man could be born a metaphysical poet, nor assume the dignity of a writer by descriptions copied from descriptions, by imitations borrowed from imitations, by traditional imagery and hereditary similes, by readiness of rhyme and volubility of syllables.

In perusing the works of this race of authors the mind is exercised either by recollection or inquiry; either something already learned is to be retrieved, or something new is to be examined. If their greatness seldom elevates, their acuteness often surprises; if the imagination is not always gratified, at least the powers of reflection and comparison are employed; and in the mass of materials, which ingenious absurdity has thrown together, genuine wit and useful knowledge may be sometimes found, buried perhaps in grossness of expression, but useful to those who know their value, and such as, when they are expanded to perspicuity and polished to elegance, may give lustre to works which have more propriety though less copiousness of sentiment.

This kind of writing, which was, I believe, borrowed from Marino and his followers,[7] had been recommended by the example of Donne, a man of very extensive and various knowledge, and by Jonson, whose manner resembled that of Donne more in the ruggedness of his lines than in the cast of his sentiments.

6. Thinness [*Editor*].
7. Giambattista Marino (1569–1625), Italian poet whose followers imitated his flamboyant, highly embellished style. His stylistic influence on subsequent literature was strong.

When their reputation was high they had undoubtedly more imitators than time has left behind. Their immediate successors, of whom any remembrance can be said to remain, were Suckling, Waller, Denham, Cowley, Cleveland,[8] and Milton. Denham and Waller sought another way to fame, by improving the harmony of our numbers. Milton tried the metaphysick style in his lines upon Hobson the Carrier. Cowley adopted it, and excelled his predecessors; having as much sentiment and more musick. Suckling neither improved versification nor abounded in conceits. The fashionable style remained chiefly with Cowley: Suckling could not reach it, and Milton disdained it.

* * *

His *Miscellanies* contain a collection of short compositions, written some as they were dictated by a mind at leisure, and some as they were called forth by different occasions; with great variety of style and sentiment, from burlesque levity to awful grandeur. Such an assemblage of diversified excellence no other poet has hitherto afforded. To choose the best among many good is one of the most hazardous attempts of criticism. I know not whether Scaliger himself has persuaded many readers to join with him in his preference of the two favourite odes, which he estimates in his raptures at the value of a kingdom. I will however venture to recommend Cowley's first piece,[9] which ought to be inscribed *To my Muse*, for want of which the second couplet is without reference. . . .

The ode on wit is almost without a rival. It was about the time of Cowley that *Wit*, which had been till then used for *Intellection* in contradistinction to *Will*, took the meaning whatever it be which it now bears.

Of all the passages in which poets have exemplified their own precepts none will easily be found of greater excellence than that in which Cowley condemns exuberance of wit:

> 'Yet 'tis not to adorn and gild each part;
>   That shews more cost than art.
> Jewels at nose and lips but ill appear;
> Rather than all things wit, let none be there.
>   Several lights will not be seen,
>   If there be nothing else between.
> Men doubt, because they stand so thick i'th' sky,
> If those be stars which paint the galaxy.'

* * *

In his poem on the death of Hervey there is much praise, but little passion, a very just and ample delineation of such virtues as a studious privacy admits, and such intellectual excellence as a mind not yet called forth to action can display. He knew how to distinguish and how to commend the qualities of his companion, but when he wishes to make us weep he forgets to weep himself, and diverts his sorrow by imagining how his crown of bays, if he had it, would *crackle* in the *fire*. It is the odd fate of this thought to be worse for being true. The bay-leaf crackles remarkably as it burns; as therefore this property was not assigned it by chance, the mind must

8. The poet John Cleveland (1613–1658) combined a fervent royalism with a taste for exaggerated metaphor [*Editor*].
9. I.e., "The Motto" [*Editor*].

be thought sufficiently at ease that could attend to such minuteness of physiology. But the power of Cowley is not so much to move the affections, as to exercise the understanding.

* * *

Cowley seems to have had, what Milton is believed to have wanted, the skill to rate his own performances by their just value, and has therefore closed his *Miscellanies* with the verses upon Crashaw, which apparently[1] excel all that have gone before them, and in which there are beauties which common authors may justly think not only above their attainment, but above their ambition.

To the *Miscellanies* succeed the *Anacreontiques*, or paraphrastical translations of some little poems, which pass, however justly, under the name of Anacreon. Of those songs dedicated to festivity and gaiety, in which even the morality is voluptuous, and which teach nothing but the enjoyment of the present day, he has given rather a pleasing than a faithful representation, having retained their spriteliness, but lost their simplicity. The Anacreon of Cowley, like the Homer of Pope, has admitted the decoration of some modern graces, by which he is undoubtedly made more amiable to common readers, and perhaps, if they would honestly declare their own perceptions, to far the greater part of those whom courtesy and ignorance are content to style the learned.

These little pieces will be found more finished in their kind than any other of Cowley's works. The diction shews nothing of the mould of time, and the sentiments are at no great distance from our present habitudes of thought. Real mirth must be always natural, and nature is uniform. Men have been wise in very different modes; but they have always laughed the same way.

Levity of thought naturally produced familiarity of language, and the familiar part of language continues long the same: the dialogue of comedy, when it is transcribed from popular manners and real life, is read from age to age with equal pleasure. The artifice of inversion, by which the established order of words is changed, or of innovation, by which new words or new meanings of words are introduced, is practised, not by those who talk to be understood, but by those who write to be admired.

The *Anacreontiques* therefore of Cowley give now all the pleasure which they ever gave. If he was formed by nature for one kind of writing more than for another, his power seems to have been greatest in the familiar and the festive.

The next class of his poems is called *The Mistress*, of which it is not necessary to select any particular pieces for praise or censure. They have all the same beauties and faults, and nearly in the same proportion. They are written with exuberance of wit, and with copiousness of learning; and it is truly asserted by Sprat that the plenitude of the writer's knowledge flows in upon his page, so that the reader is commonly surprised into some improvement. But, considered as the verses of a lover, no man that has ever loved will much commend them. They are neither courtly nor pathetick, have neither gallantry nor fondness. His praises are too far-sought and too hyperbolical, either to express love or to excite it: every stanza is

1. Clearly [*Editor*].

crowded with darts and flames, with wounds and death, with mingled souls, and with broken hearts.

* * *

In the general review of Cowley's poetry it will be found that he wrote with abundant fertility, but negligent or unskilful selection; with much thought, but with little imagery; that he is never pathetick, and rarely sublime, but always either ingenious or learned, either acute or profound.

It is said by Denham in his elegy:

> 'To him no author was unknown;
> Yet what he writ was all his own.'

This wide position requires less limitation when it is affirmed of Cowley than perhaps of any other poet: he read much, and yet borrowed little.

His character of writing was indeed not his own: he unhappily adopted that which was predominant. He saw a certain way to present praise; and not sufficiently enquiring by what means the ancients have continued to delight through all the changes of human manners he contented himself with a deciduous laurel, of which the verdure in its spring was bright and gay, but which time has been continually stealing from his brows.

He was in his own time considered as of unrivalled excellence. Clarendon represents him as having taken a flight beyond all that went before him,[2] and Milton is said to have declared that the three greatest English poets were Spenser, Shakespeare, and Cowley.[3]

* * *

It may be affirmed without any encomiastick[4] fervour that he brought to his poetick labours a mind replete with learning, and that his pages are embellished with all the ornaments which books could supply; that he was the first who imparted to English numbers the enthusiasm of the greater ode, and the gaiety of the less; that he was equally qualified for spritely sallies and for lofty flights; that he was among those who freed translation from servility, and, instead of following his author at a distance, walked by his side; and that if he left versification yet improvable, he left likewise from time to time such specimens of excellence as enabled succeeding poets to improve it.

[*Dryden*]

Of the great poet whose life I am about to delineate, the curiosity which his reputation must excite will require a display more ample than can now be given. His contemporaries, however they reverenced his genius, left his life unwritten; and nothing therefore can be known beyond what casual mention and uncertain tradition have supplied.

John Dryden was born August 9, 1631, at Aldwincle near Oundle, the son of Erasmus Dryden of Tichmersh; who was the third son of Sir Erasmus Dryden, Baronet, of Canons Ashby. All these places are in Northamp-

2. Cf. Edward Hyde, Earl of Clarendon, *Life of Edward Earl of Clarendon*, 2 vols. (Oxford, 1740), I, p. 30 [*Editor*].
3. Cf. John Milton, *Paradise Lost*, ed. T. Newton, 4 vols. (Dublin, 1773), I, pp. 49–50 [*Editor*].
4. Laudatory [*Editor*].

tonshire; but the original stock of the family was in the county of Huntingdon.

He is reported by his last biographer, Derrick, to have inherited from his father an estate of two hundred a year, and to have been bred, as was said, an Anabaptist. For either of these particulars no authority is given. Such a fortune ought to have secured him from that poverty which seems always to have oppressed him; or if he had wasted it, to have made him ashamed of publishing his necessities. But though he had many enemies, who undoubtedly examined his life with a scrutiny sufficiently malicious, I do not remember that he is ever charged with waste of his patrimony. He was indeed sometimes reproached for his first religion. I am therefore inclined to believe that Derrick's intelligence was partly true, and partly erroneous.

From Westminster School, where he was instructed as one of the king's scholars by Dr. Busby, whom he long after continued to reverence, he was in 1650 elected to one of the Westminster scholarships at Cambridge.

Of his school performances has appeared only a poem on the death of Lord Hastings, composed with great ambition of such conceits as, notwithstanding the reformation begun by Waller and Denham, the example of Cowley still kept in reputation. Lord Hastings died of the small-pox, and his poet has made of the pustules first rosebuds, and then gems; at last exalts them into stars; and says,

> No comet need foretell his change drew on,
> Whose corpse might seem a constellation.

At the university he does not appear to have been eager of poetical distinction, or to have lavished his early wit either on fictitious subjects or public occasions. He probably considered that he who purposed to be an author, ought first to be a student. He obtained, whatever was the reason, no fellowship in the College. Why he was excluded cannot now be known, and it is vain to guess; had he thought himself injured, he knew how to complain. In the *Life of Plutarch*, he mentions his education in the College with gratitude; but in a prologue at Oxford, he has these lines:

> Oxford to him a dearer name shall be
> Than his own mother-university;
> Thebes did his rude unknowing youth engage;
> He chooses Athens in his riper age.

It was not till the death of Cromwell, in 1658, that he became a public candidate for fame, by publishing "Heroic Stanzas on the late Lord Protector;" which, compared with the verses of Sprat and Waller on the same occasion, were sufficient to raise great expectations of the rising poet.

When the king was restored, Dryden, like the other panegyrists of usurpation, changed his opinion, or his profession, and published *Astrea Redux*, a poem on the happy restoration and return of his most sacred Majesty King Charles the Second.

The reproach of inconstancy was, on this occasion, shared with such numbers, that it produced neither hatred nor disgrace; if he changed, he changed with the nation. It was, however, not totally forgotten when his reputation raised him enemies.

The same year he praised the new king in a second poem on his restoration. In the *Astrea* was the line,

> An horrid *stillness* first *invades* the *ear*,
> And in that silence we a tempest fear;

for which he was persecuted with perpetual ridicule, perhaps with more than was deserved. *Silence* is indeed mere privation; and, so considered, cannot *invade*; but privation likewise certainly is *darkness*, and probably *cold*; yet poetry has never been refused the right of ascribing effects or agency to them as to positive powers. No man scruples to say that *darkness* hinders him from his work; or that *cold* has killed the plants. Death is also privation, yet who has made any difficulty of assigning to Death a dart and the power of striking?

* * *

Dryden may be properly considered as the father of English criticism, as the writer who first taught us to determine upon principles the merit of composition. Of our former poets, the greatest dramatist wrote without rules, conducted through life and nature by a genius that rarely misled, and rarely deserted him. Of the rest, those who knew the laws of propriety had neglected to teach them.

Two Arts of English Poetry were written in the days of Elizabeth by Webb and Puttenham, from which something might be learned, and a few hints had been given by Jonson and Cowley; but Dryden's *Essay on Dramatick Poetry* was the first regular and valuable treatise on the art of writing.

* * *

It was indeed never in his power to resist the temptation of a jest. In his Elegy on Cromwell:

> No sooner was the Frenchman's cause embrac'd,
> Than the *light Monsieur* the *grave Don* outweigh'd;
> His fortune turn'd the scale—

He had a vanity, unworthy of his abilities, to shew, as may be suspected, the rank of the company with whom he lived, by the use of French words, which had then crept into conversation; such as *fraicheur* for *coolness*, *fougue* for *turbulence*, and a few more, none of which the language has incorporated or retained. They continue only where they stood first, perpetual warnings to future innovators.

These are his faults of affectation; his faults of negligence are beyond recital. Such is the unevenness of his compositions, that ten lines are seldom found together without something of which the reader is ashamed. Dryden was no rigid judge of his own pages; he seldom struggled after supreme excellence, but snatched in haste what was within his reach; and when he could content others, was himself contented. He did not keep present to his mind an idea of pure perfection; nor compare his works, such as they were, with what they might be made. He knew to whom he should be opposed. He had more musick than Waller, more vigour than Denham, and more nature than Cowley; and from his contemporaries he was in no danger. Standing therefore in the highest place, he had no care to rise by contending with himself; but while there was no name above his own, was willing to enjoy fame on the easiest terms.

He was no lover of labour. What he thought sufficient, he did not stop to make better; and allowed himself to leave many parts unfinished, in confidence that the good lines would overbalance the bad. What he had once written, he dismissed from his thoughts; and, I believe, there is no example to be found of any correction or improvement made by him after publication. The hastiness of his productions might be the effect of necessity; but his subsequent neglect could hardly have any other cause than impatience of study.

What can be said of his versification, will be little more than a dilatation of the praise given it by Pope:

> Waller was smooth; but Dryden taught to join
> The varying verse, the full-resounding line,
> The long majestick march, and energy divine.

Some improvements had been already made in English numbers; but the full force of our language was not yet felt; the verse that was smooth was commonly feeble. If Cowley had sometimes a finished line, he had it by chance. Dryden knew how to choose the flowing and the sonorous words; to vary the pauses, and adjust the accents; to diversify the cadence, and yet preserve the smoothness of his metre.

* * *

Of Dryden's works it was said by Pope, that "he could select from them better specimens of every mode of poetry than any other English writer could supply." Perhaps no nation ever produced a writer that enriched his language with such variety of models. To him we owe the improvement, perhaps the completion of our metre, the refinement of our language, and much of the correctness of our sentiments. By him we were taught *sapere & fari*, to think naturally and express forcibly. Though Davis has reasoned in rhyme before him, it may be perhaps maintained that he was the first who joined argument with poetry. He showed us the true bounds of a translator's liberty. What was said of Rome, adorned by Augustus, may be applied by an easy metaphor to English poetry embellished by Dryden, *lateritiam invenit, marmoream reliquit*, he found it brick, and he left it marble.

Recent Criticism

LAWRENCE BABB

The Physiology and Psychology of the Renaissance†

I

Having rediscovered man as a physical and temporal creature, the Renaissance pursued the study of human nature with enthusiasm. The cunning complexity of man's physical and mental equipment and the excellence and efficacy of his faculties inspired scholars with wonder and pride. Man, they found, was a little world, a microcosm, the epitome of the great world, the macrocosm. He was "the head and chiefe of all that euer God wrought; the pourtraiture of the vniuersall world . . . [a] merueilous and cunning peece of worke";[1] "the last hand, the accomplishment, the perfection of the worke, the honor and miracle of Nature."[2]

The Renaissance derived its information concerning temporal man chiefly from writers of ancient times and from medieval writers indebted to classical thought. The principal authorities were Plato, Aristotle, Galen, Augustine, Avicenna, and Aquinas. Respect for authority was still profound. It occurred to only the very exceptional man to make scientific observation of human nature for himself. The rest studied philosophical and scientific works of elder times with fascinated interest. Many of them repeated the ideas which they found there in treatises of their own.

The concept of human nature which the Renaissance inherited from the past has at least one thing in common with that of modern science: the assumption that body and mind are closely related and mutually influential. Thus Renaissance psychology is a physiological psychology. It tends to explain mental conditions in terms of physical causes and vice versa. During the Renaissance, physiology and psychology were no more separable than they are today.

The principles of this physiological psychology were widely disseminated in sixteenth- and early seventeenth-century England. Many treatises on the subject, some of them translations, others original works by Englishmen, appeared in the native language. Poets did their share toward

† From *The Elizabethan Malady: A Study of Melancholia in English Literature from 1580 to 1642* (East Lansing, 1951), pp. 1–20. Reprinted by permission of Michigan State University Press. The author's notes have been abridged.

1. André du Laurens, *A Discourse of the Preservation of the Sight: of Melancholike Diseases; of Rheumes, and of Old Age*, tr. Richard Surphlet (London, 1599; Shakespeare Association Facsimiles, 1938), pp. 14–15.
2. Pierre Charron, *Of Wisdome*, tr. Samson Lennard (London, c. 1607), p. 8.

instructing their countrymen. Spenser's *Faerie Queene* contains an anatomy of human nature (II, ix, 21–58). There are expository poems devoted entirely to the nature of man, including *Nosce Teipsum* by Sir John Davies, *Microcosmos* and *Mirum in Modum* by John Davies of Hereford, *The Purple Island* by Phineas Fletcher. Various plays, such as Tomkis' *Lingua* and Nabbes' *Microcosmos*, present the currently accepted psychology in allegorical form. Scientific theories of human nature, moreover, subtly and thoroughly permeate many literary works which have no expository purpose. One gets the impression that England of the time of Elizabeth and the early Stuarts thought a great deal about its physical and psychic states.

It will be necessary to review some of the principles of Renaissance physiology and psychology as an introduction to the discussion of Elizabethan melancholy.[3] First of all, I shall outline the conception of the human soul and its faculties which was generally current in late Renaissance England. In doing so, I shall simplify somewhat and ignore the authorities' multitudinous disagreements concerning details.

II

The soul[4] is the force which animates the inert matter of the body and directs its activities. It is one and indivisible. It is nevertheless, for purposes of analysis and description, divided into three sub-souls known as the vegetative (or vegetable) soul, the sensitive (or sensible) soul, and the rational (reasonable) soul.

The vegetative soul is seated in the liver. Its principal faculties[5] are those of nourishment, growth, and reproduction; in general, it directs the humbler physiological processes below the level of consciousness. Plants and animals as well as men have vegetative souls. The sensitive soul has the faculties of feeling and motion. It has the power of perceiving objects other than itself, it evaluates them as pleasing or repellent, and it directs motions of the body calculated either to obtain or to avoid them. It is seated in the brain and heart. Animals as well as men are endowed with sensitive souls. Man is distinguished from all other created beings by the possession of a rational soul, located in the brain, which is capable of distinguishing good from evil (not merely pleasure from pain), of contemplating itself, and of knowing God. The rational soul is the "self."

3. Many of the subjects included in this chapter have been treated before by modern literary scholars. See especially P. A. Robin, *The Old Physiology in English Literature* (London, 1911); Murray Wright Bundy, "Shakespeare and Elizabethan Psychology," *Journal of English and Germanic Philology*, XXIII (1924), 516–49; Ruth Leila Anderson, *Elizabethan Psychology and Shakespeare's Plays* (Iowa City, 1927); Lily B. Campbell, *Shakespeare's Tragic Heroes: Slaves of Passion* (Cambridge, 1930), pp. 51–78; John W. Draper, *The Humors & Shakespeare's Characters* (Durham, N.C., 1945).
4. The following section is based mainly on *Batman uppon Bartholome, His Booke De Proprietatibus Rerum* (London, 1582), fols. 12–17; Philippe de Mornay, *The True Knowledge of a Mans Owne Selfe*, tr. Anthony Munday (London, 1602); Thomas Wright, *The Passions of the Minde* (London, 1601), pp. 5–43; Charron, *Of Wisdome*, pp. 22–101; Pierre de la Primaudaye, *The French Academie*, tr. T. B. C. (London, 1618), pp. 401–43; F. N. Coeffeteau, *A Table of Humane Passions*, tr. Edward Grimeston (London, 1621), "Preface"; Robert Burton, *The Anatomy of Melancholy*, ed. A. R. Shilleto (London, 1926–27), I, 176–92.
5. There are two popular classifications of the human faculties in Renaissance psychologies. The one which I am following groups them as powers of the three souls of the Aristotelian psychology; see *De Anima*, 413^a–414^a (II, ii–iii) and *Nicomachean Ethics*, 1102^a–1103^a (I, xiii). The other (see Anderson, *Elizabethan Psychology*, pp. 10–14) groups them according to their locations: natural faculties seated in the liver, vital faculties in the heart, animal faculties in the brain.

The faculties of sense and motion with which the sensitive soul is endowed are subdivided into various senses and motions. The senses are of two kinds, external and internal. There are five external senses—sight, hearing, smell, taste, and touch—and three internal senses—the common sense, the imagination (often called the *phantasy*, or *fancy*), and the memory. The internal senses are located in the brain.[6] The common sense receives impressions of the world outside from the external senses and assembles them into composite images. Its primary function, however, is apprehension. The eye does not know what it sees; the ear does not know what it hears. Sensory impressions are next conveyed to the imagination. This faculty can retain and consider them for some time. It evaluates them as pleasant or painful. It has the power of conceiving circumstances and situations other than those existing at the moment and of forming synthetic images from disparate elements as it pleases (hence, centaurs, griffons, and chimeras). This is the creative power of the imagination. It is a faculty which never rests; even when the other sensory and intellectual powers are in repose, a stream of images flows aimlessly through the imagination, and when one is asleep, this stream continues in his dreams. It is called the eye of the mind because the rational powers see the external world through it and through it alone; a new impression must pass successively through the external senses, the common sense, and the imagination before the reason may apprehend it.[7] The memory is a repository for sensory images delivered to it by the imagination and for ideas entrusted to it by the rational mind.

The motive powers of the sensitive soul are, like the senses, external and internal. The internal powers, which operate in the heart,[8] are the precedent causes of the external. They are what in modern speech we call emotions. The sixteenth and seventeenth centuries called them *motions*, *affections*, *passions*, and *perturbations*. These terms are virtually synonymous, although *perturbations* sometimes seems to imply a greater degree of intensity than the others.

The internal motions fall into two categories: *concupiscible* and *irascible*. There are six of the former and five of the latter. Concupiscible passions arise when the imagination or the reasonable will perceives or conceives an object which appeals to it as pleasing or repellent. If the object is pleasing, the motion *love* is aroused; if painful, the motion *hatred*. From love arises *desire*, the inclination to possess whatever one loves; from hatred arises *aversion*, the inclination to shun whatever is abhorrent. *Joy* follows the fulfillment of desire; *sorrow* arises when inclination is thwarted. The irascible passions motivate effort toward the satisfaction of the concupiscible passions. *Boldness* inspires one to meet difficulties and dangers with confidence; *fear* prompts him to flee from dangers with which he apparently cannot cope; *hope* encourages him to persevere in his pursuits; *despair* persuades him to abandon fruitless endeavors; *anger* is the impulse

6. The brain is divided into cells, or ventricles. According to the most common opinion, there are three of these. Imagination and common sense occupy the foremost cell, reason the middle cell, and memory the hindmost. See Robin, *The Old Physiology*, pp. 53–54.
7. This account of the imagination oversimplifies a complex and difficult subject. See M. W. Bundy, *The Theory of Imagination in Classical and Mediaeval Thought* (Urbana, 1927), Chap. IX.
8. Most authorities, following Aristotle (*De Anima*, 408[b]; *De Partibus Animalium*, 647[a], 665[a], 666[a]) place all the passions in the heart. According to Platonic tradition, the concupiscible passions are seated in the abdomen, the irascible in the breast (*Timaeus*, 69–71; *Phaedrus*, 253–54).

to fight for the fulfillment of desire or aversion. These eleven principal passions are considerably subdivided. *Ambition*, *avarice*, and sexual *love*, for example, are subdivisions of desire; *pity*, *shame*, and *remorse* are subdivisions of sorrow. There are also compound passions; *envy*, for instance, is compounded of the desire for something and the hatred of its possessor.[9]

These, then, are the faculties of the sensitive soul, the faculties which rule the conduct of beasts. In man, the rational soul is the ruling power, and the sensitive faculties are its servants. It has two divisions—intellectual and volitional, that is, *reason*[1] and *will*. The former, which looks at the world through the medium of the imagination, is capable of perceiving the essence, not merely the appearance. It seeks truth through a logical train of thought. It draws conclusions regarding truth and falsehood, good and evil; in other words, it is capable of judgment. The reason determines what is good and what is evil and informs the will of its conclusions. The will, because of an instinct implanted in it by God, desires the good and abhors the evil which the reason represents to it. The will is sometimes called the rational appetite because it desires the good just as the sensitive affections desire the pleasing, and it abhors the evil just as they abhor the displeasing. When the will conceives a desire or an aversion, a corresponding passion normally arises in the sensitive soul. Thus the will causes physical action indirectly through the sensitive passions. Often the sensitive and rational desires conflict; the pleasant is not always the good. In such a case, the sensitive nature should yield, and passions corresponding to the promptings of the will should arise. For the reasonable will is the absolute mistress of the human soul.

III

The physical life of man "is stayed vpon two pillers, which are the radicall heate and moisture," that is, heat and moisture with which the body is endowed at birth. The radical heat, or natural heat,

> is the principall instrument of the soule, for it is it that concocteth and distributeth our nourishment, which procureth generation, . . . which fashioneth all our parts, which maketh vs to liue. . . . This heate being a naturall bodie hath neede of nourishment, the humour which is called the radicall moisture, is the nourishment thereof, as the oyle which is put into the lampes, doth maintayne and feede the flame; this humour once failing, it must needes fall out, that the natural heate should perish, but this humor cannot last for euer, seeing the natural heate is daily threatning & consuming the same.[2]

9. The foregoing represents, in essence and in general outline, the classifications and definitions of the passions to be found in La Primaudaye, *Academie*, pp. 465 ff.; Charron, *Of Wisdome*, p. 74; Wright, *Passions*, pp. 41 ff.; Coeffeteau, *Passions*, pp. 32 ff.; Burton, *Anatomy*, I, 297 ff. These authors are following St. Thomas Aquinas (*Summa Theologica*, II [I], xxiii, 4). Not all of the authorities do so.
1. *Reason* is very often used to designate the entire rational soul. I shall use the term in this broader sense hereafter.
2. Du Laurens, *Discourse*, p. 170. This theory regarding the nature of life and the reason for its decay has very ancient sources. A living creature, says Aristotle, is by nature warm and humid; old men and dead bodies are cold and dry (*Parva Naturalia*, 466[a]; *Problemata*, 955[a]). Dying is extinction of heat (Parva Naturalia, 469[a]). Man "is warmest on the first day of his existence and coldest on the last."—Hippocrates (?), *The Nature of Man*, Chap. xii (*Hippocrates*, tr. W. H. S. Jones [London, 1923–31], IV, 37).

As man grows older his body becomes gradually drier and colder. When the natural moisture is consumed and the natural heat fails, he dies. Natural heat is literally the flame of life. Heat and moisture, then, are the primary qualities of a living creature. Cold and dryness are hostile to life.

The Renaissance term for digestion is *concoction*. The liver, being a hot organ, "is to the stomake, as fyre vnder the pot."[3] The product of digestion in the stomach is a viscid, whitish fluid called *chyle*. This is conveyed to the liver, and there the nutrimental matter undergoes a second concoction,[4] the products of which are the four primary humors. *Blood* is the most plentiful of these. Mingled with the blood which the liver produces is a light and effervescent fluid, *choler*, which tends to rise. There is also a heavy and sluggish fluid, *melancholy*, which tends to sink. Melancholy consists of the less pure and less nutrimental parts of the chyle and is considered semi-excremental. One writer describes it as "dregges and durte remoued aparte from the principalles of lyfe, ennemy to ioye and liberalite, and of nere kinred to age and death."[5] The fourth humor, *phlegm*, is merely chyle only half digested. Phlegm further digested by the liver would be blood.

These four humors (with their abnormal varieties, of which more later) make up nearly all of the fluid content of the body. Each has two primary qualities: blood is hot and moist, choler is hot and dry, melancholy is cold and dry, and phlegm is cold and moist. The four humors of the microcosm, therefore, are analogous to the four elements of the macrocosm, for air is hot and moist, fire hot and dry, earth cold and dry, and water cold and moist. The humors also have their secondary qualities: blood is red and sweet; choler is yellow, bitter, thin, and volatile; melancholy is black, sour, thick, and heavy; phlegm is whitish or colorless, tasteless, and watery.

Each humor has its physiological functions. The blood is the carrier of the natural heat and moisture. It warms and moistens the whole body, and it nourishes most of the fleshy parts; that is, it is turned into flesh through the process known as the third digestion. Choler nourishes the parts of the body supposed to be hot and dry and has the function of provoking the expulsion of excrements. Melancholy nourishes "the parts which are melancholickely qualified, as the bones, gristles, sinewes, &c.,"[6] and it provokes appetite in the stomach. Phlegm nourishes the cold and moist members, notably the brain and the kidneys. Each humor has its particular seat. The seat of the blood is the liver; the seat of phlegm is sometimes said to be the lungs, sometimes the kidneys; the gall is provided for superfluous and excremental choler; the spleen is provided for superfluous and excremental melancholy.

Pathological conditions (barring wounds, fractures, dislocations, etc.) are due to humoral abnormalities: to superabundance or deficiency of a humor throughout the body, to improper concentration of a humor in one

3. Sir Thomas Elyot, *The Castel of Helth* (London, 1541; Scholars' Facsimiles and Reprints, 1937), fol. 46^{r}.
4. There are three digestions. The last is the process by which humors are utilized as nutriment, that is, the process by which humors become flesh. See Robin, *The Old Physiology*, pp. 76–77.
5. *Regimen Sanitatis Salerni*, tr. Thomas Paynell (London, 1575), fol. cxxxii^{v}. The English matter in this volume consists of Paynell's translation of Arnoldus' commentary on the old Latin poem. Paynell prints the poem itself in Latin. All of my quotations from this volume are from the translated commentary.
6. Thomas Walkington, *The Optick Glasse of Humors* (London, 1639; originally published 1607), p. 130.

member, or to the presence, either through the body as a whole or in a single member, of noxious unnatural forms of choler, phlegm, or melancholy.[7] Renaissance medicine explains every disease by one of these conditions.[8] Each disease is classified as hot and dry, cold and dry, etc., according to the offending humor. A typical list of "diseases procedynge of melancolye," that is, cold and dry diseases, includes "madnesse, fallynge syckenesse [epilepsy], bleedynges [hemorrhoids?], quynces, poses, hoorsenes, coughes, lepries, scabbes, ache in the ioyntes."[9]

The fundamental principle of cure is, of course, the restoration of the normal. The most drastic method is bloodletting to evacuate the injurious humor from the veins. Purgation is supposed to serve the same purpose. Certain drugs are specific purgatives for certain humors. Black hellebore, for instance, is the favorite purgative for melancholy; rhubarb for choler. Various medicines ("alteratives") are used to change the character of a humor by moistening, drying, heating, cooling, thickening, thinning. Diet is important. A patient suffering from a hot and dry disease should eat cold and moist foods, such as lettuce and cress. In the Renaissance dietaries, the various foods are described in terms of heat, cold, moisture, and dryness[1] so that the reader may choose those foods which have a nature opposite to that of his complaint. The patient's daily manner of life also must be regulated. Idleness and sleep warm and moisten the body; labor and waking cool and dry it. The temperature and humidity of the atmosphere must be taken into account. The patient should enjoy peace of mind, for mental perturbation breeds ill humors.

IV

The two digestions, or concoctions, by which food is refined into humors have already been mentioned. A third refinement (not strictly speaking a concoction) takes place in the heart. By this process the purest blood is made into a substance subtler and rarer than any humor ("subtilis vapor . . . flammula ex purissimo sanguine in corde nata"[2]). This is called *vital spirit*, or *vital spirits*. The vital spirit is the vehicle of the natural heat and moisture which are essential to life.[3] The heart pours it into the arteries, and it is borne by the arterial blood to animate every part of the body. If for any length of time the supply of this spirit is meager, "the whole masse

7. These arise through the burning of a natural humor by unnatural heat, through the putrifaction of a natural humor, or through improper mixture of natural humors. The medical writers distinguish many unnatural humors. Elyot's list is typical (*Castel of Helth*, fols. 8–9). See also *Claudii Galeni Opera Omnia*, ed. Kühn, (Leipzig, 1821–33), V, 108–9; XIX, 364–65, 490.

8. * * * Galen, *De Humoribus Liber*, in *Opera*, XIX, 491. Cf. *The Nature of Man*, in *Hippocrates*, IV, 11–13; Elyor, *Castel of Helth*, fol. 8ʳ.

9. Elyot, *Castel of Helth*, fol. 83ʳ [85ʳ]. Quartan fever, cancer, and palsy are often listed as melancholy diseases. The authorities differ bewilderingly regarding the causes and classification of diseases.

1. I have derived my information on this subject principally from Elyot, *Castel of Helth*, fols. 17ᵛ ff.; Thomas Cogan, *The Haven of Health* (London, 1589; originally published 1584); William Vaughan, *Approved Directions for Health* (London, 1612; originally published 1600); Tobias Venner, *Via Recta ad Vitam Longam* (London, 1628; originally published 1620).

2. Philipp Melanchthon, *Liber de Anima*, in *Opera*, ed. Carolus Gottlieb Bretschneider (Halle, 1834–60), XIII, 88.

3. The authorities commonly define the vital spirit as the vehicle of natural heat. It is of necessity the vehicle of natural moisture also, for the two are not independent entities. Natural heat is "a substance moist and very vaporous."—Juan Huarte, *Examen de Ingenios*, tr. R. Carew (London, 1594), p. 59. The "*Radicall humour* . . . hath the celestiall and quickening heate brought immediately and directly vnto it: so that when this moisture is extinguished, the heate also vanisheth."—La Primaudaye, *Academie*, p. 547.

of bloud easily degenerateth" into melancholy.[4] If the flow of vital spirit is suddenly and completely interrupted, "then life ceaseth, as in a *syncope* or swooning."[5]

There is still a further step in the progressive rarification of matter, which takes place in the brain. Here the vital spirit is refined into an even subtler vapor, the *animal spirit*, or *animal spirits* (Latin *anima*). The animal spirit flows in the nerves ("in nervos infus [us] velut lumen"[6]). Its function is to act as messenger between the brain and the organs in other parts of the body. It is the link between mind and body.

For the proper functioning of mind and body, it is essential that the spirits be quick, lively, exquisitely subtle, and absolutely pure. The quality of the spirits depends naturally upon the quality of the blood. Unwise diet or ill digestion may produce blood of such a nature that good spirits may not be engendered from it. Superabundant or corrupted humors may vitiate the best spirits. By disturbing the operations of the heart, passions may prevent the production of good spirits: "manifestum est spiritum fieri meliorum in cerebro, quando bonum est cordis temperamentum, et quando cor non turbatum est ira et moesticia."[7]

V

The ideal man would have the four humors mingled in his body in a very exact proportion. Blood would be the most abundant humor, phlegm the next in quantity, melancholy the next, and choler the least. Such a man would enjoy perfect health of body and mind and would be richly endowed with capabilities and virtues. But "This golden temperature must be onely understood and seen with the internal eies of reason, seeing it hath not a reall existence."[8] In actuality each man's constitution varies more or less from the norm by a surplus of one humor or another; and his complexion, or temperament, is designated, according to the dominant humor, as sanguine, choleric, phlegmatic, or melancholy. It should be noted that, according to Renaissance physiology, the temperatures and humidities of men's bodies differ widely. The sanguine complexion is considered the most desirable, primarily because heat and moisture are the qualities of life. The melancholy temperament is usually considered the least enviable, for cold and dryness are opposite to the vital qualities and cut "in twain the thred of . . . life long before it be spun."[9] A man of hot and moist temperament is young at sixty; a man of cold and dry temperament is old at forty.[1]

The dominant humor to a large extent determines the individual's appearance and behavior. The well-informed observer, consequently, can readily classify men according to their complexions. The sanguine man is fleshy, ruddy, fair-haired, amiable of countenance and manner, gladsome

4. Timothy Bright, *A Treatise of Melancholie* (London, 1586; Facsimile Text Society Reprints, 1940), p. 249.
5. Burton, *Anatomy*, I, 170.
6. Melanchthon, *Opera*, XIII, 88.
7. Same place as note 6. "It is manifest that a better spirit is produced in the mind when the heart's temperament is good, and when the heart is not disturbed by anger and sadness."
8. Walkington, *Optick Glasse*, p. 151. Cf. Du Laurens, *Discourse*, p. 169.
9. Walkington, *Optick Glasse*, p. 126.
1. Du Laurens, *Discourse*, p. 177; Edward Edwards, *The Analysis of Chyrurgery* (London, 1636), p. 15.

of spirit, kindly, liberal, fond of good food and good wine, fond of music, amorous, intelligent, courageous. The choleric person is lean, hairy, "saffron colored," rash, quick to anger, proud, revengeful, bold, ambitious, shrewed. The phlegmatic man is short and fat, pale, torpid, slothful, mentally dull.[2] Melancholy men are "leane, dry, lank . . . crokenayled . . . the face becommeth pale, yelowyshe & swarty . . . As touching the notes & markes of their minds, they are churlish, whyning . . . obstinate, greedy . . . they vse a certaine slow pace & soft nyce gate, holdinge down their heads, with countenaunce & loke . . . grim and frowninge."[3] They are taciturn, they love to be alone, and they are continually tormented by fears and sorrows.[4] Of all the four complexions, the sanguine is the happiest, and the most miserable is the melancholic. The sanguine man is the most attractive in appearance, whereas "The most deformed is the Malancholike," who is "swarte and ill fauored."[5]

If a man is dissatified with his complexion, there are means, especially dietary means, by which he may heat himself, cool himself, moisten himself, dry himself. If he follows the voluminous advice in the dietaries, he "may in time change and alter his bad complexion into a better."[6]

Renaissance scholars are notoriously fond of analogies. One finds a very complex system of analogies built about the four humors and the four complexions. The correspondency between the elements and the humors is only one of several. These may be conveniently presented by means of Diagram A.[7] This means, to take the melancholic segment (lower left hand) as an example, that the planet Saturn, the element earth, the north wind, the season winter, old age, and the melancholy temperament are all cold and dry. It means, moreover, that Saturn, the north wind, winter, and old age cause increase of the melancholy humor in all men.

Among these various associations, that which connects melancholy with Saturn probably appears more often than any other in Renaissance works, scientific and literary. One finds it, of course, in astrological treatises. According to one astrologer, Saturn is "Cold and drie, melancholick, earthie, masculine . . . maleuolent, destroyer of life." There follows a characterization of the saturnine man (the man born under Saturn's influence) which corresponds closely with the usual conception of the melancholy man.[8] *Saturnine* and *melancholic* are virtually synonymous.

The melancholic character of old age[9] and the consequent decrepitude

2. *Regimen Sanitatis Salerni*, fols. cxxxix–cxlii.
3. Levinus Lemnius, *The Touchstone of Complexions*, tr. Thomas Newton (London, 1576), fol. 146.
4. *Regimen Sanitatis Salerni*, fol. cxliii.
5. Thomas Rogers, *A Philosophicall Discourse, Entituled, the Anatomie of the Minde* (London, 1576), fol. 79r.
6. Walkington, *Optick Glasse*, p. 61.
7. This is copied, with minor omissions, from Walkington's *Optick Glasse* (opposite p. 76 in the 1639 edition). A similar diagram appears on the title page of Robert Anton's *Philosophers Satyrs* (London, 1616). The scheme shown here must be taken only as representative. One finds a great many disagreements among the various writers as to which is the melancholy season, which the melancholy age, etc.
8. Claude Dariot, *A Briefe and Most Easie Introduction to the Astrologicall Judgement of the Starres*, tr. F. W. (London, 1598), sig. Dzr, Cf. sig. C4r. Examination of other astrological works shows that Dariot's ideas are conventional. Similar material appears also in *The Kalendar & Compost of Shepherds*, a widely circulated book of science for the layman, first published in English in 1503. See the edition of G. C. Heseltine (London, 1930), pp. 141–42.
9. In Renaissance works one finds many descriptions of the various ages, or periods, of man's life. There is great disagreement concerning the number of these. Most frequently, however, the writers list four ages corresponding to the four humors (see the diagram from Walkington's *Optick Glasse*) or seven ages corresponding to the seven planets (see *As You Like It*, II vii, 139–66), with Saturn

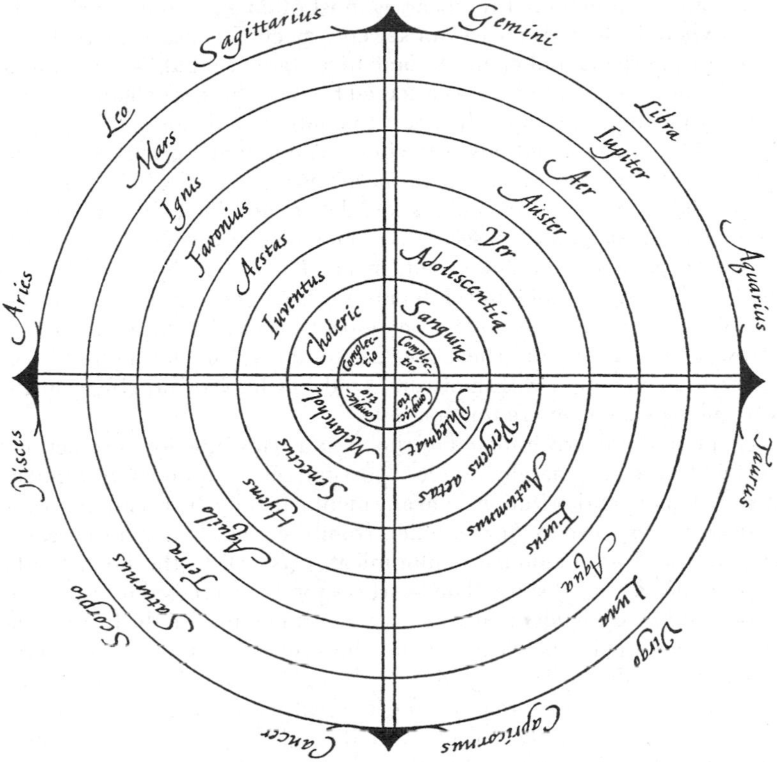

of the aged receive considerable attention in learned works. An affliction "natural to all, and which no man living can avoid," says Robert Burton, "is old age, which being cold and dry, and of the same quality as Melancholy is, must needs cause it, by diminution of spirits and substance."[1] Since melancholy is the humor most inimical to life, old men are subject to the most grievous infirmities of body and mind. Scholarly writers show deep concern for the hard lot of the aged, and in works like Du Laurens' essay "Of Old Age,"[2] Thomas Newton's *The Old Mans Dietarie* (1586), and Simon Goulart's *The Wise Vieillard*,[3] they offer advice on how to mitigate the evils of senility.

VI

I have characterized the passions as functions of the sensitive soul. They may be regarded also as physiological phenomena. A passion is a muscular expansion or contraction of the heart; the heart "doth alwaies either enlarge or shut vp it selfe according to those affections that are within it."[4]

ruling the seventh. There is fairly general agreement that youth is sanguine and old age melancholic.

1. *Anatomy*, I, 239–40. The physiology of the process of aging is discussed above.
2. *Discourse*, pp. 168–94.
3. Two issues of the English translation of this work appeared in 1621.
4. La Primaudaye, *Academie*, p. 466. Melanchthon believes "ipsum cordis substantiam adfectuum fontem esse."—*Opera*, XIII, 129.

This muscular action of the heart is most often a response to a mental state. When the mind is pleased or sees prospect of pleasure, it stimulates the heart to expand and open. A combative state of mind likewise stimulates dilation. When the mind is affected by something repellent or by the prospect of pain, it prompts the heart to contract and close.

Humors also cause motions of the heart. A hot humor provokes dilation. Tempered by moisture, heat excites passions associated with pleasure or the possibility of pleasure, such as joy, desire, and hope. These are "hot and moist," or "sanguine," passions. Accompanied by dryness, heat arouses combative passions—boldness and anger. These are "hot and dry," or "choleric," passions. Cold, in combination with dryness, provokes contraction of the heart and engenders passions associated with pain, such as sorrow, fear, and despair. These are "cold and dry," or "melancholy," passions. In combination with moisture, cold has little or no effect on the heart; phlegmatic men are unemotional.[5]

A passion is properly initiated by the reason. This function is sometimes usurped by the imagination, and it is possible for the humors to stimulate passion without authorization from any mental faculty. Normally, however, passion is a response to an injunction from the reason. When the reason sees occasion for emotion it communicates its will to the heart by the medium of the animal spirit. The heart responds as directed by expansion or contraction. Coincidentally there is a movement toward the heart of the humor whose qualities will stimulate the proper reaction in that organ (which is thus doubly stimulated). The heart does not "haue the temperature which all Passions require; for loue will haue heate, and sadnesse colde, feare constringeth, and pleasure dilateth." Thus "in pleasure concurre great store of pure [vital] spirites; in payne and sadnesse, much melancholy blood; in ire, bloud and choller; and not only . . . the heart draweth, but also the same soule that informeth the heart residing in other partes, sendeth the humours vnto the heart."[6] At the inception of a cold and dry passion, the spleen pours forth melancholy for the purpose of stimulating the heart; at the inception of a hot and dry passion, the gall pours forth choler.[7]

A passion is a definite sensation, felt first in the heart and subsequently throughout the body. Desire and joy are agreeable sensations. A joyful heart, says Melanchthon, dilates with pleasure as if to embrace the object, "ut amans laetatur amplectans puellam." In sorrow the heart suffers painful contraction: "constringitur, premitur, tremit et languefit cum acri sensu doloris."[8] When the heart is "stricken and beaten with some vnpleasant thing . . . then doth it retire, close vp it selfe & feele griefe, as if it had receiued a wound."[9] Sorrow is physical pain. In anger the heart swells belligerently and sends forth blood and spirit ("tanquam milites") to repel the offending object. In this operation it grows hot and inflames the blood and spirit, and the whole body trembles, even the bones.[1] The blood "boy-

5. The preceding paragraph is based especially on Melanchthon, *Opera*, XIII, 124–29; La Primaudaye, *Academie*, pp. 466–68, 471; Wright, *Passions*, pp. 60–68, 82–84, 101–6; Mornay, *True Knowledge*, pp. 158–60; Coeffeteau, *Passions*, pp. 15–17; Edwards, *Chyrurgery*, pp. 11, 20.
6. Wright, *Passions*, pp. 65, 83.
7. Melanchthon, *Opera*, XIII, 44, 129.
8. *Ibid.*, p. 126.
9. La Primaudaye, *Academie*, p. 466.
1. Melanchthon, *Opera*, XIII, 127.

leth round about" the heart, and "these burning flames and kindled spirits" rise to the brain[2] and vitiate the reason.

Each passion, we have noted, is associated with two of the primary qualities, namely the qualities which tend to incite it. Joy is stimulated by heat and moisture, sorrow by cold and dryness, etc. Each passion, moreover, alters the complexion of the entire body, which assumes, at least temporarily, the very qualities which excite the emotion. When the heart is opened by joy or a kindred passion, it "disperseth much naturall heate with the blood, besides great quantity of spirits."[3] The whole system is warmed and moistened. When grief or a kindred passion closes the heart, the blood and vital spirit are locked within it and thus are denied to the rest of the body. The whole system is cooled and dried both by lack of blood and vital spirit and by the melancholy humor issuing from the spleen.[4] During anger, choler issues from the gall: "ciet ardentissimum humorem scilicet rubram bilem, quae effusa, reliquum sanguinem inficit."[5] The body thus becomes hot and dry. Since any passion tends to establish the conditions which are favorable to its own continuation, it might conceivably prolong itself indefinitely.

Passions have a considerable influence upon physical health. Passions of "Content," says Edward Edwards, "dilate the heart & arteries," bring out vital spirit and natural heat, and if they are not immoderate, "comfort and strengthen all the parts of the body and minde, in all their actions."[6] Joy is "a medicine to the body: and foode to the naturall heate and moisture, in which two qualities life chiefly consisteth. . . . For this cause Phisicions alwayes exhort sicke persons to bee as merry as they may, and to auoide sorrow and sadnesse, which beeing colde and dry is contrary to life, and so consumeth men."[7]

Passions of "Discontent" divert "the vitall heat and spirits into the center of the heart." Because they deprive the system of "vitall heat and moysture," they are "destroyers" and "murtherers" "of body and minde," "hastners" of old age and death.[8] The constriction of the grief-stricken heart and the chill of the melancholy humor which surrounds the heart interfere with the production and distribution of vital spirit.[9] The blood, which should be heated and enlivened by the spirit, degenerates into melancholy; the body becomes cold and dry and withers away, "for colde extinguisheth heate, and drienesse moysture, which twoo qualities principally concerne life." Fear and sorrow "preuaile often so much with men, that they languish away and die."[1] Sorrow "is a maligne, colde and dry *Passion*" which wastes natural moisture, quenches natural heat, and withers the heart. When autopsy is performed upon "those that haue beene smothered with mel-

2. La Primaudaye, *Academie*, p. 497.
3. *Ibid.*, p. 466.
4. Fear and grief may have further physiological effects. Since the cold, dry melancholy humor has assembled about the heart, nature is "desirous to relieue and succour it [and] sendeth heat vnto it . . . she suddenly calleth backe the bloud and spirits vnto the heart, and then followeth a generall palenesse and colde in all the outward parts, and chiefly in the face, with a shiuering throughout the whole body."—*ibid.*, p. 471. This concentration of heat in the heart sometimes burns it. * * * Coeffeteau writes that the heat concentrated in the heart by fear may descend and burn the nether organs (*Passions*, p. 465). Elizabethan dramatists often associate sorrow and fear with burning.
5. Melanchthon, *Opera*, XIII, 129. The Latin phrases restate the claims that precede them.
6. *Chyrurgery*, p. 20.
7. La Primaudaye, *Academie*, p. 455; Cf. Elyot, *Castel of Helth*, fol. 68[r]; Burton, *Anatomy*, II, 137 ff.
8. Edwards, *Chyrurgery*, p. 20. Cf. Elyot, *Castel of Helth*, fol. 64.
9. La Primaudaye, *Academie*, p. 455; Wright, *Passions*, p. 105.
1. Wright, *Passions*, p. 106.

ancholy," it reveals "insteed of a heart . . . nothing but a drie skinne like to the leaues in Autumne."[2]

Any immoderate passion may be harmful. Anger "stirreth vp the naturall heat, breedeth choler, and inflameth the blood and spirits . . . it vehemently heateth the bodie, drieth it, and resolueth the strengths." Even joy, the most salutary of the passions, is harmful if it is excessive, for it "relaxeth the heart, and causeth such effusion of the spirit, as that oftentimes ensue sicknesse, and great debility of the body, swoundings. . . ."[3] Any passion, if it is very sudden and violent, may kill outright. If joy "be sodayne and feruente, it oftentymes sleeth, for as moche as it draweth to sodeynly and excessiuely naturall heate outwarde"[4] and thus leaves the heart bloodless and cold. It happens "sometimes, that present death followeth a great and suddeine feare, because all the bloud retiring to the heart choaketh it, and vtterly extinguisheth naturall heat and the spirits, so that death must needes ensue thereof."[5] Sorrow may kill in the same fashion as fear.

> For both revoke the *sp'rites, bloud,* and *kind heate,*
> And to *harte's* Center doe the same direct,
> Which place bee'ng little, and their throng so greate,
> Expels the *Vitall spirits* from their *seate.*[6]

As a result of furious anger, "Some have broken their veines, supprest their urine, whereby present death hath ensued."[7] Sudden and violent passions, moreover, may break the heart. The heart "hath all manner of fibres right, oblique and transuerse, most strong and most compact and mingled one with another . . . as well for the better performance of his motion, as for a defence against iniuries."[8] In violently expanding or contracting the heart, a passion may break the heart strings.

The reader has doubtless noticed that the old physiology of the passions has contributed many common phrases to the language: "ardent love," "blazing anger," "boiling blood," "chilling fear," "cold-blooded murder," "broken heart," and the like. These expressions were not figures of speech in Queen Elizabeth's day.

VII

The reasons for the sanguine man's characteristic gaiety, the choleric man's anger, and the melancholy man's sadness should now be clear: "euery one is most subiect to those affections that come neerest to the nature, temperature, and complexion of his body." The sanguine constitution is predisposed to certain passions and is resistant to others.

2. Coeffeteau, *Passions*, pp. 332–33.
3. Venner, *Via Recta*, pp. 225–26. Hot passions, moreover, produce a noxious "unnatural" melancholy by burning the humors.
4. Elyot, *Castel of Helth*, fol. 68.
5. La Primaudaye, *Academie*, p. 471.
6. John Davies of Hereford, *Microcosmos* (in *Works*, ed. A. B. Grosart [Edinburgh, 1878], vol. I), p. 35. Fortunately the sighs and lamentations which usually accompany grief lessen the danger of its proving fatal: "For howsoeuer griefe shutteth vp the heart . . . yet by groning, sighing, and weeping, the heart doth in some sort open it selfe, as if it would come foorth to breathe, least being wholly shut vp with sorrow it should be stifled."—La Primaudaye, *Academie*, p. 468. It is dangerous to repress grief.
7. Charron, *Of Wisdome*, p. 88.
8. Helkiah Crooke, *Microcosmographia* (London, 1616), p. 370. See Miss Anderson's discussion of heartbreak, *Elizabethan Psychology*, pp. 13, 86–87.

> As for example, the affection of ioy is hote and moist, and therefore they that are hot and moist, as children, young men, sound and healthy folkes, and idle persons, are most easily inclined to that affection. Contrariwise, sorrow is a cold and dry affection, and therefore they that are colde and drie are most giuen to that affection; and such are old folkes and they that are of a melancholy humour.[9]

Choleric men are by physical necessity inclined to be angry. Phlegmatic men necessarily are dull and passionless.

It is possible for the dominant humor to cause a passion without external stimulus. Some men "are alwayes, almost, merry, others, for the most part, melancholy, others euer angry: this diuersity must come from the naturall constitution of the body, wherein one or other humor dooth predominate."[1] Also

> wee prooue in dreames, and physitians prognosticate by them what humour aboundeth, for choller causeth fighting, blood, and wounds; melancholy disgrace, feares, afrightments, ill successe, and such like: these dreams are caused by the spirits which ascend into the imagination, the which being purer or groser, hotter or colder, more or lesse, (which diuersitie dependeth vpon the humors of the bodie) mooue diuerse passions according to their nature.[2]

Just as the temperament influences the passions, so the passions may affect the temperament. If a passion is very strong or if it continues long, it tends to establish the humor of corresponding qualities as the dominant humor, and the humor in turn may make the passion which produced it habitual. Passions may thus modify personality profoundly, even effect a permanent change in complexion. "When the *Affections' Acts* are *habits* growne," they become "*Vertues* or els *Vices*."[3]

Once more, the linguistic contribution of the old physiology should be noted. When we describe a personality as "sanguine," "choleric," or "phlegmatic," we mean something very close to what the Elizabethans meant by the same adjectives, although they have now lost their scientific connotations.

VIII

The physical dangers which lie in the passions are grave, but the moral dangers are graver. Moralists of the Renaissance subscribe to a fundamental principle of classical ethics: conduct motivated by reason is virtuous conduct; conduct motivated by unregulated passion is vicious conduct. Reason is the faculty which distinguishes man from beast. In man it is, or should be, the ruling power. If one follows its dictates, he will achieve virtue and happiness. The passions, however, are turbulently rebellious servants. Often they overrule reason and impel one into evil and misery.

> As it is . . . a poynt of treason, that suche lewed perturbations . . . shoulde rage rebell & take vpon them the rule of the hole man, con-

9. La Primaudaye, *Academie*, p. 455.
1. Wright, *Passions*, pp. 111–12.
2. *Ibid.*, p. 111. Cf. Chaucer's "Nun's Priest's Tale," ll. 103–16. The humors or fumes rising from them are sometimes said to discolor the animal spirits or even the substance of the brain. Melancholy, for example, would blacken the images in the brain.
3. John Davies of Hereford, *Microcosmos* (in *Works*, vol. I), p. 37.

> temptuously despysynge the auctorytie of the mynde, so it is extreme foly for the mynde, to be slaue vnto fonde affections, and to serue at a becke, the vyle carkeys, neyther the dignitie of nature, neyther the expresse lawe of god, any thyng regarded.[4]

This doctrine had wide currency and influence in Elizabethan and early Stuart England.[5]

The passions are strong and violent. Sometimes they compel one to act against his better judgment; "haling to ilnesse, they tosse and turmoyle our miserable soules, as tempests & waues the Ocean sea."[6] At other times they confuse or blind the reason and win its assent. They are like "greene spectacles, which make all thinges resemble the colour of greene; euen so, hee that loueth, hateth, or by anie other passion is vehemently possessed, iudgeth all things that occurre in fauour of that passion, to bee good and agreeable with reason."[7] In their insurrections against reason the passions have the imagination for an ally. The imagination, like the passions, is a sensitive faculty and is capable only of distinguishing pleasure and pain, not right and wrong. Whatever the reason can see of the world without "passeth by the gates of our imagination, the cosin germane to our sensitiue appetite." As the rising or setting moon is magnified by vapors, "euen so, the beauty and goodnesse of the obiect represented to our vnderstanding, appeareth fairer and goodlier than it is, because a clowdie imagination interposeth a mist."[8]

The sensitive powers not only may win temporary mastery over the intellect but may permanently vitiate and dominate it. They "trouble woonderfully the soule, corrupting the iudgement, & seducing the will."[9] When reason has once yielded to passion, it seeks justification for passion: "the *Wit* on the one side labours to find out reasons presently, that may countenance & grace it: and the *Imagination* on the other side, like a deceitfull Counsellor, [seeks] to blinde the eyes of the Iudge."[1] Thus the master becomes the servant. And by degrees it happens that "what was done in the beginning with some scruple and doubt, hath beene afterwards held and maintained for a veritie and revelation from heaven: that which was onely in the sensualitie, hath taken place in the highest part of the understanding."[2]

It may seem strange that, in a creature as ideally endowed as man, the lower nature should thus subvert the God-ordained order of things and win the mastery over the higher. The explanation is the corruption of man and the enfeeblement of his intellectual powers which resulted from the Fall. "The things that were made to obey vs seeme now, through the curse that followed our fall, to rebell against vs. Reason should rule our affec-

4. Juan Luis Vives, *An Introduction to Wisedome*, tr. Rycharde Morysine (London, 1540), sigs. Dii–Diii.
5. See Bundy, "Shakespeare and Elizabethan Psychology"; Anderson, *Elizabethan Psychology*, especially pp. 132–53; Campbell, *Shakespeare's Tragic Heroes*, pp. 63–72, 93–102; Theodore Spencer, *Shakespeare and the Nature of Man* (New York, 1942), pp. 21–28. The chief authorities from whom this ethical system was derived were Plato, Aristotle, Plutarch, Cicero, Seneca, Augustine, and Aquinas.
6. Wright, *Passions*, pp. 301–2.
7. *Ibid.*, p. 88.
8. *Ibid.*, pp. 91–93.
9. *Ibid.*, p. 14.
1. Daniel Tuvil, *Essaies Politicke, and Morall* (London, 1608), fol. 19v.
2. Charron, *Of Wisdome*, pp. 64–65.

tions, but now contrariwise our affections beare rule ouer reason."[3] The light of our reason is "by Mans Fall much dimmed and decayed," and "our unruly *Appetite* . . . laboureth against us . . . to deprive us of those Reliques of Sight which we yet retaine."[4]

In human nature, then, there is continual warfare between the rational and the sensitive, the human and the bestial, the intellectual and the physical. The passions are very likely to be not good servants, but intestine enemies always ready to rise and reverse the normal order of the soul. When they do so, they are diseases of the soul. Writers of the Renaissance attribute to them most of man's vices and sins. The passions, moreover, are the principal cause of human misery. Men are "slaves to their several lusts and appetite, they precipitate and plunge themselves into a labyrinth of cares, blinded with lust, blinded with ambition. . . . By giving way to these violent passions . . . they are torn in pieces, as *Actaeon* was with his dogs, and crucify their own souls."[5] Virtue and happiness are coexistent spiritual states: "happiness consisteth in a minde endued with vertue, voide of all perturbations and vnquietnesse."[6] The *summum bonum*, the greatest good possible to man in his earthly life, is "tranquillitie of the spirit. . . . This is that great and rich treasure, which . . . is the fruit of all our labors and studies, the crowne of wisdome."[7] To achieve this enviable condition, the reasonable soul must keep continual watch over the sensitive powers and must continually exert itself in curbing them.

Since man's greatest enemies lie within himself, his greatest moral problem is self-mastery. Before self-mastery must come self-knowledge, for no man can govern his lower nature without an understanding of it. For this reason the moralists write treatises on psychology, and through these there echoes the ancient exhortation *nosce teipsum*.[8] Melanchthon's *Liber de Anima*, Roger's *Anatomie of the Minde*, Wright's *Passions of the Minde*, Charron's *Of Wisdome*, Sir John Davies' *Nosce Teipsum*, Mornay's *True Knowledge of a Mans Owne Selfe*, Walkington's *Optick Glasse of Humors*, Reynold's *Treatise of the Passions*, and many other works have the avowed purpose of instructing the reader on the subject of his own nature so that he may be armed with the knowledge which is necessary to virtue and happiness. Ethical treatises are, in fact, our chief source of information on Renaissance psychology. Psychology and ethics were not distinguishable subjects in that period.

He who "throughly would know him selfe, must as well knowe his boddie, as his minde."[9] Instruction in psychology necessarily includes instruction in physiology and in the means of maintaining physical health. Treatment of diseases of the soul may involve, first of all, cure of diseases of the body. A virtuous mind is not likely to be found in a distempered

3. Sir Richard Barckley, *The Felicitie of Man* (London, 1631; originally published in 1598), p. 3.
4. Edward Reynolds, *A Treatise of the Passions and Faculties of the Soule of Man* (London, 1640), p. 63. Cf. La Primaudaye, *Academie*, p. 12; Wright, *Passions*, pp. 2–3, 322–23.
5. Burton, *Anatomy*, I, 298.
6. Barckley, *Felicitie*, p. 506. Cf. pp. 491, 513–14.
7. Charron, *Of Wisdome*, p. 346. Cf. La Primaudaye, *Academie*, pp. 14–15; Burton, *Anatomy*, II, 117–18.
8. "Know thyself," it is said, was inscribed above the portals of the temple of Apollo at Delphi. See Plato, *Charmides*, 164–65, *Phaedrus*, 229, *Alcibiades*, 129 ff.; Cicero, *Disputationes Tusculanae*, I, xxii; V, xxv.
9. Rogers, *Anatomie*, "To the Reader," p. 5.

body: "the temperance or intemperance that may be in our bodies, extendeth it selfe vnto the estate of our soule."[1]

Thus the physician shares the responsibility of the moral teacher, and many physicians are conscious of this responsibility. Timothy Bright believes that "Of all other practise of phisick, that parte most commendeth the excellency of the noble facultie, which not only releeueth the bodily infirmity, but after a sort euen also correcteth the infirmities of the mind."[2] The elaborate dietaries and regimens which medical writers offer have the twofold purpose of preventing bodily infirmity and regulating the passions of the mind. Physicians, moreover, earnestly recommend intellectual control of the emotions, for in "mediocritie" of passion "consisteth the tranquillity both of mind and body, which of this life is the chiefest happinesse . . . beware chiefly of sadnesse, for it drieth the bones; and embrace moderate ioy, for both body and minde are bettered thereby."[3]

T. S. ELIOT

The Metaphysical Poets†

By collecting these poems[1] from the work of a generation more often named than read, and more often read than profitably studied, Professor Grierson has rendered a service of some importance. Certainly the reader will meet with many poems already preserved in other anthologies, at the same time that he discovers poems such as those of Aurelian Townshend or Lord Herbert of Cherbury here included. But the function of such an anthology as this is neither that of Professor Saintsbury's admirable edition of Caroline poets nor that of the *Oxford Book of English Verse*. Mr. Grierson's book is in itself a piece of criticism, and a provocation of criticism; and we think that he was right in including so many poems of Donne, elsewhere (though not in many editions) accessible, as documents in the case of 'metaphysical poetry'. The phrase has long done duty as a term of abuse, or as the label of a quaint and pleasant taste. The question is to what extent the so-called metaphysicals formed a school (in our own time we should say a 'movement'), and how far this so-called school or movement is a digression from the main current.

Not only is it extremely difficult to define metaphysical poetry, but difficult to decide what poets practice it and in which of their verses. The poetry of Donne (to whom Marvell and Bishop King are sometimes nearer than any of the other authors) is late Elizabethan, its feeling often very close to that of Chapman. The 'courtly' poetry is derivative from Jonson, who borrowed liberally from the Latin; it expires in the next century with the sentiment and witticism of Prior. There is finally the devotional verse of Herbert, Vaughan, and Crashaw (echoed long after by Christina Rossetti

1. La Primaudaye, *Academie*, p. 456.
2. *Treatise*, dedicatory epistle.
3. Venner, *Via Recta*, p. 226.

† From *Selected Essays*, New Edition, by T. S. Eliot,

1. *Metaphysical Lyrics and Poems of the Seventeenth Century: Donne to Butler*. Selected and edited, with an Essay, by Herbert J. C. Grierson (Oxford: Clarendon Press, 1921. London: Milford).

and Francis Thompson); Crashaw, sometimes more profound and less sectarian than the others, has a quality which returns through the Elizabethan period to the early Italians. It is difficult to find any precise use of metaphor, simile, or other conceit, which is common to all the poets and at the same time important enough as an element of style to isolate these poets as a group. Donne, and often Cowley, employ a device which is sometimes considered characteristically 'metaphysical'; the elaboration (contrasted with the condensation) of a figure of speech to the furthest stage to which ingenuity can carry it. Thus Cowley develops the commonplace comparison of the world to a chess-board through long stanzas (*To Destiny*), and Donne, with more grace, in *A Valediction*, the comparison of two lovers to a pair of compasses. But elsewhere we find, instead of the mere explication of the content of a comparison, a development by rapid association of thought which requires considerable agility on the part of the reader.

> On a round ball
> A workeman that hath copies by, can lay
> An Europe, Afrique, and an Asia,
> And quickly make that, which was nothing, *All*,
> So doth each teare,
> Which thee doth weare,
> A globe, yea world by that impression grow,
> Till thy tears mixt with mine doe overflow
> This world, by waters sent from thee, my heaven dissolved so.

Here we find at least two connexions which are not implicit in the first figure, but are forced upon it by the poet: from the geographer's globe to the tear, and the tear to the deluge. On the other hand, some of Donne's most successful and characteristic effects are secured by brief words and sudden contrasts:

> A bracelet of bright hair about the bone,

where the most powerful effect is produced by the sudden contrast of associations of 'bright hair' and of 'bone'. This telescoping of images and multiplied associations is characteristic of the phrase of some of the dramatists of the period which Donne knew; not to mention Shakespeare, it is frequent in Middleton, Webster, and Tourneur, and is one of the sources of the vitality of their language.

Johnson, who employed the term 'metaphysical poets', apparently having Donne, Cleveland, and Cowley chiefly in mind, remarks of them that 'the most heterogeneous ideas are yoked by violence together'. The force of this impeachment lies in the failure of the conjunction, the fact that often the ideas are yoked but not united; and if we are to judge of styles of poetry by their abuse, enough examples may be found in Cleveland to justify Johnson's condemnation. But a degree of heterogeneity of material compelled into unity by the operation of the poet's mind is omnipresent in poetry. We need not select for illustration such a line as:

> Notre âme est un trois-mâts chercant son Icarie;

we may find it in some of the best lines of Johnson himself (*The Vanity of Human Wishes*):

His fate was destined to a barren strand,
A petty fortress, and a dubious hand;
He left a name at which the world grew pale,
To point a moral, or adorn a tale.

where the effect is due to a contrast of ideas, different in degree but the same in principle, as that which Johnson mildly reprehended. And in one of the finest poems of the age (a poem which could not have been written in any other age), the *Exequy* of Bishop King, the extended comparison is used with perfect success: the idea and the simile become one, in the passage in which the Bishop illustrates his impatience to see his dead wife, under the figure of a journey:

Stay for me there; I will not faile
To meet thee in that hollow Vale.
And think not much of my delay;
I am already on the way,
And follow thee with all the speed
Desire can make, or sorrows breed.
Each minute is a short degree,
And ev'ry houre a step towards thee.
At night when I betake to rest,
Next morn I rise nearer my West
Of life, almost by eight houres sail,
Than when sleep breath'd his drowsy gale. . . .
But heark! My Pulse, like a soft Drum
Beats my approach, tells *Thee* I come;
And slow howere my marches be,
I shall at last sit down by *Thee*.

(In the last few lines there is that effect of terror which is several times attained by one of Bishop King's admirers, Edgar Poe.) Again, we may justly take these quatrains from Lord Herbert's *Ode*, stanzas which would, we think, be immediately pronounced to be of the metaphysical school:

So when from hence we shall be gone,
  And be no more, nor you, nor I,
  As one another's mystery,
Each shall be doth, yet both but one.

This said, in her up-lifted face,
  Her eyes, which did that beauty crown,
  Were like two starrs, that having faln down,
Look up again to find their place:

While such a moveless silent peace
  Did seize on their becalmed sense,
  One would have thought some influence
Their ravished spirits did possess.

There is nothing in these lines (with the possible exception of the stars, a simile not at once grasped, but lovely and justified) which fits Johnson's general observations on the metaphysical poets in his essay on Cowley. A good deal resides in the richness of association which is at the same time borrowed from and given to the word 'becalmed'; but the meaning is clear, the language simple and elegant. It is to be observed that the language of these poets is as a rule simple and pure; in the verse of George Herbert this simplicity is carried as far as it can go—a simplicity emulated without success by numerous modern poets. The *structure* of the sentences, on the other hand, is sometimes far from simple, but this is not a vice; it is fidelity to thought and feeling. The effect, at its best, is far less artificial than that of an ode by Gray. And as this fidelity induces variety of thought and feeling, so it induces variety of music. We doubt whether, in the eighteenth century, could be found two poems in nominally the same metre, so dissimilar as Marvell's *Coy Mistress* and Crashaw's *Saint Teresa*; the one producing an effect of great speed by the use of short syllables, and the other an ecclesiastical solemnity by the use of long ones:

> Love, thou art absolute sole lord
> Of life and death.

If so shrewd and sensitive (though so limited) a critic as Johnson failed to define metaphysical poetry by its faults, it is worth while to inquire whether we may not have more success by adopting the opposite method: by assuming that the poets of the seventeenth century (up to the Revolution) were the direct and normal development of the precedent age; and, without prejudicing their case by the adjective 'metaphysical', consider whether their virtue was not something permanently valuable, which subsequently disappeared, but ought not to have disappeared. Johnson has hit, perhaps by accident, on one of their peculiarities, when he observes that 'their attempts were always analytic'; he would not agree that, after the dissociation, they put the material together again in a new unity.

It is certain that the dramatic verse of the later Elizabethan and early Jacobean poets expresses a degree of development of sensibility which is not found in any of the prose, good as it often is. If we except Marlowe, a man of prodigious intelligence, these dramatists were directly or indirectly (it is at least a tenable theory) affected by Montaigne. Even if we except also Jonson and Chapman, these two were notably erudite, and were notably men who incorporated their erudition into their sensibility: their mode of feeling was directly and freshly altered by their reading and thought. In Chapman especially there is a direct sensuous apprehension of thought, or a recreation of thought into feeling, which is exactly what we find in Donne:

> in this one thing, all the discipline
> Of manners and of manhood is contained;
> A man to join himself with th' Universe
> In his main sway, and make in all things fit
> One with that All, and go on, round as it;
> Not plucking from the whole his wretched part,
> And into straits, or into nought revert,
> Wishing the complete Universe might be
> Subject to such a rag of it as he;
> But to consider great Necessity.

We compare this with some modern passage:

> No, when the fight begins within himself,
> A man's worth something. God stoops o'er his head,

Satan looks up between his feet—both tug—
He's left, himself, i' the middle; the soul wakes
And grows. Prolong that battle through his life!

It is perhaps somewhat less fair, though very tempting (as both poets are concerned with the perpetuation of love by offspring), to compare with the stanzas already quoted from Lord Herbert's *Ode* the following from Tennyson:

One walked between his wife and child,
With measured footfall firm and mild,
And now and then he gravely smiled.
  The prudent partner of his blood
  Leaned on him, faithful, gentle, good,
  Wearing the rose of womanhood.
And in their double love secure,
The little maiden walked demure,
Pacing with downward eyelids pure.
  These three made unity so sweet,
  My frozen heart began to beat,
  Remembering its ancient heat.

The difference is not a simple difference of degree between poets. It is something which had happened to the mind of England between the time of Donne or Lord Herbert of Cherbury and the time of Tennyson and Browning; it is the difference between the intellectual poet and the reflective poet. Tennyson and Browning are poets, and they think; but they do not feel their thought as immediately as the odour of a rose. A thought to Donne was an experience; it modified his sensibility. When a poet's mind is perfectly equipped for its work, it is constantly amalgamating disparate experience; the ordinary man's experience is chaotic, irregular, fragmentary. The latter falls in love, or reads Spinoza, and these two experiences have nothing to do with each other, or with the noise of the typewriter or the smell of cooking; in the mind of the poet these experiences are always forming new wholes.

We may express the difference by the following theory: The poets of the seventeenth century, the successors of the dramatists of the sixteenth, possessed a mechanism of sensibility which could devour any kind of experience. They are simple, artificial, difficult, or fantastic, as their predecessors were; no less nor more than Dante, Guido Cavalcanti, Guinicelli, or Cino. In the seventeenth century a dissociation of sensibility set in, from which we have never recovered; and this dissociation, as is natural, was aggravated by the influence of the two most powerful poets of the century, Milton and Dryden. Each of these men performed certain poetic functions so magnificently well that the magnitude of the effect concealed the absence of others. The language went on and in some respects improved; the best verse of Collins, Gray, Johnson, and even Goldsmith satisfies some of our fastidious demands better than that of Donne or Marvell or King. But while the language became more refined, the feeling became more crude. The feeling, the sensibility, expressed in the *Country Churchyard* (to say nothing of Tennyson and Browning) is cruder than that in the *Coy Mistress*.

The second effect of the influence of Milton and Dryden followed from the first, and was therefore slow in manifestation. The sentimental age began early in the eighteenth century, and continued. The poets revolted against the ratiocinative, the descriptive; they thought and felt by fits, unbalanced; they reflected. In one or two passages of Shelley's *Triumph of Life*, in the second *Hyperion*, there are traces of a struggle toward unification of sensibility. But Keats and Shelley died, and Tennyson and Browning ruminated.

After this brief exposition of a theory—too brief, perhaps, to carry conviction—we may ask, what would have been the fate of the 'metaphysical' had the current of poetry descended in a direct line from them, as it descended in a direct line to them? They would not, certainly, be classified as metaphysical. The possible interests of a poet are unlimited; the more intelligent he is the better; the more intelligent he is the more likely that he will have interests: our only condition is that he turn them into poetry, and not merely meditate on them poetically. A philosophical theory which has entered into poetry is established, for its truth or falsity in one sense ceases to matter, and its truth in another sense is proved. The poets in question have, like other poets, various faults. But they were, at best, engaged in the task of trying to find the verbal equivalent for states of mind and feeling. And this means both that they are more mature, and that they wear better, than later poets of certainly not less literary ability.

It is not a permanent necessity that poets should be interested in philosophy, or in any other subject. We can only say that it appears likely that poets in our civilization, as it exists at present, must be *difficult*. Our civilization comprehends great variety and complexity, and this variety and complexity, playing upon a refined sensibility, must produce various and complex results. The poet must become more and more comprehensive, more allusive, more indirect, in order to force, to dislocate if necessary, language into his meaning. (A brilliant and extreme statement of this view, with which it is not requisite to associate oneself, is that of M. Jean Epstein, *La Poésie d'aujourdhui*.) Hence we get something which looks very much like the conceit—we get, in fact, a method curiously similar to that of the 'metaphysical poets', similar also in its use of obscure words and of simple phrasing.

> O géraniums diaphanes, guerroyeurs sortilèges,
> Sacrilèges monomanes!
> Emballages, dévergondages, douches! O pressoirs
> Des vendanges des grands soirs!
> Layettes aux abois,
> Thyrses au fond des bois!
> Transfusions, représailles,
> Relevailles, compresses et l'éternal potion,
> Angélus! n'en pouvior plus
> De débâcles nuptiales! de débâcles nuptiales![2]

The same poet could write also simply:

2. "O transparent geraniums, warrior incantations, / Monomaniac sacrileges! / Packing materials, shamelessnesses, shower baths! O wine presses / Of great evening vintages! / Hard-pressed baby linen, / Thyrsis in the depths of the woods! / Transfusions, reprisals, / Churchings, compresses, and the eternal potion, / Angelus! no longer to be borne [are] / Catastrophic marriages!" This passage is from *Derniers vers X* ("Last Poems," 1890), by Jules Laforgue (1860–87) [*Editor*].

Elle est bien loin, elle pleure,
Le grand vent se lamente aussi . . . [3]

Jules Laforgue, and Tristan Corbière in many of his poems, are nearer to the 'school of Donne' than any modern English poet. But poets more classical than they have the same essential quality of transmuting ideas into sensations, of transforming an observation into a state of mind.

Pour l'enfant, amoureux de cartes et d'estampes,
L'univers est égal à son vaste appétit.
Ah, que le monde est grand à la clarté des lampes!
Aux yeux du souvenir que le monde est petit![4]

In French literature the great master of the seventeenth century—Racine—and the great master of the nineteenth—Baudelaire—are in some ways more like each other than they are like anyone else. The greatest two masters of diction are also the greatest two psychologists, the most curious explorers of the soul. It is interesting to speculate whether it is not a misfortune that two of the greatest masters of diction in our language, Milton and Dryden, triumph with a dazzling disregard of the soul. If we continued to produce Miltons and Drydens it might not so much matter, but as things are it is a pity that English poetry has remained so incomplete. Those who object to the 'artificiality' of Milton or Dryden sometimes tell us to 'look into our hearts and write'. But that is not looking deep enough; Racine or Donne looked into a good deal more than the heart. One must look into the cerebral cortex, the nervous system, and the digestive tracts.

May we not conclude, then, that Donne, Crashaw, Vaughan, Herbert and Lord Herbert, Marvell, King, Cowley at his best, are in the direct current of English poetry, and that their faults should be reprimanded by this standard rather than coddled by antiquarian affection? They have been enough praised in terms which are implicit limitations because they are 'metaphysical' or 'witty', 'quaint' or 'obscure', though at their best they have not these attributes more than other serious poets. On the other hand, we must not reject the criticism of Johnson (a dangerous person to disagree with) without having mastered it, without having assimilated the Johnsonian canons of taste. In reading the celebrated passage in his essay on Cowley we must remember that by wit he clearly means something more serious than we usually mean to-day; in his criticism of their versification we must remember in what a narrow discipline he was trained, but also how well trained; we must remember that Johnson tortures chiefly the chief offenders, Cowley and Cleveland. It would be a fruitful work, and one requiring a substantial book, to break up the classification of Johnson (for there has been none since) and exhibit these poets in all their difference of kind and of degree, from the massive music of Donne to the faint, pleasing tinkle of Aurelian Townshend—whose *Dialogue between a Pilgrim and Time* is one of the few regrettable omissions from the excellent anthology of Professor Grierson.

3. "She is far away, she weeps, / The great wind mourns also." From *Derniers vers XI, Sur une défunte* ("On a Dead Woman") [*Editor*].
4. From Baudelaire's *Le Voyage:* "For the child, in love with maps and prints, / The universe matches his vast appetite. / Ah, how big the world is by lamplight! How small the world is to the eyes of memory!" [*Editor*].

WILLIAM EMPSON

Donne the Space Man†

> Why then should witless man so far misween
> That nothing is, but that which he hath seen?
> What if within the moon's fair shining sphere,
> What if in every other star unseen,
> Of other worlds he happily should hear?
> He wonder would much more, yet such to some appear.
> (Proem to Book II, *Faerie Queene*.)

Present-day writers on Donne, I have recently come to realize, have never heard of a belief about him which, twenty or thirty years ago, I though was being taken for granted. I can't believe I invented it; it was part of the atmosphere in which I grew up as an undergraduate at Cambridge. Nor, so far as I can gather, has it been refuted (though there are two old magazine articles, regularly listed in footnotes, which I have looked up and will discuss); I fancy the detailed evidence for it did not get collected because that seemed unnecessary. I myself, being concerned with verbal analysis, thought I could take this part of Donne's mind as already known; and all the more, of course, when I was imitating it in my own poems, which I did with earnest conviction. The current of fashion or endeavor has now changed its direction, and a patient effort to put the case for the older view seems timely. The text of the poems, I think, gives strong evidence, but perhaps only in a literary way; that is, the poetry becomes better, both more imaginative and more coherent, if the hints implying this opinion are allowed the weight due to a consistent use. I must begin by trying to state the position as a whole.

Donne, then, from a fairly early age, was interested in getting to another planet much as the kids are nowadays; he brought the idea into practically all his best love-poems, with the sentiment which it still carries of adventurous freedom. But it meant a lot more to him than that; coming soon after Copernicus and Bruno, it meant not being a Christian—on one specific point only, that of denying the uniqueness of Jesus. Maybe the young Donne would have denied that this denial put him outside Christianity; as would the young Coleridge for example, who arrived at it by a different route; but they both knew they had to be cautious about expressing it. In our present trend of opinion, as I understand, to impute this belief to the young Donne will be felt to show a lack of sense of history, to involve a kind of self-indulgence, and to be a personal insult to the great preacher. I shall be trying to meet these objections, but had better say at once that I think the belief makes one much more convinced of the sincerity of his eventual conversion, and does much to clear the various accusations which have recently been made against his character.

No reasonable man, I readily agree, would want space travel as such; because he wants to know, in any proposal for travel, whether he would go farther and fare worse. A son of my own at about the age of twelve, keen on space travel like the rest of them, saw the goat having kids and

† From *The Kenyon Review*—OS Summer 1957, Vol. 19, No. 3. Copyright © *The Kenyon Review*. Abridged.

was enough impressed to say "It's better than space travel." It is indeed absolutely or metaphysically better, because it is coming out of the nowhere into here; and I was so pleased to see the human mind beginning its work that I felt as much impressed as he had done at seeing the birth of the kids. One does not particularly want, then, to have Donne keen on space travel unless he had a serious reason for it.

One needs first, I think, to see that the theological dilemma is real. In our time no less than in Donne's, to believe that there are rational creatures on other planets is very hard to reconcile with the belief that Salvation is only through Christ; they and their descendants appear to have been excluded from salvation; by the very scheme of God, indefinitely and perhaps for ever. One might suppose, to preserve God's justice, that Christ repeats his sacrifice in all worlds (the curious phrase in two of the creeds, "begotten before all worlds," must have acquired a certain resonance in Donne's time), but this already denies uniqueness to Jesus, and must in some thorough way qualify the identity of the man with the divine Person. It becomes natural to envisage frequent partial or occasional Incarnations on this earth; and I understand that the young Coleridge, though boldly, was following a tradition of Platonic theorizers:

> Finally, on such a view might not Christ be the world as revealed to human knowledge—a kind of common sensorium, the idea of the whole that modifies all our thoughts? And might not numerical identity be an exclusive property of phenomena so that he who puts on the likeness of Christ becomes Christ? Hooker alludes to the idea as a well-known one in the preface to the *Ecclesiastical Policy*: "When they of the family of love have it once in their heads that Christ doth not signify any one person, but a quality whereof many are partakers . . . how plainly do they imagine that the Scripture everywhere speaketh in the favour of that sect.

The present state of scientific theory (if I may fill in the picture) almost forces us to believe in life on other planets, though the reason is different from the traditional "Great Chain of Being" so magnificently expounded by Lovejoy. Our solar system probably has no other rational inhabitants at present (if Mars has irrigation canals the builders are probably long extinct), and probably few other stars in our galaxy have habitable planets; though I gather that recent theories have tended to increase the number, and no theorist thinks the sun likely to be the only one. But there are thousands of millions of other galaxies (if not an infinite number, which I still hope can be avoided) and that decides the probability; it makes the mind revolt at any doctrine which positively requires our earth to have the only rational inhabitants. Believers in the Great Chain thought that God would be sure to fill the universe with all possible life, whereas most theorists now regard the universe as inherently capable of producing life but only through a staggering application of the laws of probability. It is thus likely to be rare; regarding stellar and biological evolution as a continuous process, you would expect fewer stars to produce life than acorns to produce oaks. But this picture gives us even less excuse than the earlier one for regarding ourselves as unique. We may feel that there is less practical danger of meeting such creatures, but not that any theoretical problem about their existence has been removed.

The problem of God's justice to men had of course long been familiar; it seemed so agonizing to Dante that he raised it in Paradise (Canto xix) saying that on earth it had long caused his mind famine; the reply seems to me only to dramatize the mystery. An Indian is already the example of a man deprived of the redeemer. But the European maritime expansion made it hit the attention of Christians much more; the number and variety of people found to be living out of reach of the Gospel, many of them not noticeably worse than Christians, came as a shock; especially to Protestant late-comers like the English, who were rather in the business of saying the Spaniards treated the natives very wickedly (to be fair to the Spaniards, they ran into the wickedest civilization built on human sacrifice then surviving). To make the problem absolute, by supposing intelligent life on other planets, gave therefore a frightful cutting edge to a problem already felt as painful. The question of such life seems to get little attention till late in the 17th Century, either in England or France, but critics cannot merely assert that it was invisible to Donne; and on the other hand Lovejoy in *The Great Chain of Being* treats it as stale, and adduces philosophers discussing it ever since Plato, but one may suspect his philosophers were such high-flying characters that they did not much affect ordinary opinion. Also a good deal of censorship may be expected. It became almost traditional to say that Copernicanism was at first resisted because it removed Man from the centre of the universe, a blow to his pride; but the centre was considered the lowest-class place, and any debasement of Man was only half of the paradox that he was also made in the image of God. I suspect that this story was often told as a deliberate evasion of the real problem. The only space-writer I know of who has handled it is the Anglican C. S. Lewis; rather brilliantly in *Out of the Silent Planet* (1938), where we find that our Earth alone required the Incarnation because it had fallen in a unique degree into the power of the Devil; but in the sequel *Voyage to Venus* (1943) we gather that all future rational creatures will have to evolve in the image of Man, throughout all galaxies, as a technical result of the Incarnation; and this feels too parochial even to be a pleasant fantasy. When we study a man in the past grappling with a problem to which we have learned the answer we find it hard to put ourselves in his position; but surely a modern Christian knows no more about this than Donne or Bruno, and has no occasion for contempt. The young Donne, to judge from his poems, believed that every planet could have its Incarnation, and believed this with delight, because it automatically liberated an independent conscience from any earthly religious authority.

The police state which uses torture to impose a doctrine was very familiar in the 16th Century (though this may come as a surprise to anyone who had adopted Christianity as an escape from Communism); and when we first find Donne discussing such matters, in the rightly praised Satire III, usually dated about 1594, when he was twenty-two or -three, the whole climax of the argument is against all Popes or Princes who do this wicked thing. The poem seems often to get regarded as a commonplace bit of Anglican liberalism, but it was not usual, or safe, then, and the licensers still doubted whether to publish the Satires after his death. The last two burnings alive for heresy in England were in 1611. In 1593 a group of anti-Puritan laws had been passed making any attack on the ecclesiastical settlement a criminal offense punishable by banishment or death, and a

Henry Barrow had been executed for having formed a sect; also Donne's younger brother had died in jail that year for having harbored a priest.

The poem apparently is using the courage of the maritime adventurers simply to argue that we should be as brave in fighting the Devil; but, considering the emphasis at the end on how much danger the seeker of the true religion may have from earthly power, they seem somehow also to give inherent argument for freedom of conscience. The poem expects heathen philosophers to be prominent in Heaven. There is nothing about the argument from planets, but the poet was clearly in a frame of mind ready to take that up with the necessary earnestness. The first hint of playing at it, as a poetical trope, comes I think in Elegy XIX, usually dated a year or two later.

A reader may suspect that problems about the inhabitants of other planets had simply not occurred to anybody in the period. But one man did write about such things; it was Bruno, who was *incommunicado* under the Inquisition from 1592 till 1600, while Donne grew from say 20 to 28; he was then burned alive at Rome. We have an account of his first deposition because he was arrested at Venice, where the Inquisition was more decent in the sense of less secretive; he was pathetically confident, but he at once confessed, or rather claimed as the real subject for discussion, that he did believe in the plurality of worlds. Eight years later (or so we are told in a gossiping letter) this belief figured in the bucketful of accusations which were read out before he was burnt alive. Such was presumably why James Joyce so greatly admired The Nolan, as he esoterically called Bruno; it seems worth pointing out, now that critics are so busy explaining that Joyce was an orthodox Catholic. However, it is not claimed that Bruno invented this belief. Mr. R. F. Johnson in his *Astronomical Thought in Renaissance England* (1937), found that the English Thomas Digges had already in 1576, for a reedition of his father's book on Copernicus, sponsored an infinite universe and a plurality of worlds. Bruno was staying in England from 1583 to 1585, and the Digges book was given two of its many reprints during that brief time. Maybe Digges was considered a crank (he appears as a prominent citizen in Leslie Hotson's *I, William Shakespeare*), but the book went on selling; at worst his position would be like the present one of Mr. Robert Graves, whose views on mythology are not prominent in universities but are in the Penguin series. Bruno's friends, such as Sidney, were interested in the book, says Mr. Johnson, and he suspects that the visit suggested the plurality of worlds to poor Bruno, who did not start the fatal process of writing about it till afterwards. There is a reason why the English should feel comparatively free here. Protestant leaders on the Continent had at once called Copernicanism absurd because it contradicted the Bible (e.g., Psalm 93: "the world also is stablished, that it cannot be moved") but seem to have thought it too absurd to require organized persecution; whereas Rome, taking the matter slowly and seeing it as a whole, eventually decided to stamp out belief in inhabitants of worlds out of reach of the Pope. But the Church of England, being a *via media*, had neither nailed its flag to a unique authority, the Pope in Council, nor to a unique text which had to be interpreted rigidly—if one is allowed to interpret the Bible in the light of Church tradition, it seems fair to interpret astronomical texts in the light of their purpose; thus the Anglicans could afford to treat the matter casually. At bottom, one would think, they too had a problem about the status of the Redeemer on other planets, but as time went on they found they were content to allow it to be more disturbing to both their opponents than to themselves. This rather accidental position probably had a decisive effect, because anything else would have made Newton impossible; but at the time it seems chiefly to have caused silence—people who were aware of the question felt both that it might be dangerous and also that it did not impose itself as one which positively ought to be raised. The Church of England has a good later record on such matters, but at the time Donne could not have known which way it would go; he might even have thought, as some critics have supposed, that the Catholics were being more liberal about it than the Protestants; but, even so, this would only give an extra twist to the gay defiance of his style.

No other poet of the time, I have to admit, betrays this excitement about the topic; not even the imitators of Donne. I quite understand that this makes scholars unwilling to recognize the topic in Donne either; indeed, anyone who has had to supervise a university thesis on "The Literary Effects of Copernicus" in the period will have been driven to conclude he had surprisingly little. But it is intelligible that Donne should be alone here. In the first place, he would know all about it; he became an adviser to Anglican officials on theological controversy while still uncommitted—"an independent and disobliged man," as he described himself to the King's favorite; and it is agreed that he read Kepler's book about a *nova* in 1606 and Galileo's about his discoveries through the telescope in 1610, as soon as they came out, which presumes that he was interested in the subject beforehand. Also, he was brought up as one of a spreading Catholic family, with martyrs, though himself doubtful as between all sects; to get himself martyred merely to please to relations would be ridiculous, but he would think it dishonorable merely to join the safer and more rewarding sect. He needed to be allowed to recognize the variety of the world, and the Anglicans were the most likely to let him do so; though it is hard to pin the matter down, as by saying that they recognized the validity of other orders, or the possibility of salvation for members of sects without orders; indeed, Donne while uncommitted might well doubt whether that Church would come to recognize its own nature firmly enough. Just how much conformity was required in a secular career is a confusing question, and one which his cast of mind would make very subtle. It is from this background that he was keenly, even if sardonically, interested in the theology of the separate planet—from fairly early, though he did not come to feel he was actually planted on one till he realized the full effects of his runaway marriage. By the time he took Anglican Orders I imagine he was thankful to get back from the interplanetary spaces, which are inherently lonely and ill-provided. I don't deny that he was very capable of casuistry—his sense of honor would work in unexpected ways; but at least he had joined the only Church which could admit the existence of his interplanetary spaces. To assume he never thought of them makes his career much less coherent.

Perhaps I should add a bit of biography, not to address this article only to specialists. Born in 1571 rather than 1572, Donne after spending his inheritance on seeing the world got a job as personal secretary to Sir Thomas Egerton, then Keeper of the Great Seal and eventually Lord Chancellor, but lost it in 1601 by secretly marrying the niece who was acting as hostess of the grand house. He couldn't have been certain when he did this that it would break his career, because it wouldn't have done if the father hadn't behaved foolishly; the father first insisted on having Donne sacked and then found he had better try to have him reinstated, which Egerton refused on the very English ground that the fuss about the matter had been sufficiently ridiculous already. Donne then had a long period of grizzling in poverty, gradually killing his wife by giving her a child every year (she died in 1617), but becoming famous in the right circles as an expert on theology in all known languages. King James sensibly enough refused to give him any job unless he became a parson, this being what he was obviously good at, and at last, the year before his patron Sir Robert Drury died, when the money position for his family was becoming hopeless, he consented to become one, early in 1615, and was at once recognized as an overwhelming preacher; though one whom Mr. T. S. Eliot has reasonably suspected of using his personality too much. These flat remarks are not at all meant to accuse him of insincerity in taking Anglican Orders, though he never denied a certain feeling of desperation about it; I am much more inclined to accept the view that he was one of the few men who constructed the intellectual platform from which later Anglicans felt able to behave moderately and well.

* * *

Theologically the most reckless of Donne's poems are those in which he presents himself as a martyr to love and thereby the founder of a religion, the Christ of all future reckless lovers (it is personally inoffensive, though the self-pity is real enough, once you realize it is meant to be general—anybody can become a Christ in this way); and here he can't easily present himself as on a separate planet, because he has to be within reach of his eventual worshippers. No doubt "The Canonization" and "The Funeral" would seem too remote to be alarming, and even in "The Relic" he only supposes it is in a time of "misdevotion" that, if a gravedigger turns up

A bracelet of bright hair about the bone

(her hair and his bone), these objects will be worshipped as relics;

Thou shalt be a Mary Magdalene, and I
A something else thereby.

Still, I was glad to see that the recent edition by Mr. Redpath of the *Songs and Sonets* (1956) is at last willing to envisage that "A Jesus Christ" is what the poet ostentatiously holds back from saying. It has been objected that Jesus left no bone behind him on earth, and indeed this clearly made Donne safer; no doubt he himself would be ready with the objection if challenged. But "*a* Jesus Christ" would be logically a very different entity from the one Jesus, and the point I am trying to make all along is that this kind of poetry continually uses the idea that the attributes of the Christ can be applied to others. The advocates of St. John, who was presumably John Donne's patron saint, neither produce a suitable anecdote nor make the line scan. The first readers of the manuscript seem likely to have thought of the more obvious meaning, however much Donne denied it even to them. One would think the process must have been dangerous; at any rate it carries to the limit the convention of comparing the hero in view to Christ.

* * *

Mr. M. F. Maloney, in a study from the Catholic point of view (*John Donne, His Flight from Medievalism*, 1944), gives a detailed argument that Donne in later life was rather irritated and suspicious at the claims of Christian mystics, and deduces that he never had any mystical experience himself. But there is another half of the religious world which believes in the Absolute rather than the personal God, and the ecstasy which Donne records in his secular love-poetry is a matter of being in contact with That. For one thing, the ideal love as he conceives it ought to be the melting of two personalities into one. The position is Asiatic rather than Christian, and no doubt he felt very unsupported in it except by the temporary exhilaration of a splendid paradox. All the same, this idea of dissolving into the Godhead, rather than seeing God, continues to crop up in his religious writing after conversion. When he begins the great "Hymn to God, my God, in my Sickness" with:

> Since I am coming to that holy room,
> Where, with thy choir of Saints for evermore,
> I shall be made thy Music . . .

it seems natural to suppose that he hardly expects a personal immortality. Mr. Clay Hunt (*Donne's Poetry*, 1954), whose very lively and intelligent book I am now to attack at various points, explains that the phrase

> implies a specific mystical doctrine which, because of its paradoxical character, seems to have appealed particularly to Donne's speculative imagination. According to this doctrine the individual soul is absorbed after death into the joys of heaven, but at the same time it retains its identity and can contemplate those joys as a spectator. Donne refers to this concept a number of times. . . . .

That seems a good case of having it both ways. I am pretty ignorant about all this, but see no reason to doubt the account given by Aldous Huxley in *The Perennial Philosophy*, that absorption into the Absolute was recurrent among Christian mystics but a good deal frowned on by the official Churches. Certainly one must not think it was unheard—of except in the East; you could hardly get more of it than in the peroration of Sir Thomas Browne:

> And if any have been so happy as truly to know Christian annihilation, ecstasies, exolution, liquefaction, transformation, the kiss of the spouse, gustation of God, and ingression into the divine shadow, they have already had an handsome anticipation of Heaven; the glory of the world is surely over, and the earth is ashes unto them.

That is very unlike Milton, for example, who seems to decide in *Lycidas* that God would give him a lot of praise in Heaven, as a first-class author, even for the books he hadn't written. Mr. Maloney, as I understand, would limit mysticism by definition to a direct relation with a personal God; whereas the later Donne, retaining contact with his past, took the opposite idea as far as he could without falling back into heresy. Such for example must be the background of the end of *Holy Sonnet IX*, which a recent coolly theological critic has found paltry:

> That thou remember them, some claim as debt,
> think it mercy, if thou wilt forget.

The idea does then "fit the separate planet" and so forth. Also it fits the universalizing of the idea of Christ, by making individuality less important.

Mr. Hunt makes a graver accusation against Donne for the religiosity of the poems written while he was unregenerate. He says for example about "The Canonization" (in which Donne pretends that posterity will worship him as a saint of true love):

> that self-defensive poem about John Donne's renunciation of worldly values, which, as I have argued, must have derived from his inclination to feel a certain private righteousness as he brooded on the suffering he had incurred by his marriage, is the most clearly Catholic in its imaginative pattern of all his major love-poems.

It was particularly unpleasant of Donne to call himself a martyr, because the broad fact was that he had ratted on the family duty of becoming one. He had, says Mr. Hunt, "the disposition, in moments of depression, to imagine a martyrdom for himself, and to think of himself at those times as a Catholic at odds with the world." This line of thought suits those who believe he was always a secret Catholic, even when he became an Anglican parson for money. How readily one can imagine this shifty character, and with what intense disgust. Surely it is much more probable, as well as more agreeable, to expect that he didn't feel committed to either sect, and saw no reason to give either of them an excuse to burn him alive. He remarked for example of Rome, Wittenberg and Geneva (*Letters*, p. 29): "They are all virtual beams of one sun, and wheresoever they find clay hearts, they harden them and moulder them into dust. . . ."; this strikes me as more strongly felt than the balancing clause "and they entender and mollify waxen." However, I agree that 1611 is remarkably late for the process to be still going on so firmly in the mind of Donne; little as he liked having to print the *Anniversaries*, I think he must have been hardened by then into feeling that the process was an imaginative convention, not a heresy; indeed, no one could seriously accuse him of believing that poor Elizabeth Drury was the Logos. His chief new cosmological opinion, as is made clear in *All Coherence Gone* (Victor Harris, 1939), is that the universe was decaying, an idea he had only played with before, and indeed played at refuting in his *Paradoxes*; he seems to have remained sure of it from now on. However, if I am accused as is now usual of "undergraduate atheism" or some such phrase for raising the doubt, meaning that it is absurdly unhistorical, I must answer that there was a good deal of undergraduate atheism knocking about the London of the 1590's; as we learn from the accusations claiming to report the talk of Marlowe, which don't sound much like Marlowe but must have served to classify him as a well-known wicked type. It was a natural result of hope and verbal expansiveness after the fierce changes in the official religion, and a historian who refuses to believe in it merely because nobody dared leave any documents about it can be deceived by any police state. As to the use of Catholic imagery in "The Canonization," its basic conceit could only be applied to the one sect which did "worship saints," and surely its only sectarian effect is a satire on that one. Maybe even the Anglicans at the time, when these matters were much less clear-cut than we now suppose, would be liable to call it blasphemous too. If you realize that Donne was showing a good deal of perky courage, as well as a secret largeness of mind. I think this particular libel against him becomes an easy one to reject.

However, it is connected in the mind of Mr. Hunt with a more general suspicion that there is something sickly about the mind of Donne. He makes a charmingly real-life approach to "The Canonization," and tries to say what he can in favor of the poem:

> the sainthood conceit and the general identification of love with religious experience . . . are intended to imply a serious philosophic statement. Donne commits himself, at least in part, to the logical implications of his central religious metaphor, and, in a sense, the analogy is actually meant as a conceptual proposition. The poem says, in effect, that, fantastic as this analogy may seem, it may contain elements of truth beneath its surface improbability.

But he has to conclude, with firm honesty, that the poem does not really come off; the last stanza is not strong enough for the basic claim:

> Even in that final stanza there are still suggestions of slick cleverness in Donne's elaboration of the sainthood conceit, so that some loose ends of levity and wit-for-wit's-sake are left dangling at the end of the poem.

He doesn't say which bits, but I think he came to the right conclusion, granting to start with that he didn't realize how big the claim was meant to be. If the private religion of Donne's love has *exactly as much* claim to "contain elements of truth beneath its surface improbability" as the official religion which it parodies, fully equipped with rack, boot, thumbscrew, and slow fire, then you can see some point in having the later congregation pray to Donne "send us back the reality which we have lost." There is an agreeable stirring of the Old Adam in Mr. Hunt when he confronts the belief that each act of sex shortens a man's life a day, a belief, he says, that must have given Donne many uneasy moments, and he is probably right in connecting it with the quaint self-importance of a sexual pun in "The Canonization":

> We die and rise the same, and prove
> Mysterious by this love.

Except the corn die in the ground, said St. Paul rather oddly, it cannot sprout; and Mr. Hunt makes some penetrating remarks:

> the mystery of the love is that the lovers are spiritualized through the bodily "death" of sexual intercourse. . . . The lovers are certainly destroying themselves physically. But their willingness so to mortify the flesh, Donne suggests, stands as evidence of their essential contempt for all material things.

That is, the quaint medical theory gives a moral weight. But surely, Mr. Hunt has himself inserted the thought about "spiritualizing"; Donne merely says that they rise "the same." Other reflections could be made about the familiar mysteries of renewal and regeneration; there was presumably a rich background to the bit of folk-lore taken over by St. Paul, and Donne recalls what it really meant ("containing some elements of truth") while firmly ignoring what St. Paul said it meant. Unless you take the intention to be so very firm and brave, here as in many other cases, it really does seem, as so many critics have felt, to be in rather bad taste. I need to try to present the thing in human terms; you might hear a top-grade lawyer (and that is more or less what Donne was in the field of theology) talk like this in his unbuttoned moments—"well, of course, the whole thing's become so frightfully technical, you'd think one twitch could send it completely haywire, but that's actually how it works"—and you wouldn't deduce from such talk that he was at all bad at his profession, nor yet at all likely to cheat at it. This I think is the basic mood which became something much more passionate and searching in the great love-poems. Their mystical doctrine was always a tight-rope-walk, a challenge to skill and courage, and after all it never pretended to offer any hope, only an assurance that people who called him wrong were themselves wrong.

The idea of man as a microcosm, goes on Mr. Hunt, searching more deeply for the point where he feels there must be something sickly about Donne, was a commonplace to the 17th Century, but (p. 176) "Donne's inclination to attitudes of withdrawn eccentricity" made him use it as "a philosophic validation of withdrawal and introversion."

> This is the conclusion which Donne derives from the concept in "The Goodmorrow," "The Canonization," and "The Sun Rising," and it obviously lurks behind "A Valediction Forbidding Mourning" as well; one is a world in oneself, or to oneself, and in that private world one can find all that other men desire; in fact—and here Donne wrests from the doctrine of the microcosm an idea which it did not normally carry—the private world of oneself is a *better* world than the world which ordinary men know.

I thought perhaps it was American of Mr. Hunt to feel you're mad if you aren't a good mixer, but it turned out that the English Mr. J. B. Leishman (*The Monarch of Wit*, 1951) had previously felt the same. What people have disliked about Donne, he recalls with full historical detail, is "a renunciation of the world, not in favor of otherworldliness, but in favor of a kind of private world," and

> Such an isolation, such a detachment from all the ordinary concerns of life, as left a man able to feel reality, to feel that he was completely alive only in and through his relationship with his wife would have seemed to Johnson something not far removed from insanity.

This at least admits he had a woman with him in his Paradise; Mr. Hunt's complaint, oddly enough, would only fit the religious poems, written when Donne was a prominent public figure. The process of judgment that we critics have gone through, in such a case, is more complex than we have to remember in summing up; we would not say that any mystic is mad, being an introvert, nor even that Blake was mad because both mystical and devoted to his wife; but we feel that the younger Donne of the love-poems hasn't somehow a reasonable claim to be sane though an introvert. Or rather, I would feel that, and would agree with Mr. Hunt, if I did not feel that the idea of the separate planet, and the explorer spirit that goes with it, make a decisive difference to the "tone." Besides, they may have corresponded to a truth; as a free-lance consultant on theological controversy, Donne though poor had rather the status of an intellectual buccaneer. One might suspect, to be sure, that he was less conscious of the psychological dangers of introversion than we have had to learn to be; as is commonly said, his period more or less invented the individualism of the private world—consider Montaigne. But no one doubts that he went on trying to get hold of money for his family from the outer world, by means of his own line of thought, which was on matters of general public concern (it is the refusal to do that which excites moral indignation against introverts); worldly and unscrupulous he has been considered, but not soft as well. In any case, the extreme intellectual interest of the idea of the separate planet seems to have been what first attracted him, before he realized its convenience as an expression of his temperament or his misfortunes. Hence this essay may now at last arrive at its topic, and I am sorry to have been so frightfully long in getting there; it is merely because I felt there were so many prejudices in the way.

If you start at * * * "The Good-Morrow," the separate planet surely leaps at you from the page. I have to argue with modern exegetists, not for the pleasure of nagging, but to understand what resistance needs to be overcome; I can claim to have selected a distinguished opponent in Mr. Hunt. It does not occur to him that any such idea is present; and I think two rather opposed presumptions are working together in his mind to shut it out. He feels that Donne was being rather neurotic (whereas space travel would feel boyish) but also that Donne was at any rate being high-minded, that is, backing spirit against matter (but Donne often tries to get out of this dichotomy).

> If every any beauty I did see,
> Which I desired, and got, 'twas but a dream of thee.
>
> And now good morrow to our waking souls
> Which watch not one another out of fear;
> For love, all love of other sights controls,
> And makes one little room, an everywhere.
> Let sea-discoverers to new worlds have gone,
> Let maps to others, worlds on worlds have shown,
> Let us possess one world, each hath one, and is one.
>
> My face in thine eye, thine in mine appears,
> And true plain hearts do in the faces rest;
> Where can we find two better hemispheres,
> Without sharp North, without declining West?
> Whatever dies, was not mixed equally;
> If our two loves be one, or, thou and I
> Love so alike, that none of slacken, none can die.

"Donne is playing in this line on two meanings of the word 'world,'" begins a footnote by Mr. Hunt, encouragingly, but, after some rather complicated evidence that the Old World was given that name, he deduces that the only New World in view was America. Why are they both in the plural then? What does the line about maps add to the line about discoverers—how could people put new continents on the map without discovering them? (It is true that they did, but a joke about bogus discoveries here would only weaken the rhetorical effect.) It was a regular thing for a long while to have a pair of globes, for the earth and the stars; the young ladies in Oscar Wilde's plays are still being taught "the use of the globes," very properly. Donne found it a natural turn of rhetoric to move from one to the other within a couplet, as in a bad poem to the Countess of Bedford:

> We have added to the world Virginia, and sent
> Two new stars lately to the firmament.

But Mr. Hunt fully recognizes the existence of the star-globe; he only wants to exclude it from this couplet. Discoverers, he thinks, are low people, symbolizing restless promiscuity, so they can't be paired with looking at a star-map, which is a spiritual thing. But it would never have occurred to Donne that you couldn't have discoveries in the stars. What Donne praises, in contrast to both these globes, is one made by combining the hemispheres of an eyeball from himself and an eyeball from his mistress, and he remarks with truth that this hasn't the usual properties of either of the public globes, for example "sharp north" where the lines of longitude come to a point (of course these would be marked out for measurement on the star-globe too). I do not have to deny that the imaginative effect is rich; you could feel with wonder that our own earth is being improved by the discovery of the New World—it is getting to know itself better, as the pair of lovers are; but this rather refined thought would not get in the way of the insistent thought about the stars.

Incidentally, Mr. Hunt remarks that the line

> Let us possess one world, each hath one, and is one

is very ugly in sound; this I think merely comes from not wanting to feel its drama. The sound requires it to be said slowly, with religious awe, as each party sinks into the eye of the other; it is a space-landing. Then there is a pause for realization, and the next verse begins in a hushed voice but with a curiously practical tone: "You know, there's a lot of evidence; we really are on a separate planet." It is never much use talking about a sound-effect unless you know what it is meant to illustrate.

The reason for the curious resistance of Mr. Hunt, I think, becomes clearer when he goes on to compare this passage to the middle of the "Valediction Forbidding Mourning," where the topic requires Donne to say that their love is refined enough to outlast a separation:

> The basic concept behind these lines is that of the contrast between the two different substances of which the earth and the heavenly spheres are composed; between matter, the heterogeneous substance of the earth, which belongs to the category of "things visible" and is gross, mutable, and mortal; and the fifth essence, the homogeneous substance of the spheres, which belongs to the category of "thing invisible" and is pure, stable, and eternal.

He deduces that in "The Good-Morrow" (his page 64)

> The world of their love is, in other words, like a celestial sphere . . . Their love for one another has enabled the two lovers to discover at last their "sphere," their natural and proper mode of existence in the ordered scheme of the cosmos.

I hope the reader realizes, what I didn't at first myself, that these spheres are Ptolemaic spheres, an imaginary series concentric with the earth, finally ten in number, most of them only concerned to carry one planet, or the sun or moon (the sphere of the fixed stars seems not to be meant). Thus the picture is now said to be invisible, whereas in the poem they are fascinated by seeing each other's eyes. It is true that in the "Valediction," where the situation required it, Donne said that such refined lovers "care less" to miss each other's bodies; but even this implies that they still care; and he goes on at once to the material analogies of the beaten gold and the compasses. Invariability (which is required for the eternity of the lovers in the last lines of "The Good-Morrow," already quoted) was imputed to visible heavenly bodies, not only to Ptolemaic spheres; that was why it was such a shocking bit of luck to have two large *novae* in the crucial period. They were considered to prove that the heavens were corruptible. Besides, it is the whole point of a microcosm to be small; it is cosy to have your own island, cave, house in a tree; this ancient sentiment is one of the reasons why the kids like space travel. Surely, to make Donne say that his "proper sphere" is the whole globe of heaven is to make him disagreeably smug, which he does not deserve. Here, as so very often, a critic who sets out to be highminded, even though in a sympathetic manner, only succeeds in looking unusually low-minded.

However, Mr. Hunt draws attention to an important point. Instead of simply backing Copernicus, Donne gets a kind of lock-grip on his reader by arguing from both Ptolemy and Copernicus at once. According to Ptolemy, the planets are more or less in heaven, and matter there is much better-class than matter here. Copernicus merely showed that it was convenient for calculation to treat the earth as one of the planets (with various learned qualifications), but the obvious deduction was that life on other planets is simply like it is here. Matter is very refined on Donne's secret planet, as in Ptolemy, and this allowed him to treat his refined lovers as still material; but without Copernicus their position in the universe would not have seemed plausible. It is a charming arrangement, but it gives us no reason to suppose that he meant by his love something purely spiritual. Nor does it imply that he positively disbelieved in life on other planets; in his last poem, according to Mr. Hunt, he reverted to medieval geography, but this doesn't prove that he disbelieved in the Red Indians.

A rather thrilling confusion about "spirit," I think, crops up when Mr. Hunt examines Elegy XIX, the one where a woman is undressing and Donne call her "O my America, my New-Found-Land." Otherwise Mr. Hunt is extremely good on the poem; I confess I had vaguely assumed, as no doubt most readers do, that the tropes are "merely emotive," whereas they tell us a good deal about Donne's attitude to theology. The poem is probably Donne's first approach to his separate planet, no doubt a rather unconscious one; he liked to make unwonted use of any convention, and this particular path was to open into a grand view:

> Off with that girdle, like heavens Zone glittering,
> But a far fairer world encompassing.

Certainly, he need only mean "Your body is more beautiful that *this* world, which is encompassed by stars as your body by that belt"; but the later lines drive home that she is a New World, and here astronomy is in view, so I expect she was starting to become a planet in his own mind. I set out to quote Mr. Hunt on "spirit":

> If the body is mere evanescent 'clothing' for the eternal reality of the spirit, the Mystic Ecstasy might be thought of as an experience in which the soul divested itself of its temporal clothes and went naked to immediate contact with God. . . . Donne's irreverent allusions to spiritual love and to the Beatific Vision in the climactic section of a poem celebrating the pleasures of merely physical sex could be intended only as ridicule of the school of Platonic Love. . . . (The lines) present the whole-hearted acceptance of a sensual satisfaction as an act which entails taking up a philosophic option, which forces one to embrace philosophic materialism and to reject completely the doctrines of philosophic idealism—to reject, in fact, the fundamental doctrines of Christianity.

I agree that the poem feels heterodox; I hope the precedent given by Mr. Hunt will save me from being thought tendentious there. But I think it very wrong to suppose that the effect is mere jeering. Surely the first fact about the poem is the surprise we feel at its having such a high moral tone. Donne, indeed, loved to argue his way out of a fix with defiant brilliance; but this temperament often goes with a certain self-righteousness, and here he feels genuinely exalted. Nor is the picture unlifelike, especially if, as seems likely, it recalls the first sexual success of a strictly-brought-up young man; furthermore, one who doubts the value of the strictness and has felt a certain shame at submitting to it. He feels proud, he feels liberated, he feels purified (the effects of unsatisfied desire excite disgust, so that release from them can excite a keen sense of purity). What have any of these feelings to do with "materialism"? What can be meant by calling the pleasure "merely physical"? I wouldn't have thought, to begin with, that philosophical idealism *was* the fundamental doctrine of Christianity, let alone that an adherent of it can never accept pleasure. My English Composition class in Peking, their eyes all shining with asceticism and idealism, would habitually write down sentences like "The Russians are very good because they are so material, and the Americans are very wicked because they are so material." When I objected to this they readily agreed it was against the rules and said, "But how *do* you say it in English then?" The word "spirit" in the *Faustus* of Marlowe regularly refers to devils (as in "Thou art a spirit: God cannot pity thee"). To revere the dichotomy between matter and spirit leads to hopeless confusion when reading Donne, because though he too is badgered by it he keeps playing tricks with it, feeling that it ought to be transcended. What is more, though I presume he knew they were tricks, he did not think of them as such completely wild tricks as the hardening of our intellectual outlook makes us do now. As Grierson pointed out long ago in his notes to "The Ecstasy," Donne continued to expound in sermons the then decent, though one might think Lucretian, belief that spirit is a subtle kind of matter:

> The spirits in a man, which are the thin and active part of the blood, and so are of a kind of middle nature, between soul and body, those spirits are able to do, and they do the office, to unite and apply the faculties of the soul to the organs of the body, and so there is a man.

I am pretty ignorant about Paracelsus, who was the latest thing in medicine at the time and the second major influence (say the recent thinkers) on Donne's mind after Copernicus, but one of his main points was the mystery of the self-healing powers of the body ("dying and rising the same"), which obviously did need attention. To take the simplest case, it is an astounding thing, once you think of it like that, that a broken bone heals of its own accord; and yet the spirit that does this isn't exactly sensible—a reasoning man has got to tie the splint right, or the bone doesn't have a chance to heal properly. You ought to learn to collaborate with spirits, but not respect them too much.

* * *

I feel I should apologize for so much "background material," but with Donne it seems to be mainly doubt about the background which makes a critic reject the arguments from the text of the poems. It is high time to return and try to be useful about the details of that. "Air and Angels" is a difficult poem; probably it has done more than any other to make the unspecialized reader think Donne rather a cad, and there has been a recent move, discussed in Mr. Redpath's edition, to make its grammar call women purer than men instead of men purer than women. The reason why one gets this uneasiness is that the final epigram seems to conflict with the story told by the poem, let alone with the tone of it. The beginning is:

Twice or thrice I had loved thee
Before I knew thy face or name;
So in a voice, so in a shapeless flame
Angels affect us oft, and worshipped be;
    Still when, to where thou wert, I came
Some lovely glorious nothing I did see. . . .

But after that, he argues for four more lines, it became the proper thing to descend to bodies, and the verse ends:

And therefore what thou wert, and who,
I bade Love ask, and now
That it assume thy body, I allow,
And fix itself in thy lip, eye, and brow.

This is both magnificent and lifelike; he is describing what Stendhal called "crystallization." The second and final verse which feels much flatter, begins by claiming that in the process he has just described, as quoted, he was trying to "ballast" his love, make the boat steadier by weighing it down with more matter, but then he found that too much matter would sink the boat (that is, the metaphor says that a balanced arrangement about matter is necessary even for high forms of life); but then the poem seems to end with a resentful sneer against loved women:

. . . . nor in nothing, nor in things
Extreme, and scattering bright, can love inhere.
    Then, as an Angel, face and wings
Of air, not pure as it, yet pure doth wear,
    So thy love may be my love's sphere;
        Just such disparity
As is twixt Air and Angel's purity
Twixt women's love, and men's will ever be.

Not a brutal sneer; indeed some critics find the poem tender and more serious than usual—Donne has managed to break out, they feel, from either over-exalting or debasing women throughout one poem, and achieved a more balanced attitude. I think that the poem does deserve this kind of praise (such a critic has got the intended tone of the poem right) but also that the critic does not deserve to say it till he has seen the point of the poem. On the face of the thing, if a man with the habits of the young Donne is trying to achieve a balanced attitude about the inferiority of women, their impurity is not a sensible item for him to pick out.

One needs to get the story of the poem clear. It goes through as many stages as a novel, and for most of the time she is the angel, not Donne. He first imagined her repeatedly—she is the ideal required by his nature—then when he saw her in public he fell into trance; afterwards he managed to get acquainted, and then her face became Love in person, a process like the Incarnation of Christ—the word *assume* makes a vague theological comparison. The whole of this first verse would appear standard to Chaucer, and naturally Donne wanted to add on something up-to-date. Between the two verses we are to assume he gets to bed with her; nothing else gives any point to the dramatic drop in the exalted tone, and at any rate this saves him from being self-righteous about his purity. After becoming accustomed to her body he still regards it as somehow unearthly, like an angel's. But he gets an uneasy feeling that he mustn't be overwhelmed by its brilliance, because he needs to protect his other interests; it may well occur to the reader, though it doesn't to the poet, that she too might want him to earn money, or in simpler times bring meat to the cave. After this change, his peace of mind still depends on being certain she loves him back, so that he can have her body when he does need it, on emerging from his reading, hunting or what not. Such is the peculiar sense in which he now incarnates his love not in her body but purely in her love, and feels an instinctive assurance that this process gives him steadiness to handle the world. It seems to me important to point out that the thoughts of Donne about love, so far from being over-subtle, were already real in the Stone Age. The anecdote cannot be called cynical; an ancient truth about the relations of men and women is recognized and glorified. All the same, the more you feel the story to be true, the more you feel Donne was cheating if he ended the poem by claiming he had proved men to be purer than women. To begin with, the poem has told us nothing whatever about the reactions of the lady. Chivalry he was by way of revolting against, but not logic and justice ; and it is a plausible view that he wrote the second verse long after the first, in a disillusioned frame of mind, but even so he must be interpreted as making one poem, unless the poem is simply to be called bad.

The explanation I think has to be that he is making his joke or his grand poetical conceit, not against the woman he loves but against "purity," that is against the suggestion carried by this word that the best kind of love requires sexual abstinence. I gather I am likely to meet resistance here, but I do not quite know what. Surely he often did do this in poems, both seriously and wittily, and felt he had proved it in experience; such is the point where you might call him Renaissance rather than Medieval, if you were trying to make sense of those terms. Perhaps this is why Professor C. S. Lewis has accused him of want of delicacy, calling Rosalind as a witness, and implying that Donne when trying to be profound about the relations of soul and body only succeeded in being coarser about them than less fussy authors. It is true that Donne when trying to be courtly often seems very much a member of the professional classes, but I am not sure that a sensible lawyer on either side would bring Rosalind into the witness-box; she would not back Lewis if he quoted the Fathers of the Church, and was not above making fairly complicated jokes herself. But Donne's poetical arguments from absurdity were drawn from learned theories now remote, and one may hope that the joke in this poem seemed better than it does now. The great dictionary is not much help, as the meanings required for alchemy and angelology were so specialized; but under "I. Physical: unmixed . . ." it has a good subhead "c. Spotless, stainless, transparent," with a quotation of 1481, "the moon is not so pure that the sun may shine through her as another star." (It also distinguishes chastity from both moral and ceremonial defilement.) A critic should step back, I think, and reflect that the theme "Air and Angels" was very fundamental to the developing sciences, however inadequately treated in the poem; chemistry depended on techniques for handling gases, beginning with distillation (the "limbeck" so prominent in Donne), especially as a means of getting substances "unmixed," and the gradual realization of the nature of the different "airs" went through much viewing of them as "essences" (principles with their inherent virtue in a concentrated form) and "spirits" (wind-and-breath by derivation, as was equally well known to Swift in the *Tale of A Tub*). The theories were applied to astronomy, but they were chiefly concerned with drugs for medicine; a man's fate may depend on the stars, but there is always a time in his life when he feels it depends on the doctor, and the doctor had to be an alchemist as well as an astrologer.

I am not sure how much this background needs to be read into the poem, but I think it lets one get into better proportion the argument that he meant to say women's love is purer than men's, and not men's purer than women's. The argument is surprisingly strong, and I should think Donne was conscious of putting in the details it relies on; but one cannot say that this was the single meaning he wanted for his final epigram. It would be so much against not only common opinion but the theories he was arguing from that it would need saying much more clearly, a point he would appreciate. The center of the argument making him praise women is that *it* in "not pure as it," among the lines last quoted, must refer to "air before being condensed by the angel to make himself a visible body," therefore to the woman; not to the angel, who at this stage of the poem has become the man. To call an angel "it" really is peculiar; I am told that it is unique in Donne, and anyhow would strike the first readers as a frank devaluation of this angel. However, you can see how Donne happened upon this piece of grammar; he has already called his love "it," though it is the child of his soul, and called his visions a nothing, and called her body, "things." Secondly, if "purity" can mean "transparency," a view which is at any rate supported by the great dictionary, then "air before it is condensed by the angel" is patently purer than the angel as a visible object. Then the next line "So thy love may be my love's sphere" is consistent in making the angel (and the man) the more solid body, because he becomes the planet moving on the Ptolemaic sphere of the woman. There is no need to disagree with Mr. Hunt that the Ptolemaic sphere was considered purer than the planet moving upon it. Mr. Hugh Sykes Davies who has been arguing for making the poem call women purer, or rather call their love "less involved in the need for physical expression," regards the *sphere* as diagrammatic rather than astronomical; but Mr. W. A. M. Murray tells me that Paracelsus made "the sphere" mean the body when regarded as uninfluenced by its own animal spirits, therefore as helplessly material; and this seems hard to combine with Mr. Davies' view. It may well be that the contrast of the Paracelsan meaning comes into many of Donne's uses of the word *sphere*; all I can say is that it would have to make a profound contradiction or joke. There seems no doubt, after surveying the uses in the poems, that Donne regularly gave the word the astronomical meaning, even if other meanings came in.

But then again, granting the astronomical meaning for *sphere*, a reader may turn round and recall that "an intelligence" was what ruled a Ptolemaic sphere, and the pure creature used the planet only as its country house. Yes indeed, that is the joke. These spirits also had the names of pagan gods, such as Mars or Venus, who did not pretend to be purer than the ether. Meanwhile the actual use found by theorists for these spirits was merely to drive the celestial sphere round at constant speed, so that they may properly be regarded as a high-grade derivative of petroleum suitable to aeroplane engines—the modern pun would be tiresome if it did not come to us directly from the theoretical confusion which Donne was satirizing. We had better go back again to "The Ecstasy" for Donne's view of the relations of soul to matter:

> On man heaven's influence works not so
>   But that it first imprints the air;
> So soul into the soul may flow
>   Though it to body first repair.

Surely this looks as if he himself felt, as a modern reader must do, that there was something very interesting to say about the relations of Air and Angels if only one could manage to say it. Grierson's note here shows that Donne had backing from Du Bartas, therefore presumably from a lot of other books he was reading, for the belief that air was pretty full of "virtue," as one would suppose since it is very nearly what "spirit" means; air need not show up at all badly against a minor angel, if you are interested in confusing the modes of being.

It seems to me clear that Donne was half guying the theories and half imaginatively enjoying them, even if I have got the details wrong. What a modern reader feels to be more immediately serious, before accepting the magic of the wit or poetry, is a simpler or more sociological matter; what Donne really did think about women, and how he behaved to them. Living as we do after change in the legal position of women, we would like to know more about his actual habits; apart from his minor poems jeering at women, the complete silence of his adored wife cannot but leave on us an impression of patient suffering. It might seem a plausible view that his habitual contempt for women merely broke out at the end of this love-poem, so that even for a reader at the time he spoilt this poem by finishing on a platitude—that is, the end always felt bad, but now feels worse. I do not think this a likely piece of clumsiness for the mind of Donne. "The Ecstasy" denies all "disparity" between the sexes, because the lovers become one soul, and the modern reader whether male or female tends to find this extremity an implausible one; but it does not strike us as treating women with a contempt for which we are now too far advanced. It seems fair to point out that he made less of a mess of his marriage than Coleridge did. The hostess of the palace of the Keeper of the Great Seal did behave splendidly under the terrible privations of life on a separate planet, whereas the girl Coleridge thought natural enough for the banks of the Susquehanna would probably not have turned out well even if he had collected his group to go there. The mind of Donne was much cluttered with learned authorities who called women inferior to men, but to say that they were wrong was equally fixed in his mind as his first gambit when describing his reception in high society. Of course he would also sometimes write satire against women, but what he seriously believed about them, I should expect, and I think normal opinion still agrees with him, was that women though not inferior to men have a deep "disparity" from men.

It therefore seems worth pointing out that this disparity is all that the end of the poem asserts; the words do not literally say either that women are less pure than men or that men are less pure than women. The phrase *not pure as it, yet pure*, if you take *as* to mean "like," positively labors to avoid comparison and means "they are pure in different ways"; also it strikes me that this reading has a period flavor, so that it was more likely then than now. In the same way *Aire and Angells puritie*, with no apostrophe for the possessive, could easily mean "the kind of purity in air and the kind of purity in angels"; indeed the 1669 editor, or the copyist he was following, probably felt that this needed making clearer when he changed *Aire* to "airs," and the change is still more needed now. Donne, no doubt, rather enjoyed ending with something that looked harsh if misunderstood, and I imagine that this is a fairly early poem, but he would not intend to be misunderstood radically. The whole poem has described a "disparity" between the loves of men and women, and seems to me to do that with massive truth; surely it is only fair to the poet to allow his final epigram to mean "such is the disparity."

However, it would be no good for me to present the poem as simple, thus claiming to outwit both the opposed groups of critics. I must not say that their problem is a mere mistake, because Donne neither intended to call women purer than men nor men purer than women. What he meant to do, when he added a second verse to his first splendid one, was to say something very teasing about purity. What has become too obscure is not the problem but the answer. I think he meant the reader first to accept the final epigram as a platitude in favor of men, then revolt against this view and realize that it might be in favor of women, then realize that the only truth told is about an actual unlikeness between the sexes. Surely, Donne was expected to be clever, by the first readers of these poems in manuscript whom he actually wished to please; it is not stretching the historical possibility to suppose that the second verse is meant to be clever. Indeed, there could be no point in arranging the words so as to make possible the present disagreement among critics except to make evident confusion of the conception of "purity." I do not pretend that my view makes the end of the poem very good (rather few jokes are eternal, and probably no technical ones) but it does save you from having to regard the end of the poem as bleakly mean-minded.

The separate planet is only in the background of the great "Nocturnal," but the tone of the poem is greatly improved if you recognize it there. I was convinced of this by a recent exegetist (Mr. Richard Sleight in *Interpretations*, 1956) who very honestly reports that the word "world" in the poem means more than he knows. At least, he says, "Most readers would probably agree that the word has some such unifying effect as has been described; the reasons for the effect are not so easy to find"; I do not think he claims to find them in his later remarks, and if he did I would think him wrong. He argues that Donne implies his own "reintegration" or recovery from grief even while pretending to describe his grief as absolute; in the line about alchemy "Donne is tilting at the alchemists and at himself taking himself too seriously," and at the end "he does not definitely commit himself to the harmony of death nor the dialectic of living"—but surely the end of the poem says he will prepare to join her in death. Mr. Sleight feels "it is unsatisfactory to believe that grief, however severe, is eternal except in Romantic poetry," and this I find rather bloodless. (Or perhaps it is one of the emotional confusions promulgated by Neo-Classicism.) I think he is right in feeling there is something to say about the tone but fails to nail it down.

The word comes into each of the first three verses; in the first for the ordinary world, now at midwinter; in the second the spring will be a "new world," because Donne cannot conceive of a recovery from this winter, and indeed speaks as if already outside mundane experience; in the third we find that Donne and his mistress till she died were a world to themselves, as if on a separate planet. However, this idea seems chiefly remembered from previous poems, and I would not go as far as Mr. Redpath, whose note makes it the meaning of the grammar:

Oft a flood
Have we two wept, and so
Drowned the whole world, us two; oft we did grow
To be two Chaosses, when we did show
Care to aught else, and often absences
Withdrew our souls, and made us carcases.

He takes *us two* as in apposition to *the whole world*, and no doubt this idea is what needs suggesting to the reader in a footnote, but the idea can only be a secondary one because the alternative grammar is too colloquial to be ignored—"and wept enough tears, just us two, to make another Flood." If we were expected to forget the hyperbole, and explain it completely away as only meaning a separate planet, there would be no point in using the trope here, where it has a rather special point. When first used, probably in the remote past, the trope was meant to have a kind of dramatic truth as the kind of nonsense that a person could only believe when half mad with pain. Donne now uses it almost playfully, so as to put the real solemnity further on: "How unhappy we used to think we were, when we were ruining ourselves for love; but looking back now, when she is dead, it seems to me we were having tremendous fun. For one thing, we felt so important, because nothing was real except our feelings for each other; but now I feel entirely unimportant—I am as if no world had ever been created." Surely this is the only human basis for saying he has become the elixir of the first nothing; he used to have a separate planet, and now it is as if it had never been. We need not doubt the mood of despair, but it is much sweetened by the glee with which he looks back on their bold love, so that he can give assurance to the next crop of lovers; and the fierce cosiness of the idea of the independent planet is I think a main source of this warmth.

There is a similar casualness about the hyperbole in "A Valediction Forbidding Mourning," where I had best begin by recalling a controversy.

> Moving of the earth brings harms and fears,
> Men reckon what it did and meant,
> But trepidation of the spheres,
> Though greater far, is innocent.

Mr. C. M. Coffin, in his *John Donne and the New Philosophy* (1927), took this as a reference to Copernicus: "Of the new astronomy, the 'moving of the earth' is the most radical principle; of the old, the 'trepidation of the spheres' is the motion of greatest complexity," and "Donne does not deny the truth of either doctrine—if he did the whole point of the argument would be wasted and futile." As time went on, this case became rather a victory for the new rigor, in its campaign to make poetry as dull as possible; Mr. W. K. Wimsatt in his essay "The Intentional Fallacy" (first published 1946) proved that the line refers to an earthquake. This would do actual *harm*, at a point of time, and afterwards (hence the past tense) men would *reckon* the damaged and invent a superstitious *meaning*, none of which applies literally to the new astronomy. Mr. Wimsatt gave a qualifying sentence before the bang of his final one, but I expect he felt that only made the bang stronger (*The Verbal Icon*, p. 14):

> Perhaps a knowledge of Donne's interest in the new science may add another shade of meaning, an overtone to the stanza in question though to say even this runs against the words. To make the geocentric and heliocentric antithesis the core of the metaphor is to disregard the English language, to prefer private evidence to public, external to internal.

The way that *private* goes with *external* is rather subtle; I remember a fellow lodger who was very cross because he found his razor had been used—a man's face, he said, is the most private part of his body. I agree that the earthquake is the chief meaning, but that is no reason to deny that Donne, when he first tasted his line and found it good, was conscious of a secondary meaning which he rather hoped to insinuate. The effect of giving the phrase both meanings is to say, "And also the sudden introduction of the idea that there may be life on other planets has affected the Churches like an earthquake." At this remove, the phrases can apply tidily to Copernicanism; the threat to the Churches' absolutism, Donne can mean, has frightened them and tempted them to persecution. It is what I call an equation, and of Type III; in the mind of Donne, the major sense of "moving of the earth" is the Copernican one, but the sense demanded by the immediate context is the earthquake, indeed this is also what the reader is likely to take as the major sense, and yet Donne thinks of Copernicanism as the subject of his equation, the part that comes first in the sentence expounding it. That is, the Copernicanism, and not the earthquake, is the one you are expected to understand better after the two have been compared. This Type tends to express a fixed belief of the speaker but to be resisted by the hearer, or only absorbed unconsciously; which seems to fit here. Of course, this theorizing only claims to show that the case is normal, not to prove that the extra meaning occurred to Donne; but we have some reason to expect so from the verse immediately before:

> So let us melt, and make no noise,
> No tear-floods, nor sigh-tempests move;
> Twere prophanation of our joys
> To tell the laity our love.

The second half takes for granted that they are a separate religion, as usual, but the first half, though less obviously, regards them as on a separate planet. It would be tiresome to use these conventional hyperboles, while the tone treats them as commonplace, without a moderating idea that the floods and tempests are only rightly so called within the private world of the lovers. She is tenderly exhorted to be patient, but he is rather prepared to laugh at her if she makes a fuss; the effect is cosy. This situation regularly suggested to him his secret planet, so naturally a Copernican idea came into his mind for the next verse; but he did not much want it for this poem, so he thrust it down to a secondary meaning. If you dislike my claiming to know so much, I have to answer that I think it absurd, and very harmful, to have a critical theory, like Mr. Wimsatt's, that a reader must not try to follow an author's mind.

In all this, I am not sure how far I am arguing for an opinion as if it were new when in fact it is accepted, or was accepted till quite recently. I was rather puzzled on looking up the article by Marjorie Nicolson, "The New Astronomy and English Literary Imagination" (*Studies in Philology* XXXII, 1935), so often given in footnotes. She seems at first strongly opposed to my thesis, maintaining that Donne only wrote about new astronomy during a short period after 1604, when Kepler discovered the second Nova (the first had been in 1572) and the pressure of controversy and discovery became hot; all the references to astronomy in the *Songs and Sonets* are "purely conventional," she says, giving as her example the one already considered about the sun "showing" the stars; though she does not say what it means. But then at the end she remarks casually:

> But only occasionally in the *Sermons* does Donne venture upon the more philosophical connotations of the Galilean discoveries. The idea of a plurality of worlds, which Donne had suggested in his earlier poetry, was indeed for a churchman a dangerous tenet, even, as it came to be called, the "new heresy." The condemnation of Bruno had listed that belief as one of the chief charges brought against him; and many orthodox Protestants, as well as Catholics, felt that such a conception struck at the roots of the Christian idea of the sacrifice of Christ, who died to save *this* world.

"Which Donne had suggested in his earlier poetry"—she seems to take it for granted, and merely feel that this general deduction from Copernicus doesn't count as a technical bit of astronomy. It counted for a good deal as part of the poems.

I also looked up "Kidnapping Donne" by Merritt Y. Hughes (*Essays in Criticism*, Second Series, California University Press, 1934), the other warning reference regularly given in footnotes; this is harder to deal with, because it works by suggestion and general assertion. The title, as you expect, means that various people up to 1934 had been trying to kidnap the young Donne by presenting him as a freethinker, whereas Mr. Hughes speaks of his "essentially Catholic mind." But I think it is the Catholics who deserve this reproach, and the case has something of the real horror of kidnapping, because they are likely to damage him so much that he is no use to them when they have got him. To suit their purpose, he has to be a sordid cheat. You might think it about as bad for me to make him nurse a special heresy, but that wouldn't involve his honor as one of a Catholic family, and Catholics will agree that it could more easily be renounced or digested before devoting himself to the Anglican Church. I do not need to deny that he spoke vaguely against Copernicanism in later life (no case is offered of his doing it decisively). When he says in sermons, for instance, that it is more wonderful to have the sun go round the earth all the time than to have it stand still once for Joshua, he is merely illustrating a general truth, equally sound whichever way round they go; it need not be called "good evidence that the new theory never disturbed the bottoms of his mind and that his emotions were deeply involved in the old cosmic scheme." Mr. Hughes is more convincing when he takes an almost opposite position, and says that Donne habitually regarded the new theory as "a portent of evil"; maybe he did feel that with part of his mind, whether the bottoms or not; it doesn't prove he didn't think the portent important, or couldn't have toyed with it recklessly in his early poems. Mr. Hughes agrees that Donne thought the universe was decaying, because the heavens had been shown to be variable (to expect the end of the world was of course quite orthodox); he quotes some lines from the third Letter to the Countess of Bedford, where Donne is saying the world is hopelessly bad compared to her (she is Virtue in person, l. 25, and a separate world, l. 87):

> As new Philosophy arrests the Sun
> And bids the passive earth about it run,
> So we have dulled our mind, it hath no ends;
> Only the body's busy, and pretends;
> As dead low earth eclipses and controls
> The high quick Moon, so doth the body, Souls.

"That way, for him, lay madness," says Mr. Hughes. I have quoted two more lines than he did to show that Donne does not imply disbelief in the new philosophy; presumably Donne believed in this explanation for eclipses of the moon, so if anything he implies that he also believes the theory which would lead to madness. Probably he came to accept the half-way theory of Tycho Brahe, which could be said to hold the field on the existing evidence; but there was nothing definite in that to disprove life on other planets, once you had got the idea into your head.

The other arguments in the article seem to me to work mainly by suggestion, as when we are told—

> The Songs and Elegies show no trace of the scientific and metaphysical scepticism which was penetrating England from Italy at the close of the 16th Century.

The strategy here seems to be to allow everybody else to be a sceptic so long as the one case in view is kept pure. Even if we had heard more about this scepticism in the period, which I am far from denying, it is hard to see how such evidence could prove that Donne did not hold a simple positive belief in life on other worlds.

> In spite of his consistent interest Donne never took natural science seriously; from first to last his attitude resembled that of Nicholas of Cusa in the *De Docta Ignorantia*. His contempt for adepts of natural philosophy can hardly be distinguished from contempt for natural philosophy itself.

Thus, in the *Problems and Paradoxes*, he spoke of "Physicians contemplating nature who, finding many abstruse things subject to the search of Reason, think therefore that all is so." Now, this quotation was presumably selected by Mr. Hughes to prove Donne's contempt; and it is remarkably weak evidence for contempt. Compare the hysterical attacks written by Pope and Swift on adepts of natural philosophy. As to Nicholas of Cusa, I have no need to deny that, for a man so well-read as Donne, the traditional philosophic attitude to such questions as that of life on other planets would give a firm support, a feeling of security, when (rather with another part of his mind) he accepted the obvious deduction from Copernicanism. But that is no reason to deny that he did accept it; all it shows is that he had ways of getting out of it, and I daresay he used them when he decided he had better get out of it. This is no argument against the direct literary evidence in the love-poems that at an earlier time he had accepted it. As to "taking it seriously," he took it seriously as a poet; and this doesn't at all mean taking it as a fancy, but concentrating on what the human consequences would be if it were true—treating it like a theologian, you might well say, though not like a scientist.

There is a rather splendid bit of strategy in Mr. Hughes when he warmly praises Satire III:

> his defence of liberty of conscience against the principle *cuius regio eius religio* deserves to be even better known than it is.

Now, the principle *cuius regio eius religio*, though not intellectually impressive, was an attempt to stop burning people alive; it said "let the Reformation lie as it has fallen; let us agree on co-existence, the way we are now." I do not see how a single word of Donne's poem could be twisted into an attack on this clumsy attempt at moderation, as apart from an attack on religious persecution in general. Donne is simply against burning people alive for their religious convictions, and Mr. Hughes has managed to praise him for it in a form of words which really means that Donne, with the warm approval of Mr. Hughes, wanted to burn people alive a great deal more. I really think this case ought to be enough to clear the minds of those humbly literary students like myself who often see a footnote referring us to a rather inaccessible article called "Kidnapping Donne" and feel, Oh well, what seems to me obvious must have been all disproved in some awfully specialist way.

I ought finally to admit that the idea of the private planet has at least once crossed the mind of the more recent critical world. It occurred to Mr. Leishman (1951), who naturally felt he was making a discovery. Grierson had suggested that "The Nocturnal" might well have been written to Donne's wife, because the third stanza speaks a stronger language than that of Petrarchan adoration; Mr. Leishman adds:

> What, though, so far as I am aware, neither Grierson nor any other commentator has noticed is the remarkable similarity between the image, or 'conceit,' in this stanza and the one in that fiendishly ingenious poem "A Valediction, Of Weeping." . . . It is natural and I think, legitimate to assume that this poem, like several others in which he speaks of her and of himself as forming two hemispheres, or one perfect world, was addressed to his wife.

He deduces that "The Nocturnal" was written in Paris on the night of the 13th December 1611; Donne was there with the Drury family, and anxious about his wife's coming child-birth (Isaac Walton says he knew by telepathy that not the wife but the child was dead, and so it was, but one can well believe there was a certain amount of confusion). As a young man I snatched at any chance to hear wisdom drop from Mr. T. S. Eliot, and he once remarked that the test of a true poet is that he writes about experiences before they have happened to him; I felt I had once passed this test, though I forget now in which poem. The doctrine makes one very doubtful of any dating of poems by internal evidence, and I should think it might be true of Donne. Otherwise the dating seems to me very plausible, and I ought to applaud Mr. Leishman here, not grumble at him. It is a most curious thing, but it is true, that a critic can decide whether a passage is "Petrarchan" or not without really knowing what it means. But still, the only definite reason for supposing that Donne refers to a separate planet in "The Nocturnal" is that he does it so often in other poems, sometimes obviously, but often so vaguely that we are only sure of it because the poem becomes better if we recognize it; whereas Mr. Leishman seems to regard the process with chill distaste, and merely to classify together, for purposes of dating, those cases of it which are particularly hard to ignore. I am much inclined to agree that Donne wrote these poems to his wife, because that makes them so much more practical for his actual situation at the time; but I can't help agreeing here just for once with the anti-biography critics that the point is rather unimportant, compared to realizing what the poems mean and deciding whether you find them beautiful after doing so.

JANEL MUELLER

Women among the Metaphysicals: A Case, Mostly, of Being Donne For†

The so-called metaphysicals trace the origins of their label to an accusation Dryden leveled against Donne's poetic treatment of women. "Not only in his satires," said Dryden, "but in his amorous verses, where nature only should reign," Donne "affects the metaphysics." He "perplexes the minds of the fair sex with nice speculations of philosophy, when he should engage their hearts, and entertain them with the softnesses of love."[1] How shall we evaluate this famous judgment passed by one major male poet of the

† From *Modern Philology* 87 (1989): 142–151. Reprinted by permission of The University of Chicago Press. The author's notes have been abridged.

1. John Dryden, *A Discourse Concerning the Original and Progress of Satire* (1693), cited in A. L. Clements, ed., *John Donne's Poetry* (New York, 1966), p. 106.

seventeenth century on another, sixty years his senior? What, more generally, can we say of women as subjects of metaphysical poetry and as readers of it?

In Donne's prose and verse letters to the select women who figured both as subjects and readers of his poetry, we glimpse a dynamics of gender and power quite unlike the one Dryden posits. Crucial initiatives for the production and reception of Donne's poetry rest with these women; they patronize him, not he them. Thus Donne writes to the cultivated Magdalen Herbert, entrusting "the inclosed *Holy Hymns* and *Sonnets* . . . to your judgment, and to your protection too, if you think them worthy of it," since she has bestowed, he says, "all the good opinion" he enjoys.[2] At a later juncture Donne declares as follows of the countess of Bedford, to whom he addressed six of his most "metaphysical" poems. She "only hath power to cast the fetters of verse upon my free meditations." He reserves "for her delight (since she descends to them) . . . not only all the verses, which I should make, but all the thoughts of womens worthiness."[3] Later still, when Donne's complexly motivated *Anniversary* poems on Elizabeth Drury broke into print, the countess of Bedford and the countess of Salisbury were much displeased. They let Donne know this. He quickly bowed to the censures of his two patronesses. A verse letter to each records Donne's struggles to redirect rather than defend the hyperboles he had lavished on a mere slip of a girl. "I confesse," run his lines to Lady Bedford.

> Since I had never knowne
> Vertue or beautie, but as they are growne
> In you, I should not thinke or say they shine,
> (So as I have) in any other Mine.[4]

For express testimony from a woman regarding the impact of this style of poetry, however, we must look to later in the century and to an area of potential response ignored altogether in Dryden's comments—that of sacred rather than amatory subjects. This woman was a poet herself, who wrote under the name of Orinda. Sometime before her death in 1664 at the age of thirty-two, Katherine Philips addressed Henry Vaughan in a verse epistle that surveyed and saluted his poetic development. Professing hope that her work would mature as his had, she seeks to confirm in Vaughan a recognition she has already reached as a reader and practitioner of his style: "From the charming rigour thy muse brings / Learn there's no pleasure but in serious things!"[5] As we in turn will have occasion to confirm in female readers—critics and one other poet—who have succeeded Orinda, these ringing notes warn usefully against joining Dryden in too narrow notions of how women might relate to or figure in "the metaphysics" in verse.

If he underestimated female capacities for response and judgment, Dry-

2. R. C. Bald, *John Donne: A Life* (Oxford, 1970), pp. 181–82, citing Izaak Walton's excerpt of a letter exchange in his *Life of Mr George Herbert* (1675).
3. John Donne, *Letters to Severall Persons of Honour* (1651), ed. M. Thomas Hester, Scholars' Facsimiles (Delmar, N.Y., 1977), p. 106.
4. "To the Countesse of Bedford. Begun in France but never perfected," lines 11–16; cf. "To the Countesse of Salisbury. August 1614," lines 37–38, both in *The Complete Poems of John Donne*, ed. C. A. Patrides (London, 1985), pp. 302, 307. Subsequent quotations from Donne's poetry are taken from this edition and cited by title and line numbers in my text.
5. "To Mr Henry Vaughan Silurist on his Poems," lines 37–38 (Catherine Cole Mambretti, ed., "A Critical Edition of the Poems of Katherine Philips" [Ph.D. diss., University of Chicago, June 1979], p. 121).

den nevertheless spoke accurately enough for his age in signaling its break with Donne's poetic sensibilities and practice. Donne now stands in our eyes as the last English poet to sustain the force of the great, centuries-old Continental tradition of love lyrics that had celebrated femininity for offering the male poet a privileged access to ideality and divinity as well as a means of grounding his selfhood through intimacy with a person figured to and by this self as other.[6] Among English metaphysicals Richard Crashaw might at first seem a conspicuous exception to the foregoing generalization. In scaling the visionary and affective heights of his best-known poetry, that addressed to women subjects, Crashaw works from a declared conviction that souls in female bodies and social positions, like Teresa of Avila's, are best situated to experience the onset of divine love and to surrender themselves to it. Again and again he urges his little coterie of Englishwomen toward the transcendent inward raptures that are the privilege and the secret of a bride of Christ. The most revelatory example in this vein, "To Resolution in Religion, & to render her selfe without further delay into the Communion of the Catholick Church," was addressed to Crashaw's patroness, the countess of Denbigh. Its octosyllabic couplets pant in serial entreaty:

Ah linger not, lov'd soul! a slow
And late consent was a long no,

. . . .

Choose out that sure decisive dart
Which has the Key of this close heart,

. . . .

Unfold at length, unfold fair flowre
And use the season of love's showre,

. . . .

O Dart of love! arrow of light!
O happy you, if it hitt right.[7]

Such elegant double entendres might pass among the small, self-exiled readership of two Paris editions, but the poem displayed too much erotic license to be suitable for London publication without toning-down and retitling as "A Letter from Mr. Crashaw to the Countess of Denbigh." On a biographical and poetic showing alike, Crashaw defines an idiosyncratic extreme in the adoption of Continental modes of sensibility. He finally corroborates far more than he defies the generalization that Donne was the last English poet of the metaphysics of heterosexual love.

We confront, then, a spread of primary texts that offer testimony so conflicting as to cry out for analysis and explanation. There is the central figure of Donne—and the eccentric, marginal figure of Crashaw—for whom female subjects and the metaphysical style are inextricably linked. In Andrew Marvell this linkage of subjects and style exhibits an inconstant hold. In Herbert, Vaughan, and Thomas Traherne, the metaphysical style is sustained by displacing from female subjects the integrating and spiritualizing functions that had formerly served to anchor the male lover-poet's

6. Still authoritative discussions are offered by J. B. Broadbent in *Poetic Love* (London, 1964); and by N. J. C. Andreasen in *John Donne: Conservative Revolutionary* (Princeton, N.J., 1967).
7. "To the Noblest & best of Ladyes, the Countesse of Denbigh," lines 13–14, 33–34, 43–44, 49–50 (L. C. Martin, ed., *The Poems of Richard Crashaw*, 2d ed. [Oxford, 1957], p. 237).

existence and expression. Why do women figure so divergently across the spectrum of figuration in this style of poetry?

Unless we reckon as integrally with their poetic absence as with their poetic presence, we may settle for a description that falls short as an explanation. If we immerse ourselves only in the ranging themes and tonalities that are Donne's great achievement in love poetry, we will be tempted to conclude that he exhausted the potentialities of women as subjects for the metaphysical style and that his successors reacted by turning in other directions. But if we attend, in these successors of Donne, to experiments with other than overtly female constructions of a poetic presence that empowers and validates lyric expression, we will be compelled to attribute more significance to their shift from secular to sacred love themes. Although Donne himself initiated this shift, he does not cast it as a choice between opposed poetic kinds. Later metaphysicals, however—Herbert in the youthful sonnets "My God, where is that ancient heat" and "Sure Lord, there is enough in thee," Vaughan in the prose preface and dedicatory verses of *Silex Scintillans*, and Marvell in "The Coronet"—repudiate secular ends when they profess sacred ones.

By virtue of chronology and the primacy he accords to female presence, Donne makes the first and longest claims on our attention. As we turn in that direction, we find Dryden, a poet looking closely at another poet's practice, again at our elbow. He points out that Donne, as he "affects the metaphysics," sweeps over the boundary between satire and amorous address and makes it of no account. Dryden's telling observation alerts us to what we soon identify as a constitutive feature—the imperiousness of the subjectivity that utters itself into being in Donne's verse. His poetic discourse is represented as springing from so deeply within the speaker's psyche that the discourse is always for and about that psyche. We owe to women critics of our century some now-classic appreciations of the nuances of thought and feeling that Donne's male discoursers manage to articulate.[8] Self-exploratory and self-revealing in equal measure, the speaker in poem after poem pronounces on the nature of love. Yet in reflecting on the union he seeks or finds or spurns with a female counterpart, the speaker continues to register the reaches and boundaries of his own gendered consciousness, his identity as a man.

Newer feminist readings have begun to show how these speakers' unwittingly negative aspects of self-disclosure can repay close study.[9] Donne acutely delineates a whole range of male attitudinizing about love. Fear of a possibly lasting relationship in "The Indifferent" prompts the fantasy of a Venusian edict against "dangerous constancie" (line 25). Phallic posturings and revulsions belie the speakers' world-weariness in "Loves Alchymie" and "Farewell to Love." Bravado fails to mask longing for a beloved never or only fleetingly possessed in "The Apparition" and "The Curse." A

8. See Joan Bennett, "The Love Poetry of John Donne: A Reply to Mr. C. S. Lewis," in *Seventeenth-Century Studies Presented to Sir Herbert Grierson* (Oxford, 1938), pp. 85–104; the introduction, notes, and appendices to John Donne, *The Elegies and the Songs and Sonnets*, ed. Helen Gardner (Oxford, 1965); Roma Gill, "*Musa locosa Mea*: Thoughts on the *Elegies*," in *John Donne: Essays in Celebration*, ed. A. J. Smith (London, 1972), pp. 47–72; and Barbara Hardy, "Thinking and Feeling in the *Songs and Sonnets*," in Smith, ed., pp. 73–88.

9. Lois E. Bueler, "The Failure of Sophistry in Donne's Elegy VII," *Studies in English Literature* 25 (1985): 69–85; Janel M. Mueller, " 'This Dialogue of One': A Feminist Reading of Donne's 'Extasie'," *Association of Departments of English Bulletin* 81 (1985): 39–42.

revealing turn at the end of "The Extasie" converts praise of perfect mutuality with a woman to instruction for a male overhearer: "Let him still marke us, he shall see / Small change, when we are to bodies gone" (lines 75–76). The arrogance of a man who thinks his woman his property is shaken to very different depths in different contexts. "I planted knowledge and lifes tree in thee, / Which Oh; shall strangers taste?" laments the speaker of "Natures lay Ideot" (Elegie 7, lines 26–27). Struggling to confront the prospect of his beloved's death, the speaker of "A Feaver" dissolves his claim in paradoxically sudden and complete self-abandon: "I had rather owner bee / Of thee one houre, than all else ever" ("A Feaver," lines 27–28).

In remarking how Donne "perplexes the minds of the fair sex with nice speculations of philosophy, when he should engage their hearts, and entertain them with the softnesses of love," Dryden rightly realizes that it is the speaker's play of mind—not social contexts, norms, and practices—that determines the roles of the women in Donne's verse. We ourselves note that whatever place Donne's lovers find or make for their love requires them to oppose the world and its concerns ("The Sunne Rising," "The Canonization") or to keep the love secret from a world that is sure to misunderstand ("The Undertaking"). Given the period standards set by the developed realism of the Jacobean theater, Donne, who has so often been termed "dramatic," can so qualify at best in his versifying of speech to reveal the shifts and nuances of a single sensibility, but not in dialogue or full delineation of character. Compared with earlier Renaissance love poetry, Donne's is also odd in eschewing pictorialism and other sensuous effects to convey the allure of a woman's body to a male speaker. Not only must readers of Donne forgo expectations of catching much of the flavor of a woman's personality, they must also learn to "Care lesse, eyes, lips, hands to misse" ("A Valediction forbidding Mourning," line 20). Women remain highly subjectivized presences in this highly subjectivized poetry; as such, as Ilona Bell explains, they prove indispensable to the poetry and to the identities of the discoursing males who are its mouthpieces.[1] Women serve these males' psyches to "ballast"—the verb from "Aire and Angels" (line 15)—and limit what is other than the self, what is otherwise finally the vastness of the world.

In Donne the female other begins to contribute crucially to male selfhood when a speaker registers the onset of desire. This cognizance of specifically sexual attraction impresses a man with his own lack as well as his longing to conjoin to himself all that a given woman has and is. "But this," exclaims the speaker of "The Good-morrow," "all pleasures fancies bee / If ever any beauty I did see, / Which I desir'd, and got, t'was but a dreame of thee" (lines 5–7). To the extent that such desire acknowledges and yearns toward value in its object, it manifests itself as love. By casting desire and love as physical operations actually endured, Donne invigorates stock tropes like the incising of the beloved's image with some new poetic life—as, for example, in "The Dampe," where an autopsy ordered after the speaker's mysteriously sudden death "Will have me cut up to survay each part" and will "finde your Picture in my heart" (lines 3–4). Donne also outgoes every precedent but Spenser's in focusing a number of his lyrics

1. Ilona Bell, "The Role of the Lady in Donne's *Songs and Sonets*," *Studies in English Literature* 23 (1983): 113–29.

on fulfilled rather than thwarted love, as Lu Emily Pearson was quick to note early in this century's critical vogue of the metaphysicals.[2] But even Spenser does not prepare us to encounter the Donnean male speaker who discourses analytically in these lyrics on the joys of fully reciprocated sexual love to his female counterpart. The yield is an astonishingly exact articulation of what man in Western culture has tended to make of woman and of himself in relation to her.[3]

We find that the onset of love unsettles and even shatters a man by destroying all illusion that he can live in self-containment and self-sufficiency; instead, he discovers that he is contingent, vulnerable, without a center.

What did become
Of my heart, when I first saw thee?
I brought a heart into the roome,
But from the roome, I carried none with mee,

marvels the speaker of "The Broken Heart" (lines 17–20). Especially disorienting are the concurrent demands that flesh and spirit make, for a man cannot sustain an axiomatic Christian subordination of his body to his soul when he is in love and feels "mixt of all stuffes, paining soule, or sense" ("Loves Growth," line 9). Yet if love is to be, as it is in Donne, the most sublime of human experiences, it must accommodate the "affections" and "faculties" of "sense" as well as "pure . . . soules," since both are tied in "that subtile knot" of our ensouled bodies ("The Extasie," lines 64–66). Once love overwhelms the Donnean male with the complexity and uniqueness of being human, he seeks to reconstitute his identity by obtaining the loving recognition of the woman who is the object of his love: "So thy love may be my loves spheare" ("Aire and Angels," line 25). Insofar as Donne's speakers associate the full mutuality of this human recognition with heterosexual intercourse freely undertaken and enjoyed, they rather strikingly represent the man and the woman as equals in love: "So, to one neutrall thing both sexes fit" ("The Canonization," line 25); "Let us possesse one world, each hath one, and is one" ("The Good-morrow," line 14).

The spiritual counterpart of this equality is the gaze enacted in "The Extasie" and invoked in a number of other lyrics. As the lovers draw close together, face to face, and see themselves reflected in the pupils of one another's eyes, one subjectivity fixes and gives back another subjectivity to itself.[4] In this connection, Aristotle's doctrine that a substance resists change and annihilation through the equal mixture of its elements acquires an emotional and intellectual resonance that brings poetic discourse to a genuinely "metaphysical" level. This doctrine provides the backdrop and perhaps also the stimulus for Donne's remarkable group of lyrics on leave-taking, the event that best verifies because it most severely tests mutuality based in heterosexual love. Of this group, however, only "A Valediction forbidding Mourning" and "A Valediction of Weeping" come close to strik-

2. Lu Emily Pearson, "John Donne's Love Lyrics," in her *Elizabethan Love Conventions* (Berkeley, 1933), pp. 223–30.
3. The fullest inventory of cultural constructions remains that of Simone de Beauvoir in her magisterial *Le deuxieme sexe: 1–Les faits et les mythes* (Paris, 1949), abridged in H. M. Parshley's translation, *The Second Sex* (New York, 1953).
4. See Wilbur Sanders's sensitive discussion of this recurring moment in *John Donne's Poetry* (Cambridge, 1975), pp. 66–72.

ing a balance between the forces of the lovers' subjectivities.[5] By contrast, the male speaker of "Sweetest love, I do not go" lapses into self-regard—" 'tis best, / To use my selfe in jest / Thus" (lines 6–7)—thus revealing at the critical moment of parting how tenuous an achievement this sexual equality is, how fearsome its counterpulls are. Finally significant are the very few settings Donne offers for his representations of sexual equality. They are limited to the "little roome" that becomes, "an every where" or to the "Pregnant banke," a kind of Renaissance lovers' lane ("The Good-morrow," line 11; "The Extasie," line 2). It seems literally inconceivable that such equality might hold elsewhere than in the most intimate aspects of the man's and woman's love.

Thus, what Natalie Davis remarks of Renaissance culture at large applies as well in Donne's poetry generally: to confront the fact of sexual difference is to engage with issues of dominance and subordination, for there seems to be no other reason for the difference to exist.[6] Donne's many cynical and libertine speakers enact their conviction of male superiority, whether or not they finally undercut themselves in what they say. But the lyrics of reciprocated love also inscribe at key points the prevailing asymmetry of outlook and sexual role that casts the male as the persuader and possessor, the female as the persuaded and the possessed: "She's all States, and all Princes, I / Nothing else is" ("The Sunne Rising," lines 21–22). To his personal credit, Donne lends no credence to essentialist views of sexual difference, for his poetry is unmarked by their major premise—that a woman's capacity to bear children defines her and her relation to a man. Yet, conditioned as Donne was to think by the norms for education and conduct in his patriarchal society, he could scarcely at all imagine or figure his analytical, ratiocinative verse as anything but a male prerogative: "my words masculine perswasive force" ("Elegie: On his Mistris," line 4).[7] Even in the poems that figure amorous equality, the male act of representation—"this dialogue of one"—reinscribes the inequality of the sexes ("The Extasie," line 74). Virginia Woolf registers as much in her equivocal tribute to Donne's "power of suddenly surprising and subjugating the reader."[8] Indeed the most conspicuous constant in Donne's verse is the monopoly on discourse enjoyed and exercised by male figures—an aspect of the "phallocentrism" whose "command" of "literary history" is at issue for feminist critics.[9] Within the cultural mainstream—ours no less than Donne's—this monopoly acquires even further valency from the intense,

5. For detailed analyses that support this generalization, see William Empson, "A Valediction of Weeping," in *John Donne: A Collection of Critical Essays*, ed. Helen Gardner (Englewood Cliffs, N.J., 1962), pp. 52–60; John Freccero, "Donne's 'Valediction: Forbidding Mourning,'" in *Essential Articles for the Study of John Donne's Poetry*, ed. John Roberts (Hamden, Conn., 1975), pp. 279–304; and Avi Erlich, "Ambivalence in John Donne's 'Forbidden Mourning,'" *American Imago* 36 (1979): 357–72.

6. Natalie Zemon Davis, "Women on Top," in her *Society and Culture in Early Modern France: Eight Essays* (Stanford, Calif., 1975), pp. 124–51, esp. p. 128.

7. Though frameworks of explanation vary, the denomination "patriarchal" characterizes Donne's era in such diverse accounts as Roberta Hamilton, *The Liberation of Women: A Study of Patriarchy and Capitalism* (London, 1978); Lawrence Stone, *The Family, Sex and Marriage in England, 1500–1800* (London, 1977); and Keith Wrightson, *English Society, 1580–1680* (London, 1982).

8. Virginia Woolf, "Donne after Three Centuries," in her *The Second Common Reader* (New York, 1932), pp. 22–37, quote on p. 24.

9. Hélène Cixous, "Sorties," in *New French Feminisms: An Anthology*, ed. Elaine Marks and Isabelle de Courtivron (New York, 1981), pp. 90–98, quote on p. 92. Also see Luce Irigaray, *This Sex Which Is Not One*, trans. Catherine Porter (Ithaca, N.Y., 1985), chaps. 2, 4, 5.

nuanced subjectivities ascribed to these male speakers and the sturdiness of their characterization as active heterosexuals.[1]

If Donne had written only love poetry, the present account of him might end here. After 1607, however, he set to work more or less concurrently in two new genres: religious lyrics and verse letters in praise of prospective or actual patronesses. While there are many obvious differences between them, these two genres proved similar to Donne in an important respect. They brought into question, as inappropriate or wholly inapplicable, the framework of sexual consummation between a man and a woman within which he had located virtually everything he had written about love. This framework had also served as one of two vital props for the compelling naturalism of Donne's poetic representations. The other was provided by the highly developed subjectivity of the male speaking figure, and this figure Donne retained unaltered. But in the new genres this figure had to discourse differently of love, or had to discourse of a different love. It is not always exactly ascertainable how Donne construed his new poetic challenge.[2]

In the Holy Sonnets it proves continuously troubling for the male speaking-figure to do without heterosexual love as a model for ideality. He pursues his self-explorations alone. They leave him overwhelmed with his sins, which he sometimes expressly equates with his former active sexuality now branded as "Idolatry" ("O might those sighes and teares," lines 5–6; "What if this present," line 9). Fear rather than love of God predominates in the Holy Sonnets, where the speaker strains to place this irrepressible reflex in a positive light: "Those are my best dayes, when I shake with feare" ("Oh, to vex me," line 14).[3] Fear persists in the late "A Hymne to God the Father," although there the speaker regards it negatively: "I have a sinne of feare" (line 13). Deprived of the resources of human intersubjectivity, he continually appears at a loss for ways to relate to God as the sole divine Other. Infrequent direct address in very general terms like "God" and "Lord" compounds with expressions of insecurity or bewilderment as this male speaker seeks engagement with his male God.

What options existed for models of personal relationship in the genre of religious lyric? Not the model of single-sex, specifically male friendship that informs Donne's verse letters to male friends, because there could be no second-self or alter-ego relation between the human and the divine in the Christian orthodoxies within which Donne confined his choice of religion.[4] The father-son model carried full biblical and theological sanction, but it is remarkable how rarely and how indirectly the Donnean speaker

1. Donne's "Breake of Day" and "Confined Love" are short, slight exercises. Only in "Sapho to Philaenis" does a Donnean woman speaker sustain discursive and imaginative force comparable to a male's in addressing the object of her passion. It cannot be accidental that she is also an imperious poetic talent. Her lesbianism, equally, cannot be accidental; see my essay, "A Letter from Lesbos: Utopian Homoerotics in Donne's 'Sapho to Philaenis'," in *Sexuality and Gender in Early Modern Europe—Multidisciplinary Essays*, ed. James Grantham Turner (Cambridge, England, 1993), pp. 182–207.
2. For a sympathetic highlighting of such continuities as can be discerned in the earlier and later phases of Donne's poetry, see Kitty Datta, "Love and Asceticism in Donne's Poetry: The Divine Analogy," *Critical Quarterly* 19, no. 2 (1977): 5–25.
3. For discussion of the theological sources and implications of this Donnean fear, see Richard Strier, "John Donne 'Awry and Squint,'" *Modern Philology* 86 (1989): 357–84.
4. For an influential reading of Donne in which his exchange of the Roman for the English Church becomes a self-determining act of apostasy, see John Carey, *John Donne: Life, Mind and Art* (New York, 1981).

uses it. Tenaciously figuring his maleness as adult manhood, he evinces the residual force of the sexualized model for love in Donne's religious poetry. Such a speaker cannot posit himself as a child. However, the most strenuous ingenuity proves incapable of adapting the sexualized model to the divine-human relationship without forfeiting the qualities that make this model so valuable and appealing in Donne's secular love poems. This speaker's two experiments along this line produce the "fearful accommodations" of a God who expresses love through torture, rape, and bondage in "Batter my heart" and a spouse who fulfills her role by behaving like a whore in "Show me deare Christ."[5] By contrast, moreover, with their analytic and elucidating functions in the secular love poems, the paradoxes of Donne's religious lyrics remain either paradoxical or blunt to theological commonplace in such characteristic instances as "Thy Makers maker, and thy Fathers mother," "Therefore that he may raise the Lord throws down" ("La Corona. Annunciation," line 12; "Hymne to God my God, in my Sicknesse," line 30).

The same cannot be said of Donne's verse letters to noblewomen and the two *Anniversaries*, which stand to each other as preparatory exercises and masterworks on the symbolic power of femininity. As Barbara Lewalski has discussed in detail, this poetry is nothing if not metaphysical; its trajectories of hyperbole often take us a great distance from any recognizable female presence.[6] Here the Donnean discourser proves capable of displacing the flesh while retaining the spirit at the center of a male-female relationship, and the verse epistles to noblewomen suggest several reasons why. The least of these seems to be the fact that such a relationship tallies in all essentials with the parting and separation—that is, the physical distancing—that figures so crucially as a test of heterosexual love for the male speakers of the love poetry. More important is the readiness shown by this discourser to love his patronesses as authority figures who, through their attentions to him, set the worth of his person and the direction of his life. Of course one can decide to dismiss such "love" as an exaction of Renaissance patronage, but Margaret Maurer has argued cogently for its centrality to Donne's own psychic and social being.[7] Even if we chalk the fact up as a vestige of Marian devotion, it is surely noteworthy that, on the evidence of this poetry, the Donnean male speaker can love a woman much more easily than he can God in a dominating role. Most interesting of all are the reflections offered on femininity. They complete what the love poetry leaves implicit or undeveloped in the Donnean representation of woman as they push to a vanishing point in her the distinction between the human and the divine.

The verse letters go far beyond the love poetry in ascribing to feminine otherness a sweeping ethical force. The judging role of the women in the

5. See William Kerrigan's incisive essay, "The Fearful Accommodations of John Donne," *English Literary Renaissance* 4 (1972): 337–63.
6. Barbara Kiefer Lewalski, *Donne's Anniversaries and the Poetry of Praise: The Creation of a Symbolic Mode* (Princeton, N.J., 1973); cf. my review article, "Death and the Maiden: The Christian Symbolism of Donne's *Anniversaries*," *Modern Philology* 70 (1973): 280–86.
7. Margaret Maurer, "The Real Presence of Lucy Russell, Countess of Bedford, and the Terms of John Donne's 'Honor is So Sublime Perfection,'" *ELH* 47 (1980): 205–34. For further probing of Donne's self-cognizance regarding the transactional character of his maneuverings for patronage and position, see Judith Scherer Herz's "'An Excellent Exercise of Wit That Speaks So Well of Ill': Donne and the Poetics of Concealment," in *The Eagle and the Dove: Reassessing John Donne*, ed. Claude J. Summers and Ted-Larry Pebworth (Columbia, Mo., 1986), pp. 8–14.

love poetry is typically confined to the specifics of the argument which the speaker is making about his or their love—for example, in "The Flea" or in "A Valediction of my Name, in the Window." In the verse letters we gain a deepened sense of what the male self seeks in a female other: not just to be acknowledged but also to be wholly ratified by her. The patroness occupies a privileged position in his construction of the world. Her outlook, unclouded (in his casting of the matter) by masculine pursuits and preoccupations, can uniquely reach a true appraisal of his character, his enterprises, and even the quality of his reasoning. Thus an epistle to the countess of Bedford begins:

> Madame,
> You have refin'd mee, and to worthyest things
> . . . now I see
> Rarenesse, or use, not nature value brings.
> (lines 1–3)

In exerting this higher power over the speaker's life, the patroness quickly assumes the aspect of divinity: "Divinity, that's you" ("Reason is our Soules left hand," line 2).

In another epistle to the countess of Bedford, her matchless understanding and practice of virtue are credited to her gender as Donne ingeniously applies pseudologic to establish the sexual double standard as an ethical standard possessed of redoubled force. Since she is a moral agent gendered female, Lady Bedford always has her "honour" to maintain. Her high attainment of goodness results from knowing, as only a lady can, how to unite prudential worldly considerations with heavenly concerns: "Discretion is a wisemans Soule, and so / Religion is a Christians, and you know / How these are one" ("Honour is so sublime perfection," lines 40–42). An epistle to the countess of Huntington also equates her femininity with divinity while disclosing the speaker's adroit manipulation of gender roles and positions. Because Lady Huntington has accepted the (subordinating) involvement with a man that gives her "a wifes and mothers name," she can be trusted not to establish norms inimical to the male speaker: "Vertue having made you vertue, 'is faine / T'adhere in these names, her and you to show" ("Man to Gods image, *Eve*, to mans was made," lines 29, 31–32).

Against this quite innovative backdrop of associations of ideality with the lives and persons of mature married women, the turn to a virgin's body and soul as the locus of all the world's value in *The Anniversaries* both looks and is more conventional. We do not have to agree with Ben Jonson that the poems should have been more conventional still, that if they "had been written of the Virgin Marie" they "had been something." For there is nothing in the poetic transmutation of the fifteen-year-old Elizabeth Drury in *The Anniversaries* that does not tally with traditional attributes of the Virgin at the same age, the age she was supposed to have borne Christ, except for the bearing of Christ. Donne more than makes good any potential deficit in his subject by assimilating the attributes of Christ as well as Mary to what he told Jonson was "the idea of a Woman, and not as she was."[8] The apotheosis of femininity as divinity in the English Renaissance, these poems demonstrate the heights to which male idealization and imag-

8. Ben Jonson, *Conversations with Drummond of Hawthornden* (1618–19), excerpted in Clements, ed., *John Donne's Poetry*, p. 103.

ination can rise when the female other is postulated purely as a blank counter. "Her death did wound, and tame thee than," says the speaker of "The First Anniversary," addressing the world—"and than / Thou mightst have better spar'd the Sunne, or Man" (lines 25–26). Donne understood well enough the wire-drawn extremities to which he had pursued virtue in female guise in his *Anniversaries* to see that any defense of them would have to be staked in the world-realizing capacities of the mind—the precincts, from first to last, of all the metaphysicals. In specifically staking out those precincts by demonstrating the centrality of gender relations to the constitution of the mind's capacities,[9] Donne has as strong a claim as he ever did to be considered the definitive poet of the English style that takes its name from his defining practices.

EARL MINER

[The Cavalier Ideal of the Good Life]†

The social character of Cavalier poetry affords one kind of testimony to the cohesive civilization behind the work. To say so much is not to say that all Cavalier poets were alike, any more than to say that all parts of England were then alike. More than that, the same men and poets changed with the times. The question of just what changes took place is one still exercising social historians. Simply put, however, Cavalier social values are those of an aristocracy and gentry that two centuries before might have struggled against the throne but that now sought to protect the King, for all his faults (Elizabeth, James I, Charles I, Charles II) against his enemies, and to preserve crown, mitre, estates, and what was often termed "our liberties." But social values often conflicted with family interests, religious belief, and ambition. There was much changing of sides, and in fact much of what happened in the century remains beyond our reach. But I see no need to worry our problems hair by hair or to subtlize them out of existence. When, on "that memorable Scene," as Marvell put it, Charles I "with his keener Eye / The Axes edge did try," he presumably found time to consider that he had enemies. And these enemies are precisely those who threw the name "Cavalier" at the King's supporters, as many of them had thrown "Puritan" at the other side. Not all who supported the King, however, were Cavalier poets. Some men turned to the more intimate alternative of Metaphysical poetry. Very many more were led by piety or indifference to disregard poetry. What deserves remark, therefore, is the variety of those who shared Cavalier poetic and human values, and the degree of agreement among them as to what their values were.

The foremost Cavalier ideal expressed in poetry is what we may call the good life, and in a sense that is the subject of all else following in this book

9. For further suggestive discussion, see Nancy Chodorow, *The Reproduction of Mothering: Psychoanalysis and the Sociology of Gender* (Berkeley and Los Angeles, 1979); Dorothy Dinnerstein, *The Mermaid and the Minotaur: Sexual Arrangements and Human Malaise* (New York, 1976); and Carol Gilligan, *In a Different Voice: Psychological Theory and Women's Development* (Cambridge, Mass., 1982).

† From *The Cavalier Mode from Jonson to Cotton* (Princeton, 1971). Reprinted by permission of Virginia Miner.

as well as of the preceding chapter. This ideal reflects many things: a conservative outlook, a response to a social threat, classical recollections, love of a very English way of life, and a new blending of old ideas. The ideal is not necessarily Christian or pagan, this worldly or otherworldly. But by comparison with Metaphysical and Restoration poetry, it probably does seem more secular and classical, pagan, or Horatian in some ways than do the other two great modes of seventeenth-century poetry. In itself, Cavalier poetry reveals a consistent urge to define and explore the features of what constituted human happiness, and of which kind of man was good.

One of the best introductions to the idea of the good life may be found in *The Compleat Angler*, whether in Izaak Walton's first part (1653 *et seq.*) or Charles Cotton the Younger's second (1676 *et seq.*).[1] The charm attributed to this work testifies not to a measurability of charm, but to a conviction of decent pleasure that Walton and Cotton carry straight to the heart of even the most indifferent fisherman. Here Walton speaks in the guise of the "angler," Piscator.

> I'll now lead you to an honest Ale-house, where we shall find a cleanly room, Lavender in the windowes, and twenty Ballads stuck about the wall; there my Hostis (which I may tel you, is both cleanly and conveniently handsome) has drest many a [chub] for me, and shall now dress it after my fashion, and I warrant it good meat. (I, ch. ii; 1653, p. 49)

England is one of the handsomest and pleasantest countries of the world, when the sun shines, and there is a real sense in which the sun shines always in *The Compleat Angler*, even when Peter tells of a rainy day.

> *Peter* . . . indeed we went to a good honest Ale-house, and there we plaid at shovel-board half the day; all the time that it rained we were there, and as merry as they that fish'd, and I am glad we are now with a dry house over our heads, for heark how it rains and blows. Come Hostis, give us more Ale, and our Supper with what haste you may, and when we have sup'd, let us have your Song, *Piscator*, and the [catch] that your Scholar promised us, or else *Coridon* will be dogged . . .
> [Viator]. And I hope the like [i.e., to be perfect] for my [song], which I have ready too, and therefore lets go merrily to Supper, and then have a gentle touch at singing and drinking; but the last with moderation. (I. ch. xi; 1653, pp. 208–09)

Walton stresses certain elements more heavily, and others more lightly, than a Jonson or a Herrick would; and what he writes turns upon the subject of angling. But his very English book does bring to view a good life, a world in which man's life possesses fullness, and satisfaction is realized.

Walton's small group of anglers exemplifies the usual social microcosm of the Cavaliers. Such another, and more properly poetic, group we find in the famous Tribe of Ben, with Jonson like Piscator the good father figure inculcating virtue, self-knowledge, and poetry (Jonson's mysterious trinity) in his Sons, as they express their praise, happiness, and devotion. And their

1. Walton especially revised his work for reprintings. Some of the best things I quote derive entirely or in their quoted form from later editions. His "naturalness" was both genuine and artistic.

disagreement. One of the wonderful things we discover about Jonson in his relations with his Tribe is his ability to take criticism. His Sons show the complete devotion expected of sons and the frankness expected (in theory, usually) of friends. The evidence, although implicit, drives again and again to show that Jonson expected his Sons to be honest (in not just the modern sense, but also in Walton's and the usual Roman senses). Here is James Howell, writing "To my Father, Mr. Ben Johnson":

> Father *Ben Nullum fit magnum ingenium sine mixtura dementiae*, there's no great Wit without some Mixture of Madness . . . it is verified in you, for I find that you have been oftentimes mad! you were mad when you writ your [*Volpone*], and madder when you writ your *Alchymist*; you were mad when you writ *Catalin*, and stark mad when you writ *Sejanus*; but when you writ your *Epigrams*, and the *Magnetic Lady*, you were not so mad; insomuch that I perceive there be Degrees of Madness in you. Excuse me that I am so free with you.[2]

Free he is, but he spent the next six months hunting out a Welsh grammar for his Father Ben. Jonson's world is, then, a tougher, more verisimilar world than Walton's, so that the goodness and grace that he won for his poetry represent victories far greater than those achieved in Walton's semi-pastoral world. His tone, his frank, manly, ethical note that led his Sons to respond so forthrightly, can be heard in that poem celebrating the rites of admission to the Tribe.

> Men that are safe, and sure, in all they doe,
> Care not what trials they are put unto;
> They meet the fire, the Test, as Martyrs would;
> And though Opinion stampe them not, are gold . . .
>
> First give me faith, who know
> My selfe a little. I will take you so,
> As you have writ your selfe. Now stand, and then,
> Sir, you are Sealed of the Tribe of Ben.[3]

A true and complete man, inviolate in his central integrity, although passionate enough, Jonson conveys as no other English poet does that sense of *integer vitae*. Reading his ethical poetry, we sense that his central claim (and one that animates us as we read) simply comes to this: "I am a man, and I am true."

Whether or not Jonson's poem just quoted from was addressed to Thomas Randolph, I cannot say, but by what seems a coincidence we have a poem by Randolph offering his gratitude for admittance to the Tribe: "A gratulatory to Mr Ben. Johnson for his adopting of him to be his Son." His gratitude is partly personal and loyal, partly derived from the debt of an artistic "mystery"—whether angling or poetry—that the young owe to their masters.

> I was not borne to *Helicon*, nor dare
> Presume to thinke my selfe a *Muses* heire.
> I have no title to *Parnassus* hill,
> Nor any acre of it by the will

2. Howell, *Epistolae Ho-Elianae*, 11th edition (London, 1754), I. V. 1 (27 June 1629).
3. *An Epistle Answering to One That Asked to Be Sealed of the Tribe of Ben*, ll. 1–4, 75–78.

Of a dead Ancestour, nor could I bee
Ought but a tenant unto Poëtrie,
But thy Adoption quits me of all feare,
And makes me challenge a childs portion there.
I am a kinne to *Hero's* being thine,
And part of my alliance is divine.
Orpheus, Musaeus, Homer too; beside
Thy Brothers by the *Roman* Mothers side;
As *Ovid, Virgil*, and the *Latine Lyre*,
That is so like thy *Horace*.

(1–14)

Randolph's grateful awe conveys part of the good life: its definition of what is good in terms of relations with contemporaries and with the immortal men of the past. Herrick, addressing Jonson, treats a different aspect of the good life, its relaxed pleasure (with, he insists, moderation, although no doubt he and Walton meant different limits by that).

Ah *Ben*!
Say how, or when
Shall we thy Guests
Meet at those *Lyrick* Feasts,
Made at the *Sun*,
The *Dog*, the triple *Tunne*?
Where we such clusters had,
As made us nobly wild, not mad . . . [4]

Whether it is Jonson, Walton, Howell, Randolph, or Herrick—or others—certain elements are shared. Most important is the premise of the good life, which involves social intercourse with like-minded people. Very frequently that relation turns on the band of friends, male equals joined in fraternal affection and esteem. But the relation may be paternal and filial, as we see in the anglers and the Tribe of Ben. Two other groups make up the four chief kinds: men and women, lord and vassal. The latter relation usually involves prince and subject, but it may be patron and artist. Since all four resemble each other in involving relationship and in representing value, they may be substituted for each other: the woman loved may be a queen, her lover her subject. In due course we shall have cause to observe that such bonds were formed as much by rites and ceremonies as by ethical concerns. We must acknowledge that on occasion some thought that there was just cause for breaking the bonds: Suckling debated the code of love in his lyrics, and most Cavaliers treated the vices of kings and even questions of justifiable regicide in their tragedies. But the usual alignment that imparts Cavalier literature its special flavor is friendship or love or small groups, in each case a relation with a code that implicitly agrees with those in the world whose opinion and principle one values. The limits of the good life and the strength of the social bonds were tested by the Cavalier poets themselves and by events. And we sometimes encounter those moments that make us believe that we are advancing at one step toward pleasure and heaven. A sentence added to later editions of *The Compleat Angler* expresses such anti-Puritanical wisdom in little.

4. Herrick, "An Ode for him," ll. 1–8.

> None of these [trout] have been known to be taken with an Angle, unless it were one that was caught by Sir *George Hastings* (an excellent Angler, now with God).[5]

It is of course the parenthesis that strikes us, a conjunction of many things, but especially of a recreation with divinity, that we may fairly grant to Walton and the Cavaliers as their discovery. Walton's pastoral notes and warmth of heart will be found, with many of the very same details we have noticed, in Cavalier religious poetry. Here is Herrick, in "A Thanksgiving to God, for his House."

> Lord, Thou hast given me a cell
>   Wherein to dwell;
> An little house, whose humble Roof
>   Is weather-proof;
> Under the sparres of which I lie
>   Both soft, and drie . . .
> Lord, I confesse too, when I dine,
>   The Pulse is Thine,
> And all those other Bits, that bee
>   There plac'd by Thee;
> The Worts, the Purslain, and the Messe
>   Of Water-cresse,
> Which of Thy kindnesse Thou hast sent; . . .
> 'Tis thou that crown'st my glittering Hearth
>   With guiltlesse mirth;
> And giv'st me Wassaile Bowles to drink,
>   Spic'd to the brink. . . .
> All these, and better Thou dost send
>   Me, to this end,
> That I should render, for my part,
>   A thankfull heart;
> Which, fir'd with incense, I resigne,
>   As wholly Thine;
> But the acceptance, that must be,
>   My Christ, by Thee.[6]

The snug house (the fire loved by the Cavaliers comes in a passage omitted), the good food and abundant drink, and the heart, "fir'd with incense," for sacrifice to Christ—all these things make up the good life for which Herrick pays God due thanks. Many will feel that there is more of the *Hesperides* in *The Noble Numbers* than of the latter in the former. There is truth in such a belief. But it is also true that in his secular poems Herrick tends to substitute pagan religious detail for Christian,[7] and that is precisely one of the things that humanists were about (and for which they were criticized by the more austerely pious). In Herrick as well as in Walton, we discover a lively strain of pleasure and joy of life.

5. Walton, I. iv; quoted from the edition of 1750, ed. Browne, p. 49.
6. Lines 1–6, 27–33, 37–40, 51–58.
7. Some of the most valuable specialized studies of Cavalier poets are the essays touching Herrick by Robert H. Deming: "Robert Herrick's Classical Ceremony," *ELH: A Journal of English History*, XXXIV (1967), 327–48; "Herrick's Funeral Poems," *Studies in English Literature, IX* (1969), 153–67; and his dissertation, 'The Classical Ceremonial in the Poetry of Robert Herrick" (Wisconsin, 1965). These studies deal with subjects important in themselves, relevant to other poets, and intimate to some of my concerns here * * *.

"Sir *George Hastings* (an excellent Angler, now with God)." Walton names a name, adding a title and what is in some sense an occupation. Once again the implication is social: we have our associates, our band of choice, like spirits. And if we seek as before for confirmation in Ben Jonson's poetry, we find him consoling Sir Lucius Cary (later Lord Falkland) for the death of their mutual friend, Sir Henry Morison.

> Call, noble *Lucius*, then for Wine,
> And let thy lookes with gladnesse shine:
> Accept this garland, plant it on thy head,
> And thinke, nay know, thy *Morison's* not dead.
> Hee leap'd the present age,
> Possest with holy rage,
> To see that bright eternall Day:
> Of which we *Priests*, and *Poëts* say
> Such truths, as we expect for happy men,
> And there he lives with memorie; and *Ben* . . . [8]

Wine and a poetic garland, priests and poets, the named members of a fraternal society—these make up the good life, these provide the marks of "happy men." Unless I am mistaken, Jonson's "happy" is a reverse Latinism of that kind peculiar to him, as when he uses "running judgements" for "current judgements." "Happy" must mean *beati*, and "happy" both in the secular sense and the religious sense of glorification. Above all, Jonson's view presumes a unity of the like-minded and a unity within individual character, *integer vitae*. And for this moral vision, he became the arbiter of his age and "lives with memorie" ever since. * * *

Our next step must be to Jonson himself: man and poet. To try to say it all at once, it is moral integrity that marks the firm center of his poetic compass. Of course we have evidence and to spare showing that Jonson was physically gross, "rocky" as he said, excessive, combative, and (by politer standards) coarse. The evidence also shows that he possessed delicacy, an element of surpassing fancifulness; that he inculcated moderation; that he was a loyal friend; that he possessed a seemingly unerring sense of decorum, beauty, and justice; and that he was admired. Without his massive animal strength, his very virtues might have been insipid. But without his consistent ideals, his integrity, he might have aroused our dislike.

What a poet praises (or criticizes) in others usually tells us something of his own ideals. When Jonson acclaimed someone for being "alwayes himselfe and even," we see very clearly the ideal of *integer vitae*. In a few lines already quoted, we see that self-knowledge is as essential to Jonson as to Socrates.

> First give me faith, who know
> My selfe a little. I will take you so,
> As you have writ your selfe.[9]

Knowing oneself and others implies a capacity to trust oneself and others. It also implies that one will remain oneself with constancy in a world of threat and change.

8. *To the Immortal Memorie, and Friendship of That Noble Paire, Sir Lucius Cary, and Sir H. Morison*, ll. 75–84. *Caveat emptor*: I shall be quoting the passage, and a few others, more than once.
9. Jonson, *An Epistle . . . the Tribe of Ben*, ll. 75–77.

Well, with mine owne fraile Pitcher, what to doe
I have decreed; keepe it from waves, and presse;
Lest it be justled, crack'd, made nought, or lesse:
Live to the point I will, for which I am man,
And dwell as in my Center, as I can.[1]

The traditional emblems are here: the vessel of the soul, the threatening waves, the center for constancy, and the circle for perfection. And what such emblems help portray is precisely a good man defining his place in the world.

In that world, and as part of the moral landscape of Jonson's poetry, there rise shapes and forces threatening the constant man. As Milton said, we are no longer capable of defining good without a knowledge of evil, and Jonson often provides ample shadowing for his bright ideals. Even his panegyrics bear warnings for princes and kingdoms.

Who, *Virtue*, can thy power forget,
That sees these live, and triumph yet?
Th' *Assyrian* pompe, the *Persian* pride,
Greekes glory, and the *Romanes* dy'de:
And who yet imitate
Theyr noyses, tary the same fate.
Force Greatnesse, all the glorious wayes
You can, it soon decayes;
But so *good Fame* shall, never:
Her triumphs, as theyr Causes, are for ever.[2]

Merlin gives to Chivalry a Jonsonian caution in matters of praising kings, in a passage coming at its end to the high ideal of integrity which Jonson set.

Nay, stay your valure, 'tis a wisdome high
In Princes to use fortune reverently.
He that in deedes of *Armes* obeyes his blood
Doth often tempt his destinie beyond good.
Looke on this throne, and in his temper view
The light of all that must have grace in you:
His equall *Justice*, upright *Fortitude*
And settled *Prudence*, with that *Peace* indued
Of face, as minde, alwayes himselfe and even.
So HERCULES, and good men beare up *heaven*.[3]

The legend of Hercules relieving Atlas of his burden of the world worked throughout the century as a political type for kings.[4] What set off Jonson's use of the type is the dominance of political and other concerns by the moral. To me, the moral element lives in Jonson's very cadence and syntax. To others, I can point to the cautioning of princes to moderate courses, the insistence on integrity ("alwayes himselfe and even"), and the equation of "good men" with the Hercules / king typology. The regal is assimilated in the individual, in the very manhood of the good man.

1. *Ibid.*, ll. 56–60.
2. Jonson, *The Masque of Queens*, ll. 764–73.
3. Jonson, *Prince Henries Barriers*, 405–14.
4. In *Mystagogus Poeticus*, p. 116, Ross writes that Hercules can be "The type of a good king." (Alexander Ross published this work in 1647 [*Editor*]).

The good life finds definition, then, in terms of other lives, whether those of kings or of commoners. But the act of defining involves the discovery of self-knowledge, and in order to be defined as a good man one must be constant. On assumptions such as these, Jonson creates an artistic fiction no less imaginative than that of the writer of love lyrics. And his fiction enables him to laugh at himself, to drop the adventitious in human life, in order to stress what is central to goodness. As he conceded in addressing Sir William Burlase ("My Answer. The Poet to the Painter"):

> Why? though I seeme of a prodigious wast,
> I am not so voluminous, and vast
> But there are lines, wherewith I might b'embrac'd. . . .
>
> But, you are he can paint; I can but write:
> A Poet hath no more but black and white,
> Ne knowes he flatt'ring Colours, or false light.
>
> Yet when of friendship I would draw the face,
> A letter'd mind, and a large heart would place
> To all posteritie; I will write *Burlase.*
>
> (1–3, 19–24)

He draws himself good humoredly as a gross man, so that what he says about himself as writer and about Burlase is accepted as truth. (Jonson also plays with the two "sister arts," of course.) By such means he creates a fiction of himself, his friends, and his King as good men. It must be stressed that that fiction is as much something made, or rather, as much a transformation of reality, as anything in Donne. But like every good fiction, it carries the stamp of artistic currency within the perfect ring of its own coinage. All these considerations join in Jonson's self-awareness.

> Let me be what I am, as *Virgil* cold,
>   As *Horace* fat; or as *Anacreon* old;
> No Poets verses yet did ever move,
>   Whose Readers did not thinke he was in love.[5]

The conviction is necessary. Jonson convinces us that, like his Prince, James I, he was a good judge of good men. More than that, and unlike James, he also had good judgment of bad men and of himself. And if the portrait I have been getting Jonson to draw of himself makes him seem too bluff, let me refer to the word "thinke" in the last line quoted, or ask if there is not some fun in the first two lines, and wonder if it might not be worthwhile to be cold, fat, and old if one could also be an English poet combining the geniuses of Virgil, Horace, and Anacreon? My aim has been to emphasize the strength of Jonson's moral architecture, because that is, to my view, the essential, the functional aspect of his art.

* * *

The good man has one further function besides knowing himself, improving himself, and conquering his passions with equanimity. He must judge good and evil in other men. Many of Jonson's poems judge evil

5. Jonson, *An Elegie*, ll. 1–4.

through the resources of satire, and others judge good through panegyric. How conscious Jonson was of the role of the good man as judge can be seen from his praise of one of the most learned men of the day in "An Epistle to Master John Selden."

> What fables have you vext! what truth redeem'd!
> Antiquities search'd! Opinions dis-esteem'd!
> Impostures branded! And Authorities urg'd!
> What blots and errours, have you watch'd and purg'd
> Records, and Authors of! how rectified,
> Times, manners, customes!
>
> (39–44)

Jonson possessed many poetic and human virtues, and some of them are at least implied there. He prized learning that brought moral experience, wisdom. He may cleverly adapt the old proverb that a wise man is at home in all countries, including Selden among those "that have beene / Ever at home: yet, have all Countries seene" (29–30). But he does not stop there, adding that his friend is

> . . . like a Compasse keeping one foot still
> Upon your Center, doe your Circle fill
> Of generall knowledge; watch'd men, manners too,
> Heard what times past have said, seene what ours doe.
>
> (31–34)

A quiet wit voices itself in the distinction between hearing what is remote and seeing what is at hand. It is as though Selden has talked with the wise men of the past. The compass image conveys a virtue important to Jonson, constancy,[6] and the circle emblem, of course, perfection.

These many aspects of the Cavalier conception of *vir bonus* and of *vita bona* seem all to come together in Jonson's regular pindaric ode, *To the Immortall Memorie, and Friendship of That Noble Paire, Sir Lucius Cary, and Sir H. Morison*. As the poem tells us, Sir Henry Morison died (*aet.* about twenty) in battle. Sir Lucius Cary, later Viscount Falkland, also later to fall in battle, was as much an ideal courtier as the legendary Sir Philip Sidney (who also died in the field). Falkland married Morison's sister and styled himself a "brother" of Ben Jonson. Such adoption of relationships enables Jonson to write with great feeling and integrity about his subject, which, in its initial stages, consists of the negative contrast (1–42) and then the positive value represented by Morison.

> Hee stood, a Souldier to the last right end,
> A perfect Patriot, and a noble friend,
> But most a vertuous Sonne.
> All Offices were done
> By him, so ample, full, and round,
> In weight, in measure, number, sound,

6. See Rosemary Freeman, *English Emblem Books* (London, 1948); there is a very full discussion of lore associated with compasses in John Freccero's essay, "Donne's 'Valediction Forbidding Mourning,'" *ELH: A Journal of English Literary History*, XXX (1963), 335–76, which touches on Jonson at n. 43. Since Jonson took for himself the emblem of the broken compass, we see that he possessed humility, after all. In my view, that image is appropriate for the world of the plays but not for the poet's vision of that world.

As though his age imperfect might appeare,
His life was of Humanitie the Spheare.
(45–52)

Like the circle, the sphere is an emblem of perfection and here is suggestive of the macrocosm. Words less obvious in import provide the crucial, distinctive features of Jonson's vision of the good man, however. "Hee stood"—the simple declaration implies constancy and self-sufficiency in a world of strife, *mens immota manet*. How meaningful this seemingly passive or defensive posture may seem to a world with values other than our own can best be judged by recalling the climax of *Paradise Regained*:

To whom thus Jesus. Also it is written,
Tempt not the Lord thy God; he said and stood.
But Satan smitten with amazement fell.
(IV, 560–62)

Repeatedly in the seventeenth century the moral crisis centers on standing or falling, or, in another version, of fleeing from the doomed city: Whither shall I fly? What shall I do to be saved? "Hee stood." That this does not mean merely passive or defensive action can be shown by what follows: Morison performed "All Offices." This, the central word of the passage, derives from the Stoic word for obligations or duties, and to anyone in the century who could understand such things it would immediately call to mind "Tully's *Offices*," the very popular *De Officiis* by Cicero.

We may recall, "For he, that once is good, is ever great," in reviewing the best known stanza of the poem, which now contrasts falling with another image.

It is not growing like a tree
In bulke, doth make a man better bee;
Or standing long an Oake; three hundred yeare,
To fall a logge, at last, dry, bald, and seare:
A Lillie of a Day,
Is fairer farre, in May,
Although it fall, and die that night;
It was the Plant, and flowre of light.
In small proportions, we just beauties see:
And in short measures, life may perfect bee.
(65–74)

The "flowre of light," that supererogatory image, runs through numerous versions in the next three stanzas, culminating in "Two names of friendship, but one Starre: / Of hearts the union" (98–99). The old trope for friendship, one heart in bodies twain, is altered here into the stellar apotheosis that emerges in Jonson's handling of the light imagery radiating from the lily. But the stanza's formal properties also deserve attention. In the central two lines (the fifth and sixth) we see the "Lillie of a Day," and these two short lines represent the "small proportions," "just beauties," and "short measures" that Jonson speaks of in the last two lines. More than that, there is a circularity of rhyme scheme, with the rhyme sounds of the first and last couplets being the same. The circularity is complete in the shift from "better bee" (66) to "perfect bee" (74). The stanza almost seems an unspoken version of Jonson's compass conceit.

The elegiac reconciliation completes itself in such perfection, so that what remains is the celebration we have partly read on earlier pages.

Call, noble *Lucius*, then for Wine,
And let thy lookes with gladnesse shine:
Accept this garland, plant it on thy head,
And thinke, nay know, thy *Morison's* not dead.
Hee leap'd the present age,
Possest with holy rage,
To see that bright eternall Day:
Of which we *Priests*, and *Poëts* say
Such truths, as we expect for happy men,
And there he lives with memorie; and *Ben*

Johnson, who sung this of him, e're he went
Himselfe to rest,
Or taste a part of that full joy he meant
To have exprest,
In this bright *Asterisme*.

(75–89)

The imagistic development from the "flowre of light" must strike every reader, and so too the introduction of the poet's name. In fact, seventeenth-century elegies from Donne's *Anniversaries* to Dryden's *Eleonora* usually do not allow names, unless pastoral appellations, in the text of the poem, Jonson is not so "classical," but he does employ the oratorical device of "ethical proof" or personal testimony in that remarkable division of his name between two stanzas. Toward the end of the second of these stanzas, Jonson speaks of Falkland's "*Harry*," that is, Sir Henry. At the beginning of the joined stanzas there appears "noble *Lucius*," at the end "his *Harry*." What bridges the two is "*Ben / Johnson*"—the man who identifies himself as priest and poet saying "Such truths, as we expect for happy men" (82–83).

Without a forfeit of social relationships, the sense of personality runs throughout the poem, and indeed throughout Jonson's poetry. No shrinking violet, he extolls himself among the flowers of light. The conviction—and the imagistic resources enabling the reader to relive the conviction—of the good man and the good life provide the firm ethical center of Cavalier poetry. Loyalty to the King, and to "the Church and the laws," as Sir Philip Warwick put it, provided Cavalier poetry with the social basis for its integrity. In a nearer concentric of that sphere there lay ideals of integrity, constancy, self-sufficiency and, if need be, self-sacrifice. The Cavaliers could not make exclusive claim to such ideals, any more than could the Puritans to faith and service in a providential cause. In fact, Falkland later went off to the wars with divided mind and with what has seemed to many a deliberate, almost suicidal excess of bravery. Such men did not return from their Battles of Newbury: Falkland was not a friend whom one needed "to Perswade . . . to the Warres." Whether to stand, to fly to death in what one knew or hoped to be a good cause, or to brighten like the "flowre of light," it was important that one be oneself and be good. As Jonson's learned friend Selden put it concerning books,

> I would call *Books* onely those which have in them either of the two objects of Mans best part, *Verum* or *Bonum*, and to an instructing purpose handled.[7]

We recognize Jonson's tone in those words, and even more wholly in a distinction Selden draws at length.

> So Generous, so Ingenuous [sincere], so proportion'd to good, such Fosterers of Vertue, so Industrious, of such Mould are the *Few*: so Inhuman, so Blind, so Dissembling, so Vain, so justly Nothing, but what's Ill disposition, are the *Most*.[8]

And it was of Jonson, to whom the Cavaliers owed their rich ethical patrimony, that Selden could write: that is, of

> my beloved friend that singular Poet M. *Ben: Jonson*, whose speciall Worth in Literature, accurat Judgement, and Performance, known only to that *Few* which are truly able to know him, hath had from me, ever since I began to learn, an increasing admiration.[9]

Sir John Beaumont caught the accent in his poem on Jonson's death, saying of him,

> Since then, he made our Language pure and good,
> To teach us speake, but what we understood . . .
> And though He in a blinder age could change
> Faults to perfections, yet 'twas farre more strange
> To see (how ever times, and fashions frame)
> His wit and language still remaine the same
> In all mens mouths . . .
> Could I have spoken in his language too,
> I had not said so much, as now I doe,
> To whose cleare memory, I this tribute send
> Who Dead's my wonder, Living was my Friend.[1]

Jonson would have taken pride in that identification with himself and goodness and right language, just as he would have recognized the imagery and the friendship of Falkland's poem in *Jonsonus Virbius*.

> I then but aske fit Time to smooth my Layes,
> (And imitate in this the Pen I praise)
> Which by the Subjects Power embalm'd, may last,
> Whilst the Sun Light, the Earth doth shadows cast,
> And feather'd by those Wings fly among men,
> Farre as the Fame of Poetry and BEN.[2]

O Rare Ben Jonson! Neither the first nor the last English poet to think that his poetry was a moral as well as a beautiful art, he alone put the good man at the center of his poetry and made us believe that he was such, for all his follies. His imagination was fanciful enough to create new forms for

7. Selden, *Titles of Honor* (London, 1614), sig. a2^{r-v}.
8. *Ibid.*, sigs. a2^{v}–a3^{r}.
9. *Ibid.*, sig. d1^{r}; I have reversed roman and italic usage.
1. "To the Memory of him who can never be forgotten, Master Benjamin Jonson," ll. 41 ff. from the collection made by Falkland, *Jonsonus Virbius*; in *Ben Jonson*, ed. C. H. Herford, Percy and Evelyn Simpson, 11 vols. (Oxford, 1925–1952), XI, 438–39.
2. *An Eglogue*, ll. 285–90; *Ben Jonson*, XI, 437.

the stage or to present to him as he lay abed the Romans and Carthaginians doing battle about his great toe. His humanity was such that he grieved as a father for the loss of son and daughter and yet could adopt others to his Tribe. But with his learning it was his conviction of the centrality of the good life to poetry that won him the unparalleled respect of his contemporaries.

RAYMOND WILLIAMS

Pastoral and Counter-Pastoral†

* * *

For it is not only a question of formal or informal pastoral, which, as I have said, are quite easily recognised. There is a more difficult case, in some important poems which have been commonly read as describing an actual rural economy: an existing social base for the perpetual peace and innocence of the neo-pastoral dream. These are the poems of country houses, which Cowley had celebrated as a part of Nature, in *Solitude*:

Hail, old Patrician Trees, so great and good!
Hail, ye Plebeian under wood!
Where the Poetique Birds rejoyce,
And for their quiet Nests and plenteous Food,
Pay with their grateful voice.

Hail the poor Muses richest Manor Seat!
Ye Country Houses and Retreat,
Which all the happy Gods so Love,
That for you oft they quit their Bright and Great
Metropolis above.

Here the wood, the birds, the poets and the gods are seen literally (the figure is so complete) as the social structure—the natural order—of seventeenth-century England. It is interesting to compare Fanshawe, writing directly of the actual situation, when the gentry were being ordered back to their estates in 1630. What he sees is

one blest Isle:
Which in a sea of plenty swam
And Turtles sang on ev'ry Bough,
A safe retreat to all that came,
As ours is now.

That is the familiar image of a smiling country,

Yet we, as if some Foe were here,
Leave the despised fields to Clowns,
And come to save ourselves as 'twere
In walled Towns.

And so they must go back:

† From *The Country and the City* (New York: Chatto & Windus, 1973), pp. 26–34. Used by permission of The Random House Group Limited.

The sap and blood o' th' land, which fled
Into the Root, and choakt the Heart,
Are bid their quick'ning power to spread,
Through ev'ry part.

It is the image that Milton more generously developed, drawing on the associated image of culture as natural growth, in his appeal for a national education: 'communicating the natural heat of Government and Culture more distributively to all extreme parts, which now lie num and neglected'. Fanshawe, in his return, foresees the breeding of another Virgil (that reference was dominant), but his main appeal is more direct:

Nor let the Gentry grudge to go
Into those places whence they grow.

It is a way of seeing the crisis of seventeenth-century rural England, but of course it also reminds us that Cowley's 'bright and great metropolis' was not quite as often or as naturally as all that.

Yet at the center of the structure of feeling which is here in question—a relation between the country houses and a responsible civilization—are the poems to actual places and men: notably Ben Jonson's *Penshurst* and *To Sir Robert Wroth*, and Thomas Carew's *To Saxham*. These are not, in any simple sense, pastoral or neo-pastoral, but they use a particular version of country life as a way of expressing, in the form of a compliment to a house or its owner, certain social and moral values.

How blest art thou, canst love the countrey, Wroth,
Whether by choice, or fate, or both;
And, though so neere the citie, and the court,
Art tane with neither's vice, nor sport.

The life of a country gentleman is thus celebrated as an explicit contrast to the life of the court and the city. The figures of city lawyer, city capitalist, and courtier are brought in to point the moral.

In Wroth's rural economy, as the poem proceeds and as

the rout of rurall folke come thronging in

there is an emphasis on the absence of pride and greed and calculation. And then Jonson can turn, positively, to identify and localize the pastoral convention:

Such, and no other, was that age of old,
Which boasts t'have had the head of gold.

But is it really so, past the lattice of compliment? Has a neo-pastoral vision acquired a social base, in a Tudor country house? Some critics have taken it so, but the complexity of *To Penshurst* would in any case make us pause. For what is most remarkable about it, in any open reading, is its procedure of definition by negatives:

Thou art not, Penshurst, built to envious show
Of touch, or marble; nor canst boast a row
Of polish'd pillars, or a roofe of gold;
Thou hast no lantherne, wherof tales are told;
Or stayre, or courts; but stand'st an ancient pile,

And these grudg'd at, art reverenc'd the while . . .
. . . And though thy walls be of the countrey stone,
They are rear'd with no man's ruine, no mans grone,
There's none, that dwell about them, wish them downe . . .
. . . Now, Penshurst, they that will proportion thee
With other edifices, when they see
Those proud ambitious heaps, and nothing else,
May say, their lords have built, but thy lord dwells.

This declaration by negative and contrast, not now with city and court but with other country houses, is enough in itself to remind us that we can make no simple extension from Penshurst to a whole country civilization. The forces of pride, greed and calculation are evidently active among landowners as well as among city merchants and courtiers. What is being celebrated is then perhaps an idea of rural society, as against the pressures of a new age; and the embodiment of this idea is the house in which Jonson has been entertained.

This is where the comparison with Carew's *To Saxham* is particularly relevant. For there too, as it happens, thee is a definition by negatives, though now in a different house:

Thou hast no Porter at the door
T'examine, or keep back the poor;
Nor locks nor bolts; thy gates have been
Made only to let strangers in.

Or again, more subtly:

The cold and frozen air had sterv'd
Much poore, if not by thee preserv'd,
Whose prayers have made thy Table blest
With plenty, far above the rest.

The island of Charity is the house where the poet himself eats; but that it is an island, in an otherwise harsh economy, is the whole point of the successive compliments.

We need not refuse Jonson and Carew the courtesy of their lucky exceptions; their Penshurst and Saxham 'rear'd', unlike others, 'with no man's ruine, no mans grone'; with none, 'that dwell about them', wishing them 'downe'. There were, we need not doubt, such houses and such men, but they were at best the gentle exercise of a power that was elsewhere, on their own evidence, mean and brutal. The morality is not, when we look into it, the fruit of the economy; it is a local stand and standard against it.

It is of course clear that in each of the poems, though more strongly and convincingly in Jonson, the social order is seen as part of a wider order: what is now sometimes called a natural order, with metaphysical sanctions. Certainly nothing is more remarkable than the stress on the providence of Nature, but this, we must see on reflection, is double-edged. What kind of wit is it exactly—for it must be wit; the most ardent traditionalists will hardly claim it for observation—which has the birds and other creatures offering themselves to be eaten? The estate of Penshurst, as Jonson sees it:

To crowne thy open table, doth provide
The purpled pheasant with the speckled side:

The painted partrich lyes in every field
And, for thy messe, is willing to be kill'd.

Carew extends this same hyperbole:

The Pheasant, Partridge, and the Lark
Flew to my house, as to the Ark.
The willing Oxe, of himselfe came
Home to the slaughter, with the Lamb,
And every beast did thither bring
Himselfe to be an offering.
The scalie herd, more pleasure took
Bath'd in the dish than in the brook.

In fact the wit depends, in such passages, on a shared and conscious point of view towards nature. The awareness of hyperbole is there, is indeed what is conventional in just this literary convention, and is controlled and ratified, in any wider view, by a common consciousness. At one level this is a willing and happy ethic of consuming, made evident by the organization of the poems around the centrality of the dining-table. Yet the possible grossness of this, as in Carew (a willing largeness of hyperbole, as in so many Cavalier poems, as the awareness of an alternative point of view makes simple statement impossible), is modified in Jonson by a certain pathos, a conscious realization of his situation:

And I not faine to sit (as some, this day,
At great men's tables) and yet dine away.
Here no man tells my cups; nor, standing by,
A waiter, doth my gluttony envy:
But gives me what I call, and lets me eate.

It is difficult not to feel the relief of that. Indeed there is more than a hint, in the whole tone of this hospitable eating and drinking, of that easy, insatiable exploitation of the land and its creatures—a prolonged delight in an organized and corporative production and consumption—which is the basis of many early phases of intensive agriculture: the land is rich, and will be made to provide. But it is then more difficult to talk, in a simple way, of a 'natural order', as if this was man in concert with nature. On the contrary: this natural order is simply and decisively on its way to table.

Of course, in both Jonson and Carew, though again more convincingly in Jonson, this view of the providence of nature is linked to a human sharing: all are welcome, even the poor, to be fed at this board. And it is this stress, more than any other, which has supported the view of a responsible civilization, in which men care for each other directly and personally, rather than through the abstractions of a more complicated and more commercial society. This, we are told, is the natural order of responsibility and neighborliness and charity: words we do not now clearly understand, since Old England fell.

Of course one sees what is meant, and as a first approximation, a simple impulse, it is kindly. But the Christian tradition of charity is at just this point weak. For it is a charity of consumption only, as Rosa Luxemburg first pointed out:

> The Roman proletarians did not live by working, but from the alms which the government doled out. So the demands of the Christians

> for collective property did not relate to the means of production, but the means of consumption.

And then, as Adrian Cunningham has argued, this version of charity—of loving relations between men expressed as a community of consumption, with the Christian board and breaking of bread as its natural images, and the feast as its social consummation—was prolonged into periods and societies in which it became peripheral or even damaging. A charity of production—of loving relations between men actually working and producing what is ultimately, in whatever proportions, to be shared—was neglected, not seen, and at times suppressed, by this habitual reference to a charity of consumption, an eating and drinking communion, which when applied to ordinary working societies was inevitably a mystification. All uncharity at work, it was readily assumed, could be redeemed by the charity of the consequent feast. In the complex of feeling and reference derived from this tradition, it matters very much, moreover, that the name of the god and the name of the master are significantly single—our Lord.

Any mystification, however, requires effort. The world of Penshurst or of Saxham can be seen as a moral economy only by conscious selection and emphasis. And this is just what we get: not only in the critical reading I have referred to, but in Jonson's and Carew's actual poems. There were of course social reasons for that way of seeing: the identification of the writers, as guests, with the social position of their hosts, consuming what other men had produced. But a traditional image, already becoming complicated, was an indispensable poetic support. It is not only the Golden Age, as in Jonson to Sir Robert Wroth, though Penshurst, in its first positive description, is seen through classical literature: the woods of Kent contain Dryads and Pan and Bacchus, and the providing deities of the charity are Penates. More deeply, however, in a conventional association of Christian and classical myth, the provident land is seen as Eden. This country in which all things come naturally to man, for his use and enjoyment and without his effort, is that Paradise:

> The early cherry, with the later plum,
> Fig, grape and quince, each in his time doth come;
> The blushing apricot, and woolly peach
> Hang on thy walls, that every child may reach.

Except that it is not seen as Paradise; it is seen as Penshurst, a natural order arranged by a proprietary lord and lady. The manipulation is evident when we remember Marvell's somewhat similar lines in *The Garden*:

> The Nectaren, and curious Peach
> Into my hands themselves do reach;
> Stumbling on Melons, as I pass,
> Insnar'd with flowers, I fall on grass.

Here the enjoyment of what seems a natural bounty, a feeling of paradise in the garden, is exposed to another kind of wit: the easy consumption goes before the fall. And we can then remember that the whole result of the fall from paradise was that instead of picking easily from an all-providing nature, man had to earn his bread in the sweat of his brow; that he incurred, as a common fate, the curse of labor. What is really happening, in Jonson's and Carew's celebrations of a rural order, is an extraction of just this curse, by the power of art: a magical recreation of what can be seen as a natural bounty and then a willing charity: both serving to ratify and bless the country landowner, or, by a characteristic reification, his house. Yet this magical extraction of the curse of labor is in fact achieved by a simple extraction of the existence of laborers. The actual men and women who rear the animals and drive them to the house and kill them and prepare them for meat; who trap the pheasants and partridges and catch the fish; who plant and manure and prune and harvest the fruit trees: these are not present; their work is all done for them by a natural order. When they do at last appear, it is merely as the 'rout of rurall folke' or, more simply, as 'much poore', and what we are then shown is the charity and lack of condescension with which they are given what, now and somehow, not they but the natural order has given for food, into the lord's hands. It is this condition, this set of relationships, that is finally ratified by the consummation of the feast. It is worth setting briefly alongside this a later description of a country feast, by one of the laborers: Stephen Duck, in the late 1720s:

A Table plentifully spread we find,
And jugs of huming Ale to cheer the Mind,
Which he, too gen'rous, pushes round so fast,
We think no Toils to come, nor mind the past.
But the next Morning soon reveals the Cheat,
When the same Toils we must again repeat;
To the same Barns must back again return,
To labour there for Room for next Year's Corn.

It is this connection, between the feast and work, that the earlier images significantly obscure, taking the passing moment in which anyone might forget labor and acquiesce in 'the Cheat', and making it 'natural' and permanent. It is this way of seeing that really counts. Jonson looks out over the fields of Penshurst and sees, not work, but a land yielding of itself. Carew, characteristically, does not even look:

Though frost, and snow, lock'd from mine eyes
That beauty which without door lyes . . .
. . . Yet (Saxham) thou within thy gate
Art of thy selfe so delicate,
So full of native sweets, that bless
Thy roof with inward happiness;
As neither from, nor to thy store,
Winter takes ought, or Spring adds more.

So that here not only work, but even the turning produce of the seasons, is suppressed or obscured in the complimentary mystification: an innate bounty: 'native sweets'. To call this a natural order is then an abuse of language. It is what the poems are: not country life but social compliment; the familiar hyperboles of the aristocracy and its attendants.

The social order within which Jonson's and Carew's poems took conventional shape was in fact directly described, in another kind of country poem, of which Herrick's *The Hock-Cart* (1648) is a good example. Here the fact of labor is acknowledged:

Come Sons of Summer, by whose toile
We are the Lords of Wine and Oile:
By whose tough labours, and rough hands,
We rip up first, then reap our lands.
Crown'd with the eares of corne, now come,
And to the Pipe, sing Harvest home.

But this is that special kind of work-song, addressed to the work of others. When the harvest has been brought home, the poem continues:

Come forth, my Lord, and see the Cart.

This lord is (in the poem's address) the 'Right Honourable Lord Mildmay, Earle of Westmorland', and Herrick places himself between the lord and the laborers to make explicit (what in Jonson and Carew had been implicit and mystified) the governing social relations. The laborers must drink to the Lord's health, and then remember all to go back to work, like the animals:

Ye must revoke
The patient Oxe unto the Yoke
And all goe back unto the plough
And Harrow (though they're hang'd up now)
And, you must know, your Lord's word's true,
Feed him ye must, whose food fills you.
And that this pleasure is like raine
Not sent ye for to drowne your paine
But for to make it spring againe.

It is crude in feeling, this early and jollying kind of man-management, which uses the metaphors of rain and spring to see even the drink as a way of getting more labor (and more pain). But what is there on the surface—

Feed him ye must, whose food fills you

—is the aching paradox which is subsumed in the earlier images of natural bounty. It is perhaps not surprising that *The Hock-Cart* is less often quoted, as an example of a natural and moral economy, than *Penshurst* or *To Saxham*. Yet all that is in question is the degree of consciousness of real processes. What Herrick embarrassingly intones is what Jonson and Carew mediate. It is a social order, and a consequent way of seeing, which we are not now likely to forget.

ANN BAYNES COIRO

Writing in Service: Sexual Politics and Class Position in the Poetry of Aemilia Lanyer and Ben Jonson†

The growing and increasingly central interest in writings by sixteenth- and seventeenth-century women is beginning to have some material effects on

† From *Criticism* 35:3 (1993): 357–76. Reprinted with the permission of Wayne State University Press. The author's notes have been abridged.

the literary profession. In the fifth edition of *The Norton Anthology of English Literature* (published in 1986), for example, a literature teacher could find a couple of poems by Lady Mary Wroth, one psalm by the Countess of Pembroke, and two poems by Queen Elizabeth. In the just-published sixth edition (1993), the number of texts by women has significantly increased, both in number and variety. One notable change is the inclusion of Aemilia Lanyer as a major author, a figure until very recently entirely absent from literary history, much less the canon.

The Norton Anthology is at once a commercially sensitive gauge of what will sell to changing populations of teachers and students and also a powerful shaping tool of the literary canon. Nevertheless, it will take at least a generation for the profession of literary studies to internalize these newly visible texts into our sense of literary history, for the only way they can be internalized is through a series of subtle and radical shifts in our assumptions about Renaissance and seventeenth-century literature and culture. An overriding assumption which must be questioned, for example, is our still-lingering sense of Renaissance writing as somehow aristocratic. One thing the archaeology of early modern women's writing can show us is the pattern of our professional attention. Twenty years ago, even ten years ago, the only Renaissance woman writer an English professor was likely to know anything at all about was Mary Sidney, Countess of Pembroke, and then only because of her editorial shepherding into print of her brother's *Arcadia*. First Elizabeth and then Lady Mary Sidney Wroth joined the Countess of Pembroke in our readings, forming a sort of vestibule to our construction of the now-assembling texts of women's writing, a vestibule which resembles in its names and its purpose the prestigious dedicatory collection at the front of a newly published Renaissance text.

In these initial stages of discovery we have also tended to group women writers together simply as women, and we have then attended to their shared difficulties of speaking in a male-dominated discourse. Without exception, current studies devoted to early modern women writers have emphasized an idealized sisterhood among them, even though these studies discuss highly varied configurations of women across several generations and even across continents. It would ultimately be a disservice to women writers and a distortion of their real power, however, to segregate them permanently as a subset of Renaissance literature and to romanticize their shared gender into a politically and intellectually univocal force. The mantra "race-class-gender" is not a unified chant, but a braided and abrading puzzle.

In an attempt to acknowledge contingencies of gender and class and, to some extent, even of race, I will focus on the politics of publication engaged in by two members of the service entourage surrounding powerful, wealthy women—a man, Ben Jonson, and a woman, Aemilia Lanyer, writing at the same time and to many of the same people. My concern is also, at least implicitly, with the politics of current literary criticism in Renaissance studies and feminist criticism in particular, politics which have left largely unchallenged the orthodoxies of traditional literary history so that women writers remain the lacy, decorative frill on the edge of a fabric that has not changed.

One of the central questions feminist criticism has asked of early modern women's writing is how a woman enters the psychomachia of writing performance. In order to begin to understand that question, however, it is important to acknowledge that it is virtually impossible to separate out gender as a category unrelated to class position. The crisscrossing of gender and class is particularly intricate and codependent in the Renaissance when writing venues themselves carry class and gender stigmas.[1] Manuscript was seen as a more private, classbound form of publication, for example, and writers like Philip Sidney or John Donne were extremely leery of appearing in print for fear of seeming common and thereby losing the insider positions they were vying for by seeming carelessly clever. The public, commodified circulation of print, on the other hand, was seen by those with court ambitions as a cheapening, chancy, even dangerous business. Spenser tried it in *The Faerie Queene* with a notable lack of success. Increasingly during this period, writing venues began to acquire gendered associations as well. As the dominance of print culture expanded decade after decade from Elizabeth's reign up through the civil war, manuscript became, in practice, a feminine mode of writing, suspect but carefully surveilled, containable and decorous; print, on the other hand, was figured as a more daring, aggressive, masculine mode. Women like the Countess of Pembroke wrote freely and at the highest level of accomplishment for class-controlled manuscript circulation, but would appear in print only as the ministering handmaiden for the body of a dead brother's works. By the middle of the seventeenth century, the axes of manuscript/aristocratic/feminine, on the one hand, and print/parliament/masculine, on the other, are strikingly visible in the print battles of the civil war; John Milton's late and agonized decision to begin to print his writing, for example, is also a decision to become somehow a man at last.[2]

In the single voices of two individual writers of the late Renaissance, Aemilia Lanyer and Ben Jonson, we may hear the complicated, self-conscious and subconscious constructing dialectic of gender and class, a dialectic which can illuminate the field of writing at the moment when women began to advance inexorably upon it. In many significant ways, Lanyer and Jonson have more in common with each other than does Lanyer with other important women writers of her generation. Mary Sidney, Countess of Pembroke and Lady Mary Sidney Wroth, for example, defined themselves not only as women, but also and very centrally as members of a powerful aristocratic family. They were so defined by their culture, and their decisions about what to circulate among their group in manuscript and when to release Sidney manuscripts into the print market were defined as much by their social status as by their gender.

Wroth, for example, was a visible figure, invested with complex significance. We need only read Jonson's epigram "To Mary Lady Wroth" where he acknowledges that we "know [her] to be a Sydney, though un-named"

1. For the intersections of gender and class in publication see Wendy Wall, "Disclosures in Print: The 'Violent Enlargement' of the Renaissance Voyeuristic Text," *SEL* 29 (1989): 35–59; and see my "Milton and class identity: the publication of *Areopagitica* and the 1645 *Poems*," *JMRS* 22 (1992): 161–89. See also J. W. Saunders's important article, "The Stigma of Print: A Note on the Social Bases of Tudor Poetry," *Essays in Criticism* 1 (1951): 139–64, and Arthur F. Marotti's *John Donne, Coterie Poet* (Madison: University of Wisconsin Press, 1986) and "Poetry, Patronage, and Print," *YES* 19 (1991): 69–82. On the freedom women could exercise in the manuscript forum, see Margaret Ezell, *The Patriarch's Wife: Literary Evidence and the History of the Family* (Chapel Hill: University of North Carolina Press, 1987).
2. On the cultural and psychosexual conflicts surrounding Milton's emergence into print, see Coiro, "Milton and class identity."

(Epigrammes, CIII); we need only remember her living presence in the landscape of "Penshurst," one of the great lord's "own" children, to realize that a feminist analysis of Wroth and of poetry addressed to Wroth must take into account not only concepts now shaping our sense of early modern women such as "dismemberment" or "voyeurism" or "silencing" but also the real power of this and other individual women as part of a social network.[3] In Jonson's representation of Wroth, she rises above the name of wife, her birth heritage so luminous in her writing that she reclaims her Sidney name. The public appearance of Wroth's *Urania* (a massive pastoral romance modeled to some extent on her uncle's *Arcadia* and incredibly detailed in its allusions to court scandals, many of them her own) was indeed a breach of social and sexual decorum. By printing her own words, Wroth disturbed the system where someone like Ben Jonson had been assigned the job of writing about someone like her in carefully muffled metaphoric terms. Nevertheless, it was a system set up to have Lady Mary Sidney Wroth within it.

For any woman writer, clearly, the risks of leaving the private world of manuscript circulation and entering the print market were high. For women who were not aristocratic, however, women who did not carry the fragile carapace of privilege and tradition, the entry into a print forum required a different series of negotiations. With whom could and did women who were not Sidneys align themselves in devising a print appearance? To what extent would a woman be breaking company with other women by publishing?

Two closely contemporary print appearances—Ben Jonson's *The Forrest*, published as one part of his 1616 *Workes*, and Aemilia Lanyer's *Salve Deus Rex Judaeorum*, published in 1611—present a near perfect test case for enriching our sense of writing performance in a system where, we must now in these latter days again acknowledge, women, as well as men, were authors. When we place Lanyer next to Jonson we learn a great deal about each of them as individual writers. We also learn more about concepts of authorship in the late Renaissance, more about the strains (both sexual and social) which, within three decades, would change English society, and more about the relationship of genre to social crisis. In other words, when Lanyer is fully in the canon, the canon will change at a number of perhaps unexpected pressure points.

Before we can think with some objectivity we must, however, look our own critical bogeys in the face. Our sense of Renaissance women, particularly of non-aristocratic Renaissance women, has been as deeply and romantically shaped by Virginia Woolf as our sense of Jacobite Scotland has been shaped by Sir Walter Scott.[4] Virginia Woolf's powerful parable in *A Room of One's Own* of Shakespeare's sister Judith has affected generations of readers, stirring the fundamental beginnings of feminist scholarship and women's studies.[5] In Woolf's telling, Shakespeare was lucky

3. These and all further references to Jonson's poetry will be from *The Complete Poetry*, ed. William B. Hunter, Jr. (New York: Norton, 1963).
4. Gilbert and Gubar's influential study, *The Madwoman in the Attic: The Woman Writer and the Nineteenth-Century Literary Imagination* (New Haven: Yale University Press, 1979), uses Woolf's various brief comments on Milton and her invented character Judith Shakespeare to construct important parts of their argument about the suppression of women in the canon. * * *
5. Woolf's parable has sufficient popular currency to be invoked in the name of a successful rock group, "Shakespeare's Sister."

enough to have a modest but sufficient education and to be able, after a charmingly rakish youth, to set off to London "where he got work in the theatre, became a successful actor, and lived at the hub of the universe, meeting everybody, knowing everybody, practicing his art on the boards, exercising his wits in the streets and even getting access to the palace of the queen."[6]

But Woolf imagines that Shakespeare had a gifted sister who remained at home, uneducated, while her parents tried to force her into a life of conventional wifehood. Woolf imagines her rebelling and fleeing to London, fleeing to the same stage door where her brother had first found his way, but there "men laughed in her face" at her wish to become an actress and the manager "hinted—you can imagine what. . . . At last, for she was very young" and because she reminded him of Shakespeare, she was taken as a mistress by the manager and became pregnant. "Who shall measure the heat and violence of the poet's heart when caught and tangled in a woman's body?"—she killed herself and was buried like a witch at the crossroads (50).

Woolf is a powerful and imaginative story-teller and her influence on feminist readings of the Renaissance has been profound, both on our sense of the wounded desperation of early modern women writers and on our sense of the damaging domination and misogyny of canonical male writers like Milton. Yet there is something worrisome about Woolf's pathetically charming and seemingly sympathetic little story, for it romanticizes, and thereby eradicates, the possibility of Shakespeare's sister's writing voice. After her story of fragile genius driven mad and destroyed by rigid sexual mores, Woolf concludes "That, more or less, is how the story would run, I think, if a woman in Shakespeare's day had had Shakespeare's genius. . . . But it is unthinkable that any woman in Shakespeare's day should have had Shakespeare's genius. For genius like Shakespeare's is not born among labouring, uneducated, servile people. It was not born in England among the Saxons and the Britons. It is not born today among the working classes. How, then, could it have been born among women?" (50).

There is now another story to be told, however, a story strikingly like Woolf's in some details but powerfully different in its conclusions. Aemilia Lanyer is one of the few early modern women writers whose work was available on the library shelf as early as the 1970s. Even as I write this in the spring of 1993 it is still not possible to find Lanyer published free-standing under her own name, however. Until a modern edition of Lanyer appears later this year, Lanyer will be found shadowed under the name of Shakespeare. In 1978 A. L. Rowse, a famously crotchety Shakespeare scholar, published a theory he had been developing for a decade, asserting that Lanyer is the Dark Lady of the sonnets. Rowse reprinted Lanyer's 1611 book, *Salve Deus Rex Judaeorum*, which he regarded as a nearly negligible piece of writing, as another bit of evidence in the endlessly fascinating hunt for Shakespeare's biography.[7] No one has since fully

6. Virginia Woolf, *A Room of One's Own* (San Diego: Harcourt Brace Jovanovich, 1929), 29. Further parenthetical references will be to this edition.
7. *The Poems of Shakespeare's Dark Lady: "Salve Deus Rex Judaeorum"* by Emilia Lanier, Introduction by A. L. Rowse (London: Jonathan Cape, 1978). Rowse assesses Lanyer's poetry in a revealingly relative frame: "What is . . . surprising is that she is a fair poet, far superior to the Queen, for example, who wrote antiquated doggerel. In fact, except for Sidney's sister, the Countess of Pembroke, Emilia is the best woman poet of the age. This is not saying much. . . . Her defect indeed

accepted Rowse's theory about Lanyer's relationship with Shakespeare, but neither is it implausible. Certainly, given the connections Rowse traces, Shakespeare would have known her. What follows, framed by a pronounced dose of irony in giving Shakespeare once again the possessive place, is the counter-story of Shakespeare's maybe mistress, Aemilia.

Lanyer was the daughter of an Italian musician, Baptista Bassani, who had come to England in the mid-sixteenth century to serve as paid amusement and polish in the rather rough-around-the-edges Tudor court and had married an Englishwoman named Margaret Johnson. It is at this point in the early modern period still fairly anachronistic to speak of a middle or working class, but clearly the Bassani family inhabited the same social sphere as Shakespeare or Ben Jonson—talented, educated people using their wits to carve out a successful life in a changing society. Aemilia Lanyer's one surviving work, *Salve Deus Rex Judaeorum*, is stridently Christian in its argument, constructing the Old Testament as a time when women might indeed bear some of the guilt for human frailty, but celebrating Christ's coming as the moment when women completely redeemed themselves from the Fall, by nurturing Christ and defending him, while men persecuted and killed one of their own in cowardly jealousy and hatred. In considering Lanyer's class position, gender position, and her startlingly feminist poem, it is also critically important to note that Aemilia Lanyer is a second-generation Jew, one of the very few people of Jewish heritage in England at this time. (In this, too, Lanyer's real story interlaces with Woolf's fantasy in elaborate and fascinating counterpoint.)

Lanyer became the mistress of the powerful Lord Hunsdon, Elizabeth's Lord Chamberlain and patron of Shakespeare's acting company. When she became pregnant by Hunsdon, however, she was married off to another musician, Alfonso Lanyer, who was a Catholic. It is really impossible to emphasize strongly enough how marginal, how unusual her position was in Renaissance England—as a Jew, converted or not, as an Italian, as the wife of a Catholic, as a woman artist making a living as a fringe member of the court. Lanyer herself makes clear that Elizabeth read her poetry and was generous in her patronage, but Alfonso Lanyer lost all her money in a series of foolish investments. By the time Aemilia Lanyer wrote *Salve Deus Rex Judaeorum* Elizabeth had been dead for almost a decade, there was a new sovereign who was much less generous to poets, and Aemilia Lanyer was forty and probably no longer in the position to sell her beauty for favors (as contemporary gossip claims she had done earlier).[8]

Lanyer serves as a strikingly de-romanticizing counter-narrative to Woolf's sad story of Shakespeare's sister. She met everyone, knew everyone, practiced her art, exercised her wit, and even got access to the palace of the queen. She got pregnant, lost everything, but she didn't kill herself, she self-consciously identified herself with the laboring classes, and she

is that she was too facile and fluent: she wrote too much, she padded out what she had to say—it would have been much more effective if shorter. (One remembers what Forman said about her talking too much, she 'can hardly keep a secret.')" (17).

8. Simon Forman records his relationship with Lanyer in his diary. She came to him, he said, to have her fortune cast to see "whether she should be a lady or no." Thereafter Lanyer and Forman began, according to Forman, some kind of a sexual relationship in which she agreed "for lucre's sake to be a good fellow." The actual details of Forman's telling, however, describe a woman who was the aggressor and controller of whatever relationship they had together (quotations from Forman taken from Rowse, 12).

wrote. And she is far from the only example of what we can tentatively call middle-class women writing at this time. *A Room of One's Own* has been a critical text in opening a still widening wedge for women in the academy, both as writers and readers. Lanyer's complex counter-story is now visible to us in part because of Woolf's elegant challenge. But *A Room of One's Own* embodies, too, the conservative class prejudices embedded in our profession. Even as it asks that we turn the house of writing open, it presumes still a serving class ministering and silent somewhere in that house. We need to question continually the story literary history has been telling us. The call to question was, after all, Woolf's manifesto. And Aemilia Lanyer's writing will call into question many old assumptions.

Lanyer's book, *Salve Deus Rex Judaeorum*, is one interwoven text constructed of, first, up to ten prefatory pieces to different aristocratic women. She had some eliminated and others rearranged in at least four separate printings in order to tailor them for presentation to different patrons; the chief focus of her hopes, however, seems to have been Margaret Clifford and her daughter Anne, who had retreated to the country as the result of a dispute with the Clifford men about Anne's right to inherit property. The next section of the book is an aggressively feminist preface, "To the Vertuous Reader"; and then the body of the poem retells the story of the fall and of Christ's passion in a way that makes women the redemptive figures in the New Testament dispensation and men the betrayers of Christ. *Salve Deus Rex Judaeorum* ends with the first country-house poem published in England, "The Description of Cooke-ham." Lanyer's poem centers on the grounds of Cooke-ham where three women—Margaret Clifford, Countess of Cumberland, Anne Clifford, Countess of Dorset and later to be Countess of Pembroke and Montgomery, and Aemilia Lanyer—wander in Christian contemplation. It is a gorgeous Eden, walled and safe from a fallen world. One of the striking things about this country-house poem is that Cooke-ham was not the ancient family seat of the Clifford family, but a temporary refuge lent or rented to these women by the king while they persisted in their stubborn fight to be allowed, as women, to inherit land, an outrageous claim.[9] For reasons that are not made clear in the poem, the Clifford women have left Cooke-ham; there are other estates for them. But for Lanyer the exclusion from paradise seems final. They have left her behind and asked her to write a poem in memory of their time there.

The two framing thirds of *Salve Deus*, the long section of poems addressed to women of rank and virtue and the concluding country-house poem, may be closely and fruitfully paired with Ben Jonson's *The Forrest*, for Jonson's book is similarly a collection of deftly panegyric poems to powerful aristocrats within which is positioned his extremely famous country-house poem, "To Penshurst." The fifteen odds and ends of lyric and epideictic poetry in *The Forrest* are gathered around the motivating factor of praise for the Sidney family. Several of these poems are addressed to women; indeed, one long poem, "To the World A Farewell for a Gentlewoman, Virtuous and Noble," is spoken in the voice of a noblewoman who renounces courtly pleasures and retreats, like the Clifford women, to the country. Jonson's country-house poem, "To Penshurst," which

9. See Barbara Lewalski, "Re-writing Patriarchy and Patronage: Margaret Clifford, Anne Clifford, and Aemilia Lanyer," *YES* 21 (1991): 87–106.

describes the ancestral home of the Sidney family in Kent, is the book's masterpiece.

The country-house poem is a genre which has attracted a great deal of critical attention, especially in recent years, and "To Penshurst" is the set-piece of this very impressive critical dialogue among Marxist, formalist, and new historicist critics. "To Penshurst" is also a bedrock of the English canon. Any conventionally trained college English major is at least glancingly familiar with the subtle and superb craftsmanship of Jonson's artful compliment that begins:

> Thou art not, Penshurst, built to envious show,
> Of touch, or marble; nor canst boast a row
> Of polish'd pillars, or a roofe of gold:
> Thou hast no lantherne, whereof tales are told;
> Or stayre, or courts; but stand'st an ancient pile,
> And these grudg'd at, art reverenc'd the while.

It is the classic example of a poem enshrined in and defining of literary history, the founding instance of an important genre in English. But in fact, it is not the first country-house poem; Lanyer's, published five years earlier, is.

The two collections, then, invite comparison: both heavy with praise of patrons, some the same people, both grounded by the two earliest country-house poems in English, both structured around the role of the poet speaking. One striking difference between the two is Lanyer's long central section on the fall of Eve and on Christ's passion and the redemption of women. The central narrative is particularly fascinating because of its pre-Miltonic subversion of the story of Christian history, and also in light of Lanyer's heritage as a Jew. *Salve Deus Rex Judaeorum* should become a text crucial in our reconfiguration of literary history not only in its conflicted narrative of gender and class but also and connectedly in its narrative of gender and race. In Lanyer's poem, it is not Jews who kill Christ, but men; at the same time, any real possibility of freedom and dignity for women begins with Christ's coming. For the purposes of comparing Lanyer and Jonson, I will emphasize the social and poetic negotiations of the panegyric poems of *Salve Deus Rex Judaeorum* and *The Forrest*, but Lanyer's bold, passionate biblical narrative lies at the vibrant center of her text, complicating her praises and sharply highlighting the containments of Jonson's poetry and his unease with religious themes. When we read Jonson's *Forrest*, we read one of the most handsome, tactful and, at the same time, melancholy works of social poetry in the Renaissance. When we read Lanyer's triptych of praise, passion, and country-house poem we read one of the most audacious, deliberate and intensely personal social critiques to be published in the early seventeenth century.

Salve Deus Rex Judaeorum is a radical poem—a poem in which Christ comes for the poor, the ignorant, those at the bottom of the English social structure, not just for the rich and well-born. It is, as Barbara Lewalski and other critics have argued, an affirmation of good women, but it is very explicitly not an affirmation of all women. A crucial part of her social radicalism is that Lanyer is writing as a woman writer to aristocratic women; her writing is as edgy, self-fashioning, and socially self-conscious as Jonson's ever is. We cannot read her right until we read her sophisticated irony about her position in a world where she is dependent on a matriarchy she often resents.

In the prefatory poems and in the closing country-house poem, Lanyer alludes to a life of cultured servitude, amusing companion in the households of Countesses—something of a Renaissance Lily Bart. To place her in the same position with the Countess of Pembroke, or Lady Mary Wroth, or Lucy, Countess of Bedford simply because she is a woman is a flattening distortion of her marginal, precarious position. Both Lanyer and Jonson lived dependent on these women and, to a large extent, their writing personalities were generated by the resentments and needs that these service relationships created. It is now a critical commonplace to discuss Ben Jonson's misogyny, his need to lash out at writing women as threats to his masculinity. Placing Jonson's anger next to Lanyer's, however, should destabilize any simple sense of gender wars.

The best-known passage in *Salve Deus Rex Judaeorum* is its feminist attack on men in Lanyer's address "To the Vertuous Reader": "evill disposed men, who forgetting they were borne of women, nourished of women, and that if it were not by the meanes of women, they would be quite extinguised out of the world, and a finall ende of them all, doe like Vipers deface the wombes wherein they were bred, onely to give way and utterance to their want of discretion and goodnesse" (77). But we should not excise the passage on men out from the long passage of which it is only a small part. It seems relatively easy for Lanyer to dismiss men, viperous Pilates that they are, but the real danger to Lanyer's project is women. She is praising women in her "little booke" because she says women have been defamed as defamers of women: "And this have I done, to make knowne to the world, that all women deserve not to be blamed though some forgetting they are women themselves, and in danger to be condemned by the wordes of their own mouthes, fall into so great an errour, as to speak unadvisedly against the rest of their sexe." Lanyer herself, of course, has been the object of ill-speaking, a woman who would, according to surviving gossip, trade a good time for a living. It may seem that she here utterly refutes my argument about her ironic, sometimes bitter tone toward women of the class above her, the class she served. Yet she is acknowledging exactly the situation to which I point. There is tense anger and danger in women's voices and women's textual interpretations, clearly. The whole point of her project in the opening of *Salve Deus Rex Judaeorum* is to shore up for herself some kind of protection from attack by women. She begs her readers to "increase the least sparke of virtue where they will finde it, by their favorable and best interpretations, [rather] than quench it by wrong constructions" (78).

Yet, in a move familiar to us from Jonson and other Renaissance writers when introducing particularly dangerous texts, Lanyer invites the very interpretations and the very danger she openly disclaims. Given our warning about seeking virtue, what kind of construction can we put on the prefatory poems? If we begin with the lead poem, "To the Queen's most excellent Majestie," it is hard to see how not to find a wrong construction.[1] Queen Anne is called on to "grace" this volume. She can do this not

1. For the first sustained analysis of the importance of Anne of Denmark and her personal court in English politics and culture, see Leeds Barroll's important forthcoming study.

because she is necessarily virtuous, but because she has "rifled nature of her store," "dispossest" all the goddesses of their "richest gifts":

> The Muses doe attend upon your Throne,
> With all the Artists at your becke and call. (41)

Anne is invited to look into this mirror and see not herself, as Elizabeth was asked to see herself in the mirror of *The Faerie Queene*, but another Majestie:

> He that all Nations of the world controld,
> Yet tooke our flesh in base and meanest berth:
> Whose daies were spent in poverty and sorrow,
> And yet all Kings their wealth of him do borrow.
> For he is Crowne and Crowner of all Kings,
> The hopeful haven of the meaner sort. (42)

The Lanyer persona, in sharp contrast, has nothing in Anne's world—her "wealth within his Region stands. . . . Yea in his Kingdome onely rests my lands/ Of honour" (43).

Anne is invited to a feast given by a great Lady, richly dressed by Lanyer with Honour, Eve herself. There is clearly a price to be paid for this feast, however. The queen is being subjected throughout the poem to a sustained critique for failing to provide the patronage to Lanyer that Elizabeth had done. Lanyer asks explicitly and repeatedly for money in this opening poem. And she plays the humility topos in gendered terms—I'm just a woman, just ignorant, please elevate my mind. The juxtaposition of the request "in a Woman all defects excuse," however, and the addressee, "peerlesse Princesse," absolutely levels either Lanyer's claim to find women defective or the queen's right to claim superiority. Lanyer's request for help from her "superiors" is as two-edged as Milton's Eve's was to be; indeed, and significantly it is couched in the same terms as Eve's censored request for knowledge from Adam about the heavens in Book 8 of *Paradise Lost*:

> For even as they that doe behold the Starres,
> Not with the eie of Learning, but of Sight,
> To find their motions, want of knowledge barres
> Although they see them in their brightest light:
> So, though I see the glory of her State,
> Its she that must instruct and elevate. (45)

In Lanyer's complicated text, there are two kinds of elevation—spiritual and worldly. The women in the prefatory company of women shift in and out of the two spheres, accompanied by dizzying switches of tone. What she insists virtuous ladies see throughout *Salve Deus Rex Judaeorum* is a leveling Christ. "Glory can end what Grace in you begun," she warns; only of "heavenly riches make your greatest horde."

We should not forget, however, that Lanyer has a specific suggestion about where these rich ladies might get rid of some of their excess money. For the irony of the prefatory poems is at least triple: criticism of the aristocratic ladies studded with inestimable wealth, promotion of a leveling Christian radicalism, and, at the same time, a wonderful degree of self-promotion. To Lady Margaret Clifford, her chief patron in times past, she begins "Right Honourable and Excellent Lady, I may say with St. Peter, 'Silver nor gold have I none, but such as I have, that give I you.'" To Lady Susan Bertie, in whose household she served as a young woman, she ends with a stinging claim for the freedom of her poem:

> And since no former gaine hath made me write,
> Nor my desertlesse service could have wonne,
> Onely your noble Virtues do incite
> My Pen, they are the ground I write upon;
> Nor any future profit is expected,
> Then how can these poor lines go unrespected? (54)

The final poem in the front matter lays aside the mockery and intermittent resentment that has rippled throughout. Addressing Lady Anne Clifford, Countess of Dorset, Lanyer is startlingly explicit:

> Greatnesse is no sure frame to build upon,
> No worldly treasure can assure that place;
> God makes both even, the Cottage with the Throne,
> All worldly honours there are counted base;
> What difference was there when the world began,
> Was it not Virtue that distinguisht all?
> All sprang but from one woman and one man,
> Then how doth Gentry come to rise and fall?
> Or who is he that very rightly can
> Distinguish of his birth, or tell at all
> In what meane state his Ancestors have bin . . . ? (72–73)

One need which propels Lanyer into print is service to women she hopes to win as patrons, but there is under that need a complicated and subverting anger against gender roles and class roles. Lanyer has addressed not only Queen Anne and the Clifford women but also, among others, the Princess Elizabeth, Lady Arabella Stuart, Mary Sidney, Countess of Pembroke and Lucy, Countess of Bedford. It would be a mistake to claim that all these women's lives were somehow secure because of their wealth and position. Lanyer pulled the poem to Arabella Stuart because of her dangerous disgrace; the Clifford women spent years fighting their own husband and father for Anne Clifford's rightful inheritance of lands. Yet their marginalization is crucially different from Lanyer's. Above all, Aemilia Lanyer is a writer, who writes in service to those above her while acutely conscious of those below. The strains of that service on her writing crisscross and undergird the poem's collage.

Ben Jonson's *The Forrest* is, by contrast, an oddly retreating book: it is, after all, Jonson's last collection of poetry crafted for and allowed a public appearance (its companion book, *Epigrammes*, being the first). It begins with "Why I Write Not of Love," that linking of tight poetic form with his own age and impotence. The collection could indeed be read as a linked meditation on fertility and impotence. "To Penshurst" hymns the generative successes of the Sidney family, but "To the World" hymns the Virtuous Gentlewoman's choice to retreat into her own bosom. The "Celia" songs from *Volpone* are wonderful with calculated lust, but *The Forrest* ends with

Jonson's rarely discussed but very moving prayer of hopelessness and despondency at the thought of ongoing life. While Lanyer is vividly excited and determined about seizing the print forum, Jonson is divided, half-hearted about *The Forrest*'s project of public praise. A book that begins with a poem like "Why I Write Not of Love" where the poet displays tightly packed irony and despair at his own failure at heat and life and ends with the loathing of the world so movingly spoken in "To Heaven" is a book structured by a weird ambivalence about public life and private life, about a poet's paying job and a poet's desire, about the poet's own physical, sexual life and his role as a crafter of public sentiments. Jonson was proudly uneasy about the service of praise he offered to those who could reward him. Yet, deeply desirous of being allowed to be enclosed within a country-house garden, Jonson publishes an edgy support of the aristocratic status quo. Lanyer stands startlingly close to Jonson in class position and formal convention, and yet her text is startlingly different. Left alone within a rented and then absented country-house garden, she publishes a radical manifesto.

Perhaps the most striking effect of comparing Lanyer and Jonson is the inescapable and disturbing pairing of "To Cooke-ham" and "To Penshurst." For one thing, such a pairing highlights the absence of Lanyer's writing from the outstanding body of critical work on the country-house poem. Because this is a genre so finely packed and so oddly short-lived, the country-house poem lends itself richly to formal, generic and sociopolitical readings. The genre has become a paradigm for central debates in seventeenth-century studies: to what extent is the genre "new" and to what extent an amalgam of classical forms? to what extent is it a "happy ethic of consuming," in Raymond Williams's words, where the existence of labor is simply extracted so as to leave the pleasures unadulterated?[2] to what extent is it a reflection of growing ostentation and the Crown's attempt to control its aristocracy? Each side would agree, however, that the genre uses vast country seats as vehicles to praise or analyze the power of the feudal structure of family property inherited through primogeniture. Labor, capital, and social change are thus the terrifying undertext that the form exists to repress.

"To Cooke-ham" must complicate the debate: a poem by a forty-year-old woman with fading prospects of court preferment; a poem to women who are claiming their right to property inheritance in the face of the entire patriarchy, including the King; a poem on an estate which is not the family seat, but a temporary, rented or borrowed refuge.

As revealing as the different extrinsic circumstances of property and inherited power are the intrinsic positionings of the poet figure within the garden in each poem. Jonson's Penshurst exists always in the now, a place where Jonson can go and be treated like an equal, can eat all he wants of the best food,

> Where the same beere, and bread, and selfe-same wine,
> That is his Lordships, shall be also mine . . .
> Here no man tells my cups; nor, standing by,
> A waiter, doth my gluttony envy:

2. *The Country and the City* (New York: Oxford University Press, 1973), 30.

But gives me what I call, and lets me eate,
He knowes, below, he shall finde plentie of meate.

The Jonson figure in the poem attributes parsimony at other houses' tables not to the lord but to the servant class who, in places less liberal than Penshurst, stint on serving less important guests like Jonson so that there will be food to go around below stairs later. Jonson structures into the poem the powerfully embracing feeling that while a guest at Penshurst:

. . . all is there;
As if thou were mine, or I raign'd here;
There's nothing I can wish, for which I stay.

Penshurst becomes a fantasy redress of Jonson's own social unease, caught between his patrons and the servants he mocks and who mock him. Lanyer's Cooke-ham, on the other hand, is a desolate place; this country-house poem is a poem of loss, the poet figure left behind in a ruptured Eden to memorialize paradise lost. The persona of the woman poet begins by describing her role as the kept writer of aristocratic women exiled in country retreat:

. . . where the Muses gave their full consent,
I should have powre the virtuous to content:
Where princely Palace will'd me to indite. (137)

One of the things for which we feel uneasy admiration in Jonson's poem is the astonishing tact with which he makes Penshurst a metaphoric vehicle for the great chain of being and a repressive class system; it takes a skilled eye to open up the ideology of his almost seamless poem. Lanyer's poem uses a strategy sharply different, making the artifice of the pathetic fallacy part of the subject of her poem. The place becomes a living tribute to Lady Clifford's power, she "From whose desires did spring this worke of Grace." "The Walkes put on their summer Liveries,/ And all things else did hold like similies" (137). And so throughout the body of the poem the garden becomes a garden of similes, the central oak, a man defending her from Phoebus's advances, for example, or the vista she saw from under the tree—hills, vales and woods—are men "as if on bended knee" (139) pleading before her.

Raymond Williams has described the ways in which similes function in the country-house poem genre to mystify the social order into the natural order. The heavy use of simile in Lanyer's poem, however, is openly subversive. After an extended list of elaborate similes comparing nature in the Cooke-ham garden with adoring subjects, the poet's voice breaks out in an address to Fortune which is clearly an address to the fortunate as well:

Unconstant Fortune, thou art most too blame,
Who casts us downe into so lowe a frame:
Where our dear friends we cannot dayly see,
So great a difference is there in degree.
Many are placed in those Orbes of state,
Parters in honour, so ordain'd by Fate;
Neerer in show, yet farther off in love,
In which, the lowest alwayes are above.
But whither am I carried in conceit?

The abrupt question addresses the essential danger and power of this poem. She begins by hymning the fated order of a society where some are privileged and some are low; she veers into a Christian critique of worldly power, and then she addresses the dangerous power of poetry itself. The passage is a microcosm of the poem. It goes on:

> My Wit too weake to conster of the great.
> Why not? although we are but borne of earth,
> We may behold the Heavens, despising death;
> And loving heaven that is so farre above,
> May in the end vouchsafe us entire love.
> Therefore sweet Memorie doe thou retaine
> Those pleasures past, which will not turne againe. (140)

Lanyer's final memory, however, is at once gaspingly funny and demeaning. Lady Clifford takes her farewell of Cooke-ham and, in a highly stylized, highly self-conscious gesture of pathetic fallacy, the poet has all the flowers and trees fade into autumn as a way of mourning the lady's grand exit. The patron lady and the poet pause under the great oak, however:

> To this faire tree, taking me by the hand,
> You did repeat the pleasures which had past,
> Seeming to grieve they could no longer last.
> And with a chaste, yet loving kisse took leave. (141–42)

We are moved by the act of sisterhood. By the next line, however, [the poem's] whole over-wrought, high art structure of ingratiating simile falls into a ludicrous joke: we realize that Lady Clifford has kissed the tree.

The poem ends with quietly scathing anger. Lanyer has indeed written the poem she has been asked to write by her patroness, but she publishes it. By the act of publication, she breaches the walls of the garden.

> This last farewell to Cooke-ham here I give,
> When I am dead thy name in this may live,
> Wherein I have perform'd her noble hest,
> Whose virtues lodge in my unworthy breast,
> And ever shall, so long as life remaines,
> Tying my heart to her by those rich chaines. (143)

In the Renaissance, women were bound by rich chains of marriage, of service. Aemilia Lanyer shows us the chains of obligation, need, love, and sometimes humiliation which bind her to the women above her. We should be moved by the sisterhood, but we should not be blind to the rich chains.

Lanyer and Jonson bear witness together to the shaping difficulties of gender, writing and service. Lanyer's anger at and fear of the power of women is in many ways greater than Jonson's. Her act of print publication is a rejection of her private role as a woman of service within a matriarchy. It must take, however, all the backing of Jesus Christ to propel her into that place. Jonson seems in many ways to be yearning for exactly the social gender expectations which Lanyer rejects. The poet in "To Penshurst" fantasizes retreat into a comforting estate where there will be clean sheets and lots of food, where he will be able to write marvelous poetry and escape the taint of the service class he feels nipping at his parvenu heels. Jonson is the poet literary history regards as the man who first took control of print culture, who laid out his writing in the physical space of the 1616 *Workes*. But Jonson is torn. In "To Penshurst" he scorns the builders of "proud, ambitious heaps" and praises an aristocratic family with a chaste wife and an immanent Lord existing somewhere out of and above the poem as a shaping force. The male narrator's voice is rather pathetically willing to be allowed to sit at table and be protected temporarily from the service class. He joins within Penshurst the women and children and ripe daughters. "To Penshurst" is a beautifully elaborated dance of social and sexual acquiescence.

In his "Penshurst," Jonson inscribes the Sidney oak within whose "writhed bark" angry or desolate men have cut the names of women they have failed to possess; in her "Cooke-ham" Lanyer inscribes the oak kissed by Lady Clifford. The sexual interplay with the oaks is, clearly, wholly different. But furthermore, in transcribing this act within her poem, Lanyer goes far beyond the delimitations of Jonson's exquisite panegyric. She wrests the (rented) oak away from the Cliffords by kissing it herself; she steals from the similes of praise the power those similes bestow upon the praised. It is Lanyer's choice to display openly the "rich chaines" even if she cannot fully throw them off. In displaying, in printing, she takes control—no longer a simile herself, one of the emblematic daughters of service or the wife who makes Penshurst such a lovely frieze of male power. For Lanyer, the act of printing is an act of defiance in several registers. When we have thought about country-house poems, we have summoned a genre of conservative pieties, poems shoring up the walls against the powerful realities of labor and capital. We can no longer think about the genre without Lanyer as one of its two originary instances. The walls of the estate had already been breached.

Finally, Milton can help us think in this instance about the costs and legacies of gender and writing. Milton's early poetry, written from the mid-1620s until the 1645 *Poems*, is heavily influenced by Jonson. In form, in classical learning, and even in its politics, Milton's early writing marks him as a son of Ben. Milton had tremendous difficulty letting go of this early writing. We see much of that anxiety dramatized in *Areopagitica*. It was the work of the feminine place, the Lady's closet, the aristocratic manuscript realm which Milton found so appealing. After the searing experience of the war, interregnum, and restoration, however, Milton's poetry changes utterly. Instead, we have a radical Christian vision of a garden within us all. That garden has been read as famously unfeminist, famously explicit in its underscoring of the patriarchy. Virginia Woolf, for one, condemns John Milton with aristocratic distaste as a woman writer's bogey. In the questioning voice of Milton's Eve, however, the woman who asks for knowledge, who accepts the responsibility of bringing Christ into the world, the woman who leads us out of the garden and into the world in the most powerful act of printed poetry yet written, we hear the voice of women writing for print—we hear the voice of Aemilia Lanyer.

GORDON BRADEN

Beyond Frustration: Petrarchan Laurels in the Seventeenth Century†

Literary history is, among other things, the history of the explication and rearrangement of certain master tropes. Here is one:

> *Thirsis* a Youth of the inspired Train,
> Fair *Sacharissa* lov'd, but lov'd in vain:
> Like *Phoebus* sung the no less amorous Boy;
> Like *Daphne* she as lovely and as Coy:
> With numbers he the flying Nymph pursues,
> With numbers such as *Phoebus* self might use.
> Such is the chase, when Love and Fancy leads,
> O're craggy Mountains, and through floury Meads;
> Invok'd to testifie the Lover's care,
> Or form some Image of his cruel fair:
> Urg'd with his fury like a wounded Deer,
> O're these he fled, and now approaching near,
> Had reach't the Nymph with his harmonious lay,
> Whom all his charms could not incline to stay;
> Yet what he sung in his immortal strain,
> Though unsuccessful, was not sung in vain:
> All but the Nymph, that should redress his wrong,
> Attend his passion, and approve his Song.
> Like *Phoebus* thus, acquiring unsought praise,
> He catcht at Love, and fill'd his Arm with Bays.
> (Edmund Waller, "The Story of *Phoebus* and *Daphne* applied")[1]

The story "applied": Waller is providing, in more than usually direct fashion, an interpretation of the myth of Apollo and Daphne. The male lover, pursuing a woman who does not love him in return, tries poetry—Apollo's art—to win her with representations of his suffering and her cruel beauty: poetry which fails to make an impression on her, but impresses everybody else, and wins the lover poetic fame, the bays—Daphne's tree. The poem invites us to see the ancient story as a parable about the compensatory origins of literary creation, and leaves us with the feeling that the trade-off is not, when you come down to it, a bad one.[2]

The classic source for the myth is of course Ovid's *Metamorphoses*, where in a comparable way Apollo's sexual frustration is consoled by his inventive appropriation of what the altered nymph has to offer:

† From *Studies in English Literature 1500–1900* 26:1 (Winter, 1986): 5–23. Reprinted by permission of the publisher. The author's notes have been abridged.

1. Waller, *Poems*, &c., 5th edn. (London, 1686; Wing W 517), pp. 37–38. The poem has a history of special regard by readers of Waller: "one of the most beautiful Poems in our own, or any other modern language": Elijah Fenton, ed., *The Works of Edmund Waller* (London, 1729), p. xl. * * *
2. Waller is clearer about the compensatory force than are several other Renaissance poets on the same subject, e.g, Marino: "se 'l frutto no, coglie le fronde"; Giambattista Marino, *Poesie varie*, ed. Benedetto Croce (Bari: G. Laterza & Figli, 1913), p. 175. See Christine Rees, "The Metamorphosis of Daphne in Sixteenth- and Seventeenth-Century English Poetry," *MLR* 66 (1971): 257. * * *

> cui deus "at, quoniam coniunx mea non potes esse,
> arbor eris certe" dixit "mea semper habebunt
> te coma, te citharae, te nostrae, laure, pharetrae."

> The god said to her, "Since you cannot be my wife, you will certainly be my tree. Forever will my hair, my lyre, my quivers carry you, laurel."
> (1.557–59)

Yet the honorific function Apollo goes on to specify is not for poetry but for politics:

> tu ducibus Latiis aderis, cum laeta Triumphum
> uox canet et uisent longas Capitolia pompas.

> You will be there for the Latin generals, when the happy voice sings their triumph and the Capitoline sees their long parades.
> (1.560–61)

Later in the same book, we can find a similar story in which the art of the Muses does come into play; Waller indeed seems to be remembering the line where Pan reaches for the nymph Syrinx only to find himself holding the material for a new musical instrument; the story goes

> Panaque cum prensam sibi iam Syringa putaret,
> corpore pro nymphae calamos tenuisse palustres,
> dumque ibi suspirat, motos in harundine uentos
> effecisse sonum tenuem similemque querenti.
> arte noua uocisque deum dulcedine captum
> "hoc mihi concilium tecum" dixisse "manebit."

> that Pan, when he thought he was about to take Syrinx, grabbed marshy reeds instead of a nymph's body; that while he sighed, the wind moving in the reeds made a soft sound, one like his complaint; and that the god, taken with the new art and the sweetness of its voice, said, "This union between me and you will last."
> (1.705–10)

And the concern with winning undying fame by the writing of love poetry is of course a strong theme in Ovid's *Amores:*

> sustineamque coma metuentem frigora myrtum,
> atque a sollicito multus amante legar.

> Let me carry on my head the myrtle that fears the cold, and let me be read often by the tormented lover.
> (1.15.37–38)

Yet if all the elements are there in classical literature, the tight nexus Waller draws among erotic frustration, poetry, and fame is not Ovidian but the heritage of a poet who himself momentously absorbed and refashioned the classical tradition at the leading edge of that large period of literary history whose close Waller helps to mark. "The Story of *Phoebus* and *Daphne* applied" is perhaps most notable as a particularly lucid summary of the central disposition of Petrarchan love poetry:

Dentro pur foco et for candida neve,
sol con questi pensier, con altre chiome,
sempre piangendo andrò per ogni riva,
per far forse pietà dopo mill' anni,
di tal che nascerà dopo mill' anni,
se tanto viver po ben colto lauro.

Inwardly fire, though outwardly white snow, alone with these thoughts, with changed locks, always weeping I shall go along every shore, to make pity perhaps come into the eyes of someone who will be born a thousand years from now—if a well-tended laurel can live so long.

(Petrarch, *Canzoniere* 30.31–36)[3]

That the course of Renaissance love poetry is to a great extent one of imitations of and reactions to Petrarch's *Canzoniere* is a large and obvious fact of literary history that we have had trouble knowing what to do with. Too much of Petrarchism strikes us as patently absurd, and too many of the poems are unrememberable if not unreadable; when someone finally says, "My Mistres eyes are nothing like the Sunne," we assume the decks are only now being cleared for real action. One reason we value seventeenth-century love poetry in particular is that it comes across as a blessedly fresh start—indeed, partly under Ovid's influence—after two ludicrous centuries of pearls and ivory and gold and roses and cryopyric oxymora: most especially after two centuries of monotonous female indifference and unattainability that come to seem no less ludicrous. But we should know better. Cultural tradition seldom merely snaps clean like that; and if we consider some of its inner workings, we can see Petrarchism as a tradition which the seventeenth century does not so much shut out as refract. Waller, looking down a retrospect of three hundred years, picks up a particular wavelength with special sensitivity: sexual frustration is deeply complicitous with at least a certain kind of poetic success, and the poet's own literary career—his pursuit of the bays—is in some sense the hidden agenda of his courtship.

Or, in the ramifying pun that spreads throughout the *Canzoniere*, Laura, the object of the poet's all-consuming desire, can be indistinguishable from *lauro*, the laurel.[4] In Petrarch's own life, his pursuit and public attainment of the latter are far better documented than his shadowy longing for the not quite identifiable woman whose name may well be fictitious; the suspicion hovers, as with most subsequent Petrarchan poets, that the woman herself could be a fiction, a mere pretext to have something to write about.[5]

3. For Petrarch's poetry, I use the text and translation of Robert M. Durling, *Petrarch's Lyric Poems: The "Rime Sparse" and Other Lyrics* (Cambridge, Mass: Harvard Univ. Press, 1976), cited by poem and line. On the innovative place of Petrarch in the history of the myth, see Yves F.-A. Giraud, *La Fable de Daphné* (Geneva: Drox, 1968), pp. 141–52. That Waller's interpretation of the myth traces back with some specificity to Petrarch is indicated by its general absence from the mythographic mainstream of the Renaissance, which is more directly tied to the Ovidian text. * * *

4. Carlo Calcaterra, *Nelle selva del Petrarca* (Bologna: Licinio Cappelli, 1942), especially pp. 35–87, remains basic; Aldo S. Bernardo, in *Petrarch, Laura, and the Triumphs* (Albany: State Univ. of New York, 1975), summarizes and advances much of the subsequent scrutiny. * * *

5. The accusation was apparently made to Petrarch in his lifetime; he specifically denies it in his *Epistolae familiares* (bk, 2, epistle 9). The most sensible conclusion seems to be that Laura was, as they say, "real," at the same time that derealizing her was a major task of Petrarch's poetry; for a sophisticated feminist account of what is going on here, see Nancy J. Vickers, "Diana Described: Scattered Woman and Scattered Rhyme," *Critical Inquiry I* 8 (1981): 265–79.

Whatever the actual case, the myth of Apollo and Daphne comes into play significantly in the *Canzoniere* to depict a decisive moment of frustrated enamorment that is simultaneously the beginning of a poetic vocation:

> sentendo il crudel di ch' io ragiono
> infin allor percossa di suo strale
> non essermi passato oltra la gonna,
> prese in sua scorta una possente Donna
> ver cui poco giamai mi valse o vale
> ingegno o forza o dimandar perdono;
> ei duo mi trasformaro in quel ch' i' sono,
> facendomi d'uom vivo un lauro verde
> che per fredda stagion foglia non perde.

> that cruel one of whom I speak [Love], seeing that as yet no blow of his arrows had gone beyond my garment, took as his patroness a powerful Lady, against whom wit or force or asking pardon has helped or helps me little: those two transformed me into what I am, making me of a living man a green laurel that loses no leaf for all the cold season.
> (23.32–40)

Indeed, the special power of Petrarch's telling comes in the hallucinatory compression whereby Daphne herself is virtually elided. The lover becomes the laurel, in a vertiginous fusion of subject and object spelled out by Petrarch with grotesque literalness:

> Qual me fec' io quando primier m'accorsi
> de la trasfigurata mia persona,
> e i capei vidi far di quella fronde
> di che sperato avea già lor corona,
> e i piedi in ch' io mi stetti et mossi et corsi,
> com' ogni membro a l'anima risponde,
> diventar due radici sovra l'onde
> non di Peneo ma d'un più altero fiume,
> e 'n duo rami mutarsi ambe le braccia!

> What I became, when I first grew aware of my person being transformed and saw my hairs turning into those leaves which I had formerly hoped would be my crown, and my feet, on which I stood and moved and ran, as every member answers to the soul, becoming two roots beside the waves not of Peneus but of a prouder river, and my arms changing into two branches!
> (23.41–49)

Such reversals are common in Petrarch; this particular *canzone* ends with the myth of Actaeon, in which, as the hunter's dogs turn on him, he again becomes the unexpected object of his own hunt. As Durling has skillfully shown, the Ovidian myth that seems to haunt the margins of the poem is that of Narcissus, who fell in love with what he only thought was somebody else.[6] The woman's distance in the *Canzoniere* may not be merely the sad

6. Durling, pp. 26–33; see further my "Love and Fame: The Petrarchan Career," in *Pragmatism's Freud: The Moral Disposition of Psychoanalysis*, ed. William Kerrigan and Joseph H. Smith (Baltimore: Johns Hopkins Univ. Press, 1986).

subject of the poet's song; it may be the very condition of its creation. Encounters with Laura herself are brief, explosive, catastrophic:

> le dissi 'l ver pien di paura;
> ed ella ne l'usata sua figura
> tosto tornando fecemi, oimè lasso!
> d'un quasi vivo et sbigottito sasso.

> I told her the truth, full of fear, and she to her accustomed form quickly returning made me, alas, an almost living and terrified stone.
> (23.77–80)

The sequence's moments of real peace come at a great physical distance from her. In her absence, the poet can wander freely alone and project his image of her onto the landscape:

> I' l'ò più volte (or chi fia che mi 'l creda?)
> ne l'acqua chiara et sopra l'erbe verde
> veduto viva, et nel troncon d'un faggio
> e 'n bianca nube, sì fatta che Leda
> avria ben detto che sua figlia perde
> come stella che 'l sol copre col raggio;
> et quanto in più selvaggio
> loco mi trovo e 'n più deserto lido,
> tanto piu bella il mio pensier l'adombra.

> I have many times (now who will believe me?) seen her alive in the clear water and on the green grass and in the trunk of a beech tree and in a white cloud, so beautiful that Leda would have said that her daughter faded like a star covered by the sun's ray; and in whatever wildest place and most deserted shore I find myself, so much the more beautiful does my thought shadow her forth.
> (129.40–48)

"*Because* she is not there, he can take charge almost entirely of her image, its appearance and disappearance";[7] what he is actually in love with may well be his own imaginative powers.

Many of the more conspicuous features of Petrarchism are answerable to that possibility. The fragmented décor that threatens to occlude our view of the woman it is said to represent, the stylized emotional extremity that all but buries the events that are supposed to prompt it—such predilections may indeed make most sense to us as part of an insistence on the claims of creative subjectivity over external reality. The involvement of such claims in this particular mode of love poetry may also help us understand the awesome but often inscrutable popularity of this mode in Renaissance culture: it is a mode that brings with it a dramatic aggrandizement of the authority of the poetic imagination, indeed offers a kind of training for the poetic ephebe in the techniques of that aggrandizement. More than one poetic career in the Renaissance begins with an episode of Petrarchism not merely in response to empty fashionability but, we may guess, because such an episode provides entry to an expanded feel for the mind's auton-

7. Mariann Sanders Regan, *Love Words: The Self and the Text in Medieval and Renaissance Poetry* (Ithaca: Cornell Univ. Press, 1982).

omy in shaping and contemplating the inner landscape of its desire. With such a beast, however obliquely, in view, the lover might well be thought to connive in his own sexual frustration; the laurel and not Daphne might well have been the real goal all along.

Yet such duplicity opens itself up to exposure. We may sense a major poetic epoch rounding off when Sor Juana Inés de la Cruz, toward the end of the seventeenth century, provides as it were the Petrarchan mistress's gentle but clear-headed response to her lover's worship:

> Vosotros me concebisteis
> a vuestro modo, y non extraño
> lo grande: que esos conceptos
> por fuerza han de ser milagros.
> La imagen de vuestra idea
> es la que habéis alabado;
> y siendo vuestra, es bien digna
> de vuestros mismos aplausos.
> Celebrad ese, de vuestra
> propia aprehensión, simulacro,
> para que en vosotros mismos
> se vuelva a quedar el lauro.

> You conceive me in your own form, and I am not surprised at its greatness: because those conceptions necessarily had to be miracles. The images of your ideal is that which you have praised; and being yours, it is very worthy of your own applause. Celebrate that semblance of your own perception, so that to yourself returns the laurel. (51.109–20)[8]

Disabuse is not always so kind. Petrarch's own conscience was tormented by the immorality of his love, as spelled out remorselessly by Augustine in the crucial last book of Petrarch's *Secretum*: "That beauty which seemed so charming and so sweet, through the burning flame of your desire, through the continual rain of your tears, has done away all that harvest that should have grown from the seeds of virtue in your soul."[9] Augustine cuts deepest when he discloses not merely the sin of lust but also the more dangerous sin of pride: "As for your boasting that it is she who has made you thirst for glory, I pity your delusion, for I will prove to you that of all the burdens of your soul there is none more fatal than this."[1] The climactic accusation ignores the woman altogether to target literary ambition itself: "I greatly fear lest this pursuit of a false immortality of fame may shut for you the way that leads to the true immorality of life."[2] Pursuit of the laurel—publicizing one's inner life as a way of gaining worldly recognition—is overtly a form of vainglory; and the subtler agenda of Petrarchan love poetry is censurable as well under the wider Augustinian understanding of what pride is: human aspiration to an illusory self-sufficiency, the

8. Text and references (opus and line numbers) from *Obras completas de Sor Juana Inés de la Cruz*, ed. Alfonso Méndez Plancarte and Alberto G. Salceda, 4 vols. (Mexico City: Fondo de Cultura Económica, 1951–1957), 1; I owe my knowledge of this poem and the translation to Luis Gamez. In context, Sor Juana is not in the simple position of Petrarchan mistress; she is declining praise for her own literary works.
9. *Petrarch's Secret, or, The Soul's Conflict with Passion*, trans. William H. Draper (1911; rpt. Norwood: Norwood Editions, 1978), p. 123.
1. Ibid., p. 124.
2. Ibid., p. 166.

attempt to live in a world of one's own creation in preference to the one God made.[3] The Petrarchan lover's problem is not just his rejection by an uncooperative woman; it is also the intrinsic problem of a narcissistic individualism, amplifying to Renaissance scale. The most important heritage of Petrarchism is a troubled concern with the place of such individualism in the larger scheme of things.

Putting it that way may help us sound the depths of a feature of Renaissance poetry often taken as merely gamesome: the rearrangement of a familiar myth to novel outcomes. English poetry of the later Renaissance is in fact particularly taken with the prospect of rewriting the myth of Apollo and Daphne, and Waller's special lucidity probably owes something to an established tradition of experiment in reassembling the pieces of that story to see what other arrangements might be possible.[4] Not the least interest is in imagining some un-Petrarchan response from that immovable female object: "Runne when you will, the story shall be chang'd: / *Apollo* flies, and *Daphne* holds the chase" (*Midsummer Night's Dream*, II.i.230–31). Such a mere turning of the tables, of course, simply preserves the frustration symmetrically. More promising is the vision that becomes possible in libertine love poetry, which defines itself so often through an incisive critique of Petrarchism: "Love's not so pure, and abstract, as they use / To say, which have no Mistresse but their Muse" (Donne, "Loves Growth," lines 11–12). The age's most extravagant poem about sexual love expresses that extremity with a picture of the Petrarchan lover, indeed Petrarch himself, having brought his courtship to its hitherto impossible end:

> *Laura* lyes
> In *Petrarchs* learned armes, drying those eyes
> That did in such sweet smooth-pac'd numbers flow,
> As made the world enamour'd of his woe.
> (Carew, "A Rapture," lines 139–42)[5]

In Carew's paradise, even Petrarch finally gets some, even Laura finally puts out. Yet the fantasy addresses its own past more searchingly than just that; in the preceding lines an even older frustration is even more movingly undone:

> *Daphne* hath broke her barke, and that swift foot,
> Which th'angry Gods had fastned with a root
> To the fixt earth, doth now unfetter'd run,
> To meet th'embraces of the youthfull Sun:
> She hangs upon him, like his Delphique Lyre,
> Her kisses blow the old, and breath new fire:
> Full of her God, she sings inspired Layes,
> Sweet Odes of love, such as deserve the Bayes,
> Which she her selfe was.
> (lines 131–39)

3. See Augustine, *City of God*, 14.12–14; I am being guided here by John Freccero, "The Fig Tree and the Laurel: Petrarch's Poetics," *Diacritics* 5 (1975): 34–40.
4. See Rees, pp. 254ff.—an important supplement to Giraud's uncharacteristically sketchy account, pp. 346–52, of Daphne's fortunes in England.
5. I quote Carew from *The Poems of Thomas Carew*, ed. Rhodes Dunlap (Oxford: Clarendon Press, 1949). * * *

The loveliness of the conceit is the implication that the pleasure had been worth the wait and even enabled by it. Carew's resolution of Ovid's myth comes in mirroring Petrarch's inversion of it: where Petrarch elides Daphne to become the laurel himself, Carew restores a Daphne who undergoes Petrarch's experience and becomes herself a poet. You learn things being a tree. She leaves paralysis not simply to service her lover, but to confront him as a new equal, interested in mutual pleasure; sexual gratification, at least at this level, comes in the engagement with an other of something like one's own talents and instincts. Narcissus finds himself reflected in something besides a mirror: "My face in thine eye, thine in mine appears" (Donne, "The Good-morrow," line 15).

The reciprocity of sexual pleasure is elsewhere in libertine poetry among the seducer's most compelling arguments:

> Did the thing for which I sue
> Onely concerne my selfe not you,
> Were men so fram'd as they alone
> Reap'd all the pleasure, women none,
> Then had you reason to be scant.
> (Carew, "To A. L.: Perswasions to love," lines 17–21)

And I think it is fair to say that seventeenth-century love poetry generally is, at its most impressive, informed by a sense of contentious mutuality—a sense that in Ovid's *Amores* coexists quite happily with the poet's aspirations to personal glory, but gets bleached out in the one-sided self-absorption of Petrarchism. John Carey has recently provoked a good deal of mixed recognition and dismay with his portrait of the imperious, self-satisfied, bullying egotism of the lover in Donne's *Songs and Sonnets* and elsewhere: "The selfishness of love is . . . defiantly affirmed . . . We are careful to talk, nowadays, as if we believed that the male ought to respect the female's individuality. Donne is above such hypocrisies."[6] But within the context of Renaissance love poetry, the lover's outsized egotism is not the new note. What is new is the feeling that Donne's wiry, ingenious hectoring is maneuvering in the face of a similarly resourceful, unpredictable response: "Tomorrow when thou leav'st, what wilt thou say?" ("Womans Constancy," line 2). I suggest that the literary historical scenario here is not the rejection of Petrarchism, but the bringing of the Petrarchan ego into the sexual arena where it must confront psychic otherness much more intimately and insistently than it previously had to do.

The most convincingly hopeful picture of human love in seventeenth-century literature is of the ego's finding its way in such confrontation, so that Petrarchan unattainability becomes simply a move in the negotiations of courtship. Before the century ends, Congreve will have one of the age's most vividly practical pair of lovers begin their major scene together by quoting, antiphonally, Waller's poem, only to herald not the usual deadlock but some wary tactical deliberation:

Millamant: Like Phoebus *sung the no less am'rous Boy.*
Enter Mirabell.
Mirabell: —Like Daphne *she as lovely and as Coy*. Do you lock your self

6. John Carey, *John Donne, Life, Mind and Art* (New York: Oxford Univ. Press, 1981), p. 100.

up from me, to make my search more Curious? Or is this pretty Artifice Contriv'd, to Signifie that here the Chase must end, and my pursuit be Crown'd, for you can flie no further.—

Millamant: Vanity! No—I'll fly and be follow'd to the last moment, tho' I am upon the very Verge of Matrimony, I expect you shou'd solicite me as much as if I were wavering at the grate of a Monastery, with one foot over the threshold. I'll be solicited to the very last, nay and afterwards.

(*The Way of the World,* IV.i.153–65)[7]

What is at issue is the relation between love and selfishness—"Ah! I'll never marry, unless I am first made sure of my will and pleasure" (IV.i.180–81)—and what follows is a session of down-to-earth prenuptial bargaining—"where ever I am, you shall always knock at the door before you come in" (IV.i.224–25)—in which this newly savvy Daphne works out the terms of the bossy surrender: "Well, you ridiculous thing you, I'll have you,—I won't be kiss'd, nor I won't be thank'd—here kiss my hand tho'—so hold your tongue now, and don't say a word" (IV.i.294–97). The zig-zags chart the lineaments of a realistically satisfying marriage between two quick-thinking individuals who know their own worth; from Waller's beginning we come to this different end, a balancing of wits in which the ego finds its territory not in withdrawal but in a quickening engagement with its equal.

At a visionary stretch, this mutuality can be seen yielding a freshly powerful joint identity: "That abler soule, which thence doth flow, / Defects of lonelinesse controules" (Donne, "The Exstasie," lines 43–44). Still, any such triumph entails the acceptance of a fundamental challenge to the ego's exclusivity; and the unexpectedly harsh change of tone that comes a few lines after the pictures of Daphne and Laura ends "A Rapture" with a version of that point. Just as the erotic bliss seems about to jump all limits, we find ourselves confronted with an attack, in a tone of stern outrage, on some of the acquisitive and competitive drives that group around the standard of "honor." They, rather than female sexual timidity, are the real threat to Carew's erotic paradise:

this false Impostor [Honor] can dispence
With humane Justice, and with sacred right,
And maugre both their lawes command me fight
With Rivals, or with emulous Loves, that dare
Equall with thine, their Mistresse eyes, or haire:
If thou complaine of wrong, and call my sword
To carve out thy revenge, upon that word
He bids me fight and kill.

("A Rapture," lines 154–61)

The sins of lust are now even more firmly than in the *Secretum* subordinated to the sins of pride: a virulent touchiness about reputation and a desire for possessive exclusivity in one's enjoyments that lead to a fearsome bloodthirstiness in both men and women. The erotic release of Carew's vision effectively depends on restraining those impulses; and for its role in

7. Text and references from *The Complete Plays of William Congreve*, ed. Herbert Davis (Chicago: Univ. of Chicago Press, 1967); I owe this reference to Michael Seidel. The first line of Waller's poem had been quoted earlier in the scene (line 63).

that, lust may be said not merely to lose its sinfulness, but indeed to become the agent of a serious kind of moral discipline. If the ego can here find a fulfillment that Petrarch himself could never admit, it can still do so only in taking on that discipline; Petrarch's Augustinianism is being less forgotten than—to use Kerrigan's term—renegotiated.[8]

The tact of Carew's fantasy is even clearer—on several levels—when set against the imagining of Daphne's defloration in what has become one of the most notorious poems of the century:

Coy Nature, (which remain'd, though aged grown,
A Beauteous virgin still, injoy'd by none,
Nor see unveil'd by any one)
When *Harveys* violent passion she did see,
Began to tremble, and to flee,
Took Sanctuary like *Daphne*, in a tree:
There *Daphnes* lover stop't, and thought it much
The very Leaves of her to touch,
But *Harvey* our *Apollo*, stopt not so,
Into the Bark, and root he after her did goe:
No smallest Fibres of a Plant,
For which the eiebeams Point doth sharpness want,
His passage after her withstood.
What should she do? through all the moving wood
Of Lives indow'd with sense she took her flight,
Harvey persues, and keeps her still in sight.
(Cowley, "Ode. *Upon Dr. Harvey*," lines 1–16)[9]

What Bush calls the "demented intricacies" of Cowley's invention in likening the pursuit of a nymph and the discovery of the circulatory system secured this ode a special place as one of the earliest poems in *The Stuffed Owl*.[1] The determination to incorporate new medical information into a poetic conceit indeed reaches giddy heights as the chase comes to its climax:

at the heart she stay'd,
Where turning head, and at a Bay,
Thus, by well-purged ears, was she o're-head to say.

Here sure shall I be safe (said she)
None will be able sure to see

8. I perhaps elide too quickly the problem of Carew's final lines: "Then tell me why / This Goblin Honour which the world adores, / Should make men Atheists, and not women Whores" (164–66). For many readers, this ending exposes something dark in what has led up to it: "it seems incredible that a sober plea for animalistic naturalism can be intended in a poem . . . which closes with the fearful brutality of this more than Swiftian couplet . . . Nowhere else in Carew have I found such black violence. Surely it reduces the entire argument of the poem to rubble"; Francis G. Schoff, "Thomas Carew: Son of Ben or Son of Spenser?" *Discourse* 1 (1958): 23–24.

9. I quote Cowley from *Poems*, ed. A. R. Waller (Cambridge: Univ. Press, 1905). This ode is not Cowley's only interesting dealing with Daphne; see Rees, pp. 259–61.

1. Douglas Bush, *Mythology and the Renaissance Tradition in English Poetry*. 2nd edn. (New York: Norton, 1963), p. 235; D. B. Wyndham Lewis and Charles Lee, eds., *The Stuffed Owl: An Anthology of Bad Verse* (1930; rpt. New York: Capricorn, 1962), pp. xviii–xix, 24–26. Hugh Kenner, in *The Counterfeiters* (1968; rpt. Garden City: Anchor, 1973), is even more emphatic about the historical significance of Cowley's poem; it signals "a wholly new way for poetry to fail, so that failure becomes a kind of positive quality. This is transcendental: is as if someone could invent a new sin" (p. 34). Robert B. Hinman, *Abraham Cowley's World of Order* (Cambridge, Mass.: Harvard Univ. Press, 1960), pp. 206–12, is more conventionally appreciative.

> This my retreat, but only He
> Who made both it and me.
> The heart of Man, what Art can e're reveal?
> A wall impervious between
> Divides the very Parts within,
> And doth the Heart of man ev'n from its self conceal.
> She spoke, but e're she was aware,
> *Harvey* was with her there,
> And held this slippery *Proteus* in a chain,
> Till all her mighty Mysteries she descry'd
> Which from his wit the attempt before to hide
> Was the first Thing that Nature did in vain.
> (lines 20–36)

For all its eccentric excess, though, the conceit is almost inevitable, one we might virtually have predicted: a revision of the Daphne myth to image the self's untrammelled victory in pursuit, its final possession of exactly what it thought it wanted on just about the terms it had in mind. It makes sense that the course of Renaissance individualism would not end without this style of egotistical conquest being so celebrated; and Cowley is finding the proper ground for that celebration in shifting the reference from sexuality to science. Harvey's discovery did indeed prove a secure possession, prophetic in a very practical way of a new age of mastery and control over the natural world. Here if anywhere we may speak of a human triumph uncomplicated in its satisfaction.

Yet even in its prophetic accuracy Cowley's revision of the myth is still disturbingly crude in its force: modern uneasiness about our technological success has in fact found common expression in the likening of the scientific triumph over nature to rape. Cowley compromises his own apparent message with the concluding information that Harvey is now suffering delayed punishment for his youthful act of violence:

> For though his Wit the force of Age withstand,
> His Body alas! and Time it must command,
> And Nature now, so long by him surpass't,
> Will sure have her revenge on him at last.
> (lines 88–91)

And the wisdom we most value in Cowley's time knows the surety of such retribution; it finds the self's most secure triumphs not in defying the constraints set to its ambition, but through accepting them. Indeed, Cowley's equation of Daphne with Nature provides a possibility elsewhere expanded into what I want to argue is the age's truest conversion of Petrarch's legacy of frustration into a victory—truest because it begins rather than ends with the strictures of Petrarch's Augustinian conscience:

> How vainly men themselves amaze
> To win the Palm, the Oke, or Bayes.
> (Marvell, "The Garden," lines 1–2)[2]

2. I quote Marvell from *The Poems and Letters*, ed. H. M. Margoliouth, 3rd edn., rev. Pierre Legouis and E. E. Duncan-Jones (Oxford: Clarendon Press, 1971). On Marvell's indebtedness to Petrarch generally, see Paulina Palmer, "Marvell, Petrarchism and 'De gli eroici furori,'" *EM* 24 (1973–1974): 19–57, though she finds no reason to discuss "The Garden."

Marvell's warning against worldly ambition includes, climactically, poetic ambition; and this dismissal of pride is followed by the dismissal of Petrarch's other sin, lust:

> No white nor red was ever seen
> So am'rous as this lovely green.
> (lines 17–18)

Yet the result is nevertheless, in the sense I have been developing here, precisely Petrarchan:

> When we have run our Passions heat,
> Love hither makes his best retreat.
> The *Gods*, that mortal Beauty chase,
> Still in a Tree did end their race.
> *Apollo* hunted *Daphne* so,
> Only that She might Laurel grow.
> And *Pan* did after *Syrinx* speed,
> Not as a Nymph, but for a Reed.
> (lines 25–32)

Something like this is what Petrarch was trying to say all along; it becomes sayable when it can be liberated from the taint of pride, when the laurel is not a civic crown but, well, a tree. What this confrontation with nature yields, though, is not scientific study but something like the imaginative expansiveness that Petrarch's mind would exercise on those solitary walks:

> Mean while the Mind, from pleasure less,
> Withdraws into its happiness:
> The Mind, that Ocean where each kind
> Does streight its own resemblance find;
> Yet it creates, transcending these,
> Far other Worlds, and other Seas;
> Annihilating all that 's made
> To a green Thought in a green Shade.
> (lines 41–48)

"Modern commentators all agree that the sixth stanza, central to the poem, is a witty Platonism, and of course this is so . . . But a green thought? This is a great bogey."[3] In Daphne's vicinity we may remember the green thought that Petrarch found so troubling even as its shade was irresistable:

> ei duo mi trasformaro in quel ch' i' sono,
> facendomi d'uom vivo un lauro verde
> che per fredda stagion foglia non perde.
> . . . .
> né per nova figura il primo alloro
> seppi lassar, ché pur la sua dolce ombra
> ogni men bel piacer del cor mi sgombra.

> those two transformed me into what I am, making me of a living man a green laurel that loses no leaf for all the cold season . . . nor for any

3. Frank Kermode, "The Argument of Marvell's 'Garden,'" *EIC* 2 (1952): 236, 239.

> new shape could I leave the first laurel, for still its sweet shade turns away from my heart any less beautiful pleasure.
>
> (*Canzoniere*, 23.38–169)

This may not qualify as a source, but it lets us know where we are. The principal means in the Renaissance for bringing the Petrarchan story to a happy end was Neoplatonic philosophy, which could promise that the lover's frustrated self-absorption was the beginning of a spiritual ascent: "To avoide therefore the torment of his absence, and to enjoy beautie without passion, the Courtier by the helpe of reason must full and wholy call backe againe the coveting of the bodie to beautie alone . . . and frame it within in his imagination sundred from all matter, and so make it friendly and loving to his soule, and there enjoy it."[4] The three centuries separating Petrarch and Marvell provide the theory for an exalted narcissism that is not entrapment but access to a higher reality: "Therefore the soule ridde of vices, purged with the studies of true Philosophie, occupied in spirituall, and exercised in matters of understanding, turning her to the beholding of her owne substance, as it were raised out of a most deepe sleepe, openeth the eyes that all men have, and few occupie."[5] Marvell's exclusion of women from his Eden—"Two Paradises 'twere in one / To live in Paradise alone" (lines 63–64)—simply moves up a gesture essential to the Neoplatonized Petrarchan career—"thus shall he beholde no more the particular beautie of one woman, but an universall, that decketh out all bodies"[6]—and may be described as the gesture of a Petrarchism newly lucid and confident about its rightness.

Marvell responds to a Petrarchan enthrallment with the mind's empire with an un-Petrarchan sense of the potential innocence of that enthrallment; his poem affirms a solitary contemplative rapture that can survive the paring away of its impure motives. Reducible to neither lust nor pride, it beckons as the true joy of our isolation. The idolatrous dead end opens up to become the gentle liminality of the freed spirit:

> like a Bird it sits, and sings,
> Then whets, and combs its silver Wings;
> And, till prepar'd for longer flight,
> Waves in its Plumes the various Light.
>
> (lines 53–56)[7]

In expectation of that genuine immortality which Petrarch dreaded he was foreclosing, the soul sweetly preens itself without guilt or fear.

4. Baldesar Castiglione, *The Book of the Courtier*, trans. Sir Thomas Hoby, intro. J. H. Whitfield (London: Dent, 1974), p. 317.
5. Ibid., p. 318.
6. Ibid.
7. Cf. ibid.: "Wherefore such as come to this love, are like to yong birdes almost flush, which for all they flitter a litle their tender winges, yet dare they not stray farre from the nest, nor commit themselves to the winde and open weather."

WILLIAM KERRIGAN

Kiss Fancies in Robert Herrick†

In a tradition stretching from Edmund Gosse to Gordon Braden, critics have intimated that something major and male is absent from Herrick's erotic verse. Although he believed that "Julia" was an actual mistress, and observed that Herrick wrote "so much that an English gentleman, not to say clergyman, had better left unsaid," Gosse also noted the "total want of passion in Herrick's language about women."[1] F. W. Moorman, writing around the electric word "passion," complained of a "lack of the genuine fire of love."[2]

Something is obviously missing in these descriptions of what is missing. It was left to Braden to elevate this tradition to the standards of twentieth-century candor: "The emphasis on foreplay and nongenital, especially oral, gratifications, the fixation on affects (smells, textures) and details (Julia's leg), and the general voyeuristic preference of perception to action . . . are all intelligible as a wide diffusion of erotic energy denied specifically orgastic focus and release. What is missing in the *Hesperides* is aggressive, genital, in other words, 'adult' sexuality."[3] Herrick was practicing a discipline, attempting to confine libido to artistic imagination, and the result is a "self-contained lyric world whose principal activity is the casual permutation of its own décor."[4]

In Braden we have an observation about the poetry and a supposition about the man. The poetry specializes in obstructed desire. "*Jocund his Muse was, but his life was chast.*" Ovid and Martial said the same thing, but there is a better case on purely internal grounds for believing the Renaissance poet: his verses are not as jocund as theirs. The man, Braden supposes, was probably living under a self-imposed sexual prohibition, using the poems to make up the deficit and simultaneously to channel his erotic feeling away from intercourse.

Now there *are* Herrick pieces, such as "Kisses," "Up Tailes All," and "To Anthea," that invite women to have intercourse with the poet. Braden would have to claim that these verses are uncharacteristic or half-hearted.[5] I believe that this claim can in fact be substantiated. The supposition can never be more than that, maybe right, maybe wrong, but the observation on which it rests seems to me sound.

† From the *George Herbert Journal* 14 (1990–91): 155–71. Reprinted by permission of the *George Herbert Journal*.

1. Edmund Gosse, *Seventeenth Century Studies* (New York: Dodd, Mead, and Co., 1897), p. 133.
2. F. W. Moorman, *Robert Herrick* (London: Thomas Nelson and Sons, 1910), p. 160. A recent critic speaks of "quintessential Herrick, taking all the delight possible in flirtation with no fear that things will go too far" (Gerald Hammond, *Fleeting Things: English Poets and Poems, 1616–1660* [Cambridge: Harvard Univ. Press, 1990], p. 295). Similar charges of fundamental sexual disinterest have been leveled at Marvell's poetry.
3. Gordon Braden, *The Classics and English Renaissance Poetry: Three Case Studies* (New Haven: Yale Univ. Press, 1978), p. 223.
4. Braden, p. 220.
5. "To Anthea" is the most convincing of the invitations to intercourse, for here Herrick, in the manner of Catullus and Martial, accumulates kisses, then alludes to a "private play" that will bring more pleasure than kissing. Even here he promises to speak the name of this act, but blushes to write it: intercourse is not fully welcomed into the poem. "To Anthea," in any case, is an anomaly. Herrick's usual attitude is consistent with "Love Me Little, Love Me Long": "desire / Grown violent does either die or tire."

Braden is a great student of decorative eroticism in the Western literary tradition. Far from consigning Herrick to triviality, his treatment of "decoration" in *Hesperides* redeems that word from its usual pejorative sense by exploring, in superb literary detail, some of the aesthetic and psychological possibilities of decorative verse. This scholar has spent long hours with somewhat imagined, perhaps imagined, and obviously imagined poetic love affairs; the charge of "imagined" hovers about nearly every mistress in the Petrarchan tradition, and Braden knows a great deal, perhaps more than any of us do, about this tradition. I think it was Braden's particular attunement to the uncertain borders between fantasy and fact that led him, in the case of Herrick, from literary response to biographical proposal. The supposition is his way of drawing closer to Herrick—our foremost scholar of imagined love placing a garland on the remains of one of its most serious practitioners. "I know you, lyricist," Braden is saying. "We were made for each other."

Yet Braden has left unfinished business here. His biographical speculation assigns a defensive and regressive role to the erotic verse without showing that these qualities are in some fashion the source or precondition of its literary value. My essay hopes to fill that gap.[6]

For to another sort of critic, this view of Herrick opens him to bluff dismissal. J.B. Broadbent, for example, finds the poet insufficiently broad bent. He celebrated "tertiary sexual characteristics," fawned over "fetishistic superficies," and was not above stooping to "snuggling infantilism":

> All Herrick's sweets are the same, and too sweet—pretty lewdness is boring. People sense something wrong, a lack of genuine sexuality. Herrick himself thought this excused him: 'Jocund his muse was, but his life was chaste,' he wrote for his own epigraph; but that's the condemnation.[7]

Away with all this cute erotic bric-a-brac (lawns, silks, nipplets, nervelets); the pansy lacked genital enthusiasm, and that's an end on it!

Today the friends of Herrick have little to fear from champions of "genuine sexuality," although odd strands of moral disapproval mar the otherwise interesting discussions of Herrick in Gerald Hammond's *Fleeting Things*. But the new political criticism, with its disdain for the personal sphere of existence, may produce a similar judgment about the triviality of sexual imagining, and especially of defensive sexual imagining. In the days when New Historicism was first in the air a prominent scholar explained to me over a beer that Herrick's lyrics on silks and petticoats were really about the vestment controversies. I must have chuckled. "What do *you* think they're about?" the scholar demanded. I shrugged. "Women's clothes?" Her icy expression let me know in no uncertain terms that great lyrics could not be attached to such unworthy objects. To be sure, *Hesperides* is not a garden of the mind, and our new awareness of seventeenth-century politics has already strengthened our grasp on the variety of concerns in Herrick's book. Yet we need a way of talking about the erotic lyrics that, rather than smashing them with inappropriate political seri-

6. Although my focus is psychological, the view of Herrick in this essay is compatible with Leah Marcus' politically informed discussion of the "trusting, childlike faith" (p. 138) expressed in *Noble Numbers*. See *Childhood and Cultural Despair: A Theme and Variations in Seventeenth-Century Literature* (Pittsburgh: Univ. of Pittsburgh Press, 1978), pp. 120–39.
7. See John Broadbent, *Poetic Love* (London: Chatto and Windus, 1964), pp. 245–46.

ousness, allows them to be what they seem to be (erotic, imagined, to some degree hobbled) and also to be major achievements, now as ever the mainstay of Herrick's reputation.

I begin with the observation that the "something missing" in these poems is also something gained. Although Herrick urges virgins to make much of time, he does not, like Sidney, Shakespeare, and Donne, negotiate with female honor. He does not oppose, subvert, or indict the honor of his poetic mistresses. If a woman resists Herrick's desire, as Corinna does, her reluctance does not seem to be principled, nor is there, on the poet's side, the bitter cycles of anger, frustration, jealousy, cynicism, and self-loathing one knows from *Astrophil and Stella*, Shakespeare's *Sonnets*, or Donne's *Songs and Sonnets*.

A great deal has indeed been removed from Herrick's range of sexual feeling. But his relative disinterest in intercourse is part and parcel of an aura of innocence that is his in abundance. Innocence and psychic defense, it seems to me, have correlative structures. Consider the dynamics of a successful repression, the most primitive of the psychic defenses.[8] It prohibits, subtracting offending material from consciousness. Yet it also stimulates the unconscious material to recombine in novel permutations that will appear "innocent" to the ego, and on that account be admitted to consciousness. Defense, then, produces the conditions for two kinds of innocence, an innocence of negative removal and an innocence of positive retrieval. The concept of innocence is marked by precisely this duality. It can be thought of as a positive quality that is lost (or in danger of being lost) and must somehow be retrieved or bestowed again. It can also be thought of as something to be achieved by a process of exclusion—what remains when bad things are subtracted from a guilty world. Milton, the only poet of the period to excel Herrick in the representation of innocent sexuality, plays on this doubleness throughout *Paradise Lost*. Adam and Eve have a virgin majesty and native honor that we have lost; viewed another way, they lack our shame, pomposity, and hypocrisy. In a less programmatic fashion, Herrick, too, convinces us (by "us" I mean "admirers of his erotic verse under Braden's description of it") that his regressive sexual imaginings, though full of retreats and expurgations, also make contact with a primal innocence.

The combination of goodness and sexuality is a rare quality in art. Freud taught us that men tend to split the image of woman into ideal asexual figures and debased sexual figures. In fact, they split themselves along similar lines, which is why Broadbent sounds like half a man. Configurations of the ideal and the sexual are almost always under some pressure to separate in male art. By the seventeenth century the Renaissance had produced two distinct traditions of love poetry—Petrarchism, celebrating an ideal but sexually unobtainable woman, and libertinism, celebrating bawdiness in complete disillusionment over the Petrarchan ideal. On the one hand, Ovid, Catullus, and Martial; on the other, Christ, Dante, and Petrarch. Both of the strands appear in Donne's work. When they fuse, as

8. Anna Freud, *The Ego and the Mechanisms of Defense*, trans. Cecil Baines (New York: International Universities Press, 1946), pp. 53–54. She also points out that repression, precisely because it "accomplishes so much," is the most dangerous of the defenses, the least adaptable, and therefore likely to produce neurotic symptoms—a fact that will be borne out in my forthcoming discussion of Herrick's kiss lyrics. See also Joseph H. Smith, "Rite, Ritual, and Defense," *Psychiatry*, 46 (1983), 16–30.

in "The Canonization," they produce sexual innocence. But Donne's is an innocence that has to be consciously secured; arguing for it is the main conceit of the poem. In Herrick the innocence is less asserted than entered into.

There it is, like the freshness of a flower:

White though ye be; yet, Lillies, know,
From the first ye were not so:
  But Ile tell ye
  What befell ye;
Cupid and his mother lay
In a Cloud; while both did play,
He with his pretty finger prest
The rubie niplet of her breast;
Out of the which, the creame of light,
  Like to a Dew,
  Fell downe on you,
  And made ye white.[9]

What a lovely fountain this would make, in downtown Devon: a splash of pure happiness, from the first and deepest source of happiness, the breast of the maternal sex goddess, landed on the world like an epigram upon a page.

Here, no doubt, is the infantile sweetness that cloys on the palate of Prof. Broadbent. The negative judgment makes a bluff kind of sense, for Herrick is indeed using the lillies to play a coy game with the human fact of unremembered sexual origins. The lyric does retreat.

One can readily plot the regressions and displacements. The poet will reveal the forgotten facts of life, the knowledge of how lillies came to be. "Where do flowers come from?" has supplanted "Where do babies come from?" This substitution allows the sexual yet infantile "play" of Venus and Cupid to replace intercourse. There is an orgasm here, perhaps the most sharply evoked in the entire *Hesperides*, but it is a maternal ejaculation in which a "ruby niplet" stands in for the penis and the role of the vagina is taken by the pressing finger of the boy-child. Avoiding the guilt and strife of the Oedipus complex, the poem regressively constructs a brief tableaux of immense polymorphous sexual innocence. Moreover, the milk is spilt, not drunk: if we think in terms of sexual transpositions, the breast of Venus is masturbated by her son. The little poem has given up sperm to douse the world with mother's milk, according to Freud the original term in all figurations of goodness.

It is everything Broadbent condemns—pretty, useless, nongenital, infantile. Like a flower, the poem is in a way beautiful and superfluous. We do not make our shelters from flowers, do not have a major industrial use for them. "Consider the lillies how they grow: they toil not, they spin not; and yet I say unto you, that Solomon in all his glory was not arrayed like one of these" (Luke 12:27). Like innocent imaginings, lillies "come white" and clothe the brazen earth.

Herrick's muse was in fact both jocund and chaste—and this is his glory, not his condemnation. Every aspect of human sexuality is suffused with

9. I quote Herrick's poetry from L. C. Martin, ed., *The Poetical Works of Robert Herrick* (Oxford: Clarendon Press, 1956).

fantasy, with every brand of fantasy, and the capacity to yield to these fantasies, including regressive ones, is a deeper form of maturity than branding them "unadult." Pretty and infantile have their place, as do rough and ready. Most of us had our first dates at a motion picture theater, where we shared the fantasy of the picture, our fantasies about stars, our opinion of the movie, which is to say, our likes and dislikes in fantasy scenarios. How easy it was to go from the group fantasy on the screen to the fantasy-for-two of necking! Lovers of both genders call their beloved "baby." Love has ever liked a diminutive. Yet of course these very same fantasies disturb us and may cause us considerable shame. Sometimes our defenses fail, subjecting us to the wishes and aggressions they have been instituted to expel. This is Herrick's major subject as an erotic poet, his peculiar version of the conflict between ideal and debased love—a war between the would-be innocence of sexual fantasy and the insistence of embarrassment.

The inner logic of Herrick's sexual imagination can be explored in the many lyrics focused on kissing. Insofar as it belongs to foreplay, *a kiss is a preliminary stage, a promise or opening deposit in a narrative directed toward the consummation of intercourse*. Thus Sidney's apostrophe in one of his four kiss sonnets: "Poor hope's first wealth, hostage of promised weal, / Breakfast of Love."[1] Yet Catullus, Martial, and various lyrics in the *Anthologia Graeca* hint that kissing might be decontextualized, and treated as an act distinct from intercourse—an end in itself precisely in its difference from intercourse.[2]

Pseudo-Petronius, in Jonson's translation, condemns intercourse for its shortness and guilty aftermath: "Doing a filthy pleasure is, and short, / And done, we straight repent us of the sport." As in Shakespeare's "The expense of spirit" and Donne's "Farewell to love," the immediate legacy of male orgasm is shame, depletion, sorrow, and a sudden debasement of the woman's value. Kissing, however, is none of that.

> Let us together closely lie, and kiss,
> There is no labour, nor no shame in this;
> This both pleased, doth please, and long will please; never
> Can this decay, but is beginning ever.[3]

Kissing is consummation's supplement, differing from orgasm in its capacity for limitless increase, and deferring orgasm by virtue of that increase. In "pleased, doth please, and long will please," Petronius/Jonson imposes on intercourse the same before/during/after grid that Shakespeare imposes on orgasm in Sonnet 129, but with kisses the market is always up, always gaining, without the aftermath of depression.

Hundreds of kiss poems were written in the English Renaissance, and most of them follow the tradition of decontextualization, isolating kissing from the solitary, poor, nasty, brutish, and short act of intercourse. The classical precedents were organized and formalized by Johannes Secundus,

1. *Astrophil and Stella* 79, in *The Poems of Sir Philip Sidney*, ed. W. A. Ringler (Oxford: Clarendon Press, 1962), p. 206. I have modernized.
2. I have in mind Catullus' famous summation of kisses in *Vivamus, mea Lesbia* and Martial's reply in *Epigrammata* 6.34. For Renaissance imitations, see Gordon Braden, "*Vivamus, mea Lesbia* in the English Renaissance," *ELR*, 9 (1979), 199–224.
3. *Ben Jonson: The Complete Poems*, ed. George Parfitt (New Haven: Yale Univ. Press, 1982), p. 251. Jonson read the poem to Drummond (Parfitt, pp. 462–63), who understood it, but could not bring himself to record what it was that kissing beat. See also Campion's "Turn back, you wanton flyer," in *Works*, ed. Percival Vivian (Oxford: Clarendon Press, 1966), pp. 9–10.

whose Latin *Basia* is a sequence of eighteen poems about kissing. "There are no poems about penises here," Secundus declares, for his Neara prefers "a book without a penis," if not "a poet without a penis."[4] Once again, obeying a familiar law, literary tradition has divided the realm of sexuality into the ideal (foreplay) and the debased (consummation).

This tradition came to the love poets of the seventeenth century, and to Herrick in particular, through the powerful filter of Ben Jonson.[5] Kissing belongs in spirit to the central imaginative energies of Jonson's verse. Stanley Fish has emphasized the peculiar logic of praise in Jonson. Virtue is its own reward; yet the ability to praise virtue, even if superfluous, is itself praiseworthy, and the ability to credit such praise is praiseworthy, and so on: "The dynamics of this exchange trace out what every society has vainly sought, an economy that generates its own expansion and is infinitely self-replenishing, an economy in which *everyone gains.*"[6] In Jonson's verse this ideal economy of praise covers over the vicious and uncertain practices of court patronage. Kissing, which like praising is shameless and infinitely expansible, performs a comparable function in the small but influential body of Jonson's love poetry.

The economy of kissing is elegantly displayed in his short sequence "The Celebration of Charis," which Herrick must have studied with unusual care. Jonson's rival eventually becomes incarnate in Charis' description of her ideal suitor. But his first opponent is embarrassment that he should, fifty and fat, love at all; when petrified by the lightning glance of Charis, the old poet is "Mock'd of all." He vows to "revenge me with my Tongue," and in two senses he does precisely that: he proceeds to write lovely lyrics, such as "Her Triumph," and writes poems to claim kisses that make use of his tongue. That the sequence will soon focus on kissing is foretold in the famous, much-imitated last stanza of "Her Triumph":

> Have you felt the wooll o' the Bever?
> Or Swans Downe ever?
> Or have smelt o' the bud o' the Brier?
> Or the Nard i' the fire?
> Or have tasted the bag o' the Bee?
> O so white! O so soft! O so sweet is she!

Feeling, smelling, tasting: the sexual act predicted by these verbs is kissing.[7]

Presumably Jonson receives a first kiss for the praises of Charis in poem 5, since poem 6 is titled "Clayming a second kisse by Desert" and ends wondering "if such a verse as this, / May not claime another kisse." How much is a kiss worth? One of Cleopatra's repays Antony for his losses at Actium. Jonson assured Celia that, should she "leave a kiss but in the cup," he'd "not look for wine": given his fondness for cups of wine, this is truly

4. I quote from the translation of the "Twelfth Kiss" by Fred J. Nichols in *An Anthology of Neo-Latin Poetry* (New Haven: Yale Univ. Press, 1979), p. 505. One of the Caroline Sons of Ben, Thomas Stanley, englished most of the *Basia*.
5. On the verge of a discussion of the English Renaissance kiss lyric, it may be worth noting that, according to Michael Drayton, the British were known for their "*Kissing Salutations*, given and accepted amongst us with more freedom than in any part of the Southern world" (*The Works of Michael Drayton*, ed. J. William Hebel, 5 vols. [Oxford: Shakespeare Head Press, 1931–41], 4, ix).
6. Stanley Fish, "Authors-Readers: Jonson's Community of the Same," *Representations*, 7 (1984), 50.
7. It is a cliche of the period that smelling a flower equals kissing, as in Othello's "I'le smell thee on the tree." Perhaps the most memorable example is the flowery kiss of *Amoretti* 59: "Comming to kisse her lyps, (such grace I found) / Me thinks I smelt a gardin of sweet flowres."

a valuable kiss. In the transactions of "The Celebration" kissing is still more dear, since a Charis kiss is worth precisely one Jonson lyric.

The equivalence of a poem and a kiss becomes a fusion in poem 8, "Begging another, on colour of mending the former." Here, adopting the role of a middle-aged kiss instructor, Jonson makes a graphic lyric of his desire for a full and unending kiss:

> Joyne lip to lip, and try:
> Each suck the others breath.
> And whilst our tongues perplexed lie,
> Let who will thinke us dead, or wish our death.

At this moment the reader becomes fully aware of the substitution of kissing for genital consummation in this lyric courtship. Moreover, this change has allowed Jonson to perform a remarkable imaginative alchemy. The embarrassment, the ridiculousness, is gone, replaced by a booming economy of innocence and delight. The lineal descendent of love's first act, born at the sweetness of the breast, kissing is a shameless ardor; imagine the darkened tone if Jonson, claiming his lyric pieces were worth Charis' sexual compliance, had described the conventional "death" of mutual orgasm in this poem. Kissing is the touch that, in the terms of "Her Triumph," does not sever the white lily or smutch the virgin snow.

Edward Herbert's lyric "Kissing" is a Puttenham-like catalogue of varieties of kisses. The one Jonson teaches Charis is, appropriately enough, "The kiss of eloquence, which doth belong / Unto the tongue."[8] Jonson knew that "Begging another" was a triumph of lyric grace; he had it by heart, and recited it for Drummond. The poem puts me in mind of early Heidegger's insistence on "the hiddenness of the obvious," since it reveals something that is both apparent and unknown. As is not the case with intercourse, the orifices joined in kissing have no gender differences. Both have lips, and both have tongues, and both are, if you will, *both*. Mouths joined in kissing fit like the halves of an equation.

This equality of the sexes, rare in Renaissance love poetry, grows from its roots in the kiss of eloquence into the full charm of the sequence. In the remaining poems the spry exuberance of the fifty-year-old kiss instructor must weather disillusionment. The perplexed tongues foreshadow the "dictamen" of Charis, who will indeed have a tongue, a lyric of her own. She turns out to want everything Jonson can offer ("the language, and the truth"), along with the youth and nobility he so conspicuously lacks. She wants, in so many words, the male counterpart of herself. Jonson does not reproach her. Rather, the sequence ends with the response of a coarse lady from the love dialogue tradition. In the final line of "The Celebration" she places a thing unmentioned thus far in these ten lyric pieces, a penis, that lower and exclusively male tongue:

> What you please, you parts may call,
> 'Tis one good part I'd lie withall.

This is another mood, another sort of poetry—the Jonson of the urban epigrams and the comedies. The penis in the last line has the force of reality, exposing the impotence of the lyric world of mere kissing. Only a

8. *The Poems of Lord Herbert of Cherbury*, ed. G. C. Moore Smith (Oxford: Clarendon Press, 1923), p. 31.

confident master of poetic fantasy could make such innocent beauty then concede at a stroke its ridiculousness.

Up to a point, the most loyal of the Sons of Ben followed after his master in lyric kissing. Yet in Herrick the economy of kisses is strangely and intriguingly disturbed. First of all, the Herrick kiss does not stay put, as he tells us in "The Kisse. A Dialogue":

> Then to the chin, the cheek, the eare,
> It frisks, and flyes, now here, now there,
> 'Tis now farre off, and then tis nere;
> And here, and there, and every where.

Unlike Jonson's, his untethered kisses roam from the mouth, and as they do encounter the general atmosphere of blush and rebuke commentators have noted. The Herrick of "The Shooe-tying" kisses the lady's instep, "And would have kist unto her knee, / Had not her Blush rebuked me." In "The Vision" a dreaming Herrick moves to kiss a goddess' thigh, at which point the spell is broken by her reprimand: "Hence, Remove, / *Herrick*, thou are too coorse to love." Rather than reveling in a kingdom free from shame, his kisses seem to seek shame out.

Probably the best poem to end in reticence and paralyzing self-exposure is "The Vine":

> I dream'd this mortal part of mine
> Was Metamorphoz'd to a Vine;
> Which crawling one and every way,
> Enthrall'd my dainty *Lucia*.
> Me thought, her long small legs & thighs
> I with my *Tendrils* did surprize;
> Her Belly, Buttocks, and her Waste
> By my soft *Nerv'lits* were embrac'd:
> About her head I writhing hung,
> And with rich clusters (hid among
> The leaves) her temples I behung:
> So that my *Lucia* seem'd to me
> Young *Bacchus* ravisht by his tree.
> My curles about her neck did craule,
> And armes and hands they did enthrall:
> So that she could not freely stir,
> (All parts there made one prisoner.)
> But when I crept with leaves to hide
> Those parts, which maids keep unespy'd,
> Such fleeting pleasures there I took,
> That with the fancie I awook;
> And found (Ah me!) this flesh of mine
> More like a *Stock*, then like a *Vine*.

The dreamer awakens, as one expelled from paradise, because of "fleeting pleasures" derived from the sexual "fancie." In a second metamorphosis, he finds his flesh "More like a *Stock*," a tree trunk stripped of its branches—presumably an allusion to an erect penis.

Although the poem is clearly structured about a contrast between the dream and the awakening, it is by no means obvious what Herrick makes of the difference. "Ah me!" signals regret. But what exactly is the disappointment? If his sorrow stems from the interruption of his "fleeting pleasures," why can imagination not resume them, albeit without the hallucinatory power of the dream? Perhaps the waking man can only return to his dream pleasure through masturbation. The "mineness" of the body is stressed in the first and penultimate lines. What Lucia is in the dream, an erect figure about which the vine circles, the stock of the erection becomes upon awakening. The nearest equivalent to the vine in the waking realm would then be the fingers of his hand. Perhaps the dream itself is somehow aware of being an accompaniment to self-stimulation that would be shameful in the waking state—hence the gender ambivalence in comparing Lucia to Bacchus, the wine-god with whom Herrick is affiliated in other poems.[9] Indeed, the poet's comparison of Bacchus and Lucia seems intended to create an anamorphosis in which Herrick encircling Lucia is simultaneously Lucia encircling Lucia. The allusion to Bacchus ravished by his tree is probably a refashioning of the story at the end of Book 3 of Ovid's *Metamorphoses*, where Bacchus protects himself against pirates by first entangling their suddenly motionless ship in vines.[1] Lucia seems to the poet a Bacchus who has, as it were, welcomed the ravishing courtship of her own instruments. Herrick has folded his own agency into the vines Bacchus/Lucia controls, and transformed them from aggressive weapons to ardent embracers; the assumption of an Ovidian backdrop would also motivate the equation of embracing and imprisoning. Upon awakening, the hints of self-stimulation in the dream itself are left implicit in the general regret of "Ay me!" Like the "one good part" in the last line of "The Celebration of Charis," the penis at the end of the poem signifies reality. But in Jonson the penis lies with another. Herrick's reality is lonesome, a tiny transmitter that only he receives.

If these shots in the dark have merit, the contrast at the heart of the poem is between two forms of solitude, one in which fancy induces the illusion of partnership and one in which, illusion shattered, the poet is alone with his desire. Put another way, it is the difference between poetry and fact. The stock stops the poem.

"The Vine" is recognizably a variation on Jonson's trick of regaining innocence by staging his own humiliation. But Jonson was an egotist who became surprisingly adept at administering to himself well-deserved doses of self-mockery. Herrick is the victim of some perverse creature in the deep pools of his fancy. Through the summary line "(All parts there made one prisoner)," the intent of the vine is to capture Lucia part by part, the poet's concentration being so intensely distributed on her parts that there is some surprise they should add up to one creature. Beginning with line 18, his

9. In another dream poem, "The Vision," a disappointed maiden gives Herrick "the wreath" of a "cup-shot" Anacreon. Ever since receiving this gift, "my brains about do swim, / And I am wild and wanton like to him." The crown of poetic success bears with it the curse of sexual impotence. Early in the poem Anacreon's wreath is referred to as "A crawling vine."

1. I am assuming that "About her head I writhing hung, / And with rich clusters (hid among / The leaves) her temples I behung" evokes, in Herrick's mind, *Metamorphoses*, Book 3, 11.666–67:

> ipse racemiferis frontem circumdatus uuis
> pampineis agitat uelatam frondibus hastam;

> [He himself had his forehead surrounded with grapes in
> bunches as he brandished a spear clothed in vine leaves]

I use the translation of D. E. Hill in *Metamorphoses I–IV* (Oak Park, Illinois: Bolchazy-Carducci, 1985).

motive shifts emphatically: now the poet-vine, rather than wishing to imprison Lucia, wants to cover the parts normally left unespied, a champion of his maiden's modesty. Clearly she cannot now move to secure her own decency; her captor, by performing this service for her, is demonstrating his civility. The moment he discovers another and self-interested motive, the "fleeting pleasures," he is ejected from the dream. As in "The Shoe-tying" and "The Vision," refined manners give leeway to a coarseness they are apparently designed to banish.

We might pause to wonder just which parts the vine tries to cover. Since the poet has already run his soft nervelets over "Her Belly, Buttocks, and her Waste," "Those parts, which maids keep unespy'd" may refer only to the breasts, the main parts as yet unmentioned in the poem.[2] But I expect that most readers assume those parts to include the vagina. It is in fact the sudden juxtaposition of poet-vine's encounter with the vagina and his immediate awakening to the stock of an erect penis that gives the poem its power and poignance. The poet is in a melancholy trance of genital research. The two things that belong together in consummated love reside in two separate worlds, and the oneiric world, where the vagina exists, does not allow contact.

I think the lyric belongs among Herrick's kiss poems. The vine is superior to the penis because it is not a penis merely, but a penis fused with a tongue (thus the "soft *Nerv'lits*" of the vine), just as the vagina for Herrick is not a vagina merely, but a vagina fused with a breast. Kissing is meant to divert erotic energy from the consummation of intercourse. But a classic psychoanalytic fate intervenes: deny one of life's formidable masters, such as genital sexuality, and it will reappear in the very terms set forth to deny it. Intercourse reemerges in the dream of "The Vine" as cunnilingus, for Herrick a forbidden and shameful kiss that would regain in the clitoris the first oral object, the nipple of the breast.[3]

Herrick's sexuality is suspended between the oral and the genital. Ordinarily, as in Jonson, these erotic zones or genres distinguish ideal lyric innocence from comic or satirical debasement. But in *Hesperides* orality itself is split into the sweet and the shameful. I know of only one poem in which Herrick explicitly and unambiguously rejects the precedent of Jonson. The piece is called "Kisses Loathsome." Even at the mouth, the home station of kissers, there is conflict:

I abhor the slimie kisse,
(Which to me most loathsome is.)
Those lips please me which are plac't
Close, but not too strictly lac'd:
Yielding I wo'd have them; yet
Not a wimbling Tongue admit:
What sho'd poking-sticks make there,
When the ruffe is set elsewhere?

2. This interpretation would be in line with the erotic temperament found elsewhere in Herrick. In "To Dianeme" ("Shew me thy feet"), the climactic revelation of her undressing is the "All" of her breasts; Herrick's imitation of Jonson's "Her Triumph" is the strawberries and cream of "Upon the Nipples of Julia's Breast." See also "Julia's Breasts."

3. References to cunnilingus in Renaissance love poetry are exceedingly rare. The only one I have encountered in seventeenth-century English verse appears in Carew's "The Rapture." On the clitoris in Herrick, see Hammond's interpretation of "To his Closet-Gods" in *Fleeting Things*, p. 286.

The kiss Jonson taught, the eloquent kiss of perplexed tongues, the kiss without gender difference, is presumably too loathsome to be considered.[4] The poem rejects a kiss in which the man's tongue enters the woman's mouth. A "wimble" is a gimlet, or in general any tool that bores into something, making a hole. A "wimbling tongue" is thus a tongue penetrating another's mouth (the *OED* entry on the verb "wimble" cites this poem). A "ruffe" is a starched linen collar into which poking-sticks are inserted.[5] Herrick does not want the woman's mouth to admit his poking-stick tongue because the ruffe is set elsewhere on her body: poking-stick penises should be inserted there, in the vagina.

Yet the loathsomeness of such a kiss appears to derive from its resemblance to intercourse in the opening of the woman's mouth, the penetration, the sliminess. Moreover, the meaning of poking-sticks in the final line, which includes both tongues and penises, inevitably (if, on the poet's part, unconsciously) evokes cunnilingus at the thought that they belong in the ruffe of the vagina. Given the direction of the kissing in "The Shoe-tying," "The Vision," and "The Vine," we may speculate that the rejected kiss awakens the fleeting interdicted pleasure of putting the oral poking-stick in the genital ruffe, a fancy that embodies all too concretely, too shamefully, Herrick's confusion of developmental zones. This odd lyric spits out a forbidden desire. It is also worth noting that the set of the woman's mouth, not the discipline of the man's tongue, is supposed to prevent this abhorrent kiss from happening: when men (or women) are most at war with their strictures, they vest another with the duties of their own uncertain self-control.

Innocence is not carefree in Herrick. As readers of his verse, we pay for the elation of "How Lillies came white" with the disgust of "Kisses Loathsome." The conflicts of "The Vine" are not those of pampered negligence: there is a huge mysterious sadness in the way that poem delivers, with no commentary besides regret, the parting image of Herrick's erection. These epigrams are a terrific resource for those interested in how civilization shapes, and is shaped by, erotic fantasy. Did they cost their maker a great deal? We tend to believe that art, especially when it appears to be joyous and even frivolous, is more valuable if in truth it grew from the loam of suffering and sacrifice. Maybe Braden, when he intuits Herrick's uneasy celibacy, is simply making up a conventional case for the dignity of the verse. But I also detect a sadness in Herrick, mixed in with the devotion, panegyric, and exhilaration of the love poetry.

I hear it in the lonely confined voice of "Corinna's going a Maying," urgently trying to rouse his mate:

> So when or you or I are made
> A fable, song, or fleeting shade;
> All love, all liking, all delight
> Lies drown'd with us in endlesse night.
> Then while time serves, and we are but decaying;
> Come, my *Corinna*, come, let's goe a Maying.

4. Other instances of male "kiss disgust" occur at the end of Edward Herbert's "Kissing" and in Hamlet's "pair of reechy kisses" (3.4.184). Examples from the female point of view turn on discomfort with the beard: *Much Ado About Nothing*, 2.1.26–28 and Marston's *The Dutch Courtesan*, 3.1.10ff.

5. Sexual plays on the ruffe and poking-stick are also found in Middleton and Dekker's *The Honest Whore, Part I*, 2.1.18–22.

They will be dead when they are made a fable or a song—and they are, and they are. Corinna is still inside. Herrick, too, is inside, writing the fable and the song. The excellence of the poem, in my view, lies in the fact that Herrick is not only trying to persuade Corinna to go a-Maying, but is also exhorting himself. His most famous poem measures the cost of his art: a sexual desire enmeshed in poetry, pressing to get out and be something under the sun.

GERALD HAMMOND

Caught in the Web of Dreams: The Dead†

Superimposing the living upon the dead and the dead upon the living is one of seventeenth-century poetry's major concerns. Having no body to bury makes Milton restore it at the end of *Lycidas*, the sea giving it back at the moment when the poet celebrates Edward King's entry into heaven. Theologically this is nice. Here are man's two bodies, the corruptible and the incorruptible. While seawater is cleaned off the first, tears are wiped away from the second. The mind's eye has to hold both in view, together if possible—otherwise, alternately, like Jonson's Cary and Morison, the one on earth and the other in heaven. Look at Cary as he ages and you see how Morison would have grown old. Remember Morison forever young and in his prime and you remember how Cary used to be: "each styled by his end, / The copy of his friend." The living shepherd heading eastward to new pastures at the end of *Lycidas* is a reflection of his dead friend, the sun dropped into the western bay. The eye holds both images together.

At its most basic this is a matter of optics. "Upon Appleton House" is the *locus classicus* for altered perspectives and superimpositions, many of them shifting from the dead past to the living present. The merging of Thwaites and Maria, Fairfax and his ancestor, is part of the same process which makes the eye see at one moment cows in a field, at another spots on a face or a constellation in the skies. While much can be described by the new science of optics, more depends upon the knowledge and expectations of the observer. Knowing the history of the Fairfax family encourages Marvell to see the nunnery from whose demolition the stones were taken for the building of the house. The stones themselves are neutral, only their context making them vicious or just. The eye sees both possibilities.

Lovelace's "Aramantha," a pastoral poem which influenced "Upon Appleton House," pins its rambling narrative upon just such a shift in perspective. Two former lovers meet by apparent chance in a wood, mistake each other to the point where violence is imminent, and then suddenly see that they are Alexis and Lucasta, not a shepherd and Aramantha. The moment of recognition is recounted with a significant parallel (298–308):

Now as in war intestine, where
I'th' mist of a black battle, each

† From "Caught in the Web of Dreams" in *Fleeting Things: English Poets and Poems, 1616–1660* (Cambridge: Harvard University Press, 1990), pp. 194–200, 208–18.

Lays at his next, then makes a breach
Through th'entrails of another whom
He sees nor knows when he did come
Guided alone by rage and th' drum,
But stripping and impatient wild,
He finds too soon his only child.
So our expiring desp'rate lover
Fared, when amazed he did discover
Lucasta in this nymph . . .

In a state in which divisions have been driven so deep that civil war has come about, the poet becomes interested in how different eyes see the same thing in different ways, and in how difficult it becomes to hold onto one view of a thing as circumstances alter radically and swiftly.

Lovelace's poetry has many such shifts in appearance and observation. The poem in praise of Lely's portrait of Charles I and his son at Hampton Court alternates between the artist's perception of a subject and a subject's (in the other sense) perception of his king. The focus is carefully blurred. One is looking through tears, sorrowing at the sight of a monarch so reduced; and one is looking at tears, admiring the artist's skill in showing them about to well up, or held back from their subjects' eyes. This is part of Lovelace's vision of the committed Cavalier in prison:[1]

Stone walls do not a prison make,
Nor iron bars a cage;
Minds innocent and quiet take
That for an hermitage;
If I have freedom in my love,
And in my soul am free;
Angels alone that soar above,
Enjoy such liberty.

The most liberated man is the one most closely confined. The very tangibility of walls and bars frees the imagination. But this is not the freedom of transcendence or detached meditation, for more than anything else the stanza registers the presence of iron and stone, rather as Jonson's imaginative recreation of the breadth of English society and history in his late plays is fixed firmly to his own immobility and confinement. The focus moves forward and backward, alternating between solid and abstract without losing sight of either. In another poem, "Lucasta's Fan With a Looking Glass in It," Lovelace has Lucasta moving across a ballroom floor in all her finery, with her ostrich-feather fan at her side, to be suddenly perceived as the ostrich itself—the eye alternating between one of creation's most elegant objects and one of its most ungainly.

Herrick's short poems often treat such visual puzzles, when nipples become strawberries or a leg becomes an egg. This is a moment of sudden illusion:

The Silken Snake

For sport my *Julia* threw a Lace
Of silk and silver at my face:

1. "To Althea From Prison," 25–32.

Watchet the silk was; and did make
A show, as if't'ad been a snake:
The suddenness did me affright;
But though it scared, it did not bite.

As usual in Herrick's poetry, the situation is entirely domestic, the ingredients of the poem as commonplace as the "Argument of his Book" promises the readers of *Hesperides*, the behavior of the protagonists entirely harmless—even flirtation would be too strong a word for it. And yet the poem is full of sexuality, violence, and death. Only a fraction of a second is occupied by such possibilities, but it takes only a fraction of a second to die. The suddenness of the whole thing is what frightens him. Within its tiny space the incident reveals her repressed aggression, their potential sexual relationship, his role as victim, and, most of all, how beneath the trained, rational practices of polite behavior there is an instinct always on the alert for the final threat. His eye responds in two ways, simultaneously: civilized man, knowing the games the sexes play, registers the details of color and material as well as motive ("for sport"); savage man sees the predator about to strike.

Milton plays skillfully on just this kind of double sight in *Paradise Lost* when Satan approaches Eve to mount the great temptation. Solitary at last, she stands doing her gardening work, in just such a way as to heighten the fallen reader's responses (9:424–427):

Eve separate he spies,
Veiled in a cloud of fragrance, where she stood,
Half spied, so thick the roses bushing round
About her glowed . . .

The immediate memory here is of Guyon's temptresses on the way in to the Bower of Bliss in *The Faerie Queene*: their eroticism is magnified by their nakedness being perceived through water. Herrick's poetry is also full of veils and thin tissues of lawn through which the object of beauty is only half or three-quarters perceived. In a brief poem called "The Lawn" this effect is transferred to the skin itself:

Would I see Lawn, clear as the Heaven, and thin?
It should be only in my *Julia's* skin:
Which so betrays her blood, as we discover
The blush of cherries, when a Lawn's cast over.

While this is a classic piece of seventeenth-century aesthetic appreciation, it is disturbing, too, in its realization of how thin is the membrane which keeps life in. Milton's Eve is veiled and half-spied in a way calculated to delight anyone who shares Herrick's delight in near transparencies: "bushing" is carefully chosen to match the flora to her pubic hair, so that we cannot be quite sure which of the two we are catching glimpses of.[2] Like Satan we are encouraged to approach her in appreciation of her beauty and, as her predator, in appreciation of her defenselessness. Because she is an unfallen creature she lacks any such double vision: Milton describes her as "mindless" (431), conveying all of her vulnerability to the Darwinian world she is soon to enter. In any garden where snakes are common, fallen

2. Most American editions of *Paradise Lost* carry the misprint "blushing" for "bushing," anticipating one of my later themes.

humans stay very mindful of their existence; even Herrick's *homo domesticus* has the instinct. After the Fall Adam soon learns to look at nature with a double eye. In the unfallen garden the human couple make no distinction between the elephant writhing his trunk and the serpent writhing his body; both are elements in the Disney park of entertainment which exists for their amusement. Now, however, the aesthete has to make space for the animal which can be both hunter and hunted (11:184–193):

> night in her sight
> The bird of Jove, stooped from his airy tower,
> Two birds of gayest plume before him drove:
> Down from a hill the beast that reigns in woods,
> First hunter then, pursued a gentle brace,
> Goodliest of all the forest, hart and hind;
> Direct to the eastern gate was bent their flight.
> Adam observed, and with his eye the chase
> Pursuing, not unmoved to Eve thus spake.
> O Eve, some further change awaits us nigh . . .

Again, we can see how attractive this poem must have been to a man beginning to formulate a theory of natural adaptation and selection.

Man's most painful adaptation is to the knowledge of his aging and death. This is Herrick's "On Julia's Picture":

> How am I ravished! When I do but see,
> The Painter's art in thy *Sciography?*
> If so, how much more shall I dote thereon,
> When once he gives it incarnation?

"*Sciography*" catches the eye: so technical a word in so slight a poem. Herrick is having fun showing how even his fragments can find room for the technicalities of art. But the word which shifts the poem from theory to the real world of life and feeling is "incarnation." The artist incarnates his sciograph by filling it in with a flesh color.[3] In doing this he slides it away from representation toward real existence, which means life, aging, and death. *Incarnation* had, and still has, as its principal sense God's taking on of human flesh. The devil in *Paradise Lost*, who parodies all of Christ's actions, takes on serpent's flesh with the same word (9:163–167):

> O foul descent! That I who erst contended
> With gods to sit the highest, am now constrained
> Into a beast, and mixed with bestial slime,
> This essence to incarnate and imbrute,
> That to the height of deity aspired . . .

Incarnating an essence is just what happens to Julia in Herrick's poem. *Sciography*, from the Greek *skia*, "shadow," is "that branch of the science of Perspective which deals with the projection of shadows."[4] Julia, sketched in outline, shadows without color, is so essentially recognizable that the image ravishes Herrick: her incarnation will be unbearably exciting. But behind this hope is the frustrating sense that all incarnations are really illusions. The closer her image is brought to a living, breathing

3. *OED*, s.v. "incarnation," 5: "Flesh-colour, carnation; a pigment or dye of this colour" (quotation from the *Art of Limning*, 1575).
4. *OED*, s.v. "sciagraphy."

human being, the further one is removed from the unchanging essence, for incarnation is a matter of subtle and constant alterations of tone. Satan dismisses it as imbrutement and mixture with bestial slime. We might agree with him about taking on the flesh of a serpent, except that at this stage in the poem the snake is still a creature who goes erect rather than crawling in the dust, and its beauty marks it out among the other beasts in the garden. It comes down to a matter of perspective, to whether we stress the spiritual sense of *incarnation*—that is, its color—or its carnal sense.

John Suckling begins his "Farewell to Love" by describing the ladies whom he abandons as a "well-shadowed landskip." His image of them soon deteriorates into Grand Guignol (21–50):[5]

Oh! how I glory now! that I
Have made this new discovery!
Each wanton eye
Inflamed before: no more
Will I increase that score.

If I gaze now, 'tis but to see
What manner of death's-head 'twill be,
When it is free
From that fresh upper skin,
The gazer's Joy and sin.

The Gum and glist'ning which with art
And studied method in each part
Hangs down the heart,
Looks (just) as if, that day
Snails there had crawled the *Hay*.

The Locks, that curled o'er each ear be,
Hang like two Master-worms to me,
That (as we see)
Have tasted to the rest
Two holes, where they like 't best.

A quick corse, methinks, I spy
In every woman, and mine eye,
At passing by,
Checks, and is troubled, just
As if it rose from dust.

They mortify, not heighten me:
These of my sins the Glasses be:
And here I see
How I have loved before,
And so I love no more.

As the eye, so the object; and when the eye is haunted by images of death, then the more beautiful the sight, the more of a *memento mori* it becomes.

5. Suckling's poems are from Thomas Clayton, ed., *The Works of Sir John Suckling*, vol. 1 (Oxford, 1971). In line 37 "heart" is often emended to "hair."

Much of Suckling's poetry is concerned with different ways of looking at the same thing, as in the supposed dialogue with Carew on "My Lady Carlisle's Walking in Hampton Court Garden," where Carew's idealism is undercut by Suckling's mental stripping of the lady; or a "Sonnet" which begins:

> Dost see how unregarded now
> that piece of beauty passes?
> There was a time when I did vow
> to that alone;
> but mark the fate of faces;
> That red and white works now no more on me
> Than if it could not charm or I not see.

There is more than mere libertinage in these poems. True, they function in part as defenses for inconstancy, but they have an edge of bafflement at the way the eye refuses to hold a stable, unchanging view of a subject whose beauty should command undeviating fidelity. Hence comes the popularity of so much *carpe diem* verse, which pretends to be concerned with seduction, but which is really only using this plea as a stratagem for exploring the processes of aging and death. Like the application of cosmetics it is a means of escaping the tyranny of the present moment. Where the one covers up wrinkles and rouges away the paleness of sickness or age, the other paints in the lines and accelerates youth into experience.

* * *

How far one's identity is bound to one's body is always a puzzle, the more so in a period when the very idea of identity was such a novel thing. It was an idea which was tested at all levels. Poems on Charles I's death took the highest view, relating not only body to soul but also king to man, and, naturally, they celebrated the concept of the two identities of the king which the Stuart propagandists had pushed so hard. Charles came to be, in the eyes of friends and enemies, a king and no king. But on lower levels poets speculated on smaller amputations than the decapitation of a monarch. Herrick has a poem on the loss of a finger; Thomas Randolph has two. Herrick's is the shortest of the three and most to the point:

Upon the Loss of his Finger

> One of the five straight branches of my hand
> Is lopped already; and the rest but stand
> Expecting when to fall: which soon will be;
> First dies the Leaf, the Bough next, next the Tree.

Trunk is the unspoken word here. Its first three definitions in the *OED* are "the main stem of a tree," "the human body," "a dead body . . . also the body considered apart from the soul or life." Herrick's poem moves through all of these meanings. Whether "expecting" includes a hope of the life to come, the expectation of heaven, or only a patient resignation to the fact of annihilation is left unanswered, but the austerity of the poem allows no room for consolation. Randolph, in contrast, is all wit and extravagance:[6]

6. Randolph's poems are from John Jay Parry, ed., *The Poems and Amyntas of Thomas Randolph* (New Haven, 1917).

On the Loss of his Finger

How much more blest are trees than men,
Their boughs lopped off will grow again;
But if the steel our limbs dissever,
The joint once lost is lost for ever.
But fondly I dull fool complain,
Our members shall revive again;
And thou poor finger that art dust
Before the other members, must
Return as soon at heaven's command,
And reunited be to th' hand
As those that are not ashes yet;
Why dost thou then so envious sit,
And malice Oaks that they to fate
Are tenants of a longer date?
Their leafs do more years include
But once expired, are ne'er renewed.
Therefore dear finger though thou be
Cut from those muscles governed thee,
And had thy motion at command,
Yet still as in a margent stand,
To point my thoughts to fix upon
The hope of Resurrection:
And since thou canst no finger be
Be a death's head to humble me,
Till death doth threat her sting in vain,
And we in heaven shake hands again.

This is the lesser known of the two poems on his lost finger, but the more amusing of the two in the variety of symbols it has the finger playing, right down to the admonitory sign in the margin. And in even so light a piece there is still room for bafflement over the identity which controls the muscles which control the finger. That little piece of flesh and bone has a separate identity, its own body and brain, rendering it capable of a handshake at the end. I suppose there is even the possibility of the finger being saved while the rest of the body, because of its later dissolute life, is damned.

One of Herrick's best death poems, only three lines long, is "On Himself." This title could introduce any kind of epigram, but this is an epitaph. So, with every word counting double in such a tight, little poem, "On" adds to its normal meaning in a title—"About"—a literal location, the inscription on the gravestone:[7]

Lost to the world; lost to my self; alone
Here now I rest under this Marble stone:
In depth of silence, heard, and seen of none.

Few poems say so much in so little space. In spite of its size, Herrick can afford repetition. "Lost," doubly emphasized by its initiating the poem and its repetition, is the other side of *restore*. To lose one's self is a haunting

7. It is common in modernizing seventeenth-century texts to change the *my self* to *myself*, but because this poem plays on a distinction between Herrick and his self, I have kept the original form.

theme of seventeenth-century lyric poetry. How one can say, as Herrick does here, that I have lost my self, is a puzzle, for an I which has no self is difficult to conceive. Riddles lie here, and we have already seen that the grave is the one place where unriddling is guaranteed. That is the job for the worms, creatures not entirely removed from poets and readers of poems who also burrow into echoing vaults and try too-long-preserved virginities. The I who writes Herrick's poem is the I who is alive in the 1630s and 1640s, while the "now" is now, all these hundreds of years after 1674. Hence the title "On Himself" rather than "On Myself," for to the readers of "now" Herrick is a third person whose identity is constructed out of the poems. In "alone" is the terrible alienation of the dead, cut off from everything which gave them their identity; the alienation of the living, also, for the continuum between life and death is virtually unbroken—in Flatman's words, "one unlucky moment" which "sever[s] / Us, and our hopes, us and our joys for ever." Milton writes about Edward King as if his corpse had the power of volition which an identity would allow it, visiting, sleeping, and looking homeward. According to the poem's argument these are no longer the "frail thoughts" of the pathetic fallacy passage, but a new realism in which the poet comes to terms with the absence of King's corpse and its humming around the oceans of the world. But perhaps a concern of *Lycidas* is to show how our frailty prevents us from looking squarely at death. As the Psalmist puts it (39:4): "Lord, make me to know mine end, and the measure of my days, what it is; that I may know how frail I am." The Authorized Version's marginal alternative to "how frail I am" is "what time I have here."

The frailest of all human notions is that the dead are only sleeping or resting. Lycidas sleeps just off Land's End, near St. Michael's Mount. Herrick rests alone under the marble stone. "Rest" is slightly tougher than *sleep* because it allows in a little more of the inanimation which a corpse has—things can rest merely by lying in or on something else, unlike animate creatures, who rest in order to wake refreshed. Herrick rests in "depth of silence." The depth is literal enough, under ground, but slides into the figurative when attached to silence. All seems to find compensation with "heard"—"In depth of silence, heard"—and our frail responses to the duplicity of Herrick's syntax raise the possibilities of some heroic survival of identity in a voice which, through his poems, outbraves the oblivion of death. But "heard" is cruelly extended into "and seen of none," a final reminder that the grave's silence is a double one: we hear nothing and we say nothing.

Herrick was just as austere when mourning others, as in his four-line poem "Upon his Sister-in-Law, Mistress Elizabeth Herrick":

> First, for Effusions due unto the dead,
> My solemn Vows have here accomplished:
> Next, how I love thee, that my grief must tell,
> Wherein thou liv'st for ever. Dear farewell.

Really, the whole statement is contained in the final two words. They fulfill the solemn vows which are introduced in lines 1–2 and declare Herrick's love for his dead relative, and explained in lines 3–4. The poem is about our responsibilities to the dead; hence the careful statement of the first line, making clear the difference between us and them. They, for all their individuality, are part of that anonymous crowd labeled "the dead," the city more populous than London itself. What we can salvage of their identity we do with our grief, but the frail illusion of their survival is cut down by the sudden following of "for ever" with "farewell," a tiny parallel to Milton's shepherd striding off toward the east, his back to the Irish Sea.

"Dear," Herrick's address to his dead sister-in-law, is a remembered intimacy. As the corpse decays it becomes ever more difficult to restore our closeness to it. Strode has a gentle poem, one of the common genre in which ladies were counseled on how to mourn their dead husbands, in which he directs "the Right Honourable the Lady Penelope, Dowager of the Late Viscount Bayning" on how to bear her loss:

> Great Lady,
>   Humble partners of like grief
> In bringing Comfort may deserve belief,
> Because they Feel and Feign not: Thus we say
> Unto Ourselves, Lord Bayning, though away,
> Is still of Christ-Church; somewhat out of sight,
> As when he travelled, or did bid good night,
> And was not seen long after; now he stands
> Removed in Worlds, as heretofore in Lands;
> But is not lost. The spite of Death can never
> Divide the Christian, though the Man it sever.
>   The like we say to You: He's still at home,
> Though out of reach; as in some upper room,
> Or Study: for His Place is very high,
> His Thought is Vision; now most properly
> Returned he's Yours as sure, as e'er hath been
> The jewel in Your Cask, safe though unseen.
>   You know that Friends have Ears as well as Eyes,
> We hear He's well and Living, that well dies.

Here death is entirely domesticated. So strong was the dead lord's personality that his identity is marked upon each room of the house, his absence felt as temporary. Surely he will soon come through the door or be glimpsed in the hallway. Strode's poem plays on the frailest of our responses to death, that the dead still haunt us, their identity being so strongly impressed on our memory that we sense their presence about and around us. The experience is at once comforting and unnerving. Lady Penelope will welcome the constant reminders of her dead husband's existence as a sign that all is not lost even if all cannot be restored; but there is an alienation built into such experiences, for they will remind her that her own identity is as insubstantial as a dream.

Sleep is where the dead haunt the living most strongly, often refusing to accept that they are different from us. Milton's nineteenth sonnet, written probably in the late 1650s, is the most moving description of such an experience:

> Methought I saw my late espoused saint
>   Brought to me like Alcestis from the grave,
>   Whom Jove's great son to her glad husband gave,
>   Rescued from death by force though pale and faint.
> Mine as whom washed from spot of childbed taint,

Purification in the old Law did save,
And such, as yet once more I trust to have
Full sight of her in heaven without restraint,
Came vested all in white, pure as her mind:
Her face was veiled, yet to my fancied sight,
Love, sweetness, goodness in her person shined
So clear, as in no face with more delight.
But O as to embrace me she inclined
I waked, she fled, and day brought back my night.

The critical dispute over which of his two dead wives Milton remembers here is unresolved, the preference possibly being for Katherine, who died in February 1658, having borne a daughter in October of the previous year, over Mary, who died three days after their daughter's birth in May 1652. These biographical facts are important to any interpretation of the sonnet's reference to the ceremony of the purification of women after childbirth. Other biographical details which affect our response to the poem are Milton's blindness—he had seen Mary but had never seen Katharine—and the possibilities that Mary is represented in the poem as the virgin Mary in line 5, who "accomplished the days of her purification" (Luke 2:22), or that Katharine, from *katharos*, "pure," is referred to throughout in the repeated insistence upon purification and cleansing. The balance of that evidence points to Katharine, and we might think, too, that "saint" is more appropriate to Katharine Woodcock than to Mary Powell if Milton is using the word in the Puritan sense of a living member of a community of believers.

It is, after all, a very Puritan sonnet in its celebration of married love and its stress on purity of body and mind. It stands as one of the most austere love poems in our literature, the more moving for that, as it harnesses an almost complete incongruity of language and syntax to the most traditional themes of love poetry—the woman coming to the bed, the wished-for embrace, and, eventually, unrequited love. Behind the image which he thinks he sees Milton is remembering Petrarch's Laura, Dante's Beatrice, perhaps Wyatt's newfangled mistress, perhaps even Shakespeare's master-mistress whose appearance in dreams makes "nights bright days," and, certainly, Odysseus' vain attempts to embrace his mother in the underworld in book II of the *Odyssey*.[8]

In this book Achilles tells Odysseus that all the visions he sees are not realities, but each is merely an afterimage, an *eidolon*; the only exception being Hercules, who has been genuinely transformed into a higher being.[9] Hercules is in Milton's sonnet too, as "Jove's great son"; but his apotheosis is certain, marked by his power to enter and return from the land of death. In Milton's poem the female vision is an *eidolon* and nothing more—"an image or unsubstantial appearance; a spectre or phantom; a mental image, an idea"[1]—which flees the imaginer's return to full consciousness. The experience is a veiled one, as befits a dream, particularly the dream of a blind man. "Methought I saw" would itself be a powerful piece of wish

8. An interesting parallel comes in Herrick's "The Vision," which begins "Me thought I saw (as I did dream in bed). . . ."
9. *Eidolon* (XI.476) is translated by Richmond Lattimore as "mere imitations of perished mortals," by Robert Fitzgerald as "the after-images of used-up men."
1. *OED*, s.v. "idolum."

fulfillment, without the addition of any specific object; so the dream is doubly fantastic, a restoration of sight as well as a restoration of the dead. From this comes the sonnet's harping on "as," the particle best suited to convey similarity while denying identity or certainty. Its use is the more striking because of the poem's apparently confident deployment of absolutes. In spite of the veil, in spite of the approximations, he can be sure he sees purity, love, sweetness, goodness, even clarity.

This mixture of vagueness and certainty is consistent with the nature of deep dreams. Entirely convincing while we are immersed in them, our waking records only a fragment, a movement, gesture, impression. And between the dream and the memory of it is the moment of waking, when the vision flees and the light crowds in. Milton's sonnet, of course, closes with an apparent reversal of this experience, for his waking is a return to our darkness; but the experience is still closely related to ours, for our sight and his blindness are only two slightly different versions of fallen man's fancied sight as opposed to the full sight which our arrival in heaven will grant us. One of the seventeenth-century religious poets' favorite images for our seeing only through a glass darkly is the veil; Henry Vaughan's poems, for instance, are packed with such images. And Milton writes of Eve, in her unfallen state, as needing no veil, being virtue-proof. Only when Satan moves in for the kill is she described as veiled, "in a cloud of fragrance."

The dream, then, offers a veiled image of a pure state in contrast with which our waking life lacks clarity and intensity. The idea is not just a religious one. A fair number of love poems follow Donne's example in lamenting the lost dream. This is one by William Cartwright, a minor poet who occasionally comes up with unexpected parallels to Milton:[2]

A Dream Broke

As Nilus' sudden Ebbing, here
Doth leave a scale, and a scale there,
And somewhere else perhaps a Fin,
Which by his stay had Fishes been:
So Dreams, which overflowing be,
Departing leave Half things, which we
For their Imperfectness can call
But Joys i' th' Fin, or in the Scale.
If when her Tears I haste to kiss,
They dry up, and deceive my Bliss,
May not I say the Waters sink,
And Cheat my Thirst when I would drink?
If when her Breasts I go to press,
Instead of them I grasp her Dress,
May I not say the Apples then
Are set down, and snatched up again?
Sleep was not thus Death's Brother meant;
'Twas made an Ease, no Punishment.
As then that's finished by the Sun,
Which *Nile* did only leave begun,

2. Text in G. Blakemoor Evans, ed., *The Plays and Poems of William Cartwright* (Madison, Wis., 1951), pp. 484–485.

> My Fancy shall run o'er Sleep's Themes,
> And so make up the Web of Dreams:
> In vain fleet shades, ye do Contest:
> Awak'd how e'er I'll think the rest.

The "Web of Dreams" is a fine phrase to describe the way most of the poets use their dream experiences. For them responsibility ends in dreams. Cartwright's typical intention is to spend his waking time making up the web, that is, restoring the experience which has trapped his imagination. Here, surely, is the power of Milton's sonnet, that while he gives full expression to the hold the past has upon him, he refuses to be trapped by or in it. It is sometimes revealing to read critics of the poem, for they tend to rewrite it slightly, making the movement toward the embrace as much Milton's as the dead wife's, rather as Cartwright's dream is full of his actions. But Milton in his sonnet is almost entirely passive, the done to rather than the doer. The vision is brought to him, and at the end his night is brought back. His one act is to wake up. In normal circumstances waking is the most passive of actions, the consequence of external stimuli, usually, as in Donne's poem, the sun peeping through the curtains—although in Milton's case the stimulus to awakening would have to be sound, smell, or touch, not sight. We should realize that in the case of this dream Milton's awakening is not passive, but an act of heroic resistance.

Whereas George Herbert chose to begin his *Outlandish Proverbs* with the one about man proposing and God disposing, whoever reprinted them in 1652 added this one to the beginning: "Old men go to Death, Death comes to Young men."[3] Milton at the time he wrote the sonnet was appreciably older than he or Edward King was when *Lycidas* was written, but he was still creatively young, his great poem probably not yet started. Very soon he would copy Hercules and go down to hell to help restore the dead to life. Doing this would involve the same effort of will as is sketched out in this sonnet, awakening from a dream possession by a female muse to a cold winter morning, encompassed by darkness and danger. The effort of *Paradise Lost* is to turn memory into prophecy. This sonnet is the first stage in this process, escaping the embrace of the dead and delivering the experience intact, with all of its pain. With "I waked" the act of resistance is sudden and complete, his refusal to be claimed by the past.

In this context the sonnet's concern with childbirth is paramount. The analogy between parturition and literary creation was a cliché when Sir Philip Sidney used it to open *Astrophel and Stella*, and frequently it was man's compensation for what a female Freud might call womb envy. In neither case, however, is the creation *ex nihilo*. The artist, too, is penetrated and possessed and, if not strong enough, will be left in silence. So many and fertile are the conceptions with which memory holds him, that the effort to render them with anything like the clarity of their original impression will leave him, at best, pale and faint. The gap between the absolute certainty of the experience and its inevitably inadequate reproduction in words is figured repeatedly in Milton's poetry—as in the paralysis of Shakespeare's reader, the lady's paralysis in *Comus*, and, eventually triumphantly, in the son's stasis in *Paradise Regained*. In this sonnet Milton

3. F. E. Hutchinson, ed., *The Works of George Herbert* (Oxford, 1941), p. 356.

is in a position very close to Jonson's: not paralyzed and bedridden, but blind and in bed, dependent upon his will to resist the siren's song.

One further element which makes the resistance so difficult is the sexual power of the dream. Appreciating it gives the clue to how Milton turned the subliminal into the sublime. The purification ceremony which monopolizes the sonnet's octave is, as he takes care to remind us, derived from the Old Testament. In Leviticus 12 the woman who has given birth to a female child, as Milton's wives had, "shall be unclean two weeks . . . and shall continue in the blood of her purifying threescore and six days." During this time "she shall touch no hallowed thing, nor come into the sanctuary." When the days of her purifying are completed, then she shall bring an offering "unto the door of the tabernacle of the congregation, unto the priest." The ceremony had its second biblical reference in the New Testament, in the passage I have already mentioned in Luke 2, where the Virgin Mary accomplishes the days of her purification. The ceremony continued into the Catholic and then Protestant churches, where it came to be known as the churching of women, the title given to it in the 1552 Book of Common Prayer.

In several curious ways Milton's sonnet is tightly bound to this ceremony, so that the veiled vision is not merely a representation of his blindness or dream state, but a literal enough description of the woman at the purification ceremony, in which a veil was traditionally worn. Then there is the psalm which, until 1662, was the centerpiece of the ceremony, number 121, *Levavi oculos*. In the Great Bible version, used in the prayer book, its closeness to Milton's sonnet comes not only in its opening image—"I have lifted up mine eyes"—but also in its description of the creator of heaven and earth as one who "shall neither slumber nor slepe"; and, more pointedly, "he that kepeth thee wil not slepe."[4] And the psalm closes with a promise that the Lord will "preserve thy going out, and thy coming in," a link between the ceremony's traditional location at the church door and the sonnet's closing with a going away and a coming back.

It is tempting now to see the ceremony of churching as yet one more example of man's contempt for woman, so that even her part in the creation of life is interpreted as something unclean from which she needs to be purified. There is probably much in this, but it needs to be added that the ceremony had a function which was of some importance to the woman. It gave her a period when, because of her "uncleanness," she could recover from childbirth without having to resume sexual relations. Therefore, the ceremony had an erotic force, a sign of the resumption of lovemaking after a long period of abstinence. In Milton's sonnet the eroticism may be signaled in his trust to have "full sight of her in heaven without restraint." "Restraint" is a word which crops up with potentially strong sexual connotations in *Paradise Lost*.[5] Here the poem touches on an idea which has never been far beneath the surface of this chapter, that of the nature of the resurrected body. In his epic Milton gives fuller consideration to the lost opportunities for continued sexuality as man is gradually refined to a state of angelic bliss. Here, in the sonnet, the real alternative is starkly

4. See *The First and Second Prayer Books of Edward VI*, Everyman edition (London, 1949), pp. 428–429.
5. In discussing angelic intercourse, 8:678.

described—that a lost lover is lost forever, never to be restored. As the gospel has it, "when they shall rise from the dead, they neither marry, nor are given in marriage; but are as the angels of God in heaven" (Matthew 22:30). One implication of these words is that "my late espoused saint" will forever be just that, to be seen but not to be touched. Indeed, it could hardly be otherwise for Milton, assuming that Mary Powell was saved too, for a polygamous heaven is not a Christian ideal. The eternal loss is conveyed by the syntax, as all the promise of "as yet once more I trust to have" is diluted to make "have" not a marker of possession, franking the "mine" which begins the sentence, but only part of a phrasal verb "have . . . sight of." The sight is full, which is a double compensation for a blind man; but poetry is the creation of the fancied sight which lays the living upon the dead and the dead upon the living.

ALDOUS HUXLEY

[The Inner Weather]†

* * *

The climate of the mind is positively English in its variableness and instability. Frost, sunshine, hopeless drought and refreshing rains succeed one another with bewildering rapidity. Herbert is the poet of this inner weather. Accurately, in a score of lyrics unexcelled for flawless purity of diction and appositeness of imagery, he has described its changes and interpreted, in terms of a mystical philosophy, their significance. Within his limits he achieves a real perfection.

* * *

W. H. AUDEN

[Anglican George Herbert]‡

* * *

* * * His poetry is the counterpart of Jeremy Taylor's prose:[1] together they are the finest expression we have of Anglican piety at its best. Donne, though an Anglican, is, both in his poems and his sermons, much too much of a *prima donna* to be typical.

Comparing the Anglican Church with the Roman Catholic Church on the one hand and the Calvinist on the other, Herbert writes: [Quotes "The British Church," lines 7–24; see p. 266.] Herbert, it will be noticed, says

† From *Texts and Pretexts* (New York, 1932), p. 13.
‡ From *George Herbert: Selected by W. H. Auden* (London, 1973), pp. 10–13.
1. Jeremy Taylor (1613–67), celebrated preacher, chaplain to King Charles I, and bishop; noted for the simplicity, lucidity, vigor, and splendor of the devotional writings, especially *The Rule and Exercise of Holy Living* (1650) and *The Rule . . . of Holy Dying* (1651). [*Editor*]

nothing about differences in theological dogma. The Anglican Church has always avoided strict dogmatic definitions. The Thirty-Nine Articles, for example, can be interpreted either in a Calvinist or a non-Calvinist sense, and her Office of Holy Communion can be accepted both by Zwinglians[2] who regard it as a service of Commemoration only, and by those who believe in the Real Presence. Herbert is concerned with liturgical manners and styles of piety. In his day, Catholic piety was typically baroque, both in architecture and in poets like Crashaw. This was too unrestrained for his taste. On the other hand, he found the style of worship practised by the Reformed Churches too severe, too 'inward'. He would have agreed with Launcelot Andrewes[3] who said: 'If we worship God with our hearts only and not also with our hats, something is lacking.' The Reformers, for instance, disapproved of all religious images, but Herbert thought that, on occasions, a stained-glass window could be of more spiritual help than a sermon.

> Doctrine and life, colours and light, in one
> When they combine and mingle, bring
> A strong regard and aw; but speech alone
> Doth vanish like a flaring thing,
> And in the eare, not conscience ring.[4]

Walton tells us that he took enormous pains to explain to his parishioners, most of whom were probably illiterate, the significance of every ritual act in the liturgy, and to instruct them in the meaning of the Church Calendar. He was not a mystic like Vaughan: few Anglicans have been. One might almost say that Anglican piety at its best, as represented by Herbert, is the piety of a gentleman, which means, of course, that at its second best it becomes merely genteel.

As a Christian, he realized that his own style of poetry had its spiritual dangers:

> . . . Is there in truth no beautie?
> Is all good structure in a winding stair?[5]

But as a poet he knew that he must be true to his sensibility, that all he could do was to wash his sweet phrases and lovely metaphors with his tears and bring them

> to church well drest and clad:
> My God must have my best, even all I had.[6]

He is capable of writing lines of a Dante-esque directness. For example:

> Man stole the fruit, but I must climb the tree,
> The Tree of Life to all but only Me.[7]

2. Followers of the Swiss Reformer Ulrich Zwingli (1484–1531), who emphasized a purely symbolic interpretation of the Eucharist, denying every form of the physical presence of Christ in the Eucharist [*Editor*.]
3. Launcelot Andrewes (1555–1626), famous preacher, bishop of Chichester, Ely, and Winchester, and one of the leaders among the translators who made the King James (or Authorized) Version of the Bible [*Editor*].
4. "The Windows," p. 252 [*Editor*].
5. "Jordan [I]," p. 247 [*Editor*].
6. "The Forerunners," p. 284 [*Editor*].
7. "The Sacrifice," p. 227 [*Editor*].

But as a rule he is more ingenious, though never, I think, obscure.

Each thing is full of dutie:
Waters united are our navigation;
Distinguished, our habitation;
Below, our drink; above, our meat;
Both are our cleanlinesse. Hath one such beautie?
Then how are all things neat?[8]

He is capable of clever antitheses which remind one of Pope, as when, speaking of a woman's love of pearls for which some diver has risked his life, he says:

Who with excessive pride
Her own destruction and his danger wears.[9]

And in a most remarkable sonnet, 'Prayer,' he seems to foreshadow Mallarmé.[1]

Church-bels beyond the starres heard, the souls bloud,
The land of spices; something understood.

Wit he had in abundance. Take, for example, 'The Church-Porch'. Its subject matter is a series of moral maxims about social behaviour. One expects to be utterly bored but, thanks to Herbert's wit, one is entertained. Thus, he takes the commonplace maxim, 'Don't monopolize the conversation,' and turns it into:

If thou be Master-gunner, spend not all
That thou canst speak, at once; but husband it,
And give men turns of speech; do not forestall
By lavishnesse thine own, and others wit,
As if thou mad'st they will. A civil guest
Will no more talk all, then eat all the fast.

A good example of his technical skill is the poem 'Denial'. He was, as we know, a skilled musician, and I am sure he got the idea for the structure of this poem from his musical experience of discords and resolving them. * * * This poem and many others also show Herbert's gift for securing musical effects by varying the length of the lines in a stanza. Of all the so-called 'metaphysical' poets he has the subtlest ear. As George Macdonald said of him:

> The music of a poem is its meaning in sound as distinguished from word. . . . The sound of a verse is the harbinger of the truth contained in it. . . . Herein Herbert excels. It will be found impossible to separate the music of his words from the music of the thought which takes shape in their sound.

And this was Coleridge's estimate:

8. "Man," p. 261 [*Editor*].
9. "Vanity [I]," p. 258 [*Editor*].
1. Stéphane Mallarmé (1842–1898), leading French Symbolist poet, whose work is often musical, evocative, and obscure.

> George Herbert is a true poet, but a poet *sui generis*,[2] the merits of whose poems will never be felt without a sympathy with the mind and character of the man.

My own sympathy is unbounded.

JOSEPH H. SUMMERS

The Poem as Hieroglyph†

Too often Herbert is remembered as the man who possessed the fantastic idea that a poem should resemble its subject in typographical appearance, and who therefore invented the practice of writing poems in shapes such as wings and altars. Herbert, of course, no more invented the pattern poem than he invented 'emblematic poetry' or the religious lyric: his originality lies in his achievement with traditional materials. 'The Altar' and 'Easter-wings,' his two most famous pattern poems, are not exotic or frivolous oddities; they are the most obvious examples of Herbert's religious and poetic concern with what we may call the hieroglyph.

A hieroglyph is 'a figure, device, or sign having some hidden meaning; a secret or enigmatical symbol; an emblem.'[1] In the Renaissance 'hieroglyph,' 'symbol,' 'device,' and 'figure' were often used interchangeably. Because of special meanings which have become associated with the other words, 'hieroglyph' seems more useful than the others today, and even in the seventeenth century it was often considered the most inclusive term.[2] 'Hieroglyphic,' the older form of the noun, was derived from the Greek for 'sacred carving,' and the root usually retained something of its original religious connotation. Ralph Cudworth[3] used it in its generally accepted meaning when he said in a sermon, 'The Death of Christ . . . Hieroglyphically instructed us that we ought to take up our Cross likewise, and follow our crucified Lord and Saviour.'[4] The hieroglyph presented its often manifold meanings in terms of symbolic relationships rather than through realistic representation. * * *

Aside from the metaphorical use of hieroglyphs common to almost all the poets of the time, the religious lyric poet could most obviously make his poem a meditation on one of the innumerable hieroglyphs in nature, art, or the Church, or he could use the hieroglyph as the central image in a meditation on some doctrine or experience. * * * Most of the poems written for the emblem books typify the first practice: the moral applica-

2. Unique, of its own kind [*Editor*].

† From chapter VI of *George Herbert: His Religion and Art* (Cambridge: Harvard University Press, 1954). Reprinted by permission of U. T. Summers. Some notes have been slightly abridged.

1. *NED*, Sb. 2. [*New English Dictionary*, second paragraph.—*Editor*.]

2. In his *Hieroglyphicorum Collectanea, ex Veteribus et Neotericis Descripta* ('In hac postrema editione recognita & expurgata'; Lvgdvni, 1626), p. 7, Giovanni Pierio Valeriano summarized the general usage: 'Ad hieroglyphica accedunt emblemata, symbola, insignia, quae quamuis nomine different, reipsa multis modis conueniri videntur.' [Hieroglyphs include emblems, symbols, devices that, while they have various names, actually correspond with each other in many respects.—*Editor*.]

3. Ralph Cudworth, 1617–1688, a leader of the Cambridge Platonists, idealists opposed to Hobbesian materialism and convinced that reason and religion were in harmony with each other.

4. Quoted in *NED*, 'Hieroglyphically,' 2, from 'Sermon I' (1642) in *A Discourse Concerning the True Notion of the Lord's Supper* (London, 1670), p. 210.

tions are drawn from the image point by point. Herbert never wrote a poem quite so crudely. * * *

* * *

In 'The Bunch of Grapes' Herbert used the hieroglyph in the second obvious fashion, as the central image in a meditation on a personal experience. The title of the poem indicates the hieroglyph, but the 'cluster' is not mentioned until the end of the third stanza. The subject of meditation is the problem of the absence of joy from the Christian's life:

> Joy, I did lock thee up: but some bad man
> Hath let thee out again:
> And now, me thinks, I am where I began
> Sev'n years ago: one vogue and vein,
> One aire of thoughts usurps my brain.
> I did towards Canaan draw; but now I am
> Brought back to the Red sea, the sea of shame.

Joy, once possessed, has now escaped. Herbert prevents any misunderstanding of the traditional imagery of Canaan and the Red Sea by explaining in the next stanza Paul's teaching that every event during the wandering of the Children of Israel from Egypt to the Promised Land was a type of the Christian's experiences in his journey between the world of sin and heaven:[5] we may discover within the ancient history the heavenly evaluations and solutions for our problems. With the third stanza, Herbert enumerates some of the parallels:

> Then have we too our guardian fires and clouds;
> Our Scripture-dew drops fast:
> We have our sands and serpents, tents and shrowds;
> Alas! our murmurings come not last.
> But where's the cluster? where's the taste
> Of mine inheritance? Lord, if I must borrow,
> Let me as well take up their joy, as sorrow.

Joy may not be fully achieved until we reach the Promised Land, but the Christian should at least experience a foretaste of it, such a rich proof of its existence as was the cluster of Eschol to the Children of Israel. But the introduction of Eshcol provides the answer. That 'branch with one cluster of grapes,' which was so large that 'they bore it betweene two vpon a staffe,' had represented a joy which the Israelites refused. To them the bunch of grapes substantiated the report that it was 'a land that eateth vp the inhabitants thereof, and all the people that we saw in it, are men of a great stature. And there we saw the giants, the sonnes of Anak, which come of the giants: and wee were in our owne sight as grashoppers, and so wee were in their sight' (Num. xiii. 23–24). From fear they turned to the rebellion which caused God to decree the wandering of forty years. Of all the adults who saw the grapes, only Caleb and Joshua entered the Promised Land. The image of the bunch of grapes suggests, then, not only the foretastes of Canaan and heaven, but also the immeasurable differences between those foretastes under the Covenant of Works and the Covenant of Grace:

5. I. Cor. x. The marginal reading for 'ensamples,' v. 11, is 'Or, Types.'

> But can he want the grape, who hath the wine?
> I have their fruit and more.
> Blessed be God, who prosper'd *Noahs* vine,
> And made it bring forth grapes good store.
> But much more him I must adore,
> Who of the Laws sowre juice sweet wine did make,
> Ev'n God himself being pressed for my sake.

The bunch of grapes is a type of Christ and of the Christian's communion. 'I have their fruit and more,' for the grapes, of which the promise was conditional upon works, have been transformed into the wine of the New Covenant: 'I' have both the foretaste and the assurance of its fulfilment. The prospering of '*Noahs* vine,' like the cluster of Eshcol, was a sign of God's blessing. It was a partial fulfilment of 'Bee fruitfull and multiply, and replenish the earth,' and of God's covenant with all flesh: 'neither shall there any more be a flood to destroy the earth' (Gen. ix. 1, 11). Yet, as at Eshcol, God's blessings under the Law could become man's occasion for the renewal of sin and the curse: Noah's misuse of the vine resulted in the curse on Ham. The bunch of grapes has furnished the image of the poet's lost joy, the image of blessings refused or perverted, and also the image of the Christian's source of joy, ever present if he will cease his murmurings. The Holy Communion is a constant reminder of Christ's sacrifice which established the joyful Covenant of Grace; it is the instrument of present grace; and it foretells the joy of heavenly communion. The examination of the Christian's lack of joy has resolved rather than explained the original problem. The blessing and adoration of the final lines indicate that joy is no longer lost.

Herbert frequently used a hieroglyph to crystallize, explain, or resolve the central conflict in a poem. 'Josephs coat,' a strange sonnet with an unrhymed first line, concerns the mixture of joy and sorrow in the Christian life, and Joseph is not mentioned in the text. The conclusion, 'I live to shew his power, who once did bring My *joyes* to *weep*, and now my *griefs* to *sing*,' is an acknowledgment of God's power, but without the title it might be construed as an acknowledgment of a powerful and inexplicable Fate. The title, a reference to a traditional Christian type, gives Herbert's interpretation of the experience of contradictory joys and sorrows. Joseph's 'coat of many colours' was the sign of his father's particular love.[6] It was also the immediate occasion for his brothers' jealousy and hatred and for his slavery and suffering; but the presentation of the coat was, finally, the initial incident in the long chain of causes which led to the preservation of the Children of Israel in Egypt. After all the suffering, the sign of Jacob's love ended in beatitude. The extraordinary mixture of joy and sorrow in the Christian's life is a particular sign of God's love. Joy has been made 'to *weep*' to forestall the self-sufficience which leads to wilful pride, and '*griefs*' have been made 'to *sing*' to preserve the soul and body from despair and death. God's 'Cross-Providences' also lead to beatitude. For Herbert, 'Joyes

6. George Ryley, 'The Temple explained and improved' [an eighteenth-century commentary on Herbert, in a Bodleian Library manuscript—*Editor*.], pp. 315–16, summarizes the biblical allusions: 'Joseph's Coat was of *many colours*; very beautifull; and it was a token of his father's peculiar affection. *Gen.* 37.3. . . . This poem speaks the language of the prophet, *Is.* 61. 10, *I will greatly rejoice in the Lord, &c. for he hath cloathed me with the garments of salvation*, and of the Apostle, 2 Cor. 6. 10, *As sorrowfull, yet always rejoicing*.'

coat,' with which anguish has been 'ticed' was evidenced by his ability to 'sing,' to compose lyrics even when the subject was grief.

At first reading 'Church-monuments' appears to belong to the group of poems which are explanations of a hieroglyph. For once the modern reader could surmise the title from the contents, for the poem is a considered meditation on 'Church-monuments' in which all their hieroglyphic applications are drawn. [Quotes text; see p. 251.] The first stanza states the purpose of the meditation, that 'my flesh . . . betimes May take acquaintance of this heap of dust.' Most obviously, the monuments form a hieroglyph worthy of the flesh's 'acquaintance' because they contain the dust of formerly living flesh. Yet, with the identification of 'heap of dust' as that 'To which the blast of deaths incessant motion . . . Drives all at last,' the meaning expands to include the dissolution of all earthly things. Through contemplating the monuments the 'bodie' 'may learn To spell his elements.' The ambiguous 'spell' (meaning both to 'divine' the elements and to 'spell out' the inscriptions) introduces as part of the hieroglyph the inscriptions on the monuments. Their 'dustie' physical state (which makes them difficult to decipher) and their intended verbal meaning cause them to serve as intermediate symbols relating the flesh of man and the contents of the tomb. The 'dustie heraldrie and lines' factually tell the genealogies of the deceased and include some conventional version of 'for dust thou art, and vnto dust shalt thou returne.' ('Lines,' associated with 'birth' and 'heraldrie,' seems to signify genealogical 'lines' as well as the lines of engraving.) The monuments are an ironic commentary on mortality; their states and messages mock at their composition of 'Jeat and Marble'—too obviously fleshly attempts to deny the dissolution of the bodies which they contain. Can there be monuments to monuments? Can monuments hope for a memorial 'When they shall bow, and kneel' as the body of the meditator is doing, or 'fall down flat' in dissolution, as his body will do and as the bodies within the monuments have already done? The flesh can learn its 'stemme And true descent' both in its origin in dust and in its decline into dust.

The figure of the hour-glass summarizes what 'thou mayst know' from the contemplation of the monuments and further enriches the meaning:

> That flesh is but the glasse, which holds the dust
> That measures all our time; which also shall
> Be crumbled into dust.

It is one of Herbert's most successful condensations, and it is difficult only if we have failed to follow the careful preparation for its introduction. The hour-glass defines the flesh in terms of what has been learned from the monuments. The monuments, like the traditional *memento mori*, have told of more than physical death. It is 'the exhalation of our crimes' which 'feeds' 'the blast of deaths incessant motion'; and the monuments, like the 'grasse' of the Psalmist and Isaiah and the New Testament,[7] have served to exemplify the vain dust of the sin and the 'goodlinesse' and 'glory' of living flesh as well as that of flesh's final dissolution. The function of proud

7. Ps. cii. 11; Isa. xl. 6; I Pet. i. 24.

flesh and proud monument is the same: to hold 'the dust That measures all our time,' whether it is the figurative dust of our vain goodliness and glory and sinful wills or the actual dust of our bodies. Dust is the true measure of 'all our time' (not our eternity): the vanity and endurance of our lives and of our ashes provide the sole significances to the flesh and the monument. Finally, the flesh and the monuments, the containers, 'shall Be crumbled into dust,' both symbolic of and undifferentiable from the dust contained. The closing address directs the flesh's attention to the 'ashes' rather than to the monuments:

Mark here below
How tame these ashes are, how free from lust,
That thou mayst fit thy self against thy fall.

The flesh can escape neither its measuring content nor its final goal. The knowledge it has gained may, however, serve as bridle to 'tame' its lust. The flesh may 'fit' itself 'against' its 'fall' in that, in preparation for its known dissolution, it may oppose its 'fall' into pride and lust.[8]

Such an analysis indicates the manner in which Herbert explained the complex meanings of the hieroglyph, but it does not explain 'Church-monuments.' The movement of the words and the lines, of the clauses and the sentences, conveys even without analysis a 'meaning' which makes us recognize the inadequacy of any such prose summary. Yvor Winters has called 'Church-monuments' 'the greatest poem by George Herbert': 'George Herbert's *Church Monuments*, perhaps the most polished and urbane poem of the Metaphysical School and one of the half dozen most profound, is written in an iambic pentameter line so carefully modulated, and with its rhymes so carefully concealed at different and unexpected points in the syntax, that the poem suggests something of the quiet plainness of excellent prose without losing the organization and variety of verse.'[9] The effect which Winters praised is achieved largely through the extraordinary use of enjambment and the looseness of the syntax. Only three lines of the poem come to a full stop, and nine of the twenty-four lines are followed by no punctuation. Many of the semi-cadences indicated by the punctuation, moreover, prove illusory: the syntax demands no pause, and the commas serve as fairly arbitrary directions for a slight voice rest, obscuring rather than clarifying the simple 'prose' meaning. Winters seems to praise 'Church-monuments' for practices which are found in no other poem in *The Temple*. Herbert characteristically considered his stanzas as inviolable architectural units. Each usually contained a complete thought, representing one unit in the logic of the 'argument,' and the great majority of his stanzas end with full stops.[1] In the form in which it was printed in 1633 'Church-monuments' provides the only example of complete enjambment between stanzas in *The Temple*, and two of the three

8. 'Against' and 'fall' are used ambiguously. 'Against' means both 'in preparation for' and 'in opposition to,' and 'fall' means both physical collapse and 'fall' into sin. These ambiguities are characteristic of Herbert's use of the device. Neither is at all recondite: 'against' in the sense of 'in preparation for' often carried something of the meaning of 'in opposition to,' and 'the fall' of man and angels had traditionally equated physical and moral movement.
9. *Primitivism and Decadence: A Study of American Experimental Poetry* (New York, 1937), pp. 10, 123.
1. On the rare occasions when a stanza ends with a colon or semicolon, modern usage would often require a period.

examples of stanzas in which the final points are commas.[2] When Herbert departs so dramatically from his usual consistent practice, it is advisable to look for the reason. It cannot be found, I believe, in an intent to suggest 'something of the quiet plainness of excellent prose without losing the organization and variety of verse.' These straggling sentences fulfil the criteria for excellence by neither Ciceronian nor Senecan nor Baconian standards of prose. They possess neither the admired periodicity, nor trenchant point, nor ordinary clarity. The series of clauses and participial phrases, each relating to a word in some preceding clause or phrase, threaten to dissolve the sentence structure. The repetitions of 'that' and 'which' give the effect of unplanned prose, a prose which seems to function more by association than by logic.

The poem is a meditation upon a *memento mori*, the hieroglyph of the monuments. One reason for the slowness of the movement and the 'concealed' rhymes might be that the tone of the meditation was intended to correspond to the seriousness of its object. The most important clue, however, is in the manuscripts: in neither the Williams nor the Bodleian MS. is the poem divided into stanzas at all. As F. E. Hutchinson remarked, 'the editor of 1633 recognized that the rhyme-scheme implies a six-line stanza,'[3] and subsequent editors followed the original edition and printed the poem in stanzas. But the manuscript arrangement was not the result of accident or carelessness. In the Williams MS., which Herbert corrected, the non-stanzaic form is emphasized by the indentation of line 17 to indicate a new paragraph.[4] The fact that Herbert established a six-line stanzaic rhyme scheme but did not create stanzas, either formally or typographically, is a minor but a convincing evidence that he intended the poem itself to *be a memento mori*, to function formally as a hieroglyph. The dissolution of the body and the monuments is paralleled by the dissolution of the sentences and the stanzas.

The movement and sound of the poem suggest the 'falls' of the flesh and the monuments and the dust in the glass. The fall is not precipitious; it is as slow as the gradual fall of the monuments, as the crumbling of the glass, as the descent of the flesh from Adam into dust. Every cadence is a dying fall. Even the question of stanza 3 contains three commas and ends with the descriptive clause, 'which now they have in trust,' carrying no interrogation. Part of the effect is achieved by obvious 'prose' means. 'Dust' re-echoes seven times in the poem, and the crucial words and phrases describe or suggest the central subject: 'intombe'; 'blast of deaths incessant motion'; 'dissolution'; 'earth with earth'; 'bow, and kneel, and fall down flat'; 'descent'; 'measures'; 'crumbled';[5] 'ashes'; 'fall.' Herbert has also used every means to slow the movement of the neutral words. With the clusters of consonants, it is impossible to read the poem rapidly.[6] The related rhymes, with their internal echoes and repetitions, both give phonetic con-

2. The third example is st. 5 of 'The Bag.' Here the comma after line 30, 'And straight he turn'd, and to his brethren cry'd,' is strong, since it precedes the two stanzas of direct quotation.
3. *Works*, p. 499.
4. *Works*, p. 65. In *B* the line begins a new page.
5. The only significant change which Herbert made after the version in *W* was to introduce 'crumbled' in line 22 for the less effective 'broken.'
6. In the twenty-four lines the sound of *t* occurs 59 times; *th* and *th*, 36; *s* and *z*, 51; *sh*, 15; *n*, 35; *d*, 27.

tinuity to the poem and suggest the process of dissolution: 'devotion' and 'motion' are mocked by 'exhalation' and 'dissolution'; 'betimes' and 'crimes' modulate to 'lines' and 'signes' as do 'learn' and 'discern' to 'birth' and 'earth.' 'Trust' and 'lust' are echoed incessantly by 'dust,' and, internally, by 'blast,' and 'last.' Continual internal repetition deprives the end-rhymes of any chime of finality: 'blast-last,' 'earth with earth,' 'bow-now,' 'they-pray,' 'that-that,' 'which-which' disguise and almost dissolve the iambic pentameter line. Three of the six sentences in the poem take up five and a half lines each, but, straggling as they are, each is exhausted before it reaches what should be the end of the stanza. Although the sentences are hardly independent (the many pronominal forms create a complex of interdependent meanings), the expiration of each sentence marks a break which requires a new beginning: after the opening of the poem, each new sentence begins with a long syllable which usually causes a break in the iambic rhythm. The sentences sift down through the rhyme-scheme skeleton of the stanzas like the sand through the glass; and the glass itself has already begun to crumble.

'Church-monuments' differs in kind as well as degree from such poems as 'The Church-floore' and 'The Bunch of Grapes.' The natural or religious hieroglyph was an eminently pleasant and profitable subject for a poem, and it could be used either as the object which the poem explained or as the image which explained the poem. Yet Herbert seems to have believed that it was more pleasant and profitable to make the poem itself a hieroglyph. To construct the poem so that its form imaged the subject was to reinforce the message for those who could 'spell'; for the others it would not distract from the statement—and if they read and meditated long enough, surely they would discover the mirroring of the meanings within the form of the poem!

There were fewer readers who could not 'spell' in Herbert's day than in ours. The attempt to make formal structure an integral part of the meaning of a poem assumed a general consciousness of traditional formal conventions. The disturbances of the rhyme schemes in 'Grief' and 'Home,' for example, depend for their effects on the reader's firm expectation of a conventional pattern. Such an expectation could be assumed in readers accustomed to Renaissance English poetry, whether the poetry of the Court or the hymns of the Church or the doggerel of the broadsides. In his hieroglyphs Herbert never attempted to abandon rational control for an 'identity' with a natural object: the poems always embody or assume a firm pattern of logic, rhyme, and rhythm. The formal organization of the subject was imitated by the formal organization of the poem.

The poems in which Herbert's 'imitations' are obvious are those which are likely to draw the fire of strict advocates either of that art which conceals art or of that upwelling inspiration which is oblivious of form. But Herbert often intended the form of a poem to be obvious. The opening stanzas of 'Deniall,' for example, picture the disorder which results when the individual feels that God denies his requests: [Quotes lines 1–10; see pp. 255–256]. The final stanza, with its establishment of the normal pattern of cadence and rhyme, is the symbol of reconstructed order, of the manner in which men (and the poem) function when God grants the request:

O cheer and tune my heartlesse breast,
Deferre no time;
That so thy favours granting my request,
They and my minde may chime,
And mend my ryme.

The stanza which had been the symbol of the flying asunder of a 'brittle bow' has become a symbol for the achievement of order. The form of the final prayer indicates that its request has already been answered. The individual and the poem have moved from fear through open rebellion and 'unstrung' discontent. 'Deniall' is overcome through renewal of prayer: the ordered prayer provides the evidence.

Of Herbert's many other formal hieroglyphs ('Sinnes round,' 'A Wreath,' 'Trinitie Sunday,' etc.) 'Aaron' is one of the most effective. [Quotes "Aaron", see pp. 283.] Herbert may have chosen the five stanzas of five lines each partially because of the five letters in 'Aaron'; if so, the technical problem may have been of importance to the poet, but it does not matter particularly to the reader. Nor does it seem that Herbert primarily intended that each stanza should 'suggest metrically the swelling and dying sound of a bell':[7] the 'bells' and the 'musick' occur only in the third line of each stanza, and the rhymes are hardly bell-like. The central meaning of those identical rhymes and those subtly transformed stanzas[8] is clearly stated in the poem. The profaneness in man's head, the defects and darkness in his heart, the cacophonous passions which destroy him and lead him to a hell of 'repining restlessnesse'[9] *can* be transformed through the imputed righteousness of Christ into the ideal symbolized by Aaron's ceremonial garments.[1] The 'clay'[2] (like the stanzas) retains its outward form, but inwardly all is changed in the divine consumption of the self. As the 'Priest for euer after the order of Melchisedec' 'dresses' the new Aaron with the inward reality for which the first Aaron's garments were but the hieroglyphs, the poem moves with a ritualistic gravity from opposition to a climactic synthesis.

When we have understood Herbert's use of form in these poems, or, say, his extraordinarily formal picture of anarchy in 'The Collar' and his divine numerology in 'Trinitie Sunday' we may see the poems which derive from the Elizabethan acrostics and anagrams in a different light. Aside from the courtiers to whom any exercise in ingenuity was welcome, this type of poem had its serious religious adherents in the seventeenth century. If biblical exegesis demanded the solution of anagrams,[3] and if the good man was truly 'willing to spiritualize everything,' the composition of such poetry was a logical result. With due appreciation of the wit involved, the good man was likely to treat such poetry seriously. The seriousness depended on a religious subject and on the assumption that the poet would draw 'true' meanings from his word-play. Herbert abided by the rules, and he never repeated the various forms. In *The Temple* there is one true ana-

7. Grierson, *Metaphysical Lyrics*, pp. 231–32.
8. Douglas Bush has remarked that in the first stanza describing the 'type,' the consonants *l*, *m*, and *r* predominate; in the second concerning the 'natural man,' *p*, *st*, *t*, *z*, and *s*; and in the final stanza the two patterns of consonants are united.
9. 'The Pulley,' p. 278.
1. Hutchinson, *Works*, p. 538, summarizes the relevant passages from Exod. xxviii.
2. Cf. 'The Priesthood.'
3. See Kenneth B. Murdock's discussion and quotations in *Handkerchiefs from Paul* (Cambridge, Mass., 1927), pp. liv–lvi.

gram (labelled as such), one echo poem, one 'hidden acrostic,' one poem based on the double interpretation of initials, one based on a syllabic pun, and 'Paradise,' which can only be described as a 'pruning poem.' For his unique example of each type, Herbert usually chose that Christian subject which was most clearly illuminated by the device.

* * *

In 'The Altar' and 'Easter-wings' Herbert extended the principle of the hieroglyph to a third level. If the natural or religious hieroglyph was valuable as content (used either as the object which the poem explained or as the image which crystallized the meaning of the poem), and if the poem could be constructed as a formal hieroglyph which mirrored the structural relationships between the natural hieroglyph, the poem, and the individual's life, it was but a further step to make the poem a visual hieroglyph, to create it in a shape which formed an immediately apparent image relevant both to content and structure.

Neither the conception of the pattern poem nor the two shapes which Herbert used were at all novel.[4] The Greek Anthology[5] had included six pattern poems (including a pair of wings and two altars), and those patterns were widely imitated in the sixteenth century. Although Thomas Nashe, Gabriel Harvey, and Ben Jonson denounced such poems, the practice flourished.[6] After the appearance of *The Temple* patterns were published in profusion. Wither, Quarles,[7] Benlowes, Joseph Beaumont, Herrick, Christopher Harvey, and Traherne were among the practitioners. Both before and after 1633 the literary quality of most of these poems was notoriously low. The poets seemed usually to consider the shapes as a superficial or frivolous attraction for the reader. As the Renaissance poets and critics never tired of reiterating, pleasure *could* be made a bait for profit, but a superficial conception of the 'bait' often resulted in very bad poems. Many of the patterns depended largely on wrenched typography, and it was a common practice to compose a poem in ordinary couplets, then chop the lines to fit the pattern.

Herbert's poems are another matter. From his knowledge of both the Greek originals and English practice,[8] Herbert chose the two patterns which could be most clearly related to the purposes of his Christian poetry. His patterns are visual hieroglyphs. The interpretation of them as naïve representations of 'real' objects has resulted in the citation of 'The Altar' as additional proof of Herbert's extreme Anglo-Catholicism. An examina-

4. In the discussion which follows I am indebted to Miss Margaret Church's 'The Pattern Poem' (Doctoral thesis, Radcliffe College, 1944), the most useful discussion of the history and development of the European pattern poem which I have found. Miss Church's Appendix C, pp. 240–247, 'includes copies of all the pattern poems discussed in the text with the exception of several *carmina quadrata* by P. Optatianus Porfirius and Hraban Maur.'
5. A compilation of Greek poetry, mostly on amorous themes, from various anthologies ranging in time from the seventh century B.C. to the tenth century A.D. [*Editor*].
6. Church, p. 161, cites the comments of Nashe, 'Have with you . . . ,' *The Works*, ed. R. B. McKerrow (London, 1900), III, 67; Harvey, *Letter-Book*, ed. E. J. L. Scott (Westminster, 1884), pp. 100–01; and Jonson, *The Works*, ed. F. Cunningham (London, 1816), III, 320, 470, 488.
7. Except for one 'lozenge,' 'On God's Law,' in the *Divine Fancies* of 1632, all of Quarles's patterns, like his emblems, were published after 1633. If there was any influence, it was Herbert who influenced Quarles.
8. See Church, pp. 297 ff. English composers of altars before Herbert included Richard Willis (1573), Andrew Willet, and William Browne of Tavistock (in *The Shepherd's Pipe*, 1614). Willet's shapes were printed at the beginning of Sylvester's *Bartas His Devine Weekes & Works* (1605–08).
* * *

tion of the poem in the light of its tradition and Herbert's formal practice shows it to be artistically complex and religiously 'low.'[9] [Quotes text; see p. 227.]

When one reads 'The Altar' it is well to remember that the word 'altar' was not applied to the Communion Table in the Book of Common Prayer, and that the canons of Herbert's time directed that the Table should be made of wood rather than stone. Throughout his English writings Herbert always used 'altar' and 'sacrifice' according to the 'orthodox' Protestant tradition of his time: 'altar' is never applied to the Communion Table nor is the Holy Communion ever called a 'sacrifice.'[1] Yet Herbert and his contemporaries cherished the conception of the altar and the sacrifice. The Mosaic sacrifices were considered types of the one true Sacrifice, in which Christ had shed blood for the remission of sins once for all time. To man were left the 'sacrifices' of praise, good works, and 'communication' (Heb. xiii. 15–16). The Hebrew altar which was built of unhewn stones was a type of the heart of man, hewn not by man's efforts but by God alone. The engraving on those stones with which 'all the words of this Law' were written 'very plainely' (Deut. xxvii. 8) was a type of the 'Epistle of Christ,' the message of salvation engraved on the Christian heart (2 Cor. iii. 3). Herbert's conceptions that the broken and purged heart is the proper basis for the sacrifice of praise and that even stones may participate in and continue that praise were firmly biblical. In his psalm of repentance (Ps. li.) David had stated that the true sacrifices of God are 'a broken and a contrite heart'; Christ had promised that 'the stones' would cry out to testify to Him (Luke xix. 40); and Paul had stated that 'Ye also as liuely stones, are built vp a spirituall house . . . to offer vp spiritual sacrifice' (I Pet. ii. 5).

There is hardly a phrase in 'The Altar' which does not derive from a specific biblical passage. Yet the effect of the poem is simple and fresh. In an important sense this, the first poem within 'The Church' (the central section of *The Temple*), *is* the altar upon which the following poems (Herbert's 'sacrifice of praise') are offered, and it is an explanation of the reason for their composition. God has commanded a continual sacrifice of praise and thanksgiving made from the broken and contrite heart. The condition of mortality as well as the inconstancy of the human heart requires that such a sacrifice be one of those works which 'doe follow them' even when they 'rest from their labours.' For the craftsman and poet, construction of a work of art resulted in that continual sacrifice and introduced the concept of the altar: the poem is a construction upon which others may offer their sacrifices; it is a 'speaking' altar which continually offers up its own

9. Hutchinson, *Works*, p. 26, notes that in *W* the word 'onely' [line 15—*Editor*] has been corrected to 'blessed.' The change is a poetic improvement, but the original word substantiates my interpretation of the poem.

1. Cf. the references cited by Cameron Mann, *A Concordance to the English Poems of George Herbert* (Boston and New York, 1927). For 'sacrifice,' see 'The Church-porch,' ll. 6, 275; 'The Sacrifice' throughout and especially 1. 19; 'Mattens,' 1. 3; 'Providence,' 1. 14; 'Love unknown,' 1. 30. For 'altar' see 'Love (I),' 1. 21 and the first of the 'Sonnets to his Mother,' 1. 6. At first reading chapter vi, 'The Parson Praying,' of *A Priest to the Temple* (*Works*, pp. 231–32), seems to provide an exception to Herbert's customary use of 'altar.' After a description of the parson's actions 'when he is to read divine services,' Herbert adds, 'This he doth, first, as being truly touched and amazed with the Majesty of God, before whom he then presents himself; yet not as himself alone, but as presenting with himself the whole Congregation, whose sins he then beares, and brings with his own to the heavenly altar to be bathed, and washed in the sacred Laver of Christs blood.' Despite the familiar imagery, there is no reference here to the Eucharist. The 'altar' and 'the sacred Laver of Christs blood' are truly *in* heaven. * * *

sacrifice of praise. The shape of Herbert's poem was intended to hieroglyph the relevance of the old altar to the new Christian altar within the heart. It was fittingly, therefore, a modification of the traditional shape of a classic altar rather than of what Herbert knew as the Communion Table. F. E. Hutchinson's description of the changes in the printing of the poem furnishes a miniature history of progressive misinterpretation.[2] From 1634 to 1667 the shape was outlined merely to draw the reader's attention to its significance. The change in religious temper and vocabulary by 1674 was indicated by 'an engraving of a full-length Christian altar under a classical canopy, with the poem set under the canopy': the assumption was that Herbert had attempted to image a 'Christian altar.' The final liturgical representation of the poem did not, however, occur until the nineteenth century: 'In 1809 there is Gothic panelling and canopy-work behind a modest altar with fringed cloth, fair linen cloth, and the sacred vessels.' Herbert's attempt to use the shape of a classical altar as a hieroglyph of his beliefs concerning the relationships between the heart, the work of art, and the praise of God failed to communicate its meaning to a number of generations. While not one of Herbert's greatest poems, 'The Altar' within its context in *The Temple* is still an effective poem if we take the pains to understand it.

'Easter-wings' had been subject to fewer misinterpretations than 'The Altar.' In the last twenty years particularly it has generally been considered a good poem, although there has been little agreement as to the meaning and effectiveness of its pattern. It is the final poem in the group concerning Holy Week, and to read it within its sequence helps to explain some of the difficulties for the modern reader. [Quotes text; see pp. 239–240.] The pattern is successful not merely because we 'see' the wings, but because we see how they are made: the process of impoverishment and enrichment, of 'thinning' and expansion which makes 'flight' possible. By that perception and by the rhythmical falling and rising which the shaped lines help to form, we are led to respond fully to the active image and to the poem. The first stanza is a celebration of the *felix culpa*.[3] Man was created in 'wealth and store,' with the capacity for sinlessness. Through Adam's sin Paradise was lost, yet from one point of view the loss was not unhappy: 'where sinne abounded, grace did much more abound' (Rom. v. 20). If man 'rises' in celebration of Christ's victories, the fall will indeed further his flight to God. The second stanza concerns the reduction of the individual by God's punishment for sins. Again, if we 'combine' with Christ 'And feel this day thy victorie,' affliction can prove an advance to flight, for it is through such affliction that souls are led to 'waite vpon the Lord' and 'renew their strength,' and the promise is specific: 'they shall mount vp with wings as Eagles, they shal runne and not be weary, and they shall walke, and not faint' (Isa. xl. 31). The New Testament had related the death and resurrection of the spirit and the body to the germinal cycle of nature, and the favourite English pun on 'son-sun' seemed to acquire a supernatural sanction from Malachi iv. 2: 'But vnto you that feare my Name, shall the Sunne of righteousnesse arise with healing in his wings.' The 'decaying' of the first stanza of Herbert's poem implies the fruitful image of the grain, and the conclusion of that stanza broadens to include

2. *Works*, p. 484.
3. "Happy fault," i.e., because Adam's sin "caused" the Redemption [*Editor*].

the rise of the 'Sun,' the 'harmonious' ascent both of the flight and the song of the larks.[4] The triumphant dichotomies are implied throughout the poem: sickness and health, decay and growth, poverty and wealth, foolishness and wisdom, punishment and reward, defeat and victory, the fall and rise of song and wings and spirit, sin and righteousness, burial and resurrection, death and life. These states are not in polar opposition. The poem and its pattern constantly insist that for man only through the fall is the flight possible; that the victory, resurrection, whether in this life or the next, can come only through the death of the old Adam.

The pattern poem is a dangerous form, and its successful practitioners before and after Herbert were few. The conception behind it, however, is neither so naïve nor so dated as some critics have assumed: writing with intentions differing greatly from Herbert's, E. E. Cummings and Dylan Thomas have created successful contemporary pattern poems.[5] For Herbert such poetry was a natural extension of his concern with the hieroglyph. Most of the other poets of his time, whether followers of Spenser, Jonson, or Donne, characteristically used hieroglyphs as the basis for their imagery in either short or extended passages. Herbert's distinction lies in his successful development of the conceptions that the entire poem could be organized around a hieroglyph and that the poem itself could be constructed as a formal hieroglyph.

The hieroglyph represented to Herbert a fusion of the spiritual and material, of the rational and sensuous, in the essential terms of formal relationships. It may have been that his delight in the power and beauty of the hieroglyphic symbol helped to keep his poems from becoming only rational exercises or pious teachings. Yet reason and piety were central, for to Herbert the hieroglyph did not exist as a total mystery or as isolated beauty, but as a beauty and mystery which were decipherable and related to all creation. The message was precise and clear even if complex and subtle. A differing conception of the religious hieroglyph led Crashaw to esctatic adoration and worship. For Herbert, however, celebration could never be divorced from examination. The hieroglyphs, whether of God's or of man's creation, were to be 'read' rather than adored, and they sent the reader back to God. The chief tool for such reading was the logical use of man's reason.

It was, moreover, delightful as well as edifying for the poet to imitate God in the construction of hieroglyphs. As Sir Philip Sidney had remarked long before, the way in which God had worked in the creation of nature was not so mysterious as marvellous; man could observe and could imitate:

> Neither let it be deemed too saucy a comparison, to balance the highest point of man's wit with the efficacy of nature; but rather give right honour to the heavenly Maker of that maker, who having made man to his own likeness, set him beyond and over all the works of that second nature; which in nothing he showeth so much as in poetry;

4. See Bennett, *Four Metaphysical Poets*, p. 66.
5. As Lloyd Frankenberg has pointed out, *Pleasure Dome: on reading modern poetry* (Boston, 1949), pp. 172–79, Cummings continually writes such poems; the fact that his patterns are based on individual and spontaneous gestures or situations or personalities rather than on symmetrical and abstract forms has disguised the fact from some readers. John L. Sweeney, *The Selected Writings of Dylan Thomas* (New York, 1946), p. xxi, has suggested that the pattern of Thomas's 'Vision and Prayer' may have been inspired by 'Easter-wings.' As Theodore Spencer once remarked, the formal effects of James Joyce's *Ulysses* are directly related to the tradition of George Herbert's poetry.

when, with the force of a divine breath, he bringeth things forth surpassing her doings, with no small arguments to the incredulous of that first accursed fall of Adam; since our erected wit maketh us know what perfection is, and yet our infected will keepeth us from reaching unto it.[6]

MICHAEL SCHOENFELDT

"That Spectacle of Too Much Weight": The Poetics of Sacrifice in Donne, Herbert, and Milton†

But how then shall I imitate thee, and
Copie thy fair though bloudie hand?
—George Herbert

If you can't imitate him, don't copy him.
—Yogi Berra

This essay began with a question that has been rattling around in my head since I first began studying devotional poetry: Why did the scenario of the Christian sacrifice prove such a vexed and perplexing subject for lyric poetry in seventeenth-century England? Why, that is, did the Passion shift from being a site of the deepest imaginative engagement for medieval Catholic writers to a comparatively marginal subject, which challenges and defeats the best efforts of mortal devotees? As Donne in "Goodfriday, 1613, Riding Westward" deliberately rides away from the east, the scene of the sacrifice, so does Protestant lyric devotion in seventeenth-century England move away from identification with the spectacularly gruesome suffering of the crucified Christ toward the apprehension of the extravagant mercy ensuing from Jesus' victory over sin and death on the cross. There are many reasons for this change, but a central reason is a renewed emphasis in Reformed religion on the Davidic and Pauline notions that the only sacrifice God desires occurs neither in sanctified architectural space nor in explicit corporeal suffering but rather in the interior spaces of the believer. Sacrifice is not so much a ritual action as a devotional state achieved in the temple that is the heart of the devout.

In *The Poetry of Meditation*, Louis Martz helped revive the study of seventeenth-century religious lyrics by locating a range of these poems amid the practices of Catholic, and specifically Ignatian, meditation. Martz demonstrates how Ignation meditational structures urge devotees to exercise their imaginations in order to envisage the Passion of Jesus, and to position themselves emotionally in relation to this vivid scene of profound suffering.[1] To exemplify this process, Martz cites texts such as Luis de la Puente's *Meditations*, a work which enjoins the believer to

6. *The Defence of Poesy, The Miscellaneous Works*, ed. William Gray (Boston, 1860), pp. 69–70.

† From the *Journal of Medieval and Early Modern Studies* 31:3 (2001): 561–84.

1. Louis Martz, *The Poetry of Meditation: A Study in English Religious Literature of the Seventeenth Century* (New Haven: Yale University Press, 1954; rev. 1962).

> set before mine eyes Christ Jesus crucified, beholding his heade crowned with thornes; his face spit upon; his eyes obscured; his armes disjoincted; his tonge distasted with gall, and vinegar; his handes and feete peerced with nailes . . . and then pondering that hee suffereth all this for my sinnes, I will drawe sundrye affections from the inwardest parte of my heart, sometimes trembling at the rigour of God's justice.[2]

Martz argues cogently that "such practices of 'composition' or 'proposing' lie behind the vividly dramatized, firmly established, graphically imaged openings that are characteristic" of poets such as Donne and Herbert.[3]

If these writers look toward the scene of the Passion, however, they do so through squinting eyes amid slumping postures, as if they were glimpsing a trauma too immense for human comprehension. The poems explored in this essay—Donne's "Good Friday, 1613," Herbert's "Sacrifice" sequence, and Milton's "Passion"—are not so much vivid dramatizations of the sacrifice as they are performances of the enormous difficulty of apprehending what is, in Donne's words, a "spectacle of too much weight for mee."[4] These writers ask how the immense suffering of the Christian sacrifice can be represented in poetry, free of the inevitable anesthesia of memory and the distorting fictions of the imagination. They record not just the immense spiritual benefits that ensue from the sacrifice of the suffering Jesus but also the prodigious psychological costs of that beneficent sacrifice for the mortal worshipper. They offer a way of engaging with the Passion that is not so much a poetry of meditation as it is a poetry of immolation.

Passion is in this context an enormously rich and elusive term, designating both the enormous agony of Jesus and the swirl of emotions that this suffering instills in the individual believer. What becomes for these poets the central subject of the Passion, then, is not the tortured body of Jesus but rather the ethical, intellectual, and finally emotional difficulty of accepting unequivocally the extravagant mercy achieved by the extravagant agony at the center of the Christian dispensation. By looking at the suffering Jesus, these writers confront the excruciating paradox of a religion of love whose central symbol is an instrument of torture and death. As Herbert remarks in his poem "The Crosse," this symbol is a "strange and uncouth thing" that makes him "sigh, and seek, and faint, and die."[5] For Herbert, the cross, emblem of Christ's suffering, spurs a series of contra-

2. Luis de la Puente, *Meditations* (1605), 1:59–60; quoted from Martz, *Poetry of Meditation*, 49. See also Anthony Raspa, *The Emotive Image: Jesuit Poetics in the English Renaissance* (Fort Worth: Texas Christian University Press, 1983); A. D. Cousins, *Catholic Religious Poets from Southwell to Crashaw* (London: Sheed and Ward, 1991); and Alison Shell, *Catholicism, Controversy, and the English Literary Imagination, 1558–1660* (Cambridge: Cambridge University Press, 1999).
3. Martz, *Poetry of Meditation*, 31.
4. "Good Friday, 1613, Riding Westward," line 16, cited from *The Divine Poems of John Donne*, ed. Helen Gardner (Oxford: Clarendon Press, 1978). All citations of Donne's sacred poems are from this edition, given by line numbers. I am not suggesting, of course, that these works are the only available lyric engagements with the Passion; rather, I wish to treat them as symptomatic of a larger trajectory of seventeenth-century devotional writings from corporeal suffering to ethical injunction. Notable poetic engagements with the Passion that I do not explore here include Amelia Lanyer's *Salve Deus Rex Iudaeorum* (1611), which I discuss in detail in "The Gender of Religious Devotion: Amelia Lanyer and John Donne," in *Religion and Culture in the English Reneaissance*, ed. Debora Shuger and Claire McEachern (Cambridge: Cambridge University Press, 1997), 209–33; and Nicholas Breton's "The Countesse of Pembroke's Passion" (n.d.).
5. "The Crosse," lines 1–2, in *The Works of George Herbert*, ed. F. E. Hutchinson (Oxford: Clarendon Press, 1941). All subsequent references to Herbert's poetry are given by line numbers from this edition.

dictory emotions that ultimately embody in the individual believer a harrowing if diminished version of the original passion of Jesus.

Donne's poem of the same name entails by contrast a breathless flow of conventional if clever quandaries, dispersing its concern about corporeal suffering into the proliferation of intellectual paradox. Even this poem dedicated to the central symbol of Jesus' suffering asserts the superiority of spiritual to material agony, announcing that the former is far more salutary for the afflicted soul.

> Materiall Crosses then, good physicke bee,
> And yet spirituall have chiefe dignity.
> These for extracted chimique medicine serve,
> And cure much better, and as well preserve;
> Then are you your own physick, or need none,
> When Still'd, or purg'd by tribulation.
>
> (25–30)

Whereas physical suffering functions like Galenic medicine, aiming at health by restoring a healthy humoral balance, spiritual suffering works like Paracelsan chemical distillations, which drive out the seeds of disease through the introduction of antagonistic alchemy.[6] For Donne, the homeopathic paradoxes of the cross prescribe terrestrial tribulation as a cure for spiritual disease.

Debora Shuger has recently argued that "Christ's agony provides the primary symbol for early modern speculation on selfhood and society. The tortured and torturing males who supply the dramatis personae of the Crucifixion . . . also haunt the interior landscape of the Puritan automachia."[7] For Shuger, passion narratives "attempt to produce a specific version of Christian selfhood—a divided selfhood gripped by intense, contradictory emotions and an ineradicable tension between its natural inclinations and religious obligations."[8] Donne, Herbert, and Milton certainly discover a kind of Reformed subjecthood in the attempt to come to terms with the Crucifixion. Whereas the goal of Catholic meditational writers is to imagine the self in the scenario of the Passion in order to cultivate the extreme passions it arouses, Donne, Herbert, and Milton discover the difficulty of that act of imagination, and stumble upon the corollary truth that the fitting object of sacrifice is the tacitly arrogant self that would claim to be able to respond appropriately to this event. Whereas the Catholic meditational writers emphasize the emotional affect the event stirs, Donne, Herbert, and Milton focus on the psychological effect of the Passion.

These poets, then, engage in a poetics of interior sacrifice, one that relocates the sacrifice from the rituals of liturgy to the labyrinths of psychology. The Reformed rejection of the Mass as an efficacious sacrifice and nonconformist criticism of the sign and symbol of the cross together

6. Donne's medical metaphor may be chosen with great care here, since the Millenary Petition, which had asked that "the cross in baptism . . . may be taken away," cited the king's own Galenic model of the king as physician to his people: "For, as your princely pen writeth: 'The king, as a good physician, must first know what pecant humours his patient naturall is most subject unto, before he can begin his cure'" (*The Stuart Constitution, 1603–1688: Documents and Commentary*, ed. J. P. Kenyon [Cambridge: Cambridge University Press, 1966], 132). The dispute over the sign of the cross in baptism is analyzed in David Cressy, *Birth, Marriage, and Death: Ritual, Religion, and the Life-Cycle in Tudor and Stuart England* (Oxford: Oxford University Press, 1997), 124–48.
7. Deborah Suger, *The Renaissance Bible: Scholarship, Sacrifice, and Subjectivity* (Berkeley: University of California Press, 1994), 127.
8. Ibid., 7.

signal a move away from Christ's suffering as the central devotional focus of the believer.[9] Much of the Reformation, particularly in England, entailed a series of questions about how to reconfigure in one's own conduct the bloody sacrifice at the core of the Christian belief in the atonement. Should one focus on the intense suffering of that sacrifice, and attempt to recreate it imaginatively? Should one focus on the ritual meal of communal love that reenacts that sacrifice? Or should one explore the immense pressures that the sacrifice places on quotidian ethical conduct? How might the sacrifice best assume a real presence in the devotional life of the individual believer?

Part of the problem has to do with a misleading early modern definition of sacrifice as it applies to the violent suffering of Jesus. In *A Christian Dictionary*, Thomas Wilson defines sacrifice as "A sacred action, wherein the faithfull Jews did voluntarily worship God, by offering some outwarde thing unto his glory, thereby to testifie his chiefe dignity and dominion over them, and their servitude and submission unto him." When applied to Christianity, though, this definition is complicated, because as Wilson writes, "Christ Jesus beeing the trueth and substance, who in the offering of himselfe once upon the crosse, hath fully apeased Gods wrath."[1] The term that had been used to describe an action that humans perform on behalf of God now designates an act of divine suffering performed on behalf of humans. It is a word, then, that assumes the burden of human obligation to God while describing a unique action that God took on behalf of humanity. Christ's unique status, as human and God at once, only complicates the definition further. Christian sacrifice entails the stunning idea that God incarnated himself into the creation so as to experience the pain of being one of his own creatures, and so to regenerate a mode of intimacy between creature and creator. As such, sacrifice obligates mortals to respond to God in a way that is by definition unavailable to them.

Sacrifice had always possessed something of an interior trajectory in the Judeo-Christian tradition. In its original meaning sacrifice was a sacred meal eaten either by the deity alone or by both deity and worshipper together. The early sacrifices were thought to provide God with his necessary food; an animal was burned on the altar so that Yahweh could enjoy its sweet savor. But in the Davidic Psalms, the psalmist bestows a symbolic and internal meaning on what had been an external ritual action: "O Lord open thou my lips, and my mouth shall shew forth thy praise. For thou desirest not sacrifice: else would I give it: thou delightest not in burnt offering. The sacrifices of God are a broken spirit: a broken and contrite heart, O God, thou wilt not despise" (51:15–17).[2] Sacrifice here is located in the believer's heart and emotions. In Romans 12:1, Paul develops this internalization of sacrifice into an ethics of self-control—"Beseech you therefore brethren, by the mercies of God, that ye present your bodies a living sacrifice, holy, acceptable unto God, which is your reasonable sacrifice." In Psalm 51 we see sacrifice taking place in the believer's emotions; in Paul, it is the believer's self-regulating actions. Sacrifice, then, can designate a ritual performance, an interior state, or a principle of self-regulation.

9. See Cressy, *Birth, Marriage, and Death*, 124–48.
1. Thomas Wilson, *A Christian Dictionary* (London, 1616), 505.
2. All biblical quotations are from the Authorized Version.

Reformed practice in England tended to deemphasize ritual and to reemphasize the affective and ethical components. In *The Saints Humiliation*, for example, Samuel Torshell glosses the passage from Psalm 51 in order to demonstrate the full nature of the internal sacrifice that the Christian God demands:

> The heart is naturally strong, proud, stiffe, and rebellious, but it must be beaten from its owne height, and layd levell and flat before Gods foot-stoole; it must be wounded and lie bleeding before God, it must shake and tremble at his presence. . . . Such humiliation . . . is called Gods sacrifice, because God himselfe is the Author of it, he onely breaks us and fits us for his owne Altar. . . .
>
> Wee must be waxe in the hand of God . . . a piece of soft waxe might be moulded to any fashion. . . . If ever wee have Comfort wee must be of ductible, following dispositions, to be . . . fashioned by his rod unto humilitie and submission. . . . To be, not what wee are, or of our selves would be but willingly what he will have us be. . . . A perfume smells sweetest when 'tis bruised or crusht, and when wee are stamped before God in the sence before declard, wee yeeld a pleasant savour to his Nosthrills.[3]

Self-fashioning here is explicitly oppose to the process by which one labors to make oneself a fitting sacrifice to God. The devotional goal is to render the self as wax in the hand of God. As a perfume releases its odor when pounded and bruised, so are God's forceful manipulations of his creatures the occasion for their becoming a pleasing sacrifice to him.[4] Where Catholic devotional writers tended to emphasize the careful composition of the place of Jesus' original sacrifice, Reformed writers stressed the necessary decomposition of self that would internalize the energies of that sacrifice.

Both Catholic and Reformed writers emphasize the immense importance of welcoming the fashioning afflictions of God; in doing so, they give the experience of pain a central place in the spiritual imagination. Elaine Scarry's *The Body in Pain* has taught us to understand the cruel calculus by which the imposition of pain is an exercise of power intended to destroy the subjective world of the sufferer.[5] While this model works wonderfully for the texts of twentieth-century torture that Scarry explores, it works less well for the early-seventeenth-century accounts of sacrificial suffering examined here. These writers, and Donne in particular, imagine pain as constitutive rather than destructive of the subject.[6] Part of the reason for this is a profound difference about where spiritual authenticity might reside. Where we imagine selfhood to reside in the experiences, memories, and desires that produce the quirks we call personality, early-seventeenth-century English writers imagine such quirks as encrustations that must be purged if true selfhood is to emerge. What is solicited, even demanded, is

3. Samuel Torshell, *The Saints Humiliation* (London, 1633), 102–3, 111.
4. Tellingly, Herbert uses the same image of fragrance released by violent manipulation both to depict his own devotional longings in "The Odour" and to describe God's delicious sacrifice in "The Banquet."
5. Elaine Scarry, *The Body in Pain: The Making and Unmaking of the World* (Oxford: Oxford University Press, 1985).
6. In *Discourses of Martyrdom in English Literature, 1563–1694* (Cambridge: Cambridge University Press, 1993), 9, John Knott argues similarly that in Foxe's martyrology "pain does not have the obliterating effects described by Elaine Scarry. Foxes's Marian martyrs affirm their identity as true Christians by gestures, such as clapping their hands in the flames, and memorable last words."

the complete and overwhelming imposition of affliction so intense that the caprices of fallen personality might be completely consumed.

It is important that we not pathologize as masochism such aspirations to corporeal suffering, however aberrational they may seem to us. It is also important that we attend to them, since these aspirations supply the scale by which we can gauge the full weight of the Passion on Donne's religious imagination. Donne's remarkable poem "Good Friday, 1613, Riding Westward" is a marvelous example of the difficulty that Donne experienced in coming to terms with the sacrifice, as well as the corollary difficulty that readers have had in coming to terms with Donne's abiding interest in corporeal suffering. Most critics have been so impressed by the rich intellectual heritage of the dazzling opening conceit, which likens the speaker's own terrestrial motions to those of the planets, that they have largely ignored the equally stunning corporeal terms in which the poem ends. This self-consciously brilliant opening has provided a consummate field on which both an older historicism in search of intellectual lineage and a new criticism in search of metaphorical ingenuity could strut its stuff.[7] About halfway through the poem, though, Donne finds himself guilty of precisely those procedures in which so much criticism of Donne is complicit—subordinating that body whose movement is the subject of the opening conceit to an obsessive concern with discursive rationalization of its motions. The poem begins with a cogent if inevitably inadequate comparison, likening a human soul to a sphere:

> Let mans Soule be a Spheare, and then, in this,
> Th'intelligence that moves, devotion is,
> And as the other Spheares, by being growne,
> Subject to forraigne motions, lose their owne,
> And being by others hurried every day,
> Scarce in yeare their naturall forme obey:
> Pleasure of businesse, so, our Soules admit
> For their first mover, and are whirld by it.
> Hence is't, that I am carryed towards the West
> This day, when my Soules form bends toward the East. (1–10)

The very facility with which Donne prosecutes this vigorous analogy, though, arouses suspicion; indeed, Donne subsequently envisages his Savior's body as encompassing, literally and metaphorically, those spheres whose soul-like motions initiated the poem. The speaker asks with a trepidation that belies the confident metaphors of the opening:

> Could I behold those hands which span the Poles,
> And tune all spheares at once pierc'd with those holes?
> Could I behold that endlesse height which is
> Zenith to us, and our Antipodes,
> Humbled below us? or that blood which is
> The seat of all our Soules, if not of his,
> Made durt of dust, or that flesh which was worne
> By God, for his apparell, rag'd and torne? (21–28)

7. I am thinking here particularly of the erudite essays of A. B. Chambers, "Good Friday, 1613. Riding Westward: The Poem and the Tradition," *English Literary History* 28 (1961): 31–53; and Chambers, " 'Good Friday, 1613. Riding Westward': Looking Back," *John Donne Journal* 6 (1987): 185–212.

As Donald Friedman has argued, "The physical reality of pain, blood, and torn flesh will [finally] supplant the self-protecting conceptual intricacies of spheres, intelligences, and irrational motions."[8] The grandiose opening is reimagined as a glorious but misleading fiction that dissolves under the stare of his suffering Savior. But even Friedman's compelling reading of the poem as a movement from "ratiocinative bloodlessness" to the Savior's blood seems unwilling to consider the speaker's ultimate turn from the suffering body of his Savior to the fervent demand that his own body suffer in like fashion. Arguing that "the light and clarity of 'remembered' wisdom" rather than the intense pain of corporeal punishment is the subject of the poem's end, Friedman allows the cerebral art of memory to supplant the corporeal discipline the poem invokes.[9]

In "Good Friday," though, the speaker concludes not by recollecting in tranquility his Savior's suffering but by asking that the suffering of his own body ultimately replace the process of rationalizing his geographical trajectory away from the direction of his suffering Savior:

> I turne my backe to thee, but to receive
> Corrections, till thy mercies bid thee leave.
> O thinke mee worth thine anger, punish mee,
> Burne off my rusts, and my deformity. . . . (37–40)

At the end of "Good Friday," then, the speaker no longer addresses himself but rather a God he does not look at, yet who watches him. Heartfelt supplication supplants meditative rationalization.

The poem's conclusion pointedly juxtaposes the speaker's horrified refusal to look at God with a sense of mortal subject's complete visibility before God. The speaker cannot return God's gaze, he says, until God has properly punished him. Although both Foucault and feminist film theory have taught us to conceptualize the gaze as an inherently intrusive, even oppressive phenomenon, Donne was fascinated by a contrary notion: the immense comfort that can emerge from a sense of complete visibility before God, and the corollary fear that God will not deign to bestow such a gaze upon him. The ultimate terror, Donne argues in a sermon, is

> that that God, who hath often looked upon me in my foulest uncleannesse, and when I had shut out the eye of the day, the Sunne, and the eye of the night, the Taper, and the eyes of all the world, with curtaines and windows and doores, did yet see me, and see me in mercy, by makeing me see that he saw me, . . . [that that God] should so turne himself from me.[1]

As the fabrics of privacy are rendered a transparent fiction before the penetrating gaze of the omniscient God, Donne finds consolation rather than paranoia in visibiliity, even in the moments of his "foulest uncleannesse." His greatest fear is not that his sins will be seen, but rather that God will turn away from him, just as he turns from God in "Good Friday, 1613, Riding Westward."

8. Donald Friedman, "Memory and the Art of Salvation in Donne's Good Friday Poem," *English Literary Renaissance* 3 (1973): 431.
9. Ibid., 426.
1. *The Sermons of John Donne*, ed. George R. Potter and Evelyn M. Simpson, 10 vols. (Berkeley: University of California Press, 1953–62), 5:266. Further citations are given in the text by volume and page numbers.

In a sermon praising the "extraordinary austerity" of John the Baptist, Donne links images of riding and corporeal punishment in ways that illuminate the dilemmas of his "Good Friday" poem:

> he that uses no *fasting*, no *discipline*, no *mortification*, exposes himself to many dangers in himselfe . . . my body is the horse I ride . . . my business lies at Jerusalem; thither I should ride . . . my horse over pampered casts me upon the way, or carries me out of the way . . . must not that be my way, to bring him to a gentler riding, and more command, by lessening his proportions of provender. S. Augustine meanes the same that S. Paul preached, *I beat down my body*, says he, *and bring it in subjection*; And, (as *Paulinus* reades that place) *Lividum reddo, I make my body blacke and blue; white* and *red* were not Saint Pauls colours. (*Sermons*, 4:152–53)

As in "Good Friday," corporeal punishment compensates for the innate misdirections of the body. The black and blue of bruised flesh are the colors under which the devout Christian rides.

As Donne turns away from his God in "Good Friday," moreover, we need to glimpse not just a spiritual trajectory but also a profound violation of social decorum, since in the liturgy of bodily demeanor, one was never supposed to turn one's back on a superior. To say "I turne my back on thee" to a figure of authority is an act of overt defiance. Indeed, when Queen Elizabeth failed to approve the earl of Essex's nomination for the position of commander of the English forces in Ireland, Essex "turned his back upon her in such a contemptuous manner as exasperated her to such a high degree, that she gave him a box on the ear, and bid him go and be hang'd."[2] Donne attempts to render this contemptuous posture as covert solicitation of a far more severe form of physical punishment than the box on the ear that Essex received. "When the Lord comes to us," Donne remarks in a sermon, "though he come in corrections, in chastisements, not to turne to him, is an irreverent and unrespective negligence" (*Sermons*, 5:370). Donne, though, never turns around in the poem. Relatedly, even the speaker's wish to be punished is stated as a command—"punish mee, / Burne off my rusts, and my deformity, / Restore thine Image." As such, it offers, and unstable blend of command and submission to the superior to whom the speaker desires to submit unconditionally.[3] Punish me, the speaker says, and only then will I offer you, the highest superior, the common respect of showing my face rather than my backside.

Donne's speaker is nevertheless able to recreate in painstaking detail the somatic details of the Passion he cannot visually confront, and in doing so participates, albeit provisionally, in the Catholic meditative practices Martz describes. Christ's hands are "pierc'd with those holes," his copious outpouring of blood makes "durt of dust," his "flesh" is "rag'd, and torne." When turning to the prospect of his own suffering, however, the speaker initially opts for euphemism: "I turne my back to thee, but to receive / Corrections." Authoritarian periphrasis, though, soon gives way to a graphic language which does not flinch from the excruciating pain it implores: "O think mee worth thine anger, punish mee, / Burne off my

2. Thomas Birch, *Memories of the Reign of Queen Elizabeth*, 2 vols. (London, 1754), 2:384.
3. The gesture is, to borrow the terms of Wilbur Sanders's discussion of a similar moment in "Batter my heart," so "fiercely willed that it destroys the possibility of its own fulfillment" (*John Donne's Poetry* [Cambridge: Cambridge University Press, 1971], 130).

rusts, and my deformity." Instruments of torture are imagined as tools of purification.

While we read these lines, we need to keep in mind the linkages that Donne would have felt acutely between Catholic religious practice and bodily punishment. The poem's fervent attention to Mary involves a proto-Catholic mode of devotion that Protestant authorities discouraged. In "The Litanie," Donne certainly had exalted Mary's role in salvation in ways that could be construed as Catholic: Mary is "That she-Cherubin, / Which unlock'd Paradise"; she is likewise a figure who can be addressed in prayer: "As her deeds were / Our helpes, so are her prayers; nor can she sue / In vaine, who hath such titles unto you" (38–39, 43–45). In a sermon, though, Donne argued against such Mariolatry: "God forbid any should say, That the Virgin Mary concurred to our good, so, as Eve did to our ruine . . . The Virgin Mary had not the same interest in our salvation, as Eve had in our destruction; nothing that she did entred into that treasure, that ransom that redeemed us" (*Sermons*, 1:200). To describe Mary as "Gods partner here, [who] furnish'd thus / Halfe of that Sacrifice, which ransom'd us"(31–32), was to risk sounding like the proscribed and persecuted religion he had ostensibly left. The poem's final request to be thought *worthy*, moreover, nudges it into the realm of Catholic theology, which emphasized merit rather than grace as the avenue to salvation, even if it is only a worthiness to be punished, not to be saved. Although Donne dares not glance eastward until properly punished by his God, then, he does dare to speak in theologically risky ways, both to his God and to those of his contemporaries who were privileged to see the poem in one of its many manuscript versions.

As John Carey has reminded us, Donne's own family had suffered greatly for espousing just the kind of proto-Catholic sentiments displayed in "Good Friday."[4] As Donne remarks in *Pseudo-Martyr*, "no family . . . hath endured and suffered more in their persons and fortunes, for obeying the Teachers of Romane Doctrine, then it hath done."[5] Carey imagines Donne poised precariously between two horrible prospects of punishment: on the one side, he was threatened by the severe corporeal sanctions against Catholics of the English government, and on the other he was confronted with the even more terrifying prospect of eternal hell as the punishment for apostasy.[6] His success at avoiding these punishments depends, in so many ways, on how he responds to the sacrifice. On one of his sermons, Donne imagines acutely the terrifying moment in which a damned soul experiences "a sodain flash of horror first, and then he goes into fire without light" (*Sermons*, 2:239). "Good Friday" hopes for a very different kind of fire, one that will "Burne off my rusts, and my deformity," but Donne nevertheless remains anxious about the similar caloric medium shared by the purifying fires of God's mercy and the horrifying fires of eternal damnation.

Purification and punishment, furthermore, are imagined in these poems as media of self-fashioning. The fires will not consume the speaker but rather will restore God's image in him in order to occasion God's recog-

4. John Carey, *John Donne: Life, Mind, and Art* (New York: Oxford University Press, 1981).
5. Quoted in Carey, *John Donne*, 20.
6. Donne's residual Catholicism is explored by Richard Strier, "John Donne Awry and Squint: The 'Holy Sonnets,' 1608–1610," *Modern Philology* 86 (1989): 357–85; and by Dennis Flynn, *John Donne and the Ancient Catholic Nobility* (Bloomington: Indiana University Press, 1995).

nition of him; he will be punished "that thou mayst know me." This is a peculiar thing to say to an omniscient being, quietly placing limits on that being's capacity to know his creatures.[7] At the same time, it implies that Donne has the perverse power to make himself unrecognizable to his maker. The poem longs for God to use pain to sacrifice the congenitally perverse subjectivity of its speaker in order to reveal a more authentic if less individuated self within. Original sin, Donne suggests in a sermon, "hath banished me out of my self" (*Sermons*, 6:116–17). God's attentive afflictions, he hopes, will end this exile. Although the opening gambit of the speaker of "Good Friday" is to divorce soul and body as an explanation of his own divided will, his solicitation of punishment intends to reunite them, since torture is an action imposed on the body but perceived in the mind. He longs to experience the pain that would wean him from the pleasant world that draws him away from his God.[8] An emphasis on how Christ suffered for humanity precipitates a devotional mode in which humanity longs to suffer for God.

Where Donne's account of the Passion concludes with a focus on the salutary and constitutive violence that God directs toward humans, Herbert's account of the Passion explores the spiritual and psychological vertigo that issues from the attempt to internalize an impossible sacrifice. Where Donne could not bear to look at his suffering Savior, Herbert ventriloquizes the bitter laments of his. In doing so, Herbert draws on a vast medieval tradition based in Jeremiah. Herbert's "The Sacrifice" has in fact been the subject of one of the major critical debates of the last century: where William Empson finds the poem exemplary of his final type of ambiguity, in which completely opposite sentiments are held in uneasy suspension, Rosemond Tuve argues that Empson's ingeniously ambiguous readings evaporate in the harsh light of the scholarly tradition. While the initial battle seems to have gone to Tuve, Empson appears to have won the war. While Tuve is correct that many of the phenomena that Empson explores are traditional, what is significant is Herbert's particular amplification and contextualization of them. As J. A. W. Bennett, no friend of Empsonian ingenuity, observes, the tone of Herbert's "Sacrifice" is "harsher and more ironic than that of any medieval antecedent, or of any contemporary presentation."[9] It is this harsh irony that Tuve would dampen, and that Empson has given us ears to hear.

Herbert, moreover, lays out such traditional liturgical patterns at the threshold of his temple of devotion in order to stage an aggressive dialogue with them. He does this first of all through sequence. The preceding poem is "The Altar," a shaped poem that welcomes the reader into the lyrics of "The Church," and which identifies through its form the symbolic place whereby the sacrifice of Jesus is reenacted in the liturgical practices of the Church of England. But it also signals the pressures of sacrificial interior-

7. In his "Hymn to God the Father," Donne would engage in a similarly outrageous version of this topos, reminding God that "when thou hast done, thou hast not done, / For I have more."
8. In Sonnets 50 and 51, Shakespeare explores a similar topos, imagining a speaker who is riding away from a friend and into affliction: "My grief lies onward, and my joy behind" (*Shakespeare's Sonnets*, ed. Stephen Booth [New Haven: Yale University Press, 1977]).
9. J. A. W. Bennett, *Poetry of the Passion: Studies in Twelve Centuries of English Verse* (Oxford: Clarendon Press, 1982), 158–59; Rosemond Tuve. *A Reading of George Herbert* (Chicago: University of Chicago Press, 1952), 19–99.

ization—the altar books like an "I," and the substance of the altar is revealed to be the hard stones of a mortal heart, stones that only God can cut. As such, the poem uses the psalmic internalization of sacrifice to align Hebraic sacrificial rituals with the sacrifice of Jesus, and with the contemporaneous liturgical practices designed to replicate that sacrifice. The speaker prays in the poem's conclusion that God will "let they blessed SACRIFICE be mine, / And sanctifie this ALTAR to be thine" (17–18). The final couplet of "The Altar," then, advertises the purpose for which the altar was constructed—it is a place where humans can reenact the sacrifice of God.

But the subsequent poem, "The Sacrifice," demonstrates just how difficult it is for a mortal to feel secure in the performance of this sacrifice. Its interrogatory refrain—"Was ever grief like mine?"—reiterates the uniqueness of the event in dramatizes, and so haunts the injunction to respond to it. There is a profound structural irony in the existence of a poem in which a mortal poet assumes the voice of the suffering God telling his creatures that they cannot appropriate the sacrifice represented therein. Throughout the poem, bitter irony underscores the vast distance between God's behavior toward his creatures and those creatures' cruel treatment of their maker. Herbert's Jesus proves quite the ironist, turning it repeatedly against the creatures who mock and torture him. "The princes of my people make a head / Against their Maker" (5–6), he laments, punning bitterly on the aggressive and creative meanings of *make*. Similar syntactic patterns and linguistic puns run throughout the poem: "They use that power against me, which I gave" (11); "At their commands / I suffer binding, who have loos'd their bands" (46–47); "Then from one ruler to another bound / They leade me" (53–54). Jesus, moreover, is charged with just the kind of violent impertinence that his creatures so grotesquely display: "Then they accuse me of great blasphemie, / That I did thrust into the Deitie" (61–62). His torturers will prove guilty of just the gesture for which they accuse Jesus, thrusting quite literally into the deity: "Nay, after death their spite shall further go: / For they will pierce my side, I full well know" (245–46).

Herbert's Jesus seems particularly offended by the social indecorum to which he is made subject:

> Herod in judgement sits, while I do stand;
> Examines me with a censorious hand:
> I him obey, who all things else command. (81–83)

Though commanding "all," Jesus is forced to defer to a petty mortal lord. Mortal treatment of Jesus here resembles the disrespect Donne performs in turning his back on his superior. Herbert's Jesus, moreover, is subjected to abuse by those creatures who are lowest on the social hierarchy—"Servants and abjects flout me" (141). He announces that

> A King my title is, prefixt on high;
> Yet by my subjects am condemn'd to die
> A servile death in servile companie. (233–35)

Herbert's Jesus here announces the political dimension of his sacrifice; rather than creatures offering a gift of gratitude to their creator, here creator and king is sentenced to death by his subjects and creatures. The universe is maliciously turned upside down.

This total ontological reversal produces a hidden propriety in the pathetic attempts of Jesus' torturers to engage in corrosive irony:

> They bow their knees to me, and cry Hail King:
> What ever scoffes or scornfulnesse can bring,
> I am the floore, the sink, where they it fling:
> Was ever grief like mine?
>
> Yet since mans scepters are as frail as reeds,
> And thorny all their crowns, bloudie their weeds;
> I, who am Truth, turn into truth their deeds:
> Was ever grief like mine? (173–80)

Mortals mock this figure who claims he is king, yet the joke is on them, because the object of their mockery is the celestial king. As the mob urges Jesus to use his power to help himself—"Now heal thy self, Physician; now come down"—Jesus again transubstantiates their mockery into truth by describing the kenosis as an occasion when he had already performed the descent they urge: "Alas! I did so, when I left my crown / And fathers smile for you, to feel his frown" (221–23).

"The Sacrifice," then, indicates repeatedly that the event which the speaker of "The Altar" prays to appropriate is unfathomable and unreachable by humanity. The final stanza of "The Sacrifice" emphasizes this point through a bitter ambiguity that renders promise and threat, gratitude and revenge, indistinguishable:

> But now I die; now all is finished.
> My wo, mans weal: and now I bow my head
> Onely let others say, when I am dead,
> Never was grief like mine. (249–52)

Is the final statement direct or indirect discourse? As Empson brilliantly argues, the last two lines contain an excruciating ambiguity.[1] Are these "others" to suffer for their sinful treatment of their Savior so that they too will lament "never was grief like mine"? Or are these others to acknowledge the uniqueness of Christ's sacrifice, and the subsequent inability of mortals to make it their own? Are the "others" his torturers, or his followers, or is this distinction sustainable in the face of indiscriminate moral arrogance? If it is taken as direct discourse spoken by others, then the poem's final utterance is Jesus' vengeful promise that others shall suffer for the way he has been made to suffer. If it is indirect discourse, then the poem's final utterance depicts the inimitable uniqueness of Christ's sacrifice. Either through terror or incapacity, mortal responses to this stunning event are quailed.

Rather than resolving the ambiguity, the poem opens out into the next poem, "The Thanksgiving," in which a mortal attempts to respond to the voice of the suffering Christ, to fulfill the wish expressed at the end of "The Altar" to make Christ's sacrifice his own. What emerges is a deeply sincere but implicitly ludicrous imitation of the "King of griefs." The speaker of "The Thanksgiving" proposes to respond to the voice of his suffering lord by imitating him: "But how then shall I imitate thee, and /

1. William Empson, *Seven Types of Ambiguity* (New York: New Directions, 1947), 226–33.

Copie thy fair though bloudie hand?" (15–16). He slowly comes to realize, though, that the *imitatio Cristi* is from a Reformed perspective an impossible and ultimately misguided form of devotion that arrogates to the self the prerogatives of God alone. As Martin Luther had proclaimed at the beginning of the Reformation,

> all hypocrites and idolators essay to do those works which properly pertain to divinity and belong to Christ solely and alone. They do not indeed say with their mouth: I am God, I am Christ, yet in fact, they arrogate to themselves the divinity and office of Christ. And so, in fact, they say: I am Christ, I am saviour, not only of myself, but also of others.[2]

By staging the voice of the sacrificial Christ and his own wish to imitate it, Herbert deliberately installs the furnishings of Catholic meditation in a deeply Reformed temple. As Ilona Bell observes, "much as Sidney and Donne raided and exploded the Petrarchan conventions, Herbert used and doomed the familiar images, postures, and goals of Catholic meditation."[3] Herbert performs a devotional imitation whose aggressive failures entail a heartfelt act of sacrifice and praise.

The speaker of "The Thanksgiving" begins as if he has just finished reading a text of the last stanza of "The Sacrifice," and is meditating upon the ambiguities contained therein. "O King of Grief," he asks, "How shall I grieve for thee, / Who in all grief preventest me?" (1, 3–4). The word *prevent* here, like the ambiguity at the end of "The Sacrifice," looks in two directions at once: the word means not only "to act before, to anticipate," but also "to forestall, balk, or baffle. . . . To cut off beforehand, debar, preclude."[4] Christ's immense sacrifice prevents the speaker not only chronologically but also qualitatively; it is a grief that is both prior and unparalleled. Linked to *prevenient*, the theological term for the manner in which God's grace anticipates human needs, *prevent* infers the way that God's sacrificial mercy places an infinite burden on the mortal devotee. The speaker of "The Thanksgiving" suggests that Jesus' moment of greatest despair—when he had cried, "My God, my God, why dost thou part from me?"—was "such a grief as cannot be" (10). He nevertheless proposes to match God's beneficence with his own pious yet misguided good works as a way to "revenge me on they love":

> If thou dost give me wealth; I will restore
> All back unto thee by poore.
> If thou dost give me honor; men shall see,
> The honor doth belong to thee.
> I will not marry; or if she be mine,
> She and her children shall be thine.
> My bosome friend, if he blaspheme thy name,
> I will tear thence his love and fame.
> One half of me being gone, the rest I give

2. *D. Martin Luthers Werke Kritische Gesamtausgabe*, ed. J. C. F. Knaake, et al. (Weimar, 1883), 40: 404; quoted in Anders Nygren, *Agape and Eros*, trans. Philip S. Watson (New York: Harper Torchbooks, 1969), 702 n. 1.
3. Ilona Bell, "Setting Foot into Divinity': George Herbert and the English Reformation," *Modern Language Quarterly* 38 (1977): 222.
4. Ibid., 228.

Unto some Chappell, die or live.
As for thy passion—But of that anon,
When with the other I have done. (19–30)

As is the case so frequently with Herbert, the verse-form participates actively in the meaning: the alternating long and short lines represent the pulse of poverty and wealth that would be part of this false spiritual economy, even as the sing-song rhythm suggests the glibness of the speaker's response. When he turns to the subject of the Passion, though, the meter falters, as the speaker stutters into authenticity, realizing that humans can never offer a sacrifice that would in any way match that of Jesus.

Among the more ridiculous proposals is the speaker's suggestion that he can imitate God's foreknowledge:

For thy predestination I'le contrive,
That three years hence, if I survive,
I'le build a spittle, or mend common wayes. (31–33)

The very claim depends upon the contingency of his survival, a contingency that completely undoes the parallel between his own actions and God's. The poem concludes with the speaker stammering at his inability to find any mode of response to Christ's sacrifice: "Then for the passion—I will do for that— / Alas, my God, I know not what" (49–50). His broken syntax represents the internal violence the sacrifice demands. The poem in some sense ends where it begins, wondering how to grieve for a figure who prevents all grief.

It is appropriate that part of the battle between Empson and Tuve over "The Sacrifice" had to do with just how original the poem is, because the speaker of "The Thanksgiving" confronts the issue of originality head-on when he asks, "How then shall I imitate thee, and / Copie thy fair though bloudie hand?" (15–16). Is the follower of Christ to parrot the words of Christian tradition, or is he or she to engage in a creative imitation which will attempt to emulate Christ's sacrifice? In "The Crosse," Herbert's poetic confrontation with the symbol of the suffering figure that utters "The Sacrifice," the speaker complains about the excoriating contradictions of his mortal existence before discovering the essence of the cross in his own psychological agony:

Ah my deare Father, east my smart!
These contrarieties crush me: these crosse actions
Doe winde a rope about, and cut my heart:
And yet since these thy contradictions
Are properly a crosse felt by thy Sonne,
With but foure words, my words, *Thy will be done*. (31–36)

His momentary conformity with God's will is expressed not only in the submissive sentiments of the last four words but also in their origin in the Lord's Prayer. Embracing the excruciating paradoxes of mortal existence as an interior version of Christ's suffering precipitates a viable response to the symbol of Christ's sacrifice. In the *Ancilla Pietatis*, Daniel Featley, a moderate conformist, had asserted the productive discipline of assimilating the phrases of the Bible into one's devotions:

> For in these we ought most of all to denie our selves, and to captivate, not onely our thought to the conceptions, but our tongs to the words and phrases of the inspired Oracles of God.[5]

Although imitating the sacrifice of God entails for Herbert a misguided mode of devotion, imitating the words of God, making them your own, entails the ultimate sacrifice—that of the self and its language. In the self-immolation of a fully biblical stylistics, Herbert points to what it might mean to "copie they fair though bloudie hand." The poem thus serves as a provisional answer to the devotional dilemma uncovered in "The Thanksgiving."

Although Christ announces in the last stanza of "The Sacrifice" that "all is finished," the problem of responding devoutly to this vexed historical moment has only just begun. The poem that follows "The Thanksgiving," "The Reprisall" (originally entitled "The Second Thanks-giving"), demonstrates that the only sacrificial offering the speaker is capable of making is surrendering any illusions he might have about his capacity to imitate Christ's sacrifice. He begins by conceding that "There is no dealing with thy mighty passion" (2) and says that even if he would die for his Savior, he would be in arrears, since Christ was blameless and died for all: "Though I die for thee, I am behind" (3). He complains bitterly that God has chosen to "outgo" him both in "eternal glorie" and in corporeal agony:

> Ah Was it not enough that thou
> By thy eternal glorie didst outgo me?
> Couldst thou not griefs sad conquests me allow,
> But in all vict'ries overthrow me? (9–12)

Herbert here allows the implicit competition of sacrificial gift-giving to emerge. It is a potlatch that mortals can never win. The conclusion, though, promises that through "confession" the speaker will "come / Into thy conquest" (13–14). He offers to turn his agonistic and competitive energies inward, bifurcating the self in order to "overcome / The man who once against thee fought" (15–16). In doing so, he inaugurates an unending division of the sinful self that becomes, ultimately, a lyrically productive liturgy of interior sacrifice.

The lyrics of *The Temple* are in many ways an extended series of such reprisals. Herbert's poem entitled "Good Friday" begins in the interrogative mode, wondering what mode of response a mortal can generate to this scene of suffering:

> O my chief good,
> How shall I measure out thy bloud?
> How shall I count what thee befell,
> And each grief tell?
>
> Shall I thy woes
> Number according to they foes?
> Or, since one starre show'd thy first breath,
> Shall all they death? (1–8)

5. Daniel Featley, *Ancilla Pietatis: Or, the Hand-maid to Private Devotion* (London, 1626), 107.

The last twelve lines of this poem, written in a different meter and originally comprising in the Williams manuscript a separate poem entitled "The Passion," transform the speaker's effort to compose a response to the sacrifice into a prayer to be made the vehicle of divine writing:

Since bloud is fittest, Lord, to write
Thy sorrows in, and bloudie fight;
My heart hath store, write there, where in
One box doth lie both ink and sinne:

That when sinne spies so many foes,
Thy whips, thy nails, thy wounds, thy woes,
All come to lodge there, sinne may say,
No room for me, and flie away.

Sinne being gone, oh fill the place,
And keep possession with they grace;
Lest sinne take courage and return,
And all the writings blot or burn. (21–32)

Herbert wittily hopes that by assimilating the sacrifice of his God into the marrow of his being, he will at once crowd out sin and invite that God to enter and to write the story of his passion in his subject's own blood. Where Donne on Good Friday interrogates the possibility of beholding his bleeding God, Herbert longs on that day to have God compose his own story in Herbert's blood.

I would like to conclude this symptomatic study of seventeenth-century sacrificial poetics by glancing at Milton's surprisingly pathetic attempt at a Passion poem, and to suggest that it has more in common with Donne's and Herbert's deservedly canonical lyrics than we might think. The poem was probably intended as a companion-piece of Milton's gorgeous "Navitity Ode"; it is written in the same meter and rhyme scheme as the opening stanzas of that poem. The precocious twenty-one-year-old poet obviously planned in these two poems to cover the birth and death of his Savior. While the subject of Christ's birth brought out the best in the young poet, the subject of his suffering and death brought out his worst. While he could strut proudly into Bethlehem, he could only steal disconcertedly around Golgotha. "The Passion" consists of eight stanzas that swaddle the subject with ludicrous clichés before the poet abandons the effort entirely. Milton begins "The Passion" by describing the subject and style of the "Navitity Ode"—

Ere-while of Musick, and Ethereal mirth,
Wherwith the stage of Ayr and Earth did ring,
And joyous news of heav'nly Infants birth,
My muse with Angels did divide to sing.[6]

This lyric exaltation is a striking contrast to the "sorrow" and "notes of saddest woe" he must now sing, a lugubrious subject he experiences as undesirable and constraining: "These latter scenes confine my roving vers,

6. *The Riverside Milton*, ed. Roy Flannagan (Boston: Houghton Mifflin, 1998), lines 1–4. All citations of Milton are from this edition.

/ To this Horizon is my Phoebus bound" (22–23). Milton seems to be trying to urge his muse to transport him to the scene of the Passion, perhaps by borrowing Ezekiel's chariot, or by asking "som transporting Cherub . . . / To bear me where the Towers of Salem stood" (39–40). But it is as if his muse were riding westward on what is probably Good Friday, 1630, and will not allow herself to be directed toward that ponderous subject. The poem ends in a bathetic image of the poet's tears impregnating a cloud; Milton here sounds like Crashaw on a bad day:

> Or should I thence hurried on viewles wing,
> Take up a weeping on the Mountains wilde,
> The gentle neighbourhood of grove and spring
> Would soon unboosom all thir Echoes milde,
> And I (for grief is easily beguild)
> Might think th'infection of my sorrows loud,
> Had got a race of mourners on som pregnant cloud.

Milton then appends an explanatory note to the poem: "This subject the author finding to be above the yeers he had, when he wrote it, and nothing satisfi'd with what was begun, left it unfinisht."

Yet Milton carefully printed the incomplete poem in both the 1645 and the 1673 editions of his poems, as if the fragment had some meaning for him. Moreover, any poet who could compose *Paradise Lost, Paradise Regained*, and perhaps *Samson Agonistes* while blind and in political defeat, could have completed a comparatively slight lyric on the highly conventional subject of the Passion if he had wanted to. But he did not, and the sacrifice recedes from the horizon of this decidedly religious poet. In *Paradise Lost*, the suffering of the cross is mentioned only briefly as an abstract figure (12.413–25); Milton is in this epic far more interested in moral rectitude than in salvific suffering. When Abdiel is welcomed back into heaven, for example, the angels salute him as one who "for the testimonie of Truth hast born / Universal reproach, far worse to beare / Then violence" (6.33–35). *Paradise Regained* is likewise focused on the Son's rejection of temptation, not on his carnal suffering. It is "one mans firm obedience fully tri'd / Through all temptation" (1:4–5) that allows paradise to be regained. In both epics Milton deliberately relocates the atonement from a scenario of corporeal martyrdom to a moment of ethical decision. Only in the vivid suffering of *Samson Agonistes* do we get some of the attention to corporeal affliction that had been a crucial element in earlier Passion narratives, and here it is far removed from a sacrificial context. With Milton, the Passion drops away as a subject of religious and poetic inquiry, its energies are absorbed by the ethical pressures of temptation and the continual persecution experienced by the one just man in a world of woe.

I want to argue that Milton cherished this short and flawed lyric in part because it participates in a subgenre of works dedicated to the idea that the sacrifice inevitably defeats human response. It is not just that Milton could not finish the poem, but that its unfinished and unsuccessful nature represents something substantial and meaningful. The subject was not just beyond the poet's years, but beyond the capacity of any Christian to fathom. In its very incompleteness, then, and even in its aesthetic inadequacy, the poem offers a formal version of the stuttering inability to respond to Christ's sacrifice that concludes Herbert's "The Thanksgiving," or of the willed avoidance of the Passion that structures Donne's "Good Friday" poem.

Golgotha, then, proved a particularly difficult hill for seventeenth-century English devotional poets to climb. Donne saunters away from it, Herbert stammers his inability to deal with it, and Milton incompletely circles it before turning his attention to the matters. If a poetics of sacrifice emerges from these poems, it is in the realization that Christ's sacrifice ultimately defeats poetry. As a poetic subject, the sacrifice demands that one perform the inexpressibility topos writ large. In the work of these three very different poets, we can see how the subject of the Passion at once elicited and discouraged lyric response. If subsequent English poetry largely follows the trajectory of Milton in pursuing other subjects for religious verse, we can nonetheless prize the remarkable lyric achievements of Donne and Herbert as they produce riveting aesthetic documents from their own spiritual and poetic impediments.

EAVAN BOLAND

Finding Anne Bradstreet†

1

This is a piece about Anne Bradstreet. But there is another subject here as well. Its nature? For want of an exact definition, it is subject matter itself: that bridge of whispers and sighs over which one poet has to travel to reach another, out of which is formed the text and context of a predecessor. That journey into the past—not just Anne Bradstreet's but my own—is the substance of this essay.

I have always been fascinated by the way poets of one time construct the poets of a previous one. It can be an invisible act, arranged so that none of the awkwardly placed struts are visible. But the discussion of invisibility is not my intention. I am interested in the actual process of reconstruction, in the clear and unclear motives with which a poet from the present goes to find one from the past; I am interested, therefore, in the actions and choices that have the power to turn a canon into something less authoritarian and more enduring: from a set text into a living tradition. The sometimes elusive, yet utterly crucial, difference between a canon and a tradition is also part of this piece. So in that sense I want the plaster work to show and the background noise to be heard.

All of this seems worth saying at the beginning because I found Anne Bradstreet first in a revealing context. Not in her own words: not in the quick, fluent, and eventually radical cadences that mark her style. My first discovery of her had an ominous irony about it, so I will begin with that.

American poetry was hard to find in Dublin when I was a young poet. It was the mid-sixties. The names of American poets and their poems were not just unavailable in the bookshops: they were unavailable in the air. Part of that was simply enclosure. In the previous decades Ireland had

† From *Green Thoughts, Green Shades: Essays by Contemporary Poets on the Early Modern Lyric*, ed. Jonathan F. S. Post (Berkeley: University of California Press, 2002), 176–90.

come through an intense, inward adventure of its own. Its own poetry, its own poets, its domestic sense of having beaten the odds in both a historic and aesthetic sense were the dominant tropes of its literary self-perception. In that sense the Irish Poetry world stood on what Arnold eloquently called "burning ground." Everyone shared in it. Everyone stood on it. It was an exciting literary culture, precisely because it was so enclosed. In a newspaper article Patrick Kavanagh made a vivid distinction between literary provincialism and parochialism. Parochialism, he wrote, was that blind conviction of being at the center of things, of knowing no other place: it was the summer crossroads where he first made up ballads on football. It was the city that talked about itself endlessly: Joyce's city, with its draped curtains, glittering coastline, and malicious jokes. Provincialism, however, was the hankering for an elsewhere, and anxious measuring of the local against some other, distant standard. In that sense Dublin was—in the best sense—parochial.

A few things got through: a random sampling of the excitements of elsewhere. One of these was *Homage to Mistress Bradstreet* by John Berryman. Published in 1953 in the *Partisan Review*—and then as a volume in 1956—it was a tour de force, a cunning mixture of eulogy and elegy. Its language and syntax, its odd and vehement music had packed its energies in Yeats's proverbial ice and salt and readied them to cross the Atlantic. Over the next decade the poem made its way into the conversations of young Irish poets. Some of this was because of Berryman himself. He came to Dublin in the mid-sixties, made friends, made enemies, caused a certain amount of mayhem, and briefly entered a poetic way of life that thrived on all three.

I remember struggling with *Homage to Mistress Bradstreet*. It was not easy to read for any student or young poet who was used to the Irish poem. It bore no resemblance to anything else. It was a rough, sinuous evocation of a snowy New England I had never seen, a Puritan rubric I had never heard of, a historical reinvention I knew next to nothing about. As a piece of information it was a lot less clear than *Lycidas* and a lot less transparent than *Adonais*. It was also stubbornly mannered, hard to follow, given to cross-jumps of tone and point of view. I was twenty years old and a bad-tempered parochial in Kavanagh's definition, and I was not at all sure I wanted to persevere with it.

Yet my first information about Anne Bradstreet came from that poem. "Born 1612 Anne Dudley, married at 16 Simon Bradstreet, a Cambridge man, steward to the Countess of Warwick & protégé of her father Thomas Dudley, secretary to the Earl of Lincoln. Crossed in the *Arbella*, 1630, under Governor Winthrop."[1] But none of those practical details arrested me. The woman, the poet, was not yet visible. What disturbed and struck me were those fifty-seven stanzas. I didn't give them up. I continued to read. I floundered around in the richly divided identities of the piece. Part ode, Part dialogue, Part harangue. Part séance. And then the poet's voice, usurping the very identity he is seeking out.

(2)
Outside the New World winters in grand dark
white lashing high thro' the virgin stands

1. John Berryman, *Homage to Mistress Bradstreet and other Poems* (New York: Noonday Press, 1968), 10.

foxes down foxholes sigh,
surely the English heart quails, stunned.
I doubt if Simon than this blast, that sea,
spares from his rigour for your poetry
more. We are on each other's hands
who care. Both of our worlds unhandled us. Lie stark,

(3)
thy eyes look to me mild. Out of maize & air
your body's made, and moves. I summon, see,
from the centuries it.
I think you won't stay. How do we
linger, diminished, in our lovers' air,
implausibly visible, to whom, a year,
years, over interims; or not;
to a long stranger; or not; shimmer and disappear.[2]

These stanzas by Berryman prove the point: using the materials of a different moment, he boldly and obstinately constructs a poet and a past. By the time the poem concludes, he has forced his way into the presence of Anne Bradstreet: that young woman who sailed from England at the age of eighteen, who found the Massachusetts winters harsher than those in Lincolnshire, who bore American children, who wrote love poems to her husband, who resolved her quest for style in a radical, domestic polemic. The problem is that by the time the poem is over, we know how the Massachusetts winter drifts down through a broken syntax, how a scalding faith may once have sounded, how musical those names and salutations were. We can even guess about John Berryman's need for a past, a place, a source. But what do we know about her?

2

Anne Dudley was born in 1612, in Northamptonshire, in an England that had been nine years without its imperious queen and would, in another four, lose William Shakespeare and the raffish ethos of the Tudor World. Post-Elizabethan England. Already sowing the wind of the Civil War that was less than thirty years away. Already feeling the pinch and reproach of real-life Malvolios.

Her father was Thomas Dudley, at first clerk to Judge Nicolls in Northamptonshire and then steward of the earl of Lincoln's estate in Sempringham. These were not great people, but they lived in the shadow and peace of greatness. Her father would have known about the fine wines and treasured books and the weighty ermines of the court. He would have talked to the ambitious builders and covetous architects of the period. Although he himself had never been to university he had been tutored by a graduate, so he was able to give his daughter some knowledge of Greek and Latin and French.

It is hardly possible to imagine that England. It was a paradox, a contradiction, a place marching toward regicide and fratricide yet still in sight of the glories and upheavals of the Elizabethan Age. Although Anne Dudley

2. Ibid., 11.

must have heard reminiscences, within the shelter of the earl of Lincoln's estates, of the Armada, of the queen, of ships returning with silks and spices and new tastes and stolen riches, her reality was darker. When the Massachusetts Bay Company was formed in 1628, she was sixteen years old. Her father and her new husband, Simon Bradstreet, were founding members. The nonconformist protest was intensifying, and rage at the taxes and restrictions of Charles I was suddenly the text for action. The old England, with its grace, pride, and remembrance, was now a life-threatening fiction.

In 1630 these founding members began their "errand into the wilderness," as Samuel Danforth called it.[3] The *Arbella* set sail from Southampton. Three months later John Winthrop wrote that "there came a smell off the shore like the smell of a garden."[4] They were safe. They landed at Massachusetts. For Puritanism it was a new context. For America a new history. For Anne Bradstreet a new story. Or half of one. As she steps onto the shore of New England, she disappears. The young woman who loved England is lost in America. "I . . . came into this country, where I found a new world and new manners, at which my heart rose."[5]

Anne Bradstreet is that rare thing: a poet who is inseparable from history. The proportions are not usually so equal and compelling. She can be located in the same way as a place name on a map, and we can judge the distance more accurately because of that. After all, it was history that swept her up, out of the graceful houses and prospects of Lincolnshire and into a three-month sea voyage. History that brought her to the shores of Massachusetts. History that included her in the rigorous self-definition of the Puritans. History that almost demoted her to a figure in the background of a turbulent time.

But when she encountered the New World, she was met not so much by history as by daily routine and hardship. The first winter was cruel and hungry. Food was scarce. "Clams, and muscles [sic], and ground-nuts and acorns"[6] must have seemed a poor diet after the feasts of Lincolnshire. Even her father wrote the bleak truth back to England: "There is not a house where is not one dead, and some houses many."[7] But her life at that moment was set in a mold of survival and compliance, both. First the hard winters, the forced adaptation. Then it was swift and relentless shifting: from Salem to Charlestown, to Cambridge, to Ipswich, and finally to Andover. With each move, each unquestioning pursuit of her husband and father, each trekking after Dudley and Simon Bradstreet, she wrote herself deeper into that difficult history.

The mid-thirties found the Dudleys and Bradstreets living in Ipswich, with a parcel of land, some more prosperity, a gradual easing of conditions. Now twenty-four years old, with two children, Anne Bradstreet had partially recovered from the lameness she had suffered during her eighteenth

3. Samuel Danforth, "Brief Recognition of New England's Errand into the Wilderness," in *American Sermons: The Pilgrims to Martin Luther King Jr.*, ed. Michael Warner (New York: Library of America, 1999), 151.
4. John Winthrop, "Journal," in *Winthrop Papers*, 5 vols. (Boston: Massachusetts Historical Society, 1929–47), 2:259.
5. *The Works of Anne Bradstreet in Prose and Verse*, ed. John Harvard Ellis (Charlestown, Mass.: A. E. Cutter, 1867), 5.
6. Alexander Young, *Chronicles of the First Planters* (Boston: Little, Brown, 1846), 381.
7. Thomas Dudley, "Letter to Countess Lincoln," ibid., 325.

year. She was raising her children, absorbing her landscape, writing in earnest. And there I leave her for the moment so as to widen the story of which she is a part.

3

The mysterious life and achievement of Anne Bradstreet—her occasionally surprising and quick-moving poems, her fresh and intense outlook—is a story I will keep circling around here. No one approach is completely satisfactory. History, culture, political change are all part of it. But not all of it. Some of her truth may have less to do with history than with social anachronism. Because Anne Bradstreet is a founding American poet, it is easy to forget that she was also a dying star in the context of European poetry: a poet writing against a background of adamant faith from a country deeply troubled by the usurpation of religion by politics. A poet of the coteries, when the wider community was becoming fashionable. A poet whose inner and outer life remained powerfully undivided, when the subtle divisions between them—from which romanticism would eventually emerge—was beginning to evolve in England.

It is ironic that had Anne Bradstreet stayed in England, her ecosystem would have been radically different. In a country with an incipient Civil War, a poisoned and politicized religious system, and, after that, an approaching Restoration, where women would be considered bait for princes rather than poets in their own right, how would she have fared? Any consideration of Anne Bradstreet's work has to take this into account: she left a poetic tradition in which she would almost certainly have remained anonymous and founded another in which she is visible, anomalous, and crucial.

4

How do I see Anne Bradstreet? The answer is not simple. To start with, there is no figure in Irish poetry like her. To read of her travels and her pieties, to consider the male power that surrounded her and to which she deferred, and finally to hear her plain-spoken and resistant voice convince me of some out-of-the-way truths. Here is one of them:

When we speak of the way a poet constructs the poets of another age—which is a good deal of my subject—certain things get missed. When I was a young poet, it was an article of faith that modernism was the watershed, the event that changed every poet's view of the recent and distant past. If I wasn't persuaded then, I am even less convinced now.

No, the real watershed—the place where poets divide—is in the version of those centuries—the sixteenth, seventeenth, and eighteenth—which are talismanic possessions for the young poet. Not just in poetry. After all, in those centuries galaxies were found and poetic forms rediscovered; faiths were changed and diseases named. Those are the centuries that divide or attach poets.

Those are the last continents of time where the hinterland of poetry lay as a gleaming, shining distance, still to be named and changed. Just to see that hinterland, just to lay claim to those possessions, is for the young poet often the first unforgettable sensing of the freedom and the grandeur of the art.

But my version of those centuries is the Irish, not the British or American one. There is a world of difference. As Anne Bradstreet was seeking the New World, Ireland was losing the old one. As the Massachusetts Bay Colony was testing its ideas of grace, Ireland was sinking deeper into its knowledge of abandonment. As Simon Bradstreet was touching the light of manifest destiny, the Gaelic order, the bards and the unlucky princes of Ireland were preparing to learn the opposite. And what Anne Bradstreet took with her into her poetry, into the New World—that upward roll of Elizabethan music—is the very cadence that poisoned the wells for the Irish poets.

So when I picture her, this figure from the time and language that dispossessed my own, how can I see her clearly? I am not John Berryman, imagining her on the deck of the *Arbella*, founding his tradition, guaranteeing his music, fearing her elusiveness—"I think you won't stay."[8] Unlike Berryman, my syntax was guaranteed by another group of poets.

But the truth is, I do see her. And somehow the fact that I do, despite not counting her century into my inheritance, seems to prove my point: that the reconstruction of the past, the reconstruction of poet by poet, is willful, inventive, compulsive. The truth is, I cannot afford not to see Anne Bradstreet. She lays her claim across every boundary, in spite of every distance. What's more, she tests my own powers of reconstruction. Pockmarked, slightly lame, outspoken and astonishing in her ability to survive the odds, she comes before me.

5

Anne Bradstreet was thirty-eight when her poetry was published. Not in her native Massachusetts, not even in America, but in an England she would never see again. Her brother-in-law arranged it. He returned to England in 1650, bringing a manuscript of her poems with him and arranging for its publication as *The Tenth Muse, Lately Sprung Up in America*. It would appear to be a strange route to publication but only if seen through modern eyes. Publication for contemporary poets has been a single and sometimes superstitious act: the first book, then the second. But I suspect that in Puritan Massachusetts, as once in eighteenth-century Ireland, the line between what was broadcast and published and locally known and communally written was not at all as clear as it became later: that there was a rich, blurred run of colors at the edge of private authorship and public faith.

The Tenth Muse was published through the efforts of her brother-in-law, the Reverend John Woodbridge, who wrote a winning and eloquent "Epistle to the Reader" at the start of the book. It is Anne Bradstreet's only publication in her lifetime. Not until she had been dead six years did a second, amended edition of *The Tenth Muse* come out. A third followed in 1758. This is a leisurely publication schedule by any standards, and not until 1867 did John Harvard Ellis produce a scholarly and complete text of this book, with more authoritative inclusions.

In his "Epistle to the Reader" Woodbridge is quick to disclaim any poetic vanity on the part of his sister-in-law. He remarks that he has "presumed to bring to publick view what she [Bradstreet] resolved should in such

8. "Homage to Mistress Bradstreet" (line 40), in Berryman, *Homage to Mistress Bradstreet*.

manner never see the sun."[9] Despite this, the poems are only partially successful. A heavy Spenserian shadow hangs over them, as if her girlhood ghost were haunting the paneled rooms of Sempringham. They pay elaborate and conventional tribute to the old heroes and graces of her past: Philip Sidney; her father, Thomas Dudley. The public tone often falters; the language rarely shines. Only *In Honour of That High and Mighty Princess Queen Elizabeth of Happy Memory* cracks open to suggest strength and craft. Despite a clumsy percussion, despite the rhymes, swerving and chasing the sentiments around the page, there is a vigor of nostalgia, something haunting and striking about this memory of a powerful woman, written by a woman just learning her own power:

Who was so good, so just, so learn'd, so wise,
From all the kings on earth she won the prize.
Nor say I more than duly is her due,
Millions will testify that this is true.
She hath wiped off th' aspersion of her sex,
That women wisdom lack to play the rex.
Spain's monarch, says not so, nor yet his host;
She taught them better manners, to their cost.[1]

There is no mystery about *The Tenth Muse*. It is the oddly confident, sometimes accomplished work of a well-born woman. The mystery comes later. After 1653, in the years following the death of her father, Anne Bradstreet's poems changed. The subjects closed in. Her feelings, her children, the life of her home, the spirit of her marriage—these, rather than elegies for lost courtiers, became her themes. The music shifted: the volume was turned down; the voice became at once more private and more intense. A quick-walking cadence accompanied the neighborly, definite voice in which she now told her story. These were cadences that came from the New England moment in which she lived. At last the complicated England of her youth was receding.

To My Dear and Loving Husband

If ever two were one, then surely we.
If ever man were loved by wife, then thee;
If ever wife was happy in a man,
Compare with me, ye women, if you can.
I prize thy love more than whole mines of gold
Or all the riches that the East doth hold.
My love is such that rivers cannot quench,
Nor ought but love from thee, give recompense.
Thy love is such I can no way repay,
The heavens reward thee manifold, I pray.
Then while we live, in love let's so persevere
That when we live no more, we may live ever.
(225)

Or this, from the last year of her life:

9. Quoted in Ellis, *Works*, 84.
1. *The Works of Anne Bradstreet*, ed. Jeannine Hensley, with a foreword by Adrienne Rich (Cambridge, Mass.: Harvard University Press, 1967), 195–98. All verse quotations are from this volume. Subsequent pagination will be indicated parenthetically in the essay proper.

In Reference to Her Children, 23 June 1659

I had eight birds hatched in one nest,
Four cocks there were, and hens the rest.
I nursed them up with pain and care,
Nor cost, nor labour did I spare,
Till at the last they felt their wing,
Mounted the trees, and learned to sing;
Chief of the brood then took his flight
To regions far and left me quite.
My mournful chirps I after send,
Till he return, or I do end:
Leave not thy nest, thy dam and sire,
Fly back and sing amidst this choir.
(232–34)

Where does this voice come from? On the surface, it seems to be earned and made by a woman caught in an unusually rich and powerful dialogue with an authoritarian tradition. Whatever name is given to that authority—maleness, Puritanism, doctrine—the dialogue is sweetened by a strange irony. It appears that the Puritan world can offer a woman poet more permission for domestic and ordinary detail than the Elizabethan one ever did. This is not to diminish the authorship. It is Anne Bradstreet's unique achievement that she could burrow into the cracks, discover the air of history, and find a breathing space to be Puritan, poet, and woman:

I washed thy face, but more defects I saw,
And rubbing off a spot still made a flaw.
I stretched thy joints to make thee even feet,
Yet still thou run'st more hobbling than is meet;
In better dress to trim thee was my mind,
But nought save homespun cloth i' th' house I find.
("*The Author to Her Book*," 221)

As Adrienne Rich wrote of her: "The web of her sensibility stretches almost invisibly within the framework of Puritan literary convention; its texture is essentially both Puritan and feminine."[2] And the Puritan spirit is more easily reconciled, it seems, within the domestic parameter, with the willful, personal intention of the earthly artist, envious of being remembered. "You once desired me," she writes to her son in 1664, "to leave something for you in writing that you might look upon, when you should see me no more."[3]

In the final years of the 1660s, when a lavish court has been reinstated in the country of her birth, Anne Bradstreet—only a few years from her death in 1672—is a world away from power and costume. She has become the author of a bold, personal narrative, mourning her grandchildren, stripping out the rhythms she once learned as ornament, making them serve true feeling:

I knew she was but as a withering flower,
That's here today, perhaps gone in an hour;
Like as a bubble, or the brittle glass,

2. Hensley, *Works of Anne Bradstreet*, xix.
3. Quoted in Hensley, *Works of Anne Bradstreet*, 271.

Or like a shadow turning as it was.
(*"In Memory of My Dear Grandchild Anne Bradstreet,"* 236)

But where did she get the permission for this? Did she really find the sustenance in a Puritan world for what looks remarkably like private and willful expression? The answer (or answers) to that question puts the most strain on the second subject of this piece: the relation between the past and present of poetry. Between the dead and living poet.

6

Anne Bradstreet not only lived in another time; she continues to dwell in a past that I could never hope to find. Strong-willed, displaced, she appears and disappears in front of me. The pock-marked young English girl, scarred by a mystery illness, becomes an American woman poet in the midst of a drama of fervor and faith, becomes the wife and daughter of powerful men, becomes mother of a powerful son to whom she confided her language and purpose.

I wish I could see her clearly. I wish I could see the pen she wrote with. I wish I could reach back to those first hurt conversations in the Massachusetts colony, to her struggles with grace and her conflict with obedience. I wish I could see her in the house in Ipswich, with her children around her. "Nor cost, nor labour did I spare."[4]

The fact is, I can't. And to overlook this simple realization may well corrupt that contact between poet and poet that I began by considering. Poets of the present may invent the poets of the past all too easily, may wrench them from the disciplines and decisions of the world they lived in with such care and pain and disfigure them in a more convenient present.

The example of Anne Bradstreet is a sobering, chastening warning to such canon making. I cannot, as I've said, reconstruct her. If the young woman is unavailable, the older one is elusive. But even the poet that she is resists, in some strange way, any easy reevaluation by the present. In this may lie one of the enduring fascinations of her work. So in summary I will try to outline some of that resistance here.

The challenge offered by Anne Bradstreeet's work is partly to do with its time and location: its origins in one world and its outcome in another. But there is more to the issue than that. In a real way her work lays bare the possible corruptions of the invention of one poet by another, of the past by the present.

If one poet returned to another with simply the prejudices of a time, it would be awkward but understandable: there might be a risk of simplification but not erasure. But this is never the case. We return as poets to the past lugging the huge wing-beams and magical engines and turbines of our age. We drag them across subtleties and differences and demand that our predecessors learn to fly as we have. Providing, of course, they use our machines to do so.

Consider Anne Bradstreet. She lived in a community and adventure of faith, at a real and figurative distance from a continent where both were fading. She struggled with the very concepts of grace, unreason, and compliance that Europe was preparing to throw over. Her first poems—those

4. From "In Reference to Her Children, 23 June 1659," In Hensley, *Works of Anne Bradstreet*, 232.

in *The Tenth Muse*—were structured, formal, and derivative. Her final ones were sharp and musical and impossible to overlook. She waits to be reconsidered. But how can it be done?

In one sense she is a compelling figure precisely because she stands outside the categories we have prepared for the dialogue between past and present. Our concepts of what constitutes the public and private poem will not do when we approach her. Above all, our postromantic definition of what is the inner life and what the outer in poetry, and who patrols the borders, will not serve in her case. If we use these catagories, we will blur the astringent angles of what she achieved. But how to do otherwise?

A quick look shows how. If we return to Anne Bradstreet with our definitions of the public and private poem and notions of nineteenth-century inner life, we will be drawn to a single and deceptive conclusion: the poems in *The Tenth Muse* are more wooden and fixed than Bradstreet's later poems. The later poems are fresh, warm, particular. How tempting it is to use our everyday categories of criticism to argue that her inner mind was freed by the death of her father; that this new freedom compelled her to negotiate the inner world of love and domesticity into a private poetry rather than an official one; that she found a private voice within the public ethos of Puritanism; that, if the truth were told, she is a subversive within the larger structures of the early American experience. These are certainly appealing propositions. But are they true?

It would be convenient if they were. It would make Anne Bradstreet immediately available to the poetic wisdoms of our own time. But I am not sure. As an Irish poet I see a flaw in those divisions between private and public. As a woman poet I see a founding inaccuracy in this blueprint of the inner life. No, to understand her at all requires a break with the norms of psychobiography—far too often employed on poets and especially women poets—and an attempt to track her in the broader context where her works belong.

It is tempting to see the girl who left England in 1628 as young and singular, almost a child bride about to travel from ease to hardship, and to read back from her poetry to catalogue her adjustments and realizations. But this view is incomplete. No individual journey can explain the woman who suddenly, in 1662, could write with spirit, with a compelling contemporary eloquence, about desire in marriage, the death of children, the burning of her house. Another explanation is necessary.

The tense and elaborate world of poetry she left behind must have seemed a faraway dream in the mid-seventeenth century on the salty coasts of New England. But her shedding of that world is not easily measurable today. It would be a mistake to look for it in one act of style or one suppression of rhetoric. It has to be judged, like a quark or quasar, by absences, negations, negative energies, suppositions of space and distance.

The England that Anne Bradstreet left behind had already assigned a place to the poet. And it is clearly identified in those poems in *The Tenth Muse* in which she herself echoes the place-making energies of that canon. The place is not to be found in style. It is a series of angles and distances, a series of inferences by which poets reveal the ground they stand on by the words they choose.

By the time Anne Bradstreet sailed for America, the English poet had in these angles and relations an inner and outer world. Like a child, that poetic world had dissociated itself out of self-protection: it had split apart the better to handle the raw, intimate relation to power that history and society had ordained for the English poet of that time. The outer world was often coded into decorums, ornaments, pieces of rhetoric. The inner world was dark, raw, nihilistic. And this dichotomy reflected the fact that the poet of Elizabethan England, and before that Tudor England, was often an artist of grace and gifts who had learned the hard way—Surrey is an obvious example—that power offered no exemption, that poets must write in the shadow of the gallows, as well as in the light of favor. Above all, they had learned how to arm themselves with the gorgeous pastoral of prothalamion—the rivers, the nymphs, the musical harmonies—the better to infer a world of exclusion and pain.

What happened to Anne Bradstreet? To put it another way, What did not happen to her? She did not learn from the young Milton, the young Marvell. She did not see how ornament might imply disorder. She did not learn that the poet's place is in a split-apart world. In fact, the opposite. She came to enact in her life and her work a world of action, faith, expression, family, and ordinary adventure. And in the process the fissure healed. And suddenly—of course not suddenly—we have a woman in middle life whose children are gone, whose house has burned down, who makes no angles, distances, or perspective among faith, event, and feeling. They are all one. They have all happened. So she generates a poem in which they are indivisible, from a sensibility that is not divided. And she changes the history of poetry.

By this interpretation Anne Bradstreet wrote—in her best and later work—in a community so scalded by change and history that the public and private were fused into one and the same. This is a rare circumstance for poetry. Nevertheless, I suspect her poems were indeed written in the crucible of that fusion: they document a privacy that was public and a public faith that was privately realized. They also presume the most intimate and exacting audience: one anxious to hear and see its own new adventures. If all this is true, then the later shift into the intimacy of poems about her husband, her children, her domestic life is not truly disruptive. The poems are merely continuations of this powerful intimacy between poet and community caught in the same dialogue of faith, duty, reflection. Anne Bradstreet's poems shift and reassemble and shimmer with the hard-won confidence of that complex historical self. They are excitingly innocent of the sense that this is, by some definition of her own past, a smaller life. Most important, by being innocent of these definitions, she questions our own.

It would be wrong to make extravagant claims for Anne Bradstreet. Her work is memorable and strange and moving but also uneven and unrealized in certain parts. Yet it would also be wrong to deny how strongly she challenges our rights over the past. However powerful the relation between poet and poet, it must always yield to a poet like Anne Bradstreet, a poet whose work comes from a world both made and suffered and not at all ready to be erased by our easy assumptions, a poet who makes it clear that any relation with her must be on her terms also.

WILLIAM EMPSON

Marvell's 'Garden'†

The chief point of the poem is to contrast and reconcile conscious and unconscious states, intuitive and intellectual modes of apprehension; and yet that distinction is never made, perhaps could not have been made; his thought is implied by his metaphors. There is something very Far-Eastern about this; I was reminded of it by Mr. Richard's discussion, in a recent *Psyche*, of a philosophical argument out of Mencius. The Oxford edition notes bring out a crucial double meaning (so this at least is not my own fancy) in the most analytical statement of the poem, about the Mind:

> Annihilating all that's made
> To a green Thought in a green shade.

'Either "reducing the whole material world to nothing material, i.e., to a green thought," or "considering the material world as of no value compared to a green thought" '; either contemplating everything or shutting everything out. This combines the idea of the conscious mind, including everything because understanding it, and that of the unconscious animal nature, including everything because in harmony with it. Evidently the object of such a fundamental contradiction (see in the etymology: turning all *ad nihil, to* nothing, and *to* a thought) is to deny its reality; the point is not that these two are essentially different but that they must cease to be different so far as either is to be known. So far as he has achieved his state of ecstasy he combines them, he is 'neither conscious nor not conscious,' like the seventh Buddhist stage of enlightenment. (It is by implying something like this, I think, that the puns in Donne's *Extasie* too become more than a simple Freudian giveaway.) But once you accept this note you may as well apply it to the whole verse.

> Meanwhile the Mind, from pleasure less,
> Withdraws into its happiness;
> The Mind, that Ocean where each kind
> Does straight its own resemblance find;
> Yet it creates, transcending these,
> Far other Worlds, and other Seas;
> Annihilating . . .

From pleasure less. Either 'from the lessening of pleasure'—'we are quite in the country, but our dullness gives a sober and self-knowing happiness, more intellectual than that of the overstimulated pleasures of the town' or 'made less by this pleasure'—'The pleasures of the country give a repose and emotional release which make me feel less intellectual, make my mind less worrying and introspective.' This is the same opposition; the ambiguity gives two meanings to pleasure, corresponding to his Puritan ambivalence about it, and to the opposition between pleasure and happiness. *Happiness*, again, names a conscious state, and yet involves the idea of things falling right, happening so, not being ordered by an anxiety of the conscious rea-

† From *Scrutiny*, I (1932), 236–40. Reprinted with permission of Curtis Brown Limited, London on behalf of the William Empson Estate.

son. (So that as a rule it is a weak word; it is by seeming to look at it hard and bring out its implications that the verse here makes it act as a strong one.)

This same doubt gives all their grandeur to the next lines. The sea if calm reflects everything near it; the mind as knower is a conscious mirror. Somewhere in the sea are sea-lions and -horses and everything else, though they are different from land ones; the unconscious is unplumbed and pathless, and there is no instinct so strange among the beasts that it lacks its fantastic echo in the mind. In the first version thoughts are shadows, in the second (like the *green thought*) they are as solid as what they image; and yet they still correspond to something in the outer world, so that the poet's intuition is comparable to pure knowledge. (Keats may have been quoting the sixth verse, by the way, when he said that if he saw a sparrow on the path he pecked about on the gravel.) This metaphor may reflect back so that *withdraws* means the tide going down; the *mind* is *less* now, but will return, and it is now that one can see the rock-pools. On the Freudian view of an Ocean, *withdraws* would make this repose in nature a return to the womb; anyway it may mean either 'withdraws into self-contemplation' or 'withdraws altogether, into its mysterious processes of digestion.' *Straight* may mean 'packed together,' in the microcosm, or 'at once': the beasts see their reflection (perhaps the root word of the metaphor) as soon as they look for it; the calm of nature gives the poet an immediate self-knowledge. But we have already had two entrancingly witty verses about the sublimation of sexual desire into a taste for Nature, and the *kinds* look for their *resemblance*, in practice, out of a desire for *creation*; in the mind, at this fertile time for the poet, they can do so 'at once,' being 'packed together.' This profound transition, from the correspondences of thought with fact to those of thought with thought, to *find* which is to be *creative*, leads on to the next couplet, in which not only does the *mind transcend* the world it mirrors, but a sea, by a similar transition, transcends both land and sea too, which implies self-consciousness and all the antinomies of philosophy. And it is true that the sea reflects the *other worlds* of the starts. Yet even here the double meaning is not lost; all land-beasts have their sea-beasts, but the sea also has the kraken; in the depths as well as the transcendence of the mind are things stranger than all the kinds of the world.

Green takes on great weight here, as Miss Sackville West pointed out, because it has been a pet word of Marvell's before; to list the uses before the satires may seem a trivial affectation of scholarship, but at least shows how often he used the word. In the Oxford text; pages 12, l. 23: 17, l. 18: 25, l. 11: 27, l. 4: 31, l. 27: 38, l. 3: 45, l. 3: 70, l. 376: 71, l. 390: 74, 1. 510: 122, l. 2. Less important, 15, l. 18: 30, l. 55: 42, l. 14: 69, l. 386:74, l. 484: 85, l. 82: 89, l. 94. It is connected here with grass, buds, children, and an as yet virginal prospect of sexuality,[1] a power of thought as yet only latent in sensibility, and the peasant stock from which the great families emerge. The 'unfathomable' grass both shows and makes a soil fertile; it is the humble, permanent, undeveloped nature which sustains everything, and to which everything must return; children are connected with this as

1. Cf. 'giving a green gown' (16th century); 'having a bit of green' (20th century).

buds, because of their contact with Nature (as in Wordsworth) and unique fitness for Heaven (as in the Gospels).

> The tawny mowers enter next,
> Who seem like Israelites to be
> Walking on foot through a green sea[2]

connects greenness with oceans and gives it a magical security; though one must drown in it.

> And in the greenness of the grass
> Did see my hopes as in a glass[3]

connects greenness with mirrors and the partial knowledge of the mind. The complex of ideas he concentrates into this passage, in fact, had been worked out separately already.

To nineteenth century taste the only really poetical verse of the poem is the central fifth of the nine; I have been discussing the sixth, whose dramatic position is an illustration of its very penetrating theory. The first four are a crescendo of wit, on the themes 'success or failure is not important, only the repose that follows the exercise of one's powers' and 'women, I am pleased to say, are no longer interesting to me, because nature is more beautiful.' One effect of the wit is to admit, and so make charming, the impertinence of the second of these, which indeed the first puts in its place; it is only for a time, and after effort among human beings, that he can enjoy solitude. The value of these moments made it fitting to pretend they were eternal; and yet the lightness of his expression of their sense of power is more intelligent, and so more convincing, than Wordsworth's solemnity on the same theme, because it does not forget the opposing forces.

> When we have run our Passions heat,
> Love hither makes his best retreat.
> The *Gods*, that mortal beauty chase,
> Still in a Tree did end their race.
> *Apollo* hunted *Daphne* so,
> Only that she might Laurel grow,
> And *Pan* did after *Syrinx* speed,
> Not as a Nymph, but for a Reed.

The energy and delight of the conceit has been sharpened or keyed up here till it seems to burst and transform itself; it dissolves in the next verse into the style of Keats. So his observation of the garden might mount to an ecstasy which disregarded it; he seems in this next verse to imitate the process he has described, to enjoy in a receptive state the exhilaration which an exercise of wit has achieved. But striking as the change of style is, it is unfair to empty the verse of thought and treat it as random description; what happens is that he steps back from overt classical conceits to a rich and intuitive use of Christian imagery. When people treat it as the one good 'bit' of the poem one does not know whether they have recognised that the Alpha and Omega of the verse are the Apple and the Fall.

2. "Upon Appleton House," stanza 49 [*Editor*].
3. "The Mower's Song" [*Editor*].

What wond'rous Life is this I lead!
Ripe Apples drop about my head;
The Luscious Clusters of the Vine
Upon my Mouth do crush their Wine;
The Nectaren, and curious Peach,
Into my hands themselves do reach;
Stumbling on Melons, as I pass,
Insnar'd with Flow'rs, I fall on Grass.

Melon, again, is the Greek for apple; 'all flesh is *grass*,' and its own *flowers* here are the snakes in it that stopped Eurydice.[4] Mere grapes are at once the primitive and the innocent wine; the *nectar* of Eden, and yet the blood of sacrifice. *Curious* could mean 'rich and strange' (nature), 'improved by care' (art) or 'inquisitive' (feeling towards me, since nature is a mirror, as I do towards her). All these eatable beauties give themselves so as to lose themselves, like a lover, with a forceful generosity; like a lover they *ensnare* him. It is the triumph of his attempt to impose a sexual interest upon nature; there need be no more Puritanism in this use of sacrificial ideas than is already inherent in the praise of solitude; and it is because his repose in the orchard hints at such a variety of emotions that he is contemplating *all that's made*. Sensibility here repeats what wit said in the verse before; he tosses into the fantastic treasure-chest of the poem's thought all the pathos and dignity that Milton was to feel in his more celebrated Garden; and it is while this is going on, we are told in the next verse, that the mind performs its ambiguous and memorable *withdrawal*. For each of the three central verses he gives a twist to the screw of the microscope and is living in another world.

JOSEPH H. SUMMERS

Marvell's "Nature"†

The similarities between the verse of Marvell and that of many modern poets are seductive. A number of Marvell's poems have been cited as evidence to support the critical assumption, based largely on modern poetic practice, that the most mature and rich works of literature are necessarily ironical. One can disagree with the assumption and still recognize that irony, not of a paralyzing variety, is central to most of Marvell's poems. Marvell's surfaces, moreover, are close to one modern ideal. The tones of the typical modern *personae* echo the sensuous richness of Marvell more often than the logical violence of Donne—that poet who wrote "To Mr. Samuel Brooke," boastfully yet accurately, "I sing not Siren like to tempt; for I / Am harsh." The "speakers" of Marvell's poems are farther removed from immediate embroilment in action than are Donne's. They approach their situations from some distance, with a wider and a clearer view. Their speech is closer to that of meditation or of a quiet colloquy in a garden than to the raised voice, the immediate and passionate argument. And the

4. The wife of Orpheus, she died from the bite of a serpent [*Editor*].
† From *ELH*, 20 (1953), 121–35.

verse which they speak shows a concern for euphony, a delicate manipulation of sound patterns suggesting Campion's[1] songs—or much of the verse of Eliot and MacLeish and many younger poets.

The differences between Marvell and the moderns, however, are equally noteworthy, and failure to perceive them has resulted in strange readings of a number of Marvell's poems. To prevent misreadings, to define any specific poem, we need to achieve some sense of the body of Marvell's work. And here is the difficulty, for our sense of that work is likely to be an impression of dazzling fragments, each brilliant and disparate. The reader may feel that the sixth stanza of "The Gallery," the poem in which the poet invites Chlora to view her portraits in his soul as "an inhumane murtheress," Aurora, "an enchantress," Venus, and "a tender shepherdess," applies more justly to the poet than to Chlora:

> These Pictures and a thousand more,
> Of Thee, my Gallery do store;
> In all the Forms thou can'st invent
> Either to please me, or torment.

Yet the poem assures us that Chlora is one, however numerous her pictures; and the poet who could take various and even contradictory positions on the claims of the active and contemplative lives, of the body and the soul, of the time-honored plea to "seize the day," of gardens ("These Pictures and a thousand more") is equally one poet. The attempts to bring intellectual order out of the apparent confusion by means of a hypothetical biographical development of the poet have been unconvincing. The development or rather break in his poetic practice after 1660 is clear. Before that time, the single poem "Upon Appleton House" indicates that Marvell was an extraordinarily sophisticated poet, capable of employing numerous traditions and multiple attitudes as occasions or moments demanded. Among the few attitudes which I have been unable to discover in Marvell's poetry, however, are those expressed in two of the modern poems which owe most to Marvell. Archibald MacLeish's "You, Andrew Marvell' concludes with the lines,

> And here face downward in the sun
> To feel how swift how secretly
> The shadow of the night comes on . . .

Robert Penn Warren's "Bearded Oaks" includes the following stanza:

> Upon the floor of light, and time,
> Unmurmuring, of polyp made,
> We rest; we are, as light withdraws,
> Twin atolls on a shelf of shade.

In Marvell's verse man is neither an atoll nor an island, and if night is anticipated, so is light.

An examination of Marvell's uses of "Nature," the world of the flowers and fruits and the green grass, provides a sketch not only of the virtuosity and multiple intellectual and moral stances within the poems, but also of the central vision which occurs most frequently in the most successful

1. Thomas Campion (1567–1620), musician and poet, composer of several books of airs, i.e., lyrics written for solo performance accompanied by lute or bass viol [*Editor*].

poems. Occasionally Marvell used nature as an image of classical order, an artfully contrived realization of the mean which man is to imitate—or, more properly, which a specific man has imitated. Jonson had shown in his ode "To the Memory of Sir Lucius Cary and Sir Henry Morison" that nature conceived as an ordered mean was a most effective source of hyperbolical compliment. In "Upon the Hill and Grove at Bill-borow," Fairfax too is at one with nature. After his active life (in which he had "thunder'd" "Through Groves of Pikes," "And Mountains rais'd of dying Men"), Fairfax has returned to the retirement of the hill and grove; the humanized landscape is both his ward and his image:

See how the arched Earth does here
Rise in a perfect Hemisphere!
The stiffest Compass could not strike
A Line more circular and like;
Nor softest Pensel draw a Brow
So equal as this Hill does bow.
It seems as for a Model laid,
And that the World by it was made.
(st. 1)

See what a soft access and wide
Lyes open to its grassy side;
Nor with the rugged path deterrs
The feet of breathless Travellers.
See then how courteous it ascends,
And all the way it rises bends;
Nor for it self the height does gain,
But only strives to raise the Plain.
(st. 3)

After this delightfully artificial description of landscape as Republican gentleman, we are not surprised that these Roman oaks should speak oracles of praise for Fairfax. In the opening lines of "Upon Appleton House," an ordered and properly proportioned nature is again the symbol for Fairfax and his dwelling, particularly in contrast to the "unproportion'd dwellings" which the ambitious have constructed with the aid of "Forrain" architects: "But all things are composed here, / Like Nature, orderly and near." Nature is also near and extraordinarily "orderly" when a natural object. "A Drop of Dew" for example, is examined as an emblem. Here we are close to Herbert, but in Marvell we are chiefly compelled by the ingenuity with which the natural is made to reflect the conceptual.

More often nature is nearer if not so orderly when it is conceived as the lost garden, whether Eden or the Hesperides or England:

O Thou, that dear and happy Isle
The Garden of the World ere while,
Thou *Paradise* of four Seas,
Which *Heaven* planted us to please,
But, to exclude the World, did guard
With watry if not flaming Sword;
What luckless Apple did we tast,
To make us Mortal, and The Wast?
("Upon Appleton House," st. 41)

The lost garden represents not measure but perfect fulfillment; its memory is an occasion for ecstasy:

And Ivy, with familiar trails,
Me licks, and clasps, and curles, and hales.
Under this *antick Cope* I move
Like some great *Prelate of the Grove*,

Then, Languishing with ease, I toss
On Pallets swoln of Velvet Moss.
("Upon Appleton House," st. 74–75)

What wond'rous Life in this I lead!
Ripe Apples drop about my head;
The Luscious Clusters of the Vine
Upon my Mouth do crush their Wine;
The Nectaren, and curious Peach,
Into my hands themselves do reach;
Stumbling on Melons, as I pass,
Insnar'd with Flow'rs, I fall on Grass.
("The Garden," st. 5)

It is in this vein that Marvell occasionally gives a sensuous particularity to his descriptions of natural objects which may remind us of Vaughan's "those faint beams in which this hill is drest, / After the Sun's remove" ("They are all gone into the world of light!"), and which has led some readers to consider him a romantic born too early. And yet the "gelid *Strawberryes*" and "The hatching *Thrastles* shining Eye" of "Upon Appleton House" contribute to a complicated vision of nature which is finally unlike the nineteenth century's; the "*Hewel's* wonders" (the activities of the woodpecker) teach the "*easie Philosopher*" who "Hath read in *Natures mystick Book*" the just relationships between sin and death:

Who could have thought the *tallest Oak*
Should fall by such a *feeble Strok'*!

Nor would it, had the Tree not fed
A *Traitor-worm*, within it bred.
(As first our *Flesh* corrupt within
Tempts impotent and bashful *Sin*.)
And yet that *Worm* triumphs not long,
But serves to feed the *Hewels young*.
While the Oake seems to fall content,
Viewing the Treason's Punishment.
("Upon Appleton House," st. 69–70)

In "The Garden," too, identification with nature is neither complete nor simple. The famous fifth stanza, which I have quoted above, expertly "imitates" the bodily ecstasy, and the following stanzas systematically portray the higher ecstasies of the mind and the soul; all, moreover, are framed with witty and civilized reversals of the ordinary civilized values, of classic myth, of the biblical account of the creation of woman, and of the idea that sexual relations are "natural." To read "The Garden" and "The Mower Against Gardens" in succession is to realize that in Marvell's poetry the man-made garden and the "natural" meadows are significant not intrinsically but instrumentally. Both poems are ultimately concerned with lost perfection. "The Garden" presents a fictional and momentary attempt to recapture what has been lost. In "The Mower Against Gardens," the garden itself is an image of the sophisticated corruption responsible for the loss of "A wild and fragrant Innocence." Marvell's image of the lost garden is as much an occasion for the recognition of man's alienation from nature as it is for remembered ecstasy.

The degree to which Marvell both followed and modified conventional practice can be seen most clearly in the "pastoral" poems in which he substituted the mower for the traditional shepherd. The life of the shepherds had imaged the pre-agricultural golden age, the paradisiacal simplicity ideally if not actually associated with the simple country life, away from cities and civilizations, wars and corruptions. When love was concerned, the passion was usually direct, uncontaminated by worldly considerations, and not much affected by age, even if the lover was unhappy or the mistress proved untrue. The good shepherd and his sheep could imply the ideal political relation between the ruler and the ruled, and the Christian poets explored the rich possibilities of the Good Shepherd and his flock and the large pastoral inheritance of the Psalms. Milton, who retained the shepherd image in "Lycidas," kept the humanist emphasis on higher man (the poet, the pastor) as the guide of less perceptive humanity through the labyrinth of nature to an ultimate goal. The shepherd followed Christ, and he also led his own sheep into the true fold. Marvell used some of this material in a direct if not very distinguished fashion in "Clorinda and Damon," and although the participants are oarsmen rather than shepherds, the spirit of the tradition is present in "Bermudas." He gave up most of these associations, however, when he chose the figure of the mower as his central image. That figure, of course, had its own traditions. As "Damon the Mower" mentions, the mower's craft had long served to picture man's greatest mystery and fear:

Only for him no Cure is found,
Whom *Julianas* Eyes do wound.
'Tis death alone that this must do:
For Death thou art a Mower too.

The mower who cut down the living grass was a natural symbol for death. Because of the seasonal nature of his activities, he was also a symbol for time. Marvell's mower does not lead; he destroys. However simple his character or sincere his love, he cuts down for human ends what nature has produced. He symbolizes man's alienation from nature:

With whistling Sithe, and Elbow strong,
These Massacre the Grass along:
While one, unknowing, carves the *Rail*,
Whose yet unfeather'd Quils her fail.
The Edge all bloody from its Breast
He draws, and does his stroke detest;
Fearing the Flesh untimely mow'd
To him a Fate as black forebode.
("Upon Appleton House," st. 50)

"The Mower's Song" is a playful and elaborately artificial lament of a lover, but it is more than that. The refrain insists that the mower-lover's relation to nature exactly parallels his cruel mistress's relation to him:

For *Juliana* comes, and She
What I do to the Grass, does to my Thoughts and Me.

Greenness in this poem, as so often in Marvell's verse, represents hope and vitality and virility, the fertile promise of life which man desires and destroys. The mower, angry that there is no true sympathy between man and nature, "fictionally" determines to destroy nature to make the symbolism more complete:

Unthankful Medows, could you so
A fellowship so true forego,
And in your gawdy May-games meet,
While I lay trodden under feet?
When *Juliana* came, and She
What I do to the Grass, does to my Thoughts and Me.

But what you in Compassion ought,
Shall now by my Revenge be wrought:
And Flow'rs, and Grass, and I and all,
Will in one common Ruine fall.
For *Juliana* comes, and She
What I do to the Grass, does to my Thoughts and Me.

The Mower poems conveniently define the crucial terms of Marvell's most frequent poetic use of nature. Marvell did not discover an impulse from the vernal wood which spoke unambiguously to the human heart and which offered a possibility for man's at-oneness with all. Nor did he, like George Herbert, usually see in nature patterns of a distinguishable and logical divine will, the *paysage moralisé* which offered a way to the understanding and imitation of God. Human moral criteria do not apply to most of Marvell's landscapes. In his poems nature apart from man is usually "green," vital, fecund, and triumphant. Since it affirms life it is, as part of the divine plan, "good," but its goodness is neither available nor quite comprehensible to man. Man is barred from long or continuous spiritual communion, and his intellect cannot comprehend the natural language. Since his alienation with the departure from Eden, man can only live in nature either as its observer or its destroyer; since he partially partakes of nature, he is, if he acts at all, also his own destroyer. His capacity for self-destruction is clearly implied by the contrast between nature's fecundity and man's harassed and frustrated attempts at love. Faced with unrequited love, man the mower only sharpens his scythe for the destruction of the grass and sharpens the "Woes" which destroy himself:

How happy might I still have mow'd,
Had not Love here his Thistles sow'd!
But now I all the day complain,
Joyning my Labour to my Pain;
And with my Sythe cut down the Grass,
Yet still my Grief is where it was:

But, when the Iron blunter grows,
Sighing I whet my Sythe and Woes.
("Damon the Mower")

But man destroys the natural and dies not only because he is inferior but also because, suspended between the natural and divine, he is superior to the green world. In "A Dialogue between the Soul and the Body" each of the protagonists charges wittily and convincingly that the other is the source of human misery; of the first 40 lines, each speaks 20, and points are made and capped so expertly as to produce a forensic stalemate. But the Body wins and ironically resolves the argument with its final additional four lines:

What but a Soul could have the wit
To build me up for Sin so fit?
So Architects do square and hew
Green Trees that in the Forest grew.

Without the soul the body would be truly a part of nature and could not sin. Yet architecture, whether external or internal, is the product and desire of a higher part of man, even though many "Green Trees" may be destroyed for it. Whether the building is used for good or ill, man's capacities for reason, for structure, for creation outside the carnal, are not natural but Godlike. Man's distinctive gifts are as destructive within the post-Eden garden as are his weaknesses and his corruption.

It is, moreover, exactly man's superiority to the vegetative world which allows him to recognize his alienation. Nature does not possess the capacity for man's choices between the active and contemplative lives: it can only act. The rival claims of those two chief modes of man's life are ever present in Marvell's poetry, and they are closely related to his themes of nature and time. Man must act and he must contemplate, and he must do each in accordance with the demands of time. Yet the contemplative life is usually the more desirable way—at least for the poet. The poet surpasses most men in the degree and consistency of his recognition of man's alienation, for he is chiefly concerned with the contemplation of the condition of man. In Marvell's poetry, significantly, natural beauty is usually described and appreciated as if it were an imitation of the works of man. The fort and artillery of the garden in "Upon Appleton House" are not simply factual or fanciful. In "The Mower to the Glo-Worms" nature is the gracious and kindly courtier to man, so lost in love "That I shall never find my home." In one of the most memorable descriptions in "Bermudas" God Himself is the manlike decorator:

He hangs in shades the Orange bright,
Like golden Lamps in a green Night.
And does in the Pomgranates close,
Jewels more rich than *Ormus* show's.

It is the artifacts, the "golden Lamps" and the "Jewels more rich than *Ormus* show's," which contribute most of the sensuous richness to the passage. In relation to the garden man is the judge and the measure as well as the accused.

Whatever the immediate resolutions, man is usually suspended between the greenness and God at the conclusions as well as at the beginnings of Marvell's poems. Within "A Dialogue between The Resolved Soul, and Created Pleasure," the Soul deftly propounds the orthodox thesis that the sensuous and worldly pleasures are only appearances, that the soul possesses the quintessence of all pleasures in his resolution. Yet the tensions are still felt, and the soul's conclusions, while "true," are also partial. At the moment of death "The rest" (both the ease and the remainder of all the pleasures) *does* "lie beyond the Pole, / And is thine everlasting Store." But before that moment, Marvell and most of his contemporaries believed that no man enjoyed fully and continuously either the flesh or the spirit, that the battle was constantly renewed so long as a living spirit inhabited a living body. This did not imply that the battle lacked interest nor that decisions and momentary achievements were impossible. Such decisions and such achievements were, in fact, the poet's subjects, not only in "A Dialogue" but also "To his Coy Mistress." The speaker of the latter poem seems to resolve clearly for sensuality: *Carpe diem* appears to be all. The image of the "birds of prey," however, makes us realize the costs of a resolution to "devour" time, to choose destructive brevity of life since eternity cannot be sensually chosen.

The reader's awareness of Marvell's complex use of nature should cast light on almost any one of the poems. Within such light, the presentation of Cromwell in "An Horatian Ode" as a force of nature seems not perplexing but inevitable. "Upon Appleton House" is Marvell's most ambitious and in many respects his most interesting poem. A full consideration of it would require another essay, and I only wish to suggest here that it is a mistake to read it as an artificial "public" poem interesting chiefly for a few "personal" passages. Similarly, "The Picture of little T. C. in a Prospect of Flowers" is not a graceful trifle which somehow goes wrong. It is a fine poem, and it elucidates Marvell's central vision of man and nature. [Quotes poem. See pp. 546–47.]

The opening stanza of the poem tells us of the child's alienation from and superiority to nature, as well as of her delight in it. Her apparently successful imposition of her own order and value on nature raises inevitably the question of the prospect of time, and we see prophetically in the second stanza her future triumph over "wanton Love"—and over man. Not a combatant, the speaker of the poem resolves to observe the dazzling scene from the shade which allows vision, for the god-like glories cannot be viewed immediately by profane man. If he is to admire her triumph, it must be from a distance where there is no fear of its destructiveness. With the "Mean time" of the fourth stanza we are back at the present prospect, and the observer from his advantageous point of view advises the present T. C. At the golden moment when "every verdant thing" charms itself at her beauty, she is instructed to prepare for her future career by reforming the "errours of the Spring." At first it seems, or perhaps would seem to a child, an almost possible command. With the talismanic power of her "fair Aspect" she already "tames / The Wilder flow'rs, and gives them names," and she tells the roses "What Colour best becomes them, and what Smell." At least within the circle of her immediate view she may, perhaps, by a judicious bouquet arrangement cause the tulips to share in sweetness, and it is possible to disarm roses of their thorns with assiduous labor. But the thing which should be "most" procured is impossible for the human orderer even within his small area. And all of it is, of course, impossible if all the "errours of the Spring" are in question. For, in comparison either with the triumph of T. C. or the vision of Eden, Spring is full of errors; the decorative details suggest exactly how far nature fails to sustain human visions of propriety, delight, and immortality. T. C. and the idealizing aspect of man wish delight and beauty and goodness to be single, but they cannot find such singleness within the promising verdancy of nature; if they desire it they must impose it on nature or must seek it in an "unnatural" or supernatural world. The tulips show how improperly the delights of the senses are separated in this world; the roses with their thorns traditionally indicate the conjunction of pain and pleasure, the hidden hurts lying under the delights of the senses; and the transience of the violets is a perpetual reminder of the mortality of life and innocence and beauty. The description of the preceding triumph is placed in a doubtful light. If T. C.'s reformation of floral errors is so doomed, how much real hope or fear can there be of her reformation of the errors of that higher order, man? Is the former description a fantasy, ideal yet frightening, of what might happen if the superhuman power as well as the superhuman virtue were granted, a fantasy proceeding from the observer's sharing for one moment the simplicity of the nymph?

In the exclamatory warning of the final stanza the observer and the reader see the picture of little T. C. in the full prospect of time which the flowers have furnished. At the present moment "Nature courts" her "with fruits and flow'rs" as a superior being; she represents the promise of an order higher than we have known. But she is also the "young beauty of the Woods," and she is a "Bud." The child of nature as well as its potential orderer, she shares the mortality as well as the beauty of the flowers; her own being, in the light of the absolute, is as "improper" as are the tulips or the roses. The former vision of her triumph implied full recognition of only one half of her relationship to the fruits and flowers. The introduction of Flora reminds us more sharply than anything else in the poem of the entire relationship. However lacking in the ideal, Flora has her own laws which man violates at the peril of self-destruction. Flora decrees that life shall continue: the infants shall not be killed "in their prime"—either in their moment of ideal promise or in their first moment of conception. The sexual concerns which have been suggested throughout the poem are made explicit in the final stanza. The picture in the central stanzas of the complete triumph of T. C., the absolute rule of human notions of propriety, has inevitably meant that "wanton Love's" bow will be broken, his ensigns torn: there will be no more marriages. With a recognition of mortality and of the power of Flora, we recognize also the doom of such a triumph, for both the ideal and the reality will soon die, and there is no prospect of renewal in future "T. C.'s." The conclusion, however, is neither a Renaissance nor a modern "naturalism." Because perfect fulfillment is impossible, man is not therefore to abandon his attempts at perfection. T. C. is allowed and even commanded to "Gather the Flow'rs," to expend her present and her future energies in ordering the natural nearer to the ideal pattern—so long as she spares the buds. The qualification is all important. Man must beware of attempting to anticipate heaven by imposing the ideal absolutely on earth. The killing of the infants in their prime is not only a crime against Flora but against all the gods, for man is never free to commit either murder or suicide in the pursuit of the abstract ideal. The human triumph must function within and wait upon the fullness of time. It must recognize the real and individual as well as the ideal and the general or it becomes a horror. The ending of the poem revalues everything which has gone before. "Ere we see" may mean something equivalent to "in the twinkling of an eye"; it certainly means, "Before we see what will become of you and the vision of a new and higher order." What will be nipped "in the blossom," in the first full flowering, unless the warning is heeded will be not only "all our hopes" (our hopes of the idealized child and of a possible new order, our hopes of love and of a new generation), but also "Thee," the living child.

"The Picture of little T. C. in a Prospect of Flowers" is characteristic of Marvell's poetry both in its complexity and in its subtle use of superficially "romantic" or decorative detail. It may remind us of modern poetry, but ultimately Marvell is both more complex and more assured of his meanings than are most of the moderns. Marvell does not present a *persona* simply and finally torn between this world and the next, distracted by the sensuous while attempting to achieve a spiritual vision. For Marvell, as for most Renaissance poets, the perception of a dilemma was not considered a sufficient occasion for a poem. Marvell made precise the differences between the values of time and of eternity. He recognized that man exists and discovers his values largely within time; he also believed that those values could be ultimately fulfilled only outside time. The recognition and the belief did not constitute a paralyzing dilemma. Each of his early poems implies the realization that any action or decision costs something; yet each presents a precise stance, an unique position and a decision taken at one moment with a full consciousness of all the costs. The costs are counted, but not mourned; the position is taken, the poem is written, with gaiety.

When we have understood what the "prospect of flowers" implies, "The Coronet" does not seem a churchly recantation of all that Marvell valued, but an artful recognition of the ultimate issues. Here the decision is taken in the full light of eternity, and, as in George Herbert's "A Wreath" (which Marvell probably remembered), the intricate and lovely form of the poem provides an index to the joy. The speaker of the poem describes his attempt to create a coronet for Christ. He dismantles "all the fragrant Towers / That once adorn'd my Shepherdesses head" to gather the necessary flowers, but he discovers that the Serpent has entwined himself into the proposed offering, "With wreaths of Fame and Interest." The poet prays that Christ would untie the Serpent's "slipp'ry knots,"

> Or shatter too with him my curious frame
> And let these wither, so that he may die,
> Though set with Skill and chosen out with Care.
> That they, while Thou on both their Spoils dost tread,
> May crown thy Feet, that could not crown thy Head.

The poem is moving as well as orthodox in its expression of willingness to sacrifice man's sensuous and aesthetic structures to a divine necessity. But Marvell's most Miltonic line, "Though set with Skill and chosen out with Care," ruefully insists that, whatever his vision of ultimate value, the living poet also values the structures of time.

LEAH MARCUS

Children of Light: Vaughan and Traherne†

Vaughan and Traherne—the two names have been closely linked ever since the discovery of Traherne's manuscripts in the 1890s and their initial attribution to Vaughan by Alexander Grosart. His mistake is understandable, for the two writers do have much in common—most notably their profound interest in the visionary capacity of children. In turning from the earlier poets to these we may sense that we have entered a strange rarefied atmosphere, a new realm of ideas remote from the ritual forms and doctrines of conservative Anglicanism. Yet both Vaughan and Traherne, as the latter's recently discovered "Select Meditations" demonstrate, considered themselves devoted to the Anglican church; both were appalled by the Civil War's destruction of its head, the English monarch. The two poets faced the same dilemma: how to regain the traditional Anglican vision of order when the traditional governmental and ecclesiastical hierarchies had disappeared. Both poets sought to resolve the dilemma through vision—in cultivating the capacity to discern beyond apparent chaos the luminous animate unity which once, according to conservative theorists, had shone so brightly in England.

And yet we must not allow our recognition of the striking similarities between the two poets to blind us to the profound differences between them. Critics are wont to elucidate Traherne by quoting Vaughan, and vice versa, thus obscuring the fact that the two approach the same problem in radically different spirits. In the precise powers they attribute to childhood, in the ways they merge it into the larger whole of human experience, Vaughan and Traherne are far apart. The dominant mood in Vaughan's poetry is pessimism, and a sense of deep loss which occasional moments of vision can only partly alleviate. Vaughan conveys a feeling of such age and world-weariness that we must remind ourselves he was writing as a fairly young man: when the first part of *Silex Scintillans* was published in 1650, its author was still in his late twenties. Traherne, on the other hand, writes in a tone of eternal and occasionally maddening optimism. He felt a profound sense of loss at the destruction of church and state but built a highly original system which restored the loss and insulated him in a most ingenious fashion against any new experience of national upheaval. While for Vaughan, nothing short of death could make up for the loss of the past, for Traherne, the absence of continuing tradition was a challenge to new synthesis.

In dealing with the marked difference between the two poets, as always we must acknowledge the factor of personal temperament; but we must also continue to explore links between the poet's personal situation vis-à-vis the national disorders and his treatment of the theme of childhood. If Vaughan's poetry seems much more rooted in the past than Traherne's, much more tied to prewar ideals of order, it may in part be because Vaughan's life was considerably more immersed in that order: he was fif-

† From *Childhood and Cultural Despair: A Theme and Variations in Seventeenth-Century Literature*, by Leah Sinanoglou Marcus, pp. 153–200. Abridged. Reprinted by permission of the University of Pittsburgh Press.

teen years older than Traherne during a period of English history when change was so rapid that fifteen years was a long time. The national peace and harmony Vaughan yearned for and connected with the period of his own childhood were things which Traherne, who was not born until 1637, scarcely knew. For Vaughan, individual and national history are intrinsically bound together; his search for childhood perception is a search for an order somehow imbedded in England and inseparable from England's past. In the writings of Traherne, on the other hand, order is not found within things but imposed upon them. The child's perception and actual conditions in England are separate; though a return to childhood perception allows Traherne to re-create a vision of English order, that order is overlaid, not intrinsic, and departs in a number of ways from the ritualized, late-medieval order the earlier poets had sought. For them, and for Vaughan, the retreat to childhood was an attempt to salvage a unity inherent in English institutions or at least upon English soil. For Traherne, who was many years their junior and who grew up during the war years, the idea of inherent unity no longer existed.

1

* * *

For Herbert and Herrick, retreat to childhood was a way of limiting and domesticating their responses to God by basing them on the common everyday relationship of a submissive child and its loving parent. But for Vaughan, childhood is anything but everyday—as far away and strange as a "Chronicle" of past history: "I cannot reach it, and my striving eye, / Dazles at it, as at eternity."[1] Childhood does not limit the powers of adulthood, but expands them, for the child is a seer who gazes steadily on the full face of God and sports with his angels:

> An age of mysteries! which he
> Must live twice, that would Gods face see;
> Which *Angels* guard, and with it play,
> Angels! which foul men drive away.
>
> (521)

"Take heed that ye despise not one of these little ones; for I say unto you, That in heaven their angels do always behold the face of my Father which is in heaven" (Matt. 18:10). Christ's beautifully ambiguous warning was often cited in the seventeenth century as biblical proof that children enjoy the protection of guardian angels who dwell in the presence of God. Thomas Fuller suggested that an infant's apparently uncaused smiles are

1. Henry Vaughan, *Works*, ed. L. C. Martin, 2nd ed. (Oxford: Clarendon, 1957), p. 520. Future quotations from this edition will be cited by page number in the text. Among the numerous critical discussions of Vaughan, Helen C. White, *The Metaphysical Poets*; M. M. Mahood, *Poetry and Humanism* (1950; rpt. Port Washington, N.Y.: Kennikat, 1967), and Louis L. Martz, *The Paradise Within* (New Haven: Yale Univ. Press, 1964), are particularly useful in defining the quality of the poet's religious experience and linking Vaughan to earlier poets like Herbert. L. C. Martin, "Henry Vaughan and the Theme of Infancy," in *Seventeenth Century Studies Presented to Sir Herbert Grierson* (1938; rpt. New York: Octagon, 1967), 243–55, is an important study of the sources and emotional impetus behind Vaughan's retreat to childhood; Martin points out that Wordsworth and Vaughan shared some of the same depression in similar political and personal circumstances. Chapter 5 of James D. Simmonds, *Masques of God: Form and Theme in the Poetry of Henry Vaughan* (Pittsburgh: Univ. of Pittsburgh Press, 1972), is the most comprehensive discussion of Vaughan's anti-Puritanism.

prompted by its secret communings with its angels.[2] But Vaughan's children behold the face of God just as their angelic guardians do: the very young are forgetful, easily distracted, and inattentive to the world of adults—not out of folly but through wisdom, since their attention is fixed on things divine.

This mysterious detachment from matters worldly makes children, not man, the proper study of mankind:

How do I study now, and scan
Thee, more then ere I studyed man,
And onely see through a long night
Thy edges, and thy bordering light!
O for thy Center and mid-day!
For sure that is the *narrow way*.
(521)

Vaughan's alchemically minded brother Thomas echoes his interest in the "Center and mid-day" of childhood. In the midst of a discussion of the interaction of fire and water in *Euphrates* he recalls his extraordinary insights into "Platonick Philosophie" as a child and digresses:

> This Consideration of my self, when I was a Child, has made me since examine Children, namely, what thoughts they had of these elements, we see about us. . . . A Child, I suppose, in puris Naturalibus, Before education alters him, and ferments him, is a Subject hath not been much consider'd, for men respect him not, till he is company for them, and then indeed they spoil him. Notwithstanding, I should think, by what I have read, that the natural disposition of Children, before it is corrupted with Customs and Manners, is one of these things, about which the Antient Philosophers have busyied themselves even to some curiosity.[3]

Just at this point Thomas abruptly recalls himself to the alchemical business at hand, but we can be sure one thing he had in mind was the interest of "Antient Philosophers" in the idea of preexistence.

This time-honored doctrine, expounded by Pythagoras and Plato and christianized by Origen and Cyril of Alexandria, was widely held in one form or another during classical and early Christian times. In its Christian form, its basic tenet was that all human souls were created by God in the beginning, along with heaven and earth, and placed in human embryos one by one as they were needed. St. Augustine gave the doctrine the dignity of his own consideration, asking God, "Did my infancy succeed another age of mine that died before it? was it that which I spent within my mother's womb? . . . and what before that life again, O God my joy, was I anywhere or any body? For this have I none to tell me, neither father nor mother."[4] St. Augustine concluded that the best answer to his questions was not to answer them at all, but St. Jerome was somewhat less charitable,

2. *A Pisgah-Sight of Palestine* (London, 1650). Dedicatory Epistle to Bk. I. Vaughan was probably acquainted with some of the writings of Jacob Boehme, who frequently describes the angels in heaven as playing children. See *The Threefold Life of Man*, tr. John Sparrow, reissued by C. J. B[arker], Intro. by G. W. Allen (London: Watkins, 1909), p. 363; and *The Aurora*, tr. John Sparrow, ed. C. J. B[arker] and D. S. H[ehner] (London: Watkins, 1914), pp. 277, 287.
3. Thomas Vaughan, *Euphrates, or the Waters of the East (1655)*, ed. W. Wynn Westcott, Collectanea Hermetica, Vol. 7 (London, 1896), pp. 28–29.
4. St. Augustine, *Confessions*, p. 5.

considering it a *stulta persuasio* that "souls were created of old by God and kept in a treasury."[5] By A.D. 543, when it was formally condemned, the doctrine of preexistence was virtually dead.

But like so many other doctrinal speculations of the early Christian period, in the seventeenth century it returned to life. It was popular among the Cambridge Platonists, above all Henry More who first suggested it in the poetic appendix to his "Song of the Soul" and later defended it with great zeal. By the 1660s More had made important converts—George Rust in *A Letter of Resolution concerning Origen* and Joseph Glanville in his *Lux Orientalis*.[6] Advocates of the doctrine could marshal in its defense not only early eastern fathers but also biblical testimony. Job 38.7 ("The morning stars sang together, and all the sons of God shouted for joy"), if it refers to the time of creation, certainly implies that human souls existed then. The Wisd. of Sol. 8:19–20 ("For I was a witty child, and had a good spirit. Yea rather, being good, I came into a body undefiled") could be interpreted as a description of the child's preexistent state. Thomas Vaughan taught the doctrine of preexistence and engaged in a voluminous and acrimonious debate with the more genial More over its precise nature. But the idea received its most compelling literary treatment in the poetry of his brother Henry.

In "The Retreate" Vaughan looks back with longing on his infancy:

> Happy those early dayes! when I
> Shin'd in my Angell-infancy.
> Before I understood this place
> Appointed for my second race.
> (419)

The phrase "second race" hints that his soul existed before his life on earth, that it dwelt in the eternal light of God's presence evoked later in the poem as "that plaine, / Where first I left my glorious traine, / From whence th'Inlightned spirit sees / That shady City of Palme trees" (419). Here Vaughan conflates Moses' vision from the heights of Pisgah of the Promised Land, the Plain of Jerico and city of palm trees (Deut. 34:1–3), with the "Plain of Truth" in Plato's *Phaedrus* where preexistent souls

> with the rest of the happy band . . . saw beauty shining in brightness—we philosophers following in the train of Zeus, others in company with other gods; and then we beheld the beatific vision and were initiated into a mystery which may be truly called blessed, celebrated by us in our state of innocence, before we had any experience of evils to come, when we were admitted to the sight of apparitions innocent and simple and calm and happy, which we beheld shining in pure light, pure ourselves.[7]

5. See W. G. T. Shedd's concise discussion of preexistence in *A History of Christian Doctrine* (New York, 1864), II, Bk. 4, Chap. 1.
6. On preexistence in seventeenth-century England, see Merritt Y. Hughes, "The Theme of Pre-Existence and Infancy in *The Retreat*," *PQ*, 20 (1941), 484–500; Marjorie Hope Nicolson, ed., *Conway Letters: The Correspondence of Anne, Viscountess Conway, Henry More, and Their Friends, 1642–1684* (New Haven: Yale Univ. Press, 1930), p. 173; and Anne Davidson [Ferry]'s unpublished dissertation, "Innocence Regained: Seventeenth-Century Interpretations of the Fall of Man," Columbia University, 1956.
7. Plato, *Phaedrus*, 250, in *Dialogues*, tr. Jowett, III, 157.

Vaughan's children, before they are sent down to earth, walk like Plato's philosophers on a shining plain in trains of glorious spirits, beholding and enlightened by the presence of God.

* * *

Being born is no small catastrophe. According to Vaughan's *Flores Solitudinis*, a newborn child weeps, despite the joy and laughter of adults around it, to protest as best it can against its earthly imprisonment: "Thou onely art the infallible diviner of thy own frail condition, who refusest it with teares, which are the most proper expressions of unwilling, & constrained nature" (287).[8] What soul could welcome such confinement of its native powers?

> *Our Eyes from henceforth shall not behold the Divine spirits, for wee shall onely peepe through two small Spheres made of grosse and corrupt humours. When we look towards Heaven, we shall have onely the liberty to grone for the presence of our Creatour, but see him we may not; for we shall see then by a Secondary light, which is the light of the lower World, and not be permitted to use our own discerning light, &c. We shall hear our* Kinred *rejoycing in the air, and mourn that we are not partakers of their liberty, &c. But thou great Father and maker of Spirits, who doest dispose of all thy works as it pleaseth thee, appoint we beseech thee some terme to our sad bondage, and let this punishment passe quickly over us, that we may be restored again to our celestiall liberty, to behold (without obstruction) the perfect beauty of all thy works.* (284)

We need not assume that Vaughan always agreed with Nierembergius, from whose works he was translating. And indeed, on the face of it, this mournful evocation of the plight of flesh-imprisoned souls seems to contradict Vaughan's celebration of the child's vision of God and converse with angels in "Childe-hood." But the contradiction is resolved if we realize that, for Vaughan, the shades of its prison house close over the soul not all at once, but subtly and slowly.

"That was the true Light, which lighteth every man that cometh into the world" (John 1:9). Newborn infants, though separated from God, are still bathed in his light. "The Retreate" describes them as having left their preexistent state so recently that they are still oriented toward it:

> When yet I had not walked above
> A mile, or two, from my first love,
> And looking back (at that short space,)
> Could see a glimpse of his bright-face;
> When on some *gilded Cloud*, or *flowre*
> My gazing soul would dwell an houre,
> And in those weaker glories spy
> Some shadows of eternity.
>
> (419)

Everywhere the poet looked as a child he could see reflections of the divine light. Even his own body seemed irradiated with it: he "felt through all this

8. The idea is of course traditional. See *Notes and Queries*, Ser. 4, Vol. 7 (1871), 211 and 394; and Ser. 4, Vol. 8 (1871), 54.

fleshly dresse / Bright *shootes* of everlastingnesse" (419). But his spirit could not long resist the burgeoning corruption of the body: "The Retreate" oscillates between the lost unity and the forces which have shut it off, forcing us to contemplate the childhood state from a perspective of ever increasing darkness and absorption in evil.[9] "Repentance" expresses the same pattern of negative development. As the poet grew, his spiritual vision was gradually eclipsed by the foulness of his body like a flower choked off by weeds:

> Lord, since thou didst in this vile Clay
> That sacred Ray
> Thy spirit plant, quickning the whole
> With that one grains Infused wealth,
> My forward flesh creept on, and subtly stole
> Both growth, and power; Checking the health
> And heat of thine.
>
> (448)

Vaughan's lines echo Herbert's "Although by stealth / My flesh get on" in "*H. Baptisme* (II)" except that Vaughan's working of the idea does not require the sacrament of baptism. The child is pure not because he has so recently been cleansed by baptism, but because the corruption of his flesh has not yet clouded and extinguished the vision of his soul.

Though Vaughan's formulation would perhaps have raised Herbert's eyebrows, there was nothing terribly recondite about it. John Earle's popular character of "A Child" sketches much the same pattern in witty capsule form: "The elder he growes, hee is a stayre lower from God; and like his first father, much worse in his breeches. . . . Could hee put off his body with his little Coate, he had got eternitie without a burthen, and exchang'd but one Heauen for another."[1] The solemn intonations of thrice-great Hermes are even closer to Vaughan:

> Look at the soul of a child, my son, a soul that has not yet come to accept its separation from its source; for its body is still small, and has not yet grown to its full bulk. How beautiful throughout is such a soul as that! It is not yet fouled by the bodily passions; it is still hardly detached from the soul of the Kosmos. But when the body has increased in bulk, and has drawn the soul down into its material mass, it generates oblivion; and so the soul separates itself from the Beautiful and Good, and no longer partakes of that; and through this oblivion the soul becomes evil.[2]

In Vaughan's poetry as in the *Hermetica*, it is the smallness and weakness of the infant's body which make possible the vision of his soul.

But once the "material mass" of the body has gained the upper hand, all the world seems to conspire to bury the soul deeper and deeper in mire. Life is shrouded in noxious mists and hurled pell-mell, a "dark contest of waves and winde" ("Quickness," 538). In "The World" Vaughan contrasts the cloudy and erratic daily pursuits of earthly beings with the great ring of eternity—"pure and endless light, / All calm, as it was bright" (466).

9. See Simmonds' reading, pp. 46–49.
1. John Earle, "A Childe" in *Micro-cosmographie* (London, 1628).
2. *Hermetica*, ed. and tr. Walter Scott (Oxford: Clarendon, 1924–36), I, 197–99.

Lovers pine for "sour delights" and "silly snares of pleasure"; statesmen thirst for power but are "hung with weights and woe / Like a thick midnight-fog"; the miser and epicure struggle frantically for "slight, trivial wares." Imprisoned in the flesh, human beings are caught in a vicious circle: their passions move them to seek their pleasures in material things which alienate them ever further from that vision of eternity which is the only solace of the spirit.

Vaughan's study of childhood creates in him a restlessness in the world, a profound homesickness for the glorious past he cannot relive. But if he must look back on his childhood with a sense of irrevocable loss, perhaps he can look forward with hope to death and renewed freedom from the flesh. Vaughan draws an imaginative parallel between the child's state before birth and the afterlife. His vision of the departed souls in "They are all gone into the world of light!" is strikingly close to his portrayal of preexistence in "The Retreate." The spirits of the dead are like angelic children "walking in an Air of glory" (484) and bright with the radiance of their celestial home. Life marks out a circle, beginning in the light of God's presence, moving into darkness, but returning at last to eternal light.

Senex bis puer as the old saying goes: old men are as forgetful and inattentive as children. For Vaughan the old man's detachment from the world is, like the child's, a positive good. As the aging poet's body weakens and its passions subside, perhaps it will lose its stranglehold over his soul so that at death he will be as pure and clearsighted as when he was born:

Some men a forward motion love,
But I by backward steps would move,
And when this dust falls to the urn
In that state I came return.
("The Retreate," 420)

Waller's lines on old age in "Of the Last Verses in the Book" provide an interesting gloss for Vaughan's and a reverse image of Vaughan's childhood decline from the light of preexistence into the darkness of the flesh:

The soul's dark cottage, battered and decayed,
Lets in new light through chinks that time has made;
Stronger by weakness, wiser men become,
As they draw near to their eternal home.
Leaving the old, both worlds at once they view,
That stand upon the threshold of the new.[3]

Vaughan can take some comfort from the fact that every step he takes away from the vision of childhood is a step back toward it. But as often as his knowledge of heaven to come inspires hope and exultation, it breeds despair:

I see them walking in an Air of glory,
Whose light doth trample on my days:
My days, which are at best but dull and hoary,
Meer glimerings and decays.
("They are all gone," 484)

3. Edmund Waller, *Poems*, ed. G. Thorn Drury (London, 1893), II, 144. Waller, however, does not combine this vision of gradual enlightenment with the doctrine of preexistence.

His perception of the happiness of the dead merely heightens his own sense of miserable imprisonment in time and decay. He wanders through life an Ishmael, an alien in a strange land.

This mortal world is a barren and dreary place by comparison with the glory of eternity. "Fire is the *Suburb* of *Heaven*: The *Earth* which is cold and dull, like an *Iland* lies most remote, and cut off (as it were) from the *neighborhood of light*" (*Flores Solitudinis*, 266). But though the light of God seems hopelessly far away and lost, Vaughan tirelessly explores for faint glimmers, finding them first within himself:

I summon'd nature: peerc'd through all her store,
Broke up some scales, which none had touch'd before,
Her wombe, her bosome, and her head
Where all her secrets lay a bed
I rifled quite, and having past
Through all the Creatures, came at last
To search my selfe, where I did find
Traces, and sounds of a strange kind.
("Vanity of Spirit," 418)

The searcher's soul is not totally eclipsed by the darkness of his flesh: he recognizes in its "weake beames, and fires" vestiges of the "sacred Ray" planted there by God. Nor are the natural creatures around him dull and dead. In "Cock-crowing" he discovers that all have souls as he does—kernels of light planted within them. For plants and animals, these sparks act as magnets lifting up their heads toward heaven in still and patient anticipation of their liberation from the flesh:

And do they so? have they a Sense
Of ought but Influence?
Can they their heads lift, and expect,
And grone too? why th'Elect
Can do no more: my volumes sed
They were all dull, and dead,
They judg'd them senselesse, and their state
Wholly Inanimate.
Go, go; Seal up thy looks,
And burn thy books.
("And do they so?" 432)

The creatures of the natural world are as absorbed in the world beyond as children are and seemingly unconscious of this world or even of themselves. The commonplace that children are like animals was usually cited in Vaughan's period as proof of the brutish obtuseness of both. But when seen in the light of the spirit, both are patterns of otherworldliness.

As so often in Vaughan, his perception creates a double response. He rejoices in the upward vision of natural things toward their Creator, but at the same time he is tortured by the awareness of his own inability for steady contemplation. Moments of spiritual intensity like the climax of "Regeneration" and "The Morning-watch" come seldom and are quickly past:

But I am sadly loose, and stray
A giddy blast each way;

O let me not thus range!
  Thou canst not change.

Sometimes I sit with thee, and tarry
  An hour, or so, then vary
Thy other Creatures in this Scene
  Thee only aym, and mean.
(432)

The same longing which attracts him to childhood impels him even further down the great chain of being, to birds, plants, and even stones:

I would I were a stone, or tree,
  Or flowre by pedigree,
Or some poor high-way herb, or Spring
  To flow, or bird to sing!
Then should I (tyed to one sure state,)
  All day expect my date.
(432)

Plants and animals never forget the world beyond and never cease longing for it, while children grow into adults too restless and aimless to remain focused on God. Yet, since human beings are not animals, the closest they come to the "sure state" of natural things is during the clear and steady theocentricity of childhood.

Ontogeny recapitulates philogeny: Vaughan pairs the golden age of childhood, "the short, swift span / Where weeping virtue parts with man" (521), and the golden age of the Old Testament patriarchs. During the childhood of the race, grown men still had precisely those visionary powers which were later limited to young children:

Sure, It was so. Man in those early days
  Was not all stone, and Earth,
He shin'd a little, and by those weak Rays
  Had some glimpse of his birth.
He saw Heaven o'r his head, and knew from whence
  He came (condemned,) hither,
And, as first Love draws strongest, so from hence
  His mind sure progress'd thither.
Things here were strange unto him.
("Corruption," 440)

Like children newly placed on earth, human beings newly fallen from Eden were still oriented toward it. They retained their communion with the angels:

Angels lay *Leiger* here; Each Bush, and Cel,
  Each Oke, and high-way knew them,
Walk but the fields, or sit down at some *wel*,
  And he was sure to view them.
(440)

Like children, the early patriarchs could see the joys of their lost estate reflected on the earth. "Still *Paradise* lay / In some green shade, or fountain" (440). Just as Vaughan himself lost sight of the light as he grew, the whole human race has gradually fallen under a cloud. As for the individual, so for all humanity: Vaughan was a lover of beginnings.

Another blessed beginning was the childhood of Christianity, a "Golden Age," an "age that loved light" before war and superstition blasted the peace of the early church (*Primitive Holiness*, 340). Like all loyal high-churchmen of his time, Vaughan identified Laudian Anglicanism as the only true follower of primitive Christianity. Writing during the Interregnum in his "Ad Posteros," he used the same pattern of light into darkness to describe the deterioration of church and state during his own lifetime:

> In order that you may be well informed about the times in which I lived, let me tell you that they were cruel. I lived when religious controversy had split the English people into factions. I lived among the furious conflicts of Church and State. At the outset, while the wretched inhabitants raged through their pleasant fields, the base weed laid low the holy rose. They disturbed the fountains, and peace perished beneath the flood, and a gloomy shadow overspread the light of heaven.[4]

After the Restoration, as before the Interregnum, conservatives preached openly what Vaughan in "Ad Posteros" could only hint—that the prerevolutionary times of Charles I had been England's golden age. The idea swept John Beaumont to great heights in one of his Restoration sermons:

> And was not the Land most blessed? . . . In civil respects; was it not the Paradise where Peace, Plenty, and Honer, securely flourished, whilst they were nipped and blasted in other Nations? Was not this the Object of the World's Envy, and yet so secured, as that all Envy could not endanger it? In ecclesiastical respects, was it not the onely Sanctuary of the truly Catholik and Apostolic Faith and Discipline? Was not God's Service amongst us happily protected from Superstition on one hand, and from profanes on the other? . . . Join both respects together, and were not the forged prerogatives of the Golden Age, I say, not copied, but really transcended, by our felicity?[5]

Even *after* the reestablishment of order in church and state, the idealization of prerevolutionary England exerted a tremendous emotional pull upon conservatives. What must Vaughan have felt, writing under the dark shadow of the Interregnum, when so many past values seemed irrevocably gone?

The poet's ideals were embodied in the life and works of his spiritual mentor George Herbert, first among "many blessed Patterns of a holy life in the *Brittish Church*, though now trodden under foot, and branded with the title of Antichristian" (*Mount of Olives*, 186). Herbert would have found this yearning for his own times profoundly ironic. Already in his day a sharp cleavage had developed between church and state, and the "rose" of Anglicanism, though not yet laid low by "base weeds" as in Vaughan's "Ad Posteros," was clearly under attack, as Herbert lamented in "*Church-Rents and Schisms*."

But despite growing dissent, an established church "triple moated" with divine grace was still available to Herbert. Through grace, he could become

4. Henry Vaughan, *The Complete Poetry*. ed. French Fogle (1964; rpt. New York: Norton, 1969), pp. 45–46.
5. Quoted from a manuscript at Peterhouse, Oxford, in Warren, *Richard Crashaw*, pp. 50–51.

a child and servant in his Father's house; its rituals and sacraments were a haven "Which I can go to, when I please."[6] For Herrick and Crashaw, too, becoming the child of God by submitting without question to ecclesiastical doctrine and discipline seemed a viable means for attaining peace and stability, though Crashaw was obliged to cross the Channel and drown himself in the symbols of Continental Catholicism to find his spiritual home. But for Vaughan, retreat into a temporal institution was not possible: as a young man he saw Herbert's sanctuary broken open and sacked. It is likely that he actually fought against the parliamentary forces in the Civil War and watched his brother William die at home as a result of war wounds;[7] it is quite evident from the anti-Puritan rhetoric which is so salient a feature of all his writings after the war that he watched with horror the gradual extinction of the earthly manifestations of Laudian Anglicanism. Her holy offices were usurped by "barbarous persons without *light* or *perfection*" (*Mount of Olives*, 171); her festivals, "those *bright columnes of light*" (*Primitive Holiness*, 379), abolished by parliamentary decree. The Puritan regime was established in South Wales as early as 1646; many of Vaughan's clerical friends were sequestered then. When his brother Thomas was evicted from his living in the local parish in 1650, Vaughan's earthly church did literally disappear, since the post remained vacant for nearly eight years.[8]

Vaughan and his fellow royalist gentry in South Wales suffered real hardship during the Interregnum. In view of his own life experience, it is hardly surprising that he associates childhood with all he calls good. When Herbert died in 1633, Vaughan was about twelve years old. His childhood years were actually passed during what he later portrayed as the golden age of Anglicanism, when divine grace, the "light of heaven," seemed to shine on Britain and her church. As he grew up he saw the end of this golden age of grace, peace, stability, and light as the country was darkened by the clouds of approaching war. Vaughan's early verse seems relatively unaffected by England's troubles; it is mostly secular, written in the Cavalier mode about the usual amatory subjects. But sometime around 1648, or perhaps a bit more gradually, the impact of the war and the overwhelming changes it wrought upon England began to hit home. In the 1654 preface to the second part of *Silex Scintillans*, Vaughan himself claimed that he had been transformed by "the blessed man, Mr. *George Herbert*, whose holy *life* and *verse* gained many pious *Converts*, (of whom I am the least)" (391). At any event, after the Civil War, Vaughan's poetry became almost exclusively religious, a highly individualized search for glimmers of divine order in a world that had been deprived of the "light" of church and monarchy. Much of the force and poignancy of Vaughan's vision of childhood must derive from his adult conviction that the very years when he had been a child were the years when his religious ideals had been best embodied on British soil.

Vaughan could not conceive of order except in the traditional terms of the *Book of Homilies*; none could exist without proper hierarchy and subordination. He wrote vehemently anti-Puritan tracts in defense of traditional order; his verse is only slightly more covert in its condemnation of

6. George Herbert, *"The H. Communion"* in *Works*, p. 53. I am indebted to Mahood, p. 28.
7. See E. L. Marilla, "Henry Vaughan and the Civil War," *JEGP*, 41 (1942), 214–26.
8. Martz, p. 13.

the warring upstarts who had destroyed that order. In "The Constellation," for example, he contrasts the hierarchies of the stars, always moving by divine command and always at peace with one another despite varying brightness, with the anarchic willfulness of the Puritan populace:

> But here Commission'd by a black self-wil
> The sons the father kil,
> The Children Chase the mother, and would heal
> The wounds they give, by crying, zeale.
>
> . . . .
>
> Thus by our lusts disorder'd into wars
> Our guides prove wandering stars,
> Which for these mists, and black days were reserv'd,
> What time we from our first love swerv'd.
>
> (470)

The poet closes by praying for a return to the Anglican ideal of the seamless cloak of Christ. If the British returned to their "first love," submitted once again to the humility of divine grace, then church and state would be repatterned to accord with the harmony of the celestial hierarchy:

> Settle, and fix our hearts, that we may move
> In order, peace, and love,
> And taught obedience by thy whole Creation,
> Become an humble, holy nation.
>
> Give to thy spouse her perfect, and pure dress,
> *Beauty* and *holiness*,
> And so repair these Rents, that men may see
> And say, *Where God is, all agree.*
>
> (470)

The poet of *Silex Scintillans*, for all his interest in the hermetic and the arcane—indeed, *through* his interest in ideas so remote from the mainstream of earlier Anglicanism—was searching for the same stasis and unity the earlier poets had sought; for Vaughan, though, these values seemed much further away.

Herbert, Herrick, and Crashaw were able to return to childhood in spirit, aided always by the grace of God. But for Vaughan, childhood and adulthood are separated by a tremendous gulf, just as the two states were divided in his own life by the dark chaos of war. Childhood seems too distant and mysterious even to be comprehended, let alone regained. When Vaughan uses the *persona* of child, it generally functions not to bring him back to his early spiritual communion with God, but to dramatize his awareness that past blessings are lost. In "The Seed growing secretly" he compares his life on earth to the progress of a plant prospering at first, but then cut off from life-giving nourishment:

> My dew, my dew! my early love,
> My souls bright food, thy absence kills!
> Hover not long, eternal Dove!
> Life without thee is loose and spills.
>
> Something I had, which long ago
> Did learn to suck, and sip, and taste,

But now grown sickly, sad and slow,
Doth fret and wrangle, pine and waste.

O spred thy sacred wings and shake
One living drop! one drop life keeps!
If pious griefs Heavens joys awake,
O fill his bottle! thy childe weeps!
(510–11)

The voice is not that of a chosen "little one" of God, but of an outcast Ishmael dying of thirst in the desert, his early spiritual food gone.

Earlier Anglicans could quench their thirst with the holy sacraments; Vaughan, deprived of the church, was obliged to look elsewhere for spiritual sustenance. What the ritual and symbolism of Anglicanism were for his master Herbert, the flora and fauna of the countryside were for Vaughan. His poetry is dominated by imagery drawn from the natural world—the elemental power of wind and rain, the secret activities of plants and animals, the great cycles of the seasons. Herbert's God was relatively approachable much of the time—the familiar Father and Master of His house, the church. But Vaughan's is modeled on the sun, that remote body which sheds down light and warmth on all of nature, yet is often shrouded in clouds. Herbert's church and her ritual were "bright and clear," beautifully ordered, and reflecting heavenly harmonies. As Claude J. Summers and Ted-Larry Pebworth have recently demonstrated, the emblematic landscape of Vaughan's "Regeneration" is a natural temple whose elements recapitulate the architectural features of an Anglican house of worship.[9] But Vaughan's temple of nature is all too often a seeming chaos of flux—wandering breezes, sudden inexplicable shiftings of light and shadow. Only occasionally and intermittently does it mirror the pattern of those "Fair, order'd lights," the stars (469). It comforts him with hints that there is a "tye of Bodyes," a unity behind the apparent chaos. But just as often, it taunts him with his own failure of vision.

Much of the power of Vaughan's lyrics derives from his ceaseless exploration of his own paradoxical situation. He longs for innocence and purity, yet he is bound by the sinfulness of his flesh. He prays for flashes of vision into the bright light of eternity, but when they come, he is unable to sustain them. He apprehends the possibility of a "heaven on earth," of a clear and constant vision of God here in this life, but his glimmers of insight into the static realm he seeks usually reveal it as far away in space and time from his earthly prison. "My Soul there is a Countrie, / Far beyond the stars" ("Peace," 430). Vaughan acknowledges his inability to transcend the paralyzing duality of his nature and achieve under his own power the heaven on earth he longs for. He can only wait in mingled hope and despair, praying that God will break through the sinful veil which covers him and grant him full sight.

Critics have generally characterized Vaughan's verse as an uneven alteration between flashes of brilliance and morose turgidity: his poems kindle into brief incandescence when he moves toward perception of a fragment of the lost unity; they lapse into relative formlessness and incoherence

9. Claude J. Summers and Ted-Larry Pebworth, "Vaughan's Temple in Nature and the Context of 'Regeneration,'" *JEGP*, 74 (1975), 351–60.

when he loses the thread of vision. With ritualism banished from the land, he was cut off from the play spirit and its potential for generating links with higher order. The poet was an exile in the fallen wilderness of Puritanism, but without the Puritans' faith in struggle toward the New Jerusalem. With no confidence in the future, he was locked into nostalgia for the past, into a need to recapture somehow—through death if not in life—the steady white light which shines upon childhood.

2

"Ye are all the children of light, and the children of the day: we are not of the night, nor of darkness," St. Paul wrote to the Thessalonians (I Thess. 5:5). Vaughan began life as a child of light but slipped into darkness with the passing years. On turning to the writing of Thomas Traherne, however, we immediately sense ourselves to be in the presence of one who has regained the light. Nearly all of his works express radiant joy and perfect fulfillment. He announces to the world, in a voice of prophetic conviction:

> Our Saviors Meaning, when He said, He must be Born again and becom a little Child that will enter into the Kingdom of Heaven: is Deeper far then is generally believed. It is not only in a Careless Reliance upon Divine Providence, that we are to becom Little Children, or in the feebleness and shortness of our Anger and Simplicity of our Passions: but in the Peace and Purity of all our Soul. Which Purity also is a Deeper Thing then is commonly apprehended, for we must disrobe our selvs of all fals Colors, and unclothe our Souls of evil Habits; all our Thoughts must be Infant-like and Clear: the Powers of our Soul free from the Leven of this World, and disentangled from mens conceits and customs.[1]

Vaughan would have found little to object to in this formulation. If we were to stop here, as some readers have, Traherne would seem almost identical to Vaughan in his conviction that childhood is a time of innocence and spiritual vision. But if we press on we will discover subtle yet basic points of disagreement between the two poets on the subject of childhood—disagreements which help account for Vaughan's failure to regain the steady light of childhood and Traherne's relative ease in doing so.

While Vaughan could retain only indistinct impressions of what childhood must have been, Traherne re-creates its "Center and mid-day" by projecting us back into his own. His imaginative reentry into childhood in *The Third Century* is based not on Vaughan's analogy between children and early man, but on the even more surprising belief that as an infant newly born on earth he was a faithful replica of Adam just placed in the Garden of Eden. The notion that the first man in the Garden was actually

1. Thomas Traherne, *Centuries, Poems, and Thanksgiving*, ed. H. M. Margoliouth (Oxford: Clarendon, 1958), I, 113. All future quotations from this edition will be cited by volume and page number in the text. The best full-length studies of Traherne are K. W. Salter, *Thomas Traherne, Mystic and Poet* (London: Arnold, 1964); and Gladys I. Wade, *Thomas Traherne* (Princeton: Univ. Press, 1946). See also Allen H. Gilbert, "Thomas Traherne as Artist," *MLQ*, 8 (1947), 319–41, for a critique of some of Wade's assumptions. Particularly useful studies of Traherne's religious ideas include Rosalie Colie's "Thomas Traherne and the Infinite: The Ethical Compromise," *HLQ*, 21 (1957), 69–82; Davidson [Ferry], n. 6 above; and Martz, *The Paradise Within*. Carol L. Marks has studied Traherne's sources in "Thomas Traherne and Cambridge Platonism," *PMLA*, 81 (1966), 521–34; and "Thomas Traherne and Hermes Trismegistus," *RN*, 19 (1966), 118–31. See also Joan Webber's discussion of Traherne's prose style in *The Eloquent "I."*

a child enjoyed a measure of popularity among early Greek and medieval authorities;[2] it was echoed by John Earle's "A Child is a Man in a small Letter, yet the best Copie of *Adam* before hee tasted of *Eue*, or the *Apple*."[3] Godfrey Goodman asked, "How credulous and easie of beliefe are the young children, as if they were fit subjects to be again seduced by the serpent?"[4] but took no interest in exploring those positive aspects of the parallel which fascinated Traherne.

Adam left posterity no record of his response on first seeing the joys of the Garden, but we may assume he was as dazzled as Traherne's infant by the beauty of his surroundings. Traherne never tires of evoking the child's sense of wonder at even the most commonplace earthly objects: "All appeared New, and Strange at the first, inexpressibly rare, and Delightfull, and Beautifull. I was a little Stranger which at my Enterance into the World was Saluted and Surrounded with innumerable Joys" (I, 110). Not the least charming aspect of his glorious surroundings is the fact that all have been created expressly for him. "All Things were Spotles and Pure and Glorious; yea, and infinitely mine, and Joyfull and Precious" (I, 110). Just as Adam was given dominion over all the earth and her creatures, the infant is monarch of all he surveys: "The Skies were mine, and so were the Sun and Moon and Stars, and all the World was mine, and I the only Spectator and Enjoyer of it" (I, 111). Traherne recaptures with remarkable accuracy the grandiosity of early childhood perception, when the infant assumes he is the center of the world, and everything in it an extension of himself made to serve his good pleasure.

Before Adam fell, he had no knowledge of death or any other evil. Jeremy Taylor thought that since knowledge removed Adam from paradise, the child's ignorance would put him back in.[5] For Traherne, too, the child's "very Ignorance was Advantageous" (I, 110). He is convinced that all he sees has been forever as he sees it, and can never change: "The Corn was Orient and Immortal Wheat, which never should be reaped, nor was ever sown. I thought it had stood from everlasting to everlasting" (I, 111). He is divided by "A learned and a Happy Ignorance" from the sins and follies of mankind ("*Eden*," II, 12). One of the happiest results of this ignorance is that, not knowing sin, the infant feels as perfect and pure as Adam was:

> But that which most I Wonder at, which most
> I did esteem my Bliss, which most I Boast,
> And ever shall Enjoy, is that within
>   I felt no Stain, nor Spot of Sin.
>
> ("Innocence," II, 14)

Andrew Willet recorded in his commentary on Genesis, "Some thinke, that there remaineth yet in children that are not ashamed of their naked-

2. Jeremy Taylor quotes Theophilus Antiochenus [Ad Autolycum lib. ii (cap. 25)]: "Adam, in that age was yet as an infant, and therefore did not understand that secret, viz., that the fruit which he ate had in it nothing but knowledge" (*Works*, VII, 322). For similar opinions in other early authorities, see George Boas, *Essays on Primitivism and Related Ideas in the Middle Ages* (Baltimore: Johns Hopkins Univ. Press, 1948), pp. 16, 25, 39, 43, and 95–96; and Davidson [Ferry], pp. 42 and 242.
3. Earle, "A Childe."
4. *The Fall of Man*, pp. 328–29 (London, 1616).
5. Taylor, *The Rule and Exercises of Holy Living*, Chap. II, Sect. VI, in *Works*, III, 107.

nes, some shadow of our first estate."[6] Adam was not ashamed of his body until he had fallen from righteousness; nor is Traherne's child. His limbs and features, fresh from the shaping power of God, seem as precious to him as the jewels in the rivers of paradise. "These little Limmes, / These Eys and Hands which here I find, / . . . Welcom ye Treasures which I now receiv. / . . . New Burnisht Joys! / Which yellow Gold and Pearl excell!" ("*The Salutation*," II, 4). One of Traherne's favorite biblical texts is Ps. 139:14: "I will praise thee; for I am fearfully and wonderfully made," expanded in his *Thanksgivings* into fifteen pages extolling the beauty and power of the human body. For Vaughan, it is the body's vileness which spoils the angelic spirit of humanity. But Traherne, inverting the great chain of being, asserts in his *Christian Ethicks* that having a body is precisely what places humanity above the angels: "IF you look into the *Nature* of Angels and *Men* you will find this mighty Difference between them, Angels are more Simple Spirits, Men are Images of GOD carefully put into a Beautiful Case. Their Souls would seem Equal to the Angels were they not to live in Humane Bodies, and those Bodies are Superadded, certainly for unspeakable and most Glorious Ends."[7]

But if the case is beautiful, how much more so the "Image of GOD" within it? Traherne occasionally disparages the body, but only by comparison with the soul. God is infinite, so a soul made in his image must be infinite as he is: "a Sphere like Thee of Infinite Extent: an Ey without walls; All unlimited & Endless Sight" ("Select Med.," I, 91). Traherne was emphatically not, as Herrick was, a lover of littleness. Christ's exhortations to humility do not at all mean human beings should be contented with small blessings and lowliness of spirit:

> Humility . . . is the way to full and perfect Sublimity. A man would little think, that by sinking into the Earth he should come to Heaven. He doth not, but is buried, that fixeth and abideth there. But if he pierceth through all the Rocks and Minerals of the inferiour World, and passeth on to the end of his Journey in a strait line downward, in the middle of his way he will find the Centre of Nature, and by going downward still begin to ascend, when he is past the Centre; through many Obstacles full of gross and subterraneous Darkness, which seem to affright and stifle the Soul, he will arrive at last to a new Light and Glory, room and liberty, breathing-place and fresh-air among the *Antipodes*, and by passing on still through those inferiour Regions that are under his feet, but over the head of those that are beneath him, finally come to another Skie, penetrate that, and leaving it behind him sink down into the depth of all Immensity.[8]

Even the lowly virtue of humility leads the soul into the sublime vastness of infinity.

6. Andrew Willet, *Hexapla in Genesis, a Sixfold Commentary upon Genesis* (London, 1608), p. 39. Willet, however, discounts the idea.
7. Thomas Traherne, *Christian Ethicks*, ed. Carol L. Marks and George Robert Guffey (Ithaca, New York: Cornell Univ. Press, 1968), p. 104. Traherne's recently discovered "Select Meditions" IV, 37 expands on man's superiority to the angels. I am greatly indebted to the late James M. Osborn for having kindly allowed me to read this as yet unpublished manuscript in the Beinecke Library, Yale University. Quotations from this manuscript will be slightly modernized, and indicated by Century (roman numerals) and Meditation (arabic numerals) in the text.
8. *Christian Ethicks*, pp. 209–10. See also "Select Med.," III, 98.

Like Adam before his fall, the infant bears God's image clear and unspoiled. Traherne celebrates the infinity of his infant soul with seemingly indefatigable bursts of hyperbole and bristling forests of exclamation points: "O Joy! O Wonder, and Delight! / O Sacred Mysterie! / My Soul a Spirit infinit! / An Image of the Deitie!" "*My Spirit*," II, 54). He delights in the old definition of God as a sphere whose center is everywhere and circumference nowhere and applies it, quite logically, to the soul of the infant itself:[9]

A Strange Extended Orb of Joy,
   Proceeding from within,
Which did on evry side convey
It self, and being nigh of Kin
   To God did evry Way
Dilate it self even in an Instant, and
Like an Indivisible Centre Stand
At once Surrounding all Eternitie.
(“*My Spirit*” II, 54)

How can a center surround? If Traherne's exposition of the power of the infant soul is something less than lucid, it may be because he is struggling to express the inexpressible, the combined though contradictory attributes of immanence and transcendence.

* * *

As the mystic sees God, little children see all things—simultaneously within them and without. Jean Piaget's research has clearly shown the inability of young children to distinguish themselves from their surroundings. The world around them seems simultaneously to flow through their minds. They cheerfully hold paradoxical beliefs—a thought or a dream is a voice in the head and at the same time outside it. What appears paradoxical to the adult is simple to the child because he has not yet learned to see boundaries between things.[1]

It is precisely this refusal to dichotomize which Traherne discovers and celebrates in the infant soul in "*My Spirit*." Like the God in whose image it was created, the soul is *one*—a unity "Simple like the Deitie" (II, 50). Like God, it is both immanent and transcendent: "In its own Centre is a Sphere / Not shut up here, but evry Where." Since it knows no "Brims or Borders," what is sees outside it is at the same time within it (II, 52); the infant is therefore unable to distinguish between a thing and a thought, between objective reality and his own mental creations:

With all she wrought,
My Soul was fraught,
And evry Object in my Soul a Thought
Begot, or was; I could not tell,
Whether the Things did there
Themselvs appear,
Which in my Spirit *truly* seemed to dwell;

9. For the ancestry of the definition, see Hiram Haydn, *The Counter-Renaissance* (New York: Scribner, 1950), p. 335; and Abel Lefranc, *Grands écrivains Français de la Renaissance* (Paris: Champion, 1914), pp. 172–81.
1. See Piaget, *The Child's Conception of the World*. Salter discusses the absence of self-object boundaries in Traherne's work, p. 32.

Or whether my conforming Mind
Were not alone even all that shind.
(II, 52)

Through tortured abstractions, Traherne struggles to communicate his remarkable insight into the undifferentiated wholeness of the infant's perception—an insight which had to wait until the twentieth century to be validated by the research of Piaget.

The mysterious "Center and mid-day" of childhood so longingly sought by Vaughan is its wholeness, its denial of all dualisms. But for Vaughan such unity could have existed with any permanence only in the "world of light" of the child's preexistent state. England once had reflected this heavenly unity, but no longer could. On earth, dichotomies are inevitable, beginning with the powerful antagonism between body and soul. As soon as a child's pure soul is placed in a body of gross and sinful flesh, the first border is drawn, the first dualism firmly established. As the child grows, dichotomies multiply rapidly. Light and dark, heaven and earth, God and humanity—all come to seem total opposites divided by unbridgeable chasms. Even to the child newly born, though God is still visible, He has lost His immanence. The child and the natural world around him are bathed in white light, but God himself, the source of the light, lies apart—in a heaven far distant from the earth.

For Traherne, the light of childhood vision is not passively received from above, but actively generated from within. Traherne's God, like Vaughan's, is modeled on the sun—an inexhaustible orb radiating light and energy throughout the universe; the infant soul, made in His image, is a sun as He is: "For Since the Sun which is a poor little Dead Thing, can at once shine upon many Kingdoms, and be wholy present, not only in many Cities and Realms upon Earth, but in all the Stars in the firmament of Heaven: surely the Soul which is a far more perfect Sun, nearer unto GOD in Excellency and Nature, can do far more" (I, 92). Little children commonly think of vision as emanating from their eyes and giving light;[2] Traherne celebrates the "*Infant-Ey*," the light of the soul, as "A simple Light from all Contagion free" that "shineth in an hevenly Sence, / And round about (unmov'd) its Light dispence" (II, 86). For Traherne, Matt. 5:14, "Ye are the light of the world," is literal truth, when applied to the infant eye.

Since the child's vision is generated from within himself, Traherne has no need for Vaughan's concept of preexistence. The spiritual powers of infancy date from conception: "Will you see the Infancy of this sublime and celestial Greatness? Those Pure and Virgin Apprehensions I had from the Womb, and that Divine Light wherewith I was born" (I, 110). The child's powers are planted within him by God: "By the Gift of GOD they attended me into the World" (I, 110). But once he has received his spiritual vision, he carries it with him everywhere.

The beams of the infant eye can shoot out through the universe and penetrate mysteries, so that the infant knows all as God does. Traherne asserts, with all due modesty, "My Knowledg was Divine" and asks, "Is it not Strange, that an Infant should be Heir of the World, and see those Mysteries which the Books of the Learned never unfold?" (I, 111). Strange indeed, and paradoxical when we remember that Traherne's infant knows

2. Piaget, *Child's Conception*, p. 49.

no evil. " 'Tis strange that I should Wisest be, / When least I could an Error see" (*"The Return,"* II, 87). But this paradox, like all others, is resolved through the wholeness of childhood perception. Since infants cannot distinguish between thoughts and things—between what they create and what exists independently of their own minds—evil does not exist for them as long as they fail to perceive it.

Traherne was no Berkeleian—he never denies the existence of things in themselves, independent of the human mind. But his writings give strong and consistent emphasis not to things in themselves, but to things as they are perceived. By seeing the world about him as Eden and his own body as beautiful and pure, the child makes them so; and by failing to perceive evil, in effect he uncreates it. His conviction that all the world's loveliness belongs to him is not megalomania, but simple truth. Beauty *is* in the eye of the beholder: "Tis not the Object, but the Light / That maketh Heaven" (*"The Preparative,"* II, 22). The wondrous kingdoms of the child are his because he has created them through the godlike and God-given power of the "Infant-Ey." Heaven, eternity, paradise—these are not places. They are a state of mind. Vaughan's child gazes toward a heaven far removed from the earth in space and time, but Traherne's sees paradise all about him: "Neither shall they say, Lo here! or, lo there! for, behold, the kingdom of God is within you" (Luke 17:21).

As Traherne grew up, however, he lost his celestial state of mind:

> The first Light which shined in my Infancy in its Primitive and Innocent Clarity was totally ecclypsed: insomuch that I was fain to learn all again. If you ask me how it was ecclypsed? Truly by the Customs and maners of Men, which like Contrary Winds blew it out: by an innumerable company of other Objects, rude vulgar and Worthless Things that like so many loads of Earth and Dung did over whelm and Bury it. (I, 114)

Like Vaughan, Traherne sees the child's soul as gradually clouded and choked off. But for Traherne, the first agent of corruption is not the sinful body, but the evil customs of men. His fall dated not from his birth, but from his first communication with other human beings.

Traherne was well aware of the effects of language and its hidden assumptions on patterns of thought. In *"Dumnesse"* he describes his infancy as a time of silent exultation over the glories within and around him. Nature created him speechless "that he / Might in himself profoundly Busied be" and deaf "that he might / Not be disturbd, while he doth take Delight / In inward Things, nor be depravd with Tongues, / Nor Injured by the Errors and the Wrongs / That *Mortal Words* convey" (II, 40). Mortal words, as much of Traherne's verse testifies, are powerless to communicate the vision of infancy—they warp what is clear and simple into gnarled tangles of paradox. When first placed on earth, the infant has no use for words. He sees himself as unique, like Adam before the creation of Eve, and enjoys his Eden in solitary splendor. Other people are not beings like himself, but decorative parts of his own unified creation: "The Men! O what Venerable and Reverend Creatures did the Aged seem! Immortal Cherubims! And young Men Glittering and Sparkling Angels and Maids strange Seraphick Pieces of Life and Beauty! Boys and Girles Tumbling in the Street, and Playing, were moving Jewels. I knew not that they were

Born or should Die" (I, 111). But as he grows, the infant gradually becomes conscious that he is not alone in his Eden. Other people like himself talk to him. Their words teach him that he is not the center of the universe, that his vision of the world is relative, not absolute—just one of myriad possible viewpoints. Words teach him new and foreign concepts like death, decay, and sin. He is forced to accept "Churlish Proprieties," bounds and divisions, and his unified vision crumbles and passes away, to be replaced by the chaotic multiplicities and discontinuities of the fallen world of adults:

> All Mens thoughts and Words were about other Matters; They all prized New Things which I did not dream of. I was a stranger and unacquainted with them; I was little and reverenced their Authority; I was weak, and easily guided by their Example: Ambitious also, and Desirous to approve my self unto them. And finding no one Syllable in any mans Mouth of those Things, by Degrees they vanishd, My thoughts, (as indeed what is more fleeting then a Thought) were blotted out. And at last all the Celestial Great and Stable Treasures to which I was born, as wholy forgotten, as if they had never been. (I, 115)

By learning to speak their language, Traherne signaled his acceptance of the world view of adults: "*I then my Bliss did, when my Silence, break*" ("Dumnesse," II, 40). By the time he was three or four, Traherne's unified vision had been destroyed by the divisive power of human beings and their language.

* * *

Traherne's adult visionary power scarcely differs from that he remembers from his infancy, except in its greater range, elaboration, and impregnability. The child's power is instinctive, but easily destroyed because it operates unconsciously. As an adult Traherne has "Collected again, by the Highest Reason" what was intuitive before his "Apostasie" (I, 110). He has experienced and rejected the vision of fallen adulthood and consciously regained his infant ability to gather the world's multiplicities into a unity. Traherne's unawareness of sin as an infant made him its easy victim. But for the adult, the evils of the world not only pose no threat—they can become an aspect of felicity. Made in the image of God, Traherne has inherited his power to "draw Order out of Confusion," to make a heaven of the fallen world (I, 129). His perception of the sufferings of sinful humanity increases his own happiness (II, 188–89), and the very pains of the damned are assimilated into his joyous unified vision, for "Hell it self is a part of GODs Kingdom, to wit His Prison. It is fitly mentioned in the Enjoyment of the World: And is it self by the Happy Enjoyed, as a Part of the world" (I, 24). Traherne, it would seem, had little sympathy for the Vaughans of his day—those who languished in sin and darkness, convinced they were powerless to escape.

Many readers have found Traherne's cheerful acceptance of the woes of others somewhat deficient in the Christian charity he preached, to say the very least. But the idea that the blessed rejoice in the sufferings of the damned is old and venerable. If we are to deal fairly with Traherne we must recognize that here, as in so many other areas, he rethought Christian commonplace: his professed enjoyment of the sufferings of fallen men by no means prevented him from trying to turn them from their mistakes. Traherne was nothing if not a missionary—for every passage about enjoying the tortures of sinners, he wrote many exhorting them to abandon their errors and seek true happiness. Much of his work, in marked contrast to Vaughan's, is open and public in tone. Now that he has regained felicity he must lead others to follow in his footsteps.

Traherne delights in pointing out that, although the world was made for him alone, it was made for every other single human being just as it was for him: "all we see is ours, and evry One / Possessor of the Whole" ("Ease," II, 66). By this paradox, God satisfies man's need to get just as well as his need to give (I, 96). In bringing others to felicity, Traherne not only gives happiness but also receives it since the happiness of others increases his own; in showing others that the world belongs to them, he does not divide his own inheritance, but multiplies it, since the worlds possessed by others belong to him as sole heir of all things. And everyone else who has regained the vision of infancy is in exactly the same position he is. Traherne's system is based on his infant conviction that all the world's treasures were made expressly for him. But he ingeniously combines infantile grandiosity with altruism so that each augments the other in an endlessly expanding spiral of joy. This infinite but ever-increasing felicity is the one grand theme which reverberates through all Traherne's writings. At its worst his work is uninspiring didacticism, incessant hammering at the same worn-out ideas. But at its best it conveys infectiously the glowing spirit behind it.

* * *

For Traherne, original sin means no more than the child's innate willingness to follow the bad examples all round him. Once he has lost his infant vision, he is a *tabula rasa*, weak, inexperienced, and easily led: "An Empty Book is like an Infants Soul, in which any Thing may be Written. It is Capable of all Things, but containeth Nothing" (I, 3).[3] Adam ate the apple because he was weak and gullible, no match for the subtle serpent. Children fall because they are equally deceived by the customs and manners of humanity. But no self-respecting theologian would consider this weakness original sin, since it is not the *result* of Adam's fall, as original sin, must be, but its *cause*.

And Traherne goes so far as to suggest that children need not fall at all. The very malleability which makes them so easily succumb to false values can be used to instill true ones. They must be taught the validity of their infant perception of the world:

> Had any man spoken of it, it had been the most easy Thing in the World, to hav taught me, and to hav made me believ, that Heaven and Earth was GODs Hous, and that He gav it me. That the Sun was mine and that Men were mine, and that Cities and Kingdoms were mine also: that Earth was better then Gold, and that Water was, every Drop of it, a Precious Jewel. And that these were Great and Living Treasures: And that all Riches whatsoever els was Dross in Comparison.

3. The idea of the *tabula rasa* was by no means invented by Locke, but a seventeenth-century commonplace, often used in discussion of education and ultimately based on Plato's comparison of the soul to a wax tablet in *Theatetus*, 191. Traherne actually uses the phrase *Rasa Tabula* in his "Select Med.," IV, 2.

> From whence I clearly find how Docible our Nature is in natural Things, were it rightly entreated. (I, 115)

Children are eager to have their instinctive knowledge confirmed by others, if only there were others in the world who would teach them.

Traherne's interest in the religious education of children allies him with the Puritans. But while John Bunyan and James Janeway call upon parents and teachers to wean children from evil, Traherne urges that children's instinctive values be rationally reinstilled before they are shattered by the beginning of speech: "By this let Nurses, and those Parents that desire Holy Children learn to make them Possessors of Heaven and Earth betimes to remove silly Objects from before them, to Magnify nothing but what is Great indeed, and to talk of God to them and of His Works and Ways before they can either Speak or go. For Nothing is so Easy as to teach the Truth becaus the Nature of the Thing confirms the Doctrine" (I, 117). We can safely assume that no child was ever kept from falling by the wayside through Traherne's proposed method. But the very fact that he could suggest such an educational program testifies to his lack of sympathy with the doctrine of the child's innate depravity. The poet was very well aware of the existence of sin, but his writings implicitly deny any recognizable form of original sin.

* * *

If Traherne cannot be entirely defended against charges of heresy, however, he can certainly be excused. His theological system is so original and full of vitality that we may at first fail to realize one of its most striking traits. He was a divine of the Church of England who, according to the contemporary who prefaced his "Serious and Pathetical Contemplation," was "much in love with the beautiful order and *Primitive* Devotions of this our excellent Church. Insomuch that I believe, he never failed any one day either publickly or in his private Closet, to make use of her publick Offices, as one part of his devotion, unless some very unavoidable business interrupted him" (I, xxxii). But the church and her rituals scarcely appear in most of his writings. Much as he may have loved Anglicanism, he built a large and coherent body of religious thought quite independent of it and, in fact, contradicting many of the chief tenets of Anglicanism.

It would be tempting to resolve this apparent paradox by discounting contemporary testimony concerning Traherne's allegiance to Anglicanism. But in the "Select Meditations" Traherne himself describes at length his devotion to the prerevolutionary pattern of English church and government and his dismay over its destruction in the Civil War:

> Besids ye Heaven and ye Earth wch ye Heathen enjoy, Thou hast brought in ye Gospel of thy Son into our land Converted our Kings Senators & Nobles, Exalted thy Name, Established thy word and worship by Laws, Builded thy Selfe Temples, and Appoynt[ed] Revenues for thy Church and Ministers, Greatly are . . . our Saviour Dignified, & our Cittys Beautified with those thy Most Glorious and Beautifull Houses wear all this to be Done againe Thou knowest ye Sweat & Bloud wherewith it was Atcheived, But O ye wickedness of Ignorant zealots! who contemn thy Mercies and Despise ye union ye Beautifull union of they Nationall church! every way thou art provoked to Anger,

> by Open profaness & Spirituall wickedness. And by ye Ignorance of both, Despising thy Mercies O Lord when our citties & Teritories are united by Laws in ye fear of thy Name: & are at one accord in Calling upon Thee; When they Move by Consent like an united Army. How Ravishing is their Beauty, How Sweet their Order! It is O my God as if ye Nation had but one Soul. In all wch while thy Glory Reigneth, she is made thy Throne; one Throne and Temple unto Thee. Be not wroth very Sore O Lord, neither remember Iniquity forever. The Holy Citties are a Wilderness, Zion is a wilderness, Jerusalem a Desolati[on] our Holy and our Beautifull house where our fathers praised Thee is burnt up with fire and all our pleasant Things are layd wast. ("Select Med.," I, 85)

The Traherne of the "Select Meditations" is staunchly if belatedly Laudian in his praise for "ye Shining Light wch a Golden candlestick giveth in a National Church" ("Select Med.," III, 23), his rejoicing in "The Saboths and festivals & ordinances of thy church" ("Select Med.," IV, 24), and his insistence on the virtue of religious uniformity: "might every man do what is right in his own Eys we should all run into confusion" ("Select Med.," III, 25).

Traherne by no means saw his own highly original and heretical system as part of the "confusion" he deplored. Rather the system was meant to counteract it. His conception of infant vision allowed him to escape old boundaries, to shatter old limits and expand into infinity. Yet this escape was made in the service of reintegrating old forms, of reviving the same seamless cloak of national religious and political unity whose decline was mourned by Herbert and Herrick and Vaughan. As in the earlier poets, we can see an important correlation between Traherne's use of the theme of childhood and his personal experience of political and social fragmentation. Traherne was only fifteen years Vaughan's junior, but those were a critical fifteen years: born in 1637, he spent his early life during the Civil War and Protectorate. The "beauty in holiness" of institutional Anglicanism which Vaughan remembered with such nostalgia had passed away before his time. Like Jeremy Taylor and many others who came to intellectual maturity during England's troubles, Traherne responded to the absence of a uniform, received theology by building his own, based on "Beauties of Inward Holiness" ("Select Med.," I, 87), which would allow each individual human being to restore through his own all-encompassing creative vision the "one Soul" of light and unity that postwar England had lost.

Vaughan still followed traditional habits of thought to the extent that he searched for an ordered unity inherent in the fallen world and found in moments of heightened perception that natural things were alive and linked by a "tye of Bodyes." But for Traherne, the ties must be imposed from without. Material objects are chaotic and diffuse without the God-given power of the infant eye to "draw Order out of Confusion" and weld them into unity.[4] They are "dead and quiet" particles (I, 123). Even the human body is a "Poor Carcase" (I, 83). But the creative vision of the infant eye brings them to life and motion much as a sudden appearance of the sun on a cloudy day kindles and transforms the landscape.

4. See *Christian Ethics,* pp. 78–79.

Since order is not discovered in things seen but created by those who see, Traherne was much more optimistic than any of the earlier poets we have discussed about the possibility of restoring England's golden age. The infant sees even the works of civilization as part of the glory of his paradise: "The Citie seemed to stand in Eden, or to be Built in Heaven. The Streets were mine, the Temple was mine, the People were mine, their Clothes and Gold and Silver was mine, as much as their Sparkling Eys Fair Skins and ruddy faces" (I, 111). In *The Third Century* Traherne condemns the creations of human beings as evil because they divide and distract the child from his true happiness in the creation of God. But once the visionary powers of infancy are regained, all the works of humanity can be perceived as beautiful and divine. Traherne's *Thanksgivings* celebrate the joys of civilized England as well as the pleasures of Eden:

> Festivals and Sabbaths,
> Sacraments and solemn Assemblies,
> Bishops, Priests, and Deacons,
> Emperors, Kings, and Princes,
> Counsellors, Physicians; Senators,
> And Captains,
> In all the Beauty of their Office and Ministry,
> Shine like Stars
> In the firmament of thy Kingdom:
> In the midst of whom
> Thy Servant liveth.
>
> (II, 252)

Whatever the actual changes in English church and state, and there were many during Traherne's short lifetime, his infant eye can effortlessly and instantaneously restore the "one Soul" of national unity.

Just as he imaginatively rebuilds English society according to the model of Richard Hooker and the *Book of Homilies*, Traherne affirms the worth of the mental powers so valued by sixteenth-century humanists. He by no means shared the anti-intellectual strain we have noted in the earlier poets. Knowledge, reason, understanding—all of these are treasures which contribute to the greatness of the human soul.

* * *

With Traherne we have come full circle. For Herbert, the demands of faith and the pursuits of secular society seemed hopelessly at odds. Retreating to childhood was a way out—a way of abandoning intellectual pride and social ambition for a narrower world which excluded them. In Herrick and Crashaw, the retreat became progressively narrower and more constricting. For Vaughan, retreat into any earthly institution seemed impossible: searching for childhood meant looking beyond the world altogether into another realm far above it and already lost. But for Traherne, childhood was not a way out, but a way back in. By regaining his infant powers, Traherne put Humpty Dumpty together again—reunited what seemed to Herbert irreconcilable. The infant eye does not establish boundaries and create limits, as Herbert tried to, but obliterates them. It does not whittle down and narrow adult experience but builds up and expands it. Through the creative vision of infancy, Traherne was able to reenter the world the other poets abandoned, to affirm the value of many activities they had been obliged to give up. In tracing the meaning of childhood * * *, we have actually traced a much larger pattern of disintegration and reintegration: the collapse of the humanist faith that the individual, the church, and English society are an orderly continuum; the gradual realization that order is not inherent within things but imposed from without; and the conscious rebuilding of the continuum, or at least those aspects of it which could be rebuilt, after the Restoration.

* * *

WILLIAM KERRIGAN

Transformations of Friendship in the Work of Katherine Philips†

After so many centuries of silence, what would she say?

Some of the male poets of the seventeenth century must have looked forward to a time when female poets would engage at long last the ideas, arguments, and conventions of their artistic tradition. In the decisive "Eighth song" of *Astrophil and Stella*, Stella had made it clear that her refusal was not personal. Astrophil was loved in return; yet this love would to their sorrow obey the higher power of honor: "Tyran honour doth thus use thee, / *Stella's* selfe might not refuse thee."[1] In seventeenth-century poetry, however, beginning with Donne's "The Dampe," "Confined Love," and "Communitie," female honor came under sustained attack as, variously, a deviation from nature, a falling off from the Golden Age, a mark of social corruption, a chimera invented to curtail pleasure. Triumphing over the defeatist Petrarchism of their predecessors, love poets were now writing verses for an Ovidian world in which sexual consummation was not just desired, but enjoyed, and not just enjoyed, but subjected to utopian elaborations. The Daphnes and Lauras of this new libertinism were finally cooperating, and this mutuality of erotic interest might one day produce a long-delayed poetic dialogue between the sexes.

In "A Rapture," the most notorious and influential of these hedonistic utopias, Carew transforms the story of Daphne and Apollo, for centuries the abiding etiological myth of male frustration in the Petrarchan tradition, into a fantasy of the birth of female poetry:

> *Daphne* hath broke her barke, and that swift foot,
> Which th'angry Gods had fastned with a root
> To the fixed earth, doth now unfetter'd run,
> To meet th'embraces of the youthful Sun:
> She hangs upon him, like his Delphique Lyre,
> Her kisses blow the old, and breath new fire:
> Full of her God, she sings inspired Layes,

† This essay appears for the first time in this Norton Critical Edition.
1. W. A. Ringler, ed., *The Poems of Sir Philip Sidney* (Oxford: Clarendon Press, 1962), p. 220.

Sweet Odes of love, such as deserve the Bayes,
Which she her selfe was.[2]

Liberated, her unfastened foot runs into poetic feet. Sexual cooperation means literary cooperation.

Carew died in 1640. The sort of female poet he imagined did in fact appear, after the Civil War and the Interregnum, in the figure of Aphra Behn. Surely the male poets of the Restoration and their audience would be curious about how a woman would treat the "imperfect enjoyment" topos explored by Rochester and others. Behn's "The Disappointment" slakes that thirst. Joining the male libertines in writing against female honor, she introduces a novelty into this masculine tradition. Whereas the masculine poets, describing the loss of easy sexual satisfaction in the state of nature, all attribute this catastrophe to a jealous male's invention of female honor, Behn uniquely proposes that female honor was the brain-child of "Some Woman sure, ill-natur'd, old, and proud, / Too ugly ever to have been deceiv'd; / Unskill'd in Love; in Virtue, or in Truth."[3]

But before there was Aphra Behn, there was Katherine Philips, "the matchless Orinda" as the title page of her 1667 *Poems* christened her: the first woman in the history of English poetry to gain large renown for her achievement. She was not at all what Carew anticipated. Philips celebrates what she calls "essential Honor" or honor "turned . . . inward," set free "From titles and popularity."[4] Deliberately rejecting the love tradition, she instead celebrates friendship, particularly (though not exclusively) friendship among women. She herself never alludes to the myth of Daphne and Apollo. But a certain "Philo-Philippa," author of one of the eulogies prefacing the 1667 *Poems*, refashions the story to provide a rebuke to Carew wholly in keeping with the new tradition Philips initiates:

Let the male poets their *Phoebus* choose,
Thee I invoke, *Orinda*, for my *Muse*;
He could but force a branch; *Daphne* her tree
Most freely offers to her Sex and thee,
And says to verse so unconstrained as yours
Her laurel freely comes, your fame secures:
And men no longer shall with ravished bays
Crown their forced poems by as forced a praise.[5]

This is excellently vigorous. If unable to ravish Daphne herself (and her successors), men have ravished the plant in order to make the laurel crown, long-time symbol of poetic achievement. This vegetable "forcing" becomes a comment on the very genre in which Philo-Philippa is writing—the prefatory poem of praise in which one versifier crowns another. Such praise is as "forced," as enjoined by convention, as the seductive poetry it would

2. Rhodes Dunlap, ed., *The Poems of Thomas Carew* (Oxford: Clarendon Press, 1949), p. 52.
3. Janet Todd, ed., *The Works of Aphra Behn*, Vol. 1: *Poetry* (London: William Pickering, 1992), p. 149.
4. See "A Friend," l. 31, and "On Mr Francis Finch," ll.53–58, in Patrick Thomas, ed., *The Collected Works of Katherine Philips*, Vol. 1: *The Poems* (Essex: Stump Cross Books, 1990). All subsequent citations of Philips' verse use this edition. Ironically, Philips' conception of female honor was also celebrated by Thomas Carew in his song "Feminine Honor" (Dunlap, p. 60).
5. I quote Philo-Philippa (having modernized her spelling and punctuation) from Germaine Greer, Susan Hastings, Jeslyn Medoff, and Melinda Sansone, eds., *Kissing the Rod: An Anthology of Seventeenth-Century Women's Verse* (New York: Farrar Straus Giroux, 1988), p. 204.

reward. But in this instance Daphne's "laurel freely comes" to a woman who would praise a female poet whose work does not seek to force her into compliance with male sexual desire. Daphne has been liberated, not to complete the love tradition, as Carew foretold, but to initiate a poetic tradition by women for women about women.

Philips' poetry fell from favor in the early eighteenth century, and despite the attention of modern scholars, has not regained the prestige it once enjoyed.[6] If she is to be retrieved for students today—and I hope for this possibility—it may well be because her poetry is intensely fixed on friendship at a moment in history when this ancient tradition was undergoing a number of momentous ideological transformations that would in time deliver a fund of liberal goods to us. Today's students, all but historyless, are prone to suppose that such enlightenments have been inexplicably bestowed on our day, and just as inexplicably denied to the stupid, benighted centuries that precede us. But it should not be a hard sell to remind them that historical achievements are best received for what they are.

Royalist Friendship

Members of Philips' "society" took names derived from plays and romances. From her lyric "Friendship in Emblem," it would appear that some of these interlocking friends were given a symbolic badge: two burning hearts merging with each other, over which was a pair of compasses (which Philips explicates in a manner somewhat reminiscent of Donne, as emblematic of constancy and the joining of souls), over which was written "Friendship."[7] A male in the group, Francis Finch or "Palaemon," was encouraged to produce a short treatise, *Friendship*, which was privately printed in 1654; the author tells us that, uninterested in fame, he destroyed most of the copies.[8] In 1657 the famous Anglican divine Jeremy Taylor published *A Discourse of the Nature, Offices and Measures of Friendship, with Rules of Conducting it*, which is in the form of a letter to "the Most Ingenious and Excellent Mrs. Katharine Philips," answering her inquiries about the status of friendship in the Christian faith. A book appeared in 1659 entitled *Some Motives and Incentives to the Love of God*, and this work too is assumed to bear some relationship to the society of friends centered on Mrs. Philips. It was the first publication of Robert Boyle, the scientist. We appear to be dealing with a coterie practicing a somewhat unusual variety of friendship—esoteric enough, in any case, to require prose works codifying and clarifying its doctrines.

But the first thing to understand is that this friendship, whatever its theological and philosophical underpinnings, was fiercely political. English interest in chaste friendship can be traced to the neoplatonic *préciosité* brought by Henrietta Maria to the court of Charles I. At the time it was often treated, no doubt justly, as a frivolous fad. James Howell, writing in

6. The best account of the fortunes of her reputation is Paula Loscocco, " 'Manly Sweetness': Katherine Philips Among the Neoclassicals," *Huntington Library Quarterly* 56 (1994): 259–279.
7. I suspect that her handling of the compass conceit owes less to Donne's "Valediction Forbidding Mourning" than to Guarini's "Risposta dell'amante," the madrigal that Donne himself so freely adapted.
8. Finch's bid for oblivion was nearly successful. A single copy survives, in the library of Christ Church, Oxford University. See W. G. Hiscock, "*Friendship*: Francis Finch's Discourse and the Circle of the Matchless Orinda," *RES* 15 (1939): 466–468.

1634, took note of a new court fashion "called Platonic love" that "sets the wits of the town on work."[9] An anonymous lyric, probably from the Caroline period, refers to the fashion as "mere Court-Frippery," a wanton misuse of the prestige of Plato.[1] But with the various conflicts of the 1640s, in which friendships were tried and often destroyed; the execution of Charles in 1649 by a movement comprising more than a few people who were once, or so it appeared, honored to call him "friend"; the Protectorate of the 1650s, where Royalists, and acquaintances of Royalists, could gain immediate advantages by betraying their intimates, the old frippery of platonic friendship acquired the force of a political cult that was not only nostalgic, a keeping of the faith, but Darwinian, a matter of survival through trust in one's fittest friends.[2] Most of Philips' best lyrics on friendship were written during the 1650s.

She was staunchly Royalist, more so than either her father or her husband. Her interest in friendship, viewed from this angle, is part of a larger political vision—a vision in which friendship itself is the Royalist model for an ideal society. The Civil War was above all an outrage to friendship, to bonds of amicability that once united the entire nation. Charles I, she writes, suffered the double misery of "Unfaithful friends, ignoble enemies" ("Upon the Double Murder of K. Charles"), and his son is also "By foes pursu'd, by friends betraid" ("Arion on a Dolphin"). Her first publication, "In Memory of Mr. Cartwright," was one of a number of poems prefacing the 1651 *Works* of William Cartwright. The volume was planned as an assertion of the values of Royalist culture, and Philips weighs in with a nifty conceit: the ghost of Cartwright must not yet return to the world, but await its renovation in a "restored Poetry." At the center of this artistic and political Restoration, she elsewhere declares, will be the subject of friendship. In place of a Golden Age of erotic fulfillment spoiled by the invention of female honor we find in the works of Philips a Golden Age of friendship spoiled by the invention of male ambition ("A Country Life"). Warring armies, she assures one of her female addressees, will one day throw down their arms at her tomb ("To Mrs. Mary Aubrey at parting").

There are suggestions that Philips may have read Hobbes. As the tutor of Charles II, he was of course much favored among intellectual Royalists. Although he does not write at length of friendship, it is clear that bonds of fellow-feeling must be necessary to prevent a society from lapsing into the all-out warfare of everyone against everyone in the state of nature, which for Hobbes is equivalent to the Civil War. A close student of Hobbes, the Earl of Rochester, is responsible for the famous remark that "if there bee a reall good upon Earth 'tis in the Name of a friend, without which all others are meerly fantastical"—something of a surprise coming from him, until one remembers the close association between Royalism and friendship.[3] In "Upon Friendship, preferr'd to Love," Wycherley cel-

9. *Epistolae Ho-Elianae*, 2 vols. (Boston: Houghton Mifflin, 1907), 2:38.
1. "Platonic Love," in Henry Lawes, *The Treasury of Musick* (London: William Godbid, 1669). Quoted from the Chadwick-Healey English Poetry Full-Text Database, © 1992. See also Cartwright, "No Platonic Love," in *The Plays and Poems of William Cartwright* (Madison: Univ. of Wisconsin Press, 1951), p. 494; John Cleveland, "The Antiplatonic," in *Poems* (London, 1657); and Abraham Cowley, "Platonick Love," in *Poems*, ed. A. R. Waller (Cambridge: Cambridge Univ. Press, 1905), p. 75.
2. See the "Biographical Note" to Thomas's edition of Philips, pp. 7–10.
3. *The Letters of John Wilmot, Earl of Rochester*, ed. Jeremy Treglown (Chicago: University of Chicago Press, 1980), p. 93.

ebrates friendship in clearly Hobbesian tones as the difference between nature and civilization: "Man's best Security, from all Distrust."[4]

Throughout her verse Philips develops conceits that move in these directions. Friendship is lost in this age, its altars decayed, and must be the central value of any good time to come. The old notion of a hard stoic selfhood immune to ill fortune becomes in Philips a chaste and loving friendship immune to ill fortune. Lovelace strikes the same chord in a famous stanza of "The Grasshopper":

> Thou best of men and friends! we will create
> A genuine summer in each other's breast;
> And spite of this cold time and frozen fate,
> Thaw us a warm seat to our rest.[5]

Herrick's main contribution to this tradition is the suggestively titled "His Age, Dedicated to His Peculiar Friend, Master John Wickes": to have a friend is also to have an understanding of one's unfriendly place in history.

Friendship for Philips is part of the complex of neoclassical values that Maren-Sophie Røstvig traced in her monumental study of *The Happy Man*. These values include retirement from the court to the country, and the discipline to substitute modest contentment for the dizzying intoxications of ambition, self-sufficiency for society, rustic quiet for urban hubbub, virtue for political calculation, friendship for rivalry, otium for intrigue, nature for art. All of these more or less Horatian values appear in such Philips poems as "A retir'd friendship, to Ardelia," "La Grandeur d'esprit," "A Country Life," "Invitation to the Country," and "An Ode upon retirement, made upon occasion of Mr. Cowley's on that subject." Sometimes the evocation of retired complacency in Philips is so extreme that Røstvig is reminded of the distant gods of Lucretius, "Far off remov'd from us and our Affairs; / Neither approach'd by *Dangers*, or by *Cares*."[6] Orinda and her friends enjoy this aloof serenity:

> Here is no quarrelling for crowns,
> Nor fear of changes in our fate;
> No trembling at the Great One's frowns,
> Nor any slavery of state.
> ("A retir'd friendship")

> At length this secret I have learn'd;
> Who will be happy, must be unconcern'd,
> Must all their comfort in their bosom wear,
> And seek their power and their treasure there.
> ("An Ode upon retirement")

> When all the stormy world doth roar,
> How unconcern'd am I?
> I can not fear to tumble lower

4. *The Complete Works of William Wycherley*, ed. Montague Summers, 4 vols. (Soho: Nonesuch Press, 1924), 3:43–45.
5. *Cavalier Poets*, ed. Thomas Clayton (Oxford: Oxford University Press, 1978), p. 262.
6. *The Happy Man: Studies in the Metamorphosis of a Classical Ideal*, Vol. 1: *1600–1700* (2nd ed.; Norway: Norwegian Universities Press, 1962), pp. 252–260. Lucretius is quoted in Rochester's translation, in Harold Love, ed., *The Works of John Wilmot, Earl of Rochester* (Oxford: Oxford Univ. Press, 1999), p. 108.

That never would be high.
Secure in these unenvied walls
I think not on the state,
And pity no man's case that falls
From his ambition's height.
Silence and Innocence are safe;
A heart that's nobly true
At all these little arts can laugh
That do the world subdue.
("A Country Life")

One can readily concede the soberer complacencies of such assertions. When friends visited Katherine at her husband's estate in Wales, their "retir'd friendship" no doubt provided shelter from the constant rain of news and gossip, "Who loses and who wins; who's in, who's out" (*King Lear* 5.3.15). But the Olympian claim to be "unconcern'd" with the world's political turbulence is of course impossible, since that unconcern is itself shot through with political defiance.

Philips is, along with Cowley, the fullest exponent among mid-century English poets of the *beatus vir* tradition. Indeed, we begin to appreciate her historical importance when we understand that this moral and political affinity explains her close association with Cowley, first as a biographical fact, then in the fate of their reputations.

Cowley wrote an ode "On Orinda's Poems" and later an elegy on her death by smallpox. Orinda, for her part, produced an ode echoing Cowley's "On Retirement," and when the male poet in fact retired to his country home at Barn-Elms, visited him and carved her name on one of his trees ("Upon the engraving"). In 1667, James Gardiner, looking back on a "fruitful age" of English poetry, declared that "*Cowley*, and bright *Orinda* do adorn it most."[7] Later on she would more usually be linked, solely on the grounds of her gender, with Aphra Behn. But her true ideological and in some respects literary affiliation is with Cowley.

He is another poet whom we now have trouble reading with pleasure, though anyone who studies the late seventeenth and the eighteenth centuries in any depth soon becomes aware of his considerable historical heft. In literary terms, Cowley, like Philips, retained aspects of the metaphysical style—its extended metaphors, its interest in the metaphysics of united souls, its ideal of the poem as a "well-wrought urn" turned inward on itself—but eschewed its abrupt syntax, its sudden transitions, its difficult compression. Both cultivated a ready ease and grace in panegyric, though perhaps neither became so deft in this mode as their contemporary, Edmund Waller. Both poets tried in their way to fuse the examples of Donne and Jonson. And so both poets moved toward the neoclassical manner—the style of noble conservation that Pope heard from the mouth of Bolingbroke: "Correct with spirit, eloquent with ease, / Intent to reason, or polite to please."[8]

But they also passed on to the Augustan Age an updated, native English version of Horatian country virtue. Philips and Cowley teach us the essen-

7. Quoted in Thomas's "Biographical Note," p. 23.
8. *An Essay on Man*, IV.381–382.

tial prehistory of the eighteenth-century ideas at the heart of two of our most admired works of cultural history. They were early architects of the "retrospective radicalism" of Raymond Williams' *The Country and the City* and the "civic republicanism" of J. G. A. Pocock's *The Machiavellian Moment*.[9]

Love, Marriage, and Friendship

It would never have occurred to Aristotle to speak of friendship between women, because friendship was above all a response to the virtuous soul, and women did not have virtuous souls. But in the middle of the seventeenth century the platonized Christianity of Henry More and others stood ready to correct this classical mistake. Philips was firm on this matter, but not agitated. She does not appear to have anticipated serious resistance to the idea of female friendship conceived in Aristotelian and Ciceronian terms, and indeed, I know of no response to her work that questions the suitability of the classical friendship tradition for women. Philips devotes one stanza only to the subject:

> If souls no sexes have, for men t' exclude
> Women from friendship's vast capacity,
> Is a design injurious and rude,
> Onely maintain'd by partial tyranny.
> Love is allow'd to us, and Innocence,
> And noblest friendships doe proceed from thence.[1]

Precisely the same argument about sexless souls would lead to one of the clearest definitions of gender equality in the early eighteenth century. "Is 't probable there will be any sexes in Heaven?" *The Athenian Oracle* was asked, and the answer was no: "this difference is only accidental, men and women being in essence the same. But in a state of bliss and perfection, all that's imperfect or accidental shall be removed, and accordingly one would think sexes should."[2]

So the dignity of female friendship is not, for Philips, a particularly difficult victory. She spends a good deal more energy on the appropriate way to conceive the relationship among friendship, love, and marriage. Here, too, she touches the nerve of major change. For in her time, and in her class, the ancient hierarchical conception of marriage was mutating into companionate marriage—marriage as a friendship based on mutual respect for mutual virtues.[3]

In her several epithalamia Philips wishes for the brides a marriage able to evolve into friendship. She addresses her husband (called "Antenor") as a friend with whom her soul is joined ("To my dearest Antenor on his Parting"). Should friendship fail, marriage holds no prospect of success:

> Nobler than kindred or than marriage band,
> Because more free; wedlock felicity

9. For a remarkable attempt to synthesize these two accounts of high Augustanism, see William C. Dowling, *The Epistolary Moment* (Princeton: Princeton Univ. Press, 1991).
1. "A Friend," stz. 4. I believe that the first line of this stanza is misprinted in the Thomas edition.
2. *The Athenian Oracle*, 4 vols. (3rd ed.; London, 1728), 1:408.
3. See Lawrence Stone, *The Family, Sex, and Marriage in England 1500–1800* (New York: Harper & Row, 1977).

It self doth only by this Union stand,
And turns to friendship or to misery.
("A Friend")

Note that friendship is assumed to appear only after a marriage. Marriages, as she knew them, were made for diverse reasons, and some of these initial designs and interests might well preclude the evolution of a friendship:

All love is sacred, and the marriage ty
Hath much of Honour and divinity;
But lust, design, or some unworthy ends
May mingle there, which are despis'd by friends.
("Friendship")

Moreover, marriage is often the death-knell of prior friendships, as she confesses in an extraordinarily penetrating letter:

> I find too there are few Friendships in the World Marriage-proof; especially when the Person our Friend marries has not a Soul particularly capable of the Tenderness of that Endearment, and solicitous of advancing the noble Instances of it, as a Pleasure of their own, in others as well as themselves. And such a Temper is so rarely found, that we may generally conclude the Marriage of a Friend to be the Funeral of a Friendship; for then al former Endearments run naturally into the Gulf of that new and strict Relation, and there, like the Rivers in the Sea, they lose themselves for ever. This is indeed a lamentable Truth, and I have often study'd to find a Reason for it. Sometimes I think it is because we are in truth more ill-natur'd than we really take our selves to be; and more forgetful of the past Offices of Friendship, when they are superseded by others of a fresher Date, which carrying with them the Plausibility of more Duty and Religion in the Knot that ties them, we persuade our selves will excuse us if the Heat and Zeal of our former Friendships decline and wear off into Lukewarmness and Indifferency; whereas there is indeed a certain secret Meanness in our Souls, which mercenarily inclines our Affections to those with whom we must necessarily be oblig'd for the most part to converse, and from whom we expect the chiefest outward Conveniences.[4]

Things change. Two of her most treasured friendships were seriously damaged when the women arranged secret marriages.

Her pragmatic, case-by-case approach to companionate marriage—hopeful yet skeptical—contrasts with the tendency of male writers to decide the question in the realm of principle. For Montaigne and Robert Burton, for example, the passionate, sexual aspect of love precludes friendship of the Aristotelian kind.[5] On the other side of the question, Jeremy Taylor maintains that marriage is by its nature "the queen of friendships, in which there is a communication of all that can be communicated by friendship: and it being made sacred by vows and love, by bodies and souls, by interest and custom, by religion and by laws, by common counsels and common fortunes; it is the principal in the kind of friendship, and the

4. Patrick Thomas, ed., *The Collected Works of Katherine Philips*, Vol. 2: *The Letters* (Essex: Stump Cross Books, 1990), pp. 42–44.
5. Montaigne, "Of Friendship," in *The Complete Essays of Montaigne*, trans. Donald Frame (Stanford: Stanford Univ. Press, 1965), p. 137; Robert Burton, *The Anatomy of Melancholy*, ed. Floyd Dell and Paul Jordan-Smith (New York: Tudor Publishing, 1927), pp. 471–472.

measure of all the rest."[6] Robert Boyle's treatise on *Some Motives and Incentives to Love of God* is addressed to a friend who has fallen into a Petrarchan obsession with a disinterested mistress. He exhorts the man to acknowledge the superior value of friendship, which is the state of the angels, and indeed of the blessed in heaven.[7] Sir Thomas Browne, as we might expect, was not programmatic on the issue:

> I confess I do not observe that order that the Schools ordain our affections, to love our Parents, Wives, Children, and then our Friends; for excepting the injunctions of Religions, I do not find in my self such a necessary and indissoluble Sympathy to all those of my blood. I hope I do not break the fifth Commandment, if I conceive I may love my friend before the nearest of my blood, even those to whom I owe the principles of life: I never yet cast a true affection on a woman, but I have loved my friend as I do virtue, my soul, my God.[8]

Schools aside, commandments aside, Browne was as he was. But things change. He would later give up friendship for sex and marriage.

There were also poems on the relative merits of love and friendship. All of the ones I have been able to locate (by Thomas Stanley, James Shirley, John Denham, Rochester, and William Wycherley) take the side of friendship.[9] This genre surely expresses male resistance to the new idea of companionate marriage. Even William Habington, one of the most considerate male love poets of the century, respectful almost to a fault of his "Castara," includes in his sequence a prose character entitled "A Friend," which opens: "A friend is a man. For the free and open discovery of thoughts to woman can not passe without an ever licentious familiarity, or a justly occasion'd suspition: and friendship can neither stand with vice or infamie."[1] The male opponents of companionate marriage identify a little paradox in the conception of it. On the one hand, marriage is to be held a friendship, even, in Taylor's words, "the queen of friendships." Yet that very idea, especially in a platonic context, installs friendship as the idea or pattern of marriage—and to that degree gives it priority over marriage.

The pro-friendship poems avail themselves of the notion, found throughout the seventeenth-century love lyric, that sexual appetite cloys upon satisfaction. Orinda herself has several poems of this kind ("Against Pleasure," "Against Love," "A married State"). The fact is that Philips does in subtle ways make contact with the male love tradition. Most straightforwardly, she adapts its *topoi* to the sphere of female friendship. There are poems occasioned by the parting of friends, and by the absence of friends. There are even a few poems, notably "Injuria amici," "To Rosania (now Mrs Mountague)," and "Rosania to Lucasia on her Letters," that develop what may fairly be termed Petrarchan friendship, in which Orinda pleads her hapless ardor in the face of a friend's coolness or disdain. But

6. *A Discourse of the Nature, Offices, and Measures, of Friendship*, in *The Whole Works of the Right Rev. Jeremy Taylor*, 15 vols. (London: Ogle, Duncan, & Co., 1822), 11:325. See also the 5th Part of Thomas Stanley's *The History of Philosophy* (London: Humphrey Moseley and Thomas Dring, 1656), p. 84: "the amatory art is a kind of friendship."
7. *The Works of the Honourable Robert Boyle*, 6 vols. (London, 1772), 1:243–292.
8. *Religio Medici* 2.6, in *The Works of Sir Thomas Browne*, ed. Charles Sale, 3 vols. (Edinburgh: John Grant, 1912), 1:94.
9. Thomas Stanley, "To Mr. W. Hammond"; James Shirley, "Friendship, or Verses Sent to a Lover"; Sir John Denham, "Friendship and Single Life Against Love and Marriage"; Rochester, "Love a *Woman*! y'are an Ass"; William Wyncherley, "Upon Friendship, preferr'd to Love."
1. *Habington's Castara*, ed. Charles A. Elton (Bristol: J. M. Gutch, n.d.), p. 282.

her main success in making common cause with the male love tradition lies in her idiosyncratic use of that tradition's peculiar suspicion of what is also its distinct innovation: sexual consummation.

Jonson translated some telling lines from Pseudo-Petronius, and in the middle of the century they were translated again by John Oldham:

> I hate Fruition, now 'tis past,
> 'Tis all but nastiness at best;
> The homeliest thing, that man can do,
> Besides, 'tis short and fleeting too:
> A squirt of slippery Delight,
> That with a moment takes its flight. . . .
> But thus, let's thus together lie,
> And kiss out long Eternity:
> Here we dread no conscious spies,
> No blushes stain our guiltless Joys:
> Here no Faintness dulls Desires,
> And Pleasure never flags, nor tires:
> This has pleas'd, and pleases now,
> And for Ages will do so:
> Enjoyment here is never done,
> But fresh, and always but begun.[2]

The Jonson version, along with some lovingly evoked Catullan kisses elsewhere in his work, inspired countless kissing lyrics in the seventeenth century.[3] It also initiated a whole batch of "anti-fruition" poems playing with the idea that a perfected sexuality should be confined to foreplay. There were "pro-fruition" poems as well, answering step by step the arguments advanced by the anti-fruition lyrics.[4]

In this context, I think, we can appreciate the wittiness of a Philips poem like "An Answer to another persuading a Lady to Marriage":

> Forebear bold Youth, all's Heaven here,
>   And what you do aver.
> To others Courtship may appear,
>   'Tis Sacriledge to her.
>
> She is a publick Deity,
>   And were't not very odd
> She should depose her self to be
>   A petty Household God?

Ostensibly this is a feminist twist to the poems preferring friendship to love and marriage. The woman being courted by this rude youth must remain free, her divine grandeur available to the world, not debased and

2. Harold F. Brooks and Raman Selden, eds., *The Poems of John Oldham* (Oxford: Clarendon Press, 1987), pp. 215–216. Jonson's version, which opens "Doing, a filthy pleasure is, and short," may be found in George Parfitt, ed., *Ben Jonson: The Complete Poems* (New Haven: Yale Univ. Press, 1978), p. 251.
3. See my "Kiss Fancies in Robert Herrick" and "Milton's Kisses," in Stephen B. Dobranski and John P. Rumrich, *Milton and Heresy* (Cambridge: Cambridge Univ. Press, 1998), pp. 117–135.
4. Con: Suckling, "Anti-Fruition (1)," "Anti-Fruition (2)"; Cowley, "Against Fruition"; Henry King, "Paradox. That Fruition Destroys Love"; Robert Heath, "To Clarastella complaining of my long kisses"; Rochester, "The Platonick Lady." Pro: Waller, "In Answer of Sir John Suckling's Verses against Fruition"; Henry Bold, "For Fruition, In Answer to Sir John Suckling," "Another for Fruition, In Answer to Sir John Suckling"; Cleveland, "The Antiplatonick"; Cowley, "Platonick Love"; Wycherley, "For Fruition. To His Platonick Mistress."

sequestered in marriage. But the opening address to the "bold youth" oddly suffuses the argument with the feelings and attitudes of the anti-fruition debate. The best-known of these poems, Suckling's "Against Fruition (1)," also begins by restraining an over-eager youth: "Stay here fond youth and ask no more, be wise."[5] The speaker of Oldham's Pseudo-Petronius hates fruition "now 'tis past." Suckling would save him the trouble. He does not use the word "bold," but might have, as we learn from the pro-fruition reply to "Against Fruition (1)" by Henry Bold, who makes Suckling's fond youth into family: "*Go* on! *Bold boy!* and put her to 't, be *wise!*"[6] Without for a moment writing unchastely, Philips deepens her low estimate of courtship and marriage by allusion to male poetry's low estimate of sexual end-pleasure. This brilliant mixture of genres invests with profounder sense "'Tis Sacrilege to her," and makes it odd indeed that "She should depose her self" in becoming the object of a pleasure that will result in the debasement of her divinity. Cowley's "Against Fruition" in fact reproduces exactly the argument of Philips' lyric:

> Keep still thy distance; for at once to me
> *Goddess* and *Woman* too, thou canst not be;
> Thou'rt *Queen* of all that sees thee; and as such
> Must neither *Tyrannize*, nor *yield* too much.[7]

The anti-fruition genre also complicates one of Orinda's most philosophical poems, "To my Lucasia, in defence of declared friendship." As the poem opens, the two friends are apparently sitting together silently, and if the reader thinks of the staring, motionless lovers of Donne's "The Extasie," the lyric turns out to be aware of such associations, and seeks to make artistic capital of them. The speaker wants conversation: "O! my Lucasia, let us speak our love." We are, of course, already in the binary opposite to love: this is a poem of chaste friendship. But the desire for speech is implicitly equivalent to the desire for consummation in male love poetry, and before long the analogy between conversation and sexual satisfaction comes to the surface:

> Nay, to what end did we first barter minds,
> Only to know and to neglect the claim?
> Or (like some wanton) our pride pleasure finds
> To throw away the thing at which we aim.

They have spoken in the past. Is their current silence an analogue to the ruined pleasure following consummation in male love poetry? She goes on to compare the silence to miserliness, a metaphor we also find in the anti-fruition poems: "Fruition adds no new wealth, but destroyes," writes a Suckling reluctant to "spend." But at this point Orinda shifts from bad conceptions of their silence to good projections of their renewed conversation.

Previously her metaphors have been suggesting the pro-fruition side of the debate. Now she wittily adopts the anti-fruition argument, for conver-

5. *The Works of Sir John Suckling*, Vol. 1: *The Non-Dramatic Works*, ed. Thomas Clayton (Oxford: Clarendon Press, 1971), p. 37.
6. Henry Bold, "Another for Fruition, In Answer To Sir John Suckling," in *Poems Lyrique Macaronique Heroique* (London, 1664), quoted from the Chadwick-Healey Database. See also John Cleveland, "The Antiplatonick," 1.44, and Carew's "Boldness in Love."
7. *Poems*, p. 99.

sation is imagined, not as end-pleasure, but as foreplay, ever increasing like the splurging kisses at the end of Pseudo-Petronius:

> Think not 'tis needless to repeat desires;
> The fervent Turtles always court and bill,
> And yet their spotless passion never tires,
> But does increase by repetition still.

Joys "by motion multiply," like perpetually renewing Catullan kisses, and to elaborate on this idea Philips develops the conceit of a river flowing into the sea. Like river and sea, these friends have joined. But the river does not cease to be, and some of its waters repeatedly curl back "on its own waves," then repeatedly flow into the sea: so the soul of a friend bounces back and forth between union and separation, object and self, ever producing new joys through this "reflux." The poem began by implying that conversation must be like consummation, which may be why we're not doing it any more, then ends by proving that conversation must instead be like foreplay, which is why we should be doing it all the more.

I obviously do not agree with modern commentators who argue that female friendship in Philips "masks" an active, genital lesbianism.[8] As her editor points out, there is only one direct reference to touching in her friendship poems, and that in a lyric of doubtful attribution.[9] But I do think she was quite aware of an erotic component in same-sex friendship, and she expresses this perception with admirable literary skill.

Friendship Poetry

"It is the most satisfying experience in the world to have someone you can speak to as freely as your own self about any and every subject upon earth."[1] The supreme pleasure of friendship, which is itself the supreme pleasure, resides for Cicero in the exchange of confidences, of feelings and opinions ordinarily kept to oneself. As Francis Finch assured the Philips circle, friendship is "secret."[2] The unpardonable crimes in friendship, according to Jeremy Taylor, are a treacherous blow and the revealing of a secret: "in the matters of friendship, which is the marriage of souls, these are the proper causes of divorce: and therefore I shall add this only, that secrecy is the chastity of friendship, and the publication of it is a prostitution and direct debauchery" (332). Philips, too, cherishes the rapture of full disclosure, conversing with another "as freely as your own self." The ideal letter from a friend is as "undisguis'd as thought" ("Parting with a Friend"). The union between two friends stems from this doubled honesty:

> Whose well acquainted minds are now as near
> As Love, or vows, or secrets can endear.
> I have no thought but what's to thee reveal'd,
> Nor thou desire that is from me conceal'd.

8. For example, Arlene Stiebel, " 'Not Since Sappho': The Erotic in Poems of Katherine Philips and Aphra Behn," in Claude J. Summers, ed., *Homosexuality in Renaissance and Enlightenment England: Literary Representations in Historical Context* (New York: Haworth Press, 1992), pp. 153–172, finds the poems "clearly erotic" (154). My own position on this question is that of Harriette Andreadis, "The Sapphic-Platonics of Katherine Philips, 1632–1664," *Signs* 15.1 (1989): 34–60.
9. Thomas, Poems, p. 398.
1. "Laelius: On Friendship," in Cicero, *On the Good Life*, trans. Michael Grant, p. 188.
2. Hiscock, p. 467.

Thy heart locks up my secrets richly set,
And my breast is thy private cabinet.
("L'amitié")

Friendship doth carry more than common trust
And treachery is here the greatest Sin:
Secrets deposed then none ever must
Presume to open, but who put them in.
They that in one Chest lay up all their stock,
Had need be sure that none can pick the lock.
("A Friend")

What are the consequences of this concealment for friendship poetry?

One can imagine a private poetry between two friends that could exemplify such absolute forthcomingness. But poetry meant to be read by anyone outside the friendship must necessarily keep its confidences secret, since otherwise the poems would be not a celebration of friendship but a betrayal of it. The poet of friendship chooses a subject whose deepest pleasure cannot be revealed to the reader in any detail whatsoever. It is by its nature a poetry of absence and generalization, proclaiming the virtue of a friend whose character cannot finally be specified and an intimacy whose value cannot finally be demonstrated. The bond of candor between author and reader is not so profound as the bond of candor between friends. There does not appear to be any way to circumvent this problem. Even if one leaps ahead through the centuries to our own age, where the imperative to confess may trump the ethic of secrecy in friendship, one is still inclined to think of such authors as spiteful and self-centered. They are literary opportunists, not friends.

But there are ways around most things, and this is no exception. The author of friendship poetry can, for example, be relatively candid about himself, and in that way convey to the reader the real stuff of friendship, the warmth of it, the actual feel of intimacy with him. Such was the manner adopted by Ben Jonson, the first great English poet to place male friendship at the center of his work.

"Inviting a Friend to Supper" is exemplary. About half way through the poem, when describing the bill of fare, Jonson admits that his main desire is to have his verse invitation accepted: "I'll tell you of more, and lie, so you will come." It is a confidence: he lies. This particular lie is a flattering one, no doubt, but his candor sets us thinking. He lies. He lies to manipulate friends. Does he lie about other things? A servant will read some classical author "Of which we'll speak our minds, amidst our meat; / And I'll profess no verses to repeat." The piece of ordinary language that is "speak our minds" comes entirely to life here, for this is to be a gathering of friends, and speaking their minds is precisely what friends do. But Jonson does not always speak his mind. He lies, and he lies in the next line. Through the magic of tone, simply because he writes "I'll profess no verses to repeat" rather than, say, "I will repeat no verses," we know immediately that the professing poet is lying. Charmingly, to be sure, for who would want to dine with Ben Jonson and not hear him recite verses? But now we know that he lies, not only to manipulate friends, but to conceal his literary vanity, his autocratic desire to have his verses heard and admired. But he also lies to reveal that vanity: self-esteem has been offered up as a topic for conversation. It will be all right to twit him about it. Twitting him about it belongs to friendship with him. The poem ends with a beautiful definition of ideal conversation during ideal drinking, both ideals a balance of liberty and restraint:

> Nor shall our cups make any guilty men:
> But, at our parting, we will be, as when
> We innocently met. No simple word,
> That shall be uttered at our mirthful board,
> Shall make us sad next morning: or affright
> The liberty, that we'll enjoy tonight.

This sounds like, and is, serious business, but we have been schooled by the poem to understand that guarding this balance will surely involve lies and jokes.

We find a convivial engagement with Jonson's vanity in some of the poems addressed to him by the Sons of Ben. Carew for instance, in one of many lyrics answering Jonson's bitter ode ("Come leave the loathed stage") occasioned by the failure of *The New Inn*: "The wiser world doth greater Thee confesse / Than all men else, than Thy selfe onely less." The wise esteem Jonson greater than all other men, which is still less than his own self-estimate. But few other friendship poets were able to put their foibles and shortcomings into play as powerfully as Jonson. Herrick tries two imitations of "Inviting a Friend to Supper," one of them a burlesque ("The Invitation"). These lines from "A Panegyric to Sir Lewis Pemberton" represent a more serious try:

> No man that's there his guilty glass
> Drinks of distemper, or has cause to cry
> Repentance to his liberty.

But this doesn't have it. The ideal of good conversation drops out, and Herrick focuses on the relatively charmless subject of how much should be drunk, how much left undrunk. Good imitations of the poem are in fact rare. I know of nothing up to the challenge until Thom Gunn's "An Invitation," which concludes superbly:

> And while food lasts, and after it is gone,
> We'll talk, without a TV on,
> We'll talk of all our luck and lack of luck,
> Of the foul job in which you're stuck,
> Of friends, of the estranged and of the dead
> Or living relatives instead,
> Of what we've done and seen and thought and read,
> Until we talk ourselves to bed.[3]

Here, as in Jonson, utopian conversation is not just defined, but invited, and the charmed reader, eager for what Cicero called "the most satisfying experience in this world," really wants to come to dinner.

Philips is never able to transform her readers, in however illusory a way, into friends. She never offers up her faults and vanities as topics of conversation. She is the philosopher of unions that remain wholly con-

3. Thom Gunn, *Collected Poems* (New York: Farrar Straus Giroux, 1994), p. 412. The poem is addressed to his brother Ander Gunn, the photographer.

cealed from the reader. The element of secrecy inherent in friendship poetry gives her verse a somewhat arid, undramatic, marmoreal, theoretical character about which critics have often complained. But of course much of what I have said about friendship as a literary subject could as well be said of love, which also has its clandestine world of intimacies. Do we know, as we know people in our lives, the lovers of "The Canonization"? Of course not: their real love is forever concealed within the well-wrought urn of Donne's great poem; all we can ever know is its pattern or idea. The good reader of friendship poetry must discipline curiosity, must learn to feel something other than impatience in the presence of its veiled rapture.

Waller's "On the Friendship betwixt Two Ladies" is instructive:

Tell me, Lovely loving pair,
  Why so kind, and so severe?
Why so careless of our Care,
  Only to your selves so dear?

By this cunning change of Hearts,
  You the pow'r of Love control;
While the Boy's deluded Darts
  Can arrive at neither Soul.

For in vain to either Breast
  Still beguilèd Love does come;
Where he finds a Foreign Guest,
  Neither of your Hearts at home.

Debtors thus with like design,
  When they never mean to pay;
That they may the Law decline,
  To some Friend make all away.

Not the silver Doves that fly,
  Yok'd in *Citharea's* Car;
Not the Wings that lift so high,
  And convey her Son so far,

Are so Lovely, Sweet, and Fair,
  Or do more ennoble Love;
Are so choicely matched a Pair,
  Or with more Consent do move.

It is as if two poems have been glued together with no transition. For four stanzas the very loveliness of the friends spawns the irritation that they are unavailable to male advances. Private, wholly intent on each other, they cannot be seduced. Suddenly, in the last two stanzas, the speaker abandons his role as the would-be destroyer of this "loving Pair." Now he champions their achievement in friendship: they are lovelier, sweeter, fairer, nobler, and their movements more perfectly synchronized than the doves of Venus. Waller, it is clear from the first four stanzas, courts women. He bears with him the entire ethos of the male love tradition in his day. But in the end this tradition can pay tribute to female friendship, can enfold and preserve it in a panegyric language already broached by Shakespeare: "And wheresoe'er we went, like Juno's swans, / Still we went coupled and inseparable," Celia says of her friendship with Rosalind in *As You Like It*.[4] One need only get over one's exclusion from it.

In that sense, I think, the lyric is helpful to readers of Orinda's friendship poetry. Philips is not Ben Jonson—or Carew, or Suckling. She is not convivial. Her reader is not her friend. She keeps her secrets. She is, like Donne, self-enwound, the creator of a two-sided language that addresses us while constantly referring to a precious interior hidden from our view. We have the idea only, and that should be enough to demand, if not our love or friendship, then our respect.

4. *As You Like It*, 1.3.75–76. For Shakespeare's version of some of themes explored in this essay—female friendship, the conflict between friendship and marriage—see my "Female Friends and Fraternal Enemies in *As You Like It*," in Valeria Finucci and Regina Schwartz, eds., *Desire in the Renaissance* (Princeton: Princeton Univ. Press, 1994), pp. 184–206.

Select Bibliography

The literature on the history, culture, and poetry of seventeenth-century England is enormous: comprehensive bibliographies of individual topics or poets—Donne, Jonson, Herbert, Milton, and Marvell, in particular—fill volumes of their own. Thus we have provided a select bibliography that highlights major studies and recent contributions. Our Jonson bibliography does not touch on his work as a playwright or as a composer of masques. Our Milton, Dryden, and Cavendish bibliographies focus on their early poetry and not on their efforts in other genres or their later poetry. Students of particular poets should always attend to the general studies of the period as well: Carew, Suckling, Lovelace, and many of the minor figures in this volume are rarely studied alone, but rather they frequently appear in book-length studies of specific themes, genres, or topics.

Major journals that publish articles on early seventeenth-century literature include *English Literary Renaissance* (ELR); *Studies in English Literature, 1500–1900* (SEL); *English Literary History* (ELH); *Modern Philology*; *Renaissance Studies*; *Texas Studies in Literature and Language* (TSLL); and *Representations*. Journals that specifically target the period include *The Seventeenth Century*, *Seventeenth Century News*, *The John Donne Journal*, *The George Herbert Journal*, *The Ben Jonson Journal*, *Milton Studies*, and *Milton Quarterly*.

• indicates a work included or excerpted in this Norton Critical Edition.

Historical and Cultural Background

Amussen, Susan Dwyer. *An Ordered Society: Gender and Class in Early Modern England*. New York: Columbia UP, 1988.

Appleby, Joyce Oldham. *Economic Thought and Ideology in Seventeenth-Century England*. Princeton: Princeton UP, 1978.

Bray, Alan. *Homosexuality in Renaissance England*. London: Gay Men's Press, 1982.

Fraser, Antonia. *The Weaker Vessel: Woman's Lot in Seventeenth-Century England*. London: Methuen, 1985.

Hall, Rupert. *The Scientific Revolution, 1500–1800*. New York: Longman, 1954.

Henderson, Katherine U., and Barbara F. McManus, eds. *Half Humankind: Contexts and Texts of the Controversy about Women in England, 1540–1640*. Urbana: U of Illinois P, 1985.

Hill, Christopher. *The Century of Revolution, 1603–1714*. 2nd ed. New York: Norton, 1980.

———. *The World Turned Upside Down: Radical Ideas during the English Revolution*. London: Maurice Temple Smith, 1972.

———. *The Collected Essays of Christopher Hill, Vol. II: Religion and Politics in 17th Century England*. Amherst: U of Massachusetts P, 1986.

Hirst, Derek. *England in Conflict, 1603–1660: Kingdom, Community, Commonwealth*. London: Arnold, 1999.

Holstun, James. *Ehud's Dagger: Class Struggle in the English Revolution*. New York: Verso, 2000.

Houlbrooke, Ralph A. *The English Family 1450–1700*. London: Longman, 1984.

Kishlansky, Mark. *A Monarchy Transformed: Britain 1603–1714*. Harmondsworth: Penguin, 1996.

MacFarlane, Alan. *The Family Life of Ralph Josselin, a Seventeenth-Century Clergyman*. New York: Norton, 1977.

Parry, Graham. *The Seventeenth Century: The Intellectual and Cultural Context of English Literature, 1603–1700*. London: Longman, 1989.

Russell, Conrad. *The Causes of the English Civil War*. Oxford: Clarendon, 1990.
Shea, William R. *Galileo's Intellectual Revolution*. London: Macmillan, 1972.
Shumaker, Wayne. *The Occult Sciences in the Renaissance*. Berkeley: U of California P, 1972.
Sommerville, J. P. *Politics and Ideology in England, 1603–1640*. London: Longman, 1986.
Stone, Lawrence. *The Crisis of the Aristocracy 1558–1641*. Abr. ed. Oxford: Oxford UP, 1967.
———. *The Causes of the English Revolution*. London: Routledge and Kegan Paul, 1972.
———. *The Family, Sex, and Marriage in England 1500–1800*. Abr. ed. New York: Harper, 1979.
Thomas, Keith. *Religion and the Decline of Magic*. London: Weidenfeld and Nicolson, 1971.
Tillyard, E. M. W. *The Elizabethan World Picture*. London: Chatto and Windus, 1943.
Trevor-Roper, H. R. *Catholics, Anglicans and Puritans: Seventeenth Century Essays*. London: Secker and Warburg, 1987.
Underdown, David. *Revel, Riot, and Rebellion: Popular Politics and Culture in England 1603–1660*. Oxford: Oxford UP, 1985.
———. *Fire from Heaven: Life in an English Town in the Seventeenth Century*. New Haven: Yale UP, 1992.
Wrightson, Keith. *English Society 1580–1680*. New Brunswick: Rutgers UP, 1982.

Literary History and Criticism: General

Alvarez, A. *The School of Donne*. London: Chatto and Windus, 1961.
Anselment, Raymond A. *Loyalist Resolve: Patient Fortitude in the English Civil War*. Newark: U of Delaware P, 1988.
Bush, Douglas. *English Literature in the Earlier Seventeenth Century 1600–1660*. 2nd ed. New York: Oxford, 1962.
Colie, Rosalie. *The Resources of Kind: Genre-Theory in the Renaissance*. Berkeley: U of California P, 1973.
Corns, Thomas N. *Uncloistered Virtue: English Political Literature, 1640–1660*. Oxford: Clarendon, 1992.
Dickson, Donald R. *The Fountain of Living Waters: The Typology of the Waters of Life in Herbert, Vaughan, and Traherne*. Columbia: U of Missouri P, 1987.
Enterline, Lynn. *The Tears of Narcissus: Melancholia and Masculinity in Early Modern Writing*. Stanford: Stanford UP, 1995.
Estrin, Barbara L. *Laura: Uncovering Gender and Genre in Wyatt, Donne, and Marvell*. Durham: Duke UP, 1994.
Goldberg, Jonathan. *James I and the Politics of Literature: Jonson, Shakespeare, Donne, and Their Contemporaries*. Baltimore: John Hopkins UP, 1983.
Guibbory, Achsah. *The Map of Time: Seventeenth-Century English Literature and Ideas of Pattern in History*. Urbana: U of Illinois P, 1986.
———. *Ceremony and Community from Herbert to Milton: Literature, Religion, and Cultural Conflict in Seventeenth-Century England*. Cambridge: Cambridge UP, 1998.
• Hammond, Gerald. *Fleeting Things: English Poets and Poems, 1616–1660*. Cambridge: Harvard UP, 1990.
Harvey, Elizabeth D., and Katherine Eisaman Maus, eds. *Soliciting Interpretation: Literary Theory and Seventeenth-Century English Poetry*. Chicago: Chicago UP, 1990.
Healy, Thomas, and Jonathan Sawday, eds. *Literature and the English Civil War*. Cambridge: Cambridge UP, 1990.
Hollander, John. *The Untuning of the Sky: Ideas of Music in English Poetry 1500–1700*. New York: Norton, 1970.
Holstun, James. "'Will you rent our ancient love asunder?' Lesbian Elegy in Donne, Marvell, and Milton." *ELH* 54:4 (1987): 835–867.
Kerrigan, William, and Gordon Braden. "Petrarch Refracted: The Evolution of the English Love Lyric." *The Idea of the Renaissance*. Baltimore: Johns Hopkins UP, 1989. 157–189.
Lewalski, Barbara K. *Protestant Poetics and the Seventeenth-Century Religious Lyric*. Princeton: Princeton UP, 1979.
Low, Anthony. *Love's Architecture: Devotional Modes in Seventeeth-Century English Poetry*. New York: New York UP, 1978.
———. *The Georgic Revolution*. Princeton: Princeton UP, 1985.
———. *The Reinvention of Love: Poetry, Politics and Culture from Sidney to Milton*. Cambridge: Cambridge UP, 1993.
MacLean, Gerald F. *Time's Witness: Historical Representation in English Poetry, 1603–1660*. Madison: U of Wisconsin P, 1990.
• Marcus, Leah S. *Childhood and Cultural Despair: A Theme and Variations in Seventeenth-Century Literature*. Pittsburgh: U of Pittsburgh P, 1978.
———. *The Politics of Mirth: Jonson, Herrick, Milton, Marvell, and the Defense of Old Holiday Pastimes*. Chicago: U of Chicago P, 1986.
Martz, Louis L. *The Poetry of Meditation*. New Haven: Yale UP, 1954.
———. *The Paradise Within: Studies in Vaughan, Traherne, and Milton*. New Haven: Yale UP, 1964.
McClung, William A. *The Country House in English Renaissance Poetry*. Berkeley: U of California P, 1977.
McColley, Diane. *Poetry and Music in Seventeenth-Century England*. Cambridge: Cambridge UP, 1997.
Miner, Earl. *The Metaphysical Mode from Donne to Cowley*. Princeton: Princeton UP, 1969.
• ———. *The Cavalier Mode from Jonson to Cotton*. Princeton: Princeton UP, 1971.

Nevo, Ruth. *The Dial of Virtue: A Study of Poems on Affairs of State in the Seventeenth Century*. Princeton: Princeton UP, 1963.
Norbrook, David. *Writing the English Republic: Poetry, Rhetoric and Politics, 1627–1660*. Cambridge: Cambridge UP, 1999.
Parfitt, George. *English Poetry of the Seventeenth Century*. New York: Longman, 1985.
Patterson, Annabel. *Censorship and Interpretation: The Conditions of Writing in Early Modern England*. Madison: U of Wisconsin P, 1984.
• Post, Jonathan F. S., ed. *Green Thoughts, Green Shades: Essays by Contemporary Poets on the Early Modern Lyric*. Berkeley: U of California P, 2002.
Potter, Lois. *Secret Rites and Secret Writing: Royalist Literature, 1641–1660*. Cambridge: Cambridge UP, 1989.
Rambuss, Richard. *Closet Devotions*. Durham: Duke UP, 1998.
Richmond, Hugh. *The School of Love: The Evolution of the Stuart Love Lyric*. Princeton: Princeton UP, 1964.
Røstvig, Maren-Sofie. *The Happy Man: A Study in the Metamorphosis of a Classical Idea*. 2 Vols. Oslo: Scandinavian UP, 1954–1958.
———. *Configurations: A Topomorphical Approach to Renaissance Poetry*. New York: Oxford UP, 1994.
Scodel, Joshua. *Excess and the Mean in Early Modern English Literature*. Princeton: Princeton UP, 2002.
Seelig, Sharon Cadman. *The Shadow of Eternity: Belief and Structure in Herbert, Vaughan and Traherne*. Lexington: UP of Kentucky, 1981.
Sharpe, Kevin, ed. *Criticism and Compliment: The Politics of Literature in the England of Charles I*. Cambridge: Cambridge UP, 1987.
Sharpe, Kevin, and Steven N. Zwicker, eds. *Politics of Discourse: The Literature and History of Seventeenth-Century England*. Berkeley: U of California P, 1987.
Shifflett, Andrew. *Stoicism, Politics, and Literature in the Age of Milton*. Cambridge: Cambridge UP, 1998.
Smith, Nigel. *Literature and Revolution in England, 1640–1660*. New Haven: Yale UP, 1994.
Stachniewski, John. *The Persecutory Imagination: English Puritanism and the Literature of Religious Despair*. Oxford: Clarendon, 1991.
Summers, Claude J., and Ted-Larry Pebworth, eds. *Classic and Cavalier: Essays on Jonson and the Sons of Ben*. Pittsburgh: U of Pittsburgh P, 1982.
———. *"The Muses Common-Weale": Poetry and Politics in the Seventeenth Century*. Columbia: U of Missouri P, 1988.
Summers, Joseph H. *The Heirs of Donne and Jonson*. Oxford: Oxford UP, 1970.
Turner, James. *The Politics of Landscape: Rural Scenery and Society in English Poetry 1630–1660*. Cambridge: Harvard UP, 1979.
Wedgwood, C. V. *Poetry and Politics under the Stuarts*. Cambridge: Cambridge UP, 1960.
Wilding, Michael. *Dragon's Teeth: Literature in the English Revolution*. Oxford: Clarendon, 1987.
• Williams, Raymond. *The Country and the City*. New York: Oxford UP, 1973.
Young, R. V. *Doctrine and Devotion in Seventeenth-Century Poetry: Studies in Donne, Herbert, Crashaw, and Vaughan*. Cambridge: Brewer, 2000.

Literary Criticism: Individual Authors

AEMILIA LANYER

Grossman, Marshall, ed. *Aemilia Lanyer: Gender, Genre, and the Canon*. Lexington: UP of Kentucky, 1998.
Hodgson, Elizabeth M. A. "Prophecy and Gendered Mourning in Lanyer's *Salve Deus Rex*." *Studies in English Literature* 43:1 (2003): 101–116.
Lewalski, Barbara K. "Imagining Female Community: Aemilia Lanyer's Poems." *Writing Women in Jacobean England*. Cambridge: Harvard UP, 1993. 213–241.
McBride, Kari Boyd. "Remembering Orpheus in the Poems of Aemilia Lanyer." *Studies in English Literature* 38:1 (1998): 87–108.
Ng, Su Fang. "Aemilia Lanyer and the Politics of Praise." *ELH* 67:2 (2000): 433–451.
Phillippy, Patricia. "Sisters of Magdalen: Women's Mourning in Aemilia Lanyer's *Salve Deus Rex Judaeorum*." *English Literary Renaissance* 31:1 (2001): 78–106.
Rogers, John. "The Passion of a Female Literary Tradition: Aemilia Lanyer's *Salve Deus Rex Judaeorum*." *Huntington Library Quarterly* 63:4 (2000): 435–446.
Seelig, Sharon Cadman. " 'To All Vertuous Ladies in Generall': Aemilia Lanyer's Community of Strong Women." *Literary Circles and Cultural Communities in Renaissance England*. Ed. Claude Summers and Ted-Larry Pebworth. Columbia: U of Missouri P, 2000. 44–58.
Woods, Susanne, ed. *Salve Deus Rex Judaeorum*. New York: Oxford UP, 1993.
———. "Aemilia Lanyer and Ben Jonson: Patronage, Authority, and Gender." *The Ben Jonson Journal* 1 (1994): 15–30.

JOHN DONNE

Andreasen, N. J. C. *John Donne, Conservative Revolutionary*. Princeton: Princeton UP, 1967.
Bald, R. C. *John Donne: A Life*. Oxford: Clarendon, 1970.
Carey, John. *John Donne: Life, Mind, Art*. Oxford: Oxford UP, 1981.

Corthell, Ronald. *Ideology and Desire in Renaissance Poetry: The Subject of Donne*. Detroit: Wayne State UP, 1997.

Empson, Sir William. *Essays on Renaissance Literature: Donne and the New Philosophy*. Cambridge: Cambridge UP, 1993.

Fish, Stanley. "Masculine Persuasive Force: Donne and Verbal Power." *Soliciting Interpretation*. Ed. Elizabeth D. Harvey and Katherine Eisaman Maus. Chicago: Chicago UP, 1990. 223–252.

Flynn, Dennis. *John Donne and the Ancient Catholic Nobility*. Bloomington: Indiana UP, 1995.

Guibbory, Achsah. "'Oh, let mee not serve so': The Politics of Love in Donne's Elegies." *ELH* 57 (1990): 811–833.

Hester, M. Thomas. *Kind Pitty and Brave Scorne: John Donne's Satyres*. Durham: Duke UP, 1982.

Lewalski, Barbara K. *Donne's "Anniversaries" and the Poetry of Praise: The Creation of Symbolic Mode*. Princeton: Princeton UP, 1973.

Marotti, Arthur F. *John Donne, Coterie Poet*. Madison: U of Wisconsin P, 1986.

Mueller, Janel. "Troping Utopia: Donne's Brief for Lesbianism." *Sexuality and Gender in Early Modern Europe: Institutions, Texts, Images*. Ed. James Grantham Turner. Cambridge: Cambridge UP, 1993. 182–207.

Norbrook, David. "The Monarchy of Wit and the Republic of Letters: Donne's Politics." *Soliciting Interpretation*. Ed. Elizabeth D. Harvey and Katherine Eisaman Maus. Chicago: Chicago UP, 1990. 3–36.

Patterson, Annabel. "All Donne." *Soliciting Interpretation*. Ed. Elizabeth D. Harvey and Katherine Eisaman Maus. Chicago: Chicago UP, 1990. 37–67.

Stachniewski, John. "John Donne: The Despair of the 'Holy Sonnets.'" *ELH* 48 (1981): 677–705.

Strier, Richard. "Essay 6. Impossible Radicalism I: Donne and Freedom of Conscience." *Resistant Structures: Particularity, Radicalism, and Renaissance Texts*. Berkeley: U of California P, 1995. 118–164.

Summers, Claude J., and Ted-Larry Pebworth, eds. *The Eagle and the Dove: Reassessing John Donne*. Columbia: U of Missouri P, 1986.

Tayler, Edward W. *Donne's Idea of a Woman: Structure and Meaning in* The Anniversaries. New York: Columbia UP, 1991.

Young, R. V. "Donne's Holy Sonnets and the Theology of Grace." *"Bright Shootes of Everlastingnesse": The Seventeenth-Century Religious Lyric*. Ed. Claude Summers and Ted-Larry Pebworth. Columbia: U of Missouri P, 1987. 20–39.

BEN JONSON

Evans, Robert C. *Ben Jonson and the Poetics of Patronage*. Lewisburg, PA: Bucknell UP, 1989.

Fish, Stanley. "Authors-Readers: Jonson's Community of the Same." *Representations* 7 (1984): 26–58.

Greene, Thomas M. "Ben Jonson and the Centered Self." *Studies in English Literature* 10 (1970): 325–348.

Helgerson, Richard. *Self-Crowned Laureates: Spenser, Jonson, Milton and the Literary System*. Berkeley: U of California P, 1983.

Kay, W. David. *Ben Jonson: A Literary Life*. New York: St. Martin's, 1995.

Marotti, Arthur F. "All about Jonson's Poetry." *ELH* 39 (1972): 208–237.

Maus, Katharine Eisaman. *Ben Jonson and the Roman Frame of Mind*. Princeton: Princeton UP, 1984.

Norbrook, David. "Jonson and the Jacobean Peace, 1603–1616." *Poetry and Politics in the English Renaissance*. Rev. ed. Oxford: Oxford UP, 2002. 155–172.

Peterson, Richard S. *Imitation and Praise in the Poems of Ben Jonson*. New Haven: Yale UP, 1981.

Riggs, David. *Ben Jonson: A Life*. Cambridge: Harvard UP, 1989.

Van den Berg, Sara J. *The Action of Ben Jonson's Poetry*. Newark: U of Delaware P, 1987.

Wayne, Don E. *Penshurst: The Semiotics of Place and the Poetics of History*. Madison: U of Wisconsin P, 1984.

LADY MARY WROTH

Dubrow, Heather. *Echoes of Desire: English Petrarchism and Its Counterdiscourses*. Ithaca: Cornell UP, 1995.

Fienberg, Nona. "Mary Wroth's Poetics of the Self." *Studies in English Literature* 42:1 (2002): 121–136.

Lewalski, Barbara K. "Revising Genres and Claiming the Woman's Part: Mary Wroth's *Oeuvre*." *Writing Women in Jacobean England*. Cambridge: Harvard UP, 1993. 243–307.

Miller, Naomi J. "Rewriting Lyric Fictions: The Role of the Lady in Lady Mary Wroth's *Pamphilia to Amphilanthus*." *The Renaissance Englishwoman in Print: Counterbalancing the Canon*. Ed. Anne M. Haselkorn and Betty S. Travitsky. Amherst: U of Massachusetts P, 1990. 295–310.

———. *Changing the Subject: Mary Wroth and Figurations of Gender in Early Modern England*. Lexington: UP of Kentucky, 1996.

Miller, Naomi J., and Gary Waller, eds. *Reading Mary Wroth: Representing Alternatives in Early Modern England*. Knoxville: U of Tennessee P, 1991.

Quilligan, Maureen. "The Constant Subject: Instability and Authority in Wroth's Urania Poems." *Soliciting Interpretation*. Ed. Elizabeth D. Harvey and Katherine Eisaman Maus. Chicago: Chicago UP, 1990. 307–335.

Roberts, Josephine A., ed. *The Poems of Lady Mary Wroth*. Baton Rouge: Louisiana State UP, 1983.

Waller, Gary. *The Sidney Family Romance: Mary Wroth, William Herbert, and the Early Modern Construction of Gender*. Detroit: Wayne State UP, 1993.

———. "Good Boys, Mad Girls: Greville, Sidney, Wroth, and the (Re)Construction of Gender in Early Modern England." *Sidney Journal* 19:1–2 (2001): 41–61.

ROBERT HERRICK

Braden, Gordon. *The Classics and English Renaissance Poetry: Three Case Studies*. New Haven: Yale UP, 1978.

Chute, Marchette. *Two Gentle Men: The Lives of George Herbert and Robert Herrick*. New York: Dutton, 1959.

Coiro, Ann Baynes. *Robert Herrick and the Epigram Book Tradition*. Baltimore: John Hopkins UP, 1988.

———, ed. *Robert Herrick*. Spec. issue of *The George Herbert Journal* 14:1–2 (1989–1990).

Deming, Robert H. *Ceremony and Art: Robert Herrick's Poetry*. The Hague: Mouton, 1974.

DeNeef, A. Leigh. *'This Poetick Liturgie': Robert Herrick's Ceremonial Mode*. Durham: Duke UP, 1974.

Moroney, Maryclaire. "Recent Studies in Herrick (1972–1997)." *English Literary Renaissance* 29:1 (1999): 154–176.

Swann, Marjorie. "The Politics of Fairylore in Early Modern English Literature." *Renaissance Quarterly* 53:2 (2000): 449–473.

———. *Curiosities and Texts: The Culture of Collecting in Early Modern England*. Philadelphia: U of Pennsylvania P, 2001.

Rollin, Roger B. *Robert Herrick*. Rev. ed. New York: Twayne, 1992.

Rollin, Roger B., and J. Max Patrick, eds. *Trust to Good Verses: Herrick Tercentenary Essays*. Pittsburgh: U of Pittsburgh P, 1977.

GEORGE HERBERT

Benet, Diana. *Secretary of Praise. The Poetic Vocation of George Herbert*. Columbia: U of Missouri P, 1984.

Braden, Gordon. "Unspeakable Love: Petrarch to Herbert." *Soliciting Interpretation*. Ed. Elizabeth D. Harvey and Katherine Eisaman Maus. Chicago: Chicago UP, 1990. 253–272.

Charles, Amy M. *A Life of George Herbert*. Ithaca: Cornell UP, 1977.

Fish, Stanley. *The Living Temple: George Herbert and Catechizing*. Berkeley: U of California P, 1978.

Harman, Barbara Leah. *Costly Monuments: Representations of the Self in George Herbert's Poetry*. Cambridge: Harvard UP, 1982.

Hodgkins, Christopher. *Authority, Church, and Society in George Herbert: Return to the Middle Way*. Columbia: U of Missouri P, 1993.

Malcolmson, Cristina. *Heart-Work: George Herbert and the Protestant Ethic*. Stanford: Stanford UP, 1999.

Pahlka, William H. *Saint Augustine's Meter and George Herbert's Will*. Kent: Kent State UP, 1987.

Roberts, John R. *George Herbert: An Annotated Bibliography of Modern Criticism, 1905–1984*. Columbia: U of Missouri P, 1988.

Schoenfeldt, Michael C. *Prayer and Power: George Herbert and Renaissance Courtship*. Chicago: U of Chicago P, 1991.

Sherwood, Stanley. *Herbert's Prayerful Art*. Toronto: U of Toronto P, 1989.

Strier, Richard. *Love Known: Theology and Experience in George Herbert's Poetry*. Chicago: U of Chicago P, 1983.

———. "Tradition." *Resistant Structures: Particularity, Radicalism, and Renaissance Texts*. Berkeley: U of California P, 1995. 13–26.

———. "Impossible Worldliness: 'Devout Humanism.'" *Resistant Structures: Particularity, Radicalism, and Renaissance Texts*. 83–108.

• Summers, Joseph H. *George Herbert: His Religion and Art*. Cambridge; Harvard UP, 1954.

Tuve, Rosemond. *A Reading of George Herbert*. Chicago: U of Chicago P, 1952.

Vendler, Helen. *The Poetry of George Herbert*. Cambridge: Harvard UP, 1975.

THOMAS CAREW

Altieri, Joanne. "Responses to a Waning Mythology in Carew's Political Poetry." *Studies in English Literature* 26:1 (1986): 107–124.

Ezell, Margaret J. M. "Thomas Carew and the Erotic Law of Nature." *Explorations in Renaissance Culture* 14 (1988): 99–114.

Hannaford, Renée. "'My Unwashed Muse': Sexual Play and Sociability in Carew's 'A Rapture.'" *English Language Notes* 27:1 (1989): 32–39.

King, Bruce. "The Strategy of Carew's Wit." *Review of English Literature* 5 (1964): 42–51.

Low, Anthony. "Thomas Carew: Patronage, Family, and New-Model Love." *Renaissance Discourses of Desire*. Ed. Claude Summers and Ted-Larry Pebworth. Columbia: U of Missouri P, 1993. 93–106.

McGuire, Mary Ann C. "The Cavalier Country-House Poem: Mutations on a Jonsonian Tradition." *Studies in English Literature* 19:1 (1979): 93–108.

Nixon, Scott. "Carew's Response to Jonson and Donne." *Studies in English Literature* 39:1 (1999): 89–109.
Parker, Michael P. "Carew's Politic Pastoral: Virgilian Pretexts in the 'Answer to Aurelian Townsend.'" *John Donne Journal* 1:1–2 (1982): 101–116.
Sadler, Lynn. *Thomas Carew*. Boston: Twayne, 1979.
Selig, Edward. *The Flourishing Wreath: A Study of Thomas Carew*. New Haven: Yale UP, 1958.

EDMUND WALLER

Alison, A. W. *Toward an Augustan Poetic: Edmund Waller's 'Reform' of English Poetry*. Lexington: U of Kentucky P, 1962.
Chambers, A. B. *Andrew Marvell and Edmund Waller: Seventeenth-Century Praise and Restoration Satire*. University Park: Pennsylvania State UP, 1991.
Chernaik, W. L. *The Poetry of Limitation*. New Haven: Yale UP, 1968.
Erskine-Hill, Howard. *The Augustan Idea in English Literature*. London: E. Arnold, 1983.
Gilbert, Jack G. *Edmund Waller*. Boston: Twayne, 1979.
Hillyer, Richard. "Better Read than Dead: Waller's 'Of English Verse.'" *Restoration* 14 (1990): 33–43.
Prichard, Will. "The Invention of Edmund Waller." *Restoration* 22:1 (1998): 1–17.
Zwicker, Steven N. *Lines of Authority: Politics and English Literary Culture, 1649–89*. Ithaca: Cornell UP, 1994.

JOHN MILTON

Boehrer, Bruce. "'Lycidas': The Pastoral Elegy as Same-Sex Epithalamium." *PMLA* 117:2 (2002): 222–236.
Di Cesare, Mario, ed. *Milton in Italy*. Binghamton, NY: SUNY P, 1991.
Dobranski, Stephen B. *Milton, Authorship, and the Book Trade*. Cambridge: Cambridge UP, 1999.
Evans, J. Martin. *The Road from Horton: Looking Backwards in "Lycidas."* Victoria: U of Victoria P, 1983.
———, ed. *John Milton: Twentieth-Century Perspectives, Volume 2: The Early Poems*. New York: Routledge, 2003.
Fish, Stanley. "What It's Like to Read L'Allegro and Il Penseroso." *Milton Studies* 7 (1975): 77–99.
Halpern, Richard. "The Great Instauration: Imagery Narratives in Milton's 'Nativity Ode.'" *Re-Membering Milton*. Ed. Mary Nyquist and Margaret W. Ferguson. New York: Methuen, 1987. 3–24.
Hanford, James Holly. "The Youth of Milton." *John Milton, Poet and Humanist: Essays by James Holly Hanford*. Cleveland: Case Reserve UP, 1966. 1–74.
Hill, Christopher. *Milton and the English Revolution*. London: Faber and Faber, 1977.
Hunt, Clay. *Lycidas and the Italian Cities*. New Haven: Yale UP, 1979.
Kerrigan, William. *The Prophetic Milton*. Charlottesville: U of Virginia P, 1974.
Lewalski, Barbara K. "How Radical Was the Young Milton?" *Milton and Heresy*. Ed. Stephen Dobranski and John Rumrich. Cambridge: Cambridge UP, 1998. 49–72.
Martz, Louis L. "The Rising Poet, 1645." *The Lyric and Dramatic Milton*. Ed. Joseph Summers. New York: Columbia UP, 1965. 3–33.
Nardo, Anna K. *Milton's Sonnets and the Ideal Community*. Lincoln: U of Nebraska P, 1979.
Norbrook, David. "The Politics of Milton's Early Poetry." *Poetry and Politics in the English Renaissance*. Rev. ed. Oxford: Oxford UP, 2002. 224–269.
Parker, William Riley. *Milton: A Biography*, 2 vols. Oxford: Oxford UP, 1968.
Patrides, C. A., ed. *Milton's Lycidas: The Tradition and the Poem*. Columbia: U of Missouri P, 1983.
Shawcross, John T. *John Milton: The Self and the World*. Lexington: U of Kentucky P, 1993.
Revard, Stella P. *Milton and the Tangles of Neaera's Hair: The Making of the 1645 Poems*. Columbia: U of Missouri P, 1997.
Rumrich, John. "The Erotic Milton." *Texas Studies in Literature and Language* 41:2 (1999): 128–144.
Sirluck, Ernest. "Milton's Idle Right Hand." *JEGP* 60:4 (1961): 749–785.
Tillyard, E.M.W. *Milton*. London: Chatto and Windus, 1930.
Womack, Mark. "On the Value of *Lycidas*." *Studies in English Literature* 37:1 (1997): 120–136.

SIR JOHN SUCKLING

Squier, Charles L. *Sir John Suckling*. Boston: Twayne, 1978.

ANNE BRADSTREET

Arner, Robert D. "The Structure of Anne Bradstreet's *Tenth Muse*." *Discoveries and Considerations: Essays on Early American Literature and Aesthetics*. Ed. Calvin Israel. Albany: SUNY P, 1976. 46–66.
Cowell, Pattie, and Ann Stanford. *Critical Essays on Anne Bradstreet*. Boston: Hall, 1983.
Daly, Robert. *God's Altar: The World and the Flesh in Puritan Poetry*. Berkeley: University of California P, 1978.

Hensley, Robert, ed. *The Works of Anne Bradstreet*. Cambridge: Belknap, 1967.
Martin, Wendy. "Anne Bradstreet's Poetry: A Study of Subversive Piety." *Shakespeare's Sisters: Feminist Essays on Women Poets*. Ed. Sandra Gilbert and Susan Gubar. Bloomington: Indiana UP, 1978.
Oser, Lee. "Almost a Golden World: Sidney, Spenser, and Puritan Conflict in Bradstreet's 'Contemplations.'" *Renascence: Essays on Value in Literature* 52:3 (2000): 187–202.
Rosenmaier, Rosamond R. "The Wounds upon Bathsheba: Anne Bradstreet's Prophetic Art." *Puritan Poets and Poetics: Seventeenth-Century American Poetry in Theory and Practice*. Ed. Peter White. University Park: Pennsylvania State UP, 1985. 129–146.
———. *Anne Bradstreet Revisited*. Boston: Twayne, 1991.
Schweitzer, Ivy. "Anne Bradstreet Wrestles with the Renaissance." *Early American Literature* 23:3 (1988): 291–312.
———. *The Work of Self-Representation: Lyric Poetry in Colonial New England*. Chapel Hill: U of North Carolina P, 1991.
Stanford, Ann. *Anne Bradstreet, the Worldly Puritan: An Introduction to Her Poetry*. New York: Franklin, 1974.

RICHARD CRASHAW

Davidson, Clifford. "The Anglican Setting of Richard Crashaw's Devotional Verse." *Ben Jonson Journal* 8 (2001): 259–276.
Mintz, Susannah B. "The Crashavian Mother." *Studies in English Literature* 39:1 (1999): 111–129.
Netzley, Ryan. "Oral Devotion: Eucharistic Theology and Richard Crashaw's Religious Lyrics." *Texas Studies in Literature and Language* 44:3 (2002): 247–272.
Parrish, Paul. *Richard Crashaw*. New York: Twayne, 1980.
———. "Moderate Sorrow and Immoderate Tears: Mourning in Crashaw." *Speaking Grief in English Literary Culture: Shakespeare to Milton*. Ed. David A. Kent. Pittsburgh: Duquesne UP, 2002. 217–241.
Praz, Mario. *The Flaming Heart: Essays on Crashaw, Machiavelli, and Other Studies*. New York: Doubleday, 1973.
Rambuss, Richard. "Pleasure and Devotion: The Body of Jesus and Seventeenth Century Religious Lyric." *Queering the Renaissance*. Ed. Jonathan Goldberg. Durham: Duke UP, 1994. 253–279.
Raspa, Anthony. *The Emotive Image: Jesuit Poetics in the English Renaissance*. College Station: Texas A&M UP, 1986.
Roberts, John R. *Richard Crashaw: An Annotated Bibliography of Criticism, 1632–1980*. Columbia: U of Missouri P, 1985.
———, ed. *New Perspectives on the Life and Art of Richard Crashaw*. Columbia: U of Missouri P, 1990.
Sabine, Maureen. *Feminine Engendered Faith: John Donne and Richard Crashaw*. London: Macmillan, 1992.
Strier, Richard. "Crashaw's Other Voice." *Studies in English Literature* 9 (1969): 135–148.
Warnke, Frank J. *Versions of Baroque*. New Haven: Yale UP, 1972.
Warren, Austin. *Richard Crashaw: A Study in Baroque Sensibility*. Ann Arbor: U of Michigan P, 1939.
Young, R. V. *Richard Crashaw and the Spanish Golden Age*. New Haven: Yale UP, 1982.

SIR JOHN DENHAM

Caldwell, Tanya. "John Dryden and John Denham." *Texas Studies in Literature and Language* 46:1 (2004): 49–72.
Curlin, Jay Russell. "'Is There No Temperate Region . . . ?' Coopers Hill and the Call for Moderation." *The English Civil Wars in the Literary Imagination*. Ed. Claude J. Summers and Ted-Larry Pebworth. Columbia: U of Missouri P, 1999. 119–129.
Guillory, John. "The English Common Place: Lineages of the Topographical Genre." *Critical Quarterly* 33:4 (1991): 3–27.
O Hehir, Brendan. *Harmony from Discords: A Life of Sir John Denham*. Berkeley: U of California P, 1968.
———. *Expans'd Hieroglyphicks: A Study of Sir John Denham's Coopers Hill with a Critical Edition of the Poem*. Berkeley: U of California P, 1969.
Rockett, William. "'Courts Make Not Kings, but Kings the Court': 'Cooper's Hill' and the Constitutional Crisis of 1642." *Restoration* 17:1 (1993): 1–14.

RICHARD LOVELACE

Anselment, Raymond A. "'Stone Walls' and 'Iron Bars': Richard Lovelace and the Conventions of Seventeenth-Century Prison Literature." *Renaissance and Reformation* 17:1 (1993): 15–34.
Hartmann, Cyril Hughes. *The Cavalier Spirit and Its Influence on the Life and Work of Richard Lovelace*. London: Routledge, 1925.
Kelly, Erna. "'Small Types of Great Ones': Richard Lovelace's Separate Peace." *The English Civil Wars in the Literary Imagination*. Ed. Claude J. Summers and Ted-Larry Pebworth. Columbia: U of Missouri P, 1999. 81–101.
Seelig, Sharon Cadman. "My Curious Hand or Eye: The Wit of Richard Lovelace." *The Wit of*

Seventeenth-Century Poetry. Ed. Claude J. Summers and Ted-Larry Pebworth. Columbia: U of Missouri P, 1995. 151–170.
Weidhorn, Manfred. *Richard Lovelace*. New York: Twayne, 1970.

ABRAHAM COWLEY

Hinman, Robert B. *Abraham Cowley's World of Order*. Cambridge: Harvard UP, 1960.
Jose, Nicholas. *Ideas of the Restoration in English Literature*. Cambridge: Harvard UP, 1984.
Mason, Tom. "Abraham Cowley and the Wisdom of Anacreon." *Cambridge Quarterly* 19 (1990): 103–137.
Nethercot, Arthur H. *Abraham Cowley: The Muse's Hannibal*. London: Oxford UP, 1931.
Revard, Stella P. "The Politics of Cowley's Anacreontiques." *Ben Jonson Journal* 4 (1997): 131–150.
Taaffe, James G. *Abraham Cowley*. New York: Twayne, 1972.
Trotter, David. *The Poetry of Abraham Cowley*. London: Macmillan, 1979.

ANDREW MARVELL

Abraham, Lyndy. *Marvell and Alchemy*. Hants, UK: Scolar, 1990.
Brett, R. L., ed. *Andrew Marvell: Essays on the Tercentenary of His Death*. Oxford: Oxford UP, 1979.
Chernaik, Warren. *The Poet's Time: Politics and Religion in the Work of Andrew Marvell*. Cambridge: Cambridge UP, 1983.
Chernaik, Warren, and Martin Dzelzainis, eds. *Marvell and Liberty*. New York: St. Martin's, 1999.
Colie, Rosalie. *"My Ecchoing Song": Andrew Marvell's Poetry of Criticism*. Princeton: Princeton UP, 1970.
Duncan-Jones, E. E. "Marvell: A Great Master of Words." *Proceedings of the British Academy*. Oxford: Oxford UP, 1976. 267–290.
Empson, Sir William. *Some Versions of Pastoral*. London: Chatto and Windus, 1935.
Friedman, Donald. *Marvell's Pastoral Art*. London: Routledge and Kegan Paul, 1970.
Haber, Judith. *Pastoral and the Poetics of Self-Contradiction: Theocritus to Marvell*. Cambridge: Cambridge UP, 1994.
Hodge, R. I. V. *Foreshortened Time: Andrew Marvell and Seventeenth Century Revolutions*. Cambridge: D. S. Brewer, 1978.
Kegl, Rosemary. "'Joyning my Labour to my Pain': The Politics of Labor in Marvell's Mower Poems." *Soliciting Interpretation*. Ed. Elizabeth D. Harvey and Katherine Eisaman Maus. Chicago: Chicago UP, 1990. 89–118.
Legouis, Pierre. *Andrew Marvell: Poet, Puritan, Patriot*. Oxford: Clarendon, 1965.
Patterson, Annabel. *Marvell and the Civic Crown*. Princeton: Princeton UP, 1978.
Rogers, John. "Marvell, Winstanley, and the Natural History of the Green Age." *The Matter of Revolution: Science, Poetry, and Politics in the Age of Milton*. Ithaca: Cornell UP, 1996. 39–69.
———. "Marvell and the Action of Virginity." *The Matter of Revolution: Science, Poetry, and Politics in the Age of Milton*. Ithaca: Cornell UP, 1996. 70–102.
Scoular, Kitty. *Natural Magic: Studies in the Presentation of Nature in English Poetry from Spenser to Marvell*. Oxford: Clarendon, 1965.
Stocker, Margarita. *Apocalyptic Marvell: The Second Coming in Seventeenth Century Poetry*. Brighton: Harvester, 1986.
Summers, Claude J., and Ted-Larry Pebworth, eds. *On the Celebrated and Neglected Poems of Andrew Marvell*. Columbia: U of Missouri P, 1992.
Wallace, John M. *Destiny His Choice: The Loyalism of Andrew Marvell*. Cambridge: Cambridge UP, 1968.
Wheeler, Thomas. *Andrew Marvell Revisited*. New York: Twayne, 1996.

HENRY VAUGHAN

Calhoun, Thomas O. *Henry Vaughan: The Achievement of* Silex Scintillans. Newark: U of Delaware P, 1981.
Durr, Robert A. *On the Mystical Poetry of Henry Vaughan*. Cambridge: Harvard UP, 1962.
Halley, Janet E. "Versions of the Self and the Politics of Privacy in *Silex Scintillans*." *George Herbert Journal* 7 (1983–84): 51–71.
Holmes, Elizabeth. *Henry Vaughan and Hermetic Philosophy*. Oxford: Blackwell, 1932.
Hutchinson, F. E. *Henry Vaughan: A Life and Interpretation*. Oxford: Clarendon, 1947.
Martin, L. C., ed. *The Works of Henry Vaughan*. 2nd ed. Oxford: Clarendon, 1957.
Martz, Louis. "Henry Vaughan: The Man Within." *PMLA* 78 (1963): 40–49.
Pettet, E. C. *Of Paradise and Light: A Study of Vaughan's* Silex Scintillans. Cambridge: Cambridge UP, 1960.
Post, Jonathan F. S. *Henry Vaughan: The Unfolding Vision*. Princeton: Princeton UP, 1982.
Rudrum, Alan. "The Influence of Alchemy in the Poems of Henry Vaughan." *Philological Quarterly* 49 (1970): 469–480.
———. "An Aspect of Vaughan's Hermeticism: The Doctrine of Cosmic Sympathy." *Studies in English Literature* 14 (1974): 129–138.
———, ed. *Henry Vaughan: The Complete Poems*. Harmondsworth: Penguin, 1976.
———, ed. *Essential Articles for the Study of Henry Vaughan*. Hamden, CT: Archon, 1987.

Simmonds, James D. *The Masques of God: Form and Theme in the Poetry of Henry Vaughan*. Pittsburgh: U of Pittsburgh P, 1972.

MARGARET CAVENDISH, DUCHESS OF NEWCASTLE

Battigelli, Anna. *Margaret Cavendish and the Exiles of the Mind*. Lexington: UP of Kentucky, 1998.
Clucas, Stephen, ed. *A Princely Brave Woman: Essays on Margaret Cavendish, Duchess of Newcastle*. Aldershot: Ashgate, 2003.
Cottegnies, Line, and Nancy Weatiz, eds. *Authorial Conquests: Essays on Genre in the Writings of Margaret Cavendish*. Madison, NJ: Fairleigh Dickinson UP, 2003.
Jones, Kathleen. *A Glorious Fame: The Life of Margaret Cavendish, Duchess of Newcastle*. London: Bloomsbury, 1988.
Price, Bronwen. "Feminine Modes of Knowing and Scientific Enquiry: Margaret Cavendish's Poetry as Case Study." *Women and Literature in Britain, 1500–1700*. Ed. Helen Wilcox. Cambridge: Cambridge UP, 1996. 117–139.
Rees, Emma. " 'Sweet Honey of the Muses': Lucretian Resonance in *Poems and Fancies*." *In-Between: Essays and Studies in Literary Criticism* 9:1–2 (2000): 3–16.
———. *Margaret Cavendish: Gender, Genre, Exile*. Manchester: Manchester UP, 2003.

JOHN DRYDEN

Cacicedo, Alberto. "Seeing the King: Biblical and Classical Texts in *Astraea Redux*." *Studies in English Literature* 32:3 (1992): 407–427.
Gordon, Scott Paul. "Endeavoring to Be the King: Dryden's *Astraea Redux* and the Issue of 'Character.' " *Journal of English and Germanic Philology* 101:2 (2002): 201–221.
Hammond, Paul. *John Dryden: A Literary Life*. New York: Palgrave Macmillan, 1991.
———. *Dryden and the Traces of Classical Rome*. Oxford: Oxford UP, 1999.
Miner, Earl. *Dryden's Poetry*. Bloomington: Indiana UP, 1967.
Winn, James A. *John Dryden and His World*. New Haven: Yale UP, 1987.
Zwicker, Steven N. *Politics and Language in Dryden's Poetry: The Arts of Disguise*. Princeton: Princeton UP, 1984.

KATHERINE PHILIPS

Andreadis, Harriette. "The Sapphic-Platonics of Katherine Philips, 1632–1664." *Signs* 15 (1989): 34–60.
Evans, Robert C. "Paradox in Poetry and Politics: Katherine Philips in the Interregnum." *The English Civil Wars in the Literary Imagination*. Ed. Claude J. Summers and Ted-Larry Pebworth. Columbia: U of Missouri P, 1999. 174–185.
Hageman, Elizabeth H. "Katherine Philips: The Matchless Orinda." *Women Writers of the Renaissance and Reformation*. Ed. Katharina M. Wilson. Athens: U of Georgia P, 1987. 566–608.
Hobby, Elaine. "Orinda and Female Intimacy." *Early Women Writers: 1600–1720*. Ed. Anita Pacheco. London: Longman, 1998. 73–88.
Mintz, Susannah B. "Katherine Philips and the Space of Friendship." *Restoration* 22:2 (1998): 62–78.
Price, Bronwen. "A Rhetoric of Innocence: The Poetry of Katherine Philips, 'The Matchless Orinda.' " *Write or Be Written: Early Modern Women Poets and Cultural Constraints*. Ed. Barbara Smith and Ursula Appelt. Aldershot: Ashgate, 2001. 223–246.
Shifflett, Andrew. " 'How Many Virtues Must I Hate': Katherine Philips and the Politics of Clemency." *Studies in Philology* 94:1 (1997): 103–135.
———. " 'Subdu'd by You': States of Friendship and Friends of the State in Katherine Philips's Poetry." *Write or Be Written: Early Modern Women Poets and Cultural Constraints*. Ed. Barbara Smith and Ursula Appelt. Aldershot: Ashgate, 2001. 177–195.
Souer, Philip W. *The Matchless Orinda*. Cambridge: Harvard UP, 1931.
Stiebel, Arlene. "Subversive Sexuality: Masking the Erotic in Poems by Katherine Philips and Aphra Behn." *Renaissance Discourses of Desire*. Ed. Claude Summers and Ted-Larry Pebworth. Columbia: U of Missouri P, 1993. 223–236.
Thomas, Patrick. *Katherine Philips (Orinda)*. Cardiff: U of Wales P, 1988.
———. *The Collected Works of Katherine Philips: The Matchless Orinda*, 3 Vols. Essex: Stump Cross, 1990.

THOMAS TRAHERNE

Clements, A. L. *The Mystical Poetry of Thomas Traherne*. Cambridge: Harvard UP, 1969.
Day, Malcolm M. *Thomas Traherne*. Boston: Twayne, 1983.
Dowell, Graham. *Enjoying the World: The Rediscovery of Thomas Traherne*. New York: Morehouse, 1990.
Margoliouth, H. M. *Centuries, Poems, and Thanksgivings*, 2 Vols. Oxford: Clarendon, 1958.
Stewart, Stanley. *The Expanded Voice: The Art of Thomas Traherne*. San Marion, CA: Huntington, 1970.
Wade, Gladys. *Thomas Traherne*. Princeton: Princeton UP, 1944.
Wallace, John M. "Thomas Traherne and the Structure of Meditation." *ELH* 25 (1958): 79–89.

Index